DATE DUE

	PRINTED IN U.S.A.

*International Encyclopedia of the
Social Sciences, 2nd edition*

International Encyclopedia of the Social Sciences, 2nd edition

VOLUME 6
OAXACA, RONALD–QUOTAS, TRADE

William A. Darity Jr.
EDITOR IN CHIEF

MACMILLAN REFERENCE USA
A part of Gale, Cengage Learning

GALE
CENGAGE Learning

Detroit • New York • San Francisco • New Haven, Conn • Waterville, Maine • London

International Encyclopedia of the Social Sciences, 2nd edition
William A. Darity Jr., Editor in Chief

For permission to use material from this product, submit your request via Web at http://www.gale-edit.com/permissions, or you may download our Permissions Request form and submit your request by fax or mail to:

Permissions Department
Gale 27500 Drake Rd.
Farmington Hills, MI 48331-3535
Permissions Hotline:
248-699-8006 or 800-877-4253 ext. 8006
Fax: 248-699-8074 or 800-762-4058

Since this page cannot legibly accommodate all copyright notices, the credits constitute an extension of the copyright notice.

While every effort has been made to ensure the reliability of the information presented in this publication, Gale does not guarantee the accuracy of the data contained herein. Gale accepts no payment for listing; and inclusion in the publication of any organization, agency, institution, publication, service, or individual does not imply endorsement of the editors or publisher. Errors brought to the attention of the publisher and verified to the satisfaction of the publisher will be corrected in future editions.

LIBRARY OF CONGRESS CATALOGING-IN-PUBLICATION DATA

International encyclopedia of the social sciences / William A. Darity, Jr., editor in chief.—2nd ed. v. cm. Rev. ed. of: International encyclopedia of the social sciences / David L. Sills, editor. c1968–c1991.
   Includes bibliographical references and index.
   ISBN 978-0-02-865965-7 (set hardcover : alk. paper)—ISBN 978-0-02-865966-4 (v. 1 hardcover : alk. paper)—ISBN 978-0-02-865967-1 (v. 2 hardcover : alk. paper)—ISBN 978-0-02-865968-8 (v. 3 hardcover : alk. paper)—ISBN 978-0-02-865969-5 (v. 4 hardcover : alk. paper)—ISBN 978-0-02-865970-1 (v. 5 hardcover : alk. paper)—ISBN 978-0-02-865971-8 (v. 6 hardcover : alk. paper)—ISBN 978-0-02-865972-5 (v. 7 hardcover : alk. paper)—ISBN 978-0-02-865973-2 (v. 8 hardcover : alk. paper)—ISBN 978-0-02-866141-4 (v. 9 hardcover : alk. paper)—ISBN 978-0-02-866117-9 (ebook : alk. paper)
   1. Social sciences—Dictionaries. 2. Social sciences—Encyclopedias. I. Darity, William A., 1953– II. Title: Encyclopedia of the social sciences.
   H40.A2I5 2008
   300.3–dc22

2007031829

0-02-865965-1 (set)
0-02-865966-X (v. 1)
0-02-865967-8 (v. 2)
0-02-865968-6 (v. 3)
0-02-865969-4 (v. 4)
0-02-865970-8 (v. 5)
0-02-865971-6 (v. 6)
0-02-865972-4 (v. 7)
0-02-865973-2 (v. 8)
0-02-866141-9 (v. 9)

This title is also available as an e-book.
ISBN 978-0-02-866117-9; 0-02-866117-6
Contact your Gale representative for ordering information.

Printed in the United States of America
3 4 5 6 7 8 14 13 12 11 10 09 08

Editorial Board

Contents

O

OAXACA, RONALD
1944–

Ronald Oaxaca is the McClelland Professor of Economics and faculty associate at the Economics Science Laboratory at the University of Arizona. Best known to many economists as the developer of the Oaxaca wage decomposition technique for examining wage differentials, he has conducted research and published extensively since the 1970s on topics such as labor economics, applied econometrics, and applied microeconomics including sex, union, and race differentials and discrimination; unemployment and unemployment insurance; and the minimum wage.

Oaxaca is perhaps best known for developing one of the most important methods used in the field of labor economics to study wage discrimination based on sex and race known as the wage gap decomposition, which he outlined in his 1973 article "Male-Female Wage Differentials in Urban Labor Markets." Also influenced by economist Alan S. Blinder, the wage gap decomposition provides a means for identifying residual differences between observed and predicted wages that are not accounted for by characteristics associated with productivity, such as education and skill, and can thus be attributed to labor market discrimination and other omitted variables. The seminal method has since been refined and elaborated upon to add other elements of analysis, such as the use of alternative wage structures as reference points for comparison; selectivity bias; comparative analysis across countries and time; the explanation of penalties associated with motherhood; and analysis of discrimination across the income distribution rather than using means. Oaxaca has also continued to utilize and improve upon the wage decomposition, notably with Michael R. Ransom in two studies conducted in 1994 and 1999 (as mentioned in Yana van der Meulen Rodgers's 2006 article "A Primer on Wage Gap Decompositions in the Analysis of Labor Market Discrimination"), further refining methods for developing the nondiscriminatory wage structure and emphasizing the importance of the reference group for estimating the unexplained or discriminatory portion of the wage gap.

More recently Oaxaca has focused on topics such as the influences of ability and family background on optimal schooling levels; the effects of dual job holding; statistical discrimination; and consistent estimators of linear probability models. His continued study of gender differentials in wages includes work to examine the impact of technology and to compare trends in the United States and Denmark. Further he is conducting research on such disparate subjects as determinants of faculty salaries, the production of engineering degrees, optimal sick pay schemes, gender bias in the criminal justice system, and measurement error in work experience. He currently serves as the coeditor of *American Economic Review*, and he is on the editorial board of the *Journal of Economic Inequality*. From 1986 to 1989 he was on the editorial board of the *Journal of Urban Economics*, and he previously coedited *Economic Inquiry*. To date he has published over seventy articles, working papers, and book reviews.

Oaxaca is also a teacher who has been a member of over seventy thesis committees since 1978. He joined the faculty of the University of Arizona in 1976 (after teaching at the University of Massachusetts from 1973 to 1976) and has been a visiting professor at a number of institutions, including Smith College (1975); Princeton

University (1982); Stanford University (1983–1984); New Mexico State University (1991), where he was a Distinguished Visiting Professor; the University of Aarhus in Denmark (1997); and ERMES at the University of Paris II (2003). He is an active member of the Association for Hispanic Economists.

Oaxaca was a fellow of the Udall Center at the University of Arizona from 1995 to 1996 and since 2001 has been a research fellow at the Institute for the Study of Labor (IZA) in Bonn, Germany. In 2005 *Hispanic Business* magazine selected Oaxaca to appear on the list of the 100 most influential Hispanics.

Oaxaca earned a bachelor's of science (summa cum laude with honors) from California State University at Fresno (1965) and a master's (1969) and doctorate (1971) in economics from Princeton University.

SEE ALSO *Blinder-Oaxaca Decomposition Technique; Econometric Decomposition*

BIBLIOGRAPHY

Oaxaca, Ronald L. 1973. Male-Female Wage Differentials in Urban Labor Markets. *International Economic Review* 14 (3): 693–709.

Rodgers, Yana van der Meulen. 2006. A Primer on Wage Gap Decompositions in the Analysis of Labor Market Discrimination. In *Handbook on the Economics of Discrimination*, ed. William M. Rodgers, III. Cheltenham, UK: E. Elgar Publishing.

Elizabeth Nisbet
William M. Rodgers III

OBEDIENCE, DESTRUCTIVE

Obedience is the act of compliance to the commands of a legitimate authority. In destructive obedience the acquiescence is to a command to harm another person. The phrase was first introduced into the social sciences in 1963 by Stanley Milgram in his article "Behavioral Study of Obedience" in the *Journal of Abnormal and Social Psychology* describing the first of a series of experiments on obedience he conducted at Yale University from 1961 to 1962.

In those experiments the subject was told to teach a learner a series of word pairs, using increasingly painful electric shocks—up to 450 volts—as punishment for each error. Although the shocks were fake and the learner was an actor who feigned his suffering, the experiment was stressful for most of the subjects. Sixty-five percent of the subjects were fully obedient to the experimenter's com-

mands, progressing to the maximum shock. The unexpectedly high rate of destructive obedience was the central and most dramatic finding in Milgram's experiments. While we did not need Milgram to tell us that people tend to obey authorities, the sheer power of that finding was revelatory: that ordinary people would act contrary to conscience and hurt an innocent person at the bidding of an authority without coercive means to enforce his or her commands.

Milgram conducted over twenty different variations in his series of experiments on destructive obedience. A second important insight is provided by a subset of those variations. In that series Milgram varied the distance between the teacher and the learner. As the distance was reduced, so was the percentage of obedient subjects. The morality of shocking an innocent victim did not change from condition to condition, but the tendency to obey the destructive orders did, demonstrating that the immediate situation can have powerful effects on behavior even at the expense of the subject's personal inclinations.

Milgram undertook his research to shed light on the Holocaust in an attempt to explain how normal people could become complicit in carrying out the murderous commands of Nazi leaders. Although early twenty-first century regulations in the United States and other countries make it virtually impossible to replicate Milgram's experiments, experiences in real life continue to affirm his findings.

For example, in 2004 two male students at a Georgia high school obeyed their teacher's orders to throw an unruly female classmate out the window. Real-life events also have broadened the scope of destructive obedience in several ways. For instance, it is known that destructive obedience can take place even when the self is the victim. A review of airplane accidents between 1978 and 1990 found that in about 25 percent of cases the first officer's reluctance to correct an error made by his or her captain was a contributing factor. Also the power of destructive obedience when the action is damaging in a nonphysical manner is as strong as or stronger than is the case when the obedient act is physically destructive, strong enough to override a person's moral or ethical principles. As a teaching exercise, a University of San Diego law professor, Steven Hartwell, had his students advise a client on how best to present her side of a rent dispute in court. Hartwell told them to advise the client to lie under oath and say that she had paid her rent. Twenty-three of twenty-four subjects complied and told the woman to perjure herself.

SEE ALSO *Authoritarianism; Authority; Conformity; Holocaust, The; Milgram, Stanley; Nazism*

BIBLIOGRAPHY

Blass, Thomas, ed. 2000. *Obedience to Authority: Current Perspectives on the Milgram Paradigm*. Mahwah, NJ: Lawrence Erlbaum.

Blass, Thomas. 2004. *The Man Who Shocked the World: The Life and Legacy of Stanley Milgram*. New York: Basic Books.

Hartwell, Steven. 1990. Moral Development, Ethical Conduct, and Clinical Education. *New York Law School Law Review* 35 (1): 131–161.

Milgram, Stanley. 1963. Behavioral Study of Obedience. *Journal of Abnormal and Social Psychology* 67 (4): 371–378.

Milgram, Stanley. 1974. *Obedience to Authority: An Experimental View*. New York: Harper and Row.

Thomas Blass

OBESE EXTERNALITY

In the late 1960s, the social psychologist Stanley Schachter (1922–1997) proposed that obese people eat (and overeat) not because of hunger, stress, or boredom, but in response to external (i.e., environmental) food cues, which drive eating in the obese until those cues are removed (or consumed). External food cues include the sight or smell of palatable food and other salient cues in the situation indicating that eating is appropriate. When external cues are absent, the obese are not motivated to eat, even if they are substantially food-deprived. This focus on internal and external cues is often seen as originating in Schachter's earlier research on emotion, although a close reading reveals significant differences in Schachter's analyses of these two domains.

Schachter's obese-externality theory achieved widespread attention because it challenged long-standing ideas about the causes of obesity by means of several innovative and dramatic experiments. These experiments showed that obese people's food intake is less affected by manipulations of food deprivation and distress than is that of normal-weight people. Obese individuals, for instance, are less disturbed by time-zone changes or by the requirements of religious fasting, as long as food cues are not prominent. These clever studies, written with great flair, were complemented by studies demonstrating that obese people are differentially affected by manipulations of external cues, ranging from varying the visual prominence of food cues (by, for example, altering the lighting or providing nuts either shelled or unshelled) to doctoring a clock (so that dinnertime arrived either early or late) to offering experimental subjects either one or three sandwiches to eat. These studies fascinated the research community, even if the data were not always robust.

Schachter's research was correlational, showing that obesity is associated with externality. He assumed that externality (in an environment rife with food cues) causes obesity. But what is the source of externality? Schachter postulated that impairment of the brain's ventromedial hypothalamus (VMH) was responsible; rats with VMH damage behaviorally resemble obese humans. This line of reasoning was extended by Schachter's student Richard Nisbett (1972), who argued that suppression of VMH functioning was a consequence of weight suppression by dieting or other means, which is common among the obese. This proposal led in turn to research by C. Peter Herman and Janet Polivy (1980) on restrained eating (dieting), which hinged on the notion that even normal-weight people who suppress their weight ought to be especially external. Work on restrained eating, however, quickly turned away from questions of internal versus external. The Eating Disorders Inventory contains a scale concerned with interoception, the perception of one's own internal states, which is weak in those with eating disorders; but again, the eating disorders literature pays scant attention to Schachter's internal/external distinction.

Challenges to the obese-externality theory include the argument that internal and external cues reciprocally influence each other and are thus inseparable. Research shows that external cues (such as social influence and portion size) exert such a powerful influence on food intake in everyone that it is misleading to identify external responsiveness exclusively with the obese. Still, Schachter's original proposal has not been disproved so much as superseded by subsequent formulations, all of which owe a debt to his groundbreaking demonstrations of how eating may be studied experimentally and creatively.

SEE ALSO *Nutrition; Obesity; Overeating; Schachter, Stanley*

BIBLIOGRAPHY

Herman, C. Peter, and Janet Polivy. 1980. Restrained Eating. In *Obesity*, ed. A. J. Stunkard, 208–225. Philadelphia: Saunders.

Nisbett, Richard E. 1972. Hunger, Obesity, and the Ventromedial Hypothalamus. *Psychological Review* 79: 433–453.

Schachter, Stanley. 1968. Obesity and Eating. *Science* 161: 751–756.

Schachter, Stanley. 1971. Some Extraordinary Facts about Obese Humans and Rats. *American Psychologist* 26: 129–144.

C. Peter Herman

OBESITY

Obesity results from chronic energy intake that exceeds energy expenditure and is characterized by "excessive" body fat. The precise assessment of an individual's body fat is an expensive and complicated procedure. Instead, body mass index (BMI), though somewhat controversial, is used commonly because it is easy to assess and correlates highly with body fat. BMI is calculated by taking an individual's weight in kilograms and dividing it by that individual's height in meters squared (kg/m^2). For adults a healthy BMI is between 18.5 and 24.9. A BMI of 25 to 29 is classified as overweight, obesity is defined as a BMI of 30 to 39, and clinically severe obesity is defined as a BMI of 40 or more. Because of the pervasive social stigma associated with the term *obesity*, it is avoided for children; *at risk for overweight* and *overweight* are the recommended terms. To account for normal age and sex differences in children's body fat, at risk for overweight is defined as a BMI at or above the 85th percentile and overweight as a BMI at or above the 95th percentile of the sex-specific BMI-for-age growth charts.

PREVALENCE OF OBESITY

Health statistics for the United States reveal a dramatic upsurge in obesity prevalence during the early 1980s, and the rates have continued to rise. U.S. national health statistics in 2007 estimated that 34.1 percent of adults were overweight, 32.2 percent obese, and 4.8 percent clinically obese; 17.1 percent of children and adolescents age six to nineteen were estimated to be overweight, and 16.5 percent were at risk for overweight. Sociodemographic risk factors for obesity include being of a racial/ethnic minority and being of low socioeconomic status.

CONSEQUENCES OF OBESITY

Obesity is associated with high morbidity and mortality rates. The medical sequelae of obesity include type II diabetes, coronary heart disease, stroke, osteoarthritis, sleep apnea, and some cancers, including breast and colon cancer.

Among the most insidious and common adverse effects are the socioemotional consequences of obesity. Obese individuals are significantly more likely to experience social stigmatization and discrimination in all domains, including education, employment, social relationships, and health care. Also, obesity is associated with low self-esteem, body image disorders, anxiety, and depression. Associations between BMI and body satisfaction vary with race/ethnicity and gender. African Americans have a higher mean BMI than do European Americans but tend also to have greater body satisfaction. Generally, females report significantly lower body satisfaction than do males regardless of race/ethnicity.

ENVIRONMENTAL EXPLANATIONS

The escalating rates of obesity since the 1980s are attributable to a complex interaction of environmental, sociocultural, behavioral, and biological/genetic factors that is not well understood. At a macrosystemic level, U.S. food policy is fundamentally at odds with the goal of healthful eating. Food is overproduced, and as a result of the abundant supply, food companies must compete aggressively for market share. Cheap, palatable, and accessible energy-dense foods are mass-marketed and offered in portions vastly disproportionate to individuals' caloric needs. A marked shift toward away-from-home and prepared food consumption probably has resulted from time constraints caused by a rise in dual-career and single-parent working families. In 1977, 9.6 percent of meals were eaten at restaurants and fast food outlets; by 1996 that proportion had risen to 23.5 percent.

Over roughly the same period consumption of high-fructose corn syrup (HFCS) increased 1000 percent or more. HFCS is used instead of sugar (glucose) as a caloric sweetener in many foods and all soft drinks; however, it is digested, absorbed, and metabolized differently than glucose is. Fructose, unlike glucose, distorts levels of insulin, leptin, and ghrelin, the hormones that act as key signals in food regulatory processes and body weight, making dietary fructose a prime suspect in the obesity epidemic.

A sedentary lifestyle is an important contributing factor, especially in light of the fact that decreased energy expenditure has been accompanied by increased energy consumption. A sedentary lifestyle is a natural consequence of a built environment characterized by urban sprawl that necessitates travel by car or mass transit and time-consuming commutes. Technological advancement that reduces energy output, low-energy office occupations, and leisure preferences such as television viewing and computer use increase the probability of a physically inactive lifestyle.

EARLY PSYCHOLOGICAL THEORIES

Two classic psychological theories of obesity predate the onset of the obesity epidemic. To explain differences in the eating patterns of obese and normal-weight individuals, in 1968 Stanley Schacter proposed the internal-external theory of obesity and in 1972 Richard Nesbitt proposed the set point theory. Schacter hypothesized that obese individuals are more likely to be responsive to cues from the external environment such as the sight and palatability of food, whereas normal-weight individuals are more likely to eat in response to internal physiological cues. Nesbitt countered with the hypothesis that each individual has a unique, biologically determined ideal weight, with obese individuals having an above-average set point. He theorized further that societal ideals of thinness cause obese individuals to restrain their intake and eat below their set points, essentially causing a chronic state of deprivation and hyperresponsiveness to external food cues. These models of obesity have faded in importance because of a lack of empirical support. However, the derivative construct of dietary restraint and its effect on individuals' eating patterns continues to generate much research and some controversy.

DIETARY RESTRAINT

Dietary restraint is defined as the deliberate and persistent restriction of food to promote weight loss. Restraint theory proposes that restrained eaters may develop disordered eating patterns as a result of the stress inherent in chronic appetitive self-control. Although research has supported a relationship between dietary restraint and disinhibited eating, the validity of the restraint measurement scales is at issue and further work on more definitive construct measurement and the role of dietary restraint in disordered eating is warranted.

BIOLOGICAL EXPLANATIONS

Obesity also is explained by reference to biological processes. Research indicates that neuroendocrinological processes, most centrally the hypothalamic-pituitary-adrenal (HPA) axis, figure prominently in obesity. The HPA axis, which consists of the hypothalamus and the pituitary and adrenal glands, is a key player in stress regulation as well as in physiological processes such as digestion, energy use, and mood. Stress, which is inherent in the daily demands of the twenty-first-century environment, causes elevated cortisol secretion by the HPA axis. Protracted stimulation of the HPA axis results in a flood of neuroendocrine-endocrine disturbances that in turn cause insulin resistance and visceral (abdominal) obesity. Visceral obesity carries the highest risk for comorbidities.

Genetic research is still in its early stages. There is substantial heritability of individual differences in BMI. However, more than twenty genes, hypothesized as working in conjunction with a wide range of environmental factors, have been linked to obesity: Clearly, obesity is causally very complex. Equally clearly, however, obesity is an urgent health problem that will continue to be a challenge for the foreseeable future.

SEE ALSO *Body Image; Body Mass Index; Disease; Overeating*

BIBLIOGRAPHY

Bjorntorp, Per, and Roland Rosmond. 2000. Neuroendocrine Abnormalities in Visceral Obesity. *International Journal of Obesity and Related Metabolic Disorders* 24 (Supplement 2): S80–S85.

Bray, George A., Samara Joy Nielsen, and Barry M. Popkin. 2004. Consumption of High-Fructose Corn Syrup in Beverages May Play a Role in Obesity. *American Journal of Clinical Nutrition* 79: 537–543.

Centers for Disease Control and Prevention. National Center for Health Statistics. 2006. *National Health and Nutrition Examination Survey Data.* Hyattsville, MD: U.S. Department of Health and Human Services, Centers for Disease Control and Prevention. http://www.cdc.gov/nchs.htm.

Nesbitt, Richard E. 1972. Hunger, Obesity, and the Ventromedial Hypothalamus. *Psychological Review* 79 (6): 433–453.

Ogden, Cynthia L., Margaret D. Carroll, Lester R. Curtin, et al. 2006. Prevalence of Overweight and Obesity in the United States, 1999–2004. *Journal of the American Medical Association* 295 (13): 1549–1555.

Ruderman, Audrey J. 1986. Dietary Restraint: A Theoretical and Empirical Review. *Psychological Bulletin* 99: 247–262.

Schacter, Stanley. 1968. Obesity and Eating. *Science* 161: 751–756.

Smith, D. E., J. K. Thompson, J. M. Raczynski, and J. E. Hilner. 1999. Body Image among Men and Women in a Biracial Cohort: The CARDIA Study. *International Journal of Eating Disorders* 25 (1): 71–82.

Stice, Eric, Melissa Fisher, and Michael Lowe. 2004. Are Dietary Restraint Scales Valid Measures of Acute Dietary Restriction? Unobtrusive Observational Data Suggest Not. *Psychological Assessment* 16 (1): 51–59.

Joan K. Orrell-Valente
Kim Jones

OBJECT-RELATIONS THEORY

SEE *Psychoanalytic Theory.*

OBJECTIVE FUNCTION

In an optimization problem, there is a (real-valued) function that is to be maximized or minimized. This function is frequently called the *objective function,* a term that seems to have arisen in the realm of planning and programming, particularly linear programming, through the work of mathematician George Dantzig (1914–2005). Prior to 1947, when Dantzig invented the linear programming problem and the simplex method for its solution, military logistical plans, called "programs," involved large-scale decision-making based on ground rules. Dantzig created mathematical models to capture the conditions that needed to be satisfied and a criterion for choosing one feasible solution over another. This made a significant contribution to a vital sphere of activity. Dantzig ushered in a new era in decision-making and brought forth the term *objective function* as a numerical mathematical expression for the *objective* that was to be achieved by the program.

Thus, an objective function measures the "goodness" of a feasible vector, that is, a vector whose coordinates satisfy all the imposed side conditions, if any. To illustrate, in a linear programming problem,

$$
\begin{aligned}
\text{maximize} \quad & p_1 x_1 + p_2 x_2 + \cdots + p_n x_n \\
\text{subject to} \quad & a_{11} x_1 + a_{12} x_2 + \cdots + a_{1n} x_n \leq b_1 \\
& a_{12} x_1 + a_{22} x_2 + \cdots + a_{2n} x_n \leq b_2 \\
& \qquad\qquad \vdots \\
& a_{m1} x_1 + a_{m2} x_2 + \cdots + a_{mn} x_n \leq b_m \\
& x_j \geq 0, \quad j = 1, 2, \ldots, n
\end{aligned}
$$

the objective function is the linear form $p_1 x_1 + p_2 x_2 + \ldots + p_n x_n$, which might, for instance, measure the total revenue resulting from sales in the amounts $x_1, x_2, \ldots, x_n$ at unit prices $p_1, p_2, \ldots, p_n$. The inequalities in this illustration represent side conditions (or constraints) on the variables $x_1, x_2, \ldots, x_n$.

This is not to say that all objective functions (or all constraints) are of this type. They may be linear or nonlinear, depending on how goodness is defined in the applied context. The function being minimized in a parameter estimation by the "least-squares" criterion is an example of a nonlinear (actually quadratic) objective function. In problems of this sort, the "variables" in question may be "free" (unconstrained) or constrained. In the nonlinear case, convexity (or lack of it) becomes an important issue from the optimization-theoretic standpoint.

The underlying concept of an objective function—under a different name or no name at all—had existed for centuries before Dantzig introduced this particular terminology. One has only to recall the method of multipliers devised by Joseph-Louis Lagrange (1736–1813) for equality-constrained optimization problems. Many synonymous terms are in use. Among the more abstract ones are *maximand* for maximization problems and *minimand* for minimization problems. These terms can be used in the respective optimization problems no matter what the application may be. In applied areas such as econometrics, one finds the term *criterion function*. Still others with an obvious connection to economics are *social welfare function*, *economic welfare function*, *loss function*, and *profit function*. Further examples coming from other fields are *distance function* and *flow value*; the point being that the term used in place of *objective function* might refer to what it is measuring.

SEE ALSO *Koopmans, Tjalling; Maximization; Preferences; Preferences, Interdependent; Principal-Agent Models; Programming, Linear and Nonlinear; Rationality; Representative Agent; Social Welfare Functions; Utility Function*

BIBLIOGRAPHY

Bergson, Abram. 1938. A Reformulation of Certain Aspects of Welfare Economics. *Quarterly Journal of Economics* 52: 310–334.

Dantzig, George B. 1963. *Linear Programming and Extensions.* Princeton, NJ: Princeton University Press.

Dorfman, Robert, Paul A. Samuelson, and Robert M. Solow. 1958. *Linear Programming and Economic Analysis.* New York: McGraw-Hill.

Koopmans, Tjalling C. 1951. Introduction. In *Activity Analysis of Production and Allocation,* ed. Tjalling C. Koopmans, 1–12. New York: Wiley.

Lagrange, Joseph-Louis. 1797. *Théorie des fonctions analytiques.* Paris: Imprimerie de la République.

Lange, Oskar. 1942. The Foundations of Welfare Economics. *Econometrica* 10: 215–228.

Wood, Marshall K., and George B. Dantzig. 1951. The Programming of Interdependent Activities: General Discussion. In *Activity Analysis of Production and Allocation,* ed. Tjalling C. Koopmans, 15–18. New York: Wiley.

Richard W. Cottle

OBJECTIVE PROBABILITY
SEE *Probability.*

OBJECTIVE VALUE
SEE *Value, Objective.*

OBJECTIVISM

Objectivism is the philosophy enunciated by the Russian-born American novelist and philosopher, Ayn Rand (1905–1982).

Rand's philosophical system begins with a realist premise: Reality is what it is, independent of what people think or feel. The concept of "objectivity" is central to Rand's theory of knowledge. A knowing subject can acquire objective knowledge of reality only through reason, a distinctively human faculty, which integrates the inductive evidence of the senses, in accordance with logical principles.

Because reason is a basic means of acquiring human knowledge and, hence, a basic tool of human survival, Rand places it at the center of her conception of ethics. In Rand's view, reason enables human beings to discover those principles and practices necessary to their sustenance as rational animals. Rand's ethical egoism proclaims the "virtue of selfishness," that it is morally right for individuals to pursue their own rational self-interests, voluntarily exchanging spiritual and material values.

Rand argues that the only social system consonant with this "trader principle" is laissez-faire capitalism, wherein individuals constitute free-market relationships. These relationships depend upon a structure of individual rights to life, liberty, property, and the pursuit of happiness. Rights can only be violated, Rand maintains, if an individual or group of individuals initiates force against others.

Rand supports a libertarian nonaggression principle that allows for the retaliatory use of force against those who initiate it. This principle informs Rand's defense of government as an institution with a monopoly on such retaliatory uses. In keeping with a classical liberal or libertarian conception of politics, Rand restricts government institutions to the role of defending individual rights, through the police, the armed forces, and the judiciary.

RAND'S LIFE AND WORK

That such a defender of capitalism and limited government was born and raised in Russia during the period in which the Bolsheviks came to power is ironic. Rand would publicly reject what she saw as the mysticism of Russia's religious culture and the collectivism and statism of its politics. But some scholars have argued that aspects of her approach to philosophical and social problems echo some of her early Russian influences. Born Alissa Zinovievna Rosenbaum in Saint Petersburg to a middle-class family, Rand witnessed a reign of Communist terror that led her to a virulent rejection of totalitarianism in all its forms. She was educated, however, during a cultural period known as the Russian Silver Age. Central to Silver Age thought, and to Rand's thought as well, is a rejection of conventional dichotomies: mind versus body, fact versus value, theory versus practice, and so forth. During this period, the influence of Friedrich Nietzsche (1844–1900) was also substantial; Nietzsche's writings had a significant effect on the young Rand's early thinking. Having graduated from the University of Leningrad in 1924, Rand had been exposed additionally to the teachings of prominent professors in both the dialectical idealist and Marxist traditions—those who emphasized, like Rand, the importance of grasping the full context of any problem as a prerequisite to its resolution.

In 1926 Rand immigrated to the United States, fully committed to pursuing a career as a writer. Her first novel, *We the Living* (1936), details communism's violent subjugation of social life. Rand said that this novel was as close to an autobiography as she would ever write. Its focus is on the individual versus the state, that is, how an oppressive state ultimately creates an "airtight" environment that must destroy individual human lives. The novel was later adapted by Italian filmmakers, who produced an unauthorized, though largely faithful, film version during World War II (1939–1945).

Rand also wrote a novella called *Anthem* (1938) that projects a primitive collectivist society of the future in which personal pronouns—and independent thinking—are prohibited. Despite that society's best efforts to stamp out individual identity, the protagonist (known as Equality 7-2521) rediscovers the "I" and, in so doing, heralds the rebirth of individualism.

In *The Fountainhead* (1943), Rand tells the story of architect Howard Roark, a trader, entrepreneur, and creator, who is a man of integrity struggling mightily against the collectivist culture and statist politics of the age. The novel enabled Rand to explore the soul of the individualist, those qualities of rationality, productiveness, independence, and authenticity that are essential to people's survival and flourishing. Adapted for the screen in 1949, directed by King Vidor (1894–1982), and starring Gary Cooper (1901–1961) as Roark, the novel was Rand's first major commercial success.

But it was in *Atlas Shrugged* (1957) that Rand first presented the philosophy of objectivism. With three parts named after the Aristotelian laws of logic—it was Aristotle (384–322 BCE) whom Rand credited as having had the greatest impact on her thought—the novel is an epic mystery, part science fiction, part fantasy. With the world on the verge of collapse, strangled by political interference with economic and social life, the productive "men of the mind" go on strike. By refusing to sanction their own victimization, and by withdrawing from the world, the strikers bring down the system of exploitation. It is only with their return to the world that a free society becomes possible.

In this novel, Rand presents her image of ideal men and women, people who are "new intellectuals," men and women of thought, who are also men and women of action. Such individuals reject the mind-body dichotomy and all of its insidious consequences—reason versus emotion, thought versus action, morality versus prudence—which fragment human existence.

This stand on the integrated individual also underlies much of the work that Rand wrote during her years as a public philosopher. Her nonfiction works, such as *The Virtue of Selfishness* (1964) and *Capitalism: The Unknown*

Ideal (1966), repudiate all modernist "false alternatives," including idealism versus materialism, rationalism versus empiricism, religious conservatism versus welfare liberalism, fascism versus communism, anarchism versus statism, and so forth. Though her political stance is libertarian, insofar as it rejects any government intervention in the economy or in people's personal lives, Rand was profoundly critical of contemporary libertarianism because many of its adherents focused on economics without regard for the larger philosophic and cultural context that would nourish the triumph of human freedom. In Rand's view, though human freedom entails free trade, it can only be fully achieved when people are free to think and to act on the basis of their own rational, independent judgment. This requires their psychological and moral liberation from exploitative ideologies that demand human sacrifice. As Rand argues in *For the New Intellectual* (1961), "*intellectual* freedom cannot exist without *political* freedom; political freedom cannot exist without *economic* freedom; *a free mind and a free market are corollaries*" (p. 25).

BIBLIOGRAPHY

PRIMARY WORKS

Rand, Ayn. 1943. *The Fountainhead.* Indianapolis, IN; New York: Bobbs-Merrill.

Rand, Ayn. 1946. *Anthem.* New York: New American Library.

Rand, Ayn. 1957. *Atlas Shrugged.* New York: Random House.

Rand, Ayn. 1959. *We the Living.* New York: Random House.

Rand, Ayn. 1961. *For the New Intellectual: The Philosophy of Ayn Rand.* New York: Random House.

Rand, Ayn. 1966. *Capitalism: The Unknown Ideal.* New York: New American Library.

Rand, Ayn, and Nathaniel Branden. 1964. *The Virtue of Selfishness, a New Concept of Egoism.* New York: New American Library.

SECONDARY WORKS

Binswanger, Harry, ed. 1986. *The Ayn Rand Lexicon: Objectivism from A to Z.* New York: New American Library.

Gladstein, Mimi Reisel. 1999. *The New Ayn Rand Companion.* Enl. 2nd ed. Westport, CT: Greenwood.

Peikoff, Leonard. 1991. *Objectivism: The Philosophy of Ayn Rand.* New York: Dutton.

Sciabarra, Chris Matthew. 1995. *Ayn Rand: The Russian Radical.* University Park: Pennsylvania State University Press.

Chris Matthew Sciabarra

OBJECTIVITY

Objectivity in the sciences, especially the social sciences, is paired implicitly or explicitly with its opposite, subjectivity. Less obvious yet commonplace pairings with the term *objectivity* are *partiality*, *relativity*, and *the arbitrary*. This entry deals primarily with objectivity in opposition to subjectivity. Subjectivity is associated with the modern concept of the self. The shift to the notion of the modern self occurred concurrently with the scientific revolution of the seventeenth century.

DESCARTES AND HIS CRITICS

René Descartes (1596–1650), who is considered the father of modern philosophy, claimed to be able to doubt systematically the existence of anything except the fact that he was doubting. Because doubt is a species of thought, he asserted, "*cogito ergo sum,*" which usually is translated as "I think therefore I am" or "I think therefore I exist." Even Descartes's body did not survive his systematic doubt; only his mind—"a thinking substance"—did. He argued that upon this rationally defended certainty rested all other claims regarding the existence of objects outside the mind. In that absolute divide the mindful inside became the subjective state and anything on which the mind exercised its cognitive power was an object. Thus, objectivity came to refer on the one hand to the subject's ability to consider or represent external objects without being influenced by subjective feelings, opinions, or prejudices and on the other hand to the description of those mind-independent objects. Despite Descartes's many detractors, modern philosophy made bringing subjective thought into concordance with objects of external reality its signal challenge.

Descartes's critics in his day and soon afterward could be divided into two camps: the idealists and the empiricists. Despite their differences, they held in common with Descartes the idea that the senses play a part in objectivity. The idealists described sensation variously as a species of thought but one that is unclear and indistinct, inferior, and unreliable or merely as confused thinking. Among those critics were Benedict Spinoza (1632–1677) and Gottfried Wilhelm Leibniz (1646–1716).

Conversely, British empiricists reinstated the sensory perception of objects in experience as the source of all reliable knowledge and the basis of objectivity. Thomas Hobbes (1588–1679) described thought as merely the faint remains left behind by sense impressions, and John Locke (1632–1704) argued that all ideas about the external world arise from sensation and reflection; if not for the sensory input made available by the senses in experience, the mind would be a blank tablet. For David Hume (1711–1776) thought was nothing but the faint copies of "impressions" left behind by the senses. In Hume's understanding, claims to objectivity are based not on reason but on habits of expectation that are developed from accumulated sense experiences.

CRITICAL PHILOSOPHY

The response to the early British empiricists can be seen as twofold: critical philosophy on one hand and the philosophy of science on the other hand. The origin of critical philosophy most commonly is identified with Immanuel Kant (1724–1804). Kant did not see objectivity-subjectivity as a proportionately inverse relation. They were distinct, and so one could not be considered an inferior form of the other or vice versa even though only together could they make objectivity possible.

Kant's concept of the object, however, was very subtle, and he used three different terms for it: *Ding, Gegenstand,* and *Objekte. Ding* referred to the metaphysical thing-hood, as in *ding an sich,* the unknowable thing in itself, making the question of objectivity moot. For even minimal experience to be possible, the contents of experience ("sensory data") must be ordered and limited in certain ways. These ways are not determined by what is given to the senses but by the synthetic activity of the faculty of intuition that possesses certain principles of form—space and time—that constitute the synthetic unity of sensory apperception. For what is given is, as Hume held, nothing but a flux of sensations and images. The synthesis of this manifold of sensory data is an a priori and necessary feature of experience and not empirical. This object of appearance that is experienced in this synthesis is the *Gegenstand*. The *Gegenstand,* this experience of appearance as object, is only a re-presentation. It is transformed into an object of recognition, thought, or knowledge by virtue of it being subsumed by the universal categories of understanding, and thereby it becomes an *objekt*. Kant described the *objekt* as "that in the concept—of the understanding—of which the manifold of a given intuition is united." (Kant [1787] 1965, p. B137). It is this *objekt* of knowledge about which the subject of the experience can make judgments that are true or false. By objectivity, then, Kant meant the object of a true judgment. However, this is not the judgment of an individual subject but that of a transcendental subject.

In the triumvirate of the great sociologists of the nineteenth and early twentieth century, Max Weber (1864–1920) is the most (neo-) Kantian of the three.

PHILOSOPHY OF SCIENCE

Whereas critical philosophy was a reaction to British empiricism, the philosophy of science was its progeny. Among the many strands in the history of the philosophy of science, positivism has been the most conspicuous. Auguste Comte (1798–1857), who invented the term *pos-itivism,* was an admirer of Hume and with Hume held that there is no objectivity beyond human objectivity. However, unlike Hume, he did not begin with an empiricist account of the contents of the mind but instead with a history of human development. According to that history, inquiry begins with theology, which is transformed into metaphysics, which is replaced by positive science.

For Comte objective science and observational science were near synonyms. Science, he held, should restrict itself to the observation of appearances and stop looking for or speculating about hidden "causes." He believed that hypotheses must be based only on phenomena that can be grasped by the cognitive and sensory faculties and be open to positive verification; this alone could guarantee objectivity. Comte saw the social world as unified with the physical and subject to laws that were identifiable by natural observation, hence sociology, the science of society. Émile Durkheim (1857–1917), the French sociologist and precursor of structuralism, considered his sociology to be in the positivist tradition and antipathetic to Kantian metaphysics, which nevertheless saturated his most important work, *The Elementary Forms of the Religious Life.*

In the twentieth century the prioritization of the sensory was channeled into logical positivism with its focus on language and logic. In logical positivism the objective world is considered a world not of things but of facts. Objectivity describes the capacity to express verifiable facts—the truth or falsity of which can be determined—in meaningful sentences. A meaningful sentence is seen as one that in some way can be related to a foundational sense experience or analytically true statements. Bertrand Russell (1872–1970) thought that he could derive the world from experience by means of symbolic logic. Rudolph Carnap (1891–1970) was determined to prove the world's verifiability, even though Ludwig Wittgenstein's (1889–1951) *Tractatus* clearly signaled the ultimate failure of that attempt. However, logical positivism persisted until it ran its course almost a decade before Carnap's death in 1970.

Georg W. F. Hegel (1770–1831) led Kantian insights even further from empiricism. For Hegel, objectivity was a matter of degree and an integral part of knowledge in which the subject is confronted with two types of objects: the external thing it desires to know and its own consciousness. In the *Phenomenology of Spirit* ([1807] 1977) Hegel's aim is to show that all claims to knowledge are best understood as historically and socioculturally situated. Empiricists hold that not only is objective knowledge—that is, knowledge that is independent of social practices—possible but that it is the only form of knowledge worthy of its name. The candidates that are proposed as being able to secure such knowledge, independent of any historically specific social practice, are "sense-certainty," "perception," and the "force of understanding," in that order. Hegel demonstrates that all three fail to provide, on their own terms, the kind of knowledge that their proponents' claim for them. In fact, under the "force of understanding" the reader is forced to acknowledge that it is our recognition of a thing that makes it real. But who is this subject that does the recognizing? While it is true that both Hegel and Kant presuppose a unified self or subject that is capable of knowing, for Kant such a self is a given, whereas for Hegel it is *we* who presuppose or construct this self. But how do we construct a self without recognizing it? This is where the "other" becomes necessary, for it is only the other who can recognize and construct one, and thereby makes one real. Moreover, the other must not take me to be a mere object of his or her self-consciousness but as a self-conscious knowing subject in my own right. It is at this point that Hegel uses his, by now famous, master-slave parable to begin the dialectical argument of why the objects of our knowledge are inter-subjectively and socioculturally constructed and known. Thus a reflective socialized and historicized self-consciousness works its way dialectically through reason and spirit, toward absolute knowledge in an ever-expanding and increasingly shared point of view that leads toward a universal point of view, which would at least theoretically serve as the standpoint from which pure objectivity, both moral and epistemological, would be possible.

Hegel was the first philosopher to historicize objectivity and chart its growth in the dialectic of history. Unlike Kant, he did not base objectivity on the abstract analysis of its conditions but on the human sociohistorical subject. Even so, Karl Marx (1818–1883) accused him of positing a method of coming to know, which lost its way in the clouds of ideas and ideologies. If human history is to be seen in its reality, Marx claimed, it is necessary to look at human labor and relations of production and domination. This is the road to objectivity in history. Paradoxically, Marx may be considered to be the closest to Hegel among the great sociologists, even if the object and the objective are viewed materially rather than ideally by Marx.

OBJECTIVITY IN TWENTIETH-CENTURY PHILOSOPHY

The influence of Kant's and Hegel's understandings of objectivity are vast and varied, sometimes reemerging under different labels. In the pragmatism of the American philosopher Charles Peirce (1839–1914), Kantianism, Hegelianism, and British empiricism are modified and compounded. Here experiences are more than what the senses report; they include anything that is forced upon one's acknowledgment, real or ideal, including sensory and cognitive surprises. Experiences are only perceptual judgments and therefore can be true or false but never

infallible; they are authoritative only because people are compelled to accept them, if not in the short run, then in the long run.

For Peirce, the so-called outer and inner worlds are only vicinities with no boundaries. Therefore, neither metaphysical theses nor so-called analytic statements are immune from empirical evidence; their truth, and hence their objectivity, depends on their ordinary observable consequences, not on their experiential origins. A correspondence theorist of truth would hold that a proposition or belief is true only if it corresponds to a mind-independent reality and as a corollary would insist that a hypothesis can be true even when its truth has no consequences for belief. A pragmatist would hold that such a view, insofar as it has no consequences, is spurious. Objectivity must be connected with the hypothesis that will survive the test of inquiry, experiment, experience, and life. As for truth, it is nothing more than the best inquiry can do.

Inquiry must begin against a background of beliefs held with or derived from a community, and therefore its objectivity can be fixed only by a community of inquirers committed to its truth, a truth that is capable of having consequences. In Peirce's theory of the Sign, the object is one of three correlates that constitute the Sign, the other two being the *representamen* and the *interpretant*. Objectivity is a significant act of which the interpretant (of which the interpreter is a subset) is an indispensable component.

The view of knowledge as human understanding that was initiated by Hegel's dialectic of self-consciousness admitted "interpretation" into the human sciences in a major way. If in Edmond Husserl's (1859–1938) early Cartesian writings there appeared aspects of sensory objects that an empiricist or positivist could have recognized as such, by the time he wrote his last work, *The Crisis of European Sciences and Transcendental Phenomenology*, consciousness had become his prime, if not sole, object of inquiry. In his phenomenology of human experience in the world Husserl saw no way of getting around the fact that consciousness is always someone's consciousness, and so he proposed that the process of investigating human capacities and faculties had to begin with the rigorous self-examination of one's self. Husserl called this the standpoint of transcendental solipsism. This methodological solipsism, however, leads one to the recognition of intersubjective communal grounding of the knowing activity as well as the ethical dimension of that intersubjectivity, how the "I" stands in the "we." He came to see objectivity as the achievement of intersubjective confirmation and acceptance in the "life-world," a pre-theoretically experienced world. The influence of Husserl's phenomenology in sociology can be seen mainly in the writings of Alfred Schutz (1899–1959), who combined that phenomenology with the interpretive sociology of Max Weber.

Among the philosophers considered thus far, objectivity was seen as possible because objects are re-cognizable. Heidegger, Dilthey, and later Gadamer became interested in understanding the unique and unrepeatable—and hence unre-cognizable—in history and culture. Wilhelm Dilthey (1833–1911) held fast to the possibility of scientific objectivity with the proviso that the method for achieving objectivity in the human sciences was different from that employed in the natural sciences. Both Weber and Dilthey had a strong influence on the interpretive anthropology of Clifford Geertz (1926–2006). Heidegger and Gadamer rejected the very notion of objectivity and the subject-object model as a vestige of Cartesianism. Hans-Georg Gadamer (1900–2002) saw understanding as an aesthetic experience of history and as being quite different from but no less valid than that of the natural sciences. Indeed, the natural sciences were no less value-free in his opinion and no less free of the art of interpretation.

NIETZSCHE AND FOUCAULT

Friedrich Nietzsche (1844–1900) spoke about objectivity in a manner that was consonant with all the historical-hermeneutic sciences. He believed that to understand objectivity as a "contemplation without interest" was nonsensical and absurd. "[L]et us be on guard," he cautioned:

> against the dangerous old fiction that posited a "pure, will-less, painless, timeless knowing subject"; let us be on guard against the snares of such contradictory concepts as "pure reason," "absolute spirit," "knowledge in itself." … There is only a perspective seeing, only a perspective "knowing"; and the more affects we allow to speak about a thing, the more eyes, different eyes, we can lend to the thing, the more complete will our "concept" of this thing, our "objectivity," be. But to eliminate the will altogether, to suspend each and every affect, supposing we were capable of this, what would that mean but to castrate the intellect. ([1887] 1967, p. 119)

In this view, if Hegel's hope for an absolute knowing that could synthesize a range of perspectives must come to naught, the rejection of objectivity by Heidegger and others who employ the hermeneutic method is premature:

> "Objectivity" [ought to be understood] as the ability to have one's For and Against under control and to disengage them, so that one knows how to employ a variety of perspectives and affective interpretations in the service of knowledge. ([1887] 1967, p. 119)

Nietzsche's subject is embodied and governed by desire and passion more than by thought, but it is still Cartesian in that it is the arbiter of being and value. Nietzsche's influence has been especially strong in the writings of Michel Foucault (1926–1984).

SEE ALSO *Empiricism; Geertz, Clifford; Hegel, Georg Wilhelm Friedrich; Hume, David; Intersubjectivity; Kant, Immanuel; Knowledge; Locke, John; Nietzsche, Friedrich; Objectivism; Phenomenology; Philosophy; Philosophy of Science; Positivism; Pragmatism; Science; Social Science; Social Science, Value Free; Subjectivity: Analysis; Subjectivity: Overview; Weber, Max*

BIBLIOGRAPHY

Descartes, Rene. [1641] 1998. *Discourse on Method and Meditations on First Philosophy*. Indianapolis, IN: Hackett.

Dilthey, Wilhelm. [1862] 1996. *Hermeneutics and the Study of History*. Princeton, NJ: Princeton University Press.

Durkheim, Émile. [1895] 1958. *The Rules of the Sociological Method*. Glencoe, IL: Free Press.

Foucault, Michel. 1984. What Is Enlightenment. In *The Foucault Reader*, ed. Paul Rabinow, 32–50. New York: Pantheon.

Gadamer, Hans-Georg. 1975. *Truth and Method*. New York: Cross Road Press.

Geertz, Clifford. 1973. *The Interpretation of Culture*. New York: Harper Collins.

Hegel, Georg W. F. [1804] 1977. *The Phenomenology of Spirit*. Oxford: Clarendon Press.

Heidegger, Martin. [1927] 1962. *Being and Time*. San Francisco: Harper.

Hume, David. [1777] 1977. *An Inquiry Concerning Human Understanding*. Indianapolis, IN: Hackett.

Husserl, Edmund. [1931] 1977. *Cartesian Meditations*. The Hague: Martinus Nijhoff.

Kant, Immanuel. [1787] 1965. *The Critique of Pure Reason*. New York: St. Martin's.

Locke, John. [1689] 1996. *Essay Concerning Human Understanding*. Indianapolis, IN: Hackett.

Marx, Karl. *The German Ideology*. [1845] 1998. Amherst, NY: Prometheus Books.

Nietzsche, Friederich. [1887] 1967. *On the Genealogy of Morals*. New York: Random House.

Peirce, Charles S. 1992–1998. *The Essential Peirce: Selected Philosophical Writings*, ed. Carl Houseman. Bloomington: Indiana University Press.

Schutz, Alfred. (1970). *On Phenomenology and Social Relations*. Chicago: University of Chicago Press.

Weber, Max. ([1922] 1949) *The Methodology of Social Sciences*. Glencoe, IL: Free Press.

Winch, Peter. 1958. *The Idea of a Social Science and Its Relation to Philosophy*. London: Routledge and Kegan Paul.

E. Valentine Daniel

OBOTE, APOLLO MILTON
1925–2005

Apollo Milton Obote became the first prime minister of Uganda when the country gained independence in 1962. He later served as Uganda's president from 1966 to 1971 and 1980 to 1985. Obote was born in the village of Akokoro in northern Uganda, and received his education in his home district of Lango, at Gulu High School in Busoga, and at Makerere University College in Kampala. Over time, Obote developed into an astute and progressive Ugandan nationalist. Overthrown by Idi Amin (1925–2003) in a military coup in January 1971, Obote went into exile for eight years in Tanzania. But he returned to Uganda in 1980 and was elected for a second term as president, only to be overthrown in yet another coup staged by Ugandan military officers Tito Okello (1914–1996) and Bazilio Okello (1929–1990) in July 1985. Obote again went into exile, this time in Zambia, where he died in October 2005 at the age of eighty. Obote's demise brought to an end a long, colorful, and controversial political career spanning nearly half a century.

During his first term as Uganda's leader, Obote supported domestic nation-building, a concept he understood to include a quickened pace of progress toward national unity in the face of Uganda's deep social cleavages. Obote also called for economic and social transformation to uproot what he saw as the evil trinity of poverty, ignorance, and disease. On the international scene, Obote stood for East African cooperation, Pan-Africanism, and Uganda's active participation in world affairs.

Obote managed Uganda's external relations successfully, with the exception of a falling out with the United Kingdom in 1971 over Britain's sale of military arms to apartheid-era South Africa. During Obote's tenure, Uganda became not only a respected, albeit small, member of the community of nations, but the country also benefited from its membership in numerous international institutions and the acquisition of new trade and development partners. But in the domestic sphere, Obote's performance was mixed. He began well, with a remarkable record of achievements in education, health, agriculture, and the building of infrastructure. In general, government was managed on a pluralist or multiparty basis, with keen constitutional oversight, as evidenced by the numerous challenges to government actions that were presented to the courts.

The situation began to deteriorate with Obote's handling of the so-called Lost Counties of Bunyoro, a part of Uganda that Britain had handed over to the kingdom of Buganda at the beginning of its period of colonial rule.

Following a referendum, Obote returned these regions to Bunyoro, despite stiff opposition from Edward Mutesa (1924–1969), Uganda's ceremonial head of state and the *kabaka* of Buganda. After a furious confrontation that culminated in the Battle of Mengo in May 1966, Mutesa fled into exile in the United Kingdom. Triumphant, Obote moved forward with a radical overhaul of the country's political system. He abolished monarchism and federalism under his new republican constitution of 1967. Shortly thereafter, he declared what has been called his "move to the Left" by introducing socialist principles and work methods to guide the country's development. Finally, he declared that his party, the Uganda People's Congress (UPC), was the only legitimate party. In the course of this overhaul, however, Obote failed to give adequate attention to the army, and in the end it was his military commanders, first Idi Amin and later Tito Okello and Bazilio Okello, who booted him from power.

In his second term as president, Obote was an older and more mellowed politician, made perhaps wiser by the trials and vicissitudes of life in exile. He left behind the political excesses of his first term, including his commitment to socialism and to a one-party system, and he accepted the aid of the World Bank and the International Monetary Fund toward the recovery of Uganda's economy, which was left shattered after the reign of Idi Amin. By the time the two Okello generals staged yet another military coup, positive results had begun to be registered. Nevertheless, during Obote's second administration, the country's sharp social cleavages, particularly between the Bantu and Nilotic ethnicities and north/south regionalism, became politically relevant, and led to civil war.

Obote's management of this conflict has been a major blot on his record, not just for his inability to resolve it quickly but because of the large number of civilian deaths and the human rights abuses that occurred. Rendered helpless as an exile in Zambia, the blame for all of these issues was laid at his feet by his chief antagonist during the conflict, Yoweri Museveni, who became president of Uganda in 1986. Obote died just as he was shaping his response to these accusations. Obote is survived by his political party, the UPC, and a large body of supporters in Uganda and elsewhere, who will, no doubt, contribute to a more profound appreciation or critique of his long political career.

SEE ALSO *Amin, Idi; Kenyatta, Jomo; Museveni, Yoweri*

BIBLIOGRAPHY

Adoko, Akena. 1983. *From Obote to Obote*. New Delhi: Vikas.

Gingyera-Pinycwa, A. G. G. 1976. *Issues in Pre-Independence Politics in Uganda, 1952–62*. Nairobi, Kenya: East African Literature Bureau.

Gingyera-Pinycwa, A. G. G. 1978. *Apollo Milton Obote and His Times.* New York: NOK.

Ingham, Kenneth. 1994. *Obote: A Political Biography.* London and New York: Routledge.

Karugire, Samwiri Rubaraza. 1996. *The Roots of Instability in Uganda.* 2nd ed. Kampala, Uganda: Fountain Publishers.

Milton Obote: My Story. 2005. Obote Focus (a series of articles by various authors.) *Daily Monitor.* http://www.monitor.co.ug/specialincludes/ugprsd/obote/index.php.

Museveni, Yoweri Kaguta. 1997. *Sowing the Mustard Seed: The Struggle for Freedom and Democracy in Uganda.* Ed. Elizabeth Kanyogonya and Kevin Shillington. London: Macmillan.

Mutesa, Edward. 1967. *Desecration of My Kingdom.* London: Constable.

Mutibwa, Phares Mukasa. 1992. *Uganda since Independence: A Story of Unfulfilled Hopes.* Trenton, NJ: Africa World Press.

Obote, Apollo Milton. 1969. *The Common Man's Charter.* Kampala, Uganda: Consolidated Printers.

A. G. G. Gingyera-Pinycwa

OBSCENITY

Throughout history, people have represented sexuality in literature and art. However, pornography, in the early twenty-first century use of the term, did not emerge as a mass industry until the late 1950s. It eventually broke into mainstream distribution outlets and had grown to a business estimated at $12 billion a year in the United States by the end of the twentieth century, with increasing acceptance in U.S. culture. While still proscribed by law in a variety of ways and considered unacceptable in many circles, pornography is used more openly, while at the same time pop culture has adopted many of the conventions of pornography.

State and federal laws in the United States uses the term *obscenity*, rather than *pornography*, to describe sexual material that can be regulated. Obscenity prosecutions in the United States were infrequent and uncontroversial in the eighteenth century and early nineteenth century. After the Civil War, obscenity became a more public issue, largely due to the work of Anthony Comstock and other conservative religious crusaders. Obscenity became increasingly politicized in the United States in the twentieth century, particularly when literary works such as James Joyce's *Ulysses* (1922) were kept out of the country.

In 1957 in *Roth v. United States*, the Supreme Court first stated clearly that obscenity was outside the protection of the First Amendment, kicking off a string of cases in which the Court wrestled with how to define and regulate obscenity. In the 1973 *Miller v. California* decision, the Supreme Court established a three-part test for iden-

tifying obscenity, defining it as: (1) material that appeals to the prurient interest; (2) material that portrays sexual conduct in a patently offensive way; and (3) material that does not have serious literary, artistic, political, or scientific value. Further the Court identified contemporary community standards as the measure of evaluation. In decisions since *Miller*, the Supreme Court has upheld the constitutionality of zoning ordinances that restrict adult theaters and the use of racketeering statutes against businesses that sell obscene materials.

A separate category is child pornography, which comprises material that is either made using children or, in the digital age, made through the use of technology that makes it appear that the sexual activity portrayed involves children. The former is illegal (under *New York v. Ferber*, 1982); the status of the latter remains uncertain (see *Ashcroft v. Free Speech Coalition* [2002], in which the Court ruled that the section of the Child Pornography Prevention Act of 1996 that banned "virtual" child pornography was unconstitutional, calling it too broad in its scope).

Indecency, a term from radio and television broadcasting, defines a broader category that can be regulated. Indecent material is defined as language or material that, in context, depicts or describes sexual or excretory organs or activities in terms patently offensive as measured by contemporary community standards for the broadcast medium. The Federal Communications Commission administers indecency regulations.

Obscenity laws tend to be enforced in places where there is political support from citizens. This prosecutorial discretion means that material for sale openly in one jurisdiction may not be available in another. However, the availability of mail-order and computer pornography means that graphic, sexually explicit material can now be obtained easily anywhere in the United States. As the enforcement of legal prohibitions has lessened, a formerly underground industry with ties to organized crime has become a routine business with its own trade magazine, *Adult Video News*.

The term used most often in the public debate over sexually explicit material is *pornography*. This term is not rooted in law and has no commonly accepted definition. It is sometimes used as a generic term for commercially produced, sexually explicit books, magazines, movies, and Internet sites, with a distinction commonly made between soft-core material (nudity with limited sexual activity that does not include penetration) and hard-core material (graphic images of actual, not simulated, sexual activity including penetration). In other contexts the term is juxtaposed to *erotica*, defined as material that depicts sexual behavior with mutuality and respect. Pornography, in contrast, is material depicting sex involving domination or degradation. In laboratory studies of pornography's effects, three categories of pornography have been created: overtly violent, nonviolent but degrading, and sexually explicit but neither violent nor degrading.

Up until the 1970s, debates over pornography pitted liberal advocates of sexual freedom against conservative proponents of traditional sexual morality. That dynamic changed with the feminist critique of pornography, which emerged out of the larger struggle against sexual violence during the second wave of the women's movement in the 1960s. Feminist critics argued that discussions of the issue should focus not on questions of subjective sexual mores but on the harm to women. Pornography, they claimed, harmed all women, not just those used in pornographic material.

SEE ALSO *Censorship; Eroticism; Feminism; Profanity; Regulation; Sexuality; Supreme Court, U.S.; Violence*

BIBLIOGRAPHY

Dworkin, Andrea. 1981. *Pornography: Men Possessing Women.* New York: Perigee.

Lane, Frederick S. 2000. *Obscene Profits: The Entrepreneurs of Pornography in the Cyber Age.* New York: Routledge.

MacKinnon, Catharine A., and Andrea Dworkin. 1997. *In Harm's Way: The Pornography Civil Rights Hearings.* Cambridge, MA: Harvard University Press.

Strossen, Nadine. 1995. *Defending Pornography: Free Speech, Sex, and the Fight for Women's Rights.* New York: Scribner.

Robert Jensen

OBSERVATION, PARTICIPANT

Participant observation was introduced into anthropology at the beginning of the twentieth century when Bronislaw Malinowski (1884–1942) challenged the traditional paradigm of researchers conducting their studies from the veranda of a missionary station, by taking accounts from individuals rather than observing situations firsthand (Wax and Cassell 1979). He exhorted his colleagues to conduct fieldwork in situ, using participant observation. This technique was used by Malinowski in his studies of the Trobriand Islands (Malinowski 1922, 1935, 1948) "to grasp the native's point of view, his relation to life, to realize *his* vision of *his* world" (Malinowski 1922, p. 25, emphasis in original). Participant observation involved a field trip of one or two years, working in the native language as a member of the community being studied. Yet Malinowski's diary illustrates the difficulties in living up to his own demands as he had identified the ideal condi-

tions in which to conduct participant observation, while many problems needed to be resolved in the field (Malinowski 1967).

This observational approach was taken up by many anthropologists in classic studies including E. E. Evans-Pritchard (1902–1973) on the Nuer (1940) and Margaret Mead (1901–1978) in New Guinea (1977). Since the 1960s, anthropologists have "come home" to research their own societies using participant observation to examine urban settings. Harry Wolcott (1973, 1982) studying elementary schools perceived the principal as if he were the chief of a small tribe. Sociologists have taken a similar approach, studying schools (Ball 1981; Burgess 1983), factories (Pollert 1981; Beynon 1973), hospitals (Roth 1963), and new religious movements (Barker 1984, 1987; Zablocki 2001). In sociology, the work of Robert E. Park (1864–1944) and the Chicago school (Park 1952) used observational methods to study homeless men, street-corner gangs, and delinquents. Like the social anthropologists, the Chicago sociologists were strangers in their own society; they were involved but also detached. An observational approach was also used in community and locality studies in the United States and in Britain (Lynd and Lynd 1929, 1937; Warner and Lunt 1941, 1942; Warner 1959; Frankenberg 1957; Stacey 1960; Kluckhohn 1940).

The hallmarks of participant observation involve the researcher living in the community being studied, participating with individuals, observing and talking with them and interpreting the situations observed. The researcher is the main instrument of data collection, and shares in the lives and activities of those being studied by learning their language and interpreting their behavior (Becker 1958). Participant observation involves examining social behavior as it occurs rather than as it is reported through interviews and questionnaires.

Much has been written on the roles used by the participant observer (Adams and Preiss 1960; Bryman and Burgess 1999; Gans 1999). Participant observation can be formal or informal, concealed or revealed, and can involve complete participation and complete observation. These ideal types have been extended by R. Gold (1958) and Buford Junker (1960) into four major roles: (1) the complete participant, (2) the participant as observer, (3) the observer as participant, and (4) the complete observer.

The *complete participant* rarely reveals that research is being conducted because the researcher does not wish to influence the conduct of the activities being studied (Festinger et al. 1956; Humphreys 1970; Homan 1978). However, in these circumstances it is difficult for the participant observer to pose questions. This puts the researcher in the role of spy and makes it impossible to distinguish everyday roles from research roles. There is also a danger of "going native" by failing to question the activities observed (Murray 2003). Because this role infringes the principle of "informed consent," it is rarely used. The *participant as observer* role involves researcher and researched being aware that their relationship stems from research activity (Roy 1970). The researcher is involved in the social situation but also detached (Cohen 2000). This role is most frequently used. The *observer as participant* consists of the observer making the research purpose clear from the start of the investigation, but there is no intense relationship with those researched (Schatzman and Strauss 1973; Hong and Duff 2002). Finally, the *complete observer* role entirely removes the researcher from any form of participation so that the purposes of the research are not revealed. All four roles are used interchangeably and can assist or impede data collection.

The role of the participant observer is influenced by his or her membership characteristics (Delaney 1988). Age and gender will influence access to groups (Whyte 1955; Patrick 1973). Gender, ethnicity, and social class will also influence the perspective from which data are collected and in some instances access will be granted to, or withheld from, certain individuals in a social setting (Golde 1970; Wax 1979; Roberts 1981; Easterday et al. 1977; Liebow 1967; Bell 1999). Participant observation also involves selection (Arcury and Quandt 1999). Many participant observers use informants in their studies to take them into social situations, explain the context in which observations occur, and provide a perspective on the social world (Casagrande 1960; Gallmeier 1988). Participant observers need to consider how informants are selected as they influence data collection (Cohen 2000).

Participant observers record data and keep detailed field notes (Lofland 1971, 1974; Schatzman and Strauss 1973; Burgess 1982, 1984). Substantive field notes provide a record of the observations, conversations, and interviews that take place (Humphreys 1970). Methodological field notes illustrate the research process and record the personal impressions of the researcher (Geer 1964; Murray 2003), the impact of roles upon data, the selection of informants and relationships with them, and an analysis of research experience. Analytic field notes record concept development throughout an investigation and contribute to data analysis and the written narrative that constitutes the article or monograph produced (Glaser and Strauss 1967; Glaser 1978; Atkinson 1990; Ashworth 1995).

Several problems have been identified when conducting participant observation. Researchers must always remember that they are located in a social setting for the purposes of social science. They are involved and yet detached. This will help them to overcome the risks of overidentifying with other participants and "going native" in the setting by no longer questioning the actions and activities that are observed. The researcher needs to collect data that are reliable and valid (Shaffir and Stebbins 1991). Ethical problems are also frequently raised for the researcher through being placed in a marginal role with the result that stress and anxiety have to be managed throughout a study. This is frequently the case in covert studies where the researcher is unable to take notes or to use a range of other methods of research and often violates principles of informed consent, privacy, and confidentiality (Burgess 1989; Lauder 2003). The participant observer therefore needs to manage the study by being aware of the problems encountered in the research process by engaging in critical self-reflection of the research experience (Bourdieu 2003) and by bringing the study to a successful close.

SEE ALSO *Anthropology; Evans-Pritchard, E. E.; Malinowski, Bronislaw; Mead, Margaret*

BIBLIOGRAPHY

Adams, Richard N., and Jack J. Preiss, eds. 1960. *Human Organization Research: Field Relations and Techniques.* Homewood, IL: Dorsey.

Arcury, Thomas A., and Sara A. Quandt. 1999. Participant Recruitment for Qualitative Research: A Site-based Approach to Community Research in Complex Societies. *Human Organization* 58 (2): 128–132.

Ashworth, Peter D. 1995. The Meaning of "Participation" in Participant Observation. *Qualitative Health Research* 5 (3): 366–387.

Atkinson, Paul. 1990. *The Ethnographic Imagination: Textual Constructions of Reality.* London: Routledge.

Ball, Stephen. 1981. *Beachside Comprehensive: A Case Study of Secondary Schooling.* Cambridge, U.K.: Cambridge University Press.

Barker, Eileen. 1984. *The Making of a Moonie: Choice or Brainwashing?* Oxford: Blackwell.

Barker, Eileen. 1987. Brahmins Don't Eat Mushrooms: Participant Observation and the New Religions. *LSE Quarterly* 1 (2): 127–152.

Becker, Howard S. 1958. Problems of Inference and Proof in Participant Observation. *American Sociological Review* 23 (6): 652–660.

Bell, E. 1999. The Negotiation of a Working Role in Organisational Ethnography. *International Journal of Social Research Methodology* 2 (1): 17–37.

Beynon, Huw. 1973. *Working for Ford.* Harmondsworth, U.K.: Penguin.

Bourdieu, Pierre. 2003. Participant Objectivation. *Journal of the Royal Anthropological Institute* 9: 281–294.

Bryman, Alan, and Robert G. Burgess, eds. 1999. *Qualitative Research.* 4 vols. London: Sage.

Burgess, Robert G., ed. 1982. *Field Research: A Sourcebook and Field Manual.* London: Allen and Unwin.

Burgess, Robert G. 1983. *Experiencing Comprehensive Education: A Study of Bishop McGregor School.* London: Methuen.

Burgess, Robert G. 1984. *In the Field: An Introduction to Field Research*. London: Allen and Unwin.

Burgess, Robert G., ed. 1989. *The Ethics of Educational Research*. London: Falmer.

Cohen, Jeffrey H. 2000. Problems in the Field: Participant Observation and the Assumption of Neutrality. *Field Methods* 12 (4): 316–333.

Delaney, Carol. 1988. Participant Observation: The Razor's Edge. *Dialectical Anthropology* 13: 291–300.

Easterday, Lois, et al. 1977. The Making of a Female Researcher: Role Problems in Field Work. *Urban Life* 6 (3): 333–348.

Evans-Pritchard, E. E. 1940. *The Nuer: A Description of the Modes of Livelihood and Political Institutions of a Nilotic People*. Oxford: Oxford University Press.

Festinger, Leon, Henry W. Riecken, and Stanley Schachter. 1956. *When Prophecy Fails*. New York: Harper.

Frankenberg, Ronald. 1957. *Village on the Border: Social Study of Religion, Politics, and Football in a North Wales Community*. London: Cohen and West.

Gallmeier, Charles P. 1988. Methodological Issues in Qualitative Sport Research: Participant Observation among Hockey Players. *Sociological Spectrum* 8: 213–235.

Gans, Herbert J. 1999. Participant Observation in the Era of "Ethnography." *Journal of Contemporary Ethnography* 28 (5): 540–548.

Geer, Blanche. 1964. First Days in the Field. In *Sociologists at Work: Essays on the Craft of Social Research*, ed. Phillip Hammond, 322–344. New York: Basic Books.

Glaser, Barney G. 1978. *Theoretical Sensitivity: Advances in the Methodology of Grounded Theory*. Mill Valley, CA: Sociology Press.

Glaser, Barney G., and Anselm L. Strauss. 1967. *The Discovery of Grounded Theory: Strategies for Qualitative Research*. Chicago: Aldine.

Gold, R. 1958. Roles in Sociological Field Observation. *Social Forces* 36 (3): 217–223.

Golde, Peggy, ed. 1970. *Women in the Field: Anthropological Experiences*. Chicago: Aldine.

Homan, Roger. 1978. Interpersonal Communication in Pentecostal Meetings. *Sociological Review* 26 (3): 499–518.

Hong, Lawrence K., and Robert W. Duff. 2002. Modulated Participant-Observation: Managing the Dilemma of Distance in Field Research. *Field Methods* 14 (2): 190–196.

Humphreys, Laud. 1970. *The Tearoom Trade: Impersonal Sex in Public Places*. London: Duckworth.

Junker, Buford H. 1960. *Field Work: An Introduction to the Social Sciences*. Chicago: University of Chicago Press.

Kluckhohn, Florence R. 1940. The Participant Observer Technique in Small Communities. *American Journal of Sociology* 46 (3): 331–343.

Lauder, Matthew A. 2003. Covert Participant Observation of a Deviant Community: Justifying the Use of Deception. *Journal of Contemporary Religion* 18 (2): 185–196.

Liebow, Elliot. 1967. *Tally's Corner: A Study of Negro Streetcorner Men*. Boston: Little, Brown.

Lofland, John. 1971. *Analyzing Social Settings: A Guide to Qualitative Observation and Analysis*. New York: Wadsworth.

Lofland, John. 1974. Analyzing Qualitative Data: First Person Accounts. *American Sociologist* 9 (3): 101–111.

Lynd, Robert S., and Helen M. Lynd. 1929. *Middletown: A Study in Contemporary American Culture*. New York: Harcourt.

Lynd, Robert S., and Helen M. Lynd. 1937. *Middletown in Transition: A Study in Cultural Conflicts*. New York: Harcourt.

Malinowski, Bronislaw. 1922. *Argonauts of the Western Pacific*. London: Routledge and Kegan Paul.

Malinowski, Bronislaw. 1935. *Coral Gardens and Their Magic: A Study of the Methods of Tilling the Soil and of Agricultural Rites in the Trobriand Islands*. 2 vols. London: Allen and Unwin.

Malinowski, Bronislaw. 1948. *Magic, Science, and Religion, and Other Essays*, ed. Robert Redfield. Boston: Beacon.

Malinowski, Bronislaw. 1967. *A Diary in the Strict Sense of the Term*. Trans. Norbert Guterman. London: Routledge and Kegan Paul.

Mead, Margaret. 1977. *Letters from the Field, 1925–1975*. New York: Harper.

Murray, Susan B. 2003. A Spy, a Shill, a Go-between, or a Sociologist: Unveiling the "Observer" in Participant Observer. *Qualitative Research* 3 (3): 377–395.

Park, Robert E. 1952. The City: Suggestions for the Investigation of Human Behaviour in the Urban Environment. In *Human Communities: The City and Human Ecology*, 13-51. Glencoe, IL: Free Press.

Patrick, James. 1973. *A Glasgow Gang Observed*. London: Eyre Methuen.

Pollert, Anna. 1981. *Girls, Wives, Factory Lives*. London: Macmillan.

Roberts, Helen, ed. 1981. *Doing Feminist Research*. London: Routledge and Kegan Paul.

Roth, Julius A. 1963. *Timetables: Structuring the Passage of Time in Hospital Treatment and Other Careers*. New York: Bobbs-Merrill.

Roy, Donald. 1970. The Study of Southern Labour Union Organising Campaigns. In *Pathways to Data: Field Methods for Studying Ongoing Social Organizations*, ed. Robert Habenstein, 216–244. Chicago: Aldine.

Schatzman, Leonard, and Anselm L. Strauss. 1973. *Field Research: Strategies for a Natural Sociology*. Englewood Cliffs, NJ: Prentice Hall.

Shaffir, William B., and Robert A. Stebbins, eds. 1991. *Experiencing Fieldwork: An Inside View of Qualitative Research*. Newbury Park, CA: Sage.

Stacey, Margaret. 1960. *Tradition and Change: A Study of Banbury*. Oxford: Oxford University Press.

Warner, W. Lloyd. 1959. *The Living and the Dead: A Study of the Symbolic Life of Americans*. New Haven, CT: Yale University Press.

Warner, W. Lloyd, and Paul S. Lunt. 1941. *The Social Life of a Modern Community*. New Haven, CT: Yale University Press.

Warner, W. Lloyd, and Paul S. Lunt. 1942. *The Status System of a Modern Community*. New Haven, CT: Yale University Press.

Wax, Rosalie H. 1979. Gender and Age in Fieldwork and Fieldwork Education: No Good Thing Is Done by Any Man Alone. *Social Problems* 26 (5): 509–522.

Whyte, William F. 1955. *Street Corner Society.* 2nd ed. Chicago: University of Chicago Press.

Wolcott, Harry. 1973. *The Man in the Principal's Office: An Ethnography.* New York: Holt.

Wolcott, Harry. 1982. Mirrors, Models, and Monitors: Educator Adaptations of the Ethnographic Innovation. In *Doing the Ethnography of Schooling: Educational Anthropology in Action,* ed. George Spindler, 68–95. New York: Holt.

Zablocki, Benjamin. 2001. Vulnerability and Objectivity in the Participant Observation of the Sacred. *Toward Reflexive Ethnography: Participating, Observing, Narrating* 9: 223–245.

Robert G. Burgess

OBSESSION

The term *obsession* is used quite liberally in current popular vernacular to indicate an intense interest in or preoccupation with a subject. Despite the prevalence of this connotation, psychologists generally use the term to indicate a more severe disturbance in cognition. As defined by the American Psychological Association's *Diagnostic and Statistical Manual of Mental Disorders,* obsessions are "recurrent and persistent thoughts, impulses, or images that are experienced … as intrusive and inappropriate and that cause marked anxiety or distress" (2004, p. 457). This definition indicates that obsessions are identified in part by their effect on the thoughts and feelings of afflicted individuals. That is, obsessions are cognitive in content and result in negative emotions. Furthermore, obsessions are involuntary in nature and may intrude into one's consciousness unexpectedly. Therefore, true obsessions exert a measure of control over the individual that nonpathological obsessive thoughts do not. Obsessions can have a profound impact on one's ability to form and nurture interpersonal relationships and can lead to conflict with friends, coworkers, and family.

Delineations between normative behavior and abnormal obsessions can be somewhat difficult to ascertain. Showing an enthusiastic interest in a particular activity, topic, or person need not reflect psychopathology. Likewise, persistent worries about realistic problems do not qualify as obsessions. However, when such a thought occurs at a very high rate and is associated with significant distress to oneself or others, it is more likely to be considered an obsession. Differentiating obsessions from normative behavior also requires that one consider the developmental stage of the individual. For example, although it is not uncommon for young children to develop intense preoccupations with or fears of specific objects or interests, such behavior would be more worrisome in older individuals. Landmark studies by researchers in the 1970s and 1980s demonstrated that many people experience intrusive thoughts in the absence of any psychological impairment (e.g., Rachman and de Silva 1978). Therefore, the presence of unwanted thoughts alone neither qualifies as obsession nor confers a risk factor for mental disorder. Furthermore, marked emotional distress must accompany the thoughts in order for them to be considered obsessions. These emotional reactions can range, though many people report feeling anxious when confronted with obsessive thoughts.

Among the psychiatric disorders most relevant to obsessions are obsessive-compulsive disorder (OCD), body dysmorphic disorder (BDD), eating disorders, and delusional disorder. Individuals with obsessive-compulsive disorder usually have both obsessions and behavioral symptoms called *compulsions,* though an obsession-only subtype exists as well. Compulsions are ritualistic actions performed to neutralize the anxiety and distress created by obsessions. For example, a patient with obsessions about contamination may exhibit compulsive hand washing, and a patient with obsessions about harm may exhibit compulsive checking behavior. Individuals with body dysmorphic disorder have persistent unwanted thoughts about a perceived defect in their physical appearance. Common obsessions include concerns about parts of one's body being misshapen, abnormally sized, or otherwise unattractive. Like obsessive-compulsive individuals, people with BDD also exhibit compulsions, such as repetitive grooming behavior. Researchers have linked obsessions to psychotic disorders such as schizophrenia and delusional disorder. A key feature of such disorders is that the afflicted individual suffers a severe impairment of his or her ability to experience rational thoughts and perceptions. If these irrational thoughts become intrusive and persistent, then one can be said to be experiencing obsessions. Eating disorders have been associated with obsessions, in that afflicted individuals often have persistent uncontrollable thoughts about food, dieting, body image, and exercise.

Obsessions can also affect one's propensity to pursue and maintain social relationships via maladaptive means, such as stalking. Stalking is defined as the deliberate following and harassing of others, and victims are most commonly former intimate partners or celebrities. Although many individuals experience a desire to maintain contact following the dissolution of an intimate relationship, those who do so by threatening means or who act on uncontrollable thoughts about the loved one may meet criteria for stalking behavior.

The treatment of obsessions differs based upon the specific disorder in which the obsessions are couched.

Psychotherapeutic techniques are often augmented by medication, as in the case of OCD and BDD, or may serve as a primary means of treatment, as in psychotic disorders. For individuals with OCD, cognitive-behavioral therapy has proven to be more effective than other forms of talk therapy. The primary technique used in this therapy as it pertains to OCD is called *exposure and response prevention.* In this method, individuals are exposed to stimuli that raise anxiety and provoke obsessions. They are instructed to tolerate this anxiety and distress without performing any neutralizing compulsive behaviors. Although patients may experience a greater deal of distress at the onset of treatment, over time obsessions wane as individuals learn that they can tolerate the anxiety without performing a compulsion. Ideally, the obsessions themselves lose potency and become less impairing. This technique is also used to treat BDD in that patients are exposed to their obsessive body concerns and prevented from performing behaviors that combat anxiety. For example, one might be prevented from applying makeup, checking mirrors, or skin-picking if these are repetitive and anxiety-reducing strategies used by the patient.

Much of the research on the biology of obsessions has been conducted by examining individuals with OCD. Basal ganglia abnormalities are the most commonly reported structural correlates of the disorder. More specifically, the head of the caudate nucleus and the orbital gyrus may play a prominent role in the dysfunction. These structures are deep below the cerebral cortex and are implicated in the regulation and coordination of movement. In terms of neurotransmitter dysfunction, both the serotonin and dopamine systems have been implicated in OCD. Pharmacological treatments for obsessions include drugs that target the serotonin system and increase the amount of this neurotransmitter available in the brain. Serotonin reuptake inhibitors, such as clomipramine or fluoxetine, have been associated with both symptom reduction and improved quality of life for patients with both OCD and body dysmorphic disorder (McDonough and Kennedy 2002; Phillips 2002). About 40 to 60 percent of obsessive-compulsive patients report significant improvement from using a drug of this type. Combining these drugs with antianxiety drugs or neuroleptics may also be beneficial for patients, depending upon the initial response to serotonin reuptake inhibitors.

BIBLIOGRAPHY

American Psychological Association. 2000. *Diagnostic and Statistical Manual of Mental Disorders.* 4th ed., Text Revision (*DSM*-IV-TR). Washington, DC: American Psychiatric Publishing.

McDonough, M., and N. Kennedy. 2002. Pharmacological Management of Obsessive-Compulsive Disorder: A Review for Clinicians. *Harvard Review of Psychiatry* 10 (3): 127–137.

Phillips, Katherine A. 2002. Treating Body Dysmorphic Disorder Using Medication. *Psychiatric Annals* 34(12): 945–953.

Rachman, Stanley, and Padmal de Silva. 1978. Abnormal and Normal Obsessions. *Behavior Research and Therapy* 16 (4): 233–248.

Amy Mariaskin

OBSESSIVE-COMPULSIVE DISORDER

Obsessive-compulsive disorder (OCD) is an anxiety disorder characterized by recurrent and intrusive obsessions and/or compulsions that are excessive or unreasonable, are time-consuming, and cause marked distress for the individual and/or significant impairment in global functioning. *Obsessions* are defined as recurrent and persistent thoughts, impulses, or images that are intrusive and inappropriate. *Compulsions* are defined as repetitive behaviors or mental acts that are performed in response to an obsession or according to rigid rules in order to prevent or reduce distress.

Common obsessions seen in individuals suffering from OCD are fear of contamination from germs, dirt, and environmental toxins; doubts about safety—having harmed the self or others; the need for symmetry, exactness, and order—having things "just right"; fear of making mistakes and acting socially inappropriate; intrusive sexual thoughts or urges; excessive religious or moral doubts—having "forbidden thoughts"; and the need to tell, ask, or confess. Common compulsions include washing and cleaning, checking, ordering and arranging, hoarding and collecting, repeating, touching, praying, counting, reassurance seeking, making mental lists, and retracing past memories.

People with OCD are sometimes overwhelmed by their disturbing obsessions, which seem uncontrollable and cause intense anxiety. To reduce the discomfort generated by the obsessions, an OCD sufferer avoids the feared situation and/or engages in compulsions repeatedly and ritualistically, which may relieve the discomfort but only temporarily. This pattern eventually develops into a vicious cycle of obsessions and a complicated web of compulsions. However, not all people with obsessions perform compulsions.

About 2 to 3 percent of Americans, as many as seven million people, have OCD at some point in their lives. OCD can happen to anyone and usually begins in adolescence or early adulthood, but the disorder can also occur in children. Seventy-five percent of those who develop it show symptoms by age thirty. OCD starts earlier in boys than in girls. In adults, men and women are affected in equal numbers. In some cases, OCD begins after a trauma. Cases involving the interplay of OCD and post-traumatic stress disorder (PTSD) precipitated by trauma need to be treated by addressing both disorders. OCD may co-occur with conditions such as Tourette's syndrome, attention deficit disorder, other obsessive-compulsive spectrum disorders, and other anxiety disorders. Depression is often a secondary symptom to OCD.

Like many psychiatric disorders, OCD appears to result from a combination of biological and psychological factors. Some people may have a biological predisposition to experience anxiety. Research suggests that abnormal levels of the neurotransmitter serotonin may play a role in OCD. Brain scans of OCD sufferers have revealed abnormalities in the activity level of the orbital cortex, cingulated cortex, and caudate nucleus. OCD tends to develop when these biological factors are combined with a psychological vulnerability to anxiety. Some individuals may have learned that the world is a potentially dangerous place over which one has little control. This learned belief of danger is then overvalued and misattributed to one's lack of control over the environment.

OCD can have disabling effects on a sufferer's life. Individuals with severe cases of OCD may need hospitalization to treat their obsessions and compulsions. People with OCD must allow a great deal of extra time to complete seemingly routine tasks. Individuals may avoid going to certain places or engaging in certain activities due to their own embarrassment about their compulsive behavior. Furthermore, family members of individuals with OCD may feel anger, frustration, and/or guilt when the sufferer's compulsive behaviors interfere with family functioning. OCD is a chronic illness that, like other psychiatric illnesses, has periods of exacerbation followed by periods of relative improvements, though a completely symptom-free interval is generally unusual. With appropriate treatment, most sufferers show considerable improvements.

Exposure and response prevention (ERP), a form of cognitive-behavioral therapy, is the most effective type of psychotherapy for OCD. Essentially, OCD sufferers are repeatedly exposed to those anxiety-provoking thoughts and situations that they fear, but are prevented from engaging in their compulsive rituals and avoidance behaviors. The basis for ERP allows an individual the opportunity to learn that simply tolerating the obsessions without avoidance or compulsions will gradually lead to reduction in anxiety and extinction of obsessive fears. In turn, the occurrence of obsessions is reduced, and the vicious cycle eventually dissipates. Intensive ERP alone is often effective enough for many individuals with OCD.

OCD treatment using certain medications may be beneficial, but generally is not as effective as intensive ERP. Medications considered for the treatment of OCD are usually antidepressants known as selective serotonin reuptake inhibitors (SSRIs), which are often effective without severe side effects. These SSRIs, which include fluvoxamine (Luvox), fluoxetine (Prozac), sertraline (Zoloft), and paroxetine (Paxil) increase the serotonin available in the brain. Clomipramine (Anafranil), a tricyclic antidepressant, is another Food and Drug Administration–approved OCD medication that is more effective than SSRIs but has unpleasant side effects. In more resistant cases of OCD, an SSRI and clomipramine may be combined. Finally, although psychotherapy using ERP is commonly integrated with the use of medication, this treatment combination has not been established as generally superior to intensive ERP alone.

BIBLIOGRAPHY

American Psychiatric Association. 1994. *Diagnostic and Statistical Manual of Mental Disorders (DSM-IV)*. 4th ed. Washington, DC: Author.

Gorbis, Eda. 1996. Effects of Trauma, on Assessment and Treatment of Obsessive Compulsive Disorder. Ph.D. diss., California Graduate Institute, Los Angeles, CA.

Kozak, Michael J., and Edna Foa. 1997. *Mastery of Obsessive Compulsive Disorder: Therapist Guide*. San Antonio, TX: Psychological Corp.

March, John S., Allen Frances, Daniel Carpenter, and David A. Kahn. 1997. The Expert Consensus Guideline Series: Treatment of Obsessive-Compulsive Disorder. *Journal of Clinical Psychiatry* 58 (4): 65–72.

Yip, Jenny C. 2005. An Integrated Approach for the Family Treatment of OCD in Children and Adolescents. Psy.D. diss., Argosy University, Washington, DC.

Eda Gorbis

OCCAM'S RAZOR

Occam's Razor (Ockham's Razor) is also known as the Law of Economy, the Law of Parsimony, or the Principle of Parsimony. It says "entities are not to be multiplied beyond necessity" (*Entia non sunt multiplicanda praeter necessitatem*). Another form of the principle is "plurality should not be posited without necessity" (*Pluralitas non est ponenda sine necessitate*).

The principle claims that to explain something, all competing explanations should be "shaved" away until only the simplest remains. When applied to the construction of theories explaining a phenomenon in the event that competing hypotheses provide contradictory explanations, the one that uses the least theoretical assumptions is probably the more accurate. If a detective is reconstructing the facts of a murder, the "theory" of the crime will be the one that best fits the facts and is usually the simplest hypothesis. This principle agrees with the philosophy of science's understanding that nature's character is simple.

The idea of parsimonious simplicity is found in limited form in the works of Aristotle. It was championed by William of Ockham (c. 1280–1349), after whom the term "Occam's Razor" was named. It was also used by Galileo Galilee (1564–1642) when discussing the data describing the orbits of the planets in support of the Copernican model.

Opponents of Occam's razor proposed anti-razors which say where fewer entities do not suffice, posit more. For example, in biblical textual analysis, if a scholar is faced with variant readings from different manuscripts the problem is which variant is the one closest to the original autograph of the biblical writer? The general rule, in the absence of evidence to the contrary, is to choose the more complicated reading. The reason is that a few scribes and others who copied the thousands of surviving manuscripts sometimes tried to "correct" an apparently unclear, complicated reading by "simplifying" it.

Occam's razor is used in philosophy, learning theory, econometrics, public policy choices and other disciplines. In public policy choices the principle is used by analysts to show that self-interest motivates voters and that the desire for reelection motives legislators, both of which are the simplest explanations for voter and legislator behavior.

Econometrics uses Occam's razor in labor economics, financial operations studies, resource allocations, and other areas as an aided method for discovery, problem solving, or learning. It is applied as the principle that what works well and is simple will probably work best in decisions concerning poverty funding for the developing world.

Currently Occam's razor is a characteristic of alife (artificial life) studies of ecological systems. Alife uses computers, simulations and other techniques in an information systems "bottom up" approach to study the ecology associated with living organisms and how they interact with their environment.

Some anti-razorists reject Occam's razor as inadequate to explain complicated phenomena. The facts of experience tell them that a complicated model may require a complicated explanation, while at other times simplicity is the most effective.

BIBLIOGRAPHY

Spade, Paul Vincent, ed. 1999. *The Cambridge Companion to Ockham.* Cambridge, U.K.: Cambridge University Press.

Zellner, Arnold. Hugo A. Keuzenkamp, and Michael McAleer, eds. 2001. *Simplicity, Inference and Modeling: Keeping it Sophisticatedly Simple.* Cambridge, U.K.: Cambridge University Press.

Andrew J. Waskey

OCCSCORE

SEE *Occupational Score Index (OCCSCORE).*

OCCULT, THE

Properly speaking, *the occult* refers to a body of traditions concerning religious practices preserved and practiced outside of organized religions. It includes alternative means of inducing religious ecstasy, contacting supernatural beings, healing, and foretelling the future. The word itself derives from a Latin term *occultus,* meaning something "covered over" or hidden from ordinary view. In this sense, it has long been used in the sciences—for example, to refer to symptoms not easy to detect, as in *occult carcinoma.* In the 1500s the term was first extended to abstract ideas that were difficult for the uneducated mind to grasp. By the mid-1600s, it had come to refer to esoteric practices, such as alchemy and astrology (the *occult philosophies*). The term *occult* soon came to imply a body of knowledge, including mastery of magical rituals, passed down in secret by a select group of masters.

In modern usage, the term is often linked to or even confused with the term *cult,* which is (as popularly understood) a group that practices a potentially dangerous religion. However, the terms are not etymologically related: *cult* is derived from the Latin verb *colere,* meaning to plant and care for crops (whence the related terms *cultivate* and *culture*). Nevertheless, even in ancient times occult religions were often defined as dangers to the state, and their followers liable to persecution.

For instance, when the Bacchanalia, a Greek mystery religion, was introduced into Italy in the second century BCE, the Roman Senate responded with an investigation. According to Livy's *History of Rome* (Book 39), they learned that its agenda was to entice large numbers of adolescents from noble families to engage in "secret and nocturnal rites" of promiscuous sex and debauchery, then use them to overthrow the state. Its secrecy was maintained, supposedly, by murdering those members whose loyalty was suspected, in some cases so discreetly that "not even the bodies could be found for burial." Similarly, in the second century CE, the early Christian church was persecuted because it was suspected of holding ritual sex orgies and baby sacrifices, motifs that have remained part of contemporary legends about "the occult" to this day.

In the seventeenth century, the rise of fraternal organizations such as the Rosicrucians and Freemasonry led to a widespread interest in esoteric mystical traditions among intellectuals. A series of pamphlets published in German from 1614 to 1616 described the "Rosicrucian Fraternity" as an occult organization, founded by one Christian Rosencreutz, who had allegedly obtained mysteries of nature and the gift of curing diseases from Arabian magi. The original pamphlets may have been a hoax; nevertheless, from this point on many groups emerged, offering mystical knowledge and access to superhuman powers to those willing to undergo initiation. The British historian Frances A. Yates (1899–1981) located a reference to such a group in a Scottish poem dated 1638:

> For what we do presage is not in grosse,
> For we be brethren of the Rosie Crosse;
> We have the Mason Word and second sight
> Things for to come we can foretell aright.

(YATES 1972, P. 211)

This is the earliest known reference to the fraternal organization of Freemasonry, which claims to maintain occult knowledge about the nature of God and the universe, deriving from the architects of Solomon's Temple in biblical times. Certainly one of its early claims was the ability to give "second sight," or the gift of divining the future. In any case, the Masonic movement that developed during the next century cautioned its initiates to keep its secrets with a solemn oath, inspiring many sinister legends about their true practices.

Such fraternal secret societies inspired many social panics from the 1600s onward, but they also influenced the revival of esoteric magic in the nineteenth century. Spiritualism, originally based on rural folk practices of divination, became a popular phenomenon among intellectuals in the mid-nineteenth century. This practice, along with the rituals of Masonry, influenced the turn-of-the-century Order of the Golden Dawn. This group, a loose association of academics and seekers in Great Britain, attempted to reconstruct the practices of earlier ceremonial magicians from scattered historical records and details of Masonic and Rosicrucian rituals. The Golden Dawn participants, who included A. E. Waite (1857–1942), the Irish poet William Butler Yeats (1865–1939), and, for a time, Aleister Crowley (1875–1947), published widely on their occult theories.

A generation later, Gerald Gardner (1884–1964) and a circle of friends created a system of rituals based on these speculations that led to the neo-pagan revival, one of the most rapidly growing new religions in the Anglo-American world. A growing body of self-help books published by modern pagans has reintroduced a general public to practices based on these and other occult traditions.

Those aligned with traditional religion have always been antagonistic to such practices, seeing them as spiritually dangerous or even satanic in nature. Naive contact with such powers, many fundamentalist Christian authors warn, could expose practitioners to demonic influence, and could even make them susceptible to cult leaders. However, there is little evidence that the rituals taught by occult movements are, in fact, much different from similar ones preserved in folklore or by non-Western religions. Anthropologist Sabina Magliocco, herself an initiate into a neo-pagan religion, has argued that the occult is a powerful, affirming means of reclaiming "traditional ways of knowing that privilege the imagination" (2004, p. 97). Occult ritual allows the participants to generate and control extraordinary experiences, she concludes.

The occult can best be characterized as a tendency within religious expression that values individual spiritual experience over theology or self-discipline. Often based on a nativistic perspective, it expresses a longing to rediscover an imaginative realm with which contemporary religion has lost touch. The result permits the worshiper to participate directly in the mythological world. Occult practices appeal to those who are bored by the tendency of mainstream religions to channel religious power vicariously through trained specialists. Paradoxically, religions often revive themselves by incorporating elements of the occult into their own practice. In fact, many contemporary charismatic factions within Christianity promote an experience-centered faith that contains elements of divination, spirit possession, and magical healing similar to those taught within occult movements.

SEE ALSO *Magic*

BIBLIOGRAPHY

Ellis, Bill. 2003. *Lucifer Ascending: The Occult in Folklore and Popular Culture.* Lexington: University of Kentucky Press.

Kerr, Howard, and Charles L. Crow, eds. 1983. *The Occult in America: New Historical Perspectives.* Urbana: University of Illinois Press.

King, Francis. 1989. *Modern Ritual Magic: The Rise of Western Occultism.* Rev. ed. New York: Avery.

Magliocco, Sabina. 2004. *Witching Culture: Folklore and Neo-Paganism in America.* Philadelphia: University of Pennsylvania Press.

Owen, Alex. 1990. *The Darkened Room: Women, Power, and Spiritualism in Late Victorian England.* Philadelphia: University of Pennsylvania Press.

Yates, Frances A. 1972. *The Rosicrucian Enlightenment.* Boston: Routledge and Kegan Paul.

Bill Ellis

OCCUPATIONAL HAZARDS

Dictionaries as well as legislation generally define occupational hazards in terms of risks that are inherent in certain types of employment or workplaces such as deep-sea diving, cutting timber, mining, high-rise steel construction, high-voltage electrical wiring, using pesticides, and painting bridges. From the perspective of the social sciences, however, occupational hazards are less an issue of inherent dangers in certain types of work than an issue of the dangers that arise from (1) structural conditions, in particular power imbalances between employees and bosses (2) poor working conditions, such as double shifts or overcrowding (3) inappropriate demands made on unsuitable employees, such as children (4) insufficient monitoring of workplace safety.

Work-related risks and illnesses throughout time have been shaped by the forces that shape the nature of work itself. Changing modes of production, shifting economic powers, and demographic changes in the workforce all impact who is injured at work, how and why the injury occurred, and to what extent—if at all—the injury is recognized and acknowledged.

Considering that almost all humans work either inside or outside the home for most of their lives, the field of occupational health has received relatively little attention from the medical profession. Occupational physician Michael Gochfeld notes that medical writers as early as Hippocrates (c. 460–c. 370 BCE) and Galen (c. 129–216 CE) sporadically acknowledged links between health problems and specific occupations (typically mining). The emerging public health movement in the mid-nineteenth century addressed the overall unhealthy living and working conditions of immigrants and slum dwellers. It was only with the rise of labor unions in the early twentieth century that significant legislative and medical notice has been given to occupational hazards.

Throughout the twentieth and into the twenty-first centuries, definitions of, responses to, and compensation for occupational injuries continue to be highly contentious. In the United States, for example, the Occupational Safety and Health Administration (OSHA), the federal agency charged with enforcing safety and health legislation, is considered by many to be underfunded and understaffed (employing less than 2,200 inspectors for over 7 million workplaces). According to industrial hygienist Lisa Cullen, OSHA is as likely to protect the "corporations responsible for maiming and sickening workers" as it is to protect the workers themselves.

In the United States, foreign-born workers increased 22 percent from 1996 to 2000, while fatal injuries among foreign-born workers increased by 43 percent, according to a 2004 analysis published in *Monthly Labor Review.* Oftentimes, the injuries sustained by foreign-born workers are not reported by employers who wish to avoid paying workers compensation benefits. Injuries may also not be reported by workers who are unaware of American policies concerning injuries on the job or fear deportation in the case that they are undocumented. Vernon Mogensen (2005) shows that pursuant to free-market globalization, "The outsourcing of jobs from high-wage to low-wage locales has the effect of transferring relatively safe jobs from developed countries, where safety standards and trade unions are well-established, to more dangerous locales like China, where bonded-, prison-, and child labor is abundant, but both safety and health enforcement and free-trade unions are virtually nonexistent."

As economies have shifted from industrial to post-industrial and from local to global, public and legislative notions of occupational hazards have not kept pace. A popular tendency to focus on dramatic occupational hazards such as coal mining or sky-scraper construction may obfuscate the many occupational settings that are permeated by illness-inducing substances (e.g., chemical pollutants) or job tasks that demand repetitive motions that can cause injury over time. The perils involved in long days spent looking at computer monitors and typing are not the stuff of cinema heroics, but they have become among the most common hazards of the post-industrial workplace. Injuries and illnesses resulting from work in the rapidly expanding service sector are good examples of occupational hazards that rarely merit financial compensation. Nurses' aids often suffer back injuries as a cumulative result of lifting patients, telemarketers experience stress and depression from the steady stream of insults from people they are assigned to call, and the growth of all-night businesses means that more workers are exposed to the hazards of disrupted sleep cycles. For the most part, these conditions are not recognized either via workers' compensation legislation or in the public eye as "official" occupational hazards.

The definition of what constitutes a "workplace" is far from uncontested. Anthropologist and historian Harriet Rosenberg argues that all three aspects of women's domestic labor—housework, motherwork, and wifework—contain potential risks ranging from heavy lifting to lack of sleep and marital rape, yet illness and injury arising from domestic labor are rarely compensated for or even recognized as injuries on the job.

SEE ALSO *Labor Law; Labor Union; Occupational Regulation; Occupational Safety; Time-and-a-Half; Wages, Compensating; Workplace Relations*

BIBLIOGRAPHY

Bellaby, Paul. 1999. *Sick from Work: The Body in Employment.* Aldershot, U.K.: Ashgate.

Cullen, Lisa. 2002. *A Job To Die For: Why So Many Americans are Killed, Injured or Made Ill at Work and What to Do about It.* Monroe, ME: Common Courage Press.

Gochfeld, Michael. 2005. A Chronologic History of Occupational Medicine. *Journal of Occupational and Environmental Medicine* 47(2): 96–114.

Loh, Katherine and Scott Richardson. 2004. Foreign-born Workers: Trends in Fatal Occupational Injuries, 1996–2001. *Monthly Labor Review* (June), 42–54.

Mogensen, Vernon. 2005. "Introduction." In Worker Safety Under Siege: Labor, Capital, and the Politics of Workplace Safety in a Deregulated World, ed. Vernon Mogensen, xiii–xxix. London: M. E. Sharpe.

Rosenberg, Harriet. 1984. The Home is the Workplace: Hazards, Stress, and Pollutants in the Household. In *Double Exposure: Women's Health Hazards on the Job and at Home*, ed. Wendy Chavkin. New York: Monthly Review Press, 219–245.

Susan Sered

OCCUPATIONAL REGULATION

Occupational regulation refers to state approved standards for either being listed as qualified or being licensed to perform certain tasks or jobs prescribed by the government. Standard forms of occupational regulation include licensure, certification, and regulation.

The most restrictive form of occupational regulation is *licensure.* The nonprofit Council on Licensure, Enforcement and Regulation (CLEAR), which is affiliated with the Council of State Governments, refers to licensing as the "right-to-practice," and under such laws it is illegal for a person to practice a profession without first meeting state standards (Brinegar and Schmitt 1992). Licensing standards usually involve detailed educational requirements, statements of good moral character, and a test.

A less restrictive form of occupational regulation is *certification,* in which states grant title (occupational "right-to-title") protection to persons meeting predetermined standards. Those without certification may perform the duties of the occupation, but may not use the title.

The least restrictive form of occupational regulation is *registration.* This form of regulation usually requires individuals to file their names, addresses, and qualifications with a government agency before practicing a specified occupation. The requirements may include posting a bond or filing a fee. The regulation of occupations in the United States and other nations falls under this continuum of less restrictive to highly restrictive forms of government regulation.

In the United States, occupational licensing is a fast-growing form of regulation. During the early 1950s, about 5 percent of the labor force was covered by licensing laws at the state level. By the 1960s, the number of persons working in licensed occupations had grown to more than 10 percent of the U.S workforce, with an even larger number if city and county licenses for occupations are included. The number and percentage of licensed occupations has continued to grow, and data from the Occupation and Employment Survey and the 2000 Census show that approximately 20 percent of the workforce in 2000 was employed in occupations licensed by states (Kleiner 2006).

In 2003 the Council of State Governments estimated that more than 800 occupations were licensed in at least one state, and more than 1,100 occupations were either licensed, certified, or registered. However, only about fifty occupations were licensed in all states. Universally licensed occupations range from doctors, dentists, lawyers, and teachers to barbers and cosmetologists. Occupations that are licensed in some states but not in others include loan officers, respiratory therapists, and electricians. However, cities and counties represent a fast-growing venue for occupational regulation. Local governments regulate many of the construction trades, such as plumbers and electricians, even though state or federal statutes often do not regulate them. There is large variation among the states in licensing occupations. For example, California licenses almost 180 occupations, whereas Kansas licenses fewer than fifty. There are similar variations in the percentage of the occupational workforce that is regulated.

During much of the nineteenth century, few U.S. states required government permission for individuals to work in an occupation. With urbanization and the increasing complexity of tasks, however, occupational affiliation became the dominant association for many workers. Evidence from the academic literature suggests that the quality of services improved when lower-quality purveyors were excluded. Demand for services grew as consumers perceived the regulated services to be of higher quality. Over time, as members of the occupation came to dominate many of the licensing boards, entry requirements tightened and mobility between states and countries was restricted. Prices for licensed services increased and earnings for practitioners became higher than for comparable occupations with similar levels of human capital investment and experience. For consumers who could afford licensed services, quality rose. One of the major controversies in the area of occupational regulation is whether such regulations in fact raise quality or simply restrict competition.

In most cases, the available empirical evidence shows that licensing causes a rise in prices, but its impact on the quality of services rendered is unclear (Cox and Foster 1990). For practitioners of the service, licensing leads to a rise in wages. For example, switching to a licensed occupation from an unregulated occupation raises wages 17 percent in comparison to switching to an unregulated occupation from a regulated one. On average, working in a regulated occupation raises the wage premium approximately 10 to 12 percent relative to similar unregulated occupations. This value is at the lower end of the range of the union wage impact in the United States. Working in the same occupation in a state that requires licensing raises wages 4 percent relative to an unregulated state. Statistical estimates of the costs of licensing show that this form of occupational regulation reduces output in the United States by less than one-tenth of 1 percent of total consumption expenditures annually. Some argue that this is a small price for the potentially enhanced quality that is generated by occupational regulation.

Regulation of occupations in the European Union focuses on restrictions following entry into an occupation to a greater extent than occurs in the United States (Garoupa 2004). In the European Union, occupational regulations generally limit prices and regulate the structure of organizations of licensed workers. Most occupational entry restrictions also regulate the number of individuals who are admitted to schools that train workers for the regulated specialty. The results from statistical estimates show that licensing has a smaller impact on earnings in the European Union than in the United States. Unlike the United States, nations such as Germany are deregulating many of their previously licensed occupations, suggesting that the practice of occupational regulation can be reversed in response to public pressure.

BIBLIOGRAPHY

Brinegar, Pamela L., and Kara L. Schmitt. 1992. State Occupational and Professional Licensure. In *The Book of the States, 1992–1993*, 567–580. Lexington, KY: Council of State Governments.

Cox, Carolyn, and Susan Foster. 1990. The Costs and Benefits of Occupational Regulation. Bureau of Economics, Federal Trade Commission. Washington, DC: Government Printing Office.

Garoupa, Nuno. 2004. Regulation of Professions in the US and Europe: A Comparative Analysis. Paper presented at the American Law and Economics Association Fourteenth Annual Meetings, August.

Kleiner, Morris. 2006. *Licensing Occupations: Ensuring Quality or Restricting Competition?* Kalamazoo, MI: Upjohn Institute for Employment Research.

Morris Kleiner

OCCUPATIONAL SAFETY

Highly publicized job accidents, such as mining disasters, create the impression that occupational safety is a haphazard enterprise. Although accidents are random events, occupational safety levels are governed by a variety of social institutions and display systematic patterns across time and across different types of industry. Thus, the probability of occupational injuries and illnesses varies in a quite predictable manner even though the occurrence of particular accidents usually cannot be foreseen.

From the standpoint of economic analysis, firms provide specific safety levels by striking a balance between the costs to the firm of accidents and the costs of providing greater safety. The differences across industries in the costs of providing safety account for the higher risk levels of industries such as mining and construction, where eliminating risks is very costly, as compared to safer industries such as banking. Firms will incur these costs to promote safety if they have a financial incentive to do so. The chief sources of the financial incentives that lead firms to provide a safe workplace are wage premiums that they pay to workers on risky jobs, workers' compensation costs, and government health and safety regulations.

The economic analysis of occupational safety dates back to Adam Smith. Workers require higher pay, or compensating differentials, to be attracted to dangerous jobs. This wage premium usually is not in the form of hazard pay but rather is part of the higher overall pay package required to attract workers to risky jobs. In the United States, these wage premiums totaled $229 billion in 2000, or about 5 percent of all worker wages. Studies have documented similar but lower wage premiums throughout the world in countries ranging from India and Taiwan to the United Kingdom.

A useful shorthand puts these wage premiums in perspective: Suppose that the average worker faces an annual occupational fatality risk of 1 in 20,000 and receives about $350 for facing that risk. Put somewhat differently, if there were 20,000 workers facing a comparable risk, there would be one expected death in the group and $7 million paid in wage compensation for risk. Thus, the total wage compensation per expected death is $7 million, which economists often refer to as the value of statistical life (VSL). This $7 million figure is the average VSL estimate based on U.S. studies.

Estimates of the VSL only pertain to the tradeoffs workers make between very small job risks and the wages they require to accept these risks. They do not imply that a worker would be willing to accept certain death for a payment of $7 million, or that a worker would have the resources to pay that amount to avoid the certainty of a job-related death.

Although the incentives that wage premiums for risk provide are often substantial, market forces may not be adequate. Market incentives will fall short if inadequate knowledge of health and safety risks impedes worker decisions. Market incentives also do not capture society's broad altruistic concerns with worker health. Finally, wage premiums alone do not address the insurance needs of injured workers.

As a result, several modes of government intervention have been developed to address these shortcomings. Since the early twentieth century, states have instituted workers' compensation plans that compensate workers for accidents irrespective of where fault lies. The workers' compensation premiums that firms pay totaled $32.9 billion in 2003. These costs create powerful incentives for safety, as firms with better safety records pay lower insurance premium rates. This linkage of premiums to accident-prevention performance is particularly strong for large firms. Statistical estimates indicate that worker fatality rates would be one-third higher than they are now in the absence of these safety incentives.

Beginning with the passage of the Occupational Safety and Health Act of 1970, there has been direct federal regulation of workplace safety in the United States. These regulations have largely taken the form of standards that either specify safe workplace technologies or set maximum limits on exposures to dangerous chemicals. In addition, there are also important informational requirements, such as standards governing the proper communication of hazards associated with various chemicals. Firms are subject to inspection to ascertain if they are meeting regulatory standards, and those firms out of compliance incur fines. The magnitude of these financial penalties has been modest but rising over time, with total fines in fiscal year 2002 equaling $149 million. Most published studies indicate an effect on occupational injury rates on the order of a 2 to 4 percent reduction in the frequency of job injuries, but the increase in penalty levels since the 1990s may generate greater effects on safety.

The net effect of these different societal mechanisms to reduce risk has been a tremendous improvement in occupational safety. The workplace fatality rate has declined steadily over the past century. The workplace fatality risk was ten times greater in 1928 than in 2003, and the 2003 figure represents a 25 percent decline over the preceding decade, though some of that improvement may be due to changes in data reporting practices.

Two contributors to this long-term improvement in safety are noteworthy. First, the rise in societal wealth has increased the value workers and society more generally place on risk reduction. This increased wealth boosts the wage premiums firms must pay to attract workers to risky jobs, thus leading firms to introduce safer workplace conditions to reduce these costs. Greater societal wealth also increases public support for government regulation, which tends to be less pronounced in less advanced economies. Second, technological improvements over time have led to the production of safer technologies and improvements in safety equipment. Consequently, the costs of promoting safety have also declined so that firms can strike a balance between the costs of safety improvements and the costs of a risky workplace that leads to lower risk levels.

These differences in wealth and technologies also contribute to differences in safety levels across countries. International differences in workplace safety levels and regulatory regimes are to be expected given differences in societal wealth. Less advanced countries also may lack access to modern, safer technologies. However, increased affluence and economic progress in these developing countries is likely to increase their safety levels over time.

SEE ALSO *Occupational Hazards; Occupational Regulation; Risk; Workplace Relations*

BIBLIOGRAPHY

Insurance Information Institute. 2005. *Fact Book 2005.* New York: Author.

National Safety Council. 2004. *Injury Facts.* Itasca, IL: Author.

Smith, Adam. [1776] 1994. *The Wealth of Nations.* New York: Random House.

Viscusi, W. Kip. 1998. *Rational Risk Policy.* Oxford: Clarendon Press/Oxford University Press.

W. Kip Viscusi

OCCUPATIONAL SCORE INDEX (OCCSCORE)

The Occupational Score Index (OCCSCORE) is a measure of occupational reward that is available across decennial census datasets from 1850 to 2000. It was developed at the Minnesota Population Center as part of the

Integrated Public Use Microdata Series (IPUMS). The index is based on 1950 occupational classifications. As a first step in constructing the index, occupation codes for each decennial census dataset were re-categorized into the 1950 classification structure. This yielded one, common occupational classification across all decennial censuses. The IPUMS staff then quantified this common occupational structure using median total income for each occupation as reported in a 1956 *Special Report* published by the Census Bureau. The values for OCCSCORE are presented in hundreds of 1950 dollars. As an example, if median total income for economists was $20,000 in 1950, OCCSCORE would equal 20 for economists in all decennial census datasets.

OCCSCORE has two major uses. First, it provides a proxy for income in decennial censuses prior to 1960 that lack individual income data. Second, it provides a consistent measure with which to compare labor market outcomes from 1850 to 2000. However, OCCSCORE has four major shortcomings. First, it does not account for changes in occupational hierarchy across time. For each decennial census dataset, OCCSCORE conveys the rank ordering of occupations by income in 1950. However, the actual rank ordering of occupations likely changes over time. Second, the index does not account for variation in income within occupations. For example, in a given decennial census year, two individuals working in the same occupation have the same OCCSCORE value. However, based on items such as tenure and education, individuals with the same occupation may have very different incomes. Third, the index does not account for cost of living differences. An individual working as an economist in San Francisco, California, has the same OCCSCORE as an economist in Omaha, Nebraska. However, their respective purchasing powers are clearly different. Finally, although the IPUMS staff has taken great care when constructing OCCSCORE, re-categorizing occupations into the 1950 classification is problematic. New occupations evolve over time, and the U.S. Census has periodically changed the occupational classification system.

The primary alternative to the OCCSCORE is a set of prestige indices. Prestige indices are typically based on regression models where income and education are used to predict responses to an occupational prestige survey. The predicted values from these models are then used to predict the prestige of an occupation. Unlike prestige indices, OCCSCORE only measures the monetary return to occupations, not status or prestige. Overall, prestige scores have been more widely used in social sciences research, because occupation augmented by information on income and education is thought to be a better indicator of socioeconomic status than just the monetary return to occupation. One disadvantage of prestige indices is uncertainty about models' predictions of prestige.

Overall, OCCSCORE is a useful measure of occupational reward for research using censuses prior to 1960. For research focused only on 1960 or later, however, individual income measures are superior.

SEE ALSO *Socioeconomic Status*

BIBLIOGRAPHY

Ruggles, Steven, Matthew Sobek, Trent Alexander, et al. 2004. *Integrated Public Use Microdata Series: Version 3.0.* http://www.ipums.org. Minneapolis, MN: Minnesota Population Center.

Jason Dietrich

OCCUPATIONAL SEGREGATION

SEE *Crowding Hypothesis.*

OCCUPATIONAL STATUS

Occupational status is a fundamental measure of social standing that reflects the distribution of power, privilege, and prestige associated with positions in the occupational hierarchy, and is a key measure of socioeconomic status (SES). Occupational status is a popular measure of SES because it can be measured reliably in surveys, is more stable over time than economic measures of SES such as individual income, and better reflects social position over the life course than educational attainment, which typically is achieved in early adulthood (Hauser and Warren 1997). Occupations are defined in the United States by the Bureau of the Census, forming a classification of several hundred categories that is modified each decade to incorporate labor market changes. Various measures of occupational status generally are linked to these census occupation categories.

EMPIRICAL MEASURES OF OCCUPATIONAL STATUS

Key empirical measures of occupational status include occupational prestige scales and socioeconomic indices. Occupational prestige measures are generated from the rankings of occupations by survey respondents on the basis of their relative "prestige" or "social standing" and have shown high consensus among individuals from different social positions, across societal contexts, and over time (Blau and Duncan 1967; Hodge, Siegel, and Rossi

1964; Treiman 1977). An early occupational prestige scale was based on Cecil North and Paul Hatt's National Opinion Research Center (NORC) survey in 1947, but it covered only ninety occupational titles. In 1971, Paul Siegel constructed a prestige scale for the entire U.S. Census occupational classification in 1960, based on surveys conducted between 1963 and 1965 by Peter Rossi and Robert Hodge. An international occupational prestige scale was developed by Donald Treiman (1977) several years later. The U.S. General Social Survey (GSS) used the Siegel prestige scale until a 1989 GSS module designed by Robert Hodge, Judith Treas, and Keiko Nakao was used to construct a new prestige scale for the 1980 census occupational classification (Nakao and Treas 1994).

The Duncan Socioeconomic Index (SEI) and later iterations of the SEI are in greater use today than occupational prestige scales because they are more highly correlated with other variables of interest and better describe socioeconomic differences between occupations (Featherman, Jones, and Hauser 1975). The initial SEI was constructed by Otis Dudley Duncan by regressing the percentage of "good" or "excellent" prestige ratings for forty-five of the 1947 NORC prestige scores on age-adjusted percentages of men in the occupation who completed high school or more and who reported at least $3,500 in 1949 income. Resulting regression coefficients were used as weights to construct an SEI score for each U.S. census-defined 1950 occupation category, with scores ranging from about 2 (ship- and boat-building laborers) to 96 (dentists). Updates to the original Duncan SEI have been constructed for the 1960 (Blau and Duncan 1967), 1970 (Stevens and Featherman 1981), 1980 (Nakao and Treas 1994), and 1990 census occupation categories (Hauser and Warren 1997), and a Standard International Socioeconomic Index of Occupational Status (ISEI) has been developed (Ganzeboom, de Graaf, and Treiman 1992).

Empirical research has shown that in general, race/ethnicity is a stronger determinant of occupational status than gender. Traditional women's jobs have a lower average status than male-dominated jobs, but few women work in extremely low-prestige jobs, resulting in similar average prestige scores for men and women (Acker 1980). By contrast, while some Asian Americans meet or exceed average white SEI scores, African Americans, Hispanics, and American Indians have significantly and persistently lower occupational status (Hirschman and Snipp 1999). Nonetheless, while men and women tend to be found in occupations throughout the occupational status hierarchy, there is more segregation between the occupations done by men and women than between the occupations done by blacks and nonblacks in the United States (Treiman and Hartmann 1981).

CRITIQUE OF OCCUPATIONAL STATUS SCALES

The use of continuous scales of occupational status to measure social standing has been criticized by social-class theorists, who classify individuals or households on the basis of their membership in one of a small number of discrete and broad social classes. The Marxist tradition divides individuals into classes based on their ownership of productive assets in the economic sphere, while Weberian approaches also incorporate dimensions of social honor within status groups and other aspects of lived experience outside the productive sphere, rather than viewing social standing as a product of one's attained education and income. Social-class theorists from across these traditions argue that continuous occupational status scales do not capture the crucial sources of power and conflict that divide social classes (e.g., owners of factories and workers in those factories), or the sense of shared class membership that could lead to collective action (Parkin 1971; Poulantzas 1975). Modern social-class typologies such as Eric Olin Wright's (1977) neo-Marxist model are used to assess how membership in a particular social class, determined on the basis of ownership of productive assets, authority on the job, and skill and training assets, influences key social outcomes such as earnings, attitudes, and life chances. However, recent research maintains that continuous and hierarchical measures of occupational status may be better predictors of these key outcomes than broad social classes in capitalist countries such as the United States and Japan (Schooler and Schoenback 1994). A further addition to the debate are the "new class maps" created by Grusky and his colleagues (Grusky and Sorenson 1998; Weeden and Grusky 2005) that employ disaggregated occupational groupings as a measure of social position preferable to either the traditional "big social classes" or continuous occupational status scales.

SEE ALSO *Blue Collar and White Collar; Employment, White Collar; Occupational Score Index (OCCSCORE); Socioeconomic Status*

BIBLIOGRAPHY

Acker, Joan R. 1980. Women and Stratification: A Review of the Literature. *Contemporary Sociology* 9: 25–39.

Blau, Peter M., and Otis Dudley Duncan. 1967. *The American Occupational Structure.* New York: Wiley.

Featherman, David L., F. Lancaster Jones, and Robert M. Hauser. 1975. Assumptions of Social Mobility Research in the U.S.: The Case of Occupational Status. *Social Science Research* 4: 329–360.

Ganzeboom, Harry B., Paul M. de Graaf, and Donald J. Treiman. 1992. A Standard International Socio-Economic Index of Occupational Status. *Social Science Research* 21: 1–56.

Grusky, David B., and Jesper B. Sorenson. 1998. Can Class Analysis be Salvaged? *American Journal of Sociology* 103: 1187–1234.

Hauser, Robert M., and John Robert Warren. 1997. Socioeconomic Indexes for Occupations: A Review, Update, and Critique. *Sociological Methodology* 27: 177–298.

Hirschman, Charles, and C. Matthew Snipp. 1999. The State of the American Dream: Race and Ethnic Socioeconomic Inequality in the United States, 1970–1990. In *A Nation Divided: Diversity, Inequality, and Community in American Society*, eds. Phyllis Moen, Donna Dempster-McClain, and Henry A. Walker, 89–107. Ithaca, NY: Cornell University Press.

Hodge, Robert W., Paul M. Siegel, and Peter H. Rossi. 1964. Occupational Prestige in the United States, 1925–1963. *American Journal of Sociology* 70: 286–302.

Nakao, Keiko, and Judith Treas. 1994. Updating Occupational Prestige and Socioeconomic Scores: How the New Measures Measure Up. *Sociological Methodology* 24: 1–72.

Parkin, Frank. 1971. *Class Inequality and Political Order: Social Stratification in Capitalist and Communist Societies*. New York: Praeger.

Poulantzas, Nicos. 1975. *Classes in Contemporary Capitalism*. London: New Left Books/Verso.

Schooler, Carmi, and Carrie Schoenback. 1994. Social Class, Occupational Status, Occupational Self-Direction, and Job Income: A Cross-National Examination. *Sociological Forum* 9: 431–458.

Stevens, Gillian, and David L. Featherman. 1981. A Revised Socioeconomic Index of Occupational Status. *Social Science Research* 10: 364–393.

Treiman, Donald J. 1977. *Occupational Prestige in Comparative Perspective*. New York: Academic Press.

Treiman, Donald J., and Heidi I. Hartmann. 1981. *Women, Work, and Wages: Equal Pay for Jobs of Equal Value*. Washington, DC: National Academies Press.

Weeden, Kim A., and David B. Grusky. 2005. The Case for a New Class Map. *American Journal of Sociology* 111 (1): 141–212.

Wright, Eric Olin, and Luca Perrone. 1977. Marxist Class Categories and Income Inequality. *American Sociological Review* 42 (1): 32–55.

Sarah A. Burgard

OEDIPUS COMPLEX

Sophocles, one of the great Greek playwrights, is best known for his Oedipus trilogy based on the tragic myth of the king of Thebes, who unknowingly slew his own father and married his own mother. When he learns of the truth of his deed, great tragedy befalls him. Some 2,500 years later, Sigmund Freud, the father of psychoanalysis, shocked the scientific world with his then radical ways of treating mental illness through a "talking cure." This cure was based on a theory of personality in which people were driven by sexual and aggressive desires, which were clearly evident in young children. In his early case histories of Anna O, Dora, and Little Hans, for example, he discerned a clear pattern—little children seemed to have sexual feelings toward the opposite-sexed parent and feelings of jealousy and hostility to the same-gender parent that he or she would like to replace. But these children often felt guilt over both the erotic and aggressive feelings that might prompt later neurotic symptoms. Freud framed his theory of neurosis as the "Oedipus complex," named after the fabled story of King Oedipus. Freud would claim that all neuroses were based on this early "family romance," which he claimed was universal.

In Freud's theory of the stages of psychological development, in which the social intersected with the developmental, he postulated that children went through an "oral stage" of dependency and attachment to the caretaker(s) via sucking the breast, an "anal stage" of learning self control, and an "Oedipal stage" in which the young child felt erotic desire for the opposite-sexed parent and resentment to the parent of the same sex whom he or she aspired to replace. Girls felt angry toward their mothers who denied this wish and were thought to have castrated the little girls, who then suffered "penis envy," which today is understood more as based on male status and power than genitalia. Little boys feared that their sexual feelings to the mother would be greeted by a violent expression of paternal revenge, castration, and were left with enduring anxiety over their masculinity. In both cases, the turmoil of the Oedipus complex eventually resolved when the child identified with its parents as role models for its personality and mediators of society's values, which were then internalized as one's conscience—the superego. Henceforth, the child would submit to the internalized voice of authority, repress its desires, and renounce the desire for the opposite-sexed parent. Thus, for Freud, the Oedipus complex was the basis of (1) the superego (conscience) and the guilt upon which civilization depended, (2) the foundation of gender identity, (3) later choices of a mate, and (4) the central core of neurosis.

Freud has been significant for social theory because of his concerns with the emotional side of socialization and development and the applications of his theory to important aspects of social life. In common with many Enlightenment thinkers who embraced a "social contract theory," he saw that passions and desires needed to be restrained in order for people to live together in relative harmony. In his early story of the origins of the Oedipus complex that were evident in primitive incest taboos, he theorized that people once lived in "primal hordes" ruled by a powerful patriarch who monopolized sexual access to the women of his group, including his daughters. When the sons reached puberty, they were excluded from the group. But, sexually deprived and outnumbering him, they banded together, overthrew and slew the father, and ate his body to incorporate his power. But soon they felt remorse over the deed and henceforth vowed to repress their desires for the sake of joint living. In Freud's theory of civilization, the Oedipus complex was the psychological foundation of civilization. Socially required constraint was maintained by the repression of desire through fear of punishment from within. People experienced this fear as guilt, as much about unconscious wishes as about actual conduct. Renunciation—at the cost of suffering—was the price of civilization that enabled collective adaptation.

Freud saw similar dynamics operating in religion, which he considered an illusion of an all-powerful, benevolent father who gratifies frustrated wishes and provides people with the happiness that actual fathers, and real-life circumstances, typically deny. His theory of group psychology suggested that people were likely to submit to the authority of a father figure to gain his love and recognition. Moreover, the common attachment to the same leader fostered unconscious attachments between group members.

Freud's theories were controversial from the start. He was attacked on scientific as well as moral grounds. His theories have been difficult to test, especially by the "objective" methods typical of social sciences. One of the earliest to examine of the Oedipus complex was anthropologist Bronislaw Malinowski ([1927] 2001), who claimed that among the Trobriand Islanders, where the maternal uncle rather than the father disciplined the (male) child, Oedipal resentment was directed to him, not to the father who had sexual access to the mother. More recent studies shed doubts on Malinowski's findings. Recent French theories such as those of Michel Foucault and Jacques Lacan have recast the theory in terms of internalized discipline mediated through language, while Gilles Deleuze and Félix Guattari suggested that the Oedipus complex is fostered by capitalism to sustain its power.

Today, the Victorian family, with the father as breadwinner and mother as sole, full-time homemaker, has practically disappeared. So, too, has the classical Oedipus complex been rethought. (See Young 2001 for a recent review of the concept.) Many families consist of single parents and children, second marriages with step-siblings, and other configurations. As with any major theoretical framework, over time psychoanalysis underwent changes in theory and practice. For example, the work of Karen Horney, Erich Fromm, and Harry Stack Sullivan stressed social life and interaction. The British "object relations" theories and the "self psychology" of the Chicago school paid more attention to earlier stages of development, with concerns about early attachments and the adequacy of early caretaking and/or the extent to which the infant's emerging self is given empathic recognition. Thus, chil-

dren need to separate from symbiotic ties with caretakers, which can overwhelm and stifle, while separation and individuation—being on one's own—brings anxiety and uncertainty. Clinicians are more likely to look at how early attachments, resentments, and identification with each parent based on such issues as their desired, if not envied, power. Thus notions of "penis envy" or "womb envy" that are salient in early childhood tend to be based less on anatomy than on the social roles and power of mothers and fathers.

For a number of reasons, psychoanalysis and sociology have been separate realms of theory and practice, though some people have worked at the intersections of the social and the personal; Freud himself offered various speculations. Today, however, those who do work at these junctures are more likely to work within the frameworks of object relations theory or self psychology. For example, Nancy Chodorow (1999) has looked at early gender differences in separation-individuation from early attachments to the mother. Young boys are able to make a more complete separation. Young girls are more likely to retain an attachment and identification with their mother, and thus "mothering is reproduced" in the shaping of their character. Jessica Benjamin (1988) has focused more on the need for recognition of self. Young girls deprived of recognition early in life are likely to seek it at any costs and are prone to masochism and humiliation to gain recognition from a man.

The most important legacy of Freudian theory in general and the Oedipus complex in particular has been to look at the emotional side of child development in general and gender socialization in particular. More sociological theories of socialization and personality development were influenced by Georg Simmel's theory of dyads and triads in which the family structure alone gave rise to tensions and conflicts in which one party, the child, might foster conflict between parents, play off one parent against the other, or join one to gang up on the other. Much of what Freud observed was a result of the emotional aspects of the family structure. Charles Cooley, George Herbert Mead, and the symbolic interactionist traditions looked at language, play, role taking, and institutional aspects of socialization that fostered the "social self," the active "I," and the socially expected "me." These approaches, however, often ignore the very powerful role of feelings and passions in the development and motivation of behavior. While few sociologists have tried to frame the major questions of civilization in terms of the Oedipus complex, some have considered some of the implications of Freud's insights on gender, desire, and morality. For Philip Slater (1970), the repression of erotic desire to the mother, frustrating basic needs for dependency and community, has fostered a lonely society prone to aggression. Philip Rieff ([1966] 1987), on the other hand, felt that Freudian theory undermined the morally based repression that society required to maintain civility and its high culture. More recently, Lauren Langman (2006a, 2006b) has suggested that the macroeconomic consequences of globalization, often experienced as "castration" (powerlessness), have inspired various compensatory strategies such as religious fundamentalisms, which privilege patriarchy and celebrate male aggression.

The nature of the Oedipus complex still fosters lively debate, which will continue as long as people have children whose personal development involves ties to parents and intense feelings, emotions, desires, defenses, and ambivalence, all of which impact the nature of their adult personality.

SEE ALSO *Adolescent Psychology; Attachment Theory; Child Development; Crime and Criminology; Culture; Developmental Psychology; Dictatorship; Foucault, Michel; Freud, Sigmund; Gender; Malinowski, Bronislaw; Maturation; Sexuality; Social Movements; Stages of Development*

BIBLIOGRAPHY

Benjamin, Jessica. 1988. *The Bonds of Love.* New York: Pantheon Books.

Chodorow, Nancy. 1999. *The Reproduction of Mothering: Psychoanalysis and the Sociology of Gender.* Berkeley: University of California Press.

Freud, Sigmund. 1921. *Group Psychology and the Analysis of the Ego.* Trans. James Strachey. New York: Liveright, 1951.

Freud, Sigmund. 1927. *The Future of an Illusion.* Trans. James Strachey. New York: Norton, 1961.

Freud, Sigmund. 1930. *Civilization and Its Discontents.* Trans. James Strachey. New York: Norton, 1961.

Freud, Sigmund. 1933. *New Introductory Lectures on Psycho-Analysis.* Trans. James Strachey. New York: Norton, 1990.

Langman, Lauren. 2006a. From the Caliphate to the Shaheeden. In *Marx, Critical Theory, and Religion: A Critique of Rational Choice*, ed. Warren W. Goldstein. New York: Brill.

Langman, Lauren, and Meghan Burke. 2006b. From Exceptionalism to Imperialism: American Character and Political Process. *Current Perspectives in Social Theory*, Vol. 24, eds. J. Lehmann and H. Dahms, 189–228. New York: JAI Press/Elsevier.

Malinowski, Bronislaw. 1927. *Sex and Repression in Savage Society.* New York: Routledge, 2001.

Rieff, Philip, 1966. *The Triumph of the Therapeutic: Uses of Faith After Freud.* Chicago: University of Chicago Press, 1987.

Slater, Philip. 1970. *The Pursuit of Loneliness: American Culture at the Breaking Point.* Boston: Beacon Press.

Young, Robert. 2001. *The Oedipus Complex.* Cambridge: Icon Books.

Lauren Langman

OFFSHORE BANKING

The term *offshore banking* has no precise definition and thus means different things to different people. In part, confusion arises because the term is applied to two separate yet related phenomena. The generally accepted view is that offshore financial markets consist primarily of the various segments of the euromarkets, a "wholesale" or interbank market that is used primarily by commercial banks. The most important characteristics of offshore banking markets are their relative freedom from direct regulation and their specialization in wholesale banking transactions. Collectively these markets tend to function as a distribution mechanism for shifting funds from lenders to borrowers or deficit spending units on a global scale. Therefore, the economic rationale for offshore banks is that they perform this distribution function efficiently.

DESCRIPTION AND TERMINOLOGY

The offshore financial market is fully integrated, internally coherent, and global in reach yet is not literally offshore. It is situated in and between different types of financial centers, all of which are in major onshore cities such as London and Tokyo or in tax havens, some of which are called offshore financial centers (OFCs). That has led to some confusion. Intergovernmental bodies such as the International Monetary Fund (IMF) and the Bank for International Settlements (BIS) apply the term *offshore banking* in a more restrictive sense to describe financial activities that take place in an offshore banking sector of an OFC, or a tax haven in colloquial usage, such as the Bahamas and the Cayman Islands. However, only some countries employ the term *offshore sector* to describe a portion of their financial sectors. Two of the best known tax havens, Switzerland and Luxembourg, for instance, do not use that term. Intergovernmental bodies thus apply the term only to those countries. Academic scholars use the term more broadly to refer to all financial activities that take place in the unregulated offshore financial market.

The offshore financial market is not entirely unregulated: It is subject to so-called self-regulation based on market principles by the banks and other financial actors that use that market. The best known among a series of self-regulating agreements was the capital adequacy agreement, or the Basle Concordant of 1988, which was followed by Basle II, whose final accord was issued in 2004. In addition, for the sake of convenience, clearing goes through New York, giving the U.S. government some control over the market.

Transactions usually are thought to be offshore from the perspective of the host country even though the banks that conduct those operations are onshore. Among the reasons for this are the following:

- Some attempt usually is made to separate offshore from onshore banking activities and the rest of the domestic financial system by means of exchange control, regulation, tax incentives, separate accounting procedures, and the like.

- The institutions in the market tend to be classified as nonresident for balance of payments purposes.

- Transactions in these markets have a significant nonresident component. In some cases transactions are restricted specifically to nonresidents, but in other cases resident access to the market is permitted to varying degrees.

- Transactions in the offshore market are restricted primarily to foreign currencies.

SPONTANEOUS OFFSHORE BANKING SITES

There are three routes by which offshore centers are set up: the so-called spontaneous offshore sites, such as London and Hong Kong; international banking facilities (IBFs) such as New York and Tokyo; and tax havens, which include over seventy states. The offshore center in the city of London originally was called spontaneous because it allegedly was created accidentally as a result of attempts by the British government to reestablish London as the center of global financial activities after World War II.

The exact origins of the offshore financial market are in dispute, but it appears to have emerged in a set of fortuitous events. In late 1956, during the Suez Canal crisis and the ensuing run on the British pound, the British government attempted to defend the currency from devaluation by imposing restraints on sterling credits on countries that engaged in third-party transactions in the sterling area and by raising the bank rate from 5 percent to 7 percent. As a result, a number of second-tier merchant banks, such as the Bank of Latin America, that specialized in third-party international loans were faced with complete cessation of their business. In response, they began actively to solicit dollar deposits to use in trade credits to replace sterling credits. They have argued that the British government's rulings explicitly prohibited the use of sterling credits in third-party loans but said nothing about other currencies, specifically American dollars. The British government allowed and perhaps encouraged the merchant banks to turn to American dollars; otherwise they would have gone out of business.

The little-known understanding between the Bank of England and the merchant banks produced a subtle but important reinterpretation of the purview of British sovereignty: It placed dollar transactions, along with all other third-party currency transactions, outside exchange rate regulation, reserve regulation, and any other regulation by the British state. However, because those transactions took place within the territorial boundaries of the United Kingdom, they were sheltered from the regulation of other states; they therefore were, de facto, under no state regulation, or "offshore."

The new understanding was applicable only to third-party transactions, that is, cases in which British banks served as intermediaries between two non-British nationals using dollars or other foreign currencies. To ensure the legality of those transactions, British banks, who soon were joined by branches of American and other foreign banks in London, kept two sets of books: one for onshore financial transactions in which at least one party to the transaction was British and the other for offshore transactions when both parties were non-British.

INTERNATIONAL BANKING FACILITIES

An IBF is a more restricted type of offshore center in which, in contrast to spontaneous offshore centers, companies must apply for a license to trade. The first IBF was the Asian Currency Units (ACUs) set up in Singapore in 1968. The better known IBFs are situated in the United States.

The first New York IBF came about as the result of prolonged and complex battles between the U.S. Treasury, the Swiss government, and a number of Caribbean tax havens. The United States government had tried hard to reregulate the euromarkets in 1979. Failing that and with the active encouragement of the New York banking community, particularly Citibank and Chase, the U.S. Treasury concluded that rather than fight the onset of offshore centers, the United States stood to gain more by encouraging the formation of its own offshore centers. A swift about-face took place, culminating in the establishment on December 3, 1981, of a New York offshore market: the New York International Banking Facilities. A decade later more than 540 IBFs had been established across the United States to take advantage of those cost and tax benefits. New York had the largest number (over 250); California had 100 IBFs, and Florida had 80. However, as a result of their restrictiveness compared with other offshore centers, interest in IBFs waned. The New York IBF spawned the creation of the Tokyo IBF. In 1982 the Hosomi plan was put forward in imitation of the New York IBF to spur domestic liberalization in Japan.

TAX HAVENS

The third category of offshore financial centers is tax havens, of which there were seventy in the first decade of the twenty-first century. Tax havens are centers that offer an array of tax and regulatory incentives for nonresident investors and complete flexibility in the management of foreign assets. There are as many varieties of tax haven laws as there are jurisdictions, but it is common practice to distinguish among four classes of tax havens: countries where there is no income tax and where foreign corporations pay only license fees; jurisdictions with low taxation, such as Liechtenstein and Jersey; countries where taxes are levied only on internal taxable events but not at all or at very low rates on profits from foreign sources; and jurisdictions that offer special tax privileges to certain types of companies and operations. Crucially, most tax havens maintain strict bank secrecy laws and prevent banks located in their territory from revealing the identity of account holders even to the tax haven government. Many tax havens have created provisions for trusts and other financial entities whose ultimate owners are difficult to identify. For these reasons tax havens are used not only for tax evasion and avoidance, but also for money laundering purposes and other criminal financial activities.

Tax havens are employed by the banking community for a number of interrelated reasons: avoiding current tax, preserving wealth, securing secrecy, avoiding regulation, and gaining easy access to the euromarkets. Banks tend to register high-volume, lucrative wholesale financial transactions through offshore subsidiaries as the financial equivalent of transfer pricing to reduce their tax bill. More important, tax havens are employed to help wealthy clients reduce current tax or preserve wealth or to secure secrecy. In addition, banks are able to avoid domestic regulation by diverting certain activities to their offshore subsidiaries. U.S. banks, for instance, employed offshore subsidiaries in the 1970s and 1980s to access other lucrative financial sectors, such as insurance and mortgages thus avoiding U.S. financial regulations.

Tax havens provide a cheap and easy way for resident companies or individuals to masquerade as nonresidents for euromarkets purposes; hence, a strong symbiotic relationship has evolved between tax havens and the euromarkets. In addition, tax havens permit companies to syndicate their profits worldwide in jurisdictions with zero or nearly zero regulation. Tax havens thus are used to accumulate dividends, interest, and other income. They also are used by multinational enterprises as central points for handling paperwork and preparing and processing trade documents. Many companies depend on tax havens for passage of title to goods to minimize red tape.

For all these reasons, tax havens have been an enormous success. On average 50 to 65 percent of all international banks' net external liabilities were routed through tax havens between 1980 and 2004; approximately 27 percent of all foreign investments by multinational corporations are routed through tax havens. Havens such as the British Virgin Islands (6.7 percent) and the Cayman Islands (2 percent) are among the most important "for-

eign" direct investors in China; they were second and seventh, respectively, in 2004.

TYPES AND USES OF OFFSHORE FINANCIAL MARKETS

Regardless of the historical and juridical origins of the different financial centers, they tend to be closely linked, with a division of labor among them. The literature distinguishes four types of offshore financial centers: Primary centers such as London and New York serve worldwide clients and act as international financial intermediaries for their market regions; booking centers such as Nassau and the Cayman Islands are used by international banks primarily as the location for "shell branches" to book both eurocurrency deposits and international loans; funding centers such as Singapore and Panama play the role of inward financial intermediaries, channeling offshore funds from outside their markets toward local or regional uses; and collection centers such as Bahrain engage primarily in outward financial intermediation. This hierarchy indicates the degree of specialization and interdependence among offshore centers.

The offshore financial market in the first decade of the twenty-first century included several markets: eurocurrency deposits, eurocurrency bank loans, euro notes, eurobonds, euro equities, and foreign exchange markets. The eurocurrency market grew very fast. According to the BIS, the gross size of the eurocurrency market increased from $US 12.4 billion in 1963 to $US 149.9 billion in 1972, $US 1,517.4 billion in 1982, $US 6,197.7 billion in 1992, and $US 24,026 billion in 2006. According to a BIS survey, average daily turnover in traditional foreign exchange markets is approximately $1,880 billion. Approximately 80 percent of all international financial transactions take place in this offshore financial market (BIS, Locational Banking statistics, 2006).

EFFECTS ON THE WORLD ECONOMY

The offshore financial market is therefore a secondary space for financial operations that has accelerated the transnationalization of the world economy. The development of offshore banking operations should be considered in the broader context of the general process of internationalization of economic activities involving trade. Because offshore financial markets have widened the access of companies to loan markets, it has been argued, they have brought down borrowing costs relative to the underlying level of interest rates. As a result of reduced costs, competition from offshore financial markets has forced the liberalization of onshore markets. As a result, only the imposition by some central banks of non-interest-bearing reserve requirements on domestic bank deposits remains as a major domestic regulation that favors eurocurrency transactions. Because costs have fallen, companies can borrow in whatever market is most advantageous to them and swap the proceeds for the currency they need.

The apparent lack of regulation and control raises concerns about whether these markets have a capacity to create credit or money beyond the domestic banking systems and the extent to which they have diffused domestic monetary controls. To what extent have they contributed to currency instability? Although offshore finance is distinguished by a relative lack of state regulation and monitoring, there are degrees of regulation and monitoring. Besides the variations among financial centers that were noted above, several agreements reached by various standing committees that meet at the BIS under the aegis of the Governors of the Group of Ten have proved to be successful. The Basle Committee on Banking Supervision is the best known of those committees, and the Euro-currency Standing Committee is the oldest, having been set up in the early 1960s to monitor and assess the implications of the newly established eurocurrency markets.

The most important long-term impact of offshore finance may have occurred elsewhere. The term *offshore* evokes images of the high seas, of a world beyond borders. However, offshore financial transactions are very much onshore, conceived, organized, and handled in the traditional financial centers of London, New York, and Tokyo. Offshore banking therefore is not outside the state system but is a juridical realm marking the differential degrees of intensity by which states apply regulation and taxation. Offshore banking therefore denotes the bifurcation of the juridical space of sovereignty into mutually dependent relative spaces.

SEE ALSO *Banking; Banking Industry; Capital Controls; Capital Flight; Corruption; Drug Traffic; Finance; Financial Markets; Globalization, Social and Economic Aspects of; Money Laundering; Tax Evasion and Tax Avoidance; Taxes*

BIBLIOGRAPHY

Bank for International Settlements (BIS). 2006. Locational Banking Statistics, April. http://www.bis.org/statistics/bankstats.htm.

Burn, Gary. 2006. *The Re-emergence of Global Finance.* London: Palgrave Macmillan.

Errioco, Luca, and Alberto Musalem Borrero. 1999. Offshore Banking: An Analysis of Micro- and Macro-Prudential Issues. *IMF Working Paper* no. 99/5.

Hampton, Mark. 1996. *The Offshore Interface: Tax Havens in the Global Economy.* Basingstoke: Macmillan.

Hampton, Mark, and Jason Abbott, eds. 1999. *Offshore Finance Centers and Tax Havens: The Rise of Global Capital.* Basingstoke: Macmillan.

Palan, Ronen. 2003. *The Offshore World: Sovereign Markets, Virtual Places, and Nomad Millionaires.* Ithaca, NY: Cornell University Press.

Ronen Palan

OGBU, JOHN U.
1939–2004

John Ogbu, one of the United States's foremost educational anthropologists, studied the educational attitudes of marginalized youth, particularly highlighting the underachievement of African American students. Ogbu depicted blacks as being the victims of their own defeatist attitudes that have evolved over years of oppression. His work was and remains controversial.

Born to a farming family in a small village in Nigeria in 1939, Ogbu completed his BA (1965), MA (1969), and PhD (1971) all at the University of California at Berkeley. He was hired into the university's department of anthropology and was promoted to professor in 1980. He died August 20, 2004, at the age of 64.

Ogbu was not the first to stress a victim blame analysis, but his theoretical propositions, written with such sophistication, elegance, and clarity, were easily translated into researchable hypotheses, and this explains why his ideas continue to generate research that both affirm and contest his stance. To Ogbu, low-income and privileged black youths shared a resistance to high achievement that is a result of the legacy of slavery as well as the racial oppression that was particularly acute up to the 1954 Supreme Court *Brown v. the Board of Education of Topeka, Kansas* decision calling for the desegregation of public schools. With the expanding opportunities achieved by blacks as part of the civil rights and black power movements of the 1960s and 1970s, Ogbu saw black resistance turn into an anachronistic coping mechanism (Ogbu 1995a; 1995b). He did not deny the effects of ongoing racism, but he felt blacks should recognize they were misreading the now more open and less oppressive U.S. society. Eschewing notions of genetic inferiority, Ogbu argued that the larger society and the black community itself had to work to help turn black educational attitudes from disengagement to an active pursuit of excellence and hope.

Because Ogbu's theories touched on educational disadvantage found across the globe, his books, chapters, and articles were translated into Spanish, Mandarin, Italian, French, German, and Croatian. Although his analysis placed heavy emphasis on the educational attitudes of individual children and their parents, his overall perspective was ecological, and he demonstrated that educational attitudes held by children were the result of complex, daily interactions within the family, neighborhood, community, workplace, and nation. Overall, his work reflected strong structural-determinism themes. His *Minority Education and Caste: The American System in Cross-Cultural Perspective* (1978) argued that the same kinds of social divisions between white and black societies in the United States are replicated in caste-society interactions across many cultures. His work with Signithia Fordham (1986) helped popularize concepts such as the burden of "acting white" and "black oppositional identity," and his career culminated with a stunning text, *Black Americans in an Affluent Suburb: A Study of Academic Disengagement* (2003), in which he showed that both low-income and middle-class black youths are hesitant to embrace academic achievement.

Much of Ogbu's research was grounded in small-scale ethnographic studies covering a limited number of participants and a constrained number of research sites. Using large samples collected in schools across a wide range of sites, other researchers have failed to find empirical support for Ogbu's key premises (Ainsworth-Darnell and Downey 1998; Cook and Ludwig 1998; Spencer et al. 2003). Even Ogbu's attempt to link contemporary trends in black education with a "legacy of slavery" has been shown to have no basis in historical fact and research (Anderson 1988; Spencer et al. 2003). It has been suggested that the small scale of Ogbu's research exaggerated the significance of educational attitudes held by only a fraction of black students while overlooking or dismissing attitudes held by the overwhelming majority of students that undercut his pejorative thesis (Foster 2004). To the very end, though, Ogbu held true to his perspective, and he accused his critics of the worst kind of cultural romanticism (2003), although he never produced findings from any large-scale study that refuted his critics' charges. Although the trend in the empirical literature is to move away from Ogbu's theorizing, figures in the popular debate about black achievement attitudes—such as the comedian-turned-social-critic Bill Cosby and the celebrated radio-television commentator Juan Williams—continue to accord Ogbu's work considerable credence (Williams 2006).

SEE ALSO *Achievement Gap, Racial; Acting White; American Dream; Americanism; Anthropology; Culture; Education, Unequal; Inequality, Racial; Oppositionality; Schooling in the USA; Underachievers*

BIBLIOGRAPHY

PRIMARY WORKS

Fordham, Signithia, and John U. Ogbu. 1986. Black Students' School Success: Coping with the Burden of "Acting White." *The Urban Review* 18 (3): 176–206.

Ogbu, John. 1978. *Minority Education and Caste: The American System in Cross-Cultural Perspective*. New York: Academic Press.

Ogbu, John. 1995a. Cultural Problems in Minority Education: Their Interpretations and Consequences—Part One: Theoretical Background. *The Urban Review* 27 (3): 189–205.

Ogbu, John. 1995b. Cultural Problems in Minority Education: Their Interpretations and Consequences—Part Two: Case Studies. *The Urban Review* 27 (4): 271–297.

Ogbu, John. 2003. *Black Americans in an Affluent Suburb: A Study of Academic Disengagement*. Mahwah, NJ: Erlbaum.

SECONDARY WORKS

Ainsworth-Darnell, James W., and Douglas B. Downey. 1998. Assessing the Oppositional Culture Explanation for Racial/Ethnic Differences in School Performance. *American Sociological Review* 63: 563–553.

Anderson, James D. 1988. *The Education of Blacks in the South, 1860–1935*. Chapel Hill: University of North Carolina.

Cook, Phillip J., and Jens Ludwig. 1998. The Burden of "Acting White": Do Black Adolescents Disparage Academic Achievement? In *The Black-White Test Score Gap*, eds. Christopher Jencks and Meredith Phillips, 375–400. Washington, DC: Brookings Institute.

Foster, Kevin M. 2004. Coming to Terms: A Discussion of John Ogbu's Cultural-Ecological Theory of Minority Academic Achievement. *Intercultural Education* 15 (4): 369–384.

Spencer, Margaret Beale, William E. Cross Jr., Vinay Harpalani, and Tyhesha N. Goss. 2003. Historical and Developmental Perspectives on Black Academic Achievement: Debunking the "Acting White" Myth and Posing New Directions for Research. In *Surmounting All Odds*, eds. Carol C. Yeakey and Ronald D. Henderson, 273–304. Greenwich, CT: Information Age Publishing.

Williams, Juan. 2006. *Enough: The Phony Leaders, Dead-End Movements, and Culture of Failure That Are Undermining Black America—and What We Can Do About It*. New York: Crown.

William E. Cross Jr.

OHLIN, BERTIL

SEE *Heckscher-Ohlin-Samuelson Model; Stockholm School.*

OIL SECTOR

SEE *Petroleum Industry.*

OKUN'S LAW

In 1962 the Council of Economic Advisers (CEA) to U.S. president John F. Kennedy (1917–1963) was trying to persuade him to stimulate an underperforming economy. Council members explained that the actual output of the economy was far below its potential or full-capacity output level. As a result, unemployment was excessive. An economy with high unemployment was not only socially unjust and oppressive, but also wasteful and inefficient. The unemployment rate was only the tip of the iceberg of a depressed economy troubled by enforced part-time work, lost overtime and promotion opportunities, discouraged job seekers, greater poverty, declining productivity, and rising government deficits. While there appeared to be a strong case to persuade policymakers of the benefits of reducing unemployment, there was only conjecture about the magnitude of the likely output and income gains. A more precise estimate of these gains was needed to clinch the argument.

The CEA settled on 4 percent unemployment as consistent with potential output. The issue was then how to use this unemployment figure to work out the value of the gap between actual and potential output that needed to be closed. The economist Arthur Okun (1928–1980), then working for the CEA, found a good shorthand approximation for the complicated interaction between employment and output: there was a three-to-one link between output and the unemployment rate so that each extra percentage point in the unemployment rate above 4 percent was associated with a 3 percent fall in output (or real gross domestic product [GDP]). This then yielded the following relationship:

$$P = A \left[1 + 0.03 \left(U - 4 \right) \right].$$

So if unemployment (U) = 4 percent, then potential GDP (P) equaled actual GDP (A). If U = 5 percent, the estimated gap between what the economy was capable of producing and what it was actually producing was 3 percent of GDP. This then provided an estimate of how much extra output and income needed to be generated to get the economy healthy again.

The relationship between unemployment and output that Okun had discovered was called *Okun's law*. The economist James Tobin (1918–2002) regarded it as "one of the most reliable and important empirical regularities of macroeconomics" (Perry and Tobin 2000, Preface), and it provided a major part of the empirical justification for Kennedy's tax cuts to stimulate the economy (Prachowny 2000). Okun's law did not have precise theoretical underpinnings. It was a widely used rule of thumb. Okun had tried alternative ways to estimate the relationship but always got roughly the same answer, and he was delighted how well it stood up over time.

THE REACTION TO OKUN'S LAW

High-output growth is typically associated with a fall in unemployment as firms hire more workers to produce output. However, output growth must at least cover the natural increase in the labor force and the increased productivity of labor to prevent unemployment from rising. Output needs to grow in excess of this rate in order to reduce unemployment. Yet there may be lags in the relationship so that even if output growth rises, firms may delay new hiring until they are certain that the increased growth will persist. Furthermore, the nature of the unemployment will determine how easily it can be absorbed into new work opportunities. If it is cyclical unemployment (associated with temporary layoffs), then it will be absorbed more rapidly than structural unemployment (associated with jobs permanently relocated elsewhere in other industries or with a different skill mix). Even then an increased labor force participation rate, from those formerly outside the labor force, will mean that unemployment may not immediately fall. The relationship then is a very complicated one, and Okun's law is only a rough forecasting tool.

Okun's relationship will vary from country to country and over time. Empirical studies suggest that the Okun's law coefficient increased over the 1981 to 2000 period compared to the 1960 to 1980 period. International comparisons find that the coefficient varies considerably across countries, with Japan in particular being an outlier, reflecting the different labor market arrangements in that country. Research has also focused on getting better estimates of the relationship using more sophisticated econometric techniques and alternative empirical specifications, and correcting for various biases in the estimation. Other studies have concentrated on breaking the relationship into its component parts or have used different measures of unemployment, such as the constant weighted unemployment rate, to account for differences in the composition of the labor force. Various lagged output measures have often been used. Some studies claim that the output-employment ratio is asymmetric; in other words, cyclical unemployment is more sensitive to falls in output growth than increases. There are even skeptics who dismiss concepts such as potential output, the output gap, and the full-employment target altogether and argue that governments should not be in the business of actively managing the economy.

Paul Samuelson acknowledged Okun as the wisest and most creative economic policy adviser of his time. Edmund Phelps called him the foremost practitioner of macroeconomics in the United States. Okun attempted to translate theoretical ideas and concepts into operational guides or computational shortcuts that would be of direct use to policymakers. His widely used rule of thumb has remained one of the most enduring stylized facts in macroeconomics. It continues to attract the interest of applied researchers and features in most macroeconomics textbooks, and it is through this "law" that generations of students come across Okun's name.

SEE ALSO *Productivity; Unemployment*

BIBLIOGRAPHY

Lodewijks, John. 1988. Arthur M. Okun: Economics for Policymaking. *Journal of Economic Surveys* 2 (3): 245–264.

Pechman, Joseph A., ed. 1983. *Economics for Policymaking: Selected Essays of Arthur M. Okun.* Cambridge, MA: MIT Press.

Perry, George L. and James Tobin, eds. 2000. *Economic Events, Ideas, and Policies: The 1960s and After.* Washington, DC: Brookings Institution Press.

Prachowny, Martin F. J. 2000. *The Kennedy-Johnson Tax Cut: A Revisionist History.* Cheltenham, U.K.: Elgar.

John Lodewijks

OLIGARCHY

The term *oligarchy* refers to a form of government in which political power is in the hands of a small minority. The word *oligarchy* derives from the Greek word *oligarkhia* (government of the few), which is composed of *oligoi* (few) and *arkhein* (to rule). This definition does not necessarily distinguish oligarchy from other forms of government. Autocracy, for example, can be viewed as a form of oligarchy in which "the few" refers to a single individual, though autocracies, especially when they take the form of dictatorships, have commonly been associated with greater use of coercion. Democracy, some argue, is also characterized by a "rule of the few" because most political decisions are made by a small section of society. The key factor differentiating oligarchy and democracy is the fact that in democracy political decisions are made by representatives who can be voted out of office by the citizens in regularly scheduled elections. Direct democracy, where the people decide on policies without the intermediation of representatives, is an exception. Therefore, it can be useful to think of the different types of government as being located along a continuum that runs from autocracy to direct democracy. Furthermore, oligarchies are not confined to national politics; oligarchies can also emerge in local government (e.g., Hunter 1953) or in other organizations, such as labor unions.

THE IRON LAW OF OLIGARCHY

The most influential treatment of the politics of oligarchy is *Political Parties* (1911) by German social scientist Robert Michels (1876–1936). The focus of Michels's work was the German Social Democratic Party, but his analysis had clear references to other types of social institutions, including national government. Michels's conclusions were highly pessimistic from a democratic point of view. He argued that the necessity of organization for any large-scale social institution would sound the death knell for democratic governance. Famously, Michels went so far as to state, "Who says organization, says oligarchy" (1962, p. 365). The need for organization concentrated political power in the hands of a select few whose position at the apex of the organization served to solidify their standing. In Michels's view, the advantages conferred upon the leaders of the organization eliminated the possibility of democratic control through leadership elections. These advantages included greater access to information, greater ability to communicate with the organization's members, and the opportunity to develop political skills. Combined with the "incompetence of the masses," evidenced by a lack of participation by ordinary members, which Michels saw as being due to the members' lower degree of education, the division of labor, and organizational obstacles, the political power of the leadership was ensured.

Differences in knowledge and education also gave the appearance that the division between the leaders and the led was natural. If democratic government is defined as a form of government that serves the interests of its members, rather than being defined in procedural terms, nothing thus far suggests that democracy is impossible. However, the final component of Michels's theory was that the interests of the leaders and the members would inevitably diverge. As the heads of the organization, the leaders' interests become identified with their institutional position rather than the interests of the organization's members. The leaders' primary concern becomes protecting their position and serving their own ends using the organization as their means.

Despite Michels's pessimistic conclusion about the prospects of democracy, it appears that relatively few governments identified as oligarchic in the literature followed the route he described. Instead, oligarchies have appeared as a consequence of, for example, the devolution of monarchical rule (e.g., in England under King John in the thirteenth century) or the concentration of economic influence (e.g., in Florence around the turn of the fifteenth century and in Chile in the 1830s).

RESEARCHING OLIGARCHY

Since Michels's seminal contribution, there have been few systematic studies of the politics of oligarchy. There are several reasons for why this has been the case. First, many of the issues raised by Michels are not specific to oligarchy as such but have far wider applicability. Representative government has been analyzed extensively in the context of democratic governments. Similarly, whether ordinary members can control their leaders is taken up in the literature on principal-agent theory. Both issues are at the core of Michels's argument. Second, while the term *oligarchy* is commonly used, there exists no clear, universally accepted definition of *oligarchy* in the literature (Payne 1968; Leach 2005). Most scholars agree that oligarchy involves the concentration of political power in the hands of a minority, but this form of government has few other universally accepted defining characteristics. Third, because oligarchy is not necessarily seen as incompatible with (free) elections, the line between oligarchy and democracy becomes blurred. The most frequently cited factor distinguishing oligarchy from democracy is that admission into the class of oligarchs is restricted in some manner to a subset of the citizenry. The Greek philosopher Aristotle (384–322 BCE) classified oligarchies on the basis of types of restrictions on participation in government, where participation depended on property qualification or heredity (Whibley 1896). South Africa during the apartheid era, where the majority was disenfranchised on the basis of race, serves as an example of another possible type of restriction.

The failure to settle on a definition of *oligarchy* means that comparative studies, such as *The Logic of Political Survival* (2004) by Bruce Bueno de Mesquita, James Morrow, Randolph Siverson, and Alistair Smith, provide perhaps the most general insights into the politics of oligarchies. Rather than classifying governments as autocratic, democratic, or oligarchic, Bueno de Mesquita and his coauthors instead focus on the size of the group that has a say in the selection of the government or leader and the size of the coalition that the government needs to stay in power. Bueno de Mesquita and colleagues find, for example, that the characteristics associated with oligarchies (i.e., smaller coalitions) tend to reduce economic growth and government expenditures but to increase corruption.

The issue of membership in the governing class also looms large in accounts of the decline of oligarchies. J. Mark Ramseyer and Frances Rosenbluth's (1995) account of Japan's Meiji oligarchy highlights two problems an oligarchy must solve to survive: it must prevent the membership from being expanded, and, at the same time, it must provide for rules of succession. Ramseyer and Rosenbluth show that oligarchies may be vulnerable to competition for political influence among the oligarchs, which may induce them to mobilize previously excluded sections of society. For the same reason, oligarchs may be unable to agree on institutions that govern succession within the oligarchy. In the Soviet Union, by contrast, the Communist Party provided institutions that checked the actions of the oligarchs, although the rules guiding succession were somewhat ambiguous (Hammer 1990).

SEE ALSO *Aristocracy; Aristotle; Democracy; Elites; Elitism; Power, Political; Republic*

BIBLIOGRAPHY

Bueno de Mesquita, Bruce, Alastair Smith, Randolph Siverson, and James Morrow. 2004. *The Logic of Political Survival.* Cambridge, MA: MIT Press.

Hammer, Darrell P. 1990. *The USSR: The Politics of Oligarchy.* 3rd ed. Boulder, CO: Westview.

Hunter, Floyd. 1953. *Community Power Structure: A Study of Decision Makers.* Chapel Hill: University of North Carolina Press.

Leach, Darcy K. 2005. The Iron Law of *What* Again? Conceptualizing Oligarchy across Organizational Forms. *Sociological Theory* 23 (3): 312–337.

Michels, Robert. [1911] 1962. *Political Parties: A Sociological Study of the Oligarchical Tendencies of Modern Democracy.* Trans. Edan and Cedar Paul. New York: Free Press.

Olson, Mancur. 1971. *The Logic of Collective Action: Public Goods and the Theory of Groups.* Cambridge, MA: Harvard University Press.

Payne, James L. 1968. The Oligarchy Muddle. *World Politics* 20 (3): 439–453.

Ramseyer, J. Mark, and Frances M. Rosenbluth. 1995. *The Politics of Oligarchy: Institutional Choice in Imperial Japan.* Cambridge, U.K.: Cambridge University Press.

Whibley, Leonard. 1896. *Greek Oligarchies: Their Character and Organisation.* London: Metheun.

Indridi H. Indridason

OLIGARCHY, IRON LAW OF

Coined by the German sociologist Robert Michels in his 1911 monograph *Political Parties*, the *Iron Law of Oligarchy* refers to the inbuilt tendency of all complex social organizations to turn bureaucratic and highly undemocratic. According to Michels, even the left-wing parties of Western Europe in the pre–World War I era, which were programmatically committed to mass democracy, popular participation, and equality within their ranks, tended to become *de facto* oligarchies. In spite of their revolutionary manifestos and formally democratic constitutions, the labor parties of his day were dominated by demagogic ruling cliques with an interest in the perpetuation and growth of the organization itself rather than in its proclaimed ideological aims. As an especially ironic example, he noted that in a fundamentally democratic organization such as his own German Social-Democratic Party (SPD)—just as in the traditional conservative parties—only a few people in executive positions actually held power and made all the important decisions. The SPD leaders, Michels argued, came to value their own prominent status and social-mobility rewards more than any commitment to the official goal of emancipating Germany's "industrial proletariat." Inevitably, their actual policies became more conservative and accommodationist seeking parliamentary compromise with the imperial authorities of Wilhelminian Germany in order to preserve the party, rather than endanger it by any confrontation in the streets. Eventually, the SPD leaders gained real legislative power and public prestige, but instead of serving the collective will of the mass membership, they were in fact dominating and directing it. For the numerically small party elite, the SPD as an organization became an end in itself, rather than a means to a revolutionary end: "It is organization which gives birth to the domination of the elected over the electors, of the mandatories over the mandators, of the delegates over the delegators. Who says organization, says oligarchy" (Michels [1911] 1968, p. 365).

Michels based his fatalistic theory on empirical observation. First of all, the day-to-day administration of any large-scale, differentiated bureaucratic organization such as the SPD by the rank-and-file majority was impossible. Given the "incompetence of the masses," there was a need for full-time professional leadership and top-down guidance. In theory, the SPD leaders were subject to control by the rank-and-file through delegate conferences and membership voting, but in reality they were firmly in command. The simple organizational need for division of labor, hierarchy, and specialized leadership roles meant that control over the top functionaries from below was "purely fictitious." The elected leaders had the experience, skills, and superior knowledge necessary for running the party and controlling all formal means of communication with the membership, including the party press. While proclaiming their devotion to the party program of social democracy, they soon became part of the German political establishment. The mass membership was unable to provide an effective counterweight to this entrenched minority of self-serving party officials, who were more committed to internal organizational goals and their own personal interests than to radical social change. Michels also felt that these inevitable oligarchic tendencies were reinforced by a mass predisposition for depending upon and even glorifying the party oligarchs, because the rank-and-file had a basic psychological need for hero-worship: "Though it grumbles occasionally, the majority is really delighted to find persons who will take the trouble to look after its affairs. In the mass, and even in the organized mass of the labor parties, there is an immense need for

direction and guidance. This need is accompanied by a genuine cult for the leaders, who are regarded as heroes" (Michels [1911] 1968, p. 88).

The Iron Law of Oligarchy was thus a product of Michels's own personal experiences as a frustrated idealist and a disillusioned social-democrat. His *Political Parties* was based upon an empirical study of the SPD and a number of affiliated German trade unions. He observed firsthand that the ordinary members of these working-class organizations were practically excluded from the decision-making process, which was effectively in the hands of the more experienced and skilled leadership cadres. This sociological analysis made Michels increasingly pessimistic about the possibility of mass democracy, until he eventually embraced the "elite theory" of his Italian contemporaries Vilfredo Pareto (1848–1923) and Gaetano Mosca (1858–1941). In a total break with the past, he also adopted Italy as his new homeland and Italian fascism as his political ideal, becoming one of Benito Mussolini's academic acolytes and favored ideologues.

Democratic theorists have ever since questioned whether the oligarchic tendencies described by Michels's overdeterministic model are indeed so universal, inevitable, and immutable to be labeled an "iron law." Michels's theory has been applied to modern-day labor unions, trying to demonstrate how, as bureaucratic organizations, they have become ends in themselves rather than a means to an end. Critics, however, have rejected Michels's message that "organizational parties" destroy democracy and turn it into oligarchy. The eminent Italian political scientist Giovanni Sartori, for one, argues that Michels may well have formulated an iron law of bureaucracy, but only a "bronze law" of oligarchy, mistakenly seeking "democracy in structures, not in interactions," and ignoring the real difference between democracies and nondemocracies (Sartori 1987, pp. 149–151). In contrast, students of post-Communist politics have noted that too many respondents in public-opinion surveys claim to have the same or even less influence on government today than under Communist rule. In this empirical sense, the Iron Law of Oligarchy is difficult either to confirm or to refute decisively.

SEE ALSO *Bureaucracy; Bureaucrat; Communism; Democracy; Elite Theory; Elites; Fascism; Left Wing; Michels, Robert; Mussolini, Benito; Oligarchy; Organizations; Pareto, Vilfredo; Political Parties; Power Elite*

BIBLIOGRAPHY

Beetham, David. 1977. From Socialism to Fascism: The Relation Between Theory and Practice in the Work of Robert Michels. *Political Studies* 25: 3–24, 161–181.

Beetham, David. 1981. Michels and His Critics. *Archives of European Sociology* 22: 81–99.

May, John D. 1965. Democracy, Organization, Michels. *American Political Science Review* 59: 417–429.

Michels, Robert. [1911] 1968. *Political Parties: A Sociological Study of the Oligarchical Tendencies of Modern Democracy*. Trans. Eden and Cedar Paul. New York: Free Press.

Sartori, Giovanni. 1987. *The Theory of Democracy Revisited*. Chatham, NJ: Chatham House.

Rossen Vassilev

OLIGOPOLY

SEE *Competition, Imperfect; Strategic Behavior.*

OLMECS

"Olmec" is the name used to designate an archaeological culture centered on the lowlands of the states of Veracruz and Tabasco on the Gulf Coast of Mexico. Olmec culture, which flourished from 1200 to 400 BCE, was the first complex culture with monumental art and architecture in ancient Mesoamerica (Mexico, Guatemala, and Belize). Later Mesoamerican cultures such as the Aztec, Maya, and Toltec built on the achievements of the earlier Olmec, especially in the areas of social organization, monumental artistic expression, and religious thought.

The hot, humid lowlands of Veracruz and Tabasco had been little explored in the 1930s when archaeologists began to uncover signs of a complex archaeological culture in the area. The initial trait that set Olmec culture apart was the presence of stone monuments that proved to be the earliest examples of monumental art in Mesoamerica. Shortly after these discoveries, archaeologists found examples of monumental architecture in the form of the Mesoamerican truncated pyramid. An early example, from the site of La Venta, rose to a height of 98 feet and was one of the largest buildings in Mesoamerica at the time. Work from the 1960s through the 1990s at the site of San Lorenzo revealed monumental sculpture together with early evidence of a residential palace, complete with a stone drainage system and massive stone columns at the entryway. Major stone monuments also survive at Laguna de los Cerros, a little explored Olmec center. Access to stone in a region with few stone resources must have been a sign of prestige, and the presence of an elaborate palace structure demonstrates that Olmec society was clearly stratified.

Later Olmec also treated access to jade as a principal elite marker. The Olmec traded for the material across a major portion of Mesoamerica, as most Olmec jade is thought to originate in the highlands of Guatemala. While the physiognomy of the colossal heads is sometimes cited as proof of transatlantic contacts, there is no clear archaeological evidence that the Olmec traded with or were contacted by Africans or any other peoples outside of Mesoamerica and Central America.

The iconography of Olmec monumental stone sculpture is varied but may be characterized by its interest in portraying rulership. Colossal stone portrait heads of the rulers were set up in the center of Olmec cities, while the earliest stelae bear the image of humans performing rites clearly associated with rulership in later Mesoamerican cultures. Massive stone thrones also point to the close relationship between monuments and rulership. A particular interest in the depiction of infants is evidenced in both small-scale ceramic and monumental stone sculpture. Other motifs and a set of supernatural beings were shared with peoples all over Mesoamerica from the earliest Olmec times. The Olmec developed hieroglyphic writing before other literate Mesoamerican cultures such as those of Monte Albán or the Maya.

Olmec centers, the largest of which held perhaps 3,000 inhabitants, were based on the highly productive agriculture possible around the waterways of Veracruz and Tabasco. Control of this land may have lead to early stratification, and the presence of extensive waterways eased travel and trade in an area that had no beasts of burden. San Lorenzo, the earliest Olmec center (flourished 1200–900 BCE), as well as its successor, La Venta (flourished 900–400 BCE), fit this pattern.

SEE ALSO *Anthropology; Anthropology, Biological; Archaeology; Pre-Columbian Peoples*

BIBLIOGRAPHY

Benson, Elizabeth P., and Beatriz de la Fuente. 1996. *Olmec Art of Ancient Mexico*. Washington, DC: National Gallery of Art.

Diehl, Richard A. 2004. *The Olmecs: America's First Civilization*. London: Thames and Hudson.

Pool, Christopher. 2007. *Olmec Archaeology and Early Mesoamerica*. Cambridge, U.K.: Cambridge University Press.

Rex Koontz

OLYMPIC GAMES

The Olympic Games are an international sporting event held quadrennially in different venues. The date of inception remains a point of conjecture among historians, but it is generally accepted that the Olympic Games found their genesis in Olympia, Greece, in 776 BCE and survived in attenuated form until 393 BCE. Inspired by the ancient Greek festival, the modern Olympic Games were revived in 1896 by Baron Pierre de Coubertin, a French nobleman who envisaged that the Games would foster a religion of patriotism by directing the new power of national identity into constructive and peaceful channels. Initially, only amateur athletes were permitted to compete in the Olympics; professional athletes were not allowed to compete until the 1970s when the amateurism requirements were extracted from the Olympic Charter. The revival of the Olympic Games was held in Athens, Greece. The Games attracted a relatively small competitive field, with about 240 athletes competing in 43 events.

In the early years of the twentieth century, the International Olympic Committee encountered an array of difficulties with the hosting of the Games. The subsequent two celebrations that followed the Athens Games failed to command popular support, partly because they were crossed with, and effectively eclipsed by, the World's Fair Exhibitions in Paris (1900) and Saint Louis (1904). The 1908 Games, though originally awarded to Rome, were held in London. The majority of the competing countries selected national teams to participate in the London Games, and the athletes were paraded by nation at the opening ceremony. The Olympic Games had institutionalized the "nation" in international athletics. After the 1912 Olympic Games, held in Stockholm, the Olympic movement entered a period of upheaval. De Coubertin may have seen the Olympics as an agent of international peace in a world moving inexorably toward war, but the ideal of the Olympics as an event that could prevent war proved ill-founded. The Games scheduled for Berlin in 1916 were abandoned because of World War I, and two other Olympiads passed without Games in 1940 and 1944 as a result of World War II.

In the aftermath of World War I, the 1920 Games were awarded to Antwerp as a mark of respect for the Belgian people after the anguish that had been inflicted on them during the war. The 1920 opening ceremony was notable for the introduction of the Olympic flag, the release of doves as a symbol of peace, and the presentation of the athletes' oath. The introduction of the flag, representing the unity of the five continents, and the symbolic release of doves also reflected the idyllic vision of the Olympic movement as standing for international peace and unity.

However, it was also in the interwar period that Olympic sport became symbolic of national struggle, with participants as representatives of their national groups. Throughout the twentieth century, John MacAloon argues, "a nascent athletic nationalism was already undermining the Olympic ideal" (1981, pp. 258–259). A notable instance of this was Adolf Hitler's use of the 1936

Olympic Games to enhance his control over the German populace and legitimize Nazi culture. The opening ceremony designed for those games was a shrewdly propagandistic and brilliantly conceived charade that reinforced and mobilized the hysterical patriotism of the German masses. The Berlin Games have also become closely associated in the popular imagination with the African American athlete Jesse Owens. Against a background of Nazi efforts to manipulate the Games to demonstrate the racial and athletic superiority of the Aryan race, Owens won four gold medals at the first Olympic Games to be broadcast on a form of television. The Berlin Games demonstrated how the hosting of the Olympic Games could be manipulated to provide a benign and uncritical backdrop for the parade of national identity.

Another political incident involving African American athletes occurred at the 1968 Summer Olympics in Mexico City. Two African American track-and-field athletes, Tommie Smith and John Carlos, bowed their heads and raised a black-gloved power salute on the victory podium during the playing of "The Star-Spangled Banner." USA Olympics officials asserted that the athletes should not have used the Games as a platform to air their political grievances, and the two athletes were immediately suspended from the U.S. team and banned from the Olympic Village. Politics was also to cast its shadow over the 1972 Summer Olympics in Munich, West Germany, when members of the Israeli Olympic team were taken hostage by the Palestinian terrorist organization Black September. The terrorists killed eleven Israeli athletes and one German police officer in an event that is conventionally referred to as the Munich Massacre.

The 1980 Olympics in Moscow were arguably the most political in the history of the Games and reflected the extremes of nationalism that had emerged as a result of the renewed cold war struggle. In 1980 the United States and sixty-four other Western nations refused to compete at the Moscow Olympics that year because of the Soviet invasion of Afghanistan. The boycott reduced the number of nations participating to only eighty, including only sixteen Western nations—the lowest number of nations to compete since 1956. The Soviet Union and fourteen Eastern bloc countries (Romania was the exception) retaliated by boycotting the Los Angeles Olympics in 1984.

In the Olympic arena, encircled by flags of various nations, the political symbolism of sport is most evident. Young nations make use of the nationalist symbolism of sport to gain recognition on the world stage; established nations do so to demonstrate their strength and prowess. The media make use of sport to construct a "battle" among nations, giving individuals a public spectacle at which they can cheer on their compatriots. The central role of the Olympics as a forum where new nations can gain acceptance is also clear from the number of nations taking part. In Antwerp in 1920, twenty-nine nations competed; by the Athens Olympics of 2004, that number had risen spectacularly to 201. The importance of the Olympic Games to cultural unity and national identity lies not only within the event as staged but in the sporting occasion as an international spectacle. Beyond the demonstration of physical strength and skill, Olympic sport as collective ritual, highlighting concepts of leadership and heroism, has become part of the language of nationalism.

SEE ALSO *Aryans; Black September; Entertainment Industry; Hitler, Adolf; Nationalism and Nationality; Nazism; Racism; Sports; Sports Industry; Union of Soviet Socialist Republics*

BIBLIOGRAPHY

Coakley, Jay, and Eric Dunning, eds. 2000. *Handbook of Sports Studies.* London: Sage.

Cronin, Mike. 1999. *Sport and Nationalism in Ireland: Gaelic Games, Soccer, and Irish Identity since 1884.* Dublin and Portland, OR: Four Courts Press.

Guttmann, Allen. 1984. *The Games Must Go On: Avery Brundage and the Olympic Movement.* New York: Columbia University Press.

Guttmann, Allen. 2002. *The Olympics: A History of the Modern Games,* 2nd edition. Urbana: University of Illinois Press.

Hill, Christopher R. 1996. *Olympic Politics.* Manchester, U.K., and New York: Manchester University Press.

Holt, Richard. 1993. *Sport and the British: A Modern History.* Oxford and New York: Oxford University Press.

Houlihan, Barrie. 1994. *Sport and International Politics.* New York: Harvester Wheatsheaf.

MacAloon, John J. 1981. *This Great Symbol: Pierre de Coubertin and the Origins of the Modern Olympic Games.* Chicago: University of Chicago Press.

Miller, David. 2003. *Athens to Athens: The Official History of the Olympic Games and the IOC, 1896–2004.* Edinburgh: Mainstream.

David M. Doyle

ONE-BIRTH POLICY

SEE *Population Growth.*

ONE-PARTY STATES

One-party states, or single-party states, are nation-states where only one specific political party has the monopoly of political power. One-party states are autocratic and nondemocratic political regimes. Examples of one-party nation-states are North Korea, Cuba, and China. In these countries the Communist Party has the legal monopoly of representing the whole of society in politics on the basis of a Communist constitution. Non-Communist one-party states can be found mainly in Africa, but these political systems are mostly linked with weak or failing states, whereas Communist single-party states are combined with a strong state apparatus and a highly centralized bureaucracy.

The main difference between a one-party state and a dominant party state is that one party has the monopoly of political representation of society in the former and a strong party is dominating within a multiparty system in the latter. A single-party nation-state is always a nondemocratic political regime. A dominant party state can be either a democratic regime or a hybrid regime, combining elements of democratic and autocratic political systems. In a dominant party state there is one strong, major political party, which dominates several small and minor political parties. Historical examples of democratic dominant party states are Italy and Japan after 1945 and India after gaining independence from the British Empire in 1947. An example of a hybrid dominant party state with democratic as well as autocratic elements is the Russian Federation under President Vladimir Putin (2000–2007), with "United Russia" as the dominant political party.

One-party states are characterized by one single party representing the whole of society, assuming that there are no particular social interests, only a general and unified political will, representing a dominant and supposedly superior social class, the working class. Communist one-party states like North Korea, Cuba, or China are characterized by long-term autocratic and charismatic leaders such as Kim Il Sung (1912–1994) in North Korea, Fidel Castro (1926–) in Cuba, and Mao Zedong (Tse-tung) (1893–1976) in China. For many decades the one-party regime in all three countries had leaders with a cult of personality, and the nations displayed gigantic portraits and statues to create a larger-than-life public image for their rulers. In the mid-2000s North Korea and Cuba were examples of unchanged Communist regimes with a centrally planned economy. China represents a Communist one-party state, which is changing the economic system from a Communist command economy to a capitalist market economy. One positive aspect of one-party states is the centralization of political power, which facilitates structural changes of the economy toward a free market economy, like in contemporary China. Negative aspects of single-party states are the lack of democratic and human rights as well as the absence of social liberties and political freedom. One-party states can be—due to the lack of democratic checks and balances—irrational actors in international politics, when their autocratic leaders decide a certain course of foreign policy. The end of the rule of the current dictators in Cuba and North Korea might be a chance for social forces and social movements in these remaining Communist states to commence a transformation toward democracy and a free market economy. China is already on a long march toward a capitalist economy with an uncertain future of its current one-party state.

SEE ALSO *Autocracy; Castro, Fidel; Mao Zedong; Nation-State; Party Systems, Competitive; Personality, Cult of; Totalitarianism*

BIBLIOGRAPHY

Brooker, Paul. 1995. *Twentieth-Century Dictatorships: The Ideological One-Party States.* New York: New York University Press.

Brooker, Paul. 2000. *Non-Democratic Regimes: Theory, Government, and Politics.* New York: St. Martin's Press.

Dalton, Russell J., and Doh Chull Shin, eds. 2006. *Citizens, Democracy, and Markets Around the Pacific Rim: Congruence Theory and Political Culture.* Oxford: Oxford University Press.

Christian W. Haerpfer

ONG, WALTER

SEE *Popular Culture.*

OPEC

SEE *Organization of Petroleum Exporting Countries (OPEC).*

OPEN MARKET OPERATIONS

Open market operations are purchases and sales of securities between a central bank (for example, the Federal Reserve in the United States, the Bank of England in the United Kingdom, and the European Central Bank in most of Europe) and the banking system. These securities are usually government-issued (mostly bonds on government debt), although they can include private and foreign securities, and gold. When the central bank buys a security from a bank it increases the bank's asset position with respect to the central bank. This allows the bank to make more loans to its clients, thus increasing the overall amount of money available to the public. By contrast, a central bank sale of securities has the converse effect.

Banks holding excess asset positions with the central bank can loan these surplus funds to banks with deficit positions. These trades are usually in the form of overnight loans at an interest rate negotiated individually between the parties of the agreement. For example, in the United States such loans are called *federal funds* and the volume weighted average of the interest rate charged is called the *federal funds rate*. In addition, most central banks have standing deposit and lending facilities so that banks that cannot find favorable counterparties can trade with the central bank instead. Standing facilities therefore limit the variability of the overnight rate charged in bilateral trades between banks.

Open market operations allow the central bank to modify the banking system's overall asset position and, hence, to control the average interest rate charged on these overnight loans. This overnight rate then serves as a reference rate for loans at longer maturities. For example, to make a borrower indifferent to the choice between a two-day loan and a one-day loan that is rolled over the next day, the loan rate charged on the two-day loan should be an average of the rates charged on the two one-day loans. Similar arbitrage arguments (with some adjustments for risk and uncertainty about the value of one-day loans in the future) link interest rates at different maturities (often referred to as the *term structure*) with the overnight rate that the central bank manages through open market operations. Ultimately, fluctuations in longer-term interest rates affect investment decisions and the future level of economic activity.

In most modern economies, independent central banks are commissioned with two main responsibilities: (1) the conduct of monetary policy, broadly meant as managing the amount of money in the economy so that it is compatible with price and exchange rate stability, and economic growth; and (2) regulation of the banking and financial systems. The central bank is the banking system's banker (as well as the government's). Its ability to conduct open market operations and modify the overall asset position of the banking system allows the central bank control over the economy's money supply and the overnight interest rate. Insofar as high levels of economic activity can generate inflation and overnight rates are linked through arbitrage to long-term rates (which ultimately determine investment and the overall level of economic activity), open market operations are the main vehicle by which a central bank implements its monetary policy objectives.

SEE ALSO *Banking; Banking Industry; Central Banks; Federal Reserve System, U.S.; Interest Rates; Money, Supply of; Policy, Monetary*

BIBLIOGRAPHY

Meulendyke, Ann-Marie. 1998. *U.S. Monetary Policy and Financial Markets*. New York: Federal Reserve Bank of New York.

Òscar Jordà

OPEN SHOP

SEE *Labor Law.*

OPERANT CONDITIONING

Learning is an important topic for the social sciences. It can explain much of development, for example, and can be used in many applied settings (such as educational or clinical). There are various perspectives on learning. One of the most useful involves operant conditioning.

An operant is a voluntary behavior that is used in order to obtain a reinforcer or avoid a punisher. Operant Conditioning uses reinforcement and punishment systematically to facilitate learning. Its unique foci include, first, its focus on voluntary behaviors ("operants"), and second, its emphasis on the consequences of behavior. Other learning theories emphasize antecedents rather than consequences and involuntary behaviors, or reflexes, rather than operants. The Classical Conditioning perspective, for instance, focuses on antecedents and reflexes. The founder of Classical Conditioning, Ivan Pavlov, used a bell as an antecedent stimulus in his well-known research with dogs. These dogs salivated after the ringing of the bell had been repeatedly associated with meat powder. Salivation is of course a reflex. Though this emphasis on reflexes implies that Classical Conditioning may not be as useful as Operant Conditioning, it did influence the development of the Lamaze birthing technique and has been adapted to the systematic desensitization of phobias and other problems that involve physiology and reflexes.

Another perspective, called Social Learning theory, is more consistent with Operant theory than is Classical Conditioning. It emphasizes modeling and observational learning but it recognizes the impact of consequences. A child might observe a hero on television, for example, who is richly rewarded for some altruistic behavior, and although the child watching the television is not reinforced, the child imitates the hero. Observational learning of this sort is sometimes described as "vicarious reinforcement."

Reinforcement makes operant behavior more likely to occur in the future. Punishment makes operants less likely to occur. Reinforcement can be used in an operant procedure known as shaping. Here reinforcement is given to behaviors that increasingly resemble a target behavior, and gradually the individual will in fact display that target behavior. It is sometimes called the Method of Successive Approximation. Fading involves reinforcing one behavior simultaneously with prompts or assistance of some kind. The assistance is gradually withdrawn, or faded, until the behavior is emitted without any prompts. Undesirable behaviors can be eliminated from behavioral repertoires by punishing them. Alternatively, it is sometimes more appropriate to identify the reinforcers that are supporting the undesirable behavior and simply eliminate them. In this fashion, punishment is unnecessary. If behavior is not supported by reinforcement, it becomes extinct. This is the rationale for time-outs; individuals are placed in a setting that does not allow them to receive reinforcement, nor support inappropriate behaviors.

Consequences are not always effective in controlling behavior. Indeed, one of the most important steps when using operant procedures involves the accurate identification of reinforcers and punishers. There are many idiosyncrasies; what controls the behavior of one person often has no impact on another. The effectiveness of consequences is in part determined by the type and amount given, but also by deprivation (hunger), the gradient (the interval between the behavior and the consequence), and the schedule (the number of behaviors that must be emitted to earn a reinforcer). In general, a shorter interval ensures that consequences are maximally effective. Early on it is also important to use a continuous schedule, with a one-to-one ratio (every single instance of the behavior earns the consequence). Larger ratios are useful to program generalization and maintenance. It is typically best to start with a continuous schedule, but then thin the schedule such that the individual may emit two, then three, then five, then ten behaviors to earn one reinforcer. Similarly, variable schedules can be used to ensure that behavior is resistant to extinction. In a variable (or intermittent) schedule the ratio of behaviors to reinforcers fluctuates (3:1, then 5:1, then 2:1, then 7:1, and so on). B. F. Skinner demonstrated each of these operant concepts using highly controlled laboratory experiments, typically with subhuman species.

At one point Skinner drew from operant principles to develop a highly controlled crib for his own daughter. It kept her environment at an ideal temperature, with controlled lighting and visual stimuli. This reflects Skinner's emphasis on environmental control. The environment sometimes influences behavior in ways that one does not even notice, such as visual distraction or temperature, and sometimes the environmental influence takes the form of obvious consequences to one's actions, such as reinforcers and punishers. Skinner felt that one could retain free will only if one maintained an awareness of the environmental and experiential influences on one's behavior. The apparatus just described is sometimes called a Skinner Box, though that name is also sometimes used to describe the operant chamber in which rats are trained via reinforcement. Operant chambers automatically monitor and reinforce particular behaviors (for example, pressing down on a bar). They provide a high level of experimental control, which was typical of Skinner's work. He felt that objectivity and experimental control were necessary if psychology was to be scientific. He once stated that sciences are only valid if they can "predict and control."

Additional research by Skinner and others has demonstrated that operant conditioning is highly effective when used systematically in educational or clinical settings. In fact, according to Skinner, operant conditioning also occurs spontaneously in the natural environment. Parents, for example, may reinforce or punish behavior without really intending to do so (or at least without relying on operant theory to make their decisions). Skinner's 1948 novel, *Walden Two*, describes a segment of the population that employs operant principles in a kind of utopia. The key idea is that consequences dramatically influence behavior and, as noted above, in order to exercise free will, people should be aware of operants' effects and use them in a systematic and beneficial fashion.

BIBLIOGRAPHY

Skinner, Burrhus Frederick. 1948. *Walden Two*. New York: Macmillan.

Skinner, Burrhus Frederick. 1953. *Science and Human Behavior*. New York: Macmillan.

Skinner, Burrhus Frederick. 1976. *About Behaviorism*. New York: Vintage.

Mark A. Runco

OPERATION BOOTSTRAP

Operation Bootstrap was a development policy implemented in Puerto Rico after World War II (1939–1945) that achieved rapid industrialization of the island's economic structure. Critics, though, contend that the policy brought about steep agricultural decline and dislocation, large-scale emigration, and increased economic dependency.

Puerto Rico, a colony that the United States took from Spain during the 1898 Spanish-American War, had until World War II an agricultural economy plagued with severe unemployment and poverty. Teodoro Moscoso (1910–1992), the first director of Puerto Rico's Economic Development Administration (popularly known as Fomento), and Luis Muñoz Marín (1898–1980), Puerto Rico's first elected governor, concluded that the best solution to the island's development problems was to promote industrial investments from the United States.

They proposed using tax exemptions, approved by Puerto Rico's legislature in 1947, to entice American corporations to set up factories on the island. Further attractive conditions for corporate investment were low labor costs, laws allowing products to enter the United States duty free, and the security of operating in an American-controlled territory.

Muñoz Marín first used the name *Operation Bootstrap* in 1949 in testimony before the U.S. House of Representatives Committee on Public Lands. "We are trying to lift ourselves by our own bootstraps," he stated. The name, though, was a disingenuous misnomer, in that it metaphorically implied endogenous development when the plan in reality relied upon foreign investment. The more accurate translation for the program's name in Spanish, *manos a la obra*, is "let's get to work."

In order to further its campaign to attract U.S. industrial investments, Fomento employed American advertising agencies, including one headed by David Ogilvy (1911–1999), to create a positive image of Puerto Rico and the idea that the island was undergoing a renaissance. American corporations responded quickly. In its first phase, which lasted up to the 1960s, Operation Bootstrap attracted low-wage, labor-intensive industries, particularly in textiles and clothing. The subsequent second phase attracted more capital-intensive industries in petrochemicals, oil refinement, and pharmaceuticals.

At the high point of Operation Bootstrap's tax-exemption policy in the 1960s, U.S. corporations could operate on the island completely exempt from all federal and local taxes and could repatriate profits tax-free to the mainland. In addition, they were exempt from federal minimum-wage requirements. Both of those conditions have since been modified. Federal minimum-wage requirements were instated on the island in 1976, and in 1996 the U.S. Congress began a ten-year phaseout of Section 936 of the Internal Revenue Code, which gave corporations credits for federal taxes paid on profits gained in Puerto Rico. Thereafter, Operation Bootstrap could only offer corporations exemption from local taxes.

Many officials saw Operation Bootstrap as transforming Puerto Rico into a showcase for what American development policy could do for Latin American countries and therefore as a model or prototype that other Latin American countries should adopt as well. Bootstrap's importance as a model for other countries became evident in the Cold War 1960s when nearby Cuba adopted an alternative socialist development model. Operation Bootstrap, by sticking to a capitalist strategy that relied upon private investment from the United States, directly countered the Cuban socialist strategy, which relied on state investment and sought independence from traditional American economic domination. That Teodoro Moscoso became the first director of John F. Kennedy's (1917–1963) Alliance for Progress, which was established in 1961 in large part to counter Cuban influence, underscores Bootstrap's importance as an early model for American development policy for Latin America.

Operation Bootstrap's basic proposals of relying on foreign, particularly American, investment and opening up economies to free trade were components of the Caribbean Basin Initiative promoted by the Ronald Reagan (1911–2004) administration in the 1980s as an answer to the 1979 Sandinista revolution in Nicaragua and revolutionary movements in El Salvador and Guatemala. They also became basic principles of the 1994 North American Free Trade Agreement (NAFTA) and attempts to develop a free trade agreement for the Americas.

More than a half century's experience, however, indicates that Operation Bootstrap has had mixed results for Puerto Rico. There is no question that within decades the profile of its labor force changed to approximate that of the United States and other developed countries with proportionately few workers remaining in agriculture, many more in industry, and the majority in services. There is also no question that Puerto Rico's living conditions improved, though they are still far from being at a par with those in the United States.

But Operation Bootstrap also increased the economic dependence of Puerto Rico on the United States, undercutting development of a self-sustaining economy and economic sovereignty. One of the policy's political consequences may well have been to undercut support for political independence, with substantial numbers of Puerto Rican voters believing that the island absolutely needed continued U.S. control for economic survival.

Operation Bootstrap never accomplished one of its promised objectives: to reduce unemployment to tolerable limits. Official unemployment figures remain much higher on the island than in the United States. Because Puerto Rico's labor-force participation rate is comparatively low, hidden unemployment is even higher. Support for the island's unemployed population requires significant transfer payments in the form of food stamps and other welfare aid from the United States. The seeming progress Bootstrap made in lowering official unemployment figures required exporting great numbers of the unemployed to the mainland United States.

As Bootstrap-stimulated industrial investments increased, labor-intensive agriculture declined. Because of improvements in transportation technologies, including air freight, brought on by World War II necessities, it became easier for American farmers to export their surpluses to the island, sell them at low prices, and thereby take markets away from Puerto Rican farmers.

The decline of Puerto Rican farming swelled the ranks of the already large unemployed population, and the growth of unemployment outpaced the creation of Operation Bootstrap's new industrial jobs. A significant proportion of the unemployed then migrated to the United States in search of work. In 1940, before the advent of Operation Bootstrap, 96 percent of all Puerto Ricans lived on the island. That percentage declined steadily as Operation Bootstrap–induced industrialization and agricultural decline progressed. By 1960, it had fallen to 72 percent; by 1980 to 61 percent; and in 2004 the line was crossed with a majority of Puerto Ricans living off the island, the vast majority in the mainland United States. The architects of Operation Bootstrap believed that the island was absolutely overpopulated and actively encouraged this emigration as a safety valve to keep unemployment from being higher than it otherwise would be. For the migrants though, life in the United States has proved to be problematic. Despite having on average higher incomes and less poverty than their island counterparts, their economic conditions remain among the lowest of ethnic groups in the United States, in large part owing to considerable discrimination and ethnic and racial prejudice.

BIBLIOGRAPHY

Dietz, James L. 1986. *Economic History of Puerto Rico: Institutional Change and Capitalist Development.* Princeton, NJ: Princeton University Press.

Fernandez, Ronald. 1996. *The Disenchanted Island: Puerto Rico and the United States in the Twentieth Century.* 2nd ed. Westport, CT: Praeger.

Maldonado, A. W. 1997. *Teodoro Moscoso and Puerto Rico's Operation Bootstrap.* Gainesville: University Press of Florida.

Weisskoff, Richard. 1985. *Factories and Food Stamps: The Puerto Rico Model of Development.* Baltimore, MD: Johns Hopkins University Press.

James W. Russell

OPIUM WARS

Opium Wars is a term referring to two wars that Britain fought against imperial China in the middle of the nineteenth century, presumably over the attempts of the Chinese authorities to stop the growing influx of foreign-produced opium. The real cause of the first Opium War (1839–1842), also called the "Anglo-Chinese War," was Chinese resistance to Britain's free-trade demands and practices, of which the unrestricted trade in opium was only the most controversial example. Seeking to end high Chinese import duties and other restrictions on foreign trading, the British found a pretext for war when China prohibited the importation of the drug and then confiscated a British shipment of opium.

Opium had long been used in China to treat some ailments, but in the seventeenth and the early part of the eighteenth centuries millions of Chinese from all social classes began to use it recreationally. Britain's East India Company was shipping large quantities of Indian-grown opium to China, which it traded for Chinese tea and other local products. The imperial government was so concerned at the growing number of Chinese opium addicts that in 1799 it forbade its import trade and even decreed the death penalty for illicit trafficking in opium. Despite this legal prohibition, the opium trade continued to thrive, as private traders from Britain and other Western countries, including the United States, made huge profits from selling the extract to Chinese "opium eaters." By the late 1830s foreign merchants were importing into China an estimated 5 million pounds of the illegal drug annually. Opium smuggling had so upset China's balance of trade that its backward economy seemed to be on the verge of collapse. The alarmed imperial authorities made opium possession illegal in 1836 and began to close down the numerous opium parlors.

In 1839 Chinese customs officials seized a shipment of opium that British merchants were planning to market in the seaport city of Canton. In response, Britain rejected the legitimacy of China's opium ban and threatened to use military force if the confiscated opium was not returned to its British owners. When China refused, the British navy shelled Canton and occupied the coastal areas around it, including Hong Kong. The war continued until China was forced to accept the humiliating terms of the 1842 Treaty of Nanking and compensate British merchants for their lost opium. The opium trade continued and even expanded under the generous import-license privileges that the Treaty of Nanking had granted to British merchants. This first of the so-called "unequal treaties" with China also ceded Hong Kong to Britain, opened five coastal cities, including Canton, to British rights of residence and trade, and imposed a very low tariff on British imports under the "most-favored-nation" principle. In 1844 the French and the Americans pressured China into granting them the same trading rights as the British.

The second Opium War (1856–1860) is sometimes called the "Arrow War" because the British, incensed by what they felt were clear treaty violations, used as a pretext to renew hostilities the boarding and seizure of the British ship *Arrow* and the arrest of its twelve crew members for opium smuggling and piracy. This time France joined the British in launching a punitive expedition inland after an initial British attack had been repelled by the Chinese. A combined Anglo-French military raid into China's hinterland led to the signing of the 1858 Treaty of Tientsin. The Chinese imperial court refused to accept the onerous terms of this second "unequal treaty" until another joint Anglo-French expedition captured the capital Peking in 1860 and forced China's total surrender. The Treaty of Tientsin allowed foreign embassies in Peking, a closed city at that time, opened eleven more coastal cities to foreign trading, and completely legitimized the opium trade. It also allowed westerners to travel in the Chinese interior, gave Christian missionaries the right to proselytize and hold property throughout China, and lowered even further import duties on British goods. In 1860 similarly imposed treaties were signed with France, the United States, and Russia.

The Opium Wars marked the beginning of China's century-long subjugation and servitude to foreign powers. The defeated Chinese were forced to legalize the importation of opium, accept unfair and unbalanced terms of foreign trade, open up China's seaports and the Yangtze River to foreign commercial penetration under the so-called "treaty port" system, and exempt westerners from China's local laws and national jurisdiction. So severely curtailed was China's independence in that period that the Chinese still view the Opium Wars as a national disgrace.

SEE ALSO *Colonialism; Drugs of Abuse; Imperialism; Protected Markets; Protectionism; Sovereignty; Trade*

BIBLIOGRAPHY

Beeching, Jack. 1977. *The Chinese Opium Wars.* New York: Harcourt Brace Jovanovich.

Fay, Peter W. 1975. *The Opium War, 1840–1842: Barbarians in the Celestial Empire in the Early Part of the Nineteenth Century and the War by Which They Forced Her Gates Ajar.* Chapel Hill: University of North Carolina Press.

Hu, Sheng. 1991. *From the Opium War to the May Fourth Movement.* Trans. Dun J. Li. Beijing: Foreign Languages Press.

Inglis, Brian. 1976. *The Opium War.* London: Hodder and Stoughton.

Rossen Vassilev

OPPORTUNITY COST

The opportunity cost of an economic decision is the value or benefit of the next best alternative to that decision. For example, if a community decides to use part of its budget to reduce classroom size in schools, it cannot use that same money to achieve another priority, such as improving the aesthetics of the downtown area. Meeting concerns of parents and having better educated residents has clear benefits, but the opportunity cost is a more pleasing downtown drawing in tourism or new business. In opting for the former, the town must sacrifice the latter, at least until the town budget expands and there are more resources to accomplish alternative goals.

The concept of opportunity cost is a core element in the field of economics, particularly within the marginal theory of value, where economic decisions are based on maximizing benefits subject to resource constraints. Consumers are said to "maximize utility," choosing the combination of goods that leads to the highest amount of satisfaction possible. However, the choices are limited by the consumer's budget, and the consumer must choose a combination available within the budget constraints that exist. If the consumer wishes to see another movie, two chocolate bars must be given up. The benefit or pleasure obtained from eating the two chocolate bars is the opportunity cost of going to another movie. Similarly, workers are assumed to maximize utility, choosing a mix of income from labor and enjoyment from leisure time that best meets their individual desires, given time constraints. Firms maximize profits by selecting what to produce, how much to produce, and how to produce, subject to resource constraints.

Whole societies also face trade-offs. Existing amounts of land, labor, and other resources, as well as the current state of technology, limit how much can be produced and therefore consumed. If the society chooses to produce and consume more of one good, it must trade off some amount of another good. The opportunity cost of having more of one good is the benefit of consuming the alternative.

Opportunity costs are different from accounting costs, for which only price is considered. A student may view the cost of attending school as the monetary value of tuition and fees, but the tuition and fees are the accounting costs. The opportunity costs include the loss of income and experience of full-time employment, as well as the benefit of other items the tuition and fees could have bought. However, if the parents of the student decide to support her studies by paying her the income she would have earned in full-time employment, the forgone income is no longer an opportunity cost for the student. Instead, the parents may have sacrificed a world tour or a new boat

in order to support their child, essentially assuming at least part of the opportunity costs unto themselves.

Opportunity costs include both private and social costs, but individual and collective decisions may not necessarily reflect the social costs. For example, if a firm chooses to invest in a new product line rather than expand its existing line, it is basing its decision on which choice will bring in the most profits given the costs of inputs. If manufacturing the new product results in more air pollution, social costs exist that are born by the larger community. These costs, which may include additional spending on health care and pollution mitigation, are opportunity costs of the firm's decision, even if the firm did not consider them or pay them. The calculation of an opportunity cost is not the sum of all alternatives. If the consumer is watching more movies but eating less chocolate, the opportunity cost is only the pleasure that would have been derived from the chocolate, not the chocolate and the licorice and the popcorn, or any other choice that was not considered. Also, if something is not an option, it cannot be an opportunity cost. If the consumer wants to buy some hunting land that is not for sale, the hunting land cannot be the opportunity cost of deciding to buy a new car.

The concept of opportunity cost is frequently used in public policy debates. A favorite textbook expression of this is the "guns versus butter" debate. A society can choose more guns (i.e., more military spending), but in the context of limited resources, it must give up butter (i.e., spending on meeting human needs). During the military build-up and wars of the George W. Bush administration, many argued that the additional military spending had large opportunity costs. The money could have been used, for example, to provide health care for the uninsured, invest in greater energy efficiency, or a number of other alternatives. The opportunity cost of the spending is the benefit that could have been achieved from the most valued of these alternatives.

SEE ALSO *Choice in Economics; Choice in Psychology; Economics; Marginalism; Microeconomics; Social Cost; Trade-offs; Utility, Objective; Utility, Subjective*

BIBLIOGRAPHY

Goodwin, Neva, Julie A. Nelson, and Jonathan Harris. 2006. *Macroeconomics in Context*. Boston: Houghton Mifflin.

Riddell, Tom, Jean Schackleford, Steve Stamos, and Geoffrey Schneider. 2005. *Economics: A Tool for Critically Understanding Society*. 7th ed. Boston: Pearson Addison Wesley.

Anita Dancs

OPPOSITIONALITY

There is a long tradition in the social sciences of examining oppositional behavior. In particular, this work has focused on the ways adolescents act in opposition to a range of authority figures, social institutions, and expected norms of behavior. Whereas much work in psychology focuses on the individual causes and consequences of oppositionality, research in sociology and education tends to characterize oppositionality as a collective cultural response to a structural condition. Debates in these fields focus on whether, as a form of resistance, oppositional culture is productive or constraining.

In one of the classic examples from this field, Paul Willis's *Learning to Labor* (1977) examined how "working class kids get working class jobs" and in particular, what role working-class "lads'" oppositional culture played in the process of social reproduction. Willis (1977) argued that working-class nonconformity and open opposition to the school's achievement ideology, rules, and authority structure functioned both as a critique that reflected lads' understanding of the limited possibility of their being upwardly mobile and simultaneously made such mobility even less likely (1977). *Learning to Labor* highlighted the central paradoxes that have been echoed in related literature in the years since: that oppositionality in various forms can be characterized as resistance and that it reflects a critique of constrained structural conditions (Giroux 1983; Macleod 1995; Weis 1990), while at the same time, youths' oppositional behavior often contributes to the reproduction of their own subordinate racial or class status.

In a related articulation of the idea of oppositionality, Douglas Massey and Nancy Denton (1993) outline what they call a "culture of segregation" that is created by external structural conditions. They write, "An alternative status system has evolved within America's ghettos that is defined in opposition to the basic ideals and values of American society" (Massey and Denton 1993, p. 167). Similar to Willis, oppositional culture here is a rational adaptation to social and economic conditions, albeit one that may also have dysfunctional consequences for the communities in question.

In recent years oppositionality often has been discussed in reference to the work of John Ogbu and Signithia Fordham (Ogbu 1978, 1987, 1990, 1991; Fordham and Ogbu 1986). Focused in part on explaining racial differences in academic achievement, Ogbu argued that discussions of racial minorities in U.S. schools need to differentiate the experiences of involuntary from voluntary minorities. Involuntary minorities are those who have been forcibly incorporated into the United States through colonization and slavery, whereas voluntary minorities are those who have come to the United States through immigration or other voluntary means. Voluntary minorities tend to compare their prospects in the United States to those in their country of origin and thus have positive estimations of U.S. institutions and their prospects within them. In contrast, involuntary or subordinate minorities view their status in comparison to whites, and understand that they face many social, political, and institutional barriers to success. Ogbu hypothesized that, out of their understanding of structural constraint, involuntary minorities would develop an oppositional culture, disengaging from mainstream institutions and limiting the effort they put forth to succeed in them.

Since the 1990s a number of critics have challenged the oppositional culture thesis, arguing, for example, that black students neither possess an oppositional orientation toward education nor reject school as a "white thing" (Ainsworth-Darnell and Downey 1998; Carter 2005; Horvat and O'Connor 2006; O'Connor 1997, 1999; Tyson 2002). For example, James Ainsworth-Darnell and Douglas Downey (1998) use national data to show that African American students frequently report optimistic educational expectations and demonstrate more "pro-school" attitudes than their white counterparts, and that high-achieving students are more likely to be viewed as "popular" among peers. The authors conclude that African American students do not exhibit the habits and styles that are rewarded in school primarily because they do not enjoy the same structural conditions as their white counterparts. Prudence Carter (2005), Karolyn Tyson (2002), Garvey Lundy (2003), and others have suggested that this theory has not given enough attention to the ways that social institutions construct and produce oppositionality, and thus has put too much emphasis on the need for students to change their behaviors rather than focusing on the need for real change within social institutions and social arrangements more generally. In many ways this recent work continues to highlight the key questions within the field: Does oppositionality represent an accurate critique of and resistance to fundamentally unequal social arrangements? Or is oppositionality better understood as a dysfunctional cultural adaptation? These are not merely theoretical questions, because discussions of oppositional culture are central to debates about how to address a whole range of pressing social problems. Should the focus of change efforts be on social institutions and on social inequality more generally, or on the oppositional behavior of certain groups of adolescents?

SEE ALSO *Achievement; Achievement Gap, Racial; Acting White; Authority; Conformity; Culture; Norms; Ogbu, John U.; Protest; Resistance; Social Movements; Values; Working Class*

BIBLIOGRAPHY

Ainsworth-Darnell, James W., and Douglas B. Downey. 1998. Assessing the Oppositional Culture Explanation for Racial/Ethnic Differences in School Performance. *American Sociological Review* 63 (August): 536–553.

Ainsworth-Darnell, James W., and Douglas B. Downey. 2002. The Search for Oppositional Culture among Black Students. *American Sociological Review* 67: 156–164.

Carter, Prudence. 2005. *Keepin' It Real: School Success Beyond Black and White.* New York: Oxford University Press.

Fordham, Signithia. 1996. *Blacked Out: Dilemmas of Race, Identity, and Success at Capital High.* Chicago: University of Chicago Press.

Fordham, Signithia, and John U. Ogbu. 1986. Black Students' School Success: Coping with the Burden of "Acting White." *Urban Review* 18: 176–206.

Giroux, Henry A. 1983. *Theory and Resistance in Education: A Pedagogy for the Opposition.* South Hadley, MA: Bergin and Garvey Publishers.

Horvat, Erin, and Carla O'Connor. 2006. *Beyond Acting White: Reassessments and New Directions in Research on Black Students and School Success.* Boulder, CO: Rowman and Littlefield.

Lundy, Garvey F. 2003. The Myths of Oppositional Culture. *Journal of Black Studies* 33 (4): 450–467.

Macleod, Jay. 1995. *Ain't No Makin' It: Aspirations and Attainment in a Low-Income Neighborhood.* Boulder, CO: Westview Press.

Massey, Douglas, and Nancy Denton. 1993. *American Apartheid: Segregation and the Making of the Underclass.* Cambridge, MA: Harvard University Press.

O'Connor, Carla. 1997. Dispositions toward (Collective) Struggle and Educational Resilience in the Inner City: A Case Analysis of Six African-American High School Students. *American Educational Research Journal* 34 (4): 593–629.

O'Connor, Carla. 1999. Race, Class, and Gender in America: Narratives of Opportunity among Low-Income African American Youths. *Sociology of Education* 72 (3): 137–157.

Ogbu, John U. 1978. *Minority Education and Caste.* New York: Academic Press.

Ogbu, John U. 1987. Variability in Minority School Performance: A Problem in Search of an Explanation. *Anthropology and Education Quarterly* 18: 312–334.

Ogbu, John U. 1990. Minority Education in Comparative Perspective. *Journal of Negro Education* 59 (1): 45–57.

Ogbu, John U. 1991. Immigrant and Involuntary Minorities in Comparative Perspective. In *Minority Status and Schooling: A Comparative Study of Immigrant and Involuntary Minorities*, eds. John Ogbu and Margaret Gibson, 3–33. New York: Garland.

Ogbu, John U. 2003. *Black American Students in an Affluent Suburb: A Study of Academic Disengagement.* Mahwah, NJ: Lawrence Erlbaum.

Tyson, Karolyn. 2002. Weighing In: Elementary-Age Students and the Debate on Attitudes toward School among Black Students. *Social Forces* 80 (4): 1157–1189.

Weis, Lois. 1990. *Working Class Without Work: High School Students in a De-Industrializing Economy.* New York: Routledge.

Willis, Paul. 1977. *Learning to Labor: How Working Class Kids Get Working Class Jobs.* New York: Columbia University Press.

Geoffrey Banks
Amanda Lewis

OPPOSITIONALITY, SCHOOLING

Oppositional identity refers to any attitudes or behaviors intended to challenge schooling. These attitudes and behaviors range from mild opposition, such as not doing homework or becoming the class clown, to more disruptive opposition, such as defying and striking teachers or walking out of class. The most extreme form of opposition is dropping out of school. The high dropout rates and low academic achievement of racial and ethnic minority and lower-class students is often explained as a result of their adoption of an oppositional identity.

An oppositional stance to school develops because students believe that education will not lead to social mobility or because school requires behaviors that are deemed incompatible with their racial, ethnic, or class identity. Historically, racial and ethnic minority and low-income students have been subjected to discriminatory practices that deny them opportunities for social mobility through education. Knowing that schooling does not lead to social mobility shapes their attitudes toward and responses to school. Since there are scant opportunities for social mobility, they develop an oppositional stance toward school that leads to disengagement and low achievement (MacLeod 1987; Ogbu 1978; Willis 1977). Oppositional identity is a form of cultural inversion in which minority and lower-income students regard certain attitudes and behaviors as "white" or "middle class" and thus inappropriate for their group. Signithia Fordham and John Ogbu (1986) identified speaking standard English, listening to white music and white radio stations, going to the opera, getting good grades, doing volunteer work, going camping, and being on time as "white" behaviors. While subscribing to these behaviors may lead to school success, it also constitutes cultural or racial suicide because it entails the rejection of their culture in favor of white culture (McLaren 1994).

Ogbu refers to the "burden of acting white" as the price that black students pay when they assume these "white" behaviors and do well in school. Fueled by peer-group pressure, fear of being accused of disloyalty, fear of losing friends, and fear of not being accepted by whites, black students engage in oppositional behaviors that lead to underachievement (Fordham and Ogbu 1986). High achievers run the risk of being perceived as "acting white" or as being "sellouts." Peer chastising can include verbal taunting, ostracism, and physical aggression. To avoid peer harassment, high-achieving students must mask their accomplishments by engaging in some form of opposition, such as hiding or downplaying their grades, clowning or acting crazy, pretending to put little effort into school, or having friends who can protect them. A more socially costly alternative, and one that can lead to social isolation, is to assume a raceless persona, disassociating and disidentifying from their group (Fordham 1988).

Many scholars argue that the effects of the "burden of acting white" may be overstated (Lundy 2003; Flores-Gonzalez 2005). Many students manage to maintain a racial, ethnic, or class identity while being academically successful. Some develop dual identities that enable them to meet peer demands at school and in their neighborhood or to act differently with different peer groups (Mehan, Hubbard, and Villanueva 1994; Horvat and Lewis 2003). Others are immersed in peer networks or academic tracks that foster academic achievement. Furthermore opposition to school is not necessarily the result of peer pressure to underachieve but of structural factors that make schooling a painful and identity threatening experience for racial and ethnic minority and low-income students (Flores-Gonzalez 2005). Discrimination ensures that these students attend highly segregated schools that are usually overcrowded, understaffed, and underfunded. There they are subjected to subtractive schooling, the practice of devaluing the students' culture by administrators and teachers who sort, select, and reward students based on their proficiency with dominant "white and middle-class" culture (Carter 2003; Valenzuela 1999). Students who display minority culture are believed by the staff to be opposing school, which leads to their being further marginalized into the lower tracks and labeled as dumb or troubled and to their punishment (detention, suspension, expulsion) for their lack of knowledge and display of the dominant culture. Prudence Carter (2003) adds that while minority students possess and make use of both dominant and nondominant culture, they often experience difficulty enacting dominant culture. It is their inadequate display of dominant culture that is found problematic and inappropriate by teachers, leading to their negative appraisals. Furthermore one must differentiate between behaviors that are truly oppositional and are intended to challenge or resist some aspect of schooling and behaviors that may be expressions of power or triggered by other issues such as sexism or racism (Giroux 1983).

Adopting an oppositional identity almost always leads to negative consequences, such as low academic per-formance, grade repetition, detention, suspension, expulsion, and dropping out of school. Yet it can also protect a student's sense of self. Michelle Fine (1991) shows that students who conform to school tend to be more depressed, less politically aware, less assertive, and more conformist than those who take on an oppositional stance. In a stratified schooling system where opportunities are structured to lead most students to failure, developing an oppositional identity may shield students from the negative effects of schooling on their sense of self and may also reinforce their sense of collective identity.

SEE ALSO *Achievement Gap, Racial; Acting White; Conformity; Education, Unequal; Identity; Ogbu, John U.; Racism; Resistance; Sexism; Stratification*

BIBLIOGRAPHY

Carter, Prudence. 2003. "Black" Cultural Capital, Status Positioning, and Schooling Conflicts for Low-Income African American Youth. *Social Problems* 50 (1): 136-155.

Fine, Michelle. 1991. *Framing Dropouts: Notes on the Politics of an Urban Public High School.* Albany: State University of New York Press.

Flores-Gonzalez, Nilda. 2005. Popularity versus Respect: School Structure, Peer Groups, and Latino Academic Achievement. *International Journal of Qualitative Studies in Education* 18 (5): 625–642.

Fordham, Signithia. 1988. Racelessness as a Factor in Black Students' School Success: Pragmatic Strategy or Pyrrhic Victory? *Harvard Educational Review* 58 (1): 54–84.

Fordham, Signithia, and John Ogbu. 1986. Black Students' School Success: Coping with the "Burden of 'Acting White.' " *Urban Review* 18 (3): 176–206.

Giroux, H. 1983. Theories of Reproduction and Resistance in the New Sociology of Education: A Critical Analysis. *Harvard Educational Review* 53 (3): 257–293.

Horvat, E. M., and K. S. Lewis. 2003. Reassessing the "Burden of 'Acting White' ": The Importance of Peer Groups in Managing Academic Success. *Sociology of Education* 76 (4): 265–280.

Lundy, Garvey. 2003. The Myths of Oppositional Culture. *Journal of Black Studies* 33 (4): 450–467.

MacLeod, J. 1995. *Ain't No Makin' It: Leveled Aspirations in a Low-Income Neighborhood.* Boulder, CO: Westview.

McLaren, P. 2007. *Life in Schools: An Introduction to Critical Pedagogy in the Foundations of Education.* 5th ed. New York: Longman.

Mehan, H., L. Hubbard, and I. Villanueva. 1994. Forming Academic Identities: Accommodation without Assimilation among Involuntary Minorities. *Anthropology and Education Quarterly* 25 (2): 91–117.

Ogbu, John. 1978. *Minority Education and Caste: The American System in Cross-Cultural Perspective.* New York: Academic.

Valenzuela, A. 1999. *Subtractive Schooling: U.S.-Mexican Youth and the Politics of Caring.* Albany: State University of New York Press.

Willis, P. 1977. *Learning to Labor: How Working Class Kids Get Working Class Jobs.* New York: Columbia University Press.

Nilda Flores-Gonzalez

OPTIMAL GROWTH

Optimal growth theory occupies a central part of modern capital theory and dynamic models of planning, macroeconomics, exhaustible resources, natural resources, development economics, finance, and dynamic games. It originated with a classic 1928 paper by the mathematician Frank Ramsey, who investigated what kind of savings policy (equal to investment) would realize the largest social welfare, defined as the sum total of utilities from current and future consumption flows. Since the choice of capital stock at any point in time can only be based upon the consumption streams the stock can yield in the future, the problem necessarily takes an open-ended form with no finite terminal date for the planning horizon.

A brief and abstract statement of the typical mathematical problem in optimal growth theory follows. Let t denote time in discrete units, $t = 0, 1, 2 ..., k_t$ the stock of goods at t, and T_t the technology set known at t, composed of pairs of vectors (x,y) such that from stocks x at t it is feasible to reach the stocks y at $t + 1$. A function u_t: $T_t \rightarrow R$ provides the maximum utility $u_t(x,y)$ that is achievable, consistent with the transition of stocks from x to y. Let k denote the historically given initial stock. A path from k is an infinite sequence $\{k_t\}_{t=0}^{\infty}$ satisfying $k_0 = k$ and $(k_t, k_{t+1}) \in T_t$ for each $t \geq 0$. Loosely speaking, a path is optimal if it maximizes $\sum_{t=0}^{\infty} u_t (k_t, k_{t+1})$ over the set of all possible paths from k.

The reduced-form model stated above, developed by David Gale (1967) and Lionel McKenzie (1968), is flexible enough to allow for changing technology and tastes with very liberal interpretations of stocks, including environmental factors, fixed resources, and unfinished goods in process, to name a few. A substantial part of the literature concentrates attention on the quasi-stationary model where technology and utility is time independent; that is, there is a set T, a function u: $T_t \rightarrow R$, and a constant discount factor δ, where $0 < \delta \leq 1$, such that $T_t = T$ and $u_t(x,y) = \delta^t u(x,y)$. A special case is the extensively studied one-sector neoclassical growth model, with one consumption cum capital good, the output of which is given by a production function f, and $T = \{(x,y) : x \geq 0, 0 \leq y \leq f(x)\}$. A utility function w is defined directly over consumption $c = f(x) - y$; so, here, $u(x,y) = w(c)$. It is noteworthy that the general reduced-form formulation may allow for direct stock effects over and above the effect of consumption on utilities and is a much richer framework.

Ramsey studied the one-sector model with time as a continuous variable and the infinite sum accordingly replaced by an integral. He obtained a remarkable rule governing the optimal savings rate at each point of time, essentially the Euler equation in the calculus of variations. Ramsey focused primarily on the undiscounted case, that is, $\delta = 1$; much later Tjalling Koopmans (1965) and David Cass (1965) treated the discounted case, that is, $\delta < 1$ thoroughly. The undiscounted case presents the problem that the welfare sum may not converge. Ramsey circumvented the problem by assuming that, due to constraints on tastes or technology, there is an upper bound on the achievable level of utility, and he sought to minimize the divergence of the utility level along paths from this bliss level. This problem received much more careful and rigorous attention later, employing variants of Carl C. von Weizsäcker's (1965) overtaking criterion, which provides only a partial ranking over paths but can still yield a workable notion of optimality. Simultaneously, following Gale and William Brock (1970), existence of an optimal program was explored carefully in multisector models. The so-called golden rule program or optimal stationary state, where the per period utility along constant feasible programs is maximized, plays a role analogous to that of the bliss level in Ramsey.

TURNPIKE THEORY

A 1945 paper by another mathematician, John von Neumann, on a general equilibrium model primarily stressing production, which established the existence of a balanced growth path with a maximal rate of expansion and associated present value prices at which the activities employed are profit maximizing, led to the turnpike property first explicated in 1958 by Robert Dorfman, Paul Samuelson, and Robert Solow. Several authors followed with rigorous proofs of turnpike theorems, which showed that planning paths, with long horizons and terminal stock accumulation as the goal, would tend to take advantage of the maximal rate of growth of the balanced path, the turnpike, by orienting stocks to those of the turnpike for most of the horizon.

In the context of optimal growth models, Roy Radner's (1961) value-loss method was adapted by authors such as Gale and McKenzie (1968) to show that the optimal stationary state plays the role of the turnpike and optimal programs converge to the golden rule, albeit with some interesting qualifications when linearities are present in the model in an essential way. This convenient property is, in general, limited to the undiscounted case. José Scheinkman (1976) showed that for large discount factors the turnpike property holds; however, for small discount factors Jess Benhabib and Kazuo Nishimura (1985) showed that optimal cycles are possible. Later

Michele Boldrin and Luigi Montruchhio (1986) showed that chaotic optimal paths are possible. These papers gave rise to the literature on the possibility of nontrivial business cycles in deterministic macromodels with a representative agent carrying out the infinite horizon optimization. Also, the effect of variations in parameters, especially of the discount factor, on the optimal policy function became a topic of considerable interest following a remarkable 1992 paper by Gerhard Sorger (in this connection, see also Mitra et al. 2006).

Following Paul Romer (1986), models allowing aspects of externalities or public goods in production, which may have many equilibrium paths, gave rise to the literature of the indeterminacy problem surveyed in Nishimura and Alain Venditti (2006). Integration of turnpike theory with general equilibrium theory began with Robert Becker (1980) who, following up on Ramsey's conjecture, investigated the long-run wealth distribution that arises in a Ramsey-type general equilibrium model with several infinitely lived agents and related it to the discount factors of the agents.

DUALITY THEORY

Since Edmund Malinvaud (1953), the well-known connection between the static theory of price and efficiency went through a major evolution in the context of efficient allocation of resources in infinite horizon models. In the context of optimal growth models, McKenzie (1986) provides a transparent version of Martin Weitzman's 1973 proof of the existence of present value prices at which in each period myopic profit maximization takes place, with utility treated as an output. These are likened to familiar individual decision rules in competitive equilibrium, and the optimality conditions are usually called the *competitive* conditions. The distinctive feature of the infinite horizon aspect of the problem is that, in general, these need to be supplemented by a transversality condition, which requires that an appropriate limit condition be satisfied by the value of stocks, a condition that cannot be interpreted as a myopic decision rule. There has been some success at obtaining alternate price characterizations of optimal paths that require only period-by-period conditions to be verified by myopic agents; that is, the optimal path is "decentralizable" (see Majumdar 1992). Indeed, in a fairly wide class of production models satisfying a reachability condition, the competitive conditions alone characterize optimality (see Dasgupta and Mitra 1999a).

Duality theory played a significant role in grounding and extending the familiar macroeconomic concept of *national product*, based upon explicit welfare considerations in dynamic models. Weitzman (1976) observed that in a continuous-time framework, national income at any time along an optimal path is a proxy measure of the hypothetical level of constant consumption that, if possible to maintain forever, provides the same level of welfare found along the optimal path. While the same is not necessarily true for competitive equilibrium paths in general, in some models involving exhaustible resources, it is possible to extend such results to paths that are not necessarily optimal but satisfy the competitive equilibrium conditions only (see Dasgupta and Mitra 1999b). The interpretation of stocks in Weitzman is very general and may include exhaustible resources, environmental factors, and the like, leading to this literature developing a strong connection with the concept of "green" national income accounting. Connections with sustainable consumption paths have also been explored following Solow (1986).

Convexity is essential for the necessity side of duality theorems. Nonconvexity arises in many models, such as those with natural resources. The qualitative properties are significantly different (see Majumdar 2006). Nonconvexity is also of importance in endogenous growth models following Romer (1986).

Optimal growth allowing uncertain technology, changing technology, and so forth have been studied. With uncertainty, the possibility of ensuring long-run survival may temper optimality considerations in interesting ways (see Olson and Roy 2006). The additive-separable form of the welfare function is a severe restriction, and the literature on recursive utility functions seeks to address that (see Boyd 2006). Introducing population growth as a control variable raises interesting questions about appropriate forms of the welfare function.

An assessment is needed of the implications, the importance, and the weaknesses of the manifold developments in optimal growth theory, especially of the literature on cycles, chaos, and indeterminacy in the context of macrodynamics and business cycles, bearing in mind that the phenomenon of excess capacity does not appear in these models. An assessment is also needed of the models' practical significance for planning, bearing in mind that practical planning is expected to be finite horizon in nature and to rely on decentralized mechanisms for its implementation. This may yield more productive directions for future research.

SEE ALSO *Economic Growth; Golden Rule in Growth Models; Maximization; Neoclassical Growth Model; Optimizing Behavior; Social Welfare Functions*

BIBLIOGRAPHY

Becker, Robert A. 1980. On the Long-Run Steady State in a Simple Dynamic Model of Equilibrium with Heterogeneous Households. *Quarterly Journal of Economics* 95 (2): 375–382.

Benhabib, Jess, and Kazuo Nishimura. 1985. Competitive Equilibrium Cycles. *Journal of Economic Theory* 35: 284–306.

Boldrin, Michele, and Luigi Montruchhio. 1986. On the Indeterminacy of Capital Accumulation Paths. *Journal of Economic Theory* 40: 26–39.

Boyd, John H. 2006. Discrete-Time Recursive Utility. In *Handbook on Optimal Growth*, eds. Rose-Anne Dana, Cuong Le Van, Tapan Mitra, and Kazuo Nishimura, 251–272. Berlin and New York: Springer.

Brock, William A. 1970. On Existence of Weakly Maximal Programmes in a Multi-sector Economy. *Review of Economic Studies* 37 (2): 275–280.

Cass, David. 1965. Optimal Growth in an Aggregative Model of Capital Accumulation. *Review of Economic Studies* 32: 233–240.

Dasgupta, Swapan, and Tapan Mitra. 1999a. Optimal and Competitive Programs in Reachable Multi Sector Models. *Economic Theory* 14 (3): 565–582.

Dasgupta, Swapan, and Tapan Mitra. 1999b. On the Welfare Significance of National Product for Economic Growth and Sustainable Development. *Japanese Economic Review* 50 (4): 422–442.

Dorfman, Robert, Paul A. Samuelson, and Robert M. Solow. 1958. *Linear Programming and Economic Analysis*. New York: McGraw-Hill.

Gale, David. 1967. On Optimal Development in a Multi-sector Economy. *Review of Economic Studies* 34: 1–18.

Koopmans, Tjalling. 1965. On the Concept of Optimal Economic Growth. *Pontificae Acadmiae Scientarum Varia* 28: 225–300.

Lucas, Robert E. 1988. On the Mechanics of Economic Development. *Journal of Monetary Economics* 22: 3–42.

Majumdar, Mukul, ed. 1992. *Decentralization in Infinite Horizon Economies*. Boulder, CO: Westview.

Majumdar, Mukul. 2006. Intertemporal Allocation with a Non-convex Technology. In *Handbook on Optimal Growth*, eds. Rose-Anne Dana, Cuong Le Van, Tapan Mitra, and Kazuo Nishimura, 171–202. Berlin and New York: Springer.

Malinvaud, Edmund. 1953. Capital Accumulation and Efficient Allocation of Resources. *Econometrica* 21: 233–268.

McKenzie, Lionel W. 1968. Accumulation Programs of Maximum Utility and the von Neumann Facet. In *Value, Capital, and Growth: Papers in Honour of Sir John Hicks*, ed. J. N. Wolfe, 348–357. Edinburgh: Edinburgh University Press.

McKenzie, Lionel W. 1986. Optimal Economic Growth, Turnpike Theorems, and Comparative Dynamics. In *Handbook of Mathematical Economics*, Vol. 3, eds. Kenneth J. Arrow and Michael D. Intriligator, 1281–1358. New York: North Holland.

Mitra, Tapan. 2006. Duality Theory in Infinite Horizon Optimization Models. In *Handbook on Optimal Growth*, eds. Rose-Anne Dana, Cuong Le Van, Tapan Mitra, and Kazuo Nishimura, 55–84. Berlin and New York: Springer.

Mitra, Tapan, Kazuo Nishimura, and Gerhard Sorger. 2006. Optimal Cycles and Chaos. In *Handbook on Optimal Growth*, eds. Rose-Anne Dana, Cuong Le Van, Tapan Mitra, and Kazuo Nishimura, 141–169. Berlin and New York: Springer.

Nishimura, Kazuo, and Alain Venditti. 2006. Indeterminacy in Discrete-Time Infinite-Horizon Models. In *Handbook on Optimal Growth*, eds. Rose-Anne Dana, Cuong Le Van, Tapan Mitra, and Kazuo Nishimura, 273–296. Berlin and New York: Springer.

Olson, Lars J., and Santanu Roy. 2006. Theory of Stochastic Optimal Growth. In *Handbook on Optimal Growth*, eds. Rose-Anne Dana, Cuong Le Van, Tapan Mitra, and Kazuo Nishimura, 297–336. Berlin and New York: Springer.

Radner, Roy. 1961. Paths of Economic Growth that Are Optimal with Regard Only to Final States: A Turnpike Theorem. *Review of Economic Studies* 28 (2): 98–104.

Ramsey, Frank. 1928. A Mathematical Theory of Saving. *Economic Journal* 38: 543–559.

Romer, Paul. 1986. Increasing Returns and Long-Run Growth. *Journal of Political Economy* 94: 1002–1037.

Scheinkman, José A. 1976. On Optimal Steady States of n-Sector Growth Models When Utility is Discounted. *Journal of Economic Theory* 12 (1): 11–30.

Solow, Robert M. 1986. On the Intergenerational Allocation of Natural Resources. *Scandinavian Journal of Economics* 88: 141–149.

Sorger, Gerhard. 1992. On the Minimum Rate of Impatience for Complicated Optimal Growth Paths. *Journal of Economic Theory* 56: 160–179.

Sorger, Gerhard. 2006. Rationalizability in Optimal Growth Theory. In *Handbook on Optimal Growth*, eds. Rose-Anne Dana, Cuong Le Van, Tapan Mitra, and Kazuo Nishimura, 85–113. Berlin and New York: Springer.

Von Neumann, John. 1945. A Model of General Economic Equilibrium. *Review of Economic Studies* 13: 1–9.

Von Weizsäcker, Carl C. 1965. Existence of Optimal Programs of Accumulation for an Infinite Time Horizon. *Review of Economic Studies* 32 (2): 85–104.

Weitzman, Martin L. 1973. Duality Theory for Infinite Horizon Convex Models. *Management Science* 19: 783–789.

Weitzman, Martin L. 1976. On the Welfare Significance of National Product in a Dynamic Economy. *Quarterly Journal of Economics* 90: 156–162.

Swapan Dasgupta

OPTIMISM/PESSIMISM

People differ in how they approach the world. Some individuals are optimistic and tend to be positive in their outlook and expectations for the future, whereas others are pessimistic and tend to have more negative expectations. Furthermore, these individual differences appear to be stable across time and context. The construct of optimism is in many ways rooted in folk wisdom, but scientific approaches have linked the concepts of optimism and pessimism to expectancy models of motivation. The optimism construct is therefore also grounded in decades of theory and research on motivation and on how such motivation is expressed through behavior.

One of the most recognized contemporary theories of optimism assumes expectancies to be dispositional, and refers to generalized expectancies that apply more or less across a person's entire life span. Michael F. Scheier and Charles S. Carver developed the dispositional optimism concept in 1985, as well as one of the most popular measures used to assess optimism and pessimism, the Life Orientation Test (LOT). The LOT and its revised version, the LOT-R, contain items measuring both positive and negative expectancies (e.g., "In uncertain times, I usually expect the best" and "If something can go wrong for me, it will"). Both of these measures therefore provide the most direct assessment of optimism and pessimism as people usually understand these constructs.

Another approach to optimism, separate from the dispositional optimism approach, assumes that expectancies are based on individual interpretations of previous experiences. Often referred to as attributional or explanatory style, this approach is based on Martin E. P. Seligman's work on learned helplessness. To account for human variation in responses to uncontrollability, the attributional reformulation of learned helplessness specifically focused on people's explanations for events. Optimists interpret bad events as temporary, limited in scope, and not resulting from personal fault. Pessimists on the other hand, are more likely to interpret bad events as long lasting, pervasive in scope, and due to their own fault. Optimists' tendency to attribute negative events to unstable, specific, and external causes contributes to their resiliency to negative experiences and helplessness.

Attributional style is measured with the Attributional Style Questionnaire (ASQ), which Chris Peterson and colleagues developed in 1982. The ASQ consists of six negative event items and six positive event items. For each event, the person gives one major cause for why the event occurred and rates the internality, stability, and globality of the cause. Attributional style can also be assessed through spoken or written material, using the content analysis of verbatim explanations (CAVE) method Peterson and colleagues developed in 1983. In this method, good and bad events are rated along three dimensions (internal, stable, global) using a seven-point continuum. On both of these scales, a person considering positive events to be happening due to internal, stable, and global events is considered to have an optimistic explanatory style. If a person considers negative events to be happening due to internal, stable, and global events, this individual is considered to have a pessimistic explanatory style.

Differences between optimists' and pessimists' attributional styles can account for different expectancies. In attributing causes to their own behavior rather than to external factors, optimists believe in their ability to influ-

ence event outcomes. On the other hand, pessimists often judge events as being caused by external factors and see no opportunity to influence the outcomes. When these attributions are stable and global, as they often are for pessimists, helplessness results.

Whereas attributional styles are generally based on interpretations of previous experiences, the construct of dispositional optimism arose from a general self-regulatory framework. Because optimists see positive outcomes as attainable, they are more likely to invest continued effort in order to achieve their goals, instead of disengaging and giving up, as pessimists might do. This tendency of optimists to expect positive outcomes and remain engaged in challenges creates a self-fulfilling prophecy in which positive outcomes and success can be actualized. For pessimists, on the other hand, the tendency to expect negative outcomes and give up on challenges creates a self-fulfilling prophesy of failure.

One of the mechanisms by which dispositional optimism and attributional style translate into better adjustment is through coping with stressors. Optimists appear to cope in active ways that help them adjust better to stressful situations. Optimists' resilience to helplessness and effortful behaviors has been found to be positively associated with approach coping strategies aiming to eliminate, reduce, or manage stressors, and negatively associated with avoidance coping strategies aiming to avoid, ignore, or withdraw from stressors. High optimism may therefore led to approach coping, which again may lead to better adjustment to stressors.

Positive outcome expectancies and optimistic explanatory styles may also be protective factors contributing to resiliency, both psychologically and physiologically. For example, high dispositional optimism has been associated with less distress, anxiety, and depression in women with breast cancer and has been found to be protective of distress in women coping with in vitro fertilization failure. Pessimistic attributional style has also been associated with depression and distress. As for physiological well-being, dispositional optimism has been associated with a faster rate of physical recovery from coronary artery bypass surgery and has been linked to lower changes of rehospitalization for cardiac patients. Dispositional optimism has also been linked to longer survival in cancer patients and to better recovery and resistance to postsurgical infection in transplant patients. Optimistic attributional style has also been positively correlated with vigorous immune reaction to an antigen challenge as well as longer survival. Clearly, the link between positive outcome expectancies and well-being is pervasive.

Carver and Scheier's pioneering research on generalized outcome expectancies and Seligman's groundbreaking work on learned helplessness have led to an enhanced understanding of the significance of positive outcome expectancies. The positive psychology movement, initiated in 1998 by American Psychological Association president Seligman, emphasizes the focus in research on positive aspects of human behavior, such as dispositional optimism. The movement highlights the importance of studying not only the negative side of human experience such as disease and distress, but also recognizing the positive aspects of human behavior such as strength and virtue. Positive psychology focuses on people's satisfaction with various aspects of their lives, and considers building positive qualities as equally important to mending the worst in life. Researchers in this area address questions relating to happiness, well-being, and human potential, among others. The positive psychology movement aims to advance the understanding of how human traits can serve to buffer against not only psychological, but also physical, ailments.

SEE ALSO *Attribution; Depression, Psychological; Expectations; Positive Psychology; Psychoneuroendocrinology; Stress*

BIBLIOGRAPHY

Carver, Charles S., and Michael F. Scheier. 1998. *On the Self-Regulation of Behavior*. Cambridge, U.K.: Cambridge University Press.

Chang, Edward C. 2002. *Optimism and Pessimism: Implications for Theory, Research, and Practice*. Washington, DC: American Psychological Association.

Diener, Ed, and Martin E. P. Seligman. 2002. Very Happy People. *Psychological Science* 13: 81–84.

Peterson, Chris, L. Luborsky, and Martin E. P. Seligman. 1983. Attributions and Depressive Mood Shifts: A Case Study Using the Symptom-Content Method. *Journal of Abnormal Psychology* 94: 165–169.

Peterson, Chris, et al. 1982. The Attributional Style Questionnaire. *Cognitive Therapy and Research* 6: 287–299.

Scheier, Michael F., and Charles S. Carver. 1985. Optimism, Coping, and Health: Assessment and Implications of Generalized Outcome Expectancies. *Health Psychology* 3: 219–247.

Scheier, Michael F., Charles S. Carver, and M. W. Bridges. 1994. Distinguishing Optimism from Neuroticism (and Trait Anxiety, Self-Mastery, and Self-Esteem): A Reevaluation of the Life Orientation Test. *Journal of Personality and Social Psychology* 67: 1063–1078.

Seligman, Martin E. P. 1991. *Learned Optimism*. New York: Knopf.

Solberg Nes, Lise, and Suzanne C. Segerstrom. 2006. Dispositional Optimism and Coping: A Meta-Analytic Review. *Personality and Social Psychology Review* 10: 235–251.

Lise Solberg Nes
Abbey Roach

OPTIMIZATION

SEE *Optimizing Behavior.*

OPTIMIZING BEHAVIOR

In mathematics, optimization refers to the general ideas of choosing some element of a set to maximize a function that is defined on the set. Abstractly, if one defines a function f (which is typically indexed by some set of parameters θ) from some general set S to the real numbers S, the function $y = f(s, \theta)$; optimization is typically nothing more than asking which element of S produces the largest value of y. Notice that the set can contain complicated objects, including infinite sequences, or functions.

In economics, the notion of optimization has been used to model individual behavior. Indeed, neoclassical economic reasoning is typically predicated on the assumption that individual actors optimize in the sense that, subject to a set of constraints and beliefs about the consequences of their actions, agents choose actions that are optimal relative to their preferences. In a classic microeconomics problem, a consumer is assumed to choose a bundle of consumption goods to maximize utility subject to a budget constraint. This problem produces a relationship between relative prices and the marginal utilities of different goods. A more complicated version of this problem can ask what consumption/saving rules maximize a lifetime notion of utility in the presence of uncertainty about the future (cf. Brock and Mirman 1972). Under appropriate convexity assumptions, this type of stochastic growth model can be used to represent intertemporal general equilibrium in an economy with a representative consumer by the device of support prices constructed from the optimization problem. This approach has been fruitful in macroeconomics.

The notion that individual agents optimize is controversial from the perspectives of other social sciences. A gross simplification of this controversy is that sociologists focus much more on how social structures influence individual preferences and beliefs whereas psychologists emphasize empirically based descriptions of individual decisionmaking which can incorporate cognitive errors and limitations in the processing of information as well as what, from the perspective of the neoclassical economic theory of choice, are inconsistencies in preferences.

These alternative perspectives have become part of current economic reasoning. Herbert Simon was an early pioneer of work on bounded rationality, which emphasized limits to the ability of individuals to optimize. Simon advocated the alternative idea that individuals satisfice, that is, make acceptable rather than optimal actions. Simon's views did not affect most economic practice. Rather, experimental research pioneered to a great extent by psychologists Amos Tversky and Daniel Kahneman created a strong case that the standard optimization assumptions in economics were flawed for many contexts. There is a rich literature that attempts to both empirically identify (again, via experiments) and formally model individual decisionmaking that accounts for limits to human reasoning in economically interesting environments. Efforts also exist to expand the formulation of preferences to account for social context and social preferences such as altruism, although this work seems less a challenge to the notion of optimization than a reconsideration of the objectives of individuals. Together, this work is known as behavioral economics.

An alternative approach to relaxing the standard optimization paradigm is to ask whether, in dynamic environments, individual behavior will evolve toward optimality. This question, which is a major theme of evolutionary game theory, does not admit a simple answer, as different models produce different results. But interesting environments have been identified where this convergence does occur.

Perhaps the appropriate lesson is that the appropriateness of optimization assumptions depends on contexts. For example, the empirically well established absence of arbitrage opportunities in financial markets suggests in modeling individual traders, they are optimizing to the extent that for the market as a whole, all such possibilities are eliminated. Also one should not underestimate the capacity of optimization models to explain seemingly irrational behaviors, as demonstrated by the Gary Becker and Kevin Murphy (1988) model of rational addiction. Efforts to move economic models away from optimization assumptions have yielded many valuable insights, but it is hardly the case that the optimization paradigm no longer has a key role to play in economic analysis.

A user-friendly introduction to mathematical methods of optimization relevant to economists is Rangarajan Sundaharam's book *A First Course in Optimization Theory* (1996). Herbert Simon's views are well summarized in his *Reason in Human Affairs* (1983). Colin Camerer's *Behavioral Game Theory* (2003) provides an overview of behavioral approaches to economics. Drew Fudenberg and David Levine's *The Theory of Learning in Games* (1998) is a standard text on learning and dynamics.

SEE ALSO *Decisionmaking; Economic Model; Evolutionary Games; Maximization; Minimization; Partial Equilibrium; Satisficing Behavior; Theory of Second Best*

BIBLIOGRAPHY

Becker, Gary, and Kevin Murphy. 1988. A Theory of Rational Addiction. *Journal of Political Economy* 96: 675–700.

Brock, William, and Leonard Mirman. 1972. Optimal Economic Growth and Uncertainty: The Discounted Case. *Journal of Economic Theory* 4: 479–513.

Camerer, Colin. 2003. *Behavioral Game Theory: Experiments in Strategic Interaction*. Princeton, NJ: Princeton University Press.

Fudenberg, Drew, and David Levine. 1998. *The Theory of Learning in Games*. Cambridge: MIT Press.

Simon, Herbert. 1983. *Reason in Human Affairs*. Stanford, CA: Stanford University Press.

Sundaram, Rangarajan. 1996. *A First Course in Optimization Theory*. New York: Cambridge University Press.

William A. Brock
Steven N. Durlauf

ORAL TRADITION
SEE *Storytelling.*

ORDINALITY

The concept of ordinality belongs to the broad issue of utility, preferences, and measurement of pleasure or consumer satisfaction. Economists and social philosophers have always aimed at explaining how to overcome the omnipresent scarcity that nature imposes upon humans, and thus to achieve a state of higher satisfaction. The concept of utility was developed to mean the quality that makes a commodity—through whose consumption the satisfaction can be achieved—desired. It has always been recognized that utility is a subjective matter, because the outside observer cannot know much about why and to what extent a commodity is desired, but originally it was believed (by early utility theorists such as H. H. Gossen, W. Stanley Jevons, and Léon Walras) that utility is measurable and additive—that is, that numbers can be attached to each intensity of satisfaction (cardinal utility theory) and can be summed up to get a "total utility." In criticizing this idea, two points were made: first, that utility is nonadditive and fundamentally unmeasureable within an individual (and much less across two individuals); and second, that one actually does not even need to assume cardinality in order to make use of utility theory in economics (though cardinal utility still may exist). It came to be understood that there is an alternative approach, represented by the concept of ranking of available options that satisfy consumer preferences—ordinal utility theory. This is done in two different ways.

The first of them was based on the principle of indifference. In a standard model, the consumer maximizes her satisfaction by spending her limited budget on two goods. Any combination of the quantities of the two goods yields the same satisfaction (level of utility) to the consumer, which is why she is indifferent in her choice between these combinations. Considering all such combinations gives rise (under certain assumptions) to an "indifference curve"—a tool widely used in twentieth-century microeconomics. A set of such curves for different levels of satisfaction is an "indifference map." Similarly, considering all combinations of the two goods that can be purchased with the same limited budget gives rise to a "budget constraint." With these tools at hand, whether the cardinal utility exists or not is immaterial for the problem of decision making, because what matters is satisfaction ranking of all the ways in which the given budget can be spent on the two goods. Thus, when seen on a graph, the best use of the budget utility-wise is the combination of the two goods represented by the intersection of the budget constraint and the indifference curve, signifying the greatest possible satisfaction (which will typically be the one that is just "touched" by the budget constraint). This approach is associated with the work of Robert Edgeworth, Vilfredo Pareto, John Hicks, and Roy G. D. Allen, among others.

In the second approach to ordinal utility, every acting person can make a ranking of his alternative ends according to his values. This ranking, rooted in the process of subjective valuation, brings about the construction of an individual preference scale. In every action a choice is made and a part of the preference scale is demonstrated, so that the external observer can get "data" about other people's utility ranking. For example, we can see that an individual who is buying a book ranks the $20 he is spending lower than he ranks the book on his preference scale, whereas a seller of the book has a reverse preference ranking—that is, she values the money more than the book, and therefore she is willing to sell. Value scales can be used to formulate the theory of exchange and build up a price theory and the whole of microeconomics. This approach was elaborated by Carl Menger and Eugen von Böhm-Bawerk and their followers of the so-called "Austrian school"—the Czech economist Franz Cuhel, the Austrian economists Ludwig von Mises and Friedrich Hayek, and their American followers Israel Kirzner and Murray Rothbard.

There is no doubt that utility theory is the cornerstone of the theory of consumer behavior, and yet there seems to be no general consensus on the underlining issues related to the nature of utility. On the one hand, defenders of value scales are criticized by those using indifference curves that working solely with ranked units of goods hinders the use of more sophisticated mathematical analysis and model building. Users of indifference curves are criticized on the other hand because indifference cannot be demonstrated in action—that is, an actor always prefers in his action A over B, so when observing actual behavior, the "data" we see is preference, not indifference. Thus, indifference should not then be a category of economics, but of psychology. Some argue, however, that utility theory needs more psychology, to provide more input into economics because actual preference ranking may be biased or uninformed. Lastly, some authors argue, the dichotomy between ordinality and cardinality is mostly artificial and does not play any significant role when policy implications are discussed.

SEE ALSO *Austrian Economics; Consumer; Consumption; Hayek, Friedrich August von; Hicks, John R.; Opportunity Cost; Pareto, Vilfredo; Scarcity; Utilitarianism; Utility Function; Utility, Subjective; Walras, Léon.*

BIBLIOGRAPHY

Rothbard, Murray N. [1956] 1997. *Toward a Reconstruction of Utility and Welfare Economics.* In *The Logic of Action One: Method, Money, and the Austrian School,* 211–255. London: Edward Elgar.

Spiegel, Henry W. 1991. *The Growth of Economic Thought.* 3rd ed. Durham, NC: Duke University Press.

Josef Sima

ORDINARY LEAST SQUARES REGRESSION

Ordinary least squares (OLS) regression is a statistical method of analysis that estimates the relationship between one or more independent variables and a dependent variable; the method estimates the relationship by minimizing the sum of the squares in the difference between the observed and predicted values of the dependent variable configured as a straight line. In this entry, OLS regression will be discussed in the context of a bivariate model, that is, a model in which there is only one independent variable (X) predicting a dependent variable (Y). However, the logic of OLS regression is easily extended to the multivariate model in which there are two or more independent variables.

Social scientists are often concerned with questions about the relationship between two variables. These include the following: Among women, is there a relationship between education and fertility? Do more-educated women have fewer children, and less-educated women have more children? Among countries, is there a relationship between gross national product (GNP) and life expectancy? Do countries with higher levels of GNP have higher levels of life expectancy, and countries with lower levels of GNP, lower levels of life expectancy? Among countries, is there a positive relationship between employment opportunities and net migration? Among people, is there a relationship between age and values of baseline systolic blood pressure? (Lewis-Beck 1980; Vittinghoff et al. 2005).

As Michael Lewis-Beck notes, these examples are specific instances of the common query, "What is the relationship between variable X and variable Y?" (1980, p. 9). If the relationship is assumed to be linear, bivariate regression may be used to address this issue by fitting a straight line to a scatterplot of observations on variable X and variable Y. The simplest statement of such a relationship between an independent variable, labeled X, and a dependent variable, labeled Y, may be expressed as a straight line in this formula:

$$Y = a + bX + e, \qquad (1)$$

where a is the intercept and indicates where the straight line intersects the Y-axis (the vertical axis); b is the slope and indicates the degree of steepness of the straight line; and e represents the error.

The error term indicates that the relationship predicted in the equation is not perfect. That is, the straight line does not perfectly predict Y. This lack of a perfect prediction is common in the social sciences. For instance, in terms of the education and fertility relationship mentioned above, we would not expect all women with exactly sixteen years of education to have exactly one child, and women with exactly four years of education to have exactly eight children. But we would expect that a woman with a lot of education would have fewer children than a woman with a little education. Stated in another way, the number of children born to a woman is likely to be a linear function of her education, plus some error. Actually, in low-fertility societies, Poisson and negative binomial regression methods are preferred over ordinary least squares regression methods for the prediction of fertility (Poston 2002; Poston and McKibben 2003).

We first introduce a note about the notation used in this entry. In the social sciences we almost always undertake research with samples drawn from larger populations, say, a 1 percent random sample of the U.S. population. Greek letters like α and β are used to denote the parameters (i.e., the intercept and slope values) representing the relationship between X and Y in the larger population, whereas lowercase Roman letters like a and b will be used to denote the parameters in the sample.

When postulating relationships in the social sciences, linearity is often assumed, but this may not be always the case. Indeed, a lot of relationships are not linear. When one hypothesizes the form of a relationship between two variables, one needs to be guided both by the theory being used, as well as by an inspection of the data.

But given that we wish to use a straight line for relating variable Y, the dependent variable, with variable X, the independent variable, there is a question about which line to use. In any scatterplot of observations of X and Y values (see Figure 1), there would be an infinite number of straight lines that might be used to represent the relationship. Which line is the best line?

The chosen straight line needs to be the one that minimizes the amount of error between the predicted values of Y and the actual values of Y. Specifically, for each of the i th observations in the sample, if one were to square the difference between the observed and predicted values of Y, and then sum these squared differences, the best line would have the lowest sum of squared errors (SSE), represented as follows:

$$SSE = \sum_i (Y_i - \hat{Y})^2 \qquad (2)$$

Ordinary least squares regression is a statistical method that produces the one straight line that minimizes the total squared error.

Using the calculus, it may be shown that SSE is the lowest or the "least" amount when the coefficients a and b are calculated with these formulas (Hamilton 1992, p. 33):

$$b = \left[\sum (X_i - \bar{X})(Y_i - \bar{Y})\right] / \sum (X_i - \bar{X})^2 \qquad (3)$$

$$a = \bar{Y} - b(\bar{X}) \qquad (4)$$

These values of a and b are known as *least squares* coefficients, or sometimes as *ordinary least squares* coefficients or OLS coefficients.

We now will apply the least squares principles. We are interested in the extent to which there is a relationship among the counties of China between the fertility rate (the dependent variable) and the level of illiteracy (the independent variable). China had 2,372 counties in 1982. We hypothesize that counties with populations that are heavily illiterate will have higher fertility rates than those with populations with low levels of illiteracy.

The dependent variable, Y, is the general fertility rate, GFR, that is, the number of children born in 1982 per 1,000 women in the age group fifteen to forty-nine. The independent variable, X, is the percentage of the population in the county in 1981 aged twelve or more who are illiterate.

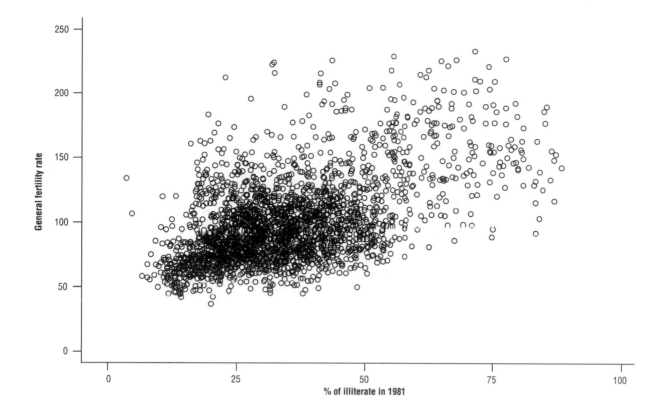

Figure 1

The relationship may be graphed in the scatterplot in Figure 1. The association between the GFR and the illiteracy rate appears to be linear and positive. Each dot refers to a county of China; there are 2,372 dots on the scatterplot.

Equation (1) may be estimated using the least squares formulas for *a* and *b* in equations (3) and (4). This produces the following:

$$\hat{Y} = 57.56 + 1.19x \qquad (5)$$

The OLS results in equation (5) indicate that the intercept value is 57.56, and the slope value is 1.19. The intercept, or *a*, indicates the point where the regression line "intercepts" the *Y*-axis. It tells the average value of *Y* when *X* = 0. Thus, in this China dataset, the value of *a* indicates that a county with no illiterate person in the population would have an expected fertility rate of 57.6 children per 1,000 women aged fifteen to forty-nine.

The slope coefficient, or *b*, indicates the average change in *Y* associated with a one-unit change in *X*. In the China example, *b* = 1.19, meaning that a 1 percent increase in a county's illiteracy rate is associated with an average GFR increase, or gain, of 1.19 children per 1,000 women aged fifteen to forty-nine.

We would probably want to interpret this *b* coefficient in the other direction; that is, it makes more sense to say that if we reduce the county's illiteracy rate by 1 percent, this would result in an average reduction of 1.2 children per 1,000 women aged fifteen to forty-nine. This kind of interpretation would be consistent with a policy intervention that a government might wish to use; that is, a lower illiteracy rate would tend to result in a lower fertility rate.

The regression line may be plotted in the above scatterplot, as shown in Figure 2.

It is noted that while in general the relationship between illiteracy and fertility is linear, there is a lot of error in the prediction of county fertility with a knowledge of county illiteracy. Whereas some counties lie right on or close to the regression line, and therefore, their illiteracy rates perfectly or near perfectly predict their fertility rates, the predictions for other counties are not as good.

One way to appraise the overall predictive efficiency of the OLS model is to "eyeball" the relationship as we have done above. How well does the above OLS equation correspond with variation in the fertility rates of the counties? As we noted above, the relationship appears to be positive and linear. A more accurate statistical approach to address the

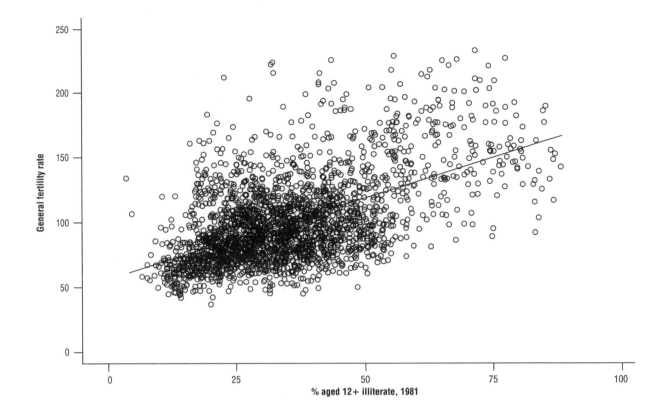

Figure 2

question of how well the data points fit the regression line is with the coefficient of determination (R^2).

We start by considering the problem of predicting Y, the fertility rate, when we have no other knowledge about the observations (the counties). That is, if we only know the values of Y for the observations, then the best prediction of Y, the fertility rate, is the mean of Y. It is believed that Carl Friedrich Gauss (1777–1855) was the first to demonstrate that lacking any other information about a variable's value for any one subject, the arithmetic mean is the most probable value (Gauss [1809] 2004, p. 244).

But if we guess the mean of Y for every case, we will have lots of poor predictions and lots of error. When we have information about the values of X, predictive efficiency may be improved, as long as X has a relationship with Y. "The question then is, how much does this knowledge of X improve our prediction of Y?" (Lewis-Beck 1980, p. 20).

First, consider the sum of the squared differences of each observation's value on Y from the mean of Y. This is the *total sum of squares* (TSS) and represents the total amount of statistical variation in Y, the dependent variable.

Values on X are then introduced for all the observations (the Chinese counties), and the OLS regression

equation is estimated. The regression line is plotted (as in the scatterplot in Figure 2), and the actual values of Y for all the observations are compared to their predicted values of Y. The sum of the squared differences between the predicted values of Y and the mean of Y is the *explained sum of squares* (ESS), sometimes referred to as the *model sum of squares*. This represents the amount of the total variation in Y that is accounted for by X. The difference between TSS and ESS is the amount of the variation in Y that is not explained by X, known as the *residual sum of squares* (RSS).

The coefficient of determination (R^2) is:

$$R^2 = \text{ESS/TSS} \qquad (6)$$

The coefficient of determination, when multiplied by 100, represents the percentage amount of variation in Y (the fertility rates of the Chinese counties) that is accounted for by X (the illiteracy rates of the counties). The R^2 values range from +1 to 0. If $R^2 = 1.0$, the X variable perfectly accounts for variation in Y. Alternately, when $R^2 = 0$ (in this case the slope of the line, b, would also equal 0), the X variable does not account for any of the variation in Y (Vittinghoff et al. 2005, p. 44; Lewis-Beck 1980, pp. 21–22).

SEE ALSO *Cliometrics; Least Squares, Three-Stage; Least Squares, Two-Stage; Linear Regression; Logistic Regression; Methods, Quantitative; Probabilistic Regression; Regression; Regression Analysis; Social Science; Statistics in the Social Sciences; Tobit*

BIBLIOGRAPHY

Gauss, Carl Friedrich. [1809] 2004. *Theory of Motion of the Heavenly Bodies Moving About the Sun in Conic Sections: A Translation of Theoria Motus.* Mineola, NY: Dover.

Hamilton, Lawrence C. 1992. *Regression with Graphics: A Second Course in Applied Statistics.* Pacific Grove, CA: Brooks/Cole.

Lewis-Beck, Michael S. 1980. *Applied Regression: An Introduction.* Beverly Hills, CA: Sage.

Poston, Dudley L., Jr. 2002. The Statistical Modeling of the Fertility of Chinese Women. *Journal of Modern Applied Statistical Methods* 1 (2): 387–396.

Poston, Dudley L., Jr., and Sherry L. McKibben. 2003. Zero-inflated Count Regression Models to Estimate the Fertility of U.S. Women. *Journal of Modern Applied Statistical Methods* 2 (2): 371–379.

Vittinghoff, Eric, David V. Glidden, Stephen C. Shiboski, and Charles E. McCulloch. 2005. *Regression Methods in Biostatistics: Linear, Logistic, Survival, and Repeated Measures Models.* New York: Springer.

Dudley L. Poston Jr.

ORGANIZATION FOR ECONOMIC CO-OPERATION AND DEVELOPMENT (OECD)

SEE *Public Assistance.*

ORGANIZATION MAN

This concept was made famous in mid-1950s America with the publication of William Hollingsworth Whyte's *The Organization Man* (1956). Sponsored by *Fortune Magazine* to do extensive interviews with chief executive officers of major companies such as General Electric, Whyte (1917–1999) studied white-collar employees of large, successful corporations in the heyday of the Eisenhower administration. These men did not simply work for the corporate world; they *belonged* to the Organization. This new stratum of American society was no longer driven by the spirit of individualism that had characterized the early Protestant settlers, the frontier, and nineteenth-century capitalism. A code was emerging that Whyte called the "social ethic," which involved a new, all-embracing fealty to the corporation. This ethic, which was associated with the growing professionalization of management and a commitment to practical expertise rather than abstract knowledge, emphasized belief in the social group as the fountain of creativity and the importance of "belongingness" for the individual. Whyte's ethnographic study was a bestseller intended for a nonacademic audience, but it had a serious purpose, which was to argue that the Protestant ethic—the ascetic individualism and sense of calling made famous by the German sociologist Max Weber—was in decline and America was changing profoundly as a result.

Weber, who visited the United States in 1904, recognized a connection between the ascetic sects of American frontier society and the European Reformation, a comparison he outlined in 1905 in *The Protestant Ethic and the Spirit of Capitalism.* Weber was impressed by the vibrant nature of local religious communities and the obvious connections between American capitalism and the asceticism and individualism of the sects. In contrast to the culture that Weber had observed, the new corporate culture, Whyte argued, did not reward thrift, hard work, and self-reliance. The organization man spent his working day in a committee and was rewarded as an administrator for working "through others for others" (p. 22). The principal influence over corporate culture was not Protestantism, but the pragmatism of John Dewey (1859–1952). Whyte's analysis formed an important social critique of corporate America, and suggested that the prospects for an energetic entrepreneurial culture were significantly diminished by the social conformism of corporate executives and their managers.

The social ethic of organization men, Whyte claimed, spilled over into their private lives. Personal saving had lost its moral imperative, and young couples in the new corporate culture saved for specific items—houses, cars, or schooling—that would give their lives more security and stability. The organization culture of 1950s suburbia created what came to be called a "lifestyle," in which couples progressed from a two-bedroom court apartment to a three-bedroom house, and subsequently to a ranch house, a split-level home, and finally, as retirement approached, back into a two-bedroom apartment. These suburbanites chose their friends from a limited social milieu, principally consisting of their suburban neighbors. Church attendance and the education of their children was key to achieving stability and security in lives that were characterized by transience, due to frequent postings to new branches of an organization. The conformist values of the organization also had implications for gender relations. Company wives were expected to be pretty but not sexy, and ambitious, but not too overtly materialistic. Even women's physical appearance expressed corporate values, which put a premium on female slenderness: As their husband's income went up, women's waistlines went down.

Whyte's ethnography now looks socially obsolete. Organizations at the beginning of the twenty-first century offer not life-long employment but short-term project-based careers, and company downsizing has produced a survival-oriented mentality among employees. Whyte's picture of the happy wives of organization men carefully managing their suburban households is also historically dated. The stability of life-long commitment to the company has collapsed in the face of intense economic competition in a global economy.

SEE ALSO *Bureaucracy; Organizations*

BIBLIOGRAPHY

Weber, Max. [1905] 2002. *The Protestant Ethic and the Spirit of Capitalism.* Trans. and ed. Peter Baehr and Gordon C. Wells. New York: Penguin.

Whyte, William Hollingsworth. 1956. *The Organization Man.* New York: Simon and Schuster.

Bryan S. Turner

ORGANIZATION OF AFRICAN UNITY (OAU)

The Organization of African Unity (OAU) was postcolonial Africa's first continent-wide association of independent states. Founded by thirty-two countries on May 25, 1963, and based in Addis Ababa, Ethiopia, it became operational on September 13, 1963, when the OAU Charter, its basic constitutional document, entered into force. The OAU's membership eventually encompassed all of Africa's fifty-three states, with the exception of Morocco, which withdrew in 1984 to protest the admission of the Saharan Arab Democratic Republic, or Western Sahara. The OAU was dissolved in 2002, when it was replaced by the African Union.

The process of decolonization in Africa that commenced in the 1950s witnessed the birth of many new states. Inspired in part by the philosophy of Pan-Africanism, the states of Africa sought through a political collective a means of preserving and consolidating their independence and pursuing the ideals of African unity. However, two rival camps emerged with opposing views about how these goals could best be achieved. The Casablanca Group, led by President Kwame Nkrumah (1909–1972) of Ghana, backed radical calls for political integration and the creation of a supranational body. The moderate Monrovia Group, led by Emperor Haile Selassie (1892–1975) of Ethiopia, advocated a loose association of sovereign states that allowed for political cooperation at the intergovernmental level. The latter view prevailed.

The OAU was therefore based on the "sovereign equality of all Member States," as stated in its charter.

AIMS AND OBJECTIVES

Article 2 of the OAU Charter stated that the organization's purposes included the promotion of the unity and solidarity of African states; defense of their sovereignty, territorial integrity, and independence; and the eradication of all forms of colonialism from Africa. Member states were to coordinate and harmonize their policies in various areas, including politics and diplomacy, economics, transportation, communications, education, health, and defense and security. Article 3 of the OAU Charter included among its guiding principles the sovereign equality of all member states, noninterference in the internal affairs of states, respect for sovereignty and territorial integrity, the peaceful settlement of disputes, and the emancipation of dependent African territories. Although the organization's primary motivation initially was the liberation struggle and the defense of the independence and territorial integrity of African states, the OAU later expanded its scope of activities to encompass economic cooperation and the protection of human rights.

PRINCIPAL INSTITUTIONS

The OAU's Assembly of Heads of State and Government was the organization's supreme organ. It normally met once a year, in a different capital city, although it could also meet in extraordinary session. Although each state had one vote, the assembly tended to operate by consensus. Except for internal matters, its resolutions were nonbinding.

The Council of Ministers, composed of government ministers (usually foreign ministers), normally met twice a year or in special session. Subordinate to the Assembly of Heads of State and Government, the council's principal responsibility was preparing the assembly's agenda. The council implemented the assembly's decisions and adopted the budget. In practice it emerged as the OAU's driving force.

The General Secretariat was headed by a secretary-general, appointed by the Assembly of Heads of State and Government. The secretariat was responsible for the administration of the OAU. The secretary-general was initially envisaged as an apolitical administrator, but over time the office assumed a proactive role, including acquiring the power under the Mechanism for Conflict Prevention to resolve disputes. The General Secretariat became mired in controversy in 1982 when the decision was taken to admit the Saharan Arab Democratic Republic to the organization. Morocco challenged the legality of this decision as it claimed that the Saharan Arab Democratic Republic was not a state. Since 1975 Morocco had occupied most of Western Sahara, a former

Spanish colony, and was engaged in a war against the Polisario Front, which had declared the Saharan Arab Democratic Republic an independent state in 1976 and was fighting for its liberation. The United Nations is still trying to settle this dispute.

The Commission of Mediation, Conciliation, and Arbitration, established as the OAU's dispute settlement mechanism, had jurisdiction over disputes between member states only. Member states, the Assembly of Heads of State and Government, and the Council of Ministers could refer disputes to the commission, but only with the prior consent of the states concerned. The commission never became operational because African governments were distrustful of third-party adjudication.

ADDITIONAL INSTITUTIONS

The African Commission on Human and Peoples' Rights, established under the African Charter on Human and Peoples' Rights (1982), became operational in 1987. Based in Banjul, Gambia, and composed of eleven individuals, the commission is a treaty monitoring body with the specific mandate of promoting and protecting human and peoples' rights. Particularly important is its competence to hear complaints from individuals and nongovernmental organizations concerning alleged violations by parties to the Charter on Human and Peoples' Rights. After an uncertain beginning, the commission is becoming a more effective defender of human and peoples' rights. The commission now functions under the auspices of the African Union and shares responsibility for the protection of human rights with the African Court on Human and Peoples' Rights.

The African Court on Human and Peoples' rights was established under a protocol to the Charter on Human and Peoples' Rights in 1998 that came into force in 2004. The court's jurisdiction over human rights treaties is broad in scope. The Commission, African Intergovernmental Organizations, and participating states can submit cases to the Court, as can individuals and nongovernmental organizations with the permission of the accused state. Its judgments are binding, but it can also give advisory opinions.

The Mechanism for Conflict Prevention, Management, and Resolution was founded in 1993 with the task of finding political solutions to disputes between OAU member states. Its primary objective was the anticipation and prevention of conflicts, with emphasis on the adoption of anticipatory and preventative measures, especially confidence-building measures. The mechanism operated subject to the fundamental principles of the OAU, especially with regard to the sovereignty and territorial integrity of member states and the principle of non-interference in their internal affairs. The mechanism's role

was therefore subject to the consent and cooperation of the warring parties. The mechanism was able to mediate in various civil conflicts and participate in election monitoring, but it never acquired the capacity to provide peacekeeping forces.

EVALUATION

The OAU had a mixed record. Its greatest success was in relation to decolonization. Other achievements included making significant contributions to the development of international law, especially in the fields of refugee law and human rights law, where several important treaties were adopted under OAU auspices, although in practice progress was slow and uneven. A court of human rights was envisaged, but the OAU was dissolved before it was established. Efforts were made to promote economic cooperation, and in 1991 it was decided to set up an African economic community, which in time was intended to lead to a customs union, a common market, and African monetary union. Little progress was made.

Overall, the failures of the OAU outweighed its successes. Arguably, its major failing was its inability to bring peace, prosperity, security, and stability to Africa. The OAU was found wanting in its responses to the tyrannies and kleptocracies ruining Africa, a deficiency that undermined its credibility. Its powers were too weak and its influence inadequate to deal with the internal and external conflicts, poor governance, human rights abuses, poverty, and underdevelopment from which much of Africa suffered. The OAU was also considered incapable of meeting the challenges of globalization. By the end of the century, reform so comprehensive was required that it was decided to start afresh with a new organization, the African Union, devoted to the political and economic integration of Africa based on respect for democratic values, good governance, the rule of law, and human rights.

SEE ALSO *Darfur*

BIBLIOGRAPHY

Amate, C. O. C. 1986. *Inside the OAU: Pan-Africanism in Practice.* London: Macmillan.

El-Ayouty, Yassin, ed. 1994. *The Organization of African Unity after Thirty Years.* Westport, CT: Praeger.

Elias, Taslim Olawale. 1964. The Commission of Mediation, Conciliation, and Arbitration of the Organisation of African Unity. *British Yearbook of International Law* 40: 336–54.

Elias, Taslim Olawale. 1965. The Charter of the Organization of African Unity. *American Journal of International Law* 59 (2): 243–67.

Evans, Malcolm, and Rachel Murray, eds. 2002. *The African Charter on Human and Peoples' Rights: The System in Practice, 1986–2000.* Cambridge, U.K.: Cambridge University Press.

Kufuor, Kofi Oteng. 2005. The Collapse of the Organization of African Unity: Lessons from Economics and History. *Journal of African Law* 49 (2): 132–144.

Magliveras, Konstantin, and Gino Naldi. 2004. *The African Union and the Predecessor Organization of African Unity.* The Hague, Netherlands: Kluwer Law International.

Naldi, Gino, ed. 1992. *Documents of the Organization of African Unity.* London and New York: Mansell.

Naldi, Gino. 1999. *The Organization of African Unity: An Analysis of its Role.* 2nd ed. London and New York: Mansell.

Gino J. Naldi

ORGANIZATION OF PETROLEUM EXPORTING COUNTRIES (OPEC)

Throughout its history, the Organization of Petroleum Exporting Countries (OPEC) has indirectly influenced oil prices in response to sharp volume fluctuations resulting from geopolitical tensions. However, as of 2006 OPEC's effect on the market, which affords member states political leverage, has changed dramatically relative to the late twentieth century, because member states now have far less excess production capacity (see Figure 1).

OPEC had more excess oil capacity in the 1980s, when crude oil prices reached close to $80 a barrel, than it did by 2006, during which prices reached as high as $75 a barrel (Figure 2). Minimal surplus capacity limits OPEC's ability to soften the blow of the high price of oil via increasing supply to meet the immense demand.

The Organization consists of eleven developing nations whose economies rely heavily on oil export revenues. OPEC seeks to maintain stable international oil prices via quotas on oil production and pursue petroleum policies that serve the national and collective interests of its members. In 2002 OPEC agreed that a fair price on crude oil should be set between $22 and $28 a barrel. Three years later, member states agreed to cap their crude oil production at 28 million barrels per day (MBPD). By 2006 Qatari Energy Minister Abdullah Attiyah maintained that a fair market price for crude oil should be in the range of $50 to $55 a barrel. However, during the

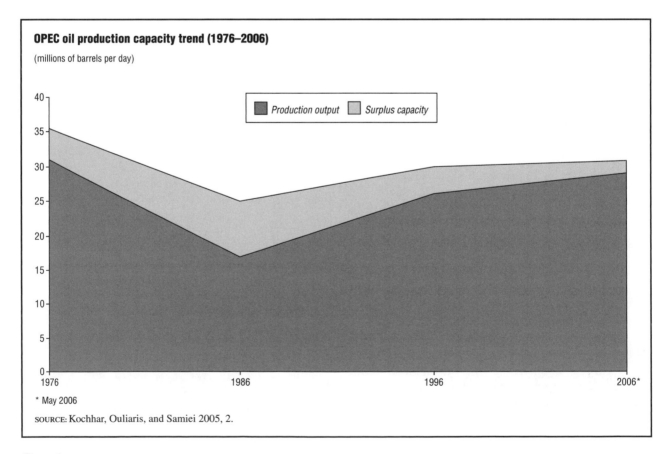

OPEC oil production capacity trend (1976–2006)

(millions of barrels per day)

Production output · Surplus capacity

* May 2006

SOURCE: Kochhar, Ouliaris, and Samiei 2005, 2.

Figure 1

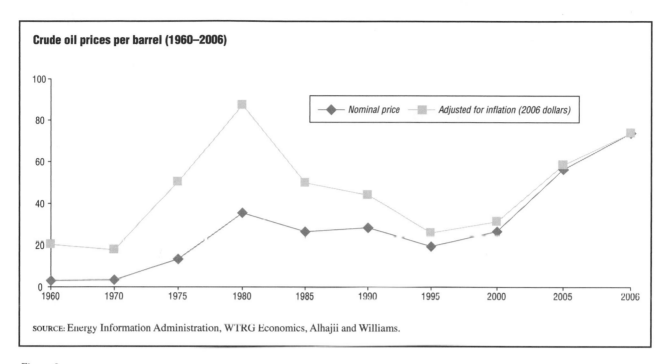

Crude oil prices per barrel (1960–2006)

SOURCE: Energy Information Administration, WTRG Economics, Alhajii and Williams.

Figure 2

same year, crude oil prices reached over $70 a barrel, and some OPEC countries often surpassed their production quotas by 2 MBPD.

Prior to OPEC, the so-called Seven Sister Companies dominated the crude oil market. Those seven companies included Esso (which later became Exxon, and is now known as Exxon Mobil), the Anglo-Iranian (previously Anglo-Persian) Oil Company (later British Petroleum, and currently known as BP), Royal Dutch Shell, Gulf Oil (most of which became a part of what is today known as Chevron), Standard Oil of New York (which became Mobil, and later merged with Exxon), Texaco, and Standard Oil of California (now part of Chevron) (see Table 1). Crude oil prices remained stable, with a range from $2.50 to $3.00 a barrel during the late 1940s through the 1960s, or $21 to $22 a barrel when adjusted to 2006 dollars.

The Seven Sister Companies remained dominant by restricting oil output and minimizing internal conflict. But competition from other world suppliers would eventually break up their control over the international oil market.

OPEC was created at the Baghdad Conference on September 10–14, 1960, by Iran, Iraq, Kuwait, Saudi Arabia, and Venezuela. Eight more countries later joined the Organization—Qatar (1961), Indonesia (1962), Libya (1962), United Arab Emirates (1967), Algeria (1969), Nigeria (1971), Ecuador (1973), and Gabon (1975). OPEC set up a secretariat in Geneva, Switzerland,

which moved to Vienna in 1965. The OPEC Statute states that countries that apply for membership must maintain "a substantial net export of crude petroleum" and "have fundamentally similar interests to those of Member Countries" (OPEC Statute, p. 3). The formation of OPEC resulted in a shift in influence over the oil market away from the Seven Sister Companies toward OPEC.

OPEC's dominance became fully evident during the 1970s as its Arab member states limited oil shipments and cut production at a time when demand was high, which resulted in a spike in oil prices. The Arab countries imposed an embargo on oil shipments to the United States

Shares in the international market of major oil companies (1946)

Seven Sister Companies	Production (%)
Esso	28
Anglo-Iranian Oil Company	22
Royal Dutch Shell	21
Gulf Oil	9
Standard Oil of New York	5
Texaco	3
Standard Oil of California	2
Total	**90**

SOURCE: Moran 1987, p. 585.

Table 1

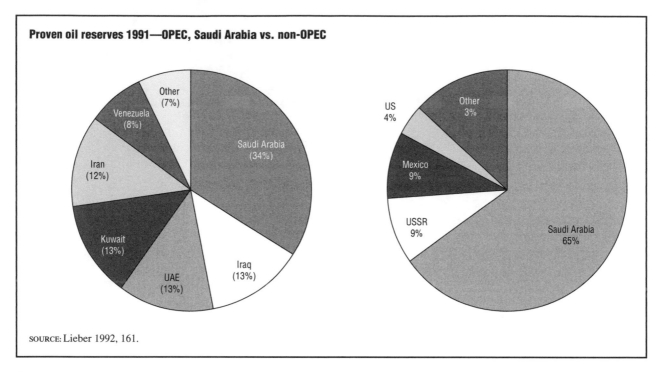

Proven oil reserves 1991—OPEC, Saudi Arabia vs. non-OPEC

SOURCE: Lieber 1992, 161.

Figure 3

and any other country that condemned Egypt and Syria's attack on Israel in 1973, which was significant considering that OPEC exports accounted for 85 percent of world oil trade at the time (Mikdashi 1974, p. 4). According to data from the *Middle East Quarterly* and *WTRG Economics*, the nominal price of oil escalated by more than 300 percent at the end of 1974 compared to prices a decade earlier. OPEC validated its authority and gained political leverage by reducing oil supply to the world market.

During this same period, Libya became a more prominent member of OPEC. Libya had undergone a regime change a few years earlier as the result of a military coup led by Colonel Muammar al Qadhafi, and had officially become known as the Great Socialist People's Libyan Arab Jamahiriya. Qadhafi encouraged Arab-nationalist and socialist policies. Many analysts have credited the new Libyan regime with shaping OPEC's measures to increase oil prices, enforce embargoes, and gain control of oil production (Anderson 1999, p. 4). For example, according to a 1973 *Time Magazine* article, Qadhafi took advantage of the high global demand for oil by forcing oil companies to increase Libya's oil royalties over 100 percent from $1.1 billion in 1969 to $2.07 billion in 1971 ("The Arab World," p. 2). Libya's influence played a partial role in OPEC's enhanced political strength on the world stage.

OPEC's reaction to the scarcity of oil supply resulting from the Iranian Revolution in 1979 and the Iraqi inva-

sion of Iran in 1980 further illustrated its strength. The new regime in Iran, which was the second largest OPEC oil exporter following Saudi Arabia, curbed oil exports to the world market driving prices upward. By 1979 Iran produced less than 1 MBPD, which was down from over 6 MBPD a year earlier ("Iran and Oil Prices," *Washington Times*, January 17, 2006; Phillips 1979, pp. 1–2). Iraq's invasion of Iran in 1980 sparked a reduction in the combined production of both countries to only 1 MBPD and a jump in prices from about $14 per barrel by early 1979 ($43.48 in 2006 dollars), to $35 per barrel by 1981 ($77.97 in 2006 dollars), according to *WTRG Economics*. Other countries within OPEC were able to offset Iran and Iraq's lower oil production by increasing their output while also maintaining a substantial amount of excess capacity. Saudi Arabia alone utilized three-quarters of its production capacity in order to make up for reduced output. Additional output from the other OPEC members helped crude oil prices to fall.

However, increased OPEC crude oil supply resulted in an oil price collapse by the mid-1980s. A Brookings Institution report entitled "Lessons from the 1986 Oil Collapse" (1986) notes that Saudi Arabia increased its market share after many of its OPEC partners failed to abide by their production quotas, thus oversupplying the market. Consequently, in 1986 crude oil prices declined from over $20 to as low as $12 a barrel ($22.17 in 2006 dollars).

Lack of cohesion among member states presented a challenge to the effectiveness of OPEC during this period.

By the early 1990s, the price of oil began to creep upward with the Iraqi invasion of Kuwait and the resultant threat of a Persian Gulf war. Saudi Arabia possessed the most oil reserves regionally and internationally (see Figure 3).

Saudi Arabia increased production by more than 3 MBPD during the Gulf War of 1991 (Lieber 1992, p. 155). This increased output to offset shortages created by the Gulf War of 1991 resulted in the stabilization of prices shortly after.

As the twenty-first century began, many geopolitical tensions further limited OPEC's oil supply and raised prices. The 2002 strike by state-owned Petroleos de Venezuela caused Venezuelan oil production to plunge so low that Venezuela still has not been able to regain its peak output capacity of 3.5 MBPD. In addition, the international military action in Iraq in 2003 caused Iraqi output to plummet to less than 1.5 MBPD. In 2006 Iran's threat to slash oil exports during its dispute with the United Nations over its nuclear missile program kept oil prices high at over $70 a barrel.

OPEC's ability to offset price increases in the early part of the twenty-first century pales in comparison to its clout during political conflicts thirty years earlier because there is far less additional oil supply in OPEC countries, including Saudi Arabia. The U.S. Energy Information Administration reported Saudi Arabia's excess capacity as being around 1.3 to 1.8 MBPD in May of 2006. Other OPEC members have zero surplus capacity in a world that consumes around 80 MBPD (see Figure 4). By the first half of 2006, oil prices jumped from $50 a barrel to a little more than $70 a barrel. Although the price per barrel is a few dollars shy of that in 1981 ($77.97 in 2006 dollars), the peak production capacity of OPEC is far less than that of the early 1980s, thus reducing OPEC's ability to manipulate the market.

OPEC's impact on the international crude oil market will continue to wane with such a tight supply. High crude oil prices have led to discussions about the possibility of tapping new oil reserves in non-OPEC countries and expanding alternative sources of energy, such as ethanol, in order to meet high demand at a much lower cost.

SEE ALSO *Energy; Energy Industry; Energy Sector; Qadhafi, Muammar al*

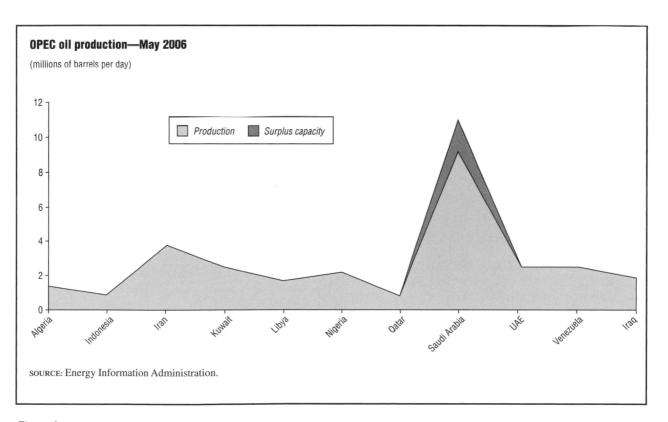

Figure 4

BIBLIOGRAPHY

Alhajji, A. F., and James L. Williams. 2003. The Coming Energy Crisis? *WTRG Economics.* http://www.wtrg.com/EnergyCrisis/EnergyCrisis.pdf.

Anderson, Frank. 1999. Qadhafi's Libya: The Limits of Optimism. *Middle East Policy* 6 (4): 68–79.

Buchbinder, David. 2003. Venezuela's Oil Strike May Be Over, but Industry Faces High Hurdles. *Christian Science Monitor,* February 19: 7.

Ceasar, Mike. 2002. Venezuelans Hit by Oil Crisis. BBC News. http://news.bbc.co.uk/1/hi/business/1913893.stm.

Energy Information Administration Web site. http://www.eia.doe.gov.

Gately, Dermot, M. A. Adelman, and James M. Griffin. 1986. Lessons from the 1986 Oil Price Collapse. *Brookings Papers on Economic Activity* 2: 237–284.

Kanovsky, Eliyahu. 2003. Oil: Who's Really over a Barrel? *Middle East Quarterly* 10 (2): 51–64.

Kliesen, Kevin L. 2001. Rising Oil Prices and Economic Turmoil: Must They Always Go Hand in Hand? *Regional Economist* (January): 4–9.

Kochhar, Kalpana, Sam Ouliaris, and Hossein Samiei. 2005. *What Hinders Investment in the Oil Sector?* Washington, DC: International Monetary Fund Research Department.

Lieber, Robert J. 1992. Oil and Power after the Gulf War. *International Security* 17 (1): 155–176.

Mikdashi, Zuhayr. 1974. Cooperation among Oil Exporting Countries with Special Reference to Arab Countries: A Political Economy Analysis. *International Organization* 28 (1): 1–30.

Moran, Theodore H. 1987. Managing an Oligopoly of Would-Be Sovereigns: The Dynamics of Joint Control and Self-Control in the International Oil Industry Past, Present, and Future. *International Organization* 41 (4): 575–607.

Oil Price History and Analysis. *WTRG Economics.* http://www.wtrg.com/prices.htm.

OPEC Statute. *OPEC Secretariat.* http://www.opec.org/library/opec%20statute/pdf/os.pdf.

OPEC Warns of Oil Crisis. 2002. BBC News. http://news.bbc.co.uk/1/hi/business/1917522.stm.

Organization of Petroleum Exporting Countries Web site. http://www.opec.org.

Peak Oil News and Message Boards. 2006. Fair Price for Oil Is 50 to 55 Dollars per Barrel: Qatari Minister. http://www.peakoil.com/article16202.html.

Phillips, James A. 1979. The Iranian Oil Crisis. Heritage Foundation. http://new.heritage.org/Research/MiddleEast/bg76.cfm.

Time Magazine. 1973. The Arab World: Oil, Power, and Violence. April 2.

Washington Times. 2006. Iran and Oil Prices. January 17.

Sarita D. Jackson

ORGANIZATION THEORY

Organization theory is a theoretical perspective which conceives of organizations as complex social actors and investigates how the structures they adopt affect their behavior. The field takes a broad view of the term "structure" including not only formal structure, but also informal and network relationships and cultural and cognitive aspects of the organizations. As such, it addresses broad questions of how and why organizations come to be, take the forms they do, behave as they do, and survive or fail. With its focus on organizations as a collective entity, organization theory complements *organizational behavior*, which focuses on individuals and small groups within the larger field of *organization studies*.

BACKGROUND AND ORIGINS

Organization theory was derived from several fields, including sociology, economics, anthropology, and political science. Many scholars in these fields have influenced organization theory, including Émile Durkheim, Karl Marx, Adam Smith, and Max Weber. Of these, Weber most directly influenced organization theory with his work on authority and bureaucracy.

Writing around the turn of the twentieth century, Weber identified two sources of authority that dominated previous social organization: *traditional authority*, vested in established patterns of behavior passed down through generations, and *charismatic authority*, vested in an individual's powers of attraction and influence over others. He also identified a third form, *rational-legal authority*, in which authority is vested in individuals selected based on rules and legally binding processes designed to identify those best qualified to exercise it. This rational-legal authority is the basis of Weber's *theory of bureaucracy*, in which he posited that organizing in this manner could generate remarkable social advances comparable in magnitude to the economic advances of the Industrial Revolution. Furthermore, Weber's ideal view of rationality comprised two types: *substantive rationality*, which determines what a social group's goals, values, and ideals should be, and *formal rationality*, which governs how a social group allocates resources and measures progress toward those goals and ideals. In an oft-quoted passage he warned that formal rationality without substantive rationality could lead to a dehumanizing "iron cage." While some critics suggest that early English translations of Weber did not sufficiently reflect the true spirit of his work, Weber has nevertheless provided a foundation upon which much of organization theory has been built.

Building on Weber and others, more recent organization theorists have generally emphasized two primary perspectives on the nature and function of organizations, which have been elaborated into a number of influential theories of organizations. The first of these perspectives considers organizations as rational and efficient solutions to various problems associated with cooperation, complexity, and uncertainty. The second perspective considers organization not on the basis of its rational structure and function but rather on the basis of its social meaning and value.

ORGANIZATIONS AS RATIONAL SOLUTIONS TO SOCIAL PROBLEMS

Some of the earliest theories of organizations emerged in the wake of the Industrial Revolution and were characterized by the search for universal organizing principles. Influential among these early theorists were Frederick Taylor and Henri Fayol, whose work can be characterized as the application of mechanical and industrial engineering principles to the management and control of human labor. However, in the 1960s organization theorists turned attention from universal organizing principles to theories that argued that ideal organization structures were not one-size-fits-all, but instead contingent on various factors within the organization and its environment.

In 1967, Paul Lawrence and Jay Lorsch introduced *contingency theory*, which claimed that the best way to organize depends upon the characteristics of an organization's environment. Lawrence and Lorsch argued that organizations' environments vary widely and that organizations come to reflect this variety by rationally adopting structures best suited to their environments. They showed that the degree of volatility and uncertainty in an organization's environment affects things like the formalization of an organization's structure, the centrality of its decision making, the time horizon upon which it focuses, and how it divides itself into departments and its tasks. Lawrence and Lorsch's emphasis on contingencies proved influential, and several other contingency-based theories of organizations emerged in the 1970s. Among these are *agency theory, transaction cost economics*, and *resource dependence theory*.

Agency theory focuses on the fact that, in organizations, one person (the *agent*) acts at the behest of another (the *principal*). This principal–agent relationship exists in organizations between stockholders and managers and between managers and employees. Agency theorists assume that both agents and principals have self-interests and that these interests frequently diverge. This creates a need for principals to monitor the agents, which is difficult and expensive since agents often have more expertise than principals and cannot be continuously and directly observed. Agency theorists therefore depict organizational structures as rational attempts to establish complex yet efficient systems of cooperation, which differ from orga-

nization to organization and task to task depending on the information asymmetry between principals and agents.

Transaction cost economics (TCE) is closely related to agency theory, but instead of emphasizing how organization structures govern internal principal–agent relationships, TCE emphasizes that organizations are rational and efficient solutions to managing the relationship between itself and other organizations in its environment. Oliver Williamson, who introduced TCE in the mid-1970s, argues that small-scale transactions (i.e., simple and immediate exchanges of goods and services) do not require organizations; however, as transactions become more complex and uncertain, organizations are needed to monitor and limit the liabilities of these risks. TCE also explains organizational boundaries on the basis of transaction costs: Functions for which the costs of external transactions are too great are brought inside the organization, while those available for less total cost elsewhere are performed externally.

The resource dependence view of organizations, like TCE, emphasizes an organization's relationship to other organizations but focuses on how an organization's structures are contingent on the nature and scarcity of the resources it needs to operate rather than on the complexity and uncertainty of its transactions. More so than the other contingency-based theories, the resource dependence view emphasizes the role of management in negotiating the dependencies resulting from an organization's resource needs, and specifies a number of strategies that firms may undertake to do this under different dependency conditions.

The rational/efficient assumptions within contingency-based theories of organizations also underlie the theories of *population ecology* and *co-evolution*, which conceptualize the environment shared by organizations in the same or related fields as an ecosystem. These theorists employ ecological and evolutionary mechanisms, (e.g., variation, selection, specialization) to explain how organizations come to be and survive or fail. In this stream of research, organizational success, failure, and form are contingent upon environmental adaptation, fit, and population density.

ORGANIZATIONS AS EMBODIMENTS OF VALUE AND MEANING

Another approach to addressing the questions of how organizations come into being and why they take the forms they do is based on the conception of organizations as embodiments of value and meaning. Many of these theories can be traced to Peter Berger and Thomas Luckmann's *The Social Construction of Reality* (1966), in which they suggest that, in the context of social science, "knowledge" and "reality" are subjectively created rather than objectively discovered. Theories based on this approach shift their emphasis from identifying efficient ways of organizing to understanding the purpose or meaning derived from organizing a particular way. The shift was essentially a move from Weber's formal rationality to substantive rationality, which critics held had been slighted by modernist social science and its natural preference for formal rationality.

One example of this branch of organization theory comes under the generic heading of *institutional theory*, which grows out of the concept of social institutions. While diverse definitions of institutions abound, reflecting the evolution and variety of theories under this rubric, common to all of them is the idea of stable patterns of social interaction that over time become vested with value and power. Within organization theory, institutions were first associated with the processes by which leaders infuse organizational structures or processes with value beyond their technical requirements, resulting in their reproduction and stability. In this stream of research, sometimes termed *old institutionalism*, the focus is on creating meaning and infusing values from within the organization.

This is contrasted with *neo-institutional theory*, or *new institutionalism*, which focuses on how external aspects of the context in which organizations exist affect their structures and processes. In a seminal piece from 1983, Paul DiMaggio and Walter Powell suggested the similarity among organizations in a field was the result of their common environment, which comprised three distinct forces for conformity: *coercive forces*, such as a common regulatory environment; *normative forces*, such as professionalization and standardized professional education (e.g., accounting); and *mimetic forces*, in which organizations copy visible or successful others when facing uncertainty. The idea that processes and structures result from passively adapting to external pressures contrasted directly with old institutionalism, which theorized they were actively infused with value from within. Later, in response to criticisms that neo-institutional conceptions of organizations were too passive and static, neo-institutionalists highlighted *institutional change*, where organizations dynamically adapt to changing institutional environments, and *institutional entrepreneurship*, where actors actively shape the institutional environments in which they exist. These advances, along with the concept of *institutional work*, have blurred the distinctions between old and new institutionalism.

These blurred distinctions are also evident in *organizational culture* and *organizational identity*, both of which focus on how organizations enact meaning within their social contexts. Organizational identity theorists address the issues of "who we are" as an organization and show a similar focus on the reproduced social meaning (i.e., what is enduring, central, and distinctive) within an organization, and how that affects the structures and processes of organizations. Work on organizational culture focuses directly on the meaning systems of organizations at three levels: *artifacts*, the rituals and symbols employed in an organization; *values*, the conscious beliefs about what should or should not be; and *assumptions*, the deeply held and often unconscious beliefs that guide how members make sense of an organization. Consistent with the work on the social construction of reality, this suggests that organizational action flows from values about what should or should not be, but is constrained by assumptions about what is or can be.

SEE ALSO *Authority; Bureaucracy; Culture; Durkheim, Émile; Industrialization; Institutionalism; Marx, Karl; Models and Modeling; Modernism; Organizations; Peace; Principal-Agent Models; Rationality; Smith, Adam; Taylorism; Transaction Cost; Values; Weber, Max*

BIBLIOGRAPHY

Astley, W. Graham, and Andrew H. Van de Ven. 1983. Central Perspectives and Debates in Organization Theory. *Administrative Science Quarterly* 28 (2): 245–273.

Berger, Peter, and Thomas Luckmann. 1966. *The Social Construction of Reality.* New York: Doubleday.

Clegg, Stewart R., David Courpasson, and Nelson Phillips. 2006. *Power and Organizations.* Thousand Oaks, CA: Sage.

DiMaggio, Paul J. and Walter W. Powell. 1983. The Iron Cage Revisited: Institutional Isomorphism and Collective Rationality in Organizational Fields. *American Journal of Sociology* 48 (2): 147–160.

Hatch, Mary Jo, and Ann L. Cunliffe. 2006. *Organization Theory: Modern, Symbolic, and Postmodern Perspectives*, 2nd ed. Oxford: Oxford University Press.

Lawrence, Paul R. and Jay W. Lorsch. 1967. Differentiation and Integration in Complex Organizations. *Administrative Science Quarterly* 12 (1): 1–47.

Lawrence, Thomas B., and Roy Suddaby. 2006. Institutions and Institutional Work. In *The Sage Handbook of Organization Studies*, eds. Stewart R. Clegg, Cynthia Hardy, Thomas Lawrence, and Walter Nord, 215–254. London: Sage.

Scott, W. Richard. 2002. *Organizations: Rational, Natural, and Open Systems*, 5th ed. Englewood Cliffs, NJ: Prentice Hall.

Tsoukas, Haridimos, and Christian Knudsen, eds. 2003. *The Oxford Handbook of Organization Theory: Meta-theoretical Perspectives.* Oxford: Oxford University Press.

Weber, Max. 1925. *The Theory of Social and Economic Organization.* Trans. by A. M. Henderson and Talcott Parsons. New York: Free Press, 1947.

Rich DeJordy
Bradley A. Almond

ORGANIZATIONS

Formal organizations are ubiquitous in modern society. Most people work in organizations, join organizations, and interact with organizations in their daily lives. The study of organizations includes an examination of the relationship between individuals and organizations, organizations and their external environments, and how corporations and other constellations of organizations exercise power and influence public policy.

INDIVIDUALS IN ORGANIZATIONS: CONTROL OVER DECISION MAKING

Organizational theorists maintain that the emergence of modern large-scale bureaucracy is an outcome of the increased application of formally rational means (e.g., written laws, rules, and regulations) to achieve the substantively rational goals (i.e., large-scale capitalism, democracy) associated with modernity. Although large-scale organizations can be used to increase the productive capability of capitalism and extend democracy to more spheres of social life, they also provide means for elites who control them to exercise power and advance their political and economic interests (Weber [1921] 1978). Scholars who examine organization control have shown that at the turn to the twentieth century capitalists hired scientific managers to experiment with techniques to increase control over the labor process. These scientific managers collected information from workers and centralized it in planning departments where engineers used it to establish formal rules to control the labor process (Braverman 1974).

In the middle decades of the twentieth century, decision-making theorists demonstrated that the capacity of elites to control managers in large and complex organizations is constrained by bounded rationality: limits on rationality that are affected by unclear preferences, limited information, and the cognitive abilities of individual decision makers (Simon 1957). These decision-making theorists showed that superordinates attempt to overcome bounded rationality and increase their control over subordinates by establishing premise controls, which limit the search for alternatives in the decision-making process (March and Simon 1958). Other organizational researchers point out that bounded rationality cannot be completely eliminated and that premise controls and other formal controls have unintended consequences (Perrow 1972; Burawoy 1979). Research in this tradition shows that formally rational controls caused widespread inefficiencies in the decision-making process in corporate American during the middle decades of the twentieth century. In response to the capital accumulation crisis in the 1970s and early 1980s, like the earlier period when elites increased their control over the labor process, capitalists and their top managers implemented scientific management principles to increase control over the managerial process. They hired engineers and other technical experts to collect information from production managers, centralize that information into computerized information processing systems, and use it to develop premise and other formal controls that limited the discretion of lower and middle-level managers (Prechel 1994).

ORGANIZATIONS AND THEIR ENVIRONMENTS

Another line of research in organizational sociology examines the relationship between the internal organizational structures and the environment. There are two distinct types of organization-environment theories. The "weak form" of the organization-environment hypothesis stresses how organizations respond to environmental forces. Organizational ecology, which borrows from the biological model of natural selection, conceptualizes organizational populations as aggregates of organizations that are alike in some respect (e.g., newspapers). Organizations are considered part of a larger system that must adapt in order to survive. This perspective stresses the importance of structural isomorphism, which denotes a fit between the organization and its environment (Carroll and Hannan 1995). However, organizational adaptation is limited by inertia, which includes internal politics and increased age, size, and complexity. In the absence of adaptation to the environment, organizations will cease to exist.

Neoinstitutional theory also represents the weak form of the organization-environment hypothesis. This perspective examines organizational fields: a recognized area of institutional life with key suppliers, resource and product consumers, regulatory agencies, and other similar organizations (DiMaggio and Powell 1983). Once an organizational field is established, three mechanisms cause organizations to become homogeneous. First, mimetic behavior occurs when organizational technologies are poorly understood, when goals are ambiguous, or when the environment creates symbolic uncertainty. When these conditions exist, organizations model themselves on the dominant organization in their field. Second, normative behavior entails professionalization, which includes efforts by practitioners of an occupation to define the conditions and methods of their work, control the supply of new producers, and establish a cognitive base and legitimation for their occupational autonomy. Third, coercive pressures emerge from political and cultural influences. This neoinstitutional perspective assumes that an autonomous state creates public policies and laws (e.g., antitrust, product safety) and is capable of making corporations and other organizations comply with those laws.

In contrast, the "strong form" of the organization-environment hypothesis suggests that corporations and other organizations are capable of influencing public policies that are designed to control and regulate them. Resource dependence theory maintains that the environment constrains organizations, and organizations depend on other organizations for resources (Aldrich and Pfeffer 1976; Pfeffer and Salancik 1978). This perspective also maintains that the key to survival is the ability to acquire and maintain resources from other organizations in the environment. To reduce dependencies that limit their prospects for autonomous action and survival, organizations set up strategies to manage their environments.

ORGANIZATIONS AND PUBLIC POLICY

The strong form of the organization-environment hypothesis is consistent with research by political sociologists who show that business elites use networks of organizations to influence public opinion and public policy (Domhoff 2006), and economic sociologists who maintain that the behavior of individuals and organizations can only be understood by examining the social relations in which they are embedded (Granovetter 1985). Other researchers maintain that the universalizing assumptions in many social theories can be misleading and that the strong form of the organization-environment hypothesis is historically contingent (Prechel 1990). Historical contingency theory of corporate political behavior maintains that although elites are always politically active, the level of elite political activity varies over time. When the condition of economic uncertainty is high (e.g., periods of low or unstable profits), corporations become more politically active, and they pressure state managers to implement policies to attain economic stability and predictability and to preserve the social relations in capitalist society (Prechel 2000). Although capitalists and their top managers do not always have a coherent conception of the relationship between their economic goals and the means to achieve those goals, they engage in political behavior to transform public policies in order to create the conditions that better advance their profit-making agendas.

Historical contingency theory explains the three major corporate form changes in the largest U.S. firms between the 1880s and 1990s. First, in the 1880s and 1890s, business elites lobbied states to pass formal laws to give industrial corporations the right to use the joint-stock holding company. This corporate form holds the majority of the stock (i.e., more than 50 percent) of legally independent subsidiary corporations. The embeddedness of the holding company in an environment with little regulatory control created opportunities for capitalists to consolidate many independent companies into giant companies such as AT&T, General Motors, and U.S. Steel Corporation. By the 1920s, stock overvaluation and other forms of malfeasance were widespread in many holding companies (Berle and Means 1932). To reinvigorate and sustain capitalism after the Great Depression, the Franklin D. Roosevelt (1882–1945) administration set up public policies to limit the use of this corporate form. These policies included a tax on the transfer of capital between subsidiary corporations and the holding company. By increasing the cost to operate the holding company, this capital transfer tax contributed to the deinstitutionalization of this corporate form. After this legislation was passed, corporations began to restructure into a *multidivisional form* where product lines are organized as divisions inside a single corporation. By 1960, the multidivisional form prevailed in corporate America (Chandler 1962).

In response to the capital accumulation crises of the late 1970s and early 1980s, corporate America mobilized politically to replace the institutional arrangements that were established during and after the New Deal. These market-driven neoliberal policies included: (1) redefining antitrust regulations that prohibited large corporations from merging with others operating in the same market; (2) eliminating the tax on capital transfers from subsidiary corporations to parent companies; and (3) dismantling regulatory control over the banking and financial industry. Now, corporations were allowed to engage in behaviors that were previously illegal or not viable, including using new forms of financing to merge or acquire other large corporations and organize their new and existing corporate entities as subsidiaries in the *multilevel-subsidiary form*. This multilevel-subsidiary form has a parent company at the top of the corporate hierarchy that operates as a financial management company, with two or more levels of legally separate subsidiary corporations embedded in it (Prechel 2000, p. 12). By 1993, 65 percent of the one hundred largest U.S. industrial corporations used this corporate form (Prechel 2000, p. 244). As occurred during the late nineteenth and early twentieth centuries, this multilevel-subsidiary form provided a means to create giant corporations such as Exxon-Mobil, Chevron-Texaco, and ConocoPhillips. The embeddedness of this corporate form in these new institutional arrangements also created opportunities to overvalue corporate stock and to conceal financial malfeasance (Prechel 2000, p. 265).

CORPORATE CRIME

Following the 2001 bankruptcy of Enron Corp., civil and legal investigations showed that Enron's management used the multilevel-subsidiary form to transfer capital between legally independent corporate entities and manipulate its financial statements (Prechel 2003). Self-interest-seeking with guile was not limited to managers in the few corporations that the media focused on. Between January 1995 and May 2005, the Commodity Futures Trading Commission, the Department of Justice, and the Securities and Exchange Commission filed 457 allegations against 151 (i.e., 30%) of the 500 largest U.S. corporations. In 2005 alone, the Federal Bureau of Investigation pursued 405 corporate fraud cases that resulted in an additional 317 convictions (FBI 2005). However, many executives who engaged in corporate malfeasance were not accused of wrongdoing or held responsible for misleading the public because deregulation made many social acts legal that were previously illegal or not viable.

Unlike in the 1920s, when most stock was owned by the upper classes, the expansion of mutual funds created means for the working classes to invest their retirement and savings into corporate securities. As a result, the working classes lost billions of dollars due to corporate chicanery and malfeasance in the 1990s. Estimates suggest that $2.1 billion was wiped out from the employee pension plan at Enron alone and that $40 billion was lost from employee pension funds in general.

ORGANIZATIONS AND INEQUALITY

Political mobilization by corporations and wealthy individuals was not limited to deregulating corporations. During the same period that public policy was changed in ways that created opportunities for corporate malfeasance, elites financed political action committees, think tanks, and lobbying organizations to transform public policy in ways that lowered taxes on wealthy individuals and corporations. This policy shift also included a reduction in social programs for the poor.

By 1990, family income inequality increased to the highest level since 1947, when the U.S. government began compiling these data, and continued to increase into the twenty-first century. The very rich benefited most in this redistribution of income and wealth. Whereas the top 1 percent of American income earners received 9.3 percent of the total income in 1979, this group received 17.8 percent of the total income in 2000 (Mishel et al. 2005, p. 62). Although the rich have always held a large percentage of the wealth in American society, wealth inequality also increased during the 1980s and 1990s. Whereas the wealthiest 1 percent of the population held 33.8 percent of the nation's total net worth in 1983, it had increased to 38.1 percent by 1998 (Mishel et al. 2005, p. 282).

SUMMARY

The strong form of the organization-environment hypothesis suggests that the power of elites is derived, in part, from their capacity to control organizations and to use organizations to change their environment. Beginning in the 1970s, corporations and wealthy individuals used their wealth and power to decrease government regulation, increase corporate property rights, and extend free markets. These new institutional arrangements resulted in a historic turning point characterized by reduced regulatory oversight, lower taxes on corporations and wealthy individuals, higher rates of corporate chicanery and malfeasance, and increased inequality.

SEE ALSO *Organization Theory*

BIBLIOGRAPHY

Aldrich, Howard, and Jeffrey Pfeffer. 1976. Environments of Organizations. *Annual Review of Sociology* 2: 79–105.

Berle, Adolf A., and Gardiner C. Means. [1932] 1991. *The Modern Corporation and Private Property*. New Brunswick, NJ: Transaction Publishers.

Braverman, Harry. 1974. *Labor and Monopoly Capital: The Degradation of Work in the Twentieth Century*. New York: Monthly Review Press.

Burawoy, Michael. 1979. *Manufacturing Consent: Changes in the Labor Process under Monopoly Capitalism*. Chicago: University of Chicago Press.

Carroll, Glenn, and Michael Hannan, eds. 1995. *Organizations in Industry: Strategy, Structure, and Selection*. New York: Oxford University Press.

Chandler, Alfred. 1962. *Strategy and Structure: Chapters in the History of the Industrial Enterprise*. Cambridge, MA: MIT Press.

DiMaggio, Paul J., and Walter W. Powell. 1983. The Iron Cage Revisited: Institutional Isomorphism and Collective Rationality in Organizational Fields. *American Sociological Review* 48: 147–160.

Domhoff, G. William. 2006. *Who Rules America? Power and Politics, and Social Change*. 5th ed. Boston: McGraw Hill.

Federal Bureau of Investigation. 2005. *Financial Crimes Report to the Public*. http://www.fbi.gov/publications/financial/fcs_report052005/fcs_report052005.htm.

Granovetter, Mark. 1985. Economic Action and Social Structure: The Problem of Embeddedness. *American Journal of Sociology* 91: 481–510.

March, James G., and Herbert A. Simon. 1958. *Organizations*. New York: Wiley.

Mishel, Lawrence, Jared Bernstein, and Sylvia Allegretto. 2005. *The State of Working America, 2004/2005*. Ithaca, NY: Cornell University Press.

Perrow, Charles. 1972. *Complex Organizations: A Critical Essay*. Glenview, IL: Scott, Foresman. 3rd ed., 1986. New York: McGraw Hill.

Pfeffer, Jeffrey, and Gerald Salancik. 1978. *The External Control of Organizations: A Resource Dependence Perspective*. New York: Harper.

Prechel, Harland. 1990. Steel and the State: Industry, Politics, and Business Policy Formation, 1940–1989. *American Sociological Review* 55: 648–668.

Prechel, Harland. 1994. Economic Crisis and the Centralization of Control over the Managerial Process: Corporate

Restructuring and Neo-Fordist Decision Making. *American Sociological Review* 59: 723–745.

Prechel, Harland. 2000. *Big Business and the State: Historical Transitions and Corporate Transformation, 1880s–1990s.* Albany: State University of New York Press.

Prechel, Harland. 2003. Historical Contingency Theory, Policy Paradigm Shifts, and Corporate Malfeasance at the Turn of the 21st Century. In *Political Sociology for the 21st Century,* eds. Betty A. Dobratz, Lisa K. Waldner, and Timothy Buzzell, 311–340. Amsterdam: Elsevier Science.

Simon, Herbert. 1957. *Administrative Behavior: A Study of Decision-Making Processes in Administrative Organization.* 2nd ed. New York: Macmillan.

Weber, Max. [1921] 1978. *Economy and Society: An Outline of Interpretive Sociology.* Eds. Guenther Roth and Claus Wittich; trans. Ephraim Fischoff et al. Berkeley: University of California Press.

Harland Prechel

ORGANIZATIONS, PEASANT

Peasants—and peasant organizations—exhibit enormous diversity across time and space. Since the origin of state societies, smallholders, tenant farmers, sharecroppers, squatters, and landless laborers have participated in local organizations—some formal and others informal—to coordinate planting, cultivation, and harvesting; to administer irrigation systems; to exchange labor; to acquire inputs and market harvests; and to demand from those in power fairer prices, lower taxes, and access to land and other resources. In many parts of the world, peasant insurgencies against elites and colonial powers involved thousands or even millions of rebels drawn from among the rural poor. Twentieth-century peasant wars—such as the Mexican and Chinese revolutions and the Vietnam War (1957–1975)—brought massive social upheavals and reshaped geopolitics at the world level. In the late twentieth and early twenty-first centuries, organizations of peasants and small farmers helped to stall global trade negotiations and to reformulate policies in such areas as poverty alleviation, genetically modified crops, agrarian reform, and environmental sustainability.

Peasant and farmer cooperatives have existed in Europe and the Americas since at least the late nineteenth century. Most have been organized around the production and marketing of particular commodities, but many have involved machinery services, input purchasing, savings and credit, transport, and retail businesses. Cooperatives in most countries are barred from political advocacy activities, but many national- and international-level coopera-

tive federations attempt to work for their members' interests in governments and multilateral institutions.

Peasant and farmer associations that lobby or employ pressure tactics to defend their members' interests are found virtually everywhere, including in developed countries where only a small portion of the economically active population works in agriculture. Unions of agriculturalists in France, the United States, and Canada exercise substantial political influence. In poorer countries, such as Ecuador and Bolivia, peasant and indigenous movements contributed to toppling national governments in the early twenty-first century. Even in China, where the government does not tolerate independent political organizations, rural unrest is widespread and has led to major administrative reforms, such as reductions in the taxes agriculturalists pay to local governments.

Scholars and activists have long debated the role of outsiders in forming peasant organizations. While rural people have had improved access to education in recent decades, through either government programs or nongovernmental organizations, a broad consensus exists that effective peasant associations usually require some outside leadership, at least in their initial stages. At the same time, it is now widely recognized that many rural people are increasingly cosmopolitan, with experience in urban areas and abroad that equips them for organizing and leading peasant movements.

Social scientists once distinguished between *farmers*, who had a commercial orientation, employed hired labor, and operated with advanced technology, and *peasants*, who were subsistence-oriented and used family labor and rudimentary technology. These ideal types have proven problematical as the rural poor adopt modern technologies, as agriculturalists in developing and developed countries collaborate around issues of common concern, as rural residents migrate to cities, and as peasants and farmers themselves emphasize their commonalities and downplay differences. Moreover, in many languages the terms equivalent to *peasant*—the French *paysan* or the Spanish *campesino*, for example—are more inclusive, meaning simply "people from the countryside" and including many farmers.

Transnational peasant organizations have a long history. The Farmers' Institutes extension program originated in Canada in the 1890s and spread to the United States and Britain. Following World War I (1914–1918), peasant political parties—termed "the Green International"—held power in several eastern European countries. The Associated Country Women of the World was founded in 1933 and claims a membership of nine million in 365 participating societies in seventy countries. The Paris-based International Federation of Agricultural Producers, formed in 1946, includes many organizations of large farmers and some peasant associations. The global farm crisis of the 1980s, marked by plummeting commodity prices and skyrocketing prices for fossil fuel–based inputs, sparked a new wave of cross-border peasant organizing, much of it directed against the General Agreement on Tariffs and Trade (GATT) and later the World Trade Organization (WTO). The Vía Campesina, or Peasant Road, a militant international peasant and farmer organization that emerged in the early 1990s, has been in the forefront of campaigns to take agriculture out of the WTO and to implement "food sovereignty" policies. The Vía Campesina has nearly one hundred member organizations in Asia, Europe, Africa, and the Americas. These include the Brazilian Landless Movement, the U.S. National Family Farm Coalition, the National Farmers Union of Canada, the Peasant Confederation of Peru, the Assembly of the Poor in Thailand, the Nepal National Peasant Women's Association, and the European Farmers Coordination.

SEE ALSO *Peasantry*

BIBLIOGRAPHY

Cooper, Frederick, Florencia E. Mallon, Steve J. Stern, et al. 1993. *Confronting Historical Paradigms: Peasants, Labor, and the Capitalist World System in Africa and Latin America.* Madison: University of Wisconsin Press.

Edelman, Marc. 2003. Transnational Peasant and Farmer Movements and Networks. In *Global Civil Society 2003*, eds. Mary Kaldor, Helmut Anheier, and Marlies Glasius, 185–220. London: Oxford University Press.

McKeon, Nora, Michael Watts, and Wendy Wolford. 2004. *Peasant Associations in Theory and Practice.* Geneva: United Nations Research Institute for Social Development.

Wolf, Eric R. 1969 *Peasant Wars of the Twentieth Century.* New York: Harper.

Marc Edelman

ORGANIZED CRIME

SEE *Kefauver, Estes; Mafia, The.*

ORICHAS

SEE *Santeria.*

ORIENTALISM

Orientalism refers principally to the academic study during the eighteenth, nineteenth, and early twentieth centuries of the peoples, languages, and cultures of North Africa, the Middle East, and, to a lesser degree, South Asia. In art history, the term refers to a school of European painters of the nineteenth century who took the peoples of these regions as their primary subjects. Since the publication of Edward Said's (1935–2003) widely influential study titled simply *Orientalism* (1978), the term has become pejorative, suggesting a critical orientation or mode of representation that privileges the Western over the Eastern or idealizes the East in a manner that reflects European desires and political and economic interests.

What is called, after Said, *orientalist discourse*, developed during the era of most active European colonialism, from the early 1800s to World War I (1914–1918). Among the first important works accurately called *orientalist* were those produced by figures associated with colonialist endeavors in North Africa and the Middle East, including the massive, twenty-four-volume *Description de l'Égypte*, produced by approximately 160 scholars who accompanied Napoléon Bonaparte (1769–1821) on his ultimately failed expedition to conquer Egypt in 1798. The *Description*, completed in 1829, is typically orientalist in, on the one hand, the idealization of Egyptian people and places in its many beautifully rendered images, and, on the other, its overall concern with defining and classifying all the cultural and physical aspects of Egypt toward the ultimate objective of controlling its people and natural resources.

The nineteenth century can rightly be called the *orientalist era* in the arts, as works across the spectrum of literature and painting drew on the myth of the Orient that was being produced by the functionaries of colonialism and the scholars of philology. While French painters such as Eugène Delacroix (1798–1863) and Jean-Léon Gérôme (1824–1904) are widely regarded as the preeminent orientalists in the visual arts, the movement was widespread and included Frederick Arthur Bridgman (American, 1847–1928), Frederick Goodall (British, 1822–1904), Louis-Joseph Anthonissen (Belgian, 1849–1913), Ludwig Deutsch (German, 1855–1935), and Leopold Carl Müller (Austrian, 1834–1892). Orientalist literary artists include Rudyard Kipling (1865–1936), Edgar Allan Poe (1809–1849), Joseph Conrad (1857–1924), and Arthur Rimbaud (1854–1891), to list only a very few.

Muslim women were a particular focus of orientalist artists. The "slave market," "harem," and "bath" received seemingly endless treatments. Gérôme's images characteristically give the impression of the voyeur who has lifted or pulled back the "veil" to reveal the hidden mystery of the Orient. Women's bodies are erotically on display, often, in fact, under examination by some Arab buyer or slave trader. The precise response of a European audience to such images is difficult to ascertain, but generally the erotic construction of an Arab "other" appealed to a patriarchal sense of superiority and interest in control.

The matters of the European sense of superiority and interest in control can also be seen in orientalist scholarship. Non-Western societies were described as backward and barbaric, fundamentally incapable of social, political, or technological modernization. An important point is that the works of orientalist scholars were often not intentionally or explicitly motivated toward the interests of Western power. The assumptions of superiority and control were embedded in the scholarship, often despite the fact that an individual scholar might regard his or her subject very sympathetically. However, it is certainly true that whatever the disposition of the orientalist scholar, his or her work was a critical part of the general body of knowledge that facilitated and justified the control and exploitation of colonized peoples.

The publication in 1978 of Said's study unleashed a fierce and continuing debate. The debate is wide ranging and contains multiple positions, though it can be roughly divided between two groups. Some believe Said's work has overly politicized the academic study of non-Western peoples and unfairly characterized the work of devoted scholars. Others, particularly the generation of scholars who pursued their graduate work in the later 1980s and 1990s, hold that Said's work is a particularly valuable contribution to the broad examination of the ideological assumptions and effects of intellectual works that purport to be disinterested.

Whatever the multiple positions in this rich debate, the influence of Said's volume has been tremendous. *Orientalism* has been translated into at least thirty-six languages, including Hebrew and Vietnamese, gone through multiple editions, and is certainly one of the most cited works in the humanities and social sciences since 1978. The critique of orientalist work is at the center of entire new disciplines, such as postcolonial studies, which is concerned with the struggle of non-Western peoples to meaningfully represent themselves and their social, political, and cultural concerns to both Western and non-Western audiences and institutions.

SEE ALSO *Colonialism; Gaze, Colonial; Imperialism; Other, The; Postcolonialism; Racism; Representation in Postcolonial Analysis; Said, Edward*

BIBLIOGRAPHY

Irwin, Robert. 2006. *Dangerous Knowledge: Orientalism and Its Discontents.* Woodstock, NY: Overlook.

Said, Edward. 1978. *Orientalism.* New York: Vintage.

Turner, Bryan S. 1994. *Orientalism, Postmodernism, and Globalism.* New York: Routledge.

Stephen A. Germic

ORIGINAL SIN
SEE *Sin.*

O-RING THEORY

Michael Kremer formulated the O-ring theory in 1993. His article, "The O-ring Theory of Economic Development," published in the *Quarterly Journal of Economics*, presents a production function in which production consists of many tasks, all of which must be successfully completed for the product to have full value. Mistakes can be extremely costly reducing the product's value. The name O-ring comes from the accident of the space shuttle *Challenger* that exploded because one of the components, the o-rings, failed.

The production function has two crucial assumptions. The first is that workers must be sufficiently imperfect substitutes for each other; that is, it is not possible to substitute several low-skill workers for one high-skill worker. Skill is defined as the probability of a worker successfully completing a task, q. The second assumption is that there are strong complementarities among inputs; that is, if there are n tasks, output, y, is given by multiplying the q-values of each of the n tasks together. Assuming that firms are risk-neutral, labor is supplied inelastically and labor markets are competitive, production is given by:

$$E(y) = y = k^{\alpha}(\Pi_{i=1}^{n} q_i)\eta B$$

where k is capital and B is output per worker with a single unit of capital if all tasks are performed perfectly. Profit maximizing firms choose a level of capital, k, and the skill of each worker, q_i, facing a wage schedule $w(q)$ and a rental rate, r. The first-order condition associated with each of the q_i is

$$\frac{dw(q_i)}{dq_i} = \frac{dy}{dq_i} = k^{\alpha}(\Pi_{j \neq i} q_i)nB$$

Thus, the increase in output a firm obtains by replacing one worker with a slightly higher skill worker, leaving everything else constant, must equal the increase in its wage bill necessary to pay the higher skill worker. Thus the wage schedule is a function of worker skill.

As the derivative of the marginal product of skill for the ith worker with respect to the skill of the other workers is positive, $\frac{d^2 y}{dq_i d(\Pi_{j \neq i} q_j)} = k^{\alpha} nB > 0$, firms with high q workers in the first $n-1$ tasks place the highest value on having high-skill workers in the nth task, so they bid the most for these workers. As a result workers of the same skill are matched together in firms.

Kremer stressed that this production function is consistent with many stylized facts such as: (1) wage and productivity differentials between rich and poor countries are enormous; (2) firms hire workers of different skill and produce different quality products; (3) there is a positive correlation among the wages of workers in different occupations within firms; (4) firms only offer jobs to some workers rather than paying all workers their estimated marginal product; and (5) income distribution is skewed to the right. Assuming sequential production in which the highest q workers are allocated to the later stages of production it is possible to show that: (1) poor countries have higher shares of primary production in gross national product (GNP); (2) workers are paid more in industries with high value inputs; and (3) the effects of efficiency wages, bottlenecks, and trade restrictions are magnified. When the number of tasks, n, is endogenized it is possible to show that: (1) rich countries specialize in complicated products; (2) firms are larger in rich countries; and (3) firm size and wages are positively correlated. Finally, when skill is endogenized as the product of investment in education or effort Kremer showed that there is some level of education subsidy that improves welfare. Although many of these predictions of the model may be due to a variety of causes, together they suggest that O-ring production functions are empirically relevant.

Kremer stressed that if strategic complementarity is sufficiently strong one may have multiple equilibria and each may be inefficient. Therefore, there is room for public policies to move the economy to a preferred equilibrium. According to Michael Todaro and Stephen Smith's 2003 work, one of the limitations of the model is that it falls short on practical policy implications.

The applications of the O-ring theory are wide. In 2006 Charles Jones adapted it to study the role of knowledge in the theory of economic development. Alberto Dalmazzo's 2002 work combines the O-ring production function with efficiency wages; the workers employed in a firm with a more complex production process should earn higher wages than identical workers that work on identical tasks in firms with less complex production processes. Tuomas Pekkarinen's 2002 estimates for the Finnish metal industry find evidence supporting this hypothesis.

In the O-ring theory productivity is associated with the job rather than with the worker, which raises questions about how workers get access to the higher productivity jobs. Peter Doeringer and Michael Piore's 1971 work shows that internal labor market analysis promotions have the role to allow workers to get access to the higher productivity jobs and firms to extract the maximum effort from workers. The economy may be characterized by dual labor markets in which one sector offers high wages, stability, and good working conditions and the other sector offers low wages, high turnover, and poor working conditions, pressing one back to the structuralist analysis.

Kremer acknowledged that his paper combines Sherwin Rosen's 1981 analysis of multiplicative quality effects with Gary Becker's 1981 analysis of matching in marriage markets. However, some of Kremer's ideas were advanced by the theory of stratification formulated by Kingsley Davis and Wilbert Moore in 1945 and developed by Arthur Stinchcombe in 1963 and Stinchcombe and T. Robert Harris in 1969. According to Davis and Moore, stratification in all societies was viewed as an unconsciously evolved device by which societies assured that the most functionally important positions would be filled by the most capable persons. Stinchcombe, focusing upon organizational rather than social stratification, hypothesized that the more complementary are individual contributions to total production, the greater will be the inequality of rewards. Stinchcombe and Harris anticipated the production function presented by Kremer in which the case of interdependence of activities in production is modeled as the product of the probability that every worker will be working.

SEE ALSO *Coordination Failure; Development Economics; Enterprise; Inequality, Income; Labor Market Segmentation; Productivity; Wages*

BIBLIOGRAPHY

Abrahamson, Mark. 1973. Talent Complementarity and Organizational Stratification. *Administrative Science Quarterly* 18: 186–193.

Becker, Gary. 1981. *Treatise on the Family*. Cambridge, MA: Harvard University Press.

Dalmazzo, Alberto. 2002. Technological Complexity, Wage Differentials and Unemployment. *Scandinavian Journal of Economics* 104: 515–530.

Davis, Kingsley, and Wilbert E. Moore. 1945. Some Principles of Stratification. *American Sociological Review* 10: 242–249.

Doeringer, Peter, and Michael Piore. 1971. *Internal Labor Markets and Manpower Analysis*. Lexington: DC Heath.

Kremer, Michael. 1993. The O-ring Theory of Economic Development. *Quarterly Journal of Economics* 108: 551–575.

Pekkarinen, Tuomas. 2002. Complexity, Wages, and the *O-Ring* Production Function: Evidence from Finnish Panel Data. *Labour Economics* 9: 531–546.

Rosen, Sherwin. 1981. The Economics of Superstars. *American Economic Review* 71: 845–858.

Stinchcombe, Arthur L. 1963. Some Empirical Consequences of the Davis-Moore Theory of Stratification. *American Sociological Review* 28: 805–808.

Stinchcombe, Arthur L., and T. Robert Harris. 1969. Interdependence and Inequality: A Specification of the Davis-Moore Theory. *Sociometry* 32: 13–23.

Todaro, Michael P., and Stephen C. Smith. 2003. *Economic Development*. 8th ed. New York: Addison Wesley.

João Ricardo Faria

ORTEGA, DANIEL

SEE *Sandinistas.*

ORTHODOXY

The concept of orthodoxy is variously used as: (1) a historically specifically located term; (2) a descriptive-analytic term to describe traditions or writers that may not describe themselves by that term; and (3) a titular self-description in various religious communities (e.g., Modern Orthodox Judaism, Greek Orthodox Church). Often, *orthodoxy* is juxtaposed with *orthopraxy*, whereby orthodoxy would apply more appropriately to *cognitivist* traditions, such as Christianity and its emphasis on faith and theology, rather than to traditions that define themselves along behavioral lines, such as Judaism and Islam with their emphases on religious law. This juxtaposition is artificial, however, since Judaism and Islam, as well as Christianity, develop discourses of orthodoxy and authenticity.

The historical origin of the concept of *orthodoxy* (from the Greek word for correct or normative faith) as the antonym of *heresy* (Greek, "faction") can be traced back to early Christian literature. Conceptually, *orthodoxy* emerges as a by-product of the early Christian practice of heresiography, whereby the two antonyms were aligned with other oppositional pairs, such as, importantly, truth and its perversions. To a large degree, the heresiographers opted to define orthodoxy by what it was not—namely, the aberrant heresies—rather than to formulate what orthodoxy actually entailed. First-century writers such as Josephus (37–c. 100 CE) could still employ the term *heresy* in the sense of "school of thought," as in his description of the various schools of thought in first-century Judaism (Pharisees, Sadducees, Essenes, and potentially Zealots). Hence, this first-century phenomenon is most often described as *sectarianism* rather than as a struggle for orthodoxy. To Josephus, none of these groups constituted an orthodox versus a heretical version of Judaism, or an exclusionary normative Judaism from which the others were to be excluded as deviant marginal groups. What distinguishes the heresiographical texts of the second half of the second century and onward from first-century writers such as Josephus is precisely this shift in meaning from *heresy* as a school of thought, still subsumed under the umbrella of the larger category term of Judaism (in Josephus's case), to *heresy* as a deviant aberration from the true religion, hence to be excluded from its boundaries of identity. Only the latter allows a notion of orthodoxy as the true, authentic version of Christianity (and subsequently Judaism) to emerge.

It may be debatable as to the degree to which the early Christian leader Paul already engaged in a heresio-graphical practice in his epistles without resorting to the concept of *heresy* when in his Epistle to the Galatians (1:6–7) he denounced his opponents as those preaching "another gospel" and thereby "perverting the gospel of Christ." However, it appears that the first author of what turned into the genre of Christian heresiography was Justin Martyr (100–165 CE) with his *Refutation of all Heresies*, a text that is no longer preserved. Subsequently, Irenaeus's treatise *Adversus omnes haereses* (Against All Heresies, 185 CE) drew on Justin's work, and from then on heresiographies present a distinct genre of Christian literature and theology. Around the same time, Jewish writers, such as the authors of the earliest Rabbinic text, known as the *Mishnah* (c. 200 CE), began to adopt heresiographical practices.

The early Jewish and Christian debates were carried out in a context in which the writers lacked the support of institutional or political authority. A case may be made that these strategies of self-representation contributed to, if not entirely caused, the institutional consolidation of the Catholic Church, ultimately backed by the political authority of the Roman Empire, and the rabbinical leadership of the Jewish community at the end of the late antique period.

The heresiographers employed a number of strategies to render persuasive their notion of the true and therefore authoritative or normative version of theology and practice. One strategy to establish authenticity was to attribute historical or chronological priority to their norms. For example, the early rabbis claim that their traditions or their "oral Torah" was already given to Moses on Sinai (Mishnah Avot 1:1), and the Christian heresiographers attribute their teachings to the first apostles and ultimately Jesus himself. The historical priority of authentic traditions is subsequently secured by chains of traditions that lead from the source to each respective heresiographical author. Heresies then are represented as groups ("them") that split off from the normative tradition and perverted it, versus the projected "us" who continue the authentic and original tradition. This classic strategy of self-representation is employed in various other religious contexts, often in order to disguise innovative practices and beliefs. In the case of early Judaism and Christianity, this strategy was so successful that modern historians have often assumed such claims to be descriptive rather than recognizing them for their rhetorical work.

Another strategy of the heresiographers was to adduce and at the same time reduce the origin of what they wished to portray as false belief to a founding figure whose name would give the denounced faith its name. Paul juxtaposes the idea of following Christ with merely following Paul, Apollo, or Cephas (Peter) in his argument against divisions in the early church communities (1 Cor. 1:12).

Subsequently, heresiographers provide lists of named and supposedly nameable groups who may not have described themselves by those names, as Justin Martyr does in his *Dialogue with Trypho* : "Some are called Marcionites, some Valentinians, some Basilideans and some Saturnalians, and some others by other names" (Martyr 1930, p. 70), just not the name Christians. This strategy allows for contrasting these marginalized categories of groups with the universal unnamed category employed to promote the appearance of authenticity, whether that is represented by terms like *orthodox* and *catholic* (Greek, "universal") in the Christian case, or "Israel" versus groups such as Sadduceans and Boethusians in the early Rabbinic case. Both these strategies—the attribution of historical priority to that which is promoted as authentic, and the reduction of opponents to marginal movements contrasted to one's own universality—are repeated in numerous other conflicts, mostly of a religious nature.

While the concepts of orthodoxy and heresy have specific historical origins, and are mostly used in the contexts of religious practices and religious studies as well as in sociology of religion, they have come to be used more broadly in various other disciplines and subject matters. Any established tradition or symbolic order perceived as truth, as the law, or as political consensus can be described as orthodoxy, and anyone diverging therefrom as heterodox or heretic. A discipline of study may be legitimated by one normative methodology, leading to a perception of innovative approaches as heterodox or heretic.

In the social sciences, Pierre Bourdieu (1930–2002) elevated the concepts of orthodoxy and heresy to methodological principle in his analysis of social behavior, accompanied by a third concept, *doxa*. In his classic work *Outline of a Theory of Practice* (1977), he defines orthodoxy as "a system of euphemisms, of acceptable ways of thinking and speaking the natural and social world, which rejects heretical remarks as blasphemies" (Bourdieu 1977, p. 169). Hence, orthodoxy is always a social fiction, a socially established convention in the realm of discourse. *Doxa*, on the other hand, refers to the "pre-verbal taking-for-granted of the world that flows from practical sense" (Bourdieu 1990, p. 68). At times, Bourdieu maps all three terms on class distinctions in that *doxa* is the product of a system of domination. Accordingly, he defines *doxa* as the viewpoint of the dominant, which disguises itself as universal, neutral, or objective, and which the dominant classes have an interest in defending, whereas the dominated have "an interest in pushing back the limits of *doxa* and exposing the arbitrariness of the taken for granted" (Bourdieu 1977, p. 169). *Doxa* is a stronger tool of domination because it is "an ensemble of fundamental beliefs which do not even need to affirm themselves in the guise of an explicit dogma, conscious of itself" (Berlinerblau 2001, p. 346), that is, orthodoxy. Hegemony and ortho-

doxy are interchangeable. The heretic then is the person, a prophet or *homo academicus*, who discovers some unrecognized belief about the world that supplies the means of thinking the unthinkable.

Bourdieu is not the first to translate the concepts of orthodoxy and heresy or heterodoxy, originally coined in a religious context, into analytic vocabulary for sociological and political analysis, but his is the most influential to date.

SEE ALSO *Bourdieu, Pierre; Christianity; Galbraith, John Kenneth; Hegemony; Judaism; Kuhn, Thomas; Religion; Revolutions, Scientific; Roman Catholic Church; Science*

BIBLIOGRAPHY

Bauer, Walter. 1971. *Orthodoxy and Heresy in Earliest Christianity*, eds. Robert Kraft and Gerhard Krodel. Trans. Philadelphia Seminar on Christian Origins. Philadelphia: Fortress.

Berlinerblau, Jacques. 2001. Toward a Sociology of Heresy, Orthodoxy, and Doxa. *History of Religions* 40 (4): 327–351.

Bourdieu, Pierre. [1971] 1988. Vive la Crise!: For Heterodoxy in Social Science. *Theory and Society* 17 (5): 773–787.

Bourdieu, Pierre. 1977. *Outline of a Theory of Practice*. Trans. Richard Nice. Cambridge, U.K.: Cambridge University Press.

Bourdieu, Pierre. [1980] 1990. *The Logic of Practice*. Trans. Richard Nice. Stanford, CA: Stanford University Press.

Boyarin, Daniel. 2004. *Border Lines: The Partition of Judaeo-Christianity*. Philadelphia: University of Pennsylvania Press.

Brooke, John, and Ian Maclean, eds. 2005. *Heterodoxy in Early Modern Science and Religion*. New York: Oxford University Press.

Cohen, Shaye J. D. 1998. *The Beginnings of Jewishness: Boundaries, Varieties, Uncertainties*. Berkeley: University of California Press.

Henderson, John B. 1998. *The Construction of Orthodoxy and Heresy: Neo-Confucian, Islamic, Jewish, and Early Christian Patterns*. Albany: State University of New York Press.

Katz. Jacob. 1998. *A House Divided: Orthodoxy and Schism in Nineteenth-Century Central European Jewry*. Trans. Ziporah Brody. Hanover, NH: University Press of New England.

Kurtz, Lester. 1983. The Politics of Heresy. *American Journal of Sociology* 88 (6): 1085–1115.

Le Boulluec, Alain. 1985. *La notion d'hérésie dans la littérature grecque II-II siècles*. 2 vols. Paris: Études Augustiniennes.

Martyr, Justin. 1930. *Justin Martyr: The Dialogue with Trypho*, ed. and trans. A. Lukyn Williams. London: Society for Promoting Christian Knowledge (SPCK).

Zito, George. 1983. Toward a Sociology of Heresy. *Sociological Analysis* 44: 123–130.

Charlotte Elisheva Fonrobert

ORTHOPRAXY

SEE *Orthodoxy.*

ORTIZ, FERNANDO
1881–1969

Fernando Ortiz was a public intellectual known for his interdisciplinary studies of Cuba's popular cultural traditions, particularly Afro-Cuban culture and its multiethnic African heritages. Recognized as the founder of the social sciences and specifically of anthropology and ethnomusicology in Cuba, he was born in Havana on July 16, 1881, but spent his youth in Minorca, Spain. After completing high school in Barcelona, he returned to Cuba in 1895 to study law at the University of Havana. Within three years he decided to complete his studies at the University of Barcelona because of the turmoil from the war of independence against Spain. Upon earning his bachelor's degree in law in 1900 and a doctorate in law from the University of Madrid in 1901, he returned to Cuba where he agreed to serve the newly established republic by accepting a three-year term as a diplomat. While in Italy, he met Cesare Lombroso (1835–1909) and Enrico Ferri (1856–1929), positivist criminologists who, along with Spanish scholars (e.g., Rafael Salillas, Manuel Sales y Ferré, Bernaldo de Quirós, and Dorado Montero), influenced his early thinking on crime.

Following his diplomatic service, Ortiz taught law at the University of Havana. Even before this academic appointment began, he investigated Cuba's criminal underworld, particularly African- and to some extent Chinese-descended criminals. His first book, *Hampa afro-cubana: Los negros brujos* (Afro-Cuban Underworld: The Black Wizards, 1906), was a "criminal anthropology" of the deviance that constituted *la mala vida* (the evil life). Ortiz's study of Havana's criminal underworld, particularly *brujería* (witchcraft) and the notorious ritual murders of white children purported to be a part of it, was grounded in the Spencerian evolutionism and biological determinism advanced by Lombroso, who wrote the book's preface. Ortiz's treatise reinforced the racist notion that lawlessness and social disorder were attributable to those of African origin, whose savagery impeded national development.

In later work, Ortiz shifted to a perspective contesting the idea that Afro-Cuban culture was inconsistent with modernity. He moved beyond a criminological approach to an ethnographically informed anthropological framework for understanding the cultural integrity of the multiple religions that were homogenized and confused with antisocial "black" magic. This important shift

was, in part, the result of influence from the Haitian-descended ethnographer Rómulo Lachatañeré (1909–1952), who pushed Ortiz to use a more culturally appropriate lexicon for Afro-Cuban religions and ritual specialists.

Ortiz developed a methodology that stressed the significance of culture and history. In *Hampa afro-cubana: Los negros esclavos* (Afro-Cuban Underworld: The Black Slaves, 1916), he began to clear the ground for an analysis that would eventually lead to the elaboration of a theory of *transculturation*, his major contribution. He introduced this neologism in *Contrapunteo cubano del tabaco y el azúcar* (Cuban Counterpoint: Tobacco and Sugar, 1940), a watershed book establishing him as Cuba's leading social scientist dedicated to illuminating the complex dialectical interplay between culture, history, and political economy. Coined as an alternative to acculturation, the more conventional concept in U.S. and British cultural and social anthropologies, transculturation elucidated the "complex transmutations of culture" (Ortiz [1947] 1995, p. 98) and the ongoing interchanges, reciprocities, and tensions in a national context in which diverse peoples have experienced "loss or uprooting" (p. 102), as well as the accomplishment of creating new cultural forms and a social system for ordering the lives of both the dominant and the dominated. Transculturation was invoked in conjunction with the analogy Ortiz often made between Cuban national identity and *ajiaco*, an always-changing stew. The centrality of Africa's contributions to that stew was a key insight discernible even in his earlier work.

Misrepresented as functionalist in Bronislaw Malinowski's (1884–1942) introduction, *Cuban Counterpoint* was an innovative work written in an allegorical style. At once a cultural and an economic history, the book interpreted Cuba's development in terms of the oppositional and mutually constituted agency of its two major commodities, sugar and tobacco. Through the poetic deployment of these entities as metaphors, he offered a holistic analysis of these paradigmatic commodities as both material objects and socially constructed historical actors in a world shaped at once by human practice and the wider structural forces that constrain it. Critical of reductionist interpretations of Cuba's colonial and neocolonial experience, Ortiz's contrapuntal method offered an alternative to the dominant canons of anthropology and history as established within the Northern Hemisphere.

Ortiz's far-ranging contributions included laying the foundations for the progressive reform of Cuba's criminal justice system, writing on the indigenous origins of Cuban culture, and serving as a Liberal Party representative in congress. The bulk of his contributions to Cuba's intellectual life and public culture stemmed from his seminal research on all aspects of Cuba's African-influenced, orally transmitted traditions. He validated the use of *Afro-Cuban* as an analytical construct while insisting that Afro-Cuban cultural forms were integral to a unified Cuban national identity. He also addressed the problem of racism and the workings of race as a social rather than biological category. Major publications in his later life included *La africanía de la música folklórica de Cuba* (The Africanity of Cuba's Folkloric Music, 1950), *Los bailes y el teatro de los negroes en el folklore de Cuba* (Black Dances and Theater in Cuba's Folklore, 1951), and the five-volume work, *Los instrumentos de la música afrocubana* (Instruments of Afro-Cuban Music, 1952–1955). These mature works reflected the comparative method Ortiz used to treat "the processes of social contact, their impact on the historical effects of the slave trade, and different African ethnic groups and their transculturation" (Font and Quiroz 2005, p. 250). Throughout his career, much of which was based at the University of Havana, he founded a number of journals, associations, and institutions to provide outlets and support for research on Afro-Cuban culture and other components of Cuban national identity. He died in Havana on April 10, 1969.

SEE ALSO *Anthropology; Crime and Criminology; Determinism; Determinism, Biological; Ethnomusicology; Functionalism; Malinowski, Bronislaw; Modernism; Racism; Slavery Industry; Sugar Industry; Tobacco Industry*

BIBLIOGRAPHY

PRIMARY WORKS

Ortiz, Fernando. 1906. *Hampa afro-cubana: Los negros brujos (apuntes para un studio de etnología criminal)*. Madrid: Librería de Fernado Fe.

Ortiz, Fernando. 1916. *Hampa afro-cubana: Los negros esclavos: Estudio sociológico y de derecho público*. Havana: Revista Bimestre Cubana.

Ortiz, Fernando. 1940. *Contrapunteo cubano del tabaco y el azúcar*. Havana: Jesús Montero. English trans: [1947] 1995. *Cuban Counterpoint: Tobacco and Sugar*. Trans. Harriet de Onís. Durham, NC: Duke University Press.

Ortiz, Fernando. 1950. *La africanía de la música folklórica de Cuba*. Havana: Ministerio de Educación, Dirección de Cultural/Ediciones Cárdenas y Cía.

Ortiz, Fernando. 1951. *Los bailes y el teatro de los negros en el folklore de Cuba*. Havana: Ministerio de Educación, Dirección de Cultural/Ediciones Cárdenas y Cía.

Ortiz, Fernando. 1952–1955. *Los instrumentos de la música afrocubana*. 5 vols. Havana: Ministerio de Educación.

SECONDARY WORKS

Castellanos, Jorge. 2003. *Pioneros de la ethnografia afrocubana: Fernando Ortiz, Rómulo Lachatañeré, Lydia Cabrera*. Miami, FL: Ediciones Universal.

Coronil, Fernando. [1947] 1995. Introduction: Transculturation and the Politics of Theory: Countering the Center, Cuban Counterpoint. In *Cuban Counterpoint: Tobacco and Sugar*, by Fernando Ortiz, trans. Harriet de Onís, ix–lvi. Durham, NC: Duke University Press.

Diaz, María del Rosario. 2005. The Tragedy of the Ñañigos: Genesis of an Unpublished Book. *New West Indian Guide* 79 (3–4): 229–237.

Font, Mauricio A., and Alfonso W. Quiroz, eds. 2005. *Cuban Counterpoints: The Legacy of Fernando Ortiz*. Lanham, MD: Lexington Books.

Palmié, Stephan. 2002. *Wizards and Scientists: Explorations in Afro-Cuban Modernity and Tradition*. Durham, NC: Duke University Press.

Faye V. Harrison

OSCEOLA
1804–1838

Osceola (ah-see-oh-la) was a warrior and chief of the Seminole Indian tribe during the Indian removal from Florida to unsettled U.S. territory in the West during the early 1800s. His significance in the academy and the social sciences is linked to issues related to Native American identity and the political relationship between Native Americans and the U.S. government. Significant as well is his historical relationship to African slaves and contemporary African Americans' tenuous relationship to Native American tribes—the Seminoles in particular, but also the Choctaw, Creek, Cherokee, and Chickasaw, who were removed from their original homelands in the southeastern United States to their present, primary home in Oklahoma.

Osceola is seen as a major figure in securing the rights of Seminoles and other native peoples during the colonial period—not through signing agreements and treaties with agents of the U.S. governments, as some tribal leaders had done, but through guerrilla warfare tactics that kept the U.S. military at bay for a long time and so slowed the removal of Seminoles and the taking of Seminole lands. Osceola has also been viewed as a symbol of the ancestral mixture that formally and informally linked African peoples to the Indian tribes, a link that fuels contemporary claims to tribal government benefits.

The Seminoles in Florida were remnants of other Indian tribes that fled to Florida and established a lifestyle, culture, and politics that were indigenous and self-governing. Osceola strenuously objected to the United States's offer to buy Seminole Florida lands in exchange for removal and settlement to open territory west of the Mississippi. Though his position differed from those of many of his tribal brethren, he found allies among another group of wanderers who had fled to Florida—free Africans and fugitive slaves who had several years before merged with the Florida Seminoles. These freedmen and fugitives—referred to by the Seminoles as *Estelusti*—joined the faction of Seminoles led by Osceola in opposing relocation, fighting alongside them in the Seminole Wars.

Although these "Black Seminoles" were loyal to the Seminole tribe, adopting many of their customs, intermarrying, and settling with them in the new Indian Territories in Oklahoma, Texas, Louisiana, and other surrounding states, neither the Seminoles nor whites during that period recognized them as official tribe members. Later, when the Dawes Act of 1887 required a census of Native American tribal members, Black Seminoles—referred to as Freemen—were counted as part of the tribal role, and received allotments of tribal lands. As a result of Jim Crow laws enacted after Oklahoma statehood, Black Seminoles were physically separated from their Seminole tribal brethren and their legal status as official tribal members was called into question. The ensuing controversy lasts until the present, in large part due to the refusal of the Bureau of Indian Affairs to grant official certificates of Indian blood to Black Seminoles not originally on the Dawes rolls. Blacks were officially enrolled as tribe members and recognized as such by the federal government. In 1991 the federal government awarded the Seminoles $56 million for their Florida lands, but nonblack members of the tribe claimed that the black members had no claim to share in the award. This prompted black members of the tribe to file suit in federal court; in one argument, they pointed to the original relationship their ancestors had with Osceola (and one of his wives who was African descent) and their loyalty in fighting with him as a reason that they should be recognized as full tribal members.

SEE ALSO *African Americans; Guerrilla Warfare; Indigenous Rights; Land Claims; Native Americans; Reparations; Resistance*

BIBLIOGRAPHY

Hartley, William B., and Ellen Hartley. 1973. *Osceola, the Unconquered Indian.* New York: Hawthorn.

Porter, Kenneth W. 1996. *The Black Seminoles: History of a Freedom-Seeking People.* Gainesville: University Press of Florida.

Charlton McIlwain

OSCHNER, ALBERT

SEE *Sterilization, Human.*

OTHER AMERICA, THE

SEE *War on Poverty.*

OTHER, THE

The term *other* is used in a variety of contexts. In the most basic sense, the other is used with a small *o* to depict the manners or processes by which perceptions of others are attained. This is the subject of much research in psychology, neurology, cognitive science, and philosophy of mind. Psychologists, particularly childhood psychologists, postulate that perceptions of the other proceed inter alia from processes of contrast, comparison, and analogy through which the self sets itself apart from, first, those who are close—mother, father, and other kin—and, second, outwardly to distant "strangers" (Klein 1964; Erikson [1950] 1993). It is thus understood that consciousness of the self depends upon processes that affect distinct characteristics to others.

Often in the social sciences and humanities the other is signified by a capital *O*. For instance, following in the footsteps of Georg W. F. Hegel ([1807] 2003) and Edmund Husserl ([1929] 1999), continental European philosophy investigates the question of otherness in conjunction with the tendency of the self to conceive all things after one's own likeness. This tendency results in the desire of the ego to "feel at home" in any philosophical speculation or scientific inquiry and yet separate or above the process of inquiry. The Other emerged in this context with either a transfigured or disfigured essence, no longer a reflection of itself and unaware of itself. This "Other" is a product of the self or at least only knowable first because of one's awareness of the self.

Post–World War II existentialists such as Jean-Paul Sartre sought to "transcend" the subjugated position of the Other by examining the role that self-consciousness plays in any inquiry (Sartre [1943] 2001). Then, from Russia and eastern Europe, Mikhail Bakhtin, Emmanuel Levinas, and Julia Kristeva brought to the terms *other* and *otherness* different inflections and connotations (Bakhtin [1986] 1993; Levinas 2000; Kristeva 1994). These authors founded their theories of the Other on personal or collective experiences in more or less cosmopolitan contexts of heterogeneous mixes of disparate languages and cultures in Europe. They stressed their own otherness based on difference, that is, either individual characteristics of persons or systematized identities of classes of people. For Levinas, the Other is the very condition of one's own existence. The Other is not any particular person, but instead an entire category that he calls "Otherness," which makes being and self or "I" possible, thus reversing the presupposition of phenomenologists such as Husserl and other continental thinkers who began all philosophical inquiry with the self. This line of argument has also concerned feminist thought, accepting the problem of the Other as the first philosophical question (Butler 2005) but insisting on the re-examination of the highly gendered notions of the ego, desire, subjectivity, and ethics (Beauvoir [1949] 1989).

The Other has not always been an interlocutor or object of reciprocal engagements. Karl Marx, Friedrich Nietzsche, Michel Foucault, and others have indicated difficulties involved in transcending the immediacy of the self in ideology or inquiry into social, political, and economic relations (Marx [1844] 1998; Nietzsche [1901] 1967; Foucault 2005). Anticolonialists and postcolonial theorists have constructed similar arguments that posit that the colonial enterprise was guided by an ideology that degraded the markers of culture, arts, and science in non-European societies to the status of folklore, myths, shamanism, and the like. Then, the colonized other was not merely different. Placed under the sign of the native (the secular equivalent of infidel), the other was deemed inferior and variably educable according to race, geography, and culture (Said 1979). It is now widely accepted that colonialists projected their own inadequacies or fears onto the colonized (Trouillot 1997). Even today, political discourse is rife with notions of rogues, failed states, and doctrines of democratic peace that assume inherent differences based on region, religion and culture, and race.

However, the stereotyping of the other(s) remains intractable because it seems to be integral to thought processes. It has benign or deadly consequences, depending on intent and circumstances, extending from simple acts of discrimination to ethnic cleansing and other crimes against humanity. As a result, neuroscientists and other specialists of the brain have undertaken inquiries on the nature of the brain, particularly how the brain generates and processes perceptions of self and the other. Indeed, scientists continue to wonder about the extent to which the brain and the mind can be made to transcend self-consciousness and affect to relate differently to desire, interest, and their pathos (Damásio 2000). For social scientists, the question of self and other centers on the means to a higher order of politics, where all might feel at home aided by scientific practices that ensure human survival (Connolly 2002).

SEE ALSO *Foucault, Michel; Marx, Karl; Marxism; Said, Edward*

BIBLIOGRAPHY

Bakhtin, Mikhail M. [1986] 1993. *Toward a Philosophy of the Act.* Austin: University of Texas Press.

Beauvoir, Simone de. [1949] 1989. *The Second Sex.* New York: Vintage.

Butler, Judith. 2005. *Giving an Account of Oneself.* New York: Fordham University Press.

Connolly, William E. 2002. *Neuropolitics: Thinking, Culture, Speed.* Minneapolis: University of Minnesota Press.

Damásio, António. 2000. *The Feeling of What Happens: Body and Emotion in the Making of Consciousness.* New York: Harcourt, Brace.

Erikson, Erik. [1950] 1993. *Childhood and Society.* New York: Norton.

Foucault, Michel. 2005. *The Hermeneutics of the Subject: Lectures at the College de France, 1981–1982.* New York: Palgrave Macmillan.

Hegel, Georg Wilhelm Friedrick. [1807] 2003. *The Phenomenology of the Mind.* New York: Dover.

Husserl, Edmund. [1929] 1999. Empathy and the Constitution of the Other. In *The Essential Husserl: Basic Writings in Transcendental Phenomenology,* ed. Don Welton, 135–160. Bloomington: Indiana University Press.

Klein, Melanie. 1964. *Love, Hate, and Reparation.* New York: Norton.

Kristeva, Julia. 1994. *Strangers to Ourselves.* Trans. Leon S. Roudiez. New York: Columbia University Press.

Levinas, Emmanuel. 2000. *Alterity and Transcendence.* New York: Columbia University Press.

Marx, Karl. [1844] 1988. *Economic and Philosophical Manuscripts of 1844.* Essex, U.K.: Prometheus.

Nietzsche, Friedrich. [1901] 1967. *The Will to Power.* New York: Random House.

Said, Edward W. 1979. *Orientalism.* New York: Vintage.

Sartre, Jean-Paul. [1943] 2001. Being-for-Others. In *Being and Nothingness: A Phenomenological Essay on Ontology.* New York: Citadel.

Trouillot, Michel-Rolph. 1997. *Silencing the Past.* Boston: Beacon.

Siba Grovogui

OTTOMAN EMPIRE

The Ottoman Empire (c. 1290–1922) provides a vivid example of durable and successful state building in world history. A late medieval creation, the Ottoman state achieved world empire status in 1453 because of its conquest of Constantinople. During the surrounding several centuries, it was among the most powerful states in the world. Although geography and luck played roles, the success of the empire mainly derived from pragmatic and flexible Ottoman policy-making and considerable openness to innovation, including military technology. At its peak, the empire covered parts of Asia, Africa, and Europe. Its extent is suggested by this partial list of successor states: Albania, Bosnia, Bulgaria, Egypt, Greece, Iraq, Israel, Jordan, Kuwait, Lebanon, Montenegro, Romania, Saudi Arabia, Serbia, Syria, and Turkey.

Expansion slowly faded into memory and territorial contraction began thanks partly to developments elsewhere in the world, notably the rise of capitalism and industrialism in Europe and then elsewhere, and to the New World wealth that poured into Europe. As wealth flowed elsewhere, the Ottoman Empire was unable to compete and lost its preeminent position; by about 1800 it had become a second-class economic, military, and political power. Within the empire innovation faded, partly because entrenched bureaucrats, statesmen, and military personnel acted to protect their children's positions and closed entry to newcomers.

During the nineteenth century a successful series of programs measurably strengthened the state and its military. The bureaucracy grew both in size and in the scope of its activities, now not merely collecting taxes and providing security but also taking responsibility for the health, education, and welfare of its subjects. Yet, the empire fell defeated in World War I (1914–1918) and was partitioned by the Great Powers, notably Great Britain and France.

In its domestic polity, the Ottoman state underwent continuous change. The Ottoman ruler, the sultan, began as one among equals, but between about 1453 and 1600, sultans ruled as true autocrats. Thereafter until about 1826, sultans reigned, but others in the imperial family and other inhabitants of the palace—often in collaboration with provincial elites—maintained real control of the state. Then, bureaucrats and sultans vied for domination of the state apparatus. In sum, the sultan presided over the imperial system for all of Ottoman history, but actually personally ruled for only portions of the fifteenth, sixteenth, and nineteenth centuries. Also, political power almost always rested in the imperial center and, depending on the particular period, extended into the provinces either through direct military and political instruments or indirectly through fiscal means.

A combination of religious and secular laws regulated the lives of Ottoman subjects. Under Ottoman state authority Muslim, Christian, or Jewish judges presided over the legal affairs of their respective communities. Often, however, subjects of all religions used the Muslim courts because rulings from such courts might have greater weight than those from Christian or Jewish sources. In addition to this religious law, the state routinely passed its own, secular, ordinances, often with lip-service adherence to Islamic principles. In the nineteenth century, when a flood of ordinances and regulations marked the presence of an expanding bureaucratic state, even the lip service frequently fell away in favor of scientific management.

This was an agrarian empire that, again, changed considerably over time. Most Ottoman subjects were and remained cultivators, raising a wide variety of different crops for subsistence and for sale. The particular mix of crops changed over time. Cereals remained dominant throughout the Ottoman period, but important new crops emerged at different times, for example, tobacco in the seventeenth century. In theory, the vast majority of land was owned by the sultan, but in practice, generally, land users enjoyed security of tenure. Sharecropping was widespread and the major vehicle by which goods came to market; most holdings were small. Commercialization of agriculture considerably developed in the eighteenth and nineteenth centuries. Ottoman manufacturing, for its part, remained largely small-scale and handcrafted, with some late mechanization. During the seventeenth and eighteenth centuries foreign markets for Ottoman manufactures fell away, but producers continued to enjoy a vast domestic market for their wares; in the nineteenth century export markets emerged for Ottoman rug makers and silk spinners, who usually were women working outside their homes. In transportation and communication there were important technological breakthroughs during the second half of the nineteenth century, including steamships, railroads, and the telegraph.

Ottoman intercommunal relations are hotly argued, and many popular stereotypes persist around the "terrible Turks" who slaughtered Ottoman Christians. For nearly all of Ottoman history, this stereotype is not true. For most of its duration, the Ottoman Empire can be characterized fairly as a tolerant political system. At times, the Ottoman state led the way in extending tolerance to minorities. For example, at the end of the fifteenth century Ottoman sultans welcomed the large Iberian Jewish population that the new Spanish monarchs were expelling from their own kingdom. More generally, the key to Ottoman success and a major reason for its longevity lay in the tolerant governmental treatment of those who did not share its professed religion. This tolerance was based both in practical politics and in the dictates of Islam. Until the 1870s the majority of Ottoman subjects were Christians and the state's official religion was Islam, which required that the Muslim state protect the religious rights of its Christian and Jewish subjects. The Ottoman Empire, for nearly all of its history, was a multinational, multireligious entity that did not seek to impose Islam on its subjects. This fact often has been forgotten in the confusion surrounding the end of the empire and the emergence of the Ottoman successor states, but it remains true nonetheless. Overall, the Ottoman system recognized difference and protected those differences so long as subjects rendered obedience and paid taxes. Until the eighteenth-century era of the Enlightenment, minorities in the Ottoman world likely were treated better than in Europe. Atrocities did occur, but they were exceptions in the rule of a generally admirable record of intercommunal relations over the 600-year life span of the Ottoman Empire.

BIBLIOGRAPHY

Imber, Colin. 2002. *The Ottoman Empire, 1300–1650: The Structure of Power.* New York: Palgrave Macmillan.

Inalcik, Halil, with Donald Quataert. 1994. *An Economic and Social History of the Ottoman Empire, 1300–1914.* Cambridge, U.K.: Cambridge University Press.

Lowry, Heath. 2003. *The Nature of the Early Ottoman State.* Albany: State University of New York Press.

Quataert, Donald. 2005. *The Ottoman Empire, 1700–1922.* 2nd ed. Cambridge, U.K.: Cambridge University Press.

Donald Quataert

OUGHT SELF

The ought self is a particular type of self-guide. Broadly, self-guides are representations of the self. Proposed by E. Tory Higgins (1987), self-guides are involved in self-regulation such that they provide standards for the self. The ought self is a self-guide attached to ideas about who persons feel they should be or should become. These selves are typically concerned with safety and responsibility. In contrast to the ought self is the ideal self, which represents who individuals want to become and is generally concerned with hopes and wishes.

Particular self-guides are associated with different affective experiences. Individuals who perceive a large discrepancy between their actual selves and their ought selves are more likely to experience an agitation-related affect, such as anxiety and guilt, while individuals who perceive their actual selves to be more proximal to their ought self–guides experience a relief-related affect, such as calmness.

Individuals may also differentiate between various sources of their self-guides. They may construe that their self-guides represent their own ideas of who they should become or that they represent their ideas of whom others think they should become. Regardless of the source of the guide, discrepancies involving the ought self are associated with an agitation-related affect.

The experience of discrepancy from an ought self incites a negative affect. This negative affect is unpleasant, and individuals generally want to avoid it. Consequently they will self-regulate or attempt to bring their actual selves more in line with their self-guides. In this way they reduce the perceived discrepancy between their actual selves and their ought selves. When the discrepancy is reduced, a less negative affect is experienced. In their 1994 study E. Tory Higgins, Christopher R. J. Roney, Ellen Crowe, and Charles Hymes found that individuals concerned with ought selves tend to use avoidance strategies in the process of self-regulation.

Individuals may differ in the extent to which they tend to use ought selves as self-guides. In his 1997 article, Higgins considers those who are more likely to use the ought self to be prevention-focused. That is, they are more likely to pursue goals that are related to safety and responsibility. In contrast, individuals who are more likely to use ideal selves as a self-guides are referred to as being promotion oriented.

Developmentally, parental factors may be associated with using ought selves in self-regulation. In 1998 Nanmathi Manian, Timothy J. Strauman, and Nancy Denney investigated the relationship between recollections of parental styles, temperament, and tendencies to use ought versus ideal selves. They found that individuals who recall their parents behaving in ways they perceived as rejecting were more likely to possess discrepancies between their actual selves and their ought selves. The researchers attribute this finding to an increase in the salience and usage of negative outcomes for these individuals. Additionally they found that both negative and positive temperament characteristics predicted actual and ideal discrepancies, while only negative temperament characteristics predicted actual and ought discrepancies.

SEE ALSO *Emotion and Affect; Parenting Styles; Personality; Self-Representation; Temperament*

BIBLIOGRAPHY

Higgins, E. Tory. 1987. Self-Discrepancy: A Theory Relating Self and Affect. *Psychological Review* 94: 319–340.

Higgins, E. Tory. 1997. Beyond Pleasure and Pain. *American Psychologist* 52: 1280–1300.

Higgins, E. Tory, Christopher R. J. Roney, Ellen Crowe, and Charles Hymes. 1994. Ideal versus Ought Predilections for Approach and Avoidance: Distinct Self-Regulatory Systems. *Journal of Personality and Social Psychology* 66: 276–286.

Manian, Nanmathi, Timothy J. Strauman, and Nancy Denney. 1998. Temperament, Recalled Parenting Style, and Self-Regulation: Testing the Developmental Postulates of Self-Discrepancy Theory. *Journal of Personality and Social Psychology* 75: 1321–1332.

Michelle Sherrill

OUT-GROUP BIASES

SEE *Identity, Social.*

OUTSOURCING

Outsourcing is a process whereby an organization contracts with an outside entity to perform some business function previously done "in-house." Practically any function can be outsourced, from manufacturing labor to customer service. The spatial distance between the core firm and the contractor can vary greatly. *Offshoring* denotes an outsourcing of business functions to a contractor located in a foreign country. Domestic outsourcing occurs within a single country, and can even involve two firms located directly adjacent to one another. The temporal relationship between core and contractor firms can also vary, from a decades-long partnership to temporary services rendered for a single day. Due to the complex nature of the phenomenon and the inadequacy of existing data, no precise metric is available with which to quantify the extent of outsourcing or its growth over time. Those interested in the issue of measurement should consult Robert C. Feenstra (1998). Social scientists generally agree, however, that outsourcing has proliferated globally since the 1970s.

To explain this proliferation of outsourcing, scholars situate it in relation to the larger phenomenon of economic globalization. In this view, the mid-twentieth century was dominated by large oligopolistic firms catering to regional markets within the nation-state. These firms were vertically integrated; that is, they controlled both supplier and distributor firms. They located their headquarters and production facilities proximate to supplier and consumer markets. Work was organized to achieve economies of scale and to maximize the volume of goods produced. Workers were in turn offered job security and generous wages.

Commencing in the 1970s, several major changes to the organization of economies and states dramatically transformed ideas of how a successful business should be designed. Business leaders now sought to "pare down" their organizations, by outsourcing all but a small core of essential functions. These streamlined firms would then be integrated into a web of strategic alliances with other firms around the world. But what were the changes that led to the emergence of what Manuel Castells (2000) calls a "network society"? First, firms experienced increased competition due to a deregulation of business relationships and the removal of barriers to trade across nations. Second, the ownership structure of firms underwent a transformation, as institutions purchased large portions of corporate stock. While individual shareholders are typically passive, institutional investors actively demand that managers maximize short-term profits. Third, advances in communications and transportation technology (especially personal computers and Internet access) enabled the coordination of production across great distances.

Intensified competition, a shareholder conception of control, and new technology increased the feasibility and attractiveness of outsourcing. As Paul Osterman (1999) documents, outsourcing decreases labor costs insofar as contracting firms pay on average lower wages and offer fewer benefits. Outsourcing also relieves the core firm from the responsibility of ensuring that working conditions meet state regulations. In the United States, for example, should a contracting firm be found to have forced employees to work overtime, it and not the core firm would be found culpable. More generally, outsourcing is believed to maximize flexibility. Temporary workers may be contracted to meet seasonal fluctuations in business activity, and production processes can be quickly reengineered to match changes in consumer demand, while relationships with suppliers can be terminated should production schedules be altered.

The proliferation over the past three decades of offshoring and domestic outsourcing has invoked considerable debate within nations. It is important to consider the points of view of two main parties: states and workers. Governments of states targeted by firms as sites of outsourcing can take a range of positions. At one extreme is a developmental state actively encouraging investment. At the other is staunch opposition to outside investment, most likely when the outsourced activity is perceived as vital to national security. For example, in April 2006 plans to outsource the inspection of incoming containers at U.S. ports to a Dubai-based company were canceled after U.S. Congressional leaders protested over potential security risks.

When confronted with proposals by domestic firms to offshore production, governments may accuse firms of behaving greedily or unpatriotically. This is especially the case when the outsourcing will entail plant closings, or when the domestic firm is outsourcing not for economic survival but to achieve a higher rate of return on investment overseas. Politicians may even pass legislation to discourage foreign investment by domestic firms. Such protectionism, however, represents what Robert Reich labels "vestigial thought" (1992, p. 154), insofar as it remains wedded to a vision of unitary firms producing and selling goods within a single nation-state. In fact, managers, when deciding to offshore production, are merely responding to the shifting rules of the larger game of global capitalism. Governments intent on protecting domestic jobs would be wiser to cooperate to reshape the rules of this game rather than demonizing individual players.

Like states, workers in existing core firms may view outsourcing as against their interests. After all, the flexible labor markets required by global capitalism entail the replacement of secure jobs offering middle-class incomes with insecure jobs and low wages. The competition among states to attract investment capital is in fact often labeled a "race to the bottom." Yet workers and their unions are hampered in their capacity to take action against individual firms, since strikes or work stoppages may only quicken the pace at which work is outsourced. As Jeffrey Sallaz (2004) has documented, unions lack the means to influence the rules of the game at a national or global level, and so fight to slow the pace at which work is outsourced from core facilities to allow older workers time to adjust to the "new economy."

To conclude, as competitive global capitalism has eclipsed oligopolistic national capitalisms, outsourcing has emerged as a strategy used by private firms to cut labor costs and increase flexibility. Of immediate interest to social scientists in the coming years will be the question of how the economic trend toward outsourcing is affected by political developments involving the global "war on terror," heightened border security, and resurgent nationalisms.

SEE ALSO *Globalization, Social and Economic Aspects of; Trade*

BIBLIOGRAPHY

Castells, Manuel. 2000. *The Rise of the Network Society.* 2nd ed. Malden, MA: Blackwell.

Feenstra, Robert C. 1998. Integration of Trade and Disintegration of Production in the Global Economy. *Quarterly Journal of Economics* 12 (4): 31–50

Osterman, Paul. 1999. *Securing Prosperity: The American Labor Market, How It Has Changed, and What to Do about It.* Princeton, NJ: Princeton University Press.

Reich, Robert B. 1992. *The Work of Nations: Preparing Ourselves for 21st-Century Capitalism.* New York: Vintage.

Sallaz, Jeffrey J. 2004. Manufacturing Concessions: Attritionary Outsourcing at GM's Lordstown, USA, Assembly Plant. *Work, Employment, and Society* 18 (4): 687–708.

Jeffrey J. Sallaz

OVERACHIEVERS

The motivational basis for human-achievement behavior has interested psychologists for decades. Research has linked basic psychological theory to applications in education, business, and industry where achievement is critical. Striving for success pervades social interaction in the classroom, in the corporate boardroom, on the playing field, and even within families and friendships. Those who achieve success are viewed as productive members of society worthy of admiration and respect.

To some extent, practical concerns, such as the need to motivate children to set satisfactory goals in school and to address underachievement, generated scientific interest in achievement issues. Historically, underachievement (and overachievement) has been defined in objective terms according to the match between expectations and life outcomes, and psychologists have usually been concerned with these objective terms. Specifically, expectations for one's performance are based on relatively objective criteria. For instance, people set expectations of their potential based on past performances or on the evaluations of significant others (e.g., parents, teachers). In Western society, standardized tests (e.g., the SAT) are common as a practical and seemingly objective basis for expectations of future performance. When someone performs below (e.g., grade point average) the level expected (e.g., by aptitude scores), that is underachievement. When underachievement is identified, educators marshal effort to help people realize their full potential.

Educators have paid little attention to the mirror image of underachievement: overachievement. When someone performs better than predicted in school (or anywhere else), that is overachievement. Overachievement presents no real problem to solve. Doing well is highly regarded, so it is not surprising that educators have neglected to study it. When someone outstrips objectively based predictions of their performance, prevailing wisdom suggests reason to celebrate, not to intervene.

This traditional emphasis on objective achievement suggests that people might be expected to work tirelessly to ensure success. Yet, everyday observation reveals that people approach achievement in their everyday lives in many ways. Some people strive mightily, but others seem lazy and disengaged; still others take credit for outcomes that they appear not to have earned, and sometimes people flee from tasks when the prospects of failure or embarrassment become too great.

Social psychologists have studied the subjective experience associated with underachievement and overachievement. Findings show that there is a great deal to be learned about these experiences. In particular, the subjective experience of overachievers may be highly stressful and unpleasant and marked by anxiety, but uniquely defined by self-doubt. Specifically, the subjective experience of chronic self-doubt, coupled with intense performance concerns, appears to inspire overachieving behavior. Overachievers may expend heroic effort to cope with their chronic doubts.

One social psychologist coined the term *John Henryism hypothesis* to describe the psychological stress associated with the social and economic challenges faced by African Americans. The research links an increased risk of hypertension and other health problems among African

Americans to the stress of persistent, effortful coping in the face of socioeconomic challenges, a parallel to the experience of the fictional character John Henry, who outpaced the steam drill but died soon thereafter from the exertion. Like John Henryism, the stress of everyday overachieving may also have adverse health implications.

Ironically, overachievement can serve to enhance rather than diminish self-doubt in one's natural talent. The effort of overachievers provides an alternative explanation to natural ability for any success they achieve. Moreover, these shaky assessments of ability generalize to shaky expectations of future potential. Sadly, overachievers may reap success beyond objective expectations but still doubt their own ability to reproduce success without enormous effort. Overachievers may ultimately enter a vicious cycle in which they cope with self-doubt by, once again, expending heroic effort to ensure that they can perform successfully again and again. High achievement and overachievement in the context of a group might even enhance self-doubt about an individual's personal contribution, and produce shaky judgments about one's individual talent and personal value to the group. The increased pressure to perform successfully in a public arena has been shown in research many times.

Some individuals experience high self-doubt without having the intense concern over performance that characterizes the overachiever. At a behavioral level, the lower concern with performance leads these individuals to employ a very different strategy than overachievers. These individuals may cope with self-doubt by employing the seemingly paradoxical strategy of deliberately sabotaging, or handicapping, their own performance. Like the overachiever, self-handicappers experience chronic self-doubt. Unlike the overachiever, however, self-handicappers are more concerned about the implications of failure as it relates to judgments about their ability; they worry that failure will be an indication (to themselves or others) that they lack ability. Thus, whereas the overachiever will expend heroic effort to avoid failure, the self-handicapper is willing to embrace failure (i.e., withdraw effort) to protect a basic perception of personal competence. They undermine their own performance in order to make the cause of their (perhaps failing) behavior ambiguous. Examples include alcohol use and abuse, procrastination, laziness, and any other behavior that could excuse failure.

Though speculative, the distinct psychological style of subjective overachievers can be traced to their early learning history. The budding overachiever may come to internalize the parental message that only successful performance can guarantee continued love and support. These early beliefs may lead overachievers to assign higher significance to successful outcomes than to exploring their actual talents.

Subjective overachievement has been distinguished in research from high achievement motivation (people show the same concern over successful performances, but seek achievement for personal satisfaction), perfectionism (people display intense preoccupation with successful performance, but do not necessarily experience self-doubt), and the imposter phenomenon (where self-doubt is present, but success is seen as unearned or illegitimate because it is due to luck, not effort).

SEE ALSO *Achievement; Underachievers*

BIBLIOGRAPHY

Arkin, Robert M., and Kathryn C. Oleson. 1998. Self Handicapping. In *Attribution and Social Interaction: The Legacy of Edward E. Jones*, eds. John M. Darley and Joel Cooper, 317-347. Washington, DC: American Psychological Association.

Elliot, Andrew J., and Carol S. Dweck. 2005. Competence and Motivation: Competence as the Core of Achievement Motivation. In *Handbook of Competence and Motivation*, eds. Andrew J. Elliot and Carol S. Dweck, 3–12. New York: Guilford.

James, Sherman A. 1994. John Henryism and the Health of African-Americans. *Culture, Medicine, and Psychiatry* 18 (2): 163–182.

Oleson, Kathryn C., Kirsten M. Poehlmann, John H. Yost, et al. 2000. Subjective Overachievement: Individual Differences in Self-doubt and Concern with Performance. *Journal of Personality* 68 (3): 491–524.

Weiner, Bernard. 1972. *Theories of Motivation: From Mechanism to Cognition.* Chicago: Markham.

Robert M. Arkin
Patrick J. Carroll

OVER-ATTRIBUTION BIAS

The over-attribution bias, also known as "correspondence bias," occurs when people attribute human behavior to whichever causal factor is most available to them. Behavior often "engulfs the field," and people draw dispositional inferences that correspond to the behavior. When a person freely expresses a certain attitude, others assume that the person believes it. The same inference is biased, however, when observers know that a powerful other asked the person to express that attitude. The bias is most striking when it is the observers themselves who constrain the respondent's behavior.

The common interpretation of the correspondence bias is that it constitutes a "fundamental attribution error"

(Ross 1977). This interpretation holds that people fail to fully discount the influence of a person's internal disposition as a cause of behavior. The error interpretation has been influential in social psychology because it implies that people are incapable of understanding the power of the typical social-psychological experiment, which is to demonstrate that subtle changes in a person's situation can dramatically change behavior.

Upon review, the idea that people fail to appreciate the power of social situations needs to be tempered. The correspondence bias reverses, for example, when people who know a person's disposition are asked to judge the strength of the situation. They continue to attribute behavior in part to the situation even when the behavior is freely chosen. Hence, the correspondence bias is generic rather than purely dispositional. People attribute behavior firstly to whichever causal factor they happen to be focused on, be it a property of the person or the situation, and then modulate this inference by considering the other, less salient causal factor. Because the former process is likely intuitive and automatic, whereas the latter is deliberate and controlled, the bias is larger when people are unmotivated or unable (e.g., because of distraction) to process all available information.

Most models of causal attribution are hydraulic in that they regard the total causal force directing behavior as a zero-sum quantity. As one causal factor is being favored, another one must yield. On this view, the correspondence bias reflects a failure to fully discount the primary and salient cause when the secondary cause is sufficient. For the explanation of everyday behavior, the hydraulic model is sometimes inadequate. For example, people often attribute aggressive behavior to an aggressive disposition. To do so, however, they require the presence of a facilitating stimulus, such as an insult or a threat. Whereas a hydraulic model suggests that inferences about an aggressive disposition should be stronger in the absence of provocation, an interactionist model recognizes that a situational cause (provocation) is necessary for a dispositional attribution. On this view, theories of personality that seek to capture individual differences by merely counting trait-related acts are likely contaminated by the researchers' correspondence biases.

The common tendency of attributing correspondence bias to people's dispositional failure to think logically may itself be an example of the very same bias. Correspondence biases are, after all, experimentally evoked when investigators limit the salience of the situational causes of behavior. Hence, it may be sufficient to attribute respondents' preference for dispositional inferences to the nature of the experimental situation.

SEE ALSO *Attribution*

BIBLIOGRAPHY

Gawronski, Bertram. 2004. Theory-Based Correction in Dispositional Inference: The Fundamental Attribution Error Is Dead, Long Live the Correspondence Bias. In *European Review of Social Psychology*, vol. 15, ed. Wolfgang Stroebe and Miles Hewstone. Chichester, U.K.: Wiley.

Jones, Edward, and Victor Harris. 1967. The Attribution of Attitudes. *Journal of Experimental Social Psychology* 3: 1–24.

Ross, Lee. 1977. The Intuitive Psychologist and His Shortcomings. In *Advances in Experimental Social Psychology*, Vol. 10, ed. L. Berkowitz, 174–221. New York: Academic Press.

Joachim I. Krueger

OVER-CONTROL
SEE *Farsightedness.*

OVEREATING

Overeating is a relative term, defined as food consumption that exceeds energy expenditure. Chronic overeating typically results in obesity and is not uncommon. In fact, obesity is at epidemic proportions for all age groups, and is seen as a growing health threat not just in Western societies but also in much of the world. Risk for obesity increased markedly during the 1980s, an increase that is attributable to a complex combination of environmental, sociocultural, genetic, and behavioral factors.

Overeating can be either active or passive. Active overeating is largely the consequence of a convergence of sociocultural factors that most notably include aggressive mass marketing of energy- or calorie-dense foods (foods high in fat, refined carbohydrates, and sugar) and disproportionately large portions of food relative to individuals' actual caloric needs. Not coincidentally, such foods are easily accessible, widely available, relatively affordable, and highly palatable. Unsurprisingly, society has fallen prey to marketing influences, and consumption of such foods is on the rise. It is noteworthy that, as of 2006, the highest rates of obesity and obesity-related disorders in the United States are found in lower-income groups for whom the marketing of energy-dense, low-cost foods is most pervasive.

Active overeating is also part of the symptom complex of conditions such as bulimia nervosa and binge eating disorder. With bulimia, individuals experience a sense of being unable to control what and how much they eat, and they engage in recurrent episodes during which they very rapidly consume an abnormally large quantity of food. This symptom is also a defining characteristic of binge eating disorder. A key distinction between bulimia and binge eating disorder is that with bulimia, individuals engage in dangerous methods of weight control (e.g., purging, fasting, and vomiting), whereas with binge eating disorder, individuals do not engage in such weight control efforts and, in fact, may be obese. Active overeating may also result from hypothalamic dysfunction, either due to genetic defects (e.g., Prader-Willi syndrome), physical injury, or pharmacological agents.

Although active overeating accounts for a substantial proportion of the high rates of obesity, passive overeating may best explain prevalence rates. There are several aspects to consider in passive overeating. First, as is perhaps obvious, individuals with an energy-dense diet who consume food equal in quantity to individuals with a lower-energy diet have an overall greater energy intake. Second, lower-energy diets are most satiating, whereas energy-dense diets are least satiating: Consumption of a greater quantity of energy-dense foods is required to achieve equal levels of satiety. Thus, passive overeating is the unintentional, but inevitable, consequence of a diet that is energy-dense. Given that it is also a prime factor in the energy balance equation, physical inactivity compounds the issue. Technological advances promote an increasingly sedentary lifestyle that, in combination with active or passive overeating, further subverts the energy equation, resulting in ever-rising obesity rates.

Although research on pharmacological interventions to treat obesity is ongoing, lifestyle changes are likely to remain central features of any intervention. It may, however, require major macrosystemic social change to effect significant improvement in our nutrition and physical activity.

SEE ALSO *Nutrition; Obese Externality; Obesity; Schachter, Stanley*

BIBLIOGRAPHY

American Psychiatric Association. 2000. *Diagnostic and Statistical Manual of Mental Disorders* (*DSM*-IV-TR). 4th ed., text rev. Washington, DC: Author.

Hill, James O., Holly R. Wyatt, George W. Reed, and John C. Peters. 2003. Obesity and the Environment: Where Do We Go from Here? *Science* 299 (5608): 853–855.

Joan K. Orrell-Valente

OVEREMPLOYMENT

Little is as damaging economically, socially, and psychologically as depriving people of income and job opportu-

nities, from unemployment and underemployment. Overemployment, however, refers to depriving the employed of desired time. Individuals are defined as *overemployed* when they are prepared to sacrifice income proportionally for a given reduction in their work hours but cannot do so at their current job or a suitable comparable job. For example, an overemployed individual would like to work no more than forty hours per week (including overtime), but he or she is forced by the employer to work fifty hours per week.

The conventional microeconomic model of individual labor supply assumes that workers desire to work a certain number of hours per week based on their expected wage rate, nonwage income, and preference for nonwork uses of time. Insightful models have incorporated the possibility that at least some workers are often not able to realize a preference for fewer work hours because of constraints that are imposed by employers or the labor market (Dunn 1996; Feather and Shaw 2000; Altonji and Oldham 2003). Employers face a variety of incentives and pressures that may lengthen the hours of work demanded from each employee (Rebitzer and Taylor 1995; Contensou and Vranceanu 2000). Whenever hours demanded exceed workers' desired number of hours supplied to their job, workers supply "surplus" hours (Lee and McCann 2004). This condition may persist indefinitely when the alternative job with shorter hours actually results in relatively lower levels of utility than working surplus hours (Kaufman and Hotchkiss 2006). Hours mismatches or inconvenient hours do not create compensating wage differentials for working (Altonji and Paxson 1992; Reynolds 2004). Overemployment becomes a wider social problem to the extent that it creates symptoms of "overwork," such as fatigue and stress, which heighten the risk of workplace accidents, illnesses, and work-family time conflict.

As with unemployment, there are cyclical, frictional, and structural macroeconomic sources of overemployment (Altman and Golden 2004). Further, measuring the overall rate of overemployment has proven tricky. The estimated rate is sensitive to the wording of survey questions and response options. Estimates range from 6 percent to over 30 percent of the U.S. workforce (Bell and Freeman 1995; Altman and Golden 2004), lower than the rate in comparable countries (Bielinski, Bosch, and Wagner 2002). Moreover, the overemployment rate may diminish with time if preferences are "endogenous." Workers unable to "get what they want … eventually want what they get" (Schor 2005, p. 46). The distribution of overemployment is highest among women with preschool children, those in professional and technical health occupations, and those with long workweeks (Golden 2005). Overemployment may take the form of an unfulfilled wish to switch from longer to standard or part-time hours or to decline mandatory overtime work.

Conventional economists discount overemployment for two reasons. One is the suspicion that stated preferences for shorter hours would actually be acted upon. In addition, the rate of overemployment is a low priority because it is dwarfed by the rate of underemployment (Kahn and Lang 2001). However, a proactive approach would favor regulatory incentives that compel employers to shift the excess hours of the overemployed toward the underemployed within their workplace or industry.

SEE ALSO *Inflation; Underemployment*

BIBLIOGRAPHY

Altman, Morris, and Lonnie Golden. 2004. Alternative Economic Approaches to Analyzing Hours of Work Regulation and Reform. In *Law and Economics: Alternative Economic Approaches to Legal and Regulatory Issues,* eds. Margaret Oppenheimer and Nicholas Mercuro, 286–307. Armonk, NY: Sharpe.

Altonji, Joseph, and Christina Paxson. 1992. Labor Supply, Hours Constraints, and Job Mobility. *Journal of Human Resources* 27: 256–278.

Altonji, Joseph, and Jennifer Oldham. 2003. Vacation Laws and Annual Work Hours. *Economic Perspectives* 3: 19–29.

Bell, Linda, and Richard Freeman. 1995. Why Do Americans and Germans Work Different Hours? In *Institutional Frameworks and Labor Market Performance: Comparative Views on the U.S. and German Economies,* eds. Friedrich Butler, Wolfgang Franz, Ronald Schettkat, and David Soskice, 101–131. London and New York: Routledge.

Bielenski, Harald, Gerhard Bosch, and Alexandra Wagner. 2002. *Working Time Preferences in Sixteen European Countries.* Dublin: European Foundation for the Improvement of Living and Working Conditions.

Böheim, René, and Mark P. Taylor. 2004. Actual and Preferred Working Hours. *British Journal of Industrial Relations* 42 (3): 149–66.

Contensou, François, and Radu Vranceanu. 2000. *Working Time: Theory and Policy Implications.* Cheltenham, U.K.: Edward Elgar.

Dunn, L. F. 1996. Loss Aversion and Adaptation in the Labor Market: Empirical Indifference Functions and Labor Supply. *Review of Economics and Statistics* 78 (3): 441–450.

Feather, Peter, and Douglass Shaw. 2000. The Demand for Leisure Time in the Presence of Constrained Work Hours. *Economic Inquiry* 38 (4): 651–662.

Golden, Lonnie. 2005. Overemployment in the US: Which Workers Face Downward Constrained Hours? In *Decent Working Time: New Trends, New Issues,* eds. Jean-Yves Boulin, Michael Lallement, Jon Messenger, and François Michon, 209–234. Geneva: International Labour Organization.

Kaufman, Bruce, and Julie L. Hotchkiss. 2006. *The Economics of Labor Markets.* 7th ed. Mason, OH: Thomson South-Western.

Lang, Kevin, and Shulamit Kahn. 2001. Hours Constraints: Theory, Evidence, and Policy Implications. In *Working Time in a Comparative Perspective.* Vol. 1: *Patterns, Trends, and Policy Implications for Earnings Inequality and Unemployment,* eds. Ging Wong and Garnett Picot, 261–290. Kalamazoo, MI: Upjohn Institute for Employment Research.

Lee, Sangeon, and Dierdre McCann. 2004. In *Working Time and Workers' Preferences in Industrialized Countries: Finding the Balance,* ed. Jon Messenger, 65–91. New York: Routledge.

Rebitzer, James, and Lowell Taylor. 1995. Do Labor Markets Provide Enough Short-Hour Jobs? An Analysis of Work Hours and Work Incentives. *Economic Inquiry* 33: 257–273.

Reynolds, Jeremy. 2004. When Too Much Is Not Enough: Actual and Preferred Work Hours in the United States and Abroad. *Sociological Forum* 19 (1): 89–120.

Schor, J. 2005. Sustainable Consumption and Worktime Reduction. *Journal of Industrial Ecology* 9: 37–50.

Lonnie Golden

OVERFISHING

Overfishing occurs when the stock (*biomass*) of a fish species has been subjected to a rate or level of fishing mortality (usually from commercial fishing) that has reduced it below its capacity to maintain an established fishing (*harvest*) yield. This yield is usually specified as the *maximum sustainable yield* (MSY), defined as the maximum amount of fish that can be removed from the biomass on a sustained basis while maintaining the same stock level, given the stock's biological growth function (*dynamics*). Overfishing is inherently a biological concept, although it is fundamentally tied to economic behavior because it involves fishing pressure or intensity beyond an optimum level. The model used to evaluate it is thus called a *bioeconomic* model.

To more specifically define overfishing it is necessary to determine what fishing level would be optimal in terms of the biological stock, or not constitute overfishing. The first step is to define the biological growth function, which is generally attributed to Milner B. Schaefer (1954; see also Anderson 1986). Given his assumption of a logistic growth equation, a sustainable yield curve can be drawn as a parabola, expressed in terms of either the biomass stock (S) or fishing *effort* (E), as shown on the left and right hand side of Figure 1, respectively.

In an unexploited state (no mortality from fishing) the fishery is in a biological equilibrium where growth is zero, at the left-hand extreme of both curves in the figure. If fishing then begins, defined in terms of increasing fishing effort (days, or boat/crew), the fish stock falls (a movement to the right on the horizontal axis in both panels). The biomass (fish) growth that may be harvested (caught) on a sustainable basis rises, however (as indicated by the increasing yield on the vertical axis with a move up the

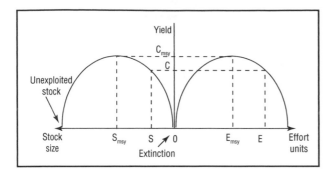

Figure 1: Sustainable yield curve

curves), because the stock will be regenerating toward the biological equilibrium.

The maximum possible sustained yield is attained at the very top of the curve(s), which shows the MSY fish stock (S_{msy}), the effort required to harvest that stock on a sustained basis if no shock changes the curves (E_{msy}), and the maximum catch attainable in that state (C_{msy}). If more fishing effort than E_{msy} is applied to harvesting, however, the stock and thus sustainable catch decline (a movement down the right hand sides of the curves), because reproduction is not proceeding fast enough to counteract the exploitation. This is a state of *overfishing*, represented by the lower sustained yield (or mortality) than possible (such as at $C < C_{msy}$). The stock is thus *overfished*, characterized by a lower stock than at the MSY point ($S < S_{msy}$), and the fishery is *overcapitalized* ($E > E_{msy}$).

Overfishing is the likely outcome in an unmanaged fishery because it is *common property* or *open access* (no one owns the fish), so fishers will keep fishing as long as they find it profitable. Such overuse is generally expected for common property or *common pool* resources, a problem often called "the tragedy of the commons" (see Hardin 1968). That is, *overexploitation* of the stock occurs because without property rights fishing will continue until the average rather than marginal benefits of harvesting are equal to marginal costs. In the standard bioeconomic model this results in an effort level on the right hand side of effort curve.

A primary goal of fishing management is thus to counteract the incentive to fish the stock down to an overexploited or overfished state. This can be accomplished by command and control polices such as limits on the total allowable catch or days at sea. Such policies still do not provide incentives for fishers to maximize the economic value of the fishery, which is best accomplished by conferring property rights on fishers to approximate a socially optimal outcome. Such programs can be difficult to implement, however, due to distributional and political issues about who is allowed to fish, how much revenue

each fisher receives, and how such rights should be conferred (e.g., for free or auctioned off with the proceeds going to the public or to support fishery management).

SEE ALSO *Coase Theorem; Externality; Tragedy of the Commons*

BIBLIOGRAPHY

Anderson, Lee. 1986. *The Economics of Fisheries Management.* Baltimore, MD: Johns Hopkins University Press.

Hardin, Garrett. 1968. The Tragedy of the Commons. *Science* 162: 1243–1248.

Schaefer, Milner B. 1954. Some Aspects of the Dynamics of Populations Important to the Management of Commercial Marine Fisheries. *Bulletin of the Inter-American Tropical Tuna Commission* 1: 25–56.

Catherine J. Morrison Paul

OVERLAPPING GENERATIONS MODEL

Like other economic models, an overlapping generations model (or as it is widely known, an OLG model) is a simplified theoretical representation of complicated economic processes through a set of identities and equations that describe the behavior of various agents interacting with each other. The most distinguishing feature of an OLG model lies in the way it captures the changing behavior of consumers over different phases of their lives. Since consumers in an OLG model are modeled as individuals who live for n periods ($n \geq 2$), people born in n different periods (or n different generations) coexist in any given period t. While consumers die at the end of n periods, reproduction assures that there will be an infinite succession of consumers, each living for n periods.

At the beginning of their economically active lives, individuals are endowed with a labor power that they can sell to firms (and may have goods or assets they inherit from the previous generation). They work when young and spend part of their labor and asset earnings on present consumption, saving the rest for financing their consumption when they are old. Thus, their old-age consumption is financed through savings they made while they were young and any returns to assets they acquired by using those savings. In other words, individuals must spread their income from the wages they earn by supplying their labor power to firms and the return on their assets over their lifetime such that they can continue to consume even after they are too old to work (or after they retire).

Consumers just starting their economic lives make their decisions on how much to spend on consumption and how much to save within each period ahead of them so as to maximize their lifetime utility. Profit-maximizing firms produce an output by employing labor supplied by young workers and capital supplied through their savings invested in physical capital. In essence, capital is part of the current output set aside to be used in production of the next period's output. Thus, the more individuals save for future consumption, the higher the expansion in the capital stock and, hence, the higher the rate of economic growth will be. As such, OLG models extend standard growth models by relating capital accumulation to savings that young adults make out of their earnings for the purpose of financing their old-age consumption. Within this framework, the long-run equilibrium (or the steady state) will be reached after the growth rate of the total capital stock in the economy has become equal to the population growth rate (or equivalently, after capital stock per worker has stopped changing over time).

Suggested first by French economist Maurice Allais in 1947, the concept of an OLG model was further developed in a 1958 article by Paul A. Samuelson (Samuelson and Allais won the 1970 and 1988 Nobel prizes in economics, respectively). While Peter A. Diamond also made a significant contribution to the OLG modeling literature through a 1965 article, the growth of this literature remained slow until the mid-1980s. The growing concerns over the upcoming burden of the retirement of baby boomers born in the 1940s and the 1950s on social security systems of industrial countries starting from the 1980s led to the realization that extending previous OLG models to incorporate social security was relatively easy, as they realistically captured the changing consumption and savings behavior of individuals before and after retirement. This development has revived interest in OLG models and attracted the attention of economists to the long-term economic effects of demographic developments.

In addition to purely theoretical models, a book by Alan Auerbach and Laurence Kotlikoff published in 1987 popularized the use of numerical solutions to large-scale OLG models with several generations in studying issues related to social security and the evolution of fiscal policy in different countries with different demographic structures. Numerous applied models were constructed thereafter to investigate the implications of changes in age profiles of populations for labor supply, savings, and fiscal balances, as surveyed by David Miles (1999). The realism of applied models has increased with the introduction of additional production sectors that produce distinct goods by employing capital and labor. (Elaborate theoretical grounds for two-sector OLG models that allow the consumption goods to be distinguished from investment goods were laid out in an article by Oded Galor published in 1992.)

Theoretical as well as applied OLG models have since proved particularly popular in analyzing the long-term economic consequences of the gradual aging of nations, a demographic process characterized by the increasing population share of the elderly due to declining fertility rates and increasing life expectancies during a country's demographic transition. As demographic projections pointed to the continuation of this trend in the decades ahead, modeling of demographics within the OLG framework became increasingly realistic. (According to the United Nations, the world's population, standing at less than 7 billion in 2006, will reach 9.3 billion by 2050. The number of people aged sixty or over is projected to more than double to nearly 2 billion during the same period. Furthermore, the elderly population itself is aging, with the eighty-plus age group making up the fastest-growing segment of the population.)

Despite variations in its timing and speed across countries, this demographic transition is expected to have important implications not only for future balances of the social security system and the time paths of age-specific public expenditures such as education and health care in a country, but also for the evolution of the supply of labor and capital. In most of the industrial countries where demographic transition started earlier than developing countries, the population shares of people older than the retirement age have already reached critical levels that signal financial trouble for publicly managed retirement systems. Likewise, the declining share of working-age population in these countries raises concern about contractions in domestic labor supply. Furthermore, because the elderly tend to spend more and save less, industrial countries are also expected to face changes in the ratio of savings to consumption in their national income, as well as in the composition of consumption.

These demographically induced developments are certain to affect not only investment and growth patterns of industrial economies but also the global allocation of resources by creating incentives for migration and by affecting the patterns of international trade and capital flows. They must, thus, have implications also for developing countries, even though these countries' own demographic transition processes lag behind industrial nations. The growing awareness of this situation prompted renewed interest in the OLG works of the early 1980s, such as the articles by Joel Fried and Willem Buiter studying issues related to trade or capital flows between nations. Oded Galor and Shoukang Lin made important contributions to the theoretical analysis of international trade using OLG models. Such authors as Andrew Mountford and Emily Cremers showed in different articles that dynamic trade equilibrium in an OLG framework may not always imply welfare gains for trading partners, contrary to predictions of static trade models. In a particularly interesting 2001 article based on results from an applied OLG model developed to study trade between a middle-income country at the beginning of its demographic transition and a group of high-income countries with aging populations, Turalay Kenc and Serdar Sayan showed that trade and capital flows serve as a channel for the middle-income country to import the effects of population aging in its trade partners ahead of time.

SEE ALSO *Insurance; Macroeconomics*

BIBLIOGRAPHY

Auerbach, Alan J., and Laurence J. Kotlikoff. 1987. *Dynamic Fiscal Policy.* New York: Cambridge University Press.

Buiter, Willem H. 1981. Time Preference and International Lending and Borrowing in an Overlapping-Generations Model. *Journal of Political Economy* 89 (4): 769–797.

Cremers, Emily T. 2005. Intergenerational Welfare and Trade. *Macroeconomic Dynamics* 9: 585–611.

Diamond, Peter A. 1965. National Debt in a Neoclassical Growth Model. *American Economic Review* 55 (5): 1126–1150.

Fried, Joel. 1980. The Intergenerational Distribution of the Gains from Technical Change and from International Trade. *Canadian Journal of Economics* 13 (1): 65–81.

Galor, Oded. 1992. A Two-Sector Overlapping Generations Model: Global Characterization of the Dynamical System. *Econometrica* 60: 1351–1386.

Galor, Oded, and Shoukang Lin. 1997. Dynamic Foundations for the Factor Endowment Model of International Trade. In *Dynamics, Economic Growth, and International Trade*, eds. Bjarne S. Jensen and Kar-yiu Wong, 151–168. Ann Arbor: University of Michigan Press.

Jelassi, Mehdi, and Serdar Sayan. 2005. Implications of Unequal Rates of Population Growth for Trade: An Overlapping Generations-General Equilibrium Analysis within the Heckscher-Ohlin Framework. *METU Studies in Development* 32: 391–408.

Kenc, Turalay, and Serdar Sayan. 2001. Demographic Shock Transmission from Large to Small Countries: An Overlapping Generations CGE Analysis. *Journal of Policy Modeling* 23 (6): 677–702.

Miles, David. 1999. Modelling the Impact of Demographic Change upon the Economy. *Economic Journal* 109: 1–36.

Mountford, Andrew. 1998. Trade, Convergence, and Overtaking. *Journal of International Economics* 46: 167–182.

Samuelson, Paul A. 1958. An Exact Consumption-Loan Interest Model of Interest with and without the Social Contrivance of Money. *Journal of Political Economy* 66 (6): 467–482.

Sayan, Serdar. 2005. Heckscher-Ohlin Revisited: Implications of Differential Population Dynamics for Trade within an Overlapping Generations Framework. *Journal of Economic Dynamics and Control* 29 (9): 1471–1493.

Tosun, Mehmet S. 2003. Population Aging and Economic Growth: Political Economy and Open Economy Effects. *Economics Letters* 81 (3): 291–296.

Serdar Sayan

OVERLENDING

Overlending describes the behavior of creditors that extend loans to borrowers that are unable or unwilling to repay the debt on its original terms. The borrowers may be individuals, firms, or sovereign countries. Creditors span the range of public and private-sector institutions, although much of the analysis of overlending focuses on the lending patterns of banks. Overlending can lead to unsustainable debt burdens for the borrower and financial losses, both for the lenders and the broader economy, particularly in cases where disruptions of debt service lead to financial crisis.

Theoretical explanations for overlending often cite imperfect information and moral hazard as factors contributing to unsustainable lending booms. Imperfect information about the borrower or economic conditions contributes to uncertainty in assessing credit risk. Moral hazard, where the existence of insurance or guarantees encourages greater risk taking, may also contribute to overlending. Overlending can also take place when excess liquidity and competitive pressures between lending institutions contribute to loosening of credit standards. Obvious profligacy, including loans to insiders, corrupt businesspersons, or relatives where the loan may be made with no expectation of repayment, may also take place in the absence of strict credit standards.

In the United States, the government has crafted policies to inhibit overlending. Bank supervision aims to contain the moral hazard associated with deposit insurance and prudential standards prohibit the most egregious lending practices. Nevertheless, the savings and loan crisis, which lasted from the late 1970s through the 1990s, included elements of overlending. While structural problems related to restrictions on lending rates and the resulting interest-rate mismatch were underlying causes of the crisis, some thrift institutions had large loan losses attributed to insider loans or to lending in riskier markets. The policy solution to the savings and loan crisis therefore involved an enhanced supervisory structure as well as an infusion of funds to recapitalize troubled thrifts institutions.

By the early 1980s, the Latin American debt crisis was vying with the savings and loan crisis as the most significant financial calamity. In a paper presented at a World Bank symposium, Jack M. Guttentag and Richard J. Herring argued that competitive pressures on banks and overoptimistic assessments of borrower capacity contributed to unsustainable levels of lending. In their book *The Loan Pushers* (1988), William A. Darity and Bobbie L. Horn pointed out that while competitive pressures can lead to overlending, moral hazard might also have played a role since commercial bankers may have viewed the International Monetary Fund (IMF) and other public-sector actors as guarantors that would orchestrate a bailout. Darity and Horn also detailed factors that might have contributed to imprudent borrowing, but recognized that policies to prevent future financial turmoil must be based on a clear understanding of the roles that creditors as well as borrowers played. Institutional weaknesses would require institutional reform.

Despite efforts at such reform, international debt service problems reemerged in the mid-1990s. These problems involved bond holders as well as banks, and came after a rapid expansion of credits to firms and sovereign borrowers in Latin America and Asia. International financial institutions also increased their lending to the least developed countries, and by the end of the 1990s many poor countries, especially in Africa, were carrying unsustainable debt burdens. There has been a concerted policy response to the events of the 1990s: debt relief, a greater share of aid in grants, and promoting compliance with international financial standards and codes. All of these policy interventions are aimed at preventing the re-emergence of overlending.

SEE ALSO *Economics; Financial Instability Hypothesis; Financial Markets; Hedging; Leverage; Liquidity; Loans; Moral Hazard; Ponzi Scheme; Wealth*

BIBLIOGRAPHY

Darity, William, Jr., and Bobbie L. Horn. 1988. *The Loan Pushers: The Role of Commercial Banks in the International Debt Crisis.* Cambridge, MA: Ballinger Publishing.

Guttentag, Jack M., and Richard J. Herring. 1985. Commercial Bank Lending to Developing Countries: From Overlending to Underlending to Structural Reform. In *International Debt and the Developing Countries*, ed. G. Smith and J. Cuddington. Washington, DC: World Bank.

Willene A. Johnson

OVERPOPULATION

When laypersons speak of overpopulation, often they are referring to exceeding the carrying capacity of the Earth. Carrying capacity is an often-used term with many definitions, a common element of which is the number of people able to sustain life within the limits of the earth's environment. A definition of overpopulation should go beyond carrying capacity per se and take into account the state of the environment—whether the condition of the natural world allows for a comfortable existence and whether the current generation will leave the Earth inhabitable for the next generation.

An issue in assessing the dynamics of overpopulation is how best to create a reliable parameter for its measurement. What level of comfort among the various alternatives—the American, the Guatemalan, the Japanese—should be the ideal? The answer to this question determines the relevant issues of the environment to be considered and the number of people who may be sustained. Consider the amount of meat in a typical diet, the culturally defined idea of personal space, or the number of comfort goods that need to be produced and the resources involved in their production. The United States is the world's biggest consumer of natural resources, though its population makes up only 5 percent of the world's population. If the world were held to the American standard, the Earth's carrying capacity would soon be exceeded.

The concern with overpopulation is not new. During the eighteenth century Thomas Robert Malthus declared that overpopulation was bound by nature to occur. He assumed that, if left unchecked, populations tend to increase geometrically and food and sustenance arithmetically. Malthus advised moral, that is, sexual restraint and late marriage as preventive checks to prevent population increase. He also noted that such positive checks as wars, pestilence, and famine would keep the death rate high, also resulting in a slowing down of population growth. In 1968 Paul Ehrlich made similar predictions in his popular book *The Population Bomb.* Unlike Malthus, he gave special attention to the degradation of the environment by humans. Ehrlich's solutions were much more dramatic. He reasoned that billions of people must starve to death for there to exist an equilibrium between population and the environment. Neo-Malthusianist concerns continued into the 1970s with the Club of Rome's report on *Limits to Growth* and E. F. Schumacher's influential 1975 book *Small Is Beautiful,* which spawned a counterculture with the same name. Benjamin Friedman noted in his 2005 study that portions of these themes are reflected presently in the anti-globalization movement.

Is the world overpopulated? The world's population in the year 2006 was estimated to be over 6.5 billion strong and growing. These growth dynamics need to be considered in any discussions about overpopulation. The Population Reference Bureau projects a world population in 2050 of 9.3 billion people (Population Reference Bureau 2006). The United Nations reports that before 2050 more than 80 percent of the world will have below-replacement fertility (U.N. 2002), and their medium population projections for 2050 are very similar to the PRB's projection.

Around 3.5 billion people were added to the world's population between 1950 and 2000; this was the fastest rate of population growth in recorded world history (UNPD 2002). By mid-century the world is expected to add another 3 billion to its population. Though the absolute number of people in the world in 2050 will have increased, its rate of growth will have slowed. There are now forty-four countries with fertility rates below the replacement level; their populations are projected to diminish in the next forty-five years. Most of the growth in the world will occur in the less developed regions of the world. Families will be smaller all over the world; indeed there has already occurred a marked decrease in average family size in most of the countries of the developing world.

If the planet is already overtaxed by 6.5 billion people, then coming decades will likely be a time of disquiet and suffering over much of the world. When considering overpopulation, one must weigh the well-being of the individual against that of all of Earth's inhabitants. Rights that form the base of many nations, such as the rights to property, reproductive rights, and economic rights, will likely be less well defined in a situation where the issue of overpopulation is paramount. The right to purchase and use land may need to be regulated in order to protect the environment. Families may be forced to limit their numbers, and individuals may have to decrease their consumption to conserve natural resources and protect the environment.

It is difficult to construct the parameters of overpopulation. Considering the health of an entire world versus a single nation seems contrary to much of human history. Population projections for the rest of the century are subject to much variation depending on fertility patterns, thus further complicating the issue. As the world competes for limited resources, it is quite possible that the issue of overpopulation will be an issue of concern in many countries.

SEE ALSO *Birth Control; Club of Rome; Demography; Depopulation; Limits of Growth; Malthus, Thomas Robert; Malthusian Trap; Natural Resources, Nonrenewable; Population Control; Population Growth; Population Studies*

BIBLIOGRAPHY

Ehrlich, Paul. 1968. *The Population Bomb.* New York: Ballantine Books.

Friedman, Benjamin M. 2005. *The Moral Consequences of Economic Growth.* New York: Knopf.

Meadows, Donella, Jørgen Randers, and Dennis L. Meadows. 2004. *Limits to Growth: The 30-Year Update.* White River Junction, VT: Chelsea Green Publishing Company.

Population Reference Bureau. 2006. 2006 World Population Data Sheet. Washington, DC: Population Reference Bureau.

Poston, Dudley L., Jr. 2006. Malthus, Thomas Robert. In *The Cambridge Dictionary of Sociology*, ed. Bryan S. Turned, 347–348. Cambridge, U.K., and New York: Cambridge University Press.

Price, David. 1999. Carrying Capacity Reconsidered. *Population and Environment: A Journal of Interdisciplinary Studies* 21 (1): 5–26.

Schumacher, E. F. 1975. *Small Is Beautiful: A Study of Economics As If People Mattered.* New York: Harper Colophon.

United Nations. 2002. *The Future of Fertility in Intermediate Fertility Countries.* New York: Department of Economic and Social Affairs, Population Division, United Nations.

United Nations Population Division (UNPD). 2002. *Expert Group Meeting on Completing the Fertility Transition.* New York: UN Population Division Department of Economic and Social Affairs.

Chris Russell
Dudley L. Poston, Jr.

OVERPRODUCTION

Say's law of markets is commonly understood, by friends and foes alike, to deny the possibility of general gluts. Overproduction theories are one of the ramifications of the opposition to this view; they evolved through direct confrontation with the proposition they were denying, in its various interpretations. These criticisms share the general standpoint that crises (or cycles) are to be explained in terms of some systematic divergence between production and consumption. Whereas Say's law only admitted accidental disequilibrating causes (such as wars or exceptionally abundant or scarce crops) or temporary imbalances (due for instance to entrepreneurial miscalculations), the dissenters insisted on the general character of market gluts and pointed at causes intrinsic to the working of the system. Where dissenting views diverge is on the specific causes of disequilibrium. Overproduction theories of crises and business cycles emphasized troubles arising from the side of production, whereas the underconsumptionists instead attributed the disharmony to lack of effective demand, often stressing distributional factors determining lack of purchasing power or excessive saving. (The first representative of the latter view was J.C.L. Simonde de Sismondi; other prominent writers in this tradition include J. A. Hobson, William Trufant Foster and Waddill Catchings, and some Marxists). The distinction, however, is somewhat artificial, for there is a certain complementarity and overlapping between the causes identified by overproductionist and underconsumptionist writers.

Say's law emerged as the winner of the "gluts debate" after the Napoleonic wars. David Ricardo's argument, that production is only undertaken with a view to sell and sales only made with the intention of purchasing other goods thereafter, with its implication that disequilibria can only be temporary states of affairs resulting from exogenous events or miscalculation, gained wide acceptance. Thomas Robert Malthus's contrary opinion, that the system's development could be hindered, and unemployment would ensue, if the accrued production were not distributed in such a way as to "occasion the most effective demand for future production," was only accepted by a minority of heretics (Malthus 1952, p. 10). From the 1840s onward, however, a growing number of writers questioned the validity of Say's law. A first step (taken by John Stuart Mill, Karl Marx, and Wilhelm Roscher) consisted in rejecting the assumption that exchange was essentially equivalent to barter, by pointing out that money separates the acts of buying and selling and thereby makes crises possible. But this is only an abstract possibility. At the time, most authors believed that the factors turning this possibility into an actuality were linked to credit and speculation. Later, processes like hoarding, liquidation, and repayment of loans were added.

Marx's theory of crises was the starting point of a number of overproduction approaches. His reproduction schemes showed that while harmonious growth is a logical possibility, it is not a necessity. One of the points on which Marx insisted was that advances in technology and organization imply an increase in productivity, and therefore diminish the value of wage-goods. If, in the short term, workers obtain increases in their real wages, the profit rate decreases below what capitalists considered customary, and production has to be stopped. The German-language branch of overproduction theories emphasizing producers' losses (prominently represented by Arthur Spiethoff) built on this view. The American counterpart of this approach grew out of the distinction between "absolute" and "relative" overproduction: While it was admitted that there cannot be overproduction with respect to human needs, it was pointed out (by David A. Wells, Uriel H. Crocker, Arthur Twining Hadley, and Constant Southworth) that production can be in excess to demand to the extent that the price is not sufficient to cover costs inclusive of a remunerative or ordinary profit—although the notion of "ordinary" profits was questioned (by Thorstein Veblen).

A second group of overproduction theories stemming from Marx's schemes of reproduction emphasized that there is no logical necessity that productive sectors grow proportionately and that maladjustments tend to amplify and spread to the whole system (M. I. Tugan-Baranovsky). Along this line we also find writers (Hans Neisser, L. V. Birck) who stressed the implications of technological progress, pointing out that when the vertical structure of production is altered, the preservation of the correct proportions becomes increasingly difficult and is likely to be disrupted by several minor causes. Another group of writers insisted instead on the fixity of fixed capital: Having acquired expensive machinery requiring maintenance costs even if not used, entrepreneurs find it rational to keep producing even at a loss (Crocker, Wells). In this view, overproduction is not so much an excess of goods as of productive capacity (William Smart, Scoville Hamlin).

Several other authors considered systematic impediments to the establishment of a stable equilibrium between supply and demand. Time lags, in particular, were invoked in this connection by Albert Aftalion and Mentor Bouniatian. They argued that a divergence between supply and demand would generate price differences inducing an adjustment, but that as production lags behind demand due to the time required to build plants, prices send the wrong signals and induce overproduction crises.

When such a view was incorporated into formal dynamics in the 1930s (in particular by Michael Kalecki), the business cycle came to be seen as resulting from the dynamic properties of the system and the need to stress overproduction gradually faded. The other contemporary business-cycle theories—the equilibrium and the real business cycle approaches—focus on equilibrium and thus dispense with an essentially disequilibriumist concept altogether.

SEE ALSO *Business Cycles, Theories; Marx, Karl; Say's Law; Underconsumption*

BIBLIOGRAPHY

Aftalion, Albert. 1913. *Les crises périodiques de surproduction.* Paris: Marcel Rivière.

Birck, L. V. 1927. Theories of Over-Production. *Economic Journal* 37 (March): 19–32.

Bouniatian, Mentor. 1908. *Wirtschaftskrisen und Ueberkapitalisation: Eine Untersuchung über die Erscheinungsformen und Ursachen der periodischen Wirtschaftskrisen.* Munich: Ernst Reinhardt.

Crocker, Uriel H. 1887. General Overproduction. *Quarterly Journal of Economics* 1 (3): 362–366.

Crocker, Uriel H. 1892. The "Overproduction" Fallacy. *Quarterly Journal of Economics* 6 (3): 352–363.

Hadley, Arthur Twining. 1896. *Economics: An Account of the Relations between Private Property and Public Welfare.* New York and London: G. P. Putnam's Sons; reprint, New York: Arno Press, 1972.

Hamlin, Scoville. 1930. *The Menace of Overproduction: Its Cause, Extent, and Cure.* New York: J. Wiley & Sons; London: Chapman & Hall.

Kalecki, Michael. 1935. A Macrodynamic Theory of the Business Cycle. *Econometrica* 3 (July): 327–344.

Malthus, Thomas Robert. 1952. Letter to Ricardo, 7 July 1921. In *The Works and Correspondence of David Ricardo*, ed. Piero Sraffa and Maurice Dobb, vol. IX, 10. Cambridge, U.K.: Cambridge University Press.

Marx, Karl. 1862–1863. *Theories of Surplus Value*. Trans. G. A. Bonner and Emile Burns. London: Lawrence & Wishart, 1964–1972.

Marx, Karl. 1867–1894. *Capital: A Critique of Political Economy*. Trans. Samuel Moore and Edward Aveling. Moscow: Progress Publishers, 1967; reprint, London: Lawrence & Wishart, 1974. (Trans. from the 3rd German ed.)

Mill, John Stuart. [1848] 1965. *Principles of Political Economy, with Some of Their Applications to Social Philosophy*. In *Collected Works*, ed. John M. Robson, vols. 2–3. Toronto: University of Toronto Press; London: Routledge.

Neisser, Hans. 1934. General Overproduction: A Study of Say's Law of Markets. *Journal of Political Economy* 42 (4): 433–465.

Roscher, Wilhelm. 1854. *Principles of Political Economy*. 2 vols. Trans. John L. Lalor. New York: Henry Holt, 1878. (Trans. from the 13th German ed. of 1877.)

Smart, William. 1895. *Studies in Economics*. London and New York: Macmillan.

Southworth, Constant. 1924. Can There Be General Overproduction? *Journal of Political Economy* 32 (6): 722–725.

Spiethoff, Arthur. 1933. Overproduction. In *Encyclopedia of the Social Sciences*, vol. 11. New York: Macmillan.

Tugan-Baranovsky, M. I. 1914. *Periodicheskiye promyshlennyie krizisy*. 3rd ed. St. Petersburg, Russia. Translated in 1954 in an abridged version as *Periodic Industrial Crises. A History of British Crises* (*Annals of the Ukrainian Academy of Arts and Sciences in the United States* 3 (3): 745–802).

Veblen, Thorstein. 1892. The Overproduction Fallacy. *Quarterly Journal of Economics* 6 (4): 484–492.

Wells, David A. 1889. *Recent Economic Changes, and Their Effect on the Production and Distribution of Wealth and the Well-Being of Society*. New York: D. Appleton.

Daniele Besomi

OVERSHOOTING

Overshooting is a term used in macroeconomics and international finance to describe the behavior of the exchange rate after the economy is hit with a shock (i.e., an unanticipated event of sufficient magnitude such that it affects aggregate income, the general level of prices, or the aggregate volume of employment). Further, overshooting is a theoretical concept and is not always observed in the data. This concept was introduced into the economics literature by Rudiger Dornbusch (1942–2002) in his 1976 article "Expectations and Exchange Rate Dynamics," which is the most-cited professional article in international macroeconomics.

Overshooting describes the fact that before the exchange rate gets to its new long-run value in response to

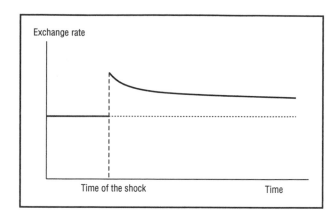

Figure 1

a shock, it may initially move past or "overshoot" the new level to which it will eventually settle.

Figure 1 represents the response of the exchange rate (measured in U.S. dollars per euro) to an increase in the U.S. money supply. As one can see, in the short run the exchange rate overshoots (moves to a point higher than) its long-run value.

Theoretically, overshooting arises in an economic model that assumes: (1) exchange rates are flexible; (2) uncovered interest parity holds (i.e., the difference between interest rates in the U.S. and euro zone is equal to the expected rate of U.S. dollar depreciation); (3) money demand depends on interest rate and output; and (4) prices are fixed in the short run but they fully adjust to offset monetary shocks in the long run. Thus, in the long run, an increase in the money supply would be fully reflected in an increase in the price level, including the price of foreign currency, the exchange rate.

Since prices are sticky in the short run, they cannot adjust immediately, and therefore an increase in money supply would instead lower the interest rate in the United States. For the uncovered interest parity to hold, people should now be expecting the U.S. dollar to appreciate. At the same time, we know that in the long run the dollar exchange rate will converge to a more depreciated value; thus, immediately after the shock, the dollar has to depreciate by more than in the long run and then start appreciating, as shown in Figure 1.

The overshooting phenomenon is common to many modern theories in international macroeconomics that assume sticky prices in the short run. Thus, it is a necessary component of any macroeconomic forecast, as well as of the analysis of possible responses of the economy to monetary policy changes. Nevertheless, not all models, and not even all sticky-price models, predict overshooting in the behavior of the exchange rates.

The concept of overshooting helps explain an important empirical regularity—the fact that exchange rates are much more volatile than price levels or interest rates. Indeed, while prices adjust slowly and monotonically to their new long-run levels, exchange rates "bounce around." In a world with numerous economic shocks, this leads to a high volatility of exchange rates and a much smaller volatility of prices.

The concept of overshooting does not help much in predicting exchange rates. This is partly due to the fact that one of the main assumptions of the model, the uncovered interest parity, is not borne out by the data. On the other hand, other models do not do a better job in predicting exchange rates than the overshooting model.

BIBLIOGRAPHY

Dornbusch, Rudiger. 1976. Expectations and Exchange Rate Dynamics. *Journal of Political Economy* 84 (6): 1161–1175.

Rogoff, Kenneth. 2002. Dornbusch's Overshooting Model After Twenty-Five Years. Mundell-Fleming Lecture. Second Annual IMF Research Conference. http://www.imf.org/external/np/speeches/2001/112901.htm.

Galina Hale

OVERTIME

Overtime work is a historical, legal, sociocultural, and economic construction. It typically refers to instances where an employee is working hours of labor in a given week (or per day or month) beyond some "standard," "regular," or "normal" hours. Overtime may be defined in terms of either national laws or workplace culture. The notion of overtime has changed over time, as these standards or norms have themselves changed. Indeed, laws place pressure on conventional norms and on the actual number of working hours (and vice versa). This explains why the connotation of overtime differs by country, time period, workplace culture, type of job, and employment contract.

In the United States, overtime work became codified as part of the 1938 Fair Labor Standards Act (FLSA). The FLSA was enacted both to counter the Depression era's prolonged unemployment and the long, grueling workdays and workweeks for wage workers that predominated during the industrialization phase of capitalism prior to the 1930s. Unlike European countries' statutory limits, the United States and other Anglo countries tend to apply only monetary incentives, the time-and-a-half pay premium requirement for hours worked by employees in excess of forty in a given week period to enforce the standard.

About one in five workers in the United States works extra hours for extra pay. Where there is no legally required pay premium for hours beyond forty hours, for those in exempt managerial, administrative, and professional jobs, the definition of what constitutes overtime work becomes hazier. About three in ten workers work longer than forty hours per week. More than one in five employees work extra hours because it is required by their employer. According to Juliet Schor's *The Overworked American: The Unexpected Decline of Leisure* (1993), there is evidence that the long-run trend toward shorter average workweeks reversed course in the mid- to late-twentieth century in the United States. In 2000 Ronald Hetrick found that overtime hours in manufacturing among hourly workers has risen. However, average hours have not so much risen as hours have polarized. A greater proportion work either fifty or more hours at the same time as a rising proportion works short hours. In addition, in 2005 Jared Bernstein and Karen Kornbluh found the rise in working hours has occurred more within families or dual-income households than among individuals. According to an article published by Daniel Hamermesh in *Industrial and Labor Relations Review* (2000), longer hours cannot be attributed to a steady replacement of hourly paid with salaried jobs.

Any trends in overtime work may be traced to the economics of labor demand and labor supply. Employers' demand for longer hours is driven by their response to economic incentives and market pressures to drive down labor costs per hour. Employers will substitute hours for employees when the fixed costs of hiring, training, and employee benefits escalate. Rising hours will be reinforced if workers prefer to allocate more time toward paid work activities because of the net income effects of falling real hourly wages, rising job insecurity, or rising consumer debt. In addition, the diminished presence, weakening, and changing priorities of the labor movement has removed an institutional pressure that once leaned against rising work hours. Unionized or not, overtime for hourly workers has often become a rationed privilege, where the legal or contracted pay premium has become an incentive to supply more hours of labor.

Nevertheless, the repercussions of overtime—usually unpaid hours for salaried workers—take its toll not only on individuals, but also on families, workplaces, and society. Studies confirm that overtime work is a dual-edged sword, providing additional income but also adverse repercussions due to the heightened risk of injury, illness, accident, and work-family time conflict, via fatigue and stress. Such risks are often magnified when overtime is imposed rather than voluntary. Early-twenty-first-century controversies in research involve the appropriate degree of annual averaging of work hours and the extent to which curbing overtime would spur employment. Policy proposals that attempt to alter the framework for regulating or enforcing overtime laws, in the United States and elsewhere, become controversial. This includes the scope of which jobs are to be covered by the FLSA's overtime pay premium, limiting mandatory overtime work, and whether compensation for overtime hours should be in the form of future promised compensatory time off rather than immediate pay.

SEE ALSO *Capitalism; Labor; Leisure; Work Week; Working Day, Length of*

BIBLIOGRAPHY

Altonji, Joseph G., and Jennifer Oldham. 2003. Vacation Laws and Annual Work Hours. *Economic Perspectives* 27 (3): 19–29.

Berg, Peter, Eileen Appelbaum, Thomas Bailey, and Arne Kalleberg. 2004. Contesting Time: Control over Working Time in Seven Industrialized Countries. *Industrial Relations* 57 (3): 531–549.

Bernstein, Jared, and Karen Kornbluh. 2005. *Running Faster to Stay in Place: The Growth of Family Work Hours and Incomes.* Washington, DC: Economic Policy Institute and New America Foundation.

Bluestone, Barry, and Steven Rose. 2000. The Enigma of Working Time Trends. In *Working Time: International Trends, Theory, and Policy Perspectives,* ed. Lonnie Golden and Deborah M. Figart. London: Routledge.

Bosch, Gerhard. 1999. Working Time: Tendencies and Emerging Issues. *International Labour Review* 138 (2): 131–150

Campbell, Iain. 2002. Puzzles of Unpaid Overtime. In *Flexible Work Arrangements: Conceptualizations and International Experiences,* ed. Isik Zeytinoglu. The Hague: Kluwer Law International.

Caruso, Claire, Edward Hitchcock, Robert Dick, et al. 2004. *Overtime and Extended Work Shifts: Recent Findings on Illnesses, Injuries and Health Behaviors.* Washington, DC: U.S. Department of Health and Human Services Centers for Disease Control and Prevention, National Institute for Occupational Safety and Health.

Cross, Gary, ed. 1989. *Worktime and Industrialization: An International History.* Philadelphia: Temple University Press.

Dembe, Allard. 2005. Long Hours, Health, and Injuries. *Perspectives on Work* 8 (2): 20–22.

Drago, Robert, Mark Wooden, and Y. Tseng. 2005. Usual and Preferred Hours in Dual Working Couples. *Journal of Family Studies* 11 (1): 46–61.

Fenwick, Rudy, and Mark Tausig. 2004. The Health and Family Social Consequences of Shift Work and Schedule Control. In *Fighting for Time: Shifting Boundaries of Work and Social Life,* ed. Cynthia Fuchs Epstein and Arne L. Kalleberg. New York: Russell Sage.

Golden, Lonnie, and Deborah Figart. 2000. Doing Something about Long Hours. *Challenge* 43 (6): 15–37.

Golden, Lonnie, and Barbara Wiens-Tuers. 2006. To Your Happiness? Overtime Work, Worker Happiness, and Satisfaction. *Journal of Socio-Economics* (35) 2: 382–397.

Hamermesh, Daniel. 2000. 12 Million Salaried Workers Are Missing. *Industrial and Labor Relations Review* 55: 649–675.

Hart, Robert A. 2004. *The Economics of Overtime Working.* New York: Cambridge University Press.

Hetrick, Ronald. 2000. Analyzing the Upward Surge in Overtime Hours. *Monthly Labor Review* 123 (February): 30–33.

Huberman, Michael. 2004. Working Hours of the World Unite? New International Evidence of Worktime, 1870–1913. *Journal of Economic History* 64: 964–1001.

Idson, Todd, and Paul K. Robbins. 1991. Determinants of Voluntary Overtime Decisions. *Economic Inquiry* 29 (1): 79–91.

Jacobs, Jerry A., and Kathleen Gerson. 2004. *The Time Divide: Work, Family, and Gender Inequality.* Cambridge, MA: Harvard University Press.

Linder, Marc. 2002. *The Autocratically Flexible Workplace: A History of Overtime Regulation in the United States.* Iowa City, IA: Fanpihua Press.

Martorana, Paul, and Paul Hirsch. The Social Construction of Overtime. *The Transformation of Work* 10: 165–187.

Nyland, Chris. 1989. *Reduced Working Time and the Management of Production* Cambridge, U.K.: Cambridge University Press.

Owen, John D. 1989. *Reduced Working Hours: Cure for Unemployment or Economic Burden?* Baltimore, MD: Johns Hopkins University Press.

Rakoff, Todd. 2002. *A Time for Every Purpose: Law and the Balance of Life.* Cambridge, MA: Harvard University Press.

Schor, Juliet B. 1993. *The Overworked American: The Unexpected Decline of Leisure.* New York: Basic Books.

Spurgeon, Anne. 2003. *Working Time: Its Impact on Safety and Health.* Geneva: ILO.

Yaniv, Gideon. 1995. Burnout, Absenteeism, and the Overtime Decision. *Journal of Economic Psychology* 16 (2): 297–309.

Lonnie Golden

OVERWEIGHT
SEE *Obesity.*

OWN RATE OF INTEREST
SEE *Interest, Own Rate of.*

OXYTOCIN
SEE *Oedipus Complex.*

P

PAASCHE INDEX

SEE *Price Indices.*

PACIFISM

The term *pacifism* is a neologism that was coined in the early twentieth century. It was invented by the French notary Emile Arnaud, who used it in a newspaper article in 1901. According to Karl Holl, Arnaud wanted to stress the peculiar determination and common ideological orientation of those who were not only "peaceful" or "peacemakers," but "pacifists," and he therefore formed an "ism" similar to other political currents, such as socialism or liberalism. The new concept was meant to incorporate all previous goals of the bourgeois peace movement—including arbitration, disarmament, and a European confederation—under a new label. The term was also meant to suggest parity with other political movements, and to play up the theoretical pretense of this current. The last point was particularly important for central European pacifists such as Alfred Hermann Fried. Older terms such as *peace movement, mouvement pacifique,* or *Friedensbewegung* were not fully displaced by the neologism.

It has been suggested that an analytical distinction be made between pacifism, a position that rejects both war and support for war, and "pacificism," which aims to reform the international system and rejects aggressive wars, but which also underlines the justification of military defensive against a foreign aggressor (Ceadel 1987, p. 5). This distinction is problematic, however, because it disregards most of the early proponents of pacifism, including most of the peace societies of nineteenth century Europe. These groups were sympathetic to the idea of national defensive warfare and promoted what the historian Sandi Cooper has called a "patriotic pacifism" (Cooper 1991). The distinction also focuses too much on the ideological ramifications of peace activism, thereby neglecting forms of agitation and group sociability as key angles for a historical interpretation.

The strength of pacifist groups in the period from 1810 to 1945 depended particularly on their ability to lay claim to a respected position within the political culture of the respective countries. The capacity for pacifist mobilization was strongest in countries with a substantial pietist community and related cultural traditions, such as the United Kingdom, Germany, Switzerland, the Netherlands, and the Scandinavian countries. The pietist mentality, with its moralistic language and its commitment to salvation for a sinful world (based on the consciousness of the individual), fed into the dominant semantic patterns of pacifist activism and its often intense moral dichotomies. Even in the predominantly Catholic country of France, most of the founding members of the Association de la paix par le droit (ADP, Association for Peace through Law) in 1887 were Huguenots and members of the Reformed Church (Ingram 1991, p. 27).

HISTORY

Religious motives (particularly from the historic peace churches of the Quakers and Mennonites in England and the United States) engendered the first peace societies in New York (1815) and London (1816), while philanthropic motives led to similar societies in Paris (1821) and

Geneva (1830). In both Europe and the United States, nineteenth-century pacifism relied on a homogeneous stratum of middle-class supporters and their characteristic patterns of sociability and associational life. International contacts between peace activists intensified in the last quarter of the nineteenth century, and these contacts were institutionalized through the International Peace Bureau in Bern, Switzerland, founded in 1892. The outbreak of war in August 1914 betrayed pacifist hopes that a growing network of international relations would prevent war. It also compromised most bourgeois pacifists, who demonstrated their readiness to support a national war effort. In a response to this perceived moral bankruptcy of "patriotic pacifism," pacifist organizations with a more radical approach emerged in various countries, including the Union for Democratic Control in the United Kingdom and the *Bund Neues Vaterland* (New Fatherland League) in Germany.

European pacifism in the 1920s and early 1930s was characterized by the coexistence of a liberal current on the one hand and a more radical or integral current on the other. The former was represented by the ADP in France, the League of Nations Union in Britain, and the liberal current in the *Deutsche Friedensgesellschaft* (German Peace Society, DFG). The latter was exemplified by groups such as the *Ligue internationale des combattants de la paix* (LICP) in France and the Peace Pledge Union (PPU), founded by the Anglican clergyman Dick Sheppard, in the United Kingdom. Toward the end of the 1920s, ideological conflicts between the two wings hardened, and sectarianism and organizational fragmentation prevailed. This was due not only to individual idiosyncrasies and the growing militancy of many radical pacifists. It also reflected the fact that the political and cultural cleavages between liberal dignitaries, with their characteristic patterns of sociability, and radical democrats, socialists, and anarchists, which represented a broader cross section of society, could no longer be reconciled.

The Italian invasion of Abyssinia in 1935, the remilitarization of the Rhineland by the Nazi government in 1936, and particularly the Spanish Civil War from 1936 to 1939 undermined the moral and political foundations of European pacifism. The tendency of the PPU to grant concessions to Nazi Germany, along with the apparent failure of the British appeasement policy, compromised its moral grounds. Italian and German military intervention against the Spanish Republic called for a revocation of a principled nonviolent stance, as powerful critics such as George Orwell argued. And with the Nazi seizure of power in 1933, German pacifists were forced into exile or became subject to police persecution. Soon, pacifists in countries such as Norway or France would have to decide whether they would participate in violent resistance against the German occupation.

In both historical and sociological perspective, pacifism ceased to exist as a major political current after World War II. In terms of sociability and mobilization, the permanent but small associations of middle-class dignitaries were transformed into the more fluctuating single-issue campaigns of peace movements, with their ability to attract highly volatile mass support. In terms of ideology and the support of nonviolent methods, some of the former pacifist impetus shifted toward an engagement in human rights campaigning. Yet since 1945 a strictly nonviolent, pacifist orientation has still consistently been displayed by organizations such as the War Resisters' International (WRI). Since its foundation in 1921, the WRI has promoted nonviolent direct action and supported conscientious objectors. It has emerged as a major transnational network of radical pacifists, with branches in various European countries, the United States, and other parts of the world.

SEE ALSO *Peace; Peace Movements*

BIBLIOGRAPHY

Brock, Peter. 1972. *Pacifism in Europe to 1914.* Princeton, NJ: Princeton University Press.

Ceadel, Martin. 1987. *Thinking about Peace and War.* Oxford: Oxford University Press.

Cooper, Sandi. 1991. *Patriotic Pacifism: Waging War on War in Europe, 1815–1914.* Oxford: Oxford University Press.

Holl, Karl. 1978. Pazifismus. In *Geschichtliche Grundbegriffe: Historisches Lexikon zur politisch-sozialen Sprache in Deutschland,* ed. Otto Brunner, Werner Conze and Reinhart Koselleck, Vol. 4, 767–787. Stuttgart, Germany: Klett-Cotta.

Ingram, Norman. 1991. *The Politics of Dissent: Pacifism in France 1919-1939.* Oxford: Clarendon Press.

Benjamin Ziemann

PAGANISM

SEE *Infidels.*

PAIN

SEE *Psychosomatics.*

PAIRED COMPARISON METHOD

SEE *Scales.*

PALEONTOLOGY

SEE *Archaeology; Johanson, Donald; Leakey, Richard.*

PALESTINE LIBERATION ORGANIZATION (PLO)

The Palestine Liberation Organization (PLO) is an umbrella political organization founded in 1964 to deal with the problems of the Palestinian Arab refugees. The 1947 United Nations Partition Plan for Palestine (UN General Assembly Resolution 181 of November 29, 1947) had divided the ex-British mandate territory of Palestine into a Jewish state and an Arab-Palestinian state, with the Greater Jerusalem area, including Bethlehem, placed under international administration. But the first Arab-Israeli war (1948–1949) led to a three-way partition of Palestine and the problem of the so-called occupied Palestinian territories. Egypt took the Gaza Strip, the kingdom of Transjordan (later Jordan) took the West Bank (of the River Jordan), and the rest of Palestine was incorporated into the newly formed State of Israel, prompting the exodus of hundreds of thousands of Palestinian Arabs who were dispersed to refugee camps all over the Arab world. The PLO emerged from the angry despair of the homeless and impoverished Palestinian refugees and their desire to establish an independent Palestinian state in the "occupied territories."

The PLO is governed by a legislative body called the Palestinian National Council (PNC), which elects an executive committee to assume leadership of the organization between its sessions. The PNC meets every two years and passes resolutions by a simple majority with a two-thirds quorum. The first PNC, composed of 389 nominated representatives from Palestinian diaspora communities in Jordan, Gaza, Egypt, Syria, Lebanon, Kuwait, Iraq, Qatar, Libya, and Algeria, met in East Jerusalem, Jordan, on May 29, 1964, and adopted the Palestinian National Covenant (Palestine's constitutional charter). It established the PLO as the political voice of the Palestinian people and elected Ahmad Al-Shuqeiry (1908–1980) as the first chairman of the PLO Executive Committee.

Fatah, an Egyptian-backed guerrilla movement led by Yasser Arafat (1929–2004), joined the PLO in 1968. It was followed by other Palestinian guerrilla groups (*fedayeen*) such as the pro-Syrian As Saiqa, the Marxist-oriented Popular Front for the Liberation of Palestine (PFLP), and the leftist Democratic Front for the Liberation of Palestine (DFLP), among others. The PLO's military wing, the Palestine Liberation Army (PLA), began staging acts of guerrilla warfare against military and civilian targets inside Israel, as well as Jewish targets in third countries; the

Israeli government has branded these acts "terrorism." Arafat became PLO leader in 1969 and declared himself the only legitimate spokesman for the Palestinian people. For much of its history, the PLO regarded Israel as an illegitimate foreign presence in Palestine, because neither the local Palestinian Arabs nor any neighboring Arab country have ever agreed to the creation of a Jewish state in their midst. The PLO leadership has accused Israel of illegally occupying the Arab lands in Palestine, especially the Gaza Strip and the West Bank, including East Jerusalem, which were captured by Israel during the Six-Day War of June 1967. The PLO has also insisted on the "right to return" to their ancestral homes for hundreds of thousands of Palestinian refugees (and their descendants) who were forced into exile in 1948.

The PLO was expelled from its guerrilla bases in Jordan after a bloody confrontation with the army of Jordanian King Hussein I (1935–1999) in September 1970 (which became known as "Black September" because as many as 3,400 Palestinians were killed in the conflict). The defeated PLO relocated most of its fighting force to refugee camps in Lebanon and Syria. In 1974 the Arab League proclaimed the PLO the "sole legitimate representative" of the Palestinians, with Jordan and Egypt giving up their claims to the West Bank and Gaza, respectively. In the same year, Arafat called for a democratic, secular Palestinian state, and the United Nations recognized the PLO as the government-in-exile responsible for all Palestinian affairs, according it the status of a permanent observer to the UN. Since then, more than 100 non-Arab states have also extended diplomatic recognition to the PLO as the legitimate representative of the Palestinian people. The PLO was granted full membership in the Arab League in 1976.

The PLO became embroiled in the first phase of the bloody Lebanese Civil War (1975–1977), but suffered defeat at the hands of the Syrian army, which in 1976 invaded Lebanon in support of the Christian-dominated government in Beirut. Arafat rejected the Camp David Accords of 1977 and accused Egyptian president Anwar Al Sadat (1918–1981) of betraying the Palestinian people and all other Arab nations, but at the same time called for diplomacy to resolve the Palestinian problem. The PLO suffered another setback in 1982 when the Israeli invasion of Lebanon forced some 8,500 of its fighters to leave their stronghold in West Beirut and resettle in other Arab countries, such as Tunisia and Syria. In 1985 the Israeli air force bombed the PLO headquarters in Tunisia, inflicting significant losses of life, but missing Arafat. The PLO was caught by surprise by the first Palestinian intifada (1987–1993), and while it was trying to help and direct the anti-Israeli uprising from abroad, the local radical Islamic groups Hamas and Islamic Jihad challenged its leadership position within the occupied territories. The

PLO also lost financial support from wealthy Arab Gulf states for backing Iraq during the First Gulf War (1990–1991).

With U.S. support, Israel refused to negotiate with the PLO, insisting that it would only talk to Palestinian representatives from the occupied territories, which complicated and delayed the peace process. In reaction to the intifada, the PLO unilaterally declared an independent "Arab state of Palestine" at the nineteenth PNC session held in Algiers in 1988. Arafat expressed support for a UN Security Council resolution calling for a two-state settlement on the pre-1967 borders (which had been vetoed by the United States in January 1976), with Israel and Palestine living side by side, provided that East Jerusalem became the capital of the Palestinian state and Palestinian refugees were given the right to return to their pre-1948 homes in Israel. On September 13, 1993, after months of U.S.-brokered back-channel negotiations, Arafat signed an historic peace agreement with Israel in Oslo, Norway, even though such an accommodation was vehemently opposed by radicals within the PLO's own ranks and by irreconcilable Palestinian groups such as Hamas and Islamic Jihad. The agreement, known as the Oslo Accords, involved mutual recognition, with security guarantees to and from Israel, and the gradual introduction of Palestinian self-government and autonomy in Gaza and parts of the West Bank until a final peace settlement was signed. A year later, Arafat appointed a provisional government, the nineteen-member Palestinian Authority, to administer the areas of Palestinian self-rule. He was elected president of the Palestinian-controlled territories in 1996. The PLO convened a PNC session in Gaza in April 1996, which voted with 504 votes in favor and 54 against to recognize Israel's right to exist.

Mahmoud Abbas (b. 1935), a moderate Fatah politician, was appointed Palestinian prime minister in 2003 in the midst of the second intifada (2000–2006). In the same year, Palestinians and Israelis agreed to new negotiations based on the U.S.-proposed "roadmap to peace," although this failed to stop the daily violent attacks and reprisals. However, Abbas soon resigned after clashing with Arafat over control of the PLO's security forces. Following Arafat's death in November 2004, Abbas succeeded him as PLO leader and was elected Palestinian Authority president in January 2005.

In an unexpected blow to Abbas, Hamas swept the Palestinian parliamentary elections in January 2006 and formed a Hamas-led Palestinian Authority cabinet that promised to rid Palestinians of the rampant corruption, mismanagement of foreign aid, and endemic abuses of power under Fatah's rule. The result was an escalating conflict between President Abbas and Palestinian prime minister Ismail Haniyeh (b. 1963) of Hamas over many issues, including Hamas's retaliatory missile attacks on Israeli territory and Abbas's plan to hold a referendum to force Hamas to recognize Israel. To end sporadic armed clashes between Hamas members and the Fatah-controlled security forces, a Hamas-led coalition government with the participation of several Fatah-supported ministers was formed in March 2007. But the Hamas-Fatah coalition collapsed in June 2007 when a military confrontation between the two rival groups led to Hamas's victory and takeover of Gaza. Without the consent of the Hamas-dominated Palestinian parliament, Abbas dissolved the coalition government and appointed an emergency cabinet led by pro-Fatah prime minister Salam Fayyad (b. 1952) on June 17, 2007, signaling a newly divided Palestine ruled by the Iranian-backed Hamas in Gaza and the American-backed Fatah in the West Bank.

SEE ALSO *Arab-Israeli War of 1967; Arafat, Yasir; Intifada, The; Palestinian Authority; Palestinian Diaspora; Palestinians; Peace Process*

BIBLIOGRAPHY

Khalidi, Rashid. 2006. *The Iron Cage: The Story of the Palestinian Struggle for Statehood.* Boston: Beacon.

Mussalam, Sami. 1988. *The Palestine Liberation Organization: Its Function and Structure.* Brattleboro, VT: Amana.

Nassar, Jamal R. 1991. *The Palestine Liberation Organization: From Armed Struggle to the Declaration of Independence.* New York: Praeger.

Reische, Diana L. 1991. *Arafat and the Palestine Liberation Organization.* New York: F. Watts.

Sela, Avraham, and Moshe Ma'oz, eds. 1997. *The PLO and Israel: From Armed Conflict to Political Solution, 1964–1994.* New York: St. Martin's Press.

Smith, Charles D. 1996. *Palestine and the Arab-Israeli Conflict.* New York: St. Martin's Press.

Rossen Vassilev

PALESTINIAN AUTHORITY

The establishment of the Palestinian Authority (PA) in 1994 was a culmination of a process dating back to the Madrid Conference of October 1991 when Israelis and Palestinians engaged in official direct negotiations for the first time. The Declaration of Principles (DOP), which was officially signed by Israel and the Palestinian Liberation Organization (PLO) in September 1993 in Washington, D.C., gradually led to Palestinian self-government in about 42 percent of the West Bank and the whole Gaza Strip.

THE ESTABLISHMENT OF THE PALESTINIAN AUTHORITY

The DOP, also known as the Oslo Accords, are the first sustained effort sponsored by the international community led by the United States and Russia to find a peaceful solution to the Israeli-Palestinian conflict on the basis of United Nations resolutions 242 and 338. The marginalization of the PLO after the first Gulf War and the impacts of the first intifada (a Palestinian uprising directed against Israel) on Israeli perceptions of the Palestinians made both sides more willing than ever to directly negotiate with each other. The DOP was based on the Israeli recognition of the PLO as the legitimate representative of the Palestinian people in exchange for the PLO's recognition of the State of Israel.

The DOP envisioned the creation of Palestinian autonomous government in Gaza and the West Bank as a three-stage process in five years. The Cairo agreement between Israel and the PLO in 1994 established Palestinian self-rule in Gaza and the West Bank city of Jericho. The second stage was initiated with the signing of the "Oslo 2 Accord" in September 1995 when Palestinian self-rule was extended to the West Bank, which was divided into three zones. PA would control all civilian and security affairs in Zone A, which would cover cities populated by the Palestinians. Zone B would consist of Palestinian villages, and Israel would have final authority in external security in this zone. Zone C would include Jewish settlements, strategic roads, and sparsely populated areas (which made up 70 percent of the West Bank) and would remain under Israeli control. There were no restrictions on the further expansion of Jewish settlements in this zone. While the PA gained control of about 30 percent of the West Bank, only 3 percent of this area was in Zone A.

The Oslo Process continued with additional agreements in the 1990s. The Hebron Agreement in January 1997 divided the city of Hebron into two and resulted in the redeployment of Israeli soldiers to a smaller section of the city. In October 1998 Israel and the Palestinians signed the Wye Memorandum that called for further redeployment of the Israeli military in the West Bank and the PA to fight against terrorism against Israel. The third and final stage was originally scheduled to take place in 1999 and would have led to a peace treaty solving all core issues, such as the status of East Jerusalem, Jewish settlements, refugees, security arrangements, and water rights. While Palestinians consider East Jerusalem as the capital of their future state, Israel, which annexed East Jerusalem, refused to relinquish its sovereignty over the city. Israel and the Palestinians reasserted their commitment to the resumption of permanent status negotiations by signing the Sharm el-Sheik Memorandum in September 1999.

However the outbreak of the second intifada in September 2000 ultimately derailed the process.

The creation of the PA was a major step toward the fulfillment of Palestinian national aspirations. However the PLO's recognition of Israel and the Oslo Process did not enjoy universal approval among Palestinians. A rejectionist front that included Hamas and Islamic Jihad denounced the Oslo Process. Terrorist attacks by militant Palestinian groups and Israeli retaliations undermined the process and fueled the mutual suspicions between Israel and the Palestinians. Furthermore, the Palestinian support of diplomatic negotiations with Israel was not sustainable. The partial Israeli withdrawal from Gaza and the West Bank did not necessarily translate into independence, security, freedom of action, and economic well-being for the Palestinians. The PA was not sovereign and was highly dependent on Israeli cooperation for its survival. It had no control over its external borders, customs, airspace, water, and minerals. Israel collected the PA's custom duties, taxed Palestinian citizens working in Israel on behalf of the PA, and remained the market for its export and the source of its imports. Foreign assistance made a substantial portion of the PA's budget. From the Israeli perspective, the main task of the PA was the establishment of order and security in the Palestinian territories and the end of attacks against Israeli military and citizens. From the Palestinian perspective, the Oslo Process would ultimately result in the establishment of a Palestinian state in Gaza and the West Bank. By 2000 neither side achieved its goals.

1996 ELECTIONS AND THE STRUCTURE OF THE PA

The DOP specified that free and general elections should be organized in the West Bank and Gaza to enable the Palestinians to govern themselves according to democratic principles. The elections for the Palestinian legislative council (PLC) and the presidency took place in January 1996 after Israeli military withdrew from Zones A and B in December 1995. Yasser Arafat (1929–2004), who was the leader of both Fatah (the Palestinian National Liberation Movement, a branch of the PLO) and the PLO, was elected president by capturing around 88 percent of the vote. Fatah dominated the legislative council elections, which was boycotted by Hamas, by capturing a majority of the seats.

Despite having popular legitimacy, the PA was characterized by authoritarian practices. Power was personalized in the hands of Arafat who thwarted the PLC's attempts to make him more accountable and to end his ruling by decree. While the PLC ratified the Basic Law in 1997, which was intended as an interim constitution, Arafat did not ratify it for five years. He populated senior positions mostly with comrades from Fatah who had been in exile for decades at the expense of local leaders and grassroots organizations. The tension between "outsiders," who did not participate in the intifada, and "insiders," who had public support, fostered discontent with the PA. Public positions were distributed according to personal connections, histories, family relations, and patronage considerations. Distinction between personal and public budget blurred and the administration was beset by widespread corruption and incompetent management. The establishment of multiple layers of security forces facilitated the suppression of dissent. The PA's intimidation of the Palestinian press contributed to the rise of self-censorship. The PA entered into strategic alliances with local notables by co-opting and assigning them positions in the administration. All these practices diminished the prospects for a vibrant civil society and eroded the rule of law.

The PA's obligations to Israel and the Palestinian people were hardly compatible. On the one hand, Israel demanded the PA to prevent security threats to Israeli civilians and military from the areas it controlled. On the other, Palestinians expected that the establishment of the PA would stop Israeli incursions, blockades, and expansion of settlements. The PA's performance in combating attacks against Israeli targets was not satisfactory for Israel and the latter continued its policies of retaliation and intimidation against the Palestinians. As a result both Palestinian and Israeli support for the PA diminished.

THE SECOND INTIFADA AND THE COLLAPSE OF THE OSLO PROCESS

The official deadline for conclusion of Israeli-Palestinian formal settlement negotiations passed on May 4, 1999. It appeared to all parties that the Oslo Process was reaching a dead end. In July 2000 U.S. president Bill Clinton invited Arafat and Israeli prime minister Ehud Barak to a summit at Camp David to achieve a breakthrough. However, the summit was terminated without an agreement. After the Israeli Likud leader Ariel Sharon visited the Temple Mount, sacred for both Muslims and Jews, in September 2000, Israeli Arabs and Palestinians in the West Bank rioted. Younger generation Fatah members created Tanzim, an armed wing of Fatah, and confronted the Israeli military. The Oslo Process was in shambles. The conflict escalated to a new level in April 2002 when Israel conducted "Operation Defensive Shield" and reoccupied the parts of the West Bank and Gaza it had previously withdrawn from. Arafat was surrounded in his compound in Ramallah, in the West Bank. Israel accused Arafat of igniting the intifada and sponsoring terrorism and demanded his dismissal. In the same year, Sharon who won the Israeli elections in 2001, began constructing a barrier intended to separate the Palestinian West Bank from Israel and stop suicide terrorism employed by the

militant Palestinian groups. As a result of Israeli operations and blockades the PA was in crisis. Unemployment skyrocketed among the Palestinians and the economy collapsed. Meanwhile, U.S. president George W. Bush declared that he would conditionally support the establishment of a Palestinian state in June 2002. His conditions included a comprehensive reform of the PA, the replacement of Arafat, and Palestinian agreement to a ceasefire. In 2003 the PLC amended the Basic Law as part of the reform initiative. A post of prime minister was created and the number of seats in the PLC was increased from 88 to 132. Arafat appointed Mahmoud Abbas as prime minister and gave away some of his extensive powers to him in March 2003. However, Abbas resigned in October complaining about his lack of power.

THE ROAD MAP AND TRANSITION OF POWER IN THE PA

Bush's declaration ultimately resulted in the Road Map for Peace, which was released in April 2003. The Road Map was issued by the Quartet—the United States, the European Union, Russia, and the United Nations—and was intended to end the Israeli-Palestinian conflict by 2005. It required the PA to make democratic reforms and end its support of terrorism. The conditions seemed positive for progress toward peace negotiations as two developments in 2004 abated the level of violence. In February 2004 Sharon announced that Israel would unilaterally withdraw from Gaza, and in November 2004 Arafat died. Following Arafat's death, presidential elections were held in January 2005. Hamas boycotted the elections and Marwan Barghouti, who was a popular leader of Tanzim, retired from the race several weeks before voting was to occur. Consequently, the Fatah candidate Abbas easily won the elections with 62 percent of the votes cast. Abbas's election to the presidency led to a thaw in relations with the United States and Israel. A month after his election, he met with Sharon and they both declared their commitment to work together to end the violence. In May Abbas visited the White House and received Bush's support for an independent Palestine and promise of direct aid in exchange for the PA's crackdown on terrorism. In August Israel dismantled the Jewish settlements and disengaged from Gaza.

The second Palestinian presidential and parliamentary elections were originally scheduled for 2001; however, the elections were indefinitely delayed after the outbreak of violence. After the death of Arafat in November 2004, Palestinian factions met in Cairo, Egypt, in March 2005 to discuss how to replace him. Fatah consented to have elections, and Hamas agreed to a ceasefire with Israel. After the adoption of a new electoral system the same month, the parliamentary elections eventually took place in January 2006. This time Hamas did not boycott the elections and defeated Fatah by capitalizing on public discontent with the PA's past ten-year performance. Hamas captured 74 of the 132 seats to Fatah's 45 seats in the PLC. Hamas formed a new cabinet in March and Ismail Haniya became the prime minister. The relationship between Hamas and Fatah remained tense and skirmishes took place between militants in October 2006.

Hamas, which does not officially recognize Israel, isolated the PA in the international arena and ended the thaw between the PA and Israel. The U.S. administration refused to deal with Hamas until it renounced its terrorist tactics and recognized Israel's right to existence. Both the United States and the European Union cut all aid to the PA, and Israel declined to hand over tax receipts it had collected on behalf of the PA. As a result the PA was unable to pay the salaries of its civil servants, which had disastrous consequences for Palestinian society. In June 2006 Israeli military reentered Gaza following an attack that killed two Israeli soldiers and abducted one. Israel detained Hamas members including ministers and PLC representatives. This most recent conflict further undermined the prospects for diplomatic negotiations between the PA and Israel.

SEE ALSO *Arab-Israeli War of 1967; Arabs; Arafat, Yasir; Bush, George W.; Colonialism; Jews; Palestine Liberation Organization (PLO); Palestinians; Peace Process; Sharon, Ariel*

BIBLIOGRAPHY

Brown, Nathan J. 2003. *Palestinian Politics after the Oslo Accords: Resuming Arab Palestine.* Berkeley: University of California Press.

Khalidi, Rashid. 2006. *The Iron Cage: The Story of the Palestinian Struggle for Statehood.* Boston: Beacon.

Khan, Mushtaq Husain, ed., with George Giacaman, and Inge Amundsen. 2004. *State Formation in Palestine: Viability and Governance during a Social Transformation.* New York: RoutledgeCurzon.

Klein, Menachem. 2003. By Conviction, Not by Infliction: The Internal Debate Over Reforming the Palestinian Authority. *Middle East Journal* 57 (2): 194–212.

Parsons, Nigel. 2004. *The Politics of the Palestinian Authority: From Oslo to al-Aqsa.* New York: Routledge.

Robinson, Glenn E. 1997. *Building a Palestinian State: The Incomplete Revolution.* Bloomington: Indiana University Press.

Rubin, Barry. 1999. *The Transformation of Palestinian Politics: From Revolution to State-Building.* Cambridge, MA: Harvard University Press.

Shikaki, Khalil. 2006. Sweeping Victory: Uncertain Mandate. *Journal of Democracy* 17 (3): 116–130.

Gunes Murat Tezcur

PALESTINIAN DIASPORA

There is an increasing literature that describes as diasporic the twentieth-century dispersion of the Palestinian people from their historical homeland in the Middle East. However, the question arises whether celebrating the hybridity and the challenge to notions of nation-state and the dominant culture inherent in diaspora cultures does not detract from legitimate political claims to the homeland that was lost. This is particularly obvious in the case of the Palestinians. Thus, the literature on Palestinian diaspora communities and their experiences of dispersal and uprootedness demonstrates some unease in using the term *diaspora* precisely because it implies the possibility of permanence and the denial of return. The terms *exile* and *refugee* are more prominent in the discourses on Palestinians and in the Palestinians' own usage. Both terms put a much stronger emphasis on the forced nature of the dispersal and the intent to return to the homeland, however symbolic or realistically impossible such a return may be. Using the term *diaspora* for the Palestinian experience can, on the other hand, allow comparison with other communities in order to contextualize the Palestinian experience in a global political, social, and cultural framework.

The term *diaspora* has historically been linked exclusively to the experience of the Jewish people and their dispersal from the "promised land." The Greek word means "the scattering or sowing of seeds." More emotionally charged for Jews than *diaspora* is *exile*, linked to suffering, displacement, and physical distance from the homeland, while the term *diaspora* can connote the potentially beneficial scattering of seeds and thus the possibility of growth and improvement.

It is only in the later twentieth century that the term *diaspora* came to be used more widely for other groups of migrants with a history of dispersal and global networks of communities. In this more recent usage, it has come to denote a specific field of migration studies, namely *diaspora studies*. Within this field the exact meaning of the term has been subject to debate concerning the criteria that define a diaspora. The emerging consensus requires the following features: interconnected communities in at least two places in the world; a shared collective attachment to the homeland; and a sense of collective history of displacement or expansion, a common identity combined with a more or less uneasy relationship with the host societies. Some scholars insist that the cause of the dispersal has to be related to force or to another form of trauma; others argue that this would limit the definition too much. Arguably, many of these characteristics can be found in the history and present situation of the Palestinian people.

HISTORY OF PALESTINIAN MIGRATION

Palestinian migration from the area of historical Palestine can be traced to the beginning of the twentieth century. Palestine had been one of the remote provinces of the Ottoman Empire, economically underdeveloped but politically touched by ideas of Arab nationalism, which resulted in the emergence of a sense of Palestinian identity parallel and overlapping with other local identities and awareness of being Ottoman subjects. Between the world wars and after the collapse of the Ottoman Empire, Arabs emigrated from Palestine to Europe and the Americas in search of better employment and fortune, or they sought higher education after being introduced to Western ideas and education through missionary schools.

Regional migration, as well as economic exchange and trade between Syria, Lebanon, Palestine, and Jordan, was unrestricted, as the area was considered the unified region of Greater Syria. The first major event that caused a larger emigration movement was the 1936–1939 Arab revolt. In their protest against the British mandate and the increasing numbers of Jewish immigrants (supported by Britain), Palestinians were involved in armed clashes and subject to British persecution, while the economic situation deteriorated further and led especially younger males to seek employment, education, and fortune outside of the Middle East.

The war of 1947 to 1948 and its result, the creation of the State of Israel, simultaneously experienced as *An-Nakba* (the catastrophe) for Palestinians, created the Palestinian refugee problem, turning approximately 750,000 Palestinians (75 percent of the Palestinian Arab population) into refugees. Many of them fled their villages in fear of massacres and battles; others were forcibly evicted or barred from returning to their homes. Ultimately, most of them were prevented from returning to the territory that became the State of Israel. They took refuge in the West Bank (which was controlled by Jordan during the war and declared Jordanian territory in 1950) or in the Gaza Strip under Egyptian control. Many others fled to Lebanon and Syria.

In 1949, in response to the desperate humanitarian situation and the growing needs of the Palestinian refugees, the United Nations founded the UN Relief and Works Agency (UNRWA) with the mandate to administer aid to the Palestinian refugees in Jordan, Syria, Lebanon, the West Bank, and Gaza. Refugee camps under UNRWA control were set up, for the most part physically separating Palestinian refugees from the surrounding host societies. Arab countries and Palestinians shared political agreement in their refusal to permanently resettle Palestinians in any country other than Palestine.

During the 1950s and 1960s Palestinians left Israel, as well as the West Bank and Gaza, in search of employment. The economic situation was extremely depressed, further complicated by political oppression in Israel, where Arab towns and villages stayed under military control. Palestinians also went from Gaza to Egypt for education, while others sought employment in the Gulf states, where the discovery of oil demanded skilled laborers and professionals. On the political level, the Palestine Liberation Organization (PLO) was founded in 1964 by Palestinians outside of Palestine, in the diaspora.

The Six-Day War of 1967, in which Israel occupied the West Bank, East Jerusalem, and Gaza, turned many Palestinians into refugees for the second time. An estimated 250,000 West Bank residents and 75,000 residents of Gaza were driven from their homes between June 1967 and December 1968. They fled to Jordan, Egypt, Lebanon, and Syria, often moving several times. The rate of emigration slowed between 1969 and 1974 when a strong sense of holding on to the land based on the ideology of *sumud* (steadfastness) emerged and the Palestinian liberation movement, which had consolidated its organizational structure outside of Palestine, instilled a renewed sense of political pride and Palestinian identity.

Relatively steady numbers of Palestinians left the Occupied Palestinian Territories from the mid-1970s onward. They responded to Israeli policies of political and cultural oppression and land confiscation. Family and chain migration, as well as the immigration policies of potential host countries, became important factors for Palestinian patterns of temporary settlement in countries throughout the world. Major political events, such as the first Intifada (from 1987) and the second Intifada (from 2000), and their negative effects on safety, the political climate, the economy, and education, forced more Palestinians to leave the Occupied Territories and prevented many others from returning.

Palestinians living in Arab countries, however, developed their own patterns of migration, closely linked to political developments inside and outside the region. On one level, such population movement was caused by changes in the relationship between Arab host governments and the Palestinian leadership. In addition, PLO cadres and their families followed the PLO leadership to various Arab countries or were sent to other countries for organizational purposes.

At other times, Palestinians in Arab countries were caught up in larger political and military conflicts, such as the Lebanese Civil War (1975–1990) and the first Gulf War (1991). The civil war in Lebanon and the forced removal of the PLO and its military units from Lebanon in 1982 after the Israeli invasion was a major cause of migration. During the war, Palestinians who sought safety and wanted to escape the volatile situation were accepted by Western countries as refugees or asylum seekers. In the wake of the 1982 events, PLO officials, their staffs, and their families left for Tunisia, where the PLO had reached an agreement with the government to temporarily establish its headquarters.

The Gulf War of 1991 resulted in the expulsion of a large number of Palestinians and their families from Kuwait, mainly as punishment for the Palestinian support for Iraq during the war. Many attempted to settle into a difficult life in Jordan after losing their livelihood and savings in Kuwait. Some held the necessary documents to return to the Occupied Territories, and others sought a new life elsewhere in the world.

The fall of Iraqi president Saddam Hussein in 2003 and subsequent developments in Iraq have contributed to the deterioration of the situation of Palestinians in Iraq who were politically favored by the Iraqi regime. They have experienced severe hardships and marginalization, and many have reportedly attempted to leave Iraq permanently.

PALESTINIAN DIASPORA COMMUNITIES

In 1947 the Arab population of historical Palestine numbered approximately 1.3 million people. In 2000 estimates of the number of Palestinians in the world ranged from 7.7 to 9 million. In the absence of a Palestinian state to issue passports, Palestinians in Palestine and the diaspora carry refugee travel documents or, where available, passports of current or past host countries. Thus reliable data on Palestinian demographics is scarce. Nevertheless, demographics play an important role in the political discourse on the Palestinian refugee problem and its possible solutions, and thus carry tremendous symbolic weight.

Four main groups of Palestinians can be distinguished according to location: those living in Israel, in the West Bank and Gaza, in Arab countries, and in Western countries. The reason that some of those living in the territory of historical Palestine are included in this overview is the fact that many who were internally displaced during the wars perceive their lives as shaped by a sense of inner diaspora, a temporal and special dislocation from their place of origin. This is a sentiment that should not be discounted and that has shaped various expressions of Palestinian national and cultural identity.

The Palestinians inside Israel number less than one million people and constitute approximately 20 percent of the total population of Israel. A significant number of the Palestinians in Israel are internally displaced and consider themselves internal refugees. Many of them have repeatedly attempted to return to their villages or resettle in close proximity to their place of origin; they live in unrec-

ognized villages without access to Israeli health care, education, or social welfare services.

Palestinians in the West Bank and Gaza are divided into refugees and nonrefugees. In June 2005 the total refugee population of the West Bank (registered with UNRWA) was 690,988 with 26 percent (or 182,191) living in nineteen official refugee camps. In the Gaza Strip, UNRWA offered assistance to 969,588 refugees, 49 percent of whom lived in the eight official refugee camps. The number of refugees who need UNRWA assistance has dramatically increased since the beginning of the second Intifada, which led to the Israeli reinvasion of Palestinian territories, economic isolation, and political violence. Since 2000, unprecedented numbers of Palestinian refugees in the West Bank and Gaza have been pushed into poverty.

The largest of the Palestinian diaspora communities is situated in Jordan and numbers approximately 2.6 million. UNRWA reported 1,795,326 registered refugees in Jordan as of June 2005, 16 percent of whom lived in the ten official refugee camps. They are refugees from both the 1948 and 1967 wars and their descendants. A significant number of Palestinians in Jordan carry Jordanian passports, have the right to vote and hold office, enjoy full rights to public services such as higher education, and can work in the government sector. The legal, economic, and social situation of Palestinians in Jordan can be considered far better than in other countries, and some scholars even speak of a virtual merge of Palestinian and Jordanian identity. The Palestinians in Jordan are widely expected to stay in Jordan, even if the right of return may be achieved during future negotiations. Generally, it is assumed that return to a Palestinian state established in the West Bank and Gaza will be a more likely option for the 1967 refugees, while many of the 1948 refugees insist on the literal right of return to homes and villages now in Israel.

The number of Palestinians in Lebanon is widely debated and the only numbers available are limited to registered refugees (401,071) and the camp population (53%). Palestinians in Lebanon face the harshest socioeconomic conditions: their Lebanese travel documents are not recognized by most countries in the world, and they must obtain work and travel permits issued by the Lebanese authorities and are not allowed to work in the public sector and a long list of other professions. Changes in existing laws are closely linked to Lebanese domestic politics. Lebanon has with very few exceptions rejected any permanent settlement or naturalization of Palestinian refugees.

The exact number of Palestinians in Syria is unknown, but 426,919 Palestinians are registered as refugees, 27 percent of whom live in the ten UNRWA administered camps. Most refugees enjoy rights similar to those of Syrian citizens, but they are not allowed to vote, hold office, or carry Syrian passports. The travel documents issued by the Syrian government are not recognized by most states.

Palestinian refugees living in other countries of the Arab world, such as Saudi Arabia, the Gulf states, Libya, Egypt, and Iraq, are not assisted by UNRWA. Many of these Palestinians are work migrants who relocated after leaving their initial country of refuge in hope of finding better education and employment.

Palestinians in Western countries are divided into European communities and those in the Americas. The estimated numbers vary widely, but less than 6 percent of the Palestinian people live in Western diaspora communities. Many countries, such as the United States, Canada, and Australia, have, because of their status as immigration countries, over the years provided Palestinians with work and residency permits and also citizenship. Others have been accepted as refugees and asylum seekers. European countries tend to accept refugees at times of acute crises, but do not generally favor integration or naturalization of refugees.

PALESTINIAN DIASPORIC IDENTITIES AND CULTURES

A distinct feature of diaspora communities is a sense of collective identity, often linked to the events surrounding the loss of the homeland and the hardships of living separated from its territory and culture. The Palestinian diaspora is characterized by strong intercommunity networks on many levels, such as family ties, global communication, frequent migratory moves, organizational structures, and cultural exchange. These connections facilitate the preservation and negotiation of Palestinian national identities.

On one hand, scholars celebrate the emergence of new hybrid intellectual and cultural dimensions of diaspora communities. Palestinian communities have both features. Case studies of Palestinian diaspora communities in different parts of the world indicate that the more Palestinians are allowed to integrate into a host society on political, social, economic, and cultural levels, the more their Palestinian identity becomes part of a hyphenated set of identities. On the other hand, many Palestinian refugees in Lebanon or Iraq have no other identities to choose from; thus they remain in a sense more strongly Palestinian. The same correlation can be detected for integration and return wishes. The right of return is subject to heated political debate among Palestinians and internationally, and will have to be resolved as part of a final settlement of the Palestinian-Israeli conflict.

Discussion of the Palestinian diaspora is not complete without mentioning the importance of Palestinian cultural and intellectual production throughout the world and the significance of commemorating the events (in particular the 1948 war) that led to the expulsion of the Palestinians from their homeland. In the absence of national museums, school textbooks, and a state, these collective memories have been shaped by memoirs, oral history, and artistic expression. Palestinian writers, visual artists, musicians, and poets have contributed to Palestinian national culture and the cultures of their respective host countries. Palestinian intellectuals and scholars have not only shaped or challenged the field of Palestine studies but have also contributed to many areas of the social and natural sciences without denying their Palestinian diasporic identities. Such identities are by definition in flux, in a constant state of redefinition and adjustment, and one can argue that future generations of Palestinians will have to renegotiate how, where, and to what extent they want to be part of the Palestinian diaspora.

SEE ALSO *Intifada, The; Palestinians*

BIBLIOGRAPHY

Christison, Kathleen. 2001. *The Wound of Dispossession: Telling the Palestinian Story.* Santa Fe, NM: Sunlit Hills.

Cohen, Robin. 1997. *Global Diasporas: An Introduction.* London: University College.

Gröhndal, Mia. 2003. *In Hope and Despair: Life in the Palestinian Refugee Camps.* Cairo, Egypt: American University in Cairo Press.

Hammer, Juliane. 2005. *Palestinians Born in Exile: Diaspora and the Search for a Homeland.* Austin: University of Texas Press.

Jayyusi, Salma Khadra, ed. 1992. *Anthology of Modern Palestinian Literature.* New York: Columbia University Press.

Karmi, Ghada, and Eugene Cotran, eds. 1999. *The Palestinian Exodus: 1948–1998.* Reading, U.K.: Ithaca.

Lindholm Schulz, Helena, and Juliane Hammer. 2003. *The Palestinian Diaspora: Formation of Identities and Politics of Homeland.* London: Routledge.

Mattar, Philip. 2005. *Encyclopedia of the Palestinians.* Rev. ed. New York: Facts on File.

Morris, Benny. 2004. *The Birth of the Palestinian Refugee Problem Revisited.* Cambridge, U.K., and New York: Cambridge University Press.

Said, Edward. 1986. *After the Last Sky: Palestinian Lives.* New York: Pantheon.

United Nations Relief and Works Agency for Palestine Refugees in the Near East (UNRWA). http://www.unrwa.org.

Juliane Hammer

PALESTINIANS

Historically, the term "Palestinian" has been associated with the inhabitants of the south of ancient Syria west of the Jordan River between Lebanon and Sinai. The name "Palestinian" is related to the "Philistines," an Indo-European group that invaded the southern coast of ancient Syria from the sea in the fourteenth century BCE. The Palestinians, however, are descendants of the Canaanites, a Semitic group that migrated from the Arabian Peninsula between 3000 and 2500 BCE and settled the coastal areas of Palestine. The Arabic language and Islamic religion spread among the Palestinians with the Arab migrations from the Arabian Peninsula between 630 and 650 CE. Throughout four hundred years of Muslim Ottoman rule, Palestinians maintained an Arab identity and included Muslim, Christian, and Jewish communities. At the turn of the twentieth century, the Palestinian population was composed of a Muslim Sunni majority and minority populations of Christians (10 percent) and Jews (less than 5 percent).

After World War I (1914–1918), the Palestinians were provisionally recognized as independent under a British mandate that was supposed to provide advice and maintain their status quo until self-rule. The British, however, began to resettle European Jews in Palestine as a way of supporting the Zionist solution to the Jewish question created by the anti-Semitism of Europe. The increase in the European Jewish population from 4.8 percent in 1882 to 28 percent in 1936 created economic hardships for the indigenous population because the lands purchased were in the arable, coastal, and urban centers of Palestine. Moreover, the uneven economic policies of the British that favored the Jewish sector increased Palestinian unemployment, rural outmigrations, landlessness, and thus a cheap labor force. Palestinian discontent culminated in a general strike and protests between 1936 and 1939, which were brutally suppressed by the British army and the Jewish militia.

Palestinian lives have been shaped since mid-twentieth century by two main events, their repercussions, and the attempted solutions: Al Nakba (Arabic for "the catastrophe") of 1948, which marked Palestinian dispossession and exile coinciding with the establishment of the Israeli state; and Al Naksa (Arabic for "the tragedy") of 1967, which marked the beginning of the Israeli occupation in the West Bank, the Gaza Strip, and East Jerusalem. Al Nakba caused the exodus of 750,000 Palestinians from the land on which the state of Israel was established into the nearby Arab countries of Jordan, Lebanon, and Syria, as well as into the West Bank and the Gaza Strip; and Al Naksa created an additional 350,000 refugees who fled to Jordan, of whom 15,000 were allowed to return. The indigenous Palestinian population that remained on the

land under Israeli control was put under military rule until 1966 and was later incorporated into Israeli society as a minority with citizenship but not equality.

After 1948 Palestinian society emerged divided between the West Bank, a kidney-shaped area of approximately 2,270 square miles whose population doubled with the arrival of refugees, and the Gaza Strip, a tiny strip of land of approximately 140 square miles absorbing a refugee population that outnumbered its inhabitants. Between 1948 and 1967, the Palestinians in the West Bank, annexed then by Jordan, could get Jordanian passports listing their citizenship as Jordanian, while the Palestinians in Gaza, under Egyptian rule, were given Egyptian travel documents listing their nationality as undetermined.

The Palestinians in both the West Bank and the Gaza Strip were united after 1967 through their status as occupied subjects sharing a history under Israeli occupation while struggling against its oppressive conditions. The contention included a guerrilla resistance in the first couple of years of occupation in the refugee camps of Gaza. It was suppressed when the camps were subjected to martial law. Sporadic protests took place in the 1970s and 1980s, a mass uprising took place in 1987, and a second uprising began in 2000.

Under occupation, all aspects of Palestinian life were subject to the Israeli military authorities' approval, from economic activity to the right of movement, and monitored through a hierarchically ordered color-coded identity card system— to be carried at all times—differentiating Palestinian residents of East Jerusalem (blue), the West Bank (orange), and the Gaza Strip (red). The Palestinians of East Jerusalem, which was annexed by Israel after the 1967 war while remaining integral to the West Bank, were assigned the status of residents, situating them hierarchically above occupied subjects but lower than citizens. Nonetheless, the mid-1990s uncovered their shaky status when the Israeli government demanded that East Jerusalemites prove that the center of their activities continued to revolve around the city if they wanted to keep their residency rights. The residency status of close to two thousand East Jerusalemites was revoked.

The Palestinian economy, underdeveloped on the eve of the 1967 war, deteriorated under the Israeli occupation policies of control of mobility of Palestinian labor and commodities and confiscation of land for building and expanding Israeli Jewish settlements in the occupied territories. By 1993, a survey of living conditions found that Palestinian households in the territories are mostly dependent on wage labor. Moreover, Palestinians preferred to work in Israel because of higher wages even as they are paid less than the average wages of the Jewish workers. Under a general exit system in 1967, Palestinians could cross the border to work as day laborers but were not allowed to stay after sunset. Thus, Palestinian chances for making a living in the territories largely have depended on Israeli border policies since 1967.

Peace negotiations between Palestinians and Israelis to end the occupation started in 1993 yet coincided with Israel closing its border and imposing a permit policy restricting Palestinian movement with repercussions for Palestinian livelihood. Although the peace process brought a Palestinian National Authority to Gaza and Jericho and redeployed the Israeli military from main Palestinian towns, it did not end Israeli control. Israel retained 59 percent of the West Bank lands and 20 percent of the Gaza Strip, and maintained security control over most of the West Bank. In the years following the arrival of the Palestinian Authority to the territories in 1994, Palestinians faced more mobility restrictions—between Gaza, the West Bank, and East Jerusalem, within the West Bank. Additionally, the construction of a wall between the West Bank and Israel has had significant consequences for Palestinian social life.

SEE ALSO *Arab League, The; Arab-Israeli War of 1967; Intifada, The; Islam, Shia and Sunni; Muslims; Palestine Liberation Organization (PLO); Palestinian Authority; Palestinian Diaspora; Peace Process; Suicide Bombers*

BIBLIOGRAPHY

Farsoun, Samih, and Christina E. Zacharia. 1997. *Palestine and the Palestinians.* Boulder, CO: Westview Press.

Heiberg, Marianne, and Geir Ovensen, eds. 1993. *Palestinian Society in Gaza, West Bank, and Arab Jerusalem: A Survey of Living Conditions.* Oslo, Norway: FAFO.

McDowall, David. 1998. *The Palestinians: The Road to Nationhood.* London: Minority Rights Group International.

Roy, Sara. 2001. *The Gaza Strip: The Political Economy of De-Development,* 2nd ed. Washington, DC: Institute for Palestinian Studies.

Mary Hovsepian

PAN-AFRICAN CONGRESSES

Pan-African congresses is the name given to seven international meetings planned by W. E. B. Du Bois between 1919 and 1929, of which four actually materialized, and another meeting in 1945 in which he participated only peripherally in planning and organizing, but over which he presided. At the 1945 congress, he called for another to take place nine years later. This materialized only in 1974,

after his death. Another congress took place in 1994, with another proposed a few years later.

THE ORIGIN OF THE TERM *PAN-AFRICAN*

Pan-African was coined, it is claimed, by the Trinidadian lawyer Henry Sylvester Williams in an 1899 letter concerning the Pan-African Conference of 1900. It appears, however, that Du Bois had a much greater claim to the term. It is plausibly derived from the Pan-Slav, Pan-German, and Pan-American movements, of which the most influential for residents of the Western Hemisphere would logically be the Pan-American movement.

Du Bois is the only major participant to link explicitly in print all four of these pan-movements. In 1888 he gave as his valedictory address at Fisk University a speech titled "Bismarck"; Du Bois said that Otto von Bismarck, the German chancellor, was his hero because of his feat in organizing the reunification of Germany. While at the University of Berlin from 1892 to 1894, Du Bois wrote a PhD dissertation in economics under the Pan-German Gustav von Schmoller. Heinrich von Treitschke, whom Du Bois described as a "fire-eating Pan-German," was the philosophical leader of the Pan-German League, and discussed its tenets in class. During this period, Du Bois also traveled to Pan-Slav centers in Prague, Bohemia; "the borders of Russia"; and Krakow, Poland. The movement held a demonstration in Prague in 1898. Du Bois wrote of these travels in his letters from Europe to the *New York Age*, a weekly newspaper, from 1892 to 1894 and in his 1940 and 1968 autobiographies. Also in his autobiographies, Du Bois wrote of James G. Blaine, the U.S. secretary of state in 1881 and from 1889 to 1892, and the architect of the U.S. government's Pan-American policy. Thus, Du Bois mentioned in published writings the individuals or sites associated with all three prior pan-movements. The European pan-movements differed from the American movement, which was based on the unity of independent territorial states only, without regard to language or ethnicity.

By contrast with Du Bois, Williams used the term *Pan-African* only in one unpublished letter and in the documents promoting the 1900 conference. For him, there is no indication of the provenience of the term.

Three other aspects of Pan-African conferences/congresses are considered in this entry: (1) the participants; (2) the public resolutions and other documents; and (3) the organizations established to continue the movement.

CONFERENCE PARTICIPANTS

It should be noted that continuity from congress to congress was guaranteed, because each of the meetings from

1919 to 1974 was organized by participants from previous meetings. Du Bois, as stated, participated in every meeting between 1900 and 1945. C. L. R. James, Amy Ashwood Garvey, T. Ras Makonnen, and Adam Clayton Powell Jr. provided direct links between the 1945 and 1974 congresses. However, the Seventh Pan-African Congress, held in Kampala, Uganda, in 1994, had no participants from previous congresses.

PUBLIC RESOLUTIONS, MANIFESTOS, AND MESSAGES

The documents produced by the Pan-African meetings through 1945 include:

- 1900: "Address to the Nations of the World"
- 1919: the Du Bois "Memorandum" and the "Resolutions of the Pan-African Congress"
- 1921: the "Manifesto of the Second Pan-African Congress" and "The Pan-African Association Declared the 8 December 1921 Statutes"
- 1923: "Resolutions"
- 1927: "Announcement of the Fourth Pan-African Congress," "About the Pan-African Congress," and a press release on the resolutions
- 1945: a "Memorandum to the U.N.O." and "Resolutions"

Du Bois wrote most of these documents. Several themes in them stand out. Perhaps most striking is his use of the term *Africa for the Africans*, which appeared from 1921 to 1927. Second, Du Bois always began with a demand for self-government in the African colonies. Third, with the exception of 1919, he always addressed the plight of those of African descent in the Americas, and elsewhere in the African diaspora. Brazil, however, was addressed only in 1921 and 1923. In 1927 his horizons extended beyond Africa to China and India. The 1945 documents contained no reference to the plight of the African diaspora, but in his own speech, Du Bois did stress that theme repeatedly. Fourth, he always spoke of the plight of black labor, and of black access to land and capital.

The "General Declaration" of the 1974 congress acknowledged the need to "consolidate the unity between the peoples of Africa and of African descent," as had Du Bois. That congress's "General Statement on Economics" declared that the purpose of economic development was "the liberation of our people at home and in the diaspora." The "Resolution on Democratisation of International Institutions," also from the 1974 congress, recommended that African regional and subregional organizations permit the participation of "counterpart organizations in the Caribbean and North America."

CONTINUING ORGANIZATIONS

The international Pan-African meetings held between 1900 and 1945 established four organizations intended to be permanent. These were the Pan-African Association, 1900–1902; the International Pan-African Association, 1921–1925; the New York Pan-African Congress Committee, 1923–1927; and the Pan-African Federation, 1944–1947. The headquarters of these four organizations were located in the very capitals of the colonial countries the conferees wished to displace: London, Paris, and New York.

POST-MANCHESTER CONGRESSES

Between 1945 and 1974 most Pan-African activity took place on the African continent. The 1945 congress was organized by George Padmore and Kwame Nkrumah, the latter of whom was inspired by black nationalist Marcus Garvey. A native of Trinidad, Padmore was a former law student at Howard University who became an important official of the Communist International. Nkrumah, who graduated from Lincoln University and the University of Pennsylvania, became the first president of an independent Ghana in 1957, the foremost advocate of Pan-Africanism during this period, and the principal founder of the Organization of African Unity (OAU) in 1963. The Sixth Pan-African Congress resulted from the long-term actions, sometimes in concert, but often not, of three men: Julius K. Nyerere (1922–1999) of Africa, Adam Clayton Powell Jr. (1908–1972) of North America, and C. L. R. James (1901–1989) of the Caribbean. At the Cairo summit meeting of the Organization of African Unity (OAU) held in July 1964, which was attended by Malcolm X, Nyerere, then president of Tanzania, introduced and negotiated to passage a resolution recognizing the Afro-American struggle as a concern of the OAU. In an October 17, 1967, address titled "After the Arusha Declaration," Nyerere invited foreigners, including African Americans, to come to Tanzania to assist in nation building. In the late 1960s Nyerere went to Harlem and issued an invitation to African Americans to come to Tanzania to assist in building a socialist African state. As a result of these efforts, the number of African Americans in Tanzania increased rapidly to about eight hundred in 1974. Among the most important for the Sixth Pan-African Congress were Sam Dove and Bill Sutherland. Dove served as a consultant to the Tanzanian government on the sixth Pan-African congress. Sutherland was the founder of the Congress of Racial Equality (CORE), a founder of the American Committee on Africa (ACA), a consultant of President Nkrumah, and a liaison between the Tanzanian government and the African American community in Tanzania. Also resident in Dar es Salaam at this time was Walter Anthony Rodney, a Guyanese.

The Black Power Conferences were initiated in Washington, D.C., in 1966 by Powell, a U.S. congressman who had participated in the 1945 Manchester congress. The Newark Black Power Conference of July 1967 resolved to sponsor "an International Black Congress." Chairing the economics workshop was Robert S. Browne of Fairleigh Dickinson University. The Philadelphia Black Power Conference of the late summer of 1968 resolved to thank the government of Tanzania for its invitation to hold the Fourth Black Power Conference in Tanzania. This could not be arranged, however, and so at the Bermuda Black Power Conference of July 1969, C. L. R. James chaired a workshop on "Politics," including a sub-workshop on "Pan-Africanism." His closing address to the conference advocated a new Pan-African congress. James, a Trotskyite socialist, was a professor at the Federal City College and Howard University, both in Washington, D.C., from 1966 to the mid-1970s, and from this base he began preparing a new congress in 1970.

James formed an entirely new group consisting of the principal survivors of the Manchester congress, or their widows and ex-wives, and some of his students. Most important of the veterans were T. Ras Makonnen, Amy Ashwood Garvey (1897–1969), and Shirley Graham Du Bois (1907–1977), who lent their names as sponsors of the new congress. James's students included Walter Rodney; Courtland Cox, formerly of the Student Nonviolent Coordinating Committee; and Marvin Holloway. The organizing group, based in Washington, D.C., styled itself the Provisional Secretariat for a Sixth Pan-African Congress.

The group organized itself into regional committees for North America, the Caribbean and South America, and Africa. European, Asian, and Pacific organizations and individuals were recognized by the secretariat on an ad-hoc basis. In 1972 the organizing committee issued a "call" to the Sixth Pan-African Congress, written largely by James, Rodney, and Cox. Two years later it issued a briefing paper. Rodney contributed a paper, "Toward the Sixth Pan-African Congress: Aspects of the International Class Struggle in Africa," which was distributed by the organizers in April 1974. A 1945 Du Bois speech, "The Pan-African movement," was reprinted and issued by the organizers, also in 1974.

Three regionwide meetings took place in North America—at Kent State University, at the Center for Black Education (CBE) in Washington, D.C., and in Atlanta. The Temporary Organizing Committee for a Sixth Pan-African Congress was established, with head-quarters in Washington. Cox of the CBE was elected

international secretary-general by acclamation. Sylvia Hill of the CBE was elected secretary-general for North America, and Julian Ellison of Columbia University and the Black Economic Research Center (BERC) was elected associate secretary-general for North America. This trio was denominated the Temporary Secretariat. James Turner of Cornell University accepted a Secretariat invitation to head the actual North American delegation, which had not yet been selected. At a regionwide meeting in Atlanta, Cox, Hill, and Ellison were formally elected as permanent officers. Cox then left for Dar es Salaam, taking with him several staff workers, including Geri Stark, who served as information officer.

North American delegates included "Queen Mother" Audley Moore, Julianne Malveaux of the Massachusetts Institute of Technology, Gay McDougall of Yale University, William Sales of Columbia, Matthew Meade of Yale, Carroll Clarke of Brooklyn College, Wentworth Ofuatey-Kodjoe of the City College of New York, Barbara Britton of BERC, Owusu Sadaukai of Malcolm X Liberation University, Amiri Baraka of the Congress of African Peoples, Haki Madhubuti of Black Books Bulletin, and Oba T'Shaka of San Francisco State University. At a final meeting of the delegates at Columbia University on June 9 and 10, Clarke and Ellison finalized drafts of North American position papers.

In March 1974 the Caribbean and South American Regional Steering Committee elected Eusi Kwayana chairman, with Tim Hector and Maurice Bishop among those selected as delegates. However, no official nongovernmental delegation from this region was finally permitted.

The Sixth Pan-African Congress opened on June 20, 1974, in Nkrumah Hall at the University of Dar es Salaam. In the first order of business, Nyerere was elected president of the congress by acclamation. Conducting the opening plenary session as co-masters of ceremonies were Cox and Aboud Jumbe, the vice president of Tanzania. A taped message from Ahmed Sékou Touré, president of Guinea, was played. Papers were presented on the three major issues of the congress—politics, science and technology, and economics—the last of which Ellison persuaded the Secretariat to add. Two speeches, by Samora Machel and Peter Onu, deputy secretary-general of the OAU, were devoted to politics. The economics paper was by D. M. Nomvete of the United Nations Economic Commission for Africa. The congress proceeded with daily plenary sessions followed by simultaneous sessions of committees A, B, and C, for political; economic development; and African science, technology, education, and culture, respectively.

The Seventh Pan-African Congress convened in April 1994 in Kampala, Uganda. The organizers, led by Naiwu

Osahon of Lagos, Nigeria, included no one who had participated at the Dar es Salaam or earlier congresses.

THE AFRICAN UNION

In 2002 the OAU was replaced by a new organization, the African Union (AU), which was a more politically and economically integrated confederation of African states. By this time, all former colonies on the continent, as well as South Africa, were ruled by Arab or black governments, as were all colonies in the Caribbean except those of France. The AU represented the near accomplishment of the dream of Williams, Du Bois, Marcus Garvey, George Padmore, James, and Kwame Nkrumah.

SEE ALSO *Black Nationalism; Black Power; Colonialism; Decolonization; Du Bois, W. E. B.; James, C. L. R.; Malcolm X; Marxism, Black; Nyerere, Julius; Pan-Africanism; Rodney, Walter*

BIBLIOGRAPHY

Aptheker, Herbert, ed. 1973–1978. *The Correspondence of W. E. B. Du Bois.* 3 vols. Amherst: University of Massachusetts Press.

Bankie, B. F., ed. 2001. *Globalising Africans: Towards the Seventh Pan-African Congress.* Cape Town, South Africa: Centre for Advanced Studies of African Society.

Broderick, Francis L. 1959. *W. E. B. Du Bois: Negro Leader in a Time of Crisis.* Stanford, CA: Stanford University Press.

Cronon, Edmund David. 1955. *Black Moses: The Story of Marcus Garvey and the Universal Negro Improvement Association.* Madison: University of Wisconsin Press.

Du Bois, W. E. B. 1968. *The Autobiography of W. E. B. Du Bois.* New York: International Publishers.

Logan, Rayford W. 1962. The Historical Aspects of Pan-Africanism, 1900–1945. In *Pan-Africanism Reconsidered*, ed. the American Society of African Culture, 37–52. Berkeley: University of California Press.

Makonnen, Ras. 1973. *Pan-Africanism from Within*, ed. Kenneth King. Nairobi: Oxford University Press.

Martin, Tony. 1976. *Race First: The Ideological and Organizational Struggles of Marcus Garvey and the Universal Negro Improvement Association.* Westport, CT: Greenwood.

Martin, Tony. 1997. Discovering African Roots: Amy Ashwood Garvey's Pan-Africanist Journey. *Comparative Studies in South Asia, Africa, and the Middle East* 17 (1): 118–126.

Mathurin, Owen Charles. 1976. *Henry Sylvester Williams and the Origins of the Pan-African Movement, 1869–1911.* Westport, CT: Greenwood.

Nascimento, Elisa Larkin. 1980. *Pan-Africanism and South America: Emergence of a Black Rebellion.* Buffalo, NY: Afrodiaspora.

Padmore, George. 1971. *Pan-Africanism or Communism.* Garden City, NY: Doubleday.

Taylor, Ula Yvette. 2002. *The Veiled Garvey: The Life and Times of Amy Jacques Garvey.* Chapel Hill: University of North Carolina Press.

Thompson, Vincent Bakpetu. 1969. *Africa and Unity: The Evolution of Pan-Africanism.* London: Longmans.

Wilcox, Preston, ed. 1970. *Black Power Conference Reports.* New York: Action Library, Afram Associates.

Julian Ellison

PAN-AFRICANISM

Pan-Africanism is a political, ideological, and cultural movement centered on the liberation of Africa and Africans both on the continent and in the diaspora. The primary tension in the history of the movement has been the precise nature and relative importance of race and class, and their relation, in this struggle (Allen 1969).

There are many definitions of Pan-Africanism, and even debate about when it began and what actors and actions constitute the movement. These different conceptions hinge largely on whether one is referring to an organized historical movement self-identified as "Pan-Africanism" that began in the late nineteenth century and continues into the twenty-first. The alternative is a "general sentiment of international black kinship" (Weisbord 1973, p. 7n), sometimes written with a lowercase *p* (i.e., "pan-Africanism"; cf. Shepperson 1962), identified as existing as far back as ancient Egypt (Nantambu 1998), including slave revolts and (inter)nationalist tendencies in the Caribbean and Americas in the eighteenth and nineteenth centuries associated with such names as Nat Turner, Paul Cuffee, Denmark Vesey, Toussaint-L'ouverture, Joseph Cinque, Martin Delaney, David Walker, Edward Blyden, and many others. The remainder of this entry focuses primarily on the first, the contemporary organized movement, though their predecessors have always been explicitly recognized and honored.

The first Pan-African conference, held in London in 1900, was organized by Henry Sylvester Williams, a Trinidadian barrister, and attended by W. E. B. Du Bois. The group had previously formed under the title of "African Association" but changed it to "Pan-African Association" and committed to a conference every two years, the next to be held in the United States (Esedebe 1994, p. 44). The movement, a response to racism and colonialism, promoted civil and political rights for and cooperative development among all those of African descent—on the continent and in Europe, the Caribbean, and the rest of the Americas (Legum 1962).

Du Bois organized and led the second conference, often regarded as the "first" Pan-African *Congress*, in 1919, followed by congresses in 1921, 1923, and 1927. The nineteen years between the first and second meeting were not without activity, however. Debates between those who did and did not support repatriation, between those who saw the issue primarily in racial terms and those who gave more weight to economic considerations, and between conservative accommodationists and liberal or radical liberationists were all lively, and included not only Du Bois but Marcus Garvey and Booker T. Washington. But the period from the end of World War I to the end of World War II marked an important and intensive growth of the organized movement, with its concerns reflecting developments worldwide. This activity included, but was not limited to, a number of important publications by leading Pan-Africanists, such as C. L. R. James (*The Black Jacobins*), Jomo Kenyatta (*Facing Mount Kenya*), and George Padmore (*How Britain Rules Africa*).

Many participants and observers alike have remarked on the changes that came with the first post–World War II Congress, the Fifth Pan-African Congress, held in Manchester, England, in 1945. As Kwame Nkrumah emphasized, for example:

> For the first time, there was strong worker and student participation, and most of the over two hundred delegates who attended came from Africa. They represented re-awakening African political consciousness; and it was no surprise when the Congress adopted socialism as its political philosophy.... Two declarations were addressed to the imperial powers, one written by Du Bois, and the other by myself. Both asserted the right and the determination of colonial peoples to be free, and condemned capitalism. (Nkrumah 1973, pp. 42–43)

At the same time, the interwar period had been one in which the Communist Party attacked Pan-Africanism as "petit bourgeois nationalism," while official U.S. and European governments and the media portrayed the movement as completely under the control of Moscow and the Communists. The Fifth Congress, then, was seen as the end of the "coming-of-age" period of Pan-Africanism, whose leaders and proponents were now consciously "seeking a way of achieving national liberation and economic emancipation without allying themselves with the Communists" (Padmore 1971, p. 130). The formation and mobilization of colonial liberation movements in the postwar period led to Ghana's independence in 1957, when "Pan-Africanism moved to Africa, its real home, and Pan-African Conferences were held for the first time on the soil of a liberated African state" (Nkrumah 1973, p. 43).

In the period of decolonization that began with Ghanaian independence, a growing continental Pan-Africanism in which continental political and economic unity was envisioned was strongly promoted by Nkrumah (1963), Cheikh Anta Diop ([1960] 1978), and others. One of the issues hotly debated in this period regarded the relation of North Africa to sub-Saharan Africa. Continental Pan-Africans viewed the North as African, while "sub-Saharan" Pan-Africanists, concerned with Pan-Negroism versus Pan-Arabism, did not include the North in their proposals. This debate also overlaps with and touches on many issues relevant to cultural Pan-Africanism, in which all Africans—continental and diasporan—are seen as sharing many cultural and even linguistic characteristics that distinguish them from other non-Africans, especially Europeans (Marah 1998, p. 80). Some of the divisions were represented on the continent by the rivalry between the Brazzaville and Casablanca groups, which resulted in a "compromise" with the creation of the Organization of African Unity (OAU) in 1963. In the diaspora, these divisions were reflected in the debates between cultural nationalists (some who eventually embraced Afrocentricity) and political (or revolutionary) nationalists, including those coming out of the civil rights and Black Power movements, such as Stokely Carmichael (Kwame Ture).

But the tradition of continental and diasporan alliance was continued as Malcolm X, founder of the Organization of Afro-American Unity (OAAU) attended the OAU's Cairo Summit in 1964, where he spoke in favor of the inseparable connections between Africans "at home" and abroad that could not be ignored, and author Richard Wright attended the Bandung Conference in 1955. These developments were also played out in the rise of black studies courses and curricula in the 1960s, including the establishment of the Afro-Asian Institute at Temple University in Philadelphia in 1969, later reorganized and renamed the Department of Pan-African Studies (including its Pan-African Studies Community Education Program, or PASCEP) in 1972. Bandung, the Non-Aligned Movement, and the Afro-Asian Institute are examples of what Mazrui identified as the growing "Global Pan-Africanism" uniting not only continental and diasporan Africans but other colonized or previously colonized peoples of ASIA and the Americas (Mazrui 1977). Malcolm X's experiences in Mecca and elsewhere and Martin Luther King Jr.'s position on Vietnam later in life, even the haiku and tanka poetic forms of Richard Wright and Sonia Sanchez, were all manifestations of global Pan-Africanism.

In the twenty-first century, the Pan-African notions of African political unity and continued discussion of the relation and relevance of racism and capitalism remain alive. With the fall of the apartheid government in South Africa, political independence has been achieved, but neocolonialism remains alive and gives no indication of withering away on its own. In the diaspora, although there remains tremendous racial residential segregation and strong evidence of ongoing discrimination, those of African descent have obtained positions of authority and power in the political and economic spheres, resulting in what might be viewed as "domestic neocolonialism." In the face of all these developments, Pan-Africanists such as Shivji are promoting "an alternative Pan-Africanism of the People, rooted in anti-imperialism and liberation. In other words, the nationalism of the twenty-first century is Pan-Africanism rooted in anti-imperialism" (Shivji 2006).

SEE ALSO *African Diaspora; African Studies; Anticolonial Movements; Black Power; Caribbean, The; Civil Rights; Civil Rights Movement, U.S.; Diop, Cheikh Anta; Du Bois, W. E. B.; Garvey, Marcus; Haitian Revolution; James, C. L. R.; Kenyatta, Jomo; Malcolm X; Nationalism and Nationality; Nkrumah, Kwame; Organization of African Unity (OAU); Pan-African Congresses; Pan-Arabism; Pan-Caribbeanism; Rastafari; Turner, Nat; Vesey, Denmark*

BIBLIOGRAPHY

Allen, Robert L. 1969. *Black Awakening in Capitalist America: An Analytic History.* Garden City, NY: Doubleday.

Diop, Cheikh Anta. 1978 [1960]. *Black Africa: The Economic and Cultural Basis for a Federated State.* Trans. Harold Salemson. Westport, CT: Lawrence Hill.

Esedebe, P. Olisanwuche. 1994. *Pan-Africanism: The Idea and Movement, 1776–1991*, 2nd ed. Washington, DC: Howard University Press.

James, C. L. R. 1938. *The Black Jacobins: Toussaint L'Ouverture and the San Domingo Revolution.* New York: Dial Press.

Kenyatta, Jomo. 1965. *Facing Mount Kenya: The Tribal Life of the Gikuyu.* New York: Vintage. (Orig. pub. 1938).

Legum, Colin. 1962. *Pan-Africanism: A Short Political Guide.* New York: Praeger.

Marah, John K. 1998. *African People in the Global Village: An Introduction to Pan African Studies.* Lanham, MD: University Press of America.

Mazrui, Ali. 1977. *Africa's International Relations: The Diplomacy of Dependency and Change.* Boulder, CO: Westview Press.

Nantambu, Kwame. 1998. Pan-Africanism Versus Pan-African Nationalism: An Afrocentric Analysis. *Journal of Black Studies* 28 (5): 561–574.

Nkrumah, Kwame. 1963. *Africa Must Unite.* New York: Praeger.

Nkrumah, Kwame. 1973. *Revolutionary Path.* New York: International Publishers.

Padmore, George. 1936. *How Britain Rules Africa.* New York: Lothrop, Lee & Shepard.

Padmore, George. 1971. *Pan-Africanism or Communism.* Garden City, NY: Doubleday.

Shepperson, George. 1962. Pan-Africanism and "Pan-Africanism": Some Historical Notes. *Phylon* 23 (4): 346–358.

Shivji, Issa G. 2006. From Neo-liberalism to Pan-Africanism: Towards Reconstructing an Eastern African Discourse. *Transformation: Critical Perspectives on Southern Africa* 61: 108–118.

Weisbord, Robert G. 1973. *Ebony Kinship: Africa, Africans, and the Afro-American.* Westport, CT: Greenwood Press.

Mathew Forstater

PAN-ARABISM

Pan-Arabism is a Western term for the ideological and political project Arabs refer to as *Arab nationalism.* This project's central premise is that all those who speak Arabic, from Iraq in the east to Morocco in the west, share a common history, heritage, and culture, and are therefore members of a single nation whose destiny it is to overcome the artificial boundaries imposed by colonialism and achieve independence and unity.

Like all nationalisms, Arab nationalism claims ancient roots but is actually of relatively recent origin. The term *Arab* was used by neighboring peoples to designate an ethnos based in the central and northern Arabian Peninsula from well before the emergence of Islam in the seventh century CE, and among Muslims the Arabs enjoyed a distinctive status as the people to whom God chose to send his final and most complete revelation, transmitted by an Arab prophet, Muhammad (c. 570–632), in the Arabic language. But in the later Ottoman period, the term was often used by literate urban folk to denote the uncultured nomads of the desert. Premodern identities in what is today called the Middle East were generally framed in religious, kinship, tribal, occupational, and local or regional terms, or in terms of one's loyalty or subjection to a particular ruler or state, such that before the nineteenth century no one in what is now referred to as the Arab world would have considered oneself an Arab in the modern national sense of the term.

Arab nationalism was a product of the social, cultural, and political transformations that the predominantly Arab provinces of the Ottoman Empire underwent in the second half of the nineteenth century and the first decades of the twentieth century. These transformations included the disruptive effects of the region's growing integration into a Europe-centered world economic and political order; efforts by the Ottoman ruling elite to centralize power and create a modern state that could withstand European encroachment and counter separatist movements among its subject Christian peoples; the spread of modern schools; and the complex encounter with European ideas, institutions, and practices, disseminated and mediated largely through new print media. These processes helped foster what would come to be called the *nahda*, the Arab cultural "renaissance" that was centered in Ottoman-ruled geographic Syria (encompassing the present-day states of Syria, Lebanon, Israel/Palestine, and Jordan) and in Egypt, which opened the way to a protonational and largely cultural "Arabism."

After the Ottoman constitutional revolution of 1908, politically active Arabs (largely from the educated upper and middle classes) tended to advocate greater autonomy for the Ottoman Empire's Arab provinces while remaining loyal to the Ottoman framework, seen as the only bulwark against European colonial domination; only a few marginal groups and individuals went so far as to call for Arab independence from Ottoman rule. But after the outbreak of World War I in 1914, Ottoman repression and centralization, as well as wartime hardships, alienated many Arabs from Ottoman rule. Meanwhile the British, seeking local allies against the Ottomans, established secret links with Husayn (c. 1854–1931), the quasi-autonomous ruler of the holy city of Mecca, who hoped to escape Ottoman control and carve out a state for himself and his Hashemite clan, and through him with Arab nationalist activists in Syria. In 1915, bolstered by Britain's promise to support postwar Arab independence under Hashemite rule and equipped with British weapons, money, and advisors, the Hashemites and their allies revolted against Ottoman rule in the name of "the Arab nation" and participated in the Allied military campaign that eventually defeated the Ottoman forces.

It was only with the end of Ottoman rule over the Arab provinces that significant numbers of their inhabitants began to see themselves as Arabs in a new national sense, though that identity was never uniform, uncomplicated, or uncontested. Arab nationalist hopes for independence and unity were soon frustrated as the victorious Allies reneged on their wartime promises and instead divided the former Ottoman Arab provinces into several new states ruled by Britain or France as "mandates," which their new subjects accurately perceived as a thinly disguised form of colonialism. Arab nationalists held fast to their vision of a unified Arab nation; yet over time distinctive national identities (Syrian, Lebanese, Iraqi, Palestinian, and so on) took root in these new states, often in tension with a widespread and persistent but contingent sense of common pan-Arab identity. This tension was further complicated by the fact that many of the new "Arab" states contained substantial minorities that were either non-Arab (e.g., the Kurds in Iraq) or non-Muslim (e.g., Christians in Lebanon), or came to be dominated by minority groups (e.g., the Alawites in Syria, the Sunnis in Iraq).

As the eastern Arab lands won independence from colonial rule in the 1930s and 1940s and many Egyptians began to see their country as part of a wider Arab world, the question of Arab unity came to take center stage. The League of Arab States, established in 1945, proved ineffectual, and in the 1950s the cause of Arab unity was championed by a new pan-Arabist movement based in Syria and Iraq (the *Ba'th*, from an Arabic term for "renaissance") and by the new regime in Egypt led by Gamal Abdel Nasser (1918–1970). Despite the rhetorical commitment of key Arab leaders to pan-Arab unity, however, the only real experiment in unification—the merger of Egypt and Syria into the United Arab Republic in 1958 under Nasser's leadership—foundered after just three years. Israel's victory in the June 1967 Arab-Israeli War was a major defeat for the radical Arab nationalism espoused by both Nasser and his Ba'thist rivals. Thereafter, Pan-Arabism as a political project went into decline, sidelined by authoritarian regimes (whether monarchical or republican) concerned mainly with their own survival and rejected by the Islamist movements that emerged as those regimes' main opposition.

Nonetheless, thanks to transnational migration, the spread of literacy and mass communications, and more recently pan-Arab satellite television broadcasting, many Arabic speakers today participate in a common cultural-political field in which the same cultural products are consumed and what are perceived to be common problems are addressed, including autocracy, economic underdevelopment, social inequality, the plight of the Palestinians, and U.S. hegemony and intervention. As a result, despite the continuing salience of separate state nationalisms, distinctive local forms of spoken Arabic, the deep divisions within the Arab world, and its failure to achieve even a modicum of equitable economic integration, much less pan-Arab political unity, a variable and contingent but nonetheless significant sense of common Arab identity (and sometimes solidarity) persists.

SEE ALSO *Nationalism and Nationality; Pan-Africanism*

BIBLIOGRAPHY

Jankowski, James, and Israel Gershoni, eds. 1997. *Rethinking Nationalism in the Arab Middle East.* New York: Columbia University Press.

Kayali, Hasan. 1997. *Arabs and Young Turks: Ottomanism, Arabism, and Islamism in the Ottoman Empire, 1908–1918.* Berkeley: University of California Press.

Khalidi, Rashid. 1991. Arab Nationalism: Historical Problems in the Literature. *American Historical Review* 96 (5): 1363–1373.

Khalidi, Rashid, Lisa Anderson, Muhammad Muslih, and Reeva S. Simon, eds. 1991. *The Origins of Arab Nationalism.* New York: Columbia University Press.

Zachary Lockman

PAN-CARIBBEANISM

The emergence of Pan-Caribbeanism—a movement dedicated to regional economic and political integration—can only be understood in the context of the Caribbean's history, from plantation system and slavery, to anti-colonialist struggles and eventual independence. The attempt to integrate the region economically and politically dates back to the eighteenth century, when British colonial authorities sought confederation of the Leeward Islands. Other attempts occurred in the late nineteenth century and early twentieth century, but met with no success. Indeed, no serious consideration of West Indian Federation was made until the mid-1940s.

Some scholars suggest that the idea of the West Indian Federation originated with colonial officials and that federation was thought of as a way of reducing the cost of governing the colonies. Other analysts believe that the plan was hatched by West Indians living in the region and abroad, and was intended as a transitional phase leading to independence. Whoever was behind the idea of the British West Indies Federation, it was conceived as an attempt to centralize the economy and political administration of the region. Prominent West Indians, including businessmen, union leaders, and local politicians, saw the plan as a viable solution to the challenging economic situation facing the region. It was not, however, until the Montego Bay conference of 1947 that serious consideration was given to federation. A combination of factors contributed to Britain's stronger interest in the plan. First, between the two World Wars, Great Britain had experienced a series of setbacks that had forced the reorganization of its empire and the loss of some of its colonies. Independence movements in Australia, Canada, New Zealand, the Union of South Africa, India, and other British colonies were exerting pressure on the home government. Second, the West Indian colonies had seen widespread disturbances and rebellions by workers during the 1930s, and labor union leaders were becoming increasingly militant. West Indian workers' demands included better working conditions, better salaries, universal suffrage, self-government, and federation. British colonial officials saw these demands as necessitating changes in colonial policy.

West Indian leaders, however, were suspicious of British intentions. As a result, it took several meetings over a ten-year period for all concerned parties to even agree on an agenda. These meetings and dispatches from West Indian leaders and British colonial officials reveal the frustration and ambivalence of many of the proponents of federation. The Moyne Commission report of 1940 exposed the persistent economic neglect experienced by the British West Indies, but argued that the islands were not ready for economic federation. Indeed, federalism was never presented as a viable path to the economic and political development of the region; it was simply a way to cover up for failed colonial policy. It was also perceived by West Indians as a British attempt to sabotage the decolonization process.

In 1956 a conference was convened in London in which it was debated whether the federation would facilitate the eventual achievement of the islands' self-government. Some argued that if Britain accepted the idea of a federation, it would surrender its imperial authority. Despite the debate, a federal constitution was drafted. It established that the unit members of the federation would be under the mandate of a governor-general appointed by the crown. The government would consist of a prime minister, a cabinet, a council of state, a house of representatives—in which the number of representatives from any given island would be based on that island's population—and a senate. Trinidad was selected as the federal capital.

The West Indian Federation took effect in 1958. It included the islands of Antigua and Barbuda, Barbados, Dominica, Grenada, Jamaica, Montserrat, Saint Kitts-Nevis-Anguilla, Saint Lucia, Saint Vincent, and Trinidad and Tobago.

From its conception to its implementation, the West Indian Federation was destined to fail. Some analysts observe that the federation of fifteen scattered islands, separated by hundred of miles, was an inherently difficult process. These islands' leaders also had to overcome insular attitudes and regionalism. More importantly, the real test of the federation was whether the larger islands were prepared to help the smaller islands escape their desperate economic plight. Unfortunately, the weak economy of the smaller islands became a burden for Jamaica and Trinidad. Some have suggested that federation failed because narrow nationalism prevailed over Pan-Caribbeanism. The call for federation emerged at a time when some of the islands were caught up in intense nationalist fervor. For example, achieving national independence dominated the agenda of Jamaica's People's National Party (PNP), despite party leader Norman Manley's support for federation. As a result, neither the PNP nor the Jamaican people embraced federalism. Nationalism also exacerbated tensions between Trinidad and Jamaica. The Jamaicans expressed their discontent with the federal constitution and with representation in the federal parliament. Jamaica, with a population of 1.5 million, held seventeen seats—whereas Trinidad, with 750,000 inhabitants, held seven seats, and Barbados, with 230,000 inhabitants, had five seats. Nationalist fervor in Jamaica pushed the Jamaica Labour Party, led by Alexander Bustamante, to call for a referendum, and in 1961 Jamaicans decided to leave the federation. Inevitably, with Jamaica's withdrawal from the federation, Trinidad decided there was no reason for it to remain either at a time when its economy was taking off.

The withdrawal of the largest islands from the federation stalled progress for the rest of the islands. Economic integration was achieved by the creation of a less ambitious organization called the Caribbean Free Trade Area (CARIFTA), which later was transformed into the Caribbean Community (CARICOM). In 1962 the West Indian Federation was dissolved. After its dissolution, there was some discussion of creating an Eastern Caribbean Federation, with Trinidad as the leading country. Arthur Lewis, then the vice-chancellor of the University of West Indies, led discussions with Trinidadian Premier Eric Williams, British colonial officials, and the rest of the leaders of the islands involved about forming this new federation. However, when the scheme was welcomed in London, Williams decided to take Trinidad out of the proposed federation.

The West Indian Federation lasted for less than four years, but despite its brief existence it strengthened West Indians' yearning for political independence. The dissolved federation triggered a movement toward independence in the British West Indies, including the separation of the University of the West Indies from the University of London. Regardless of whether the West Indian Federation was an attempt to paper over the shortcomings of British colonial policy or a failed attempt to create regional cooperation, it helped lead to the decolonization of the Caribbean.

SEE ALSO *Caribbean, The; Federalism; Lewis, W. Arthur; Nationalism and Nationality; Williams, Eric*

BIBLIOGRAPHY

Augier, F. R. 1989. Federations: Then and Now. *Caribbean Quarterly* 35 (3): 16–23.

Campbell, Jock. 1963. The West Indies: Can They Stand Alone? *International Affairs* 39 (3): 335–344.

Hurwitz, Samuel J. 1966. The Federation of the West Indies: A Study in Nationalisms. *Journal of British Studies* 6 (1): 139–168.

James, C. L. R. 1933. *The Case for West-Indian Self-Government*. London: Hogarth Press.

Killingray, David. 2000. The West Indian Federation and Decolonization in the British Caribbean. *Journal of Caribbean History* 34 (1–2): 71–87.

Knight, Franklin W. 1990. *The Caribbean: The Genesis of a Fragmented Nationalism*. 2nd ed. New York: Oxford University Press.

Lewis, Gordon K. 1957. The British Caribbean Federation: The West Indian Background. *Political Quarterly* 28 (1): 49–65.

Lewis, Gordon K. 1968. *The Growth of the Modern West Indies*. New York: Modern Reader Paperback.

Proctor, Jesse H., Jr. 1957. The Development of the Idea of Federation of the British Caribbean Territories. *Caribbean Quarterly* 5 (1): 5–33.

Schneider, Fred D. 1959. British Policy in West Indian Federation. *World Affairs Quarterly* 30 (3): 241–265.

Skelton, Tracey, ed. 2004. *Introduction to the Pan-Caribbean*. New York: Arnold Publishers.

Springer, Hugh W. 1962. Federation in the Caribbean: An Attempt That Failed. *International Organization* 16 (4): 758–775.

Wallace, Elizabeth. 1996. The Break-Up of the British West Indies Federation. In *Caribbean Freedom: Economy and Society from Emancipation to the Present*, eds. Hilary Beckles and Verene Shepherd, 455–475. Princeton, NJ: Markus Wiener Publishers.

Williams, Eric. 1970. *From Columbus to Castro: The History of the Caribbean, 1492–1969*. New York: Harper & Row.

Williams, Eric. 1973. A New Federation for the Commonwealth Caribbean? *Political Quarterly* 44 (3): 242–256.

Milagros Denis

PANEL STUDIES

A panel study is a type of nonexperimental longitudinal study design that samples (using random or stratified random methods) a population to identify a set of respondents, then recontacts the *same* respondents repeatedly over time. A traditional panel study differs from a trend study in that a trend study samples the same population repeatedly but with *different* respondents at each time point. A panel study is similar to a traditional epidemiologic cohort study in that a sample or cohort is followed over time. However, the purpose of following participants in a traditional cohort study is to allow enough time to be able to observe a particular outcome and determine how exposure to a certain variable is associated with the outcome. In contrast, the purpose of following participants in a panel study is typically to observe changes on a particular variable over time to potentially relate those changes to an outcome of interest or explain what factors may lead to the changes in the variable over time. Thus, a panel study often includes multiple measurements of variables, usually at regular intervals, over a circumscribed period of time.

Compared to other nonexperimental study designs such as case-control or cross-sectional studies, a carefully conducted panel study can strengthen the case for inferring causation because temporality (i.e., the cause precedes the effect in time) is more accurately preserved. In panel studies, a researcher is also able to determine the strength of an association between an explanatory variable and an outcome. However, specificity or the degree to which a cause leads to a single effect is not as high as it is in a randomized controlled trial or experimental study. Thus, in panel studies statistical controls for group non-equivalence are often employed. A further advantage of panel studies is that they allow for complex statistical modeling of dynamic phenomena (e.g., latent growth modeling and other types of trajectory analyses) that may more accurately reflect reality.

One primary disadvantage of panel studies is the problem of selective attrition over time. Participants who remain in the panel over time may be qualitatively different from the participants who are lost to follow-up due to relocation, lack of interest, or death. Another disadvantage is that panel studies can be quite costly as they require measurements at multiple time points, and tracking highly mobile respondents can be a challenge. Panel studies are strengthened when the measurement protocol or instrument remains the same over time. However, this can be difficult to maintain because of emerging technological advances in instruments or measurements or the difficulty in measuring the same phenomena during developmentally different phases of life. A change in the measurement protocol or instrumentation makes it difficult to determine if an observed change in the data is the result of measurement protocol changes or of actual changes. Finally, panel surveys can also be fatiguing to participants, leading to selective attrition, or participants may become primed to the instrument or measurement protocol, leading to atypical responses. Large scale, well-conducted panel studies include the Panel Study of Income Dynamics, National Longitudinal Surveys, the Health and Retirement Survey, the National Longitudinal Study of Adolescent Health, Coronary Artery Risk Development in Young Adults, and the Framingham Heart Study.

SEE ALSO *Data, Longitudinal; Data, Pseudopanel; National Education Longitudinal Study; National Longitudinal Study of Adolescent Health; National Longitudinal Survey of Youth; Panel Study of Income Dynamics; Sample Attrition; Survey; Surveys, Sample*

BIBLIOGRAPHY

Baltagi, Badi H. 2005. *Econometric Analysis of Panel Data.* 3rd ed. West Sussex, U.K.: Wiley.

Institute of Social Research. University of Michigan. Panel Study of Income Dynamics. http://psidonline.isr.umich.edu.

National Heart, Lung, and Blood Institute of the National Institutes of Health. Coronary Artery Risk Development in Young Adults (CARDIA). http://www.cardia.dopm.uab.edu/.

National Heart, Lung, and Blood Institute of the National Institutes of Health. Framingham Heart Study. http://www.nhlbi.nih.gov/about/framingham/index.html.

National Institute on Aging. The Health and Retirement Study. A Longitudinal Study of Health, Retirement, and Aging. http://hrsonline.isr.umich.edu.

University of North Carolina. The National Longitudinal Study of Adolescent Health: AddHealth. http://www.cpc.unc.edu/projects/addhealth/.

U.S. Department of Labor. Bureau of Labor Statistics. National Longitudinal Surveys. http://www.bls.gov/nls.

Bernard F. Fuemmeler

PANEL STUDY OF INCOME DYNAMICS

The Panel Study of Income Dynamics (PSID) is a longitudinal study of a representative sample of U.S. individuals and the families in which they reside. The PSID emphasizes the dynamic aspects of family economics, demography, and health. Data have been collected since 1968, making the PSID the longest running panel on family and individual dynamics. It has consistently achieved response rates of 95 to 98 percent, and as of 2005, 8,041 families were currently participating in the survey. Over the years, the PSID has collected information on nearly 70,000 individuals spanning as much as thirty-seven years of their lives.

Through multiple waves collected over long time periods, these data are the only data ever collected on life course and multigenerational health, well-being, and economic conditions in a long-term panel representative of the full U.S. population. The PSID has collected data on employment, income, housing, food expenditures, transfer income, and marital and fertility behavior annually between 1968 and 1997, and biennially between 1999 and 2005. Additionally PSID collects data on health status, health behaviors, health care utilization, health insurance, and philanthropy. Beginning in 1985 comprehensive retrospective fertility and marriage histories of individuals in the households have been assembled.

The PSID sample, originating in 1968, consists of two independent samples of the U.S. population: a cross-sectional national sample and a national sample of low-income families. The Survey Research Center (SRC) drew the cross-sectional sample (known as the "SRC sample"), which was an equal probability sample of households from the forty-eight contiguous states designated to yield about 3,000 completed interviews. The second sample came from the Survey of Economic Opportunity (SEO) conducted by the Bureau of the Census for the Office of Economic Opportunity. In the mid-1960s, the PSID selected about 2,000 low-income families with heads under the age of sixty from SEO respondents. The PSID core sample combines the SRC and SEO samples.

From 1968 to 1997 the PSID interviewed individuals from families in the core sample every year, whether or not they were living in the same dwelling or with the same people. Adults have been followed as they have grown older, and children have been interviewed as they advance through childhood and into adulthood, forming families of their own. In 1997 the PSID changed from every-year interviewing to every-other-year interviewing. Moreover, a sample of 441 immigrant families was added to enhance the representativeness of the sample.

In 1997 and again in 2002, the PSID supplemented its main data collection with information on PSID parents and their children in order to study the dynamic process of early life experiences. The supplement, called the Child Development Supplement (CDS), included a broad array of development measures, including: (a) age graded assessments of cognitive, behavioral, and health status of children obtained from the caregivers and the child/youth; (b) a comprehensive accounting of parental/caregiver time inputs to children as well as other aspects of the ways in which children and adolescents spend their time; (c) teacher-reported time use in elementary school; and (d) other-than-time use measures of additional resources, for example, the learning environment in the home, teacher reports of school resources, and decennial-census-based measurement of neighborhood resources. In 1997 CDS-I collected data on 3,563 children aged zero to twelve in 2,394 families. Five years later, CDS-II re-interviewed 2,021 of the CDS-I families, providing data on 2,907 CDS children and youth.

In calendar year 2005 alone over 5,500 unique users (i.e., unique IP addresses) downloaded more than 32,000 data sets from the PSID Data Center. The PSID Web site received over 1.6 million hits in 2005. Since its inception, over 2,000 journal articles, books, book chapters, and dissertations have been based on the PSID, and today a paper is published in a peer-reviewed outlet roughly every four days. The study was named one of the National Science Foundation's (NSF) "Nifty Fifty," the most notable NSF-funded inventions and discoveries in NSF history, 1950–2000.

It is difficult to briefly summarize the scientific impact of the PSID. Additional detail is provided on the PSID Web site. Areas of significant contribution include intergenerational transmission of economic status, children's time use, the dynamics of poverty and economic status, resource sharing among extended family members, the interconnection between well-being and marriage and fertility, and neighborhood effects on individual social and economic outcomes.

SEE ALSO *National Assessment of Educational Progress; National Family Health Surveys; National Longitudinal Study of Adolescent Health; National Longitudinal Survey of Youth; Survey; Surveys, Sample*

BIBLIOGRAPHY

Altonji, Joseph G., Fumio Hayashi, and Laurence Kotlikoff. 1992. Is the Extended Family Altruistically Linked? Direct Tests Using Micro Data. *The American Economic Review* 82 (5): 1177–1198.

Brooks-Gunn, Jeanne, et al. 1993. Do Neighborhoods Influence Child and Adolescent Development? *American Journal of Sociology* 99 (2): 353–395.

Gottschalk, Peter, and Robert Moffitt. 1994. The Growth of Earnings Instability in the U.S. Labor Market. *Brookings Papers on Economic Activity* 2: 217–272.

Hofferth, Sandra L., and John F. Sandberg. 2001. How American Children Spend Their Time. *Journal of Marriage and the Family* 63 (2): 295–308.

McLanahan, Sara, and Gary Sandefur. 1994. *Growing Up with a Single Parent: What Hurts, What Helps.* Cambridge, MA: Harvard University Press.

Solon, Gary. 1992. Intergenerational Income Mobility in the United States. *The American Economic Review* 82 (3): 393–408.

Robert F. Schoeni

PANIC

The term *panic* is used with a vast variety of meanings by the population at large, as well as by professionals and research scientists in different disciplines. For example, economists talk of financial or stock market panics, scholars of popular culture discuss moral panics or widespread public anxieties about deviant behaviors, and journalists sometime refer to certain kinds of hoarding or buying activities as an expression of panicky behavior. However, this entry confines itself to the two major usages of the term in the scientific and professional literature, which have little to do with the examples just given.

Even the two major usages differ. Along one line, there is an identification of panic with certain kinds of overt behavior by a number of people, such as rapid physical flight from a situation perceived as highly and personally dangerous to individuals in the collectivity involved. Sociologists have primarily used the term this way, and to a lesser extent so have psychologists. The other use of the term has reference to a mental state characterized by a sudden and extreme anxiety attack, with the person being unable to perceive any obvious reason for the reaction. Psychiatrists and other mental health professionals, who have been the primary students of this phenomenon, call it *panic disorder*.

Apart from using the same term, *panic*, there is otherwise very little in common between the two approaches. Interest in and study of the phenomena have had radically different origins and have involved different kinds of research by different specialties. In addition, the end goal of the research has differed. Those looking at panic disorder have increasingly come to believe that the mental problem can be dealt with through therapeutic and other measures. Those interested in flight behavior initially thought that understanding such behavior would be useful for disaster planning and crisis management purposes. However, as more empirical studies of disasters have been undertaken, many researchers have increasingly argued that the very concept of panic should be abandoned as a useful concept for scientific research. They argue that what occurs can be much better understood through other concepts, such as social roles and social relationships.

PANIC AS A SUBTYPE OF ANXIETY DISORDER

Panic disorder involves unexpected and repeated episodes of intense anxiety attacks accompanied by physical symptoms that may include chest pain, shortness of breath, heart palpitations, abdominal distress, trembling, dizziness, and a sense of unreality. An attack generally peaks within ten minutes, although some symptoms may last much longer. Many of those suffering from the disorder develop intense anxiety between episodes because they worry when and where the next one will strike. Routines of everyday life can be totally disrupted.

According to the U.S. National Institute of Mental Health, in any given year 1.7 percent of the American population will have a panic disorder. Females are twice as likely as males to develop panic disorders. Panic disorder usually occurs in early adulthood. Roughly half of all people who have panic disorder develop the condition before the age of twenty-four. Such statistics ought to be treated with caution, however; panic attacks are sometimes misdiagnosed and missed because many of the symptoms resemble heart attacks. Also, not everyone who experiences a panic attack will develop panic disorder; people can experience one attack but never have another.

What exactly causes the disorder is unknown. Heredity is probably involved, since the disorder seems to run in families. But there is also evidence that very stressful life events are a factor.

Fortunately, two types of treatment are available for panic disorder. There are medications that can keep symptoms under control as long as the prescribed medication is used. There are also specific kinds of psychotherapy that can teach sufferers how to view panic attacks differently, as well as ways to deal with the anxiety between attacks. Reports on success rates vary considerably, but it appears that a majority of those treated are helped. However, since panic disorder often coexists with other disorders and physical ailments, restoration to a less stressful life is also dependent on treatment of these other problems. Information on panic disorder and its treatment is available on the Internet, but care should be taken to insure that such reports are from legitimate medical sources.

PANIC FLIGHT AS A FORM OF COLLECTIVE BEHAVIOR

In the 1920s, sociologists interested in the study of collective behavior (which looks at nontraditional or emergent behavior) began discussing instances of panic in certain risky situations, such as a fire in a crowded theater. The prevailing idea was that panic involved extreme and groundless fear that spread in a contagion-like way, resulting in irrational flight behavior, with individuals trampling one another. This view of panic is still commonly depicted in disaster movies and television shows.

However, the emergence of systematic disaster studies in the mid-twentieth century led to some reformulations about the nature of panic and the conditions necessary for its emergence. Research has shown that panic flight, while not unknown, is extremely rare in disasters and similar kinds of crises. The notion that panic behavior spreads through contagion has been widely discredited. The behavior is not irrational from the viewpoint of those involved. There is no evidence that certain kinds of people are more likely to flee in panic. At worst, panic is asocial rather than antisocial in that people do not regress to an animal-like response.

Panic flight also occurs only under specific conditions. Potential participants must believe that there is an immediate and certain risk to their own life. Contrary to stereotypic views, flight will not be attempted if there is a belief that one is completely trapped. In other words, there must be hope that escape is possible. Persons who break in panic know what they are afraid of, and they are moving away from a specific location (in contrast to a stampede, which involves convergence). It is fear, not anxiety, that prevails. Finally, what others are doing around a person is crucial. This social interaction can work both ways, but usually reinforces a tendency not to flee.

SEE ALSO *Anxiety; Psychotherapy; Psychotropic Drugs*

BIBLIOGRAPHY

Aguirre, Ben. 2005. Emergency Evacuations, Panic, and Social Psychology. *Psychiatry* 68 (2): 121–129.

Johnson, Norris. 1987. Breakdown of Social Order: Popular Myth, Social Theory, Empirical Evidence. *Sociological Focus* 20: 171–183.

National Institute of Mental Health. 1999. Facts About Panic Disorders. http://www.nimh.nih.gov/publicat/panicfacts.cfm.

National Institute of Mental Health. 2000. Anxiety Disorders. http://www.nimh.nih.gov/publicat/anxiety.cfm.

Quarantelli, Enrico. 2001. Sociology of Panic. In *International Encyclopedia of the Social and Behavioral Sciences*, eds. Neil Smelser and Peter Baltes, 11020–11023. Oxford: Elsevier.

Enrico L. Quarantelli

PANICS

Panics are social-psychological reactions to fear. Financial panics occur when investors react to the fear of capital losses by dumping assets, thus causing the collapse of a financial institution or financial market. *Moral panics*, as Stanley Cohen (1972) coined the term, are situations in which the public expresses not fear but righteous indignation in opposition to a deviant activity of a subgroup, perceived to threaten society and its values. As either social-psychological reactions or financial events, panics are commonly thought to evoke irrational escape-mob behavior—such as stampeding to escape a threatening situation—when rationally one would have less chance of injury with an orderly exit.

Exits in financial panics involve the mass conversion of real or less-liquid financial assets into liquid (or more-liquid) assets, typically money instruments. A sudden high volume of selling—as investors scramble to escape further anticipated capital losses—can abruptly depress or cause a "crash" in the price of illiquid assets. Financial panics known as *bank runs* entail the mass withdrawal of bank deposits precipitated by a fear that the bank may be unable to meet such a demand in the future. The bank run may be either a *lobby run*—with retail depositors lining up to convert bank deposits into cash—or it may be an attempt by wholesale and other institutional depositors to transfer funds out electronically. Such fears of illiquidity can, by forcing a distress sale of assets to meet liquidity demands, cause illiquidity and insolvency. As in all financial panics, a fear that the event will happen motivates action that increases the likelihood of the feared event occurring.

A run on a bank that forces insolvency and the suspension of credit facilities, or a market crash that impedes the operation of a significant financial market, heightens the risk of an economic crisis. The breakdown of a market or the sudden withdrawal of credit can adversely affect, on a large scale, the day-to-day commercial operations of organizations in the nonfinancial sectors of the economy. As Milton Friedman and Anna Schwartz (1963) suggest in their explanation of the Great Depression of the 1930s,

financial panics can precede, both temporally and causally, economic crises in employment, production, and trade—crises that may extend well beyond the boundary of the original panic. The possibility exists, however, that causality runs instead from economic activity out to money and credit, as Peter Temin (1976) suggests. The historical evidence is sufficiently ambiguous to leave scope for much debate.

Theories of panics as the manifestation of a "crowd mind" turn on whether the observed collective behavior is contagious, convergent, or emergent. Theories of financial panics parallel loosely these psychosocial theories of panics, though such links most often appear only in motivational narratives.

The idea of a distinct crowd mind was introduced in 1895 by Gustave Le Bon with his psychological law of mental unity. Le Bon posited a view of the crowd as distinctly different from the individuals composing it. Through contagion—the spread of behavior from one participant to another—a distinct and distinctly irrational collective mind is formed. Special characteristics of crowds include "impulsiveness, irritability, incapacity to reason, the absence of judgment and of the critical spirit, the exaggeration of the sentiments, and others besides" (Le Bon 1896, bk. 1, chap. 2, p.17). In contagion theories of panics, the "individual" is lost, transformed into a member of a "herd," acting irrationally in the common-sense meaning of the term articulated above.

Douglas Diamond and Philip Dybvig (1983), in the tradition of Friedman and Schwartz, model bank runs as an equilibrium outcome of random withdrawal and contagious panic. In their model, a sufficiently large withdrawal of bank deposits can threaten bank liquidity, spark a fear of insolvency, and thus trigger a bank run that in the absence of deposit insurance or some other means to ensure reimbursement will yield the feared outcome.

Rejecting Le Bon, Floyd Allport (1924) posited that the crowd mind was simply the aggregated, possibly intensified, feelings of individual participants subjected to the same external stimulant. Like-minded people converge to a crowd rationally in the sense that the crowd mind is wholly consistent with independent individual preferences. Unlike contagion theories, no transformation takes place, and observed similarities across crowd participants cause the collective, not vice versa.

Some authors have attempted to explain financial panics as the result of rational convergent behavior on the part of individuals who fear bank-system insolvency because of some external financial shock. Charles Calomiris and Joseph Mason (1997), for example, suggest that when depositors can observe a financial shock that threatens bank portfolios but cannot identify which banks are at risk, they run collectively on all banks. This asymmetric information theory of bank runs as financial panics is, like Allport's symbolic convergent theory of crowd minds, "rational" in the sense that the collective run on banks is nothing more than prior shared motivations resulting in the clustering of like-minded depositors acting similarly.

As a third explanation of the crowd mind, the emergent norm theory of Ralph Turner and Lewis Killian (1987) permits convergence insofar as similarities draw people together. But Turner and Killian suggest that there is then the emergence of distinct collective features when unusual situations challenge traditional norms and social interactions shape crowd behavior.

Brenda Spotton Visano (2006) explicitly links the emergent norm theory of crowd mind to a socioeconomic explanation of financial panics. In a framework that adopts a credit theory of the business cycle similar to that which grounds Charles Kindleberger's (1989) historical study of manias and panics, the panic emerges in a demoralized environment created by the combination of prevailing financial distress and a sudden actual loss of liquidity.

All agree that financial panics involve a substantial and typically abrupt change in asset liquidity. All agree as well that the beliefs of depositors motivate behavior that is self-fulfilling. The debate is over which theory best explains a given financial panic, with history again sufficiently ambiguous, leaving the question wide open for debate.

SEE ALSO *Banking; Bubbles; Economic Crises; Great Tulip Mania, The; Manias*

BIBLIOGRAPHY

Allport, Floyd. 1924. *Social Psychology.* Boston: Houghton Mifflin.

Calomiris, Charles W., and Joseph R. Mason. 1997. Contagion and Bank Failures During the Great Depression: The June 1932 Chicago Banking Panic. *The American Economic Review* 87 (5): 863–883.

Cohen, Stanley. 1972. *Folk Devils and Moral Panics: The Creation of the Mods and Rockers.* London: MacGibbon and Kee.

Diamond, Douglas, and Philip Dybvig. 1983. Bank Runs, Liquidity, and Deposit Insurance. *Journal of Political Economy* 91 (3): 401–419.

Friedman, Milton, and Anna Jacobson Schwartz. 1963. *A Monetary History of the United States, 1867–1960.* Princeton, NJ: Princeton University Press.

Kindleberger, Charles P. 1989. *Manias, Panics, and Crashes: A History of Financial Crises.* Rev. ed. New York: Basic Books.

Le Bon, Gustave. [1895] 1896. *The Crowd: A Study of the Popular Mind.* http://etext.virginia.edu/toc/modeng/public/BonCrow.html.

Spotton Visano, Brenda. 2006. *Financial Crises: Socio-economic Causes and Institutional Context.* London: Routledge.

Temin, Peter. 1976. *Did Monetary Forces Cause the Great Depression?* New York: Norton.

Turner, Ralph H., and Lewis M. Killian. 1987. *Collective Behavior.* 3rd ed. Englewood Cliffs, NJ: Prentice-Hall.

Brenda Spotton Visano

PAPACY

SEE *Vatican, The.*

PARADIGM

A *paradigm* is a template, model, or framework. Paradigms can be used to create new objects, just as templates can be used as patterns when outlining or designing something new. In fact, the word *paradigm* has its roots in the Greek term for a side-by-side comparison. Within the philosophy of science, a paradigm is a general but distinct worldview or theory. The history of science is characterized by paradigm shifts.

The seminal work on paradigm shifts is that of Thomas Kuhn (1922–1996). His 1962 monograph, *The Structure of Scientific Revolutions,* described what is essentially a form of nonlinear progress within the sciences. Put simply, during phases of what Kuhn called "normal science," individuals working in a scientific field share assumptions, perspectives, and methods, and knowledge accumulates in a linear fashion. There is progress, but all of the knowledge and information is constrained by the same set of premises and assumptions. It is in this sense that it is conceptually linear. Eventually the assumptions are brought into question and the inadequacies and limitations of the theories being used are recognized. At that point one or more assumptions may be questioned, and new empirical results may be difficult or impossible to explain. It is not just one theory or method that is inadequate; instead, the fundamental assumptions of a field are brought into question. A bit later an alternative perspective or paradigm is introduced that is so dramatically different from what came before it that the shift is clearly not just an extension of what came before, but a fundamental and overarching change within the field. Examples of major paradigm shifts underscore the magnitude of these paradigm shifts: Einstein's theory of relativity is enormously different from the Newtonian physics that preceded it; Copernicus initiated a revolution of a similar magnitude; Darwin changed the way biologists thought about the Homo sapiens, and stimulated modern reconsideration of humanity's role within nature.

In his review of paradigm shifts in the 1999 *Encyclopedia of Creativity*, Thomas Nickles suggested that research produced within a paradigm is highly convergent, whereas that produced when a shift between paradigms is occurring is highly divergent. Convergent thinking is not very original nor creative. It involves finding conventional or correct answers and solutions to fairly well-defined questions and problems. Divergent thinking, in contrast, is often original and creative. It involves exploring new options; the thinking moves in different and often original and unconventional directions. Various theories of divergent thinking are also described in the *Encyclopedia of Creativity* (Runco 1999).

Kuhn (1963) also referred to the convergent and divergent thinking involved in normal science and in paradigm shifts. He felt there was "an essential tension" between them, and one that stimulated creative thinking as well as paradigm shifts. Kuhn wrote: "Something like convergent thinking is just as essential to scientific advance as is divergent. Since those two modes of thought are inevitably in conflict, it will follow that the ability to support tension that can occasionally become almost unbearable is one of the prime requisites for the very best sort of scientific research" (1963, p. 342).

Paradigm shifts introduce new rules and new problem-solving techniques. In fact, they often introduce new problems as well as solutions. This may sound odd, but such problem discovery is distinct from problem solving, and is an important part of the creative process. Psychologists studying creativity even include problem-finding skills as part of the creativity complex. There is more to paradigm shifts: They also introduce new taxonomies, new classifications of the phenomena under study, and new ideas. Significantly, much of the new thinking that characterizes new paradigms is preconscious. Indeed, many of the differences between paradigms (e.g., Newton's and Einstein's) reflect assumptions, which of course are by definition not consciously processed.

Nickles used two tree metaphors to describe the reclassifications that occur during normal science and those that occur during paradigm shifts. The former can be viewed as branching, where new findings and ideas suggest additional specific branches to the tree of knowledge (or perhaps remove an old branch). The research on creative thinking can itself be used as an example. At one point, creative thinking was equated with problem solving. That was the tree, so to speak, and new theories merely identified new kinds of problem solving. Then behavioral scientists realized that thinking is often the most creative when the individual actually identifies a new problem, rather than merely solves an existing problem. Nickles referred to this kind of breakthrough as "tree switching" because an entirely new tree—not just a new branch—is introduced. In dramatic paradigm shifts such as Einstein's, the old tree is completely dismissed. Nickles gave Mendeleev's theory of the periodic table of elements and Darwin's theory of evolution as examples of tree switching and true paradigm shifts.

Kuhn himself described normal science as progressing by working with exemplars. The basic idea here is that problem solving during a period of normal science depends on identifying similarities among problems and questions; and once the similarity is identified, a solution (which is itself analogous to previous solutions) is suggested. Kuhn even applied this to science education, where instruction and the curriculum rely on exemplars, analogies, and similarities. Paradigm shifts, in contrast, involve what Kuhn called "new disciplinary matrices." This was Kuhn's way of describing tree switching and entirely new perspectives within the sciences.

Note that disciplinary matrices are, for Kuhn, within the sciences. Indeed, Kuhn's theory of paradigm shifts initially focused on the hard sciences. The example above, concerning problem-solving and -finding extends this to the social and behavioral sciences. But the concept of paradigm shifts is now used much more broadly, even outside the sciences. The idea of paradigm shifts and the suggestion of questioning assumptions and nonlinear progress has proven to be very useful in organizational theory and management, for instance, and a large number of articles and programs outlined in business periodicals tie paradigm shifts to innovation. According to Nickles (1999), political debates and advertisements also regularly refer to paradigm shifts. Whether or not these meet the criteria presented by Kuhn is dubious, but the assumption that dramatic shifts of some sort are useful for creativity and innovation is obviously quite useful.

Criticisms of the theory of paradigm shifts underscore the retrospective and even post hoc method used by Kuhn, as well as the implication that normal science relies so heavily on analogies and "acquired similarity relations" (exemplars). Critics often note that normal science is much more inventive and creative than the original theory of paradigm shifts allowed. Alternative conceptions of scientific progress include the evolutionary perspective whereby changes do occur but they are more linear, perhaps the result of a natural selection process. If this is accurate, progress—even highly creative advance—is more gradual and less sudden than described by paradigm shifts. Of course, the interesting thing here is that the evolutionary perspective is itself an analogy, taken from the biological sciences. Still, it is no doubt useful to recognize that paradigm shifts themselves represent one theoretical framework and one set of assumptions. The theory is enormously useful, but not the final word on progress. If it was the final word, the theory of paradigm shifts would, in a manner of speaking, refute itself.

SEE ALSO *Discourse; Epistemology; Foucault, Michel; Kuhn, Thomas; Mannheim, Karl; Philosophy of Science; Revolutions, Scientific; Science*

BIBLIOGRAPHY

Kuhn, Thomas S. 1962. *The Structure of Scientific Revolutions.* Chicago: University of Chicago Press.

Kuhn, Thomas S. 1963. The Essential Tension: Tradition and Innovation in Scientific Research. In *Scientific Creativity: Its Recognition and Development*, eds. Calvin W. Taylor and Frank Barron, 341–354. New York: Wiley.

Nickles, Thomas. 1999. Paradigm Shifts. In *Encyclopedia of Creativity*, eds. Mark A. Runco and Steven Pritzker, 335–346. San Diego, CA: Academic Press.

Runco, Mark. 1999. Divergent Thinking. In *Encyclopedia of Creativity*, eds. Mark A. Runco and Steven Pritzker, 577–582. San Diego, CA: Academic Press.

Mark A. Runco

PARADOX OF VOTING

The most common form of the paradox of voting refers to a situation where the outcome of majority-rule voting over a discrete set of candidates produces no clear winner, even though each individual voter has a clear and transitive rank ordering of preferences over the alternative options. The paradox is that although individual preferences are transitive, the preferences of the majority are cyclical. Thus, although each individual voter has a most preferred candidate, a "reasonable" majority-rule method of voting produces no clear winner.

To see the paradox at work, consider this example. Adam, Bala, and Chen are three candidates for a position on the school committee. There are three voters, whose preferences are as follows:

First Voter: 1. Adam, 2. Bala, 3. Chen;

Second Voter: 1. Chen, 2. Adam, 3. Bala;

Third Voter: 1. Bala, 2. Chen, 3. Adam.

Who should be declared the winner if each voter declares their rankings? Two out of three voters (First Voter and Second Voter) prefer Adam over Bala. Similarly, two out of three voters (Second Voter and Third Voter) prefer Chen over Adam. Should Chen be declared the winner? Not quite. Two out of three voters (First Voter and Third Voter) prefer Bala over Chen, thereby leading to no clear resolution.

The potential for such a paradox was first noted by the marquis de Condorcet (1743–1794), the French mathematician, philosopher, and social scientist, in his *Essai sur l'application de l'analyse à la probabilité des décisions rendues à la pluralité des voix* (*Essay on the Application of Analysis to the Probability of Majority Decisions*, 1785). The voting method used in the example is the so-called Condorcet method, which can be summarized as follows: First, rank each candidate in order of preference (tied ranking is allowed), and then compare each candidate with every other candidate and find a winner for each pair-wise comparison. The candidate that tallies the biggest wins across all pair-wise comparisons wins the election; however, as suggested by the term *paradox*, there is no guarantee of a winner.

Since Condorcet, other scholars have discussed the paradox and its broader implications, most notably Kenneth Arrow in his seminal work *Social Choice and Individual Values* (1951). Arrow postulated five "rational" and "ethical" criteria that any social-welfare function must meet, and showed that there is no method of aggregating individual preferences over three or more alternatives that satisfies these criteria and always produces a fair and logical result. Much of the work on social choice theory that has followed Arrow's results either validates his conclusions or attempts to find a way around them.

Subsequent authors have attempted to resolve the original paradox of voting in various ways, including one that involves using the Condorcet method first, and if it produces no resolution, then using an alternative such as the "Borda count." In a Borda count, each voter assigns points to candidates in order of his or her preference: If there are n candidates, each voter gives n points to his or her top ranked candidate(s), $n - 1$ points to the second ranked candidate(s), and so on. There are different formulae for assigning points to each voter's preferences, with higher points being assigned to higher ranked candidates. The candidate with the highest number of points aggregated across all voters wins.

Other approaches involve taking a multistage approach to finding a winner. In the first stage, if there is no clear winner, a second voting method is used whereby the candidates are restricted in some way, for example with the smallest set such that every candidate in the set beats all candidates not included in this restricted set (the "Smith set"). Other approaches involve the farsightedness of voters. Ariel Rubinstein (1980) introduced the "stability set," which produces a winner when voters not only make pair-wise comparisons, but also think one step ahead. Yet, Bhaskar Chakravorti (1999) has shown that this notion is itself limited, and if voters do not ignore farsightedness on the part of other voters and are "consistently" farsighted (that is, they can consider comparisons arbitrarily far ahead in the chain), then the paradox returns.

Many alternative voting systems have been proposed to ensure a fair resolution in most practical situations. Common alternatives include run-off elections; approval voting, where voters cast a vote for all the candidates of whom they approve; and the Borda count.

A second version of the paradox of voting is attributed to Anthony Downs (1957). According to Downs's construct, a rational voter will refrain from voting because the costs of voting usually exceed the expected benefits. The probability of casting an election's decisive vote is too small to make the benefits worthwhile, whereas the cost of going out to vote and forgoing other activities is positive and quite tangible. The fact that voters do, indeed, participate in elections to vote is paradoxical, given such a rational calculation. Various theories have been put forward to resolve or explain the Downs paradox. Some have suggested that voters consider factors other than the private cost-benefit analysis to decide whether or not to vote. Some vote because they consider it a responsibility and a social duty, whereas others vote to gain satisfaction from the fact they have registered their preferences in some way, even if it is not decisive, and derive utility from participating in a democratic process.

SEE ALSO *Arrow Possibility Theorem; Arrow, Kenneth J.; Condorcet, Marquis de; Public Choice Theory; Voting*

BIBLIOGRAPHY

Arrow, Kenneth. 1970. *Social Choice and Individual Values.* New Haven, CT: Yale University Press.

Chakravorti, Bhaskar. 1999. Far-Sightedness and the Voting Paradox. *Journal of Economic Theory* 84 (2): 216–226.

Downs, Anthony. 1957. *An Economic Theory of Democracy.* New York: Harper.

Rubinstein, Ariel. 1980. Stability of Decision Systems under Majority Rule. *Journal of Economic Theory* 23: 150–159.

Bhaskar Chakravorti

PARANOIA

Paranoia is a term commonly used to describe people who are preoccupied with the idea that others are "out to get them" or "talking about them." This common usage of the term by the lay public reflects a key feature of the concept in the social and behavioral sciences, particularly in the mental health literature. Constant worry about harm to the self is self-referential thinking. Self-referential thinking is a major feature of the paranoid condition. A paranoid person is also mistrustful, suspicious, and has an exagger-

ated sense of self-importance. These are the basic elements of paranoid thinking. The various ways that paranoia is discussed in the social and behavioral science literature include psychiatric classification, causal theories, and symptom-level approaches.

PSYCHIATRIC CLASSIFICATION

The fourth edition of the *Diagnostic and Statistical Manual of Mental Disorders*, or DSM-IV (American Psychiatric Association 1994), defines *paranoia* as a symptom of mental illness. The DSM-IV includes three types of mental illnesses or syndromes of which paranoia is a significant symptom: paranoid personality disorder, delusional disorder, and paranoid schizophrenia. Paranoid personality disorder involves strong feelings of suspiciousness, jealousy (in romantic relationships), and defensiveness without justification or evidence, but the individual does not have a psychotic illness such as schizophrenia. Delusional disorder is more severe and involves psychotic thinking, but the themes of the delusions are not bizarre. Instead, the themes of the paranoid delusions involve situations that can occur in real life such as a spouse cheating, being poisoned, or contracting an infectious disease. Finally, paranoid schizophrenia is the most severe form of mental illness in this category. The delusions are more bizarre, such as the belief that other people can read the patient's thoughts or take them out of his or her head.

Attempts have been made to conceptualize paranoid personality disorder, delusional disorder, and paranoid schizophrenia as reflecting a continuum from mild to severe psychopathology, respectively. This perspective assumes that the type of delusional symptom defines the relationship between the different types of psychiatric disorders. Genetic studies of patients with delusional disorder using the family history method are one line of research that does not support the continuum perspective (Kendler, Masterson, and Davis 1985; Schanda et al. 1983). Schanda et al. (1983) found that risk for "atypical psychosis" was higher in the first-degree relatives of delusional disorder patients than in those of patients with paranoid schizophrenia. Kendler et al. (1985) found that paranoid personality disorder may have a stronger familial link to delusional disorder than to schizophrenia. These two findings are at odds with the notion that there is greater genetic vulnerability among patients with schizophrenia. Thus it may be more useful to consider paranoid symptoms apart from diagnoses.

CAUSAL THEORIES

Causal theories of paranoia fall into three basic categories: biological, psychological, and social. Biologically, Strider et al. (1985) claim that various neuropsychological impairments such as memory problems and hearing loss associated with brain injuries or the cognitive decline that accompanies old age may engender paranoia because individuals may attribute their inability to find misplaced objects and inaudible conversations to the deliberate attempts of others to keep things from them. Moreover, both clinical and experimental data indicate that injury to the right hemisphere of the brain is more likely to produce paranoid thinking because of the inability verbally to label sensory and emotional experiences (Strider et al. 1985). Thus paranoid thinking may be manifested as a result of damage to the brain.

There may also be a genetic component to paranoia. Genetic studies of patients with delusional disorder using the family history method indicate that the percentage of first-degree relatives (i.e., parents, siblings, or offspring) with schizophrenia ranges from 0 percent to 3 percent and affective disorder ranges from 3 percent to 6 percent (Kendler, Masterson, and Davis 1985; Schanda et al. 1983). Bentall et al. (2001) argued that because diagnoses include multiple symptoms that involve multiple genes, heritability estimates may be higher for diagnoses than for paranoid symptoms alone. Taken together, these findings suggest that paranoid conditions have very limited inheritability, which may manifest differently in various forms of psychopathology.

Classical and modern psychological theories view paranoia as a defense against threats to the self. The classical theory of Freud defines paranoia as an unconscious defense against repressed homosexuality, chronic problems of self-esteem regulation, and sensitivity to narcissistic injury (Bone and Oldham 1994). The idea that paranoia protects against threats to self-esteem is the only aspect of Freudian theory that survives in modern theories of paranoia. Bentall et al. (2001) propose an attribution–self-representation model of persecutory delusions (i.e., paranoia). In their model, individuals make attributions for positive or negative events based on available self-representations stored in memory, which, in turn, influence future attributions in an ongoing cycle. Paranoia occurs when the individual attempts to engage in self-esteem regulation after experiencing a negative event, where the cognitive search does not yield a negative self-representation to explain the event, resulting in a shift to external-personal causes (Bentall et al. 2001). In other words, the person maintains a positive view of the self because those self-representations could not account for the negative event.

Social theories of paranoia emphasize that it is a reaction to threatening environments or inadequate resources (Mirowsky 1985; Marcus 1994). Marcus (1994) extends the psychoanalytic perspective to paranoid tendencies expressed by social groups in organizational contexts. He considers the paranoid reaction in social groups and organizations a manifestation of a survival instinct when there are behavioral constraints on members because of unequally distributed resources that are hidden or protected (Marcus 1994). Mirowsky (1985) proposes a similar theoretical explanation for paranoia in social groups. It is a form of self-protection from exploitation and oppression among social groups that are powerless. He demonstrated that paranoid beliefs in the general population are the product of interactions between feelings of mistrust and exposure to social environments that are threatening (Mirowsky 1985). This may be why paranoia appears to be more common among individuals in the lower social classes and among ethnic/minority groups (Mirowsky 1985; Whaley 1998). Self-protection is a theme that links biological, psychological, and social theories of paranoia. In this way, paranoia may be a coping response that is adaptive. However, extreme paranoia as evidenced in paranoid schizophrenia with no basis in social reality is dysfunctional.

SYMPTOM-LEVEL APPROACHES

Paranoia is not an all-or-none condition. It is best to think of paranoid symptoms as falling on a continuum of severity, with the mild end being represented by suspiciousness, mistrust, and self-consciousness and the severe end represented by delusions of persecution often involving hallucinatory experiences (Fenigstein 1996; Whaley 1998). Both mentally ill patients and normal persons have these types of paranoid tendencies, and the difference between them is a matter of degree or severity (Fenigstein 1996). Whether a person recovers from a mental illness depends more on the diagnosis (e.g., paranoid personality disorder versus schizophrenia) than on the presence of paranoid symptoms. The notion "once paranoid—always paranoid" is not correct; people with paranoid conditions can recover (Retterstol 1991). Finally, the types of cultural experiences that people have may influence whether they exhibit paranoid behaviors.

Immigrants are at increased risk for developing paranoid responses (Kendler 1982). Social groups that have been oppressed or discriminated against such as African Americans also develop paranoid-type coping responses (Whaley 1998). The social and psychological theories of paranoia provide some insight into why this may be the case (Bentall et al. 2001; Marcus 1994; Mirowsky 1985). Under these circumstances, the responses to real threats in the environment or adjustment to new experiences may appear similar to conditions of clinical paranoia, but these expressions often are normative and not pathological. Understanding that paranoia falls on a continuum from mild to severe, as opposed to a symptom that is either present or absent, allows us to appreciate that just because someone is paranoid does not always mean that the person's reaction is sign of mental illness.

SEE ALSO *Coping; Mental Illness; Psychotropic Drugs; Schizophrenia*

BIBLIOGRAPHY

American Psychiatric Association. 1994. *Diagnostic and Statistical Manual of Mental Disorders*. 4th ed. Washington, D.C.: Author.

Bentall, R. P., R. Corcoran, R. Howard, et al. 2001. Persecutory Delusions: A Review and Theoretical Integration. *Clinical Psychology Review* 21: 1143–1192.

Bone, S., and J. M. Oldham. 1994. Paranoia: Historical Considerations. In *Paranoia: New Psychoanalytic Perspectives*, eds. J. M. Oldham and S. Bone, 3–15. Madison, CT: International Universities Press.

Fenigstein, A. 1996. Paranoia. In *Personality Characteristics of the Personality Disordered*, ed. C. G. Costello, 242–275. New York: Wiley.

Kendler, K. K. 1982. Demography of Paranoid Psychosis (Delusional Disorder): A Review and Comparison with Schizophrenia and Affective Illness. *Archives of General Psychiatry* 39: 890–902.

Kendler, K. S., C. C. Masterson, and K. L. Davis. 1985. Psychiatric Illness in First-Degree Relatives of Patients with Paranoid Psychosis, Schizophrenia, and Medical Illness. *British Journal of Psychiatry* 147: 524–531.

Marcus, E. R. 1994. Paranoid Symbol Formation in Social Organizations. In *Paranoia: New Psychoanalytic Perspectives*, eds. J. M. Oldham and S. Bone, 81–94. Madison, CT: International Universities Press.

Mirowsky, J. 1985. Disorder and Its Context: Paranoid Beliefs as Thematic Elements of Thought Problems, Hallucinations, and Delusions under Threatening Social Conditions. In *Research In Community Mental Health*, ed. J. R. Greenley, 5: 185–204. Greenwich, CT: JAI Press.

Retterstol, N. 1991. Course and Outcome in Paranoid Disorders. *Psychopathology* 24: 277–286.

Schanda, H., P. Berner, E. Gabriel, et al. 1983. The Genetics of Delusional Psychosis. *Schizophrenia Bulletin* 9: 563–570.

Strider, M. A., C. Chu, C. Golden, and R. J. Bishop. 1985. Neuropsychological Dimensions of Paranoid Syndromes. *International Journal of Clinical Neuropsychology* 7: 196–200.

Whaley, A. L. 1998. Cross-Cultural Perspective on Paranoia: A Focus on the Black American Experience. *Psychiatric Quarterly* 69: 325–343.

Arthur L. Whaley

PARAPRAXIS

SEE *Psychoanalytic Theory.*

PARDO

Pardo is a Brazilian Portuguese term that translates as the color "brown." It is an official census category used by the Brazilian Institute of Geography and Statistics (IBGE) to refer to all individuals who either self-identify or have been classified by interviewers as not "white" (*branco*) and not "black" (*preto*). It is a term that is not typically heard in speech or social interactions. *Pardo* is an umbrella term that can include all individuals of mixed or multiracial ancestry. It is also a synonym for the term *moreno*, a racially ambiguous term that can refer to all individuals who have black or dark brown hair. Self-identification as *pardo* can reflect ancestry, culture, wealth, education, and socialization.

Pardo is a term used by individuals to "whiten" or "darken" themselves when self-reporting on government census forms. France Winddance Twine (1998) has referred to this practice as "white inflation." *Pardo* is a racially ambiguous term that can be employed by dark-skinned individuals of visible or predominant African ancestry who possess forms of educational, social, or economic capital to avoid being classified as black (*preto*). The term *pardo* can also be used by all individuals of predominant or exclusive European ancestry to "darken" themselves. Consequently, individuals who would otherwise be classified as white based on ancestry or appearance but who possess little or no education, wealth, or social capital may self-identify as *pardo* rather than as *blanco* (white).

Terms that indicate color or race have been employed on the Brazilian census since 1940. In 1970 the Brazilian military decided that race was not statistically meaningful, so data related to color or race was not reported for this year. In contrast to the United States and South Africa, the criteria for inclusion in specific racial or color categories has not been legally defined in Brazil. This absence of legal classifications to precisely define race in Brazil facilitates discrepancies between how individuals are classified by appearance and how they may self-identify by race or color on the census and how others would racially classify them in local communities. In statistical analyses of the Brazilian national surveys that involve the self-reporting of race, U.S. sociologist Edward Telles (2002) found that consistency in racial classification varies from 20 to 100 percent depending on age, level of education, sex, and local racial composition. Inclusion in the category *pardo* is based on a combination of physical characteristics such as hair texture, nose shape, lip size and shape, and skin color, as well as achieved social characteristics such as education, occupation, and wealth.

SEE ALSO *Blackness; Colorism; Moreno/a; Negro; Race; Racism; Trigueño; Whiteness; Whitening*

BIBLIOGRAPHY

Telles, Edward. 1995. Who Are the Morenas? *Social Forces* 73 (4): 1609–1611.

Telles, Edward. 2002. Racial Ambiguity among the Brazilian Population. *Ethnic and Racial Studies* 25 (3): 415–441.

Telles, Edward, and Nelson Lim. 1998. Does It Matter Who Answers the Race Question?: Racial Classification and Income Inequality in Brazil. *Demography* 35 (4): 465–474.

Twine, France Winddance. 1998. *Racism in a Racial Democracy: The Maintenance of White Supremacy in Brazil*. New Brunswick, NJ: Rutgers University Press.

France Winddance Twine

PARDO, ITALO
SEE *Anthropology, Urban.*

PARENT-CHILD RELATIONSHIPS

Of all the interpersonal relationships humans develop across their life spans, none is more enduring or important than the parent-child relationship. The nature of the parent-child relationship is a primary factor underlying one's personality, social, and cognitive development. Although there is little debate among family researchers regarding the importance of the parent-child relationship to later adult life, the attributes of a good parent-child relationship are still debated.

HISTORICAL VIEW OF PARENT-CHILD RELATIONSHIP RESEARCH

Throughout most of human history, parents have been concerned primarily with their children internalizing parental values and cultural norms. Thus, parenting was heavily focused on teaching children to be obedient to parental authority and the social and religious order through strict discipline and harsh punishments for disobedience. Most parent-child relationship research has focused on explaining the ways in which parents achieve these goals.

Behaviorists in the early part of the twentieth century argued that children learn how to behave in a culturally normative way through a series of punishments for unwanted behaviors and rewards for desired behaviors. These reinforcers were posited to lead to the development of behavioral habits in children. The major behaviorists of the time instructed parents not to show too much affection to children because they would develop habits of dependence and weakness. Behaviorists admonished parents who did not maintain firm control and a strict regiment of rules and structure.

Many schools of thought emerged that directly challenged these ideas of emotional distance and harsh punishment. For example, psychodynamic theory was based on the idea that children are born with innate drives and impulses for pleasure and self-fulfillment that may conflict with parental goals. Psychoanalysts suggested that parents learn to channel the energy from children's unmet desires instead of repressing them. This led to the idea that parents should be less rigid, more accepting of children's behavior, and emotionally available to children.

Based primarily on psychodynamic thought, Benjamin Spock (1903–1998) wrote the most influential parenting book in history, *The Common Sense Book of Baby and Child Care* (1945). In it, Spock advocated unconditional love, allowing children freedom to explore their surroundings, and limited use of parental authority. Spock, as well as other psychodynamic theorists, stressed increasing disciplinary reasoning and reducing parental power assertions such as spanking.

The research by Kurt Lewin (1890–1947) in the 1930s on group atmospheres was also influential to later ideas of effective parenting. In one of the most important studies, Lewin and colleagues examined the effects of autocratic, laissez-faire, and democratic leadership styles on preadolescent boys' motivation and behavior. Autocratic leaders were trained to have a rigid structure in which they made all the decisions with little input from group members. Laissez-faire leaders were trained to not provide any structure or direction: The boys had complete freedom to work on their group projects as they saw fit. The democratic leaders were taught to provide structure, make suggestions, and list the goals, but seek input from the boys for most decisions. The results showed that the boys in the democratic group were more motivated and more cooperative, they produced a better final project, and they were more likely to work in a constructive manner when the leader left the room. The boys in the autocratic group produced an adequate final project, but when the leader left the room, chaos ensued. Those in the laissez-faire group produced the worst group project and displayed little interaction or cooperation.

Alfred Baldwin later applied these ideas to parents in the 1940s. In a longitudinal study, Baldwin found that parents he described as emotionally warm and who allowed their children a great deal of freedom had children with the best intellectual development. He argued that emotionally detached, authoritarian parenting was detrimental to children. Separate research into the authoritarian personality around this same time echoed these same concerns.

Probably the most ardent opponents of the behaviorist approach to child rearing were the attachment theorists. Based on ethology, cybernetics, and psychodynamic principles, the groundbreaking theory developed by John Bowlby (1907–1990) and Mary Ainsworth (1913–1999) in the 1950s and 1960s made it explicitly clear that the best parent-child relationship is one in which there is mutual trust, respect, and an emotional bond. Furthermore, the attachment theorists argued that a mother's degree of responsiveness to her infant's needs and demands dictated the nature of the relationship. Highly responsive mothers tended to have infants who formed secure attachments with them. Less responsive mothers tended to have infants with ambivalent, avoidant, or disorganized attachments. A large body of research has shown that those with secure attachments to their primary caregivers tend to have better relationships with others, perform better in school, and are on the whole better adjusted than those with nonsecure attachments.

These different strands of research and theory on authoritarian parenting, psychodynamic theory, attachment theory, and other influential work in humanistic psychology all came to the same basic conclusion—the best parents are emotionally responsive to their children's needs and desires. This new trend in parenting led to the common belief that parents should be less concerned with discipline and child obedience and instead focus on the emotional climate of the relationship, accepting children for who they are, and not stifling their individuality. Although Spock and other psychodynamic theorists warned against spoiling children by avoiding disciplinary encounters and even picking up crying infants too much, and Lewin clearly warned against laissez-faire leaders, many in the general public took this to mean that punishment should give way to unconditional acceptance of child behavior.

This new focus on parental responsiveness and child freedom was in stark contrast to the behaviorist and religious fundamentalist focus on structure, order, and firm discipline. At the heart of this controversy were differing socialization goals. The authoritarian's goals were to have children comply with rules of existing social structures, as well as develop an emotional resiliency that would allow them to handle the challenges of life. Those who focused on parental responsiveness were more concerned with developing children's self-esteem and agency, as well as their cognitive development. Thus, they were fearful of stifling children's potential, whereas authoritarians were fearful of creating emotionally fragile and disobedient children. The political controversies surrounding these opposing views remain as virulent today as ever. However, the influential research on parenting styles by Diana Baumrind and similar models have helped to rectify much of the controversy in mainstream research.

PARENTING STYLES

Probably the most influential research-based parenting theory to date, Baumrind's authoritative model revolutionized the study of parenting when it was first proposed in the 1960s. Based on several studies, principles from behaviorism, psychodynamic theory, attachment theory, Lewin's leadership styles, and critical theoretical contributions from Eleanor Maccoby and John Martin (1983), Baumrind argued that there were four dispositional parenting styles, distinguished by their levels of parental demandingness and parental responsiveness.

According to Baumrind, parental demandingness refers to the degree to which parents facilitate structure in their children's lives, have control of the parent-child relationship, monitor children's behavior and whereabouts, use firm and consistent discipline, set high maturity demands for their children, and are willing to confront noncompliance by children. Based on concepts from attachment theory and psychodynamic theory, Baumrind defined parental responsiveness as the degree to which parents are warm, emotionally connected, and supportive of their children, as well as the amount of freedom and decision-making they allow children, their use of disciplinary reasoning, and their tendency to acquiesce to their children's needs and demands. Baumrind examined both major parenting dimensions simultaneously in defining the authoritarian, permissive, authoritative, and neglectful parenting styles.

Authoritarian parents are defined as being high on demandingness but low on responsiveness. Thus, authoritarian parents attempt to maintain firm parental control by confronting disobedience and restricting the amount of decision-making and general freedom a child has. Authoritarian parents do not usually reason with children or explain the rules, believing that a child should accept the rules without necessarily understanding them. Many have equated this style with certain behaviorist and religious fundamentalist views of parenting.

Permissive parents represent the antithesis of the authoritarian parents. They are low on demandingness and high on responsiveness. They attempt to be emotionally connected and have a warm relationship with their children, and they tend to be accepting of children's impulses and behaviors. Permissive parents also assert very little direct power to get their children to comply with their authority. Instead of direct confrontation, permissive parents often use various forms of psychological control as a means of getting their children to comply. Many have equated the permissive style with Spock's model of optimal parenting.

Authoritative parents essentially combine the best attributes of the authoritarian and permissive parenting ideas. They are high on both demandingness and responsiveness. They value independence in their children, but maintain firm control. Authoritative parents attempt to achieve the goals of behavioral compliance as well as psychological autonomy and agency by judiciously allowing freedom and decision-making in their children, and by giving them age-appropriate maturity demands and structure.

Neglectful parents are low on both demandingness and responsiveness, and they have chaotic and dysfunctional relationships with their children. Whereas the other parenting styles develop primarily from parents' child-rearing goals and philosophy about what is best for children, the neglectful parents' behavior is more a consequence of social circumstances than of philosophy. Neglectful parents tend to have the most children, the least income and education, and more mental health problems than other parents. Consequently, most of their parenting can be explained by dire social circumstances that prevent them from fulfilling their parenting duties.

As Baumrind predicted, European American youth with authoritative parents are more competent, well-adjusted, and high achieving, and less likely to use illicit drugs or engage in risky behaviors compared to those with nonauthoritative parents. In authoritarian homes, boys tend to be aggressive, and girls tend to be low in independence and dominance. Those with permissive parents tend to have problems with self-confidence, impulse control, and achievement. Not surprisingly, those with neglectful parents are at risk for virtually every negative outcome researchers have measured.

CULTURAL DIFFERENCES IN PARENTING STYLES

The research on parenting styles has shed much light on the most effective parenting strategies for European American youth, but the research on other groups is less clear. For instance, European Americans are more likely to have authoritative parents than Asian Americans, and Asian Americans are more likely than European Americans to have authoritarian parents, even though Asian Americans have higher overall academic achievement. Furthermore, some studies in the 1980s and early 1990s found no relation between parenting style and African American youth's academic achievement. Others found that authoritarian parenting was not as detrimental to Asian American and African American youth as it was for European American youth.

Based on these findings, many suggested that the effects of parenting styles could only be understood in a specific cultural context. Often referred to as the "cultural specific model," its proponents argue that African American youth may do better with authoritarian parenting because firm parental control is adaptive in the more dangerous inner cities. Similarly, Ruth Chao (1994) proposed the idea that Baumrind's authoritative model was not a good description of the optimal parenting strategies for Asian American youth because it did not take into consideration the important cultural traits of filial piety, communalism, or other beliefs about expressions of emotion. The basic premise of the cultural specific approach to parenting styles is that the cultural context gives parenting behaviors meaning, so it is not the specific behaviors that matter, but the meaning that youth ascribe to the behaviors.

Counter to this perspective, the cultural equivalence model suggests that the effects of parenting styles are consistent across cultural groups. According to this model, all children, regardless of their ethnic background, gender, or other demographic factors, have the need for warmth, support, connection to others, structure, and autonomy. Consequently, the authoritative parenting practices such as reasonable behavioral control, provisions of emotional support and warmth, and psychological autonomy are important for all children. More recent studies in Asian countries and with African Americans lend support to this idea, finding that those Asian and African American youth with authoritative parents perform better in school and in other areas compared to those with other types of parents.

In conclusion, the study of parent-child relationships has changed dramatically since the beginning of the twentieth century, but many of the same controversies remain. Ultimately, the parenting goals of the authoritarian and the permissive groups are both desirable. Modern parents must find a balance between getting children to conform to parental authority and control their impulses and encouraging them to develop a sense of independence, agency, and critical thinking abilities. However, the empirical evidence is strikingly clear: Both the traditional authoritarian and more modern permissive methods for achieving those goals are limited. A combination of demandingness and responsiveness is best for achieving most pro-social parental goals. Although differences among cultural groups might lead to some variation in effective strategies for rearing children, given children's universal needs for both affection and direction, authoritative parenting is most likely an optimal strategy for rearing all children.

SEE ALSO *Ainsworth, Mary; Attachment Theory; Authority; Baumrind, Diana; Behaviorism; Bowlby, John; Child Development; Children; Developmental Psychology; Leadership; Lewin, Kurt; Norms; Parenthood, Transition to; Parenting Styles; Peer Influence; Spock, Benjamin*

BIBLIOGRAPHY

Baldwin, Alfred L. 1955. *Behavior and Development in Childhood.* New York: Dryden.

Baumrind, Diana. 1971. Current Patterns of Parental Authority. *Developmental Psychology* 4: 1–103.

Baumrind, Diana. 1996. The Discipline Controversy Revisited. *Family Relations: Journal of Applied Family and Child Studies* 45: 405–414.

Bretherton, Inge. 1992. The Origins of Attachment Theory: John Bowlby and Mary Ainsworth. *Developmental Psychology* 28: 759–775.

Chao, Ruth K. 1994. Beyond Parental Control and Authoritarian Parenting Style: Understanding Chinese Parenting through the Cultural Notion of Training. *Child Development* 65: 1111–1119.

Dobson, James. 1992. *The New Dare to Discipline.* Wheaton, IL: Tyndale House.

Grusec, Joan E., and Paul D. Hastings, eds. 2007. *Handbook of Socialization: Theory and Research.* New York: Guilford.

Lamborn, Susie D., and Amanda J. Felbab. 2003. Applying Ethnic Equivalence and Cultural Values Models to African-American Teens' Perceptions of Parents. *Journal of Adolescence* 26: 605–622.

Lewin, Kurt, Ronald Lippitt, and Ralph K. White. 1939. Patterns of Aggressive Behavior in Experimentally Created "Social Climates." *Journal of Social Psychology* 10: 271–299.

Maccoby, Eleanor E., and John Martin. 1983. Socialization in the Context of the Family: Parent Child Interaction. In *Socialization, Personality, and Social Development.* Vol. 4 of *Handbook of Child Psychology,* ed. Paul H. Mussen and E. Mavis Hetherington, 1–101. New York: Wiley.

Spock, Benjamin. 1946. *The Common Sense Book of Baby and Child Care.* New York: Duell, Sloan, and Pearce.

Steinberg, Laurence, Sanford M. Dornbusch, and B. Bradford Brown. 1992. Ethnic Differences in Adolescent Achievement: An Ecological Perspective. *American Psychologist* 47: 723–729.

Jelani Mandara

PARENTHOOD, TRANSITION TO

In many cultures, the transition to parenthood takes place within a traditional marital relationship: When a woman becomes pregnant, she and her husband (or significant other) begin to prepare for the arrival of their new baby. Different cultures and ethnic groups sanction different means and timetables for such preparations, and evolving technologies and changing social norms have diversified the family structure. First-time parents may be single or attached to a same-sex partner; they may be adopting or conceiving using various reproductive technologies or with the help of a surrogate mother. However the child arrives and whatever the parents' age, family structure, socioeconomic status, or ethnicity, new parents face a complex and vital transition into a novel, challenging, and ultimately rewarding life role.

Defining this new role and identifying the principal factors that contribute to a smooth transition can be elusive. Family-systems models identify multiple influences on the adaptation to parenting, including an individual's biological, psychological, and sociological characteristics and those of family members, as well as the relationship between the new parents, between the parents and their extended families, and between the parents and the child. Levels of anxiety or confidence, for example, might be influenced by the new parents' culture, their own parents' parenting styles, and their infant's temperament.

Social support from partners and friends appears to be one key variable in the successful transition to parenthood, particularly for new mothers. New parents must adjust not only to a set of novel responsibilities pertaining to child care, but also to challenges to many aspects of their personality and intelligence, including self-efficacy and personal control, patience and understanding, and problem solving and decision-making. The type of social support available to new parents frequently reflects the contributions of their own families as much as their community and culture. Social support systems function as critical sources of information about parenting and child development.

Parents generally begin the search for information long before the arrival of a baby; information gathering on labor and child care tends to increase in the second and third trimesters of pregnancy. New parents often struggle with anxiety or postpartum depression; education and strong parent partnerships both help to alleviate parental stress. Gathering information about parenting and child development helps new parents gain an understanding of "normal" development and set realistic expectations for their children. Understanding child development also helps improve parent performance and augments parental satisfaction. Information gathering helps individuals prepare psychologically for the coming responsibilities of child care and define their identity as a parent.

Relationships between partners change with the arrival of a child: While satisfaction with the level of emotional support between parents often improves, general marital satisfaction usually declines following a birth. Couples who adopt children rather than bear biological children suffer less deterioration in marital satisfaction, perhaps due in part to the additional preparation and planning that accompanies adoption. Satisfaction with participation in and effectiveness of child care increases as men become comfortable in the role of father and a healthy co-parent partnership develops.

In some couples, maternal and paternal roles follow traditional patterns. This is less common if both parents are employed, and these couples need to arrive at a stable division of labor in the family. Not all parents make the transition well. Adolescent parents in particular have not fully matured themselves and are less likely to have a realistic grasp of child development, further complicating their already demanding transition to parenthood.

Historically, evaluations of parenting have been biased toward the positives of parenthood, sometimes leaving aside the realities of parental feelings of guilt and failure after (inevitable) negative parenting experiences. Parents must continually adjust their parenting; as a child develops, the parent–child relationship changes continually as well. Acknowledging parenthood's challenges and negative aspects signifies a positive change in social attitudes about parenthood. Only full awareness allows adults to prepare properly for the transition.

SEE ALSO *Child Development; Family Functioning; Maturation; Parent-Child Relationships; Parenting Styles*

BIBLIOGRAPHY

Bornstein, Marc H., ed. 2002. *Handbook of Parenting.* 2nd ed. 5 vols. Mahwah, NJ: Erlbaum.

Cowan, Carolyn P., and Philip A. Cowan. 1992. *When Partners Become Parents: The Big Life Change for Couples.* New York: Basic Books.

Demick, Jack. 2002. Stages of Parental Development. In *Handbook of Parenting*, Vol. 3, *Being and Becoming a Parent*, ed. Marc H. Bornstein. 2nd ed., 389–413. Mahwah, NJ: Erlbaum.

Heinicke, Christoph M. 2002. The Transition to Parenting. In *Handbook of Parenting*, Vol. 3, *Being and Becoming a Parent*, ed. Marc H. Bornstein. 2nd ed., 363–388. Mahwah, NJ: Erlbaum.

Michaels, Gerald Y., and Wendy A. Goldberg. 1988. *The Transition to Parenthood: Current Theory and Research.* New York: Cambridge University Press.

Lea Bornstein
Marc H. Bornstein

PARENTING STYLES

Parenting or child rearing styles are parents' characteristic, consistent manner of interacting with their children across a wide range of everyday situations. Research on parenting styles has demonstrated their influence on children's developmental outcomes, including academic skills and achievement, aggression, altruism, delinquency, emotion regulation and understanding, moral internalization, motivation, peer relations, self-esteem, social skills and adjustment, substance abuse, and mental health.

CLASSIFICATION SYSTEMS

Researchers have developed three primary ways of classifying parenting styles. In the late 1950s and early 1960s, Earl Schaefer and Wesley Becker proposed circumplex models of parenting. Their models have in common two independent dimensions proposed as important in understanding parenting style (see Figure 1). One dimension involves parents' emotional or affectionate attitude toward the child; the other, parents' exertion of control over the child's behavior. Because each dimension forms a continuous measure, parents' individual styles may be mapped anywhere within the circumplex.

The system developed by Jeanne Humphries Block in the mid-1960s is multifaceted. Block noted that the structure of parenting or childrearing styles may vary across groups of parents; thus, defining a universal set of parenting dimensions may be neither desirable nor possible. Nonetheless, like Schaefer and Becker, Block's work has identified dimensions related to parental control or restriction of children's behavior, and to parents' emotional attitude or responsiveness to the child. Additionally, Block noted that the degree to which parents find childrearing to be satisfying and are involved with their child, among other dimensions, may be important in understanding parenting styles and their influence on children's outcomes. In the late 1980s, William Roberts and Janet Strayer conducted further work with Block's measurement system that suggested five dimensions: (1) parents' warmth and closeness rather than coolness and distance; (2) parental strictness and use of punishment; (3) parental encouragement of children's boldness and maturity; (4) parents' enjoyment of and involvement in parenting; and (5) parents' encouragement or discouragement of children's emotional expressions. Composition of these dimensions differed somewhat between mothers and fathers.

In the late 1960s, Diana Baumrind formulated a typology including three distinct parenting styles: authoritative, authoritarian, and permissive. These parenting styles vary according to parents' demand that their children meet standards for behavior and their responsiveness to their children's needs. Authoritative parents are high in both demand and responsiveness. They communicate to their children about expectations and standards in a warm and responsive manner. Authoritarian parents are highly demanding but are neither warm nor responsive to their children's behavior. Their expectations and demands are communicated with little to no rationale or warmth. Permissive parents are moderate in responsiveness and warmth and low in demand, tending to accept children's

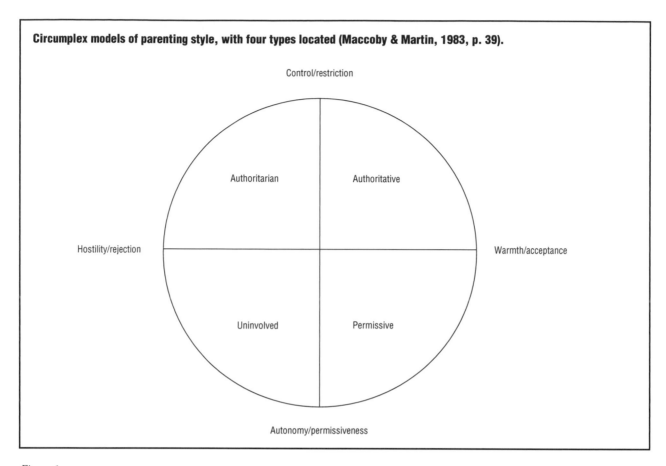

Circumplex models of parenting style, with four types located (Maccoby & Martin, 1983, p. 39).

Control/restriction

Authoritarian   Authoritative

Hostility/rejection   Warmth/acceptance

Uninvolved   Permissive

Autonomy/permissiveness

Figure 1

impulses. There is an absence of parental enforcement of expectations or standards for children's behaviors.

In 1983 Eleanor Maccoby and John Martin integrated extant theory and research and proposed four parenting styles, differing along the two dimensions of control or demand and warmth or responsiveness that are held in common in all three preceding systems and incorporating parental involvement into those dimensions. Maccoby and Martin's reconceptualization proposes three styles similar to Baumrind's typology, and in addition a fourth style, uninvolved or neglectful parenting, which is characterized by both a low degree of parental demand that the child meet behavioral expectations and by low warmth and responsiveness to children's needs (see Figure 1). These parents may appear distant and uninterested in their children, or may respond to children in a manner designed only to end children's requests rather than to help their child develop. These four parenting styles are generally used.

ASSESSMENT METHODS

Parent and child self-report and naturalistic observations have been used to assess parenting style. Q sort tasks, in which parents or outside observers (i.e., researchers, teachers) divide a set of statements into piles according to how characteristic they are of the parents' typical style, have been popular in measuring parenting or childrearing style because they may reduce some self-report or observer bias. One area of controversy in measurement is whether parents should be assigned to mutually exclusive categories (typological approach) or whether parents' extent of using each parenting style or dimension (dimensional approach) should be measured. For example, using the typological approach, a parent would be described as authoritative if most of his or her parenting behaviors fit that style, even if he or she showed frequent authoritarian and occasional permissive behaviors. Using the dimensional approach, the same parent would receive scores for each parenting style, high for authoritative, moderate for authoritarian, and low for permissive, reflecting the extent to which they were used. In 1994 Laurence Steinberg and colleagues described the typological approach as most appropriate for assessing short-term child outcomes because parents' predominant style is emphasized. Conversely, because the dimensional approach includes measurement of all parenting styles, in their 1989 work Wendy Grolnick and

Richard Ryan noted the advantage of investigating independent and joint effects of parenting styles on children's outcomes.

RELATIONS TO CHILDREN'S DEVELOPMENTAL OUTCOMES

Parenting styles are often used in investigating diverse developmental outcomes, such as academic competence, achievement, self-esteem, aggression, delinquency and substance abuse, moral reasoning, and social adjustment. Research suggests that authoritative parenting is conducive to optimal development. Specifically, children reared by authoritative parents demonstrate higher competence, achievement, social development, and mental health compared to those reared by authoritarian or permissive parents. Negative effects of authoritarian parenting on children's outcomes include poorer self-esteem, social withdrawal, and low levels of conscience. Permissive parenting has been related to negative outcomes such as behavioral misconduct and substance abuse. The worst outcomes for children are associated with neglectful parenting. This lack of parenting is associated with delinquency, negative psychosocial development, and lower academic achievement. Longitudinal research by Steinberg and colleagues supports these concurrent associations such that children raised by authoritative parents continued to display positive developmental outcomes one year following measurement of parenting style, whereas those raised by neglectful or indifferent parents had further augmented negative outcomes.

From Baumrind's framework, in authoritative homes children's adaptive skills are developed through the open communication characteristic of parent-child interactions. Parents' clear expectations for children's behavior and responsiveness to children's needs provide an environment that supports children's development of academic and social competence. Authoritative parenting does seem to be robustly associated with positive outcomes across ethnically and socioeconomically diverse populations, though the strength of the association varies.

Less clear is whether permissive and authoritarian parenting styles have negative effects on children's development in varying contexts. In 1981 Catherine Lewis questioned whether the positive outcomes associated with authoritative parenting were due to the combination of demand and responsiveness, or rather to the warm and caring parent-child relationship. When a parent-child relationship has few conflicts, and therefore there is little need for parents to exert control over children's behavior, permissive parenting might be as effective as authoritative parenting. Indeed, from an attribution theory framework, parents' absence of controlling children's behavior would be expected to lead to children's internalization of behav-

iors and values. Research in the United States and in China in the 1990s and 2000s suggested that the combination of greater parental warmth or support and less parental control or punishment is related concurrently or retrospectively to positive outcomes such as self-esteem, prosocial behavior, socioemotional skills, and family harmony.

Lewis proposed that the firm but not punitive control characteristic of authoritative parenting might be more reflective of children's willingness to obey than of parents' style. In 1994 Joan Grusec developed a theoretical model that elaborated children's role in accurately perceiving and choosing to accept or reject their parents' communication of behavioral standards through disciplinary practices and parenting style. Few researchers have investigated such bidirectional child effects on parenting styles. An exception is Janet Strayer and William Roberts's 2004 research, in which they statistically tested whether children's anger elicited parents' control and lack of warmth and found greater evidence for parenting style leading to children's anger and thereby impacting children's empathy.

Some research indicates a lack of negative or even positive outcomes for children whose parents are highly strict and authoritarian, depending on the family's ethnicity (e.g., African American, Clark et al. 2002; Palestinian-Arab, Dwairy 2004). In 2004 Enrique Varela and colleagues found that it was not ethnicity per se (nor assimilation, socioeconomic status, or parental education), but rather ethnic minority status that was related to greater endorsement of authoritarian parenting by Mexican immigrant and Mexican American families living in the United States compared to both white, non-Hispanic families living in the United States and Mexican families living in Mexico. Varela and colleagues have called for research to examine ecological influences on parenting style and on the effects of parenting style on children's outcomes.

Finally, reminiscent of Block's perspective, some research suggests that additional or redefined parenting styles and dimensions may be necessary to understand parenting cross-culturally. Filial piety and individual humility, which involve emphasizing family or group obligations, achievements, and interests over individual goals and expressions, are two parenting values that have been identified in Hong Kong and mainland Chinese families. Peixia Wu and colleagues (2002) cautioned that, despite seeming similarities between Chinese parenting dimensions such as directiveness and maternal involvement and the demand and responsiveness characteristic of authoritative parenting, the meaning of the dimensions and their relations to one another seem to vary considerably between Chinese and American mothers. Thus, although parenting style may provide a useful framework for understanding developmental outcomes, it is critical to consider the meaning of parenting practices and styles within the family's cultural context.

SEE ALSO *Attachment Theory; Child Development*

BIBLIOGRAPHY

Baumrind, Diana. 1967. Child Care Practices Anteceding Three Patterns of Preschool Behavior. *Genetic Psychology Monographs* 75 (1): 43–88.

Chao, Ruth K. 1994. Beyond Parental Control and Authoritarian Parenting Style: Understanding Chinese Parenting through the Cultural Notion of Training. *Child Development* 65 (4): 1111–1119.

Darling, Nancy, and Laurence Steinberg. 1993. Parenting Style as Context: An Integrative Model. *Psychological Bulletin* 113 (3): 487–496.

Grusec, Joan E. 2002. Parenting Socialization and Children's Acquisition of Values. In *Handbook of Parenting*, Vol. 5: *Practical Issues in Parenting*, 2nd ed., ed. Marc H. Bornstein, 143–167. Mahwah, NJ: Lawrence Erlbaum Associates.

Maccoby, Eleanor E., and John A. Martin. 1983. Socialization in the Context of the Family: Parent-Child Interaction. In *Handbook of Child Psychology*, Vol. 4: *Socialization, Personality, and Social Development*, eds. Paul H. Mussen and E. Mavis Hetherington, 1–101. New York: Wiley.

Spera, Christopher. 2005. A Review of the Relationship among Parenting Practices, Parenting Styles, and Adolescent School Achievement. *Educational Psychology Review* 17 (2): 125–146.

Steinberg, Laurence et al. 1991. Authoritative Parenting and Adolescent Adjustment across Varied Ecological Niches. *Journal of Research on Adolescence* 1 (1): 19–36.

Steinberg, Laurence, et al. 1994. Over-time Changes in Adjustment and Competence among Adolescents from Authoritative, Authoritarian, Indulgent, and Neglectful Families. *Child Development* 65 (3): 754–770.

Strayer, Janet, and William Roberts. 2004. Children's Anger, Emotional Expressiveness, and Empathy: Relations with Parents' Empathy, Emotional Expressiveness, and Parenting Practices. *Social Development* 13 (2): 229–254.

Wu, Peixia, Clyde C. Robinson, and Chongming Yang. 2002. Similarities and Differences in Mothers' Parenting of Preschoolers in China and the United States. *International Journal of Behavioural Development* 26 (6): 481-491.

Julie C. Dunsmore
Pa Her

PARETO, VILFREDO
1848–1923

Vilfredo Pareto was born in Paris on July 15, 1848, the son of Raffaele (a marquis originally from Genoa, republican political exile, and hydraulic engineer) and Marie Metenier, the daughter of a winegrower from Moulins, a small city in the department of Allier in central France. Vilfredo was therefore perfectly Italian-French bilingual. He could also read English but did not know any other modern language, although he had a good knowledge of ancient Greek and Latin (and their respective cultures).

He studied in Turin, where in 1867 he obtained a degree in mathematics, and in 1870 a degree in engineering. From his university studies he derived not only an up-to-date mathematical and technological preparation but also his scientific method: the logical-experimental method. It is likely that he acquired this method from Dutch physiologist Jakob Moleschott (who in that period was teaching at the University of Turin), and then refined it by studying John Stuart Mill's *System of Logic* in its French edition (1866).

Pareto thought that the explanation (that is, the theoretical reproduction) of reality can never be perfect but can always be improved by drawing the hypotheses of the theory from the observation of reality, by developing them with the help of mathematics, and by obtaining in this way some propositions that must then be compared with reality (through statistics and history). From the discrepancies that one inevitably finds, one can deduce some refinements for the starting hypotheses, and so on.

From 1873 until 1890, Pareto managed one of the first Italian ironworks, situated in San Giovanni Valdarno near Florence. After resigning in 1890 because of differences with the owners, he devoted himself to journalism as a vehicle for his views in favor of pacifism and free trade.

Through Maffeo Pantaleoni and above all Léon Walras, he became interested in mathematical economics, which he initially intended to use to provide economic liberalism with new theoretical foundations. Pareto was offered the chair of political economics at the University of Lausanne, where he replaced Walras, who had resigned for health reasons. There he taught, albeit with increasing irregularity, from May 12, 1893, to June 9, 1909. From Walras he only took the concept of General Economic Equilibrium (GEE) because of its methodological property of encompassing the whole of economic phenomena. He developed it by applying it to reality and above all by giving it a new foundation in the theory of choice, which seemed to him more compatible with his methodology than the theory of utility, a concept that could not be easily measured and was therefore unbearably metaphysical.

In the same framework Pareto places his well-known definition of economic optimum as an allocation of resources such that if, as one moves away from it, the ophelimity, or economic satisfaction, of at least one individual increases and the ophelimity of at least one other individual decreases. The sources of this definition are

Walras's demonstration of the optimality of free competition and some criticisms by Pantaleoni and Enrico Barone about a first tentative Pareto's treatment of the subject.

The failure of European economic liberalism at the end of the nineteenth century did nevertheless reinforce his idea that economic theory was unable to explain the whole of social reality. Many more concepts were required for that, and Pareto took them from sociology. In this way he integrated GEE in a general social equilibrium whose main elements, alongside interests, are: passions (which he called residues); the diversity of human beings, which generates the division of every society into a majority of dominated people and a minority of dominating people, that is, the elite, with the elites following one another in power in rather rapid succession; and derivations (that is, the pseudological motivations that human beings give for actions—and they are the majority of all actions—that are in fact only inspired by passions). The main criticisms of Pareto regard the static nature of his systems of general (economic and sociological) equilibrium, and his idea that human nature cannot be modified. In the last months of his life Pareto sympathized with fascism, as many Italian liberals did at the time, since in it he saw the timely restorer of Italian public order, which had been disrupted by the local supporters of bolshevism. On the other hand, he noticed and condemned the first authoritarian trends of Mussolini's regime.

Pareto died in Céligny, Canton Geneva, Switzerland, on August 19, 1923.

SEE ALSO *Authoritarianism; Elites; Fascism; Free Trade; Lausanne, School of; Liberalism; Marginalism; Mathematical Economics; Mill, John Stuart; Pacifism; Pareto Optimum; Sociology; Utility Function; Walras, Léon*

BIBLIOGRAPHY

Busino, Giovanni. 1989. *L'Italia di Vilfredo Pareto. Economia e Società in un carteggio del 1873–1923*. 2 vols. Milan, Italy: Banca Commerciale Italiana.

Pareto, Vilfredo. 1906. *Manual of Political Economy*. Trans. Ann S. Schwier, eds. Ann S. Schwier and Alfred N. Page. London: Macmillan, 1972.

Pareto, Vilfredo. 1916. *Mind and Society*. Trans. Andrew Bongiorno and Arthur Livingston with the advice and the cooperation of James Harvey Rogers. London and New York: Routledge, 2003.

Pareto, Vilfredo. 1964–2005. *Oeuvres Complètes*. 32 vols. Geneva, Switzerland: Droz.

Fiorenzo Mornati

PARETO OPTIMUM

In further developing French economist Léon Walras's 1874 demonstration of the optimality of free competition, at first Italian economist Vilfredo Pareto studied the problem of optimal allocation of resources in terms of maximization of utility for a representative agent, which he described in his 1892 article "Considerazioni sui principi fondamentali dell'economia politica pura." In a later article titled "Il massimo di utilità dato dalla libera concorrenza.I" (1894a), he re-analysed the question by determining the production coefficients that maximize the utility of a collectivistic society and demonstrated that they are exactly those of free competition (this is the real origin of the story of the second theorem of economic welfare). It was only at an even later stage, and as a consequence of some criticisms by Italian economists Maffeo Pantaleoni and Enrico Barone, that this theorem was redemonstrated by Pareto in 1894 and 1909. To reconfirm his theorem, Pareto started from the hypothesis of the incomparability of individual ophelimities, in flagrant contrast with his methodological position according to which every science—and therefore economics as well—is a science of averages. From this there directly ensues the proposition that an allocation of resources is optimal (i.e., it is a pareto optimal point), if, as one moves away from it, the ophelimity of at least one individual increases and the ophelimity of at least one other individual decreases. On the other hand, this proposition cannot obviously be made operational from the point of view of economic policy, because the entire availability of resources of a society can be allocated in an infinite number of Pareto optimal points (described by the contract curve), from which the *maximum maximorum* (i.e., the best of the pareto optimal points) cannot therefore be extracted. Pareto more or less understood this difficulty and resolved it by stating in a 1913 article that if one wishes to give indications in terms of economic policy, one has to move into the realm of sociology, where the optimal allocation of resources can be univocally identified starting from a comparison between personal ophelimities arbitrarily carried out by the government.

The question of the economic unclassifiability of Pareto optimal points was authoritatively tackled in later years. As a solution, John Hicks and Nicholas Kaldor both published articles in 1939 that proposed a criterion of compensation that is conceptually similar to Pareto's sociological criterion. Abram Bergson in his 1938 article "A Reformulation of Certain Aspects of Welfare Economics" and Paul Anthony Samuelson in his 1947 publication *Foundations of Economic Analysis* attempted to solve the problem by maximizing a social well-being function that was constructed, however, starting from cardinal individual functions of utility made comparable by resorting to value judgments.

While giving rise to outstanding formal analyses by such economists as Aldo Montesano (1990), Maurice Allais (1989), and Mark Blaug (1992), the subsequent literature developed around the theme of the either positive or normative nature of the Pareto optimum. While P. Hennipmann in his 1976 article "Pareto Optimality: Value Judgement or Analitical Tool" and G. C. Archibald in his 1959 article "Welfare Economics, Ethics, and Essentialism" defended the thesis that Pareto's postulates do not reflect value judgments, Alan T. Peacock and Charles K. Rowley, in their 1972 and 1974 articles, weakened it by differentiating between economic liberalism and Pareto optimality, even though they attempted to portray the latter as a simple tool of economic reasoning. The normative thesis was taken to its extreme and—considering Pareto's unwavering political-intellectual militancy—paradoxical consequences by Amartya Sen in 1970 and 1971 in articles where he demonstrated that in order to be logically consistent social choice cannot at the same time be liberal (respect of other people's preferences, once one's own have been reaffirmed) and Paretian (incomparability of individual preferences and therefore necessary unanimity of social choices). Sen has been criticized in the literature for his too narrow definition of liberalism. By relaxing it, the compatibility between Pareto's principle and liberalism would be restored. On the other hand, it should be pointed out that no ordinalistic theory of economic welfare based on a definition different from Pareto's has yet been developed.

SEE ALSO *Income Distribution; Pareto, Vilfredo*

BIBLIOGRAPHY

Allais, Maurice. 1989. *La théorie générale des surplus.* Grenoble, France: Presses Universitaires.

Archibald, G. C. 1959. Welfare Economics, Ethics, and Essentialism. *Economica* 26 (104): 316–327.

Bergson, Abram. 1938. A Reformulation of Certain Aspects of Welfare Economics. *Quarterly Journal of Economics* 52 (2): 310–334.

Blaug, Mark. 1992. *The Methodology of Economics, or, How Economists Explain.* 2nd ed. Cambridge, U.K.: Cambridge University Press.

Fine, Ben. 1975. Individual Liberalism in a Paretian Society. *Journal of Political Economy* 83 (6): 1277–1281.

Hennipman, P. 1976. Pareto Optimality: Value Judgement or Analitical Tool. In *Relevance and Precision: From Quantitative Analysis to Economic Policy*, eds. J.S. Cramer, A. Heertje, and P. Venekamp, 39–69. New York: North-Holland.

Hicks, John. 1939. The Foundations of Welfare Economics. *Economic Journal* 69: 696–712.

Hillinger, Claude, and Victoria Lapham. 1971. The Impossibility of a Paretian Liberal: Comment by Two Who

are Unreconstructed. *Journal of Political Economy* 79 (6): 1403–1405.

Kaldor, Nicholas. 1939. Welfare Propositions of Economics and Intertemporal Comparisons of Utility. *Economic Journal* 49: 549–552.

Montesano, Aldo. 1991. Il massimo di ofelimità per la collettività: definizioni, analisi, interpretazioni di Pareto e loro generalizzazione. In *Pareto oggi*, ed. G. Busino, 115–138. Bologna, Italy: Il Mulino.

Ng, Yew-Kwang. 1971.The Possibility of a Paretian Liberal: Impossibility Theorems and Cardinal Utility. *Journal of Political Economy* 79 (6): 1397–1402.

Osborne, D. K. 1975. On Liberalism and the Pareto Principle. *Journal of Political Economy* 8 (6): 1283–1287.

Pareto, Vilfredo. 1892. Considerazioni sui principi fondamentali dell'economia politica pura. *Giornale degli Economisti* (August): 151–157.

Pareto, Vilfredo. 1894a. Il massimo di utilità dato dalla libera concorrenza.I. *Giornale degli Economisti* (July): 48–57.

Pareto, Vilfredo. 1894b. Il massimo di utilità dato dalla libera concorrenza.II. *Giornale degli Economisti* (July): 57–66.

Pareto, Vilfredo. 1909. *Manuel d'économie politique.* Paris: Giard et Brière.

Pareto, Vilfredo. 1913. Il massimo di utilità per una collettività in sociologia. *Giornale degli Economisti* (avril): 338–341.

Peacock, Alan T., and Charles K. Rowley. 1972. Pareto Optimality and the Political Economy of Liberalism. *Journal of Political Economy* 80 (3): 476–490.

Rowley, Charles K., and Alan T. Peacock. 1975. *Welfare Economics: A Liberal Restatement.* London: Martin Robertson.

Samuelson, Paul Anthony. 1947. *Foundations of Economic Analysis.* Cambridge, MA: Harvard University Press.

Sen, Amartya. 1970. The Impossibility of a Paretian Liberal. *Journal of Political Economy* 78 (1): 152–157.

Sen, Amartya. 1971. The Impossibility of a Paretian Liberal: Reply. *Journal of Political Economy* 79 (6): 1406–1407.

Walras, Léon. 1874. *Eléments d'économie politique pure ou thèorie de la richesse sociale.* Lausanne, Switzerland: Rouge.

Fiorenzo Mornati

PARIS PEACE CONFERENCE

SEE *Interwar Years.*

PARK, ROBERT E.
1864–1944

The American sociologist Robert Ezra Park was a leading figure in the "Chicago school" of sociology. He was born February 14, 1864 in Harveyville, Pennsylvania. His mother, Theodosia Warner, was a schoolteacher and his father, Hiram Asa Park, was a soldier in the Union army. Soon after the Civil War the family moved to Red Wing, Minnesota, where Park grew up.

Park attended the University of Michigan and received a Ph.B. in philosophy in 1887, studying under the young John Dewey (1859–1952). From 1887 until 1898 he was a reporter on daily newspapers in Minneapolis, Detroit, Denver, New York, and Chicago. In 1894 Park married Clara Cahill, and they had four children: Edward, Theodosia, Robert, Jr., and Margaret (Raushenbush 1979).

In 1899 Park entered Harvard University, where he studied under William James (1842–1910) and Josiah Royce (1855–1916). He then took his family to Germany, where he studied with Georg Simmel (1858–1918) and took the only formal course on sociology he ever had. He completed his Ph.D. in 1904 at Heidelberg with his dissertation, "Masse und Publikum" (The Crowd and the Public). He returned to Harvard for a year, but soon became bored with academic life and accepted the position of secretary of the Congo Reform Association. He later met Booker T. Washington (1856–1915) and worked for seven years at Tuskegee Institute studying the American Negro.

At the invitation of W. I. Thomas (1863–1947), Park joined the faculty at the University of Chicago in 1914 and remained there until he retired in 1929. Between 1929 and 1932 he traveled extensively, researching race relations in other countries and teaching. He was a guest professor at Yenching University in Peking and at the University of Hawaii. From 1936 until his death in 1944 he lectured at Fisk University in Nashville, Tennessee (Hughes 1968).

Park was not a prolific writer, but he produced several books and numerous articles. His articles have been published in three volumes by his students as *The Collected Papers of Robert Ezra Park*, vol. 1: *Race and Culture* (1950), vol. 2: *Human Communities: The City and Human Ecology* (1952), and vol. 3: *Societies* (1955). Perhaps his most influential publication was the pathbreaking *Introduction to the Science of Sociology*, published with Ernest W. Burgess in 1921, which has been described as the most influential sociological textbook ever produced in the United States (Martindale 1960; Coser 1971).

In Park's view, society is best seen as the interactions of individuals controlled by traditions and norms. Park was keenly interested in social psychology, and his favorite topics were collective behavior, news, race relations, cities, and human ecology (Raushenbush 1979). Park defined sociology as "the science of collective behavior," which suggests the need for analysis of social structures with the study of more fluid social processes (Coser 1971, p. 358).

These processes are divided into four major categories: competition, conflict, accommodation, and assimilation. Park held that "competition is the elementary universal and fundamental form of social interaction" (Park and Burgess 1921, p. 507). It is as universal and continuous in human society as it is in nature, and it assigns persons their position in the division of labor. Conflict is intermittent and personal. Competition determines the position of the individual in the community; conflict fixes his place in society (Coser 1971, p. 359). Accommodation is a cessation of conflict that is fragile and easily upset. Assimilation "is a process of interpenetration and fusion in which persons and groups acquire the memories, sentiments, and attitudes of other persons and groups, and, by sharing their experiences and history, are incorporated with them in a common culture" (Park and Burgess 1921, p. 735). Then when assimilation is achieved it does not mean that individual differences are eliminated or that competition and conflict end, but that there is enough unity of experience so that a "community of purpose and action can emerge" (Coser 1971, p. 360). Social distance refers to "the degree of intimacy that prevails between groups and individuals. The degree of intimacy measures the influence which each has over the other" (Park 1950, p. 357). The greater the social distance between individuals and groups, the less they influence each other.

Although Park's theory fit with the prevailing assimilationist view of his time, there are several criticisms of his race-relations cycle: (1) Park did not set a time frame for the completion of the assimilation process—making it essentially untestable; (2) Park could not cite any racial group that had passed through all four stages of his cycle—instead, he and other assimilation theorists explained the lack of assimilation as the result of interference in the process, resulting in a tautological theory that can neither be proved nor disproved; (3) Park did not describe the assimilation process in much detail (Healey 2007; Parrillo 2005).

Park described sociology as the "abstract science of human nature and experience" that included the "applied science" of his four social process to analyze "those modifications in human beings that are due to the human environment."

> The same social forces which are found organized in public opinion, in religious symbols, in social conversation, in fashion, and in science ... are constantly recreating the old order, making new heroes, overthrowing old gods, creating new myths, and imposing new ideals. And this is the nature of the cultural process of which sociology is a description and an explanation (Park and Burgess 1921, quoted in Raushenbush 1979, p. 82).

Park's sociology "always focused analytical attention on those processes or situations which foster the emergence of novel forms that upset or render obsolete previous adjustments and accommodations" (Coser 1971, p. 366).

Although Park has sometimes been accused of making racist remarks, his interest in the problem of race relations stems from a desire for a deeper understanding of the human situation. In a letter to Horace R. Cayton, another Chicago school sociologist, Park elaborated on his work with Negroes, demonstrating his broader analytical views of the problems involved:

> Democracy is not something that some people in a country can have and others not have, something to be shared and divided like a pie—some getting a small and some getting a large piece. Democracy is an integral thing. If any part of the country doesn't have it, the rest of the country doesn't have it (quoted in Raushenbush 1979, p. 177).

Park stimulated his students to learn from their own experiences and observations: "Park's teaching always gave the sense of something in the making" (Raushenbush 1979, p. 184).

There is no better testimony to the impact of Park's teaching than the imposing roster of his students. Everett C. Hughes, Herbert Blumer, Stuart Queen, Leonard Cottrell, Edward Reuter, Robert Faris, Louis Wirth, and E. Franklin Frazier all became presidents of the American Sociological Society. Helen McGill Hughes, John Dollard, Robert Redfield, Ernest Hiller, Clifford Shaw, Willard Waller, Walter C. Reckless, Joseph Lohman and many other students of Park became leading social scientists. It is hard to imagine the field of sociology without the contribution of the cohort of gifted men whom Park trained at Chicago. What higher tribute can be paid to a teacher? (Coser 1971, p. 372).

Charles S. Johnson, one of Park's students, noted that "his mind never ceased to work with ideas and he had not lost his zest for life and work and the still uncharted frontiers of human behavior even when, in his final illness, he could no longer speak" (Raushenbush 1979, p. 176). Park died at his home on February 7, 1944, seven days before his eightieth birthday.

SEE ALSO *Assimilation; Blumer, Herbert; Chicago School; Cox, Oliver C.; Drake, St. Clair; Frazier, E. Franklin; Park School, The; Sociology, American; Sociology, Urban*

BIBLIOGRAPHY

PRIMARY WORKS

Park, Robert E., and Ernest W. Burgess. 1921. *Introduction to the Science of Sociology.* Chicago: University of Chicago Press.

Park, Robert E. 1950. *Race and Culture: The Collected Papers of Robert Ezra Park*, vol. 1, ed. Everett C. Hughes, et al. Glencoe, IL: Free Press.

SECONDARY WORKS

Coser, Lewis A. 1971. *Masters of Sociological Thought: Ideas in Historical and Social Context.* Fort Worth, TX: Harcourt Brace Jovanovich.

Healey, Joseph F. 2007. *Race, Ethnicity, and Gender.* Thousand Oaks, CA: Pine Forge Press.

Hughes, Helen MacGill. 1968. Robert E. Park. In *International Encyclopedia of the Social Sciences*, vol. 11, ed. David L. Sills and Robert K. Merton, 416–419. New York: Macmillan.

Martindale, Don. 1960. *The Nature and Types of Sociological Theory.* Boston: Houghton Mifflin.

Parrillo, Vincent N. 2005. *Strangers to These Shores: Race and Ethnic Relations in the United States.* 8th ed. Boston: Allyn and Bacon.

Raushenbush, Winifred. 1979. *Robert E. Park: Biography of a Sociologist.* Durham, NC: Duke University Press.

Larry R. Ridener

PARK SCHOOL, THE

The concept of a school includes having "a central figure around whom the group is located, who is an inspiring and effective leader, whose school it essentially is, and without whom the school eventually begins to break-up" (Harvey 1987, p. 3). Robert Ezra Park (1864–1944) was that essential figure during his tenure in the Sociology Department at the University of Chicago. Park had been a newspaper journalist prior to becoming a sociologist. He brought the practice of immersing oneself into a situation as a participant observant to his new field and taught his students to do the same (Harvey 1987). A great deal of Park's work was undertaken in conjunction with Ernest W. Burgess (1886–1966), Park's colleague and friend. Park's sociology, which includes his reliance upon field research as well as much of the novel theory that he and Burgess espoused coupled with Park's ability to attract quality graduate students, is often referred to as the Park school of thought or the "Park School."

HUMAN ECOLOGY

One of Park and Burgess's major contributions to sociology is the use of ecology in the study of human groups. Borrowing from animal ecology and economics, Park hypothesized that, much like plant and animal life, human groups carve out niches for themselves based on competition for space (Park 1950). For example, key tenets of Burgess and Park's concentric zone theory are that businesses need a central location and that communities build around these business districts to form biotic or mutually interdependent relationships. Additionally, the zones are populated and repopulated via a cycle of invasion and succession much like that found in plant life (Coser 1971).

The social or moral order differentiates human and plant or animal negotiation of the ecological system. Human society is composed of both the biotic (interdependence) and the culture that encompasses the ability to communicate. Humans engage in collective action to create a society that is composed of a common will. Population, material culture, nonmaterial culture, and natural resources interact to create a social hierarchy or social order that maintains biotic balance and social equilibrium. Park's race relations theory is a human ecology theory that exemplifies social order in transition or social change (Park 1950).

Park posits that there is a cycle of events that repeats itself in every initial encounter or contact between racial groups. The cycle includes four stages: contact/conflict, competition, accommodation, and assimilation. He identified contact as the first stage, while other researchers use contact and conflict interchangeably (Park 1950). Although Park assumed that each minority group would eventually fully assimilate into the dominate group, he theorized that each group could possibly go through a series of accommodations first.

Borrowing from Georg Simmel and preceding Emory Bogardus's social distance scale, Park suggested that social distance is the level of intimacy experienced between diverse racial groups or the etiquette of knowing one's group's place in the social order (Coser 1971). Compromised social distance etiquette or conflict between groups for space and life's rewards disturbs the moral order or ecological equilibrium. Social change readjusts the balance in three stages: dissatisfaction, social unrest and mass movements, and finally a new accommodation (Coser 1971). The new accommodation, which is often assimilation, is a social change (Park 1950).

Through his students, Park's influence extends further than his individual contributions to the discipline. Eight of his students became president of the American Sociological Association. Many more of his students became leading sociologists and took Park's work in many directions (Harvey 1987). Clifford Shaw's work with concentric zone theory birthed theories of criminology of place as well as social disorganization theories; E. Franklin Frazier expounded on that line of research to develop sub-

culture theory; and Louis Wirth's research contributed to the foundation of twentieth-century urban sociology. Similarly, Park's critics span the generations as well.

CRITICS AND THE DECLINE OF THE SCHOOL

In her 1988 book, Mary Jo Deegan suggests that human ecology theory is a pathological marriage between sociology and Darwinism. Others posit that human ecology theory ignores the influence of the social environment and does not consider the impact of human diversity (Brown 2006). Park's contemporaries, including many University of Chicago sociology scholars, criticized his resistance to the use of quantitative methods (Harvey 1987). Although Chicago also always had quantifiers, Chicago never lived Park's qualitative reputation down. Despite the criticism, Park's retirement was a big factor in the decline of the department. No one else could inspire students like Park, nor was anyone else as devoted to their intellectual and research success as was Park (Harvey 1987). In addition, to outsiders, sociological research done at Chicago was the sociology *of* Chicago or the "Park School." Without Park, the research ethos was lost. Finally, while Chicago would never dominate sociology again, no other department ever held the dominance that the University of Chicago held during Park's tenure (Harvey, 1987).

BIBLIOGRAPHY

Brown, Nina. 2006. Robert Park and Ernest Burgess: Urban Ecology Studies, 1925. Center for Spatially Integrated Social Science. http://www.csiss.org/classics/content/26.

Coser, Lewis A. 1971. *Masters of Sociological Thought.* New York: Harcourt Brace Jovanovich.

Deegan, Mary Jo. 1988. *Jane Addams and the Men of the Chicago School: 1892–1918.* New Brunswick, NJ: Transaction Books.

Harvey, Lee. 1987. *Myths of the Chicago School of Sociology.* Brookfield, WI: Avebury.

Park, Robert Ezra. 1950. *Race and Culture.* Glencoe, IL: Free Press.

Yolanda Y. Johnson

PARLIAMENT, UNITED KINGDOM

The United Kingdom Parliament has one of the longest histories of any representative assembly in the world and is often referred to, mistakenly, as the "mother of parliaments." The modern U.K. parliament consists of representatives from the four countries of England, Northern Ireland, Scotland, and Wales and is located in the Palace of Westminster in central London, England. Hence, it is commonly referred to as the Westminster parliament.

After the 2005 U.K. general election there were 646 elected members of Parliament: 529 representing English constituencies, 18 from Northern Ireland, 59 from Scotland, and 40 from Wales. The U.K. parliament is bicameral. In addition to the elected members who sit in the lower chamber, the House of Commons, there are also some 700 members of the upper chamber, the House of Lords, who are known as "peers." The numerical composition of both houses of Parliament had been subject to change as a result of the constitutional reforms of the post-1997 Labour governments. The creation of a devolved parliament in Scotland in 1999, alongside representative assemblies in Northern Ireland and Wales, led to a reduction in the size of the House of Commons from 659 to 646 in 2005; whereas the abolition of hereditary peers, under the provisions of the House of Lords Act 1999, virtually halved the total membership of the upper chamber from 1295 to 695. After the implementation of this act, some 80 percent of the members of a new "interim House" were "life peers" who were appointed for their lifetimes, 4 percent were bishops or archbishops of the established Church of England, 4 percent were law lords, and 12 percent were "elected hereditary" peers. The 92 elected hereditary peers were to be removed after the second phase of reform, and the law lords and their associated judicial functions were to be removed upon the creation of a separate supreme court in 2008. Following the changes to the composition of the House of Lords, an independent public body, the House of Lords Appointment Commission, was established in May 2002 to scrutinize nominations made by political parties and to recommend nonpolitical appointees to the Queen. Formally, life peers are appointed by the monarch on the advice of the prime minister.

In addition to the two chambers—the Commons and the Lords—the monarch is also part of Parliament and, in fact, the legally precise institutional term for the body is the *Crown-in-Parliament*. Indeed, the history of the U.K. parliament reflects the changing relationships between monarch, political executive, and legislature, and between the constituent nations of the United Kingdom.

HISTORY

The origins of the English parliament can be traced back to the eleventh and twelfth centuries in the institutional forms of the Anglo-Saxon *Witenagemot*, a national assembly of freemen, and the medieval king's court, the *Curia Regis*. In the thirteenth century, monarchs became more reliant for the consent and authorization of their policies, particularly taxation policies, upon intermittent meetings of the feudal magnates, the great earls and barons (who

controlled private armies), the archbishops, bishops and abbots (who represented the church as the major landowner of the time), and eventually, between 1265 and 1295, representatives of urban citizens and commercial classes. In 1265 the Simon de Montfort parliament (named after the most powerful baron) met for the first time in Westminster Hall, in the Royal Palace of Westminster. In 1295 the "model parliament," summoned by King Edward I, extended the base of representation formally to members of the "Commons." Initially representatives of the Commons were not allowed to speak in the presence of their more powerful feudal superiors and, for this reason, began to meet separately from the Lords, and after 1377 elected a "Speaker" to speak on their behalf to the monarch. Importantly, the principles of consent and representation were invoked at the time in support of, and not as a challenge to, strong monarchical (executive) government. Parliamentary government in Britain has historically been conceived, and functioned, as a means of legitimating executive power.

The inversion of the power relationship between the Crown and Parliament eventually came during the civil war in the seventeenth century and reflected a wider transformation of economic, social, and political forces in the English state. Attendant upon these wider economic and social transformations came institutional change. These changes found confirmation, eventually, in the Constitutional Settlement of 1689. After 1689 legal supremacy rested in Parliament rather than in any other state institution—whether monarch or law courts. The boundaries of legitimate state power were thus marked out. The subsequent history of parliamentary development in Britain (in 1707 the Act of Union merged the separate English and Scottish parliaments into a single parliament of Great Britain) saw Parliament retained at the center of the state but, inevitably, it was not to be sustained as *the* central institution of state decision making—which became focused upon the prime minister, cabinet, and executive.

MODERN FUNCTIONS

The U.K. parliament is a multifunctional institution. As a representative body Parliament has served the functions of providing consent, legitimation, and authorization for executive actions. Modern governments derive their authority from their majority party position within a democratically elected House of Commons. Conventionally government ministers are recruited primarily from the Commons, but may also be members of the Lords. Parliament serves, therefore, to recruit ministers and also to hold them accountable by requiring them to explain and defend their actions. A key role of Parliament, therefore, is to examine government policy and administration and to inform the public about what the government is doing and why. A variety of procedures are available to perform these scrutiny and informing functions: debates; questions; and committees—"standing committees" that process legislation and "select committees" that scrutinize and investigate executive actions more broadly. Although the U.K. parliament is a legislature, its primary legislative role is to scrutinize, amend, improve, and authorize laws proposed by the executive. Each house has a similar five-stage legislative process, and all laws have to be agreed by both houses. Although the Lords actively proposes and makes legislative amendments, ultimately, the final decision rests with the government in the House of Commons. Under the Parliament Act of 1949, if the Lords does not approve a bill it can only delay its passage into law for up to one year. Given the control of the majority party in the House of Commons, the average success rate of government proposals becoming law is some 95 percent. The final stage of the legislative process in Parliament is the royal assent, whereby legislation is accepted with the symbolic words "*La Reyne le veult*"—"the queen wills it." These words underline the continued significance of "the Crown-in-Parliament" and point to the institutional complexity of the United Kingdom as both a parliamentary democracy and a constitutional monarchy.

SEE ALSO *Magna Carta; Participation, Political; Political Parties*

BIBLIOGRAPHY

Blackburn, Robert, and Andrew Kennon. 2003. *Parliament: Functions, Practice, and Procedures.* 2nd ed. London: Sweet and Maxwell.

Judge, David. 1993. *The Parliamentary State.* London: Sage.

Rush, Michael. 2005. *Parliament Today.* Manchester, U.K.: Manchester University Press.

David Judge

PARLIAMENTS AND PARLIAMENTARY SYSTEMS

Parliaments are representative institutions that link political decision makers with citizens affected by the decisions taken. Representative institutions have a variety of names in different countries—Parliament (a term usually associated with the United Kingdom and often adopted in its former colonies, for example, in Australia, Canada, and India); Congress (for example, the United States,

Argentina, Brazil, China, Mexico); Assembly (for example, Cuba, Slovenia, and the Russian Federation); Cortes (Spain); Diet (Japan); Folketing (Denmark); Sejm (Poland); and Storting (Norway)—and are often subsumed under the generic term "legislature." In total, throughout the world in 2006, the Inter-Parliamentary Union listed 189 national parliaments with over 44,000 members. These ranged in size from the 2,980 members in the Chinese National People's Congress to 15 members in the Parliament of the Tuvalu Islands in the South Pacific. Seventy-five parliaments were bicameral, having an upper house or a senate alongside a lower house or representative assembly. In addition, there are also a large number of regional or subnational parliaments, with seventy-four in western Europe, thirty in India, and fifty in the United States. At a supranational level the European Parliament, after January 1, 2007, had 785 members representing over 375 million voters from twenty-seven member states in the European Union.

Yet not all parliaments in the twenty-first century are democratic institutions—in the sense that their members are chosen through the processes of free and competitive elections. In 2006, the United Nations Development Programme identified only 140 countries in which competitive multiparty elections were held for national parliaments.

ORIGINS AND HISTORIC PRINCIPLES

The Icelandic Althingi has a claim to be the oldest parliament, as it met for the first time around 930 CE and served as a general assembly of the most powerful leaders, where legislative acts were made and justice was dispensed. Other parliaments emerged in Europe in the twelfth and thirteenth centuries, when monarchs convened meetings of representatives of the most powerful sections of feudal society to authorize specific royal policies and taxes. The English Parliament, the Spanish Cortes, the French States-General or Estates-General, and the Scandinavian parliaments all trace their roots back to such medieval advisory bodies. Although the subsequent institutional trajectories of these parliaments differed markedly, and while most parliaments were in abeyance for long periods, nonetheless, the principles of authorization and representation marked the common and continuing hallmarks of parliamentary institutions. By the beginning of the twentieth century most western European countries had parliamentary systems, and such systems proved to be resilient. Even those countries that endured authoritarian regimes at some stage in that century (Germany, Italy, Greece, Portugal, and Spain) subsequently reestablished parliamentary systems.

In their contemporary forms, parliaments still institutionalize the principles of representation and authorization, but now these ideas are normally associated also with the electoral principle and notions of accountability. In turn, elections and accountability invoke ideas of "representative and responsible" government—where decision makers are representative of those for whom decisions are to be made and are responsible to those affected by the decisions. In this sense, parliaments occupy pivotal institutional positions in the linkage between citizens and governors. Indeed, parliaments face in two directions: first, toward the "people," the "represented," or the "governed"; and, second, toward the "government" or the "political executive." In this pivotal position, parliaments can be seen as part of an institutional nexus of government—as a "parliamentary system."

PARLIAMENTARY SYSTEM

Like any other system, a parliamentary system is a complex whole that comprises of a set of connected parts. Frequently, parliamentary systems are defined in contrast to presidential systems and categorized by the distinctive institutional configurations that link the electorate, the legislature, and the executive. In a parliamentary system the electorate votes for representatives who, when assembled together, collectively constitute the representative institution of parliament. In turn, the political executive, or government, is then derived from the representative institution. Viewed as an ideal-typical process of delegation, a parliamentary system thus enables citizens to delegate decision-making capacity, through the medium of elections, to their representatives. In this process representatives, as the "agents" of electors, are authorized to act on behalf of citizens as "principals" (in the terminology of delegation theory). From this single direct act of delegation to representatives in parliament flows a sequential and serial process of delegation, whereby representatives in parliament then delegate the routines of decision making to a related institution—the political executive—which acts as the agent of the "principal" of parliament. In turn, the political executive (whether termed "cabinet" or "government" and normally headed by a chief executive known as a "prime minister") delegates further to other "agents" in the institutional form of the bureaucracy or civil service. In contrast, in a presidential system, citizens elect and directly authorize both a political executive, either through elections or through an electoral college, and representatives in a legislature. In presidential systems, therefore, the electorate has two agents. Moreover, in presidential systems there is a separation of powers between the legislature and the executive, whereas in parliamentary systems there is a fundamental fusion of parliamentary and executive institutions.

LEGISLATIVE–EXECUTIVE RELATIONSHIPS

In a parliamentary system political executives are authorized by parliaments. This can take the form of a formal investiture vote before an executive takes office (Germany, Hungary, Greece, Ireland, Portugal, Spain, and Sweden) or immediately after an executive assumes office (Belgium, Italy, and Luxembourg). The outcomes of such votes are heavily dependent upon bargaining among political parties. In other parliamentary systems, executives are deemed to be authorized tacitly unless the executive loses the confidence of parliament (for example, in Australia, Austria, Denmark, Finland, France, Iceland, Japan, the Netherlands, New Zealand, Norway, and the United Kingdom). Using the concept "authorization" avoids using notions of the "selection" or "emergence" of executives from parliaments. In practice, few parliaments actively select leaders from their ranks, and in several states membership of the executive is incompatible with membership in parliament (for example, Austria, the Netherlands, Norway, and Sweden). Only in the UK and Ireland, among western European parliaments, are cabinet members required to be members of parliament.

In a parliamentary system executives are also accountable to parliament; in turn, parliaments are accountable to citizens. In the twenty-first century, ideas of parliamentary accountability are rooted predominantly in free competitive elections. In the strongest sense, executives are accountable to parliaments insofar as there are "no-confidence" procedures by which cabinets or governments can be collectively dismissed by parliament. In a weaker sense, executives may be held to account in terms of "informing" parliament and "explaining" their actions through oversight procedures such as questions, debates, and statements and by providing evidence to parliamentary committees. In an intermediate sense, executives may also be accountable where ministers are prompted by parliamentary scrutiny to accept culpability and to consider remedial action or redress.

The reciprocal relationship of accountability finds further reflection in the dissolution powers normally conferred upon prime ministers individually or cabinets collectively. In most countries the no-confidence procedures in parliament are counterbalanced by the executive's capacity to invoke a confidence vote or to dissolve parliament directly. In all western European states since 1945 (as well as, for example, in Japan and Canada) executives have, on at least one occasion, dissolved parliaments before completion of the full electoral term. In Denmark, Greece, and Ireland some two-thirds of modern parliaments have been dissolved early. Upon dissolution, parliaments and political executives then face their ultimate accountability to the electorate.

PARLIAMENTARY SYSTEMS AND LEGITIMATION

As noted earlier, the terms *parliament* and *legislature* tend to be used synonymously and interchangeably. Yet few parliaments are legislatures in the literal sense of "lawmaker" (derived from the Latin words *legis*, meaning "law," and *lator*, meaning "carrier" or "proposer"). The formulation of legislative proposals in most parliamentary systems is conducted largely beyond parliaments, in executives operating in broader institutional networks of organized interests and political parties. In this case, the prime role of parliaments in the legislative process is the authorization of laws. Legislative outputs are legitimated through procedures of parliamentary deliberation, scrutiny, amendment, assent, and, ultimately, monitoring. Through processes of representation, the opinions and interests of wider civil society—variously in the form of individual constituents, territorial electoral districts or constituencies, political parties, or civil society associations—are brought to bear in the parliamentary processing of legislation. And, through these processes, popular authorization and legitimation of legislative outputs is secured. Indeed, in some systems, supreme legislative authority is deemed to reside in parliament (as in the concept of "parliamentary sovereignty" in the UK). In most parliamentary systems, however, the people are held to be "sovereign"—with authority delegated temporarily and contingently to representatives in parliament.

Much has been made in academic writings of a distinction between "deliberative assemblies"—with an emphasis on debate (linguistically the term *parliament* derives from the French verb *parler*, meaning "to talk")—and "working assemblies"—with the emphasis on legislative functions. The former type of assembly is commonly associated with parliamentary systems and the latter with presidential systems. In practice, however, such distinctions are of restricted value. A more effective way of identifying and categorizing parliaments is encapsulated in the notions of "representation," "authorization," "accountability," and "legitimation." In linking citizens with their government, parliaments serve, in the first instance, to represent "the people" (however constituted in different countries) and also, indirectly, to authorize executive action. In the second instance, however, parliaments hold executives accountable for their actions and so provide an institutional mechanism for the public control, and ultimately, the legitimation, of government.

SEE ALSO *Authority; Bicameralism; Democracy; Democracy, Representative; Elections; Government; Knesset, The; Parliament, United Kingdom; Participation, Political; Political Parties; Voting*

BIBLIOGRAPHY

Beetham, David. 2006. *Parliament and Democracy in the Twenty-First Century: A Guide to Good Practice.* Geneva, Switzerland: Inter-Parliamentary Union.

Norton, Philip, ed. 1990. *Legislatures.* Oxford: Oxford University Press.

Strøm, Kaare, Wolfgang C. Müller, and Torbjörn Bergman, eds. 2003. *Delegation and Accountability in Parliamentary Democracies.* Oxford: Oxford University Press.

David Judge

PARNES, HERBERT
1919–2006

Herbert Saul Parnes was a consummate social scientist, though his official title was professor of economics. Educated at the University of Pittsburgh (BA and MA) and Ohio State University (PhD), he spent most of his distinguished career as a labor and human resources economist at Ohio State, studying and teaching others about the experiences of people in American labor markets. His career also involved visiting professorships at Princeton and the University of Minnesota, a stint as an Organization for Economic Cooperation and Development (OECD) consultant in Paris, and three years at Rutgers following his retirement from Ohio State. Later, he returned to Ohio State as a National Institute on Aging grantee to continue his study of the labor market experiences of the elderly. His legacy as recounted below relates only to his substantive research, his pathbreaking contributions to the field of empirical labor market analysis, and his emphasis on a multidisciplinary focus. However, it must be noted that there are scores of economists and other social scientists to whom he was a teacher and mentor and whose own work bears witness to the significance of his scholarly contributions.

Parnes began his academic life as a political science major, and he never strayed from the idea that understanding human experiences in labor markets was valuable not only for its own sake but also for what it could contribute to the sensible formation of public policy. He was never a devotee of pure theory and recounts in his memoir, *A Prof's Life* (2001), several instances when he undertook jobs and occupations to acquire a solid understanding of how workers really interacted with their jobs, coworkers, and employers. Although he acknowledged in the preface to *PEOPLEPower: Elements of Human Resource Policy* (1984) that his appreciation for the value of microeconomic theory grew during his career, he always believed that only the collection and analysis of data could provide the understanding needed to undergird policy recommendations.

The signal accomplishment of his career was initiating and overseeing the single largest labor market research project ever funded by the U.S. Department of Labor, the National Longitudinal Surveys of Work Experience (NLS). It began in 1966 and has continued in modified forms into the twenty-first century. Literally thousands of scholarly articles, monographs, theses, and dissertations have been completed using what in the earliest years were known as the *Parnes data.* Parnes authored or coauthored more than fifty of those during his prolific career. Before that, he had published several significant works. In *Research on Labor Mobility: An Appraisal of Research Findings in the United States,* he synthesized everything known empirically to that point (1954) about worker mobility in American labor markets. He updated that synthesis a decade and half later in *A Review of Industrial Relations Research* (1970). His collaboration with other social scientists began early in exploring the economic, psychological, and sociological elements of a critical aspect of human decision-making in "Occupational Choice: A Conceptual Framework" (1956). This belief in the importance of multidisciplinary approaches carried over into the research team that he assembled at Ohio State's Center for Human Resource Research to design and analyze the NLS data, which dismayed critics who believed it resulted in an underemphasis on economic theory.

Attesting to the policy importance of the NLS-based research are many studies of race and sex discrimination in labor markets, the salient factors related to the changing labor force participation of adult women, the impacts of schooling and training on the labor market success of various age-sex groups, and the correlates of changing retirement behavior among adult American men. Critical to the ability to offer policy recommendations on these and related issues is the longitudinal and detailed microeconomic character of the data that comprise the NLS. Furthermore, the collection of data on attitudes and a variety of schooling and training experiences enable testing of hypotheses about which only speculations were possible before the NLS existed. Among the attitude measures in which Parnes had profound scholarly interest were questions designed to tap into mobility as a propensity to move (by changing employers or occupations or geographic locations) as a predictor of later actual movement. This was, in part, born of his skepticism of the standard theoretical assumption that all workers are always seeking to improve their position in the marketplace and are always searching for information to enable such improvement. Though he coauthored several published studies using the data from these questions, many opportunities to exploit them exist for newer generations of social scientists, thus adding to Parnes's contribution to our understanding how people really behave in labor markets and what social policies might be invoked to improve their well-being and the effectiveness of the economy in allocating and utilizing scarce human resources.

SEE ALSO *Economics; Economics, Labor; National Longitudinal Survey of Youth; Occupational Status; Social Science; Work*

BIBLIOGRAPHY

Blau, Peter, John Gustad, Richard Jessor, Herbert Parnes, and Richard Wilcock. 1956. Occupational Choice: A Conceptual Framework. *Industrial and Labor Relations Review* 9 (4): 531–543.

Parnes, Herbert S. 1954. *Research on Labor Mobility: An Appraisal of Research Findings in the United States.* New York: Social Science Research Council.

Parnes, Herbert S. 1970. Labor Force Participation and Labor Mobility. In *A Review of Industrial Relations Research*, vol. 1, 1–70. Madison, WI: Industrial Relations Research Association.

Parnes, Herbert S. 1975. The National Longitudinal Surveys: New Vistas for Labor Market Research. *American Economic Review* 65 (2): 244–249.

Parnes, Herbert S., ed. 1981. *Work and Retirement: A Longitudinal Study of Men.* Cambridge, MA: MIT Press.

Parnes, Herbert S. 1984. *PEOPLEPower: Elements of Human Resource Policy.* Beverly Hills, CA: Sage.

Parnes, Herbert S. 2001. *A Prof's Life: It's More than Teaching.* San Jose, CA: Writer's Showcase.

Andrew I. Kohen

PARODY

Parodic practices carry implications for the study of social institutions and cultural frameworks because, especially when allied with satiric critique, they can lead to the clearing away of older modes of thought, and the opening up of alternate paradigms of cultural understanding. Not all forms of parody accomplish this skeptical questioning, emptying out, or overturning of an official perspective; normative parodies attack dissidents and divergences from the dominant cultural ideology and enforce established values. But parodies that reverse accepted hierarchies of value can serve as indicators of or even contributors to cultural change.

Parody—from the Greek *para,* "beside," and *odos,* "song" or "derived from another poem"—involves both the repetition and inversion of some elements of an established work or genre, usually so as to lower what has been elevated or respected. Aristophanes, the first great parodist in the tradition, implies conservative cultural allegiances in his comedies (written between 427 and 385 BCE), which parody the style and thought of Euripides, the last of the great Athenian tragedians, the philosopher Socrates, and the Sophists, the new, professional teachers of rhetoric.

The *Satyricon* of Petronius (early 60s CE) probably constitutes the best example from the ancient world of the use of satiric parody to empty out established canons of value. The longest surviving episode of this novel, "Trimalchio's Feast," satirizes the vulgar pretensions and mangled learning of the immensely rich former slave Trimalchio. But the dinner conversation of Trimalchio's guests, who are obsessed with money, mortality, and the passing of the good old days, also parodies the dinner conversation of the aristocratic Athenians in Plato's dialogue, the *Symposium*. Contrasting the honest vulgarity and materialism of Trimalchio and his guests with the corruption and hypocrisy of the educated narrator and his friends, Petronius achieves a portrayal of the lowborn, newly rich class that is neither caricatural nor condescending, and implicitly places them on a level with Plato's high-minded Greeks.

In *Gargantua* and *Pantagruel* (first two books, 1532 and 1534), François Rabelais satirically parodies as illogical, ungainly, and repetitive the scholastic learning of the medieval universities that was authorized by the Catholic Church, and proposes by contrast the graceful, thoughtful, and persuasive eloquence of students trained in the new humanistic model of education. Where Rabelais criticizes a system buttressed by religious authority, Miguel de Cervantes, like Petronius, achieves in *Don Quixote* (Part 1, 1605; Part 2, 1615) a satiric critique of a previously dominant aristocratic culture, through parody of the romance epics of the Middle Ages and the Renaissance. Cervantes adopts the episodic structure of such works and their concerns with love and adventure; however, by making Don Quixote, the reader who believes in the literal truthfulness of these romances, repeatedly collide with contemporary social reality, he suggests the inadequacy of this narrative form in the more commercial world of his own time. He thus opens up a cultural space for the development of the new genre of the modern novel. In *Gulliver's Travels* (1726), Jonathan Swift parodies travelers' tales in general and Daniel Defoe's *Robinson Crusoe* (1719) in particular to satirize the arrogance of Englishmen and of Europeans in relation to the inhabitants of other parts of the world they were encountering through their voyages of discovery, commerce, and empire. In a similar way, *Ubu Roi* (1896), Alfred Jarry's parody of the high genre of tragedy, and particularly of Shakespeare's *Macbeth*, produces an acidic critique of middle-class intellectual and artistic culture that opened the way to such twentieth-century movements as dadaism and absurdism. Finally, to take a contemporary example, Thomas Pynchon's novels from *V.*

(1963) to *Mason & Dixon* (1997) consist almost entirely of parodic reworkings of established genres and discourses—from travel guides and spy novels to captivity narratives—to suggest a radical skepticism toward received understandings of history, technology, and power in the modern world.

Satiric parody has also affected cultures through popular media such as comics and television in the last half-century. *MAD* magazine made a mark in American culture during the 1950s and 1960s, puncturing pretensions by means of its irreverent parody of hit films and television shows. It was joined in doing so by a new form, the weekly satiric television news program, first with *That Was The Week That Was* (U.K., 1963; U.S., 1964–1965), then with "Weekend Update" (beginning in 1975 as a regular feature of *Saturday Night Live*). The latter lasted longer, but was more limited formally, consisting largely of comic anchors reading items based on stories in the news. The next most significant instances of parodic satire of politics and journalism in America consist of *The Daily Show* with Jon Stewart, followed by *The Colbert Report* with Stephen Colbert, which appear back-to-back four nights a week on Comedy Central. Stewart usually maintains a smile as he reports, often verbatim, the statements of newsmakers, spokesmen, journalists, and commentators; only occasionally does he let outrage show. By contrast, Colbert's adoption of the persona of a hard-right cable talk-show host enables him to say what others find impossible to express: by zealously criticizing even the most well-grounded skepticism of government officials, their policies, and their bullying manipulation of mainstream media, he makes clear what the authorities believe but do not say, and allows the commonsense criticism to be expressed along the way.

In a famously controversial argument first published in 1984, Fredric Jameson maintained that in the postmodern period parody had become divorced from satiric critique. For Jameson, all that remained of parody was pastiche, a toothless, complacently unhistorical mixing of incongruous fragments from earlier styles. A year after Jameson's essay, Linda Hutcheon by contrast argued that twentieth-century parodic forms do not possess a fixed and unfluctuating ideological persuasion: parody can be conservative or transgressive, or can even combine the two in an authorized transgression. Although, as Hutcheon and others have pointed out, the thought of Mikhail Bakhtin could be utopian in its emphasis on the possibilities for inversion and renewal through parody, most critics would agree that Bakhtin's works (written from the 1930s through the 1960s) constitute the essential and seminal reflections on the renovating cultural work performed by satiric parody from the ancient world to the present.

SEE ALSO *Satire*

BIBLIOGRAPHY

Bakhtin, Mikhail. [1934–1935] 1981. Discourse in the Novel. In *The Dialogic Imagination: Four Essays.* Trans. Caryl Emerson and Michael Holquist, 259–422. Austin: University of Texas Press.

Hutcheon, Linda. 1985. *A Theory of Parody: The Teachings of Twentieth-Century Art Forms.* New York: Methuen.

Jameson, Fredric. 1991. *Postmodernism, or, The Cultural Logic of Late Capitalism.* Durham, NC: Duke University Press.

Frank Palmeri

PARSIMONY
SEE *Occam's Razor.*

PARSONS, TALCOTT
1902–1979

American sociologist Talcott Parsons, the youngest of five children, was born in Colorado Springs in 1902. His father was a Congregational minister, professor, and university president, and his mother was a progressive and a suffragist. Parsons completed his undergraduate studies in biology at Amherst College in Massachusetts. He also attended the London School of Economics, where he studied with Bronislaw Malinowski (1884–1942), inheriting his view of society as a system of interrelated parts. In 1926 Parsons attended the University of Heidelberg, where he studied the theories of Max Weber (1864–1920). He translated Weber's *The Protestant Ethic and the Spirit of Capitalism* (1904–1905) into English in 1930. Parsons was initially an instructor of economics at Harvard University, where he was mentored by Pitirim Sorokin (1889–1968), then became an inaugural member of the sociology department. In 1945 Parsons established Harvard's Department of Psychology and Social Relations, an interdisciplinary collaboration in the behavioral sciences and economics. He served as chair of the department until its dissolution in 1972. He continued teaching as a visiting professor upon his retirement in 1973 from Harvard. Parsons died in May 1979.

Parsons was the major American social theorist until about 1969, and some claim that social theory since then has been in conversation with Parsons. Parsons attempted to develop a "grand theory" of society that explains all social behavior, everywhere, throughout history, and in all contexts, with a single model called *structural functionalism.* This approach considers values to be the core of cul-ture, because values give meaning to what people do, direct people's lives, and bind people together. These "cultural traits" thus function for the operation of society (Parsons 1966). Parsons believed that all lasting social systems strive for stability or equilibrium with a strong sense of social order and institutional interdependence. Influenced by Sigmund Freud (1856–1939), he was interested in how actors choose goals and means in relation to internalized norms and values, and argued for an objective external world that is understood empirically with concepts created by the ideas, beliefs, and actions of those under study. This is a modernist approach because it assumes an absolute developmental process.

Parson's early theorizing on social action, influenced by Weber, focused on active, creative mental processes that have an important subjective component. In *The Structure of Social Action* (1937), Parsons developed his empirical approach of analysis based on observation, reasoning, and verification, and explored the difference between the concepts of behavior (a mechanical response to stimuli) and action (an inventive process and analysis of the subjective aspect of human activity) (Ritzer 2000). For Parsons, the basic unit of study is the *unit act*, which involves the following criteria: an actor/agent motivated to action; an end toward which action is oriented and means to reach this end; a situation where the action takes place; and norms and values that shape the choice of means to ends. Actions consist of the structures and processes from which humans are motivated to form meaningful intentions (through available goal-attaining means) that are put into practice within the social system (Parsons 1966). Parsonian "action" is considered from all of the following perspectives: culture (values), society (norms), personality (source of motivation), and organism (source of energy). For Parsons, people cannot choose goals and means without society in the background, and they cannot make sense of agency or action without enforced or expected social norms. This means people must have an intention and awareness of society's norms, and they cannot escape these norms. Parsons is sometimes criticized for this position because he cannot account for social change.

Parsons was concerned with the integration of structure and process, and defined a social system as comprised of the interactions of many individuals within a situation, where the system itself includes commonly understood cultural norms. These cultural norms are within a system of generalized symbols and their associated meanings (Parsons 1951). These social systems have parts, or subsystems of varying complexity, that represent organizational structures. Additionally, social structures have social functions, which are the consequences of any social pattern for the operation of society as a whole. For Parsons, society is a complex system whose parts work together to promote solidarity and stability (they strive for equilibrium), and hence he defines the social structure as any relatively stable pattern of social behavior. An analysis of the social system is thus a consideration of ordered processes of change in the interactive patterns of actors within a structure (the norms behind the goals and means). Actors have status roles or positions within the structure itself, and in relation to other actors via interactions. However, these statuses and roles are units of the social system, and are not qualities of the actors themselves.

Parsons and Robert F. Bales (1916–2004) apply this analysis of status based on hierarchy and power to the family (a small social unit) with Parson's notions of feminine-expressive and masculine-instrumental leadership roles. For Parsons, men assume through socialization a more technical, executive, and "judicial" role, and women a more supportive, integrative and "tension-managing" role (Parsons and Bales 1955). These stereotypical views result in a narrow and limited view of gender.

Parsons later developed pattern variables that categorize expectations and relationship structures that allow for understanding universal social action. These are: how much emotion to invest into any social phenomena (affectivity-affective neutrality); whether to orient oneself to part or all of a social phenomena (specificity-diffuseness); how to judge a social phenomena, either in terms of emotional or general standards (universalism-particularism); whether to judge a social action by its intentions or results (ascription-achievement); and whether to pursue self-interest or the interest of the collectivity (self-collectivity).

Additionally, Parsons claimed that for any given system of action, there were four functional components that were necessary for a system to exist, function, and maintain equilibrium: a social system must adapt and be able to exist in a changing environment; must have clearly stated goals; must involve actors within a subsystem of a greater organizational system; and must define and maintain a set of norms and values, which in turn legitimates action within the system itself.

C. Wright Mills (1916–1962) mocked Parsonian theory in his book *The Sociological Imagination* (1959), and postmodernists disagree paradigmatically with Parsons and his "grand theory" approach to understanding an ordered society.

SEE ALSO *Culture; Family; Femininity; Functionalism; Malinowski, Bronislaw; Masculinity; Mills, C. Wright; Norms; Postmodernism; Psychology; Sociology; Sociology, Parsonian; Structuralism; Values; Weber, Max*

BIBLIOGRAPHY

Parsons, Talcott. [1937] 1949. *The Structure of Social Action: A Study in Social Theory with Special Reference to a Group of Recent European Writers.* 2nd ed. Glencoe, IL: Free Press.

Parsons, Talcott. 1951. *The Social System.* Glencoe, IL: Free Press.

Parsons, Talcott. 1954. *Essays in Sociological Theory.* Glencoe, IL: Free Press.

Parsons, Talcott. 1960. *Structure and Process in Modern Societies.* New York: Free Press.

Parsons, Talcott. 1964. *Social Structure and Personality.* New York: Free Press.

Parsons, Talcott. 1966. *Societies: Evolutionary and Comparative Perspectives.* Englewood Cliffs, NJ: Prentice Hall.

Parsons, Talcott. 1969. *Politics and Social Structure.* New York: Free Press.

Parsons, Talcott. 1971. *The System of Modern Societies.* Englewood Cliffs, NJ: Prentice Hall.

Parsons, Talcott, and Robert F. Bales. 1955. *Family, Socialization, and Interaction Process.* Glencoe, IL: Free Press.

Parsons, Talcott, Robert F. Bales, and Edward Shils. 1953. *Working Papers in the Theory of Action.* Glencoe, IL: Free Press.

Ritzer, George. 2000. *Classical Sociological Theory.* 3rd ed. Boston: McGraw Hill.

Ryan Ashley Caldwell

PARTIAL AUTOCORRELATION FUNCTION

SEE *Time Series Regression.*

PARTIAL EQUILIBRIUM

With the publication of the first edition of his *Principles of Economics* in 1890, Alfred Marshall developed partial equilibrium analysis as a method for turning economic theory into a form that could be used to formulate policy and aid in the analysis of actual problems. He wanted economics to be "an engine for the discovery of concrete truth" (Hausman 1992, p. 152). In partial equilibrium each market or section of the economy is considered as a separate entity, and so its interdependence with other markets is not considered. This often is described as *ceteris paribus*, that is, other things do not change. To bring some order and understanding to an extremely complex world in which everything affects everything else, partial equilibrium concentrates on key relations, holding the rest constant (Hausman 1992). It is not that these factors are believed to be unchanging but that they are held in the ceteris paribus "pound." As Marshall stated in 1922:

The forces to be dealt with are however so numerous, that it is best to take a few at a time: and to work out a number of partial solutions.... Thus we begin by isolating the primary relations of supply, demand and price in regards to a particular commodity. We reduce to inaction all other forces by the phrase "other things being equal": we do not suppose that they are inert, but for the time being we ignore their activity.... In the second stage more forces are released from the hypothetical slumber that had been imposed on them. (Marshall 1922, pp. xiv–xv)

Marshall suggested that, in each stage of the analysis, more factors could be allowed to vary.

The element of time is a chief cause of those difficulties in economic investigations which make it necessary for a man with limited powers to go step by step; breaking up a complex question, studying one bit at a time, and at last combining his partial solutions into a more or less complete solution of the whole riddle. In breaking it up, he segregates those disturbing causes, whose wanderings happen to be inconvenient, for the time in a pound called *Cæteris Paribus*. The study of some groups of tendencies is isolated by the assumption *other things being equal*.... With each step more things can be let out of the pound. (Marshall 1922, p. 366, emphasis in original)

INTERDEPENDENCE IN PRICES AND MARKETS

Marshall was fully aware of the interdependence between most markets and prices in the economy, as is apparent from notes XIV and XXI of the Mathematical Appendix to his *Principles*, where he outlined the basis of a general equilibrium system. However, he realized that attempting to analyze that interdependence would render the economic problem so complex that the main causal factors could not be isolated. Hence he regarded partial equilibrium analysis and the use of ceteris paribus as important approximations that allow casual inferences to be made and real-world problems to be studied.

In particular Marshall concentrated on the role of price in individual markets as the main determinant of the quantities supplied and demanded. To illustrate this, one can examine the demand for oranges (D_0), which will depend on their price (P_0), all other prices in the economy ($P_1, ..., P_n$), the income of all individuals in the economy ($Y_1, ..., Y_m$), the weather, people's tastes, international factors, and so forth:

$$D_0 = f(P_0, P_1, ..., P_n, Y_1, ..., Y_m, \text{weather, tastes,}$$
etc.).

Some of these factors, such as weather and tastes, are not economic variables, and so they normally are considered exogenous. This does not mean that it is assumed that they do not change but that their changes cannot be explained within economics, and so they are unlikely to be influenced significantly by economic variables. What is left is the general equilibrium demand function for oranges in terms of all prices and incomes in the economy. Clearly this is extremely complex because in general equilibrium everything affects everything else. Therefore it is difficult to use the theory to make meaningful statements about policy or causality.

In partial equilibrium analysis each market is considered in isolation. When each market is concentrated on individually and when part of the economy is broken off and relations within that part are considered, causal inferences can be made. In addition it is assumed that demand and supply are separable and can be represented as independent curves, with price determined as the balance of those forces. To calculate the partial equilibrium demand function for oranges, the price of oranges is considered as the main determinant, other things being equal. In other words, all variables that are not determined within that market, particularly all other prices and incomes, are assumed for the analysis to be given and constant. This leaves the partial equilibrium demand curve for oranges:

$$D_0 = f(P_0)$$

MARSHALL'S FOUR TIME PERIODS

According to Marshall, the question of which factors are left in the ceteris paribus pound depends on the time allowed for those factors to respond to changes in the market. In particular the length of time that is allowed for supply to respond to changed conditions will exert an important influence on the operation of the market. Accordingly Marshall distinguished four time periods that are appropriate for economic analysis, determined on the basis of which factors are held constant in each situation. The first is the very short run, or the market period in which it is assumed that goods are already at market and must be sold, so that supply cannot vary and price is determined mainly by demand. In the short period, quantity supplied is allowed to vary as a result of variations in production through changes in the variable factors, but the quantity and structure of fixed capital goods cannot be varied. As plants are fixed, firms can neither enter or exit the market, and so a supernormal profit can be made even in competitive industries. In the long period, plants can be varied, and firms can enter or exit from the market, and so all factors are variable. In this case no supernormal profit can be sustained in a competitive market. Finally, in what Marshall referred to as the "secular long period" knowledge, population, technology, and tastes all can vary.

APPLICATIONS AND PROBLEMS

Clearly, in evaluating partial equilibrium it is not relevant to consider the question of whether the underlying assumptions are realistic. As approximations, they are intended to focus on key relations, intentionally abstracting from secondary ones, which are held constant in the ceteris paribus pound. Demand and supply are determined by more than just the price of a commodity. However, in evaluating assumptions it is necessary to look at whether they capture the key aspects of any relationship, whether what is assumed away is as important as what is included, whether the variables that are assumed to be constant vary systematically with the variables included in the analysis, and whether the variables that are assumed to be independent, in this case supply and demand, are in fact interdependent.

As a result of these considerations, partial equilibrium can be applicable only to commodities that are relatively unimportant in terms of household budgets and that have neither close substitutes nor complements. If a commodity has close complements or substitutes, changes in its price will lead to changes in demand conditions in other markets, which will lead to changes in prices in those markets. This means that the variables that are being held constant will change as a result of changes in the endogenous variables. This contradicts the ceteris paribus clause because ceteris are not paribus. Any change in price will lead, through its effect on other markets, to a shift in the demand curves in the market that is being considered. The things that are being held constant vary systematically with the ones being looked at, and this undermines the basis of partial equilibrium. In addition if the commodity was an important part of the household budget, changes in its price would lead to changes in the household's real income, thus changing another of the variables that have been held constant. In other words, for partial equilibrium it must be assumed that the income effect of a price change is very small. This means that the partial equilibrium framework is relevant only for goods on which only a relatively small proportion of the household budget is spent and for which there are no close substitutes or complements.

Further problems arise when the partial equilibrium framework is utilized to determine prices and outputs in competitive industries. A competitive industry will produce at that price for which aggregate demand for its output is equal to aggregate supply. In a partial equilibrium framework supply and demand must be independent of each other. The individual firm is assumed to face a U-shaped cost curve, and in perfect competition it faces an infinitely elastic demand curve. In long run equilibrium, price will cover costs exactly so that there are no economic profits.

In 1926 Piero Sraffa published an article that showed that there are severe logical problems in the use of the partial equilibrium framework for the analysis of perfectly competitive industries. He demonstrated that some elements of the analysis are inconsistent with partial equilibrium analysis and other elements are inconsistent with perfect competition.

Also, there are the standard problems associated with partial equilibrium analysis, specifically, the fact that demand and supply are often interdependent rather than independent and that the analysis is relevant only for unimportant markets. In other words, it is rare that one can break away part of the economy and assume that the interdependencies between it and the rest of the economy are negligible. Nevertheless, partial equilibrium analysis remains important in macroeconomics, particularly the distinctions between the short period, the long period, and the secular long period.

SEE ALSO *Equilibrium in Economics; General Equilibrium; Market Clearing; Markets; Maximization; Minimization; Optimizing Behavior; Prices*

BIBLIOGRAPHY

Hausman, Daniel M. 1992. Supply and Demand Explanations and Their Ceteris Paribus Clauses. In *Essays on Philosophy and Economic Methodology*. Cambridge, U.K., and New York: Cambridge University Press.

Marshall, Alfred. 1922. *Principles of Economics: An Introductory Analysis*. 8th ed. London: Macmillan.

Persky, Joseph. 1990. Retrospectives: Ceteris Paribus. *Journal of Economic Perspectives* 4 (3): 187–194.

Sraffa, Piero. 1926. The Laws of Return under Competitive Conditions. *Economic Journal* 36: 535–550.

Peter Kriesler

PARTICIPANT OBSERVATION

SEE *Observation, Participant.*

PARTICIPATION, POLITICAL

Sidney Verba and Norman Nie define political participation as, "those activities by private citizens that are more or less directly aimed at influencing the selection of government personnel and/or the actions they take" (1972, p.

2). This definition is broad in that it takes into account many activities beyond voting in elections, including being active in organizations, working on campaigns, contacting officials, attending political meetings, and being a member of a political organization (Verba and Nie 1972, p. 31). Other scholars adopt broader definitions. For example, Lester Milbrath (1965) incorporates passive behavior (i.e., taking part in ceremonial activities), some psychological orientations (i.e., becoming informed about politics), and protests and demonstrations. Scholars of nondemocratic systems include legal and nonlegal participation and mobilized participation, as well as activities more appropriate to these contexts, such as complaining through bureaucratic channels (Friedgut 1979; Huntington and Nelson 1976; Shi 1997).

Milbrath (1965) was the first to argue that political participation follows a hierarchical structure in that individuals who engage in activities at the top level also engage in activities at lower levels. The bottom rung includes those who do not engage in any type of activity. The "spectator" level consists of activities such as voting, exposure to political stimuli, and talking to others about politics. The "transitional" level includes attending meetings, donating money, or contacting an official. And the "gladiator" engages in activities such as running for office, soliciting funds, and working on a campaign.

Another way to look at the various types of participatory actions is with respect to the level of input required from citizens, the type of information the act conveys to leaders, and how much pressure they place on policymakers to pay attention (Verba and Nie 1972; Verba et al. 1995). Working on a campaign and directly contacting officials requires a great deal of initiative, while activities like voting do not entail as much time or energy. Direct contact sends a clear message to leaders about a citizen's preferences, whereas voting only conveys an ambiguous message. Finally, activities vary with respect to the pressure they put on leaders, with voting exerting a high degree of pressure since electoral support is necessary for reelection.

WHO ENGAGES IN PARTICIPATORY ACTIVITIES

A prominent finding in the early literature, especially in the United States, was that socioeconomic factors, such as income and education, have the strongest effects on increasing the likelihood of turnout (Campbell et al. 1960). With respect to a broader range of participatory activities, those higher in socioeconomic status (SES) are also more likely to engage in the more difficult and time-consuming participatory activities (Milbrath 1965; Verba and Nie 1972), including nonconventional forms of participation such as demonstrations (Barnes et al. 1979).

However, Verba, Nie, and Jae-On Kim (1978) find that the relationship between SES and voting is not as strong across all countries, which they attribute to differences in institutions and social cleavages. Furthermore, in authoritarian regimes, individuals higher in SES are actually more likely to abstain from political participation, since abstention can be a form of protest (Shi 1997).

One of the problems with the SES explanation is that it does not explain why those lower in SES do participate in politics. Verba, Kay Schlozman, and Henry Brady (1995) provide answers to this puzzle in their *civic volunteerism model*. They argue that participation is a function of three factors—resources, psychological engagement, and recruitment—with resources being further divided into time, money, and civic skills. Civic skills are "the communications and organizational abilities that allow citizens to use time and money effectively in political life" (Verba et al. 1995, p. 304) and that can be obtained on the job, in nonpolitical organizations, and in church. It is especially in this latter domain that individuals lower in SES obtain civic skills. The authors find that civic skills play the biggest role in time-based participatory activities, such as contacting officials, while they are not as important for other participatory activities, such as voting, in which SES and psychological engagement play a more important role.

Steven Rosenstone and John Mark Hansen (1993) propose mobilization as another factor that can help resolve the puzzle of why those low in SES may be inclined to participate. They argue (and find) that direct contact by political elites, such as direct mail or door-to-door canvassing, has a positive influence on the likelihood of turnout, and that this effect is more pronounced among those least likely to vote, since mobilization offsets the costs of participation. Rosenstone and Hansen also find positive effects of mobilization with respect to working on a campaign, donating money, and trying to persuade others to vote a certain way. Many scholars have subsequently demonstrated that direct contact increases the likelihood of turnout among minority groups (Leighley 2001) and is more effective than other types of mobilization, such as mailings and phone banks (Gerber and Green 2000).

IMPLICATIONS OF POLITICAL PARTICIPATION

Normatively, political participation has a long tradition of being considered important to the concepts of legitimacy and authority in democratic political systems. Whether one assumes an authorization view of representation, in which a leader is accountable to those who selected or appointed him or her, or an accountability view, in which the representative is bound to a free public, the standards for achieving both in a democracy are free and fair elections (Pitkin 1967). Thus, a political system is considered legitimate only given the participation of citizens in the voting booth. One problem with this conceptualization is that it tends to consider democracies as the only political system that provides legitimate representation (Rehfeld 2006). Participation is still relevant to the legitimacy of nondemocratic regimes, since citizen support is often necessary for the proper functioning of the system (e.g., Davis 1976; Friedgut 1979; Shi 1997).

Empirically, participation is important for the quality of representation in democratic systems: "democratic responsiveness depends on citizen participation, and equal responsiveness depends on equal participation" (Verba 1996, p. 2). Thus, inequality with respect to who participates can lead to biases in representation (Lijphart 1997). For example, scholars find that counties with higher turnout rates receive more appropriations from Congress (Martin 2003), and states with higher levels of upper-class representation have lower levels of welfare spending (Hill and Leighley 1992). Finally, Senator roll-call votes are responsive to the ideology of voters in a state, but not to nonvoters (Griffin and Newman 2005).

SEE ALSO *Autocracy; Citizenship; Democracy; Electoral Systems; First-past-the-post; Parliament, United Kingdom; Parties, Political; Pluralism*

BIBLIOGRAPHY

Barnes, Samuel H., Max Kaase, Klause R. Allerbeck, et al. 1979. *Political Action: Mass Participation in Five Western Democracies.* Beverly Hills, CA: Sage.

Campbell, Angus, Philip Converse, Warren Miller, and Donald Stokes. 1960. *The American Voter.* New York: Wiley.

Davis, Charles L. 1976. The Mobilization of Public Support for an Authoritarian Regime: The Case of the Lower Class in Mexico City. *American Journal of Political Science* 20 (4): 653–670.

Friedgut, Theodore H. 1979. *Political Participation in the USSR.* Princeton, NJ: Princeton University Press.

Gerber, Alan S., and Donald P. Green. 2000. The Effects of Canvassing, Telephone Calls, and Direct Mail on Voter Turnout: A Field Experiment. *American Political Science Review* 94 (3): 654–663.

Griffin, John D., and Brian Newman. 2005. Are Voters Better Represented? *Journal of Politics* 67 (4): 1206–1227.

Hill, Kim Quaile, and Jan Leighley. 1992. The Policy Consequences of Class Bias in State Electorates. *American Journal of Political Science* 36 (2): 351–365.

Huntington, Samuel P., and Joan M. Nelson. 1976. *No Easy Choice: Political Participation in Developing Countries.* Cambridge, MA: Harvard University Press.

Leighley, Jan E. 2001. *Strength in Numbers? The Political Mobilization of Racial and Ethnic Minorities.* Princeton, NJ: Princeton University Press.

Lijphart, Arend. 1997. Unequal Participation: Democracy's Unresolved Dilemma. *American Political Science Review* 91 (1): 1–14.

Martin, Paul S. 2003. Voting's Rewards: Voter Turnout, Attentive Publics, and Congressional Allocation of Federal Money. *American Journal of Political Science* 47 (1): 110–127.

Milbrath, Lester W. 1965. *Political Participation: How and Why Do People Get Involved in Politics?* Chicago: Rand McNally.

Pitkin, Hanna Fenichel. 1967. *The Concept of Representation.* Berkeley and Los Angeles: University of California Press.

Rehfeld, Andrew. 2006. Towards a General Theory of Political Representation. *Journal of Politics* 68 (1): 1–21.

Rosenstone, Steven J., and John Mark Hansen. 1993. *Mobilization, Participation, and Democracy in America.* New York: Macmillan.

Shi, Tianjian. 1997. *Political Participation in Beijing.* Cambridge, MA: Harvard University Press.

Verba, Sidney. 1996. The Citizen as Respondent: Sample Surveys and American Democracy. *American Political Science Review* 90 (1): 1–7.

Verba, Sidney, and Norman H. Nie. 1972. *Participation in America: Political Democracy and Social Equality.* New York: Harper.

Verba, Sidney, Kay Lehman Schlozman, and Henry E. Brady. 1995. *Voice and Equality: Civic Voluntarism in American Politics.* Cambridge, MA: Harvard University Press.

Verba, Sidney, Norman H. Nie, and Jae-On Kim. 1978. *Participation and Political Equality: A Seven-Nation Comparison.* Cambridge, U.K.: Cambridge University Press.

Jennifer Merolla

PARTICULARISM

Particularism is a philosophical position that, in brief, claims that reasoning can be rational and noncapricious without being structured using principles. (*Noncapricious* in this context means that we do not decide on a whim that a case is of a certain sort; there has to be consistency between it and other cases.) The opponents of particularists, *generalists*, deny this claim in various ways. Particularism has commonly been applied to reasoning concerned with what people should believe (epistemological reasoning) and how people should act (moral and prudential reasoning). It has attracted much attention, and the debate is carried out at a high level of abstraction. This has led to some splintering of the position; so much so that the definition given in this entry's opening sentence is a controversial formulation. Jonathan Dancy has been the leading exponent of particularism.

Imagine that any element of a possible course of action—for example, that an *action* is a stabbing; that it would be performed on a Tuesday—is a *feature*. *Situations* are collections of features. The debate raised by particularists concerns the nature of the contribution that features make to the value of the situations of which they are a part. Is it true that stabbings are always wrong, as crude generalists argue? According to particularism, sometimes stabbings are permissible, even obligatory, as in the case of self-defense. Even so, is it true that stabbings are always *wrong-making*, as more sophisticated generalists hold? That is, does the fact that an action is a stabbing always count against performing it, even though sometimes there are enough reasons to justify the action? Particularists deny that this has to be the case. By employing various arguments, distinctions, and examples, they argue that it is possible for the type of reason generated by a feature to change from situation to situation depending on the other features with which it is conjoined. Sometimes stabbings can be *right-making*. Particularists borrow a term from chemistry and claim that features can change their *valency*. (Some particularists make this claim about such features as justice, kindness, and the like.) If particularists are right, it means that there are no true moral principles apart from those with vague caveats such as "stabbing is often wrong-making." (Particularists are trying to understand how such caveats work.) In other words, particularists think that reasoning can still be consistent, but this consistency is not captured by principles.

Particularism is not relativism. Particularists claim that the valencies of features can alter, while the reason generated by a feature on any occasion is an absolute, non-relative matter.

Particularism has important implications beyond abstract philosophy. If the particularist view is true, how does it affect our interpretation of the reasoning practices of judges in legal contexts? And should it alter how ethics are taught to various groups of people, such as those in the medical profession?

SEE ALSO *Ethics; Relativism*

BIBLIOGRAPHY

Dancy, Jonathan. 1993. *Moral Reasons*. Oxford: Blackwell.

Dancy, Jonathan. 2004. *Ethics Without Principles*. Oxford: Oxford University Press.

Hooker, Brad, and Margaret Little, eds. 2000. *Moral Particularism*. Oxford: Oxford University Press.

McKeever, Sean, and Michael Ridge. 2006. *Principled Ethics: Generalism as a Regulative Ideal*. Oxford: Oxford University Press.

Simon Kirchin

PARTIDO REVOLUCIONARIO INSTITUCIONAL

The Partido Revolucionario Institucional (PRI; Institutional Revolutionary Party) had been an imprint in Mexican political life for more than seven decades when the Partido Acción Nacional (PAN; National Action Party) swept into power in 2000 and again in 2006. During its seventy-one years in political power, the PRI's ideology rested with revolutionary nationalism and state-led economic development. The party also encouraged a welfare state, anticlericalism, land reform, and autonomy from the foreign-policy influences of the United States (Russell 1994, pp. 77–78). The divergence of the PRI's undemocratic practices from the party's democratically ideological platform became the tool that ripped through its veil of political domination. Consequently the PAN victory in 2000 represented a historically significant moment for Mexico in which the true nature of democracy in terms of fair elections, candidates winning based upon popular vote, and a government led by other political parties besides the PRI had finally been realized. This illustration of democracy continued with the PAN's slight victory over the Partido de la Revolución Democrática (PRD; Democratic Revolutionary Party) in 2006. So the question remains as to what future role the PRI will play in Mexican politics.

HISTORY, SUCCESSES, AND CHALLENGES OF THE PRI

The PRI began in 1929 under Mexican president Plutarco Elías Calles, who served from 1924 to 1928. Calles founded what was known as the Partido Nacional Revolucionario (PNR; National Revolutionary Party) in an effort to organize the political elite and establish an institutional mechanism ensuring the smooth transition of authority from one president to another. Prior to the PNR, a number of presidents who were also leaders of the Mexican Revolution, such as Francisco Madero, Venustiano Carranza, and Álvaro Obregón, were murdered by opponents. Thus Calles, who also actively participated in the Mexican Revolution, found it necessary to "replace individuals with institutions" (Fuentes 1996, p. 70). That institution would exist in the form of one leading political party. Calles also pushed for a constitutional amendment that eliminated presidential reelections. It was the long-running abuse of power by one president— Porfirio Díaz—for over three decades that ignited the Mexican Revolution, which left Mexico in political and economic chaos and instability. The ultimate goal was to end the violent struggle for power between individuals of the Mexican Revolution.

The new system succeeded in shifting the struggle for power away from the use of bullets toward the use of the newly devised electoral system. However, the system also produced a more authoritarian regime. Electoral fraud became characteristic of the one-party system from the beginning. For example, the 1929 election between PNR candidate Pascual Ortiz Rubio and opposition candidate and Mexican educator Jose Vasconcelos, who received support from the Christeros, or followers of Christ, was plagued with blatant acts of ballot-box stuffing and intimidation among other fraudulent activities that led to Ortiz's victory (Castañeda 2000, p. xii). The Mexican novelist Carlos Fuentes described the stolen presidency as the result of "the first superfraud of the government party" (Fuentes 1996, p. 70).

By 1938 the PNR became known as the Partido de la Revolución Mexicana (PRM; Party of the Mexican Revolution) under President Lázaro Cárdenas, who ruled from 1934 to 1940. Cárdenas advanced upon Calles's efforts to create a more peaceful transfer-of-power process by establishing the mechanism that allows Mexican presidents to choose their successors while also discouraging them from staying in power for longer than one six-year term. Naturally the party leader would choose a successor from within the party, which perpetuated the long cycle of one-party rule in Mexico's political history.

This form of presidential succession became a point of controversy for the party. Although presidential elections took place in Mexico every six years, the process failed to fit the mold of a democratic political system. The journalist Philip Russell wrote, "The PRI maintains the fiction of democratic candidate selection" (Russell 1994, p. 76). Unlike the democratic system in the United States, for example, Mexico did not include primaries in which the public selected presidential candidates for each party prior to the national elections. Therefore the presidential succession mechanism allowed the incumbent president from the dominant party to wield more influence than the populace on the outcome of presidential elections.

Moreover the PRM underwent a structural transformation under Cárdenas known as corporatism. The new structural system was an alliance between the party and three other sectors—peasant, labor, and popular. Scholars have argued that this system of state-structured interest groups played a key role in determining political and economic results (Collier and Collier 1979). The three sectors functioned to keep the party in power by advancing the objectives of and voting for the party in return for special benefits for its members.

The influence of each corporatist branch under the leftist populist regime evolved over time. The peasant sector carried the most weight because of its large numbers. However, the sector's clout declined as Mexico's urban population surpassed that of the rural poor. The demographic shift enhanced the role of labor unions. As a result the party later relied upon the Mexican Federation of Workers to carry out its labor policies. Finally, the popular sector has been viewed as the most influential of the groups (Russell 1994, p. 79). The popular sector, which consisted of a broad range of groups from trade unions to slum organizations to professional organizations, had a large population and was organized under the National Confederation of Popular Organizations in 1943. Cárdenas envisioned that the three sectors would continue to carry out the revolutionary policies of the party and strengthen the alliance between them and the state. As a result the separation of powers in Mexico was more symbolic than actual.

State influence under the corporatist structure also spilled over into other areas of Mexican political life, thus threatening the democratic principles of checks and balances. The legislative and judicial branches as well as the media all followed the president rather than the rule of law and ethics most of the time (Castaneda 2000, pp. xii–xiii). The PRM dominated both the house and the senate because the president chose for congress PRM candidates who remained loyal to the party. The president along with the attorney general also selected judges who pledged allegiance to the presidential head of the party. The media outlets remained controlled and limited by the state until the late 1990s, even though newspapers and radio and television stations were mostly independently owned. The corporatist system became less effective as the country later moved away from a state-led government and economy toward a more liberal political and economic ideology.

Although the democratic nature of the Mexican political structure under Cárdenas remained questionable, Cárdenas also implemented successful social reform programs to ensure the equal treatment of all Mexican citizens. Fuentes described this period, stating, "And even if the upper and middle classes were favored, the working and peasant classes also received larger slices of the national pie than they ever had before or ever have had since" (Fuentes 1996, p. 71). Cárdenas carried out agrarian reform by returning to the Indian and peasant communities land that they had lost prior to the Mexican Revolution under the Spanish-controlled hacienda system. (Haciendas had been part of Mexico's colonial economy since the sixteenth century. They were large pieces of land upon which the Spanish employed workers, predominantly of Indian origin. The Indian workers depended on the land for their survival. They lived and worked on the haciendas and were usually paid low wages.)

Cárdenas also promoted health, education, and other reform programs with the objective of alleviating poverty among Mexican citizens, including the Indian population, which often faced discrimination and suffered from inequality. The history of the PRI is not completely mired in corruption and failure.

Moreover in 1938 Cárdenas nationalized Mexico's strongest export sector—oil—which contributed to the country's economic success for a substantial period. The state control over Mexico's petroleum protected the economy from the competitive forces of the global market for another four decades. Cárdenas's approach contributed to 6 percent annual growth for the next forty years and increased salaries and purchasing power (Fuentes 1996, p. 71; Castaneda 2000, p. xv). Mexico was successful, relative to the rest of Latin America, at maintaining social peace and political stability. As a result the party under Cárdenas was characterized as promoting both social justice and economic growth while lacking in political democracy.

The party name changed to PRI and underwent another structural change under President Miguel Alemán Valdés in 1946. Alemán served as president from 1946 to 1952. Whereas the party under Cárdenas mostly emphasized social change, the new PRI's dominant focus shifted toward economic development. By the mid-1950s until the late 1970s the Mexican state controlled the economy and instituted mechanisms to protect domestic producers from foreign competition. The goal of aligning social justice with economic development began to fade, and the gap between the wealthy and the poor continued to widen thereafter. The populist aspect of industrial development disappeared while the role of the state in the economy grew even more. The state's alternative development goal included advancing the interests of private investors, both domestic and foreign (Walker 1995).

The departure from the measures put in place during the 1940s showed an even uglier side of the Mexican political system under the PRI. Social injustice and human rights abuses became even more overt by the late 1950s and continued well into the 1960s and 1970s. The alliance that civil society groups enjoyed with the state disintegrated. For example, workers' movements were confronted, strikes were broken, labor leaders were incarcerated, civil society leaders were murdered, and student groups were attacked. Some cases include the murder of agrarian leader Rubén Jaramillo and the killing of students in the Tlatelolco Square massacre in 1968 right before the Mexico City Olympics.

Electoral fraud by the PRI did not continue only at the executive level. Rather, corruption plagued legislative elections as well. For instance, Félix Salgado Macedonio, opposition candidate for deputy in the second electoral district of the state of Guerrero and representative of the Frente Democrático Nacional (FDN; National Democratic Front), the antecedent of the PRD, exposed the fraud associated with the 1988 national elections before the congress. Macedonio presented the congress with a large number of ballots marked in his favor that authorities had partially or wholly burned, costing him an electoral victory over PRI candidate Filiberto Vigueras (Fuentes 1996, p. 60). The congress eventually allowed Salgado to take his well-deserved seat while offering Vigueras another congressional position.

THE DAWNING OF THE OPPOSITION POLITICAL PARTY

By the end of the twentieth century Mexico had experienced a profound change in its political system that demonstrated a move toward a more representative democracy. President Ernesto Zedillo of the PRI pushed for the first primary in Mexico starting with the 1999 elections. Zedillo's break from political tradition, which kept the PRI in power at all levels of government, set the stage for other parties to have a fair opportunity and the people to have a real voice during national elections. As a result of these changes, a candidate from PAN was voted into the presidential office in fair, democratic elections. Many Mexicans compared the election to the fall of the Berlin Wall (Kaye 2000).

Vicente Fox Quesada, a former Coca-Cola business executive and former governor of the Mexican state of Guanajuato, won the Mexican presidency in 1999. He surpassed Francisco Labastida Ochoa, who was chosen to represent the PRI during the primary, with 43 percent of the vote to 37 percent. Cuahtémoc Cárdenas Solórzano, the candidate for the PRD and son of former Mexican president Cárdenas, followed with only 17 percent of the popular vote. Fox's message of addressing the failures of the previous administration under Zedillo, such as resolving the conflict in the southern Mexican state of Chiapas and cracking down on drugs, resonated well with voters who had vivid memories of the problems under the PRI. For example, the 1990s were plagued with charges of corruption, political ties with powerful drug lords, the collapse of the Mexican peso, and an economic recession. PAN, in the words of the Mexican foreign minister Jorge Castañeda during an interview, served as the party "of prosperity, of modernization, of democracy, of respect for human rights" (Kaye 2000). The ideas of modernization and prosperity did not stray too far from the efforts of Mexican president Carlos Salinas de Gortari of the PRI during the early 1990s. Salinas pushed Mexico into a different direction economically by opening the country's market and substantially reducing state involvement in the Mexican economy through the signing of the North American Free Trade Agreement (NAFTA) with the United States and Canada in 1994.

The PRI suffered an even more embarrassing defeat in the 2006 national elections. The PRI candidate Roberto Madrazo Pintado garnered only a little over 20 percent of the vote. However, the majority of the popular vote was split between two other opposing parties. The PAN candidate Felipe Calderón won the election by an extremely small margin relative to the PRD candidate Andres Manuel Luis Obrador, with 36 percent and 35 percent respectively. Most analysts anticipated that Manuel Luis Obrador would win the election with his left-wing populist ideology, which emphasized social improvement, since early poll numbers showed him leading the national election. His campaign did not sound very different from the policies of Cárdenas fifty years before. It must be noted that Manuel Luis Obrador was a member of the PRI under the Mexican president Luis Echeverría's administration from 1970 to 1976, but he left after being frustrated with the party's inability to produce change (Castañeda 2006).

FUTURE OF THE PRI

Although the PRI lost the presidential elections in 1999, it continued to govern seventeen out of Mexico's thirty-one states and dominated the congress. Under President Fox, the PRI still maintained a significant amount of authority in both houses of congress. The PRI was able to stall a number of Fox's reform initiatives and even blocked one of Fox's trips to the United States in 2002 (Peters 2002).

The PRI merely tried to remain afloat in Mexico's political waters after badly losing its grip in both houses of congress in 2006. The party lost the majority of its seats in congress for the first time since its founding. PAN dominated both the executive and legislative branches of Mexican government as of 2007.

The future of the PRI remained bleak as the party suffered from internal turmoil. For the party to remain important in Mexican political life, it would have to redefine itself, emphasize coalition building, and establish a clear ideology and focus. In that the Mexican populace has become divided along the lines of left and right ideology, some analysts have even presented the possibility that the PRI, which is also divided along left and right ideological lines, may split into two separate political parties (Grillo 2006).

SEE ALSO *Corporatism; Mexican Revolution (1910–1920)*

BIBLIOGRAPHY

Castañeda, Jorge G. 2000. *Perpetuating Power: How Mexican Presidents Were Chosen.* New York: New Press.

Castañeda, Jorge G. 2006. Latin America's Left Turn. *Foreign Affairs*, May–June. http://www.foreignaffairs.org/20060501faessay85302-p40/jorge-g-castaneda/latin-america-s-left-turn.html.

Collier, Ruth Berins, and David Collier. 1979. Inducements versus Constraints: Disaggregating "Corporatism." *American Political Science Review* 73 (4): 967–986.

Fuentes, Carlos. 1996. *A New Time for Mexico.* Trans. Marina Gutman Castaneda and Carlos Fuentes. New York: Farrar, Straus, and Giroux.

Grillo, Ioan. 2006. Once Powerful PRI Now Trying to Survive. Associated Press. http://www.boston.com/news/world/latinamerica/articles/2006/07/03/once_powerful_pri_now_trying_to_survive/.

Kaye, Jeffrey. 2000. A Mandate for Change. PBS Online Newshour, November 29. http://www.pbs.org/newshour/bb/latin_america/july-dec00/fox_11-29.html.

Peters, Gretchen. 2002. In Mexico, War between Fox and Congress Escalates. *Christian Science Monitor*, April 16. http://www.csmonitor.com/2002/0416/p07s02-woam.html.

Primer: Mexican Elections. 2006. *Washington Post.* http://www.washingtonpost.com/wp-srv/world/interactives/mexico06/.

Russell, Philip. 1994. *Mexico under Salinas.* Austin, TX: Mexico Resource Center.

Vigueras, Armando Reyes. 2006. La Noche en que Ganó Fox. *La Nación.* http://www.pan.org.mx/?P=182&ArtOrder=ReadArt&Article=205960.

Walker, David. 1995. Review of *War, Diplomacy, and Development: The United States and Mexico, 1938–1954*, by Stephen R. Niblo. East Lansing, MI: H-LatAm. http://www.h-net.org/reviews/showrev.cgi?path=28093851271592.

Sarita D. Jackson

PARTIES

SEE *Political Parties.*

PARTITION

To paraphrase Winston Churchill, partition is the worst solution to political conflict, perhaps, except all others. Partition is an inadequate political tool whose time always comes when other solutions seem to be lacking. Often employed to resolve conflict and restore stability, partition frequently tends to exacerbate that which the division was intended ameliorate. In light of the tendency for partition to rise to the top of a list of options and the unintended consequences of partition, consider: What is partition, when does it succeed, and when does it fail?

Partition is the political division of territory. It is usually employed to resolve violent ethnic or religious strife. By physically separating conflicting groups, those who advocate partition stress its conflict-resolution benefits and downplay its unforeseen costs. It is most often precipitated by armed conflict, which in several notable cases has invited some manifestation of international intervention. However, partition is not a panacea and often tends to increase rather than ease tensions.

Partition succeeds when the following occur: (1) both sides accept (albeit sometimes grudgingly) the division; (2) violent conflict has been permanently suspended; and (3) stability is restored, and a lasting peace can be guaranteed. All these factors considered, however, partition is often an inappropriate and unsuccessful method of conflict resolution. Indeed, partition may intensify differences, inflame ethnic rivalries, damage domestic infrastructure, and be accompanied by forced mass migrations. The desire to separate warring groups or factions to avert further violence may appear to be a rational response, but history has demonstrated that partition is an imperfect solution. Perhaps with the exception of the comparatively peaceful "Velvet Divorce," in which the former Czechoslovakia was split into separate, homogenous, mutually consenting Czech and Slovak nations, one would be hard-pressed to locate an example of a truly successful partition (see Kumar 2003).

Partition fails when the following occur: (1) a partition agreement fails to meet the demands of opposing sides; (2) violence is not significantly diminished or eliminated (i.e., a permanent ceasefire has not been reached); 3) relations between opposing groups are not improved but rather deteriorate, culminating in renewed conflict. In this respect, partition has proven an ineffective political instrument. Conflicts are aggravated, rivalries are intensified, and in some instances violence continues uninterrupted. To explore why partition fails, consider its historical applications.

The partition of Palestine, while not only one of the most controversial territorial divisions in contemporary history, demonstrates the degenerative effect partition can have on ethnic violence. The eruption of violence between Jewish settlers and indigenous Arabs convinced the international community of the need to establish two independent states within the territory of Palestine: one Jewish and the other Arab. The partition was reluctantly accepted by the Jewish Agency but rejected by Arab leaders, who believed their right to national self-determination had been unjustly abrogated.

Following the 1948 war, Israel seized more land than had been provided under the United Nations Partition Plan, and as a result, hundreds of thousands of Palestinian refugees were displaced. The partition did little to mitigate the subsequent Arab-Israeli conflict; the division inflamed tensions, leading to several wars between Israel and its Arab neighbors. The occupation of Palestinian territory by the Israel Defense Forces followed the 1967 war. The occupation led to the emergence of Palestinian extremism, which in its various phases has waged a nearly interminable terrorism campaign against Israel. Although the partition of Palestine resulted in the establishment of an independent state of Israel, violence between Israel and Palestine, while abated by intermittent periods of calm, has continued almost without pause since partition.

Partition was not only the rage in Palestine; it was also the proposed British solution to the question of India. Two authors, Larry Collins and Dominique Lapierre, offer insightful examinations of both the partition of Palestine and partition of India in *O Jerusalem* (1988) and *Freedom at Midnight* (1997), respectively.

Like the partition of Palestine, the partition of India was both promising and problematic. To relieve itself of its colonial responsibilities in India, which had become increasingly onerous because of growing civil unrest and the high costs of maintaining a large colony, the British initiated the process of partitioning India into distinct, homogenous Hindu and Muslim nations. While the 1947 partition created independent Indian and Pakistani states, the division also resulted in a large-scale migration and widespread violence, displacing and killing multitudes of civilians.

The legacy of the partition of India has contributed to several long-term problems. These include myriad border disputes and the seemingly interminable conflict over the predominantly Muslim but Indian-controlled region of Kashmir. As of the end of the twentieth century, both states were in possession of nuclear weapons. This situation not only conjures up ever more nightmarish scenarios of Indo-Pakistani wars but has also served to attenuate stability on the subcontinent.

In other cases, partition was used by regional and global powers to create "spheres of influence" (Samaddar 2003). New states were suddenly being carved out and molded in the political and ideological image of more dominant states. Partition, therefore, is not only an instrument of conflict resolution but also a means of securing greater influence and political leverage in geostrategic regions of the world. On the Korean peninsula, the Soviet Union and the United States created proxies in North and South Korea. On Cyprus, an intense rivalry between Greece and Turkey split this tiny island into a modern Greek-supported state and a fledgling Turkish one, recognized only by the government in Ankara. And while armed conflict has not occurred in these areas for some time, the prospect of another Korean War or Greco-Turkish conflict remains. The Demilitarized Zone between the two Koreas is the most heavily fortified border in the world, and Greece and Turkey continue to devote significant portions of their national budgets to defense expenditures.

Partition is also a potential solution to the ongoing conflict in Iraq, in which the country would be divided into separate Kurdish, Sunni, and Shiite governments. At the center of the discussion are commentators such as Leslie Gelb and Senator Joseph Biden (Delaware), who have proposed decentralizing Iraq into autonomous ethnically homogenous Kurdish, Sunni, and Shiite federations. The plan assumes that fundamental ethnic differences, particularly between Iraqi Sunnis and Shiites, are what is fueling the insurgency and pushing Iraq perilously close to total civil war. Gelb and other proponents of this plan argue that by allowing each group to control its own affairs, sectarian conflict would diminish and U.S. forces would be allowed to withdraw and redeploy in smaller numbers to avoid a long-term American military commitment in Iraq.

But like most partition plans, the Iraqi partition plan is both promising and problematic. Partition may succeed in separating warring groups and reducing sectarian strife, but the creation of independent Kurdish, Sunni, and Shiite states presents a host of other problems. A Kurdish state is guaranteed to upset Turkey, which has been engaged in an ongoing struggle against Kurdish separatists; a Sunni state would likely be a source of further tension as very little oil is located in the area, which would be allocated to Iraq's Sunnis; and finally, a Shiite state has the potential to become a radical theocracy aligned with Iran. Again, there are benefits to the solutions but there are also very dire and troublesome costs.

In the absence of more effective solutions, partition is often the only viable remedy remaining. Partition, though, is usually an insufficient method of conflict resolution because rather than reduce or eliminate conflict, it tends to exacerbate tensions. The purpose of conflict resolution, of which partition is a method, is to formulate a solution whose principal objective is to facilitate the cessation of further hostilities. Partition aims to resolve conflicts by separating opposing groups or factions that have demonstrated that they are incapable of coexisting within the same borders. But the employment of political division does not eliminate these problems as the architects of partition intend, but in many cases amplifies them.

SEE ALSO *Communalism; Conflict; Decolonization; Ethnic Conflict; Ethnic Fractionalization; Ethnocentrism; Nationalism and Nationality; Negotiation; Peace; Secession; Separatism*

BIBLIOGRAPHY

Biden, Joseph R., and Leslie H. Gelb. 2006. Unity through Autonomy in Iraq. *New York Times.* May 1: sec. A, p. 2.

Collins, Larry, and Dominique Lapierre. 1988. *O Jerusalem: Day by Day and Minute by Minute: The Struggle for Jerusalem and the Birth of Israel.* New York: Simon and Schuster.

Collins, Larry, and Dominique Lapierre. 1997. *Freedom at Midnight: The Epic Drama of India's Struggle for Independence.* New York: HarperCollins.

Kumar, Radha. 2003. Settling Partition Hostilities: Lesson Learnt, the Options Ahead. In *Divided Countries, Separated Cities: The Modern Legacy of Partition,* ed. Ghislaine Glasson Deschaumes and Rada Ivekovic. New Delhi: Oxford University.

Samaddar, Ranabir. 2003. The Last Hurrah that Continues. In *Divided Countries, Separated Cities: The Modern Legacy of Partition,* ed. Ghislaine Glasson Deschaumes and Rada Ivekovic. New Delhi: Oxford University Press.

Raymond Tanter
Nicholas Jakobson

PARTY SYSTEMS, COMPETITIVE

Competitive party systems can be defined in two ways. They may be defined as all party systems in democratic countries, where competition among parties is at least theoretically possible. Alternatively, they may include only those party systems in which elections involving actual competition among two or more parties routinely takes place. For the sake of a broader focus of competitive party systems, the alternative definition is more encompassing and defined further in this entry. Competitive party systems differ from one-party systems primarily in terms of the number of parties that are able to seriously compete for power during elections. In one-party systems, a single dominant party routinely wins elections by a wide margin while all other parties receive quite small vote shares. In competitive party systems, by contrast, two or more parties generally receive substantial numbers of votes during elections. Hence, there is the possibility of alternation in power, in which the party that governs the country at the point of the election loses to an opposition party.

Because one or more opposition parties can meaningfully threaten the governing party with removal from power, elections in competitive party systems can serve as contests among various visions for the future of the country. Anthony Downs, in *An Economic Theory of Democracy* (1957), showed that, under certain conditions, the competitive nature of elections causes party systems to become extremely responsive to the ideological and policy desires of the electorate. If elections are decided primarily on the basis of parties' alternative platforms and proposals, then, competitive party systems may outperform one-party systems in terms of representation.

Elections in one-party systems are often thought to be characterized by patronage politics; that is, gifts of goods or services from the political party to voters. However, patronage politics play an important role in competitive party systems, as well; parties may use patronage to win voters who prefer another party's ideology or policy proposals. At the extreme, elections can become a contest to see which party can offer more patronage to a larger number of voters, with ideology and policy issues entirely neglected. Hence, patronage threatens to undermine the advantage that competitive party systems have over one-party systems in terms of representation.

The majority of party systems in democratic countries throughout the world are competitive rather than one-party systems. Democratic one-party systems have proven viable for long periods of time in several countries, such as Japan, Botswana, and Sweden. In other countries, such as Mexico and Singapore, maintenance of a one-party system depended on the ability of the government to impose restrictions on democracy. However, most party systems in democratic Europe and in the Western Hemisphere have been competitive, as have the party systems of some democratic countries in other regions.

KINDS OF COMPETITIVE PARTY SYSTEMS

The most common approach to differentiating among kinds of competitive party systems is to distinguish by the number of parties that have a meaningful chance of winning elections. By definition, competitive party systems contain at least two important parties, but they sometimes have many more. Hence, the simplest distinction to make is between two-party and multi-party systems. Giovanni Sartori's *Parties and Party Systems* (1976) extends this typology, dividing multiparty systems into limited pluralist systems with three to five important parties and extreme pluralist systems with more than five significant parties. Two-party and limited-pluralist systems lead political parties to moderate their ideologies and policy proposals in order to win the support of centrist voters during elections. Extreme pluralist systems, by contrast, are said to encourage parties to radicalize their proposals in order to differentiate themselves from the many competitors within the party system.

Since the publication of Sartori's work, discussion has focused on a quantitative classification of the number of effective parties in a competitive party system, typically denoted as N. Because N is a continuous measure of the number of meaningful parties in a system, it allows precise descriptions of differences in party systems across coun-

tries and over time. If S_i represents the vote share of the ith party in a given election, the formula for N in that election is:

$$N = \frac{1}{\sum S_i^2}$$

Other analysts have proposed that competitive party systems be distinguished according to their degree of institutionalization. A highly institutionalized party system is one in which the same set of specific political parties persists across elections, the parties have well-developed organizational and psychological connections to the electorate, and party leadership succession is handled by well-specified intra-party procedures. By contrast, a weakly institutionalized party system consists of parties that appear and disappear as organizations on a relatively regular basis; parties form only weak, temporary ties with voters; and party leadership is intensively concentrated in specific individuals, creating a major party crisis each time that a new leader is needed. Most party systems in developed countries are relatively institutionalized, whereas many party systems in less-developed countries and in the post-Soviet world are more weakly institutionalized.

CAUSES OF DIFFERENCES IN PARTY SYSTEMS

What factors determine the kind of competitive party system that a democratic country will have? Scholars have offered two major explanations of observed divergences in the number of parties within a party system: the number of major divisions within society, and electoral rules.

In their essay "Cleavage Structures, Party Systems, and Voter Alignments: An Introduction" (1967), Seymour Martin Lipset and Stein Rokkan argued that European party systems have been profoundly shaped by the resolution that each society has found to a series of shared challenges, each of which encourages a new segment of voters to form a lasting attachment to some specific political party. For example, if the society resolves debates over the proper relationship between church and state early on by allowing religious liberty, then the party system is likely to lack political parties based on divides among religious denominations. If, however, state sponsorship of one particular church persists, then political parties may be expected to form along religious divisions in order to either contest or protect the established church's privileges. A major implication of this idea is that societies with a larger number of major social divisions will have more political parties than societies that are divided along fewer important social lines.

Maurice Duverger's *Political Parties, Their Organization and Activity in the Modern State* (1954) explains differences in the number of political parties within a competitive party system in terms of electoral rules. He argues that electoral systems in which only one candidate per electoral district can win produce two-party systems. On the other hand, electoral systems that allow multiple winners per district result in multi-party systems. Hence, decisions about electoral rules are one of the major tools that societies have for managing the kind of competition that emerges among parties within a party system.

To date, no meaningful consensus has emerged about the factors that cause party systems to become institutionalized. Scholars have argued that greater length of democratic experience and higher levels of economic prosperity may encourage the institutionalization of competitive party systems, but these arguments are understood to be at best partial explanations of the phenomenon of institutionalization among competitive party systems.

BIBLIOGRAPHY

Cox, Gary W. 1997. *Making Votes Count: Strategic Coordination in the World's Electoral Systems.* Cambridge, U.K.: Cambridge University Press.

Downs, Anthony. 1957. *An Economic Theory of Democracy.* New York: Harper and Row.

Duverger, Maurice. 1954. *Political Parties, Their Organization and Activity in the Modern State.* New York: Wiley.

Lipset, Seymour M., and Stein Rokkan, eds. 1967. *Party Systems and Voter Alignments: Cross-National Perspectives.* New York: Free Press.

Mainwaring, Scott P. 1999. *Rethinking Party Systems in the Third Wave of Democratization: The Case of Brazil.* Stanford, CA: Stanford University Press.

Sartori, Giovanni. 1976. *Parties and Party Systems: A Framework for Analysis.* Cambridge, U.K.: Cambridge University Press.

Jason Seawright

PASINETTI, LUIGI
1930–

Luigi Lodovico Pasinetti was born in Zanica, Italy (near Bergamo), on September 12, 1930. Since 1962 he has been a professor of economic analysis at the Catholic University of Milan, where he had obtained his degree in economics in 1954 under the tutelage of Francesco Vito (1902–1968) and Siro Lombardini (b. 1920).

Pasinetti moved to Cambridge University in 1956. He completed his PhD there in 1962 and later became a reader in economics. Study at Cambridge, with research visits at Oxford, Cambridge (Massachusetts), and elsewhere, allowed him to gain access to the top economic

journals. His early paper on Ricardian economics (Pasinetti 1960; Pasinetti 1974) remains a classic.

Pasinetti's own research is, first and foremost, an inquiry into the dynamic theory of economic growth and income distribution. His doctoral dissertation, "A Multi-Sector Model of Economic Growth," developed into a well-known piece of analysis (Pasinetti 1965), which would further develop into his 1981 book *Structural Change and Economic Growth* (see also Pasinetti 1993). His entire body of work, in a characteristic Cambridge fashion, is explicitly rooted in classical economic analysis. Pasinetti, who has always felt a deep attachment to Cambridge, became the senior heir of the Cambridge post-Keynesian school (Pasinetti 2006). He was closely associated, in particular, with Richard Kahn (1905–1989), Nicholas Kaldor (1908–1986), Joan Robinson (1903–1983), and Piero Sraffa (1898–1983). From 1976 onward, Pasinetti turned full-time to his Milan Chair at the Catholic University, where he was elected dean of the faculty of economics. A dedicated teacher, he is also the author of a well-known textbook on the theory of production (Pasinetti 1977).

During the 1960s Pasinetti's theoretical hits were outstanding and surprising. His 1962 theorem (also in Pasinetti 1974) on the *Cambridge equation* would soon become famous and give rise to a vast literature. This equation is a long-run equilibrium relationship between the rate of profit and the rate of growth, usually given as $rs_c = n$, where r is the rate of profit, n is the rate of growth of the population, and s_c is the rate of savings of capitalists. Pasinetti's contribution demonstrated that, surprisingly, the workers' rate of savings has no effect whatsoever on the equilibrium rate of profit. Pasinetti's creative insight thus provided a correction and an intriguing generalization of the Kaldor model of growth and distribution. This theorem has also been called the *Pasinetti paradox.* Thereafter, it became customary to speak of the Kaldor-Pasinetti model of growth and distribution. Mauro Baranzini and G. C. Harcourt (1993, pp. 12–17) discuss in detail the various strands of analysis to which the Pasinetti paradox has given rise.

Pasinetti was an important participant in the Cambridge capital controversies. In 1965 David Levhari, a student of Paul Samuelson, published a paper that sought to demonstrate that some of the paradoxes in capital theory that had emerged in the literature and had been brought into full light in 1960 by Sraffa only had limited validity. However, Pasinetti proved conclusively that there were no grounds for such an attack on Sraffa and the Cambridge view. Pasinetti's paper was first presented in 1965 in Rome at the First World Congress of the Econometric Society. The following year it opened a special issue of the *Quarterly Journal of Economics* (Pasinetti

1966), where Levhari's theorem was acknowledged to be false by the author and by Samuelson himself. It was an impressive showdown that honors the economic profession and has since given rise to a full range of insights in the theory of capital (Pasinetti 1969).

Pasinetti's scientific contributions focus on two main issues: (1) the critique of the neoclassical system; and (2) the completion of the Keynesian system and its extension to distribution and growth. Pasinetti's most significant contribution on both accounts is found in *Structural Change and Economic Growth* (1981), one of the outstanding achievements in economic dynamics. Along with his dissatisfaction with aggregate dynamic models and the deceiving character of a number of disaggregated models (e.g., John von Neumann's model), it is the historical fact of the widespread unevenness of development processes—Pasinetti himself argues—that provides the drift to structural dynamics.

Pasinetti's contribution to economic growth theory has a special place: His system provides the only theory focusing on the conditions under which an economic system will reach and maintain full employment and full capacity utilization in the long run when the system is subject to structural change. Classical economic analysis, here again, provides the foundation to his framework. But Pasinetti has no interest in establishing a canon or dogma on value and distribution: Rather, by building on the open and innovative side of the classical tradition, his schemes of structural economic dynamics focus on technical progress and human learning and form a pathbreaking contribution to growth theory.

SEE ALSO *Cambridge Capital Controversy; Pasinetti Paradox*

BIBLIOGRAPHY

Baranzini, Mauro, and G. C. Harcourt, eds. 1993. *The Dynamics of the Wealth of Nations: Growth, Distribution, and Structural Change: Essays in Honour of Luigi Pasinetti.* London: Macmillan.

Pasinetti, Luigi L. 1960. A Mathematical Formulation of the Ricardian System. *Review of Economic Studies* 27 (2): 78–98.

Pasinetti, Luigi L. 1962. Rate of Profit and Income Distribution in Relation to the Rate of Economic Growth. *Review of Economic Studies* 29 (4): 267–279.

Pasinetti, Luigi L. 1965. A New Theoretical Approach to the Problems of Economic Growth. *Pontificiae Academiae Scientiarum Scripta Varia* 28: 571–677. Reprinted in *The Econometric Approach to Development Planning*, 572–696. Amsterdam: North Holland.

Pasinetti, Luigi L. 1966. Changes in the Rate of Profit and Switches of Techniques. Paradoxes in Capital Theory: A Symposium. *Quarterly Journal of Economics* 80 (4): 503–517.

Pasinetti, Luigi L. 1969. Switches of Techniques and the "Rate of Return" in Capital Theory. *Economic Journal* 79: 508–531.

Pasinetti, Luigi L. 1974. *Growth and Income Distribution: Essays in Economic Theory.* Cambridge, U.K.: Cambridge University Press.

Pasinetti, Luigi L. 1977. *Lectures on the Theory of Production.* London: Macmillan.

Pasinetti, Luigi L. 1981. *Structural Change and Economic Growth: A Theoretical Essay on the Dynamics of the Wealth of Nations.* Cambridge, U.K.: Cambridge University Press.

Pasinetti, Luigi L. 1993. *Structural Economic Dynamics: A Theory of the Economic Consequences of Human Learning.* Cambridge, U.K.: Cambridge University Press.

Pasinetti, Luigi L. 2006. *Keynes and the Cambridge Keynesians.* Cambridge, U.K.: Cambridge University Press.

Pasinetti, Luigi L., and Bertram Schefold, eds. 1999. *The Impact of Keynes on Economics in the 20th Century.* Cheltenham, U.K: Elgar.

Pasinetti, Luigi L., and Robert M. Solow, eds. 1994. *Economic Growth and the Structure of Long-term Development: Proceedings of the IEA Conference Held in Varenna, Italy.* London: Macmillan.

Teixeira, Joanílio R. 1998. Luigi L. Pasinetti. In *Italian Economists of the 20th Century*, ed. Ferdinando Meacci, 272–294. Cheltenham, U.K.: Elgar.

Pier Luigi Porta

PASINETTI PARADOX

The Pasinetti Paradox arises in a model of an idealized economy inhabited by two distinct classes: workers who save a fraction of their wages and of any profit income (also called interest) earned by their past savings; and capitalists who live exclusively off the profits generated by their wealth, saving a fraction, s_c, of their profit income. All wealth is held in the form of capital, and the ratio of profit to capital is called the rate of profit (or the rate of interest by some writers), r. The growth rate of capital is equal to the growth rate of the labor force, n, so that the economy remains in a state of full employment. Under these conditions, Luigi L. Pasinetti showed that a very simple equation describes the long-run (or steady state) relationship between the rate of profit and the rate of growth: $r = n/s_c$. This remarkable equation implies that the rate of profit is determined by the rate of growth and the saving rate of the capitalists, independently of the saving of workers or the underlying technology of the economy, which constitutes the Pasinetti Paradox. It has been at the center of a lively controversy between two different schools of economic thought since its discovery.

One might find it paradoxical that an increase in the saving rate of workers would have no effect on the rate of profit since this, by making capital (e.g., machines and factories) more abundant in relation to labor, might bid up wages and drive down the rate of profit. Pasinetti (a leading classical or neo-Ricardian economist) showed that this effect will not persist into the long run. The rate of profit will decline temporarily, but that would reduce the income of capitalists, allowing the share of wealth owned by workers to increase. Because workers are, by assumption, less thrifty than capitalists, this redistribution will eliminate the need for any change in the rate of profit in the long run. Profits thus have a privileged status in the classical theory of income distribution, for capitalists receive a rate of profit that is just high enough, after deductions for their own consumption, to support the saving necessary for sustained full employment; wages emerge as a kind of residual.

The neoclassical economists find it paradoxical that the rate of profit is not in some way determined by technology, as this seems to refute their marginal productivity theory of income distribution. Paul Samuelson and Franco Modigliani (leading neoclassical economists) pointed out that the Paradox only applies to an economy in which the workers' saving rate is low relative to the capitalists' saving rate. When workers save so much that their wealth grows permanently faster than the capitalists' wealth, the system will tend toward a one-class economy in which the capitalists' share of wealth becomes vanishingly small. This discovery led to an ongoing controversy about whether the two-class or one-class model better describes existing capitalist economies. While the early debates were often tied up with the validity of the marginal productivity theory, it has become evident that even when marginal productivity theory fails, it is usually possible for an economic model to have two possible outcomes, depending on whether the workers' saving propensity exceeds or falls short of some well-defined threshold value.

SEE ALSO *Cambridge Capital Controversy; Economic Growth; Income Distribution; Modigliani, Franco; Neoclassical Growth Model; Pasinetti, Luigi; Samuelson, Paul A.; Solow, Robert M.*

BIBLIOGRAPHY

Darity, William A., Jr. 1981. The Simple Analytics of Neo-Ricardian Growth and Distribution. *American Economic Review* 71 (5): 978–993.

Pasinetti, Luigi L. 1962. Rate of Profit and Income Distribution in Relation to the Rate of Economic Growth. *Review of Economic Studies* 29 (4): 267–269.

Samuelson, Paul A., and Franco Modigliani. 1966. The Pasinetti Paradox in Neoclassical and More General Models. *Review of Economic Studies* 33 (4): 269–301.

Thomas R. Michl

PASSING

Passing refers to a person changing his or her racial or ethnic identity. The term entered the common vocabulary under Jim Crow—the regime of racial segregation in the United States that emerged in the late nineteenth century and lasted into the 1960s. During this time period, many U.S. states and communities adopted the "one drop rule," which held that a person with any African ancestry whatsoever—no matter how remote—would be classified as "Negro." Under Jim Crow, many people with "one drop of black blood" chose to identify as white to evade racial discrimination. Numerous novels and films of this period portrayed the phenomenon, usually in the form of a tragedy.

Two types of individual passing occurred under Jim Crow. In "situational passing," a person of color presented a white identity only in certain situations—for example, to obtain employment in a white-only workplace or to gain entry into a white-only public facility such as a theater or train car. The situational passer retained his or her minority identity at home. The temptation of situational passing was generally understood and tolerated among the African American population.

Some people engaged in full-time passing, commonly referred to as "crossing over" or "passing over." A person who permanently crossed over the color line into a white identity cut most social ties with African American family members and friends. Avoiding contact with other blacks was necessary to prevent arousing suspicions within a new, white social milieu. Because people who crossed over were lost to the African American community, this type of passing was widely condemned by black editorialists and political activists.

In the United States, the Jim Crow–era conception of "passing" implied some degree of subterfuge, in which the person who passed was seen as an impostor who deceived his unsuspecting audience. This conception of passing emerged in the historical context of scientific racism and the one-drop rule, which made the color line seem a rigid boundary based on science rather than a social construction.

In other times and places, changing racial-ethnic identity was commonly done out in the open, often in the court system or as part of a public appeal. Caribbean and Latin American countries did not develop the rigid, one-drop conception of nonwhiteness that existed in the United States under Jim Crow. The saying "money whitens" is a bit of folk wisdom that observes the conflation of class with race, that a rich man is more likely to be accepted as an honorary white than a poor man. In the Spanish colonies, it was possible to purchase through the court system a *cédula de gracias al sacar*—an expensive document that was valuable because it officially removed legal disabilities from the document's bearer, such as illegitimate or multiracial birth status.

Such "passing by permission" was possible in situations where the color line was less clearly defined and thus more permeable. Passing by permission was occasionally available in the United States prior to the Jim Crow era. Some courts granted status as an honorary white to individuals of sufficiently light complexion and sufficiently respectable social status. However, this type of passing became rare in the post–Civil War era. By the early twentieth century, as the one-drop rule gained sway, passing by permission was mostly defunct in the United States.

Although individuals could not pass by permission in the United States under Jim Crow, "group passing by permission" did occur. In rural areas of the southern Atlantic seaboard, communities of mixed ancestry who had been free before the Civil War were occasionally permitted to convert to an American Indian identity and given a slightly higher status than freed slaves (Berry 1963). The motivation for the white community was to pretend that racial mixing between whites and slaves had never occurred by recategorizing the offspring of such unions as Indians. Another motive for conservative white politicians prior to black disfranchisement was that they were able to co-opt lighter-complected voters by making them honorary Indians, thereby gaining support for Jim Crow from a portion of the nonwhite population.

As the Jim Crow era ended in the 1960s, racial-ethnic identities became seen more as an option that each individual could choose for him or herself (Waters 1990). For people of mixed ancestry, self-identification became an acceptable standard, replacing the rigid one-drop system to some extent. As a consequence, reports of African Americans passing as white have mostly disappeared today.

By the late twentieth century, a new phenomenon had emerged—"reverse passing"—in which people raised with a white identity would claim a minority identity to benefit from minority set-asides in business, education, or government. For example, a federal court determined that the Malone brothers of Boston had falsely claimed to be African American to gain employment in the city's fire department under affirmative action criteria (Ford 1994).

More common is the phenomenon of the white "wannabe" passing as American Indian. In one notable case, a former white segregationist politician named Asa Carter adopted a new identity as Forrest Carter and achieved best-seller status as a Cherokee author. In the academy, Ward Churchill was exposed as having falsely claimed to be enrolled in the Keetowah Cherokee Nation in order to advance his career as an ethnic studies professor at the University of Colorado. Genealogical research revealed no evidence of Churchill's claimed American Indian ancestry. After complaints by a group of American Indian professors in the early 1990s, some universities now require that applicants must show proof of tribal enrollment when requesting affirmative action review as American Indians. However, racial-ethnic self-identification remains the de facto standard in most workplaces today, which makes passing mostly a thing of the past.

SEE ALSO *Acting White; Blood and Bloodline; Race; Whiteness*

BIBLIOGRAPHY

Berry, Brewton. 1963. *Almost White: A Study of Certain Racial Hybrids in the Eastern United States.* New York: Macmillan.

Burma, John H. 1946. The Measurement of Negro "Passing." *American Journal of Sociology* 52 (1): 18–22.

Day, Caroline Bond, and Earnest Albert Hooton. 1932. *A Study of Some Negro-White Families in the United States.* Cambridge, MA: Harvard University.

Dominguez, Virginia R. 1986. *White by Definition: Social Classification in Creole Louisiana.* New Brunswick, NJ: Rutgers University Press.

Ford, Christopher A. 1994. Administering Identity: The Determination of "Race" in Race-Conscious Law. *California Law Review* 82 (5): 1231–1285.

Waters, Mary C. 1990. *Ethnic Options: Choosing Identities in America.* Berkeley: University of California Press.

Thomas F. Brown

PASSION

SEE *Eroticism.*

PASSIVE RESISTANCE

Passive resistance commonly refers to actions of nonviolent protest or resistance to authority. The central feature is the conscious choice by the actors to abstain from a violent response even in the face of violent aggression. The term came into common use during the independence struggle in India between the 1920s and 1948. It has been used widely by groups who lack formal authority or position and has sometimes been called the "weapon of the weak."

The term is misleading, however, in that it implies passivity. In fact, passive resistance can be thought of as an active, but nonviolent, mode of struggle in a social conflict. The actions that fall under the term *passive resistance* include many forms of civil disobedience and noncooperation—such as sit-ins, boycotts, blockades and occupations of buildings, tax refusal, and alternative publications and media. More active forms of passive resistance include strikes, walkouts, protest marches, theatrical protests, and hunger strikes.

Passive resistance is rooted in a relational view of political power that sees the rulers of a community or nation as dependent on at least the acquiescence of those who are ruled. Thus, even a dictator's power rests to an important extent on some level of cooperation by the population. This view was articulated by Étienne de la Boétie (1530–1563) in the sixteenth century, as well as by John Locke (1632–1704). The premise that governance derives its legitimate authority only from the consent of the governed is the foundational idea of modern democracy.

One of the foremost contemporary scholars of the political perspective of passive resistance is Gene Sharp. Sharp argues that nonviolent struggle may reflect a moral commitment to pacifism by leaders or activists in a movement (Mohandas Gandhi [1869–1948] and Martin Luther King Jr. [1929–1968] are prominent examples), but pacifism is not a necessary condition. Passive resistance can be explicitly calculating, practical, and strategic and used effectively by those with no moral commitment to pacifism. In the long view of history, it is likely that very few practitioners of passive resistance have been moral pacifists. Arguably, the social power wielded through passive resistance also is democratizing, because it disperses power broadly in society. Like moral pacifism, however, nonviolent struggle does not depend on democracy to be used.

Seen in this broad scope, passive resistance has a long and varied history. Techniques of passive resistance are evident in Aristophanes' play *Lysistrata* (411 BCE), where the women refuse to have sexual relations with their husbands until the men cease their war making. During the War of Independence (1775–1783) in the United States, colonists refused to obey British demands for stamp taxes or for the billeting of troops. Henry David Thoreau (1817–1862) famously articulated his call for civil disobedience with his act of tax refusal during the Mexican War in the 1840s. Suffragists held demonstrations in major cities in the United States and Great Britain in the early years of the twentieth century; a few participated in hunger strikes.

Examples of passive resistance are easily found in many societies in the late twentieth and early twenty-first centuries. Student protestors occupied Tiananmen Square in Beijing in 1989. Nonviolent movements across Eastern Europe brought down Communist governments in the same year. In 2000 a nonviolent movement in Serbia ended the dictatorship of Slobodan Milošević (1941–2006). Civilians on both sides of the Israeli-Palestinian conflict have periodically employed the technique. Indigenous peoples forced the collapse of the government in Bolivia in 2005 with protests and work stoppages.

The most important development of the concepts of passive resistance came from Mohandas Gandhi and the Indian campaigns for independence. As a young lawyer in South Africa at the turn of the twentieth century, Gandhi organized Indians to resist discrimination and unequal treatment. Claiming their rights as citizens of the British Empire, they refused to carry passes and held public acts where they burned the government-issued passes. Out of these experiences, Gandhi developed his idea of *satyagraha*, which is often translated as "soul force" or "truth force."

One of the key principles of Gandhi's use of passive resistance was to find opportunities to publicly confront unjust laws or authority. Protestors, or *satyagrahis*, defied the laws, but sought to maintain a posture that treated the agents of authority with respect and even compassion. Gandhi argued that the means of struggle must be morally compatible with the ends being sought. Protestors often submitted to arrest and even violence, but did not resort to violence themselves. In a protest march to the gates of the saltworks in Dharsana in 1931, for example, protestors willingly walked up to the waiting police, who beat them brutally.

Passive resistance gained a broad public recognition in the United States as the civil rights movement exploded in the 1950s and 1960s. Throughout the movement years, techniques of passive resistance were used both to assert a moral position about rights and equality and to apply economic and political pressure. Martin Luther King Jr. drew on Gandhi and his own Christian tradition to formulate a strategy of nonviolence. Like Gandhi's *satyagrahis*, civil rights activists marched peacefully and publicly in Birmingham, Alabama, in Selma, Alabama, and elsewhere. They also accepted upon themselves the costs of their actions, including discomfort, arrest, beatings, and even death.

Nonviolent actions often also exerted economic and political leverage. Boycotts of busses and department stores pressured private business to end their policies of exclusion. Sit-ins at segregated lunch counters disrupted business until owners relented. Defiant demonstrations often led to mass arrests, which encumbered the police and judicial systems. Provocations of the police to brutality gained national and international political sympathy for the movement.

In the late twentieth and early twenty-first centuries, the uses of passive resistance in many conflicts around the world became more overtly strategic and less concerned with the moral character of the tools. Passive resistance, one of many forms of nonviolent action, provides a source of power to those disenfranchised from traditional politics. When used as part of broader strategy, it has contributed to powerful movements for social change.

SEE ALSO *Civil Disobedience; Civil Rights; Civil Rights Movement, U.S.; Gandhi, Mohandas K.; King, Martin Luther, Jr.; Mexican-American War; Morality; Protest; Resistance; Thoreau, Henry David; Violence*

BIBLIOGRAPHY

Ackerman, Peter, and Christopher Kruegler. 1993. *Strategic Nonviolent Conflict: The Dynamics of People Power in the Twentieth Century.* Westport, CT: Praeger.

King, Martin Luther, Jr. 1958. *Stride toward Freedom: The Montgomery Story.* New York: Harper and Row.

Sharp, Gene. 2005. *Waging Nonviolent Struggle: 20th Century Practice and 21st Century Potential.* Boston: Porter Sargent.

Shridharani, Krishnalal. 1939. *War without Violence: A Study of Gandhi's Method and Its Accomplishment.* New York: Harcourt, Brace.

William B. Vogele

PATH ANALYSIS

Path analysis is a widely used technique for modeling plausible sets of causal relations among three or more observed variables. In the social sciences path analysis has been widely used especially in sociology, and also in psychology (most notably in areas of child or lifespan development or other longitudinal research); elsewhere, it has proven useful in biology, particularly in genetics (including behavioral genetics).

PATH DIAGRAMS

Path models are typically represented in the form of path diagrams, but also be modeled as a set of regression equations. A path model can include any number of independent (or exogenous) variables, any number of dependent (endogenous) variables, and any number of intermediate variables, which are both dependent on some variables and predictive of others. In a path diagram, each variable is represented. The hypothesized links among variables are shown by arrows, representing predictive or correlational relations.

In most cases all of the exogenous variables are modeled with all possible correlations among them represented. A failure to include such a correlation would in effect be a hypothesis that that correlation equals zero, which is rarely applicable to measured variables. Endogenous variables (those with predictive arrows, or *paths*, leading to them) cannot be included in correlational relations. Typically each endogenous variable will

have one additional path leading to it from an unspecified source, representing all sources of variance in the endogenous variable that are not already modeled, called the residual or the disturbance. The absence of this arrow indicates a hypothesis that all of the variance is accounted for in the model which, again, is rarely the case. These residual variance sources are unmeasured exogenous variables that can be correlated with each other or with observed exogenous variables.

MODEL ESTIMATION

When the path model has been established, the next step is to estimate the path coefficients. In conventional multiple linear regression, two or more independent (or exogenous) variables are modeled as predicting one dependent (endogenous) variable. The coefficients derived in multiple regression are partial regression coefficients: the regression of the dependent variable on each independent variable, holding the other independent variables constant. Path analysis is much the same. Each path coefficient is a partial regression coefficient: again, the regression of the specified endogenous variable on the specified "upstream" variable, controlling for the other variables that have paths leading to the endogenous variable. And thus the path coefficients are interpretable as partial regression coefficients: the change in the downstream variable per unit change in the upstream variable, holding all other variables constant. Certain hypotheses involving the path coefficients can be tested as in regression, such as the null hypothesis that the path coefficient equals zero, which is tested by the ratio of the coefficient to its standard error. In fact, if the path model is a recursive system, such that the predictions of downstream variables from upstream can be depicted in a block triangular matrix (where the matrix elements are the effects of the upstream variables [columns] on the downstream variables [rows]—i.e., no variable is both upstream and downstream of a given other variable), then the path analysis can be completely conducted as a series of sequential ordinary least squares regression analyses. In more complex models, other algorithms such as maximum likelihood are needed.

More commonly the path model is estimated in software for structural equation modeling. Structural equation modeling is an extension of path analysis, in which the paths of interest are typically among latent (unmeasured) variables, or factors, with an explicit measurement model linking the factors to observed variables. As a special case of structural equation models, path models can easily be fit in the more sophisticated software.

An important benefit of such software is that it calculates a number of indices of fit of the model. A fitted path model allows for the calculation, from the various path coefficients and estimated variances, covariances, and residual covariances, of a model-implied variance/covariance matrix of the original variables—that is, a covariance matrix that is consistent with the fitted model. Broadly speaking, the fit of the model is an assessment of how well the model, with its estimated coefficients, implies a covariance matrix that matches the original matrix from the data. If there is no significant discrepancy, as measured by a chi-squared statistic, then it may be concluded that the path model is consistent with the data. Note that this does not necessarily indicate that the model is an accurate depiction of causation in reality, but only that it is not inconsistent with reality as indicated by the covariance matrix.

There has been, however, much debate over the utility of the chi-squared statistic. It is widely agreed that a non-significant chi-squared results in a failure to reject the model. However, there may be cases where the chi-squared statistic is sensitive to small deviations between the actual and implied covariance matrices that are not of practical importance to the researcher; this is especially true when the sample size is large. As a result, numerous statistics have been developed to assess approximate or close fit. Among the more prominent of these are the Comparative Fit Index, the Tucker-Lewis Index, and the Root Mean Squared Error of Approximation.

HYPOTHESIS TESTING

The test of model fit is one of the primary results of fitting a path model. Other hypotheses of interest in path analysis frequently involve constraints on the path coefficients: for example, that two path coefficients are equal to each other, or that a set of three coefficients are all equal to zero. These can readily be tested in structural equation modeling software by the estimation of nested models. In this situation the fit of a full model (without the constraints) is compared with a restricted model (with the constraints applied in the estimation process). Two such models are nested if the restricted model can be created strictly by imposing constraints on the full model. If the full model fits the data well, then the difference between the chi-squared statistics for the two models is itself distributed as a chi-squared, with degrees of freedom equal to the number of constraints applied. A significant chi-squared statistic indicates that the restricted model fits significantly less well than the full model.

APPLICATIONS

Path analysis has found utility in a number of areas of the social sciences. Two areas in which it is most prominently featured are behavioral genetics and longitudinal research. In behavioral genetics, one of the most common tools for evaluating heritability is the ACE model, a path model which allows partitioning of variability in twin studies into additive genetic effects, common (shared) environmental effects, and non-shared environmental effects. In child development or lifespan development—or any longitudinal study—path analysis is well suited as the causal direction between variables is typically unambiguous: The hypothesized causation is from the temporally prior variable. Finally, path analysis can be especially useful in intervention studies to identify mechanisms that may mediate the effects of the intervention on the outcomes.

SEE ALSO *Research, Longitudinal; Structural Equation Models*

BIBLIOGRAPHY

Bollen, Kenneth A. 1989. *Structural Equations with Latent Variables.* New York: Wiley.

Loehlin, John C. 1992. *Latent Variable Models: An Introduction to Factor, Path, and Structural Analysis.* 2nd ed. Hillsdale, NJ: Lawrence Erlbaum Associates.

Marsh, Herbert W., and John Balla. 1994. Goodness of Fit in Confirmatory Factor Analysis: The Effects of Sample Size and Model Parsimony. *Quality and Quantity* 28: 185–217.

Patrick S. Malone

PATHOLOGY, SOCIAL

Social pathology is a concept developed in modern social science to refer both to aspects of social structures and to the behaviors and values attributed to particular social categories. Definitions of *social pathology* are particular to specific times and reflect the dominant moral concerns of the era. This concept fits within the ideas of anthropologist Mary Douglas. In *Purity and Danger* (1966) she examines the universality of cultural explanations of things considered "out of order" as polluting and dangerous. These cultural constructions emerge in specific contexts. Regarding social pathology, prior to the Enlightenment in Europe, social transgressions (pathologies) were attributed to supernatural forces exerted by spirits (e.g., possession) or evil humans (witchcraft). As the Enlightenment focused on human reason and scientific understanding of the natural world, early social scientists began to objectify what they defined as natural laws of "society" that explained undesirable human behaviors as transgressions of natural law.

Modern social science developed during a period of rapid social change produced by expanding industrial capitalism and colonialism. Such processes created increased migration and a growing wealth gap between, on the one hand, colonial nations and colonized territories, and on the other, wealthy industrialist/financiers and European working classes. These social changes produced dislocations and inequalities that led to fears among established groups of moral and social danger. In the nineteenth century, following parallel developments in the advancing science of biology, social theory often used either biology (e.g., racial types) or biological analogies to the physical body and biological processes to explain the social system.

Émile Durkheim, a French sociologist, created the foundation for the modern sociological study of society by focusing on social facts, structures, and systems rather than individuals. His profound ideas generated many concepts and laid the basis for many fields of study. Like other foundational social theorists confronting rapid change, he privileged solidarity and cohesion as normal. Durkheim introduced two analogies for a smoothly functioning social order characterized by solidarity: the machine (mechanical) and the body (organic). He envisioned society as a system seeking equilibrium with norms for behavior. *Anomie* was a pathological condition of moral breakdown at the societal level.

Throughout the early twentieth century, this emphasis on social equilibrium or structural functionalism, further developed by such thinkers as Talcott Parsons, dominated U.S. social theory. In defining equilibrium and stasis (status quo) as desirable, it was implied that change and disorder were abnormal and threatening. These pathologies were not attributed to the differential nature and value of individuals but rather to aspects of structure. Nonetheless, such ideas emphasized the value of returning to the status quo over change.

The idea of declaring the behavior of individuals in particular social categories as socially pathological followed a different trajectory. In the post-Darwin nineteenth century, Darwin's theories of evolutionary change were applied loosely in ways that misinterpreted his theory. Particular social categories or populations were seen as having an essential, innate, and immutable behavioral inferiority leading to criminal and dangerous behaviors. While Darwin saw natural selection occurring in a random, purposeless way with no implied hierarchy of worth, Social Darwinism saw different classes and races as arrayed in terms of inferiority and superiority.

The development of race studies occurred as new nation-states were restructured from former European imperial monarchies, creating a need to build national unity and loyalty among diverse citizens. This led to preoccupations with the dangers of difference and an interest in the scientific study of race. Throughout the new nations of Europe and in the United States, nascent disciplines emerged such as the now-repudiated anthropological "science" of race and the racially tinged science of criminology, which used race to predict and explain crim-

inal behavior and justify policies of "social hygiene." In the twentieth century, the racial ideas of scientific racism and criminology continued, especially in Germany. There they culminated in Nazi racial theory, which advocated a removal of categories of people defined as biologically debased, such as Jews, Gypsies, and homosexuals.

As such racial thinking was repudiated in the twentieth century, concepts of culture and cultural relativism, as well as concepts related to the self, psychic states, and personal identity, developed. Behaviors viewed as pathological for society relied less on innate racial attributes. While they continued to be associated with specific social categories, the new link between populations and pathology emphasized cultural learning and personal experience rather than biology. While biological attributes retained explanatory power for differences between genders and sexualities (e.g., homosexuality), behavioral pathologies were more associated with improper values, choices, and psychological states.

Ideas such as the culture of poverty first promulgated by Oscar Lewis blamed poor people for perpetuating their condition through inappropriate values and "weak ego structures." A whole series of "social pathologies," from dependence on welfare to substance abuse and inner-city gang violence, were linked to having learned improper values through substandard parenting in single-parent households. Yet these explanations, which blamed specific populations for social pathology, merely replaced racial determinism with cultural determinism.

Because stability and order are privileged as natural and normal and the profound and rapid social changes of recent decades are relegated to the sphere of the abnormal and dangerous, people who are the most disadvantaged and excluded in dominant ideologies and representations, such as single mothers ("welfare queens"), nonwhites, and nonheterosexuals, are blamed for their own situations. They also function as popular scapegoats for broader social problems and "moral decline." In this way, they carry the weight of social problems not only through their personal circumstances of material and political deprivation but also through their symbolic representation as stigmatized and despised people.

Social science critiques of the culture of poverty examine ways to represent poor people as varied individuals with competence and awareness who cannot be categorized in terms of innate biology or culture. Particular behaviors of the poor can be analyzed in terms of the extremely constrained options of disadvantaged social positions, as rational strategies, or as political opposition rather than social pathology.

Moreover, in the second half of the twentieth century U.S. sociologists such as C. Wright Mills and William Ryan began to point out the role that dominant elite interests play in defining normalcy and pathology as the status quo as well as the way this masks the relationship between structural relations of power and the social production of inequality. Blaming the victims (stigmatized and disadvantaged groups such as the poor) was shown to not only hide the effects of power and privilege but also to stifle recognition of a need to address social problems through sociopolitical change. Late-twentieth-century European social theories developed by such thinkers as Michel Foucault, Pierre Bourdieu, and others have brought issues of differential power and inequality to the fore. After continued world wars and the cold war as well as social movements advocating anticolonial independence, socialism, feminism, and civil and human rights, these ideas have emerged and have led to reexamining the ideological uses of social pathology as a way of reinforcing current inequalities in the social order.

SEE ALSO *Benign Neglect; Bourdieu, Pierre; Crime and Criminology; Culture of Poverty; Darwin, Charles; Darwinism, Social; Determinism, Cultural; Durkheim, Émile; Foucault, Michel; Inequality, Gender; Inequality, Income; Inequality, Political; Inequality, Racial; Inequality, Wealth; Lewis, Oscar; Mills, C. Wright; Morality and Inequality; Neighborhood Effects; Poverty; Social Science; Sociology*

BIBLIOGRAPHY

Bellah, Robert, ed. 1973. *Émile Durkheim: On Morality and Society: Selected Writings.* Chicago: University of Chicago Press.

Douglas, Mary. 1966. *Purity and Danger: An Analysis of the Concepts of Pollution and Taboo.* London: Routledge and Kegan Paul.

Goode, Judith, and Jeff Maskovsky, eds. 2001. *The New Poverty Studies: The Ethnography of Power, Politics, and Impoverished People in the United States.* New York: New York University Press.

Horowitz, Irving L. 1966. *Power, Politics and People: The Collected Essays of C. Wright Mills.* New York: Oxford University Press.

O'Connor, Alice. 2001. *Poverty Knowledge: Social Science, Social Policy and the Poor in Twentieth Century U.S. History.* Princeton, NJ: Princeton University Press.

Ryan, William. 1971. *Blaming the Victim.* New York: Pantheon.

Judith Goode

PATINKIN, DON
1922–1995

Don Patinkin was born in Chicago on January 8, 1922, to Russian Jewish immigrants, and he died in Jerusalem on August 6, 1995. His main contribution was the integration of the theories of value and money developed in *Money, Interest, and Prices*, the most influential book on monetary macroeconomics in the 1950s and 1960s. That book grew out of Patinkin's PhD thesis, submitted to the University of Chicago in 1947 after an academic year as research assistant at the Cowles Commission for Economic Research, where he interacted with well-known economists such as Lawrence Klein, Kenneth Arrow, Trygve Haavelmo, and Jacob Marschak, among others. In 1949, after a brief period as assistant and associate professor at the Universities of Chicago (1947–1948) and Illinois (1948–1949) respectively, Patinkin moved to Israel to take up a position as lecturer in the newly created department of economics at the Hebrew University, where he stayed until the end of his life. Apart from his academic appointments at the university (as full professor after 1957 and emeritus after 1989), Patinkin also served as the first director of the Maurice Falk Institute for Economic Research in Israel from 1956 to 1972.

REAL BALANCE EFFECT

Patinkin's 1956 book may be regarded as the most important contribution to the neo-Walrasian synthesis (named after French economist Léon Walras)—that is, the attempt to build the theoretical framework of macroeconomics on a developed general equilibrium system—after John Hicks's 1939 *Value and Capital.* The process of adjustment to equilibrium was firmly grounded by Patinkin on the "method of successive approximation," Walras's theory of *tatonnement,* which had been largely neglected in the literature. Together with Paul A. Samuelson's stability analysis, the *tatonnement* provided the backbone of Patinkin's discussion of how the market solves the excess-demand equations. He criticized traditional "classical" monetary analysis for assuming that the equations of excess demand for goods determine relative prices (called the "homogeneity postulate"), while the price level is determined by the equation of exchange in the market for money. Partly motivated by the work of his former Chicago teacher Oskar Lange, Patinkin showed that this "dichotomization" of the economy into real and monetary sectors was logically inconsistent. In particular he was the first to realize that if the demand for money depended on the price level then—because of the budget constraint of agents—the demand for goods also depended on that level. Logical consistency required that the equations of excess demand for goods include real money balances as an argument in the individual utility functions, named "real balance effect" by Patinkin. The invalid dichotomization described above should be, according to Patinkin, distinguished from the "valid dichotomy" between the real and monetary sectors, expressed by the quantity theory of money as formulated in his book: Under the assumption the agents are free of money illusion, changes in the quantity of money affect only nominal variables and leave the equilibrium value of real variables unaffected (i.e., money is neutral in the long-run).

Although the stabilizing effect of changes in the price level on real balances and, therefore, on aggregate demand had been discussed before, specifically by Gottfried Haberler in his 1937 book *Prosperity and Depression* and by A. C. Pigou in his 1943 article "The Classical Stationary State," they did not work out its implications for the integration of monetary and value theory. According to Harry G. Johnson in his 1962 article "Monetary Theory and Policy," Patinkin's criticism of classical monetary theory sparked off a debate about the accuracy of his historical account and the import of his theoretical claims, known as "the Patinkin controversy." A few years later, Frank Hahn argued in his 1965 article "On Some Problems of Proving the Existence of an Equilibrium in a Monetary Economy," that Patinkin left unsolved a fundamental problem of monetary theory: to prove the existence of a general equilibrium with a positive value for money.

DISEQUILIBRIUM MACROECONOMICS

Patinkin's second main theme was the contrast between the Keynesian model (named after British economist John Maynard Keynes)—where markets do not clear and quantities respond to quantities—and the Walrasian system, which assumes that trades are only made at a market-clearing price vector. According to Patinkin, unemployment is a disequilibrium phenomenon that should be understood as the result of the effect of aggregate demand constraint on the behavior of firms and workers. Patinkin's disequilibrium analysis of the labor market, with both firms and workers off their respective labor demand and labor supply curves, was later complemented by Robert W. Clower's analogous interpretation of consumption as a function of income in the goods market in his 1965 publication "The Keynesian Counter-Revolution: A Theoretical Appraisal." In their 1971 article "A General Disequilibrium Model of Income and Employment," Robert J. Barro and Herschel I. Grossman combined Patinkin's and Clower's analyses in a fixed-price model that quickly became the most influential exposition of disequilibrium macroeconomics. It was largely thanks to the Barro-Grossman model—which may be regarded as an outgrowth of chapter 13 of *Money, Interest, and Prices*—that Patinkin's approach to unemployment finally penetrated the macroeconomic literature. After this theoretical contribution to Keynesian economics, Patinkin became engaged in the 1970s and 1980s in an extensive investiga-

tion of the historical development of Keynes's thought. He concluded that the "central message" of Keynes's macroeconomics was the role of changes in aggregate income in bringing the goods market to less than full employment equilibrium, based on the assumption that the marginal propensity to consume is less than one.

PATINKIN'S IMPACT

Patinkin's search for the microfoundations of macroeconomics has had a deep impact on economic theory. His contribution to the money-in-the-utility-function approach has become part of modern monetary theory mainly through the work of Miguel Sidrauski (1967). Although the real balance effect has lost space to substitution effects in monetary economics—its acceptance nowadays depends on the theoretical assumption that the intertemporal utility function is not separable in consumption and money balances, and on the empirical evidence about its size at business-cycle frequencies—according to Richard J. Sweeney (1988) and Peter N. Ireland (2005) it still plays a role as part of the broader wealth effect in models with specified intertemporal budget constraints and forward looking agents. In the same vein, despite the diminishing interest on disequilibrium macroeconomics since the late 1970s, Patinkin's pathbreaking search for the compatibility of macroeconomics and microeconomics has left its mark on the research agenda of Keynesian and neoclassical economists alike.

SEE ALSO *Arrow, Kenneth J.; Barro-Grossman Model; Economics, Classical; Economics, Keynesian; Economics, New Keynesian; Equilibrium in Economics; General Equilibrium; Hicks, John R.; IS-LM Model; Klein, Lawrence; Macroeconomics; Market Clearing; Microeconomics; Microfoundations; Tatonnement; Walras' Law; Walras, Léon*

BIBLIOGRAPHY

PRIMARY WORKS

Patinkin, Don. 1948. Price Flexibility and Full Employment. *The American Economic Review* 38 (4): 543–564.

Patinkin, Don. 1949a. The Indeterminacy of Absolute Prices in Classical Economic Theory. *Econometrica* 17 (1): 1–27.

Patinkin, Don. 1949b. Involuntary Unemployment and the Keynesian Supply Function. *Economic Journal* 59 (235): 360–383.

Patinkin, Don. 1959. *The Israel Economy: The First Decade.* Jerusalem: The Maurice Falk Institute for Economic Research in Israel.

Patinkin, Don. 1972. *Studies in Monetary Economics.* New York: Harper & Row.

Patinkin, Don. 1976. *Keynes' Monetary Thought: A Study of Its Development.* Durham, NC: Duke University Press.

Patinkin, Don. 1981. *Essays On and In the Chicago Tradition.* Durham, NC: Duke University Press.

Patinkin, Don. 1982. *Anticipations of the General Theory? And Other Essays on Keynes.* Chicago: University of Chicago Press.

Patinkin, Don. 1989. *Money, Interest, and Prices: An Integration of Monetary and Value Theory.* 2nd ed., abridged. Cambridge, MA: MIT Press. (Orig. pub. 1956.)

Patinkin, Don. 1993. Israel's Stabilization Program of 1985, Or Some Simple Truths of Monetary Theory. *Journal of Economic Perspectives* 7 (2): 103–128.

SECONDARY WORKS

Barkai, Haim, Stanley Fischer, and Nissan Liviatan, eds. 1993. *Monetary Theory and Thought: Essays in Honour of Don Patinkin.* London: Macmillan.

Barro, Robert J., and Herschel I. Grossman. 1971. A General Disequilibrium Model of Income and Employment. *American Economic Review* 61 (1): 82–93.

Boianovsky, M. 2006. The Making of Chapters 13 and 14 of Patinkin's *Money, Interest, and Prices. History of Political Economy* 38 (2): 193–249.

Clower, Robert W. 1965. The Keynesian Counter-Revolution: A Theoretical Appraisal. In *The Theory of Interest Rates*, eds. F. Hahn and F. Brechling, 270–297. London: Macmillan.

De Vroey, Michel, and Pascal Bridel, eds. 2002. Patinkin and the Development of Modern Economic Theory. Special issue of the *European Journal of the History of Economic Thought* 9 (2).

Haberler, Gottfried. 1937. *Prosperity and Depression: A Theoretical Analysis of Cyclical Movements.* Geneva, Switzerland: League of Nations.

Hahn, F. H. 1965. On Some Problems of Proving the Existence of an Equilibrium in a Monetary Economy. In *The Theory of Interest Rates*, eds. F. Hahn and F. Brechling, 126–135. London: Macmillan.

Hicks, Sir John Richard. 1939. *Value and Capital: An Inquiry into Some Fundamental Principles of Economic Theory.* Oxford: Clarendon Press.

Ireland, Peter N. 2005. The Liquidity Trap, the Real Balance Effect and the Friedman Rule. *International Economic Review* 46 (4): 1271–1301.

Johnson, Harry G. 1962. Monetary Theory and Policy. *American Economic Review* 52 (3): 335–384.

Lange, Oskar. 1944. *Price Flexibility and Employment.* Bloomington, IN: The Principia Press.

Pigou, A. C. 1943. The Classical Stationary State. *Economic Journal* 53 (212): 343–351.

Sidrauski, Miguel. 1967. Rational Choice and Patterns of Growth in a Monetary Economy. *American Economic Review* 57 (2): 534–544.

Sweeney, Richard J. 1988. *Wealth Effects and Monetary Theory.* New York: Blackwell.

Weintraub, E. Roy. 1979. *Microfoundations: The Compatibility of Microeconomics and Macroeconomics.* Cambridge, U.K.: Cambridge University Press.

Mauro Boianovsky

PATRIARCHY

Patriarchy is a social structural phenomenon in which males have the privilege of dominance over females, both visibly and subliminally. This phenomenon is manifested in the values, attitudes, customs, expectations, and institutions of the society, and it is maintained through the process of socialization. Some societies are more patriarchal than others, but virtually all are characterized by the phenomenon in one form or another. Patriarchy is a function of male physical, social, economic, and political power. Females and children, along with any individuals with a nontraditional gender identity, suffer from subordination to men.

The term *patriarchy* comes from the Latin *pater* (father) and *arch* (rule). Historically, "rule of the father" was the more appropriate definition of patriarchy. Valentine Moghadam has written that under classic patriarchy, "the senior man has authority over everyone else in the family, including younger men, and women are subject to distinct forms of control and subordination" (2004, p. 141). Furthermore, property, residence, and descent all proceed exclusively through the male line. Today, however, this definition may be considered an overly simplistic description because the phenomenon has evolved substantially over time.

As already mentioned, to varying degrees, patriarchy is nearly universally prevalent. Although, as Gerda Lerner (1986) has noted, anthropologists have found societies in which sexual differences are not associated with practices of dominance or subordination, patriarchy does exist in the majority of societies. Often, *patriarchy* is associated more strongly with nations characterized by religious fundamentalism. Yet male domination and female subordination are salient features of social structure in virtually all societies, regardless of the race, ethnicity, class, or religion of the members. Most patriarchal societies have adopted characteristics associated with male domination, namely, aggression and power, as well as the consequences of these characteristics, namely, war and destruction.

Because the subordination of women to men is a feature in the majority of all societies, patriarchy is often argued to be due to biology, such as women's principal role in childbearing. However, many scholars today hold that patriarchy is a social construction. Lerner has written that there are indeed biological differences between men and women, but "the values and implications based on [those differences] are the result of culture" (1986, p. 6).

The existence of patriarchy may be traced back to ancient times. Lerner has stated that the commodification of women's sexual and reproductive capacity emerged at about the same time as the development of private property, thus setting the stage for patriarchal social structures. The Bible is sometimes cited as exemplifying the original "father-rule" form of patriarchy in many of its stories. An example is the Adam and Eve story of creation, in which Adam is created first, followed by all the animals. Then Eve is created from part of Adam so that, in a sense, he may be considered her parent (Pateman 1989, p. 451). As such, Adam is clearly in the dominant position. This is consistent with Lerner's explanation that "men learned to institute dominance and hierarchy over other people by their earlier practice of dominance over the women of their own group" (1986, p. 9). The sexual subordination of women was subsequently written into the earliest system of laws, enforced by the state, and secured by the cooperation of women through such means as "force, economic dependency on the male head of the family, class privileges bestowed upon conforming and dependent women of the upper classes, and the artificially created division of women into respectable and not-respectable women" (Lerner 1986, p. 9).

The classic form of patriarchy decreased in its prevalence during the seventeenth century. The transition to what Teresa Meade and Pamela Haag have described as a broader fraternal-right patriarchy or "domination of society by the 'brotherhood of men'" (1998, p. 92) is often associated with the rise of "capitalist rationalism" because the prior standard of fathers ruling over sons was not compatible with the demands of capitalism. Meade and Haag also note that "the defeat of classic patriarchy in the Enlightenment era meant that the father's absolute power over sons was lost and patriarchy moved to the broader civil society" (1998, p. 92). This transformation occurred to the detriment of women whose work in the home was suddenly separated from what was considered to be the larger economy.

Modern patriarchy is structural, meaning that it underlies the foundations of all of society's institutions. In most societies, any accomplishments in the direction of gender equality must be made within a larger patriarchal structure. This is one reason why women are at such a constant disadvantage socially, politically, and economically. In the world today, the vast majority of leaders are men. Moreover, Laura Bierema has noted that while women make up over half the workforce, they fall far short of men in terms of pay, promotions, benefits, and other economic rewards. She has also observed that those women who are successful economically often reach their goals by emulating men, thus reproducing the masculine traits and characteristics that are associated with success. By doing so, the patriarchal systems "that discriminate against women and people of color" are reinforced (Bierema 2003, p. 3). Those women who actually become world leaders or advance to high positions in the business world tend often to do so on terms that accommodate the needs and characteristics of males, hence necessitating the need for them to make significant sacrifices (e.g., having a

family versus a career). Otherwise they would be viewed as distinctly different from their male peers, and this would be disadvantageous.

SEE ALSO *Gender; Power*

BIBLIOGRAPHY

Bierema, Laura L. 2003. The Role of Gender Consciousness in Challenging Patriarchy. *International Journal of Lifelong Education* 22: 3–12.

Lerner, Gerda. 1986. *The Creation of Patriarchy.* New York: Oxford University Press.

Meade, Teresa, and Pamela Haag. 1998. Persistent Patriarchy: Ghost or Reality? *Radical History Review* 71: 91–95.

Moghadam, Valentine M. 2004. Patriarchy in Transition: Women and the Changing Family in the Middle East. *Journal of Comparative Family Studies* 35: 137–162.

Pateman, Carole. 1989. "God Hath Ordained to Man a Helper": Hobbes, Patriarchy, and Conjugal Right. *British Journal of Political Science* 19: 445–463.

Christine Guarneri
Dudley L. Poston Jr.

PATRICIANS

The word *patrician* is an adjective derived from the Latin word for "father," which was also a term for a senator. In the later republic of the second and first centuries BCE, certain families were recognized as patrician by their distinctive clothing and the reservation of certain priesthood positions for them. The Roman historical tradition (formed in the third and second centuries BCE) held that patricians consisted of families granted this title at various times during the Roman kingdom and that these families had a monopoly on political office at the start of the republic. There ensued a long political conflict known as the Struggle of the Orders, in which non-patricians, known individually as the plebeians and collectively as the plebs, sought to attain the redress of economic grievances and the right to hold office. The upshot was that in the period from c. 367–c. 287 BCE the patrician monopoly of office holding was broken. The wealthy plebeian families then fused with the patricians to form a ruling class known as the nobility.

Examination of the list of the earliest chief magistrates of the republic (the consuls) shows that the traditional story of the origin of the patricians cannot be true. For the first half century of the republic (starting c. 509 BCE), a number of families that were later of plebeian status appear among the consuls. It is only from around 450 BCE onward that patricians tend to monopolize the office, and this monopoly seems established by the end of the

400s. It is a phenomenon attestable elsewhere (e.g., the city-states of Archaic Greece and the free cities of late medieval Germany) for the office-holding families of a given period to establish for themselves a legal monopoly on office, a situation that eventually breaks down as some of the monopolizing families fall into economic decline while new families attain wealth and wish to end the monopoly.

While some Roman patricians eventually sank into obscurity, a number of the most prominent senatorial families of the mid- and late republic were of patrician status, and this status conferred great prestige. The patricians suffered many deaths during the civil wars that saw the decline of the republic (88–31 BCE) and ushered in the autocratic form of government known as the Roman Empire. There were not enough patricians to fill the priesthood positions reserved for them. Both Julius Caesar (c. 100–44 BCE) and his adopted son Augustus, the first emperor (ruled 27 BCE–14 CE), were authorized to create new patrician families (from prominent senatorial families of plebeian status). As part of his effort to conceal his power by restoring some of the forms (but not the substance) of the old republican government, Augustus promoted the careers of the remaining patricians. The old patrician families continued their decline as they died out naturally and fell victim to prosecution under the Julio-Claudian emperors, and the emperors continued to create new patricians. Men with this status enjoyed swifter advancement in their careers, but the status died out in the third century.

SEE ALSO *Class; Heredity; Hierarchy; Stratification*

BIBLIOGRAPHY

Cornell, Tim. 1995. *The Beginnings of Rome: Italy and Rome from the Bronze Age to the Punic Wars (c. 1000–264 BC).* London and New York: Routledge.

Mitchell, Richard E. 1990. *Patricians and Plebeians: The Origin of the Roman State.* Ithaca, NY: Cornell University Press.

Raaflaub, Kurt A., ed. 2005. *Social Struggles in Archaic Rome: New Perspectives on the Conflict of the Orders.* 2nd ed. Malden, MA: Blackwell.

Christopher Mackay

PATRIOTISM

The word *patriotism* derives from the Latin *patria,* meaning "country." Patriots are citizens joined by a love of country and a readiness to sacrifice, perhaps even die, for their country. Such patriotism was emphatically characteristic of the Spartans of classical antiquity. They were citizens in the strict sense of the term: They shared an identity with others to whom they were related by nationality, as well as by blood, and a sense of belonging to a community for which they bore responsibility. In a word, they were public-spirited.

The Spartans' sense of public-spiritedness did not develop by accident. Spartan boys were trained, almost from birth, to be soldiers, and Spartan girls were required to exercise naked (in public), with a view to producing sons capable of being soldiers, as well as daughters capable of giving birth to them. Their readiness to fight (and perhaps give their lives) for their country is best exemplified by the legendary King Leonidas and the three hundred Spartan soldiers who fought the Persians and died at Thermopylae in 480 BCE. For good reason, then, the word *Spartan* has come to be associated with *patriot.*

In one respect at least, it was easy for Spartans to be patriots, easier than it would prove to be for later generations of Greeks, or Europeans generally. Spartans could be *for* their city without reservation or equivocation, because there was nothing else in Sparta to be for: no gods other than the city's gods, and no life other than the life in and provided by the city. As George Grote suggests, the subordination of the individual to the state has had no parallel in the history of the world.

The likes of Sparta were surely not to be found anywhere in the West after the advent of Christianity. By effecting a separation of the "things that are Caesar's" and the "things that are God's," Christianity made it more likely that a person's loyalties would be divided, and sometimes come into conflict.

Such conflict became even more likely after Martin Luther (1483–1546) launched the Reformation. Before Luther, there had been one church, but now there were several: Lutherans and Calvinist, as well as Roman Catholic. This development had political consequences. Could a devout Roman Catholic such as Thomas More (1478–1535) obey his sovereign, Henry VIII (1491–1547), after the sovereign broke with the papacy in Rome? Could the Calvinist (or Presbyterian) Scots obey their king, Charles I (1600–1649), who commanded them to worship according to the Anglican Book of Common Prayer? Not likely and, in the event, impossible; the pious More preferred the scaffold and the stubborn Scots a civil war.

The seventeenth century was not a propitious time for the making of patriots. Almost everywhere in Europe, the rulers were princes and the people subjects, not citizens. This may explain why the first recorded use in English of the word *patriotism* did not occur until 1726, when it was defined as "public-spiritedness." Generally speaking, only citizens (not subjects) could be expected to be public-spirited.

Thus, patriotism became linked with the rise of popular sovereignty. This development, in turn, depended on the discovery or pronouncement of new universal and revolutionary principles respecting the rights of man—see, for example, Thomas Hobbes's *Leviathan* (1651) and John Locke's *Two Treatises of Government* (c. 1690). From these new principles came new governments—first in America, then in France—and with them a new understanding of patriotism, or an understanding other than the sort of filial piety associated with Sparta.

Alexis de Tocqueville (1805–1859) was the first to recognize this new form of patriotism, or at least to speak of it. In his *Democracy in America* (1835–1840), Tocqueville argued that this patriotism was more rational than the simple love of one's native land; this patriotism, he said, was "born of enlightenment" and grows with "the exercise of rights." Abraham Lincoln (1809–1865), in his 1852 eulogy on the American statesman Henry Clay (1777–1852), declared that Clay "loved his country partly because it was his own country, but mostly because it was a free country; and he [worked zealously] for its advancement, prosperity and glory, because he saw in such the advancement, prosperity and glory of *human* liberty, *human* rights, and *human* nature" (Lincoln [1852] 1989, p. 264). There is nothing parochial about this patriotism; Lincoln made that very plain. Clay is praised not so much for loving his country, but rather for loving the *idea* of his country, or its principles. Those principles are scientific and, therefore, universal principles. Any country might adopt them.

This was of particular concern to Edmund Burke (1729–1797), the Anglo-Irish statesman and political theorist. He understood that the French Revolution (1789–1799) was something new and (to him) something alarming, especially because its principles appeared to be readily exportable; those abstract, scientific, and universal principles, if exported—and unleavened by the unique experiences or traditions of a country—would reduce not only the French but the people of all Europe to "one homogenous mass."

Something like this did in fact begin to happen, but the French Revolution, and what Pierre Manent has called the enormous Napoleonic enterprise, "unleashed a contrary movement of particularization and national separation" (Manent 1998, p. 187). In a word, the attempt to export these universal principles gave rise to the glorification of the nation, which is to say, nationalism and a politics of ethnicity, where what matters is blood, not the political principles associated with patriotism. "I speak *for* Germans simply, *of* Germans simply," said the philosopher Johann Fichte (1762–1814) in 1807, a sentiment repeated by many another Europeans (Fichte 1807, p. 3).

Since then, in intellectual circles, the very idea of the nation—as well as that of patriotism—has been discredited. This process began in 1848 when Karl Marx (1818–1883) declared in *The Communist Manifesto* that "working men have no country" (Marx and Engels [1848] 1932), and they would refuse to fight for country. This proved not to be true when World War I broke out in 1914. Then, after World War II (1939–1945), Europeans set about the task of divesting themselves of their sovereignty in favor of the European Union. It remains to be seen if the citizens of the European Union will love it, let alone fight for it.

It seems that patriotism has become unfashionable among some intellectuals. One prominent American university professor, Martha Nussbaum, suggests that the times require that people get rid of patriotism and, to that end, become citizens of the world and lovers of humanity. But humanity does not have a government, and there is no reason to believe that, if it had a government, it would be lovable.

SEE ALSO *Citizenship; Nationalism and Nationality*

BIBLIOGRAPHY

Berns, Walter. 2001. *Making Patriots.* Chicago: University of Chicago Press.

Fichte, Johann Gottlieb. [1807] 1922. *Address to the German Nation.* Trans. R. F. Jones and G. H. Turnbull. London: Open Court.

Grote, George. 1851–1867. *History of Greece.* Vol. 2. New York: The Bradley Company, Publishers.

Lincoln, Abraham. 1989. Eulogy on Henry Clay, July 6th, 1852. In *Abraham Lincoln: Speeches and Writings 1832–1858,* ed. Don E. Fehrenbacher. New York, NY: The Library of America.

Marx, Karl, and Friedrich Engels. [1848] 1932. *The Communist Manifesto.* New York: Modern Library.

Manent, Pierre. 1998. *Modern Liberty and Its Discontents,* ed. and trans. Daniel J. Mahoney and Paul Seaton. Lanham, MD: Rowman and Littlefield.

Nussbaum, Martha Craven. 1996. *For Love of Country: Debating the Limits of Patriotism.* Boston: Beacon.

Tocqueville, Alexis de. [1835–1840] 2000. *Democracy in America.* Vol. 1 (Pt. 2, chap. 6). Trans. Harvey C. Mansfield and Delba Winthrop. Chicago: University of Chicago Press.

Walter Berns

PATRONAGE

The term *patronage* describes the practice of distributing public sector posts in exchange for political support. In the absence of binding civil service rules, a party boss (patron) rewards loyal partisans (clients) by providing them with public sector employment. Patronage therefore can be included among a broad range of clientelistic political practices in which parties use public resources to deliver private and club benefits to particular groups of voters in order to maximize electoral support. Different from other types of clientelistic practices, patronage provides the client with a steady source of income whose stability depends on the reelection of the patron.

To successfully develop a patronage system requires: (1) the selection of political leaders through elections, (2) mass adult suffrage, (3) a high degree of electoral competition within or between parties, and (4) weak civil service rules. The first three requirements—elections, mass political participation, and party competition—lead to increasing demands on political elites by their core constituency. In the absence of civil service rules, the distribution of public sector posts becomes an appealing strategy that ties the survival of the voter (client) to the survival of the party boss (patron).

Because patrons can only sustain a limited number of clients, two crucial functions of the patronage exchange are the selection and monitoring of clients. In selecting clients, patrons seek to either maintain their vote or to expand it. For maintaining their vote, patrons target loyal voters. For expanding their vote, patrons target swing voters and invest considerable more resources in monitoring the patronage exchange. The practice of patronage is intimately connected to the rise of political machines specialized in organizing and allocating political influence by controlling the supply of public sector jobs and by monitoring the vote of large constituencies. Because the cement that binds the patron and the client is not ideological, political allegiance to the machine is based on the distribution of particularistic, material rewards over different types of political personnel.

A widespread political phenomenon, patronage is also known in the United States by the term *spoils system*, where the "spoils" of the political system go to the "victor" of the electoral contest. The spoils system that emerged during the Gilded Age was eventually dismantled by the enactment of the Pendleton Act in 1883 and the creation of the Civil Service Commission, which introduced meritocratic rules for the recruitment and promotion of public service employees. The introduction of these rules significantly reduced the available pool of public jobs that political machines could allocate to voters. Such reforms also weakened the political grip of party bosses, such as William M. "Boss" Tweed in New York, Huey P. Long Jr. in Louisiana, and Edward H. Crump in Chicago. Since the late twentieth century, as an increasing number of countries have democratized, comparative scholars have emphasized the negative consequences of patronage for the development of an independent citizenship capable of holding politicians accountable for their performance in office.

SEE ALSO *Political Parties*

BIBLIOGRAPHY

Cox, Gary W., and Matthew D. McCubbins. 1986. Electoral Politics as a Redistributive Game. *Journal of Politics* 48 (May): 370–389.

Fox, Jonathan. 1994. The Difficult Transition from Clientelism to Citizenship: Lessons from Mexico. *World Politics* 46 (January): 151–184.

Scott, James C. 1969. Corruption, Machine Politics, and Political Change. *American Political Science Review* 63 (4): 1142–1158.

Ernesto F. Calvo

PATTERN MATCHING
SEE *Campbell, Donald.*

PAVLOV, IVAN
1849–1936

Ivan Petrovich Pavlov, a Russian physiologist, received a Nobel Prize for his experimental studies of the interactions of gastrointestinal secretions with the activities of the pancreas and other glands. His observations on the role of the nervous system led him to explore what he called "psychic reflexes"—secretions of stomach acids elicited not by food itself but by stimuli such as the smells or tastes preceding food ingestion. He is best known for this discovery of conditioned, or conditional, reflexes and his subsequent experimental analyses of them. He created preparations using the salivary glands of dogs in which he could conveniently measure salivation elicited by metronomes or other arbitrary stimuli presented in various temporal relations to subsequent food deliveries.

Research inspired by Pavlov's work has been extended to applications such as the modification of emotional responding through behavior therapies. Pavlov was a principled scientist and an outspoken critic of the Soviet system in Russia, and it is unfortunate that brainwashing and other coercive methods have sometimes been attributed to his influence. These attributions are inappropriate and inaccurate because such methods are neither procedurally nor historically derivative of Pavlov's scientific contributions.

PAVLOV'S LIFE

Pavlov was the son of a parish priest. Some personal characteristics appeared early and remained with him throughout his life: a passion for physical work (especially in the garden), a love of books and learning, and an unshakable integrity. His experience in working with his hands stood him in good stead later in the speed, efficiency, and delicacy of his surgical skills. His readings led him to chemistry and biology, and he came to regard as two of his intellectual heroes the physiologist Ivan M. Sechenov (1829–1905), for construing conscious as well as unconscious activity as reflexes of the brain, and the naturalist Charles Darwin (1809–1882), for his theory of natural selection. Pavlov attended a religious seminary but in 1870 dropped theology in favor of physiology and then a medical degree in Saint Petersburg. In 1881 he married Seraphema (Sara) Vasilievna. They raised two sons, Vladimir and Vselvolod, and a daughter, Vera (a third son, Mirchik, died as a child). Sara was both devout and devoted to Pavlov, and he envied her religious faith.

After completing his dissertation, Pavlov studied in Germany and then began independent research on cardiac physiology in the Saint Petersburg laboratory of the physiologist Sergei P. Botkin (1832–1889), who soon entrusted the direction of his laboratory to Pavlov. This allowed Pavlov to devote all of his time to research. He involved himself thoroughly in all details of an experiment and even in his earliest experimental work regarded it as essential to work with the intact organism in order to maintain as far as possible the natural conditions of the physiological systems he chose to study. He had no patience with people with motives other than knowledge, such as those who saw research as a way to satisfy nonscientific agendas. The motto in Pavlov's laboratory was "Observation and observation," and he meant the direct observation of nature itself, not what someone had written about it.

Pavlov received his Nobel Prize in 1904. By the time of the Russian Revolution in 1917, his international reputation protected him from external intrusions on his research. Though he did not study the nervous system directly, he interpreted his findings in terms of changes in the irradiation of brain areas and attempted to extend his thinking to theories of language and of psychiatric disorders such as psychoses. In contrast to his contributions in physiology and conditioning, these theories did not fare well.

Pavlov maintained regular schedules of activity throughout his life, including outdoor exercise in the form of games and swims. Even during Joseph Stalin's purges, he was outspoken in his denunciation of the Communist system, going so far as refusing admission to his laboratory to the Communist commissar of education and writing a letter of criticism to Stalin. Pavlov worked in his Saint Petersburg laboratory until shortly before his death of pneumonia in February 1936.

PAVLOV'S WORK

The term *conditioned*, from the Russian phrase for "conditioned reflexes," might better have been translated as "conditional," because the name was applied to reflexes conditional upon relations among stimuli. In respondent conditioning, one stimulus, the conditional stimulus (CS), signals the presentation of another, the unconditional stimulus (US). The responses respectively elicited by these stimuli are the conditional response (CR) and the unconditional response (UR). Pavlov's conditioned salivary reflexes provide the prototypical example. When an originally neutral bell repeatedly signals food in the mouth of a hungry dog, it becomes a CS as salivation begins to be elicited by this signaling stimulus as well as by the US, the food itself.

Ironically, Pavlov may never have used a bell in his experiments; his rare mention of bells occurs only in later work, where it probably refers to electrically operated devices. The ubiquitous references to Pavlov's bell probably originated with a common example of a conditioned reflex in popular writings about Pavlov's research: a dinner bell eliciting salivation in those called to the table (Pavlov's own bell was kept on his desk, presumably for summoning servants).

Pavlov's conditioning procedure has been called "respondent," "Pavlovian," and "classical conditioning," distinguishing it from procedures studied especially by the American psychologists Edward L. Thorndike (1874–1949) and later B. F. Skinner (1904–1990). In Pavlov's procedure the important features are the relations between two stimuli, whereas in Thorndike's and Skinner's instrumental or operant procedures they are the relations between a stimulus and the response that has produced it.

Pavlov arranged various temporal relations between the CS and the US. For example, in both trace and delay conditioning, a relatively long time elapsed between CS and US; they were distinguished by whether the CS turned off or remained present in the interim. In both types conditional responding began shortly after the start of the CS, but with successive trials it gradually moved closer to the time of the US. Trace conditioning acquired its name from Pavlov's assumption that the CS had to leave some trace in the nervous system to be effective.

Attention to Pavlovian conditioning followed from how easily it could be related to the concept of association, a learning principle with substantial precedent in philosophy and psychology. Learning was said to take place through associations of ideas, and conditional reflexes seemed to represent a primitive example of their formation. In a kind of mental chemistry, ideas were thought to be associated through such properties as having common elements or occurring together in time. Thus conditioning was regarded as at the root of all learning.

During Pavlov's lifetime, conditioning was seen as a sort of stimulus substitution in which, through CS-US pairing, the CS acquires power to elicit the UR. But it is now clear that this account misrepresents what happens in at least three ways. First, conditioning depends not on CS-US pairings but rather on whether the CS predicts the US. If the CS is as often followed by no US as by the US, the two are often paired, but conditioning does not occur because the CS does not predict a US delivery. Second, in many preparations the CR differs in form or other properties from the UR. For example, with an intravenous opiate as the US, the CR is a diminished pain threshold, whereas the UR is a heightened pain threshold; the CS does not substitute for the US (similarly, if a metronome becomes a CS, the dog does not try to eat it). Third, preparations in which the typical latency between US and UR is long enough that a CS can be presented after the US but either before or after the UR show that conditioning depends on the CS-UR rather than the CS-US sequence. Conditioning occurs as long as the CS precedes the UR, so the relation of the CS to responding is more important than its relation to stimuli.

SEE ALSO *Classical Conditioning; Empiricism; Operant Conditioning; Psychology; Skinner, B. F.; Thorndike, Edward; Union of Soviet Socialist Republics*

BIBLIOGRAPHY

Babkin, Boris P. 1949. *Pavlov: A Biography.* Chicago: University of Chicago Press.

Catania, A. Charles, and Victor G. Laties. 1999. Pavlov and Skinner: Two Lives in Science. *Russian Journal of Physiology* 85 (Pavlov Sesquicentennial Issue): 1307–1313.

Donahoe, John W., and Rocio Vegas. 2004. Pavlovian Conditioning: The CS-UR Relation. *Journal of Experimental Psychology: Animal Behavior Processes* 30: 17–33.

Pavlov, Ivan P. 1927. *Conditioned Reflexes.* Trans. G. V. Anrep. London: Oxford University Press.

Rescorla, Robert A. 1988. Pavlovian Conditioning: It's Not What You Think It Is. *American Psychologist* 43: 151–160.

Siegel, Shepard, Riley E. Hinson, Marvin D. Krank, and Jane McCully. 1982. Heroin "Overdose" Death: The Contribution of Drug-Associated Environmental Cues. *Science* 216: 436–437.

A. Charles Catania

PAX BRITANNICA

Usually applied to the era between the end of the Napoleonic Wars in 1815 and the start of World War I in 1914, the term *Pax Britannica* has both geopolitical and economic connotations. That period, in contrast to preceding and subsequent periods, was comparatively free of military conflict between major powers (with notable exceptions: the Crimean War, the Franco-Prussian War, the Spanish-American War, and the Russo-Japanese War). It was also relatively free of full-blown trade wars. Britain was unquestionably the strongest country, militarily and economically. But there is no consensus among international relations scholars and economists over the extent to which British power and statecraft should be credited with the century-long "pax."

The idealized picture of Pax Britannica features nineteenth-century England as a benign global hegemon, providing the international public goods of peace and unrestricted commerce primarily through the instrumentality of its superior navy and (after the repeal of the protectionist Corn Laws in 1832) its policy of international free trade. The realist version roots the policies of naval superiority and global free trade in the self-interest of an industrializing island country dependent on a far-flung empire of raw-material producers.

Successive British governments employed the navy and the country's economic power to intimidate, if not coerce, nations—not only in the British Empire but also sovereign states—to open up their ports and domestic markets to British goods and investors. Nor was Britain willing to tolerate challengers to its ability to "rule the waves." Determined to maintain a fleet capable of defeating the combined fleets of any two countries, London took umbrage at Berlin's decision in the 1890s to significantly augment the German navy in order to support the kaiser's growing imperial appetite. In response, Britain entered into spheres-of-influence agreements with France to preempt German ambitions in Africa and elsewhere.

In theory, not only did Britain's free trade policy require the peace (which the Royal Navy was supposed to enforce), but also unrestricted global commerce, as conceptualized by Adam Smith (1723–1790), David Ricardo (1772–1823), and their disciples, would itself advance world peace. Free trade would deepen the interdependence of nations—each of which, according to the principle of comparative advantage, would specialize in producing most efficiently products that would advance the commonweal. But by the start of the twentieth century, with other major powers seeking, like Britain, to comprehensively industrialize and to modernize their militaries, mercantilistic rivalries again became the order of the day, and Pax Britannica was now widely castigated as a cover for unbridled British imperialism.

SEE ALSO *Colonialism; Imperialism*

BIBLIOGRAPHY

Ferguson, Niall. 2003. *Empire: The Rise and Demise of the British World Order and the Lessons for Global Power.* New York: Basic Books.

Imlah, Albert Henry. 1958. *Economic Elements in the Pax Britannica: Studies in British Foreign Trade in the Nineteenth Century.* Cambridge, MA: Harvard University Press.

Kennedy, Paul M. 1998. *The Rise and Fall of British Naval Mastery.* Amherst, NY: Humanity Books.

Porter, Andrew ed. 1998. *The Oxford History of the British Empire.* Vol. 3, *The Nineteenth Century.* Oxford and New York: Oxford University Press.

Williams, Judith Blow. 1972. *British Commercial Policy and Trade Expansion 1750–1850.* Oxford, U.K.: Clarendon Press.

Seyom Brown

PEACE

Peace is a key concept in the social sciences and a central concern in the field of international relations. There is much focus on peace in the world with many entities working to promote or to protect peace. At the same time, there are many disagreements surrounding it. Definitions of peace, traditional explanations of peace between states, intrastate wars, reconciliation, and the role of third parties are discussed below.

DEFINITIONS

Peace is often defined as the absence of violence. However, there is considerable disagreement over what forms of violence need to be absent. This disagreement is reflected in the list of winners of the Nobel Peace Prize, which includes statesmen, such as U.S. secretary of state Henry Kissinger (the 1973 laureate along with Le Duc Tho of Vietnam); spiritual leaders, such as the fourteenth Dalai Lama, Tenzin Gyatso (the 1989 laureate); and various international organizations. These actors have made vastly different contributions to world peace, and their recognition as Nobel laureates demonstrates the diversity of opinion on what peace is and how it is promoted.

In the social sciences, some scholars of peace, such as Johan Galtung of Norway, maintain that peace needs to encompass equality, socioeconomic factors, and social justice. In fact, there is a growing interest in the role of non-violent social movements, particularly in struggles for equality in domestic political situations, in achieving and maintaining peace. A more minimalist definition of peace focuses on the absence of physical, primarily military, vio-

lence between political entities, particularly states. This latter definition lies at the heart of the criticism seen in some circles for the choice of Kenyan Wangari Maathai as the 2004 Nobel Peace Prize laureate for her work in sustainable development and environmentalism.

For the most part, social science research has focused on the absence of military violence when discussing peace. This is particularly true for international relations scholars who were influenced by the tone of the cold war and the major interstate wars of the twentieth century.

TRADITIONAL SCHOOLS OF THOUGHT

Liberalism and realism, the dominant schools of thought in peace studies and international relations, both accept that anarchy (which is defined in international relations as the lack of a central government) is a major concern for states. However, these schools diverge on the implications of this situation on interstate cooperation and conflict. Peace studies also encompasses various lines of thoughts, with such emphases as Marxism (capitalism), feminism (gender), and constructivism (identity and meanings).

One finding that has received much attention is that democracies do not go to war with each other. Researchers trace this argument back to the views of the German philosopher Immanuel Kant (1724–1804) in his essay "Towards Perpetual Peace" (1795), and today it is identified with the liberal school of thought. This type of "democratic peace" has received much support in countless empirical studies, as well as consideration from policy circles, particularly in the West. A democratic country is essentially in a state of stable peace—that is, military violence against another democracy is removed as an option from the mindsets of leaders. In some parts of the world, this status extends to entire regions, as illustrated by pluralistic security communities such as exist in contemporary western Europe. Developments in western Europe, specifically the formation of the European Union, highlight other important elements that are identified with Kant's vision of what it takes to attain peace, such as economic development, economic ties with other countries, and international organizations.

There is another school of thought where the focus is on the role of alliances, threats, and power. This approach falls primarily within the power politics or "realist" school in international relations. Thus, in the case of western Europe, external threats and powerful opponents, particularly the Soviet Union, contributed to the coming together of European countries after World War II (1939–1945). In this view, peace emerges when there is a balance of power. That is, power deters power and in the process maintains the peace. Some have even argued that a world in which more states possess nuclear weapons might result in less bloodshed.

WARS

As shown above, the traditional schools of thought have much to say about interstate peace and war. Although some scholars suggest that interstate wars are becoming obsolete, states continue to justify the need to use violence for survival as seen in interactions between developed and developing countries. In contrast, there is little expectation that intrastate wars—that is, civil wars—may become obsolete.

Intrastate wars are more common than interstate wars, and they result in greater devastation. Civilians are particularly vulnerable in intrastate wars, and the international system has been more averse to intervening in such conflicts. Periods of respite after such wars are short, as many actors involved in intrastate conflicts return to fighting because wars leave people with few options. For this reason, there are growing calls for attention to development and institution building after intrastate wars.

Conflicts over control of governments and territory tend to play central roles in warfare. In a positive development, the international community since the end of World War II has generally not recognized territorial aggrandizement attempts. However, international norms change over time and there is no guarantee that this situation will last. Disagreements among major powers over the "rules" of the game are of particular importance because considerable global violence may occur when powerful countries are no longer satisfied with the rules and act more unilaterally.

LEVELS OF PEACE AND RECONCILIATION

There is an increasing focus on improving relations following hostility between political units. In this regard, it is useful to identify varying levels of peace. A "low level" of peace between former belligerents describes a situation where there is little more than a halt to fighting—that is, a "frozen war." In contrast, a "high level" of peace encompasses institutionalization of relations and mutually beneficial interactions between former opponents. This approach is related to the topic of reconciliation, which involves the study of how harmonious relations come about after extensive violence.

Particularly important in reconciliation is the willingness of former opponents to improve their relations. In this regard, leadership plays a crucial role. Leaders who would rather rally the public against a former foe for domestic political gain certainly do not contribute to the improvement of relations. Leaders in democracies face a

tougher atmosphere because domestic opposition can be particularly fierce and hard to ignore. As such, former warmongers have sometimes played important roles in improving relations with an opponent because their credentials lead to the belief that they will defend vital interests. One of the potential reasons for this change in heart toward a former foe is the presence of a greater security threat.

Postwar relations are influenced by the war itself and may set in motion a cycle of violence. Existing empirical research suggests that the contents of the terms of peace treaties influence the prospects for future violence. This is true for both interstate and intrastate wars. However, an important difference between interstate and intrastate wars is that forgiveness and truth-seeking play a more central role in contributing to intrastate reconciliation.

This difference brings to the forefront the positions of morality and power. Can there be peace without justice? Can peace be imposed? The lack of an international tribunal with significant authority limits what can be expected. Justice has been a major issue following intrastate wars, where public trials may occur. Yet the fear of going back to war, weak judiciaries, and the complicated task of determining culprits has resulted in the generous distribution of amnesty, and societies often seem willing to accept less than full justice. After interstate wars, justice is even more tied to power, as the defeated are the only ones on trial. This situation generally arises when one side is able to impose its will on the other, and in some contexts such impositions have been followed by the attainment of high levels of peace between states, as occurred following World War II. Yet an imposition of peace by an imperial force, a party in a civil war, or an international force is generally associated with a low level of peace and an eventual return to arms.

THIRD PARTIES

There is a considerable role for third parties. Some countries have contributed to United Nations peacekeeping operations, which have traditionally acted to keep belligerents away from each other after a cease-fire without taking sides and generally with the prior consent of the opposing parties. Third-party military (and police) deployment is particularly important after intrastate war situations where there is much suspicion and where former belligerents are likely to interpret the moves of the other as hostile and take actions to increase their security that are likely to make the other side fear them, a situation known as a security dilemma. While peacekeeping is fairly uncontroversial, such actions have had mixed records. Other third-party efforts, such as peace enforcement, are more hotly debated because they involve coercing the opposing sides to stop fighting through the use of massive force. Most of the time, third-party military involvement occurs after considerable violence has already taken place, but since the 1990s there has been a shift toward preventive diplomacy. Such efforts include the United Nations Preventive Deployment Force in Macedonia, which was deployed in early 1993 before a breakdown into chaos emerged.

Not all third-party efforts involve military might. Nongovernmental organizations play a role in socioeconomic development and in strengthening institutions and building ties before and after violence. In addition, while many entities work out their differences through bilateral means, there are other options, including adjudication and mediation. Yet, as with many other aspects that characterize attempts to foster peace, mediation does not guarantee success, given the array of elements to consider, such as timing and leverage.

Thus, the study of peace continues. Much more is understood about peace as the absence of military violence. At the same time, there is still much to be done in the area of reconciliation and in efforts to formulate a broader definition of peace.

SEE ALSO *Nobel Peace Prize; War*

BIBLIOGRAPHY

Doyle, Michael W. 1997. *Ways of War and Peace: Realism, Liberalism, and Socialism.* New York: Norton.

Galtung, Johan. 1975. *Essays in Peace Research.* Copenhagen: Ejlers.

Kacowicz, Arie, Yaacov Bar-Siman-Tov, Ole Elgström, and Magnus Jerneck. 2000. *Stable Peace Among Nations.* Lanham, MD: Rowman and Littlefield.

Kant, Immanuel. [1795] 1996. Towards Perpetual Peace. In *Practical Philosophy*, trans. and ed. Mary J. Gregor, 317–351. Cambridge, U.K.: Cambridge University Press.

Long, William J., and Peter Brecke. 2003. *War and Reconciliation: Reason and Emotion in Conflict Resolution.* Cambridge, MA: MIT Press.

Wallensteen, Peter. 2006. *Understanding Conflict Resolution: War, Peace, and the Global System.* 2nd ed. Thousand Oaks, CA: Sage.

Reşat Bayer

PEACE MOVEMENTS

In scholarly literature and public discourse, the term *peace movement* is often used as a synonym for pacifism. But in discussing peace movements, it is helpful to differentiate between the periods before and after 1945. Since World War II, peace movements have had distinctively new patterns of mobilization and organization, and many of them have been protests against certain wars or armaments, but not necessarily against violence or the military per se.

In sociological terms, peace movements can be defined as social movements that aim to protest against the perceived *dangers* of political decision-making about armaments, military alliances, and war. They stress the possibly violent fallout from these decisions (which the decision makers perceive as mere *risk*), and advocate nonviolent solutions. For these purposes, they use a variety of communication media and public performances of both an instrumental and a symbolic nature. It is one of the distinctive features of peace movements in the contemporary media society that their capacity for mobilization depends to a large degree on their resonance in public opinion and in the mass media, and that many of their protests are primarily calculated with regard to public reaction. As social or protest movements, peace movements evolved at least since the 1960s together with environmental and women's movements, often including considerable overlap and cross-fertilization in terms of aims, ideologies, institutional networks, and individual supporters.

SOCIOLOGICAL APPROACHES

According to Thorsten Bonacker and Lars Schmitt in their 2004 study, both historical and sociological research on peace movements reflects the conceptual changes within the "social movement"-approach from the 1970s to the present. Frank Parkin's 1968 study was one of the first interpretations of the British Campaign for Nuclear Disarmament (CND). Here he analyzed it in terms of its social constituency as a form of "middle class radicalism." This focus on the social characteristics of protest actors ties in with the concept of a value change from materialistic (i.e., working-class) to post-materialistic (i.e. middle-class) values as a key prerequisite for peace movement mobilization. The empirical validity of this concept has been repeatedly challenged.

During the 1980s many studies relied on the "resource mobilization" concept and tried, with a focus on the organizational capacities of protest elites, to identify the successes or failures of peace movement mobilization. Much historical research in this fashion tended to conceptualize the history of armaments and warmongering in the simplifying dichotomy of "doves" and "hawks," and to exaggerate the impact of peace protests on decision-making processes, without putting this issue under careful scrutiny. Peace movements since 1945 have, in fact, yielded their most substantial results not in opposition against any particular war, but in turning forms of civil unrest and nonviolent disobedience into a legitimate means of political mobilization. They have thus broadened, together with the feminist and environmental movements, the scope of democratic participation in American, European, and some Asian societies.

Since the 1990s constructivist approaches have gained currency in both sociological and historical research on peace movements. These concepts do not focus on the social resources of collective actors or on the political system as an external variable for movement mobilization. Rather, they stress the importance of the protests themselves as communicative events and the capacity of these events to construct reasons for protest through the attribution of possible dangerous consequences to political decisions. According to Michael S. Foley in his 2003 book *Confronting the War Machine: Draft Resistance during the Vietnam War*, characteristic elements of peace movements are in this perspective performative forms of protest, particularly those that use the bodies of the protesters to display their personal commitment and consternation, as in the draft resistance movement against the Vietnam War.

Another important feature is the moralistic codes of protest communication with its stark, sometimes eschatological or bleak dichotomies, which accentuate the difference between risk/danger, either/or. Constructivist approaches stress the importance of frames—collective semantic patterns that provide a coherent interpretation of social reality—for the transformation of latent conflicts into manifest peace protests. In a 1992 article Jürgen Gerhards and Dieter Rucht differentiate between *diagnostic* frames (what is the problem?), *prognostic* frames (how can it be solved?), and *motivational* frames, which trigger and channel the protest communication. According to this approach, "masterframes" are necessary to make the identity of protest communication plausible and visible and to determine its place in the context of society.

PROTESTS AGAINST NUCLEAR WEAPONS DURING THE 1950s AND 1960s

Peace mobilization after 1945 was mainly triggered and influenced by the dangers and the unprecedented destructive potential of nuclear technology, unleashed for the first time in the atomic bombings of the cities of Hiroshima and Nagasaki in August 1945. Particularly during the first postwar decade, mobilization against atomic armaments fell prey to the emerging cold war confrontation between the military blocs in the East and West. Communist parties worldwide were quick to seize the opportunity. The World Congress of Intellectuals for Peace met in the Polish city of Wrocław in August 1948 and was the first in a string of carefully orchestrated meetings meant to demonstrate the genuinely peace-loving policies of the socialist countries and to launch vitriolic attacks against the United States.

Toward the end of the 1950s, non-aligned protest movements against the possession, proliferation, testing, and employment of nuclear weapons gained momentum in various Western European countries. CND was founded in February 1958 by leading left-wing intellectuals such as the philosopher Bertrand Russell (1872–1970) and the historian A. J. P. Taylor (1906–1990). Its basic tactic was to renew the pressure on the parliamentary Labour Party to advocate unilateral disarmament with the means of extra-parliamentary public protest. From the early 1960s CND also adopted the aim of Britain's exit from the North Atlantic Treaty Organization (NATO, a military alliance of countries in Europe and North America). CND and subsequent movements in other countries professed a concern for peace as a global issue and for "humanity" as its subject. But in its rhetoric and commitment, the respective nation state remained the focal point. Antinuclear peace activism was thus an international, but not a strictly transnational, movement, as were later the campaigns against the Vietnam War and the Euromissiles.

CND invented and employed an annual march from the nuclear weapons facility in Aldermaston, England, to London during the Easter weekend as the major form of public protest. This example was subsequently added to the symbolic repertoire of peace movements in various European countries, as was the symbol of a circle encompassing a broken cross, representing the semaphore signals for the *n* and *d* of "nuclear disarmament." The tactics and symbols of CND were copied and emulated in many Western European countries, but also in southern Europe, for example in Greece.

THE ANTI-VIETNAM WAR MOVEMENT

Both Catholic and Communist circles in France had already protested against the attempts of the French military to regain control over the Democratic Republic of Vietnam (which was founded in 1945 in the northern part of the former French colony) since 1946. But the fate of the Vietnamese people became a focal point for massive antiwar mobilization in western European countries, Japan, and the United States only after the U.S. army had started massive attacks against the operations of the communist guerrilla NFL in South Vietnam and a systematic aerial bombing of North Vietnam in 1964 and 1965. The Norwegian Solidarity Committee for Vietnam established in December 1965 was among the first concerted efforts to organize material support for the people in North Vietnam and to call for a peaceful solution of the conflict. As similar committees and movements in other countries, it demanded an immediate stop of the American aerial bombing and the strict application of the Geneva Accords of 1954, which had divided Vietnam with a demilitarized zone around a demarcation line along the seventeenth degree of latitude. Whereas these aims could still be supported by pacifist groups such as the War Resisters International, they remained distant from the subsequent radicalization of antiwar protests, particularly its relation to the use of violence. With a peak during the years from 1967 to 1970, the anti-Vietnam War movement attracted a large, but also highly volatile, group of followers particularly among the student population in Europe, Japan, and the United States, which was involved in parallel protests against the system of higher education, the "establishment," and the anti-Communist postwar consensus in their respective countries and U.S. "imperialism" in the Third World.

The radicalization of the movement made its position with regard to the use of violence ambivalent. A growing number of antiwar protesters not only supported a military victory of the NFL, but showed also a readiness for the use of violence in clashes with the police during rallies. More generally, confrontational tactics and the calculated use of spectacular protest forms such as sit-ins, the locking of persons to buildings, or the burning of national flags were almost without precedent in the history of peace activism. Only the Committee of 100, a group of radicals that had separated itself from CND in 1960, had already practiced spectacular sit-downs of protesters in Whitehall, England, or at missile sites and had attracted a lot of media coverage with these actions. With the trend toward only loosely coordinated and more disruptive forms of public protest, the mobilization against the Vietnam War indicated a major shift in the organizational patterns and tactics of peace movements in the United States, Europe, and Japan. It thus marked a major change in the history of peace movement mobilization.

PROTESTS AGAINST EUROMISSILES DURING THE 1980s

In December 1979 NATO finalized its "double track solution" for intermediate range nuclear missiles, which combined an offer to the Soviet Union to negotiate a reduction or elimination of nuclear missiles in Europe with the announcement to deploy cruise missiles and Pershing II missiles in five Western European nations in the autumn of 1983. This decision offered, paradoxically, an unprecedented window of opportunity for peace movement mobilization, which gained momentum in all Western European countries by the spring of 1981. France was the only exception, due to the domestic consensus about the need to maintain its own nuclear weapons arsenal. The protests against the Euromissiles were not organized or orchestrated by some of the established or freshly mushrooming organizations of peace activists—according

to an estimate about 2,300 local, national, and international groups in 1982—but only loosely coordinated in a network structure. A major attempt for transnational coordination on the European level was European Nuclear Disarmament (END), founded by the historian E. P. Thompson and other veteran members of the British peace movement in April 1980. Mobilization against the Euromissiles reached its peak between June 1982 and October 1983, when the movement organized protest marches with several hundred thousand participants each in various European capital cities. Even during this climactic period, though, the peace movement was not able, with the one exception of Greece, to gather a majority of the population behind its major aim, a unilateral nuclear disarmament of NATO.

The tactics of the Euromissiles movement included two distinctive features. In contrast to the antinuclear protests of the 1950s and 1960s, this wave of mobilization did not so much employ famous novelists or intellectuals as popular figureheads and symbolic icons, but brought a new generation of experts from the sciences to the forefront. Physicians and physicists in particular briefed the mass media about the dangers of nuclear weapons and about their environmental consequences. This gradual shift from a moral to a more cognitive approach went together with a policy orientation of the Euromissiles movement. More than earlier peace movements, these new activists tried to engage in a dialogue with the respective governments about possible alternatives to existing defense policies. The public discourse of the Euromissiles campaign was highly gendered and contrasted the "male power craziness" of "Reagan-Haig-Weinberger" (then the U.S. president and two of his leading cabinet members) with the need for a more feminine empowerment in favor of peaceful solutions, encapsulated in the slogan "Petting instead of Pershing." Both as a cultural current and a political aversion, anti-Americanism provided a masterframe for the peace movements of the 1980s in Western Europe and Japan. American peace movements since the 1950s made, on the other hand, much effort to describe their activities as the embodiment of the genuine progressive tendencies of American identity and popular culture, to avoid accusations of being "un-American."

Starting in the late 1970s, an independent peace movement emerged also in the Warsaw Pact countries (those in Eastern Europe), although only on a limited scale and in constant fear of police repression. Groups such as the Moscow Trust Group in the Soviet Union, Charter 77 in Czechoslovakia, and the Protestant peace groups assembled behind the slogan "swords into ploughshares." They organized meetings and distributed unauthorized literature. Their basic aim was to restore elements of an unregulated civil society by nonviolent means and to foster a "détente from below," after the Helsinki

Agreement on Security and Cooperation had ratified *détente*, or an easing of tensions, between the Eastern and Western bloc countries in 1975.

SEE ALSO *Colonialism; Diplomacy; Disarmament; Imperialism; Left and Right; Militarism; Pacifism; Passive Resistance; Peace Process; Protest; Radicalism; Social Movements; Vietnam War; Weaponry, Nuclear*

BIBLIOGRAPHY

Bonacker, Thorsten, and Lars Schmitt. 2004. Politischer Protest zwischen latenten Strukturen und manifesten Konflikten. Perspektiven soziologischer Protestforschung am Beispiel der (neuen) Friedensbewegung. *Mitteilungsblatt des Instituts für soziale Bewegungen* 32: 193–213.

Foley, Michael S. 2003. *Confronting the War Machine: Draft Resistance during the Vietnam War*. Chapel Hill: University of North Carolina Press.

Gerhards, Jürgen, and Dieter Rucht. 1992. Mesomobilization: Organizing and Framing in Two Protest Campaigns in West Germany. *American Journal of Sociology* 98 (3): 555–596.

Giugni, Marco. 2004. *Social Protest and Policy Change: Ecology, Antinuclear, and Peace Movements in Comparative Perspective*. Lanham, MD: Rowman and Littlefield.

Kaltefleiter, Werner, and Robert L. Pfaltzgraff, eds. 1985. *The Peace Movements in Europe and the United States*. London: Croom Helm.

Nehring, Holger. 2005. National Internationalists: British and West German Protests against Nuclear Weapons, the Politics of Transnational Communications and the Social History of the Cold War, 1957–1964. *Contemporary European History* 14 (4): 559–582.

Parkin, Frank. 1968. *Middle Class Radicalism. The Social Bases of the British Campaign for Nuclear Disarmament*. Manchester: Manchester University Press.

Wittner, Lawrence S. 2003. *Toward Nuclear Abolition. A History of the World Nuclear Disarmament Movement. 1971 to the Present*. Stanford, CA: Stanford University Press.

Ziemann, Benjamin. 2004. Peace Movements in Western Europe, Japan and USA since 1945: Introduction. *Mitteilungsblatt des Instituts für soziale Bewegungen* 32: 5–19.

Benjamin Ziemann

PEACE PROCESS

A peace process is a series of persistent diplomatic and political initiatives to negotiate a resolution to a protracted conflict between political entities. The term was first used consistently during the 1970s to describe the efforts to negotiate peace agreements between Israel and its Arab neighbors. Its use has spread since, both geographically and across social categories. *Peace process* today, thus, can refer to an interstate conflict (e.g., India and Pakistan); to a conflict between a state and some politically defined group within it, such as an ethnic (e.g., South Africa and its black population), religious (e.g., Sudan and its Christian south), or ideological movement (e.g., Guatemala and the Guatemalan National Revolutionary Unity); or to a conflict between two such opposing groups within a state (e.g., Catholics and Protestants in Northern Ireland).

Aside from the protagonists, other actors are often involved, in various roles, in peace processes. Third parties in peace processes can be divided into two types. The first are weak and, at least ostensibly, neutral actors. These actors could be states (e.g., Norway in its role in the Oslo Accords between Israel and the Palestine Liberation Organization, as well as in the negotiation between the Sri Lankan government and the Tamil Tigers), nongovernmental organizations (e.g., the International Committee of the Red Cross, which is often involved in negotiations, though usually with regard to cease-fires and interim measures, not comprehensive peace agreements), or even some individuals (e.g., former U.S. president Jimmy Carter and former South African president Nelson Mandela). Although such actors are not necessarily devoid of self-interest (in boosting their prestige, for instance), they are usually perceived as nonpartisan, and therein lies their strength as peace facilitators. Weak and neutral third parties are most likely to succeed in cases where the main task involves coordination of the protagonists and supply of "good offices" (i.e., the venue for talks, facilities needed, and the diplomatic channels).

Weak actors, however, are limited in their ability to foster peace when the protagonists' positions are far apart and where mere coordination is not enough. In such cases, the involvement of the second type of mediator—a global or regional power—is often needed to enable a successful peace process. The role of the United States in the Egyptian-Israeli peace is a good example of a global power involvement, and Syria's centrality to negotiation of the 1989 Taif Accord among the warring factions in Lebanon is an example of the role a regional power has played in peacemaking. A power-wielding international organization can also play a similar role, although it usually requires the backing of strong states in such an effort. NATO in the Balkans and the Organization of American States in El Salvador have both played such a role.

Powerful third parties usually have more tools at their disposal than do weaker ones when it comes to peace negotiations, because they can bring to bear their own resources and power in order to pressure the sides towards agreement and, if necessary, to enforce their compliance with the agreements (by creating, funding, or manning verification mechanisms, or by involving their own prestige and supplying security guarantees for the agreement's implementation). To be sure, global or regional powers are less likely to be neutral in conflicts, as their more immediate self-interests are more likely to come into play, but neutrality is not always a necessary condition for successful third-party mediation. Instead, it is very important that third parties are willing to invest time, energy, prestige, and sometimes money in the peace process. They also should be willing to pressure both parties, including their allies, to make compromises and comply with agreements.

A peace process typically involves four phases. The first phase, prenegotiation, often held secretly, deals with setting the agenda for the negotiation. The second phase usually involves a cease-fire and perhaps other acts of good will, such as prisoner exchange or a return of forces to a status-quo-ante position. The third phase is the negotiation phase, which, ideally, ends in a formal peace accord. In the last phase, the parties to the agreement are required to implement their share. Although this schedule is useful for analytical purposes, the reality, of course, is much more complicated. Phases are often mixed or overlap. Whereas the Egyptian-Israeli peace process more or less followed this classic program, for instance, the Palestinian-Israeli process has a more complex structure, with many phases of negotiations and interim agreements.

Time is a crucial factor in a peace process, as the gradual pace of the process allows for construction of "confidence building measures" in order to increase mutual trust. It also allows both parties to climb down from their war-inciting rhetoric and start educating their people about the possible dividends of peace. In practice, however, the record of success of peace processes is not too encouraging: At least as many processes fail as succeed, and it is hard to distinguish a success from a temporary truce.

In a sense, this relatively poor success rate for peace processes is to be expected. Most of the cases in which a peace process is tried are very protracted and complex conflicts that are, by definition, hard to solve. There are also reasons intrinsic to the idea of the peace process that make it vulnerable to failure. First, the mere term *peace process* raises expectations in the protagonists' populations, and when progress is slow (e.g., if violence continues or the economic dividends of peace are not forthcoming), it can be difficult to secure the support of a frustrated population. Second, in order to gain approval for the process in their respective communities, leaders often exaggerate the benefits and gloss over the pitfalls of the process. Finally, another major reason for the failure of peace processes is the role of "spoilers," those actors in the two opposing camps who see peace as a threat to their positions or their interests. Spoilers are able to sour the peace process by playing on the public's frustrations. Moreover, the structure of negotiations, especially in cases that post-

pone the final accord to the end of the process, is such that the leaders often have strategic incentives to cooperate with their own spoilers as a way of pressuring their opponents to give up more concessions.

None of these problems should suggest that peace processes should be abandoned altogether, but just that they should be approached carefully, with caution not to raise expectations too high, and with a structure that minimizes the opportunities for the spoilers. One option would be to establish an accord about the final shape of the peace early on in the process, while designing a gradual and verifiable implementation to allow for trust to rebuild.

SEE ALSO *Diplomacy; International Nongovernmental Organizations (INGOs); Peace Movements; United Nations*

BIBLIOGRAPHY

Darby, John, and Roger MacGinty, 2003. *Contemporary Peacemaking: Conflict, Violence and Peace Processes.* New York: Palgrave Macmillan.

Quandt, William B., ed. 2001. *Peace Process: American Diplomacy and the Arab-Israeli Conflict Since 1976.* Washington, DC & Berkeley, CA: Brookings Institution & California University Press.

Zartman I. William, and J. Lewis Rasmussen, eds. 1997. *Peacemaking in International Conflict: Methods & Techniques.* Washington, DC: United State Institute of Peace Press.

Boaz Atzili

PEACEFUL COEXISTENCE

During the cold war the Soviet Union and China developed the concept of peaceful coexistence as a mechanism for communist states to coexist with capitalist states and, in the case of China, with regional powers. It was in direct contrast with theories of mutual antagonistic aggression that supposed the two regimes could not live in peace. However it was applied differently by the Soviet Union and the People's Republic of China and debates over differing interpretations of peaceful coexistence contributed to one aspect of the Sino-Soviet split in the 1950s and 1960s. Since the end of the cold war, peaceful coexistence has been used to describe proposed solutions to the Arab-Israeli conflict in the Middle East, Wall Street's view of regional instability following the Asian financial crisis of the late 1990s, relations between the West and Islam, relations between Jews and Christians and Muslims, and relations among the different Christian churches. The concept of peaceful coexistence has been adopted by many international documents and has become a widely accepted norm of international relations.

THE INTERPRETATION OF THE SOVIET UNION

Vladimir Lenin, revolutionary leader, head of the Communist Party, and first premier of the Soviet Union, first put forth the concept of peaceful coexistence after the Bolshevik Revolution in Russia in 1917. At that time he issued a Decree on Peace that called for World War I (1914–1918) participants to immediately open negotiations for peace. Leon Trotsky, the people's commissar of foreign affairs, followed this decree by proclaiming an official doctrine of peaceful coexistence with all peoples. However, in the early years of the Soviet Union the doctrine of world revolution was also proclaimed, especially by Lenin. The two policies, peaceful coexistence and world revolution, would appear to conflict for several decades.

In 1943 Joseph Stalin dissolved the Comintern and disbanded the Communist International, a Moscow-based organization of communist parties around the world that promoted revolution. This action was an attempt to appease the Western allies during World War II (1939–1945) and secure a wartime pact, but was ultimately a precursor to the formal adoption of peaceful coexistence as a part of Soviet foreign policy. In 1949, still under Stalin's leadership, the Soviet Union founded the World Peace Council to organize a global peace movement to promote the concept of peaceful coexistence internationally. This was meant to assuage Western concerns that the Soviet Union was driven by world revolution, as had been advocated by the Bolsheviks.

Nikita Khrushchev first fully enunciated peaceful coexistence following the Twentieth Congress of the Soviet Communist Party when he denounced crimes committed by Stalin. As Soviet premier, beginning in 1953 Khrushchev promoted the concept of peaceful coexistence as a way to ease tensions between the Soviet Union and the United States in light of the possibility of nuclear war. Beginning in 1956 peaceful coexistence was proclaimed the cornerstone of Soviet foreign policy. For the Soviet Union peaceful coexistence had one main assertion: that the United States and the Soviet Union and their respective ideologies could co-exist together without war. It had three elements: socialism in one country (the total commitment of Soviet resources in the home country, first introduced by Stalin in 1924); the Iron Curtain (sealing off the people of the Communist world from the people of the capitalist world); and the arms race (with military might substituting for political struggle). Khrushchev argued that while socialism would eventually triumph over capitalism this would occur without war, which was neither necessary nor inevitable.

Khrushchev explained the doctrine of peaceful coexistence as early as 1957 in a speech at the Albanian Embassy. In 1960 in an address to the United Nations General Assembly, Khrushchev underlined the policy: "The peoples of the Soviet Union and the Soviet Government are striving unremittingly to have the principles of peaceful coexistence firmly established in relations between States.... The policy of peaceful coexistence assumes a readiness to solve all outstanding issues without resort to force, by means of negotiations and reasonable compromises." The reasoning behind the policy was Khrushchev's aim to "catch up and overtake" the West in economic development, and thereby prove the superiority of the Soviet system. In a speech to the Supreme Soviet on October 31, 1959, Krushchev explained that conflict between the two systems, communist and capitalist, must be resolved, and that peaceful coexistence was a real method to this end based on human society.

In a 1959 article in the prominent American journal *Foreign Affairs* Khrushchev offered American readers a detailed exposition of the Soviet viewpoint, and maintained that the Soviet Union professed a policy of peaceful coexistence since its creation following the revolution in 1917: "From its very inception," Khrushchev argued, "the Soviet state proclaimed peaceful coexistence as the basic principle of its foreign policy. It was no accident that the very first state act of the Soviet power was the decree on peace, the decree on the cessation of the bloody war" (Khrushchev 1959, p. 1). Khrushchev tried to demonstrate his commitment to peaceful coexistence by participating in international peace conferences such as the Geneva Summit, and by traveling internationally, such as visiting Camp David in the United States in 1959.

The Soviet Union applied the concept of peaceful coexistence to its relations with industrialized countries, particularly its relations with the United States and relations between member countries of the North Atlantic Treaty Organization (NATO) and Warsaw Pact member countries (also termed the Communist Bloc in Eastern Europe).

THE INTERPRETATION OF THE PEOPLE'S REPUBLIC OF CHINA

During the 1960s and 1970s China applied the concept of peaceful coexistence to its relations with nonsocialist countries in the developing world while arguing that a belligerent attitude should be maintained toward "imperialist" capitalist countries. In the early 1980s China extended its interpretation of the concept of peaceful coexistence to include its relations with all countries, including capitalist countries.

In December 1953, during negotiations with India over Tibet, Chinese premier Zhou Enlai (1898–1976) proposed the Five Principles of Peaceful Coexistence. These were written into the Agreement Between the People's Republic of China and the Republic of India on Trade and Intercourse Between the Tibet Region of China and India signed in April 1954 by Zhou Enlai and Indian prime minister Jawaharlal Nehru following the Sino-Indian War in Tibet. The Five Principles were reiterated by Zhou in 1954 in joint declarations issued with the prime ministers of India and Myanmar during Zhou's visit to the two countries in June 1954, and again at the Bandung Conference of 1955, the first conference of Asian and African countries, where they were incorporated into the conference declarations. In 1982 the Five Principles were written into the Constitution of the People's Republic of China as applied to all sovereign nations. The Five Principles of Peaceful Coexistence as promoted by China are:

- Mutual respect for sovereignty and territorial integrity (government free from external control)
- Mutual nonaggression
- Noninterference in each other's internal affairs
- Equality
- Mutual benefit

There are three notable consequences of the Chinese concept of peaceful coexistence, as differentiated from the Soviet concept of peaceful coexistence. First, the Chinese concept includes the expansion of free trade. Second, the Chinese concept emphasizes national sovereignty, territorial integrity, and noninterference in internal affairs; thus American moves to promote democracy and human rights are seen as hostile actions. Third, the concept precludes support of Communist insurgents in other countries. One major consequence of this policy was that China would not support Communist insurgencies in Southeast Asia, particularly Indonesia and Malaysia, and would distance itself from overseas Chinese in those nations. The Chinese concept of peaceful coexistence does not extend to Taiwan, which is considered a part of China and thus an internal affair in which other nations, particularly the United States, should not interfere.

The concept of peaceful coexistence remains a part of Chinese foreign policy in the beginning of the twenty-first century. On September 3, 2005, Chinese president Hu Jintao called for promoting peaceful coexistence of different civilizations to draw upon each other's strengths.

SEE ALSO *Cold War*

BIBLIOGRAPHY

Aboltin, V. 1958. Economic Aspects of Peaceful Coexistence of Two Social Systems. *American Economic Review* 48 (2): 710–722.

Allen, Richard V. 1966. *Peace of Peaceful Coexistence?* Chicago: American Bar Association.

Kende, Istvan. 1968. Peaceful Coexistence: Its Interpretation and Misinterpretation. *Journal of Peace Research* 5 (4): 352–364.

Khrushchev, Nikita. 1959. On Peaceful Coexistence. *Foreign Affairs* 38 (3): 1–18.

Lerner, Warren. 1964. The Historical Origins of the Soviet Doctrine of Peaceful Coexistence. *Law and Contemporary Problems* 29 (4): 865–870.

Pittman, John. 1964. *Peaceful Coexistence: Its Theory and Practice in the Soviet Union.* New York: International Publishers.

Rees, David. 1989. *Peaceful Coexistence: A Study in Soviet Doctrine.* Washington, DC: International Security Council.

Anastasia Xenias

PEANUT INDUSTRY

Peanut (Latin, *Arachis hypogaea, Fabaceae*), often referred to as groundnut, is a leguminous plant that produces fruit below ground. The growth habit of the peanut is indeterminate, indicating that vegetative and reproductive growth occur simultaneously on the same plant throughout a significant period of the plant's life cycle. Peanut gynophores, which ultimately produce kernels enclosed by pods, are born above ground and move to the soil due to physiological processes where development and maturation occurs. Three botanical classifications of peanuts include Virginia, Spanish, and Valencia, which vary in vegetative and reproductive morphology. Pod and kernel size of peanuts belonging to these botanical classifications influence utilization and marketing.

Peanuts originated in South America in the region of northern Argentina, Bolivia, and Paraguay. Domestication of peanuts occurred slowly, in a manner similar to that of many other crop plants. During the early colonial period peanuts moved from South America to other areas, and they are now grown in many regions of the world, most notably Argentina, China, India, Indonesia, numerous countries in Africa, and the United States. Production per unit land area varies considerably across regions, and is affected by climate; soil and natural resources; production, pest management, and storage technology and capacity; management skills; and stability of governments and key infrastructure.

Peanut kernels contain 35 to 55 percent triacylglycerols (fresh weight) and 21 to 36 percent protein. Carbohydrate constitutes approximately 15 percent of peanuts, and key vitamins including ascorbic acid, niacin, riboflavin, and thiamin are found in peanuts. In addition to the positive attributes of peanut nutrition, peanuts act as an allergen in some segments of the human population.

The nutritive value and possible allergic reaction influence peanut utilization and marketing.

The primary use of the peanut is for oil production. Peanuts are also used for human consumption in pastes and peanut butter, snack foods including a component in candies, and direct consumption with little to no additional processing after harvest. In developing countries, peanuts often are consumed directly or used as a component in local diets. In countries with intricate marketing systems, peanuts are often shelled, blanched, roasted, and in some cases salted. Components originating from these processes are also used in nonfood categories. However, its uses as oil and in products for direct human consumption are by far the most important uses of peanuts around the world.

The noted scientist George Washington Carver (c. 1864–1943) was responsible for an explosion in the number of uses for peanuts while he worked at the Tuskegee Institute in the United States. Over his distinguished career, Carver developed numerous uses and products derived from or containing peanuts. Perhaps the most notable product he helped introduce to a large segment of the population was peanut butter, which accounts for approximately half of peanut utilization in the United States. These products were important in establishing markets and supporting rural farming communities, and in combating poverty around the world, especially with respect to child development and health.

Production practices vary considerably around the world. In many regions of Africa, peanuts are produced at subsistence levels, yielding less than 1,000 kg/ha, using slash-and-burn techniques. In other regions, peanut yields can exceed 6,000 kg/ha when managed with intensive fertility and pest-management programs using modern machinery, and scientifically based principles and technology. Peanuts are susceptible to a wide range of insect and disease pests, nematodes, and weed interference, and they require essential elements, most notably calcium, and fertile soils with adequate drainage, to optimize yield. Because peanuts are consumed directly by humans, with limited post-harvest processing, it is important that peanut farmers develop strategies to minimize human and environmental exposure to pesticides.

Because peanuts are considered a staple in many regions of the world, the nutritive value of peanuts offers the possibility of its cultivation as a cash crop for local, regional, national, and international trade. In many countries, especially the United States, peanuts are grown primarily for domestic consumption. In contrast, some countries such as Argentina export a high percentage of peanuts produced domestically. Government legislation and farm programs, as well as regional agreements such as the North American Free Trade Agreement (NAFTA) and more inclusive agreements such as GATT (General Agreement on Tariffs and Trade), affect domestic and export marketing of peanuts. Relationships between the three major segments of the peanut industry—farmers, shellers, and manufacturers—can be complex and at times strained in free-market economies.

Peanuts have long been a key component of human diets around the world, especially with respect to providing oil and essential protein and vitamins, and they continue to be a staple food source, especially in rural regions of developing countries. Ensuring that final peanut products do not contain aflatoxin, a mycotoxin caused by the organism *Aspregillus flavus*, is important to protect human health. Additional research and education designed to minimize the negative effects of peanut allergens are also important in the utilization and marketing of peanuts. Increasing technology development and transfer to increase yield, improve quality, and minimize storage loss will continue to be important as human populations rise and concerns over environmental impacts increase. Developing fair-trade agreements and arrangements between major peanut-producing countries, especially those with export potential, is a continuing challenge.

SEE ALSO *Agricultural Industry; Food; Industry; Third World*

BIBLIOGRAPHY

Coffelt, T. A. 1989. Peanut. In *Oil Crops of the World: Their Breeding and Utilization*, eds. Gerhard Robbelen, R. Keith Downey, and Amram Ashri, 319–338. New York: McGraw-Hill.

Jordan, David L., Jack E. Bailey, J. Steven Barnes, et al. 2002. Yield and Economic Return of Ten Peanut-based Cropping Systems. *Agronomy Journal* 94 (6): 1289–1294.

Jordan, David L., C. W. Swann, Jan F. Spears, et al. 2000. Comparison of Virginia and Runner Market Type Peanut (Arachis hypogaea L.) Grown in the Virginia-Carolina Area. *Peanut Science* 27: 71–77.

Jordan, David L., Gail G. Wilkerson, and David W. Krueger. 2003. Evaluation of Scouting Methods in Peanut (Arachis hypogaea) Using Theoretical Net Returns from HADSS. *Weed Technology* 17 (2): 358–365.

Melouk, Hassan A., and Frederick M. Shokes, eds. 1995. *Peanut Health Management*. St. Paul, MN: The American Phytopathological Society.

Pattee, Harold E., and H. Thomas Stalker, eds. 1995. *Advances in Peanut Science*. Stillwater, OK: American Peanut Research and Education Society.

Pattee, Harold E., and Clyde T. Young, eds. 1982. *Peanut Science and Technology*. Yoakum, TX: American Peanut Research and Education Society.

Spears, Jan F. 2000. Germination and Vigor Response to Seed Maturity, Weight, and Size within the Virginia-type Cultivar, VA-C 92R. *Seed Technology* 22: 23–33.

Spears, Jan F., and G. A. Sullivan. 1995. Relationship of Hull Mesocarp Color to Seed Maturity and Quality in Large-seeded Virginia-type Peanut. *Peanut Science* 22: 22–26.

David L. Jordan
Jan F. Spears

PEARL HARBOR

In the 1920s and 1930s, Americans had become strongly isolationist, many believing that America's involvement in World War I (1914–1918) had been a political mistake. Moreover, the Great Depression focused people's attention on the economy. Against this backdrop, the U.S. Congress had passed neutrality acts in 1935 and 1936. The tipping point that rallied public opinion toward involvement in World War II (1939–1945) came on December 7, 1941.

The Japanese leadership had sought to drive U.S. and U.K. forces out of Asia. To Japan, the attack on Pearl Harbor was seen as merely a "strategic necessity"—part of the grand strategy to secure the Pacific for oil shipments to fuel the empire's efforts to dominate Asia. However, as history has shown, the plan backfired.

In the attack, 21 American ships were sunk or badly damaged, 188 planes were lost, and 155 planes were damaged. In addition, 2,403 American lives were lost and 1,178 persons injured. Fortunately for the U.S. Navy, no aircraft carriers were in port. While the attack produced a substantial military loss, the main effect of the attack was to crystallize Americans' public opinion against the Axis Powers. On December 8, 1941, the United States declared war on Japan.

Prior to the attack on Pearl Harbor, President Franklin Delano Roosevelt had battled with Congress to expand American support for England's struggle against Germany. But once Americans saw themselves as victims, resistance to entering the war melted away. German führer Adolf Hitler's declaration of war against the United States on December 11, 1941, provided the linkage necessary to associate pro-war sentiment generated by Pearl Harbor to Germany, and the United States declared war on Germany and Italy on the same day.

Public sentiment toward Japanese Americans was low prior to the attack at Pearl Harbor, as evidenced by the 1924 Immigration Act that halted Japanese immigration. The attack on Pearl Harbor sparked war hysteria. In 1942 Roosevelt signed Executive Order 9066, which authorized the internment of 120,000 individuals of Japanese ancestry, two-thirds of whom were U.S. citizens. These people were removed from their homes along the West Coast and relocated to inland camps.

President Roosevelt declared December 7 "a date that will live in infamy." As a term, "Pearl Harbor" has come to represent foreign treachery, the perils of U.S. isolationism, and of potential vulnerability of American military forces. The specter of Pearl Harbor helped to fuel the nuclear arms race between the United States and Union of Soviet Socialist Republics during the twentieth century. But Pearl Harbor also constrained U.S. power. Robert Kennedy persuaded his brother, President John F. Kennedy, not to execute a surprise air strike against Cuba during the 1962 Missile Crisis because it would appear to the world as "Pearl Harbor in reverse."

In Japan, the attack is sometimes viewed as the mistake that awoke a "sleeping giant." Others associate it with a dishonorable period of aggression in the nation's history.

Though Pearl Harbor happened more than sixty years ago, the incident carries a great deal of weight in American political rhetoric. Political analysts and media personnel compared the terrorist attacks on the United States of September 11, 2001, to Pearl Harbor. While similar in some respects, the Pearl Harbor analogy, along with other thinly veiled language such as "axis of evil," permitted President George W. Bush to build support for the War on Terror by framing it in terms reminiscent of World War II.

SEE ALSO *Hitler, Adolf; Roosevelt, Franklin D.; World War II*

BIBLIOGRAPHY

Jespersen, T. Christopher. 2005. Analogies at War: Vietnam, the Bush Administration's War in Iraq, and the Search for a Usable Past. *Pacific Historical Review* 74 (3): 411–426.

Prange, Gordon W. 1991. *At Dawn We Slept: The Untold Story of Pearl Harbor.* New York: Penguin.

Todd L. Belt

PEARLIN PERSONAL MASTERY SCALE

SEE *Motivation.*

PEARSON, KARL
1857–1936

Karl Pearson was one of the principal architects of the modern theory of mathematical statistics. His interests ranged from mathematical physics, astronomy, philosophy, history, literature, socialism, and the law to

Darwinism, evolutionary biology, heredity, Mendelism, eugenics, medicine, anthropology, and crainometry. His major contribution, however, by his lights and by posterity's, was to establish and advance the discipline of mathematical statistics.

The second son of William Pearson and Fanny Smith, Carl Pearson was born in London on March 27, 1857. In 1879 the University of Heidelberg changed the spelling of his name when it enrolled him as "Karl Pearson"; five years later he adopted this variant of his name and eventually became known as "KP." His mother came from a family of seamen and mariners, and his father was a barrister and Queen's Counsel. The Pearsons were a family of dissenters and of Quaker stock. By the time Carl was twenty-two he had rejected Christianity and adopted "Freethought" as a nonreligious faith that was grounded in science.

Pearson graduated with honors in mathematics from King's College, Cambridge University in January 1879. He stayed in Cambridge to work in Professor James Stuart's engineering workshop and to study philosophy in preparation for his trip to Germany in April. His time in Germany was a period of self-discovery, philosophically and professionally. Around this time, he began to write *The New Werther*, an epistolary novel on idealism and materialism, published in 1880 under the pseudonym of Loki (a mischievous Scandinavian god). In Heidelberg Pearson abandoned Karl philosophy because "it made him miserable and would have led him to short-cut his career" (Karl Pearson, Letter to Robert Parker, 17 August 1879. Archive reference number: NW/Cor.23. Helga Hacker Pearson papers within Karl Pearson's archival material held at University College London). Though he considered becoming a mathematical physicist, he discarded this idea because he "was not a born genius" (Karl Pearson, Letter to Robert Parker, 19 October 1879. Archive reference number/922. Karl Pearson's archival material held at University College London). He stayed in Berlin and attended lectures on Roman international law and philosophy.

He returned to London and studied law at Lincoln's Inn at the Royal Courts of Justice. He was called to the bar at the end of 1881 but practiced for only a very short time. Instead, he began to lecture on socialism, Karl Marx, Ferdinand Lassalle, and Martin Luther from 1880 to 1881, while also writing on medieval German folklore and literature and contributing hymns to the *Socialist Song Book*. In the course of his lifetime, he produced more than 650 publications, of which 400 were statistical; over a period of twenty-eight years he founded and edited six academic journals, of which *Biometrika* is the best known.

Having received the Chair of Mechanism and Applied Mathematics at University College London (UCL) in June 1884, Pearson taught mathematical

physics, hydrodynamics, magnetism, electricity, and elasticity to engineering students. Soon after, he was asked to edit and complete William Kingdom Clifford's *The Common Sense of Exact Science* (1885) and Isaac Todhunter's *History of the Theory of Elasticity* (1886).

THE GRESHAM LECTURES ON STATISTICS

Pearson was a founding member of the Men's and Women's Club, established in 1885 for the free and unreserved discussion of all matters concerning relationships of men and women. Among the various members was Marie Sharpe, whom he married in June 1890. They had three children, Sigrid, Helga and Egon. Six months after his marriage, he took up another teaching post in the Gresham Chair of Geometry at Gresham College in the City of London (the financial district), which he held for three years concurrently with his post at UCL. From February 1891 to November 1893, Pearson delivered thirty-eight lectures.

These lectures were aimed at a nonacademic audience. Pearson wanted to introduce them to a way of thinking that would influence how they made sense of the physical world. While his first eight lectures formed the basis of his book *The Grammar of Science*, the remaining thirty dealt with statistics because he thought this audience would understand insurance, commerce, and trade statistics and could relate to games of chance involving Monte Carlo roulette, lotteries, dice, and coins. In 1891 he introduced the *histogram* (a type of bar chart), and he devised the *standard deviation* and the *variance* (to measure statistical variation) in 1893. Pearson's early Gresham lectures on statistics were influenced by the work of Francis Ysidro Edgeworth, William Stanley Jevons, and John Venn.

Pearson's last twelve Gresham lectures signified a turning point in his career owing to the Darwinian zoologist W. F. R. Weldon (1860–1906), who was interested in using a statistical approach for problems of Darwinian evolution. Their emphasis on Darwinian population of species, underpinned by biological variation, not only implied the necessity of systematically measuring variation but also prompted the reconceptualization of a new statistical methodology, which led eventually to the creation of the Biometric School at University College London in 1894. Earlier vital and social statisticians were mainly interested in calculating averages and were not concerned with measuring statistical variation.

Pearson adapted the mathematics of mechanics, using the *method of moments* to construct a new statistical system to interpret Weldon's asymmetrical distributions, since no such system existed at the time. Using the method of moments, Pearson established four parameters for curve fitting to show how data clustered (the mean), and spread (the standard deviation), if there were a loss of symmetry (*skewness*), and if the shape of the distribution was peaked or flat (*kurtosis*). These four parameters describe the essential characteristics of any empirical distribution and made it possible to analyze data that resulted in various-shaped distributions.

By the time Pearson finished his statistical lectures in May 1894, he had provided the infrastructure of his statistical methodology. He began to teach statistics at University College in October. By 1895 he had worked out the mathematical properties of the *product-moment correlation coefficient* (which measures the relationship between two continuous variables) and *simple regression* (used for the linear prediction between two continuous variables). In 1896 he introduced a higher level of mathematics into statistical theory, the *coefficient of variation, the standard error of estimate, multiple regression,* and *multiple correlation,* and in 1899 he established *scales of measurement* for continuous and discrete variables. Pearson devised more than eighteen methods of correlation from 1896 to 1911, including the *tetrachoric, polychoric, biserial, and triserial correlations* and the *phi coefficient.* Inspired and supported by Weldon, Pearson's major contributions to statistics were: (1) introducing standardized statistical data-management procedures to handle very large sets of data; (2) challenging the tyrannical acceptance of the normal curve as the only distribution on which to base the interpretation of statistical data; (3) providing a set of mathematical statistical tools for the analysis of statistical variation, and (4) professionalizing the discipline of mathematical statistics. Pearson was elected a Fellow of the Royal Society in 1896 and awarded its Darwin Medal in 1898.

Pearson's ongoing work throughout the 1890s with curve fitting signified that he needed a criterion to determine how good the fit was. He continued to work on improving his methods until he devised his *chi-square goodness of fit test* in 1900 and introduced the concept of *degrees of freedom.* Although many other nineteenth-century scientists attempted to find a goodness of fit test, they did not give any underlying theoretical basis for their formulas, which Pearson managed to do. The overriding significance of this test meant that statisticians could use statistical methods that did not depend on the normal distribution to interpret their findings. Indeed, the chi-square goodness of fit test represented Pearson's single most important contribution to the modern theory of statistics, for it raised substantially the practice of mathematical statistics. In 1904 Pearson established the *chi-square statistic* for discrete variables to be used in contingency tables. Pearson published his statistical innovations from his Gresham and UCL lectures in a set of twenty-three papers, "Mathematical Contributions to the

Theory of Evolution," principally in Royal Society publications from 1893 to 1916. He established the first degree course in statistics in Britain in 1915.

PEARSON'S FOUR LABORATORIES

In the twentieth century Pearson founded and managed four laboratories. He set up the Drapers' Biometric Laboratory in 1903 with a grant from the Worshipful Drapers' Company (who funded the laboratory until 1933). The methodology incorporated in this laboratory involved the use of his statistical methods and numerous instruments. The problems investigated by the biometricians included natural selection, Mendelian genetics and Galton's law of ancestral inheritance, crainometry, physical anthropology, and theoretical aspects of mathematical statistics. A year after Pearson established the Biometric Laboratory, the Worshipful Drapers' Company gave him a grant to launch an Astronomical Laboratory equipped with a transit circle and a four-inch equatorial refractor.

In 1907 Francis Galton (who was then eighty-five years old) wanted to step down as director of the Eugenics Record Office, which he had set up three years earlier; he asked Pearson to take over the office, which Pearson subsequently renamed the Galton Eugenics Laboratory. Pearson had, by then, spent the previous fourteen years developing the foundations of his statistical methodology. His work schedule was so demanding that he took on this role only as a personal favor to Galton. Because Pearson regarded his statistical methods as unsuitable for problems of eugenics, he further developed Galton's actuarial death rates and family pedigrees for the methodology of the Eugenics Laboratory. The latter procedure led to his twenty-one-volume *Treasury of Family Inheritance* (1909–1930). In 1924 Pearson set up the Anthropometric Laboratory, made possible by a gift from his student, Ethel Elderton. When Galton died in January 1911, his estate was bequeathed to UCL and he named Pearson as the first professor of eugenics. The Drapers' Biometric and the Galton Eugenics laboratories, which continued to function separately, became incorporated into the Department of Applied Statistics.

Although Pearson was a eugenicist, he eschewed eugenic policies. For him and his British contemporaries (e.g., Herbert Spencer, George Bernard Shaw, H. G. Wells, Marie Stopes, and Virginia Woolf), eugenics was principally a discourse about class, whereas in Germany and America the focus was on racial purity. The British were anxious that the country would be overrun by the poor unless their reproduction lessened; the middle classes were thus encouraged to have more children. In any case eugenics did not lead Pearson to develop any new statistical methods, nor did it play any role in the creation of his statistical methodology.

His wife, Marie Sharpe, died in 1928, and in 1929 he married Margaret Victoria Child, a co-worker in the Biometric Laboratory. Pearson was made Emeritus Professor in 1933 and given a room in the Zoology Department at UCL, which he used as the office for *Biometrika*. From his retirement until his death in 1936, he published thirty-four articles and notes and continued to edit *Biometrika*.

SCHOLARSHIP ON PEARSON

Pearson's statistical work and innovations, his philosophy and his ideas about Darwinism, evolutionary biology, Mendelism, eugenics, medicine, and elasticity have been of considerable interest to innumerable scientists and scholars for more than a century. Throughout the twentieth century, many commentators viewed Pearson as a disciple of Francis Galton who merely expanded Galton's ideas on correlation and regression. Consequently, a number of scholars have falsely assumed that Pearson's motivation for creating a new statistical methodology arose from problems of eugenics. Among writers who have taken this view are Daniel Kevles, Bernard Norton, Donald Mackenzie, Theodore Porter, Richard Soloway, and Tukufu Zuberi. However, using substantial corroborative historical evidence in Pearson's archives, Eileen Magnello (1999) provided compelling documentation that Pearson not only managed the Drapers' Biometric and the Galton Eugenics laboratories separately but also that they occupied separate physical spaces, that he maintained separate financial accounts, that he established very different journals, and that he created two completely different methodologies. Moreover, he took on his work in the Eugenics Laboratory very reluctantly and wanted to relinquish the post after one year. Pearson emphasized to Galton that the sort of sociological problems that he was interested in pursuing for his eugenics program were markedly different from the research that was conducted in the Drapers' Biometric Laboratory.

Juxtaposing Pearson alongside Galton and eugenics has distorted the complexity and totality of Pearson's intellectual enterprises, since there was virtually no relationship between his research in "pure" statistics and his agenda for the eugenics movement. This long-established but misguided impression can be attributed to (1) an excessive reliance on secondary sources containing false assumptions, (2) the neglect of Pearson's voluminous archival material, (3) the use of a minute portion of his 600-plus published papers, (4) a conflation of some of Pearson's biometric and crainometric work with that of eugenics, and (5) a blatant misinterpretation and misrepresentation of Pearsonian statistics.

Continuing to link Galton with Pearson, Michael Bulmer (2003) suggested that the impetus to Pearson's sta-

tistics came from his reading of Galton's *Natural Inheritance*. However, Magnello (2004) argued that this view failed to take into account that Pearson's initial reaction to Galton's book in March 1889 was actually quite cautious. It was not until 1934, almost half a century later, when Pearson was 78 years old, that he reinterpreted the impact Galton's book had on his statistical work in a more favorable light—long after Pearson had established the foundations to modern statistics.

The central role that Weldon played in the development of Pearson's statistical program has been almost completely overlooked by most scholars, except for Robert Olby (1988) and Peter Bowler (2003), who gave Weldon greater priority than Galton in Pearson's development of mathematical statistics as it related to problems of evolutionary biology. Weldon's role in Pearson's early published statistical papers was acknowledged by Churchill Eisenhart (1974), Stephen Stigler (1986), and A. W. F. Edwards (1993). In all her papers, Magnello addressed Weldon's pivotal role in enabling Pearson to construct a new mathematically based statistical methodology.

Norton (1978a, 1978b) and Porter (2004) argue that Pearson's iconoclastic and positivistic *Grammar of Science* played a role in the development of Pearson's statistical work. However, Magnello (1999, 2005a) disputed this and argued that while *The Grammar of Science* represents his philosophy of science as a young adult, it does not reveal everything about his thinking and ideas, especially those in connection with his development of mathematical statistics. Thus, she maintains, it is not helpful to see this book as an account of what Pearson was to do throughout the remaining forty-two years of his working life.

Although long-standing claims have been made by various commentators throughout the twentieth and early twenty-first centuries that Pearson rejected Mendelism, Magnello (1998) showed that Pearson did not reject Mendelism completely but that he accepted the fundamental idea for discontinuous variation. Moreover, Philip Sloan (2000) argued that the biometricians' debates clarified issues in Mendelism that otherwise might not have been developed with the rigor that they were to achieve.

Additionally, virtually all historians of science have failed to acknowledge that Pearson's and Galton's ideas, methods, and outlook on statistics were profoundly different. However, Bowler (2003) detected differences in their statistical thinking because of their different interpretations of evolution, and Stigler acknowledged their diverse approaches to statistics in his *The History of Statistics* (1986). Magnello (1996, 1998, 1999, 2002) explained that whereas Pearson's main focus was goodness of fit testing, Galton's emphasis was correlation; Pearson's higher level of mathematics for doing statistics was more mathematically complex than Galton's; Pearson was interested in very large data sets (more than 1,000), whereas Galton was more concerned with smaller data sets of around 100 (owing to the explanatory power of percentages); and Pearson undertook long-term projects over several years, while Galton wanted faster results. Moreover, Galton thought all data had to conform to the normal distribution, whereas Pearson emphasised that empirical distributions could take on any number of shapes.

Given the pluralistic nature of Pearson's scientific work and the complexity of his many statistical innovations twinned with his multifaceted persona, Pearson will no doubt continue to be of interest for many future scholars. Pearson's legacy of establishing the foundations of contemporary mathematical statistics helped to create the modern world view, for his statistical methodology not only transformed our vision of nature but also gave scientists a set of quantitative tools to conduct research, accompanied with a universal scientific language that standardized scientific writing in the twentieth century. His work went on to provide the foundations for such statisticians as R. A. Fisher, who went on to make further advancements in the modern theory of mathematical statistics.

SEE ALSO *Chi-Square; Regression Analysis; Statistics*

BIBLIOGRAPHY

Bowler, Peter J. 2003. *Evolution: The History of an Idea.* 3rd ed. Berkeley: University of California Press.

Bulmer, Michael. 2003. *Francis Galton: Pioneer of Heredity and Biometry.* Baltimore, MD: Johns Hopkins University Press.

Edwards, A. W. F. 1993. Galton, Pearson and Modern Statistical Theory. In *Sir Francis Galton, FRS, The Legacy of His Ideas,* ed. Milo Keynes. London: Palgrave Macmillan.

Eisenhart, Churchill. 1974. Karl Pearson. In *Dictionary of Scientific Biography* 10, 447–473. New York: Scribner's.

Hilts, Victor. 1967. *Statist and Statistician.* New York: Arno Press, 1981.

Kevles, Daniel. 1985. *In the Name of Eugenics: Genetics and the Uses of Human Heredity.* New York: Knopf.

Mackenzie, Donald. 1981. *Statistics in Britain 1865–1930: The Social Construction of Scientific Knowledge.* Edinburgh: Edinburgh University Press.

Magnello, M. Eileen. 1996. Karl Pearson's Gresham Lectures: W. F. R. Weldon, Speciation and the Origins of Pearsonian Statistics. *British Journal for the History of Science* 29: 43–64.

Magnello, M. Eileen. 1998. Karl Pearson's Mathematisation of Inheritance: From Galton's Ancestral Heredity to Mendelian Genetics (1895–1909). *Annals of Science* 55: 35–94.

Magnello, M. Eileen. 1999. The Non-correlation of Biometrics and Eugenics: Rival Forms of Laboratory Work in Karl Pearson's Career at University College London. Part 1. *History of Science* 37: 79–106; Part 2, 38: 123–150.

Magnello, M. Eileen. 2002. The Introduction of Mathematical Statistics into Medical Research: The Roles of Karl Pearson,

Major Greenwood and Austin Bradford Hill. In *The Road to Medical Statistics,* eds. Eileen Magnello and Anne Hardy, 95–124. New York and Amsterdam: Rodopi.

Magnello, M. Eileen. 2004. Statistically Unlikely. Review of *Francis Galton: Pioneer of Heredity and Biometry,* by Michael Bulmer. *Nature* 428: 699.

Magnello, M. Eileen. 2005a. Karl Pearson and the Origins of Modern Statistics: An Elastician Becomes a Statistician. *The Rutherford Journal: The New Zealand Journal for the History and Philosophy of Science and Technology.* http://rutherfordjournal.org/. (Vol. 1, December).

Magnello, M. Eileen. 2005b. Karl Pearson, Paper on the Chi-Square Goodness of Fit Test. In *Landmark Writings in Western Mathematics: Case Studies, 1640–1940,* ed. Ivor Grattan-Guinness, 724–731. Amsterdam: Elsevier.

Norton, Bernard. 1978a. Karl Pearson and the Galtonian Tradition: Studies in the Rise of Quantitative Social Biology. PhD diss., University College London.

Norton, Bernard. 1978b. Karl Pearson and Statistics: The Social Origin of Scientific Innovation. *Social Studies of Science* 8: 3–34.

Olby, Robert. 1988. The Dimensions of Scientific Controversy: The Biometrician-Mendelian Debate. *British Journal for the History of Science* 22: 299–320.

Pearson, Egon. 1936–1938. Karl Pearson: An Appreciation of Some Aspects of His Life and Work. Part 1, 1857–1905. *Biometrika* (1936): 193–257; Part 2, 1906–1936 (1938): 161–248. (Reprinted Cambridge, U.K.: Cambridge University Press, 1938).

Pearson, Karl. 1914–1930. *The Life, Letters and Labours of Francis Galton.* 3 vols. Cambridge, U.K.: Cambridge University Press.

Porter, Theodore M. 1986. *The Rise of Statistical Thinking: 1820–1900.* Princeton, NJ: Princeton University Press.

Porter, Theodore M. 2004. *Karl Pearson: The Scientific Life in a Statistical Age.* Princeton, NJ: Princeton University Press.

Sloan, Philip R. 2000. Mach's Phenomenalism and the British Reception of Mendelism. *Comptes Rendus de l'Académie des sciences* 323: 1069–1079.

Soloway, Richard A. 1990. *Demography and Degeneration: Eugenics and the Declining Birthrate in Twentieth-Century Britain.* Chapel Hill: University of North Carolina Press.

Stigler, Stephen M. 1986. *The History of Statistics: The Measure of Uncertainty before 1900.* Cambridge, MA: Belknap Press.

Stigler, Stephen M. 1999. *Statistics on the Table: The History of Statistical Concepts and Methods.* Cambridge, MA: Harvard University Press.

Zuberi, Tukufu. 2001. *Thicker Than Blood: How Racial Statistics Lie.* Minneapolis: University of Minnesota Press.

M. Eileen Magnello

PEASANT MOVEMENTS

SEE *Peasantry.*

PEASANTRY

Peasantry refers to peoples and communities who are peasants. The modern English term *peasant* comes from French and Latin terms referring to residents of an administrative district. In modern times the term has come to refer primarily to small-scale agriculturalists who live in villages and small towns in rural areas. Peasant communities are typically based economically on the cultivation of grains and other high yielding plant foods. Wheat, barley, and oats were first domesticated in the area where Syria, Palestine, and adjacent areas of Northern Iraq are now located and the first peasants appeared in Ancient Mesopotamia (present day Iraq).

The basis of peasant agriculture began with varieties of rice and wheat in Asia, corn and beans in what is now Southern Mexico, and potatoes in the Central Andes (Peru). The grains of Mesopotamia spread into Europe; rice spread into other areas of Asia; the cultivation of corn and beans spread north and south from their centers of origin; and potatoes and some grains domesticated in the Central Andes spread throughout the Andean region. These areas became the bases for the growth of peasantries. Peasants typically produce their crops with simple technology in which the work is done by human labor and the use of farm animals. Unlike farmers who usually employ some hired labor to cultivate large crops primarily for sale in markets, peasants are typically small-scale producers who consume much of each crop that they produce.

The rise of the first civilizations and the economies of most urban areas throughout history were primarily dependent in three ways on rural peasantries. The first way was for food. Due mainly to market systems and taxation, surplus peasant production was typically transferred from rural production areas to towns and cities where food was consumed by non-peasants. The second way in which urban areas were dependent on peasants was demographic. Prior to the development of modern public health practices in the nineteenth century, more people tended to die in cities than were born in them. Throughout history peasants have tended to have relatively high death rates, but have offset their death rate by an even higher birth rate. But due mainly to the inability of peasant communities to economically support growing populations, some percentage of every generation typically migrated to cities and maintained urban populations or caused them to grow. The third form of urban dependency on peasants was for labor. When peasants migrated into cities, they usually occupied the lowest rungs of the social order and provided much of the cities' manual labor and menial services.

CLASS AND CLASS RELATIONS

An essential component in the sociology, economics, and politics of peasants is the way in which they are positioned in relation to non-peasants. In terms of social class relations, peasants tend to be at or near the lower end of socioeconomic hierarchies and related to non-peasants by forms of uneven exchange whereby they render up more economic value to non-peasants than they receive in exchange. One of the basic features that make possible such uneven exchange between peasants and non-peasants is land tenure. The political importance of land tenure to peasants is expressed in the slogan of the Mexican Revolution, "Tierra y Libertad," which signals that access to land (tierra) takes precedence over liberty (libertad).

Because they make their living as small-scale cultivators, peasants must have access to land on which to grow crops and raise animals. There is wide variation in the legal, political, and economic aspects of land tenure. The concept of private property, in which land can be bought and sold in a real estate market, is a modern concept. Throughout history it has been common for peasants to live on and work land that is controlled by non-peasants and to whom the peasants are politically subordinate. In non-capitalist state societies the land is typically controlled by a central government that levies taxes on its rural communities. In many other societies, peasant lands are controlled by landlords who charge rent.

State governments also extract surplus from peasants in a number of ways. One of the most common ways is taxation on the crops that the peasants produce or on the land that they use. But taxation of peasants also takes other forms. For example, the monumental architecture of ancient societies, such as the great pyramids of Egypt and Mexico, were built mainly by peasants who had to work on them, typically without pay or other compensation. In feudal societies, peasants may have labor obligations to their lords, whereby they are required to work so many days each year on their farmland or render other services to their landlords. Sharecropping is another form of rent, whereby peasants are given access to land controlled by a landlord, who then receives some fraction of each crop that the peasants working that land produce. In economies with well-developed markets, the peasants may sell part of their harvests to raise money to pay their rents or taxes. In some societies, peasants are required to work lands of the government and also possibly render other services. Also, until recently, peasant conscripts were required to do military service in the armies of kingdoms and states, and of feudal lords. Indeed, until modern times, most of the rank and file members of armies have been of peasant origin.

POLITICS AND THE FUTURE OF PEASANTRIES

Peasants periodically rise up against the lords and governments that impose taxes and rent and other forms of uneven economic exchange on them. However, the potential for peasant rebellions and political organizing in general is often weakened by internal competition and distrust, which is a result of struggle for scarce resources within peasant communities. Indeed, it was these characteristics that moved German revolutionary Karl Marx (1818–1883) to refer to peasants as like "potatoes in a sack" ([1852] 1972) implying that they were too individualistically oriented to organize as revolutionaries.

But peasantries have on a number of occasions been involved in large-scale regional and national rebellions and revolutions. For example, from 1524 to 1526 German peasants in Franconia, Swabia, and Thuringia joined with impoverished town dwellers (many of whom were no doubt of peasant origin) to mount the "Peasant War," to redress exploitive relations with non-peasants. This movement was largely unsuccessful, but peasants have been major actors in other major conflicts that have had varied outcomes in the twentieth century, such as the Mexican and Russian Revolutions, the formation of contemporary China, and the Vietnam War of independence against France and the United States.

Until the mid-twentieth century, most of the world's population could be characterized as peasant, but since that time peasant communities have tended to become more complex, due largely to ever increasing rates of permanent and circular migration from agricultural communities to urban areas. It became common for many formerly-peasant households to be largely dependent on seasonal migration of some of their members who seek salaried work or self-employment. Much of this migration is across national borders, typically from areas and nations of lesser to higher levels of economic development. Such high rates of migration have increased social, economic, and cultural complexity in formerly peasant communities.

SEE ALSO *Agricultural Economics; Agricultural Industry; Common Land; Dual Economy; Land Claims; Land Reform; Landlords; Lewis, W. Arthur; Maximization; Subsistence Agriculture*

BIBLIOGRAPHY

Kearney, Michael. 1996. *Reconceptualizing the Peasantry: Anthropology in Global Perspective.* Boulder, CO: Westview Press.

Marx, Karl. [1852] 1972. *The Eighteenth Brumaire of Louis Bonaparte.* New York: International Publishers.

Nagengast, Carole. 1991. *Reluctant Socialists, Rural Entrepreneurs: Class, Culture, and the Polish State.* Boulder, CO: Westview Press.

Otero, Gerardo. 1999. *Farewell to the Peasantry: Political Class Formation in Rural Mexico.* Boulder, CO: Westview Press.

Shanin, Teodor, ed. 1987. *Peasants and Peasant Societies*, 2nd ed. Oxford: Basil Blackwell.

Wolf, Eric. 1966. *Peasants.* Englewood Cliffs, NJ: Prentice-Hall.

Michael Kearney

PEDAGOGY

At the present time, more is known about how people learn than ever before in human history, and breakthroughs in research are occurring with increasing frequency. The social sciences have contributed enormously to this body of theoretical knowledge, but the diffusion of pedagogical innovations remains problematic. New theories and practices usually do not completely displace existing pedagogies but are simply added to teachers' instructional repertoire. Moreover, the translation of theory into classroom practice depends heavily on how well individual teachers understand the theories they were taught and how they put them into practice.

During the twentieth century psychologists and educational theorists developed a wide variety of models to explain how humans learn, and it is clear that ongoing basic research has begun to have an impact on pedagogical practice at all levels of the educational system. Recent research in neuroscience has also added a biological dimension to our understanding of the learning process, although the pedagogical implications of this research are still not clear.

Several important themes have emerged from this body of research. For example, there is substantial agreement that in order for deep learning to occur, learners must construct new knowledge themselves, through experience, reflection, and integration. Learners also must build on what they already know and believe, so they must reconcile existing knowledge with new knowledge and correct mistaken beliefs. Metacognitive skills, such as critical thinking and problem solving, are primary goals of learning, but mastery of factual knowledge is also essential to critical thinking. Factual knowledge is best learned within conceptual frameworks that organize it in meaningful ways, and since subject disciplines use different frameworks, students need to learn a variety of approaches for organizing their knowledge.

These theories suggest that students must engage in learning tasks that require inquiry, experimentation, and active engagement in real-world problem solving. Group-based activities and projects are commonly used teaching methods in this paradigm, since cooperation and collaboration seem to facilitate the desired outcomes. The teacher's content expertise is still important, but it is used in novel ways. Questioning and dialogue largely replace lecturing, and the teacher becomes an instructional coach who designs learning activities, facilitates discussion, and guides students through the process of learning.

With various adaptations, these principles can be applied at all levels of instruction, from early childhood to adult education. For example, in an elementary school, students use models of the sun, the earth, and the moon, and a bright lamp to conduct an experiment to explain the phases of the moon. At the end of the exercise, they write up their conclusions and take a test on the essential astronomical concepts. In a college biology course, student groups are presented with a case study on stream pollution. They work collaboratively to pool their biological knowledge, pose researchable questions, develop a learning plan that includes readings for the group, conduct an investigation of the questions, and finally produce scientifically defensible solutions. The product of their work is evaluated on the accuracy of their knowledge, the thoroughness of their research, and the quality of their scientific reasoning.

Although empirical research clearly supports the effectiveness of these pedagogical approaches, only the most progressive educational institutions promote and support them as the primary mode of instruction. Typically, selected activities and projects occur only sporadically within the context of traditional didactic instruction. The reasons these theories have not been more pervasive in education are related to some of the fundamental problems of translating theory into practice.

Beyond the difficulties of mastering new instructional methods and techniques, teachers often find it hard to abandon the role of expert didact and the instructional paradigm of drill and practice under which they were taught. Indeed, educational researchers have found that the intuitive beliefs of teachers about learning have a greater impact on their instructional practices than theoretical models derived from research. Outside the academy, parents and school boards often do not understand these new approaches and may resist their incorporation into their schools. In some cases, state education standards and curriculum guides may contradict new pedagogical models suggested by research. Finally, governments and school systems increasingly require standardized end-of-grade tests as part of school accountability, and teachers can find that "teaching to the test" is more important to their career success than considerations of effective pedagogy.

It is not sufficient for social scientists to demonstrate the effectiveness of new teaching methods and techniques, since pedagogical change requires attention to the gamut of social, cultural, and political forces that mitigate the translation of theory into practice.

SEE ALSO *Curriculum; Education, Unequal; Freire, Paulo; Hegemony; Neuroscience; Schooling; Teacher Expectations; Teacher-Child Relationships; Teachers*

BIBLIOGRAPHY

Bransford, John D., Ann L. Brown, and Rodney R. Cocking, eds. 2000. *How People Learn: Brain, Mind, Experience, and School*, expanded ed. Washington, DC: National Academy Press.

Edward M. Neal

PEER CLIQUES

Friendships can foster important psychological and social growth. During late childhood and early adolescence, friends start to gather in a loose-knit collection of members called a *peer group*. Within these larger peer groups are smaller, tightly organized peer *cliques*. Peer cliques consist of a small group of close friends, about three to ten, whose members typically resemble one another in family background, attitudes, and values (Ennett, Bauman, and Kock 1996). Cliques, by their likes and dislikes and social status, for example, often constitute "the popular" and "unpopular" groups. Cliques provide a context for acquiring new social skills and for experimenting with values and social roles in the absence of parental monitoring.

Cliques formed early in childhood typically consist of same-sex members; they later begin to diversify, with an increase in mixed-gender cliques in middle and later adolescence (Dunphy 1963; Hartup 1996). Dexter Dunphy's classic study of Australian adolescent cliques suggests that cliques prepare adolescents for the heterosocial world. Cliques vary in size, but remain small enough to allow frequent interaction among members. Researchers have identified different membership positions within a clique, including a member who affiliates exclusively with the group and a liaison who connects with various other cliques (Ennett and Bauman 1994). Organized around activities, ethnicity, or self-selected friendships, cliques appear to remain stable; instead of dissolving as members leave, cliques replace old members with new members who uphold the group norms (Brown and Klute 2003). Paul Zisman and Vernon Wilson found that when cliques were more tightly organized, they are less likely to include multiple ethnic groups (1992). In most peer cliques a group leader (or leaders) emerges to exercise authority over the group and enforce group norms (Adler and Adler 1995; Dunphy 1963).

A peer clique can be a powerful socializing agent. In a seven-year study of peer cliques of middle-class, European American fourth, fifth, and sixth graders, Patricia and Peter Adler found that clique leaders ridiculed and belittled outsiders and low-status group members, and encouraged other members to act in a similar manner (Adler and Adler 1995). Likewise, Jay Macleod's 1987 observation of late adolescent boys revealed similar teasing and ridicule of outside members. Group norms and socialization become more precarious when they are marked by homogenous aggressiveness and delinquent behaviors (Cairns and Cairns 1994). Research has demonstrated that antisocial behavior is associated with involvement in deviant peer cliques from early to middle adolescence (Stormshak et al. 2005). Young adolescents form groups based on their similarities in terms of deviance and delinquency.

Importantly, not all cliques are negative or socialize children to act aggressively. Some research suggests that cliques can be a significant predictor of adolescents' psychological well-being (Hansell 1985; Gauze, Bukowski, Aquan-Assee 1996; Ladd, Kochenderfer, and Coleman 1997). According to researchers, friendships and peer acceptance into the larger group can provide social and emotional support and create a sense of connectedness to the group. Thus, social development and well-being, apparent in factors such as decreased loneliness, are enhanced in positive peer relations. According to Jeffery Parker and Steven Asher, children benefit from being accepted by the group (1993).

SEE ALSO *Acting White; Peer Relations Research*

BIBLIOGRAPHY

Adler, Patricia A., and Peter Adler. 1995. Dynamics of Inclusion and Exclusion in Preadolescent Cliques. *Social Psychology Quarterly* 58 (3): 145–162.

Brown, B. Bradford, and Christa Klute. 2003. Friendships, Cliques, and Crowds. In *Blackwell Handbook of Adolescence*, eds. Gerald R. Adams and Michael D. Berzonsky, 330–345. Malden, MA: Blackwell.

Cairns, Robert B., and Beverley Cairns. 1994. *Lifelines and Risks: Pathways of Youth in Our Time*. New York: Cambridge University Press.

Dunphy, Dexter C. 1963. The Social Structure of Urban Adolescent Peer Groups. *Sociometry* 26: 230–246.

Ennett, Susan T., and Karl E. Bauman. 1994. The Contribution of Influence and Selection to Adolescent Peer Group Homogeneity in: The Case of Adolescent Cigarette Smoking. *Journal of Personality and Social Psychology* 67: 653–663.

Ennett, Susan T., Karl E. Bauman, and Gary G. Kock. 1996. Variability in Cigarette Smoking within and between Adolescent Friendship Cliques. *Addictive Behaviors* 19: 295–305.

Gauze, Cyma, William M. Bukowski, and Jasmine Aquan-Assee. 1996. Interactions between Family Environment and Friendship and Associations with Self-Perceived Well-Being during Adolescence. *Child Development* 67: 2201–2216.

Hansell, Stephen. 1985. Adolescent Friendship Networks. *Social Forces* 63: 698–715.

Hartup, Willard W. 1996. The Company They Keep: Friendships and Their Developmental Significance. *Child Development* 67 (1): 1–13.

Ladd, Gary W., Becky J. Kochenderfer, and Cynthia C. Coleman. 1997. Classroom Peer Acceptance, Friendship, and Victimization: Distinct Relational Systems That Contribute Uniquely to Children's Social Adjustment? *Child Development* 68: 1181–1197.

Macleod, Jay. 1987. *Ain't No Making It: Leveled Aspirations in Low Income Neighborhoods*. Boulder, CO: Westview.

Parker, Jeffery G., and Steven R. Asher. 1993. Friendship and Friendship Quality in Middle Childhood: Links with Peer Group Acceptance and Feelings of Loneliness and Social Dissatisfaction. *Developmental Psychology* 29: 611–621.

Stormshak, Elizabeth A., Thomas J. Dishion, John Light, and Miwa Yasui. 2005. Implementing Family Centered Interventions within the Public Middle School: Linking Service Delivery to Change in Student Problem Behavior. *Journal of Abnormal Child Psychology* 33: 723–733.

Zisman, Paul, and Vernon Wilson. 1992. Table Hopping in the Cafeteria: An Exploration of "Racial" Integration in Early Adolescent Social Groups. *Anthropology and Education Quarterly* 23: 199–220.

Pa Her

PEER EFFECTS

Although researchers have studied children's peer relationships since the 1930s (Ladd 2005), the end of the twentieth century marked a flurry of psychological inquiry into the impact of peers on development and behavior. Traditionally, adults, especially parents, were considered the primary socializers, responsible for assimilating the child into society. However, according to developmentalists like Jean Piaget and Willard Hartup, children grow up in two distinct social worlds characterized by different types of relationships—the world of adults and the world of peers. Adult-child relationships are hierarchical, with power residing largely with the adult, whose greater experience and knowledge are essential for socializing the child as a new member of society. Yet peer relationships are also critical, though organized quite differently. Contemporary peer relationships are between age-mates of roughly equal power, operating at similar developmental levels, both cognitively and physically. The egalitarian nature of peer relationships makes them unique contexts for developing skills like negotiation, perspective-taking, cooperation, problem solving, and so on.

Peers can serve as socializers in the *absence* of adults, as shown in Anna Freud and Sophie Dann's (1951) studies of peer rearing among children during World War II (1939–1945) and in Stephen Suomi and Harry Harlow's (e.g., 1972) studies of nonhuman primates. Even when adults are available, however, peer influences are now understood to be significant. Judith Rich Harris has questioned traditional notions of the socialization process, emphasizing the impact of peers and community in her *group socialization theory* (GST). Using behavioral genetics research that attempts to specify the relative influence of hereditary versus environmental influences, Harris points out that about 40 to 50 percent of one's personality is attributable to genetics, but only 10 percent or less can be attributed to family and parenting factors, leaving about 40 percent to environmental influences that are unique to each individual. Harris proposes that the peer group is a significant contributor here, challenging us to consider socialization forces beyond the family.

In understanding peer effects, researchers like Wyndol Furman and Philip Robbins (1985) distinguish between the role of dyadic friendships, which fulfill one's need for intimacy, affection, and reliable alliance, and relations within the peer group, which meet one's need to belong in a larger social context. Both friendships and peer group acceptance contribute to development across the life span, though their impact may differ. For example, Catherine Bagwell, Andrew Newcomb, and William Bukowski (1998) found that children's friendships were associated with better attitudes toward family relationships, greater self-esteem, and lower risk for depression more than a decade later in early adulthood. Being accepted by the peer group also predicted later adjustment associated with higher educational aspirations, better school performance, and job success.

At the dyad level, research by Hartup and others has shown that children and adolescents who have friends are more socially competent, report more positive well-being, and exhibit fewer psychosocial problems than children without friends. Having friends seems particularly important in school adjustment, as the presence of friends facilitates initial school entry (Ladd 1990), helps students navigate later academic transitions (e.g., Berndt et al. 1999; McDougall and Hymel 1998), and impacts students' school engagement and motivation (e.g., Kinderman et al. 1996; Ryan 2000).

The impact of friends can be positive or negative, depending on who those friends are, or rather how they behave. Young people whose friends exhibit antisocial or problem behavior are far more likely to exhibit negative behaviors themselves (e.g., Brendgen et al. 2000). Thomas

Dishion and colleagues (1999) have shown that peer "deviancy training" happens subtly, not just through modeling, but through conversational and behavioral rewards (e.g., laughing when peers describe deviant acts they committed). For children who are already at risk for antisocial behavior due to socioeconomic disadvantage or poor family functioning, the likelihood of going down this path appears to be increased by association with deviant friends (e.g., Ary et al. 1999; Fergusson et al. 1999; Kim et al. 1999). In addition, research by Frank Vitaro and colleagues (e.g., 2001) shows that the success of interventions for high-risk youth is enhanced by *less* association with deviant peers and *more* association with nondeviant peers who provide alternative role models and support socially acceptable behavior.

In understanding peer effects, it is important to move beyond popular thinking about "peer pressure" as stemming from power based on *coercion* (e.g., threat of punishment for noncompliance) or *rewards* (e.g., influencing behavior by controlling rewards). Peer influences can also be indirect, based on *referent* power (French and Raven 1959), affecting young people's attitudes and behaviors simply because others admire them and want to be like them or affiliated with them. As Harris suggests, peers do not just "push"; they also "pull."

Perhaps the strongest evidence for peer effects comes from research on peer rejection. Since the 1930s, studies have compared individuals who experience good peer relations with those who are disliked or rejected by peers. This research shows that peer rejection predicts later maladjustment in academic (e.g., poor achievement, school dropout), externalizing (e.g., aggression, criminality), and internalizing (e.g., loneliness, depression) realms (McDougall et al. 2001). To explain the effects of peer rejection, Jeffrey Parker and Steven Asher (1987; see also Parker et al. 1995) propose that deviant social behaviors (e.g., aggression, social withdrawal) often lead to peer difficulties and peer rejection, which in turn places a child at serious risk for a host of poor adjustment outcomes, not only because of opportunities for peer-deviancy training, but also because of missed positive peer-socialization experiences that promote healthy development.

Peer group rejection has also been linked to both poor achievement and school dropout (see Juvonen and Wentzel 1996; McDougall et al. 2001), although the process begins in the early years of school. When Eric Buhs, Gary Ladd, and Susan Herald (2006) followed children through elementary school, they found that early peer rejection affected later school engagement and, in turn, achievement. Children rejected in kindergarten were more likely to avoid school and participated less in class over time, but the outcome depended on the peer treatment received. Rejected children who were abused by their peers were more likely to avoid school. Those who were excluded by peers were less likely to participate, which in turn lead to lower achievement. A critical challenge for educators (see CASEL) as well as parents (see Rubin 2002) is to recognize the interface of peer relationships on academic and life success.

SEE ALSO *Achievement; Adolescent Psychology; Child Development; Depression, Psychological; Deviance; Friendship; Loneliness; Piaget, Jean; Schooling; Social Isolation; Socialization*

BIBLIOGRAPHY

Ary, Dennis, Terry Duncan, Susan Duncan, and Hyman Hops. 1999. Adolescent Problem Behavior: The Influence of Parents and Peers. *Behavior Research and Therapy* 37: 217–230.

Bagwell, Catherine, Andrew F. Newcomb, and William M. Bukowski. 1998. Preadolescent Friendship and Peer Rejection as Predictors of Adult Adjustment. *Child Development* 69: 140–153.

Berndt, Thomas J., Jacquelyn A. Hawkins, and Ziyi Jiao. 1999. Influences of Friends and Friendships on Adjustment to Junior High School. *Merrill Palmer Quarterly* 45: 13–41.

Brendgen, Mara, Frank Vitaro, and William Bukowski. 2000. Stability and Variability of Adolescents' Affiliation with Delinquent Friends: Predictors and Consequences. *Social Development* 9: 205–225.

Buhs, Eric S., Gary W. Ladd, and Susan L. Herald. 2006. Peer Exclusion and Victimization: Processes that Mediate the Relation between Peer Group Rejection and Children's Classroom Engagement and Achievement. *Journal of Educational Psychology* 98 (1): 1–13.

CASEL (Collaborative for Academic, Social, and Emotional Learning). http://www.casel.org.

Deater-Deckard, Kirby. 2001. Annotation: Recent Research Examining the Role of Peer Relationships in the Development of Psychopathology. *Journal of Child Psychology and Psychiatry* 42: 565–571.

Dishion, Thomas J. 1990. The Peer Context of Troublesome Child and Adolescent Behavior. In *Understanding Troubled and Troubling Youth: Multiple Perspectives*, ed. Peter Leone, 128–153. Newbury Park, CA: Sage.

Dishion, Thomas J., Joan McCord, and François Poulin. 1999. When Interventions Harm: Peer Groups and Problem Behavior. *American Psychologist* 54: 755–764.

Fergusson, David M., Lianne J. Woodward, and John Horwood. 1999. Childhood Peer Relationship Problems and Young People's Involvement with Deviant Peers in Adolescence. *Journal of Abnormal Child Psychology* 27: 357–369.

French, John R. P., and Bertram Raven. 1959. The Bases of Social Power. In *Studies in Social Power*, ed. Dorwin Cartwright, 150–167. Ann Arbor: University of Michigan Press.

Freud, Anna, and Dann, Sophie. 1951. An Experiment in Group Upbringing. *Psychoanalytic Study of the Child* 6: 127–168.

Furman, Wyndol, and Philip Robbins. 1985. What's the Point? Issues in the Selection of Treatment Objectives. In *Children's Peer Relations: Issues in Assessment and Intervention*, ed. Barry Schneider, Kenneth H. Rubin, and Jane E. Ledingham, 41–54. New York: Springer-Verlag.

Harris, Judith Rich. 1995. Where Is the Child's Environment? A Group Socialization Theory of Development. *Psychological Review* 102: 458–489.

Harris, Judith Rich. 1998. *The Nurture Assumption: Why Children Turn Out the Way They Do.* New York: Free Press.

Harris, Judith Rich. 2006. *No Two Alike: Human Nature and Human Individuality.* New York: Free Press.

Hartup, Willard W. 1999. Peer Experience and Its Developmental Significance. In *Developmental Psychology: Achievements and Prospects*, ed. Mark Bennett, 106–125. Philadelphia: Psychology Press.

Hartup, Willard W., and Nan Stevens. 1997. Friendships and Adaptation in the Life Course. *Psychological Bulletin* 119: 355–370.

Juvonen, Jaana, and Kathryn R. Wentzel. 1996. *Social Motivation: Understanding Children's School Adjustment.* Cambridge, U.K.: Cambridge University Press.

Kim, Jungmeen E., E. Mavis Hetherington, and David Reiss. 1999. Associations among Family Relationships, Antisocial Peers, and Adolescents' Externalizing Behaviors: Gender and Family Type Differences. *Child Development* 70: 1209–1230.

Kinderman, Thomas A., Tanya L. McCollam, and Ellsworth Gibson Jr. 1996. Peer Networks and Students' Classroom Engagement During Childhood and Adolescence. In *Social Motivation: Understanding Children's School Adjustment*, ed. Janna Juvonen and Kathryn R. Wentzel, 279–312. Cambridge, U.K.: Cambridge University Press.

Ladd, Gary W. 1990. Having Friends, Making Friends, Keeping Friends, and Being Liked by Peers in the Classroom: Predictors of Early School Adjustment? *Child Development* 61: 1081–1100.

Ladd, Gary W. 2005. *Children's Peer Relations and Social Competence: A Century of Progress.* New Haven, CT: Yale University Press.

McDougall, Patricia, and Shelley Hymel. 1998. Moving into Middle School: Individual Differences in the Transition Experience. *Canadian Journal of Behavioural Science* 30: 108–120.

McDougall, Patricia, Shelley Hymel, Tracy Vaillancourt, and Louise Mercer. 2001. The Consequences of Early Childhood Rejection. In *Interpersonal Rejection*, ed. Mark Leary, 213–247. New York: Oxford University Press.

Parker, Jeffrey, and Steven Asher. 1987. Peer Relations and Later Personal Adjustment: Are Low-accepted Children at Risk? *Psychological Bulletin* 102: 357–389.

Parker, Jeffrey, Kenneth H. Rubin, Joseph Price, and Melissa E. DeRosier. 1995. Peer Relationships, Child Development, and Adjustment: A Developmental Psychopathology Perspective. In *Developmental Psychopathology*, Vol. 2: *Risk, Disorder, and Adaptation*, ed. Dante Cicchette and Donald Cohen, 96–161. New York: Wiley.

Piaget, Jean. 1932. *The Moral Judgment of the Child.* Glencoe, IL: Free Press.

Rubin, Kenneth H., William M. Bukowski, and Jeffrey G. Parker. 1998. Peer Interactions, Relationships, and Groups. In *Handbook of Child Psychology*, ed. William Damon. 5th ed. Vol. 3: *Social Emotional and Personality Development*, ed. Nancy Eisenberg, 619–700. New York: Wiley.

Rubin, Kenneth H., with Andrea Thompson. 2002. *The Friendship Factor: Helping Our Children Navigate Their Social World and Why It Matters to Their Success and Happiness*. New York: Penguin.

Ryan, Allison M. 2000. Peer Groups as a Context for the Socialization of Adolescents' Motivation, Engagement, and Achievement in School. *Educational Psychologist* 35 (2): 101–111.

Smith, Peter, and Craig Hart. 2002. *Blackwell Handbook of Childhood Social Development*. London: Blackwell.

Suomi, Stephen J., and Harry F. Harlow. 1972. Social Rehabilitation of Isolate-reared Monkeys. *Developmental Psychology* 6: 487–496.

Vitaro, Frank, Mara Brendgen, and Richard E. Tremblay. 2001. Preventive Intervention: Assessing Its Effects on the Trajectories of Delinquency and Testing for Mediational Processes. *Applied Developmental Science* 5 (4): 201–213.

Shelley Hymel
Patricia McDougall
Tracy Vaillancourt

PEER INFLUENCE

The study of peer influence has an important place in the social sciences, particularly in social psychology and developmental psychology. In a now classic series of studies conducted in the 1950s, Solomon Asch (1907–1996), a Polish-born American social psychologist, showed groups of eight to ten college students a set of three lines that differed clearly in length and asked them to indicate out loud which of the three lines was the same length as a fourth line. Only one of the group members was an actual experiment participant; the other group members were associates of the experimenter who were trained to respond incorrectly about the length of the line. In scenarios when the other group members provided unanimously incorrect responses, the experiment participants voiced the same opinion as the other group members one-third of the time. When they were later asked why they responded as they did, the experiment participants generally stated that they knew the group members were wrong in their choice of the matching line but said that they did not want to be ridiculed, ostracized, or thought peculiar by the rest of the group if they gave an opinion that went against the majority view. The many variants of Asch's experiments have been taken as evidence that peers exert considerable influence on the behavior of one another.

One of the difficulties that studying peer influence has encountered is the question of whether peers actually do influence one another or whether individuals who are similar to one another simply seek each other out. Although there is evidence that young people who engage in deviant behaviors seek out peers who also engage in deviant behaviors, studies that have been able to control for the effects of peer selection have shown that once deviant peers are together in a group, they do incrementally increase one another's engagement in deviant behavior (e.g., Matsueda and Anderson 1998).

NEGATIVE PEER PRESSURE AND POSITIVE PEER INFLUENCE

When thinking of peer influence, what comes readily to mind for most people is negative peer pressure. For example, parents, teachers, and other adults worry that adolescents will be pressured by their peers to smoke cigarettes, drink alcohol, have sexual intercourse, or engage in risky behaviors. Indeed, peers can and do influence one another to behave in more deviant ways. In several studies, the best predictor of whether an adolescent will engage in antisocial behavior has been found to be whether he or she affiliates with peers who engage in antisocial behavior (see Pratt and Cullen 2000).

On the other hand, peer influence can also be positive. For example, adolescents can study together, encourage each other to join an extracurricular activity, or provide a fun peer context that does not promote using drugs or engaging in risky behaviors. In fact, the premise of peer mentoring programs is that being paired with a well-adjusted peer can be a positive influence on a youth who is at risk for behavioral or psychological problems.

MECHANISMS OF PEER INFLUENCE

Several influential theories have attempted to explain how peers influence one another. Reinforcement theories emphasize that peers exert influence because they control (consciously or not) rewards that are meaningful. Individuals will behave in ways that are likely to maximize their rewards. Therefore, if an individual perceives that engaging in behavior promoted by peers will result in desired outcomes (e.g., acceptance by the group, high status, access to material possessions), he or she will be more influenced by peers.

Psychologist Thomas J. Dishion's work on deviancy training has led to a better understanding of the mechanisms through which peers reinforce one another's behavior during social interactions. Adolescent boys were observed with their best friend in a laboratory setting. The interactions were coded for whether one boy provided positive responses (such as laughter) when the other boy talked about deviant behavior. Boys whose interactions were characterized by this process of deviancy training were found to engage in subsequently higher levels of substance use, violence, and delinquency, even controlling for previous levels of problem behaviors (e.g., Dishion et al. 1996). Nondeviant boys typically ignored rather than reinforced deviant talk.

Modeling is another mechanism that has been proposed to explain how peers influence one another in either positive or negative ways. Peer mentoring programs often count on this mechanism as mentors model prosocial behavior in the hope of eliciting prosocial behavior from their mentees. On the other hand, observing others engage in deviant behaviors might lift an adolescent's own inhibitions against behaving deviantly. For example, if adolescents observe that many of their classmates drink alcohol or skip school, a given adolescent may feel that social barriers against his or her own drinking or skipping school have been lifted. Fads in clothing or music preferences can also be explained through the mechanism of modeling, which can occur not just between individuals but also at the level of entire schools or neighborhoods.

INDIVIDUAL DIFFERENCES IN SUSCEPTIBILITY TO PEER INFLUENCE

Not all individuals are equally susceptible to peer influence. Age is a key factor that relates to individuals' susceptibility to peer influence. Peer influence begins in the preschool years and increases in importance over time, generally peaking in early adolescence before decreasing as individuals enter later adolescence. Not only does the power of peer influence change with development, the outcomes that peers influence are likely to change as well. For example, peer influence has been found to affect aggression among preschoolers, aggression and covert anti-social behavior among children in elementary school, and substance use and sexual behaviors among adolescents.

In addition to age, other individual differences may contribute to susceptibility to peer influence as well. For example, youth who have a history of being rejected by their peers are more susceptible to later negative peer pressure than are youth who have a history of being accepted by their peers. Youth who have positive, supportive relationships with adults are also less susceptible to influence by their peers than are youth who are not positively connected with adults. Temperamental characteristics, such as the ability to self-regulate, may also contribute to one's susceptibility to peer influence. Research suggests that youth who have already begun to experiment with deviant behaviors are the most susceptible to peer influence toward further deviance. In contrast, youth who are already heavily involved in deviant behavior likely do not need additional peer influence to keep them on this path,

and youth who are strongly oriented against deviant behavior may be able to resist negative peer pressure. Social contexts can also alter the extent to which peers exert influence on one another. For example, in social situations that are unstructured and unsupervised by adults, adolescents are more susceptible to peer influence than they are in more structured and supervised contexts.

To summarize, despite the ability of peers to influence one another in negative ways, peers can also influence one another positively. Mechanisms through which peers influence one another include reinforcement, deviancy training, and modeling. Furthermore, not all individuals are equally susceptible to peer influence. This entry has focused on peer influence during adolescence because it is at this age when individuals are the most susceptible to peer influence; however, as Asch's pioneering work demonstrated, peer influence persists into adulthood and can lead individuals to act in ways contrary to how they would be expected to behave in the absence of peers.

SEE ALSO *Adolescent Psychology; Asch, Solomon*

BIBLIOGRAPHY

Asch, Solomon E. 1951. Effects of Group Pressure upon the Modification and Distortion of Judgments. In *Groups, Leadership, and Men: Research in Human Relations*, ed. Harold Guetzkow, 177–190. Pittsburgh, PA: Carnegie Press.

Dishion, Thomas J., Kathleen M. Spracklen, David W. Andrews, and Gerald R. Patterson. 1996. Deviancy Training in Male Adolescents Friendships. *Behavior Therapy* 27 (3): 373–390.

Matsueda, Ross L., and Kathleen Anderson. 1998. The Dynamics of Delinquent Peers and Delinquent Behavior. *Criminology* 36 (2): 269–308.

Pratt, Travis C., and Frances T. Cullen. 2000. The Empirical Status of Gottfredson and Hirschi's General Theory of Crime: A Meta-Analysis. *Criminology* 38 (3): 931–964.

Jennifer E. Lansford

PEER PRESSURE

SEE *Peer Influence.*

PEER RELATIONS RESEARCH

Peer relations research examines the types and quality of social interactions among same-aged peers. Researchers typically focus their investigation on the quality of each individual's peer interactions within a given social unit.

The particular social unit under investigation can range from a dyadic relationship (e.g., best friendship) to a small group (e.g., clique) to a large peer group. Dyadic relationships are characterized as close, intimate, bidirectional social relationships where the peers choose to interact with one another. In contrast, a peer group is loosely defined as a large set of peers who interact with one another as a matter of opportunity (e.g., all students in fifth grade). Cliques are small groups within a peer group whose membership is typically based on perceived areas of similarity. Cliques include both a network of bidirectional relationships as well as a group identity (e.g., *nerds, jocks*).

Within a given social unit, researchers have examined a wide variety of dimensions that typically fall within one of three broad categories: social behavior; social support; and liking. Antisocial interactions (e.g., aggression), prosocial interactions (e.g., cooperation), and social connectivity (e.g., withdrawal) are commonly assessed social behaviors. For example, researchers may measure the amount of conflict that occurs within a friendship or how socially isolated a child is within a peer group. In contrast, social support research focuses on the functional attributes of a relationship, such as trust, intimacy, and aid. For example, researchers may examine the degree to which members of a clique provide companionship and advice for one another.

Numerous studies have been devoted to assessing the level of liking within a social unit. In large part, this emphasis is based on evidence that the experience of liking versus disliking significantly impacts social behavior as well as a broad array of functional outcomes ranging from self-esteem to delinquency to use of mental health services. In a cyclical fashion, liking, social support, and social behavior influence one another over time. For example, poor social skills interfere with the formation of social support networks and decrease liking within the peer group that, in turn, decreases opportunities to practice social skills with peers and exacerbates social behavior problems.

Traditionally, four sources of information have been used to study peer relations: (1) *observation;* (2) *self-report,* where persons evaluate the state of their own peer relations; (3) *other-report,* where key, non-peer adults (e.g., parents, teachers, counselors) evaluate the state of another's peer relations; and (4) *peer-report,* where peers evaluate the peer relations of members of the same social unit. With observation methods, social interactions of interest (e.g., cooperative play) are observed (in real-time or via taped archives) within a targeted environment (e.g., playground). The observer is an impartial third party who is trained to evaluate the interactions along dimensions of interest (e.g., frequency, duration, quality).

Self- and other-reports are commonly gathered through paper-and-pencil questionnaires with descriptive items (e.g., troublemaking friends) rated along some scale (e.g., five options ranging from Never to Always). In addition to rating scale questionnaires, sociometrics are a common peer-report methodology through which members of a peer group nominate those peers who match specific social descriptors (e.g., fights a lot). The number of peer nominations received for a particular item is totaled for each member and standardized across the nominating group. Thus a given member's social functioning is assessed relative to that of the entire peer group (e.g., highly aggressive). Sociometrics have the advantage of increased reliability and validity due to multiple informants as well as increased sensitivity to variations within a specific group context.

A unique feature of sociometrics is the ability to assess peer group structure. By comparing liking and disliking nominations, researchers can distinguish a member's place within the social structure, including salience within the peer group (i.e., Social Impact = liking + disliking nominations) and degree of acceptance versus rejection across peers (i.e., Social Preference = liking – disliking nominations). Further John Coie and his colleagues' (1982) sociometric algorithms identify distinct social status groups: (1) Average = some liking and disliking nominations, but no extreme level of either; (2) Popular = many liking and few disliking nominations; (3) Controversial = many liking and disliking nominations; (4) Neglected = few liking or disliking nominations; and (5) Rejected = few liking and many disliking nominations. Social status is highly predictive of patterns of adjustment over time. In particular, rejection is a significant risk factor for maladjustment across social, emotional, and behavioral areas of functioning.

Development, gender, and group-level factors also need to be considered in the study of peer relations. Peers provide different social functions at different stages of life. Males and females have different social needs and interaction styles. Reputational biases within the peer group can also serve to exacerbate particular social patterns.

SEE ALSO *Peer Cliques; Socialization; Soft Skills*

BIBLIOGRAPHY

Cillessen, Antonius H., and William M. Bukowski. 2000. Conceptualizing and Measuring Peer Acceptance and Rejection. In *Recent Advances in the Measurement of Acceptance and Rejection in The Peer System,* eds. Antonius H. Cillessen and William M. Bukowski, 3–10. San Francisco: Jossey-Bass.

Coie, John D., Kenneth A. Dodge, and Heide Coppotelli. 1982. Dimensions and Types of Social Status: A Cross-Age Perspective. *Developmental Psychology* 18 (4): 557–570.

Kupersmidt, Janis B., and Melissa E. DeRosier, 2004. The Role of Peer Relations in the Development of Negative Outcomes: Explanatory Processes. In *Children's Peer Relations: From Development to Intervention*, eds. Janis B. Kupersmidt and Kenneth A. Dodge, 119–138. Washington, DC: American Psychological Association.

Melissa E. DeRosier

PEIRCE, CHARLES SANDERS

SEE *Semiotics.*

PENETRATION, EXPORT

SEE *Export Penetration.*

PENETRATION, IMPORT

SEE *Import Penetration.*

PENIS ENVY

SEE *Oedipus Complex.*

PENN WORLD TABLE

The Penn World Table (PWT) evolved from the International Comparison Program (ICP), which was begun in 1968 at the University of Pennsylvania under the auspices of the United Nations Statistical Office. The ICP benchmark comparisons were built up from 150 expenditure headings related to gross domestic product (GDP), for which detailed price comparisons were made for about three to six items per basic headings. These benchmark comparisons permitted estimates of purchasing power parities (PPPs) for the heading levels and aggregates such as food, government, and all of GDP. The initial benchmark comparisons were for 10 countries in 1970 and 34 countries in 1975. These numbers increased to 65 in 1985 and 150 in 2005. Between 1985 and 2005, the European Union countries moved to annual benchmark comparisons, while the OECD (Organization for Economic Cooperation and Development) and associate countries went to three-year benchmarks.

The early ICP comparisons developed a framework and methods but covered relatively few countries. Because there was a strong interest both in wider coverage and estimates over longer periods, the group at Penn, led by Irving Kravis, began to experiment with reduced information methods to extend the estimates to nonbenchmark countries. Robert Summers and Sultan Ahmad developed an early short-cut method to move to more countries, and in 1978 Kravis, Summers, and Alan Heston elaborated the method and published estimates for 100 countries (referring to 1970). The basic method applied the relationship between per capita income and prices for benchmark countries to estimate PPPs of nonbenchmark countries. Summers and Heston took this effort still further, developing estimates for benchmark and nonbenchmark countries that extended forward and backward in time. By the early 1980s the original relationship among the PPP, exchange rate, and per capita income became much less reliable as countries moved to free up exchange rates. In response, Summers and Heston developed an estimating equation based on alternative price sources (e.g., post-adjustment allowances) and per capita income that improved estimates of nonbenchmark countries. PWT version 6.2 covers 178 countries for some or all the years from 1950 to 2004, with 2000 used as the base year. All of the expenditure estimates are expressed in international dollars, which have the purchasing power over GDP of the U.S. dollar.

The level of detail in PWT includes consumption, investment, government, and the net foreign balance. Estimates are provided in current and constant prices, with both chain, Laspeyeres, and terms-of-trade-adjusted GDP series. Per capita, per worker, and per equivalent adult comparisons are provided, along with comparative price levels for GDP and the major components. In PWT 5.6, estimates of the physical capital stock were provided, and this will be resumed in 2007 using an improved methodology.

PWT is widely used as both a research and a teaching resource in development and econometric courses. However, the OECD provides PPP estimates that are more reliable for their member countries than PWT. The main advantage of PWT is that it covers a wider range of countries for a longer time period. The World Bank also provides PPP estimates each year in their *World Development Report*, but it is only at the GDP level and is not a time series. In PWT, quality grades are provided depending on the number of benchmark comparisons in which a country has participated, and on the consistency of their estimates over previous versions of PWT.

The wide use of PWT reflects the fact that the use of PPPs for the conversion of national currency expenditures to a common currency has proved a more reliable explanatory variable in many applications than the alternative converter, the exchange rate. Over time it has been used in a number of cases—such as the appreciation of the Japanese yen and the more recent appreciation of the Euro against the U.S. dollar—when there have been no underlying changes in PPPs or real income levels. The implication is that conversions at exchange rates would have greatly overstated changes in the GDP levels in Japan and the Euro countries relative to the United States. Thus, while PPP conversions were first thought to be an improvement because they better captured differences in real product across countries, it turns out that they are also more desirable for changes over time.

Another advantage of PPP conversions is that they take account of differences in relative prices across countries. The importance of this frequently shows up in comparisons of shares of expenditures in national currencies. There is a systematic tendency for the national currency share of investment of GDP to be overstated for low-income countries and understated for more affluent countries, compared to comparisons at international prices where relative prices of investment to GDP have been taken into account. One consequence is that it appears that low-income countries get less additional output from their investment at exchange rates compared to PPPs.

Similarly, energy consumption in physical units like BTUs, as a ratio to GDP from PWT, provides a much more acceptable measure of energy efficiency than if exchange-rate-converted GDPs are used. This has important implications for the projection of energy consumption and fossil fuel emissions for fast-growing low income countries like China and India. PWT has also been widely used in growth studies testing the hypothesis that per capita incomes of countries will converge over time.

Researchers have used PPP-converted GDP from PWT measures of both production and welfare, but it is an imperfect measure of both. As an indicator of well-being, it is but one important element, and researchers look to other variables as well, such as climate, crime rates, and air and water quality. The United Nations uses literacy and health measures in addition to per capita GDP for its Human Development Index of the Human Development Report of the United Nations Development Programme. Productivity comparisons based on PWT can only be carried out at the GDP level, whereas much greater interest attaches to productivity in sectors of production like manufacturing, retail and wholesale trade, or agriculture. The Groningen Growth and Development Centre (GGDC) has carried out such PPP-based productivity comparisons by sector for a significant number of countries, and in PWT 7.0 (for 2008 or 2009) there will be an attempt to integrate their estimates on a consistent basis with the PWT aggregates.

PWT 7.0 will also undergo a major revision as it integrates the 2005 ICP benchmark comparison. It will provide more expenditure detail, such as actual household consumption, including government-provided health and education expenditures. Alternative methods of aggregation will also be explored, and there will be a more detailed treatment of the net foreign balance, so as to distinguish between production and income of a country. This version of PWT will involve collaboration between other centers, including GGDC and the International Data Center at the University of California at Davis.

SEE ALSO *Exchange Rates; Purchasing Power Parity*

BIBLIOGRAPHY

Center for International Data, Institute of International Affairs. http://cid.econ.ucdavis.edu/.

Groningen Growth and Development Center (GGDC). http://www.ggdc.net/.

Kravis, I., R. Summers, and A. Heston. 1978. Real GDP Per Capita for More Than One Hundred Countries. *Economic Journal* 88 (350): 215–242.

Kravis, I., R. Summers, and A. Heston. 1982. *World Product and Income: International Comparisons of Real GDP.* Baltimore, MD: Johns Hopkins University Press.

Summers, R. and A. Heston. 1991. Penn World Table (Mark 5): An Expanded Set of International Comparisons, 1950–88. *Quarterly Journal of Economics* 106: 327–368.

World Bank. International Comparison Program (ICP). http://web.worldbank.org/wbsite/external/datastatistics/icptext/.

Alan Heston

PEN'S PARADE
SEE *Probability Distributions.*

PERCEPTION, PERSON

Person perception has been variously assigned such labels as social perception, interpersonal perception, social inference, person cognition, and ordinary personology (Bruner and Tagiuri 1954; Gilbert 1998). Person perception refers to how people perceive and make inferences about other people. Perception differs from sensation in that sensation is the feeling that results from sensory receptors, whereas perception is the interpretation of what is sensed. Person perception also differs from object perception or nonsocial perception because human beings are not invariant and inanimate objects. As targets of our perception, people are dynamic entities endowed with emotions, motives, and complexity (Heider 1958).

Person perception is influenced by the characteristics of (1) the perceiver, (2) the situation, and (3) the target person (Jones 1990). Research on perceiver characteristics shows that perceivers are not objective observers of their social world but are active agents whose cognitive and motivational biases color their interpretations of others. Knowledge structures, such as schemas, scripts, or stereotypes, assist perceivers in processing information efficiently. Overreliance on these cognitive structures, however, may create bias and lead to errors in person perception. With knowledge structures providing convenient summary expectations and beliefs about others, perceivers may reach hasty and incorrect judgments, or they may ignore information that disconfirms their expectations (Snyder and Swann 1978). Perceivers do not search thoroughly for information to form impressions of others (Gilbert 1998). Moreover, expectations about a target person can lead perceivers to engender behaviors from the target that confirm perceivers' initial expectation (i.e., self-fulfilling prophecy) (Rosenthal and Jacobson 1968). In addition, a perceiver may be motivated to form judgments of others that protect the perceiver's sense of self-worth (Klein and Kunda 1993).

Characteristics of the situation are often overlooked by perceivers when they form judgments of target persons. Perceivers have a tendency to underestimate the importance of situational influence and to overestimate the importance of dispositional factors when they interpret the actions of other people. This tendency is called the *fundamental attribution error* or *correspondence bias* (Ross 1977; Gilbert 1998). Perceivers also tend to see that their own failure is caused by external circumstances, while their own success is internally caused. But they are less likely to show this bias when interpreting the success or failure of others, a phenomenon known as the *self-serving bias*. Person perception research has also focused on the dynamic interpersonal perception between a perceiver and a target person (Kenny 1994) and the cultural influences on these interpersonal processes (Markus and Kitayama 1991).

Certain target-person traits (e.g., the central traits of *warm* and *cold*) have more impact than other traits (e.g., the peripheral traits of *polite* and *blunt*) on perceivers' impressions of others (Asch 1946). Negative information also tends to be more heavily weighted in person perception because of information diagnosticity (Skowronski and Carlston 1989). Research has shown that perceivers have implicit personality theories about others, such that an interferential relationship is assumed by perceivers to exist, regarding which target traits seem to co-occur to form a coherent whole (Schneider 1973).

Inferences in impression formation occur not only intentionally but also unintentionally (Anderson and Glassman 1996; Bargh 1997; Uleman 1999). Person perception includes nonverbal communication as well as cognitive inference processes (attribution or social cognition). Representative nonverbal cues are facial expression, voice tone, gaze, interpersonal spacing, touch, and gesture (DePaulo and Freidman 1998). Current work on person perception is also aimed at exploring the implicit associations perceivers have between traits and stereotyped groups.

SEE ALSO *Attribution; Jones, Edward Ellsworth; Prototypes; Schemas; Self-Serving Bias; Stereotypes*

BIBLIOGRAPHY

Andersen, Susan M., and Noah S. Glassman. 1996. Responding to Significant Others When They Are Not There: Effects on Interpersonal Interference, Motivation, and Affect. In *Handbook of Motivation and Cognition: Foundations of Social Behavior*, eds. Richard M. Sorrentino and E. Tory Higgins, vol. 3, 262–321. New York: Guilford.

Asch, Solomon E. 1946. Forming Impression of Personality. *Journal of Abnormal and Social Psychology* 41: 258–290.

Bargh, John A. 1997. The Automaticity of Everyday Life. In *The Automaticity of Everyday Life*, ed. Robert S. Wyer Jr., vol. 10, 1–61. Mahwah, NJ: Erlbaum.

Bruner, Jerome S., and Renato Tagiuri. 1954. The Perception of People. In *The Handbook of Social Psychology*, ed. Gardner Lindzey, vol. 2, 634–654. Reading, MA: Addison-Wesley.

DePaulo, Bella M., and Howard S. Friedman. 1998. Nonverbal Communication. In *The Handbook of Social Psychology*, eds. Daniel T. Gilbert, Susan T. Fiske, and Gardner Lindzey, vol. 2, 3–40. 4th ed. New York: McGraw-Hill.

Gilbert, Daniel T. 1998. Ordinary Personology. In *The Handbook of Social Psychology*, eds. Daniel T. Gilbert, Susan T. Fiske, and Gardner Lindzey, vol. 2, 89–150. 4th ed. New York: McGraw-Hill.

Greenwald, Anthony G., and Mahzarin R. Banaji. 1995. Implicit Social Cognition: Attitudes, Self-Esteem, and Stereotypes. *Psychological Review* 102 (1): 4–27.

Heider, Fritz. 1958. *The Psychology of Interpersonal Relations*. New York: Wiley.

Jones, Edward Ellsworth. 1990. *Interpersonal Perception*. New York: Freeman.

Kenny, David A. 1994. *Interpersonal Perception: A Social Relations Analysis*. New York: Guilford.

Klein, William M., and Ziva Kunda. 1993. Maintaining Self Serving Social Comparisons: Biased Reconstruction of One's Past Behaviors. *Personality and Social Psychology Bulletin* 19: 732–739.

Markus, Hazel Rose, and Shinobu Kitayama. 1991. Culture and the Self: Implications for Cognition, Emotion, and Motivation. *Psychological Review* 98: 224–253.

Rosenthal, Robert, and Lenore Jacobson. 1968. *Pygmalion in the Classroom: Teacher Expectations and Pupils' Intellectual Development*. New York: Holt, Rinehart, and Winston.

Ross, Lee. 1977. The Intuitive Psychologist and His Shortcomings. In *Advances in Experimental Social Psychology*, ed. Leonard Berkowitz, vol. 10, 173–220. New York: Academic Press.

Schneider, D. J. 1973. Implicit Personality Theory: A Review. *Psychological Bulletin* 79: 294–309.

Skowronski, John J., and Donal E. Carlston. 1989. Negativity and Extremity Biases in Impression Formation: A Review of Explanations. *Psychological Bulletin* 105: 131–142.

Snyder, Mark, and William B. Swann Jr. 1978. Hypothesis-Testing Processes in Social Interaction. *Journal of Personality and Social Psychology* 36: 1202–1212.

Uleman, Jim S. 1999. Spontaneous versus Intentional Inferences in Impression Formation. In *Dual-Process Theories in Social Psychology*, eds. Shelly Chaiken and Yaacov Trope, 141–160. New York: Guilford.

Scott T. Allison
JongHan Kim

PERESTROIKA

SEE *Glasnost; Gorbachev, Mikhail.*

PERFORMANCE

Performance, as understood in the context of the social sciences, is a process by which individuals (actors) display for others (the audience) the meaning of their social situation. During the last decades, the term *performance*, which originates from the theatrical context, has become extremely prevalent in various fields and disciplines such as art, literature, and the social sciences. In the United States it has even developed into a specific field of scholarly work, with departments specializing in performance studies. However, performance remains a highly contested concept, one that raises disagreements and divides among scholars.

HISTORICAL DEVELOPMENT

The idea that all social behavior is at least partially a performance is hardly new. It has been with us since the time of the ancient Greeks and the Greek theater, reemerging as a central motif during the Renaissance and the Baroque periods. One of the most famous speeches in William Shakespeare's play *As You Like It* reflects this understanding, opening with the words:

All the world's a stage,
And all the men and women merely players;
They have their exits and their entrances,
And one man in his time plays many parts.

This insightful metaphor was developed into an academic subject of study during the second half of the twentieth century, mainly by the fields of anthropology and sociology. The subject of "cultural performance" (a term coined in 1959 by Milton Singer) became a matter of increased interest among anthropologists during the 1960s. Victor Turner stands out as the anthropologist who probably made the most important contribution to the convergence of culture and theater, with his concept of *social drama*. This concept, based on the early-twentieth-century work of anthropologist Arnold Van Gennep, expanded the use of drama as a metaphor for nontheatrical cultural manifestations. Working closely with Turner, Richard Schechter, who came from a theatrical background, called for an infusion of theater theory with the work of the social sciences and suggested that traditional drama tends to echo the stages of social drama. Other prominent anthropological contributions to the field were made by Clifford Geertz, who suggested a distinction between "deep play" and "shallow play" in performance; and by Dwight Conquergood, who represents a shift from the anthropological preoccupation with the performer and the performative act to a greater consideration of the audience, the reporter, and the social and political implications of the performance.

ERVIN GOFFMAN AND DRAMATURGY

Sociological interest in the application of theatrical concepts to social life emerged in the second half of the twentieth century. While not the first to write on the theatrical aspects of everyday life (Nikolas Evreinoff, for example, published in 1927 a book named *The Theatre in Life*, and Kenneth Burke has also importantly written on the subject), it is the work of sociologist Erving Goffman that has really paved the way for the study of social performance. In his seminal and still highly influential book *The Presentation of Self in Everyday Life* (written in 1956 and reprinted in 1959), Goffman expands many of the ideas discussed by his predecessors. He organizes these ideas into a coherent and well-written dramaturgical analysis of social life in its entirety as a theatrical performance. In this view, we are all actors, playing a role on changing stages in front of various others, who themselves serve simultaneously as our audience and as actors who play a role, to which we are audience. Goffman takes the metaphor of the theater even further. He claims that, as in the theater, social life is guided by scripts and is divided into "front-stage," where one performs in the presence of others, and "back-stage," where the individual practices his act.

This presentation of things begs a subsequent question: Why are we all acting instead of just "being ourselves"? To this Goffman offers a clear answer: It is in our interest to perform in a way that guarantees that others will assess us favorably. In other words, we are constantly working on what Goffman calls impression management, in which we seek to influence the collective definition of the situation by convincing others to accept a positive impression of ourselves. Furthermore, according to Goffman, the self (or rather selves) is shaped and constructed through interactions with others and the various roles one plays in these interactions.

While the dramaturgical perspective seems to convey the idea that people are constantly seeking to deceive others, Goffman does not hold such a position. Rather, he believes that there is nothing inherently fake or inauthentic about the roles we play. In fact, in his view these roles are often part of who we really are. Moreover, the acting itself is not always conscious. People convey impressions both knowingly and unknowingly, and the fact they are always acting does not mean that they are always aware of their act (in fact, all too often they are not). Since there is a mutual dependency between actors and audiences, it is the goal of both sides to protect the performance and maintain its integrity, not to expose its failure.

In later writings (mainly in his 1974 book, *Frame Analysis*) Goffman expands his analysis, introducing the concept of frames—principles by which the social world is organized, which constrain and limit the possible range of performances and definitions of the situation. By this Goffman expresses the understanding that people cannot simply choose whatever performance they wish and fashion it according to their whim, but are rather constrained by the social context and their position in the social world.

RECENT DEVELOPMENTS

The writings of Turner and Goffman still offer the foundations of performance studies in the social sciences. But other scholars have suggested criticisms and extensions to their pioneering analyses. Most notably, Turner and Goffman were both criticized for focusing on the point of view of the actor and neglecting that of the audience (a challenge that was partially met by the work of Dwight Conquergood and of semiotic perspectives, most notably those of Umberto Eco). Goffman was also criticized for not expanding his theory enough to macrosociological domains and to the mass media. Scholarly work has since attempted to confront some of these challenges and expand the usage of performance ideas in the social sciences. (For example, Jeffery Alexander in a 2006 co-edited volume, *Social Performance*, offers an innovative cultural analysis of social performance.)

Turning to other disciplines, the contribution of Judith Butler emerges as an original break from former work of Goffman and other sociologists. In her well-known book *Gender Trouble* (1990) and in subsequent writings, Butler, who takes Goffman as her point of departure, uses the ideas of performance to explore the issues of gender and sexuality. Rejecting naturalistic notions of inherent sexual or gendered essences, Butler argues that the distinctions between homosexual and heterosexual and those between female and male are no more than social constructions. Since they are not based on a real essence, these distinctions are always at risk of disruption and subversion and must be maintained through recurring sexual and gender performances. In other words, rather than simply *being* a girl or a boy, people constantly act these parts and maintain the distinctions through repetitive performances. Unlike Goffman, Butler emphasizes the discursive parts of performance rather than the actions of individuals. For her there is no self or ontological body, which precede the performance. Thus, in her analysis she uses the term *performativity*, rather than performance.

The ideas of social performance were also stretched to the study of racial identities and constructions (Majors and Billson 1992), to the study of organizational and political behavior, and to other fields. Many of these accounts reveal an important aspect of social performance—through performance, previously silenced individuals and groups may receive a voice and become visible. As the study of performance continues to evolve, such issues will surely remain at the heart of the debate.

SEE ALSO *Anthropology; Anthropology, Linguistic; Communication; Essentialism; Ethnicity; Geertz, Clifford; Gender; Goffman, Erving; Identification, Racial; Identity; Linguistic Turn; Literature; Media; Race; Script Models; Self-Presentation; Sexual Orientation, Social and Economic Consequences; Social Constructionism; Social Constructs; Social Science*

BIBLIOGRAPHY

Alexander, Jeffrey C., Bernhard Giesen, and Jason L. Mast, eds. 2006. *Social Performance: Symbolic Action, Cultural Pragmatics, and Ritual.* Cambridge, U.K.: Cambridge University Press.

Brickell, Chris. 2005. Masculinities, Performativity, and Subversion: A Sociological Reappraisal. *Men and Masculinities* 8 (July): 24–43.

Butler, Judith. 1990. *Gender Trouble: Feminism and the Subversion of Identity.* New York: Routledge.

Carlson, Marvin. 1996. *Performance: A Critical Introduction.* New York: Routledge.

Goffman, Erving. 1959. *The Presentation of Self in Everyday Life.* New York: Doubleday.

Goffman, Erving. 1974. *Frame Analysis: An Essay on the Organization of Experience.* Cambridge, MA: Harvard University Press.

Majors, Richard, and Janet Mancini Billson. 1992. *Cool Pose: The Dilemmas of Black Manhood in America.* New York: Lexington Books.

Eran Shor

PERFORMANCE STUDIES

SEE *Performance.*

PERIOD EFFECTS

Researchers who investigate human development or social trends face the difficulty of disentangling various effects that lead to change. In such analyses, scientists note that change may occur for three reasons. The first type of change involves social and environmental forces related to the passage of time. These changes are termed secular effects; in this context, *secular* simply refers to the passage of time and does not imply a contrast with religion or a lack of religion. The second type of change is due to age effects, reflecting physiological changes in individuals. The final type of change relates to cohort effects, the macro conditions that birth cohorts experience over the life span. Because of the close interconnection between age, period, and cohort effects, researchers have noted the importance of teasing apart the relative contributions of these effects. Each effect can contribute independently to change, and there may be interactions among the effects that are not predictable from age, period, and cohort effects individually.

Scientists have developed a number of approaches to identifying the varying causes of change. In some research, investigators may ignore one effect (e.g., age), instead focusing only on the other two (e.g., cohort and period). The obvious drawback here is that one cannot always safely assume that the effect being ignored has not influenced the outcome measure. In other cases, the investigators may examine two of the three effects successively, one effect being temporarily ignored. In this approach, one can identify the relative contribution to an outcome measure by noting whether an effect's absence in one of the

models changes the adequacy of a prediction of the outcome.

One frequent topic associated with age, period, and cohort effects is the prevalence of suicide. An example of such research that reveals the importance of period effects, differentiated from age and cohort effects, compared suicide rates in Australia, the United States, and Canada. John Snowdon and G. E. Hunt (2002) identified an increase in suicide rates for successive cohorts in the United States and Canada in the mid- and late twentieth century. A change in Australian legislation limiting the availability of sedatives led to a different pattern. The historical change regarding therapeutic drugs, a period effect, is important in understanding suicide rates in the population. When such period effects were taken into account, estimates of suicide rates among certain cohorts were comparable in the three countries.

In much of the research, the cohort identified is the birth cohort. Some research creates different categories within the birth cohort. Studies of suicide are again instructive in this regard. In the United States blacks have traditionally been at relatively lower risk for suicide than some other groups in the United States (e.g., whites). Since the early 1980s, however, the rate of attempted and completed suicide has risen among blacks. Research has revealed a higher rate among younger black cohorts, as compared to older cohorts perhaps, as Sean Joe (2006) suggests, because of changing religiosity and greater acceptance of suicide.

With any complex social dynamic, however, period effects are not sufficient to characterize all aspects of a phenomenon. For example, in assessing alcohol consumption across the life span, researchers have documented that drinking decreases as people get older. Some of this effect is attributable simply to age. At the same time there is also evidence that cohort effects are important because of socialization factors. Finally, period effects emerge as important; relevant factors can include, as Mary Gilhooly (2005) notes, availability of alcohol, changes in drinking age, the extent of discretionary time in which to drink, and price.

Psychological and sociological studies have used age-period-cohort analysis, but other disciplines also consider these effects. For instance, research has revealed a cohort-period interaction in the voting patterns of citizens of countries formerly part of the Soviet Union. The data showed that, with the fall of communism, older voters tended to resist change, voting for candidates from the old regime. Younger voters, in contrast, embraced a more liberal approach in their voting. In this case, the period effect related to the introduction of a new economic system. Age as a factor was important, but only, as Sara Schatz (2002) shows, as it interacted with different macro experiences of the various birth cohorts.

Ann Crouter and A. E. Pirretti (2006) observe that in this type of research there are inevitable methodological concerns involving validity of data. Most researchers rely on secondary analyses, using existing datasets. As such researchers studying age, period, and cohort effects have to rely on questions that may not be ideally worded for a given project. Furthermore slight changes in wording across time may have notable effects on results. For instance, in studies on happiness by the Gallup organization, respondents answered a question whose three responses included "very happy," "fairly happy," and either "not very happy" or "not at all happy." When the final response was "not at all happy," respondents chose "fairly happy" more frequently than when the third alternative was "not very happy." People were more comfortable declaring that they were "not very happy" but more reluctant to assert that they were "not at all happy." Such dynamics, as Norval Glenn (2005) notes, complicate the long-term study of behaviors in age, period, and cohort research.

SEE ALSO *Alcoholism; Data, Longitudinal; Pollsters; Public Health; Religiosity; Research, Longitudinal; Socialization; Stages of Development; Suicide; Survey; Voting; Voting Patterns*

BIBLIOGRAPHY

Crouter, Ann C., and A. E. Pirretti. 2006. Longitudinal Research on Work and Family Issues. In *The Work and Family Handbook: Multi-Disciplinary Perspectives, Methods, and Approaches*, eds. Marcie Pitt-Catsouphes, Ellen Ernst Kossek, and Stephen Sweet. Mawhah, NJ: Lawrence Erlbaum.

Gilhooly, Mary L. M. 2005. Reduced Drinking with Age: Is It Normal? *Addiction Research and Theory* 13 (3): 267–280.

Glenn, Norval D. 2005. *Cohort Analysis*. 2nd ed. Thousand Oaks, CA: Sage Publications.

Joe, Sean. 2006. Explaining Changes in the Patterns of Black Suicide in the United States from 1981 to 2002: An Age, Cohort, and Period Analysis. *Journal of Black Psychology* 32 (3): 262–284.

Portrait, France, Rob Alessie, and Dorly Deeg. 2002. Disentangling the Age, Period, and Cohort Effects Using a Modeling Approach. Tinbergen Institute Working Paper no. 2002-120/3. Social Science Research Network, http://ssrn.com/abstract=360780.

Schatz, Sara. 2002. Age Cohort Voting Effects in the Breakdown of Single-Party Rule. *Journal of Aging Studies* 16 (2): 199–219.

Snowdon, John, and G. E. Hunt. 2002. Age, Period, and Cohort Effects on Suicide Rates in Australia, 1919–1999. *Acta Psychiatrica Scandinavica* 105 (4): 265–270.

Bernard C. Beins

PERIODIZATION

Periodization is an intellectual process that seeks to divide a continuous time interval into parts. Periodization is most frequently used in the social sciences and humanities, especially in such disciplines as economics, sociology, history, and literature. There are two ways to proceed when forming a periodization. One is to divide an entire era into smaller periods that share some homogeneity within them. This is the most common procedure in history periodization, but it is also found in economics and other social sciences. The second procedure is to identify cycles in a historical era, then break the era into phases that can be considered a full cycle. This approach is common in economics.

The origin of the idea of periodization is rooted in the old philosophical principle that there are possible quantitative variations in most concepts associated with social phenomena. Such quantitative variations can lead to qualitative changes in some features of social reality that can be used to define different periods. For example, in a particular period, a given society can be composed mainly of peasants and landlords, but it can also have a small number of artisans. The state in such a society could be controlled by landlords, and most laws would favor the ownership of land and the relationships prevailing in rural areas, with low taxes on land and so on. If the number of artisans grows, they can end up seizing state control. Then, all laws and order could change and become biased to support artisanal production. In this example, a quantitative change in the number of artisans in the society led to a qualitative change in the structure of power and institutional order. A simple periodization in this case would be to divide the history of this society into two parts: One covers the period when political power was under the control of landlords; the second covers the period when political power was controlled by artisans.

More rigorously, suppose that social reality is composed of two sets: One is a set of beings and the other is a set of relationships among them. Any being can potentially be measured, so the relationships among them define relations among quantities of the beings involved. These relationships or beings can have threshold values that change their nature. For example, one being can have two measurable dimensions, A and B; so that $A = 0$ for $B \leq B_1$, where B_1 is a specific threshold value. If $B > B_1$, A can jump so that $A = 1$. This rupture of behavior clearly creates the possibility for identification of two periods.

In economics, there is an additional notion of periodization that does not necessarily involve qualitative changes. If some economic variable presents a cyclical behavior, such as a cosine function, it is possible to identify a full cycle as a period, and a periodization emerges from such a procedure. In this case, the moment identified as the beginning of any cycle is totally arbitrary. Often the date identified as the end of a period, even when the beginning is defined, is also arbitrary, as economic variables are not well behaved. Their stochastic nature jeopardizes the simplicity of cycle identification.

The idea of arbitrariness that arises from the discussion of periodization in continuous variables, which are not subject to qualitative changes, can be extended to social phenomena that contain variables subject to discontinuous behavior. Suppose that there is a set of n variables and m relationships defining a social reality, so that $n > 3$ and $m > 3$. If all the variables are subject to noncontinuous variations, any particular variable or combinations of them may be taken as parameters to define ruptures that could characterize change in periods. Therefore, different researchers could take distinct variables or their potential combinations to identify periods, and distinct periodizations would emerge.

In addition to the imprecision resulting from the selection of different criteria for the identification of periods, it is also possible for disputes to emerge concerning the moment in which one criterion exhibits enough change to lead to a period break. Measurement of many social variables is not easy, and most of the time variables have a stochastic component that makes it difficult to identify the moment they actually reached the relevant value that generated the qualitative period change.

Periodization also tends to be historically determined, as each culture and each era has its own set of most relevant social phenomena that normally serve as the basis from which to draw criteria. Such difficulty in establishing a periodization, along with the other problems discussed above, have caused some researchers to condemn the practice of periodizing history.

SEE ALSO *Economic Model; Economics; Models and Modeling; Social Science*

BIBLIOGRAPHY

Besserman, Lawrence. 1996. *The Challenge of Periodization: Old Paradigms and New Perspectives.* New York: Garland.

Davis, Joseph H. 2005. An Improved Annual Chronology of U.S. Business Cycles since the 1790's. NBER Working Paper 11157.

Alexandre Rands Barros

PERMANENT INCOME HYPOTHESIS

The permanent income hypothesis (PIH), introduced in 1957 by Milton Friedman (1912–2006), is a key concept in the economic analysis of consumer behavior. In essence, it suggests that consumers set consumption as the appropriate proportion of their perceived ability to consume in the long run. Wealth, W, is defined as the present discounted value of current and future total income receipts, inclusive of income from assets. Under the assumption that the household is infinitely lived, *permanent income* can be defined as that level of income which, when received in perpetuity, has a present discounted value exactly equal to the wealth of the household. Equivalently, permanent income, denoted y^P, may be regarded as the amount it is believed possible to consume while maintaining wealth intact; it is therefore expressed as equal to the "annuity value of wealth," $y^P = rw$, where r is the real interest rate (assumed fixed).

More specifically, the PIH decomposes *measured* total disposable income, y, into a *permanent* component, y^P, and a *transitory* component, y^T. The permanent income component is deemed systematic but unobservable, reflecting factors that determine the household's wealth, while the transitory component reflects "chance" income fluctuations. Similarly, measured consumption, c, is decomposed into a permanent component, c^P, and a transitory component, c^T. Assuming these relationships to be additive, for simplicity: $y = y^P + y^T$ and $c = c^P + c^T$. It is also important to note that the PIH defines consumption in a "use sense," through the enjoyment or destruction of consumer goods by use, rather than the expenditure upon them, so that consumption is regarded as a service flow.

In giving the hypothesis empirical substance, Friedman assumes the transitory components to be uncorrelated across consumption and income, and with their respective permanent components. The second of these assumptions follows from the definitional decomposition and the nature of transitory components. The first implies that *irregular* income will not result in unplanned consumption. Friedman defends this assumption by arguing that transitory income changes are likely to be reflected in changes in asset holdings. Further, since the consumption definition includes only the flow of services from goods, transitory income disbursed on durable goods may still be classified as unplanned savings. Moreover, zero correlation implies only that the *average* association is zero, and positive associations in some instances may well be offset by negative associations in others.

The formal relationship between consumption and income is derived from a standard intertemporal utility-maximizing framework under the assumptions of infinite life, perfect capital markets that permit borrowing and lending of unlimited amounts (subject to solvency) at the same real interest rate, and the condition that the utility function is homogeneous of positive degree in consumption for current and all future periods, such that an expansion in the feasible budget set (arising from increased income in any period) leads to an equal proportionate change in present and planned future consumption. As a consequence, at the level of the household, permanent consumption is a proportionate function of permanent income. That factor of proportionality is dependent on tastes, age, and the real interest rate (and, with allowance for uncertainty, on the ratio of financial assets to permanent income, on the basis that financial assets provide more substantial collateral than "human wealth" in the form of discounted unearned future income). The aggregate consumption function then depends on the distribution of these factors across households. If it is further assumed that the distribution of households by income is independent of their distribution by these factors, then aggregate permanent consumption obeys a simple proportionate relationship to aggregate permanent income: $c^P = q\, y^P$.

This proportionate relationship between the permanent components of consumption and income is readily reconciled with the nonproportionate aggregate relationship typically observed empirically in cross-sections and short-run aggregate data studies. This is as a consequence of low-income brackets including a greater proportion of households with negative transitory income, and high-income brackets including a greater proportion of households with positive transitory income. However, without

any impact on consumption, which is still proportionate to the permanent income of those households, the observed consumption-income relationship is shallower than the underlying proportionate relationship between the permanent components (see Figure 1). More specifically, for zero mean transitory components and a random transitory income distribution, the cross-section average income group consumes cross-section average permanent income. For the above-average "high" income group, transitory income will typically be positive but not reflected in consumption, though assets will be accumulated. Similarly, below-average "low" income groups are more likely to have experienced negative transitory income, which reduces income below the permanent income level, associated with negative changes in asset holdings. Thus, the asymmetric incidence of transitory income generates an observed consumption-income relationship that is disproportional and lies away from the underlying proportionate behavioral relationship. Note that the exact shape of this observed relationship will depend on the actual distribution of transitory income in practice, while its positioning in the diagram will depend on the true cross-section average transitory income and transitory consumption values, which may not be zero as illustrated. Over time, as aggregate average permanent income grows

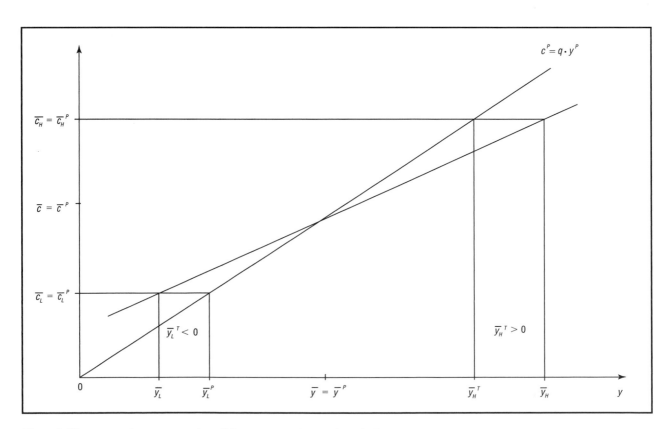

Figure 1: The cross-section representation of the permanent income hypothesis.

along trend, the cross-section consumption function shifts up, tracing out a long-run time series of aggregate average consumption and income that exhibit a constant ratio with respect to each other.

A major difficulty in attempting to test the PIH empirically is that permanent income is not observable. This necessitates the use of some proxy or means of estimating permanent income. In the empirical implementation of the permanent income hypothesis using time-series data, Friedman utilized an adaptive mechanism to relate permanent income to current and past measured income, with the greatest weight attached to current income and declining weights attached to income further in the past. That is, permanent income is represented by an exponentially weighted average of all observed measured incomes, with the weights summing to unity. This approach, with some truncation of the influence of past incomes, enabled Friedman to estimate the weight attached to current income in contributing to permanent income at around one-third (and therefore far less than unity, as would be implied by the *absolute income hypothesis*) and to demonstrate the long-run proportionality of consumption and income, as implied by the PIH.

It is also of some note that the infinite distributed lag formulation of permanent income may also be expressed equivalently in terms of a finite *adaptive expectations* representation for permanent income, such that if current measured income exceeds the previous period's estimate of permanent income, then the estimate of permanent income for the current period is revised upwards, the extent of the adjustment depending on the size of an adjustment parameter in the adaptive expectations mechanism. Algebraically, taking the infinite distributed lag formulation of permanent income, making use of the *Koyck transformation* and the definition of permanent consumption as the difference between measured and transitory consumption, it is then possible to express current measured consumption as a function of current measured income, measured consumption in the previous period, and an error term. However, this time series representation is "observationally equivalent" with the implications of alternative theories of consumption, such as the *relative income hypothesis*, thus weakening the distinctiveness of the permanent income approach (though it should be noted that this criticism is less damning to tests of the cross-sectional implications of the PIH noted above).

An ensuing criticism of the PIH is centered on the assumption of an adaptive relationship between permanent and measured income, which implies an underlying adaptive expectations mechanism, as discussed above. This criticism hinges on the observation that such expectations are entirely "backward-looking," in the sense that expectations are only revised in response to past move-

ments in income, and such revisions are in general sluggish, which suggests the possibility of systematic expectation errors. However, it is not a tenable proposition that rational economic agents, who are assumed to be optimizing subject to constraints in all other regards, would not seek to revise their expectation formation mechanism, and the information on which it draws, in such circumstances. The essence of the *rational expectations hypothesis* (REH) is that agents should utilize all relevant and available information in avoidance of systematic error, and the incorporation of the REH into the PIH therefore has considerable ramifications. Predominant amongst these is the implication that consumption should follow an approximate *random walk*, such that knowledge of previous values of any variable other than the immediately preceding level of consumption should have no predictive power for consumption, since all information available in the previous period should have been incorporated in determining the previous level of consumption. However, the available empirical evidence is not generally supportive of this proposition in its strict form, and the ensuing debate has reinforced the view that the validity of the results of tests of the PIH depend as much on the method used to represent permanent income, and in particular the relationship between current and expected future income, as on the validity of the PIH itself.

From a policy perspective, the PIH asserts that current income plays only a minor role in consumption determination, as just one element of the entire spectrum of current and expected future income, and emphasizes the assumed desire of consumers to smooth consumption flows in the face of variable income flows. In particular, conventional Keynesian demand-management policy, as might be conducted through countercyclical fiscal policy in the form of temporary income tax changes, will lead to little or no change in consumption and be relatively ineffective, since only changes perceived by households as leading to revisions in their permanent incomes will impact significantly on their consumption. Thus, transitory income movements are largely reflected in saving changes. Moreover, the economic system is consequently inherently more stable in that the income-expenditure multiplier effects of exogenous changes are reduced, so that the change in national income following a temporary change in private investment or government expenditure, for example, is correspondingly much smaller than when consumption is directly responsive to current income alone, as is the case under the Keynesian absolute income hypothesis.

However, a caveat to the preceding policy discussion is warranted in that it must be remembered that the PIH is concerned with consumption as a flow of services, as distinct from the implications for consumer expenditure, which includes expenditure on durable goods, and it is this latter concept that is important in income-expenditure analysis. Thus, while transitory income movements are reflected in savings and asset changes under the PIH, such assets include durable goods, and the potential for a sizeable multiplier effect to operate is opened through the relationship between current income and durable-good expenditures. Moreover, to the extent that capital markets are imperfect and consumers do not have good short-term lending and borrowing opportunities, the tendency toward holding transitory income in durable goods is strengthened. The issue of countercyclical policy effectiveness then becomes one of determining what form asset accumulation and associated expenditures take, and what factors influence those expenditures.

Perhaps most critically, the PIH embodies the assumption that capital markets are perfect in the sense that lenders are prepared to extend credit on the basis of repayments financed out of future income yet to be received, at a fixed rate of interest irrespective of loan size, and equivalent to the loan rate payable to deposits. However, where consumers are unable to borrow freely on perfect capital markets, possibly as a result of *adverse selection* and *moral hazard* under limited and asymmetric information, *liquidity*, as the ability to finance consumption, and *liquidity constraints*, involving limitations on the volume of borrowing as well as divergences between rates of interest on borrowing and lending, become paramount. In such circumstances, increases in current income are likely to be used to finance increased consumption, thus accentuating the observed consumption-income relationship, particularly where lenders select current income as the credit rationing device from among the observable characteristics conveying information on ability to repay debt.

SEE ALSO *Absolute Income Hypothesis; Consumption Function; Life-Cycle Hypothesis; Relative Income Hypothesis*

BIBLIOGRAPHY

Friedman, Milton. 1957. *A Theory of the Consumption Function.* Princeton, NJ: Princeton University Press.

Alan E. H. Speight

PERÓN, EVA
SEE *Peronism.*

PERON, JUAN
SEE *Peronism.*

PERONISM

Peronism is the name of the most important political force in contemporary Argentina. It emerged from the first and second presidencies of Juan Domingo Perón, who was democratically elected in 1946 and, after winning elections in 1952, was overthrown by a military coup in 1955. Beyond being a political party, Peronism has been a social and political movement firmly entrenched in the organization and political identity of Argentine society, and has given birth from the 1970s to the 2000s to different political factions with conflicting ideologies and programs.

Perón's election to the presidency in 1946 represented a reaction to the economic and industrial changes introduced by military regimes following an oligarchic restoration (1930–1939). Peronism emerged as a working- and lower-class movement, and survived an eighteen-year ban on the party, the exile of its leader (1955–1973), decades of repression, and the 1974 death of Perón, then serving his third presidential term.

Even though there is general agreement that the changes implemented by Perón transformed Argentine society, politics, and culture forever, the true character of Peronism has been widely disputed. While it has been presented as one of the paradigmatic cases of Latin American populism (De la Torre 1992), it has also been seen as a political movement with certain affinities with fascism, due to the dictatorial style of Perón's government and Perón's open admiration for Benito Mussolini. Peronism has also been studied as a strategic alliance of the working classes with the state (Murmis and Portantiero 1971), among other interpretations.

According to Daniel James (1988), one of the constitutive elements of Peronism was a belief in the essential virtue of the people. Perón considered the organization of labor vital for the success of the state in asserting workers' rights against the interests of the oligarchy. Peronism was associated with the achievement of higher wages, the generalization of a system of collective bargaining, greater levels of unionization, and better living conditions for the working classes and the poor. Peronism represented an expanded notion of the meaning of citizenship, and challenged the accepted forms of social hierarchy and traditional symbols of authority.

At the same time, Peronism was characterized by nationalism and corporatism, an emphasis on class harmony and the central role of the leader, and the overwhelming presence of a paternalistic state. Industrialization was one of the most important goals of Perón's government (Rock 1987).

The impact of Peronism on the working classes' organization was ambiguous, and thus did not have a single meaning for those classes. As James notes, the Peronist state made great efforts between the late 1940s and the mid-1950s to institutionalize and control the workers' movement, whose demands Perón had earlier encouraged, and to absorb it into the framework of a new state-sponsored orthodoxy. From this perspective, Peronism can be seen as a demobilizing force encouraging passivity among workers, who were limited in their actions by a powerful and controlling state. However, efforts to control the unions from above did not prevent the emergence of a strong oppositional culture among workers, which was the foundation of "rank-and-file resistance to the post-1955 regimes and became the basis for the reassertion of Peronism as the dominant force within the Argentine workers' movement" (James 1988, p. 40). As a political movement, Peronism drastically changed the way in which the Argentine working classes behaved politically, and how they related to other groups. Most workers saw in Peronism the promise and possibility of a better society in which they would have a vital role.

More than fifty years after its emergence, Peronism remains linked to the image of Perón, and his second wife, Eva Perón, known as Evita. Although both Perón and Evita were strong, charismatic leaders, Evita played a particularly important role in gaining the devotion and unconditional loyalty of the working classes through her speeches and actions. Her direct distribution of aid to the poor is still remembered among Argentines, and her image serves as a model for many women politicians.

Peronism not only divided Argentine society in two groups—namely, Peronists and anti-Peronists—it also has divided itself into many "Peronisms," with competing ideological perspectives, including socialist, nationalist, and conservative tendencies. Drawing rhetorically on Peronist ideals, symbols, and myths, and counting on the organizational support of the Peronist party, Carlos Menem—president of Argentina from 1989 to 1999—shaped a neoliberal project that was in fact antithetical to the original Peronism. In contrast, in 2003 Néstor Kirchner became president following a campaign based on the same kind of Peronist themes, but set out to establish a completely different political and social program, probably closer to the original Peronist ideals.

BIBLIOGRAPHY

De la Torre, Carlos. 1992. The Ambiguous Meanings of Latin American Populisms. *Social Research* 59 (2): 385–414.

James, Daniel. 1988. *Resistance and Integration: Peronism and the Argentine Working Class, 1946–1976.* New York: Cambridge University Press.

Levitsky, Steven. 2003. *Transforming Labor-Based Parties in Latin America: Argentine Peronism in Comparative Perspective.* New York: Cambridge University Press.

Murmis, Miguel, and Juan Carlos Portantiero. 1971. *Estudios sobre los orígenes del peronismo* [Studies on the Origins of Peronism]. Buenos Aires: Siglo XXI.

Rock, David. 1987. *Argentina, 1516–1982: From Spanish Colonization to Alfonsín.* Rev. ed. Berkeley and Los Angeles: University of California Press.

Diana E. Baldermann
Javier Auyero

PERRON-FROBENIUS THEOREM

SEE *Eigen-Values and Eigen-Vectors, Perron-Frobenius Theorem: Economic Applications.*

PERSON MEMORY

The term *person memory* came into common usage around 1980 in conjunction with the advent of the contemporary field of *social cognition,* with the two labels sometimes used interchangeably. As described by Reid Hastie and colleagues in their 1980 book, person memory is an attempt to "extend accounts of the formation, representation, and retrieval of first impressions of other people" (p. 1) by borrowing extensively from the field of cognitive psychology. From the beginning these extensions have relied heavily on cognitive concepts such as the *information processing* model, *schemas,* and associative network models of memory representation and retrieval.

The information processing model distinguishes stages of attention, perception, memory storage, retrieval, and judgment. Prior to 1980 researchers in social psychology had developed an extensive literature on person perception and attribution, which focused primarily on the earliest of these stages, the formation of impressions, without much regard for issues relating to memory representation or retrieval. Consequently, the term *person memory* came to apply principally to post-1980s work that extended impression formation work to the later stages of information processing.

The earliest research in person memory demonstrated that people's impressions of others comprise separate trait and episodic representations, and that these affect each other in complex ways. For example, researchers suggested that inferred traits serve to organize behavioral episodic representations, and that this actually facilitates recall for behavioral information. Subsequent research examined the effects of a variety of processing goals on the way that impressions and memories are organized and retrieved from memory.

Other person memory work examined an implication of schema theory, that people ought best to recall behavioral episodes that are congruent with their trait impressions. Person memory researchers actually found the opposite, with recall being best for episodes that contradicted prior trait impressions. Applying associative network models popular in that era, theorists suggested that as perceivers attempt to reconcile incongruent evidence with their trait impressions, they create a rich network of interconnections among these episodic memories, facilitating their ultimate retrieval. Of course, as the amount of incongruent information increases, it becomes more likely that perceivers will eventually abandon their initial trait impression. However, research indicates that first impressions tend to have persisting effects even in the face of substantial contradictory evidence.

Later work in person memory suggested that because of the incongruity effect and other such memory processes, people's memories of their trait impressions will not always correspond exactly with their memories for relevant facts and events. In fact, such correspondence is to be expected primarily when people actually base their trait impression on recalled facts and events, which is most likely when they failed to form an impression as those facts and events were initially encountered. Contemporary research on social cognition continues to examine issues surrounding the way that impressions are represented in memory, with some additional interest in the spontaneity of impression formation and the degree of conscious awareness that people have of their impressions.

SEE ALSO *Attribution; Memory; Network Analysis; Networks; Perception, Person; Schemas; Self-Schemata; Social Cognition; Social Information Processing; Social Psychology*

BIBLIOGRAPHY

Hastie, Reid, et al., eds. 1980. *Person Memory: The Cognitive Basis of Social Perception*. Hillsdale, NJ: Lawrence Erlbaum Associates.

Donal E. Carlston
Tay Hack

PERSONAL CONSTRUCTS

According to *personal construct psychology*, developed by the American psychologist and personality theorist George Alexander Kelly (1905–1967), individuals create *personal constructs* to organize ongoing experience and anticipate future events. A personal construct is a *bipolar* mental template, consisting of something and its perceived opposite. For example, one person might develop the personal con-

struct dimension of "safety versus adventure," in which safety is seen as objectionable and boring. Another person might develop a personal construct of "safety versus terror," in which safety is desirable and soothing. Clearly, these two people mean different things when they report feeling safe. Personal construct psychology contends that in order to organize experience coherently and understandably, each person develops a set of unique personal constructs. One's personal construct system is structured hierarchically, with some constructs more central and influential to how the world is understood than others. Accordingly, people often construe the same circumstances in vastly different ways. This reflects personal construct theory's notion of *constructive alternativism*, which holds that there are an infinite number of personal constructs available. People often mistakenly believe their manner of construing things is the only correct way, when all situations can be construed in countless ways.

Kelly most fully developed personal construct psychology in a two-volume work, *The Psychology of Personal Constructs*. Originally published in 1955, the volumes present personal construct psychology in a formal manner intended to be least offensive to the professional sensibilities of 1950s psychology. Kelly presented his theory as a fundamental postulate and eleven corollaries. The fundamental postulate states that people organize their psychological experience in ways that help them most effectively anticipate events. Kelly stressed *viability* over *validity* in personal construct psychology. Because people only access the world indirectly through their personal constructs, they can never be certain that their constructs match reality; the validity of constructs can never be fully established. However, people can know whether their constructs work adequately and help them to successfully navigate life. Thus, the viability of constructs takes center stage in personal construct psychology.

Kelly's eleven corollaries explain how people's personal construct systems function. For example, the *individuality corollary* maintains that each individual creates a unique set of personal constructs, while the *fragmentation corollary* contends that different subsections of one's personal construct system may be contradictory—after all, in different areas of their lives, people are often inconsistent. The *choice corollary* holds that people choose the poles of constructs that they think will be most likely to help them make productive sense of new situations. Once people choose to apply certain constructs to anticipate a situation, the *experience corollary* explains how they judge the effectiveness of the constructs they applied. When constructs are not found to be effective, people often revise them. As a final example, the *sociality corollary* asserts that when two people construe each other's construction processes, they can come to understand one another and form a close relationship—which Kelly referred to as a *role relationship*.

Clinically, Kelly developed a psychotherapy technique called *fixed-role therapy*. In fixed-role therapy, the therapist asks the client to adopt a different identity for a two-week period. The client is asked to act the part of someone whose constructions and behaviors are significantly different from the client's. Because the client is only playing a role, any threat that might occur as a result of violating one's own personal identity are minimized. After all, the client is simply playing a part. However, in so doing the client experiments with alternative ways of construing and behaving that may produce personal growth.

Personal construct psychology has become associated with theories of constructivism, which emphasize that people know the world indirectly through constructed understandings. *Radical constructivism* views the person as a closed system, one in which a person's internal psychological structure determines experiential reality. One's structure is only sensitive to specific kinds of stimulation from the external world. People do not experience the world as it is, but rather experience it only in the ways their internal structure allows. On the other hand, *social constructionism* deemphasizes individual knowledge construction and instead stresses that human understandings spring from ongoing relationships. Through discussion and interaction with each other, people negotiate and reach consensus about what is real and true. Discourses, defined as ways of talking about reality, shape human experience. As people use discourses in novel ways over time, shared constructions of reality evolve. Whether individually or socially focused, constructivist theories stress human involvement in knowledge construction, maintaining that people can only know the world indirectly via their constructions.

SEE ALSO *Constructivism; Personality; Psychoanalytic Theory; Psychotherapy; Terror*

BIBLIOGRAPHY

Burr, Vivien. 2003. *Social Constructionism.* 2nd ed. London: Routledge.

Gergen, Kenneth J. 1999. *An Invitation to Social Construction.* London: Sage.

Kelly, George A. [1955] 1991. *The Psychology of Personal Constructs.* 2 vols. London: Routledge.

Kelly, George A. 1969. *Clinical Psychology and Personality: The Selected Papers of George Kelly.* Ed. Brendan Maher. New York: Wiley.

Maturana, Humberto R., and Francisco J. Varela. 1992. *The Tree of Knowledge: The Biological Roots of Human Understanding.* Rev. ed. Trans. Robert Paolucci. Boston: Shambhala.

von Glaserfeld, Ernst. 1995. *Radical Constructivism: A Way of Knowing and Learning.* London: Falmer.

Jonathan D. Raskin

PERSONALITY

Personality most commonly refers to the psychological features that distinguish one individual from another—regularities in the way an individual thinks, feels, and behaves. Although other characteristics may also distinguish individuals (for example, hair color, nationality, or job title), it is the psychological differences that fall under the umbrella of personality. These differences may be broad in nature, such as whether a person is outgoing or shy, emotional or calm, or they may be narrower in scope, reflecting finer grained patterns of beliefs, attitudes, and behaviors that may emerge only in certain situations. A person's total collection of these characteristics defines his or her personality.

Personality also refers to a separate subfield of psychology that uses the scientific method to investigate people's defining characteristics—what the characteristics are, how best to measure them, and the consequences for individuals who embody them. The young field of personality psychology was influenced by several early movements of the nineteenth century, starting with the European and North American philosophical tradition of individualism. Personality psychology emerged most prominently in the 1930s with the publication of the highly influential 1937 textbook *Personality: A Psychological Interpretation*, written by the psychologist Gordon Allport (1897–1967). The first personality inventory was conceived during World War I to predict who would be more emotionally fit for warfare. Since that time personality psychology has continued to emphasize sound measurement to capture a variety of aspects of human personality.

LEVELS OF PERSONALITY

Given the multitude of psychological differences among people, it is helpful to organize these differences into levels. For example, the psychologist Dan McAdams (b. 1954) has organized personality at three levels.

Traits At the broadest level, individuals differ in what are called *dispositional traits*. Traits outline the coarsest differences among people and reflect the most general and enduring orientations on the world.

Although different traits have been proposed throughout history, the earliest of which subdivided individuals into groups based on prominent bodily fluids or "humors" like blood (sanguine), yellow bile (choleric), black bile (melancholic), and phlegm (phlegmatic), in the early twenty-first century there appears to be some consensus on a trait taxonomy, commonly referred to as the "big five." The big five personality traits are: extraversion (social, outgoing, energetic, and able to experience positive emotions), agreeableness (yields to and trusts others), conscientiousness (productive and follows through on tasks in an organized fashion), neuroticism (high anxiety, emotional instability, and hostility), and openness to experience (willingness to explore and engage in novel ideas, experiences, and feelings). These traits are continuous rather than categorical, with fewer people on the extremes and most people falling in between these extremes. Traits are controversial because they do not always predict how a person will behave or feel in a given situation because situations often constrain behavior. Instead, traits are more like statements about the probability that a person will behave in a certain way. Traits do predict important outcomes over longer periods of time, however. For example, extraversion predicts the time it takes people to develop a network of friends in a new environment. Likewise neuroticism is a risk factor for cardiac problems. Traits also have a strong genetic component, with evidence that about half of the variability in personality traits derive from genetic factors (that is, heritability quotients of 40 to 50 percent for most of the big five traits).

Consensus regarding the big five comes after decades of research, beginning in the 1930s with a painstaking search for terms in *The Oxford English Dictionary* that could be used to describe individuals. This task, undertaken by the prominent early personality theorists Gordon W. Allport and Henry S. Odbert, was guided by the principle that all of the important ways of characterizing people will be encoded in natural language use. Using this word list as a starting point, personality researchers like James Cattell and Hans Eysenck reduced the list into a smaller and more manageable number of categories using statistical techniques like factor analysis. In analysis after analysis, five personality dimensions consistently emerged, which came to be known as the big five. Other taxonomies have been proposed, for example, Eysenck focused on the big three, extraversion, neuroticism, and psychoticism (a combination of agreeableness and conscientiousness). Since the big five was developed, taxonomic analyses have yielded fairly good cross-cultural consistency in the five dimensions.

Other popularly known personality traits include type A and type B personalities. Type A individuals are typically driven, impatient, competitive, aggressive, and hostile, whereas type B individuals are the opposite—they are relaxed, patient, noncompetitive, and less hostile. The A/B distinction originated in the 1950s with a team of cardiologists who observed fast-paced aggressive behaviors in patients with coronary heart disease. Studies have subsequently confirmed type A as a cardiovascular risk factor—an association that appears driven by the hostility component and its negative physiological effects on blood pressure. Perhaps because of its intuitive appeal, "type A personality" moved into popular jargon fairly quickly. Fortunately the popular understanding of type A appears fairly true to the original concept.

Other related personalities include the controversial type C or "cancer prone" personality, which is characterized by emotion suppression. The associated type C coping style is characterized by denial of distress in spite of physiological evidence of distress. Evidence linking these characteristics to the incidence and recovery from cancer is mixed, however. Lastly, there is type D or distressed personality, characterized by negative emotionality, an inability to express emotions, and social isolation, which has been linked to greater cardiovascular disease and increased mortality.

Characteristics Adaptations At the next level of personality differences are mid-level *characteristic adaptations*, which comprise nuanced differences among people. Unlike traits, many of these adaptations are learned through experience, are readily influenced by culture, and reflect a dynamic interplay between people's current contexts and situations. It is at this level that conditional theories of personality emerge as alternatives to trait theory.

One of the issues with defining personality solely as traits is that traits lead us to expect people will behave in a regular way across all situations. Yet empirical data do not show this. Typically the correlation between traits (as measured by standard trait questionnaires) and behaviors measured across situations is relatively modest—with correlations of .30. This observation, made by the personality psychologist Walter Mischel (b. 1930) in his influential 1968 text *Personality and Assessment*, sparked a decades-long debate in personality known as the person-situation debate. This debate threatened the field of personality because it undermined the influence of personality traits on behavior and elevated the influence of situations on behavior, a perspective favored by social psychologists. One consequence of the debate is that it stimulated a more contextualized and conditional approach to personality, exemplified in Mischel's research with his colleague, the psychologist Yuichi Shoda. From their perspective, personality emerges as *situation-specific behavioral signatures*—regularities in behavior that manifest in certain situations, not in all situations. Thus two people who are similar at the trait level (for example, high in neuroticism) may manifest different behavioral signatures. One person may react with hostility when confronted by authority, and another may react that way when confronted by a subordinate.

Central to a conditional approach to personality are people's interpretations or *construals* of their immediate environments. This theme derives from a social-cognitive perspective on personality, which emphasizes the operation of acquired beliefs and expectations about the world in personality functioning. Within this social-cognitive perspective, there are several other types of individual differences that contribute to people's behavioral signatures. Of particular importance are people's beliefs regarding their *self-efficacy*, whether they believe they are capable of achieving desired outcomes through their actions. Formalized in theory by the psychologist Albert Bandura (b. 1925), self-efficacy beliefs are shaped from people's experiences in the world and influence motivation, expectations, and the explanations people give for their outcomes. Self-efficacy and other human strengths, such as optimism, wisdom, and empathy, have received increased focus among personality and social psychologists. Also important are our *implicit theories* about the rigidity versus mutability of self-attributes. Some individuals, referred to as "entity theorists," view their attributes, such as intelligence, as fixed and unchangeable, whereas others, "incremental theorists," view their attributes as more malleable and able to be cultivated. These personal theories, which are heavily influenced by parenting, set up characteristic styles for how people approach and respond to challenging tasks, with incremental theorists being more likely to persist at tasks requiring effort.

Mid-level differences also include motives and drives. Within each culture, individuals differ in several *higher-order motives*—whether they are driven to achieve, affiliate with others, or have power over them. At the individual level, a person may also have his or her set of *personal strivings*—the idiosyncratic ways in which an individual tries to implement his or her goals in everyday life. For example, a person with strong affiliation motives might regularly get together with friends. A person with strong achievement motives might work long nights to achieve professional goals. Individuals may not always be aware of what motivates them. "Unconscious motives" are quite common and occur when a person regularly exhibits behaviors consistent with a motive but is unaware of having this motive. In these circumstances an external observer can often see these patterns more clearly than can the person.

Other mid-level aspects of personality, not just motives, can operate at an unconscious level. It is known that individuals possess considerable knowledge about themselves and their past experiences that they cannot verbalize or represent in consciousness but that shapes their feelings and behaviors. Such knowledge is often associative in nature and measured indirectly in ways that bypass self-report (for example, using computerized tasks adapted from cognitive psychology). This knowledge may be different from other reflective forms of self-knowledge that people can verbalize and report using questionnaires. Understanding the functions and interplay between associative and reflective components of personality appears to be among the major tasks of twenty-first-century science in personality. Another example of unconscious personality processes is found in defense mechanisms, which reflect patterns of thinking that minimize conscious

awareness of threatening thoughts or feelings. With repeated and frequent use, defense mechanisms can become part of a person's characteristic style of thinking.

Personal Narratives In addition to traits and characteristic adaptations, individuals differ in their *integrative life narratives*. Life narratives are the unique person-specific stories people create about their experiences to provide coherence and meaning to their lives. A life story encompasses who a person is, how this person came to be, and what the future holds. Although each story is unique, common themes do emerge—despair, resurrection, and triumph—that are often culturally bound. Narratives also have important psychological consequences, as evidence suggests that writing about a traumatic experience in a way that gives the experience coherence and meaning speeds recovery and improves mental and physical health.

PERSONALITY DEVELOPMENT AND CHANGE

Change depends on whether personality is conceived of as traits, characteristic adaptations, or life narratives. Traits exhibit the most stability and are the hardest to change, which is consistent with traits being partly heritable and rooted in infant temperament. Early learning environments can play some role in shaping the expression of traits, however. For example, temperamentally introverted children who are exposed to intensive social environments early in life, such as day care, evidence less introversion later in life, but they may never be as outgoing as children who exhibited extraverted behaviors prior to socialization.

Traits crystallize between ages twenty-one to thirty, after which they show consistency through older adulthood. Of course people are dynamic, and they can change across their lifetime. Such changes, however, appear to occur at the level of characteristic adaptations and life narratives. Indeed therapy is often targeted at changing people's beliefs, motivations, coping strategies, and life stories rather than changing enduring dispositions. Personality also changes through adult maturational stages characterized by decreasing impulsivity, maturing defenses, changing identities (for example, parenthood), and a shift in orientation from self to other.

BIOLOGICAL SUBSTRATES OF PERSONALITY

Personality psychologists have begun to understand the neurobiological underpinnings of traits such as extraversion and neuroticism. For example, extraversion and its associated qualities of impulsivity and sensation seeking appear most strongly linked to the behavioral activation system (BAS), which consists of dopamine-transmitting pathways in the brain and neural structures that modulate the extent to which people feel pleasure in response to cues for reward. By contrast, neuroticism appears most strongly linked to the behavioral inhibition system (BIS), a set of neural structures and processes involved in anxiety and the processing of aversive outcomes such as punishment.

New avenues of research in molecular genetics hold promise for investigating links between genes and personality. For example, emergent research suggests that variation in a gene related to dopamine function (DRD4) is associated with personality differences in novelty seeking, just as variation in a gene related to serotonin function (5-HT transporter) has been linked to differences in neuroticism. The mechanisms of action between genes and personality are complex and not yet known, however. Research in genetics will likely yield important advancements in the years to come, particularly with respect to multiple gene contributions to personality, mechanisms of action, and gene-environment interplay.

DISORDERED PERSONALITY

Personality disorders appear to represent the extremes of normal variation in broad personality traits. Many of the personality disorders described in the 2000 *Diagnostic and Statistical Manual of Mental Disorders*, fourth edition text revision (DSM-IV-TR), correspond to extreme variants of the big five personality factors. For example, borderline personality disorder—characterized by impulsivity, self-destructive behavior, and emotional instability—may be a maladaptive form of the anger and hostility subfacets of neuroticism; obsessive-compulsive disorder may be related to extreme conscientiousness, with an extreme focus on order, perfectionism, rules, and structure; and paranoid personality disorder may be related to extremely low agreeableness, reflecting a wariness and mistrust of others.

SEE ALSO *Allport, Gordon; Bandura, Albert; Individualism; Mental Illness; Neuroscience; Obsessive-Compulsive Disorder; Optimism/Pessimism; Psychology; Self-Defeating Behavior; Self-Efficacy; Temperament; Trait Theory*

BIBLIOGRAPHY

American Psychiatric Association. 2000. *Diagnostic and Statistical Manual of Mental Disorders*. 4th ed. Washington, DC: American Psychiatric Association.

Canli, Turhan, ed. 2006. *Biology of Personality and Individual Differences*. New York: Guilford.

Epstein, Seymour, and Edward J. O'Brien. 1985. The Person-Situation Debate in Historical and Current Perspective. *Psychological Bulletin* 98 (3): 513–537.

Funder, David C. 2001. Personality. *Annual Review of Psychology* 52: 197–221.

Heatherton, Todd F., and Joel L. Weinberger, eds. 1994. *Can Personality Change?* Washington, DC: American Psychological Association.

McAdams, Dan P. 2006. *The Person: A New Introduction to Personality Psychology*. 4th ed. Hoboken, NJ: Wiley.

McCrae, Robert R., and Paul T. Costa Jr. 1997. Personality Trait Structure as a Human Universal. *American Psychologist* 52 (5): 509–516.

Mischel, Walter, and Yuichi Shoda. 1995. A Cognitive-Affective System Theory of Personality: Reconceptualizing Situations, Dispositions, Dynamics, and Invariance in Personality Structure. *Psychological Review* 102 (2): 246–268.

Pervin, Lawrence A., and Oliver P. John, eds. 1999. *Handbook of Personality: Theory and Research*. 2nd ed. New York: Guilford.

Wilson, Timothy D. 2002. *Strangers to Ourselves: Discovering the Adaptive Unconscious*. Cambridge, MA: Belknap Press of Harvard University.

Tamlin S. Conner
Howard Tennen

PERSONALITY, AUTHORITARIAN

The rise of fascist ideology and virulent anti-Semitism in Europe during the 1930s posed important questions for social scientists. Psychologists suggested explanations that drew on both psychoanalysis and Marxism. Wilhelm Reich (1897–1957) proposed that capitalism and sexual repression produced sadomasochistic personalities blending aggression toward the weak and vulnerable with deferential submission to power and authority. Abraham Maslow (1908–1970) and Erich Fromm (1900–1980) also described broadly similar authoritarian personalities whose basic needs attracted them to fascism. The most theoretically developed and empirically based of these explanations was proposed in 1950 by Theodor Adorno (1903–1969), Else Frenkel-Brunswik (1908–1958), Daniel Levinson (1920–1994), and R. Nevitt Sanford (1909–1995) in a monumental book, *The Authoritarian Personality* (1950). This book reported a program of research that began with the aim of explaining anti-Semitism, but culminated in a far more ambitious theory, which for a time dominated social scientific inquiry into the psychological bases of prejudice and ethnocentrism.

Their first major finding was that anti-Semitic attitudes were not held in isolation, but were part of a broader ethnocentric pattern involving a generalized dislike of out-groups and minorities, excessive and uncritical patriotism, and politically conservative attitudes. Their research suggested that this pattern of attitudes seemed to be an expression of a particular personality syndrome consisting of nine tightly covarying traits. These were:

1. Conventionalism (rigid adherence to conventional middle-class values).

2. Authoritarian submission (submissive, uncritical attitudes toward authorities).

3. Authoritarian aggression (the tendency to be on the lookout for, condemn, reject, and punish people who violate conventional values).

4. Anti-intraception (opposition to the subjective, imaginative, and tender-minded).

5. Superstition and stereotypy (belief in mystical determinants of the individual's fate, and a disposition to think in rigid categories).

6. Power and toughness (preoccupation with the dominance-submission, strong-weak, leader-follower dimension; identification with power; exaggerated assertion of strength and toughness).

7. Destructiveness and cynicism (generalized hostility, vilification of the human).

8. Projectivity (a disposition to believe that wild and dangerous things go on in the world; the projection outward of unconscious emotional impulses).

9. Sex (exaggerated concern with sexual "goings-on").

Psychometric questionnaire items were developed in order to assess each of these traits, and these culminated in the famous F ("fascist") scale, which was used to measure this "authoritarian personality" dimension. Research did indeed show that that the F scale was powerfully correlated with measures of prejudice, ethnocentrism, conservative attitudes, and extremist right-wing politics.

Adorno and his colleagues theorized that authoritarian personalities originated from childhood socialization characterized by strict, punitive parental discipline and conditional affection. This creates an inner conflict between resentment and hostility toward parental authority and a fearful need to submit to that authority, which culminates in identification with, and submissive idealization of, parental authority, and by extension all authority. This aggression is repressed and displaced onto targets sanctioned by authority. These psychodynamics are expressed in the nine surface traits of the authoritarian personality, the pattern of ethnocentric, conservative, chauvinistic social attitudes, deference to established authority, and pervasive hostility and prejudice against out-groups, minorities, and other socially deviant targets.

This theory attracted enormous attention initially, and the F scale became widely used. Critics, however, noted methodological flaws in the research, and pointed out that the theory ignored authoritarianism of the Left. The F scale was found to have serious psychometric flaws, most notably the all positive formulation of its items so that scores were heavily contaminated by the response style of acquiescence (the general tendency for people to agree rather than disagree). When this was corrected, the items of "balanced" versions of the F scale lacked internal consistency, and so could not be measuring a single unitary syndrome or dimension. As a result of this, and other nonsupportive findings, interest in the theory and the F scale largely collapsed during the 1960s.

Since the mid-1980s, however, interest in the issue has revived with the identification of two distinct "authoritarian" individual difference dimensions that seem to underlie prejudice, intolerance, and ethnocentrism. First, in the 1980s Bob Altemeyer showed that three of Adorno and colleagues' original traits—conventionalism, authoritarian aggression, and authoritarian submission—did constitute a unitary individual difference dimension, which he named *right-wing authoritarianism* and characterized as "submissive" authoritarianism. Second, in the 1990s Jim Sidanius and Felicia Pratto identified a second, "dominant," authoritarian dimension, seemingly relating to Adorno and colleagues' original traits of power, toughness, destructiveness, and cynicism, which they called *social dominance orientation.* The idea that these might be personality dimensions, however, has been challenged, and it has been argued that they seem better viewed as ideological attitude or value dimensions that are influenced by personality, but are not in themselves personality dimensions.

SEE ALSO *Anti-Semitism; Dictatorship; Fascism; Frankfurt School; Fromm, Erich; Jingoism; Leadership; Marxism; Maslow, Abraham; Nativism; Patriotism; Personality; Personality, Cult of; Psychoanalytic Theory; Scales; Social Dominance Orientation; Social Psychology*

BIBLIOGRAPHY

Adorno, Theodor W., Else Frenkel-Brunswik, Daniel J. Levinson, and R. Nevitt Sanford. 1950. *The Authoritarian Personality.* New York: Harper.

Altemeyer, Bob. 1998. The Other "Authoritarian Personality." In *Advances in Experimental Social Psychology*, Vol. 30, ed. Mark P. Zanna, 47–92. San Diego, CA: Academic Press.

Duckitt, John. 2001. A Dual-process Cognitive Motivational Theory of Ideology and Prejudice. In *Advances in Experimental Social Psychology*, Vol. 33, ed. Mark P. Zanna, 41–113. San Diego, CA: Academic Press.

John Duckitt
Chris G. Sibley

PERSONALITY, CULT OF

Cult of personality is a pejorative term implying the concentration of all power in a single charismatic leader within a totalitarian state and the near deification of that leader in state propaganda. Totalitarian regimes use the state-controlled mass media to cultivate a larger-than-life public image of the leader through unquestioning flattery and praise. Leaders are lauded for their extraordinary courage, knowledge, wisdom, or any other superhuman quality necessary for legitimating the totalitarian regime. The cult of personality serves to sustain such a regime in power, discourage open criticism, and justify whatever political twists and turns it may decide to take. Among the more infamous and pervasive cults of personality in the twentieth century were those surrounding Hitler, Mussolini, Stalin, Mao Zedong, Francisco Franco, Chiang Kai-shek, Ho Chi Minh, Kim Il Sung, Juan and Evita Peron, Pol Pot, Augusto Pinochet, Kim Jong Il, and Saddam Hussein. The term is occasionally—if idiosyncratically—applied to national leaders who did not seek similar godlike adulation during their lifetime or term in office but have been later glorified by the government or in the national mass media. Examples might include George Washington, Napoléon Bonaparte, Abraham Lincoln, Vladimir Lenin, Mustafa Kemal Atatürk, Charles de Gaulle, Ronald Reagan, Margaret Thatcher, and others.

A cult of personality differs from Thomas Carlyle's "hero worship" in the sense that it is intentionally built around the national leader and is often used to justify authoritarian rule. In one of the more idiosyncratic usages, it is sometimes applied by analogy to refer to the public veneration of famous leaders of social movements such as Karl Marx, Mahatma Gandhi, Martin Luther King Jr., Che Guevara, Malcolm X, Nelson Mandela, and others. In fact, the term itself derives from Karl Marx's critique of the "superstitious worship of authority" that had developed around his own personality, acclaimed merits, and contribution to the work of the First Socialist International in the latter half of the nineteenth century.

Historically, numerous rulers have promoted their own cults of personality. Absolute monarchies were the prevalent form of government for much of recorded history, and most traditional monarchs were held in public awe and adoration. For example, pharaonic Egypt, Imperial China, and the Roman Empire accorded their crowned sovereigns the status of revered god-kings. The doctrine of the divine right of kings claimed that absolutist monarchs such as Henry VIII, Louis XIV, or Catherine the Great sat on their thrones by the will of God. The democratic revolutions of the eighteenth and nineteenth centuries made it increasingly difficult for traditional autocrats to retain their divine aura. However, the development of the modern mass media, state-run public education, and government propaganda has enabled some more recent national leaders to manipulate popular opinion and project an almost equally extolled public image. Cults of personality developed around some of the most notorious totalitarian dictators of the twentieth century such as Hitler, Stalin, and Mao, who at the peak of their

personalistic power were lionized as infallible, godlike creatures. Their portraits were hung in every private home or public building, while the country's artists and poets were expected to produce works of art idolizing the hero-leader.

Many lesser known autocrats have engaged in similar self-glorification, subordinating nearly all aspects of national life to their fickle vanity, megalomania, and conceit. In post-Soviet Turkmenistan, for instance, the late president-for-life Saparmurat Niyazov encouraged his own cult of personality, dotting the local landscapes with public monuments to himself and even renaming the months of the year to pay homage to himself and his family. After declaring Turkmenistan's independence in October 1991, the former chairman of the Soviet-era Council of Ministers and first secretary of the Turkmen Communist Party quickly established himself as the center and source of all political authority in the new country. Niyazov became the first president of independent Turkmenistan and won the uncontested 1992 election, which was the only presidential election held during his rule. He assumed the title of *Turkmenbashi* ("head of all the Turkmen"), and the country's obedient legislature proclaimed him president for life. He even authored a book—the *Ruhnama*, or "Book of the Spirit"—that became a compulsory part of the curricula at all levels of the national educational system.

The term *cult of personality* became a buzzword after Soviet leader Nikita Khrushchev bitterly denounced Stalin's near deification before a closed session of the Twentieth Party Congress on February 25, 1956:

> The cult of personality acquired such monstrous dimensions mainly because Stalin himself, using all conceivable methods, supported the glorification of his own person.... One of the most characteristic examples of Stalin's self-glorification and of his lack of even elementary modesty is the edition of his *Short Biography*, which was published in 1948. This book is an expression of the most unrestrained flattery, an example of making a man into a god, of transforming him into an infallible sage, "the greatest leader," "sublime strategist of all times and nations." Ultimately, no more words could be found with which to praise Stalin up to the heavens. We need not give here examples of the loathsome adulation filling this book. All we need to add is that they all were approved and edited by Stalin personally and some of them were added in his own handwriting to the draft text of the book. (Khrushchev 1989)

In a country long known for its traditional worship of religious saints and czars, the public exaltation of Soviet leaders was deliberately pursued as necessary for building national unity and consensus. The result was Stalin's cult of personality—the total loyalty and dedication of all Soviet citizens to the all-powerful leader, whose demigod personality exemplified the heroism and glory of "building socialism in one country." Khrushchev's "Secret Speech" was a major break by the post-Stalin leadership with the oppressive dominance of Stalinism. "Big Brother," a fictional character in George Orwell's famous novel *Nineteen Eighty-Four*, is widely believed to be a satire of Stalin's cult of personality (even though it is equally likely to have been based on Britain's ubiquitous Lord Kitchener).

SEE ALSO *Authoritarianism; Autocracy; Divine Right; Hitler, Adolf; Khrushchev, Nikita; Mao Zedong; Peronism; Social Movements; Stalin, Joseph; Stalinism; Totalitarianism*

BIBLIOGRAPHY

Bown, Matthew C. 1991. The Cult of Personality: The Apotheosis of Stalin, 1945–56. In *Art under Stalin*. New York: Holmes and Meier.

Chandler, David P. 1999. *Brother Number One: A Political Biography of Pol Pot*. Boulder, CO: Westview.

Hollander, Paul. 2002. The Cult of Personality in Communist States. In *Discontents: Postmodern and Postcommunist*. New Brunswick, NJ: Transaction.

Khrushchev, Nikita S. 1989. О культе личности иего последствиях [On the Cult of Personality and Its Consequences]. Известия Ц ПСС [The News of the Central Committee of the Communist Party of the Soviet Union] 3 (March).

Overy, Richard J. 1997. The Cult of Personality: Stalin and the Legacy of War. In *Russia's War: Blood upon the Snow*. New York: TV Books.

Ryan, Louise. 2001. The Cult of Personality: Reassessing Leadership and Suffrage Movements in Britain and Ireland. In *Leadership and Social Movements*, ed. Colin Barker, Alan Johnson, and Michael Lavalette, 196–212. Manchester, U.K.: Manchester University Press.

Rossen Vassilev

PERSONALITY, TYPE A/TYPE B

The roles that personality and behavior play in illness and disease can sometimes be difficult to determine. Because specific personality or lifestyle characteristics cannot be randomly assigned to people, researchers must rely on longitudinal and prospective studies. In these studies, factors that are suspected to be related to disease proneness must be shown to predict health outcomes, sometimes by following participants for a period of many years. In the late 1950s, two California cardiologists named Meyer Friedman (1910–2001) and Ray Rosenman proposed a specific personality type that, based on their clinical experiences, seemed to be associated with high frequencies of cardiovascular disease. In 1960, Friedman and Rosenman began the Western Collaborative Group Study. In this longitudinal study, the researchers followed over 3,000 healthy adult males aged 39 to 59 for more than eight years. Their goal was to determine the relationships among personality, behavior, and the development of heart disease.

At the start of their study, Friedman, Rosenman, and their colleagues conducted 15-minute structured interviews that focused on both verbal and nonverbal behaviors. Participants answered questions about everyday events, such as waiting in lines, driving in traffic, and dealing with problems at home. In addition, interviewers assessed how loud and fast participants spoke during the interview and how they reacted when they were deliberately interrupted during the interview. Based on these taped interviews, the researchers identified different patterns based on a combination of physical, emotional, psychological, and behavioral indicators. Among these patterns was what the researchers called the Type A pattern, the Type B pattern, and mixtures of the two types.

TYPE A AND TYPE B

Physical indicators of Type A Behavior Pattern (TABP) include excess perspiration; facial muscle tension and tics; high levels of alertness and hyperactivity; high levels of epinephrine and norepinephrine (hormones associated with stress); and increased heart rate and levels of diastolic and systolic blood pressure. Emotional indicators include high levels of stress, irritation, hostility, anger, and aggression (especially under provoking conditions). Psychological indicators include impatience; strictness, rigidity, and perfectionism; low tolerance for mistakes; low self-esteem; personal insecurity; compulsiveness; and a high need for control. Finally, examples of behavioral indicators include a general sense of time urgency; losing one's temper while driving; speaking loudly and quickly; interrupting other people's speech; teeth and tongue clicking; a chronic focus on success, ambition, competitiveness, and achievement; and workaholism.

Early proponents of TABP sometimes referred to it as the "hurry sickness," in order to highlight those factors related to the perception of and use of time. Several TABP indicators are thought to be influenced by European and North American social, cultural, and economic values. For example, job promotions and social prestige may often be tied to how much Type A behavior a person shows. The work climate and demands of many kinds of jobs may also reinforce Type A behaviors.

In contrast to the Type A pattern, Type B behavior pattern is characterized by a more calm and even-tempered demeanor. With regard to physical indicators, Type B individuals show more muscle relaxation and lower levels of activity and alertness. Emotionally, such personality types show less frequent irritation, anger, hostility, and aggression than Type A individuals. Psychologically, Type B persons are methodical, tolerant of mistakes, and personally secure. Finally, Type B individuals are more cooperative and relaxed and less achievement-oriented than their Type A counterparts. In the Western Collaborative Group Study, the TABP proved to be a significant predictor of coronary heart disease (CHD), with Type A men showing almost twice the risk of developing CHD than Type B men. In that study, the TABP predicted increased incidence of CHD independent of other risk factors such as smoking, exercise frequency, and parental history of heart disease.

REFINEMENT OF THE TYPE A CONCEPT

As these findings were publicized and tested more fully, several concerns arose regarding the original conception of TABP. First, questions about the best way to assess the pattern emerged. In an effort to assess TABP more efficiently than through the time-consuming individual structured interviews, researchers developed several self-report measures. For example, the multiple-choice Jenkins Activity Survey (JAS), developed in 1979, assesses many of the attitudes and behaviors originally identified as comprising the TABP. However, concerns have arisen about how well the JAS and other measures capture the major dimensions of TABP. For instance, the JAS devotes less attention to the hostility component than seems to be warranted, and scores on the JAS are only weakly related to incidence of CHD. Nonetheless, this measure continues to be the most frequently used instrument in studies of the TABP. More recently, some researchers have utilized videotaped structured interview protocols.

Although the original formulation of TABP was intuitively appealing, one of the problems with such a broad and overly inclusive definition is that many (sometimes the majority) of participants in a study had been labeled as meeting the diagnostic criteria of TABP. As researchers continued to examine the links between personality and CHD, some studies were also unable to replicate the earlier findings of Friedman and Rosenman. In addition to facilitating the development of new and different measures, the concerns about diagnostic criteria led to a detailed examination of the major components of TABP. Given the large number of behaviors that can make up the Type A pattern, it is not surprising that some of these do not necessarily occur together with others. Researchers

thus began to focus their attention on which components of the original multifaceted TABP were (and were not) associated with negative health outcomes.

With these more sophisticated studies, researchers discovered that hostility, especially antagonistic or angry hostility, appeared to be the TABP component that was most strongly related to CHD. In other words, people showing chronic levels of anger and hostility as well as negative affect (in particular depression and anxiety) are more likely to develop CHD. On the other hand, levels of achievement motivation, impatience, and workaholism failed to predict CHD. In addition, subsequent research showed that the perception and use of time turned out to be less predictive of negative health outcomes than other parts of TABP. A 2006 study showed that negative affectivity (i.e., the frequency of negative emotions) and a socially dominant interpersonal style can play a role in a variety of poor health outcomes.

Researchers have also attempted to determine how the psychological components of the TABP develop and how they contribute to the development of CHD. Along these lines, some research suggests that Type A children react more strongly to stress than do Type B children. Researchers have also demonstrated that hostility and aggression are related to cardiovascular response and future risk level in children. Other research suggests that Type A characteristics are likely to develop through a combination of children's temperaments and parental behaviors. For example, children who show the competitiveness associated with the TABP may be encouraged by their parents to perform well in achievement settings, possibly making them more prone to anger and hostility.

In the last decade, researchers have examined how the TABP might be related to social behaviors that are not specifically related to illness or disease. Examples of these behaviors include marital dissatisfaction, driving behavior, group performance, and work-related stress. Some researchers have attempted to apply TABP to companies and organizations. In addition, research has examined how TABP might interact with situational factors, specific kinds of stressors, and various demographic variables (such as age and gender) in determining negative health outcomes. For example, Type A persons might be more likely than Type B persons to find themselves in situations or settings that create frustration, impatience, or irritation. Researchers have also begun to examine whether certain aspects of TABP might be caused by specific disease processes and to identify possible pathways through which personality might increase the likelihood of unhealthy behaviors that could contribute to disease frequency.

In other words, efforts to assess the relationships among personality, behavior, and disease have become more sophisticated and complex than the original TABP concept. As such, the interest, excitement, and promise relating to the original formulation TABP has waned considerably. This has led many modern day personality and health researchers and theorists to consider TABP concept to be no longer useful. Nonetheless, the initial study that identified Type A and Type B personalities, and the publicity it received, helped to energize the emerging fields of behavioral medicine and health psychology.

SEE ALSO *Aggression; Behaviorism; Disease; Lifestyles; Medicine; Mental Health; Mental Illness; Overachievers; Personality; Psychology; Replicability, Statistical; Stress*

BIBLIOGRAPHY

Houston, B. Kent, and C. R. Snyder, eds. 1988. *Type A Behavior Pattern: Research, Theory, and Intervention.* Oxford: John Wiley & Sons.

Matthews, Karen A. 1982. Psychological Perspectives on the Type A Behavior Pattern. *Psychological Bulletin,* vol. 91 (2): pp. 293–323.

Rosenman, Ray H. 1990. Type A Behavior Pattern: A Personal Overview. *Journal of Social Behavior & Personality,* vol. 5 (1): pp. 1–24.

Smith, Timothy W. 2006. Personality as Risk and Resilience in Physical Health. *Current Directions in Psychological Science,* 15 (5): pp. 227–231.

Thomas M. Brinthaupt

PERSON-SITUATION DEBATE

Many social scientists strive to understand why people do what they do. One traditional perspective in personality psychology suggests that people do what they do because of their personality traits. A trait psychologist might suggest, for example, that a person behaves talkatively because she has a high level of extraversion. Trait psychologists traditionally assume that traits are stable psychological characteristics, remaining quite consistent across situations and time. By implication, the trait approach assumes that an individual's behavior should be fairly consistent across situations and time.

In 1968 Walter Mischel published a book challenging the foundations of the trait perspective. Mischel reviewed empirical examinations of behavioral consistency, and he claimed that results revealed surprisingly low levels of cross-situational consistency. He concluded that a theoretical perspective based on broad, context-free personality traits was too simplistic, and his conclusions became the

basis of the "situationist" position that human behavior is strongly determined by situational forces.

The debate between those sympathetic to traditional personality psychology and those representing a situationist position became known as the *person-situation debate.* The nature of the debate ranged widely, with protagonists from both sides taking positions of varying extremity, accusing each other of undue extremity and of misinterpretation or misrepresentation of the opposing position. For example, proponents of the "situationist" side variously suggested, or at least were *accused* of variously suggesting, that the traditional trait approach was too simplistic, that traits do not exist, or even that personality itself does not exist. Despite such ambiguity on both sides, at its heart the debate concerned two important issues— the nature of the behavioral phenomena to be explained and nature of the theories offered as explanations of behavior.

One fundamental issue in the person-situation debate was the degree to which stable individual differences in behavior exist alongside cross-situational variability in behavior. At least two developments advanced the field's understanding of the empirical realities of behavioral stability and variability. First, research demonstrated that individuals do manifest stable differences in their general behavioral trends, if behavioral observations are aggregated across situations (Epstein 1979). Second, research demonstrated that considerable levels of behavioral stability and variability coexist (Fleeson 2001; Funder and Colvin 1991). That is, an individual does behave differently across a variety of situations; however, individuals differ from each other in their average levels of behavior, and these individual differences are indeed stable. These findings are important because they empirically demonstrate, within a single set of behavioral data, the validity of the assumptions of both the trait position (that people manifest stable differences from each other in their behavior) and the situationist position (that people's behavior varies across situations). The fact that both the trait side and the situationist side are empirically tenable legitimizes the theoretical basis of both.

A second important issue in the person-situation debate was the theoretical basis of personality psychology. Psychologists debated the appropriate ways to conceptualize personality and its ties to behavior. Emerging from two or three decades of debate, most theories are "interactionist" because they acknowledge the fact that behavior results from an interaction between personality and situational forces. Despite the general agreement that personality and situational forces affect behavior, such theories differ in terms of the nature and relative importance placed on such factors. Some theorists are sympathetic to an expanded trait perspective. Such theorists acknowledge the role of situational forces in shaping specific behaviors, but they emphasize the utility of traits as predictors of important behavioral trends and outcomes such as psychological well-being, physical health, social relationships, occupational performance, and political attitudes (e.g., Costa and McCrae 1998; Ozer and Benet-Martinez 2006). Other theorists reconceptualize personality in terms other than "traits." For example, the social-cognitive approach emphasizes the importance of cognitive characteristics affecting the way people process information about social situations. From this perspective, cognitive personality characteristics such as one's expectations, beliefs, or self-concept are indeed stable, but different situations trigger different aspects of the cognitive system, leading to variability in behavior (Mischel and Shoda 1995). Finally, some theorists recognize the need for greater attention to the psychological nature of social situations (Funder 2005).

The person-situation debate was a challenging yet ultimately constructive argument for personality psychology (Fleeson 2004). By forcing psychologists to think carefully about the links between behavior, personality, and situations, the person-situation debate was a catalyst for a deeper appreciation of the importance of personality and for a more sophisticated understanding of why people do what they do.

SEE ALSO *Personality; Schemas; Trait Theory*

BIBLIOGRAPHY

Epstein, Seymour. 1979. The Stability of Behavior: I. On Predicting Most of the People Much of the Time. *Journal of Personality and Social Psychology* 37: 1097–1126.

Fleeson, William. 2001. Towards a Structure- and Process-Integrated View of Personality: Traits as Density Distributions of States. *Journal of Personality and Social Psychology* 80: 1011–1027.

Fleeson, William. 2004. Moving Personality Beyond the Person-Situation Debate: The Challenge and Opportunity of Within-Person Variability. *Current Directions in Psychological Science* 13: 83–87.

Funder, David C. 2005. Toward a Resolution of the Personality Triad: Persons, Situations, and Behaviors. *Journal of Research in Personality* 40: 21–34.

Funder, David C., and C. Randall Colvin. 1991. Explorations in Behavioral Consistency: Properties of Persons, Situations, and Behaviors. *Journal of Personality and Social Psychology* 60: 773–794.

Mischel, Walter. 1968. *Personality and Assessment.* New York: Wiley.

Mischel, Walter, and Yuichi Shoda. 1995. A Cognitive-Affective System Theory of Personality: Reconceptualizing Situations, Dispositions, Dynamics, and Invariance in Personality Structure. *Psychological Review* 102: 246–268.

Ozer, Daniel J., and Veronica Benet-Martinez. 2006. Personality and the Prediction of Consequential Outcomes. *Annual Review of Psychology* 57: 401–421.

R. Michael Furr

PERSPECTIVE-TAKING

Perspective-taking—viewing the world from something other than one's habitual vantage point—covers a broad range from the literal to metaphorical. One can literally take a visual perspective by physically positioning oneself and gazing in a particular direction, often replicating another person's physical position and directional gaze in an attempt to see what that person sees (e.g., "Stand here and you can see the tower between the hills"). Alternatively, one can imagine a particular visual perspective (e.g., "These steps must look very tall to someone as short as a toddler") or mentally construct a visual perspective (e.g., "Let's see … facing east, I can see the house, so if I were to face west, I would see the street"). However, perspective-taking often goes beyond the visual, referring to attempts to adopt an overall mindset that differs from one's default mindset ("Imagine what the rabbi must have thought when the caterers brought out all those trays of ham!" or "I can see your point—you could have used more time to prepare").

A cornerstone of Swiss developmental psychologist Jean Piaget's (1896–1980) theory of cognitive development was that human infants have just one perspective—their own. They are profoundly egocentric: unable to even comprehend that someone else may have a different mental experience from their own and thus unable to take another person's perspective. As young children develop, they not only learn that other perspectives exist, but also how to take those perspectives and use them. Children who can recognize that other people have their own minds and can thus have other perspectives are said to have developed a *theory of mind.* In a typically developing child, a coherent theory of mind emerges between ages three and five (although rudiments of this skill, such as following another person's gaze to understand what he or she is looking at, appear earlier). Theory of mind and perspective-taking deficits are among the hallmark symptoms of autism, a psychological disorder that usually appears early in life (other psychological disorders or brain injuries can also produce perspective-taking deficits).

Some scholars have argued that a true understanding of theory of mind may be unique to the human species. However, even for adult humans, perspective-taking requires effort and presents a challenge. Easy or perfectly accurate perspective-taking is hindered by the "other minds problem"—that is, we can never know from a first-person perspective exactly how things are perceived by another person with another mind.

Perspective-taking has a variety of social implications. In both children and adults, perspective-taking is associated with greater empathy, prosocial behavior, and more favorable treatment of the person (or group) whose perspective is taken. The exact mechanism by which perspective-taking produces these outcomes is debated, with a variety of options proposed, including suppression of the usual "self"-ish perspective, a heightened desire to help the other person, attempts to relieve negative feelings aroused by perceiving another person in distress, and the cognitive merging of one's representation of the self with that of the person whose perspective is being taken. Research consistently demonstrates that instructing people to take the perspective of another person in need leads to increased feelings of compassion and empathy and often results in offers to help the person whose perspective was taken. However, perspective-taking can also be used for malevolent purposes (e.g., anticipating a rival's next move and taking steps to thwart it).

Since Piaget's day, developmental researchers (e.g., Janet Astington, Simon Baron-Cohen, John Flavell, Alison Gopnik, Andrew Meltzoff, Joseph Perner, and Henry Wellman) have continued to ask questions about perspective-taking and its relationship to other aspects of human development. Social psychologists have also pursued perspective-taking and its effects on social behavior (notably Daniel Batson's work on links between perspective-taking and altruistic behavior, and William Ickes's work on adults' accuracy in guessing others' thoughts). Most recently, neuroscientists (e.g., Jean Decety) have used brain-imaging techniques to explore perspective-taking.

SEE ALSO *Empathy; Piaget, Jean; Role Theory; Theory of Mind*

BIBLIOGRAPHY

Flavell, John H. 1992. Perspectives on Perspective Taking. In *Piaget's Theory: Prospects and Possibilities*, eds. Harry Beilin and Peter B. Pufall, 107–139. Hillsdale, NJ: Erlbaum.

Malle, Bertram F., and Sara D. Hodges, eds. 2005. *Other Minds: How Humans Bridge the Divide Between Self and Others*. New York: Guilford.

Sara D. Hodges

PERSUASION

Every day we are exposed to hundreds of attempts to change our opinions. Consider how often you come across an advertisement—in a magazine or newspaper, on television, the radio, or a Web site. But marketers are not the only ones trying to influence us. Family members, religious leaders, politicians, and friends all try to convince us to do things, agree with them, or support their cause. Although persuasive attempts are pervasive, they are not always successful.

Persuasion can be defined as an active attempt by a person, group, or entity (such as a corporation), usually through some form of communication, to change a person's mind. Although we use the term *mind* here, often what we are referring to are attitudes or opinions. Persuasion has been a central focus of the social psychology literature at least since the mid-twentieth century—perhaps because persuasive attempts are so common. Furthermore, if attitudes can be changed, behavior can be changed as well.

THE MESSAGE LEARNING APPROACH

In the 1940s a group of researchers led by the psychologist Carl Hovland (1912–1961) at Yale University spearheaded a comprehensive program of research on persuasion. The catalogue of persuasive factors that they examined is now referred to as the *message learning approach*. The Yale group also proposed a sequence for the process of persuasion: in order for persuasion to occur, a person needs to be exposed to the persuasive message, as well as pay attention to, comprehend, accept or yield to, and remember the message. Although more recent researchers have argued that not all of these steps are absolutely necessary (particularly remembering the message), this basic process has been supported in numerous studies.

The Yale group also found that the source of the persuasive communication is an important determinant of success. The expertise and trustworthiness of the source are critical. For example, in an advertisement for basketball shoes, a professional athlete may be an expert but may not be trustworthy because he is being paid to sell the shoes. Thus the advertisement may not be effective. The attractiveness of the source is also important. This is why clothing advertisers use attractive models in their advertisements. The implicit message is: "If you buy these clothes, you will look good too." Furthermore, the more you like someone and the more you are attracted to that person, the more likely you are to buy the product he or she is selling.

Characteristics of the persuasive message have also been explored. Factors that have been found to influence persuasion include: a one-sided versus a two-sided message (i.e., providing one or both sides of an argument); the order of messages; the comprehensibility of the message content; and the number of arguments presented. In terms of the sidedness and order of messages, which is superior depends on the situation. Nonetheless, it is clear that if people do not understand the message they are exposed to, they will not be persuaded. For this reason, print advertisements for complex products (such as computers or stereos) are often more effective because people have the time to read and understand them. With regard to the number of arguments, more arguments usually result in more persuasion.

Characteristics such as the intelligence, self-esteem, and gender of the recipient have all been explored as factors affecting persuasion, but the results of these studies are mixed. In general, the more intelligent a person is, the more likely it is that he or she will comprehend a message, but the less likely it is that the person will accept the message. Early studies found that women tend to be more easily persuaded, but more recent research suggests that one's knowledge about a topic is more important than gender.

TWO ROUTES TO PERSUASION

Despite hundreds of studies exploring the variables discussed above, results have not always been consistent. Sometimes variables matter and sometimes they do not. Furthermore, the change in attitude achieved by persuasive communication is often transitory. To address these issues, Richard Petty and John Cacioppo developed the *elaboration likelihood model*, which proposes that persuasion typically happens by one of two routes. They argue that the extent to which message-relevant arguments are elaborated is a key determinant of the success of a persuasive appeal. Elaboration is not simply the learning of the arguments, but involves scrutinizing, making inferences about, and evaluating the quality of those arguments.

In a number of experiments, researchers have shown that when elaboration is low, persuasion tends to occur through *peripheral route* processes. That is, persuasion occurs through features or characteristics of the persuasion context (referred to as *cues*) that are not directly related to the central merits of the arguments. Such cues include the attractiveness or expertise of the message source, the mood of the participants, and the number of arguments presented.

When elaboration is high, however, people attend to the central merits of the arguments (*central route* processing). If the arguments are of high quality (i.e., strong), people's attitudes are likely to change. However, if the arguments are weak, people will be able to counter them, and the message will not be effective. In order for elaboration to occur, however, two conditions must be met: (1) people must be *motivated* to scrutinize the message (they need to be involved, feel a sense of personal responsibility, or enjoy engaging in cognitive tasks); and (2) people must

be *able* to scrutinize the message (they must have the requisite knowledge to process the information, and must not be distracted). Perhaps this is why most advertisements on television, billboards, and Web sites are structured around peripheral cues (using expert, trustworthy, attractive sources, or humor); since people do not typically scrutinize these types of advertisements, peripheral approaches may be more successful.

Attitude-change research continues to enjoy a central role within the social psychological literature. Furthermore, it is clear from the numerous applications of the attitude-change literature to our daily lives (for advertisers, marketers, politicians, and many others) that persuasion research will continue to be at the forefront of the field.

SEE ALSO *Attitudes; Social Influence*

BIBLIOGRAPHY

Eagly, Alice H., and Shelley Chaiken. 1993. *The Psychology of Attitudes.* Fort Worth, TX: Harcourt.

Petty, Richard E., and John T. Cacioppo. [1981] 1996. *Attitudes and Persuasion: Classic and Contemporary Approaches.* Boulder, CO: Westview.

Petty, Richard E., and Duane T. Wegener. 1998. Attitude Change: Multiple Roles for Persuasion Variables. In *The Handbook of Social Psychology*, eds. Daniel T. Gilbert, Susan T. Fiske, and Gardner Lindzey, 323–390. 4th ed. New York: McGraw-Hill.

Wood, Wendy. 2000. Attitude Change: Persuasion and Social Influence. *Annual Review of Psychology* 50: 539–570.

Steven M. Smith

PERSUASION, MESSAGE-BASED

Does advertising plant product images in people's minds? Do the media influence outcomes of elections? Why do so many attempts to scare teenagers into protecting their health fail abysmally? Is persuasion a social good or a malevolent agent used by cunning connivers?

These questions strike to the heart of persuasion theory and research, a time-honored academic field that dates back to fourth century BCE when the ancient Greek philosopher Aristotle (384–322 BCE) developed the first systematic approach to persuasion, or rhetoric as it was known then. From Aristotle's era to our own, persuasion endlessly fascinates people because of its uncanny ability to powerfully influence human attitudes and the elusive relationship with truth and morality.

Persuasion is defined as "a symbolic process in which communicators try to convince other people to change their attitudes or behavior regarding an issue through the transmission of a message, in an atmosphere of free choice" (Perloff 2003, p. 8). Persuasion is fundamentally self-persuasion. We persuade ourselves to go along with what communicators suggest; unfortunately, self-persuasion can be both benevolent and malevolent, with the determination of what is malevolent or benevolent a function of the consequences of the action, the persuader's intentions, and social context.

The basic component of persuasion is the *attitude*, which the entity persuaders hope to form, influence, and reinforce. We have attitudes toward all sorts of topics, from politics to religion. Attitudes have a cognitive structure and serve psychological functions for individuals. Attitudes can be weak (e.g., one's attitude toward the candidate running for state auditor) or strong (e.g., prejudice against African Americans). Attitudes predict behavior when the attitude is strongly held and is measured at the same level of specificity as the behavior.

Persuasive communications can change attitudes by employing appealing communicators, by developing a convincing message, or by containing features that attract attention but are peripheral to the message (e.g., music that accompanies an advertisement).

The key characteristic of effective communicators is credibility. Credible communicators are perceived to possess expertise, trustworthiness, and good will. Communicators also change attitudes because they are likable, physically attractive, or perceived as similar to the audience. Because charming, likable persuaders can take advantage of naïve individuals, psychologist Robert Cialdini (2001) refers to these communicator traits collectively as "the friendly thief."

What you say and how you say it are aspects of the persuasive message. Evidence and statistics strengthen the persuasiveness of a message. Emotional factors, such as fear, also can sway audiences. A speech arousing fear (e.g., on cigarette smoking or drugs) can influence audience members if it scares them, points out negative consequences of performing a behavior, and identifies ways to avoid these consequences. Communications are also persuasive when they provoke inconsistencies—or arouse cognitive dissonance—between attitudes people harbor and their behavior.

Language is a key component of the persuasive message. The words you use, how fast you speak, and the metaphors you employ to frame your message can influence attitudes. Communicators who do not qualify or hedge their verbal statements are seen as more credible than unassertive speakers. Messages containing metaphors produce greater attitude change than those without

metaphoric statements. We all can think of books, movies, and songs that changed the way we looked at the world, in large part due to the metaphors they employed and the stories they told (Green and Brock 2005).

Persuasion occurs in different contexts—one-on-one, as when a salesperson tries to sell you a car, and in groups, such as a business meeting or a jury. Interpersonal persuasion frequently occurs in stages, and persuasion professionals frequently resort to such techniques as foot-in-the-door, door-in-the-face, and lowballing. Today, much persuasion occurs through mass media, and a great deal of money is spent on research to understand consumers' attitudes toward products and politics. Advertisements link products with fantasies in the hopes of convincing people that the product will bring them happiness or success. Politicians hire consultants who help them frame messages in politically palatable ways.

Scholars study persuasion by developing theories and testing hypotheses through empirical research. Contemporary theories, such as the *elaboration likelihood model* focus on process, emphasizing that persuaders cannot develop an effective message unless they appreciate how audiences think about the topic at hand. When individuals lack motivation to consider an issue, they process the message superficially, which suggests that simple messages with appealing images will carry the day. When people are more psychologically invested in a topic, they think more deeply about underlying issues. Under these circumstances, more complex or value-based messages influence attitudes (Petty and Cacioppo 1986).

Persuasion has great potential to help people change prejudiced attitudes and adopt healthier lifestyles. Unfortunately, human nature being what it is, unsavory communicators will continue to exploit persuasion to achieve their own ends. An educated citizenry should understand the processes by which persuasive communications induce individuals to alter their attitudes and behavior.

SEE ALSO *Advertising; Media; Medium Is the Message; Subliminal Suggestion*

BIBLIOGRAPHY

Cialdini, Robert B. 2001. *Influence: Science and Practice.* 4th ed. Boston: Allyn & Bacon.

Green, Melanie C., and Timothy C. Brock. 2005. Persuasiveness of Narratives. In *Persuasion: Psychological Insights and Perspectives,* 2nd ed., eds. Timothy C. Brock and Melanie C. Green, 117–142. Thousand Oaks, CA: Sage.

Perloff, Richard M. 2003. *The Dynamics of Persuasion: Communication and Attitudes in the 21st century.* 2nd ed. Mahwah, NJ: Erlbaum.

Petty, Richard E., and John T. Cacioppo. 1986. The Elaboration Likelihood Model of Persuasion. In *Advances in Experimental*

Social Psychology, Vol. 19, ed. Leonard Berkowitz, 123–205. New York: Academic Press.

Richard M. Perloff

PETROLEUM INDUSTRY

The documentary evidence for the human use of petroleum begins with the Old Testament books of Genesis and Exodus and the works of the ancient Greek historian Herodotus (c. 484–430/420 BCE). In addition archaeologists found pitch in the tombs of the Egyptian kings Tutankhamen (c. 1370–1352 BCE) and Seti II (c. 1200 BCE). The Toltecs of Mexico used bitumen to set tiles as early as 1200 CE, and Native Americans dug oil wells in what are now Pennsylvania, Kentucky, and Ohio.

Still, until the 1850s there was no petroleum mining or production. In that decade oil wells were drilled specifically seeking petroleum in Poland, Canada, and the United States. By 1900 petroleum had been discovered in Baku (in present-day Azerbaijan), Poland, France, Scotland, Italy, Romania, Egypt, Canada, the United States, Mexico, Sumatra, Trinidad, and Peru. In the twentieth century discoveries were made on every continent and in most countries.

THE MODERN PETROLEUM INDUSTRY

The first modern use of petroleum was for kerosene, discovered in 1852. A kerosene lamp was invented in 1857, and the first kerosene factory was built near Baku in 1859. Gasoline was a by-product of kerosene production. After 1901 most petroleum was used for fuel oil to heat and light buildings and for gasoline to power automobiles with internal combustion engines.

From a macroeconomic perspective, petroleum is important because the industrial systems of Western nations and Japan all are based upon its use as a major source of cheap energy and of chemicals for other uses. About 30 percent of the top fifty industrial firms in the United States are petroleum or chemical firms. A similar proportion of the top fifty non-American industrial firms also produce petroleum or chemical products. Petroleum has become essential for fueling production facilities in all industries and for powering, heating, cooling, and lighting buildings and illuminating streets. It thereby makes possible the high-density urban agglomerations so characteristic of western Europe and North America. Without it Western societies would have had to develop either a more efficient energy source or an extensive form of land use rather than the intensive form now practiced. Such a use

of land for living space, given a growing population, would threaten food production by depleting the acreage of farmable land. Moreover, because petroleum fuels the vast bulk of industry, virtually all employment in the West depends in the final analysis on its use. Petroleum fuel shortages mean unemployment, and large-scale unemployment can have catastrophic political consequences. Paradoxically, another use of petroleum since the mid-twentieth century has been to encourage decentralization of massive urban agglomerations into the suburbs, requiring the use of petroleum to fuel vehicles. A sustained shortage of petroleum thus would halt this trend toward decentralized land use.

From a macroeconomic perspective, petroleum is an intermediate good, consumed only to produce final consumption items. Despite the emphasis in the mass media on gasoline consumption and prices, the most extensive use of petroleum products since 1949 according to the U.S. Energy Information Administration has been for combined heat and power for homes and industry. Petroleum products thus enter the production functions of every home and industry in the economy. The amount value of petroleum products consumed in the United States in 2005 was 1,836,392 thousand barrels per day.

Industry Structure The modern petroleum industry is structured into four types of organizations: (1) state enterprises, (2) multinational corporations, (3) the Organization of Petroleum Exporting Countries (OPEC), and (4) legally organized commodity exchanges. In most petroleum-producing countries in the early twenty-first century, the state owns a petroleum company with a legal monopoly on the production and distribution of crude petroleum. The largest of these after 1918 was the Soviet state petroleum enterprise.

Most crude petroleum is produced by Western companies. In 1870 the Standard Oil Company was created by the Rockefeller brothers and two other partners. In 1893 the Standard Oil Trust was formed in New Jersey to evade an antitrust suit brought by the state of Ohio. Gulf Oil Corporation was formed in 1901 by the Richard K. Mellon family. Texaco was founded as the Texas Company in 1901 by Joseph S. Cullinan, Walter B. Sharp, and Arnols Shaect. The U.S. Supreme Court in 1911 ordered Standard Oil Trust dissolved. The component companies, still with the plurality of shares owned by the former Rockefeller shareholders, continued to operate as ostensibly separate companies. These companies were Standard Oil of Ohio, Standard Oil of Indiana, Standard Oil of New York, Standard Oil of New Jersey, Standard Oil of California, Standard Oil of Kentucky, Atlantic, and the Ohio Oil Company (later Marathon).

The Royal Dutch Company for the Exploration of Petroleum Sources in the Netherlands Indies was established in 1890. It merged in 1907 with Shell Transport and Trading Company, a British company, to form Royal Dutch Shell. The British government formed the Anglo-Iranian Oil Company in 1914. This company ultimately became British Petroleum. In 1924 the Compagnie Française des Pétroles was established by the French government. ELF began before World War II (1939–1945) with the establishment of three small companies to explore for gas near oil seepages in Aquitaine. Italy in 1926 formed Agencia Generale Italiani Petroli (AGIP). In 1953 ENI was founded as a conglomerate of thirty-six subsidiaries, including AGIP.

These companies all were multinational, multidivisional, and vertically and horizontally integrated firms. Within each company, five major functions were performed—exploration, drilling and production, transportation, refining, and distribution to final consumers. Subsidiaries were responsible for each function. Transfers of product among these subsidiaries and other divisions of the companies were accomplished using shadow pricing or some other form of transfer pricing. Actual payments were made only for transactions with outside firms.

OPEC was established in Baghdad in September 1960 as an intergovernmental organization of five original member states—Iraq, Iran, Kuwait, Saudi Arabia, and Venezuela. Its charter required that each member acquire an increasing level of control of production. By 1970 each member state was required to own a minimum of 55 percent of foreign petroleum companies operating within its jurisdiction. Iraqi production has not been part of OPEC quota agreements since March 1998 due to U.S. and United Nations controls. Other OPEC members have included Qatar (joined 1961), Indonesia and Libya (1962), Ecuador (1963–1993), Trucial States of Oman (now United Arab Emirates, 1967), Algeria (1969), Nigeria (1971), Gabon (1975–1995), and Angola (2007). The OPEC cartel was formed to control the world oil supply so as to increase revenue to member states. It operates by assigning members an annual supply quota for crude oil production and export. In 2005 it controlled about 41.7 percent of world production. OPEC also sets prices.

THE ERA OF THE SEVEN SISTER COMPANIES, 1911–1980

The name *seven sisters* was coined in a 1961 *Time* magazine article to refer to the dominant firms in the world oil industry: Royal Dutch Shell, Anglo Persian Oil (Anglo-Iranian Oil/British Petroleum/BP), Gulf Oil, Texaco, and three of the Standard Oil companies from the 1911 trust dissolution—Standard Oil of New Jersey (Humble Oil [Esso]/Exxon), Standard Oil of New York (Socony/Socony-Vacuum/Socony-Mobil/Mobil), and Standard Oil of California (Socal/Chevron). With the exception of Royal Dutch Shell, which is British and Dutch, these are all U.S. or British companies. Only the U.S. companies had their own significant domestic supply sources in the founding period of the industry from 1850 to 1950. The British and Dutch thus undertook a worldwide search for sources, beginning with their colonies and extending after World War I (1914–1918) to the League of Nations territories mandated to their administration. The seven sisters and Atlantic Richfield (ARCO), called *majors*, were vertically integrated, and all had similar structures. They had separate subsidiaries for exploration, production, refining, and distribution and geographic subsidiaries for operations in different areas.

The most important "independent" or nonintegrated companies, which did not operate in at least one of the areas defining the integrated companies, in this period included Getty, Phillips, Signal, Union, Continental, Sun, Amerada Hess, Cities Service, Marathon, Compagnie Française des Pétroles, Occidental, ENI, Tenneco, and Skelly Oil. In 1983 Occidental acquired Cities Service. Texaco acquired Getty in 1984.

Soviet Petroleum Industry The petroleum industry in Russia prior to the Bolshevik Revolution of 1917 was operated largely by U.S., British, and Swedish companies. During the seven sisters period, the Soviet state owned and operated the industry. The industry returned to private hands after 1991. ConocoPhillips acquired 16.8 percent of Lukoil, the largest Russian oil company. BP-Amoco invested in both Lukoil and Sidanko.

NATIONALIZATION, 1970–2000

Around 1912 producing countries began nationalizing or expropriating the ownership of foreign companies. The theoretical basis for expropriation was provided by Marxism-Leninism. The acceleration of this policy after 1970 was due more to nationalism, although the regimes that instituted it were almost always leftist. Majority or full expropriation took place in Argentina (1912), the Soviet Union (Baku, 1918), Mexico (1938), Iran (1951), Indonesia (1950s–1960s), Egypt (1961–1964), Peru (1968), Libya (1971), Nigeria (1971), Iraq (1972), Algeria (1972), and Saudi Arabia (1973).

CONCENTRATION AND CENTRALIZATION

Since the 1980s there has been an acceleration in the rate of concentration and centralization in the world oil industry with the development of what are referred to as *supermajors*, *majors*, and *independents* or *jobbers*. Supermajors consist of BP-Amoco, Chevron-Texaco, Exxon-Mobil, ConocoPhillips, and Shell. This category of companies is defined as having a capitalization of $100 billion or more. Majors are defined as companies having a capitalization of $30 to $100 billion. Independents and jobbers include those with a capitalization of less than $30 billion. Supermajors have largely abandoned their traditional function of exploration, 80 percent of which now is conducted by independents. They receive most of their profits from the refining and petrochemical industries and also have diversified into alternative sources of energy, including atomic energy.

Simultaneously with this centralization and consolidation, many countries opened up their petroleum industries again to private international companies. Conflicts between source countries and companies extracting crude petroleum have been endemic from the beginning of the modern era, and examples such as the conflict in southeastern Nigeria and the war in Iraq are manifestations of this phenomenon.

Environmental issues in the extraction and transportation phases of the industry's operation are less visible and perhaps less important than in the consumption phase. For this reason this issue has been the most recent to emerge. However, the environmental impact of the international industry is difficult to measure systematically, for no international statistics on this issue are collected. The number and volume of oil spills are available, but these represent only extraordinary occurrences, not the everyday degradation of the environment due to operations.

THE POLITICAL ECONOMY OF THE PETROLEUM INDUSTRY

During World War I and continuing into the early twenty-first century, Western countries transformed their economies and their military forces to use petroleum as the primary fuel source. As they did so diplomatic and military conflicts arose over control of the known sources of petroleum. Because this transformation was not far advanced until after World War I, that war cannot be characterized as a war over oil.

Most of the known sources at the beginning of this period were in the United States. Elsewhere oil production began in Baku in the 1870s, in the Dutch East Indies in 1883, in Iran in 1908, in Egypt in 1910, in Venezuela in 1914, in Kurdistan (now part of Iraq) around 1915, in Iraq in 1927, in Saudi Arabia in 1935, in Libya in 1959, in Egypt in 1966, in Sudan in 1974, and in Kazakhstan in 2000. These sources were discovered by Western oil companies, which have involved their governments in protecting their exploitation of these resources.

Local and Regional Conflicts Many of the conflicts that arose were local or regional, involving antagonistic political and military forces internal to countries with petroleum reserves, or between neighboring countries with at least one having reserves. These conflicts took the form of rebellions, revolutions, coups d'état, civil wars, and border wars. For example, in the failed 1905 revolution in Russia, the Baku fields were set afire. The Kurds, representing Turkey, massacred millions of Armenians during World War I. In 1929 and 1989 civil wars occurred in Afghanistan. In 1945 a coup in Venezuela gave control of the oil fields to a different power group in the country. Petroleum has been associated with two civil wars (1955–1972 and 1983–2005) and an armed rebellion in Sudan. The Nigeria-Biafra civil war (1967–1970) involved petroleum fields in the Niger Delta. The Angolan civil war (1976–2002) involved petroleum reserves in the Cabinda enclave. And a rebellion that began in Darfur in 2003 involved the South Darfur fields. Local and regional conflicts increased significantly after Britain withdrew its naval forces from the Indian Ocean and the Persian Gulf in 1971.

Multinational and Global Conflicts Other conflicts involved the major European political powers of the day—the large petroleum-consuming countries—in conflicts that were considered to be major set-piece "wars." Britain and Afghanistan fought three wars (1838–1842, 1878–1881, and 1919), the British attempting to thwart perceived Russian designs on British India, then including Pakistan. At that time petroleum had not been discovered in or near Afghanistan and so played little role in these wars.

After World War I, Turkey captured a part of the territory of the ethnic Kurds. Another part was given to Britain by the League of Nations as part of the Iraq mandate. A section of this territory was given to the French in the Syrian mandate. The Soviet Union captured the Azerbaijan part in 1920. Kurdistan was made a semiautonomous region of Iraq, the only Kurdish political entity internationally recognized. Turkey and the Soviet Union captured parts of the territory of the ethnic Armenians, other parts of which lie in northern Syria, Iraq, and Iran.

During the 1890s the British attempted to expand the border of their colony British Guiana (now Guyana) westward to include parts of Venezuela, where indications of oil had been discovered. This was probably unnecessary, because Guyana is a geologic sink, a lower-than-sea-level basin into which petroleum flows by gravity from Venezuela on the west and Dutch Guiana (now Surinam) on the east, so wells drilled in Guyana would draw from pools shared with Venezuela and Surinam. Nevertheless, British and German warships blockaded the ports of Venezuela until the United States, citing the Monroe

Doctrine, forced them to cease. Oil was discovered in 1914, and by 1928 Venezuela was the world's largest exporter of oil. Thus one sees the hand of Britain in the Afghanistan, Kurdistan, and Venezuela conflicts between the two world wars.

The most important of these major conflicts was World War II, the first war that might be characterized as an "oil war," with the petroleum resources of the Caspian Sea, the Persian Gulf, the Gulf of Mexico, the Caribbean Sea, Lake Maracaibo, and the Dutch East Indies being strategic targets of all combatants. As part of its strategy to defend the Caribbean Sea and the Gulf of Mexico from German attack, the United States concluded a deal with Britain in 1940 by which the United States gave Britain used destroyers in exchange for the right to use or build bases in the British Caribbean colonies.

North Africa was the location of battles between Italy and Germany on one side and Britain and the United States on the other to secure Persian Gulf oil, even though no oil had yet been discovered in Libya or the Western Desert of Egypt, where most of the battles were fought. On August 1, 1941, before its entrance into the war, the United States imposed an oil embargo on the Axis powers—Germany, Italy, and Japan. The Netherlands and Britain followed suit. The 1941 embargo reduced Germany's supply from Mexico and Venezuela and reduced Japan's supply from the Caspian Sea, the Persian Gulf fields, and the Dutch East Indies. The U.S. entrance into the war was largely due to its embargo of petroleum supplies to Japan. After negotiations with the United States, Britain and Holland failed to reverse this decision, and Pearl Harbor was attacked in December 1941 to reduce the U.S. capacity to enforce the embargo. Japan then invaded and occupied the Dutch East Indies (Sumatra, Java, and Borneo) from 1942 to 1946 to secure petroleum to fuel its war effort.

A few months after the war ended in 1945, a military coup took place in Venezuela, with control of revenues from oil production a major motivation for the conflict. The Dutch also fought wars in Indonesia to regain control of its colony but was forced to grant it independence in 1948. The cold war between the United States and the Soviet bloc from 1945 to 1991 involved the same strategic oil issues as World War II but did not rise to the level of open warfare. The Korean War (1950–1953) and the Vietnam War (1954–1975) were proxy wars for the United States and the Soviet Union but were less conspicuously concerned with control of petroleum reserves and their transportation to world markets. Importantly, however, with the exception of World War II, all conflicts over oil, both regional and global, took place in the countries in which the reserves lay, and not in the consuming countries. This changed dramatically with the onset of "terrorism."

Terrorism The rise of terrorism since the airplane hijackings in 1968—including especially the attacks on New York City in 1993 and 2001 and on the Pentagon in 2001, the bombings of U.S. embassies and ships in 1998 and 2001, and the bombings on Spanish and British trains and buses and other facilities in 2004 and 2005—changed the location of conflicts. Terrorism may be considered a form of guerrilla warfare, in contrast to a set-piece war. In response to this shift in theaters and tactics, Western governments alleged that certain Arab Muslim states were "sponsors" of these acts of terror or gave safe haven to terrorists. Western states directed military and economic sanctions against these states, which included Iran, Libya, Sudan, Somalia, Afghanistan, and Iraq. It is not without significance that all these states either have petroleum reserves or stand athwart transportation routes to world petroleum markets. Somalia, for example, controls the approach to the Red Sea and the Suez Canal.

Since 1980 five major wars have been fought in the region: the Soviet-Afghanistan War (1979–1989), the Iraq-Iran War (1980–1988), the Persian Gulf War (1990–1991), the U.S.-Afghanistan War that began in 2001, and the U.S.-Iraq War that began in 2003. In addition since 1980 U.S. naval ships and aircraft have blockaded and threatened to attack Libya, accusing it of being a state sponsor of terrorism.

In 1991 the former republics of the Soviet Union became independent. Several of them gave concessions to Western companies to explore for petroleum. With these discoveries, proposals were made for pipelines to carry the petroleum to shipping points for export to world markets. Three feasible routes exist for exporting Caspian Sea petroleum to world markets: west through Azerbaijan, Armenia, and Georgia to the Black Sea; south through Iraq and Iran to the Persian Gulf; or southeast through Afghanistan and Pakistan to the Arabian Sea. Overland markets are north into Russia and east into China.

All wars have as an objective the conquest of territory and its resources and assets, a major part since 1900 being petroleum reserves. Thus all wars since 1900 may be considered, to some extent, wars to control oil. This objective has attained the highest priority since World War II, leading to increased military and diplomatic conflict. Petroleum wars may be expected to continue to arise until a different energy source is discovered and widely employed or until an effective international nonviolent conflict resolution method is found and employed.

SEE ALSO *Energy Industry; Industry; Iran-Iraq War; Iraq-U.S. War; Nationalization; Organization of Petroleum Exporting Countries (OPEC); Resource Economics; State Enterprise*

BIBLIOGRAPHY

Bilkadi, Zayn. 1994. Bulls from the Sea. *Saudi Aramco World* 45 (4): 20–31.

Blair, John M. 1976. *The Control of Oil.* New York: Pantheon.

Ellison, Julian. 1974. The Petroleum Industry in Africa and America. Occasional Paper no. 1974–1. New York: Black Economic Research Center.

Engler, Robert. 1961. *The Politics of Oil: A Study of Private Power and Democratic Directions.* New York: Macmillan.

Library of Congress Business References Service. 2005–2006. History of the Oil and Gas Industry. *Business and Economics Research Advisor* (BERA) 5/6. http://www.loc.gov/rr/business/BERA/issue5/history.html.

Mir-Babayev, Mir Yusif. Azerbaijan's Oil History: A Chronology Leading Up to the Soviet Era. 2002. *Azerbaijan International* 10 (2).

Razavi, Hossein, and Fereidun Fesharaki. 1991. *Fundamentals of Petroleum Trading.* New York: Praeger.

Sampson, Anthony. 1975. *The Seven Sisters: The Great Oil Companies and the World They Shaped.* New York: Viking.

Snow, Keith Harman. 2007. The New Old "Humanitarian" Warfare in Africa, Part II. *Somali Times,* February 7.

U.S. Department of Commerce, Census Bureau. 1975. *Historical Statistics of the United States: Colonial Times to 1970.* Bicentennial ed., pt. 1. Washington, DC: U.S. Government Printing Office.

Wirth, John D. 1985. *Latin American Oil Companies and the Politics of Energy.* Lincoln: University of Nebraska Press.

Wirth, John D., ed. 2001. *The Oil Business in Latin America: The Early Years.* Washington, DC: Beard.

Julian Ellison

PETTIGREW, THOMAS. F.
1931–

The American civil rights researcher and activist Thomas Fraser Pettigrew is one of the leading experts in the social science of race and ethnic relations to emerge in the post–World War II (1939–1945) period. Pettigrew received his B.A. in psychology from the University of Virginia in 1952 and both his M.A. (1955) and PhD (1956) in social psychology from Harvard University in the Department of Social Relations. His graduate training, requiring courses in sociology, social psychology, and anthropology, is reflected in the interdisciplinary perspective he has brought to over five decades of research on intergroup conflict. Pettigrew's approach to social psychology was shaped by his mentor, psychologist Gordon Allport (1897–1967), and his classic 1954 text, *The Nature of Prejudice.* Other intellectual influences included sociologist and survey researcher Samuel Stouffer (1900–1960) and sociologist Talcott Parsons (1902–1979). Pettigrew's

experience of growing up white in the segregated South in the 1930s and 1940s further influenced his approach to prejudice and intergroup conflict by bringing him into close contact with the plight of African Americans.

Initially, Pettigrew studied the differences among white Americans in different regions of the United States. His research showed that psychological factors alone, in this case authoritarianism, could not account for the greater hostility toward blacks found among southerners. For a more complete picture, he argued for the importance of examining the structural components and the way in which societal norms hold bigotry in place. Pettigrew's work continued to build on this insight, and he has argued throughout his career for the importance of studying social issues at several levels of analysis.

Pettigrew consolidated his theoretical position by developing a multilevel approach to social issues that combined the individual, the situational, and the societal levels, and the links among them. In the case of prejudice, there is the micro level of analysis, which includes individual attitudes, cognitions, and personality dynamics. There is also the macro level of analysis, including structural aspects of one's society, its norms, and its mores. And finally, there is the meso level of analysis, in which the immediate situation of social interaction plays a key role. Throughout his career, Pettigrew has studied each level of analysis and its interaction with other levels, arguing that none is sufficient alone. Consequently, he has pursued research on authoritarianism and its relationship to prejudice, subtle prejudicial attitudes and their involvement in undermining societal desegregation, and the importance of friendship in his reformulation of contact theory and intergroup conflict. Pettigrew's research is international in scope, with attention always paid to racial norms guiding the societies and their institutions (e.g., South Africa, the Netherlands, Germany) in which micro and meso factors are played out.

Pettigrew came into the study of social psychology with the intention of combining both scientific work and social activism. Throughout the 1960s and 1970s, he argued for an "honest broker" approach to the study of social issues, whereby social scientists, in a two-way dialogue with policymakers, would bring research to bear on social issues through, for example, pro bono expert testimony to courts and Congress, as well as policy-relevant research. Pettigrew has provided expert testimony on the positive effects of school desegregation to municipal, state, and federal levels of government. He has conducted research and consulted directly on implementation of policies and plans for desegregated schooling. Pettigrew's work has always reflected the pulse of change in the United States for African Americans, as well as the resistance to change. He has researched, for example, white

INTERNATIONAL ENCYCLOPEDIA OF THE SOCIAL SCIENCES, 2ND EDITION attitudes to African American breakthroughs in public life at the grassroots level (e.g., the 1960s sit-in movement) and their candidacies as mayoral "firsts" in Gary, Indiana; Newark, New Jersey; Cleveland, Ohio; and Los Angeles. In his earliest books, *A Profile of the Negro American* (1964) and *Racially Separate or Together?* (1971), as well as more recent writings, Pettigrew has argued for an integrated society with data supporting its benefits in information and access for minorities.

As incoming president of the Society for the Psychological Study of Social Issues in 1967, Pettigrew pressured a reluctant American Psychological Association to provide a suitable forum for Martin Luther King Jr. (1929–1968) to address its annual convention, which King did to an overflow crowd of five thousand psychologists. Working with noted civil rights activist and scholar Kenneth B. Clark (1914–2005) on this and other civil rights projects through the latter's Metropolitan Applied Research Center (MARC), Pettigrew continued research in the public domain at a time when the majority of social psychologists were focused on micro-level analyses of individual social behavior.

Pettigrew has never retreated from debate in both the academic and the public arena, and he is one of the most articulate defenders of the need for social scientists to engage with and make explicit their values. In 1975, at the beginning of the resegregation era, James Coleman (1926–1995) published a widely publicized study showing that school desegregation resulted in "white flight" to the suburbs. Pettigrew is well known for his critique of the Coleman Report, both its flawed science and the recommendations that ensued. While "white flight" was neither universal nor as damaging as thought, it provided judges with an acceptable reason for opposing urban school desegregation, turning back the gains of the desegregation era (1930–1973) and dismissing effective metropolitan solutions.

In the late 1970s, Pettigrew challenged the claim that race was declining in its significance relative to the rising role of social class, a claim put forward by sociologist William Julius Wilson. Pettigrew drew attention to the importance of the interaction of race and class, making racial discrimination only more subtle for upper-class African Americans. Reflecting back on the fiftieth anniversary of the U.S. Supreme Court's landmark 1954 ruling in *Brown v. Board of Education*, Pettigrew argued for a rededication to efforts for preventing further resegregation in American society. By combining the best research with political and historical analyses, Pettigrew has demystified legal arguments for segregation, showing instead that separate educational facilities are inherently unequal and that intense residential segregation is a key element in the continued resistance to integrated schooling.

Pettigrew has maintained a prominent place as a scientist, teacher, public intellectual, and activist for over five decades. He has mentored numerous doctoral students, many of whom are renowned in their fields, including John Jemmott III, Howard Schuman, and Eliot Smith. He has collaborated with numerous colleagues internationally on issues of prejudice and discrimination toward immigrants in western Europe, most notably with Roel W. Meertens in the Netherlands and Ulrich Wagner in Germany. In addition, Pettigrew has held several appointments in sociology and social psychology, including appointments at Harvard University (1957–1980), the University of California, Santa Cruz (1980–1994), and the University of Amsterdam (1986–1991). He has been honored at many points in his career: as a fellow of the Center for Advanced Study in the Behavioral Sciences, Stanford University (1975–1976); with the Kurt Lewin Award of the Society for the Psychological Study of Social Issues (1987); with the Distinguished Scientist Award from the Society for Experimental Social Psychology (2002); and as a New Century Scholar, Fulbright Foreign Scholarship Board (2003). He served as president of the Society for the Psychological Study of Social Issues (1967–1968) and has been a longtime member of that organization, as well as of the American Sociological Association and the American Psychological Association.

SEE ALSO Brown v. Board of Education, *1954; Achievement Gap, Racial; Allport, Gordon; American Sociological Association; Authoritarianism; Bigotry; Clark, Kenneth B.; Ethnicity; Parsons, Talcott; Prejudice; Psychology; Race; Racism; Segregation; Social Psychology; Sociology; Stereotypes; Wilson, William Julius*

BIBLIOGRAPHY

Pettigrew, Thomas F. 1964. *A Profile of the Negro American.* New York: van Nostrand.

Pettigrew, Thomas F. 1971. *Racially Separate or Together?* New York: McGraw-Hill.

Pettigrew, Thomas F. 1993. How Events Shape Theoretical Frames: A Personal Statement. In *A History of Race Relations Research: First-generation Recollections,* ed. John H. Stanfield II, 159–178. Newbury Park, CA: Sage.

Pettigrew, Thomas F. 1997. Personality and Social Structure: Social Psychological Contributions. In *Handbook of Personality Psychology,* eds. Robert Hogan, John A. Johnson, and Stephen R. Biggs, 417–438. New York: Academic Press.

Pettigrew, Thomas F. 1998. Intergroup Contact Theory. *Annual Review of Psychology* 49: 65–85.

Pettigrew, Thomas F. 2004. Justice Deferred: A Half Century after *Brown v. Board of Education. American Psychologist* 59 (6): 521–529.

Frances Cherry

PHALANGISTS

Phalangists are members of the Lebanese Phalanges Party (Hizb Al-Kata'ib Al-Lubnaniyyah). The Phalanges Party was founded in November 1936 by pharmacist Pierre Gemayel (1905–1984) and four other Christians in the wake of a visit to Germany, where Gemayel was a member of the Lebanese delegation to the infamous 1936 Olympic Games in Berlin. Gemayel never denied his desire to replicate the youth organizations of Nazi Germany, and the name was taken from Francisco Franco's (1892–1975) Falange Española, a fascist political party. The Phalanges Party was founded as a response to the rise of "unionist" calls among Muslims and some Christian groups in Lebanon who sought the unity of Lebanon with either Syria or another Arab country as part of a larger Arab nation. *Al-Kata'ib* means "battalions," a term that underlined the military purpose of the organization. In 1943 Phalanges leaders broke with Émile Edde (1886–1949), who wanted to preserve French rule in Lebanon, supporting instead the rising tide of popular sentiment that called for immediate independence. This position gave the party national legitimacy.

The party first fielded candidates in the by-election of 1945, but failed to win parliamentary seats until 1958, when the civil war boosted the popularity of the party among Lebanese Christians. As sectarian polarization tore the country apart, the Phalanges emerged as a well-organized party with a militia. Its recruitment and propaganda techniques became more sophisticated, and the party won six parliamentary seats in the 1960 election. It emphasized the ostensible uniqueness of Lebanon and resisted the Arabization of Lebanese culture and foreign policy. A Phalanges ideologue published a manual in 1966 pledging strict dedication to traditional values: God, homeland, and family. According to the manual, the party is also dedicated to democracy, private property, and the free enterprise system, and is opposed to individualism, leftism, and communism. Membership in the party was predominantly Christian, specifically Maronite, and the leadership was tightly in the hands of its founder, Pierre Gemayel.

The Phalanges Party established the most powerful militia in Lebanon as early as the 1950s, and the party attracted followers in the 1960s and 1970s by provoking clashes with Palestine Liberation Organization (PLO) forces. The clashes increased in the late 1960s when Phalanges armed men would ambush PLO trucks and cars in Kahhalah, a strategic Phalanges city on the Damascus-Beirut highway. The party was the major fighting force of the right-wing coalition during the 1975 civil war and received aid and weapons from Israel while its enemies were receiving aid from the PLO and other Arab countries. The rise of Bashir Gemayel (1947–1982, the son of Pierre) marginalized the party, although Bashir was also a leading member of the party. The civil war had many dimensions, but one of them entailed a PLO-Phalangist conflict. Many of the episodes of the conflict, including the siege of the Tal Az-Za'tar camp (and its destruction) and the Dbayy refugee camp in 1976, were Phalangist campaigns to root out the Palestinian presence in East Beirut.

The year 1982 was a watershed in the history of the party. First, Bashir Gemayel was elected president of Lebanon, but he was assassinated before he took office. After his assassination, militias loyal to the Lebanese Forces (a collation of right-wing militias under the control of the Phalanges) entered the Sabra and Shatila refugee camps and massacred hundreds of Palestinian (and some Lebanese) civilians. Bashir's brother, Amin, became the first Phalangist to assume the presidency of the republic. In 1984 Pierre Gemayel died, and Amin insisted that Pierre's deputy, Elie Karamah, a Greek Catholic, become the permanent leader of the party. Karamah's tenure marked the ultimate marginalization of the party in Lebanese politics. In 1986 Georges Sa'adah, a Maronite, was elected to the presidency of the party, and he remained president into the 1990s, despite efforts to unseat him by his opponents and by a splinter faction headed by Karamah and supported by Amin Gemayel. The party boycotted the 1992 parliamentary election and did not win seats in the 1996 election. The Syrian government helped engineer a takeover of the party by a pro-Syrian faction headed by Karim Pakradoni, who served as a minister during the administration of Émile Lahhud. In 2005 Pakradoni all but surrendered the party to Amin Gemayel in recognition of his loss of popular support among Christian voters.

SEE ALSO *Arab-Israeli War of 1967; Elections; Genocide; Lebanese Civil War; Olympic Games; Palestine Liberation Organization (PLO); Spanish Civil War*

BIBLIOGRAPHY

Entelis, John. 1974. *Pluralism and Party Transformation in Lebanon: Al-Kata'ib, 1936–1970.* Leiden, Netherlands: Brill.

Ishtay, Shawkat. 1981. *Ash-Shuyu'iyyun wa-l-Kata'ib: Dar Al-'Amal, Tarikh Hizb Al-Kata'ib.* 2 vols. Beirut: Dar Al-'Amal.

Naji, Amin. 1966. *Falsafat Hizb Al-Kata'ib.* Beirut: Al-Kata'ib.

Shruru, Fadl. 1981. *Beruit: Dar Almasirah.*

As'ad Abu Khalil

PHARMACEUTICAL INDUSTRY

The modern pharmaceutical industry in the United States originated during the 1818 to 1822 period when less than a dozen fine chemical manufacturers constructed factories in Philadelphia. History records Robert Shoemaker, producer of glycerin, as the first large-scale manufacturer in the period from 1818 to 1840. Medicines were previously manufactured in the laboratories of pharmacies where doctors and pharmacists compounded and administered drugs to patients and observed drug reactions. The Food and Drug Administration (FDA), which originated in 1902 by an act of U.S. Congress, regulates the modern pharmaceutical industry. (The agency is also a scientific and public health agency with oversight for the safety of most food products, radiation-emitting consumer products, cosmetics, and animal feed.)

Pharmaceutical firms are engaged in the discovery, manufacturing, and marketing of legal drugs, biologics (viruses, toxins, serums, and analogous products), vaccines, and medical devices such as pacemakers and prosthetics. Products are made for both humans and animals. Pharmaceutical products, both prescription and over the counter (OTC), account for a large share of the aggregate health care spending and represent major account items in international trade transactions of developed countries.

Pharmaceuticals as a percentage of total health care spending during 2002 comprised 12.8 percent in the United States, 14.5 percent in Germany, 15.8 percent in the United Kingdom, and 22.4 percent in Italy. Pharmaceutical spending in the United States grew at an average annual rate of 11 percent between 1970 and 2005. The industry is global and led all other industries in rent-seeking activities by spending nearly $1 billion from 1998 to 2004 on lobbying. Profit-seeking firms engage in strategic lobbying, a special case of rent seeking. Rent seeking is a selfishly motivated effort of one party (pharmaceutical firms) targeted at influencing another party's (government regulators) decision. Economic agents will decide to invest in rent-seeking activities, such as lobbying, if the expected net present value of the effort is profitable at the margin. Global pharmaceutical trade grew at an average annual rate of 23 percent from 2000 to 2003 and was valued at $200 billion in 2002. More than 80 percent of pharmaceutical production and consumption occurs in North America, Western Europe, and Japan.

GENERAL CHARACTERISTICS

Several characteristics distinguish the pharmaceutical industry from other industries. A newly released pharmaceutical agent is usually available only by physician prescription. Patients in effect transfer decision-making authority on the appropriateness of medications for their ailments to the gate-keeping physicians (or pharmacists and nurses in some countries). Generally, a prescription may become available OTC (i.e., without physician prescription) for a non-chronic condition that is rel-

atively easy to self-diagnose and has low potential for harm from self-medication under conditions of widespread availability.

Another important industry characteristic is the availability of health insurance coverage for prescribed medications. Most often, private insurers or government entities subsidize retail drug purchases. Consumers make a co-payment (a fixed sum for each prescription regardless of the full price) or pay a coinsurance (a fixed percentage of the full price) that is less than the full market price. Co-payments tend to vary depending on the drug classification. Consumer payment of far less than full cost of prescriptions creates the familiar "moral hazard" (excessive use) problem.

INDUSTRY GROWTH

The Centers for Disease Control (CDC) estimated that in 2005 more than 130 million Americans got prescriptions monthly. Physicians acting as the decision maker for patients and health insurance coverage of prescriptions create a market with fairly "inelastic product demand." An inelastic product demand means that buyers' percentage change in quantity purchase decisions are relatively insensitive to a given percentage price change that brought it about. Pharmaceutical product demand elasticity estimates vary depending on many factors, including the setting (e.g., inpatient versus outpatient or military versus noninstitutional population), brands versus generics, stringency of regulatory and provider reimbursements, and the strength of the consumption habits of consumers.

Some experts predict that the rise in insurance coverage is a major culprit in the undisciplined rising consumption of prescribed drugs. Other experts contend that the growth in prescription drug use is partly a function of greater marketing efforts of the drug firms. The pharmaceutical industry in 2003 spent $3.3 billion on direct-to-consumer advertising and marketing expenditures totaled $25.3 billion. Doctors' prescribing habits are directly influenced by the probability of patient noncompliance, and advertising targeted at doctors and patients. Direct-to-consumer advertising reportedly slowed noncompliance rates. The U.S. drug firms spend a similar percentage of their sales revenue on advertising as on research and development.

The pharmaceutical industry manufactures innovative products with government-granted patent rights that may be extended after application approval from the FDA. Patents give researchers and inventors exclusive rights to market an invention for twenty years before others may duplicate and sell it. Therefore, producers of new drugs are free to limit the supply and set prices that reflect profit-maximizing mark-ups with exclusive marketing rights. Most pharmaceutical manufacturers in the United

States are multinational enterprises operating globally across countries. In 2004 the Pharmaceutical Research and Manufacturers of America (PhRMA) recorded drug sales of $159 billion within the United States and $79 billion abroad. The industry boasts investment rate of return that is four times the magnitude of the typical Fortune 500 firm. Technological progress in this industry and in the broader health care sector has led experts to project the global pharmaceutical market sales to be $842 billion in 2010.

There were more than 700 companies operating in the "pharmaceutical preparations" industry in 2006. The leading ten firms accounted for more than 40 percent of total industry sales. Other factors in this industry include retail pharmacies, health care provider institutions, and wholesalers. According to a 2000 report, the pharmaceutical industry earned 80 percent of the drug sales directly from wholesalers, 12 percent from retailers, and 4 percent from hospitals. Consumers typically buy drugs from retail pharmacies but there has recently been a rising trend in purchased drug activities via the Internet and from mail-order services within and outside the United States. Prescription drug buyers consider nontraditional purchasing outlets more convenient and private relative to traveling to a retail drugstore. Physicians may suggest Internet pharmacies to some homebound patients in order to improve compliance.

RESEARCH AND DEVELOPMENT (R&D)

In the United States new drugs must be approved by the FDA. In order to satisfy safety and benefit considerations of the FDA, pharmaceutical companies conduct on average ten to fifteen years of research on a new medication. Approval of a new drug is a rigorous process and for every 5,000 to 10,000 compounds tested, only one receives FDA approval and becomes a new or improved treatment. The entire U.S. pharmaceutical industry spent an estimated $51.3 billion on research and development in 2005. Nearly 80 percent of global R&D spending takes place in the United States and the major portion of the remaining 20 percent occurs in Europe.

The drug discovery process begins with the screening of thousands of compounds and modifying them to raise disease-fighting activity and/or minimize undesirable side effects for patients. Both laboratory and animal studies may be used to evaluate a drug's safety and efficacy during pre-clinical testing. Investigational new drugs go through a rigorous review by the FDA before moving to the clinical trials stage. Clinical trials of new medicines occur in three testing phases. Phase I includes drug tests in a small group of about 20 to 100 healthy volunteers to determine safety. During Phase II, 100 to 500 volunteer patients participate in controlled trials to determine whether the medicine effectively treats the disease. Phase III includes 1,000

to 5,000 patients taking the new drug and being monitored to confirm effectiveness and identify any side effects with comparison to patients in the placebo (inactive substance) group.

Drug development responds to the urgency and intensity of consumer demand, and economic harm, measured by disease-specific mortality, in the United States largely motivates the global distribution of drug development. The FDA approved 28 new drugs in 2005 and more than 350 medications became available for treating patients in the last decade. New medicines in development in 2006 included 682 to treat cancer, 531 to treat neurological disorders, 341 to treat infections, and 303 to treat cardiovascular disorders. One study in 2005 reported that new drugs generated 40 percent of the two-year gain in life expectancy achieved in 52 countries from 1986 to 2000.

When a company's patent rights expire, other companies can imitate the drug and produce generic brands of the medication. According to PhRMA, the generics' share of the U.S. prescription drug market was 57 percent in 2005. This share is expected to rise within the next decade as the rate of brand patent expirations increases.

ECONOMIC FEATURES

The discovery and manufacture of new drugs is a risky business without guaranteed profitability. The cost of developing one new medicine is estimated to be about $800 million (higher if genetically engineered) and on average, only three of every ten prescription medications available to treat Americans generate revenues that meet or exceed average R&D costs.

In the absence of patent protection, imitators could copy the new medication and manufacturers would lack practical incentives to invest millions of dollars on R&D of new drugs. Although patents nominally last for 20 years, the average effective patent life of prescribed medicines is only about 11.5 years due to time lost during the development and distribution of the new medicine to the market. Patent protection gives pharmaceutical manufacturers a monopoly status although generic drug makers can start preparing copies of drugs for FDA approval before patent expiration. A monopoly provides the patent owner with the sole right to manufacture the drug and determine the quantity to supply (hence the market price) according to its projected profit margin. The Treaty of Marrakech, signed in 2004 during the international trade negotiations, provided full patent protection for pharmaceutical products across industrialized nations as well as in the less-developed nations.

The pharmaceutical sector is controlled or strictly regulated by the government acting as a single buyer (payer) or a monopsony in countries with nationalized health systems (e.g., Canada, the United Kingdom). There are many end-users but they buy at government-regulated prices. Governments can regulate drug prices in a variety of ways. The most common methods of price regulation are reference pricing, formula pricing, capping or budgetary control, profit regulations and item-by-item negotiation. *Reference pricing* is a reimbursement rule where the government sets the maximum reimbursement for one drug by reference to the price of a comparable drug in the same market. Under *formula pricing*, governments use a wide criteria set, such as therapeutic novelty, to set drug prices. Capping or budgetary control would involve limiting reimbursement to the providers at a certain capitated level.

Other regulatory instruments generally target the profit margins of pharmaceutical companies and quality of manufacturing practices. For example, a 1990 law in the United States required drug manufacturers to apply on retail Medicaid prescriptions the largest discount they give any purchaser (the Medicaid drug rebate program). The U.K. government has used a rate of return regulation in which each firm negotiates with the government an allowed before-tax rate of return on its assets. Germany has used aggregate budget constraints and rollbacks. In this application, the government sets a tight overall budget and any amount above this budget would be deducted from payments to a third party (e.g., from the incomes of physicians, from the reimbursements to the drug manufacturers). These are all examples of government regulations to control drug prices and regulate excess profitability in the pharmaceutical industry.

The future pharmaceutical industry faces multi-faceted challenges that include setting and enforcing manufacturing standards; rapid patent expiration of widely used brand drugs; unregulated parallel trades (re-importation in the European context) that ignores intellectual property rights; highly fluid and unregulated Internet sales; shortage of pharmaceutical scientists; biotechnology drugs and genetically engineered products (As of 2006 the FDA had no generics approval process in place for patented biotechnology drugs whose patents are about to expire.); ineffective post-marketing surveillance; foreign manufacturing, regulatory, and pricing challenges of drugs for major diseases afflicting developing countries (e.g., AIDS and malaria); and counterfeit products.

Intellectual property abuse and counterfeiting, the fastest growing economic crime, is a $200 to $400 billion global industry. In 2006, the National Association of Boards of Pharmacy (NABP) reported that the prevalence of counterfeit medicines can range to over 10 percent of the drug supply globally. A dramatic growth of global counterfeit and piracy activities would seriously threaten the economic well-being of international pharmaceutical companies.

SEE ALSO *Drugs; Industry; Medicine*

BIBLIOGRAPHY

Armantier, Olivier, and Soiliou Daw Namoro. 2006. Prescription Drug Advertisement and Patient Compliance: A Physician Agency Approach. *Advances in Economic Analysis & Policy* 6(1). Article 5.

Civan, Abdulkadir, and Michael T. Maloney. 2006. The Determinants of Pharmaceutical Research and Development Investments. *Contributions to Economic Policy & Analysis* 5(1), Article 28.

DiMasi, Joseph A., Ronald W. Hansen, Henry G. Grabowski, and Louis Lasgna. 1991. Cost of Innovation in the Pharmaceutical Industry. *Journal of Health Economics* 10: 107–42.

Landsman, P. B., W. Yu, X. Liu, M. Teutsch, and M. L. Berger. 2005. Impact of 3-tier Pharmaceutical Benefit Design and Increased Consumer Cost-sharing on Drug Utilization. *The American Journal of Managed Care* 11(10): 621–628.

Lichtenberg, Frank R. 2005. The Impact of New Drug Launches on Longevity: Evidence from Longitudinal, Disease-Level Data from 52 Countries, 1982–2001. *International Journal of Health Care Finance and Economics* 5 (1): 47–73.

Lichtenberg, Frank R. 2006. Did CMS' Functional Equivalence Decision Result in Equitable Payments? *Journal of Pharmaceutical Finance, Economics & Policy* 15(1): 7–20.

Okunade, Albert A. 2001. Cost-output Relation, Technical Progress, and Clinical Activity Mix of U.S. Hospital Pharmacies. *Journal of Productivity Analysis* 16(2): 167–193.

Okunade, Albert A. 2001. The Impact of 1990 Medicaid Drug Rebates Policy on Access to Prescription Drugs. *Journal of Health & Social Policy* 12 (3): 33–51.

Okunade, Albert A. 2003. Are Factor Substitutions in HMO Industry Operations Cost Saving? *Southern Economic Journal* 69(4): 800–821.

Okunade, Albert A., and Chutima Suraratdecha. 2006. The Pervasiveness of Pharmaceutical Expenditure Inertia in the OECD Countries. *Social Science & Medicine* 63 (July): 225–238.

Okunade, Albert A., and Murthy Vasudeva. 2002. Technology as a "Major Driver" of Health Care Costs: A Cointegration Analysis of the Newhouse Conjecture. *Journal of Health Economics* 21(1): 147–159.

Ringel, Jeanne S., Susan D. Hosek, Ben A. Vollaard, and Sergej Mahnovski. 2001. The Elasticity of Demand for Health Care. A Review of the Literature and Its Application to the Military Health System. Prepared for the Office of the Secretary of Defense. National Defense Research Institute. RAND Health.

Seget, Steven. 2006. *Pharmaceutical Market Trends, 2006-2010: Key Market Forecasts and Growth Opportunities.* London: URCH Publishing.

Albert A. Okunade
Mustafa C. Karakus

PHASE DIAGRAMS

Phase diagrams display the characteristics of dynamical systems. They include *fixed points* (equilibrium points); *isoclines*, which subdivide the phase space into different vector forces; *trajectories*, which show particular paths of the system over time; and information on the stability/ instability properties of the dynamical system. Phase diagrams have been employed in a number of areas in the social sciences. In economics, for example, they have been used in environmental economics, growth theory, and macroeconomics—most recently in structural macroeconomics. They can be one-dimensional (called a *phase line*) or two-dimensional, involving a two-dimensional phase space. Phase diagrams can also be used to display discrete systems of difference equations or continuous systems of differential equations—although the latter is the most common.

A deterministic dynamical system has three elements: (1) a set of equations showing the direction of motion; (2) a set of parameters; and (3) a set of initial conditions. Given these elements, the trajectory of the system is defined and can be plotted in a phase diagram. To illustrate these concepts, consider the simple continuous dynamical system in Figure 1.

$\dot{x}(t)$ and $\dot{y}(t)$ define the system's motion for the variables x and y, which are a continuous function of time, t. The system has a set of parameters a, b, c, d, e, and f. The initial condition is $x(0) = x_0$ and $y(0) = y_0$. This system is *autonomous* since it does not involve time as a separate variable. A nonautonomous system, for example, might have an equation such as $\dot{x}(t) = a + bx(t) + cy(t) + he^{gt}$. This is important because the mathematical properties of dynamical systems apply largely to autonomous systems.

One of the first considerations of a dynamical system is whether it has a fixed point: an equilibrium point. A fixed point for a two-dimensional system is where $x(t) = x^*$ and $y(t) = y^*$ for all t. In other words, the system remains at this position. When systems represent economic or social systems, such fixed points identify equilibrium states: They denote a balance of forces and so remain in that position unless something exogenous, such as a shock, disturbs the system. Fixed points are identified by the conditions $\dot{x}(t) = 0$ and $\dot{y}(t) = 0$. In the example in Figure 1, therefore, the equilibrium is where $x^* = 6$ and $y^* = 9$. Because this example is linear, there is only one equilibrium point.

But far more meaning can be given to the equations in the example when they refer to economic or social systems. For example, the first equation may refer to the goods market in a macroeconomic model of the economy, and the second equation may refer to the money market. Each of these markets can be in equilibrium separately or simultaneously. The first is in equilibrium when $\dot{x}(t) = 0$ for all t, while the second is in equilibrium when $\dot{y}(t) = 0$ for all t.

Such conditions for equilibrium in each market separately identify isoclines. Isoclines represent partitions in the phase plane. Each side of the isoclines represents a disequilibrium state. More importantly, each side of the isocline represents vector forces pushing one of the variables in a particular direction. In the example in Figure 1, there are two isoclines. Along the $\dot{x}(t) = 0$ -isocline market, x is in equilibrium; along the $\dot{y}(t) = 0$ -isocline market, y is in equilibrium. The system is in total equilibrium when x and y are simultaneously in equilibrium. This must be where the two isoclines intersect. Figure 2(a) illustrates this example, and point E denotes the fixed point of the system. This figure also shows a typical phase diagram in two-dimensional space. The initial point is denoted A. The differential equations indicate the conditions by which x and y will increase or decrease over time. But exactly whether x is increasing (decreasing) or y is increasing (decreasing) will depend on the sign of $\dot{x}(t)$ and $\dot{y}(t)$ at some time t. For this reason we need to identify the vector forces in each of the quadrants.

The isoclines in this example divide the phase plane into four quadrants (areas). In each quadrant the market for x (or y) is in disequilibrium. When the market is in disequilibrium, it will change over time according to the nature of the differential equations (for continuous systems) or the difference equations (for discrete systems). The vector forces are shown by the arrows in the diagrams. They supply qualitative information about the movement of the system over time. For example, the vector forces in Figure 2(a) show that the system will move in a counterclockwise direction over time. Although the system will move between the vector forces in any quadrant, only a detailed specification of the equations can indicate whether the horizontal force or the vertical force is dominant. With autonomous systems there is only one trajectory through point A, and this is the path AE.

Consider another example illustrating a different application. Europeans discovered the Polynesian civiliza-

	Example
$\dot{x}(t) = \dfrac{dx(t)}{dt} = a + bx(t) + cy(t)$	$\dot{x}(t) = 24 - x(t) - 2y(t)$
$\dot{y}(t) = \dfrac{dy(t)}{dt} = d + ex(t) + fy(t)$	$\dot{y}(t) = 15 + 2x(t) - 3y(t)$
$x(0) = x_0$ and $y(0) = y_0$	$x(0) = 1$ and $y(0) = 1$

Figure 1

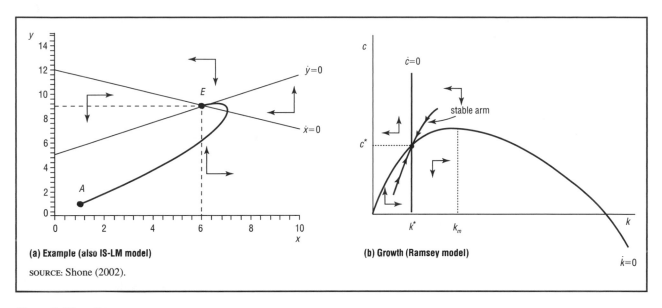

(a) Example (also IS-LM model)

SOURCE: Shone (2002).

(b) Growth (Ramsey model)

Figure 2: Phase Diagrams

tion of Easter Island in 1722 with a population of about three thousand and a set of enormous statues (*moai*). The island itself was first settled around 400 CE, when there was a large palm forest, although the island was virtually treeless in 1772. The palm was a natural resource used for a variety of purposes, and it sustained the population. However, the island's rising population, which at its height built the enormous statues, led to deforestation and, along with violent conflict, to the eventual collapse of the Easter Island civilization. Based on information about population and resources, the rise and fall of this civilization has been modeled, and is illustrated in the phase diagram in Figure 3(c) and the time profile in Figure 3(d).

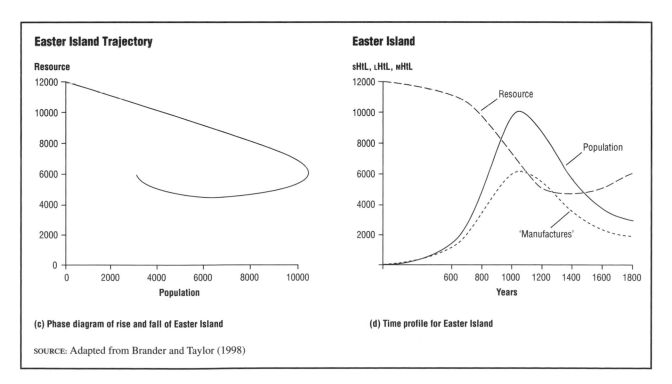

Easter Island Trajectory

(c) Phase diagram of rise and fall of Easter Island

Easter Island

(d) Time profile for Easter Island

SOURCE: Adapted from Brander and Taylor (1998)

Figure 3: Phase Diagrams

The trajectory illustrates that as the population expanded, the resource base declined, with the population reaching a peak of about ten thousand around 1400 CE. Analytically, we have a stable clockwise spiral. Sociologically, what was so particular about Easter Island? A major characteristic is that the forest involved a slow-growing palm (the Jubea palm), which grew nowhere else in Polynesia. The other Polynesian islands grew the coconut palm and the Fiji fan palm, which have a much shorter fruit-growing age—and none of these islands exhibited the same rise and fall noted on Easter Island.

A feature of dynamical social systems is asymmetric behavior. If, for example, the variable on the *x*-axis adjusts more quickly than that on the vertical axis, then the system will move in a more horizontal direction in any given quadrant. Another feature illustrated by the vector forces is the possible existence of *saddle-path* solutions. Systems can generate unstable paths except for a saddle-path, which directs the system to the equilibrium. Such saddle-paths are a particular feature of economic systems that postulate rational expectations. In example (b) of Figure 2, the saddle-path for the Ramsey growth model denotes a balanced growth path. Saddle-path solutions, however, highlight an unsatisfactory feature of such modeling. There is no reason for the system to initially be on the saddle-path, and if it is not, there needs to be some mechanism to move the system to the one and only path that will take the system to equilibrium. A third feature that dynamical systems highlight is the possibility that systems will follow orbital paths around the equilibrium, never actually moving away from or toward the equilibrium. A major consideration, therefore, of dynamical systems is whether they are stable or not. Many of the features just mentioned, however, are more likely to occur in systems that involve nonlinear isoclines, such as the Ramsey growth model.

SEE ALSO *Comparative Dynamics; Cumulative Causation; Differential Equations; Hume Process; North-South Models; Stability in Economics; Taylor, Lance*

BIBLIOGRAPHY

Azariadis, Costas. 1993. *Intertemporal Macroeconomics.* Oxford: Blackwell.

Brander, James A., and M. Scott Taylor. 1998. The Simple Economics of Easter Island: A Ricardo-Malthus Model of Renewable Resource Use. *American Economic Review* 88 (1): 119–138.

Lynch, Stephen. 2001. *Dynamical Systems with Applications Using MAPLE.* Boston: Birkhäuser.

Sandifur, James T. 1990. *Discrete Dynamical Systems: Theory and Applications.* Oxford: Clarendon.

Shone, Ronald. 2002. *Economic Dynamics: Phase Diagrams and Their Economic Application.* 2nd ed. Cambridge, U.K.: Cambridge University Press.

Taylor, Lance. 1983. *Structuralist Macroeconomics: Applicable Models for the Third World.* New York: Basic Books.

Ronald Shone

PHENOMENAL CONSCIOUSNESS

SEE *Consciousness.*

PHENOMENOLOGY

At the beginning of the twentieth century the philosopher Edmund Husserl (1859–1938) formulated phenomenology both as a philosophical perspective and as a theory of knowledge. It had a great impact on a variety of social sciences. To Husserl, reality is not given, but is constituted. It is thus apprehended in human experience and given meaning and form. Humans look upon their reality as given in a natural and unquestioned way. It is the task of the philosopher to penetrate beyond the taken-for-grantedness of the world of experience (*Lebenswelt*) through a bracketing procedure (*epoché*) in order to arrive at a deeper understanding of the essence of phenomena. For example, the phenomenologist may look at the multiple ways in which humans experience the color red and how they give meaning to it. He or she then has to "bracket" the definitions of red as phenomena or appearances of essential redness.

In his endeavor to establish the basis for an interpretative sociology, Alfred Schutz (1899–1959) critically adopted Max Weber's insistence that understanding social action was the methodological and epistemological foundation of sociology. However, understanding involved the two perspectives of the actor and observer, and the sociologist most frequently occupies the latter position. Taking Husserl's notion of the everyday world of experience characterized by the natural attitude of uncritical acceptance, Schutz accounted for social reality as one in which people cognitively suspend doubt. This is the domain of first order constructs. The sociologist, on the other hand, suspends belief in the way Husserl bracketed the world of appearances. This is the domain of second order constructs resulting from sociological reflection. Schutz laid bare the structure of the life world in terms of typifications people make in everyday life along the axes of familiarity and strangeness in space and time. On the basis of these first order constructs the sociologist embarks on the construction of ideal types through a rigorous procedure. Good examples of these ideal typifications can be found in his essays titled "The Stranger" (1944) and "The Homecomer" (1945).

Schutz laid the foundations of social constructionism for a wide range of social, cultural, and feminist studies. Widening the perspective beyond the social domain was one of the main contributions of his students, Peter Berger and Thomas Luckmann. In their seminal work *The Social Construction of Reality: A Treatise in the Sociology of Knowledge* (1966), they positioned phenomenology as a perspective rather than as an alternative paradigm in sociology. In their rendering of a sociology of knowledge from a phenomenological perspective, they demonstrate how reality as such, not just social reality, is constructed and installed as objective reality, which in turn affects society's members subjectively through processes of internalization and socialization. Other social thinkers such as George Psathas adhere to the idea of a phenomenological sociology as an alternative paradigm to functionalism.

Ethnomethodology seeks to problematize the everyday world taken for granted. Its objective is not the interpretation of first order constructs, but exploring how and by what methods people achieve and sustain a sense of order, normality, and morality in their lives. Aaron Cicourel and Harold Garfinkel pioneered this approach. Garfinkel adopted a methodological procedure akin to bracketing through his breaching experiments, during which the investigator acts as a stranger in familiar situations. Society's members' reaction to the breaching of social order and rules demonstrate their background expectations about this order and their desire to restore rule-governed situations.

The phenomenological perspective's focus on the subjective and everyday aspects of human existence proved attractive to investigators from a spectrum of inquiry including medicine, law, architectures, literature, the environment, ethnicity, gender, embodiment, history, and technology. Methodologically phenomenological investigations rely heavily on ethnographies and other qualitative measures.

With its emphasis on reality as a social construct, phenomenologically oriented social science provides fresh insights on local and global issues. Looking at race and racism, for example, it exposes racial orders, in whatever society they occur as historically constructed entities objectified as real. To society's members it demonstrates how a specific racial order appears cognitively as commonsense and legitimated as natural and how they are made to believe in its inevitability and normality. Finally it throws light on how empowered insiders construct and maintain racial hierarchies and their predominance in them by remaining racially invisible while racializing other groups and assigning them to their "proper place" in society.

Some have criticized phenomenological approaches as conservative due to their preoccupation with the mundane and commonsense aspects of life. This may be true for some studies, but phenomenology's insistence on a radical critique of knowledge resists any social structure's self-interested appropriation of social science.

SEE ALSO *Ethnomethodology*

BIBLIOGRAPHY

Berger, Peter, and Thomas Luckmann. 1972. *The Social Construction of Reality: A Treatise in the Sociology of Knowledge.* Harmondsworth, U.K.: Penguin Books.

Crowell, Steven, Lester Embree, and Samuel J. Julian, eds. 2001. *The Reach of Reflection, Issues for Phenomenology's Second Century.* Available from http://www.electronpress.com.

Garfinkel, Harold. 1967. *Studies in Ethnomethodology.* Englewood Cliffs, NJ: Prentice Hall.

Psathas, George, ed. 1973. *Phenomenological Sociology: Issues and Applications.* New York: John Wiley.

Schutz, Alfred. 1967. *The Phenomenology of the Social World.* Evanston, IL: Northwestern University Press.

Gerhard Schutte

PHENOTYPE

Variations in phenotypic characteristics skin complexion, hair texture, facial features, and stature—play a central role in racial stratification processes throughout the world. Historically, groups that are western European in physical appearance have been privileged over people of color socially, politically, and economically. Within communities of color, individuals who are more European in appearance have been accorded higher status and more opportunities than co-ethnics who are more indigenous in appearance. These overlapping systems of phenotype-based stratification are rooted in the European conquest, colonization, and enslavement of visibly different people from Africa, Asia, and Latin America beginning near the end of the fifteenth century. To justify expansion into these newly discovered lands and the subjugation of their inhabitants, Europeans established boundaries between themselves and others based on phenotype and constructed ideologies supporting their own cultural superiority. White, European appearance became equated with civilization, beauty, and competence, while indigenous appearance became equated with savagery, ugliness, and incompetence. Miscegenation resulted in a continuum of phenotypic types in these societies, and this ideological framework sometimes supported more a privileged treatment of mixed-raced subordinates. Structural and social-psychological consequences of phenotypic hierarchies are still evident to varying degrees in communities of color in the Americas and in other parts of the world.

PHENOTYPE AND STATUS ATTAINMENT

At the structural level, there is a strong link between phenotypic appearance and status attainment, which has been studied most systematically in the Americas. In the United States, where the rule of hypodescent declared that an individual with any degree of African ancestry was black, the burden of blackness has not been equally shared. It is widely held, although not uncontested, that African American slaves and free persons of color with visible white ancestry had greater access to material goods, education, and cultural capital and, consequently, emerged as social and economic elites within African American communities after emancipation in the mid-1800s. More contemporary analyses of longitudinal and cross-sectional data show that lighter skin, which is usually associated with other Eurocentric facial features, is positively correlated with education, employment, occupational prestige, and income among African Americans. Indeed, some research suggests that educational and occupational differences between the darkest and lightest African Americans are nearly equal to the differences between whites and African Americans. A study published in 2006 suggested that the advantage of light skin disappeared for African American cohorts born in the mid-1940s, but it is not clear if these analyses included adequate controls for sample attrition where African Americans with darker skin and a lower socioeconomic status may have been lost to the study due to higher mortality. Thus, the most convincing evidence to date is that phenotype continues to matter for African Americans.

The link between phenotype and socioeconomic status is also evident within the Mexican-origin population in the United States and Mexico. The conquest of Mexico by the Spaniards resulted in a caste-based society that placed light-skinned, European-looking persons at the top of the social and economic hierarchy, the darker native inhabitants of Mesoamerica at the bottom, and the mestizos or persons of mixed race in an intermediate position. As a consequence of racial intermixture during the colonial era, phenotype in the contemporary Mexican-origin population ranges on a continuum from those who appear white to those who have dark skin, indigenous facial features, and shorter height than average. In contemporary Mexico and the United States, anecdotal and rigorous empirical analyses show that Mexican-origin persons with more indigenous complexions and appearance have lower levels of educational attainment, lower occupational status, and lower incomes.

Brazil has long touted that it is a racial democracy where social, economic, and political inequalities are present but are not based on race. Unlike the United States, Brazil did not implement legal segregation, and its racial ideology encouraged racial mixing with the latter resulting in a tri-racial system consisting of whites, browns, and blacks. Yet, in spite of its "alleged" tolerance for racial differences and a fluid racial classification system, phenotypic appearance is an important determinant of Brazilian life chances. As carefully documented by Edward Telles in *Race in Another America: The Significance of Skin Color in Brazil* (2004), brown and black Brazilians are disadvantaged on all socioeconomic indicators relative to whites, and the gap between browns and blacks is quite small. He reports that even among siblings in multi-phenotypic households, those who are white are less likely to drop out of school than those who are darker. Similar to other Latin American countries, limited social mobility of mixed raced individuals blunts recognition of phenotype-based inequality. Collectively, the research on status attainment in the United States and Latin America argues that phenotypic discrimination is widespread throughout the Americas. The closer individuals of color resemble white institutional gatekeepers, the more comfortable their material lives are likely to be on average.

Interestingly, a growing mixed race population in the United States, along with other factors, suggests that the U.S. racial stratification system is moving closer to the Latin American model where an intermediate group will serve to buffer racial conflict between whites at the top and black Americans and other "symbolically" black groups positioned at the bottom of the race hierarchy. This idea is buttressed by widespread adherence to a color-blind discourse that mistakenly asserts that racism is no longer a problem in the United States. A tri-racial system does not mean the end of racism, but it does mean that phenotype is likely to become even more important in racial dynamics.

PHENOTYPE AND SOCIAL-PSYCHOLOGICAL PROCESSES

The phenotypic-based reward structure imposed by racially dominant elites has also affected social-psychological processes internal to communities of color. Phenotypic evaluations and biases are embedded in ethnic identity, complexion preferences, and concepts of beauty. Latin Americans in the United States tend to eschew black identity in favor of white identity even when their complexions are dark and their country of origin has a high proportion of Afro Latinos and Afro Latinas. Some research indicates that in countries like Brazil, great pains are taken to avoid or hide African ancestry. Thus, despite claims that racism does not exist in Latin America, it is clear that blackness and indigenous appearance are devalued. Preference for white or lighter skin is found in many communities of color. Among African Americans, there are indications that uniform preference for very light skin has diminished, but very black skin is not especially desired. Preferences for light skin have also been documented in Asian countries, in the Asian Diaspora, and among Americans of Mexican origin.

Among all people of color, phenotypic preferences disproportionately impact women because they define who is physically attractive, and expectations of attractiveness are applied more stringently to women than men. In many societies around the world, idealized beauty and femininity are constructed to incorporate white or light skin, long hair, thin bodies, and European facial features. Women whose phenotype places them at a distance from this ideal sometimes turn to cosmetic enhancements. African American women, for example, straighten their hair, wear colored contact lenses, and have attempted to become lighter by bleaching their skin. Modern skin bleaches often contain harsh chemicals that cause severe skin damage, and despite substantial health risks and attempts to ban them, bleaching products are a major problem in African countries and the West Indies. In Asian countries, women are bombarded with ads for facial creams that promise to lighten and brighten. Cosmetic surgeries, marketed under the guise of enhancing one's ethnicity, are increasing among women of color in the United States, but these procedures seem to erase rather than enhance ethnic phenotype. Women engage in these practices because attractiveness operates as a form of social capital that translates into economic rewards such as access to employment and upward mobility through marriage. In some South Asian groups light skin complexion is referenced in ads for prospective spouses, and among the Kerala of India light skin can be important in dowry negotiations. Light-skinned African American women also tend to marry more economically successful males than their darker-skinned sisters. For women, looking good counts, and looking good is heavily influenced by Eurocentric facial features and light complexion.

A CONTINUING FACTOR

Phenotypic appearance is the basis for racialized processes that privilege some groups over others and some individuals within groups. As nations become more racially and ethnically diverse and European cultural and aesthetic forms are exported around the world, it is likely that phenotype will continue to shape human interactions.

SEE ALSO *Audits for Discrimination; Blackness; Colorism; Correspondence Tests; Discrimination; Discrimination, Racial; Preference, Color; Racism; Whiteness*

BIBLIOGRAPHY

Bonilla-Silva, Eduardo. 2004. From Bi-Racial to Tri-Racial: Towards a New System of Racial Stratification. *Ethnic and Racial Studies* 27 (6): 931–950.

Goldsmith, Arthur H., Darrick Hamilton, and William Darity Jr. 2006. Shades of Discrimination: Skin Tone and Wages. *American Economic Review* 96 (2): 242–245.

Hernández, Tanya Kateri. 2001-2002. Multiracial Matrix: The Role of Race Ideology in the Enforcement of Antidiscrimination Laws, A United States-Latin America Comparison. *Cornell Law Review* 87: 1093–1176.

Herring, Cedric, Verna M. Keith, and Hayward Derrick Horton. 2004. *Skin Deep: How Race and Complexion Matter in the "Color-Blind" Era.* Chicago: University of Illinois Press.

Hill, Mark E. 2000. Color Differences in the Socioeconomic Status of African American Men: Results of a Longitudinal Study. *Social Forces* 78 (4): 1437–1460.

Hunter, Margaret L. 2005. *Race, Gender, and the Politics of Skin Tone.* New York: Routledge.

Murgia, Edward, and Edward E. Telles. 1996. Phenotype and Schooling among Mexican Americans. *Sociology of Education* 69 (4): 276–289.

Philips, Amali. 2004. Gendering Colour: Identity, Femininity, and Marriage in Kerala. *Anthropologica* 46 (2): 253–272.

Telles, Edward E. 2004. *Race in Another America: The Significance of Skin Color in Brazil.* Princeton, NJ: Princeton University Press.

Verna M. Keith

PHILANTHROPY

The word *philanthropy* derives from the Greek word *philanthrōpos*, meaning "love of mankind." In more conventional terms, it is the act of giving money to charitable causes. Although among western cultures giving has its roots in Judeo-Christian notions of tithing, or contributing to one's church, philanthropy has also been linked to capitalism.

Philanthropy has become a cultural norm in the United States. Americans give their money at a higher rate than any other country in the world. Approximately 2 percent of the U.S. gross domestic product (GDP) is given to nonprofits (Gaudiani 2003). Although corporations and foundations practice philanthropy, the real power of American giving lies with individuals. According to the Association of Fundraising Professionals (2003), individual gifts represented approximately 76 percent of the money raised by U.S. nonprofits in 2002.

Philanthropy is seen by some as a supplement to government, and by others as a way to effect change without involving government. Much of the funding for religious, artistic, educational, and health-related causes comes from philanthropic sources. In fact, many cultural, religious, and artistic organizations are almost entirely dependent on philanthropic donations. The government gives these organizations tax-exempt status in the United States. Scholars of philanthropy have identified these nonprofit organizations as the "third sector," as they are neither public nor private in nature (Payton 1991).

Throughout history there have been many critics of philanthropy. On a theoretical level, Marxists have argued that philanthropy is another aspect of capitalism that serves the interests of the rich; on an empirical one, social scientists such as C. Wright Mills showed how a small group of families control the wealth in capitalist nations, and any notion of creating social mobility through philanthropic assistance may be a mere illusion. More recently, scholars have considered race as a factor in philanthropic issues of control (Anderson 1988; Watkins 2001). In this regard there are many examples of philanthropists exerting pressure on recipients of their gifts. The oil tycoon John D. Rockefeller Sr. often tied rigid stipulations to his donations, especially those given to African American education. According to historian James D. Anderson (1988), during the late nineteenth and early twentieth centuries Rockefeller and his associates funded only vocational and manual arts education for blacks, while supporting the liberal arts for whites. Philanthropists such as the steel magnate Andrew Carnegie and Sears and Roebuck founder Julius Rosenwald followed Rockefeller's lead (Anderson 1988; Watkins 2001). In addition to their philanthropic efforts in the United States, the Carnegie, Rockefeller, and Ford foundations participated (and continue to participate) in extensive overseas initiatives, including school building in many African countries, health-related efforts in South America, and housing and agricultural programs throughout Africa, Asia, and South America. Many have questioned whether these efforts truly help the recipient nations, or merely serve the interests of U.S. foreign policy and global capitalism. On occasion, foundations have been publicly criticized for the projects that they fund both in the United States and abroad. For example, in 2003 the Jewish Telegraphic Association, a New York wire service, accused the Ford Foundation of funding organizations that supported anti-Semitic behavior. Initially, Ford denied the allegations, but the sometimes controversial foundation later learned that some of their grantees were, in fact, promoting anti-Semitic attitudes. This realization forced the foundation to make policy changes and caused discontent in the foundation world as these nonprofits worried about government interference in their grant making.

Over the course of U.S. history some have felt that the nation must choose between government-controlled and private solutions to social problems. This perspective was especially prevalent during the Roosevelt administration. Angered by Franklin D. Roosevelt's New Deal policies, many of the country's wealthy individuals refused to give because they felt the government had taken over the domain of philanthropy—a domain that they believed was rightfully theirs (Cutlip 1965). Some factions continue to hold this view today. However, most philanthropists see their gifts as a supplement to the support that government provides.

According to the conventional view, a philanthropist is a wealthy person who gives to those with less. Yet this definition tends to obscure acts of giving by middle- and lower-income people; moreover, it depicts philanthropy as primarily a white male enterprise. In response, some scholars, including Andrea Walton (2005), Emmett D. Carson (1993), Kathleen McCarty (1991), and Marybeth Gasman and Katherine Sedgwick (2005), have expanded the definition to include the giving of small monetary sums, time, and goods. Under this new definition, American philanthropists include the very wealthiest (e.g., Andrew Carnegie, George Eastman, Bill Gates, and John D. Rockefeller) and those with barely enough to make ends meet. In fact, individuals in the lowest income brackets tend to donate as much or more than their higher-waged counterparts as a percentage of their income. And in this view, minorities and women are as much philanthropists as white men. For example, a survey conducted by the *Chronicle of Philanthropy* in 2003 found that African Americans in particular give 25 percent more of their discretionary income to charity than whites (Anft and Lipman 2003).

The March of Dimes is an excellent example of the power of collective and small donors. From 1938 to 1954, 4 billion dimes, many of them collected one at a time from all sectors of the U.S. population, paved the way toward a cure for polio. Another example of vast philanthropic giving from small donors can be seen in the black churches, where parishioners, often nearly destitute themselves, donate more than 10 percent of their income. In recent times, the tragedy of September 11, 2001 spurred renewed interest in philanthropy among ordinary Americans. Besides the $2.9 billion in monetary contributions that citizens gave in the wake of the disaster, there were enormous in-kind contributions as well. For example, in the initial days after the tragedy, more than 500,000 people donated blood at American Red Cross centers across the fifty states, even after blood supplies were deemed adequate.

An innovative form of philanthropy that has emerged from the newest generation of American entrepreneurs and capitalists is venture, or "high-engagement" philanthropy. In this approach, the donor is engaged beyond providing financial support to the nonprofit organization. Venture philanthropists often require their grantees to craft, with their assistance, strategic and long-term plans, find other sources of funding, and create new partnerships. As it is a recent development, few scholars have been able to assess venture philanthropy's effectiveness and value. However, some skeptics have likened this "new" form of philanthropy to that of the turn-of-the-century industrial philanthropists—large sums of money accompanied by large amounts of interference.

BIBLIOGRAPHY

Anderson, James D. 1988. *The Education of Blacks in the South.* Chapel Hill: University of North Carolina Press.

Anft, Michael, and Harvy Lipman. 2003. How Americans Give: Chronicle Study Finds That Race Is a Powerful Influence. *Chronicle of Philanthropy*, May 1.

Association of Fundraising Professionals. 2003. http://www.afpnet.org.

Carson, Emmett D. 1993. *A Hand Up: Black Philanthropy and Self-Help in America.* Lanham, MD: University Press of America.

Cutlip, Scott. 1965. *Fund Raising in the United States: Its Role in American Philanthropy.* New Brunswick, NJ: Rutgers University Press.

Gasman, Marybeth, and Katherine V. Sedgwick, eds. 2005. *Uplifting a People: African American Philanthropy and Education.* New York: Peter Lang Publishers.

Gaudiani, Claire. 2003. *The Greater Good.* New York: Times Books.

Letts, Christine W., William Ryan, and Allen Grossman. 1997. Virtuous Capital: What Foundations Can Learn from Venture Capitalists. *Harvard Business Review* 75 (2): 36–44.

McCarty, Kathleen, ed. 1990. *Lady Bountiful Revisited: Women, Philanthropy, and Power.* New Brunswick, NJ: Rutgers University Press.

Payton, Robert. 1991. The Third Sector. *Leadership News* 9: 6–8.

Walton, Andrea, ed. 2005. *Women and Philanthropy in Education.* Bloomington: Indiana University Press.

Watkins, William. 2001. *White Architects of Black Education.* New York: Teachers College Press.

Marybeth Gasman
Noah D. Drezner

PHILISTINES
SEE *Palestinians.*

PHILLIPS, A. W. H.
1914–1975

Alban William Housego ("Bill") Phillips was born in New Zealand in 1914. Reflecting a boyhood interest in electronics, he became an electrical engineering apprentice and then wandered through Australia and Russia during the Great Depression years. He continued to study for the Institution of Electrical Engineers examinations by correspondence, and passed the examinations in 1938. During World War II (1939–1945) he served in the Royal Air Force in Asia, where he was captured and imprisoned. His experiences in the prison camp led him to study sociology at the London School of Economics after the war. One of the required units was economics, which led to an interest in macroeconomics.

Keynesian economics, which required the study of a complete system, was then coming to the fore. Phillips recognized that there were similarities between the systems studied by engineers and those by economists. Because economists were unfamiliar with systems, he recognized the utility of having a visual demonstration of the response of a miniature economic system after it was disturbed by a shock, and of how this response might be modified. Consequently, he built a hydraulic model of an idealized economy—the "Phillips machine." This was initially done for Leeds University, but improved models were later constructed for a number of universities around the globe. The machine was a great success, influencing many researchers, including Nobel Laureate James Meade (1907–1995). Today, simulations on digital computers have replaced the Phillips machine, but the ideas underlying it appeared in a number of Phillips's classic papers. These emphasized the difficulties that could arise when attempts were made to control an economic system, since economic policy actions often take a long time to have an effect upon targets. In these papers, Phillips studied the performance of an economic system when policy was envisaged as being set in a (then) novel way—according to a set of *rules*.

After this early work, Phillips's research focused upon examining relationships in the economic system and propounding methods for estimating the parameters that characterize them. His best-known paper determined a relation between inflation and the rate of unemployment that became known as the *Phillips curve*. The original curve linked the rate of wage inflation with the unemployment rate. It was transmuted into a relationship between price inflation and unemployment, particularly by Solow and Samuelson in the 1960s.

Phillips was appointed lecturer to the London School of Economics in the 1950s and rapidly rose to the position of Tooke Professor. In 1967 he moved to the Australian National University in Canberra but within a few years he suffered a stroke. Retiring to Auckland, New Zealand, he died in 1975. That Phillips's ideas have had an enduring legacy is apparent from the structure of a very popular model used for policy discussion in central banks—the *new Keynesian policy model*. Two of the three equations in its closed-economy variant are a Phillips curve and an interest-rate rule for describing how interest rates are set in response to inflation and excess demand.

SEE ALSO *Economics, Keynesian; Phillips Curve*

BIBLIOGRAPHY

Leeson, Robert. 2000. *A. W. H. Phillips: Collected Works in Contemporary Perspective.* Cambridge, U.K.: Cambridge University Press.

Phillips, A. W. H. 1954. Stabilisation Policy in a Closed Economy. *Economic Journal* 64: 290–323.

Phillips, A. W. H. 1958. The Relation between Unemployment and the Rate of Change of Money Wage Rates in the United Kingdom, 1861–1957. *Economica* 25: 283–299.

Adrian Pagan

PHILLIPS CURVE

The term *Phillips curve* originated in the work of New Zealand–born economist A. W. Phillips (1914–1975). In a 1958 article, Phillips plotted annual observations on wage change against unemployment in the United Kingdom for the 1861–1957 period, and he fitted a nonlinear curve by trial and error to the six grouped observations on wage change and unemployment (using an unusual technique, as noted by Desai [1975]). The resulting equation of $w = -0.900 + 9.638\,U^{-1.394}$, where w is the (annual) rate of change of money wages and U is the unemployment rate, displays the negative relationship between wage change and unemployment. The equation also places a floor under money-wage annual change of −0.9 percent.

The term *Phillips curve* has subsequently been used in a variety of ways and to invoke a number of mechanisms. Paul Samuelson and Robert M. Solow (1960) converted the curve into a relationship between price inflation and unemployment by deducting the presumed rate of growth of productivity from growth of wages to provide a presumed growth of prices. Later, there was an appeal to the links between output and unemployment to derive an equation linking price inflation and output (or capacity utilization or output gap).

Precursors can be found: For example, Irving Fisher's 1926 article "A Statistical Relation between Unemployment and Price Changes" was reprinted in 1973 under the heading "I Discovered the Phillips Curve." Fisher argued that "surprises" in inflation (i.e., unanticipated inflation) lead to supply responses, with the postulated positive effect of unanticipated inflation on economic activity. Anthony Thirlwall (1972) argues that

Arthur Brown (1955) has a strong claim to the discovery of an empirical relationship between wage changes and unemployment. His diagram (Brown 1955, p. 199) maps out the wage change–unemployment observations for the United Kingdom from 1880 to 1914. Even earlier, Karl Marx (1818–1883) argued that the industrial reserve army of the unemployed regulated the movement of wages.

Richard Lipsey (1960) provided a theoretical justification for the Phillips curve on the basis of a labor-market adjustment process whereby wages change in response to the level of excess demand for labor, and unemployment is viewed as a (negative) proxy for excess demand for labor. Milton Friedman argued that "Phillips' analysis of the relation between unemployment and wage change … contained a basic defect—the failure to distinguish between *nominal* and *real wages*" (1968, p. 8). This observation led to the *expectations-augmented Phillips curve*, such as $w = p^e + f(U - Un)$ (abstracting from the general trend upward of real wages), where p^e is the expected rate of inflation and Un is the "natural rate of unemployment," with the significant property that money wages would rise in line with expected inflation when $U = Un$. When unemployment was below this "natural rate," then wages would rise faster than prices, and inflation overall tends to rise. The "natural rate" was viewed as "the level that would be ground out by the Walrasian system of general equilibrium equations, provided there is embedded in them the actual structural characteristics of the labor and commodity markers, including market imperfections, stochastic variability in demands and supplies, the cost of gathering information about job vacancies and labor availabilities, the costs of mobility, and so on" (Friedman 1968, p. 8).

Edmund Phelps introduced "a sort of Phillips Curve in terms of the rate of price change, rather than wage change, that shifts one-for-one with variations in the expected rate of inflation" (1967, p. 254) with "the rate of inflation depend[ing] upon the utilization ratio and upon the expected rate of inflation" (p. 261). Using the idea that expectations were adaptive, Phelps developed the idea of a vertical long-run relationship between inflation and output, with output at the level determined by the "equilibrium utilization ratio."

Expressing the argument in terms of wage changes and unemployment, in the short-run, with a given state of expectations, there is a trade-off between wage change and unemployment. But expectations will adjust to (or even anticipate) the experience of wage inflation (and the subsequent price inflation). When expected price inflation fully incorporates wage inflation, then $p^e = p = w$, and hence $f(U - Un) = 0$: This became known as the *vertical long-run Phillips curve*. This has enormous policy implications: The economy has to operate at the "natural rate" if continuously rising or falling inflation is to be avoided. Specifically, unemployment below the "natural rate" would see escalating inflation, leading to hyperinflation.

Many of the arguments developed by Friedman were anticipated by David Champernowne. Champernowne concluded that "no period of monetary employment or of monetary unemployment is likely to last for very long. We expect there to be alternate periods of monetary employment and of monetary unemployment, so that the actual level of unemployment would oscillate above and below the level of basic unemployment" (1936, p. 206), where "basic unemployment is the amount of unemployment that there would be in that situation if each man demanded neither more nor less than his basic real wage" (p. 203). But a significant difference was that Champernowne postulated responses from the monetary authorities through interest rates as the mechanism by which actual unemployment moved to the level of "basic unemployment."

INFLATION AND THE OUTPUT GAP

The term *Phillips curve* is now widely used to signify the relationship between price inflation, expected price inflation, and the output gap, which feature heavily in the new consensus macroeconomics (e.g., Meyer 2001; Woodford 2003). The new Keynesian approach to the Phillips curve is based on price decisions being forward looking, and at the level of the individual firm price decisions depend on the expectations of prices to be charged by other firms in the future. But price decisions are staggered (following Calvo 1983), and only a proportion of firms change their price in any given period. Each firm is postulated to produce a differentiated product, and faces a constant price elasticity of demand curve for its product. In each period, a proportion of firms change price (but others do not). In each period, the probability that a firm changes price is α, which is independent of any change of price in the preceding period. The aggregate price level is then a weighted average of the lagged price level and the optimal price (derived from forward-looking profit maximization) set by those changing price. These considerations yield an equation involving prices and marginal costs: A typical form would be (from Galí and Gertler [1999], equation 3): $p_t = \lambda mc_t + \beta E_t\{p_{t+1}\}$, where mc is real marginal costs, β is the subjective discount factor, and λ depends on the frequency of price adjustments and β. Some approximations and the assumption that marginal cost is positively related with output yield an equation of the form: $p_t = \lambda \kappa x_t + \beta E_t\{p_{t+1}\}$, where κ is the output elasticity of marginal cost, and x is the output gap.

EVIDENCE

The origins of the Phillips curve were empirical rather than theoretical. Throughout its history, there have been claims and counterclaims on the extent of the empirical support for the Phillips curve, and on its disappearance and its reappearance. The initial proposition from the Phillips curve literature was a negative relationship between wage changes and unemployment. This was augmented by a proposition that the coefficient on expected price inflation was unity and there was a "natural rate of unemployment" consistent with constant inflation. Although the "natural rate" has often been treated as a constant, it can rather be seen, reflecting the quote from Friedman above, as influenced by a range of supply-side factors, but viewed as independent from the course of the level of aggregate demand or economic activity.

Although the Phillips curve as a single equation features in much theoretical literature, the empirical approach generally draws on a two (or more) equation approach involving both wage and price determination. This entry limits its discussion to the single-equation approach of a Phillips curve. The differences in the empirical results are reflected by the following. Robert Gordon (1997) considered a basic model (for the United States) in which inflation is regressed on lagged inflation, current and lagged "demand" (unemployment gap, output gap), change in productivity, in relative import price, and in relative price of food and energy (and Nixon incomes policy on/off). Gordon tried three alternative price indices. He reports that "estimated sums of coefficients on the inflation inertia variable are very close to unity, while those on the unemployment gap are always highly significant and of the correct sign. The significance of the various supply variables differs, but with two exceptions of insignificant coefficients, they all have the correct sign" (Gordon 1997, p. 24). "Taken as a group, the inclusion of the supply side variables makes a substantial difference, especially during the 1973–1981 period, which is influenced by adverse supply shocks" (p. 25). The sum of coefficients on lagged inflation is 1.01 (but 24 lags on quarterly basis) and on the unemployment gap the sum is –0.61 (current plus four lags).

In contrast, Robert Eisner separated out the effects of high and low unemployment and found "great disparities in the relations involving high and low unemployment" (1996, p. 118). For example, he found that unemployment had a negative impact on inflation when unemployment was high, but a positive effect when unemployment was low. Furthermore, the coefficients on lagged inflation were below unity when unemployment was low. Overall, Eisner concluded that "there may indeed be no stable universal relation among unemployment and all the various factors that may contribute to inflation, let alone accelerating inflation" (1996, p. 128).

For the *new Keynesian Phillips curve*, N. Gregory Mankiw argued that it "has many virtues, [but] it also has one striking vice: It is completely at odds with the facts" (2001, p. C52). In a similar vein, "attractive though the need to establish a direct inflation-output link may be, as an empirical framework for explaining inflation over the business cycle, the New Keynesian Phillips Curve … in inflation-output space has not been particularly successful" (Chadha and Nolan 2004, p. 271). Jordi Galí and Mark Gertler noted that "it is often difficult to detect a statistically significant effect of real activity on inflation using the structural formulation implied by the theory, when the measure of real activity is an output gap (i.e., real output relative to some measure of potential output). Failure to find a significant short-run link between real activity and inflation is unsettling for the basic story" (1999, p. 196; see also Galí et al. 2005).

The experience since the beginning of the 1990s, at least in the United States and the United Kingdom, could be characterized by a rather stable rate of inflation as unemployment declined substantially (at least until 2001), which some have described as akin to a horizontal (rather than a vertical) Phillips curve.

The shifts in estimates of the "natural rate of unemployment" were illustrated by Stephen Nickell (1990), who estimated the equilibrium rate of unemployment in the United Kingdom as having risen as follows (with actual rates of unemployment given in parenthesis):

1956–1959: 2.2 percent (2.24 percent)

1960–1968: 2.5 percent (2.62 percent)

1969–1973: 3.6 percent (3.39 percent)

1974–1980: 7.3 percent (5.23 percent)

1981–1987: 8.7 percent (11.11 percent)

1988–1990: 8.7 percent (7.27 percent)

Richard Layard, Nickell, and Richard Jackman (1991, p. 436) report actual and equilibrium unemployment for nineteen countries for each of three decades, and an essentially similar pattern is provided—namely, the two types of unemployment move together. Oliver Blanchard remarks that "the natural rate is at best a weak attractor" and that "the natural rate is often as much an attractee as it is an attractor" (1995, p. xiii). The "natural rate of unemployment" is seen to vary over time, but that leaves open the question of why it does so.

SEE ALSO *Friedman, Milton; Inflation; Phillips, A. W. H.; Policy, Fiscal; Policy, Monetary; Samuelson, Paul A.; Solow, Robert M.; Unemployment*

BIBLIOGRAPHY

Ball, Laurence, and N. Gregory Mankiw. 2002. The NAIRU in Theory and Practice. *Journal of Economic Perspectives* 16 (4): 115–136.

Blanchard, Oliver. 1995. In *The Natural Rate of Unemployment: Reflections on 25 Years of the Hypothesis*, ed. Rod Cross, XIII–XIV. Cambridge, U.K.: Cambridge University Press.

Brown, Arthur J. 1955. *The Great Inflation, 1939–1951*. Oxford: Oxford University Press.

Calvo, Guillermo A. 1983. Staggered Prices in a Utility Maximizing Framework. *Journal of Monetary Economics* 12: 383–398.

Chadha, Jagjit, and Charles Nolan. 2004. Output, Inflation, and the New Keynesian Phillips' Curve. *International Review of Applied Economics* 18 (3): 271–288.

Champernowne, David G. 1936. Unemployment, Basic and Monetary: The Classical Analysis and the Keynesian. *Review of Economic Studies* 3 (3): 201–216.

Desai, Meghnad. 1975. The Phillips Curve: A Revisionist Approach. *Economica* 42 (1): 1–19.

Eisner, Robert. 1996. The Retreat from Full Employment. In *Employment, Economic Growth, and the Tyranny of the Market: Essays in Honour of Paul Davidson*, vol. 2, ed. Philip Arestis, 106–130. Aldershot, U.K.: Edward Elgar.

Eisner, Robert. 1998. The Decline and Fall of the NAIRU. In *The Keynesian Revolution, Then and Now*, 454–487. Cheltenham, U.K.: Edward Elgar.

Fisher, Irving. 1926. A Statistical Relation between Unemployment and Price Changes. *International Labor Review* 13 (6): 785–792. Reprinted as "Lost and Found: I Discovered the Phillips Curve." 1973. *Journal of Political Economy* 81 (2): 496–502.

Friedman, Milton. 1968. The Role of Monetary Policy. *American Economic Review* 58 (1): 1–17.

Galí, Jordi, and Mark Gertler. 1999. Inflation Dynamics: A Structural Econometric Analysis. *Journal of Monetary Economics* 44 (2): 195–222.

Galí, Jordi, Mark Gertler, and David López-Salido. 2005. Robustness of the Estimates of the Hybrid New Keynesian Phillips Curve. *Journal of Monetary Economics* 52: 1107–1118.

Gordon, Robert. 1997. The Time-Varying NAIRU and its Implications for Economic Policy. *Journal of Economic Perspectives* 11 (1): 11–32.

Layard, Richard, Stephen Nickell, and Richard Jackman. 1991. *Unemployment: Macroeconomic Performance and the Labour Market*. Oxford: Oxford University Press.

Lipsey, Richard G. 1960. The Relation between Unemployment and the Rate of Change of Money Wage Rates in the United Kingdom, 1861–1957: A Further Analysis. *Economica* 27 (105): 1–31.

Mankiw, N. Gregory. 2001. The Inexorable and Mysterious Tradeoff between Inflation and Unemployment. *Economic Journal* 111: C45–C61.

Meyer, L. H. 2001. Does Money Matter? *Federal Reserve Bank of St. Louis Review* 83 (5): 1–15.

Nickell, Stephen. 1990. Inflation and the UK Labour Market. *Oxford Review of Economic Policy* 6 (4): 26–35.

Phelps, Edmund S. 1967. Phillips Curves, Expectations of Inflation, and Optimal Employment over Time. *Economica* 34 (3): 254–281.

Phillips, A. W. 1958. The Relation between Unemployment and the Rate of Change of Money Wages in the United Kingdom. *Economica* 25 (4): 283–289.

Samuelson, Paul, and Robert Solow. 1960. Analytical Aspects of Anti-inflation Policy. *American Economic Review* 50 (2): 177–194.

Thirlwall, Antony. 1972. The Phillips Curve: An Historical Note. *Economica* 39 (155): 325.

Woodford, Michael. 2003. *Interest and Prices: Foundations of a Theory of Monetary Policy.* Princeton, NJ: Princeton University Press.

Malcolm Sawyer

PHILOSOPHY

Philosophy is the systematic inquiry into fundamental questions about the nature of reality, knowledge, and behavior. As an academic discipline, philosophy has three central areas of inquiry and a number of other related subdisciplines that follow from these three areas. The three core areas are metaphysics, epistemology, and ethics. Other important branches of philosophy include logic, the philosophy of science, the philosophy of mind, the philosophy of language, aesthetics, political philosophy, and the philosophy of religion. Each of these areas can be further broken down into subspecialties; so for instance, the philosophy of science includes the philosophy of physics, the philosophy of biology, the philosophy of math, the philosophy of the social sciences, and so on. Furthermore, given what is generally taken to be the systematic nature of philosophical inquiry, the boundaries between the different areas of study and how each area relates to others are themselves matters of some disagreement. Is the philosophy of science to be regarded as a subdiscipline of epistemology or as a separate area of study? What is the relation of the philosophy of mind to metaphysics, on the one hand, and to the philosophy of psychology, on the other? What is the relation of political philosophy to ethics and to the philosophy of law, and should all of these areas be considered subdisciplines under a broader rubric such as value theory? Indeed, most philosophers would agree that the question "what is philosophy?" is itself a philosophical issue about which there is no one accepted answer, regardless of whether philosophy is taken as a method of inquiry, a way of understanding and living in the world, or as an academic discipline.

THE FUNDAMENTAL QUESTIONS OF PHILOSOPHY

Perhaps, then, a better way of characterizing philosophy is in terms of the fundamental questions that concern the three core areas. Metaphysics traditionally asks questions about the fundamental nature of reality. What really exists? What are the fundamental constituents of reality? Are there two (or more) fundamental and mutually irreducible substances, for instance, mind and matter? What is the nature of identity, of causation, and of time? How should we characterize the difference between persons and bodies? Metaphysical questions cross over into what might seem to be other areas of philosophy. For instance, the question of the existence of God is a metaphysical question that is at the heart of the philosophy of religion. Likewise, the metaphysical question of the relation of mind and body has traditionally been the central focus of the philosophy of mind. One might regard questions about the nature of truth as metaphysical, but the nature of truth is a central concern in both the philosophy of language and logic. The problems of freedom and determinism and the nature of freedom are generally taken to fall within metaphysics, but they have obvious and important implications for ethics, political philosophy, and the philosophy of law.

Epistemology is the study of knowledge, what it is, and how we acquire it. What can we know? What are the limits of knowledge? Can we really know anything? Or is skepticism of some variety true? If we cannot know anything, if genuine knowledge (in a particular domain or in general) is impossible for humans, then some sort of skepticism must be the case. The traditional challenge of the skeptic going back at least as far as Plato is to the assertion that we are justified in claiming to know something (in particular or in general as the case may be), the claim to have secure knowledge. So the options, in a crude and simplified way, are between having secure knowledge or skepticism. What is the difference between mere belief and knowledge? Is true belief the same as knowledge? Is there a fundamental difference between empirical knowledge and knowledge of a priori entities such as concepts and numbers? Questions about the nature of justification and justified belief, as opposed to mere opinion, also are part of epistemology.

Some questions are both epistemological and metaphysical. Such questions often have to do with the nature of perception. For example, the question of the relation of appearance to reality, that is, of how the world appears to us versus how it really is in itself, is at once both a question in epistemology (what we can know of how the world really is) and metaphysics (the nature of the real). Hovering over these epistemological concerns are questions about rationality and what it means to be, think, and act rationally. The concept of rationality might be taken to be in part epistemological and in part metaphysical, but it also is important in normative domains such as ethics and in logic.

Ethics, or moral philosophy, has three traditional questions at its core: How should one live? What is the good? What is the right? These questions have to do with, in turn, the nature of virtue, value, and duty or right action. One can approach ethics, as the Greeks typically did, by thinking about the first question: how a person should live. What is the proper or best life for a human being? What kind of person should I be? What kind of virtues or disposition of character should I attempt to cultivate in myself? Answering these questions allows one to determine what is good (what adds value to a life) and what is right (what duties one has and how one should act in certain situations).

In the modern period, philosophers have typically started with one of the other questions and moved from it to the other two concerns. One approach, consequentialism including utilitarianism, starts with a theory of the good or what has value, and then determines right action in terms of what will bring the most good into the world. Virtues are understood as those character traits that will help one best promote the good. The other major approach, often called deontology, starts with a theory of duty or right action. Certain actions are taken to be dutiful or right because of some feature they possess. The good is understood in terms of the promotion of such actions, or if there is an independent theory of the good, promoting the good is seen as subservient to doing one's duty. A third contemporary approach, virtue theory or neo-Aristotelianism, attempts to revive the approach of the Greeks and make virtue the fundamental normative concept.

These questions are all considered part of normative ethics, or the theory of how one should act. When these sorts of questions are asked of specific sorts of cases or problems, normative ethics shades into applied ethics, which includes a number of subfields such as medical ethics or bioethics, environmental ethics, and business ethics. Another important area of ethical inquiry is metaethics, or the theory of the nature of ethics. Metaethics is the inquiry into metaphysical and epistemological issues about normative ethics and the nature of moral language. Metaethical issues include questions about the nature of value and truth in ethics; epistemological issues about ethical judgments such as whether ethical assertions admit of truth, how we can come to have knowledge in ethics, and the nature of justification in ethics; and philosophy of language concerns about the nature of specifically moral language such as the moral ought and good.

The discipline of philosophy as practiced in the English-speaking world and most of Europe is primarily the tradition of the West starting with the Greeks. Non-Western traditions, including Chinese philosophy, Indian philosophy, African philosophy, and Islamic philosophy, receive some attention but remain largely on the margins of the field. In the twentieth century, a major and rather complicated division developed in European philosophy between two schools or approaches to the subject generally known as Analytic philosophy and Continental philosophy. Both approaches share the same history of the discipline, even with somewhat different readings of certain figures such as Immanuel Kant until at least Georg Wilhelm Friedrich Hegel. The Analytic tradition sees its specific roots in Gottlob Frege, Bertrand Russell, G. E. Moore, and Ludwig Wittgenstein in the early twentieth century, whereas the Continental tradition traces its origins to such figures as Franz Brentano, Edmund Husserl, Friedrich Nietzsche, and Martin Heidegger. The Continental tradition includes such philosophical subdisciplines as phenomenology, existentialism, and postmodernism. By the middle of the twentieth century the Analytic approach was dominant in Anglo-American philosophy, and the Continental approach held sway in France, Germany, and most of Western Europe.

Unlike many disciplines, in particular the natural sciences, the history of philosophy is itself an important field within philosophy. Although the history of physics might be of some interest to physicists, most would not consider it an important field of current research or inquiry within physics. Philosophers, however, regard some mastery of the history of their discipline as an essential part of current work in most areas of philosophy. More than in most other subjects, philosophers recognize that how one tells the history of the field often affects how one understands the very nature of the problems that seem of greatest contemporary interest. Discussions of the major figures in the history of Western philosophy such as Plato, Aristotle, René Descartes, David Hume, Kant, and John Stuart Mill are directly relevant to current work in ethics, epistemology, and many areas of metaphysics so much so that positions in current debates are often labeled as Kantian or Humean or Cartesian.

THE RELEVANCE OF PHILOSOPHY TO THE SOCIAL SCIENCES

Historically, the social sciences have either been offshoots of philosophy or very closely connected to philosophical discussions. In some sense the social sciences have their roots, as do the natural sciences, in Greek thought. Plato and Aristotle can lay claim to being the first political scientists and economists. Not until the modern period, however, starting with seventeenth-century figures such as Thomas Hobbes and Giambattista Vico, did the social sciences begin to emerge in their modern form. Still, it was only in the late eighteenth century and into the nineteenth century that thinking about the nature of society and social behavior began to be seen as an area of investigation separable from thinking about the deep normative issues of ethics and political philosophy. The great figures regarded as among the fathers of modern social science such as Adam Smith, Karl Marx, Émile Durkheim, Max Weber, and William James were all trained in philosophy. Only in the twentieth century, largely as a result of the influence of positivism and the specialization of the academy, did a split between the investigation of the nature of social life and processes and the traditional concerns of philosophy clearly emerge.

A subdiscipline of contemporary philosophy of particular relevance to the social sciences is the philosophy of the social sciences. A central question of this subdiscipline concerns how to situate the social sciences in relation to the other disciplines. To what degree should the social sciences on the model of the natural sciences, such as physics, be understood? Or should they rather be viewed as closer to the humanities? Or should the social sciences be regarded as different in important respects from both the natural sciences and the humanities? Part of the difficulty in answering this question is that the social sciences span a broad spectrum of types and areas of investigation, from the study of the mind and of individual behavior in different arenas of social existence such as the economic or political, to understanding alien cultures, to social and political theory on the broadest scale. Can one expect to find epistemological, metaphysical, or methodological unity across all areas of investigation that are generally regarded as social sciences?

Still, there are central questions that remain at the core of philosophical interest in the social sciences. Since the Greeks, philosophers have speculated about whether society and the institutional norms and rules that govern human life are natural or the result of convention. Thinking about this question leads naturally into questions about diverse cultures and to epistemological and methodological issues concerning how one understands alien cultures. These questions about the nature of foreign cultures and the possibility of our understanding cultures different from our own are central to anthropology and the philosophy of anthropology, a subfield of the philosophy of the social sciences.

A different, but related, epistemological issue concerns how we explain social behavior. The standard model of explanation in the natural sciences is causal explanation. This model assumes that there are lawlike generalizations in terms of which we can understand particular occurrences or phenomena. But are there comparable laws or generalizations in the social sciences, especially that hold across cultures? Many doubt that there are. Alternatively, some have tried to attempt to explain social phenomena in terms of functional explanation, where the explanation appears to be in terms of the effects brought about rather than the causes of those effects. There are, however, serious questions about the relation of causal and functional explanation. A third important position holds that neither causal nor functional explanation is appropriate in the social sciences. Rather, the goal of the social sciences is understanding in the sense of the recovery of the meaning of individual or social behavior and phenomena from the point of view of the agents themselves. This debate has traditionally been referred to as that between *Eklaren* (explanation) and *Verstehen* (understanding).

Another central debate in the philosophy of the social sciences concerns the relation of social structures, institutions, and practices on the one hand, and individual behavior and meaning on the other. Can all social phenomena be reduced to the aggregation of individual behaviors and meanings, in which case the goal of the social sciences should be to explain everything on the level of the individual? Or is the social ultimately irreducible to the level of the individual? In the latter case, the social sciences, or at least some of them, seem to occupy a conceptual space separate from the natural sciences, psychology, and the humanities. The position that holds that reduction of the social to the individual is possible and epistemologically required can be called methodological individualism. The position that resists this reduction and holds for a separate conceptual space for the social can, accordingly, be referred to as methodological holism.

One final and important issue should be mentioned: the relation of fact and value in the social sciences. The natural sciences are concerned with facts, the facts out of which the world is constructed, and regard themselves and are generally regarded as value neutral. The relation of fact and value is much more problematic in the social sciences in at least two ways. Although natural science can be used in ways that might be judged good or bad, social scientists more often seem to bring value judgments and commitments to their work, making it harder to separate purely scientific judgments from value judgments. On a more basic philosophical level, there is a question about whether the very subject matter of the social sciences can be constituted independently of values. Although some hold that all theory, regardless of whether it is in the natural or social sciences, is value-laden, those in the natural sciences have traditionally thought of themselves as concerned with a realm of fact independent of values. Whether there are social facts with anything similar to the same degree of value independence has long been and remains a much more controversial claim. The constitution of social facts may inescapably involve normative assumptions, in which case the object domain of the social sciences would be significantly different from that of the natural sciences.

SEE ALSO *Aristotle; Epistemology; Ethics; Hobbes, Thomas; Hume, David; James, William; Kant, Immanuel; Knowledge; Marx, Karl; Meaning; Meta-Analysis; Mill, John Stuart; Nietzsche, Friedrich; Philosophy of Science; Philosophy, Moral; Philosophy, Political; Plato; Positivism; Reality; Reductionism; Revolutions, Scientific; Sartre, Jean-Paul; Science; Smith, Adam; Social Science; Weber, Max*

BIBLIOGRAPHY

Audi, Robert. 2002. *Epistemology: A Contemporary Introduction to the Theory of Knowledge.* New York: Routledge.

Cutrofello, Andrew. 2005. *Continental Philosophy: A Contemporary Introduction.* New York: Routledge.

Darwall, Stephen. 1998. *Philosophical Ethics.* Boulder, CO: Westview.

Grayling, Anthony C., ed. 1995. *Philosophy: A Guide Through the Subject.* Oxford: Oxford University Press.

Grayling, Anthony C., ed. 1998. *Philosophy 2: Further Through the Subject*, Vol 2. Oxford: Oxford University Press.

Kagan, Shelly. 1997. *Normative Ethics.* Boulder, CO: Westview.

Kim, Jaegwon. 2005. *Philosophy of Mind.* Boulder, CO: Westview.

Root, Michael. 1993. *Philosophy of Social Science.* Oxford: Blackwell.

Rosenberg, Alexander. 1995. *Philosophy of Social Science.* Boulder, CO: Westview.

Stroll, Avrum. 2001. *Twentieth-Century Analytic Philosophy.* New York: Columbia University Press.

Van Inwagen, Peter. 2002. *Metaphysics.* Boulder, CO: Westview.

Lawrence H. Simon

PHILOSOPHY, MORAL

Moral philosophy is roughly the same as ethical philosophy—morals and ethics are virtually indistinguishable, *moral* being Cicero's translation of the Greek term *ethics* or *ethos,* which meant the customs and manners characteristic of a country or city-state. Typically, one distinguishes the concrete level of moral behavior and judgments from a higher theoretical level where one reflects upon this concrete level and proposes higher-order ethical principles about ethical behavior and judgment (ethical theory).

Moral philosophy is ordinarily divided into three levels: applied ethics, normative ethics, and meta-ethics. Normative ethics is primarily concerned with two questions: (1) What actions should an individual perform? and (2) what states, properties, things, and persons are (morally) good or valuable? Ordinarily, a normative ethicist will propose answers to these questions in terms of normative principles—principles specifying what one

ought to do. Applied ethics is concerned with the application of these normative principles to concrete areas such as social science ethics. Meta-ethics is concerned with the theory of normative ethics: Are ethical propositions true or false? What is the meaning of moral terms? What kind of reasoning can be advanced in support of ethical arguments? In the twentieth century meta-ethics dominated the field until midcentury, when normative theory made a gallant return. Since then all three areas have been actively pursued. The present discussion will be limited to normative ethics.

INTRODUCTION

Beginning with Socrates and Plato, philosophers have been concerned with the question of the nature of the good life and how one should attain it. It was the characteristic Greek view that an individual could reach this ultimate goal only as part of a larger social entity—the *polis*—of which he was an integral part. There was, therefore, little if any conflict between the individual's real interests and the welfare of the larger community. In short, as Plato argued in *The Republic,* it pays to be moral because an individual can be happy in life, and thus attain the ultimate state of well-being, only if the individual has the property of justice. This view was characteristically Greek, and widely shared among Greek thinkers. For example, the Stoics believed that a concern for the well-being of all human beings was developmentally built into human nature, and that even though humans begin their lives as self-centered animals, they mature to the point where they are (and should be) concerned about all humankind; this constitutes natural law theory.

Such a view was denied or undercut by Christian thinkers, who tended to separate self-interest and altruism sharply and to argue for the importance of the latter to the detriment of the former. At the same time, however, Christian thinkers such as Augustine (354–430) appropriated the ethics of Plato together with Stoicism to form the characteristic Christian view of ethics that Friedrich Nietzsche later reviled in the nineteenth century. In the thirteenth century, Thomas Aquinas appropriated the ethical views of Aristotle and wed them with the natural law tradition of the Stoics to argue that being ethical was built into human nature, where being ethical meant obeying the laws of God.

NATURAL LAW VERSUS SOCIAL CONTRACT

Historically, therefore, the key issue of ethics has concerned the self-interest of the individual (egoism) in relation to the welfare of others (altruism), with ethics pertaining primarily to actions that involve the welfare of others. A key distinction was that between natural law theory and social contract theory, which maintained that morality was conventional, not natural, and tied to the social conventions of one's larger society. Hence, being moral was not part of human nature, but rather imposed upon human nature by society.

Both of these issues—egoism versus altruism, and natural law theory versus social contract theory—emerge in clear relief in modern times in the views of Hugo Grotius (1583–1645), Samuel von Pufendorf (1632–1694), and especially Thomas Hobbes (1588–1679), the most important ethical theorist of the seventeenth century. In his immensely influential work *Leviathan* (1651), Hobbes clearly set forth an influential version of the social contract theory, in which he maintained that people originally existed in a state of nature without social laws or morals. This is a state of "all against law," unbridled egoism, in which life was "solitary, poor, nasty, brutish and short" (p. 92). People come together, Hobbes said, and agree to a social contract whereby they give up some of their liberties and rights in exchange for the security lodged in a larger system of law and order, which protects their interests. According to Hobbes, one behaves morally because of the benefits one receives from doing so; in short, because it is rational to do so. However, if one could benefit oneself by disobeying a moral convention without getting caught, it would be rationally defensible to do so. In a sense, therefore, morality is based upon rationality, and the kind of rationality present here is the economic rationality present in rational choice theory—pursuing those behavioral means that are most likely to result in the ends one desires.

Similar social contract theories can be found, in substantially different forms, in the works of John Locke, Jean-Jacques Rousseau, David Hume, and even Immanuel Kant. These are the main representatives of the social contract tradition.

The natural law theory also has its famous modern agents. Locke, who was also a representative of the social contract tradition, argued that human beings had certain "natural rights" given to them by their creator, who had hardwired these rights, as it were, into human nature. There is, Locke argued, a natural psychological law governing how human beings act, based upon their desires. It is natural for humans to strive to satisfy these desires, and it is the duty of others to allow them to pursue these interests. Locke is thus a classical liberal (like John Stuart Mill) and the inspiration for later libertarianism.

UTILITARIANISM

Hobbes said individuals behave morally out of fear of the government, but one could also argue that there are elements of human nature that support this. This was the view of David Hume and Adam Smith, who argued

against both the natural law tradition and the social contract tradition. According to Hume and Smith, humans are born with certain moral sentiments or feelings of sympathy for their fellow creatures. These feelings, a basic part of human nature, motivated individuals to care about others and to take into consideration their interests and needs. Hence, it was not rationality so much as it was emotional makeup that turned us into moral creatures.

For subsequent, post-Enlightenment thinkers, the conflict between natural law and social contract theory gave way to what is one of the major moral philosophies of modern times: utilitarianism. Although the writings of earlier individuals such as Hume contained utilitarian themes, it was Jeremy Bentham and John Stuart Mill who set forth the theory of utilitarianism: One should always act so as to produce the greatest benefit for the greatest number of individuals. This is a version of consequentialism, the view that it is the consequences of an action (or a rule governing that action) that determine its moral acceptability. As such, it has been interpreted as a commitment not to egoism, nor to altruism, but to universalism—treat everyone (including oneself) as an individual and determine the total amount of happiness to be produced by an action. Twentieth-century thinkers proposed several important modifications in this formulation, notably "rule utilitarianism," which maintains that an action is right or wrong in virtue of the good or bad consequences of the rule under which it falls.

DEONTOLOGY

In Enlightenment and post-Enlightenment thought, the philosophical debate about ethics has, until fairly recently, turned on the question of the adequacy of utilitarianism in relation to its historical rival—deontology (sometimes called "formalism"). Deontology is the view that there are fundamental human duties that are independent of their good or bad consequences; some actions are morally right or morally wrong by virtue of certain inherent properties in the actions themselves, for example, by virtue of their possessing or not possessing certain rational properties such as universalizability, reversibility, and so on. Immanuel Kant is the most famous deontologist (although in the twentieth century other individuals such as W. D. Ross championed a somewhat similar cause). Kantian ethics is concerned with advocating absolute duties (prohibitions) against lying, killing, and so on. The basis of such absolute duties derives, Kant thought, from the moral agent's rational nature pure and simple, by virtue of one's unique nature as a universal lawgiver (prescriber). There are several formulations of Kant's famous "categorical imperative": "Act as though the maxim of your action becomes by your will a universal law of nature" (2002, p. 222). and "Act in such a way that you treat humanity, whether in your own person or in any other person, always at the same time as an end, never merely as a means" (2002, pp. 229–230). Both formulations of the categorical imperative were rooted in our rational nature as autonomous agents.

VIRTUE THEORY AND RATIONAL CHOICE THEORY

The classic moral debate typically has been presented to be between utilitarianism and deontology, although recently virtue theory has become a third contender. According to virtue theory, exemplified especially by Aristotle, a morally proper action is one that flows from an internal moral virtue or good character trait of the moral agent. From the point of view of social science (especially psychology and economics), the status of moral principles has always been somewhat problematic. Assuming that such social sciences are empirical ("positive") sciences and hence concerned with ascertaining the factual nature of the social world, how can normative principles fit into such an empirical science?

According to the now-classic distinction championed by Hume and Kant and pressed even further by G. E. Moore (1873–1958), the fact-value (is-ought) distinction is a categorical one in which one can never proceed to draw an inference from a factual statement to a statement about values, or "oughts." Hence, if the social sciences are concerned exclusively with factual matters, the status of ethics in the social sciences has always remained problematic. If one is to have a unified, consistent empirical social science, committed to naturalism (in which only the natural world exists, and one can obtain knowledge only by employing the methods of the natural sciences), one might study ethical behavior empirically, describing how people actually behave or think about morality, or one might avoid ethical principles altogether (because they fall outside the realm of positive science). The latter course is problematic because the social sciences are knee-deep in value judgments and normative principles (e.g., don't fake your data, don't harm your research subjects, etc.). Furthermore, at least in the case of economics, assumptions about rationality are unavoidable: Economic behavior seems to presuppose that the economic agent is a rational one pursuing one's preferences (desires, utilities) in a rational (instrumental) way. The only possibility, therefore, would seem to be a naturalistic ethics: Produce and rationally defend a set of normative principles, but do so in a completely naturalistic way. One candidate for such a naturalistic ethics is modern contractarianism.

Rational choice theory is a descendant of utilitarianism, with a change from interpersonal preference functions to Pareto preference functions (this occurred in the early twentieth century). Contractarianism is a descendant of the social contract theory of Hobbes and has two versions: Hobbesian contractarianism and Kantian contractarianism. John Rawls (1921–2002) is the best-known Kantian contractarian (or "contractualist"), who attempts to establish a set of normative principles involving justice on the basis of what individuals would agree to in an original state of nature (the original position). However, this position begins with normativity already built in (because individuals are under "a veil of ignorance"). For many individuals, such a view is not sufficiently naturalistic. The other view is Hobbesian contractarianism, in which the goal is to derive normative principles involving justice from an original position in which nothing normative is presupposed, except the notion that the agents are rational agents attempting to maximize their utilities (preferences, desires). The main philosophical representative of this theory is David Gauthier (b. 1932), although there are social scientists who also advocate a similar position.

Beginning with the "prisoner's dilemma," Gauthier (and others inspired by this approach) attempt to show that certain kinds of prisoners' dilemmas (e.g., iterated versions) will necessarily result in cooperation, promise keeping, and justice. In short, according to this model, it is possible to show that it is rational to engage in moral behavior—understanding "rationality" in something like the standard economic sense (i.e., instrumental rationality). If such a proposal were plausible, and many doubt that it is, one would have a naturalistic ethics for the social sciences. An alternative account, one going back to Hume and Smith, would be to argue that altruism is innate in humans, that we are born with feelings of sympathy, and that such feelings are a sufficient ground to justify moral principles. There are, of course, other versions of naturalistic ethics, and many moral philosophers are skeptical of such attempts to construct a naturalistic ethics. This applies, for example, to contemporary Kantians who reject all attempts to naturalize ethics. If they are correct, then insofar as the social sciences depend upon moral principles, the social sciences would be unable to rationally ground such principles using standard social science methods and methodology. This would, once again, raise the question of the adequacy and hegemony of the social sciences—at least a certain conception of them—and thus, indirectly, of our scientific worldview. Needless to say, such an issue remains a crucial one to address in reflections upon the status of the social sciences in the twenty-first century.

SEE ALSO *Bentham, Jeremy; Economics, Classical; Enlightenment; Ethics; Hobbes, Thomas; Hume, David; Kant, Immanuel; Libertarianism; Locke, John; Maximin Principle; Mill, John Stuart; Philosophy; Plato; Prisoner's Dilemma (Economics); Prisoner's*

Dilemma (Psychology); Rawls, John; Scottish Moralists; Smith, Adam; Social Contract; State of Nature; Utilitarianism

BIBLIOGRAPHY

Aristotle. 1999. *Nichomachean Ethics*. Trans. Terence Irwin. Indianapolis, IN: Hackett.

Axelod, Robert M. 1984. *The Evolution of Cooperation*. New York: Basic Books.

Bentham, Jeremy. [1789] 1948. *An Introduction to the Theory of Morals and Legislation*. Oxford, U.K.: Basil Blackwell.

Danielson, Peter. 1992. *Artificial Morality: Virtuous Robots for Virtual Games*. London: Routledge.

Frankena, William K. 1963. *Ethics*. Englewood Cliffs, NJ: Prentice Hall.

Gauthier, David. 1986. *Morals by Agreement*. Oxford, U.K.: Clarendon.

Grotius, Hugo. [1625] 1925. *The Law of War and Peace*. Trans. Frank W. Kelsey. Oxford, U.K.: Clarendon.

Hausman, Daniel, and Michael E. McPherson. 1996. *Economic Analysis and Moral Philosophy*. New York: Cambridge University Press.

Hobbes, Thomas. [1651] 2004. *Leviathan*. New York: Barnes and Noble.

Hume, David. [1739–1740] 1978. *A Treatise on Human Nature*, ed. L. A. Selby-Bigge and P. H. Niddith. Oxford, U.K.: Clarendon.

Hume, David. [1772] 1965. The Original Contract. In *Hume's Ethical Writings*, ed. Alasdair MacIntyre, 255–273. London: Collier.

Kant, Immanuel. [1785] 2002. *Grounding for the Metaphysics of Morals*. Trans. Thomas E. Hill Jr. and Arnulf Zweig. Oxford, U.K.: Oxford University Press.

Kant, Immanuel. [1793] 1991. On the Common Saying, "This May Be True in Theory, But It Does Not Apply in Practice." *Kant's Political Writings*. Trans. H. B. Nisbet. Cambridge, U.K.: Cambridge University Press.

Locke, John. [1690] 1980. *Second Treatise on Government*, ed. C. B. Macpherson. Indianapolis, IN: Hackett.

Mill, John Stuart. [1863] 2002. *Utilitarianism*, ed. George Sher. Indianapolis, IN: Hackett.

Moore, George. 1904. *Principia Ethica*. Cambridge, U.K.: Cambridge University Press.

Nietzsche, Friedrich. [1886] 1989. *Beyond Good and Evil*. Trans. Walter Kaufmann. New York: Random House.

Plato. 2004. *The Republic*. Trans. C. D. C. Reeve. Indianapolis, IN: Hackett.

Pufendorf, Samuel. [1672] 1964. *On the Law of Nature and Nations*. Trans C. H. Oldfather and W. A. Oldfather. Oxford, U.K.: Clarendon.

Rawls, John. 1971. *A Theory of Justice*. Cambridge, MA: Harvard University Press.

Reynolds, Paul. 1982. *Ethics and Social Science Research*. Englewood Cliffs, NJ: Prentice Hall.

Rousseau, Jean-Jacques. [1762] 1950. *The Social Contract and Discourses*. Trans. G. D. H. Cole. New York: Dutton.

Schelling, Thomas C. 1960. *The Strategy of Conflict*. Cambridge, MA: Harvard University Press.

Skyrms, Brian. 1996. *Evolution of the Social Contract*. Cambridge, U.K.: Cambridge University Press.

Smith, Adam. [1759] 2002. *A Theory of Moral Sentiments*. Cambridge, U.K.: Cambridge University Press.

Ullman-Margalit, Edna. 1977. *The Emergence of Norms*. Oxford, U.K.: Clarendon.

Richard F. Kitchener

PHILOSOPHY, POLITICAL

The scholarly analysis of politics, as the realm where human beings interact and associate with each other, tends to be approached through two partly overlapping but distinct disciplines: political science and political philosophy. While political science seeks to impose order or meaning upon phenomena in the real world through observation, experimentation, and measurement, political philosophy covers more abstract and more fundamental thoughts about politics. Hence, while political science may be interested in analyzing the workings of the democratic process in a particular society (e.g., the factors that determine voter behavior in democratic elections), political philosophy takes a step back and asks second-order questions about the political concepts we use in those analyses: What is actually meant by *democracy*? What rights and duties should be bestowed on the individuals living in a democracy? And do we need political institutions such as a state, a government, or the law to ensure that these rights are upheld and the duties honored? Although infinitely more could be added, these are the questions that have proved enduringly important to human life in general and the discipline of philosophy in particular, today as much as two hundred or two thousand years ago. The student of the discipline is therefore exposed to concepts, ideas, and philosophers that often date back to Greek antiquity.

AUTHORITY, THE STATE, AND THE SOCIAL CONTRACT

Arguably, the most fundamental concern of political philosophy is the question of *political authority*. In its broadest sense, authority is the means by which one person can make others do what they would otherwise not have done. It is usefully distinguished from the related concept of *power*, in that both may be forms of control, but the latter refers to the *ability* to influence the behavior of others (through persuasion or coercion), whereas the former defines the *right* to do so (expressed through the moral duty on the part of the ruled to obey). While thus "might does not make right," the question remains when we should regard authority over us as rightfully exercised by the ruler and therefore morally justified and, crucially, what the source of that authority should be. In the view of some, notably *anarchists*, authority is always impermissible, and the only form of human association is one in which there are no persons or institutions issuing commands. Others believe in *divine authority*, whereby God's supreme might or goodness is granted, initially by God to Adam in the Garden of Eden and subsequently to God's descendants on earth who then claim unquestionable rule, for example as king over Egypt or as pope over Christendom.

The most common justification of authority, however, is the idea of the social contract as developed in various versions by philosophers such as Thomas Hobbes (1588–1679), John Locke (1632–1704), Jean-Jacques Rousseau (1712–1778), Immanuel Kant (1724–1804), and even Plato (427–347 BCE). The writings of the first three in particular had considerable impact on the creation of democratic states in the seventeenth and eighteenth centuries. Significant differences between them notwithstanding, these thinkers ask us to imagine a hypothetical "'state' of nature" before there is any political authority. Individuals are on their own, in the sense that there is no higher authority that would command their obedience or protect their interests and possessions. Since their self-interested behavior may lead to a situation of conflict between them, individuals agree to establish institutions that define and impartially enforce binding decisions on them so that their lives are preserved in a physically and economically more secure environment. They enter a voluntary agreement, the social contract, to create a state to which they hand over their power and whose laws and actions they pledge to abide by. In return, the state guarantees the protection of individuals' liberties at home and against aggression from abroad. Most democracies possess features that guarantee the legitimacy of this form of authority, such as constitutional governments, regular elections, a competitive party system, and checks and balances between the executive, legislature, and judiciary.

UTILITARIANISM, JUSTICE, AND THE INTERNATIONAL REALM

Once individuals have agreed to live in a state so depicted, the question arises as to what sorts of institutions they ought to try to bring about politically. In the nineteenth century, the British philosopher Jeremy Bentham (1748–1832) and his student John Stuart Mill (1806–

1873) established a broad consensus, commonly referred to as *utilitarianism*, according to which the yardstick in assessing political institutions is the happiness, or pleasure, of the people affected by them. On this view, all human beings are motivated by self-interest, which can be defined as the desire to avoid pain and maximize pleasure. Institutions should therefore act so as to promote the greatest happiness of the greatest number of people, which is made possible by measuring happiness in terms of its intensity and duration (and calling the resulting metric *utility*).

By virtue of its mathematical and therefore ostensibly objective approach to making moral judgments, utilitarianism succeeded in having a lasting impact upon political issues in real life, most notably the social, political, and legal reforms in nineteenth-century Britain. Yet, it also became heavily criticized for its individualistic view of human nature, which is both asocial and ahistorical, as well as its disregard for the divergent concerns, agendas, needs, powers, and wealth of individuals. What is more, the focus on utility maximization makes utilitarianism endorse acts widely considered to be unjust. To use a simplified example, it is morally wrong and a violation of human rights to harvest someone's organs, and kill one life in the process, even though in numeric terms utility is maximized because three patients could be saved by the donor's liver, heart, and lung respectively.

It took more than a century before a similarly comprehensive theoretical framework emerged as an alternative ordering principle of society. In 1971 the American philosopher John Rawls (1921–2002) published *A Theory of Justice*, in which he developed a contract-based argument of how to arrive at the principles by which members of a just society would want to distribute rights, duties, and goods amongst each other. To prevent asymmetries of power and wealth bringing about unjust contracts and principles, he asks us to imagine an "original position" where individuals exist behind a "veil of ignorance" and are deprived of any knowledge about their own particular properties, including their social status, wealth, talents, gender, and race. Free and rational agents, so he argues, would then agree to commit to two basic principles: a liberal principle according to which each person is to have an equal right to the most extensive liberty compatible with a similar liberty for others, and an egalitarian "difference principle," whereby social and economic inequalities are only justified if they are to the greatest benefit of the least advantaged. With this device, Rawls seeks to ensure that individuals are not penalized for factors over which they have no control, such as gender, race, and genetic inheritance, while still maintaining a level of inequality that provides them with sufficient incentive for economic enterprise.

The technological, social, and political developments the world saw in the second half of the twentieth century induced political philosophy to extend its thematic and geographical scope and engage with issues beyond the immediate set-up of the individual society. Not only were attempts made to transfer Rawls's conception of justice from the domestic to the international realm, but other cross-border issues began to be explored as well, such as the protection of ethnic minorities; the right of nations to wage (just) wars; secession and national self-determination; the universal applicability of human rights; as well as environmentalism and sociobiology. These topics have since come to define the research frontier of the discipline, and should continue to do so for the foreseeable future.

POSTMODERNISM AS A CHALLENGE TO THE DISCIPLINE

Political philosophy of the type described above is driven by a rigid analytical methodology, and hence it is often referred to as *analytical philosophy*. Yet, as a scholarly discourse it dominates the academic community much more in the Anglo-American sphere than in other regions. In continental Europe, for example, a school of thought called *postmodernism* holds that because society in the twentieth century is increasingly based on shared information and communication, all knowledge must be dependent on discourse and language and can by definition only be partial and local. What is more, language itself is a product of complex relations of power (on the part of the media, politicians, businesses, and other interest groups). Postmodernists such as Martin Heidegger (1889–1976), Michel Foucault (1926–1984), and Jacques Derrida (1930–2004) therefore deny that philosophy is capable of standing above such power relations. It cannot represent a moral or rational high point from which claims about knowledge, universally applicable values, and objective truths can be made. Rather, philosophy is an intrinsic part of the power relations it purports to analyze.

The postmodern disruption serves as a useful reminder to us that philosophy consists of many legitimate ethical and political positions and that the concepts employed by the discipline may not always be as neutral as they appear to be.

SEE ALSO *Arendt, Hannah; Enlightenment; Foucault, Michel; Justice; Justice, Distributive; Justice, Social; Locke, John; Philosophy, Moral; Plato; Rawls, John; Rousseau, Jean-Jacques; Smith, Adam; Social Constructionism; Social Contract; State of Nature*

BIBLIOGRAPHY

Goodin, Robert E., and Philip Pettit, eds. 1993. *A Companion to Contemporary Political Philosophy.* Malden, MA: Blackwell.

Hobbes, Thomas. [1651] 1982. *Leviathan.* London: Penguin.

Locke, John. [1689] 1986. *The Second Treatise on Civil Government.* London: Prometheus.

Plato. 1985. *The Republic.* New York: Norton.

Rawls, John. 1999. *A Theory of Justice.* Rev. ed. Cambridge, MA: Harvard University Press.

Wolff, Jonathan. 2006. *An Introduction to Political Philosophy.* 2nd ed. New York: Oxford University Press.

Dirk Haubrich

PHILOSOPHY OF SCIENCE

Everyone takes for granted scientific progress in the natural sciences, but the topic raises controversy about the social sciences. Philosophy of science attempts to answer questions like: What makes some practice scientific? Why is science so successful? Why is there unevenness in the success of science? But it also attempts to explain what these questions might mean. Because social scientists so often deal with difficult and controversial topics—the role of religion in human welfare, tolerance for cultural difference, psychological bias and stereotyping—they routinely turn to philosophy of science for guidance.

PHILOSOPHY OF SCIENCE IN THE SOCIAL SCIENCES

Three systematic theories in the philosophy of science emerged at different times in the twentieth century—*logical empiricism, scientific realism,* and *social constructivism.* Each position is designed to explain apparent scientific development or progress. Logical empiricism—in many ways the dominant outlook among methodologically reflective psychologists and social scientists in the twentieth century—states that scientific knowledge is restricted to observable phenomena, and that theories are mere instruments for generating hypotheses to be tested by observation (for the modern version, see van Fraassen 1980). Scientific Realism, as elaborated by J. J. C. Smart (1968), Hilary Putnam (1975), and Richard Boyd (1984), is the alternative view that the best scientific theories should be understood as approximately accurate descriptions of a mind-independent reality, in both its observable (empirical) and unobservable (theoretical) aspects. Social constructivism (Kuhn 1962) is the doctrine that scientific knowledge depends so deeply on theory that it is best understood as the result of a construction rather than a discovery procedure. There are also complicated hybrids of these three views, such as Arthur Fine's *natural ontological attitude* (Fine [1986] 1996).

Many social scientists accept another philosophical doctrine: *philosophical naturalism.* Naturalism is the doctrine that philosophy is methodologically and perhaps (meta)physically continuous with the natural sciences. According to this view, a philosophical doctrine about the social sciences gets tested and confirmed or disconfirmed in the same way hypotheses in the natural sciences do—by prediction and measurement.

Traditional methods in the social sciences did not emphasize prediction and measurement; the social sciences were typified by narrative methods (Martin and McIntyre 1994). Narrative methods typically describe the course of behavior by appealing to actors' intentions and construct a story of how an effect came about. Narration has been a central method in social sciences such as anthropology and history, where a chief goal is to describe the course of behavior in a particular cultural setting or epoch. The anthropological writings of Bronislaw Malinowski, such as *Coral Gardens and their Magic* (1935) or *Argonauts of the Western Pacific* (1922), and E. E. Evans-Pritchard's *Witchcraft, Oracles, and Magic Among the Azande* (1937) are prime examples of the narrative method, as are Garrett Mattingly's *Armada* (1959) and classics by Oswald Spengler (*The Decline of the West* [1928]) and Edward Gibbon (*The Decline and Fall of the Roman Empire* [1776–1788]) in history. Most of the social sciences have developed clever methods to expand the methodological power of their fields (Joseph Henrich, Richard Thaler, Steven Leavitt), but much contemporary work in anthropology, history, and the clinical arm of psychology remains in the narrative tradition. Because such appeals would be wholly inappropriate for explanations in physics, chemistry, and biology, narrative methods are unique to the social sciences.

Measurement has always played an important role in the natural sciences, from Isaac Newton's (1642–1727) laws of motion to Robert Boyle's (1627–1691) law based on the measurement of heat, pressure, and the volume of an enclosed container. The social sciences make room for another method of inquiry that uses the tools of statistical measurement. Sociology uses such techniques as causal modeling. Economics also uses causal models, as well as a wide range of regression techniques. Psychology uses experimental design and the standard array of statistical tests: analysis of variance, t-tests, multivariate analysis, and so on.

So there are some differences between the methods of inquiry in the natural and social sciences, but there is also broad agreement about such topics as the importance of measurement (Trout 1998). Other shared norms place a premium on observability and testability, however unevenly applied. Testability—at least in the experimental sense—is not a practical requirement in evolutionary theory, for example. But the testability criterion does represent an ideal. Scientific assertions, and the theories that recommend them, are testable: There is a well-established generalization in psychology that words that are more frequent in a language are identified more quickly, and in economics that markets clear, to cite just two examples.

Early philosophy of science made testability, verifiability, and falsifiability a necessary condition for scientific status—and this was a mistake. The philosophy of science has a regrettable record when it dictates the standards of science; it performs much better when it extracts lessons from reliable scientific practice. So, while it makes sense to ask what the ideal norms are in the philosophy of science, the intellectual trend runs in the opposite direction: What features of the practice of science are so successful that they deserve to be elevated to a normative standard in the philosophy of science?

METHODOLOGICAL DISPUTES IN SOCIAL INQUIRY

The logical positivists, following their interpretation of David Hume's (1711–1776) dictum that all nontautological knowledge arises from experience, attempted to formulate a way of distinguishing claims that have empirical content—and thus could be adjudicated objectively by appeal to observable evidence—from those that do not have empirical content. Fortified by the meaning-atomism of the early Rudolph Carnap (1891–1970) and Ludwig Wittgenstein (1889–1951), the logical positivists hoped to catch and identify those claims that are metaphysical, that describe conditions that are beyond experience and thus empirically meaningless. The *principle of verifiability* was formulated in a variety of ways (for the scientific rationale that was in the air at the time, see Schlick [1932–1933] 1991). But ultimately, the principle of verifiability could not accommodate the actual, epistemically reliable practices of scientists; indeed, it contradicted those practices. Scientists made patently metaphysical assertions, and no amount of "rational reconstruction" could cleanse that vocabulary. Indeed, it is now an adage that, when reliable scientific practice meets exacting philosophical principle, philosophical principle either yields or faces embarrassment. (For an excellent introductory overview of twentieth-century philosophy of science, see Godfrey-Smith 2003.)

With similar concerns about identifying and diagnosing intellectually disreputable practices, Karl Popper (1902–1994) proposed the principle of falsifiability—that the hallmark of a scientific theory is that it is falsifiable under empirical testing. Put more formally: a theory is potentially scientific if and only if there are possible observations that would falsify or refute it. According to

Popper's vision, that is what scientists do—they make conjectures and attempt to refute them.

Although Popper's proposal proved enormously influential, it turned out that neither verifiability nor falsifiability captured the practices of science. Scientists attempt to confirm and not refute their hypotheses. Moreover, their expressions are not meaningless without an experimental test to verify their hypotheses. In addition, Popper's notion of corroboration—the tendency of a hypothesis to survive repeated attempts at refutation—was too weak to capture the scientific practice of confirmation.

Thomas Kuhn (1922–1996) was a classic social constructivist. He argued that science is not progressive or even continuous, but is typified by a series of "ruptures" in the normal process of science. These ruptures, produced by scientific revolutions, make theories and the items they refer to "incommensurable," to use Kuhn's term. Scientists separated by fundamentally different theories "see different worlds."

Imre Lakatos's (1922–1974) philosophy of science deemed Kuhn's view too much of a concession to holism and relativism. Departing from Carnap's and Popper's focus on testing individual hypotheses, however, Lakatos took the entire theory as the unit of analysis. When confronted with falsifying evidence, scientists will protect the core of their favored theory from refutation by introducing auxiliary hypotheses. In response to Kuhn, Lakatos argued that a progressive (rather than stagnating) research program reflects growth, as well as findings that are novel and surprising.

LESSONS FROM PHILOSOPHY OF SCIENCE TO SOCIAL SCIENTISTS

Social scientists have long desired to extract information from catalogs of demographic data. But the reigning philosophical and social science standards in hypothesis testing had prohibited the search for correlations after the fact; all hypothesis tests have to be a priori. With new, powerful data-storing capacities, social scientists have developed sophisticated post hoc search and "data-mining" methods (Spirtes et al. 2001). These methods have allowed the social sciences to extract causal information from correlation data about important social issues, such as the efficacy of the Head Start program for low-income children.

Philosophy of science has built its theories—such as realism, empiricism, and constructivism—not just on methodological success but also on historical evidence of scientific progress. This evidence consists of case studies, often casually assembled and intuitively interpreted. But philosophers of science have been alert to the findings in the psychology of problem solving establishing the inac-

curacy of intuitive judgments. Accordingly, philosophy of science has adopted a more quantitative focus, one that replaces narratives with models, and stories about episodes with data.

Earlier antimetaphysical philosophy of science was profoundly suspicious of causal notions. But with the demise of antimetaphysical philosophy of science, the causal properties of scientific items have received close attention. Moreover, individual causal properties—like being wealthy, a Democrat, or a member of a union—can be involved in different disciplines. These causal properties produce not only unified explanations of phenomena, but also a more unified image of the world. In a roundabout way, then, contemporary philosophy of science, by focusing on causal properties generally rather than observable properties specifically, completed the unity of science program begun by the logical positivists.

The logical positivist model was one of unification by reduction, of higher-level to lower-level sciences. According to this view, sociology and economics are reducible to psychology, psychology is reducible to biology, biology to chemistry, and chemistry to physics. But the course actually taken by the social sciences has not confirmed this logical positivist account. Instead, adjacent portions of the disciplines appear to get integrated rather than assimilated, reduced, or eliminated. If anything, the social sciences have undergone a proliferation of durable specialization, a model of unification confirmed by the increasing interdisciplinary activity in these disciplines.

SEE ALSO *Revolutions, Scientific*

BIBLIOGRAPHY

Ayer, Alfred Jules. 1946. *Language, Truth, and Logic.* 2nd ed. London: Gollancz.

Boyd, Richard. 1984. On the Current Status of the Issue of Scientific Realism. *Erkenntnis* 19 (1–3): 45–90. Reprinted in Boyd, Gasper, and Trout (1991).

Boyd, Richard, Philip Gasper, and J. D. Trout, eds. 1991. *The Philosophy of Science.* Cambridge, MA: MIT Press.

Fine, Arthur. [1986] 1996. *The Shaky Game: Einstein, Realism, and the Quantum Theory.* 2nd ed. Chicago: University of Chicago Press.

Gibbon, Edward. [1776–1788] 1952. *The Decline and Fall of the Roman Empire.* Abridged ed. New York: Viking.

Godfrey-Smith, Peter. 2003. *Theory and Reality: An Introduction to the Philosophy of Science.* Chicago: University of Chicago Press.

Henrich, Joseph, Richard McElreath, Abigail Barr, et al. 2006. Costly Punishment Across Human Societies. *Science* 312: 1767–1770.

Kuhn, Thomas. S. 1962. *Structure of Scientific Revolutions.* Chicago: University of Chicago Press.

Lakatos, Imre. 1976. *Proofs and Refutations: The Logic of Mathematical Discovery.* Cambridge, U.K.: Cambridge University Press.

Leavitt, Steven, and Stephen Dubner. 2005. *Freakonomics: A Rogue Economist Explores the Hidden Side of Everything.* New York: Morrow.

Martin, Michael, and Lee McIntyre, eds. 1994. *Readings in the Philosophy of Social Science.* Cambridge, MA: MIT Press.

Mattingly, Garrett. 1959. *The Armada.* Boston: Houghton Mifflin.

Popper, Karl. 1962. *Conjectures and Refutations: The Growth of Scientific Knowledge.* New York: Basic Books.

Putnam, Hilary. 1975. Explanation and Reference. In *Philosophical Papers.* Vol. 2: *Mind, Language, and Reality,* 196–214. New York: Cambridge University Press.

Schlick, Moritz. [1932–1933] 1991. Positivism and Realism. In *The Philosophy of Science*, eds. Richard Boyd, Philip Gasper, and J. D. Trout, 37–55. Cambridge, MA: MIT Press.

Smart, J. J. C. 1968. *Between Science and Philosophy: An Introduction to the Philosophy of Science.* New York: Random House.

Spengler, Oswald. 1928. *The Decline of the West.* Vol. 2. Trans. Charles Francis Atkinson. New York: Knopf.

Spirtes, Peter, Clark Glymour, and Richard Scheines. 2001. *Causation, Prediction, and Search.* 2nd ed. Cambridge, MA: MIT Press.

Thaler, Richard. 1991. *The Winner's Curse: Paradoxes and Anomalies of Economic Life.* New York: Free Press.

Trout, J. D. 1998. *Measuring the Intentional World: Realism, Naturalism, and Quantitative Methods in the Social and Behavioral Sciences.* New York: Oxford University Press.

van Fraassen, Bas. 1980. *The Scientific Image.* Oxford: Clarendon.

J. D. Trout

PHOBIA

Phobias are morbid, irrational fear reactions to specific objects and situations. Phobias are among the most prevalent mental disorders worldwide. The term *phobia* comes from the name Phobos, the son of Aries, the Greek war god. Phobos was so fearsome-looking that enemies on the battlefield became panic-stricken when they saw him. Specific phobias are named by combining the Greek word for the object or situation with *phobia*. Thus, fear of thunder becomes *brontophobia*, and fear of closed spaces becomes *claustrophobia*. Phobias have been described for at least 2,500 years, going back to the ancient Greek physician Hippocrates (c. 460–377 BCE), the "father of medicine."

Table 1: List of Phobia Names

arachnophobia	spiders
astraphobia	lightning and stars
belonephobia	needles
catagelophobia	ridicule
ophidiophobia	snakes
ereuthophobia	blushing
kyklonasophobia	tornadoes
mysophobia	contamination
ornithophobia	birds
pediophobia	dolls
scriptophobia	writing
trichophobia	hair
xenophobia	strangers

Phobias are classified as types of anxiety disorders by the American Psychiatric Association's *Diagnostic and Statistical Manual of Mental Disorders* (*DSM*-IV-TR, 2000). The major diagnostic characteristics of a phobia are that an individual consistently reacts to some object or situation with intense fear and seeks to escape or avoid that stimulus; this fear is sufficiently strong that it interferes with the person's normal functioning. Three types of phobias are differentiated by the nature of the circumstances that precipitate the strong fear reaction: specific phobia, social phobia, and agoraphobia.

Specific phobias include fears of clearly identifiable objects or situations, such as looking down from a tall building or seeing a snake. There are four basic subtypes of specific phobia: natural environment (water, storms); animals (snakes, spiders); situations (enclosed places, bridges); and blood, injections, and injuries (dentistry). Specific phobias that do not fall into these four subtypes are classified as *other*.

Social phobia, also called *social anxiety disorder*, is defined by a persistent and intense fear reaction and avoidance of social and performance situations in which one might be embarrassed or negatively evaluated by others. Common social phobic situations include public speaking, meeting strangers or persons of the opposite sex, using public restrooms, and writing one's name in public. Social phobias typically begin in adolescence or young adulthood.

Agoraphobia, literally "fear of open spaces," is more accurately the fear of having a panic attack in a public place, such as a shopping mall or a theater, from which one might have difficulty escaping to safety. Due to this fear, agoraphobics avoid public situations and, in many cases, become totally housebound.

Phobias share many characteristics with other anxiety disorders. For example, a person with panic disorder experiences intense panic attacks that are similar to what phobics experience, except that these attacks seem to come out of nowhere and are not clearly attached to specific circumstances. The majority of agoraphobics will be diagnosed as having panic disorder with agoraphobia. *Posttraumatic stress disorder* is also similar to phobias in that following a severely traumatic experience in which people believe that they or someone else might die (such as war or rape), some people continue to react with intense fear and avoidance when reminded of the original trauma.

Although the exact details of how phobias develop are not clear, there is a broad consensus that classical or Pavlovian conditioning-like processes are involved, in which an individual experiences a strong fear reaction in the presence of a specific object or situation, forming an associative link. Subsequently, when the object is reexperienced, it triggers a panic attack. Recent theories suggest that cognitive or thinking processes contribute to some phobia development. For example, the mere observation of another person being injured or frightened can initiate a phobia. Although most phobias develop via conditioning or observation, a considerable number of phobics have no recollection of having been frightened or injured in the presence of their phobic stimulus, either directly or vicariously.

Evolutionary theory enters in as well to explain why some objects are more frequently found to be phobic stimuli than others. American psychologist Martin Seligman's theory of biological preparedness hypothesizes that due to their evolutionary significance as potential dangers, we are prone (prepared) to develop conditioned responses more readily to objects that were dangers in our evolutionary past, such as small, poisonous animals (e.g., snakes). We are less prone to develop conditioned responses to more modern but equally dangerous stimuli, such as guns.

Specific phobias are the most successfully treated of the anxiety disorders. The basic paradigm guiding most successful treatment follows from the conceptualization of the phobia's origin as a conditioning-like process. To overcome or to extinguish a conditioned fear reaction, the phobic must engage the stimulus that elicits the panic reaction. With repeated exposure to the triggering stimulus, the panic reaction diminishes progressively until it is extinguished. The engagement with the triggering stimulus can be done gradually in small increments, or the phobic can be immersed or confronted with the stimulus full-strength. When presented in small increments, an *anxiety hierarchy* can be constructed that consists of a series of graded representations of the feared stimulus. Starting at the bottom, each item is presented to the phobic, who tolerates the fear until it diminishes, after which the phobic moves up to the next item in the hierarchy. Alternately, a phobic might be immersed in the feared stimulus through a procedure called *flooding*. Here the stimulus is presented at full strength, eliciting a strong fear reaction that diminishes over time.

These exposures can be accomplished with direct, live confrontation with the feared stimulus or through a procedure in which the patient brings elements of the anxiety hierarchy to mind as mental images. In a version of this treatment, called *systematic desensitization*, patients learn deep relaxation, which helps them remain relaxed as each item of the hierarchy is imagined. With repetition, each item is progressively mastered. Although systematic desensitization was the first method found to be truly efficacious in treating phobias, it requires an average of eleven one-hour treatment sessions. Live, direct exposure to the stimulus elements extinguishes the fear reaction more quickly. Swedish psychologist Lars-Goran Öst has shown that a single five-hour session of live exposure is highly effective for treating many phobias. More recently, computer-generated stimuli presented as virtual reality have been shown to be effective for treating phobias.

In practice, several of these approaches are often combined with cognitive mechanisms that help phobics believe that they can tolerate the feared stimulus. One method, called *modeling*, is particularly effective with children. Dog-fearful children, for example, observe nonfearful children playing safely with dogs, and this exposure by observation diminishes the phobic child's fear.

Similar methods using live or imagined exposure to a feared situation are also effective for social phobia and agoraphobia. However, in contrast to specific phobias, where psychotropic drugs are generally ineffective, some medications can assist in the treatment of social and agoraphobia. A class of antianxiety drugs called *benzodiazepines* can be useful adjuncts to exposure treatments, but such drugs must be used with caution because they are addictive. Another class of medication, *selective serotonin reuptake inhibitors*, can also assist in some cases by diminishing the number of panic attacks among social phobics and agoraphobics. Although effective, the exact psychological mechanisms underlying these phobia treatments remain unclear.

SEE ALSO *Anxiety; Post-Traumatic Stress*

BIBLIOGRAPHY

American Psychiatric Association. 2000. *Diagnostic and Statistical Manual of Mental Disorders* (*DSM*-IV-TR). 4th ed., text rev. Washington, DC: Author.

Craske, Michelle G. 2003. *Origins of Phobias and Anxiety Disorders: Why More Women than Men?* London: Elsevier.

Craske, Michelle G., Martin M. Antony, and David H. Barlow. 1997. *Mastery of Your Specific Phobia.* Boulder, CO: Graywind.

Rachman, Stanley J. 1990. *Fear and Courage.* 2nd ed. New York: Freeman.

Ronald A. Kleinknecht

PHOTOGRAPHY AND PAINTING

SEE *Visual Arts.*

PHYSICAL ANTHROPOLOGY

SEE *Anthropology, Biological.*

PHYSICAL CAPITAL

Capital is a contested concept and thus its components are contested. *Physical capital* generally refers to plant and equipment, while *financial capital* refers to money. The first is a matter of physics and biology. The latter is an understanding among people allocating opportunities—an institution. Financial capital is part of the social system controlling the physics of production and the distribution of income. Physical capital is a produced good used in further production—not used up when a consumer good is made. But, the relevant time period needs definition. Stocks of raw materials and inventory of finished goods are usually referred to as circulating capital. Capital has a beneficent connotation in modern societies and thus many adjectives are added to capital, such as *social* capital, *cultural* capital, and *human* capital.

Some aggregative measure of physical capital is necessary if one is to relate its quantity to cross-country or time series differences in physical output (economic growth). But there is no way to measure a collection of physical things that differ in quality. How is one to add up a computer and a blast furnace and the change in their capacity over time? This presents an index number problem. At first glance, it appears that capital might be aggregated in terms of money invested. But a unit of money invested in the past may buy a quite different machine today. There are no convenient or unambiguous units of technology. Counting the number of scientists or patents or putting an increasing weight on investment over time only hints at changing technology. If physical capital is measured by its value today, the aggregate is influenced by the rate of profit and interest, making the measure circular. The quantity of capital would be sensitive to the business cycle and capacity utilization. In short, the money value of plant and equipment cannot be used as a proxy for the amount of physical things used in production. If capital cannot be measured unambiguously, it is impossible to determine its marginal value product and use it to justify factor shares.

Alternative capital theories and definitions are part of the history of legitimating distribution. The payment of interest was justified to motivate waiting by owners of financial assets. If the rate of interest reflected the marginal value product of capital, it could justify the income of capitalists. But the argument becomes circular if the value of capital stock is influenced by income distribution. The value of capital cannot be ascertained independently of the rate of interest.

Harrod-Domar models of growth held the ratio of financial capital to labor constant, in spite of empirical contradiction. It would be useful if investments could be ranked according to the marginal product of capital. The so-called Cambridge capital theory controversy arose over another long-held notion that a falling rate of profit would lead to more capital intensive techniques. However, it was noted that a technique profitable at one rate of interest might not be at another and may then become profitable again at still higher rates. This *reswitching* phenomena upset the conception of a unique equilibrium. The conceptual problem turns on the fact that capital is not homogeneous. It is questionable to claim that the rate of profit equals the marginal value product of financial capital.

Harrod-Domar models led to policy recommendations emphasizing saving as the means to economic growth. Poor countries were encouraged to save more. When it was clear that it was hard for the poor to save, development aid took the form of loans and capital grants. Growth then depended on exogenous inputs. The results were uneven and many countries had little growth, but huge debts. Modern growth theory has shifted attention to endogenous factors such as research and development—changing the quality of physical capital and preventing diminishing returns. New growth theory suggests that less-than-perfect competition and the promise of extraordinary profits may be necessary to entice innovation. The empirical record is mixed. The "Asian Tigers" had high savings rates, but little research and development of their own. The United States has high growth, but saves little. In rich countries such as the United States, the asserted relationship between the rate of profit and physical capital formation is used to justify tax breaks for the wealthy, even though the higher profit may be used to acquire other financial assets rather than build new plant and equipment.

Increasing the volume of financial capital transferred to poor countries may not increase growth if it is used for consumption (or fraudulently stolen by the elite) rather than investment. And, even if it is invested, it may not be invested in the most advantageous physical projects and sectors, or it may be poorly managed. Modern technology may be in place, but inputs may not be available in a timely fashion. The picture is complicated by the fact that some sources of growth, such as computers, are not capital intensive, while such things as petrochemicals and power-generation plants are. Both physical labor and physical capital have problems of aggregation because of different qualities. An hour of work from illiterate laborers is not the same as an hour from skilled workers. This led to the conceptualization of human capital. But, again, readily available measures of years of education beg many qualitative problems, as was the case for technology over time. Even land (natural resources) is difficult to aggregate because of differences in quality and kind. The ecological system can degrade without a production or financial impact in the short run.

The coordination of physical inputs to production and its distribution is a matter of institutions affecting learning and incentives. In short, the distribution of income is not some natural result of supply and demand, but of the distribution of power. It would be convenient for growth accounting and legitimation of income distribution if it were easy to clearly relate increments of physical and financial capital to increments of growth, but alas this problem has not been solved. Confusion arises when financial and physical capital inputs are mixed together in empirical studies.

SEE ALSO *Cambridge Capital Controversy; Capital; Cultural Capital; Human Capital; Natural Resources, Nonrenewable; Social Capital*

BIBLIOGRAPHY

Cohen, Avi J., and G. C. Harcourt. 2003. Whatever Happened to the Cambridge Capital Theory Controversies? *Journal of Economic Perspectives* 17 (1): 199–214.

Easterly, William. 2001. *The Elusive Quest for Growth: Economists' Adventures and Misadventures in the Tropics.* Cambridge, MA: MIT Press.

Keen, Steve. 2001. The Holy War over Capital. In *Debunking Economics: The Naked Emperor of the Social Sciences,* 129–147. New York: St. Martin's Press.

Romer, Paul. 1994. The Origins of Endogenous Growth. *Journal of Economic Perspectives* 8 (1): 3–22.

A. Allan Schmid

PHYSICAL QUALITY OF LIFE INDEX

Rapid economic growth raised average living standards in many countries around the globe in the 1960s and the early 1970s, but inequality also emerged as an issue. Prosperity bypassed large segments of the population, especially in developing countries, which stimulated a search for meaningful measures of poverty that were readily calculable. Some people saw progress in the segments of the population that lacked essential human needs, such as clean water, basic medical care, suitable housing, and adequate calories. Although interesting and useful, this approach also required considerable survey evidence, which was expensive and often unreliable.

At the behest of the Overseas Development Council, Morris David Morris created the physical quality of life index (PQLI), which assessed conditions in a country from its infant mortality rate, adult literacy rate, and life expectancy at age one (Morris 1979). Nearly all countries routinely reported these data by the 1970s.

The technique first scales each ingredient from 0 to 100, with the end points set to capture the range of historical experience. The infant mortality rate extends from a high of 229 to a low of 7 per thousand (a span of 222); life expectancy at age 1 from a low of 38 to a high of 77 years (a span of 39); and the literacy rate from 0 to 100 (a span of 100). For example, the index value of life expectancy = (100) (life expectancy − 38)/39, which means that an increase in life expectancy of 0.39 years raises the index value by 1 point. Then the indexes of the components are averaged to obtain the overall PQLI.

In principle one could use the PQLI in much the same way as any measure of human welfare, including policy design and assessment, or as a phenomenon to be explained by economic or social models. Econometric work, however, has been limited, in part because imitators and successors have crowded the field. Although the PQLI was designed as a minimal measure of social performance and partly as an antidote to undue emphasis on gross national product (GNP) per capita, its critics have noted that health is counted twice (infant mortality and life expectancy at age one are highly correlated) and that the index omits the material side of the quality of life. Soon other indexes appeared, some with more than 40 components or indicators, including crime, pollution, and suicide rates. Among these, the Human Development Index (HDI) of the United Nations has been the most widely discussed and applied. Created by the economist Mahbub ul Haq in 1990, this index was designed to register the "expansion of choice" provided by good health, knowledge, and access to material goods (United Nations Development Programme 1990). It soon was criticized for lack of attention to inequality and for incorporating a poor measure of knowledge. Thus researchers continue to debate the components of quality of life indexes and the weights that should be given to each. What is suitable, however, depends heavily on how the index will be used.

SEE ALSO *Education, USA; Inequality, Income; Morbidity and Mortality; Welfare Analysis; Welfare Economics*

BIBLIOGRAPHY

Morris, David Morris. 1979. *Measuring the Condition of the World's Poor: The Physical Quality of Life Index.* New York: Pergamon.

United Nations Development Programme. 1990. *Human Development Report.* New York: United Nations.

Richard H. Steckel

PHYSIOCRACY

The term *physiocracy* means law or rule of nature. It derives from a collection of essays by François Quesnay edited by Pierre Samuel du Pont de Nemours and published in two volumes in 1767–1768 in which the name *Physiocratie* figures prominently. Quesnay was the uncrowned leader of what was perhaps the first school of thought in economics. The school was highly influential on economic policy matters in France in the period from 1756 to the beginning of the 1770s during the reign of Louis XV. Even more important, it had a decisive impact on the emerging new scientific field of political economy. The school's relatively small number of followers and their strict adherence to the teachings of Quesnay are presumably responsible for the school also being known as a "sect." The school's major members, apart from those already mentioned, were Abbé Nicolas Baudeau, Victor Riqueti, Marquis de Mirabeau, Le Mercier de la Rivière, and François Guillaume Le Trosne. On the natural law underpinnings of physiocratic thought, see Hanz Rieter (1983).

On the physiocrats' recommendation, in 1763 and 1764 the corn trade, both domestically and abroad, was liberalized in France. The second half of the 1760s saw substantial increases in the corn price, which the public took to have been caused by the liberalization policy. However, there is reason to think that the price increase was the result not so much of grain exports as a series of bad harvests. The experiment was terminated in 1770, and since its failure was blamed on the physiocrats, it comes as no surprise that their influence declined as quickly as it had risen (Weulersse 1910; Hecht 1958). In other countries the ideas of Quesnay and his followers remained important, at least for a while, including especially Germany and Russia.

Quesnay, a surgeon and medical doctor of the king and of Madame de Pompadour, the king's favorite, came to economics rather late. In 1756 and 1757, in his early sixties, he published entries on *Fermiers* (tenant farmers) and *Grains* (corn) for the *Encyclopédie* edited by Denis Diderot and Jean d'Alembert. Yet his most important contribution to economics was the *Tableau économique.* Its first version, in 1758, was difficult to understand because of a confusing table with three columns and numerous zigzag lines joining them. Two further editions came out in 1759 (Quesnay 1972). In 1766 came the publication of a substantially revised and improved version of the *Tableau* in a work titled *Analyse de la formule arithmétique du Tableau économique de la distribution des dépenses annuelles d'une Nation agricole.* This latter version of the *Tableau* is the best known (Institut National d'Études Démographiques 1958; Quesnay 1972). It contains the first attempt to describe the intertwined processes of the production, distribution, exchange, and disposal of the riches of a nation in terms of a scheme with two large sectors of the economy—primary production and manufacture—and three social classes—the propertied class (landlords), the "productive class" (farmers), and the "sterile class" (artisans). The economy under consideration is supposed to generate a *surplus* of commodities over and above what is used up in production in terms of raw materials, tools, and means of subsistence or *produit net.* However, the surplus concerns only products of the primary sector of the economy, which explains why the people employed there are called "productive."

The idea at hand may be illustrated in the following way. To produce 1,000 bushels of corn, farmers need 200 bushels for seed, 200 bushels to support themselves and agricultural workers, 100 bushels to feed animals (horses, oxen), and 200 bushels as payment for plows bought from the manufacturing sector. The remaining 300 bushels constitute the net product. Its value in money will be paid as rent to the proprietors of the land (king, nobility, church) for the lease of their lands. The proprietors in turn will buy with money worth 150 bushels precisely that amount of corn from the productive class, and with the remaining money-rent worth another 150 bushels they will buy goods from the sterile class. The sterile class in turn will use the money to buy raw materials and means of subsistence for its artisans worth 150 bushels and transform them into manufactured goods and luxuries sold to the propertied class. The manufacturing sector is "sterile" because, while it uses part of the net product of the agricultural sector and transforms it into some other goods, it does not add to the (value of the) net product (Meek 1962; Pressman 1994).

An important aspect to be stressed is that while only the wealthy proprietors of land get the net product, their revenue is the only source from which the public administration, the army, investments in infrastructure, improvements in the conditions of production in agriculture, and the like are financed. This is secured by levying a tax—an *impôt unique*—on the propertied classes, thus relieving the tenant farmers from burden.

The *Tableau* has frequently been interpreted as involving an analogy to William Harvey's (1578-1657) scheme of blood circulation. However, as Rieter (1990) has shown, there is reason to suppose that it involves an analogy with the mechanics of a particular type of clock.

The *Tableau* contains the first description of an economic system in a state of "simple reproduction," to use Karl Marx's concept, or more precisely, of a large kingdom in a state with the highest level of agriculture. Year after year the economy could continue to reproduce itself at the same level, without expansion or contraction, provided there is neither technical progress nor regress and the agricultural and manufacturing products exchange for one another in the market as implied by the *Tableau*. In fact Quesnay assumed that the "fundamental price" of a product, a concept that anticipates Adam Smith's concept of "natural price," covers all physical real costs of production (materials used up, means of subsistence in the support of labourers) and reflects in addition the rule according to which the social surplus product is distributed among different claimants (Vaggi 1987, 1998). The *Tableau*, however, was only a first step in the physiocrats' analysis. Concerned with first identifying and then putting to use the potential for growth of the French economy among competing nation states, the physiocrats embarked on an analysis of capital accumulation, the modernization of French agriculture, and more generally the role of technical, organizational, and educational innovations. Hence with the inception of systematic economic thought at the time of the transition from feudalism to capitalism in France, the problem of the dynamism of the economic system immediately made an appearance. The physiocrats opted especially in favor of productivity-enhancing measures in agriculture and against sterile luxury consumption. Therefore the *Tableau* contained not only an ex-post analysis (national income accounting, input-output) and ex-ante analysis (circular flow and a much disputed discussion of development and growth) but also a manual for economic and social policy; see especially Quesnay's thirty "maximes générales du gouvernement d'un Royaume agricole" (Du Pont de Nemours, vol. 1, pp. 99ff.).

The physiocrats were criticized by, among others, Achille-Nicolas Isnard (1781), who argued that the impression they generated that only agriculture was productive was closely related to the system of prices underlying their schema. These prices were such that the entire net product was indeed appropriated by the landowners. Other rules of distribution would immediately reveal the peculiarity of the physiocratic doctrine and the untenability of its proponents' concept of productivity. Smith was full of praise for Quesnay and his disciples and for a while tinkered with the idea of dedicating *The Wealth of Nations* (1776) to Quesnay. However, he too found the particular form of the physiocratic concept of productivity difficult to sustain and explicitly reckoned manufactures to those industries in which "productive" labor is performed. "Unproductive" labor is now essentially identified with services that generate products that cannot be accumulated. Marx considered the physiocrats "the true fathers of modern political economy" (Marx 1963, p. 44) and dubbed the *Tableau* "an extremely brilliant conception" (Marx 1956, p. 344). He developed his own schemes of simple and extended reproduction taking it as a starting point (Gehrke and Kurz 1995). Wassily Leontief (1941) saw his own input-output analysis as following in the direct lineage of the *Tableau*. For an attempt to locate the *Tableau* in the prehistory of input-output analysis, see Heinz D. Kurz and Neri Salvadori (2000). Piero Sraffa (1960) saw his return to the classical viewpoint in the theory of value and distribution as rooted in the *Tableau*.

SEE ALSO *Input-Output Matrix; Laissez-faire; Leontief, Wassily; Liberalization, Trade; Marx, Karl; Quesnay, Francois; Smith, Adam; Surplus*

BIBLIOGRAPHY

Du Pont de Nemours, Pierre Samuel, ed. 1767–1768. *Physiocratie*. 2 parts. Part 2, 1767: *Discussions et Développmens sur quelques-unes Des Notions de L'Économie Politique. Pour servir de seconde Partie au Recueil intitulé: Physiocratie* [Discussions and Developments of Several Ideas in Political Economy. To Serve as the Second Part of the Collection Titled: Physiocracy]. Part 1, 1768: *Physiocratie, ou Constitution naturelle du gouvernement le plus avantageux au genre humain* [Physiocracy or the Natural Constitution of Government Being the Most Advantageous for Mankind]. Leyden and Paris: Merlin.

Gehrke, Christian, and Heinz D. Kurz. 1995. Karl Marx on Physiocracy. *European Journal of the History of Economic Thought* 2 (1): 53–90.

Hecht, Jacqueline. 1958. *La vie de François Quesnay*. Paris: Institut National d'Études Démographiques (INED).

Institut National d'Études Démographiques. 1958. *François Quesnay et la Physiocratie*, ed. E. Salleron, 2 vols. Paris: Institut National d'Études Démographiques (INED).

Isnard, Achille-Nicolas. 1781. *Traité des richesses*. 2 vols. London and Lausanne: F. Grasset.

Kurz, Heinz D., and Neri Salvadori. 2000. "Classical" Roots of Input-Output Analysis: A Short Account of Its Long Prehistory. *Economic Systems Research* 12 (2): 153–179.

Leontief, Wassily. 1941. *The Structure of American Economy, 1919–1939*. Cambridge, MA: Harvard University Press.

Marx, Karl. 1963. *Theories of Surplus Value*. Part 1. Trans. Emile Burns. Moscow: Progress Publishers.

Marx, Karl. 1974. *Capital*. Vol. 2. London: Lawrence and Wishart.

Meek, Ronald L. 1962. *The Economics of Physiocracy: Essays and Translations.* London: Allen and Unwin.

Pressman, Steven. 1994. *Quesnay's Tableau Économique. A Critique and Reassessment.* Fairfield, NJ: Augustus M. Kelley.

Quesnay, François. 1972. *Tableau économique.* Trans. and eds. Marguerite Kuczynski and Ronald Meek. London: Macmillan.

Rieter, Heinz. 1983. Zur Rezeption der physiokratischen Kreislaufanalogie in der Wirtschaftswissenschaft. In *Studien zur Entwicklung der ökonomischen Theorie,* vol. 3, ed. Harald Scherf, 55–99. Berlin: Duncker and Humblot.

Rieter, Heinz. 1990. Quesnays *Tableau Economique* als Uhren-Analogie. In *Studien zur Entwicklung der ökonomischen Theorie,* vol. 9, ed. Harald Scherf, 57–94. Berlin: Duncker and Humblot.

Smith, Adam. 1976. *An Inquiry into the Nature and Causes of the Wealth of Nations.* In Vol. 2 of *The Glasgow Edition of the Works and Correspondence of Adam Smith,* eds. R. H. Campbell, A. S. Skinner, and W. B. Todd. Oxford: Clarendon. (Orig. pub. 1776).

Sraffa, Piero. 1960. *Production of Commodities by Means of Commodities: Prelude to a Critique of Economic Theory.* Cambridge, U.K.: Cambridge University Press.

Vaggi, Gianni. 1987. *The Economics of François Quesnay.* Basingstoke, U.K.: Macmillan.

Vaggi, Gianni. 1998. Physiocracy. In *The Elgar Companion to Classical Economics,* vol. 2, eds. Heinz D. Kurz and Neri Salvadori, 199–203. Cheltenham, U.K., and Northampton, MA: E. Elgar.

Weulersse, Georges. 1910. *Le mouvement physiocratique en France (de 1756 à 1770).* 2 vols. Paris: Félix Alcan.

Heinz D. Kurz

PIAGET, JEAN
1896–1980

Considered by many to be the founder of modern developmental psychology, the Swiss psychologist Jean Piaget devoted his researches to children's distinctive ways of knowing and to the process of developmental change leading toward adult thought. He charted a sequence of stages in children's intellectual development whose manifestations encompass domains ranging from logical reasoning to emotional development. Trained in biology and philosophy, Piaget extrapolated from his studies of mollusks in their natural habitat to a conception of the development of intelligence in children as a progressive adaptation, tending toward ever greater equilibrium, with its reciprocal aspects of the "assimilation" of new information to existing concepts and the "accommodation" (i.e., modification) of the concepts to the new information. He viewed the development of intelligence, in turn, as the foundation of a "genetic epistemology," a theory of knowledge that conceived the development of ideas as part of their essence. On the basis of his observations of children's cognitive development and his claim that children's own action catalyzes that development, Piaget altered the face of psychology and education.

BASIC CONCEPTS: DEVELOPMENTAL STAGES

Piaget became convinced that children exhibit a distinctive type of thinking, as opposed to simply flawed adult thought, when, as a young associate working on intelligence testing in the laboratory of Alfred Binet (1857–1911), he noticed that when children answered items incorrectly, they tended to give the same wrong answer. He inferred that the children must have approached the problems methodically, only the method differed from that of adults. After altering the testing methods to include the exploration of children's answers and devising many probes of his own, he set about determining the intellectual organization of what he eventually conceived as four broad stages of development, each embodying a progression toward increasingly flexible, systematic, and complex thought: sensorimotor, preoperational, concrete-operational, and formal operational.

During the *sensorimotor* period, extending from birth to approximately eighteen months, intelligence manifests in action. Action develops within the period from reflexive movement to means-ends behavior that comes, by the last of six substages, to incorporate tool use, foresight, and detours ([1936] 1952). The advent of *representational intelligence* in the sixth substage manifests in additional ways, including deduction based upon remembered events, the imitation of events witnessed previously, symbolic play, and language. Thought now progresses to some degree independently of what is seen or otherwise directly experienced. For example, an eighteen-month-old child who sees a toy hidden in a box, then sees the box moved under a cloth, and then finds the box empty, will spontaneously search under the cloth for the missing toy, evidently having inferred that the toy left the box when the box was under the cloth (an instance of deduction). Children at this age might also imitate a funny face someone made the day before (an instance of deferred imitation) or slide a leaf along the countertop as though the leaf were a car (an instance of symbolic play). Although any of these representational activities might occur in the absence of language, language, which also depends upon conceptual connections, normally begins at around the same time.

These symptoms of nascent representational thought mark the beginning of Piaget's second broad stage, of *pre-operational* or *intuitive* intelligence, which extends roughly from two to seven years of age. Piaget found that, despite the advances it embodied, thought during this interval exhibited limitations, in particular with respect to the property of what he termed *reversibility*. The limitation is apparent in Piaget's best-known experiment with school-age children, his probe of what he called the "conservation" of quantity. When water, for example, is poured from a wide flask into a thin one, although adults or older children know the water level must rise, children under the age of (approximately) seven years sometimes anticipate that the water level will remain the same. Alternatively, when confronted with the raised water level after the water is poured, they may assert that the new (thin) flask contains more water than did the original (wide) flask ([1941] 1965).

By comparison, when presented with the same problem, children between seven and twelve years, normally the stage of *concrete-operational* thought, say the amount of liquid must remain the same because, for example, if one returned the water to the original flask, the water would rise to the level it reached initially. Or, they might say that although the level is higher in the second flask than it was in the first, the second flask is also narrower, or that nothing was added or taken away. Piaget perceived in these arguments the imagined reversal of an observed state of affairs and the construction of compensations between different variables of the problem.

The state of affairs had to be concrete and observable, however, whereas from roughly twelve years onward, during the *formal operational* stage, individuals can reason about hypothetical states and solve both abstract and concrete problems systematically, by taking account of, and if necessary manipulating, all variables pertinent to a problem. Thus, as a scientist would do, a child at this stage confronted with the problem of determining which of a series of chemicals was responsible for altering the color of a solution, for instance, would systematically vary each possible combination of liquids to isolate the necessary reaction (Inhelder and Piaget [1955] 1958).

Development through the stage of concrete operations is believed to be universal, whereas only a fraction of even well-educated teenagers from the United States exhibit formal operational reasoning when they are given the problems originally employed by Piaget. As suggested by Jean Retschitzki (1989) in a study of expert players of a popular game in the Ivory Coast, however, evidence exists that formal-operational reasoning may be employed even by members of undeveloped countries with low literacy when people participate in culturally indigenous activities in which they are expert.

Piaget characterized these tiers of development in a second way, as embodying three "Copernican revolutions" ([1964] 1968), in which children, initially "egocentric" at

the level in question, gradually progressed toward the ability to take alternative perspectives into account. Although Piaget eventually retracted the term *egocentric* in response to its apparent misconstrual by other psychologists, he retained the substantive theses underlying it.

During the sensorimotor period of infancy, as conceived within this second scheme, children come gradually to acknowledge a self, a world, and their separation. They come to recognize, for example, that their caregivers come and go on their own and that the external world generally operates independently of them ([1937] 1954).

During the preoperational period of early childhood, children progress from an obliviousness to the perspective of others to the awareness that others may perceive things differently from what they perceive, and they anticipate the alternative perspective. Thus, for instance, whereas when an interlocutor's back is turned, a four-year-old might point to the location of an object for which the interlocutor is searching, an older child would describe the location ([1923] 1955).

Corresponding to the advent of the capacity for formal operations is an interest in abstract ideals and, according to Piaget, a progression during adolescence from the view that the world should submit to one's schemes to the understanding that one does not know everything ([1964] 1968).

Piaget believed his stage sequences extended to many areas of cognition, including logical thought and children's conceptions of objects, space, time, causality, number, chance, and probability, as well as aspects of perception and memory. He perceived their manifestations also in areas of social life, especially morality. Corresponding to the progression he observed toward concrete operations, for example, he documented the emergence of an understanding of and interest in social rules and an appreciation of their purpose in regulating people's relations and protecting their welfare. He also documented a trend from the negative moral valuation of people whose actions produce bad outcomes to the negative valuation of those whose intentions are bad ([1932] 1965).

In delineating the myriad developments he did, Piaget ascribed greater importance to the sequence of developments he described than to the uniformity of development across areas of activity. He believed, however, that the capacity for more primitive types of reasoning remained in all areas throughout life and, especially in the case of morality, were more evident in some individuals and groups than in others.

BASIC CONCEPTS: THE PROCESS OF DEVELOPMENT

All of the developments Piaget described resulted, he believed, from natural, spontaneous development. With the possible exception of moral judgment, whose early stages he suggested reflected the influence of adult disciplinary tactics, the developments were not taught or otherwise prompted by the environment, which at most afforded (or limited) opportunities for growth. He contended, moreover, that the advances he charted arose through feedback from children's own action, as opposed to from the maturation of innately given abilities.

Piaget was sufficiently convinced of the potential of the mind to construct itself that he believed the entire series of developments he described evolved from a starting point of only reflexive action and the "invariant functions" of assimilation, accommodation, and the progressive storage of their results, which Piaget called organization. Merely by sucking, grasping, listening, and looking—initially reflexively—and repeating these behaviors, as followed from the inborn tendency to repeat experiences (the most primitive manifestation of assimilation), the resulting chance effects would eventually bring about change in the actions. Further changes would follow from there, until individuals reached the final equilibrium of adult forms of thought ([1936] 1952).

CRITICISM OF THE THEORY

Piaget's studies of children have been replicated worldwide, in both developed and undeveloped countries. Many have also extended his sequences to domains he did not investigate, such as attachment relations in infancy and friendships during childhood.

The theory has also been challenged by researchers who, after modifying the measures Piaget used to assess the abilities he investigated, have produced results the researchers believe attest to children's grasp of mature concepts at an earlier stage than Piaget specified. Some of this work appears in reviews by Paul Harris (1989) and John Flavell and colleagues (2002). The researchers assert that the results warrant a different model of development in which, rather than gradually developing the concepts in question, as Piaget described, children begin development in possession of the concepts' essentials and progressively "access" the essentials in increasingly reflective thought and over ever broader areas of application; Paul Rozin lays out a version of the model in "The Evolution of Intelligence and Access to the Cognitive Unconscious" (1976). According to the general view, younger children falter on Piaget's tasks not because they lack the concepts under examination, but because they become confused by nonessential features of Piaget's experiments. With age, the view says, as children's working memory and attentional capabilities increase, children became better able to negotiate Piaget's tasks.

Some researchers in the foregoing line have challenged Piaget's theory based not upon new experimental procedures, which most of the aforementioned studies employ, but upon naturalistically occurring behavior, a focus more in keeping with Piaget's original observations. For example, in 1973 Marilyn Shatz and Rochel Gelman reported that, contrary to the idea that preschoolers fail to take in others' perspectives when addressing them, four-year-olds simplify their speech when they talk to two-year-olds. More recently, Debra van Ausdale and Joseph Feagin (2001) found evidence in preschoolers' social interactions of racist ideas and practices that the authors believe possible only with the "operational" thought Piaget ascribed to middle childhood.

Another line of criticism questions the cogency of Piaget's theoretical constructs independently of the data, as exemplified by works by Sophie Haroutunian (1983) and Susan Sugarman (1987a), or the formalisms he used to represent the constructs, as argued by Daniel Osherson (1974).

Few dispute Piaget's sequences as measured by his own tests. Controversy continues about the equivalence of the concepts measured by newer tests to the concepts assessed by Piaget's procedures. The two bodies of work differ fundamentally in method. Whereas the work that challenges Piaget's norms replaces his tests at younger ages, Piaget extrapolated to his sequences from developmental changes in children's behavior on the same measure at all ages he tested; the strategy dates to Piaget's days as a researcher in intelligence testing. The difference makes it difficult to render any final conclusion about the import of the apparently conflicting results (see Sugarman 1987b for discussion of this).

With respect specifically to the challenges brought by fresh observations of naturally occurring behavior, evidence can be found within Piaget's own observations of allegedly "preoperational" thought more complex than that ascribed by his account of preoperational thinking (Sugarman 1987a). Nonetheless, the particular complexities Piaget associated with "operational" thinking, in the abstract reflective thought in which he sought them, do not appear in either Piaget's or newer data. The claim that the racist ideas and practices of some preschoolers require operational thought presents the additional problem that racism bears precisely the hallmarks of preoperational mentality as Piaget originally defined it. These properties include a one-sided point of view, often based upon appearances, that does not take account of alternative vantage points, is impervious to contradiction, and consequently remains unaware of itself as a point of view. Especially in the moral domain, which, as Piaget discusses in *The Moral Judgment of the Child* ([1932] 1965), draws upon incompletely comprehended adult influences, thought can become rigid and nearly mystical as a result of these tendencies. Given the persistence of these characteristics into adult morality, the telling question raised by the observation of racism in preschoolers might be not how preschoolers manage to exhibit racism, but why adults remain susceptible to it, given their apparent possession of more sophisticated forms of thought.

Despite the empirical challenges to his theory, Piaget's developmental milestones in children's thought dominate research in developmental psychology and retain a strong influence in education. Although conceptual critiques of the theory suggest the presence of gaps in the edifice, Piaget's general philosophy of how development occurs, namely through the exertions of a knowing subject, remains widely embraced.

SEE ALSO *Cognitive Dissonance; Intelligence*

BIBLIOGRAPHY

PRIMARY WORKS

Inhelder, Bärbel, and Jean Piaget. [1955] 1958. *The Growth of Logical Thinking from Childhood to Adolescence: An Essay on the Construction of Formal Operational Structures.* New York: Basic Books.

Piaget, Jean. [1923] 1955. *The Language and Thought of the Child.* Trans. Marjorie and Ruth Gabain. New York: Meridian.

Piaget, Jean. [1932] 1965. *The Moral Judgment of the Child.* Trans. Marjorie Gabain. New York: Free Press.

Piaget, Jean. [1936] 1952. *The Origins of Intelligence in Children.* Trans. Margaret Cook. New York: International Universities Press.

Piaget, Jean. [1937] 1954. *The Construction of Reality in the Child.* Trans. Margaret Cook. New York: Basic Books.

Piaget, Jean. [1941] 1965. *The Child's Conception of Number.* Trans. Caleb Gattegno and F. M. Hodgson. New York: Norton.

Piaget, Jean. [1964] 1968. *Six Psychological Studies.* Trans. Anita Tenzer. New York: Vintage Books.

SECONDARY WORKS

Cole, Michael. 1996. *Cultural Psychology: A Once and Future Discipline.* Cambridge, MA: Harvard University Press.

Flavell, John H., Patricia H. Miller, and Scott A. Miller. 2002. *Cognitive Development.* Englewood Cliffs, NJ: Prentice-Hall.

Haroutunian, Sophie. 1983. *Equilibrium in the Balance: A Study of Psychological Explanation.* New York: Springer-Verlag.

Harris, Paul L. 1989. Object Permanence in Infancy. In *Infant Development,* eds. Alan Slater and Gavin Bremner, 103–121. Hillsdale, NJ: Lawrence Erlbaum.

Osherson, Daniel N. 1974. *Organization of Length and Class Concepts: Empirical Consequences of a Piagetian Formalism.* Vol. 1 of *Logical Abilities in Children.* Hillsdale, NJ: Lawrence Erlbaum.

Retschitzki, Jean. 1989. Evidence of Formal Thinking in Baoule Awele Players. In *Heterogeneity in Cross-Cultural Psychology: Selected Papers from the Ninth International Conference of the International Association for Cross-Cultural Psychology,* eds.

Daphne M. Keats, Donald Munro, and Leon Mann, 234–243. Amsterdam and Rockland, MA: Swets and Zeitlinger.

Rozin, Paul. 1976. The Evolution of Intelligence and Access to the Cognitive Unconscious. In *Progress in Psychobiology and Physiological Psychology,* vol. 6, eds. James M. Sprague and Alan D. Epstein, 245–280. New York: Academic Press.

Shatz, Marilyn, and Rochel Gelman. 1973. The Development of Communication Skills: Modifications in the Speech of Young Children as a Function of Listener. *Monographs of the Society for Research in Child Development* 38 (5): 1–38.

Sugarman, Susan. 1987a. *Piaget's Construction of the Child's Reality.* New York: Cambridge University Press.

Sugarman, Susan. 1987b. The Priority of Description in Developmental Psychology. *International Journal of Behavioral Development* 10: 391–414.

Van Ausdale, Debra, and Joe R. Feagin. 2001 *The First R: How Children Learn Race and Racism.* Lanham, MD: Rowman and Littlefield.

Susan Sugarman

PILOT NATIONAL ASIAN AMERICAN POLITICAL STUDY (PNAAPS)
SEE *Race and Political Science.*

PIMPS

A pimp is commonly defined as a person who lives off the income of a prostitute. More often than not, the prostitutes are female. Pimps often lure their victims into prostitution under the pretense of a love relationship, specifically targeting adolescents who have escaped physical or sexual violence at home and are vulnerable economically, socially, and sexually. Assuming the role of a "boyfriend," a pimp might eventually suggest to his girlfriend to have sex with his friend as a favor, and eventually might resort to violence to "break her" (including beatings, death threats, rape, gang rape, false imprisonment), often also introducing her to drugs to make the person dependent on him.

Pimps might have prostitutes engage in sex work in various venues, such as brothels, escort services, massage parlors, or strip clubs. The more prestigious the establishment, the less brutal and direct is the pimp's abuse of prostitutes. Sex workers dependent on crack tend to occupy the lowest rank of all, demanding the least pay—usually in the form of crack—and providing the most high-risk sexual services. In a way symbolic of the dependency of the prostitute on the pimp, for these prostitutes the "crack pipe is the pimp."

A pimp might secure the area in which a prostitute pursues customers. A pimp prides himself on "managing" all financial and economic matters prostitutes experience in their work, including marketing (finding customers) and workplace protection (controlling an area of the street from competition, fighting dangerous or nonpaying customers, or paying off police). He might also post bail for prostitutes who have been apprehended by police.

A pimp demands all or the majority of the money prostitutes generate through their work for himself. By having more than one prostitute, a pimp multiplies his income capabilities, and experienced pimps boast about the size of their "stables," or the number of prostitutes working for them.

Ostensibly, women "trade" part or all of their income to the pimp in exchange for protection from abusive customers or those who refuse to pay, or from other pimps who might try to force them to work for them. To what extent women actively and willingly participate in a relationship with a pimp is a point of debate. Some feminists and human-rights advocates consider any sex work as sexual oppression of women and challenge the idea that someone agrees to being managed by a pimp. Their opponents argue that sex work needs to be legalized and protected. But even advocates of prostitution often request that pimping remain illegal.

A critical psychological requirement to become a successful pimp is to "learn how to reverse the pussy game." In other words, rather than sexually desiring the prostitutes who work for him, and thus becoming sexually vulnerable if they withhold their affection from him, the pimp has to learn to subjugate his sexual desires to his financial desires. In this regard, the pimp is regarded as the ultimate hustler and manipulator.

In the social milieu of the underworld, pimps enjoy high status by exhibiting many traits of hegemonic masculinity—conspicuous consumption (fancy clothes, jewelry, accessories, cars) and other evidence of a successful economic position, control over women, and sexual access as well as opportunity. Although the pimp has enjoyed a long history as an iconic figure in certain subcultures of the United States (for example, Iceberg Slim), the pimp has become a mainstream persona only since the mid-1990s, when gangsta rappers such as Snoop Dogg made the pimp a staple of their lyrics and a persona they also try to cultivate offstage. Since then, it has become a broadly used term of approval and endearment across all youth cultures, with ever-growing appeal in commercial venues, including such popular shows as "Pimp My Ride" (Staiger 2005). But while in the racial imagination of the United States pimps are thought to be primarily African American, pimping is not limited to any particular race or ethnicity.

Notwithstanding this widespread perception of the pimp, current research reveals a more complex picture of pimps and their relationship to prostitutes. A comparative ethnographic study in Canada's major cities found that many prostitutes do not have pimps at all, while a study of New Jersey streetwalkers found that pimps are in fact often boyfriends or husbands. Further, the emotional attachment between the pimps and prostitutes can be strong and supportive, with prostitutes sometimes lovingly referring to their pimps as "Daddy." As the New Jersey study found, prostitutes tend to consider their sexual interaction with customers not as a form of making love but merely as a sexual transaction with instant compensation, while reserving their emotions of sexual intimacy for their sexual relations with their pimps. This factor also explains why prostitutes who are meticulous about using condoms with customers often refuse to use condoms with their pimps, as the condom is equated with sex as a commercial transaction. This semantic separation of lovemaking with the pimp versus tricking the john suggests the psychological significance of the pimp as a means to "normalize" the sexual identity of the prostitute, an emotional attachment that of course can also give the pimp additional power.

The potential for violent relationships, however, is always there, and some pimp–prostitute relations have characteristics of battered-batterer relations on one hand or sadomasochistic relations on the other. According to the autobiography of Iceberg Slim, a legendary pimp from the 1930s to the 1950s, successful pimps "train" their prostitutes through the use of well-calculated torture. How realistic Iceberg Slim's alleged autobiography is remains questionable, but following the popularity of this text in the United States and worldwide as a handbook on how to pimp and as a bible for the gangsta rap of the 1990s, it is to be expected that many imagine pimps and prostitutes in this way, if not practice pimping accordingly.

Another pressing issue is the growing phenomenon of human trafficking fueled by the increasing profitability and the growing divide between poor countries that send prostitutes and high-demand, wealthy countries that receive them. In this manifestation of pimping, the socioeconomic role of the pimp is tilted to the extreme of economic exploitation, where pimps subject prostitutes to brutal sexual, physical, and mental abuse to "condition" them into docility and resignation, before selling them again to other pimps or end users. In such contexts, pimps take on characteristics of slave traders, "buying" individuals "in bulk" and "reselling" them to other pimps/traffickers within a relatively short period of time before finally "dumping" them if they are too sick or too old to generate further profits. This form of pimping has no traces of emotional attachment between pimp and prostitute, except for the terror of physical and sexual violence. This phenomenon of pimping has been described for traffickers from eastern Europe.

Theoretically, pimps can also be women. The trend, however, has been that women who reap profits from the prostitution of another tend to do so in brothels, with greater formal security. These women are called madams. Often they are ex-prostitutes themselves, but contrary to common perceptions, a nineteenth-century case study from St. Paul, Minnesota, showed that these madams were little older than the prostitutes who worked in their establishments, enjoyed considerable wealth and influence in the community, and often engaged in friendly relationships with the women who worked for them. As a contemporary British study has found, their crime rates associated with prostitution tend to be substantially lower and their crimes substantially less violent than those of their male counterparts.

The violence caused by pimps, from sexual and physical abuse to torture, murder, drug dealing, and the like, constitute crimes significantly more dangerous than prostitution. While this is generally recognized, pimps tend to be charged much less frequently than prostitutes, with streetwalkers, who constitute the bottom of the sex work industry, being the ones most likely to be arrested. Many self-help and advocacy groups have raised the charge that the laws and legal enforcement against prostitution victimize sex workers significantly more (and women more so than men) than the pimps, who are reaping the lion's share of their profits. Responding to the growing movement of sex workers for their right to self-determination, and in the hope of eliminating the violence and crime associated with prostitution, several countries (for example, the Netherlands and Germany) have legalized prostitution. However, even in countries where prostitution is legal, pimping remains illegal. Whether legalizing prostitution in fact eliminates or diminishes the crimes associated with prostitution and the existence of pimps remains a hotly debated issue and awaits further study.

SEE ALSO *Crime and Criminology; Drug Traffic; Economies, Transitional; Inequality, Gender; Prostitution*

BIBLIOGRAPHY

Iceberg Slim (Robert Beck). 1987. *Pimp: The Story of My Life.* Los Angeles: Holloway House.

Malarek, Victor. 2003. *The Natashas: Inside the New Global Sex Trade.* New York. Arcade.

Staiger, Annegret. 2005. Hoes Can Be Hoed Out, Players Can Be Played Out, but Pimp Is for Life: The Pimp as Strategy of Identity Formation. *Symbolic Interaction* 28 (3): 407–428.

Annegret Staiger

PITKIN, HANNA
1931–

Hanna Fenichel Pitkin is one of the most influential political theorists of the twentieth century. While best known for her seminal book *The Concept of Representation* (1967), Pitkin has composed several works of lasting relevance to the study of politics. She has shed light on such diverse topics as democracy, justice, gender, action, and the tension between political philosophy and political theory.

In *The Concept of Representation*, Pitkin utilizes the methods of linguistic analysis, developed by Oxford philosophers such as J. L. Austin (1911–1960), to focus on representation as a concept rather than a set of actual practices. She defines *representation* ideally as "re-presentation, a making present again" (1967, p. 8), but then moves on to show how this meaning has been distorted and contorted throughout the history of modern philosophical discourse. Every attempt to capture the complexity of the concept misleadingly conveys *part* of the meaning of representation as if it were the whole meaning. Pitkin surveys the various theoretical approaches to the term *representation* and finds them all lacking, including the authorization view, expressed by Thomas Hobbes (1588–1679); the trustee theory, expressed by Edmund Burke (1729–1797); and the liberal view, associated with James Madison (1751–1836), among others. Each vision is shown to be incomplete by the central paradox of representation—that is, the competing demands of the representative and the represented. Pitkin aims to preserve rather than to reconcile this paradox, and her book culminates in the recommendation that citizens safeguard both the capacity of the represented to authorize decisions and the capacity of the representatives to act independently.

Pitkin's book has been a touchstone for subsequent work in the area of representation theory. Some contemporary scholars, however, find Pitkin's insights to be anachronistic for a globalizing world in which practices of representation seem to stretch beyond the boundaries of the nation-state (Mansbridge 2003). Furthermore, scholars sensitive to issues of diversity and cultural heterogeneity have highlighted the ways in which every representative formation can obscure or suppress minority voices (Young 2000).

In many ways, the lasting relevance and importance of Pitkin's early work has overshadowed her subsequent development as a thinker and theorist. In 1972 she further articulated her interest in conceptual analysis as a fruitful method of political philosophy through an examination of the late work of Ludwig Wittgenstein (1889–1951). She pays close attention to Wittgenstein's central notion of "forms of life," the matrices of human behavior that define the contexts in which a discourse acquires meaning. For Pitkin, political philosophy should proceed to analyze these contexts to enhance our conceptual clarity on terms such as justice, membership, and action. Political theory, on the other hand, is concerned with advocating a change in our current conceptions, as the contexts in which we live and the needs of the human community transform through time.

Pitkin's *The Attack of the Blob: Hannah Arendt's Concept of the Social* (1998) exemplifies her recommended trajectories for both political philosophy and theory. She explores Hannah Arendt's (1906–1975) use of the *social* through contextual and psychobiographical analysis, and discusses the ways in which Arendt's concerns for action are compromised by a residual fear of social conformity. In the end, Pitkin implores her readers to discover ways in which they can become more reflective and critical as agents and actors in the world. In so doing, she echoes concerns born with her 1967 book, and reveals herself ultimately as a committed theorist of democracy.

SEE ALSO *Representation*

BIBLIOGRAPHY

Mansbridge, Jane. 2003. Rethinking Representation. *American Political Science Review* 97 (4): 515–528.

Pitkin, Hanna. 1967. *The Concept of Representation.* Berkeley: University of California Press.

Pitkin, Hanna. 1972. *Wittgenstein and Justice: On the Significance of Ludwig Wittgenstein for Social and Political Thought.* Berkeley: University of California Press.

Pitkin, Hanna. 1998. *The Attack of the Blob: Hannah Arendt's Concept of the Social.* Chicago: University of Chicago Press.

Young, Iris Marion. 2000. *Inclusion and Democracy.* Oxford: Oxford University Press.

David W. McIvor

PLACAGE

SEE *Mulattos.*

PLAGUE AND BLACK DEATH

SEE *Disease; Nursery Rhymes; Public Health.*

PLAGUES

SEE *Morbidity and Mortality.*

PLANNING

Planning represents the process of looking into the future, establishing something out there, creating a vision of a future state of affairs, and determining means of actualizing that state. A plan is something one intends to do or achieve, as when someone asks, "Do you have any plans for the weekend?" As a construct, a plan may mean activities that have to be performed to achieve something (objective). Plans therefore are predetermined, preceding action, and constitute programs of activities (means) considered valid for achieving predetermined aims and objectives.

TYPES OF PLANNING

Planning can take place in a variety of areas, for plans take varied forms: policy choice, manpower plans and incentive strategies, community action plans, site plans, comprehensive plans, building plans, economic development plans, disaster containment plans, housing and community development plans, and transportation plans, among others. However, urban planning has received attention in academic discussions perhaps because of its potential for improving the welfare of people and communities as well as the added impetus given to it since the nineteenth century by the formalized disciplines of architecture and engineering. Thus planning has tended to combine rationality and stylistic approaches to solving community problems by means of physical designs. Urban planning, city planning, regional planning, or community planning are concerned with ordering and designing human settlements with a view to creating more convenient, healthy, and aesthetically pleasing places for people.

Planning generally is people and community oriented. For instance, planning for economic development is vital to the process of building sustainable community. Housing and community development planning is concerned with creating accessible and equitable communities, sensitizing people to community and development issues, and generally seeking to develop strategies to address the needs of the homeless and the handicapped. Transportation planning also tends to show similar concerns for people and communities as it aims at revitalizing suburban commercial corridors to improve accessibility and mobility and, importantly, strike a balance between community needs and the interests of transporters.

Planners construct a broad vision of the community or help communities identify their goals or create a particular vision. They develop strategies by which communities can accomplish their goals and vision. They actively participate in the implementation of plans and monitor and coordinate the work of several groups of people.

THE PLANNING PROCESS

On plans and planning, Henri Fayol wrote "'The plan of action is, at the same time, the result envisaged, the line of action to be followed, the stages to go through and the methods to use" (Fayol 1949, p. 130). George Steiner observed that planning is "a process that begins with objectives, defines strategies, policies and detailed plans to achieve them" (Steiner 1969, p. 20). It follows therefore that the planning process has three distinct phases, namely, definition of basic objectives and goals; developing strategies and means (or strategic plans) and policies to implement objectives; and developing detailed tactical and operational plans, such as work procedures and practices, time schedules, and budgets.

Planning, no matter in what area it takes place, generally follows this characteristic pattern. The first and basic aspect of planning is setting objectives. While it is possible for individuals and organizations to have goals and objectives, it is equally possible for them not to have any. Peter Drucker highlighted the importance of objectives: "Few companies have any clear idea of what their mission is and that is one of the major causes of their worst mistakes.... Managers have no feeling for what the company is really good at and conversely what it is not good at" (Drucker 1954, p. 4). Aims and objectives are necessary not only to ensure effective performance by focusing energies, time, and other resources but also to ensure that strategies are related to objectives. Goals and objectives vary, however, and depend on the planning area and institution concerned. Common institutional goals include profitability, growth, market share, innovation, survival, social responsibility, worker and employee welfare and development, service to customers, and provision of public services.

Planning is also concerned with decisions about methods, that is, about means or strategies for achieving identified aims and objectives. Strategic planning (or developing strategies and policies for achieving objectives) describes processes involved in producing plans, often called strategies, that identify the basic objectives and concrete actions necessary to implement them. This aspect of planning calls for auditing of the planning environment to identify needs, constraints, opportunities, and the organization's internal strengths, weaknesses, resources, and capabilities.

The experience of California Union Bank provides apt example of a firm scanning its rather crowded competitive environment. When Harry Volk accepted an offer to become president of the bank in 1957, he surveyed the banking industry and perceived a vigorous race to create more retail or consumer-oriented branches. Rather than join the race, he decided to pursue a different strategy. Volk had observed that no bank concentrated exclusively on businesses, particularly fairly risky business loans. He reasoned that if he charged higher-than-normal interest rates on weaker credit risks, it was possible to suffer higher-than-normal loan losses and yet have a profitable business. Consequently, Union Bank opted to pursue a strategy of becoming a wholesale- or business-oriented bank.

Another aspect of planning is determination of the manner in which plans must necessarily be carried out. This is essentially a matter of conduct generally governed by such written documents as mission statements, policy statements, customer charters, and the like. Policies provide guides to decision-making, reflect company objectives, and generally guide managers and employees toward objectives in situations where judgment and discretion are required. However, conduct may also either be determined by influence or by informal standards that lie beneath organizational behavior.

The next phase preceding action in the planning process is developing tactical plans, which involves making specific commitments and providing details for methods (work practices and procedures), money (budgets), and time (time schedules). While policy provides guides for deciding, procedures provide guides for doing, for concrete actions. Procedures refer to methods of carrying out activities and might prescribe steps to be followed in doing work a kind of checklist for action. Procedures produce programmed responses to organizational problems and apply mainly to routine repetitive work.

PUBLIC-SECTOR PLANNING

Planning in the public sector is essentially embodied in public budgets, so public-sector planning emphasizes project-based financial plans. Because plans are problem-solving mechanisms, they design solutions to public-sector problems. The process in the public sector presents a distinctively different scenario from private-sector or business planning. While mathematical optimization models and computer formulations and simulations may be developed under the philosophy of obtaining "the answer," that is, the best or optimal solution for business problems, such models, including multiobjectives models, when applied to public-sector planning, may not be useful because there is a multitude of local optima and because important planning elements are not captured in the formulations. The omitted elements may actually imply that the optimal planning solution lies within the inferior region of multiobjective analysis rather than along the noninferior frontier. The choice of action, selection of public programs, or decision option may be far from the best, what is most rational, or what makes an economic sense, but it remains a political choice. The roles of these optimization methods have been to generate planning alternatives and to facilitate their evaluation and elaboration as well as to provide useful insights and to serve as catalysts for human creativity.

Business planning is relatively new to public-sector and nonprofit organizations. Approaches to business planning in provincial, municipal, federal, or board-governed organizations are different from those in the private sector, although the language and concepts remain the same. The emphasis remains on establishing the vision, goals, strategies, and performance measures for high-performance organizations.

Such plans develop strategies for performance measurement, create benchmarks, and set standards. They may also include implementation strategies with emphasis on service excellence and must necessarily involve people in the decisions that affect them. However, many rational planning models applied in the public sector appear to focus on efficiency objectives and suffer from two lingering limitations: failure to consider equity or distribution of income and the empirical limitation of calculating costs and benefits. This has meant that achieving planning's intended roles in the public domain may require the use of several models as well as new types of optimization formulations and modified algorithms and computer codes. Optimization models are important because they help generate planning alternatives and facilitate comparison between them. Thus in the public sector it may be desirable to use several different models to aid the planning process.

Because plans are strategic instruments for goal attainment, their nature and form tend to be determined by the type and nature of objectives and goals established. While goals tend to differ from one individual and organization to another and while individuals and groups generally operate under varying conditions, the effectiveness of plans and planning appears to depend on the total planning situation, consisting of several sometimes complex variables, such as the knowledge, skill, and expertise of planners, available resources and technology, and the nature of the environment, among others. It means that plans must be related to objectives and adapted to the circumstances of the planning institution. Therefore plans that enable organizations to cope with relatively stable conditions will differ in significant respects from plans that suit relatively unstable conditions. For instance, extrapolative planning may be appropriate for stable conditions, enabling forecasts of revenue and expenditure to be made based on current conditions that are assumed to remain unchanged from the previous planning period. While its major purpose may be to ensure control over costs and legality of action, extrapolative planning is unsuitable for long-range planning and incapable of dealing with turbulence and the constraints of unstable conditions. On the contrary, unstable conditions, where there

are uncertainties and where the environment is characterized by turbulence and complexities, warrant a rational comprehensive planning approach able to address long-term goals and contend with the various environmental forces. Planning, programming, and budgeting systems, one approach often used in the public sector, offer great potential for dealing with the present-day world of uncertainties. It is an integrated planning-budgeting system that is program based and relates expenditures to performance and outcomes.

Public-sector planning calls for access to budget information and the ability to understand that such information is capable of promoting public involvement in and scrutiny of the budget process. Public access to government policy initiatives, priorities, and implementation can promote popular participation. Public planners therefore necessarily need to look out for and respond to forces from the popular sector if social rationality in the public planning process is to be achieved. While the aim of rational public planning may be economic prosperity, the elimination or reduction of poverty, and the provision of public goods, good health, environmental sanity, and security, or in a nutshell, provision of general happiness, to exclude the public in this process totally contradicts the requirements of long-term comprehensive planning, which calls for active participation, cooperation, and the support of all stakeholders and clientele groups in society. In a democratic society, a theoretical and empirical if not political question has often remained: Who determines or takes part in determining what constitutes general interests? The public will probably remain indispensable in answering these questions.

Public access to information on public policy issues recommends itself for effective national comprehensive planning because it guarantees both government accountability and civil society participation in the budget process. This enables planners to use feedback arising from internal and external sources to bring about necessary adjustments in plans and, through public criticism or external performance evaluation, to remain focused.

SEE ALSO *Cities; Development Economics; Metropolis; Policy Analysis; Public Policy; Regions; Regions, Metropolitan*

BIBLIOGRAPHY

Brill, D. E., Jr. 1979. The Use of Optimization Models in Public Sector Planning. *Management Science* 25 (5): 413–422.

Drucker, Peter. 1954. *The Practice of Management.* New York: Harper.

Fayol, Henri. 1949. *General and Industrial Management.* Trans. Constance Storrs. London: Pitman.

Hampton, D. R. 1977. *Contemporary Management.* New York: McGraw-Hill.

Steiner, George. 1969. *Top Management Planning.* New York: Macmillan.

Frederick Ugwu Ozor

PLANTATION

Often defined as a "total institution," even as a prison camp, the plantation has been represented as both a type of social institution and an agricultural organization. The historical significance of this socioeconomic complex stems largely from its function in capitalist agricultural production, where it has been considered instrumental both in the creation and persistence of economic underdevelopment of those tropical areas where it dominated, and in the industrialization of northern Atlantic economics. In his influential text *Persistent Poverty* (1972), agricultural economist George Beckford, building on the seminal ideas of Lloyd Best (1968), argued that while the plantation incorporated all regions where it dominated in the larger developing world economy, as a type of economic organization it did so unevenly, driving the modernization of regions of the northern Atlantic, particularly Britain, at the expense of those in the south, including the U.S. South. However, other scholars, notably Robert Fogel and Stanley Engerman (1974), countered this perspective and held that U.S. southern plantation economies were a variant of capitalism. Such plantations, they argued, were highly productive and profitable, and the U.S. South's comparative advantages as an agricultural zone accounted for its limited or nonindustrialization.

The plantation economies of the Americas incorporated thousands of mainly African laborers, unskilled and enslaved, both free and indentured, who produced for the home and/or export market, as occurred in the U.S. South, the Caribbean, and South America. They labored on both small plantations as in the U.S. South with enslaved labor locked into paternalistic or overtly coercive relationships and large-scale, highly regimented, exploitative factory-like labor-force control. Plantation agriculture thus bespoke a peculiar mix of capital and labor processes. Consequently, debates emerged over its economic modus operandi and labor organization. These "modes of production" debates, prevalent during the mid-1970s through the 1980s, turned on whether slaves were proletarians or an in-between labor form, and whether the plantation was capitalist or not. While no scholar disputed the triangulated relationship between plantations and areas of the proto-industrializing Atlantic, differences emerged about how to characterize its relationship to the emergent capitalist economic system. Generally, several analysts saw the plantation as articulated with capitalism

but distinct from it, while primarily non-Marxists viewed the emergent global market (then mercantile) as *the* critical defining element of the capitalist world system, given slavery's facilitation of wage labor and the circulation of commodities primarily from then-emergent industrialized countries. This view was particularly prevalent among world-system theorists such as Immanuel Wallerstein (1979), who stressed relational historical developments.

Hotly debated also were questions centering on the cultures and personalities found on plantations. For example, Eric Williams (1944) saw racialization as an outcome of plantation slavery. Others averred that plantation slavery was itself a product of racialized thinking. These provocative positions were joined by questions about the social consequences of slavery's economic and racial divisions. Comparing Latin America and the U.S. South in his influential 1959 text, *Slavery: A Problem in American Institutional and Intellectual Life*, Stanley Elkins compared the "closed" authoritarian system of the plantation to Nazism's psychic destruction and concluded that plantation slavery resulted in a psychological stripping of the slave, thereby producing an infantile Sambo mentality or personality. Elkins's Sambo-type personality resonated with stereotypical representations of blacks found in earlier American classics, such as the films *Birth of a Nation* and *Gone with the Wind*, the latter adapted from Margaret Mitchell's 1936 best seller. In the former, freed and out-of-control Sambos visited disorder and chaos upon a highly racialized, gendered, and segregated South ostensibly preoccupied with protecting the virtues of white womanhood, while in the latter, blacks were stereotyped props for a melodramatic Southern romance. But these representations of the docile slave were swiftly undercut by other studies documenting modes of resistance that spelled agency rather than passivity, and later there emerged other perspectives that complicated those notions as well.

Eugene Genovese's *Roll, Jordan, Roll: The World the Slaves Made* (1976) would shift the discussion toward more detailed research on the sociocultural nature of plantation life and its impact on the U.S. South. In this seminal work, Genovese explored the master–slave relationship, arguing that masters' and slaves' transactions were paternalist in nature. For him such a hegemonic relation yielded a tacit realization and acceptance by both slave and master of their symbiotic roles within the slavery complex. In other words, slaves and masters realized their dependence on each other, and the so-called exploitative relation stressed by other analysts was shaped *essentially* by familial practices that tempered the incidence of slave revolts.

Several scholars have contested Genovese's conclusions and highlighted the need to distinguish between physical domination and hegemony, thereby undermining his romanticization of the planter class and his thesis of slaves' willful participation in the plantation-slavery complex. Moreover, analysts point to the pitfalls of reading slaves' practices within the slave system from generalized conclusions culled from too few planters in a large-scale plantation-slave complex that covered the U.S. South. Such perspectives suggest that dependent connections do not negate the incidence of exploitative relationships, nor do they prohibit the development of spaces for creating and articulating futures that are different from those the planters may have envisioned. Subsequent scholarship, which has focused on strategies of maneuver and on processes of culture building by the enslaved, tends to bear this out.

SEE ALSO *Slave Trade; Slavery Industry*

BIBLIOGRAPHY

Anderson, James D. 1976. Aunt Jemima in Dialectics: Genovese on Slave Culture. Review of *Roll, Jordan, Roll: The World the Slaves Made*, by Eugene D. Genovese. *Journal of Negro History* 61 (1): 99–114.

Beckford, George L. 1972. *Persistent Poverty: Underdevelopment in Plantation Economies of the Third World*. Oxford: Oxford University Press.

Best, Lloyd. 1968. The Mechanism of Plantation Type Economies: Outlines of a Model of Pure Plantation Economy. *Social and Economic Studies* 17 (3): 283–326.

Elkins, Stanley. 1959. *Slavery: A Problem in American Institutional and Intellectual Life*. Chicago: University of Chicago Press, 1968.

Fogel, Robert W., and Stanley L. Engerman. 1974. *Time on the Cross: The Economics of American Negro Slavery*. Boston: Little, Brown.

Genovese, Eugene, D. 1976. *Roll, Jordan, Roll: The World the Slaves Made*. New York: Vintage.

Mintz, Sidney. 1978. Was the Plantation Slave a Proletarian? *Review* 2 (1): 81–98.

Mitchell, Margaret. 1936 [1961]. *Gone with the Wind*. New York: Macmillan.

Thompson, Edgar T. 1975. *Plantation Societies, Race Relations, and the South: The Regimentation of Populations: Selected Papers of Edgar T. Thompson*. Durham, NC: Duke University Press.

Tomich, Dale. 2004. *Through the Prism of Slavery: Labor, Capital and World Economy*. Lanham, MD: Rowman and Littlefield.

Wallerstein, Immanuel. 1979. *The Capitalist World-Economy: Essays*. Cambridge, U.K. and New York: Cambridge University Press.

Williams, Eric. 1944. *Capitalism and Slavery*. London: Andre Deutsch, 1967.

Michaeline A. Crichlow

PLANTATION ECONOMY MODEL

The theory of plantation economy and society has been developed to explain the experience and evolution of societies subjected to European-controlled sugarcane production by an enslaved African labor force and later by indentured Asian laborers (mostly Indians). As the historian Philip Curtin observes, "The plantation complex … ultimately stretched from Rio Grande do Sul in south eastern Brazil to the Mason-Dixon line and it had outliers in the Indian Ocean islands of Reunion and Mauritius" (Curtin 1998, p. xii).

The plantation economy model posits that plantation slavery and specialization in export of primary commodities has marked the evolution of the societies in which it existed. The plantation economy theorist Lloyd Best hypothesizes, "The legacy of institutions, structures and behaviour patterns of the plantation system are so deeply entrenched that adjustment tends to take place as an adaptation within the bounds of the established framework" (Best 1968, p. 32). The Caribbean economist Norman Girvan contends that the transnational corporation (TNC) is an institution that exists within the "rules of the game" of the plantation economy. He points out that the historic continuity of foreign ownership, terminal stage of production, limited domestic linkages, repatriation of profits, and persistence of the incalculability of value flows with transfer pricing by TNCs are similar to slave plantation–metropole flows.

The plantation school is not fatalistic but perceives the need to understand the grip of the founding institution of the plantation in order to remove its stranglehold on the dynamic for change within the interstices of the system. The role of the Maroon, or runaway slave, culture of resistance and non-plantation production by the peasantry, for example, is central to transformation of the plantation economy. Plantation economies continue to reflect the historic legacy with plantation-type enterprises operating in primary, natural resource sectors, such as oil, gas, bauxite, bananas, sugar, and tourism. Nontraditional producing sectors compete with these export sectors and with import sectors. Fiscal, monetary, exchange rate, and industrial policy do not favor such nontraditional, residentiary-type activities. The term *residentiary sector* was developed by the plantation economy theorists to describe non-plantation production that sprang up after the end of slavery.

A subtext is the contribution of plantation economies to the industrial transformation of the slave-owning metropolitan countries themselves. Curtin notes that "the Europeans who ran the (plantation) complex learned a great deal from the experience—in ocean shipping, tropical agriculture and economic management at a distance. All this is a part of the background of the industrial age" (Curtin 1998, p. 204).

Plantation economy theory has become diffused in a range of courses offered at the University of the West Indies, including economics, sociology, and political science. Many economists incorporate plantation economy theory in an evolving theory of Caribbean economy and society. These economists include Michael Witter, Mark Figueroa, Claremont Kirton, Vanus James, and Dennis Pantin of the University of the West Indies and Eric St. Cyr. The plantation economy model differs from the Arthur Lewis model of transformation by its focus on the potential within residentiary sector peasant production. Lewis emphasizes dismantling the traditional sector and replacing it with a modern sector. Some adherents of the plantation economy share the Guyanese historian Walter Rodney's concept of the underdevelopment of both Africa and the Caribbean, while others, notably Lloyd Best, argue that Rodney's view is static and mechanistic in nature.

Critics of the plantation model include Adlith Brown and Havelock Brewster, who contend that the school has not produced a theory but rather a recounting of the history of the Caribbean. Trevor Sudama questions the historic accuracy of the model when applied to Trinidad and Tobago. Denis Benn, Thomas, and Pantin raise questions on the model's method and theory.

SEE ALSO *Lewis, W. Arthur*

BIBLIOGRAPHY

Beckford, George. 1972. *Persistent Poverty: Underdevelopment in Plantation Economies of the Third World.* Oxford: Oxford University Press.

Benn, Denis. 1974. The Theory of Plantation Economy and Society: A Methodological Critique. *Journal Of Commonwealth and Comparative Politics* 12 (3): 249–260.

Best, Lloyd. 1968. Outlines of a Model of the Pure Plantation Economy. *Social and Economic Studies* 17 (3): 283–323.

Best, Lloyd, and Kari Levitt. 1968. *Externally Propelled Industrialisation and Growth in the Caribbean.* 4 vols. Mimeo. Montreal: McGill Centre for Developing Area Studies.

Brown, Adlith, and Havelock Brewster. 1974. A Review of the Study of Economics in the English-Speaking Caribbean. *Social and Economic Studies* 23 (1): 48–68.

Curtin, Philip D. 1998. *The Rise and Fall of the Plantation Complex: Essays in Atlantic History.* New York: Cambridge University Press.

Girvan, Norman. 1971. Making the Rules of the Game: Country-Company Agreements in the Bauxite Industry. *Social and Economic Studies* 20 (4): 378–419.

Pantin, Dennis. 1980. The Plantation Economy Model and the Caribbean. *IDS Bulletin* 12 (1): 1980: 17–23.

Williams, Eric. 1964. *Capitalism and Slavery.* London: Andre Deutsch.

Dennis A. Pantin

PLATO
427–347 BCE

Plato was born in Athens in 427 BCE just as the Peloponnesian War between Athens and Sparta was beginning. His mother was related to one of the oligarchs who ruled Athens after the Spartan victory in 404 BCE, and his father died when Plato was very young. The most important shaping influence in Plato's early life, however, was the philosopher Socrates (469–399 BCE). Plato was among the young men of Athens who regularly engaged Socrates in dialogue and who took the Socratic challenge to "know thyself" very seriously. Plato, then twenty-eight, was present at the trial of Socrates, an event that clearly made a deep and lasting impression on Plato and which is reflected in all of his work. Socrates is widely regarded as the hero of the Platonic dialogues, a literary form that Plato preferred for most of his works. Following Socrates' death, Plato traveled throughout Italy, Sicily, and parts of northern Africa before returning to Athens, where he founded the Academy in about 387 BCE. Among Plato's pupils there, for twenty years, was Aristotle (384–322 BCE). Late in life, Plato traveled to Syracuse to educate and inspire a new young king, Dionysius II, though the attempt ended in failure. Plato died in Athens in 347 BCE at the age of eighty-one.

Among the more famous of Plato's dialogues are the *Apology, Crito,* and *Euthyphro,* on the trial and death of Socrates; the *Gorgias,* which explores the way of life of the *sophist;* the *Symposium,* which focuses on love and beauty; the *Phaedrus,* on rhetoric; and the *Timaeus,* a study of cosmology. Other dialogues of note that are still widely read and studied today are the *Meno, Protagoras, Phaedo, Thaetetus,* and the *Sophist.* All of these deal in various ways with Plato's famous theory of *forms,* according to which aspects of the physical world, because subject to decay and death, are inferior to eternal forms such as the true, the good, and the beautiful. But Plato's most famous dialogues, and those that continue to shape international discussion and research in the social sciences, in some measure at least, particularly in political science, are the *Republic,* the *Statesman,* and the *Laws.*

The *Republic* is considered one of the great works of world literature. It is often referred to as an example of utopian literature, which sketches an ideal *polis,* or city-state. Such a view distorts, however, what Plato clearly intended as an exploration of what human beings mean when they appeal to justice and to good rule or government. Similarly, the *Republic* is frequently summarized as an appeal for the rule of philosopher kings. This too obscures, at a minimum, Plato's belief in gender equality among *philosopher rulers,* not necessarily *kings.* Like any classic work, it is difficult to condense and summarize Plato's *Republic.* But there are key aspects that may be sketched along the following lines. At the center of Plato's political theory is a concept of the *cardinal virtues*. These virtues are moderation, or temperance, courage, wisdom, and justice. Following a procedure according to which the state (city-state) is the human person "writ large," Plato examines the cardinal virtues both with respect to the individual person and with respect to the larger city-state. Ultimately, a just society for Plato is a society of just persons. And individuals are just according to their capacity with respect to each of the cardinal virtues. Another important concept in the *Republic* is the *three waves*, which refer to perennial issues in all societies at all times. These waves represent the issues of gender, property relations, and who should rule. In the dialogue, Socrates argues on behalf of gender equality; for a community of goods and spouses for the guardians of the *polis*, a group further divided according to warriors (*auxiliaries*) and rulers (*philosopher rulers*); and for the rule of philosophers. A full measure of justice is possible for Plato only when philosophers become rulers or rulers become philosophers.

Perhaps the most famous passages in the *Republic* are those that present the allegories of the *divided line*, from Book VI, and the *cave*, from Book VII. According to the divided line, human consciousness develops well or poorly according to a progression from imagination, to belief, to understanding, to reason based on consciousness of the good. This same progression is illustrated in the famous cave allegory, where we must *imagine* human beings chained and facing a cave wall, see them *believe* in the images projected on that wall from a fire behind their backs, *understand* that there might be more to reality than what such images suggest to the cave dwellers, and have the courage and capacity, unlike most of those in the cave, to turn around, see the drama to our backs, and theirs, and make our way out of the cave to a transcendent reality that, for Plato, must ultimately inform human *reason*. These allegories come toward the end of the *Republic* and summarize and condense what is explored through dialogue in the previous five books (chapters). Toward the end of the dialogue, Plato presents his thoughts on *declining forms* and *censorship*. According to the first, regime forms decay over time, such as from *aristocracy* (rule of the virtuous), to *timocracy* (rule of those who love honors), to *oligarchy* (rule of the wealthy), to *democracy* (rule of those who love freedom), to *tyranny* (rule of the lustful despot). The final book, Book X, explores the role of the artist in society, among other topics, and the need for some form of censorship.

The *Statesman* and the *Laws* represent significant departures from Plato's views and style of presentation in the *Republic*. In the *Statesman*, for example, an outsider from Elea takes the place of Socrates as the primary spokesperson and the dialogue form is all but abandoned.

More significantly, Plato emphasizes a rule of law, or legal codes, as preferable to the rule of philosophers. This shift of emphasis in the *Statesman* puts Plato more in the tradition of constitutional democracy, with its emphasis on well-constructed constitutions and institutions, characteristic of modern and postmodern approaches to the science of politics. Yet, in the *Laws*, among Plato's last works, which otherwise places a similar emphasis on the need for good laws, one encounters a *nocturnal council* that would be the final authority in the city-state. Many critics point to this dimension of Plato's work to support the idea that Plato was ultimately something of a totalitarian.

The twentieth-century philosopher Alfred North Whitehead (1861–1947) once famously observed that the European philosophical tradition could be characterized as but a "series of footnotes to Plato." Though his influence is not as great in the modern social sciences, there is continuing debate, especially among theorists within the discipline of political science, regarding Plato's insights on the role of intellectuals in society; the role of government in promoting excellence, or virtue; the educative function of the state; gender relations; property relations; the role of religion in the state, if any; and the perennial question regarding who should rule and why. And these are but a few of the modern issues regarding which Plato's works continue to inspire creative approaches. Some modern scholars, most famously Karl Popper (1902–1994), see in Plato's political theory the seeds of modern tyranny and closed societies. Others, such as John H. Hallowell (1913–1991), Eric Voegelin (1901–1985), and James M. Rhodes, see a more balanced and humane approach to the study and practice of politics. Because of his depth of insight and his creative approach to the perennial issues of human beings in their social and political dimensions beyond temporal and cultural considerations, Plato and his legacy will continue to be debated among scholars in all of the modern social sciences into the distant future.

BIBLIOGRAPHY

Hallowell, John H. 1965. Plato and his Critics. *The Journal of Politics* 27 (2): 273–289.

Popper, Karl R. 1966. *The Spell of Plato*. Vol. 1: *The Open Society and Its Enemies*. 5th rev. ed. Princeton, NJ: Princeton University Press.

Rhodes, James M. 2003. *Eros, Wisdom, and Silence: Plato's Erotic Dialogues*. Columbia: University of Missouri Press.

Strauss, Leo. 1964. *The City and Man*. Chicago: Rand McNally.

Voegelin, Eric. 2000. *Plato and Aristotle*. Pt. 1: *Plato*. Columbia: University of Missouri Press.

Timothy Hoye

PLEASURE PRINCIPLE
SEE *Psychoanalytic Theory.*

PLESSY, HOMER
SEE *Separate-but-Equal.*

PLESSY VS. FERGUSON
SEE *Separate-but-Equal.*

PLUMBING

The progress of a society may be judged by the way in which it disposes of its human waste material, and thus by the quality of its sewerage system (Mumford 1961, chap. 8). In the ancient world, the Greeks and Romans put great emphasis upon town planning. Roman cities were famed for their sewers, drains, aqueducts, paved streets, and roads. Domestic plumbing ranged from marble bathrooms with under-floor heating and indoor toilets in upmarket villas to basic latrine provision for the Roman army, as found, for example, alongside Hadrian's Wall in northern Britain (Greed 2003). Following the decline of the Roman Empire, waste disposal returned to more primitive methods. Most ordinary people used an outdoor "privy," while nobles often had an "indoor" toilet built out from the wall of their castle, hanging over the moat. In the Christian West during the Middle Ages, indoor plumbing, or for that matter personal hygiene and privacy, were not highly esteemed marks of civilization or progress, although washing and bathing, and bathhouses, were given higher priority in the Muslim East (Bonneville 1997).

In urban areas, the emptying of chamber pots straight into the street, and the accumulation of piles of human waste, resulted in disease and an unpleasant urban environment. Night-soil men were often employed to collect excreta, which was spread on the fields as fertilizer. Although Sir John Harrington had developed an indoor flushing toilet for Queen Elizabeth I in 1596, it was not until the rise of mass industrialization and urbanization in the nineteenth century that domestic toilets were mass-produced in northern England. Flushing technology was improved through the efforts of inventive manufacturers such as John Shanks, George Jennings, Alexander Cummings, and Thomas Crapper in the United Kingdom

(Reyburn 1969) and Thomas Maddocks, John Randall Mann, William Campbell, and Henry Demarest, among others, in the United States (Palmer 1973). Early toilet manufacturers were generally companies that had first made their name in the manufacture of china and earthenware. Such English companies as Minton, Twyford, and Doulton adapted their production processes to make porcelain toilet bowls and pans. Toilet design was based upon the "sit" rather than "squat" mode of excretion (which required nothing more than a hole in the ground). The sit approach required a specific and highly marketable consumer product, the "pedestal" toilet, along with all the plumbing fixtures, such as taps (faucets), cisterns, basins, and fittings that together made up the "bathroom." Interestingly, urinals for men, although a common feature of public toilets, are not generally a feature of private domestic bathrooms. These artifacts were exported from Britain to the rest of the world as a sign of modernity and Western progress, and were rapidly adopted for fear of being seen as "backward" or "dirty," in spite of the fact that the majority of the world's population squats when eliminating waste, a position that is ergonomically more healthy and efficient.

Compartmentalization of production was marked by separate metal-manufacture companies specializing in lead piping, plumbing fixtures, and other nonporcelain components. Nowadays, international toilet companies such as Armitage Shanks, Ideal Standard, and Geberit have diversified to offer a wide range of toilet technologies and materials. Synthetic materials now predominate; piping is made of plastic and the "porcelain" is more likely to be polymer. Old and widely used lead piping has been condemned as a potential cause of poisoning. (Plumbing gets its name from *plomb*, the medieval word for lead, as plumbers were essentially lead workers.)

While in the past, mains drainage and indoor plumbing were a sign of modernity, today people want "designer" bathrooms, luxury fixtures, power showers, fitted kitchens, and the latest technology. There has been a "restroom revolution" in Asia in particular, with companies such as Toto producing complete prefabricated bathroom units for the Japanese housing market, all the components being made together. Colored polyester resins, modern plastics, and marble and granite composites feature strongly in these modern bathroom modules (Greed 2003). Likewise, modern automatic public toilets are fully integrated, prefabricated systems that often use stainless steel and pathogen-resistant polymer materials. However, user-end toilet innovation must be matched by provider-end infrastructural sewerage system provision. The functionality of domestic toilets is dependent on there being a working sewerage system to take away output. Alternatively, the output from a luxury bathroom, as is the case in some affluent areas in developing countries, might end up in a cesspool under the house for collection by traditional night-soil operatives. Alternatively, as in some parts of the Americas and Australasia, even upmarket private houses are not served by a municipal sewerage and drainage system, and depend upon their own cesspits, generators, and water tanks.

Both public and domestic toilet design is becoming increasingly technologically driven, with automatic flushes and sensor-controlled washing-and-drying facilities becoming commonplace. In parallel, environmental sustainability requirements to save water have resulted in a range of dual-flush cisterns, waterless urinals, and human-waste recycling innovations. High levels of toilet provision in every home, along with highly developed sewerage systems, are no longer necessarily seen as signs of progress and economic development. Such assumptions are now being questioned. Many parts of the world are not economically or environmentally in a position to build modern, expensive water and sewerage systems: It is not a high priority. Water is becoming an increasingly expensive and scarce resource; some see it as "the new oil" in terms of future geopolitical tensions. Far from being a sign of economic development, many see the emphasis upon water-based sewerage systems and flushing toilets as old fashioned, colonial, and unsustainable. Instead, new, more sustainable solutions are being developed, especially within prosperous advanced Asian countries that can afford such research. Such systems will incorporate the most modern technological and scientific advances in the fields of engineering, pathogen control, and urban governance (Chun 2002; Mara 2006).

SEE ALSO *Civilization; Developing Countries; Development; Modernization; Planning; Public Health; Sanitation; Toilets; Urbanization; Water Resources*

BIBLIOGRAPHY

Bonneville, Françoise de. 1997. *The Book of the Bath.* London: Thames and Hudson.

Chun, Allen. 2002. Flushing in the Future: The Supermodern Japanese Toilet in a Changing Domestic Culture. *Post Colonial Studies Journal* (The Toilet Issue) 5 (2): 153–170.

Greed, Clara. 2003. *Inclusive Urban Design: Public Toilets.* Oxford: Elsevier.

Kira, Alexander. 1976. *The Bathroom.* London: Penguin.

Mara, Duncan. 2006. Modern Engineering Interventions to Reduce the Transmission of Diseases Caused by Inadequate Domestic Water Supplies and Sanitation in Developing Countries. *Building Services and Engineering Research and Technology* 27 (2): 75–84.

Mumford, Lewis. 1961. *The City in History: Its Origins, Its Transformations, and Its Prospects.* London: Penguin.

Palmer, Roy. 1973. *The Water Closet: A New History.* London: David and Charles, Newton Abbot.

Reyburn, Wallace. 1969. *Flushed with Pride: The Story of Thomas Crapper.* London: Macdonald.

Clara Greed

PLURALISM

Pluralism denotes more than one or two of anything and is contrary to monism, or the view that there is only one kind of a thing. *Pluralism* refers to a philosophical approach to the world as well as a theory of political and social power and, finally, to an empirical and normative focus on plural groups and group-based identities. Pluralism is central to liberal democracy in that it assumes that a diversity of views and identities, or a plurality of power centers, is essential to ensure democratic outcomes.

Contemporary debates over social and political pluralism tend to center on issues of identities in the context of multiethnic, multiracial, and multi-religious societies. This sense of pluralism is discussed in greater depth in the section below. Earlier theoretical formulations of pluralism reflected an evolving notion of competing interests in a democratic society and the role of non-state associations.

BRITISH AND AMERICAN PLURALISM

In twentieth-century Western thought, pluralism has at least two dominant strands. The first found expression is in works of British political philosophy such as those of Frederic William Maitland, John Neville Figgis, G. D. H. (George Douglas Howard) Cole, and Harold J. Laski, as well as in the work of the German theorist Otto Friedrich von Gierke. The unifying theme of these works was the plurality of associations and groups of various kinds that operate independently of the state but are vital for a functional government. The argument was that centralized power in the state ought to be lessened or "pluralized" to meet the needs of citizens in a free society. In order to preserve liberty it was preferable to disperse state power among a variety of distinct and functionally autonomous groups that could better reflect the specific and diverse interests of citizens. The English pluralists rejected the sovereignty of the state but differed in their conception of the relationship between citizens and the state, with some arguing that the state is composed of groups rather than individuals and that belonging to the state is mediated through membership in other groups. These thinkers generally considered the ideal to be a limited and constrained state with a proliferation of free associations. World politics in the post–World War I era led to a resurgence of interest in a strong and effective state, thereby weakening the pluralist argument.

American theorists of pluralism shared an interest in the multiplicity of voices acting upon the state but focused on competing interest groups or pressure groups and their efforts to exert influence on the state. Notions of pluralism and its contribution to democracy originated in Alexis de Tocqueville's *Democracy in America*, in which Tocqueville argued in part that democracy depends on a plurality of secondary associations outside of the state that prevent majoritarian democracy from becoming tyrannical. Particularly since the 1950s, American pluralists have used theories of pluralism to describe a model of minimum democratic competition for influence and office. The role of the state in this view is as something of an arbiter, seeking balance among semiautonomous, often opposed and self-interested interest groups.

One prominent pluralist, Nelson W. Polsby, described American society in 1980 as a collection of "hundreds of small special interest groups, with incompletely overlapping memberships, widely differing power bases and a multitude of techniques for exercising influence on decisions salient to them" (p. 118). American theorists argued that U.S. society was differentiated and fractured into many interest groups. One of the most influential thinkers in this group was Robert A. Dahl, whose work reflected an interest in "a plurality of relatively autonomous (independent) organizations (subsystems) within the domain of a state" (Dahl 1982, p. 5). A democracy can be called a "polyarchy" if it meets certain specific conditions, especially that it contains plural centers of interest, each of which has some influence on policy making, and that no group has a monopoly of influence. Particularly relevant to the discussion below, Dahl and other pluralists argued that pluralism of identity (race, ethnicity, religion) is generally a feature of less competitive political systems, while pluralism of interests is a feature of a democracy. Dahl also posited that a democratic society is stronger if it is made up of citizens with crosscutting identity cleavages (rather than reinforcing cleavages), which reflect common interest on some issues and opposing interest on others. This means that a democratic society is one in which a broad array of issue-oriented movements draw together new constituencies that cut across identity lines.

Pluralism in this sense also stands in contrast to corporatist politics. Pluralist interest groups are made up of multiple associations focusing on a single interest issue, and the groups are voluntary, decentralized, and separated from the government. Corporatist politics is generally more organized and is characterized by a single association for each societal interest, typically with compulsory and universal membership and with central organization. For pluralists like Dahl (1998) the associations should be relatively independent and autonomous. In all respects, pluralists focus on power dispersal as a check on all centers of power, including the state.

Critics of American pluralist theory have challenged the ideal of pluralism as well as the empirical fact that such a process operates as it has been theorized in the United States. They point to the systematic inequality among interest groups that runs counter to the pluralist vision of equal and competing associations. For instance, critics such as C. Wright Mills have argued that American politics is dominated by an economic elite and that a discussion of a mere plurality of associations does not account for the hierarchies of power present in political life. In 1970 Peter Bachrach and Morton S. Baratz highlighted the importance of nondecision-making processes, those individuals or groups that seek to limit decision-making to relatively uncontroversial issues, thereby influencing political decisions in significant ways. Their work pointed to the manner in which political systems are characterized by inequality that tends to persist over time, and how subordinated groups then are "often unable to convert their demands for change into important political issues" that are ever considered by policymakers (p. 105). Henry Kariel saw classic studies of American pluralism as elevating one particular institutional system, American pluralism, as both "irreducible, beyond analysis and critique" and objectively good, preventing systematic analysis of American institutions (p. 136).

Finally, Dianne M. Pinderhughes's critical study of Chicago politics, *Race and Ethnicity in Chicago Politics: A Reexamination of Pluralist Theory* (1987), provided rich historical data on labor and housing markets, political participation, education, and the criminal justice system for black, Polish, and Italian immigrants, all of whom came to the city at roughly the same time and for similar reasons but had strikingly different patterns of social and political integration some decades on. Her work demonstrated that pluralist assumptions of black integration into American life based on the evolution of specific issue sets did not occur because of the substantial discrimination inherent in American political institutions and because black citizens' own political attitudes led to a rejection of conventional American institutions and authority symbols. The assumptions about bargaining that undergird pluralist theories of issue-oriented politics cannot occur when the issues are not bargainable and the parties to the bargain are not equal.

CONTEMPORARY PLURALISM

Pluralism in political thought underwent something of a revival in the last two decades of the twentieth century. Building on the body of work such as that of Pinderhughes, pluralists have put the concept to use in defense of multiculturalism and diversity that run counter to assimilationist nation-building projects. Pluralists have charged that modern majoritarian democratic institutions and laws privilege dominant racial, ethnic, or cultural groups and should be thoroughly democratized by giving greater attention to inclusion of these plural identity groups. Unlike earlier forms of pluralism, the diversity of groups is not composed of voluntary associations or civil society groups in the strict sense. Neither are these issue-focused interest groups. Rather, "plural" identities in this conceptualization are communal groups, typically understood to include ethnic, racial, religious, or cultural characteristics and based on identities that, while situational and fluid, are not easily acquired or discarded.

The roots of this strain of pluralist theory are to be found in part in the writings of social anthropologists and historians of the colonized world in the first half of the twentieth century. Studies of colonial empires in South Asia and Africa in particular led to a focus on "traditional societies," which were plural in the sense of being composed of ethnic groups who retained strong attachments to their distinct religions, culture, languages, and community life and were held together by pressure and even force from the colonial power and, in the postcolonial period, by the newly independent state. These distinct social segments, living side by side but rarely interacting, led to the types of heterogeneous societies found in newly independent states. Theorists typically argued that the state was captured by one minority segment within the plural society. Kuper summarized these as societies "characterized by cultural diversity, social cleavage and dissensus" (Kuper and Smith 1969, p. 12). While the focus was often empirical and descriptive, the normative tone suggested ways to reduce the plurality, which was presumed to cause political and social conflict through assimilationist nation-building policies.

Subsequent studies in comparative pluralism have widened this contemporary understanding of pluralism by emphasizing that nearly all states in the modern world are heterogeneous and plural in the sense that M. G. Smith and Leo Kuper had argued colonial societies were. Pierre L. Van den Berghe suggested that pluralism can encompass not only subcultural ethnic and communal identities but also differences based on race, caste, and class. This signaled a transition in two somewhat distinct but conceptually related subfields of social and political inquiry: race and ethnic stratification in the Western democracies, and the various ethnic (and sometimes racial) cleavages found in the former colonies of the Middle East, Africa, Asia, and Latin America.

A flourishing interest in the empirics and theory of racial and ethnic differences in North America and western Europe has produced many strands of thought on pluralism, most with a focus on group-based citizenship.

Scholars argued that the notion of a homogeneous Western nation-state was more a fiction than a reality. Michael Omi and Howard Winant's concept of racial formation described the historical creation, deployment, transformation, and destruction of racial categories. Critical race theorists pointed to the distinct role that racial identities play in the context of a "racial state" and the social, political, and economic significance of group-based identities on life prospects for members. Philosophers such as Linda Martín Alcoff (2006) defended the attachment to cultural identities as ontologically real and fully defensible within a tradition concerned with individual autonomy and rationality. Political theorists asserted that political struggles over cultural diversity are at least as important in the West as elsewhere, and that only through "multicultural citizenship" (as Will Kymlicka put it in 1995) or "differentiated citizenship" (in Iris Marion Young's 1991 formulation) can democracy or a just constitutional order be achieved. Critics of this approach, such as Brian Barry (2001), do not argue that there is a plurality of identity groups, but they insist that there is only one status of citizenship in a liberal democracy. Rights are, and should be, assigned to individuals as such, rather than to particular groups.

Paralleling this shift in Western thought on pluralism, and reflecting greater attention not just on a plurality of groups but specific kinds of groups (racial, ethnic, religious), was a deepening of theoretical attention to the nature of communal diversity in non-Western contexts. These theorists challenged perspectives like that of Kuper and Smith, which had focused on the conflict-prone nature of groups and seemed to point toward assimilationist nation-building projects. Donald L. Horowitz's seminal study *Ethnic Groups in Conflict* (1985) attempted to explain not only the material and political basis of ethnic identities but also the psychosocial importance of relative group worth in plural societies. A wealth of literature has developed on the topic, much of it focusing on institutional engineering and conflict management in ethnically diverse societies (Lijphart), as well theoretical approaches accounting for the diverse citizenship models that emerge in the context of this kind of diversity (Berman, Eyoh, and Kymlicka).

What is increasingly clear is that various forms of pluralism, however constituted, are critical to the deepening of democracy. Pluralism disperses power and contributes to the vitality of the democratic community by acting as a check on a strong state. Further, it can support identification with the democratic state by recognizing and valuing the diverse communities to which citizens belong.

SEE ALSO *Cleavages; Community Power Studies; Consensus; Dahl, Robert Alan; Democracy; Discrimination, Racial; Elites; Ethnic*

Fractionalization; Ethnicity; Interest Groups and
Interests; Kariel, Henry S.; Lindblom, Charles
Edward; Nondecision-making; Politics, Urban;
Polyarchy; Power Elite; State, The

BIBLIOGRAPHY

Bachrach, Peter, and Morton S. Baratz. 1962. Two Faces of
Power. *American Political Science Review* 56 (4): 947–952.

Bachrach, Peter, and Morton S. Baratz. 1970. *Power and Poverty:
Theory and Practice.* New York: Oxford University Press.

Barry, Brian. 2001. *Culture and Equality: An Egalitarian Critique
of Multiculturalism.* Cambridge, MA: Harvard University
Press.

Berman, Bruce, Dickson Eyoh, and Will Kymlicka, eds. 2004.
Ethnicity and Democracy in Africa. Athens: Ohio University
Press.

Crenshaw, Kimberlé, ed. 1995. *Critical Race Theory: The Key
Writings that Formed the Movement.* New York: New Press.

Dahl, Robert A. 1971. *Polyarchy: Participation and Opposition.*
New Haven, CT: Yale University Press.

Dahl, Robert A. 1982. *Dilemmas of Pluralist Democracy:
Autonomy vs. Control.* New Haven, CT: Yale University Press.

Dahl, Robert A. 1998. *On Democracy.* New Haven, CT: Yale
University Press.

Furnivall, J. S. 1948. *Colonial Policy and Practice: A Comparative
Study of Burma and Netherlands India.* Cambridge, U.K.:
Cambridge University Press.

Goldberg, David Theo. 2002. *The Racial State.* Malden, MA:
Blackwell.

Hirst, Paul Q. 1989. *The Pluralist Theory of the State: Selected
Writings of G. D. H. Cole, J. N. Figgis, and H. J. Laski.* New
York: Routledge.

Horowitz, Donald L. 1985. *Ethnic Groups in Conflict.* Berkeley:
University of California Press.

Kariel, Henry S. 1961. *The Decline of American Pluralism.*
Stanford, CA: Stanford University Press.

Kuper, Leo, and M. G. Smith, eds. 1969. *Pluralism in Africa.*
Berkeley: University of California Press.

Kymlicka, Will. 1995. *Multicultural Citizenship: A Liberal
Theory of Minority Rights.* Oxford, U.K.: Clarendon Press.

Lijphart, Arend. 1977. *Democracy in Plural Societies: A
Comparative Exploration.* New Haven, CT: Yale University
Press.

Mills, C. Wright. 1956. *The Power Elite.* New York: Oxford
University Press.

Nicholls, David. 1974. *Three Varieties of Pluralism.* New York:
St. Martin's.

Omi, Michael, and Howard Winant. 1994. *Racial Formation in
the United States: From the 1960s to the 1990s.* 2nd ed. New
York: Routledge.

Pinderhughes, Dianne M. 1987. *Race and Ethnicity in Chicago
Politics: A Reexamination of Pluralist Theory.* Urbana:
University of Illinois Press.

Polsby, Nelson W. 1980. *Community Power and Political Theory:
A Further Look at Problems of Evidence and Inference.* 2nd,
enlarged ed. New Haven, CT: Yale University Press.

Taylor, Charles. 1992. *Multiculturalism and the Politics of
Recognition.* Princeton, NJ: Princeton University Press.

Tully, James. 1995. *Strange Multiplicity: Constitutionalism in an
Age of Diversity.* New York: Cambridge University Press.

Young, Iris Marion. 1990. *Justice and the Politics of Difference.*
Princeton, NJ: Princeton University Press.

Lahra Smith

PLURALITY

As a mechanism for deciding political contests, elections
held under plurality rules have the great apparent advantage of simplicity. Plurality elections are most commonly
used to elect one candidate for one position. When the
number of positions to be filled is one, the candidate with
more votes than any other candidate is declared the winner. In some plurality elections, however, the number of
positions to be filled is more than one—for example, four.
In such elections, the positions are filled by the four candidates who win more votes than the other candidates.

But plurality elections are not as simple as they seem.
Candidates are elected under plurality rules with more
votes than the losing candidate or candidates. But when
there are many more candidates standing for election than
positions to be filled, successful candidates may receive far
less than half the votes: For example, in an election in a
single-member district for which there are 100 voters and
five candidates, the winner might receive only 21 votes,
three losers 20 votes, and the other 19. Sometimes the difference in number of votes between the winning and losing candidate in a single-member plurality election is
called the *majority*. But more accurately, a majority is 50
percent plus one of all votes cast. In this case, in the election example above, the winner would receive 51 votes
and the losing candidates 49 votes between them.
Therefore, candidates elected under plurality systems
where many more stand than can be elected do not necessarily have majority support.

Electoral theory posits that the number of candidates
likely to be competitive in a plurality election is the number that can be elected plus one: where the position is for
a single member, therefore, this equals two (Cox 1997),
but this does not always happen. This claim is often
extrapolated from a single election in one district to a general election across an entire country where parties compete. Thus plurality electoral systems are said to generate
two-party systems, and, in particular, they tend to increase
the number of successful candidates for the winning party

beyond its share of the votes cast nationally. Plurality elections, in this context, are said to produce *manufactured majorities* among the persons elected. In this sense, plurality elections produce majority outcomes, and are thus often labelled *majoritarian*. Certain theories of democracy value this aspect of plurality elections because the consequent two-party systems are said to make possible alternation of office between moderate parties and enhance the stability, decisiveness, and accountability of governments.

However, this strength of plurality elections is most apparent where societies have one major social division and related political preferences are distributed across electoral districts in a way that can generate balanced two-party competition. Plurality elections worked successfully in many democratic societies during the twentieth century under these conditions. But if social divisions and preferences are distributed similarly in all districts, one party can in theory win all seats. And if there is more than one social division and associated sets of preferences are separated spatially among districts, a multiparty system will emerge (Kim and Ohn 1992). In essence, plurality elections privilege social divisions that are distributed spatially, but provide poor representation of those that are not. Given this, it remains debatable whether plurality can operate as a system of election in the increasingly socially heterogeneous societies of the twenty-first century as successfully as it did in the past.

SEE ALSO *Elections; Electoral Systems; First-past-the-post; Voting*

BIBLIOGRAPHY

Cox, Gary W. 1997. *Making Votes Count: Strategic Coordination in the World's Electoral Systems.* Cambridge, U.K.: Cambridge University Press.

Kim, Jae-On Kim, and Mahn-Guem Ohn. 1992. A Theory of Minor-Party Persistence: Election Rules, Social Cleavages, and the Number of Political Parties. *Social Forces* 70: 575–599.

Jack Vowles

POGROMS

The term *pogrom* is derived from the Russian *pogromit* (to create a desert) and describes forcible excursions and plunder against a specific ethnic or religious minority. Outbreaks of this kind occasionally occur spontaneously but are initiated by local or national forces. It is common for a significant portion of the majority population to take part in these persecutions; as a rule the authorities do not intervene to halt the violence.

The term is used in the twenty-first century to designate a variety of events, such as the persecution of the Armenians by Sultan Abdulhamid II (1842–1918) in the Ottoman Empire from 1894 to 1896; the attacks on Greeks in Istanbul, Turkey, in 1955; the murder of ethnic Chinese in Indonesia after the fall of President Ahmed Sukarno (1901–1970) in 1965; the harrying of the Ibo people in northern Nigeria in 1967; the agitation against the Sikhs in India following the assassination of Prime Minister Indira Gandhi (1917–1984); and the excesses against the Armenians in Baku, Azerbaijan, in 1990. The word gradually became part of the international vocabulary toward the end of the nineteenth century. Originally it meant only the anti-Semitic excesses of czarist Russia. Hence consideration of the pogroms directed against Jews in central and eastern Europe is key to the following discussion, along with consideration of their political and socioeconomic context and background.

EUROPEAN POGROMS: FROM THE MIDDLE AGES TO THE EARLY MODERN ERA

During the first two Crusades (1096–1102 and 1147–1149), the Jews of central Europe, especially in Germany, fell victim to persecutions and sacrifices. The initial nature of the conflict was religious. The persecutors justified their action with the argument that the liberation of the Holy Land should be preceded by the murder of the "murderers of Christ" in Europe. The actual motives of the perpetrators were more economic, however. The burgeoning religious fanaticism of the time presented a suitably legitimate opportunity to get rid of some economic competitors, because many Jews were involved in credit trades at the time. Yet it would be a mistake to equate the history of the Jews in medieval Europe with persecution and discrimination. There were certainly longer periods of relatively peaceful coexistence with the Christian world. Nonetheless, relations between Christians and Jews were precarious. Famines and epidemics inflamed the Christian majority against religious and social minorities. Thus the great epidemic and plague of the late Middle Ages in the mid-fourteenth century resulted in pogroms against the Jewish population. The Jews were accused of causing the plague by poisoning wells and streams. Hence the initial motive for the persecution was an attempt to explain the sudden appearance of the rapidly spreading illness. At the same time the hatred of the Jews this stirred up played into the hands of Christian debtors and merchants.

Mobilization against the Jews was further spurred by accusations of ritual murder. These assertions claimed that Jews stole Christian children and slaughtered them in order to use their blood for ritual purposes. This accusation, among others, served as a reason for the destruction and plunder of the Prague Ghetto in 1389, which at the time contained the largest and wealthiest Jewish population in Europe.

Because the threat of persecution and expulsion constantly hung over their heads, beginning in the thirteenth century large segments of the Jewish population moved farther to the east. The Polish kings encouraged the settlement of Jews and guaranteed their security and economic privileges. The Jews soon became indispensable for the Polish economy, mediating as traders and brokers between town and country. The Polish nobility came to prefer leaving the administration of their property to Jews, which dragged the latter into conflicts between nobility and peasantry. In 1648 these tensions finally resulted in a pogrom of hitherto unseen magnitude, when Ukrainian peasants joined with Cossacks, Russian cavalry, led by Hetman Bogdan Chmelnicki (1595–1657) and attacked Polish cities. As many as 125,000 Jews fell victim during these massacres. As a rule the Jews could not count on the support of their Polish neighbors, and it took decades for the Jewish communities to rebuild. One reaction to the catastrophe was the rising popularity of cabalistic doctrine among eastern European Jews and the spread of messianic apocalyptic sects. The eventual outcome of these movements was Hassidism, one of the most significant mystical-religious movements in Judaism.

POGROMS IN RUSSIA UNDER THE CZARS AND DURING THE REVOLUTION

A rise in anti-Semitism in Russia coincided with the shaking off of Mongolian rule and the strengthening of the Orthodox Church in the late Middle Ages. Czar Ivan IV (1530–1584) forced religious conversion on the Jews in the newly conquered territories and severely restricted Jewish trade. By the middle of the seventeenth century, Russia had become a great power in the region and annexed Poland in 1772, lending the "Jewish question," that is, the question of how to deal with the unpleasant minority, a new urgency. Under pressure from Russian merchants fearful of Jewish competition, Catherine II (1729–1796), who ruled Russia from 1762 to 1796, issued a decree forbidding Jews from living in the Russian interior. Their territory was restricted to the so-called Pale of Settlement—the former territory of Poland and the area north of the Black Sea.

The nineteenth century saw a profound socioeconomic transformation of Russian society that also affected the life and economic activity of Jewish communities. The Jewish population concentrated itself in the cities inside the Pale of Settlement, focusing on trade; skilled trades and the cultivation of the land had become less profitable and therefore lost their appeal for most Jews. Although a small portion of the population established itself in banking and credit, most Jews became impoverished. From this point on Jews attempted to succeed as petty merchants, peddlers, and handicraftspeople. They thus found themselves in bitter, destructive competition with their Christian neighbors, which led to a rise in anti-Semitism. The Russian upper classes and nobility also became increasingly anti-Semitic, associating the Jews with modernization and capitalism (i.e., with movements that threatened the traditional social order). Thus anti-Semitism came to be associated with anticapitalism and antisocialism.

The hostility toward Jews was widespread in the Russian Empire: between 1881 and 1921 there were three devastating waves of pogroms. The first followed the assassination of Czar Alexander II (1818–1881), when anti-Semitic circles blamed his death on the Jews. The rumor spread like wildfire and gave an anti-Semitic mob justification for attacks on the Jewish community. Pogroms regularly ensued until 1884, primarily in southeastern Ukraine, but also in White Russia (later Belarus) and Lithuania. The Ukrainian pogroms were perpetrated primarily by migrant workers and railway employees. The local population, especially in the Ukraine, passively observed the plunder and violence and left the mobs unhindered, seeing these pogroms against an unloved minority as a suitable release for the pressures of unresolved social issues. Czar Alexander III (1845–1894) blamed the pogroms on the Jews themselves and drafted a series of discriminatory edicts against them in order to unite a divided population behind him. In their struggle for legitimacy, the Russian upper classes fanned the flames of already widespread anti-Semitism, misusing it as an ideology of social integration.

The outbreak of the second wave of pogroms, from 1903 to 1906, was linked directly to political developments in the czarist empire. In order to try to contain growing revolutionary sentiment, the government fanned anti-Semitism by inciting the conservative press against the Jewish population. The first pogrom of this era took place at the Jewish holiday of Passover in 1903 in the town of Kishinev, with roughly 1,500 Jewish houses and businesses looted. These pogroms were organized by the so-called Black Hundreds, an association of reactionary monarchist groups. The government instructed local authorities not to proceed against the perpetrators. Representatives of the czarist secret police wrote and disseminated anti-Semitic pamphlets, such as the infamous *Protocols of the Elders of Zion*, which blamed the Jews for all the country's ills. After the Reform Edicts of 1905, which extended suffrage to the Jews and established the Duma (i.e., the Russian parliament), the most devastating pogrom to date occurred involving sixty-four cities and six hundred villages. More than eight hundred Jews fell victim to its violence.

The wave of pogroms from 1917 to 1921 occurred in the context of world war, revolution, and civil war. Even before the end of World War I (1914–1918), deserters committed terrible massacres and robberies of Jewish property in villages near the front. After the Bolshevik October Revolution in 1917, units of the Red Army and more particularly counterrevolutionary forces (the so-called White Russian, anti-Bolshevik armies) fell on the Jewish population in towns and cities. The worst pogroms took place in the Ukrainian Republic. Before the pro-Bolshevik Red Army's victory in 1920, over sixty thousand Jews lost their lives in the violence.

As a result of the constant pogroms and growing legal and social discrimination, from the 1880s onward many young Jews joined the socialist opposition. A Jewish national consciousness also developed, culminating in Zionism. The Zionists believed that Jewish integration into eastern European society had failed and that the sole solution to the "Jewish question" was the creation of a Jewish national state. During this time also Jewish emigration to the United States (and also to Palestine) rose steadily.

POGROMS IN GERMANY

German Jews only achieved full civil rights with the creation of the Second German Empire, following the French defeat in the Franco-Prussian War in 1871. But the path was a bumpy one. In 1819 some manual workers, merchants, and students took the discussions instigated by Jewish emancipation as an occasion for pogroms in several German cities. During the nineteenth century a large portion of the Jewish population in Germany was able to achieve some social progress; however, by the 1870s several anti-Semitic parties had formed with the explicit aim of reversing the social equality and integration of the Jews. After the beginning of the twentieth century, most of these parties sank into insignificance. Although anti-Semitism was as widespread and significant a political force in Germany as in surrounding European states, it was considerably less powerful than in eastern European states.

Extreme nationalism during World War I had already led to a growing climate of anti-Semitism. After the end of the war, nationalist and populist groups, such as the right-wing extremist party the National Socialist German Workers' Party (NSDAP), blamed German Jewry for the defeat as well as the succeeding economic misery. For many members of the NSDAP Judaism and bolshevism (anticapitalism) were synonymous; both phenomena were treated as dangerous to traditional social and political order.

The systematic disenfranchisement and exclusion of German Jews began soon after the NSDAP's seizure of power in January 1933. The first pogrom against the Jews during this period broke out on 9 and 10 November 1938 and was referred to as *Reichskristallnacht* or *Kristallnacht* (night of broken glass). But this incident was anything but a spontaneous expression of violence. Members of the NSDAP and the Gestapo (the secret security police of the NSDAP) as well as paramilitary organizations such as the Sturmabteilung (SA) started fires in synagogues across Germany and plundered Jewish businesses. In the process they murdered one hundred German Jews. The German police had received orders that under no circumstances were they to intervene on behalf of the Jews. A small portion of the population participated in the pogrom, especially the plunder, while most Germans observed the events passively without participating. The NSDAP government had attempted to portray the pogrom as a spontaneous reaction by the Germans to the assassination of a German diplomat by a Jewish conspirator in Paris. The NSDAP government had three goals in the November pogrom. Initially forces within the party for whom existing anti-Jewish measures were insufficiently radical were to be mollified. Moreover the Nazi leadership sought to further intimidate the Jews and encourage their emigration. Finally, the pogrom accelerated the systematic persecution and dispossession of the Jews, a process referred to as "aryanization."

During World War II members of the NSDAP, or Nazi Party, committed countless pogroms against Jewish populations in occupied areas of eastern Europe. The local populations generally cooperated willingly with the occupiers and permitted themselves to be dragged into deeds of violence against their Jewish neighbors. On occasion, such as in the Polish town of Jedwabne, the local population did not wait for the arrival of the German conquerors and murdered the Jewish population on their own initiative. The prospect of taking over Jewish property was every bit as much to blame for this turn of events as historically deep-rooted anti-Semitism.

The czarist pogroms in Russia and the November 1938 pogrom in Germany all occurred with government participation in the planning and the violence. Nonetheless, the involvement of the population in Russia was considerably greater than in Germany, since the integration of Jews into German society was considerably more advanced than in Russia. Thus the aim of the 1938 pogrom was not so much to push social and political problems into the background and unite a politically and socially divided populace.

SEE ALSO *Anti-Semitism; Bolshevism; Christianity; Concentration Camps; Ethnic Conflict; Ethnic Fractionalization; Ethnocentrism; Ghetto; Hitler, Adolf; Holocaust, The; Jews; Nazism; Riots; Russian Revolution; Shtetl; Terrorism; Violence; World War II*

BIBLIOGRAPHY

Friedländer, Saul. 1997. *The Years of Persecution, 1933–1939.* Vol. 1 of *Nazi Germany and the Jews.* New York: Harper Collins.

Gross, Jan T. 2001. *Neighbors: The Destruction of the Jewish Community in Jedwabne, Poland.* Princeton, NJ: Princeton University Press.

Judge, Edward H. 1992. *Easter in Kishinev: Anatomy of a Pogrom.* New York: New York University Press.

Klier, John D., and Shlomo Lambroza, eds. 1992. *Pogroms: Anti-Jewish Violence in Modern Russian History.* Cambridge, U.K.: Cambridge University Press.

Dominik J. Schaller

POISSON, SIMEON DENS

SEE *Distribution, Poisson.*

POL POT
1925?–1998

Pol Pot was the ruler of Cambodia from 1975 to 1979 and presided over one of the worst genocides of the twentieth century. In approximately 1925 (the exact date of this birth remains unclear), he was born Saloth Sar to a fairly well-to-do family in Kompong Thom Province, Cambodia. Although Pol Pot's political zest developed while he was in his home country, his path to political leadership began to be forged after his arrival in Paris in 1949 to study radio electronics. There he became a member of the French Communist Party and met other Cambodian intellectual elites who would become powerful figures in the years 1975 to 1979.

Having failed his exams three years in a row, Pol Pot (a nom de guerre, short for the French *politique potentielle*) returned to Cambodia in January 1953. He had, however, become well-versed in socialism and communism—his intellectual models were Vladimir Ilyich Lenin, Leon Trotsky, Joseph Stalin, and Mao Tse-tung—and his opposition to the government of Prince Norodom Sihanouk led him to join the Communist resistance. Pol Pot became a member of the Indochina Communist Party, which was dominated by Viet Minh, within a month after his return. He then joined the Cambodian Communist Party Group, whom Sihanouk named the Khmer Rouge or Red Cambodians, and became secretary general in 1962. This group then started agitating against the Phnom Penh government. Ultimately, through armed rebellion, the Khmer

Rouge gained full control of the country. The party took power on April 17, 1975, less than two weeks before the fall of Saigon ended the Vietnam War, and renamed the country Democratic Kampuchea. One of the Khmer Rouge's first acts was to implement a complete evacuation of Phnom Penh to the countryside.

Under his four-year plan, Pol Pot's stated aim was to turn Cambodia into a Maoist agrarian utopia; he planned to nationalize all industry and finance the economy through increased agricultural exports. His regime seized all legislative and judicial powers. Every Cambodian was forced to become an unpaid agrarian laborer and was allowed limited food and rest. Under the four-year plan, at least one million Cambodians died as a result of starvation, disease, or murder. Anyone suspected of betraying the government was killed.

Throughout the late 1970s relations with Vietnam worsened. Pol Pot's government was toppled on January 7, 1979, by the invading Vietnamese army. Pol Pot himself never surrendered; he fled into the jungle near Thailand and led a Khmer Rouge guerrilla war from there. As Cambodia worked to return to normalcy, it remained under threat from the Khmer Rouge, which never recognized the Phnom Penh government and claimed some western provinces on the border with Thailand. Pol Pot maintained his opposition to the new coalition government until the national elections of 1993. Never brought to justice for having decimated his country, he died on April 15, 1998, in the Thai-Cambodian border area.

SEE ALSO *Communism; Dictatorship; Genocide; Khmer Rouge; Killing Fields; Socialism; Vietnam War*

BIBLIOGRAPHY

Kiernan, Ben. 2002. *The Pol Pot Regime: Race, Power, and Genocide in Cambodia under the Khmer Rouge, 1975–1979.* New Haven, CT: Yale University Press.

Short, Philip. 2004. *Pol Pot: Anatomy of a Nightmare.* New York: Henry Holt.

Lay Vicheka

POLICING, BIASED

Biased policing refers to the practice of law enforcement officers or agencies of systematically targeting certain groups in society for suspicious activities. Instead of being judged as innocent until proven guilty, targeted groups tend to be considered guilty first and questioned about their innocence later. Police biasing often takes the form of racial and ethnic profiling. However, biased policing may also be directed at gay men and lesbians, people who occupy the lower-class rungs of society, or groups that do not exemplify the normative behaviors expected in society (e.g., biker gangs, religious cults). In the past, research on biased policing was typically centered on local and state law enforcement agencies, such as city and state police and sheriff's departments. However, since about the mid-1990s there has been increasing research on federal law enforcement agencies that engage in biased policing (e.g., the Federal Bureau of Investigation, the Department of Homeland Security).

Biased policing is a form of institutional and systemic racism. Using Eduardo Bonilla-Silva's (2006) notion of the "racialized social system," biased policing can be seen as one form of social control against groups who are considered "outsiders." As such, biased policing helps to maintain the white middle-class structure that dominates U.S. society. This form of negative profiling has existed in American society since the slavery era, when "black codes" were institutionalized to regulate both free and enslaved blacks (Jordon 1968; Marable 2000). Both groups were heavily monitored by slave patrols, whose duties included not only punishing runaway slaves but also free blacks who were considered threatening to whites. These slave patrols were usually organized groups of three to six white men who patrolled plantations, state borders, and state roads, profiling people who did not fit the skin color and phenotype of white Europeans.

Although most law enforcement agencies have policies that clearly state that any form of biased policing, including racial profiling, is deemed unacceptable, the American Civil Liberties Union maintains that tens of thousands of Americans face some sort of biased policing everyday. Furthermore after the September 11, 2001, terrorist attacks on the World Trade Center in New York City and the Pentagon in Virginia, biased policing and, more specifically, racial profiling reached a new high in regard to the number of people who are affected by these extreme forms of social control.

The form that biased policing takes varies depending on the law enforcement agencies involved, the personal characteristics of the law enforcement officers, whether state or federal laws are involved, and the location. For example, after the passage in 2001 of the Patriot Act, designed to expand the authority of U.S. law enforcement agencies for the purpose of fighting the threat of terrorism in the United States, an increase in racial profiling against Arab and Muslim Americans took place and was justified under the guise of fear (Muneer 2002). Forms of biased policing include the stopping of motorists, the detention of a person or group of people, or the searching of a person's vehicle, home, or body based on any number of characteristics, including race, ethnicity, gender, age, or income status. Common forms of biased policing include

harassment of specific groups of people at malls, workplaces, and even political gatherings. For example, numerous blacks reported being harassed by local police on their way to voting booths during the 2000 presidential election in Florida. In addition a large number of Latinos report harassment by law enforcement officers on their way to work, school, or home as a result of controversies concerning immigration in the United States.

RACIAL PROFILING

Of the various forms of biased policing, the most notable and well researched concerns discrimination by race or ethnicity. This type of biased policing is known as *racial profiling* and refers to the systematic targeting of a person or group based solely on race or ethnicity. In other words, other than a person's race or ethnicity, there is no reasonable justification for stopping or detaining him or her. The issue of racial profiling has been such a frequent problem for blacks and Latinos in the United States that new slang terms have been created to describe such instances (Lundman and Kaufman 2003). For example, the stopping and searching of blacks and Latinos for "suspected" traffic violations is commonly referred to as DWB (i.e., driving while black) or DWM (i.e., driving while Mexican).

After the 2001 terrorist attacks, U.S. law enforcement agencies slightly shifted their focus on blacks and Latinos to include Arabs and Muslim Americans and even South Asian Americans as racially profiled targets. The matter has become increasingly complex as poll data indicate that a majority of blacks and Latinos may support racial profiling against Arab and Muslim Americans.

COUNTERARGUMENTS

Although numerous studies indicate that biased policing and racial profiling continue to be a major issue in the United States, a number of studies argue that the issue of racial profiling has been overstated or that such practices are necessary given the terrorist threat. For instance, Michael Smith and Matthew Petrocelli (2001) argued that while black drivers were pulled over more frequently than white drivers, there was no data that suggested that vehicles driven by blacks were more frequently searched. Moreover, controlling for certain variables, blacks were more likely to be issued a warning, whereas white drivers were more likely to be ticketed or arrested. In addition to research that favors biased policing, numerous articles in the mainstream press argue that racial profiling does not occur. For example, Heather MacDonald (2003) reported in the *Los Angeles Times* that police officers who were labeled as racist were in fact just doing their jobs. MacDonald further argued that what appeared to be racial profiling was really just "good policing." However, the problem with the majority of such studies and articles resides in their limited sampling techniques; as such, they do not reflect the overwhelming data that find that biased policing and racial profiling continue to be major issues in the United States.

SEE ALSO *Colorism; Crime and Criminology; Discrimination; Discrimination, Racial; Discrimination, Statistical; Inequality, Racial; Law and Order; Phenotype; Race-Blind Policies; Race-Conscious Policies; Racism; September 11, 2001; Signals; Stereotypes*

BIBLIOGRAPHY

Bonilla-Silva, Eduardo. 2006. *Racism without Racists: Color-blind Racism and the Persistence of Racial Inequality in the United States.* 2nd ed. Boulder, CO: Rowman and Littlefield.

Eberhardt, Jennifer L., Paul G. Davies, Valerie J. Purdie-Vaughns, and Sheri Lynn Johnson. 2006. Looking Deathworthy: Perceived Stereotypicality of Black Defendants Predicts Capital-Sentencing Outcomes. *Psychological Science* 17: 383–386.

Jordon, Winthrop D. 1968. *White over Black: American Attitudes toward the Negro, 1550–1812.* New York: Norton.

Lundman, Richard J., and Robert L. Kaufman. 2003. Driving While Black: Effects of Race, Ethnicity, and Gender on Citizen Self-Reports of Traffic Stops and Police Actions. *Criminology* 41 (1): 195–220.

MacDonald, Heather. 2003. What Looks like Profiling Might Just Be Good Policing. *Los Angeles Times,* January 19.

Marable, Manning. 2000. *How Capitalism Underdeveloped Black America: Problems in Race, Political Economy, and Society.* 2nd ed. Cambridge, MA: South End.

Muneer, Ahmad. 2002. Homeland Insecurities: Racial Violence the Day after September 11. *Social Text-72* 20 (3): 101–115.

Smith, Michael R., and Matthew Petrocelli. 2001. Racial Profiling? A Multivariate Analysis of Police Traffic Stop Data. *Police Quarterly* 4 (1): 4–27.

David G. Embrick

POLICY, FISCAL

Fiscal policy is the use of a government's spending, taxing, and debt issuance authority for the purpose of influencing economic activity. The origins of fiscal policy are rooted in the worldwide economic depression of the early twentieth century (1929–1939). Prior to that time, there was little in economic theory or practice suggesting the deliberate use of the government's authority to achieve particular economic ends. Rather, emphasis was placed on the government's role in creating a favorable environment for private economic activity.

DYNAMIC PRINCIPLES

A tool for understanding fiscal policy is government's intertemporal budget constraint. This constraint relates the path of government spending to the path of government receipts. It highlights the fact that a government's budget need not be balanced each time period. However, the present value of current and future government spending must equal the present value of government revenue.

To fix the ideas, let G equal current government spending, G^f equal future government spending, T equal current taxes imposed on the private sector, T^f equal future taxes imposed on the private sector, and r equal the real rate of interest. Further, let D equal the government's current budget deficit. That is, $D = G - T$. The government finances the deficit by selling an equal amount of government bonds.

In the future, the government must collect enough taxes to repay the debt (including interest) and to pay for future government purchases. That is, $T^f = (1 + r)D + G^f$. Substituting into this latter equation the expression for D and rearranging yields a government's intertemporal budget constraint:

$$G + G^f / (1 + r) - T + T^f / (1 + r)$$

The left-hand-side of this expression is the present value of government purchases. The right hand side is the present value of government taxes. A fundamental fiscal policy lesson learned from this analysis is that all government spending ultimately must be reconciled with current and/or future government taxes so that the government's intertemporal budget constraint is satisfied.

Recognition of the government's budget constraint is crucial for assessing the impact of fiscal policy on long run economic growth. Neoclassical growth theory suggests that fiscal policy's only impact is on the level of output per capita and the transition dynamics from one per capita output level to another. On the other hand, endogenous growth models suggest that fiscal policy can affect the steady state rate of economic growth. Key to this prediction is the distinction between distortionary and non-distortionary taxation and productive and nonproductive expenditures. Using data from twenty-two Organisation for Economic Co-operation and Development (OECD) member countries, in 1999 Richard Kneller, Michael Bleaney, and Norman Gemmell demonstrated that if appropriate account is taken of the implicit financing of government spending, then the evidence suggests that distortionary taxation (income, profit, property, and payroll taxes) reduces growth and productive government expenditure (education, health, housing, and transportation spending) enhances growth.

STABILIZATION CAPACITIES

Because the government is not constrained to balance its budget period-by-period, it may adopt other objectives for its spending and taxing authority in the short run. One short-run objective that has been adopted is stabilization of the macroeconomy. Discretionary fiscal policy seeks to moderate fluctuations in overall economic activity by adjusting government expenditure or taxes. (Whether there is much scope for effective discretionary fiscal policy is controversial.) Traditional macroeconomic theory suggests that for a closed economy performing below its potential, an increase in government expenditure will stimulate aggregate expenditure. Private business firms respond to the increase in expenditure by raising production and employment. The total rise in production exceeds the increase in government spending because of a chain reaction of private consumption spending induced by the initial government expenditure. This chain reaction of spending is called the multiplier. An alternative, though slightly less potent, way for the government to trigger a chain reaction of spending is to reduce the amount of taxes it collects from the private sector. These policies also work in reverse. Therefore, if the economy is performing above its potential, the government can reduce its expenditures or raise taxes to prevent the economy from overheating.

Empirical evidence from the United States in the post–World War II period suggests that shocks to government spending and taxes effect real gross domestic product (GDP) in a manner that is broadly consistent with the aforementioned description. According to a 2002 study by Olivier Blanchard and Roberto Perotti, increases in government spending raise real GDP contemporaneously and over time. The peak dynamic effect of the increased spending on GDP occurs between one and fifteen quarters in the future. Tax increases, on the other hand, lower real GDP contemporaneously and over time. The peak dynamic effect of tax increases on GDP occurs between five and seven quarters in the future.

In order to detect the impact of discretionary fiscal policy, it is necessary to account for important yet passive changes in spending and taxation by a government. Automatic stabilizers are changes in spending and taxation that occur in response to changes in economic activity. They do not require initiative by a government. Transfer payments such as unemployment insurance and tax payments linked to income are examples of automatic stabilizers. Net tax payments (taxes minus transfers) tend to rise during economic expansions and fall in recessions.

OPEN ECONOMY CONSIDERATIONS

The effectiveness of fiscal policy in economies open to international trade depends on several factors, including whether a country is large or small relative to the size of the world economy, whether capital can flow freely in and out of the country, and whether a country's exchange rate is fixed or floating.

Consider, for example, the case of a small country with capital mobility and a flexible exchange rate. Such a country takes the world interest rate as given. Further, the domestic interest rate equals the world interest rate plus a risk premium. An increase in government expenditure increases aggregate spending. The rise in spending will cause an incipient rise in the domestic interest rate. Capital from abroad will be attracted to the domestic country causing the country's exchange rate to appreciate. Net exports will fall in response to the appreciation, thereby choking off the expansion of domestic production. In the end, there will be no expansion of total output. Fiscal policy's only impact will be to change the composition of the initial level of output. The government sector is larger. The export sector is smaller. The theoretical prediction that fiscal policy is totally ineffective in this case stands in stark contrast to the closed economy case previously discussed.

Canada is a relatively small country whose characteristics closely match those described. The evidence from Canada suggests that the impact of fiscal policy on economic activity at the business cycle frequency is small at best. In 2005 Perotti estimated that the cumulative response of real GDP to positive shocks to government spending is positive but less than one, suggesting that there is no multiplier effect. In fact, in the post-1980 period, the cumulative response of real GDP to positive shocks to government spending is actually estimated to be negative. Tax cuts are estimated to stimulate economic activity in Canada. This finding, however, appears to be particular to Canada as it was not the case in any of the other OECD countries studied by Perotti.

DIFFICULTIES WITH FISCAL POLICY

Several issues make the theory and practice of fiscal policy controversial and difficult. First, there is uncertainty as to how fiscal policy should be measured. A generational accounting approach, such as the one taken by Laurence Kotlikoff, would focus on the lifetime tax burden born by different age cohorts. Second, lags in the recognition of the need for a policy change, the design of a new policy, and the implementation of a new policy may render fiscal policy too ponderous to be timely. Third, private sector expectations may thwart fiscal policy. According to a 2003 article published by Alan Auerbach in *Brooking Papers on Economic Activity*, tax changes known to be temporary, for example, are likely to have different affects than those that are permanent. Finally, fiscal policy makers may not be able to resist the temptation to renege on tax and spending promises in order to realize short-term gains. According to Edward Prescott's 2004 work, this time inconsistency problem may cause more damage to the economy in the long run because the private sector may lose confidence in the government.

SEE ALSO *Business Cycles, Real; Multiplier, The; Phillips Curve; Policy, Monetary; Shocks; Treasury View, The*

BIBLIOGRAPHY

Auerbach, Alan. 2003. Fiscal Policy, Past and Present. *Brooking Papers on Economic Activity* 34 (1): 75–122.

Blanchard, Olivier and Roberto Perotti. 2002. An Empirical Characterization of the Dynamic Effects of Changes in Government Spending and Taxes on Output. *The Quarterly Journal of Economics* 117 (4): 1329–1368.

Kneller, Richard, Michael Bleaney, and Norman Gemmell. 1999. Fiscal Policy and Growth: Evidence from OECD Countries. *Journal of Public Economics* 74 (2): 171–90.

Kotlikoff, Laurence. 1992. *Generational Accounting*. New York: Free Press.

Perotti, Roberto. 2005. Estimating the Effects of Fiscal Policy in OECD Countries. *Center for Economic Policy Research (CEPR) Discussion Papers.* 4842.

Prescott, Edward. 2004. The Transformation of Macroeconomic Policy and Research. *The Region, 2004 Annual Report*. Federal Reserve Bank of Minneapolis. http://minneapolisfed.org/.

Philip N. Jefferson

POLICY, FOREIGN

SEE *Foreign Policy.*

POLICY, MONETARY

Monetary policy is the management of money, credit, and interest rates by a country's central bank. Unfortunately, this short definition is clearly inadequate. What is money? What is credit? What is an interest rate? What is a central bank and how does it control them? And, most importantly, why should anyone care? The purpose of this entry is to answer these questions (for more detail, see the relevant chapters of Stephen G. Cecchetti [2006]).

A FEW BASICS

Money is an asset that is generally accepted as payment for goods and services or repayment of debt; money acts as a unit of account, and serves as a store of value. That is, people use money to pay for things (it is a means of payment); quote prices in dollars, euros, yen, or the units of our currency (it is a unit of account); and use money to move purchasing power over time (it is a store of value). *Credit* is the borrowing and lending of resources. Some people have more resources than they currently need (they are savers) while others have profitable opportunities that they cannot fund (they are investors). Credit flows from the savers to the investors. And an *interest rate* is the cost of borrowing and the reward for lending. Since lenders could have done something else with their resources, they require compensation—interest is rent paid by borrowers.

THE CENTRAL BANK

The U.S. Federal Reserve System, the Bank of Japan, and the Bank of England are all central banks. Nearly every country in the world has a central bank. It is easiest to understand a central bank by looking at what it does (for a history of money and central banks, see Glyn Davies [2002]). A modern central bank both provides an array of services to commercial banks (it is the bankers' bank) and manages the government's finances (it is the government's bank). While not universally true, we will assume that only banks and governments have accounts at central banks. As the bank for bankers, the central bank holds deposit accounts and operates a system for interbank payments that enables commercial banks (the ones the public uses) to transfer balances in these accounts to one another. The central bank is also in a unique position to provide loans to commercial banks during times of crisis—more on this shortly.

Like any individual or business, the government needs a bank to make and receive payments. So, the central bank keeps an account for the government. When the government wants to make or receive a payment, it needs a bank just like the rest of us. The central bank does that job. In addition, the government gives the central bank the right to print money—that is the paper currency that people use in everyday life.

At its most basic level, printing money is a very profitable business. A $100 bill costs only a few cents to print, but it can be exchanged for $100 worth of goods and services. It is logical then that national governments create a monopoly on printing money and use the revenue it generates to benefit the general public. Also, government officials know that losing control of the money printing presses means losing control of inflation.

CONTROLLING MONEY, CREDIT, AND INTEREST RATES

The fact that the central bank has the license to issue money makes it unique. If individuals want to make a purchase, they need to have the resources to do it. So, for example, someone using a debit card to purchase groceries will have to have sufficient balances in a commercial bank account to cover it. If the grocery purchaser does not have sufficient resources of his own, he will need the financial assistance of someone who is willing to make him a loan. The central bank is different. If the central bank wants to buy something—say a government-issued bond—it can just create the liabilities to do it. Essentially it can issue the money. Importantly, the central bank can expand the size of its balance sheet at will. No one else can do this.

The central bank uses its ability to expand (and contract) its assets and liabilities to implement monetary policy. Figure 1 is a simple version of the central bank's balance sheet, stripped of a number of incidental items (like buildings and gold). When looking at any balance sheet, the most important thing to remember is that assets equal liabilities, so any change in one side must be matched by a change in the other. When a central bank purchases a government security, increasing its assets, this is normally matched by an increase in commercial bank reserve liabilities. Banks hold these reserves both because they are required by law and in order to make interbank payments.

At its technical, day-to-day level, monetary policy is all about buying and selling securities to control the quantity of reserves in the commercial banking system. Modern central banks, like the Federal Reserve or the European Central Bank, use their monopoly over the supply of commercial bank reserves to control an interest rate of their choosing. In some, like the Reserve Bank of Australia, it is the deposit rate the central bank pays commercial banks on the balances in their reserve account. In the United States, it is the *federal funds rate*—the rate banks charge each other for overnight loans of reserves. The Federal Reserve decides on its target for the federal funds, and then buys and sells securities to set the supply of reserves to hit this target. Twenty-first century monetary policy is not about controlling the quantity of money or its growth rate; it is about interest rates. (For a technical discussion of the use and the abandonment of money

as a target, see Laurence Meyer [2001a]. For a detailed discussion of the monetary policy of the European Central Bank, see Otmar Issing et al. [2001]).

It is important to note that some central banks decide to use their ability to control the size of their balance sheet to target something other than interest rates. The natural alternative is the exchange value of their currency—that is, the value of the number of dollars it takes to purchase the currency issued by another central bank. But, by the beginning of the twenty-first century, this had become increasingly rare. A central bank cannot control the total quantity of money and credit in the economy directly, and no modern central bank tries.

Finally, in addition to the size of their balance sheet, central banks have two additional tools. During times of financial stress, the central bank stands ready to provide loans to banks that are illiquid (so they cannot make payments) but still solvent (so their net worth is positive). Policymakers set interest rates on these loans. When the lending is done properly, this eliminates financial systemwide panics. In addition, central banks in many countries are given the power to set requirements governing how banks hold their assets. So, for example, they may require a certain level of reserve deposits, or prohibit the holding of common stock.

MONETARY POLICY OBJECTIVES

The central bank is part of the government. Whenever an agency of the government involves itself in the economy, people need to ask why. What makes individuals incapable of doing what they have entrusted to the government? In the case of national defense and pollution regulation, the reasons are obvious. Most people will not voluntarily contribute their resources to the army, nor will a country's citizens spontaneously clean up their own air.

The rationale for the existence of a central bank is equally clear. While economic and financial systems may be fairly stable most of the time, when left on their own they are prone to episodes of extreme volatility. In the absence of a central bank, economic systems tend to be extremely unstable. The historical record is filled with examples of failure, such as the Great Depression of the 1930s, when the American banking system collapsed and economic activity plummeted.

Central bankers adjust interest rates to reduce the volatility of the economic and financial systems by pursuing a number of objectives. The three most important are: (1) low and stable inflation; (2) high and stable real growth, together with high employment; and (3) stable financial markets. Let's look at each of these in turn.

The rationale for keeping the economy inflation-free is straightforward. Standards, everyone agrees, should be standard. A pound should always weigh a pound, a mea-

---

The Central Bank's balance sheet

	Assets	Liabilities
Government's bank	Government securities	Currency
	Foreign exchange reserves	Government's account
Banker's bank	Loans	Accounts of the commercial banks (reserves)

Figure 1.

suring cup should always hold a cup, a yardstick should always measure a yard, and one dollar should always have the same purchasing power. Maintaining price stability enhances money's usefulness both as a unit of account and as a store of value.

Prices are central to everything that happens in a market-based economy. They provide the information individuals and firms need to ensure that resources are allocated to their best uses. When a seller can raise the price of a product, that is supposed to signal that demand has increased, so producing more is worthwhile. Inflation degrades the information content of prices, reducing the efficient operation of the economy.

Turning to growth, central bankers work to dampen the fluctuations of the business cycle. Booms are good; recessions are not. In recessions, people lose their jobs and businesses fail. Without a steady income, people struggle to make their auto, credit card, and mortgage payments. Consumers pull back, hurting businesses that rely on them to buy products. Reduced sales lead to more layoffs, and so on. The longer the downturn goes on, the worse it gets.

Finally, there is financial stability. The financial system is like plumbing: when it works, it is taken for granted, but when it does not work, watch out. If people lose faith in banks and financial markets, they will rush to low-risk alternatives, and the flow of resources from savers to borrowers will stop. Getting a car loan or a home mortgage becomes impossible, as does selling a bond to maintain or expand a business. When the financial system collapses, economic activity also collapses.

THE POLICY FRAMEWORK

Central banks use their ability to control their balance sheet to manipulate short-term interest rates in order to keep inflation low and stable, the growth high and stable, and the financial system stable. But what makes monetary policymakers successful? Today, there is a clear consensus that to succeed a central bank must be: (1) independent of political pressure; (2) accountable to the public; (3) transparent in its policy actions; and (4) clear in its communications with financial markets and the public.

Independence is the most important of these elements. Successful monetary policy requires a long time horizon. The impact of today's decisions will not be felt for a while—not for several years, in most instances. Democratically elected politicians are not a patient bunch; their time horizon extends only to the next election. Politicians are encouraged to do everything they can for their constituents before the next election—including manipulating interest rates to bring short-term prosperity at the expense of long-term stability. The temptation to forsake long-term goals for short-term gains is simply impossible to resist. Given the ability to choose, politicians will keep

interest rates too low, raising output and employment quickly (before the election), but resulting in inflation later (after the election).

Knowing these tendencies, governments have moved responsibility for monetary policy into a separate, largely apolitical, institution. To insulate policymakers from the daily pressures faced by politicians, governments must give central bankers control over their budgets, authority to make irreversible decisions, and long-term appointments.

There is a major problem with central bank independence: It is inconsistent with representative democracy. Politicians answer to the voters; by design, independent central bankers do not. How can people have faith in the financial system if there are no checks on what the central bankers are doing? The economy will not operate efficiently unless policymakers are trusted to do the right thing.

The solution to this problem is twofold. First, politicians establish the goals for the independent central bankers, and second, monetary policymakers publicly report their progress in achieving those goals. Explicit goals foster *accountability* and disclosure requirements create *transparency*. While central bankers are powerful, elected representatives tell them what to do and then monitor their progress.

The institutional means for assuring accountability and transparency differ from one country to the next. In some countries, such as the United Kingdom and Chile, the government establishes an explicit numerical target for inflation. In others, such as the United States, the central bank is asked to deliver price stability as one of a number of objectives (for a discussion of the structure of central bank objectives, see Laurence Meyer [2001b]).

THE FUTURE OF MONEY AND MONETARY POLICY

In the early 1980s, nearly two out of three of the countries in the world were experiencing inflation in excess of 10 percent per year. In the early twenty-first century, this is one in six. Two decades ago nearly one country in three was contracting. By 2005, five in six countries were growing at a rate in excess of 2 percent per year. But not only has inflation been lower and output higher, both inflation and output appear to be more stable. And careful empirical analysis shows that monetary policy is a likely source of this low, stable inflation and high, stable growth (see Cecchetti, Flores-Lagunes and Krause [2006]).

Central bankers' success can be traced to their ability to control interest rates. And their ability to manipulate interest rates relies on their control of the size of their balance sheet. This, in turn, requires that banks and individuals actually demand central bank liabilities. That is, people have to want to hold the currency issued by central banks, and commercial banks have to demand reserves. Won't the day come when no one wants this stuff anymore? And when that happens, won't monetary policy disappear?

The answer is almost surely no. While it is true that the creation of a secure and anonymous substitute for paper currency will ultimately cause dollar bills and euro notes to disappear, reserves are different. The central bank operates an interbank payments system based on reserves. It does this to ensure that, even during periods of crisis, banks can continue to make payments. And to ensure that commercial banks use their payments system, the central bank offers cheap access to this system—that is, it subsidizes the cost of the system's operation. So long as banks want reserves, there will be monetary policy (for a discussion of the challenges facing monetary policy makers, see Gordon Sellon and Chairmaine Buskas [1999] and Laurence Meyer [2001c]).

SEE ALSO *Business Cycles, Real; Inflation; Policy, Fiscal; Treasury View, The; Unemployment*

BIBLIOGRAPHY

Cecchetti, Stephen G. 2006. *Money, Banking, and Financial Markets*. New York: McGraw Hill–Irwin.

Cecchetti, Stephen G., Alfonso Flores-Lagunes, and Stefan Krause. 2006. Has Monetary Policy Become More Efficient? A Cross-Country Analysis. *Economic Journal* 116 (4): 408-433.

Davies, Glyn. 2002. *The History of Money from Ancient Times to the Present Day*. 3rd ed. Cardiff, U.K.: University of Wales Press.

Issing, Otmar, Ignazio Angeloni, Vitor Gaspar, and Oreste Tristani. 2001. *Monetary Policy in the Euro Area: Strategy and Decision-Making at the European Central Bank*. Cambridge, U.K.: Cambridge University Press.

Meyer, Laurence H. 2001a. Does Money Matter? The 2001 Homer Jones Memorial Lecture, Washington University, Saint Louis, Missouri, March 28. http://www.federalreserve.gov/boarddocs/speeches/2001/20010328/default.htm.

Meyer, Laurence H. 2001b. Inflation Targets and Inflation Targeting. Remarks at the University of California at San Diego Economics Roundtable, San Diego, California, July 17. http://www.federalreserve.gov/boarddocs/speeches/2001/20010717/default.htm.

Meyer, Laurence H. 2001c. The Future of Money and of Monetary Policy. Remarks at the Distinguished Lecture Program, Swarthmore College, Swarthmore, Pennsylvania, December 5. http://www.federalreserve.gov/boarddocs/speeches/2001/20011205/default.htm.

Sellon, Gordon H., Jr., and Chairmaine R. Buskas, eds. 1999. *New Challenges for Monetary Policy: A Symposium Sponsored by the Federal Reserve Bank of Kansas City*. Kansas City, MO: Federal Reserve Bank of Kansas City.

Stephen G. Cecchetti

POLICY, PUBLIC
SEE *Public Policy.*

POLICY ANALYSIS

Policy analysis is the art and science of determining which public policy, from among alternatives, will most likely achieve a determined set of goals. The art of policy analysis involves putting together pieces to determine what will work in public policy. Central to policy analysis is an understanding of the evolutionary process of policy development as policymakers strive to improve the policymaking process in general and specific policies in particular. Policy analysis is the activity of generating knowledge both *of* and *in* the policymaking process. Creating such knowledge includes the examination of the causes, consequences, and performance of public policies and programs. Unless this knowledge is shared with decision makers and the relevant public, the process of policy analysis is unfinished.

Policy analysis is a relatively young field of study. Traditionally, institutions and the processes of public policymaking were the primary concern of social scientists and political scientists. In 1951 sociologist Daniel Lerner (1917–1980) and political scientist Harold Lasswell (1902–1978) introduced the concept of "the policy sciences." Their work is often cited as the foundation for the evolution of how public policies are studied. Over time, the traditional approach expanded to include analysis of the content and process of actual policies, a discipline that is now commonly referred to as *policy analysis*.

Policy analysis, a part of the larger field of policy studies, evolved and developed in the 1960s and 1970s. Various stimuli have been cited as promoting the growth of the field. Social concerns over civil rights, women's liberation, the Vietnam War (1957–1975), the politics of the Middle East, rising energy costs, inflation, and environmental protection were among the stimuli. The expanding relationship between government and the academic community, along with government's increasing reliance on the assistance of the academic community for developing methods of maximizing output in the face of diminishing resources, also facilitated the expansion of the field. Additionally, government offered expanding research funding and job opportunities as it sought assistance in addressing the above-mentioned social issues. New analytical and interdisciplinary methods allowed academics and think tanks to capitalize on government expansion. The Keynesian revolution in economics (1930s and 1940s) is one such development. This revolution allowed for public sector intervention in the economic decision-making process. Applied policy research continues to play a major role in contemporary government decision making around issues of efficiency, effectiveness, and equity.

Although heavily influenced by the disciplines of political science, policy analysis is eclectic as it borrows from and lends to a myriad of academic disciplines. Economics, for example, contributes cost-benefit analysis and models relating to the optimal allocation of resources. Policy analysis also incorporates the emphasis in economics on prescriptive conclusions. Psychology lends to policy analysis the research paradigm of experimental and control groups and various techniques of statistical inference. Additionally, psychology provides theories and insights on the application of rewards and punishment as tools for promoting specific behaviors. Sociology's concern with social problems has also added to the development of the study of public policies. In addition, the comparative analysis of public policies has roots in anthropology, geography, and history.

Methods of policy analysis vary from analyst to analyst. Various schools of thought, such as behaviorist, post-behaviorist, and rational choice theory, among others, influence analysts in terms of what types of questions are asked and what methods are employed to answer these questions. Public policy analysts rely on a number of different approaches. Analysts can take an empirical approach, designed to primarily determine the causes and consequences of public policies. A central goal of such an approach is to understand a policy problem. Such an approach tends to yield more descriptive and predictive information. An analyst can also use an evaluative approach, where the central question concerns the value or worth of past or future policy prescription. Finally, analysts using a normative approach ask what *should* be done. Their work thus yields more prescriptive types of knowledge. Analysts can also study policy content or the policy process itself.

Over the years, different methodological tools and approaches have been employed in the analysis of public policy. Theories derived from management, organization development, and psychology, in conjunction with the use of economic and political models, influence the techniques used by policy analysts. Analysts draw from a bank of both qualitative and quantitative methods. These include, but are not limited to, case studies, economic modeling, quasi-experimental approaches, causal-path analysis, operations research, and correlations analysis.

SEE ALSO *Public Policy; Public Sector*

BIBLIOGRAPHY

Lerner, Daniel, and Harold D. Lasswell, eds. 1951. *The Policy Sciences: Recent Developments in Scope and Method.* Stanford, CA: Stanford University Press.

Nagel, Stuart S. 1975. *Policy Studies and the Social Sciences.* Lexington, MA: Lexington Books.

Nagel, Stuart S. 1984. *Contemporary Public Policy Analysis.* University: University of Alabama Press.

Wildavsky, Aaron. 1979. *Speaking Truth to Power: The Art and Craft of Policy Analysis.* Boston: Little, Brown.

Julia S. Jordan-Zachery

POLICY EXPERIMENT
SEE *Social Experiment.*

POLICY PROCESS
SEE *Public Policy.*

POLITICAL BUSINESS CYCLES
SEE *Business Cycles, Political.*

POLITICAL CONVENTIONS

National political party conventions have been the scene of some of the most dramatic moments in U.S. electoral history and have often changed the course of that history. These weeklong gatherings, held in the summer months every four years, enable delegates of the major political parties to meet and officially nominate their candidates for the presidency and vice-presidency and adopt a statement of principles. Despite this rich history, various circumstances fostering a more egalitarian nominating process and the explosion of instantaneous modern media coverage of events have rendered modern national party conventions less relevant than those of the past.

ORIGINS

Early in the nation's history, the congressional leaders of political parties met in party *caucuses* to select presidential candidates. These meetings were sometimes held in secret. In the 1824 presidential election, Andrew Jackson (1767–1845) won 43.9 percent of the popular vote, but because no candidate had received the requisite number of electoral votes to win the presidency, the election was thrown into the House of Representatives as directed by the

Constitution. Thanks to some adroit political dealing, John Quincy Adams (1767–1848), who had won just over 30 percent of the popular vote, was elected president. Supporters of Jackson decried *King Caucus* and accused Congress of ignoring the will of the people. Presidential nominating caucusing disappeared after the 1824 election in favor of national nominating conventions. The first such convention was held by a single-issue party, the Anti-Mason Party, at Baltimore, Maryland, in 1831. Other than being the first party to hold a national convention and running a candidate who won seven electoral votes in the election, the Anti-Mason Party faded from the scene after its significant historical contribution. The Democratic and Whig Parties held national conventions in 1832, and the Republican Party did so in 1854 after replacing the defunct Whigs as a national party.

Ideally national conventions were to be a transparently democratic nominating setting. This was hardly the case, however. Delegates to party conventions were almost always selected by and/or under the control of the party *boss*, or individual who had risen to power via enormous networks of support or through less-than-ethical methods. In the late nineteenth century, New York state politics were controlled by Senator Thomas Platt (1833–1910). His dislike of, and inability to control, New York governor Theodore Roosevelt (1858–1919) led Platt to demand enough delegates to the 1898 Republican Convention to nominate Governor Roosevelt for the vice-presidency, in effect removing him from office in New York. Although Roosevelt was eventually elected vice president and Platt and his colleagues congratulated themselves on their successful tactics, the plan backfired when President William McKinley (1843–1901) was assassinated, and Roosevelt became president of the United States in 1901.

Often, party conventions presented previously unknown individuals to head presidential tickets. These *no-names* resulted from deadlocked ballots and political dealing and intrigue behind closed doors. In 1844, the Democratic Convention nominated James K. Polk (1795–1849) after nine ballots. Polk was not even mentioned on the first seven of those ballots, but was seen as an acceptable compromise and, finally, the nominee. Polk won the general election. Similarly Franklin Pierce (1804–1869) was not even a candidate entering the 1852 Democratic Convention, but became the nominee and won the presidency. Intrigue became absurdity when, during the 1924 Democratic Convention, John W. Davis (1873–1955) emerged as the nominee after 103 ballots, a drama that was closely followed by Americans across the land via a new technological development called the radio.

One traditional function of national party conventions is the debate over, and eventual adoption of, a party platform. The platform is a statement of party principles and the purported foundation upon which the party's candidates will conduct their campaigns, and upon which the party stands for the subsequent four years. The proposals approved by the delegates and the stated goals are called planks. Platforms are now often ignored both by the candidates and the public at large, though they were much more useful in outlining a party's views for the public before the evolution of mass media. Platform committees construct a platform document for delegate approval. At times, planks relating to difficult issues such as abortion have divided delegates, but not enough to make a significant mark during a convention. More often than not, platform planks are not even proposed as policy, yet the adoption of a platform remains an integral part of national conventions.

Although conventions gave at least the appearance of a more open selection process, the 1912 Republican Convention was an early example of an increasing demand for the formation of a primary election system to determine delegate support and party nominees. Theodore Roosevelt, troubled by policies he viewed as overly conservative on the part of his successor, President William Howard Taft (1857–1930), decided to challenge Taft for the Republican nomination in 1912. Roosevelt campaigned in states holding presidential primaries, and swamped Taft everywhere, including the incumbent's home state of Ohio. Taft, however, still controlled enough delegates to carry him to victory at the convention and was the party nominee despite Roosevelt's electoral strength. Roosevelt and his supporters (who chanted Thou shalt not steal! after Taft was nominated) fled to form a third party, and took enough Republican support away from Taft to help make Woodrow Wilson (1856–1924), the Democratic nominee, the next president. No such drama has occurred at modern conventions. The last nomination in doubt during a national convention was the 1976 Republican Convention, in which former California governor Ronald Reagan (1911–2004) nearly toppled incumbent President Gerald Ford (1913–2006). History was made at the 1984 Democratic National Convention when the party nominated the first female candidate for the vice-presidency, Geraldine Ferraro (b. 1935), though her selection was not a surprise before the convention convened.

CONVENTIONS AND THE PRIMARY SYSTEM

Since 1936, every successful presidential candidate has been nominated by his party convention on the first ballot. The advent of television and live coverage of conventions by the major networks, however, did capture some of the traditions of old. Conventions in the 1950s and early 1960s retained the spectacle of the delegates choosing the ticket, and often the presidential nominee would throw the choice of his running mate to the convention floor. At the 1956 Democratic Convention, Adlai Stevenson (1900–1965) let the delegates choose and a dramatic race ensued between Senator Estes Kefauver (1903–1963) and Senator John F. Kennedy (1917–1963). Kennedy lost, but the nation watched as he delivered a graceful concession speech that many believed propelled him as a favorite for the 1960 nomination, which he eventually won. Even in 1960, though, Kennedy had to fend off a convention-week challenge from Lyndon B. Johnson (1908–1973), who did not participate in primaries as Kennedy had. Johnson was eventually the vice-presidential nominee.

Demand for a national primary system for choosing presidential nominees reached its peak at the 1968 Democratic National Convention in Chicago, Illinois. Senator Eugene McCarthy (1916–2005) of Minnesota had won much primary support for his stances against the Vietnam War and the increasingly unpopular incumbent Democratic president, Lyndon B. Johnson. Johnson, who declined to run for reelection, favored his vice president, Hubert H. Humphrey (1911–1978), who controlled the delegates and won the nomination. Humphrey's nomination and his alliance with Chicago mayor and political boss Richard J. Daley (1902–1976), whose Chicago police forcefully repelled antiwar demonstrations throughout the convention—all of it seen on live television across the country—led to the formation of a committee that revamped the nominating process of the Democratic Party in favor of primary elections preceding the national convention. The Republican Party followed suit.

The Democratic and Republican parties, of course, differ in how each allocates delegates to the national convention. Democrats divide delegates according to how each state voted in the previous three elections; party leaders and certain elected officials hold 15 percent of the total number of delegates. Republicans assign delegates who are already pledged to vote for a certain candidate in proportion to the votes the candidates received in the primaries. The primary election season begins in January of the election year, usually with the New Hampshire primaries and Iowa caucuses (in which voters gather in schools, homes, and community centers to debate and vote), and continues in many other states until June. Most of the primary votes are cast before April, and the nominations of each party are not in doubt by the time the last primaries are held.

While the primary system is a more democratic method for selecting a presidential nominee in that it places the selection in the hands of voters rather than convention delegates, it has relegated the nomination function of the national convention to mere formality.

Reliance upon the primary system to find a party's presidential nominee has meant that presidential campaigns now begin two and sometimes three years ahead of the date of the election, and candidates are obliged to raise millions of dollars in campaign contributions to remain competitive in such a long process. The amount of money that changes hands during a presidential election has led many lawmakers and commentators to call for more legislation governing the influence of campaign contributions on candidates and officeholders. However, few—if any—in either major party have suggested a return to the convention as the sole nomination process. Thus conventions have taken on a role of showcasing important members of the national party, writing and adopting a party platform, and presenting the presidential and vice-presidential nominees, who give acceptance speeches that attempt to persuade the voting public to support their campaigns.

SEE ALSO *Elections; Primaries; Voting*

BIBLIOGRAPHY

Boller, Paul F. 2004. *Presidential Campaigns: From George Washington to George W. Bush.* New York: Oxford University Press.

Eldersveld, Samuel J., and Hanes Walton. 2000. *Political Parties in American Society.* Hampshire, UK: Palgrave Macmillan.

Farber, David. 1988. *Chicago '68.* Chicago: University of Chicago Press.

Goodwin, Doris Kearns. 2005. *Team of Rivals: The Political Genius of Abraham Lincoln.* New York: Simon and Schuster.

Halberstam, David. 1994. *The Fifties.* New York: Ballantine Books.

Kendall, Kathleen. 2000. *Communication in the Presidential Primaries: Candidates and the Media, 1912–2000.* Westport, CT: Praeger Publications.

Maisel, L. Sandy. 2002. *The Parties Respond: Changes in American Parties and Campaigns.* Boulder, CO: Westview Press.

West, Darrell M. 2005. *Air Wars: Television Advertising in Election Campaigns 1952-2004.* Washington, DC: CQ Press.

Matthew May

POLITICAL CORRECTNESS

The term *political correctness* was first used in the innumerable and acrimonious discussions among Communist ideologues that took place, both in Russia and among members of Communist parties abroad, after the Bolshevik Revolution of 1917. The term was used, without any irony, to judge the degree of compatibility of one's ideas or political analyses with the official party line in Moscow. Because the Kremlin position kept twisting in response to nationalist and personal interests much more than to ideological consistency, staying politically correct required agile intellectual gymnastics.

After the demise of international Communism around 1990, when there no longer was a correct, official line to be measured against, *political correctness* took on a second life as a term of derision used mostly by ideologues on the Right. The term was now meant to ridicule or stigmatize conformity with the opinions, or simply the vocabulary, of liberal or leftist intellectuals, mostly in academic circles. The principal targets of that ridicule were generally movements aiming to reduce prejudice and stigmatization against racial and ethnic groups, women, homosexuals, people with disabilities, and other marginalized groups.

Since the most noticeable change brought by such movements was the adoption and diffusion of neologisms and euphemisms aimed at enfranchising such groups, the semantics of tolerance became the main butt of ridicule, notably "gender-neutral" language (e.g., *chairperson*); the use of new ethnic labels (such as *Native American* for *American Indian*, *Roma* for *Gypsy*, or *Inuit* for *Eskimo*); or euphemisms (such as *differently abled* for *disabled*, or *educationally challenged* for *slow learner*).

Soon, however, the critics of political correctness extended the scope of their attacks from the relative trivia of semantics to what they saw as a stultifying climate of hypocrisy and conformity, rampant, they alleged, on college campuses. Political correctness, they argued, stifled intellectual discourse in and out of academia, or, worse, punished the pursuit of legitimate research on, for example, the genetic bases of human behavior, sexual orientation, or gender differences.

Some scholars found themselves under assault from both the Left and the Right. For instance, the few social scientists who tried to suggest (and show) that human behavior was the product of biological as well as cultural evolution were simultaneously berated as "secular humanists" by fundamentalist Christians and as racist and sexist by their colleagues in the mainstream of their disciplines.

Intellectual climates keep changing, however, so that what may appear to be the menacing shadow of political correctness from the Left may eventually be neutralized by a rising tide of conservatism from the religious Right and the "intelligent design" movement. Reason and sanity, it seems, are always under attack, from the Left, from the Right, or, indeed, from both simultaneously. The university campus is the main theater for such jousts, and thus, also, the main depository of much nonsense. In the end, each swing of the ideological pendulum leaves a little residue of good sense. We must, however, be vigilant that the university remains the one venue where anything can be said fearlessly, and, thus, where political correctness has no place. Any restriction on intellectual discourse, even when internally generated, clashes with the central mission of the university, namely the critical examination of ideas and the diffusion of knowledge.

BIBLIOGRAPHY

Feldstein, Richard. 1997. *Political Correctness: A Response from the Cultural Left*. Minneapolis: University of Minnesota Press.

Friedman, Marilyn, and Jan Narveson. 1995. *Political Correctness: For and Against*. Lanham, MD: Rowman & Littlefield.

Newfie, Christopher, and Ronald Strickland, eds. 1995. *After Political Correctness: The Humanities and Society in the 1990s*. Boulder, CO: Westview.

Pierre L. van den Berghe

POLITICAL CULTURE

Although insights into political culture have been part of political reflection since classical antiquity, two developments in the context of the French Revolution laid the groundwork for modern understandings. First, when members of the Third Estate declared "We are the people," they were overturning centuries of thought about political power, captured most succinctly by Louis XIV's infamous definition of absolutism: "*L'etat, c'est moi*" ("I am the State"). Henceforth, sovereignty was seen to reside in society rather than in the monarch and his divine rights. A century later, Max Weber turned this political claim into a scientific one when he defined legitimacy as that which is considered to be legitimate—not only by elites but by the population in general; to understand the political power of the state, social science must therefore attend to its reception and sources in society. Second, when Jean-Jacques Rousseau retheorized the social contract as one in which individual interests were taken up in an overarching "General Will" of the collectivity, he raised the question of how social solidarity could be maintained in the absence of recourse to divine right. His answer was "civil religion," symbols and rituals that establish and dramatize the sense of collective belonging and purpose. A century later, Émile Durkheim took up these themes when he questioned whether modern, complex societies could generate sufficient solidarity to function in a stable manner. Durkheim's interest in what he called collective effervescence (generated in and through communal rituals) and collective representations (embodied in symbols as well as more abstractly in "collective conscience") extended Rousseau's concerns and has underwritten contemporary analyses of political culture as the sets of symbols and meanings involved in securing and exercising political power.

Contemporary work on political culture, however, dates more directly to the mid-twentieth century, particularly in the United States. In the wake of World War II (1939–1945), social scientists were motivated to explain why some nations had turned to authoritarianism while others supported democratic institutions. Before and during the war, anthropologists such as Margaret Mead and Ruth Benedict were proponents of a "culture and personality" approach, which asserted that members of different societies develop different modal personalities, which in turn can explain support for different kinds of political programs and institutions. In a somewhat different vein, the German exile philosopher Theodor Adorno and colleagues undertook a massive study during the war into what they called, in the title of their 1950 work, *The Authoritarian Personality*, continuing earlier research by critical theorists into the structure of authority in families, which they believed had led Germans to support authoritarian politics and social prejudice. In a similar vein, Harold Laswell described a set of personality traits shared by "democrats," including an "open ego," a combination of value-orientations, and generalized trust.

Perhaps the most important work on political culture in this period was Gabriel Almond and Sidney Verba's 1963 *The Civic Culture: Political Attitudes and Democracy in Five Nations*, which combined Laswell's description of the democratic personality with at least two strands of social science theory at the time. First, the predominant sociological theory in the United States was that of Talcott Parsons, who explained social order in terms of institutions that inculcated individuals with coherent sets of norms, values, and attitudes—what Parsons called culture—which in turn sustained those institutions through time. In contrast, the so-called behavioral revolution in political science argued that such accounts neglected extra-institutional variables as sources of social order (a concern that could be traced back to Montesquieu in the mid-eighteenth century, who sought external factors—in his case climate—to explain the different forms of law in history); in Parsons, moreover, critics charged that norms, values, and attitudes were more often simply assumed as necessary integrative features of social systems rather than measured empirically (hence the appeal to behaviorism, which in psychology held observability to be the only relevant criterion for science).

The major point of Almond and Verba's comparative study was to address the role of subjective values and attitudes of national populations in the stability of democratic regimes. This fit clearly within the behavioral revolution because it turned to extra-institutional variables (norms, values, and attitudes) to explain political outcomes. Nonetheless, the work was presented as a study of political *culture*, defined as the aggregate pattern of subjective political dispositions in the populace, thus incorporating and, indeed, operationalizing, the Parsonsian concept of culture. On the basis of extensive survey research, *The Civic Culture* theorized three basic orientations toward political institutions and outcomes: parochial, where politics is not differentiated as a distinct sphere of life and is of relatively little interest; subject, in which individuals are aware of the political system and its outcomes but are relatively passive; and participant, where citizens have a strong sense of their role in politics and responsibility for it. *The Civic Culture* rated five countries on these qualities, finding Italy and Mexico to be relatively parochial, Germany to be subject, and the United States and the United Kingdom to be participant political cultures.

Subsequent work in this tradition by Ronald Ingelhart and others has shown that the effect of basic satisfaction with political life and high levels of interpersonal trust (what would later be called "social capital") are analytically distinct from economic affluence, thus arguing forcefully that democracy depends on cultural as well as economic factors. Contemporary authors such as Samuel Huntington have extended this kind of argument about norms, values, and attitudes to the world stage, where they describe a "clash of civilizations" in terms of basic "cultural" differences understood in this way.

Nevertheless, there have been many criticisms of the approach developed by Almond and Verba and their colleagues. These ranged from methodological concerns about the survey instruments to the claim that the approach normatively privileged American-style democracy as the model against which all others must be judged. Still others argued that political culture was being used as a residual category for all that cannot be explained by other theories, and thus has no theoretically defensible conceptual ground of its own. Most trenchant, however, were charges that the way Almond and Verba defined political culture—in terms of subjectivity—eviscerates the importance of culture as symbols and meanings: Without a richer understanding of symbols, meanings, rituals, and the like, critics charged, political culture could not be distinguished conceptually from political psychology: "What 'theory' may be found in anyone's head is not," one set of critics charged, "culture. Culture is interpersonal, covering a range of such theory.... Political culture is the property of a collectivity" (Elkins and Simeon 1979, pp. 128–129).

Indeed, since the 1970s, political culture theory has been radically transformed by a more general cultural turn in social science, brought about by such influences as the symbolic anthropology of Clifford Geertz and the rise of semiotics, structuralism, and poststructuralism in European anthropology and literary theory. In contrast to older subjectivism, as well as to those who ignore culture altogether, newer work on political culture in the 1980s and 1990s argued that, in Geertz's words, "culture is public because meaning is" (Geertz 1973, p. 12). This work reformulated political culture as a system of meanings sui generis, as "a form of structure in its own right, constituted autonomously through series of relationships among cultural elements" (Somers 1995, p. 131), or as "codes," which could be either manifest or "deep." In this view, political culture can be measured only crudely by survey analysis; instead, it must be excavated, observed, and interpreted in its own terms as an objective structure, on the analogy of language.

However, the rise of various structuralisms in political culture analysis—emphasizing the Rousseau-Durkheim more than the Montesquieu-Weber axis—has required some modifications since the 1990s, when structuralist approaches in general have fallen somewhat out of favor. More recently, many historians, sociologists, and anthropologists have embraced a "practice" approach that emphasizes meaning making rather than meaning systems. While in no way a return to the earlier subjectivism in political culture theory, the practice approach recognizes the limitations of structuralism, in which agents seem to drop out of the picture, or serve only as enactors or carriers of structure. Instead, recent work has emphasized "the activity through which individuals and groups in any society articulate, negotiate, implement, and enforce competing claims they make upon one another and upon the whole. Political culture is, in this sense, the set of discourses or symbolic practices by which these claims are made" (Baker 1990, p. 4).

In sum, political culture theory makes empirical sense out of the French Revolution's claim that sovereignty derives from society rather than the state. One temptation with this recognition, however, is to assume that while states are about power, societies are about meaning and the reception of power. One solution, inspired by Michel Foucault, among others, has been to declare society the true locus of power. The problem is that this misses the ways in which states do indeed set agendas for societies. Recent analyses have thus returned to the political culture of the state (e.g., Bonnell 1997). But they do so without supposing that societies are mere recipients of such productions.

In contrast to much work in political sociology, which has drawn a facile distinction between "merely" symbolic politics and "real" politics, recent political culture theory has thus demonstrated that social life is an ongoing reproductive process. New political culture analysts in particular have focused not only on how political acts succeed or fail to obtain some material advantage but also on how in doing so they produce, reproduce, or change identities. The struggle for position that constitutes politics, we now understand, is always simultaneously strategic and constitutive: As Lynn Hunt has written, "Political symbols and rituals were not metaphors of power; they were the means and ends of power itself" (Hunt 1984, p. 54). Interpreting them and understanding how they are generated and how they work is thus of paramount importance.

SEE ALSO *Almond, Gabriel A.; Civilizations, Clash of; Culture; Dahl, Robert Alan; Discourse; Foucault, Michel; French Revolution; Geertz, Clifford; Huntington, Samuel P.; Ideology; Institutionalism; Kariel, Henry S.; Lasswell, Harold; Norms; Parsons, Talcott; Philosophy, Political; Political Science; Postmodernism; Power; Semiotics; Social Capital; Sociology, Political; State, The; Symbols; Verba, Sidney*

BIBLIOGRAPHY

Baker, Keith M. 1990. *Inventing the French Revolution: Essays on French Political Culture in the Eighteenth Century.* Cambridge, U.K.: Cambridge University Press.

Bonnell, Victoria E. 1997. *Iconography of Power: Soviet Political Posters under Lenin and Stalin.* Berkeley: University of California Press.

Elkins, David J., and Richard E. B. Simeon. 1979. A Cause in Search of its Effect, or What Does Political Culture Explain? *Comparative Politics* 11 (2): 127–145.

Geertz, Clifford. 1973. *The Interpretation of Cultures; Selected Essays.* New York: Basic Books.

Hunt, Lynn. 1984. *Politics, Culture and Class in the French Revolution.* Berkeley: University of California Press.

Somers, Margaret. 1995. What's Political or Cultural about Political Culture and the Public Sphere? Toward an Historical Sociology of Concept Formation. *Sociological Theory* 13 (2): 113–144.

Jeffrey Olick
Tatiana Omeltchenko

POLITICAL DEVELOPMENT

SEE *Research, Democracy.*

POLITICAL ECONOMY

The phrase *political economy* came into currency in the seventeenth and eighteenth centuries. It is natural to think that the name refers to a discipline that studies how politics affects the economy and vice versa. Yet the fundamental idea of the original political economists—Adam Smith, David Ricardo, Thomas Malthus—was that an economy works best when governed least. They believed that there were economic principles that tended to produce the common good if government generally left people alone in their material endeavors. Adam Smith's (1776) famous remark about "the invisible hand" puts the idea succinctly: an individual, through his industry,

> intends only his own gain, and he is in this, as in many other cases, led by an invisible hand to promote an end which was no part of his intention.… By pursuing his own interest he frequently promotes that of the society more effectually than when he really intends to promote it. (p. 456)

This invisible coordination of individual interest will result in the general welfare only if government allows the market to run on its own principles. It is ironic that the founders of political economy—the "classical economists," as they are now called—rejected a large role for politics in the economy.

While there is irony in calling this view *political* economy, it nonetheless has a rationale. The term *economics* derives from the Greek word for "household." For much of human history, the individual household was expected to meet the needs of its members through its own efforts, without significant help from the state. Nation-states came into being only in the sixteenth and seventeenth centuries, and they were soon expected to have the ability and duty to improve economic well-being. Mercantilist and physiocratic theories were the first expressions of this concern. Both of these, but especially mercantilism, demanded significant intervention in the economy, including protectionist measures to improve a nation's balance of trade.

The political economists reacted to these earlier theories. Their aim was to reveal the proper aim of political activity in economic life. The name *political economy* still made sense for their discipline, even though the proper aim was negative, a matter of minimizing interference.

MARXISM

The next iteration in the life of the phrase *political economy* came with the work of Karl Marx in the mid-nineteenth century. For Marx, the economy dominates politics. In every era (until the final era of communism) there is an economic structure that benefits certain classes and exploits others. The rest of social life, including the state, the law, culture, and dominant ideas and values, exists only to promote the economic structure and to further the interests of those on top. Marx is reasonably categorized as a political economist, given the linkage he sees between economics, politics, and the rest of social life.

There is, however, another irony about the use of the phrase *political economy* here. Marx's most important economic work, *Capital*, is subtitled *A Critique of Political Economy*. His central ideas about society are most clearly laid out in the famous preface to a different work entitled *A Contribution to the Critique of Political Economy*. Marx thus took himself to be rejecting political economy. He was rejecting ("critiquing") the ideas of the classical economists such as Smith and Ricardo. Nevertheless, since he linked economy, politics, ideology, and culture, it became reasonable for later generations to think of Marxism as the archetype of political economy. For many today, political economy means Marxist and nonorthodox explanations of political, legal, and cultural phenomena, and also mainstream ideas by reference to the economic forces they are said to uphold.

NEOCLASSICAL ECONOMICS

By the end of the nineteenth century the phrase *political economy* gave way to the word *economics*. Marginal utility theory, also known as neoclassical economics, developed. Perhaps the strongest ground for the name change was the desire to develop a discipline both independent and scientific, based on the rigorous mathematical tools and laws that marginal utility theory put forth to explain production and exchange. Neoclassical economic thinkers wished to disentangle their discipline from the normatively tinged areas of politics, philosophy, and the moral sciences generally. Thus the concept of political economy slowly gave way to the more scientific-sounding idea of economics. The phrase *political economy* has, however, remained in favor among those who want to resist the narrowness of modern neoclassical economic theory and insist that economic phenomena can only be fully understood through an understanding of the roles played by politics and culture.

Another use of the term *political economy* has developed in the last half century in the work of public choice theorists such as James Buchanan, Gordon Tullock, and Mancur Olson. These scholars seek to explain the behavior of groups, especially governments, on the basis of the idea, central to modern economic theory, that people tend to act as individual utility maximizers. Roughly put, public choice theorists argue that through the political process, politicians attempt to capture benefits for specific groups from the resources of the population generally ("rent seeking"). Thus, citizens are taxed to pay for benefits they do not receive, and the economy is made inefficient. Public choice theorists tend to respond to this "government failure" by returning to the original idea of the classical economists—the less government the better.

In recent years, the idea of political economy has come into use among those interested in global problems. International political economy studies national development and the planetary distribution of wealth. It examines the effects of economic globalization on human well-being, politics, law, culture, the environment, national sovereignty, and religion. Perhaps the most important question is the effect of economic globalization on the rich and poor. Thinkers scrutinize such organizations as the International Monetary Fund, the World Bank, and the World Trade Organization. Some argue that these represent a modernized version of neoclassical economics, labeled neoliberalism, that tends to work in favor of the rich and powerful and against the weak and poor. Others argue that free trade and liberalized flows of capital and labor will eventually improve the prospects of the global poor. The continuing debate about these issues gives *political economy* a new meaning in the global context.

SEE ALSO *Collective Action; Economics; Economics, Classical; Free Rider; Game Theory; Malthus, Thomas Robert; Political Theory; Public Choice Theory; Ricardo, David; Smith, Adam*

BIBLIOGRAPHY

Bhagwati, Jagdish. 2004. *In Defense of Globalization.* New York: Oxford University Press.

Buchanan, James, and Gordon Tullock. 1965. *The Calculus of Consent: Logical Foundations of Constitutional Democracy.* Ann Arbor: University of Michigan Press.

Marshall, Alfred. 1890. *Principles of Economics.* 8th ed. New York: Macmillan, 1949.

Marx, Karl. 1867. *Capital.* Trans. Samuel Moore and Edward Aveling. New York: International Publishers, 1967.

Olson, Mancur. 1965. *The Logic of Collective Action.* Cambridge, MA: Harvard University Press.

Ricardo, David. 1817. *The Principles of Political Economy and Taxation,* ed. R. M. Hartwell. Harmondsworth, U.K.: Penguin, 1971.

Smith, Adam. 1776. *An Inquiry into the Nature and Causes of the Wealth of Nations.* 2 vols. Ed. R. H. Campbell and A. S. Skinner. Oxford: Oxford University Press, 1976.

Stiglitz, Joseph. 2002. *Globalization and Its Discontents.* New York: Norton.

Bruce Landesman

POLITICAL INEQUALITY

SEE *Inequality, Political.*

POLITICAL INSTABILITY, INDICES OF

Political instability can be defined in at least three ways. A first approach is to define it as the propensity for regime or government change. A second is to focus on the incidence of political upheaval or violence in a society, such as assassinations, demonstrations, and so forth. A third approach focuses on instability in policies rather than instability in regimes (i.e., the degree to which fundamental policies of, for instance, property rights are subject to frequent changes).

INDICES OF POLITICAL STABILITY

Just as there are a number of definitions of political instability, there are also a number of indices designed to measure the level of political instability in countries. Some of these indices have been developed primarily for academic or policy purposes, such as the POLITY indices and the World Bank governance indices. The inclusion of objective data on political violence, such as the number of assassinations and demonstrations, in data sets for academic studies is common.

There are a number of other indices that have been developed primarily to inform international investors of the political risk involved in investing in various countries. A number of companies and institutions offer these types of indices; they include the Political Risk Services (PRS) group's International Country Risk Guide [ICRG] indices; Business Environment Risk Intelligence (BERI); the Economist Intelligence Unit; Moody's and many more.

Finally, there are a number of more specialized indices of phenomena that relate to political instability, such as the Corruption Perceptions Index of Transparency International, and the political risk and civil liberties indices of Freedom House.

The available indices relate to the various definitions of political instability in different ways. The POLITY data contain indices of regime transition and durability, reflecting the first definition. The objective indices of political violence included in the 1997 dataset of William Easterly and Ross Levine are more in line with the second definition. Indices such as those in the ICRG encompass several of the definitions, including instability in terms of potential policy volatility.

The indices broadly fall into two categories in terms of how they are developed. On the one hand there are the objective indices, which typically collect count data on the incidence of certain phenomena (e.g., demonstrations, revolutions, assassinations, and more). On the other hand, perceptions indices, which use expert opinion or surveys, gauge the assessments and insights of certain groups on the degree of political stability in a country.

PERCEPTIONS INDICES

The design of objective indices of political instability does not require much explanation. For perceptions indices, however, the methodology must be examined more closely. Following is a detailed account of two sets of indices that are frequently used in academic studies; the ICRG indices and the World Bank governance indices developed by Daniel Kaufmann and his colleagues.

The ICRG rating comprises three subcategories of risk: political, financial, and economic. The political risk rating includes twelve weighted variables covering both political and social attributes. The twelve variables are: government stability; socioeconomic conditions; investment profile; internal conflict; external conflict; corruption; military in politics; religious tensions; law and order; ethnic tensions; democratic accountability; and bureaucracy quality. The score on each variable is set by experts based on available information, and is thus based on subjective judgment. The ICRG indices provide monthly data for 140 countries, starting in 1984.

The World Bank governance indices measure six dimensions of governance: voice and accountability; political instability and violence; government effectiveness; regulatory quality; rule of law; and control of corruption. The index of political instability and violence measures the likelihood of violent threats to, or changes in, government, including terrorism. The indices are based on 352 individual variables measuring perceptions of governance, drawn from thirty-seven separate data sources constructed by thirty-one organizations. The sources include inter alia the ICRG indices. The governance indices cover 209 countries and territories for 1996, 1998, 2000, 2002, and 2004.

USE OF INDICES IN ACADEMIC WORK

Indices of political instability are employed in many cross-country empirical studies, which are generally of two types. In one type of studies, political instability is the dependent variable, whose variation is explained by other variables. These kinds of studies are typically conducted in the discipline of political science. In other studies, political instability is an independent variable. This type of analysis is common in the field of economics, where political instability is related to such dependent variables as growth or investment.

In the first type of study, researchers, for instance, seek to establish a link between inequality and political instability. Early studies of this kind use objective indices of political violence as their dependent variable. In later studies such as that of Philip Nel in 2003, objective indices of violence are complemented by the Kaufmann political stability index.

A similar development is apparent in economic studies using political instability as an independent variable. Such studies have shifted emphasis from analyzing politi-

cal stability in the traditional sense towards institutions. Early studies of growth, such as the 1992 work of Levine and David Renelt, find that the number of revolutions and coups has a robust influence on investment, which in turn influences growth. Daron Acemoglu and his colleagues used indices from the PRS group and POLITY to test the impact of institutions on growth. In the investment literature, Alberto Alesina and Roberto Perotti and Jakob Svensson use indices of political unrest and violence, and indices of government change, as independent variables. Aymo Brunetti and Beatrice Weder, however, include both objective measures and perceptions indices such as those of the ICRG. Moreover, in early-twenty-first century studies of foreign direct investment (FDI), researchers frequently use perceptions indices. Steven Globerman and Daniel Shapiro use the Kaufmann governance indices to explain the pattern of FDI across countries, while Philipp Harms and Heinrich W. Ursprung use a set of ICRG indices for the same purpose.

SEE ALSO *Conflict; Ethnic Fractionalization; Political Science; Revolution; World Bank, The*

BIBLIOGRAPHY

Acemoglu, Daron, Simon Johnson, and James A. Robinson. 2001. The Colonial Origins of Comparative Development: An Empirical Investigation. *American Economic Review* 91 (5): 1369–1401.

Alesina, Alberto, and Roberto Perotti. 1996. Income Distribution, Political Instability, and Investment. *European Economic Review* 40: 1203–1228.

Brunetti, Aymo, and Beatrice Weder. 1998. Investment and Institutional Uncertainty: A Comparative Study of Different Uncertainty Measures. *Weltwirtschaftliches Archiv* 134 (3): 513–533.

Easterly, William, and Ross Levine. 1997. Africa's Growth Tragedy: Politics and Ethnic Divisions. *Quarterly Journal of Economics* 112: 1203–1250.

Globerman, Steven, and Daniel Shapiro. 2002. Global Foreign Direct Investment Flows: The Role of Governance Infrastructure. *World Development* 30 (11): 1899–1919.

Harms, Philipp, and Heinrich W. Ursprung. 2002. Do Civil and Political Repression Really Boost Foreign Direct Investment? *Economic Inquiry* 40 (4): 651–663.

Kaufmann, Daniel, Aart Kray, and Massimo Mastruzzi. 2005. *Governance Matters IV: Governance Indicators for 1996–2004*, World Bank Policy Research Paper 3630. Washington, DC: World Bank.

Levine, Ross, and David Renelt. 1992. A Sensitivity Analysis Of Cross-Country Regressions. *American Economic Review* 82 (4): 942–963.

Muller, Edward N., and Mitchell A. Seligson. 1987. Inequality and Insurgency. *American Political Science Review* 81 (2): 425–452.

Nel, Philip. 2003. Income Inequality, Economic Growth, and Political Instability in Sub-Saharan Africa. *Journal of Modern African Studies* 41 (4): 611–639.

Svensson, Jakob. 1998. Investment, Property Rights and Political Instability: Theory and Evidence. *European Economic Review* 42: 1317–1341.

Wang, T. Y., William J. Nixon, Edward M. Muller, and Mitchell A. Seligson. 1993. Inequality and Political Violence Revisited. *American Political Science Review* 87 (4): 979–994.

Ivar Kolstad

POLITICAL PARTIES

Political parties are organizations subscribing to an ideology or formed around a special interest, with the aim of attaining power within government. They participate in elections, select candidates for public office, mobilize voters, raise funds, articulate political positions, coordinate policy making, develop campaign strategies, and generate symbols of party identification and loyalty. Parties are rooted in political, religious, sectional, ethnic, racial, and/or economic class interests. Parties are frequently coalitions of groups espousing disparate interests. Persons who support a party's candidates, espouse its policies, and work to advance its political objectives are *partisans*. An opposition party does not challenge the legitimacy of the government, but only its policies.

EARLY POLITICAL PARTIES

European political parties formed during the seventeenth and eighteenth centuries to advise the monarchy. The model of a political party can be traced to Great Britain as the Tory and Whig parties fought for control of Parliament. Alexander Hamilton (1755–1804) founded the first U.S. political party, the Federalists, in 1792 to support his fiscal and political policies.

Although a competitive party system is considered to be an essential prerequisite for political freedom today, seventeenth- and eighteenth-century Anglo-American thinkers were wary of political parties, faulting them for serving special interests rather than the public good. Parties often were associated with treason and conspiracy. George Washington (1732–1799), the first president of the United States, in his "Farewell Address" deplored "the baneful effects of the Spirit of Party" (Washington 1796, p. 226). John Adams (1734–1826), the second president, held that "a division of the republic into two great parties … is to be dreaded as the greatest political evil under our Constitution" (Adams 1851, p. 508). Political leaders who serve only the interests of their parties rather than the common good were condemned as corrupt. The

Federalists and Jeffersonian Republicans did not regard each other as legitimate opposition parties, but as threats to the republic that should be eliminated. When the Federalist Party collapsed in 1814, the political consensus that ensued—the "Era of Good Feeling"—was cited as evidence that the U.S. system had succeeded.

Others wrote more sympathetically and prophetically about the positive role that parties played in political life. Edmund Burke (1729–1797) saw party competition as a necessary good. Famously defining a party as "a body of men united for promoting by their joint endeavors the national interest upon particular principle in which they are all agreed," Burke declared that "[p]arty divisions whether operating for good or evil are things inseparable from free government" (Burke 1925, p. 229). One of the authors of the U.S. Constitution, James Madison (1751–1836), following the English philosopher David Hume (1711–1776), held in *Federalist Paper* number 10 that parties, or "factions," could not "be removed" because they are rooted in man's natural propensity to differ. The "mischief" of factions that cause, though, could be curbed by fostering a multiplicity of "factions and parties" that would render unlikely "that a majority of the whole will have a common motive to invade the rights of citizens." If they do, sufficient impediments, such as bad roads and poor communications, would make it difficult for them "to act in unison" (Madison 1787, pp. 55–61).

Although there is no mention of political parties in the U.S. Constitution, political parties are a logical outcome of the constitutional system. The First Amendment of the Constitution guarantees freedom of speech and assembly, both necessary conditions for the emergence of voluntary political organizations. The Constitution's delegation of legislative power to elected representatives encouraged the formation of political parties. Parties, in turn, transformed and democratized the constitutional system. Thomas Jefferson (1743–1826) is credited with having created the first popular political party—the Democratic-Republicans later known as the Democratic Party. For his election to the presidency in 1828, Andrew Jackson (1767–1845) transformed this party into the first national, massed-based party.

TYPES OF PARTIES AND PARTY SYSTEMS

Because power is shared between the central government and the individual states, the U.S. federal system of government impedes the development of the type of unified, cohesive parties found in, for example, the European parliamentary systems. A parliamentary system demands greater party discipline because the majority party in Parliament forms the government. Except when the Democrat and Republican parties gather every four years at their national conventions to nominate candidates for the offices of president and vice president and to write their platforms, they are not in any meaningful way national parties. Rather, each is really a coalition of state parties that are themselves confederations of semiautonomous local governmental parties. Even presidents or candidates for the presidency have only feeble control over state and local party members and elected officials. Under the U.S system, a divided government is possible, when one or both houses of Congress and the presidency are held by different parties.

The ideological spectrum of political parties typically runs from left to right. Right-wing political parties espouse conservative or reactionary views, whereas left-wing parties are associated with progressive or radical policies. The Conservative Party of Canada and the United Kingdom and the Republican Party of the United States are right-wing parties, and the Labour Party of the United Kingdom, the Liberal Party of Canada, and the Democratic Party of the United States are generally considered to be left-wing parties. The British National Front Party and the Front National of France are examples of far right-wing parties, and the Green, Communist, and Socialist parties are all on the extreme left.

Political party systems vary across the world. Nonparty states, such as Saudia Arabia and the United Arab Emirates, have no political parties at all. Single-party states, such as the People's Republic of China, North Korea, and Cuba, allow only one-party rule. The constitution of the former Soviet Union officially established the primacy of the Communist Party. The prohibition against the formation of opposition parties is evidence of the absence of liberty. In contrast, dominant-party states do allow other parties, but one party, such as the People's Action Party of Singapore and African National Congress Party of South Africa, typically wins most if not all elections. In the U.S. South until the 1970s, the Democratic Party won nearly all the general elections.

Two-party states, such as the United States, have two dominant national parties that vie for power. The system for electing the president in the United States entails an indirect election in which the electorate votes for a slate of electors who cast their votes for the president and vice president in an electoral college. This system impedes the formation of third parties: Because the slate of electors for the electoral college are elected in winner-take-all state elections, minor party candidates rarely win sufficient electoral college votes to have an impact on a national election. The election of legislative representatives in winner-take-all district elections further discourages the development of third parties. The principle that the single-member district plurality voting system results in a two-party system has been called Durverger's law, after the

French sociologist, Maurice Duverger (b. 1917), who formulated it. The two parties tend to resemble each other because each party gravitates toward the middle in an effort to capture the independent vote.

Multiparty states, such as the United Kingdom, Israel, and Canada, have a number of parties that compete for power. A multiparty system commonly exists in states with a parliamentary form of government. If no party wins a majority of seats in a parliamentary election, a coalition government is formed between two or more parties. The majority of the members of Parliament vote for a leader who serves as the head of the government. Proportional Representation, a scheme of voting used in several European states, encourages further proliferation of parties. Under this system, legislative seats are allocated according to the percentage of popular votes that the party received in the most recent election.

POLITICAL PARTIES AND DEMOCRACY

Modern political scientists regard political parties as beneficial avenues through which political interests and opinions can be channeled. "Democracy," political scientist E. E. Schattschneider (1892–1971) concluded, "is unthinkable save in terms of parties" (Schattschneider 1942, p. 124).

Other thinkers, though, were more cautious in their assessment of the democratic influence of political parties on government. Most significantly, the Italian anarcho-syndicalist sociologist Robert Michels (1876–1936) proposed the iron law of oligarchy which stipulated that no matter how democratic an organization may be initially, it will eventually develop into an oligarchy. All large organizations, to attain greater efficiency and decision-making coordination, tend to concentrate power into the hands of a few. As parties grow in size and complexity, they become more hierarchically organized. True democracy, given the premises of Michels's argument, is practically and theoretically impossible.

The noted American sociologist C. Wright Mills (1916–1962) observed that the top of the American political system was becoming more unified and powerful. He described in his most famous book, *The Power Elite* (1956), the interconnecting relationship between corporate, military, and government leaders. His controversial argument was that there was a growing power gap between a class of people Mills called "the power elite" and the increasingly manipulated and controlled masses.

Not all theorists agreed with the pessimistic implications of these arguments. The popular definition of democracy as "government by the people," Schattschneider contended, exaggerates the power of the public. Rather, a more realistic definition that emphasizes organization and leadership rather than spontaneous grass-roots politics is needed. "Democracy is a competitive political system," he observed, "in which competing leaders and organizations define the alternatives of public policy in such a way that the public can participate in the decision-making process" (Schattschneider 1960, p. 141).

WEAKENING OF PARTY LOYALTY

Some of the factors that weaken the power and influence of political parties include declining patronage, the direct primary, the role of the media, the proliferation of non-partisan political action committees, and the growing importance of the Internet as a tool for raising campaign funds and disseminating information about candidates and issues. The direct primary diminishes the ability of party leaders to select preferred candidates to run for political office. Patronage induces voters to support the party's candidates by handing out jobs, contracts, or promotions for political reasons rather than merit. As easily accessible information about candidates and issues becomes available to voters through the mass media and the Internet, voters become less dependent on parties. Better informed voters tend to be less deferential to parties and more likely to split their votes among candidates from two or more parties.

Many analysts of the U.S. political party system detect a continuing trend toward party dealignment. A growing number of voters are declining to affiliate with any political party, preferring instead to identify themselves as independents. Since 1988 the plurality of independent voters has steadily increased. In 2004 39 percent of the American voters identified themselves as independents. Polls suggest that a large portion of the American public is allergic to partisan politics. They want candidates who promise to rise above partisan bickering and party loyalty to work on enacting legislation that will effectively solve the nation's most pressing social and economic problems.

The most important function of the national political parties today is to raise funds for candidates and wage "get-out-the vote" campaigns.

SEE ALSO *Burke, Edmund; Campaigning; Centrism; Cleavages; Constitutions; Dahl, Robert Alan; Dealignment; Democracy; Elections; Electoral Systems; Federalism; Hamilton, Alexander; Hume, David; Ideology; Interest Groups and Interests; Left and Right; Left Wing; Madison, James; Michels, Robert; Mills, C. Wright; Oligarchy, Iron Law of; One-Party States; Pluralism; Political Science; Politics; Power Elite; Representation; Right Wing; Schattschneider, E. E.; State, The; Washington, George*

BIBLIOGRAPHY

Adams, John. 1850–1856. *The Works of John Adams, Second President of the United States*, vol. 1, ed. Charles Francis Adams. Boston: Little, Brown.

Aldrich, John H. 1995. *Why Parties? The Origin and Transformation of Political Parties in America*. Chicago: University of Chicago Press.

Burke, Edmund. 1925. *Works*, ed. C. F. Adams. London: Oxford University Press.

Duverger, Maurice. 1964. *Political Parties: Their Organization and Activity in the Modern State*. Trans. Barbara and Robert North. New York: Wiley and Sons.

Hofstadter, Richard. 1969. *The Idea of a Party System: The Rise of Legitimate Opposition in the United States, 1780–1840*. Berkeley: University of California Press.

Madison, James, Alexander Hamilton, and John Jay. 1941. *The Federalist*, ed. Edward Mead Earle. New York: Modern Library Press. (Orig. pub. 1787–1788).

Michels, Robert. [1911] 1915. *Political Parties: A Sociological Study of the Oligarchical Tendencies of Modern Democracies*. Trans. Eden Paul and Cedar Paul. New York: Free Press.

Mills, C. Wright. 1956. *The Power Elite*. New York: Oxford University Press.

Patterson, Kelly D. 1996. *Political Parties and the Maintenance of Liberal Democracy*. New York: Columbia University Press.

Schattschneider, E. E. 1942. *Party Government*. New York: Holt.

Schattschneider, E. E. 1960. *The Semisovereign People: A Realist's View of Democracy in America*. New York: Holt, Rinehart, and Winston.

Washington, George. 1931–1941. *The Writings of George Washington*. Vol. 35. Washington, D.C.: U.S. Government Printing Office.

White, John Kenneth, and Daniel M. Shea. 2004. *New Party Politics: From Jefferson and Hamilton to the Information Age*. 2nd ed. Belmont, CA: Wadsworth.

W. Wesley McDonald

POLITICAL PSYCHOLOGY

Political psychology is an interdisciplinary academic field that emphasizes the psychological dimension of political life. Its practitioners use psychological constructs, such as personality, attitudes, beliefs, values, needs, goals, and expectations, to explain political behavior and to examine the complex and reciprocal relationship between politics and psychology. Political psychologists presume that political actions, like all other forms of human behavior, are the result of interplay between the individual and the environment. Because the scientific study of politics investigates relations and interactions among individuals behaving as political actors, it is inevitably linked with psychology, which is concerned with human thinking and behavior. Political analysts throughout the ages and across civilizations have been interested in the interrelation between personality traits and political contexts. They have employed many concepts and theories to explain why rulers and subjects think and act as they do, and how their thoughts and actions shape the course of politics. Hence, political psychology focuses on the important role of psychological factors in determining the individual's responses to various contextual/environmental stimuli.

Born in the decades between World Wars I and II, modern political psychology has developed to cover a wide variety of subjects. It traces its intellectual roots back to the eminent American political scientist and communications theorist Harold D. Lasswell (1902–1978). His classic writings, such as *Psychopathology and Politics* (1930), *World Politics and Personal Insecurity* (1935), *Politics: Who Gets What, When, and How* (1936), *Power and Personality* (1948), and *Power and Society* (1950), centered on the impact of individual and social psychological processes—perception, motivation, conflict, cognition, learning, socialization, attitude formation, and group dynamics—as causal factors influencing politics. It was Lasswell's pioneering work in political psychology that contributed to the field's initial unidirectional nature, characterized by a specific focus on how the individual psyche shapes political behavior and values.

Several leading members of the Institute for Social Research at the University of Frankfurt (the so-called *Frankfurt school*) who had arrived in the United States as refugees from Nazi Germany—Max Horkheimer (1895–1973), Erich Fromm (1900–1980), Herbert Marcuse (1898–1979), and Theodor Adorno (1903–1969), among others—developed the concept of *authoritarian personality*, which deals with the causal relationship between political views and personality types. Their ideas inspired Adorno and his associates at the University of California at Berkeley to conduct a seminal empirical study, *The Authoritarian Personality* (1950), based on the F(ascism)-scale measurement, which linked right-wing authoritarianism ("implicit antidemocratic tendencies and fascist potential") to a family pattern of rigidity, discipline, strict rules, and fearful subservience to the demands of parents. Even though it has been widely criticized, including for its heavy reliance on the psychoanalytical perspectives of Freudian theory, this now classic work reveals how certain politically relevant aspects of the psyche lead to fascist or authoritarian belief systems. The F-scale describes a personality type characterized by ethnocentric nationalism, extreme in-group conformity, rigid adherence to conventional values, submissiveness to authority, a readiness to punish, opposition to the free-thinking and kind-hearted, arrogance toward those considered inferior, and other authoritarian attitudes that explain major polit-

ical outcomes (for instance, the rise of archconservative, ultranationalist, and fascist ideologies and war in twentieth-century Europe).

Political psychology received a significant impetus from and, in turn, was a major contributor to the "behavioral revolution" that swept the field of political science in the 1950s and 1960s. Behavioralist-oriented researchers directed their scholarly attention to new issues such as analyzing the impact of personality characteristics upon political participation and party preference. Lasswell, for one, came up with eight psychological reasons for participation in politics: power, wealth, well-being, skill, enlightenment, affection, rectitude, and respect. Similarly, Robert E. Lane in his *Political Life: Why and How People Get Involved in Politics* (1965) argued that political participation serves a number of conscious and unconscious needs and motives, including power, economic and material gain, friendship and affection, self-esteem, relief from psychic tensions, and a need to understand the world. Thanks to the behavioral revolution, survey methods showed marked improvement from early studies such as *The People's Choice* (1944), the classic study of the 1940 U.S. presidential election conducted by the famous Austrian-born sociologist Paul F. Lazarsfeld (1901–1976), to later ones such as *The American Voter* (1960), the best-known research study of American voting behavior by Angus Campbell, Philip Converse, William Miller, and Donald Stokes. Electoral behavior was examined in relation to various demographic and population variables (age, gender, level of education, type of employment, social class, ethnicity, race, religion, and ideology). The increased sophistication of public opinion polling led to numerous in-depth analyses of belief systems at both the mass and elite level, such as Philip Converse's influential study, "The Nature of Belief Systems in Mass Publics" (in David Apter's *Ideology and Discontent*, 1964), which found that mass public opinion tends to be inconsistent, fickle, and poorly informed.

Largely under Lasswell's influence, early political psychology had centered on the unidirectional impact of individual and social psychological processes upon the polity, but in later decades attention began to be devoted also to the reverse effect of politics on personality systems. Studies of political culture and political socialization, such as Gabriel Almond and Sydney Verba's *The Civic Culture: Political Attitudes and Democracy in Five Nations* (1963), looked at how political systems inform individual behavior and values. By the 1980s most political psychologists had accepted the "bidirectional" nature of the interaction between individual psychology and the polity:

> [T]he perceptions, beliefs, motives, opinions, values, interests, styles, defenses, and experiences of individuals—be they citizens, leaders, group

members, bureaucrats, terrorists, or revolutionaries—are seen as influencing what they do politically; and, in turn, the political culture, political system, mechanisms of political socialization, political movements and parties, and the international system are perceived as having an impact on what people are like. (Hermann 1986, p. 2)

Political psychology finally took shape as an academic discipline in its own right when the International Society of Political Psychology was founded in 1978 and began holding annual scientific meetings and publishing a quarterly journal, *Political Psychology*. Today, political psychology is a key component of the political behavior subfield of political science. Its diverse objects of analysis range from the psychobiography of political leaders (for example, the 1997 psychobiography of President Richard Nixon by Vamik D. Volkan, Norman Itzowitz, and Andrew W. Dod) to inquiries into the "postmaterial" bases of identity politics (e.g., Ronald Inglehart's seminal work, *Silent Revolution: Changing Values and Political Styles among Western Publics*, 1977). Psychological terminology is now an important and pervasive part of political science discourse, as numerous psychological concepts have been incorporated into political studies at both the national and international level. Psychological concepts are widely used in research on voting behavior, political socialization, political leadership, the dynamics of public opinion, political attitudes, political conflict and cooperation, international negotiation, decision-making, and, more recently, political information processing.

The two empirical research methods most often employed to study psychological variables are the sample survey and the in-depth interview. For example, political psychologists frequently use attitude surveys to probe the connections among personality structures, demographic and population variables, and dispositions toward political participation and party preference. Other more innovative but less frequently utilized research tools include simulation, projective techniques, content analysis, focus groups, and the controlled experiment. The application of psychological insights to political inquiry remains a widespread and growing trend, as many political psychology studies continue to appear within the framework of related social-science disciplines, especially political science. Although no underlying scientific paradigm or even a single basic theory provides unity and coherence to this eclectic interdisciplinary field, political psychology has already acquired a permanent, if rather heterogeneous and pluralistic, presence within the discipline of political science.

SEE ALSO *Almond, Gabriel A.; Attitudes, Political; Authoritarianism; Authority; Behaviorism; Cognition; Communication; Fascism; Frankfurt School; Lay*

Theories; Left Wing; Persuasion; Political Science; Politics; Preferences; Prejudice; Psychoanalytic Theory; Psychology; Right Wing; Stereotype Threat; Stereotypes; Tolerance, Political; Verba, Sidney

BIBLIOGRAPHY

Ascher, William, and Barbara Hirschfelder-Ascher. 2005. *Revitalizing Political Psychology: The Legacy of Harold D. Lasswell.* Mahwah, NJ: Erlbaum.

Cottam, Martha L., et al. 2004. *Introduction to Political Psychology.* Mahwah, NJ: Erlbaum.

Elster, Jon. 1993. *Political Psychology.* Cambridge, U.K., and New York: Cambridge University Press.

Hermann, Margaret G., ed. 1986. *Political Psychology.* San Francisco: Jossey-Bass.

Knutson, Jeanne N. 1973. *Handbook of Political Psychology.* San Francisco: Jossey-Bass.

Monroe, Kristen Renwick, ed. 2002. *Political Psychology.* Mahwah, NJ, and London: Erlbaum.

Sears, David O., Leonie Huddy, and Robert Jervis, eds. 2003. *Oxford Handbook of Political Psychology.* New York: Oxford University Press.

Rossen Vassilev

POLITICAL REPRESENTATION

SEE *Constituency; Democracy; Representation.*

POLITICAL SCIENCE

The first efforts to systematically study politics can be traced to Plato's *Republic* (c. 427–c. 347 BCE) and Aristotle's *Politics* (384–322 BCE). Their works were later incorporated into Christianity through neo-Platonists, such as St. Augustine (354–430 CE), and neo-Aristotelians, such as St. Thomas Aquinas (c.1225–1274 CE). The classical and Christian traditions of political philosophy postulated metaphysical first principles and relied on a process of deductive reasoning that sought to derive the moral and ethical principles of an ideal-state. Whether the ideal-state was ever achieved by any civilization was considered secondary to discovering the "highest good" that ought to guide citizens and statesmen.

The political writings of Niccolò Machiavelli were the first to break with these traditions of political philosophy. Machiavelli believed that the study of political history could yield general principles to guide statesmen in the conduct of politics, diplomacy, and war. He studied existing and historical political institutions, and the actions of great statesmen, not for the purpose of discerning a morally ideal-state, but to identify institutional arrangements that would maintain social order and political stability. The separation of politics from any metaphysical or theological foundation led subsequent political philosophers to seek a new basis for legitimate political authority, although, in the end, solutions such as reason, natural law, custom, and tradition were superseded by the idea that sovereignty resides in a nation's people.

FROM POLITICAL PHILOSOPHY TO POLITICAL SCIENCE

Francis Lieber (1798–1872) is considered the first modern political scientist. He was a liberal German émigré to the United States, who from 1827 to 1832 devoted himself to writing and editing the thirteen-volume *Encyclopedia Americana*. Its major contribution was to establish "the idea of the state," or *Staatswissenshaft*, as the organizing concept of political science. The idea of the state was gaining wide currency in Europe, particularly in Germany, but it was Lieber who first argued in the United States that the "idea of the state is the basis of a class of sciences, and gives them a distinct character as belongs to the various classes of history, philosophy, theological, medical, &c., sciences" (1838, Vol. 10, p. 225). He drew a distinction between idea of the state and the "form of government," which was "merely a means of obtaining the great objects of the state" (1838, Vol. 11, p. 568). Against the backdrop of events leading up to the U.S. Civil War, Lieber articulated a distinctly idealistic theory of the state which identified the state as an abstract and organic sovereign society that was the source of governmental authority and the basis of its legitimacy. Lieber's appointment as professor of history and political science at Columbia University in 1857 made him the first person to hold that title in the United States.

THE DOMAIN AND METHODS OF POLITICAL SCIENCE

After Lieber, political science was established as a broader discipline when John W. Burgess, a professor of constitutional law, founded the Faculty of Political Science at Columbia in 1880. Burgess's school became the leading graduate faculty in political science during the 1890s along with the Department of History, Politics, and Economics, which had been established by Henry Baxter Adams at Johns Hopkins University in the 1870s. Burgess and Adams were both adherents of the *Staatswissenshaft* doctrine, but they shifted the discipline's methodological emphasis from political ethics to history.

In 1886 Columbia's faculty founded the *Political Science Quarterly (PSQ)*, which was the new discipline's

first scholarly journal. In its first issue, Edmund Munroe Smith, a professor of international law, announced that it would "recognize but one political science—the science of the state" (1886, pp. 2–3). However, the *PSQ* also facilitated a new departure in *Staatswissenshaft* by emphasizing that it was one thing to describe the state's development, comparatively and historically, but more was required to *explain* changes and development in the state. Smith argued "if we seek to trace through history the evolution of the state, we find each step in its development recorded in the evolution of law and explained to a great degree by economic changes" (p. 7). This methodological principle, which was called "the economic interpretation of history" was developed first by James E. Thorold Rogers (1823–1890), a professor of political economy at Oxford University, whose work stimulated the next advances in the discipline.

THE ECONOMIC BASIS OF POLITICS

The Populist revolt and the Progressive movement were fertile political environments for an intellectual revolt against the formalist-idealism of the early discipline. The method of economic interpretation led to a new iteration of *Staatswissenschaft* that seemed better able to explain the political conflicts of the era. During the 1890s, there were several miscues in the effort to define "the method of economic interpretation," including both skirmishes and dialogues with Marxian historical materialists. The major breakthrough came from Edwin R. A. Seligman, a political economist in Columbia's Faculty of Political Science. Seligman's general statement of the economic interpretation of history is that:

> The existence of man depends upon his ability to sustain himself; the economic life is therefore the fundamental condition of all life. Since human life, however, is the life of man in society, individual existence moves within the framework of the social structure and is modified by it....To economic causes, therefore, must be traced in the last instance those transformations in the structure of society which themselves condition the relations of social classes and the various manifestations of social life (1967, p. 3).

The method of economic interpretation was widely adopted by political scientists in the early twentieth century, particularly after Seligman had differentiated it from Karl Marx's historical materialism. Nevertheless, the method of economic interpretation is most often identified with the work of Charles A. Beard, one of Seligman's students, and the author of *An Economic Interpretation of the Constitution of the United States* (1913). In its political context, the book became an intellectual lightning rod, because according to Beard capitalistic interests had dominated the U.S. Constitutional Convention of 1787 and, consequently, they authored a founding document that appealed "directly and unerringly to identical interests in the country at large" (p. 188). Beard later sought to generalize this doctrine in *The Economic Basis of Politics* (1922).

Beard exerted a powerful influence on the discipline over the next two decades, partly by authoring the first introductory textbook on *American Government and Politics* (1910), which became a standard text in political science for nearly four decades. In 1926, Beard's soaring reputation secured his election as president of the American Political Science Association (APSA). By the mid-1930s, his economic interpretation of the American state had achieved orthodox status among scholars as the Great Depression forced economic considerations to the forefront of government and political science.

However, developments in political science and other disciplines put the doctrine of *Staatswissenschaft* under pressure from the outset. In 1895 the American Historical Association was established by historians seeking to institutionalize Leopold von Ranke's methodological program of historical positivism. Frank J. Goodnow, who had been a member of *PSQ*'s editorial board, led the founding of the American Political Science Association in 1903, along with its new journal, the *American Political Science Review*. As the APSA's first president, Goodnow reaffirmed that the domain of political science is "that political organization of society which is termed 'the State' " (Ross 1991, p. 282). Nevertheless, the vision for a science of the state, anchored by political economy, started to fragment as one social science after another splintered into separate disciplines and, after World War I, began exploring the new positivist philosophy as an alternative methodological foundation.

THE POSITIVIST MOVEMENT

During the 1920s, political science began a paradigm shift that culminated in the behavioral revolution of the 1950s. The first aspect of this paradigm shift was a redefinition of the meaning of "science." The positivist movement sought to place political science on the same methodological foundations as the natural sciences. This movement was also promoted by the federal government, which was anxious to bring about the same types of technical success in the social sciences as had been achieved in the physical, life, and behavioral sciences (psychology) during World War I. Positivists claim that all research is similar in method and differs only in the specific problems to be solved by a particular science. Thus, there is a single "scientific method" that starts with the formulation of a hypothesis, followed by empirical observation or experi-

mentation, which leads to a falsification or verification of the initial hypothesis. Knowledge is accumulated incrementally as hypotheses are rejected or accepted as a result of empirical tests.

The Social Science Research Council (SSRC) was chartered in 1923 as an independent nonprofit organization, and funded by private foundations, specifically to encourage "behavioral research" in economics, sociology, and political science that employed empirical and statistical methods of the type advocated by positivists. The University of Chicago, which was among the first to pioneer such methods, was designated as the SSRC's showcase institution. The SSRC distributed funds to political scientists and political science departments for fellowships and training in the new empirical methods, for the development of new courses in statistics and behavioral research design, and general department building along the Chicago model. Charles E. Merriam, a professor of political science at Chicago, is often called the father of behavioral political science. In his *New Aspects of Politics* (1925), Merriam called for a science based on the observation of real governments and political behavior, although he remained skeptical about an overly quantitative political science. This skepticism was retained by Harold D. Lasswell and V. O. Key, who were both students of Merriam and important transitional figures between the positivist movement of the 1920s and the behavioral revolution of the 1950s. Lasswell called for an applied political science oriented toward solving the problems of democracy as opposed to a discipline that emulated natural science in a quest to discover "universal laws" of political behavior without respect to their practical applications. In 1951 Lasswell proposed that "policy scientists" should conduct research that was directly and immediately useful to decision makers, while employing "appropriate" quantitative methodologies that acknowledged the limits of data availability and the pressures of time and scarce resources in the decision-making process. Key is best known for his work on political parties, interest groups, electoral behavior, and public opinion. Although he disagreed with the behavioralists' fundamental tenets, he pioneered many of the statistical techniques and analytic concepts later employed by them.

THE BEHAVIORAL REVOLUTION

The positivist influence reached its apogee in the "behavioral revolution" of 1950s, which consolidated the discipline's paradigm shift, first, by codifying behavioral methodology and, second, by finally rejecting outright the concept of the state. The behavioralists broke with the earlier practice of political scientists by claiming to have discovered a "value-neutral" science and by viewing all earlier works on politics as merely a storehouse of hypotheses for empirical falsification or verification. This attitude toward political philosophy widened the long simmering rift between empirical political science and normative political theory with the latter regarded as an "unscientific" legacy of the discipline's past.

Behavioralism's main methodological claim was that uniformities in political behavior could be discovered and expressed as generalizations, but that such generalizations must be testable by reference to observable political behaviors, such as voting, public opinion, or decision making. Most behavioralists equated observation with quantification to a degree that went beyond what Merriam, Key, or Laswell had considered "appropriate quantification." Finally, the behavioralists proposed a "pure science" where the theoretical explanation of political behavior was to precede the solution of urgent practical policy problems in society.

The concept of the state, which had been central to political science, was also displaced in the 1950s by a concept of the "political system" that is mainly associated with Talcott Parsons's systems analysis. Parsons's sociology identified the political system with behaviors and institutions that provide a center of integration for all aspects of the social system. David Easton echoed this view by declaring, "neither the state nor power is a concept that serves to bring together political research" and instead defined the political system as "those interactions through which values are authoritatively allocated for a society" (1953, p. 106). Systems analysis was tied closely to various theories of decision making, but most notably to pluralist theory, which viewed decision making as the outcome of peaceful bargaining between interest groups in society. Easton emphasized that to account for the persistence of political systems, one had to assume that they successfully generate two "system outputs": (1) the political system must successfully allocate values for a society (decision making); and (2) the political system must induce most members to accept these allocations as binding, at least most of the time (legitimacy). These "policy outputs" feed back into the social, economic, international, and natural systems to generate new inputs and demands that must be continually processed by the political system.

Easton's model of the political system stimulated a great deal of research over the next two decades on decision making, interest groups, political communications, political parties, elections and voting behavior, legislative behavior, political socialization, political beliefs, and the policy process. These fields of research have also been characterized by ever increasing levels of sophistication in the use of statistical techniques and concepts. However, the systems model was often limited in applicability by its emphasis on system stability and the assumption of insti-

tutional arrangements peculiar to Western democracies. These limitations were partly addressed by the functionalists, who employed a modified concept of the political system that focused on "functions" and "processes," while acknowledging that the same functions could be fulfilled in various political systems through different processes or institutions. Functionalism was particularly influential in the study of comparative politics and non-Western political systems, where there were different institutional arrangements or where the use of statistical techniques was hampered by the absence of data and technology.

During the 1950s the political science discipline also assumed its current form as a collection of distinct subfields with most political scientists specializing in one or two subfields, while having less and less interaction with practitioners in other subfields of the discipline. The standard subfields are American government, comparative politics, international relations, political theory, public administration, and public policy, although the two latter "applied" fields have often been shifted into separate academic units, such as schools of public administration or public policy, while political theory is now actually practiced as often by historians, philosophers, and literary critics as by political scientists.

THE POSTBEHAVIORAL REVOLUTION

Political science entered a postbehavioral revolution amidst the political rebellions of the late 1960s and the new social movements of the 1970s and 1980s. New intellectual currents, such as neo-Marxism, postpositivism, poststructuralism, and postmodernism were conjoined with a variety of political movements, including pacifism, feminism, environmentalism, postcolonialism, and the gay and lesbian liberation movements. Easton identified the source of the postbehavioral revolution as a "deep dissatisfaction with political research and teaching, especially of the kind that is striving to convert the study of politics into a more rigorously scientific discipline modeled on the methodology of the natural sciences" (1969, p. 1051). The behavioral persuasion remains the dominant orientation of the official discipline, but it has been challenged numerous times since the late 1960s.

One of the most significant intellectual challenges to the behavioralist paradigm and to pluralist theory was the return to the state initiated in the late 1960s by Marxists, such as Ralph Miliband and Nicos Poulantzas and then carried forward by the "new institutionalists." Nicos Poulantzas's *Pouvoir Politique et Classes Sociales* (1968), and Ralph Miliband's *The State in Capitalist Society* (1969) directly challenged systems analysis and pluralist theory by drawing on a radical tradition identified with the writings of Karl Marx, Friedrich Engels, V. I. Lenin, and Antonio Gramsci. These authors developed theories of the state that questioned the basic assumptions of the dominant political science, particularly its assumption that political power is distributed more or less equally among different social groups. At the height of his popularity in the mid-1970s, Miliband was recognized as one of the leading political scientists in the English-speaking world, while Nicos Poulantzas was arguably the most influential political theorist in the world for a time.

However, the interest in state theory waned temporarily as many political scientists abandoned the quest for grand theory in the context of a more widespread intellectual disillusionment with grand scale metanarratives, such as state theory and their attendant transformational political projects. The shift from Marxist to post-Marxist to poststructuralist and postmodernist theory shifted the analysis of power from macroscopic to microscopic forms of power and, therefore, to the multiple "technologies of power" such as language, family, interpersonal relationships, culture, leisure and entertainment, and the configurations of repressed desire (Foucault 1972, p. 12).

The growing discontent among a minority of political scientists led to the establishment of the Caucus for a New Political Science in 1967. The Caucus includes political scientists of many diverse viewpoints, but it is united by the idea that the discipline should abandon "the myth of a value-free science" and advance a progressive political agenda. While originally founded as an alternative to the APSA, it won recognition as the first organized section of the APSA with the right to sponsor its own panels, collect dues, and to publish its own journal *New Political Science.* Members of the Caucus have authored numerous commentaries on "the tragedy" of political science, "the crisis" in political science, and "the flight from reality in political science." In 2000, these discontents again resurfaced in the "perestroika" rebellion, which denounced the APSA as an organization controlled by "East Coast Brahmins," which promotes a "narrow parochialism and methodological bias toward the quantitative, behavioral, rational choice, statistical, and formal modeling approaches" (Monroe 2005, pp. 1, 9).

While Caucus members remain a small proportion of the APSA's membership, it established a precedent that has resulted in the proliferation of "organized sections" to represent the interests of political scientists in interdisciplinary, subfield, and methodological research outside the official discipline. There are now 37 organized sections in the APSA, whose combined membership is greater than that of the discipline as a whole and attendance at "section" panels of the APSA's annual meeting tends to be higher than at the "disciplinary" panels. Political science is now fragmented into so many subfields, methodological

approaches, area specializations, and theories that "political scientists apparently come together at APSA meetings, but only in spatial terms" (Yanow 2003, p. 398). The future of the discipline in the next century is not clear, but its development over the last century has been characterized by the accretion of multiple approaches. Despite major paradigm shifts, no conception of the discipline is ever completely displaced by another approach and the discipline is now clearly marked by a lack of consensus concerning its basic concepts, theories, and methodology.

SEE ALSO *Campbell, Angus; Dahl, Robert Alan; Data; Data, Longitudinal; Economics; Empiricism; Enlightenment; Experiments; Game Theory; Methodology; Methods, Qualitative; Methods, Quantitative; Methods, Research (in Sociology); Methods, Survey; Philosophy, Political; Plato; Political Psychology; Political Science, Behavioral; Politics; Politics, Comparative; Regression; Regression Analysis; Reliability, Statistical; Research, Cross-Sectional; Research, Longitudinal; Research, Survey; Scientific Method; Social Science; Validity, Statistical*

BIBLIOGRAPHY

Almond, Gabriel A., and G. Bingham Powell Jr. 1966. *Comparative Politics: System, Process, and Policy.* Boston: Little, Brown.

Barrow, Clyde W. 1993. *Critical Theories of the State: Marxist, Neo-Marxist, Post-Marxist.* Madison: University of Wisconsin Press.

Beard, Charles A. 1913. *An Economic Interpretation of the Constitution of the United States.* Glencoe, IL: Free Press.

Burgess, John W. 1897. Political Science and History. *American Historical Review* 2 (3): 401–408.

Burgess, John W. 1930. The Founding of the School of Political Science. *Columbia University Quarterly* 22: 351–396.

Burgess, John W. 1993. The Idea and Forms of the State. In *Discipline and History: Political Science in the United States,* eds. James Farr and Raymond Seidelman, 49–62. Ann Arbor: University of Michigan Press. (Article orig. pub. 1891).

Dahl, Robert A. 1956. *A Preface to Democratic Theory.* Chicago: University of Chicago Press.

Easton, David. 1953. *The Political System: An Inquiry into the State of Political Science.* New York: Alfred A. Knopf.

Easton, David. 1965. *A Framework for Political Analysis.* Englewood Cliffs, NJ: Prentice-Hall.

Easton, David. 1965. *A Systems Analysis of Political Life.* Chicago: University of Chicago Press.

Easton, David. 1969. The New Revolution in Political Science. *American Political Science Review* 63 (4): 1051–1061.

Foucault, Michel. 1972. *The Archaeology of Knowledge & The Discourse on Language.* New York: Harper and Row.

Furner, Mary O. 1975. *Advocacy and Objectivity: A Crisis in the Professionalization of American Social Science, 1865–1905.* Lexington: University of Kentucky Press.

Goodnow, Frank J. 1905. The Work of the American Political Science Association. *Proceedings of the American Political Science Association* 1: 35–46.

Gunnell, John G. 1993. *The Descent of Political Theory.* Chicago: University of Chicago Press.

Lerner, Daniel, and Harold D. Lasswell, eds. 1965. *The Policy Sciences: Recent Developments in Scope and Method.* Stanford, CA: Stanford University Press.

Lieber, Francis, ed. 1838. *Encyclopaedia Americana.* 13 vols. Philadelphia: Thomas, Cowperthwait, & Co.

Lyotard, Jean Francois. 1984. *The Postmodern Condition: A Report on Knowledge.* Minneapolis: University of Minnesota Press.

Merriam, Charles E. 1925. *New Aspects of Politics.* Chicago: University of Chicago Press.

Merriam, Charles E. 1993. Recent Advances in Political Methods. In *Discipline and History: Political Science in the United States,* eds. James Farr and Raymond Seidelman, 129–146. Ann Arbor: University of Michigan Press. (Article orig. pub. 1923).

Monroe, Kristen Renwick, ed. 2005. *Perestroika! The Raucous Rebellion in Political Science.* New Haven, CT: Yale University Press.

Ricci, David. 1984. *The Tragedy of Political Science.* New Haven, CT: Yale University Press.

Rogers, James E. Thorold. 1888. *The Economic Interpretation of History.* New York: G. P. Putnam's Sons.

Ross, Dorothy. 1991. *The Origins of American Social Science.* Cambridge, U.K.: Cambridge University Press.

Seidelman, Raymond. 1985. *Disenchanted Realists: Political Science and the American Crisis 1884–1984.* Albany: State University of New York Press.

Seligman, Edwin R. A. 1967. *The Economic Interpretation of History.* 2nd ed. New York: Gordian Press.

Smith, Munroe. 1886. Introduction: The Domain of Political Science. *Political Science Quarterly* 1 (1): 1–8.

Yanow, Davora. 2003. Practicing Discipline. *PS: Political Science and Politics* 36 (3): 397–399.

Clyde Barrow

POLITICAL SCIENCE, BEHAVIORAL

Behavioral political science is an approach to the study of politics that claims to be more "scientific" and methodologically sophisticated than the older, so-called "traditional" political science. Although the study of politics and government dates back to Plato and Aristotle, Greek philosophers in the fourth century BCE, political science only emerged as a separate academic discipline toward the end of the nineteenth century. Since that time, the science of politics has shifted from a descriptive focus on political history, formal institutions, and legal codes to a more "behavioral" emphasis upon decision-making processes, the political behavior of individuals and groups, and their informal relationships. Methodologically, behavioral political science has replaced the predominantly historical, legalistic, and institutional studies of the traditional approach with the more empirical methods of modern social science, borrowed mostly from the field of psychology.

Broadly defined, the traditional approach of political science was concerned with the purpose, nature, and organization of the "state," stressing humanistic, ethical, and philosophical perspectives. The traditionalists shared a preference for intensive case studies and other qualitative observations in which inferences were derived on the basis of subjective norms and values. Quantitative methods were only rarely used, because the traditionalists doubted that the "scientific method" of the natural sciences could be successfully applied to the investigation of the more indeterminate human behavior. Research typically focused on the detailed description of historical data, political institutions, constitutions, and legal systems, earning traditionalists the label of "hyperfactualists."

Traditionalist political scientists regarded both empirical and normative questions as equally worthy of scholarly attention, often undertaking their studies because of strongly held personal opinions about the nature of politics. Many of their inquiries showed a normative or prescriptive slant, trying to describe the general principles and best-suited institutions of "good" government. They were also inclined to examine the influence of human values in politics and prescribe specific public policies.

In contrast, behavioral political science has attempted to apply the methodologies of empirical natural sciences to the study of politics and government. In response to the influential political scientist Heinz Eulau's (1915–2004) call for political scientists to study behavior, not institutions, the field has focused analysis on the political behavior of individuals and groups, rather than on their formal roles or the structures within which they function. Although little consensus exists about the exact characteristics of the so-called "behavioral revolution" in political science, the scientific method of the behavioralists emphasizes the collection of observable data and the use of statistical analysis based on many recorded cases. Behavioral political science claims to be "value-neutral" in the sense of separating fact from value and describing political phenomena without judging their goodness or morality.

Behavioralist-oriented political scientists try to be more rigorous and disciplined in their research, seeking scientific precision by the quantification and measurement of collected data. Through the formulation and systematic testing of empirical hypotheses, they attempt to discover regularities and uniformities in political behavior, which can be expressed in generalizations or theory. Behavioralists see a close relationship between theory and empirical research in the sense that theory should be "verifiable" by analysis of observed behavior, while the process of seeking and interpreting empirical data should be guided by theory. Behavioral political science is concerned with the cumulative acquisition of law-like generalizations about human behavior and suggests a close relationship with the other social sciences.

The "behavioral revolution" in the science of politics emerged as a major force in the 1950s and won over much of the field during the 1960s. For years its supporters and detractors debated whether or not behavioralism represented a Kuhnian "scientific revolution," producing a "paradigm shift" in the basic values and objectives concerning the nature of political science and how the pursuit of systematized knowledge about politics should be conducted. According to Thomas Kuhn (1922–1996), one of the most famous philosophers of science, a *scientific revolution* is a noncumulative revolutionary development in which an older scientific (paradigm) is supplanted by an entirely new, incompatible tradition that does not build on preceding knowledge. As the behavioralist approach gradually established itself, a new emphasis on methodology and the use of quantitative tools of analysis swept the field and increasingly became the preferred instrument of research, as reflected in refereed academic journals, scholarly books, and professional conferences. The behavioralist approach has made some remarkable contributions to the discipline, especially in providing political theory with a strong empirical basis and in dissecting the "social bases" of politics, as well as in examining comparatively the "political culture" of average citizens, as in the classic study by Gabriel Almond and Sydney Verba, *The Civic Culture: Political Attitudes and Democracy in Five Nations.*

By the late 1960s, however, the behavioral mode of inquiry came under heavy attack for its preoccupation with methodology at the expense of substance and public-policy orientation. Many younger political scientists criticized the distinction between fact and value, or "value-free" science, as abstract, sterile, and irrelevant in the age of the Vietnam War and the Watergate scandal. Far from being value-free and scientific, behavioralism was seen as static, pro-status quo, imbued with conservative values, ethnocentric, and presenting a highly idealized model of American politics. Behavioral political scientists were accused of focusing on trivial subjects of inquiry (such as analyzing accumulated statistics from elections, public-opinion surveys, legislative votes, and other easily quantifiable data), while ignoring the great ideological struggles of the day. The new movement, which the renowned Canadian-born political scientist David Easton called the "postbehavioral revolution," reaffirmed the

obligation of political scientists to be more problem-oriented and concerned with class relations and conflict, as well as to use their expertise about politics to improve public life. Postbehavioralists wanted to reverse some of the "excesses" of the behavioral school by placing substance before technique, policy orientation before ahistorical "pure science," and the service of society before academic neutrality and moral relativism.

While the fundamental changes wrought in political science by the behavioralist emphasis on empirical theory and quantitative methods now seem irreversible, what emerged from the postbehavioralist revolt of the early 1970s was a widespread recognition that practical relevance and ethical evaluation of politics are equally important. The discipline has since moved to a "postbehavioral synthesis" of the traditional and behavioralist approaches, combining the empirical perspectives and statistical tools of behavioralism with renewed concern for change-oriented values and the use of specialized political knowledge to solve societal problems.

SEE ALSO *Almond, Gabriel A.; Behaviorism; Easton, David; Kuhn, Thomas; Revolutions, Scientific; Scientific Method; Social Science, Value Free; Verba, Sidney; Vietnam War; Watergate*

BIBLIOGRAPHY

Almond, Gabriel A., and Sydney Verba. 1963. *The Civic Culture: Political Attitudes and Democracy in Five Nations.* Princeton, NJ: Princeton University Press.

Easton, David. 1965. *A Framework for Political Analysis.* Englewood Cliffs, NJ: Prentice Hall.

Easton, David. 1969. The New Revolution in Political Science. *American Political Science Review* LXIII (December): 1051–1061.

Eulau, Heinz. 1963. *The Behavioral Persuasion in Politics.* New York: Random House.

Kirn, Michael E. 1977. Behavioralism, Post-Behavioralism, and the Philosophy of Science: Two Houses, One Plague. *Review of Politics* XXIX (January): 82–102.

Rossen Vassilev

POLITICAL STRATIFICATION

SEE *Stratification, Political.*

POLITICAL SYSTEM

Political system refers broadly to the process by which laws are made and public resources allocated in a society, and to the relationships among those involved in making these decisions. The term, however, has acquired not only a descriptive meaning but also a methodological one. In the first case, "political system" describes how the institutions of a government function together to translate the desires, or "preferences," of a society's citizens into laws governing that society. Descriptions of the political system of the United States, for example, focus on how the Congress (House and Senate), the executive (the president and the bureaucracy), and the judiciary (the Supreme Court and lower courts) collectively make, implement, and enforce public policy. They also tend to describe how citizens make their preferences known to members of these institutions through voting and interest-group advocacy and how citizens respond to the policies actually produced. Though undergraduate textbooks often claim to use a political systems approach in their organization, in practice they tend to describe the structure and behavior of citizens and institutions in relative isolation from each other. By contrast, a true systems approach would emphasize *process*, or how these institutions function together and how their relationships and the policies they produce change (or fail to change) as the preferences of citizens change.

Political systems, however, need not conform to the American descriptive model. Other systems may receive citizen input in different manners or process it into policies through different institutions and relationships. The British political system, for example, is perhaps a simpler system because it does not possess separate legislative and executive institutions (the prime minister is also the majority party leader in Parliament). Political systems in other nations may listen only to the preferences of a few privileged citizens. Perhaps the most degenerate political system is the dictatorship, where preferences and lawmaking authority are vested in only a single individual.

Political system as a methodological concept grew out of efforts to scientifically study politics and predict political behavior using the "systems approach," an intellectual movement arising late in the first half of the twentieth century advocating the application of physical and biological systems models to the study of human behavior (Hammond 2003). In the wake of Talcott Parsons's (1951) argument that society is best understood as layers of systems, several leaders of the Behavioral Revolution, most notably David Easton (1965, 1981), advocated a systems approach to studying the processes of lawmaking and the function of institutions. Broadly speaking, the approach required researchers to differentiate the system from its larger social environment, identify its key components (institutions) and the relationships binding them together, learn how citizen preferences were communicated to them, and identify the "homeostatic" mechanisms that kept the resulting policy outputs stable and the

system in equilibrium when these inputs remained constant. More importantly, systems analysts were concerned with whether and how policy outputs would change as different social groups mobilized and articulated new demands on government and how great the difference between these inputs and policy outputs, the feedback loops, would have to be to stimulate resistance and even revolution. Classifying states by different systems was even promoted by Gabriel Almond (1956) as the key to comparative political research.

Political systems theory was largely abandoned as an overarching methodology for a couple of reasons. On one hand, opponents of empiricism in political science criticized it for its focus on steady-state equilibria and search for generalizable behavior over the study of the unique, as well as its emphasis on quantification and hypothesis testing (Wilson 1961). On the other hand, proponents of empirical analysis also found its use as a unifying methodology to be cumbersome and overreaching. Difficulties in identifying the system's boundaries, testing the functions of individual institutions and their interaction with each other as hypotheses, and measuring concepts such as feedback loops with the linear analysis methods commonly employed proved too intractable. Instead, political science has adopted a more reductionist approach by studying the political system's pieces, meaning various institutions, interest groups, and voters, in relative isolation. Although the last decade has seen some renewed interest in linking these pieces, political science is still a long way from returning to the political system as a unified theory.

SEE ALSO *Autocracy; Democracy; Dictatorship; Easton, David; Government; Law; Nation-State; Parsons, Talcott; Pluralism; Political Science; Political Theory; Politics; State, The*

BIBLIOGRAPHY

Almond, Gabriel A. 1956. Comparative Political Systems. *Journal of Politics* 18 (3): 391–409.

Easton, David. 1965. *A Framework for Political Analysis.* Englewood Cliffs, NJ: Prentice-Hall.

Easton, David. 1981. The Political System Besieged by the State. *Political Theory* 9 (3): 303–325.

Hammond, Debora. 2003. *The Science of Synthesis: Exploring the Social Implications of General Systems Theory.* Boulder: University Press of Colorado.

Parsons, Talcott. 1951. *The Social System.* Glencoe, IL: Free Press.

Wilson, Richard B. 1961. System and Process: Polar Concepts for Political Research. *Western Political Quarterly* 14 (3): 748–763.

Thomas T. Holyoke

POLITICAL THEORY

Political theory lies at the intersection of the contemporary disciplines of philosophy and political science. Among philosophers, political philosophy is often distinguished by its preoccupation with practical matters. Among political scientists, political theory is often understood as the least practically relevant of the major subfields. In truth, self-identified political theorists are engaged in a wide range of activities, both normative and empirical, scientific and spiritual, esoteric and practical. In addition, the history of political thought encompasses many people who would not necessarily understand themselves to be primarily political thinkers or philosophers (e.g., Julius Nyerere, Sophocles, and the Buddha).

The meanings and purposes of political theory are contested within the academic discipline because a great deal of political theory involves thinking about the nature of politics itself. Therefore, rather than describing what political theory is, it is more appropriate to describe what it has been concerned with thus far, with the understanding that the contours of the history of political thought are also part and parcel of the discussion of what constitutes "politics."

In general, political theory attempts to understand and form the human character, with particular emphasis on how people coordinate their ways of life, aims, needs and desires, and their potential to act together as a collective. One of the most important insights of political philosophy is the notion that human beings have the capacity to explore, imagine, and implement associations configured in various ways. Across cultures and throughout recorded history, at least three important and interrelated themes recur in such configurations:

1. *Femininity and masculinity.* Notions of gender often divide labor, determine the distribution of goods, and create and order the public and private spheres.

2. *The spiritual and material worlds.* Understandings of the interplay between God or gods and human beings, along with the idea that the spiritual world does not exist, often shape the nature of authority and rule.

3. *Human beings and the environment.* Ideas about the place of human beings in the natural world, and the idea that people can be distinguished from it, typically undergird various political orientations.

As these themes suggest, political theory often intersects with philosophical perspectives in sociology, economics, ethics, and theology. However, political theory lays special claim to understanding and developing ideas about formal and informal rules of collective action and interaction, such as when and how decisions are made, who can and cannot speak, and what kinds of actions are required, sanctioned, or prohibited. This interest in institutions involves the study and development of certain concepts, including justice, power, consent, citizenship, duty, legitimacy, sovereignty, freedom, equality, punishment, property, oppression, rights, liberation, and deliberation. In the last two centuries, approaches to these concepts have often been framed in terms of ideologies, including nationalism, fascism, authoritarianism, democracy, theocracy, communism, secularism, socialism, liberalism, Islamism, republicanism, colonialism, and postcolonialism.

Such concepts form the parameters of governance and law, habits and customs, appropriateness, and virtue in a wide variety of groupings. Such groupings are themselves the subject and creation of political thought and include families, extended kinship relations, castes, factions, interest groups, tribes, parties, communities, cities, classes, ethnicities, nations, races, confederations, states, genders, caliphates, dynasties, empires, colonies, international organizations, and the relations between these entities. Indeed, the idea of "humanity" itself is a primary subject, and some would argue a creation of, political thought. Deconstructing and reconfiguring such arrangements is also an important task of political theory.

Political theorists often posit new ideas through the resuscitation and reinterpretation of old ideas, frequently by analyzing the thought of a particular thinker or thinkers. Examples include: Socrates, Plato, Aristotle, and the Stoics, in the ancient Greek tradition; al-Kindi, al-Farabi, Avicenna, and Sohravardi, in the Islamic tradition; Saint Augustine, Nyerere, Nkrumah, and Sékou Touré in the African tradition; Confucius, Mencius, Mo-tzu, Chuang-tzu, Han Fei-tzu, and numerous thinkers influenced by Taoism and Buddhism in the Chinese tradition; Aquinas, Machiavelli, Hobbes, Montesquieu, Wollstonecraft, Marx, and Mill in the European tradition; Bartolomé de las Casas, Jefferson, Madison, Bolivar, and José Marti, in the American tradition; and the Vedas, written by many seers, as well as the Buddha (Siddhartha Gautama) and Mahatma Gandhi, in the Indian tradition. A full accounting of influential contemporary political thinkers would include hundreds of names from various philosophical schools and political movements (e.g., existentialism, feminism, the Frankfurt school, postcolonial studies, and environmental philosophy). Listing individual thinkers also raises questions about the proper conduct of political theory and, in particular, its relationship to political action by necessarily excluding the oral traditions of many cultures both living and dead.

SEE ALSO *Party Systems, Competitive; Philosophy, Political; Political Science; Political System; Politics*

BIBLIOGRAPHY

Arendt, Hannah. 1998. *The Human Condition.* 2nd ed. Chicago: University of Chicago Press.

Lipset, Seymour Martin, ed. 2001. *Political Philosophy: Theories, Thinkers and Concepts.* Washington, DC: CQ Press.

Dustin Ells Howes

POLITICS

The term *politics* derives from the ancient Greek word *polis*, meaning "city-state," the main form of political community in ancient Greece. We continue to use the term even though few city-states remain in existence. A commonsense understanding of the term is illustrated by this analogy: Politics is to the polis what athletics is to athletes. Just as the world of athletics is subdivided into different types of sport, politics comes in numerous modes and orders: democratic, tyrannical, constitutionalist, oligarchic, theocratic, bureaucratic, fascist, authoritarian, and so on.

However, everyday language is not a reliable guide to defining politics, because we regularly apply the term to practices that are not political. We speak of office politics, locker-room politics, or the politics of high school cliques. These usages are too broad and fail to distinguish politics as a unique activity, distinct from business, sports, social interactions, and so on. In order to gain a more comprehensively scientific understanding of the meaning of politics, it is helpful to consider two basic components: (1) the character of political activity and (2) the scope of political activity.

THE CHARACTER OF POLITICAL ACTIVITY

Politics has been defined in numerous ways. The philosopher Plato (c. 428–348 BCE) defined it as the art of caring for souls, meaning that the duty of political rulers is to cultivate moral virtue or excellence in their citizens. Numerous thinkers throughout history have reiterated Plato's view. The medieval theologian Saint Thomas Aquinas (c. 1224–1274), who closely studied the philosophy of Plato's student Aristotle (384–322 BCE), characterized politics as the activity of bringing together diverse individuals and groups, including doctors, economists, professors, and priests, each with their own talents and characteristics, into a unity: "The object for which a community is gathered is to live a virtuous life. For men to consort together that they may thus attain a fullness of life which would not be possible to each living singly: and the full life is one which is lived according to virtue" (Fuller

2000, p. 85). Both Plato and Aquinas were concerned with cultivating virtue and living a good life. Aquinas further emphasizes the synthetic or "architectonic" dimension of politics as the activity of building coalitions and maintaining harmony among the constituent parts of political society. Politics for Plato and Aquinas reflects humanity's sociable nature.

Ancient and medieval thinkers emphasized the moral purpose of politics (the why) and the means of reaching that purpose (the how), while modern thinkers, including contemporary political scientists, are more likely to emphasize only means (the how). For example, the Renaissance thinker Niccolò Machiavelli (1469–1527) wrote in *The Prince* that it is unrealistic for princes to provide moral guidance to citizens because politics requires rulers to perform unjust deeds to ensure the security and glory of the state, including such acts as treating one's friends as subjects and killing family members if necessary. Machiavelli thus introduced what would later become known as the fact-value distinction into the study of politics. It states that facts are the only objects that can be analyzed empirically and with certainty, while values are less certain. Thomas Hobbes (1588–1679) provided what in the early twenty-first century one would consider a more scientific understanding of politics. His method was to deduce political principles from general and abstract theories. In his view humans resembled atoms, and human behavior was "matter in motion," whose principle mode of behavior was self-preservation. Unlike Plato and Aquinas, Hobbes regarded humans not as social but as asocial. He sums this up in his famous formulation of human behavior:

> So that in the first place, I put for a general inclination of all mankind, a perpetual and restless desire of power after power that ceaseth only in death. And the cause of this is not always that a man hopes for a more intensive delight than he has already attained to, or that he cannot be content with a moderate power, but because he cannot assure the power and means to live well, which he hath present, without the acquisition of more. (Hobbes 1996, p. 70)

This general principle of human behavior leads Hobbes to characterize the activity of politics as the pursuit of peace and security, not as the perfection of human social inclinations. While Hobbes was not what in the early twenty-first century one would call a liberal democrat, his theory laid the foundations for liberal democracy by making consent the basis of government. He also placed politics on a lower (and in his eyes, more stable) ground than earlier thinkers by making peace and security its purpose, not the cultivation of virtue and community.

Machiavelli and Hobbes's distinction between the moral purpose of politics and the pragmatic pursuit of power can be seen in some twentieth-century definitions of politics, which deemphasize moral excellence in favor of the use of power and the distribution of goods within a community. The French thinker Bertrand de Jouvenel (1903–1987) defined politics as the activity of gathering and maintaining support for human projects: "We should regard as 'political' every systematic effort, performed at any place in the social field, to move other men in pursuit of some design cherished by the mover" (Jouvenel 1963, p. 30). Allan Ball emphasizes conflict in his definition: "[Politics] involves disagreements and the reconciliation of those disagreements, and therefore can occur at any level. Two children in a nursery with one toy which they both want at the same time present a political situation" (Ball 1971, p. 20). Harold Lasswell emphasizes distribution in his treatment of politics, as reflected in the title of his 1936 treatise *Politics: Who Gets What, When, and How*.

While these definitions have their benefits, they fail to distinguish political activity from other forms of activity. This is especially true for Ball's definition, which provides little guidance on the difference between a nursery and a nation-state like the United States. More promising is Bernard Crick's definition of politics as "the activity by which different interests within a given unit of rule are conciliated by giving them a share in power in proportion to their importance to the welfare and the survival of the whole community" (Crick 1972, p. 22). This definition recalls Aquinas's characterization of politics as unifying different parts of society. By mentioning survival, Crick also alludes to the fact that a political society requires a large degree of autonomy, in a way that a smaller unit, such as a family, lacks. By mentioning welfare, which is broader than survival, he also indicates that a political society is organized around a set of goals and principles.

THE SCOPE OF POLITICAL ACTIVITY

The activity of politics, then, consists of a continuous attempt to fashion a unity from a diverse set of competing interests and talents. Beyond this, any analysis of politics needs to move to a more concrete level. Politics, as the activity of the polis, depends on the form the political community takes. Political actions such as the conciliation of interests would take different forms in Nazi Germany, for example, and a liberal democracy like the United States. In the former, power is based on a personality cult surrounding Adolf Hitler for the purpose of furthering the utopian ideal of a Third Reich. In the latter, coalitions of interests form and compete with one another in a law-based constitutional system. In the former, politics is seen as something that will in fact cease once the utopia is

reached (this is true of any utopian system). In the latter, politics is assumed to be a never-ending activity of negotiation and bargaining, on the assumption that a diversity of opinions and interests will always exist.

Political thinkers have devised a variety of methods for evaluating the differences among political systems. Plato distinguished five regimes, ranked according to the degree to which each is just. In descending order, they are the just city governed by philosopher kings, timocracy (ruled by warriors), oligarchy (ruled by the wealthy), democracy (ruled by the many), and tyranny (Plato 1991, pp. 449a–592b). Aristotle distinguished six different regimes according to who rules and for what purpose. He identified three good and three corrupt systems: (1) monarchy and tyranny, (2) aristocracy and oligarchy, (3) polity, or constitutional democracy, and mass democracy (Aristotle 1984, pp. 1288b10–1296b15).

Plato and Aristotle's typologies are based on the polis. Modern scholars have developed typologies that attempt to organize the different forms the modern state takes. Three separate axes can be identified: (1) the interpenetration of state and society, (2) whether the state is presidential or parliamentary, and (3) whether the state is federal or unitary (Dickerson and Flanagan 1998, pp. 209–310; Finer 1999, pp. 1473–1484).

The first axis considers the extent to which state institutions and civil society are autonomous. For example, liberal democracies prize pluralism, which requires a multiplicity of political parties competing for power as well as a wide array of independent schools, newspapers, and other sources of opinion. Totalitarian governments—for example, that of Hitler—attempt to control all facets of society, including universities, newspapers, unions, and businesses. Totalitarian states permit only one party, which purportedly speaks for the nation.

The second axis considers the composition of the representative institutions. In a presidential system like the United States, the central government is divided into three branches: executive (the president), legislative (Congress), and judicial (the Supreme Court). These three branches balance one another to ensure that no single branch of government possesses complete power. In a parliamentary system like that of Great Britain, executive power (the prime minister and cabinet) is more fused with legislative (the House of Commons). According to the doctrine of responsible government, the prime minister and cabinet must continually maintain the confidence of the House of Commons, which has the power to dissolve the government. Dissolution can occur at any time, in contrast to the U.S. presidential system, where members can only be removed by election or, in extreme circumstances, by impeachment.

The third axis reflects the territorial size of a society. In ancient Greece the polis was not divided into states or provinces because city-states were small enough for government to exert control over its territory and maintain solidarity among its citizens. Modern nation-states are considerably larger in size, which poses special challenges for controlling territory and promoting social solidarity. A federal state splits up the nation-state into states or provinces and hands over to those small units specific powers appropriate to them while maintaining the powers necessary to address national concerns. Large nations such as the United States and Canada have a federal system, while smaller nations such as Great Britain are unitary. Federal systems are based on the view that citizens will have greater solidarity with those who live nearby and who share common ways of life, though this view is less salient when a society has a highly mobile population.

THE STUDY OF POLITICS

The political analysis of major thinkers like Plato, Aristotle, Machiavelli, and Hobbes attempted to combine the empirical study of politics with normative concerns, though the latter two dissolve that combination somewhat. Politics is studied in the early twenty-first century at the academic level in departments of political science. While the term *political science* is a translation of Aristotle's *politike episteme*, modern usage, with the emphasis on "science," reflects the attempt, begun by Hobbes, to study politics according to the methodologies of the physical sciences.

The division of most departments of political science into four subfields of analysis reflect this methodology. Political philosophy, which focuses on normative questions of political life, is one subfield. International relations considers the complexities of the international order, including law, organizations, war, and political economy. Comparative politics examines the politics of various countries and regions of the world. A fourth subfield examines the politics of the native country, so, for instance, every political science department in the United States has an American politics subfield, and their counterparts in Canada have Canadian politics subfields.

Political scientists frequently step outside of their subfields. This is most true of political philosophy and its relation to other fields, as few political phenomena can be separated from their normative dimensions. For instance, the study of power requires one to consider why a political actor seeks power, and these reasons usually depend on that actor's particular understanding of justice. As a result, political science involves the study of the good society, just as it did for Plato 2,500 years ago.

SEE ALSO *American Political Science Association; Aristotle; Campaigning; Conflict; Elections; Electoral Systems; Elites; Hobbes, Thomas; Lasswell, Harold; Machiavelli, Niccolò; Participation, Political; Party Systems, Competitive; Plato; Political Science; Political System; Political Theory; Power Elite; Power, Political*

BIBLIOGRAPHY

Aristotle. *Politics.* 1984. Trans. Carnes Lord. Chicago: University of Chicago Press.

Ball, Alan R. 1971. *Modern Politics and Government.* London: Macmillan.

Crick, Bernard R. 1972. *In Defense of Politics.* 2nd ed. Chicago: University of Chicago Press.

Dickerson, Mark O., and Thomas Flanagan. 1998. *An Introduction to Government and Politics: A Conceptual Approach.* 5th ed. Scarborough, ON: International Thomson Publishing.

Finer, Samuel E. 1999. *The History of Government.* Oxford: Oxford University Press.

Fuller, Timothy, ed. 2000. *Leading and Leadership.* Notre Dame, IN: University of Notre Dame Press.

Hobbes, Thomas. 1996. *Leviathan,* ed. Richard Tuck. Cambridge, U.K.: Cambridge University Press. (Orig. pub. 1651.)

Jouvenel, Bertrand de. 1963. *The Pure Theory of Politics.* New Haven, CT: Yale University Press.

Lasswell, Harold D. 1958. *Politics: Who Gets What, When, and How.* New York: Meridian Books.

Machiavelli, Niccolò. 1998. *The Prince.* 2nd ed. Trans. Harvey C. Mansfield. Chicago: University of Chicago Press. (Orig. pub. 1532.)

Minogue, Kenneth. 1995. *Politics: A Very Short Introduction.* Oxford: Oxford University Press.

Plato. 1991. *The Republic of Plato.* 2nd ed. Trans. Allan Bloom. New York: Basic Books.

John von Heyking

POLITICS, ASIAN AMERICAN

Americans of Asian heritage have been one of the fastest growing population groups in the United States over the last several decades. According to the U.S. Census Bureau, there were fewer than one million U.S. residents in 1960 who identified themselves as Asian, or less than 0.5 percent of the total population ("Asian" here refers to Americans with a Far Eastern, Southeast Asian, or subcontinent Indian background). By July 2004, this number grew to 14 million, or roughly 5 percent of the total U.S. population (based on individuals who identify as "Asian alone or in combination" with other racial groups, according to the current census classification system). This trend is expected to continue, with current census projections of 33.4 million Asians in America by midcentury. This population, moreover, is highly concentrated in particular states and cities in America. For example, Asian Americans make up 58 percent of Hawaii's population and 12 percent of California's population. Asian Americans also make up 68 percent of Honolulu's population, 33 percent of San Francisco's population, and, in the two largest "gateway" cities, 11 percent of the population of both New York and Los Angeles.

Many observers of this demographic growth predict that Asian Americans will soon be a rising political force in the United States. Several Asian Americans have already ascended to prominent elected and appointed offices, including former Democratic governor of Washington Gary Locke, Democratic senators Daniel Akaka and Daniel Inouye (both from Hawaii), members of Congress Bobby Jindal (R-LA), Mike Honda (D-CA), Doris Matsui (D-CA), and David Wu (D-OR), and Bush Administration appointees Elaine Chao (U.S. Secretary of Labor) and Norman Mineta (U.S. Secretary of Transportation). At the same time, Asian Americans in elected and appointed office are conspicuously underrepresented relative to their numbers in the general population.

More importantly, a group's political fortunes often depend critically on the number of its members who vote and the number of those votes that can be delivered to a particular political party. In this instance, the power of Asian American electorate is far less clear. Based on 2004 data from the Current Population Survey, only 69 percent of Asian Americans are eligible to vote (as citizens), 36 percent are registered to vote, and only 31 percent report having voted in the last election. The proportions in the general population, by comparison, are 91 percent citizens, 66 percent registered to vote, and 58 percent reported voting. Much attention has thus turned to the question of why Asian Americans "underparticipate." The most commonly mentioned answer is that Asian Americans are simply less interested in politics and less invested in their long-term future in the United States. This view, while perhaps true in isolated instances, gives an incomplete portrayal that almost certainly evokes insidious stereotypes of Asian Americans as inscrutable, insular, and perpetually foreigners.

Roughly two of every three Asians in the United States are foreign born. As such, factors specific to the immigrant experiences and institutional inclusion of Asian Americans better explain their (under)participation. For one thing, Asian American political participation generally rises with one's immigrant generation and length of stay in the United States. Furthermore, contrary to the perceived wisdom, the availability of dual nationality does not divide the loyalties of Asian Americans or diminish

their political engagement; if anything, Asians in the United States who come from countries allowing for dual nationality are more likely to be U.S. citizens and to vote than their counterparts from countries that make no such allowances. A third important factor is language. In particular, the availability of language assistance or multilingual ballots is key to the participation of many Asians in the United States.

As for mediating institutions, the mobilization of voters by political parties has been and still remains a decisive factor. Whereas parties in the era of urban "political machines" played a central role in the political mobilization of immigrants from European shores, parties in the mid-2000s were strong as national organizations but much weaker as local institutions that bring new Americans into their partisan fold. In their place, civic associations such as places of worship, unions, ethnic organizations, and community-based organizations were increasingly central as institutional forces that mobilize Asian American communities.

The relative absence of political parties as mobilizing institutions is also often reinforced by the prevailing belief that Asian Americans do not cast their collective political fates behind a political party. This belief is true in the sense that a plurality of Asian Americans, when given a choice, opt to affiliate with neither the Democratic nor the Republican Party. But it is untrue (and increasingly emphatically so) that Asian Americans have *no* preferences between the Democratic and Republican parties. In the 2004 presidential election, an exit poll conducted by the Asian American Legal Defense and Education Fund found 74 percent of its Asian American respondents who reported voting for John Kerry; 57 percent of poll respondents identified themselves as Democrats, compared to only 15 percent who identified as Republicans and 26 percent who did not affiliate with a party.

A final important consideration is that the political interests and identities of Asian Americans remain relatively ambiguous and amorphous by comparison, say, to that of African Americans. Only a small proportion of Asians express a strong sense of panethnic solidarity as "Asian Americans," exhibiting instead far stronger ties to ethnicity or national origin (i.e., as Japanese, Korean, Vietnamese, Pakistani, Taiwanese, and so on). This is the result in part of Census Bureau classifications that bring together a dizzying phenotypic, national, linguistic, religious, and ideological, inter alia, diversity of peoples under the common rubric of "Asian American." It is also the result in part of the mythical status of Asian Americans as "model minorities"—hard-working, law-abiding, family-oriented, education-revering people who embody the virtues of the American Dream. This model minority myth essentializes and homogenizes the diversity of Asian American experiences. It functions ideologically to reproduce racial hierarchy in the United States by exaggerating the prosperity of Asian Americans while continuing to cast them as "perpetual foreigners" and exploiting the hard-earned gains of Asian Americans as a foil to denigrate the lesser fortunes of African Americans and Latinos.

At the same time, there have been moments of successful panethnic collective action. In the Vincent Chin case in 1982, two white autoworkers in Detroit who clubbed the Chinese American to death while calling him a "Jap" were acquitted of any crime. In the Wen Ho Lee case in 1999, a naturalized U.S. citizen from Taiwan was wrongfully accused of sharing nuclear secrets with the mainland Chinese government. These were two notable instances of "reactive identity formation" that drew a national outcry of protest from Asian Americans. Perhaps the most sustained case here was the decades-long legal challenge and political campaign for "redress and reparations" for the nearly 120,000 Japanese Americans who were forcibly removed from their homes and sent to internment camps during World War II. These efforts contributed to the passage into law of the Civil Rights Act of 1988, which provided $20,000 to each surviving internee and led to the issuance of a formal apology from President George H. W. Bush. It is important, then, to remember that panethnic categories such as "Asian American" are political and social constructions that respond to a collective memory and contemporary experiences of exclusion and racialization—from the 1882 Chinese Exclusion Act and the 1907 "Gentlemen's Agreement" between the United States and Japan to the U.S.A. Patriot Act and the post–9/11 debates over restrictionist immigration policies.

SEE ALSO *Immigrants to North America; Immigrants, Asian; Model Minority; Politics, Black; Politics, Latino; World War II*

BIBLIOGRAPHY

Ancheta, Angelo. 1998. *Race, Rights, and the Asian American Experience.* New Brunswick, NJ: Rutgers University Press.

Aoki, Andy, and Don T. Nakanishi, eds. 2001. Symposium on "Asian Pacific Americans and the New Minority Politics." *PS: Political Science and Politics* 34 (3): 605–644.

Chang, Gordon, ed. 2001. *Asian Americans and Politics.* Washington, DC: Woodrow Wilson Center, and Stanford, CA: Stanford University Press.

Espiritu, Yen Le. 1992. *Asian American Panethnicity.* Philadelphia: Temple University Press.

Kim, Claire Jean. 2000. *Bitter Fruit: The Politics of Black-Korean Conflict in New York City.* New Haven, CT: Yale University Press.

Kim, Thomas. 2007. *The Racial Logic of Politics: Asian Americans and Party Competition.* Philadelphia: Temple University Press.

Lai, James, and Don T. Nakanishi, eds. 2002. *Asian Americans and American Politics.* Lanham, MD: Rowman and Littlefield.

Lien, Pei-te, M. Margaret Conway, and Janelle Wong. 2004. *The Politics of Asian Americans: Diversity and Community.* New York: Routledge.

Prasad, Vijay. 2000. *The Karma of Brown Folk.* Minneapolis: University of Minnesota Press.

Ramakrishnan, S. Karthick. 2005. *Democracy in Immigrant America: Changing Demographics and Political Participation.* Palo Alto, CA: Stanford University Press.

Wong, Janelle. 2006. *Democracy's Promise: Immigrants and American Civic Institutions.* Ann Arbor: University of Michigan Press.

Taeku Lee

POLITICS, BLACK

Black politics refers to the collective struggle of people of African descent to gain power and influence in the processes and institutions of government as a way of securing and protecting a diverse array of interests that allow them to attain and maintain the rights afforded them as American citizens. It includes not only the actions of black people to assure these rights but also those of other individuals and collective groups with whom these interests and outcomes are negotiated. Research throughout various disciplines of the social sciences have sought to understand the conditions in which black politics have emerged, as well as the wide array of problems, challenges, successes, and failures that have resulted from its pursuits.

HISTORY

Insofar as it is at its core a struggle for and negotiation of power, black politics was initiated within the American institution of slavery. Though dictated for them by both law and custom, African slaves' identity, status, and relationship to America's white citizenry represented the beginnings of blacks' struggle for recognition, power, and legitimacy within the confines of plantation life. While there was no real sense of slaves' involvement in the formal governments of the nation, slavery was a system in which blacks, though stripped of power generally, nevertheless used means available to them (religious gatherings, informal and secret attempts to educate themselves, underground escape from plantation life, insurrection, and even forging relationships with their white slave masters) to achieve their first steps toward a more perfect realization of a good life—freedom, and recognition as full and equal citizens of America.

However, blacks found that the freedom granted in law by Abraham Lincoln's Emancipation Proclamation did little to guarantee their equal status as full citizens. The years immediately following emancipation were years of uncertainty regarding the status of blacks, particularly in the South—years in which black codes extended the same system of subjugation blacks experienced throughout slavery. Yet soon, the project of Reconstruction, with its Congress-led protections and opportunities for blacks, would show signs for hope and optimism. W. E. B. Du Bois characterized blacks' political struggle for equality during this period (1867–1877) as the "mystic years"; blacks seemed to be on the fast track toward equality. Newly instituted policies such as the creation of the Freedmen's Bureau in 1865–1866, the passage of the Civil Rights Act in 1866 and the Fourteenth Amendment the same year and ratified in 1868, and others granted legal protections and opportunities for blacks to participate in American life. Blacks were afforded educational opportunities through public schools, some of which were integrated. Perhaps the greatest opportunity for blacks to forge their own political destinies was the granting of the right to vote by the Fifteenth Amendment, ratified in 1870 (giving them the ability to determine election outcomes) and the inclusion of blacks in state and federal elected office, including the 1870 election of both Hiram Revels as America's first black senator and Joseph H. Rainey as the first African American to serve in the U.S. House of Representatives.

However, the promises of Reconstruction would prove hollow after a few short years. White violence against blacks was rampant among such groups as the Ku Klux Klan and in historic riots such as those in New Orleans and Memphis in 1866 or the 1876 Hamburg Massacre in South Carolina. Informal and state-sanctioned barriers to black education and voting became prevalent, black elected officials were either stripped of their power or were made to support policies counter to their interests, and black political and social leaders were cast as buffoons, carpetbaggers, and unscrupulous opportunists in the American imagination, in large part through the white press of the time. By the end of Reconstruction, blacks found themselves stripped of many of the freedoms, opportunities, and means for political engagement they had received a brief taste of in the preceding few years. However, despite the beginnings and persistence of the Jim Crow era in the South that followed Reconstruction, blacks continued to mount considerable political and social influence: through the educational leadership of those such as Booker T. Washington and George Washington Carver, among many others; through the legal profession and such prominent legal figures as

Thurgood Marshall and organized legal/political groups such as the National Association for the Advancement of Colored People, founded in 1909; and through the institution of the black press (which had its roots in the pre–Civil War and Reconstruction eras), which spawned more than 500 newspapers between 1880 and 1890.

The 1950s and 1960s ushered a new era of black politics—one born of new struggles and resulting in new political, economic, and social opportunities. Through a variety of "unlawful" channels and struggles engaged in by Martin Luther King Jr. and organizations such as the Congress on Racial Equality (CORE), the Student Nonviolent Coordinating Committee (SNCC), and others, blacks gained much in the 1960s that would lay a foundation for the continued pursuit of black politics. This included landmark legislative initiatives passed in three consecutive years: the Civil Rights bill brought before Congress in 1963, the 1964 Civil Rights Act, and the 1965 Voting Rights Act. Although this legislation opened doors previously closed and locked to black Americans, they did not completely ensure full access to and fulfillment of the rights enshrined on its pages. Yet it was these victories, along with the beginning of a cultural shift in American society to what political scientist Tali Mendelberg refers to as a "norm of racial equality" (2001), that made possible the growth of the idea, movement, symbols, and actions of black political life.

Following these legislative gains, the late 1960s saw a marked increase in the numbers of black representatives in Congress. With the addition of three representatives to the six already seated, the 1970 Congress had the most concurrent black members serving in its ranks. This watershed of black representation led to the eventual formation of the Congressional Black Caucus, which, according to William Clay, "constituted a power-bloc deserving respect within the institution" organized around the idea of a "solidarity of purpose and program [that] would enable the nine of us to wield a significant amount of influence in the House" (1993).

Outside of this official body, a host of other individuals and organizations were working to secure a sense of black solidarity to help ensure that the earlier legislative victories were not hollow. These ranged from "militant" groups such as the Black Panthers, Malcolm X, and the Black Muslim movement to a host of black pride and similar movements that sprang up within the academy. Included were movements to form the first department of Black Studies by sociologist Nathan Hare at San Francisco State University in 1968. Soon, similar departments were begun on college campuses across the country, aimed at understanding the culture and politics of African Americans. Their inauguration would spawn similar departments geared to study the social, political, and cultural life of other American ethnic groups—departments of Latin American Studies, Asian American Studies, and others under the general rubric of ethnic studies. Each of these movements worked in formal and informal ways to secure the idea and trajectory of black politics that developed into a sense of black solidarity and collective action around securing black interests. And although the nature and substance of these interests and means of securing them have changed, the fundamental nature of black politics remains to this day.

CORE CONCERNS

There are a number of what might be called "core concerns" related to black politics. Many of these areas of scholarly investigation are related to what is perhaps a single most central concern: equal representation. Despite its presence and protections in civil rights legislation, it is an ideal that many feel has yet to be reached. Social scientists have generally focused their attention on this issue by investigating two broad related areas: the drawing and redrawing of legislative districts in ways that either allow or prohibit the election of blacks to legislative office, and the persistent nature of racial prejudice as it impacts the political process designed to ensure black representation.

Initiated by the Voting Rights Act of 1965, the practice of racially gerrymandering congressional and state legislative districts became a legal way of creating districts with a majority black population, thereby increasing the election hopes of blacks running for political office. Social scientists investigating the effectiveness of such policies have demonstrated strong arguments on both sides of this issue. Scholars who suggest the persistent need for racial redistricting policies focus on a number of research findings: the propensity for white voters to harbor deep-seated prejudices; resentments and fears of blacks; the reality that when primed by racial appeals, whites are likely to be less sympathetic to African American public-policy interests and infer that such would be the case in evaluating black candidates; and that, in general, whites tend to evaluate black political candidates less favorably than their white counterparts. The implication of such studies is that public-policy guidelines such as ensuring "safe" districts for black politicians may be necessary to mitigate the white prejudice that erects a barrier to what political scientists refer to as racial crossover voting.

Scholars whose research suggest that racial gerrymandering is not needed and may even hinder the pursuit of black political interests point to a different set of conclusions: studies of recent elections that demonstrate that white voters are sophisticated enough to sublimate racial attitudes when making voting decisions; research indicating that political ideology and political party affiliation—not negative racial attitudes—are the primary cause for

whites' unwillingness to vote for black candidates; and arguments that suggest that racial redistricting provides for a modicum of "descriptive representation" but does not likely translate into "substantive representation." This is to say, it ensures that someone who is black will quite likely be elected, but it cannot ensure that the person elected, though black, will necessarily work in the interest of his or her black constituents.

This array of competing conclusions by political scientists, sociologists, and legal and communication scholars writing in the late twentieth and early twenty-first centuries suggests that both the ideal of equal representation for African Americans and the most effective means for securing it are still an open question, persisting as one of the most significant debates within the arena of black politics.

RECENT TRENDS

Beyond research surrounding the principal concern of equal representation, much research from the early 1990s to 2006 has demonstrated some interesting trends that have a direct bearing on the present and future state of black politics. These include the shift in policy concerns of African Americans, the growing number of blacks elected to government bodies, and the nature of black participation in the political process.

According to political scientists and communication scholars such as Donald Kinder, Nicholas Valentino, Katherine Tate, Michael Dawson, and others, public opinion on national public-policy concerns continues to be divided between blacks and whites and, increasingly, among blacks themselves. For instance, studies in the early 2000s demonstrated waning—barely a majority—support among blacks for affirmative action policies in hiring practices. Research shows that diminished support from earlier decades has been influenced by gaps among blacks in terms of economic class, levels of in-group identification, and out-group racial resentment. In addition to this, public-opinion surveys conducted around the same time period by the Joint Center for Political and Economic Studies, a think-tank that has researched trends in black politics since the early 1970s, show that although blacks still by and large support policy issues that have long been central interests—social welfare policy, affirmative action, education, and others—few of these concerns rate highly in terms of what blacks say are the issues that most concern them. Thus, it seems that while the public-opinion divide between blacks and whites persists, there is a growing fragmentation of black policy interests and concerns. This has led to a number of related developments, including, but not limited to, waning (although slow) affiliation of blacks with the Democratic Party (always overwhelmingly supported by blacks) and renewed interest in and strategies by the Republican Party to recruit black political support.

Along with these public-opinion trends, the country has also seen an increase in the number of black elected officials since 1980. While most of these increases have been in state legislative bodies, there has also been a rise in blacks elected to Congress, as well as an increase in the number of black congressional hopefuls running against white opponents (some successfully) in non-majority-black districts. The increased numbers at the state level are likely to translate into continued increases in the numbers elected to higher levels and add to the debate about equal representation and the effectiveness of strategies used to ensure it.

A final area of social science scholarship has paid close attention to trends in black political participation. Research by many scholars in sociology and political science, particularly, has shown that generally the level of African American political participation has steadily declined in the years following the dawn of the civil rights movement. Research has sought to determine the precise causes and consequences of this declining participation. One set of arguments among many supported by the extant literature demonstrates that neighborhood isolation, in conjunction with states of extreme poverty, leads to political isolation—the feeling of being disconnected from the political system and of having no or little political power, which therefore sublimates motivations for political involvement. Other research suggests that a declining sense of black racial group identification has led to decreased interest in black political participation. Much of this research also relates to the increased socioeconomic stratification existing in black communities—a result, to some extent, of affirmative action policies that dramatically increased the size of the black middle class in the 1970s and 1980s.

However, there is much social-scientific evidence to suggest that black political activism and participation in social movements that coalesce around black interests—and increasingly shared interests with other minority groups—is still relatively strong. In this arena, much of the literature has focused on the issue of religious participation, most specifically on the continued relevancy of the black church as a motivating factor for, and conduit of, black political life. The influence of the church has been seen to impact the nature of black political participation in explicitly political activities such as voting and political campaign involvement, as well as less explicit forms of political participation such as volunteerism.

Social science research in the arena of black politics has tackled many significant and controversial issues in the more than four decades since the beginning of the civil rights era. While focusing on specific issues and problems, this area of scholarly inquiry has served to create and influence larger discourses about race in America. It has influenced American public opinion as well as the policy-making decisions that have occurred at every level of government that seek to protect the highest ideals of American democracy.

SEE ALSO *Attitudes, Racial; Bunche, Ralph Johnson; Civil Rights; Civil Rights Movement, U.S.; Desegregation, School; Du Bois, W. E. B.; Education, Unequal; Education, USA; Gerrymandering; Immigrants, Black; Immigrants to North America; Politics, Asian-American; Politics, Gender; Politics, Latino; Politics, Southern; Politics, Urban; Politics: Gay, Lesbian, Transgender, and Bisexual; Race; Racism; Reconstruction Era (U.S.); Slavery; Terrorism; Violence*

BIBLIOGRAPHY

Clay, William L. 1993. *Just Permanent Interests: Black Americans in Congress, 1870–1991.* New York: Amistad Press.

Dawson, Michael C. 2001. *Black Visions: The Roots of Contemporary African-American Political Ideologies.* Chicago: University of Chicago Press.

Kinder, D. R., and N. Winter. 2001. Exploring the Racial Divide: Blacks, Whites, and Opinion on National Policy. *American Journal of Political Science* 45 (2): 439–453.

Mendelberg, Tali. 2001. *The Race Card: Campaign Strategy, Implicit Messages, and the Norm of Equality.* Princeton, NJ: Princeton University Press.

Peterson, Paul E., ed. 1995. *Classifying by Race.* Princeton, NJ: Princeton University Press.

Reeves, Keith. 1997. *Voting Hopes or Fears? White Voters, Black Candidates and Racial Politics in America.* New York: Oxford University Press.

Valentino, N. A., V. L. Hutchings, and I. White. 2002. Cues That Matter: How Political Ads Prime Racial Attitudes During Campaigns. *American Political Science Review* 96 (1): 75–90.

Charlton D. McIlwain

POLITICS, COMPARATIVE

Comparative politics designates a distinct subfield in political science. Although Aristotle's political writings were arguably some of the first works in comparative political inquiry, the field has been most influenced by the writing of nineteenth- and twentieth-century thinkers including Gabriel Almond, Hannah Arendt, Robert Dahl, Harry Eckstein, Samuel Huntington, Seymour Martin Lipset, Karl Marx, and Max Weber. Research in comparative politics seeks to account for the observed variation over time and among political units on consequential social, political, cultural, and economic outcomes by examining, describing, modeling, and predicting continuity and change resulting from the dynamics among international, national, and subnational actors.

The subfield's methodological orientation is catholic in its use of quantitative and qualitative techniques. Historically, the subfield has emphasized the use of case studies, often employing John Stuart Mill's methods of difference and similarity, but statistical analysis (mostly on cross-sectional, time-series, and multilevel data), computational methods, and formal modeling have become more prevalent in recent years. Gary King, Robert Keohane, and Sidney Verba (1994) and Henry Brady and David Collier (2004) offer introductions to some recent issues in comparative political methodology.

The field is organized around substantive topics, though disagreement on these canonical elements remains considerable. However, two broad dimensions can be delineated: the statics of political systems and the dynamics of political conflict and cooperation. The study of political systems evolves around the conditions and prerequisites for the establishment and survival of various regime types. Some of the crucial questions include: What distinguishes democracies from nondemocracies and from what lies in between? What explains the successful transition from one political system to another? What is the nature of liberal democracy?

A core debate in the study of democracy is the relationship between wealth and democracy: Some claim that wealth induces democracy, others that wealth simply accompanies democracy but is causally unrelated to it, and still others (e.g., Adam Przeworski) have suggested that wealth sustains democracy once it has taken root. Closely related is the study of democratic institutions and competitive elections, which has focused on the relationship between political institutions and political outcomes, such as collective mobilization, party formation, and policy preferences (e.g., in the work of Gary Cox, Robert Dahl, Richard Katz and Peter Mair, Herbert Kitschelt, and Giovanni Sartori). The study of autocracies has focused largely on developing typologies of authoritarian regimes and on the strategic interaction of elites during the transition to democracies. The comparative study of political liberalism across countries and over time has also received sustained attention in, for example, the work of Ira Katznelson.

Gabriel Almond and Sidney Verba's *The Civic Culture* (1963) was an early cross-national comparative study of democracy in which the authors linked civic attitudes and democratic stability using a tripartite typology of political cultures—parochial, subject, and participant. The cultures spanned from purely passive to highly engaged attitudes toward the political system and civic life. Almond and Verba argued that political cultures adhere to the principle of congruence between a political structure and the attitudes of its citizens. The study concludes that competent, active citizenries sustain democracies.

The literature on democratization has vacillated between an emphasis on the structural determinants of sustainable democracy and elite incentives and capabilities to modify the political order (Skocpol 1979). The work of Samuel Huntington derives the preconditions for political order both from socioeconomic changes and political institutions. Guillermo O'Donnell and Philippe Schmitter's work challenges structuralism and represents an actor-centered approach, which argues that the elite split followed by negotiated pacts (which incorporate the preferences of the military) is a necessary precondition for the successful transition from authoritarianism to democracy. Since 1989, the transitions from authoritarian regimes have produced a variety of political outcomes in the gray zone between autocracy and democracy. The study of competitive authoritarianisms (or illiberal democracies) is an emerging field of comparative study.

The study of linkages and distributional conflicts that arise at the intersection between politics, economics, and society has led to the development of an area of inquiry often dubbed "political economy." The "varieties of capitalism" literature is a prime example (e.g., Hall and Soskice 2001; for discussions of corporatism, see Schmitter 1975). The analysis of advanced capitalist democracies (OECD states) was induced by the oil shocks and the collapse of the Bretton Woods system. Political economy, in the work of Torben Iversen, for example, has since focused on the conditions for growth, stability, wage equality, and redistribution and seeks to untangle the ties between political systems, inequality, and policy formation. One line of inquiry focuses on domestic responses to international challenges, such as global economic competition, trade openness, and international institutions.

The study of dynamics among and within political systems focuses on conflict, revolutions, ethnic tensions, and order in society. The study of revolutions, for example, identifies the sources of state collapse and patterns of group alignment and mobilization. Studies of ethnicity and political culture analyze identity formation and the conditions under which identity is or can be mobilized for political purposes. Comparative politics intersects with international relations in many ways, but most often at the interface of ethnic conflict (e.g., Horowitz [1985] 2000). According to such writers as Donald Horowitz, Arend Lijphart, and David Laitin, the causes and consequences of state failure, intercommunal violence, and the institutional conditions under which ethnically divided societies can coexist remain core questions in comparative politics.

The third wave of democratization has raised new questions about the relationship between electoral competition and economic reforms and has moved the field closer, in some ways, to international relations in debating the push-and-pull effects of international organizations (e.g., the European Union) or of global economic strategies (e.g., foreign direct investment). New agendas in comparative politics are emerging at the intersection of ethnic- (and culturally) based identities and political mobilization. Topics and subjects developed in the study of the OECD countries are beginning to migrate outside the region to address related issues. Methodologically, the field has benefited from the massive increase in computing power now available to social scientists, but it has not abandoned altogether its reliance on a small number of in-depth case studies. The field appears to be moving recognizably toward the potentially fruitful cross-pollination of quantitative and qualitative research methods and strategies.

SEE ALSO *Almond, Gabriel A.; Arendt, Hannah; Aristotle; Authoritarianism; Autocracy; Class; Democracy; Government; Keohane, Robert; Marx, Karl; Methods, Qualitative; Methods, Quantitative; Mill, John Stuart; Political Science; Politics; Socioeconomic Status; Stratification; Verba, Sidney; Weber, Max*

BIBLIOGRAPHY

Almond, Gabriel, and James S. Coleman, eds. 1960. *The Politics of the Developing Areas*. Princeton, NJ: Princeton University Press.

Almond, Gabriel, and Sidney Verba. 1963. *The Civic Culture: Political Attitudes and Democracy in Five Nations*. Princeton, NJ: Princeton University Press.

Brady, Henry, and David Collier, eds. 2004. *Rethinking Social Inquiry: Diverse Tools, Shared Standards*. Lanham, MD: Rowman and Littlefield.

Cox, Gary. 1997. *Making Votes Count: Strategic Coordination in the World's Electoral Systems*. Cambridge, U.K.: Cambridge University Press.

Dahl, Robert. 1961. *Who Governs? Democracy and Power in an American City*. New Haven, CT: Yale University Press.

Eckstein, Harry 1961. *A Theory of Stable Democracy*. Princeton, NJ: Princeton University Press.

Hall, Peter, and David Soskice, eds. 2001. *Varieties of Capitalism: The Institutional Foundations of Comparative Advantage*. Oxford: Oxford University Press.

Horowitz, Donald L. 1985. *Ethnic Groups in Conflict*. Berkeley: University of California Press, 2000.

Horowitz, Donald L. 2001. *The Deadly Ethnic Riot*. Berkeley: University of California Press.

Huntington, Samuel. 1968. *Political Order in Changing Societies*. New Haven, CT: Yale University Press.

Huntington, Samuel. 1991. *The Third Wave: Democratization in the Late Twentieth Century*. Norman: University of Oklahoma Press.

Iversen, Torben. 2005. *Capitalism, Democracy, and Welfare*. Cambridge: Cambridge University Press.

Katz, Richard, and Peter Mair. 1994. *How Parties Organize: Change and Adaptation in Party Organizations in Western Democracies*. London: Sage.

Katznelson, Ira. 1996. *Liberalism's Crooked Circle*. Princeton, NJ: Princeton University Press.

Katznelson, Ira, and Helen Milner, eds. 2002. *Political Science: State of the Discipline*. New York: Norton for the American Political Science Association.

King, Gary, Robert O. Keohane, and Sidney Verba. 1994. *Designing Social Inquiry: Scientific Inference in Qualitative Research*. Princeton, NJ: Princeton University Press.

Kitschelt, Herbert. 1989. *Logics of Party Formation: Ecological Politics in Belgium and West Germany*. Ithaca, NY: Cornell University Press.

Kitschelt, Herbert, with Anthony J. McGann. 1995. *The Radical Right in Western Europe: A Comparative Analysis*. Ann Arbor: University of Michigan Press.

Laitin, David. 1986. *Hegemony and Culture: The Politics of Religious Change Among the Yoruba*. Chicago: University of Chicago Press.

Laitin, David. 2004. Comparative Politics: State of the Subdiscipline. In *Political Science: The State of the Discipline*, eds. Ira Katznelson and Helen Milner, 630–659. New York: Norton.

Lijphart, Arend. 1977. *Democracy in Plural Societies: A Comparative Exploration*. New Haven, CT: Yale University Press.

Lipset, Seymour Martin. 1960. *Political Man: The Social Bases of Politics*. Garden City, NY: Doubleday.

Lipset, Seymour Martin. 1996. *American Exceptionalism: A Double-Edged Sword*. New York: Norton.

O'Donnell, Guillermo. 1979. *Modernization and Bureaucratic: Studies in South American Politics*. Berkeley: University of California Press.

O'Donnell, Guillermo, Philippe C. Schmitter, and Laurence Whitehead, eds. 1986. *Transitions from Authoritarian Rule: Comparative Perspectives*. Baltimore, MD: Johns Hopkins University Press.

Przeworski, Adam, Michael E. Alvarez, Jose Antonio Cheibub, and Fernando Limongi. 2000. *Democracy and Development: Political Institutions and Well-Being in the World, 1950–1990*. Cambridge, U.K. Cambridge University Press.

Sartori, Giovanni. 1976. *Parties and Party Systems: A Framework for Analysis*. New York and Cambridge, U.K.: Cambridge University Press.

Schmitter, Philippe C. 1975. *Corporatism and Public Policy in Authoritarian Portugal*. London: Sage.

Skocpol, Theda. 1979. *States and Social Revolutions: A Comparative Analysis of France, Russia and China*. New York: Oxford University Press.

Soskice, David, and Peter Hall, eds. 2003. *Varieties of Capitalism*. New York: Oxford University Press.

Zuckerman, Alan S., and Mark Irving Lichbach. 1997. *Comparative Politics: Rationality, Culture, and Structure.* New York: Cambridge University Press.

Lenka Bustikova Siroky
David S. Siroky

POLITICS: GAY, LESBIAN, TRANSGENDER, AND BISEXUAL

The politics of sexual diversity became a subject of scholarly interest soon after a surge in lesbian and gay activism in the late 1960s and early 1970s. Writers publishing in the 1970s and early 1980s on such activism or state response to sexual diversity worked at the margins of publishing and academic disciplines and often outside the academy. In the 1990s, as sexual diversity came to be more publicly recognized, there was a major opening up of publishing opportunities for social science writing on lesbian, gay, bisexual, and transgender issues, though political science was slow to recognize their relevance.

PIONEERING CONTRIBUTIONS

The activism of the 1970s brought visibility to gay liberationist challenges to the gendered foundations and sexual repressiveness of European and North American societies. Gay community magazines and newspapers such as Toronto's the *Body Politic*, London's *Gay Left*, and Boston's *Gay Community News* provided means for nonfiction writers to focus their political visions through a new radical lens. One current of this writing reflected a belief in a clearly demarcated gay and lesbian population with distinctive social and cultural norms. Most writers, however, held that homosexuality was a social and political construct and that only in relatively modern times did it shift from labeling a form of sexual behavior to describing a distinct category of person. The British sociologist Mary McIntosh had articulated such a "constructionist" view in an influential article published in 1968 ("The Homosexual Role").

The Australian writer Dennis Altman's *Homosexual: Oppression and Liberation* (1971) was a liberationist manifesto. Altman was one of the few political scientists to publish on gay issues before the late 1980s, and many years passed before his work was considered a legitimate part of that discipline. In the decade that followed most work on lesbian and gay politics was by historians, sociologists, and independent scholars. One was Jeffrey Weeks's *Coming Out: Homosexual Politics in Britain, from the Nineteenth Century to the Present* (1977); another was the U.S. historian John D'Emilio's *Sexual Politics, Sexual Communities: The Making of a Homosexual Minority in the United States, 1940–1970* (1983), which was notable for having been published by an established academic house (University of Chicago Press). Both books pointed to radical questioning of social and political repression in earlier periods, and both adopted "social construction" views by linking the development of homosexual identities to advanced forms of capitalism.

Most lesbian activism was quite separate from gay male activism, and this was soon reflected in published work. Lillian Faderman's *Surpassing the Love of Men: Romantic Friendship and Love between Women from the Renaissance to the Present* (1981) was an early example of American writing that sought to claim lesbian visibility. Writers such as Gayle Rubin, Carole Vance, and Estelle Freedman used lesbian feminism as a lens for theorizing the interplay of gender and sexual inequalities and for outlining a distinctive political agenda. At the end of the decade the political theorist Shane Phelan published *Identity Politics: Lesbian Feminism and the Limits of Community.*

THE IMPACT OF AIDS

The spread of AIDS in the 1980s posed a new threat of stigma but also enhanced the visibility of sexual minorities, reradicalized activism, provoked engagement with state institutions, and created openings to mainstream political processes. It also highlighted issues of workplace discrimination and the formal recognition of the same-sex partners of those who were infected.

This increased intellectual interest in the interdisciplinary analysis of the politics of sexual difference. Altman was one who chronicled the expansion of AIDS activism and the public response to the epidemic from its early stages. A few years later David Kirp and Ronald Bayer produced books on public and bureaucratic responses using more established political science frameworks, and together they edited a collection of essays from several European and North American countries on the politics of AIDS.

It was in the late 1980s that the first comprehensive survey of lesbian, gay, bisexual, and transgender (LGBT) activism was published, *The Rise of a Gay and Lesbian Movement* by Barry Adam, who like Altman had a comparative vision that extended across and beyond the American and British experiences. This work coincided with a surge of academic interest in social movements, though little of this material was by political scientists and even less of it addressed LGBT activism.

Much of the coverage of the movement in later years emphasized gender divisions or the distinct experience and political agendas of lesbians. Work by Vera Whisman and Becki Ross pointed to widespread fluidity in women's emotional and sexual experiences and to conscious, politically informed shifts away from men and toward other women. At the same time most accounts noted that wariness of bisexuality was more widespread among lesbians than among gay men, though it was common enough across the gender line to hamper the emergence of bisexual activism for years.

Some of the important analyses of the movements in Britain, Canada, and the United States came from the pens of activists, including Urvashi Vaid, formerly head of the Washington-based National Lesbian and Gay Task Force, and Tom Warner, long involved in the Coalition for Lesbian and Gay Rights in Ontario. Vaid, Adam, and the British sociologist Kenneth Plummer were among those students of the movement who discussed social class inequalities. Most published work on the movement extensively covered divisions within it but focused most often on gender and race or ethnicity more than class.

QUEER THEORY

The early 1990s saw a dramatic growth of publishing on sexual diversity, though legitimacy within the academy was slower to develop. One of the most prominent new bodies of literature was in queer theory, taking up a traditionally derogatory term that had been proudly adopted by young Queer Nation activists at the beginning of the decade. *Queer* was used in many different ways but usually was intended to indicate a provocative rejection of assimilitionist politics and to reflect the wide range of sexual practices and identities rejecting "heteronormativity."

Writers such as Eve Kosofsky Sedgwick (author of the influential *Epistemology of the Closet*, 1990), Michael Warner, Judith Butler, and the political theorist Mark Blasius were heavily influenced by the French philosopher Michel Foucault and particularly by the first volume (1978) of his *History of Sexuality*. They saw "homosexual" and other sexual categories as the products of a regulatory and controlling impulse. Language itself was seen as one of the fields on which power was exercised, though also where resistance was mobilized. Queer theory, like other forms of poststructural analysis, resisted the notion of a universal narrative or a common human experience of sexual difference. Within any particular time and setting too, practices were variable and identities unstable. Not surprisingly writers in such veins often paid particular attention to sexual practices and identities that crossed gender boundaries.

A current of critical legal studies was growing at this time; among the most prolific writers were the British legal scholars Didi Herman and Carl Stychin. The frameworks and very language of law, according to this view,

structured the way claims are presented and narrowed the impact of the "victories" gained. Alongside queer theory then, this writing raised critical questions about what was thought to be the assimilationism of mainstream lesbian and gay activism.

DIFFERENCES ACROSS CULTURES AND SOCIETIES

Queer theory's rejection of universalism dovetailed with discussions of racial and cultural inclusiveness among European and North American activists and the emerging profile of sexual diversity politics in minority communities in European and North American countries and in Asia, Africa, and Latin America (often propelled by AIDS). By the end of the 1990s more writers were taking up questions of cross-cultural and cross-national difference, though not necessarily through a queer theoretical lens. The activist Keith Boykin began writing about African American gay experience, and the political scientist Cathy Cohen then published *The Boundaries of Blackness: AIDS and the Breakdown of Black Politics* (1999). Both explored the erasure of African Americans in mainstream chronicles of the epidemic and within African American political circles.

At the beginning of the twenty-first century two collections brought together articles on the politics of sexual diversity covering a wide range of countries, one edited by the British activist and political scientist Peter Drucker, the other by Adam and colleagues. This new literature pointed to the influence of Euro-American "identity" models on other regions of the globe but alongside persistent local patterns of sexual practice and self-perception. The best of this writing resisted the temptation to romanticize sexual practices and beliefs about them in precolonial non-Western societies and to homogenize the West itself.

THE POLITICS OF RIGHTS

Activist claims for equality secured major gains in the 1990s, propelled partly by the visibility of sexual minorities in an expanding range of countries and partly by the public policy prominence of the issues associated with AIDS. Openly gay candidates for public office were winning elections in the 1980s for the first time, and in the following decade their numbers grew significantly in the United States, Britain, the Netherlands, and other industrialized countries.

In the United States especially, gay and lesbian rights issues became much more prominent as religious conservatives and the Republican Party intensified their opposition to such rights. President Bill Clinton's 1993 attempt to lift the ban on lesbians and gays serving in the military provoked a firestorm of protest (and some scholarly attention, such as in a collection edited by Craig Rimmerman). A successful court challenge to Hawaii's marriage law in that same year led to an even greater focus on homosexuality by the Religious Right—a focus sustained for well over a decade. Under George W. Bush's presidency, the Republican Party was as ready as ever to use the marriage issue to attack Democrats, and a series of state constitutional amendments to bar same-sex marriage was successfully introduced on election ballots in the mid-2000s.

Nevertheless, steady gains were being made in recognizing families led by same-sex couples. As activists in North America and Europe made progress in state systems, writing on their access and impact expanded. Work that deals with legal rights received substantial attention in the United States, which is not surprising given the political importance of litigation. Writers such as David Richards, William Eskridge, Daniel Pinello, William Rubenstein, and Jason Pierceson examined the highly uneven record of U.S. courts in terms that provided at least some hope for activists. The influence of critical legal studies is more evident in writings about Canadian law by writers such as Kathleen Lahey, Miriam Smith, Bruce McDougall, Brenda Cossman, and Susan Boyd.

The spread of legal recognition of sexual diversity in Europe has received somewhat less attention but more as issues related to relationship recognition have come to the fore. Robert Wintemute, Kees Waaldijk, and Yuval Merin have chronicled the rapid spread of national regimes of same-sex relationship recognition in the late 1990s and early 2000s as well as the slow march toward equity within European Union institutions.

In the late 1990s and the early 2000s dramatic shifts toward recognizing same-sex relationships (in some cases including marriage) occurred in Canada, Spain, the Netherlands, and several other northern European countries. Most reformed regimes initially excluded or compromised parenting rights for lesbian and gay couples (Canada and Spain being notable exceptions), though greater inclusiveness on that front was slowly spreading in the 2000s.

In no other country has controversy over challenges to family regimes been as sustained as in the United States. Consequently there has been only modest scholarly attention to tracking these changes outside the United States apart from the writings of Waaldijk, Wintemute, and David Rayside.

The enactment of rights measures at the state and regional government levels has received some attention in the United States, where local and state authorities have greater jurisdictional reach in areas related to sexual diversity than in almost any other system. Bob Bailey, Kenneth Wald, Barbara Rienzo, James Button, Steven Haeberle,

and Donald Haider-Markel are among the contributors to this field exploring what factors explain rights advances.

Family policy began receiving analytical attention in the United States following the emergence of same-sex marriage as a front-burner political issue during the 1990s and the early 2000s. Writers such as Eskridge and Richards argued for the importance of the issue; others such as Valerie Lehr are more skeptical of the "normalizing" dangers of seeking entry to the traditionally inequitable institution of marriage.

The prioritization of gay-related issues by the U.S. Religious Right eventually produced an analytical literature on that opposition, including work by Wald, Herman, and Clyde Wilcox. As struggles over public recognition intensified, greater analytical attention was paid to public attitudes (for example, by Sherrill). The prominence of the marriage issue in the United States led to a proliferation of analytical treatment on that issue in particular by such writers as Daniel Pinello, William Eskridge, Martin Dupuis, Jonathon Goldberg Hiller, and Andrew Sullivan. Many other issues, such as those related to schooling, policing, and parenting, should have received substantial academic attention but did not.

Transgender politics gets little space in these strands of literature on rights politics. The theorist Paisley Currah is among the few social scientists and is possibly the only political scientist who has written in a sustained way on this topic. Empirical treatments of activist movements or public policy engagement with transgenderism and bisexuality are exceedingly rare, despite the spread of a rhetorical commitment to inclusion.

ACADEMIC LEGITIMACY?

In general the legitimacy of academic attention to the politics of sexual diversity has not kept pace with the readiness of publishers to produce works in the area. To be sure, the surge of work during the 1990s was matched by a growth in academic profile. The American Political Science Association (APSA) recognized a Committee on the Status of Lesbians and Gays in the Profession in the early 1990s, following the earlier formation of an LGBT caucus. This produced more equitable policies, studies of scholarly inclusiveness (by the APSA in 1993–1995), and increased room for specialists in LGBT issues to present their work. The 1990s and 2000s also saw the creation and growth of academic programs and research centers focusing on sexual diversity, the largest and most successful being the Center for Lesbian and Gay Studies (CLAGS) at the City University of New York.

Well into the 2000s, however, sexuality was still viewed as a marginal area, much as gender had been in previous decades. Undergraduate texts in political science in all countries only rarely referred to LGBT issues. Social science literature on these questions has routinely been pigeonholed with other gay-related material and seldom seen as contributing to more general understanding of public policy, social movements, voting behavior, or legislative politics.

SEE ALSO *American Political Science Association; Civil Rights; Gender; Gender, Alternatives to Binary; Human Rights; Liberation Movements; Marriage, Same-Sex; Politics; Politics, Gender; Politics, Identity; Queer Studies; Sexual Orientation, Social and Economic Consequences; Sexuality*

BIBLIOGRAPHY

Adam, Barry. 1995. *The Rise of a Gay and Lesbian Movement*. Rev. ed. Boston: Twayne.

Adam, Barry D., Jan Willem Duyvenkad, and André Krouwel, eds. 1999. *The Global Emergence of Gay and Lesbian Politics: National Imprints of a Worldwide Movement*. Philadelphia: Temple University Press.

Altman, Dennis. 1971. *Homosexual: Oppression and Liberation*. New York: Outerbridge and Dientsfry.

Boykin, Keith. 2005. *Beyond the Down Low: Sex, Lies, and Denial in Black America*. New York: Carroll and Graf.

Cohen, Cathy. 1999. *The Boundaries of Blackness: AIDS and the Breakdown of Black Politics*. Chicago: University of Chicago Press.

Cook, Timothy E. 1999. The Empirical Study of Lesbian, Gay, and Bisexual Politics: Assessing the First Wave of Research. *American Political Science Review* 93 (September): 679–692.

Currah, Paisley, Richard M. Juang, and Shannon Price Minter, eds. 2006. *Transgender Rights*. Minneapolis: University of Minnesota Press.

D'Emilio, John. 1983. *Sexual Politics, Sexual Communities: The Making of a Homosexual Minority in the United States, 1940–1970*. Chicago: University of Chicago Press.

Drucker, Peter, ed. 2000. *Different Rainbows*. London: Gay Men's Press.

Faderman, Lillian. 1981. *Surpassing the Love of Men: Romantic Friendship and Love between Women from the Renaissance to the Present*. New York: William Morrow.

Foucault, Michel. 1978. *The History of Sexuality*. Vol. 1, *An Introduction*. New York: Random House.

Gay Left Collective, ed. 1980. *Homosexuality: Power and Politics*. London: Allison and Busby.

Herman, Didi, and Carl Stychin, eds. 1995. *Legal Inversions: Lesbians, Gay Men, and the Politics of Law*. Philadelphia: Temple University Press.

Kirp, David L., and Ronald Bayer, eds. 1992. *AIDS in the Industrialized Democracies: Passions, Politics, and Policies*. New Brunswick, NJ: Rutgers University Press.

McIntosh, Mary. 1968. The Homosexual Role. *Social Problems* 16, no. 2 (Fall): 182–192.

Phelan, Shane. 1989. *Identity Politics: Lesbian Feminism and the Limits of Community*. Philadelphia: Temple University Press.

Rayside, David. 1998. *On the Fringe: Gays and Lesbians in Politics*. Ithaca, NY: Cornell University Press.

Rimmerman, Craig A., Kenneth D. Wald, and Clyde Wilcox, eds. 2000. *The Politics of Gay Rights*. Chicago: University of Chicago Press.

Ross, Becki L. 1995. *The House that Jill Built: A Lesbian Nation in Formation*. Toronto: University of Toronto Press.

Sedgwick, Eve Kosofsky. 1990. *Epistemology of the Closet*. Berkeley: University of California Press.

Seidman, Steven, ed. 1996. *Queer Theory/Sociology*. Oxford: Blackwell.

Smith, Miriam. 1999. *Lesbian and Gay Rights in Canada: Social Movements and Equality-Seeking, 1971–1995*. Toronto: University of Toronto Press.

Stychin, Carl F. 1998. *A Nation by Rights: National Cultures, Sexual Identity Politics, and the Discourse of Rights*. Philadelphia: Temple University Press.

Weeks, Jeffrey. 1977. *Coming Out: Homosexual Politics in Britain, from the Nineteenth Century to the Present*. London: Quartet.

Whisman, Vera. 1996. *Queer by Choice: Lesbians, Gay Men, and the Politics of Identity*. New York: Routledge.

Wintemute, Robert, and Mads Andenaes, eds. 2001. *Legal Recognition of Same-Sex Partnerships: A Study of National, European, and International Law*. Oxford: Hart.

David Rayside

POLITICS, GENDER

Gender politics is a multifaceted concept in the social sciences. As a term it is used to refer to a wide range of phenomena, stemming from multiple and even competing meanings of *gender* and *politics*. Its definition is further complicated by the emergence of similar and related phrases like *women and politics*, *gender and politics*, and the *politics of gender*. This complexity indicates ongoing conceptual debates within research on gender and politics. At the same time, it reflects theoretical and empirical developments as the study of gender politics has evolved and grown to encompass a broad and heterogeneous set of topics.

DEFINITIONS

Several definitions are necessary in order to grasp the scope and content of gender politics as a concept and a field of study. At the most basic level, it is crucial to distinguish between sex, gender, and sexuality. In their most common usages, *sex* denotes biological differences between men and women as male and female, *gender* describes the social meanings given to sexual differences through notions of masculine and feminine, and *sexuality* refers to sexual relations and questions of sexual orientation. However, definitions of all three of these terms, as well as the connections between them, are subject to a great deal of confusion and debate.

First, there is a tendency to identify all three terms with only one side of the dichotomies they represent: sex is often equated with *female*, gender with *feminine*, and sexuality with *homosexuality*. The result is that sex and gender are often treated as synonymous with women, while sexuality is considered only in relation to gays, lesbians, bisexuals, transsexuals, and transgendered individuals. Second, there are important disagreements on the ways in which sex, gender, and sexuality inform and are linked to one another. Although the binaries of sex and gender assume heterosexuality, for example, other sexual orientations raise questions about the necessary connections between male and masculine and female and feminine. These patterns intersect with debates about the causal relations between these terms: Although some argue that sex produces gender which leads to sexuality, others suggest that gender and compulsory heterosexuality give rise to distinctions on the basis of sex.

Parallel to these discussions, feminists and others have pioneered new uses for the term *politics*. Although many people employ this word to refer to formal political processes, like government and elections, *politics* has assumed at least two additional meanings in the last several decades. On the one hand, women's movement activists have expanded its range to encompass informal politics and the dynamics of everyday life. They insist that social movements are a form of political participation on a par with engagement inside the state. At the same time, they draw attention to the power relations that permeate all levels of social life, including relations within the private sphere of home and family. For them, "the personal is political." On the other hand, feminist and postmodern theorists have adopted a broader notion of politics as any instance or manifestation of power relations. They are thus interested not only in the politics of the state and the politics of social movements, but also in the politics of language, the politics of exchange, and the politics of representation, to give but a few examples.

These debates, in turn, lead to a range of different understandings of the term *gender politics* and cause it to be confused with related terms like *women and politics*, *gender and politics*, and the *politics of gender*. Although many people use these phrases interchangeably, it is possible—on the basis of the theoretical distinctions outlined above—to carve out some general differences between them. *Women and politics* involves the study of various aspects of women's political activity, whether this entails engagement in social movements, political parties, elected assemblies, or the state. *Gender and politics* covers many of these same topics, but in addition, implies attention to masculinities and femininities, as well as relations between

men and women, as they operate in various political arenas. The *politics of gender*, finally, comprises a closer look at the power relations behind definitions of—and presumed causal relations between—sex, gender, and sexuality. In comparison, *gender politics* may refer to any and all of these distinct foci of investigation.

Individual disciplines take up the study of gender politics in various ways, depending on their core research interests and theoretical frameworks. Because various currents in sociology, anthropology, and philosophy embrace broad definitions of *politics*, scholars in these fields use the term *gender politics* in many different ways to refer to the study of women and politics, gender and politics, and the politics of gender. Ironically, political scientists tend to adopt a much narrower definition of gender politics to refer only to the study of women and politics and gender and politics, where the term *politics* encompasses only formal and informal political processes, to the exclusion of questions about broader power relations. Even this more restricted focus, however, has produced a wide range of literature that over time has expanded and evolved in terms of theoretical approaches and fields of empirical research.

APPROACHES

As feminist theorists have developed *sex* and *gender* as analytical categories, scholars in political science have elaborated a series of approaches for analyzing the sexed and gendered nature of political life. The first phase of research on gender politics involved highlighting women's exclusion from formal politics and then incorporating women into existing political frameworks. It was thus guided by an "add women and stir" approach: Using sex and gender as synonyms for *women*, it sought to include women but did not question the male norm implicit in reigning understandings of political processes.

Recognizing the limits of this approach, the second phase shifted its attention to the activities of women as women and analyzed their participation in formal and informal politics. Although many scholars continued to employ the term *gender* when they discussed only women, a growing number also began to use it to refer to relations between men and women in order to study how the form and content of politics reflect and shape inequalities. The third and current phase extends these insights to explore how ideas about sex and gender permeate all aspects of political life, sometimes—but not always—with the intent to break down these dichotomies. This work introduces, for the first time, the importance of studying masculinities as well as femininities in politics. It also investigates how political science itself may be gendered in terms of its concepts, definitions, theories, and methods.

The main theoretical innovation that emerges over the course of these stages is a multifaceted shift in focus from *sex* to *gender*. In light of the different definitions attributed to these terms, analysts ascribe at least three distinct meanings to this shift. The first is a move away from biological sex, or the notion that men and women are binary opposites, toward socially constructed gender identities, or the idea that masculinity and femininity constitute features that exist along a continuum. The second is a move away from exclusive concern with women in politics and public policy toward greater attention to the impact of masculinities and femininities, as well as relations between men and women, on political inputs and outcomes. The third is a move away from sex as one of many possible variables in political science toward gender as a concept that forces a fundamental reexamination of core features of political life.

All three aspects of the shift from sex to gender, nonetheless, are in some sense incomplete. For one, mainstream and feminist researchers find that while indicators for sex are relatively straightforward to incorporate into political analysis, those for gender are much more complicated. This is partly because sex refers to biological markers that are relatively unambiguous, while gender denotes social meanings that may vary a great deal within and across particular contexts. However, this is also due to difficulties that many people experience in grasping that the relationship between sex and gender is not a perfect one. Secondly, many feminists are hesitant to abandon sex in favor of gender. As the two concepts are not equivalent, these scholars argue that both are crucial to good research design, whether the purpose is to analyze men and women or masculinities and femininities as these play out in various kinds of political arenas.

FIELDS OF RESEARCH

Attempts to expand the scope of *politics* to include formal and informal political processes are reflected in the areas of empirical research on gender politics in political science. Seeking to break down dichotomies of public versus private spheres and formal versus informal politics, these scholars have explored the effects of sex and gender on a broad range of political activities. Focused on women specifically, they have examined women and voting, in terms of the right to vote, the implications of delayed suffrage, and gender gaps in voting support; women and social movements, in terms of participation in social movements, women's movements, and feminist movements; women and political parties, in terms of candidate selection and other aspects of party politics; and women and parliaments, in terms of access to political office, behavior in political office, and impact on public policy.

Turning to the products of political processes, gender politics researchers have theorized the role of the state in reflecting and shaping gender relations. They analyze how states contribute to the reproduction of gender hierarchies, or alternatively, lead to changes in patterns of inequality through different kinds of public policies. Attentive to variations across countries, they note the ways in which such policies make implicit or explicit assumptions about men and women and identify—or ignore—certain questions as *women's issues*. The possibilities of exploring other definitions of *politics* and incorporating interactions with other identities, combined with the already multifaceted nature of sex and gender, ensure that all six of these areas will remain vibrant areas for future research.

SEE ALSO *Abortion Rights; Femininity; Feminism; Feminism, Second Wave; Gender; Gender, Alternatives to Binary; Gender Gap; Inequality, Gender; Masculinity; Patriarchy; Politics; Politics: Gay, Lesbian, Transgender, and Bisexual; Politics, Identity; Sexual Orientation, Determinants of; Sexual Orientation, Social and Economic Consequences; Sexuality; Suffrage, Women's; Women and Politics*

BIBLIOGRAPHY

Bacchi, Carol Lee. 1999. *Women, Policy, and Politics: The Construction of Policy Problems.* Thousand Oaks, CA: Sage.

Butler, Judith. 1990. *Gender Trouble: Feminism and the Subversion of Identity.* New York: Routledge.

Carver, Terrell. 1996. *Gender Is Not a Synonym for Women.* Boulder, CO: Lynne Rienner.

Lovenduski, Joni. 1998. Gendering Research in Political Science. *Annual Review of Political Science* 1: 333–356.

Randall, Vicky. 2002. Feminism. In *Theory and Methods in Political Science*, ed. David Marsh and Gerry Stoker, 109–130. New York: Palgrave Macmillan.

Sapiro, Virginia. 1991. Gender Politics, Gendered Politics: The State of the Field. In *Political Science: Looking to the Future.* Vol. 1. *The Theory and Practice of Political Science*, ed. William Crotty, 165–187. Evanston, IL: Northwestern University Press.

Mona Lena Krook

POLITICS, IDENTITY

Identity politics is a term that first came into usage in the 1970s to refer to the view that social identities, such as race, ethnicity, sexuality, and gender, have an important influence on an individual's political motivations, affiliations, and political commitments. The term quickly moved from a neutral description to primarily a pejorative and began to refer to the practices of narrow interest-group politics, separatism, and the practice of assessing a person's politics on the basis of his or her identity alone.

In the 1990s both the concept and the practice of identity politics began to be vigorously defended primarily by theorists working on identity-based political movements or movements against identity-based forms of oppression.

Most consider the locus classicus of the concept of identity politics to be the Combahee River Collective Statement written in 1978. The term had been used in public discourse in the Left before this time, but this was the first place that it received an explicit formulation. In this statement, identity politics refers to the idea that the identity of political agents and theorists will have an impact on both the political work they choose to pursue and also on its effectiveness.

The Combahee River Collective was composed of African American women who believed that there did not yet exist a social theory or political movement that fully and accurately reflected the conditions of African American women's lives. They argued that African American women needed to develop such a theory and movement themselves, that they would be the group most motivated to do so, and that they would be the group with the knowledge base from which to develop the specific social analyses applicable to their form of intersectional oppression. They made a specific point of stating that they were not separatists and in fact supported coalition work, particularly with those in the feminist and antiracist movements. They also stated that they did not reject the utility of more general social theories of oppression, such as Marxism. Yet they held that a special focus on black women's lives by black women themselves was necessary to yield new insights and practices. Their defense of this latter claim was based on the state of the social movements of that time, in which the specific oppression of African American women was not pursued by either feminism in general or by the antiracist movements.

The concept of identity assumed by the Combahee River Collective was an intersectional and complex one. They did not assume that all women or all African Americans have the same political motivations or goals, hence their formation of this separate group. Many members also were lesbians and experienced marginalization as well as homophobia in other groups. Despite their experience with the complexities of group identity, they nonetheless asserted that "we believe that the most profound and potentially the most radical politics come directly out of our own identity, as opposed to working to end someone else's oppression" (Combahee River Collective 1978, p. 365).

From this rather careful and cautious explanation of the relationship between identity and politics—a relationship conceived of as philosophical as well as political—the term *identity politics* began to be associated with the identity-based splits and sectarianism that rippled throughout the civil rights, gay and lesbian, women's, and student movements of the 1960s and 1970s. Most notably this included the removal of whites from the Student Nonviolent Coordinating Committee that occurred in the mid-1960s and the gay-straight split that occurred in the women's movement in the early 1970s. Splitting organizations along identity lines was attributed to identity politics. This connotation of the term may already have been in circulation when the Combahee River Collective first formed, motivating them to give an explanation and defense of the identity-based form their collective took.

CRITICS OF IDENTITY POLITICS

From the 1980s on both liberal and left political theorists began to critique the concept as based on simplistic notions of identity and narrow conceptions of solidarity and as maintaining a focus on victimization rather than on effective solutions. These theorists argued that identity politics was an obstacle to the work of creating trust across differences of identity, which is necessary for coalitions and class-based movements. They argued further that it had detrimental effects within identity defined groups themselves, such as enforced conformism within the group, a policing of the group's boundaries, and a hampering of the expression of and debate over internal political differences within groups.

Leading liberals such as Arthur Schlesinger Jr. criticized identity politics for making a cult of identity that derailed the trend that had been growing up until the 1960s toward a melting-pot society. Other liberals also worried that identity politics in a multiethnic society would disable democracy by transforming the arena of public political discourse from a shared concern over the common good to a negotiation between interest groups locked in battle. Liberals also predicted that identity politics would lead to a Balkanization of the political landscape and an increase in civil strife, possibly including the kind of violence that occurred in the former Yugoslavia in the 1990s.

Leftists expressed the concern that identity politics had derailed the possibility of forming a class-based progressive movement that could unite around critical issues of economic injustice. Race- and gender-based movements are multi-class, they argued, and so cannot take up a working-class agenda. Many philosophers also entered the debate, especially those influenced by French poststructuralism, to argue that the concept of identity being assumed by proponents of identity politics is an illusion of coherence and unity based perhaps on a form of psychological pathology. Identity concepts assume a homogeneity of experience and political interests where none exists, and this is why identity-based movements must enforce homogeneity and police the borders around identities to keep out those with intersectional identities who might have a different set of political priorities. Some ethnic theorists, such as Paul Gilroy, united with this critique, arguing that identity politics is an understandable but pointless reaction to modernist pressures that transform identities and diminish their significance.

IDENTITY-BASED AND PROGRESSIVE

In response to these concerns a number of theorists, especially in ethnic studies, argue that identity-based political movements—such as the abolitionist movement and civil rights movement—have been among the main forces expanding democratization and developing progressive politics. Identity-based movements have improved the inclusiveness of class-based movements so that the interests of nonwhite and women workers are also represented. The white male union leaders would not have come to these more inclusive agendas on their own without being pushed by the various caucus groups within the labor movement that were organized around identity. Identity politics was a necessary part of the strategy to overcome identity-based forms of oppression, to ensure an inclusive political agenda, to develop a more thorough analysis of social oppression, and to show the equality of all people as leaders and intellectuals.

A number of ethnographic studies reveal that identity politics do not always lead to separatism or enforced conformity and that we need to develop a typology of identity-based movements in order to distinguish between different forms with different effects. Mobilizing on the basis of identity can bring new actors to political participation and thus work against the passivity of victimized notions of identity. Under extreme repression, identity groups may curtail the expression of internal differences, but this is not inherent to identity-based movements.

The concepts of identity assumed by the parties to this debate vary widely. Some theorists on both sides of the debate assume that identities are like interest groups with uniform political interests or that members of identity groups are identifiable by their shared practices, preferences, and beliefs. Other theorists, such as Satya P. Mohanty, Paula M. L. Moya, and Linda Martín Alcoff, argue that identities are historically fluid, intersectional, and heterogeneous and thus a starting place rather than the endpoint of politics. Nonetheless, identities are important indices of experience and provide epistemic resources for social analysis.

SEE ALSO *African Americans; Civil Rights Movement, U.S.; Class; Democracy; Ethnicity; Gender; Gender Gap; Identity; Individualism; Liberalism; Poststructuralism; Race; Sexual Orientation, Social and Economic Consequences; Social Movements; Women's Movement*

BIBLIOGRAPHY

Alcoff, Linda Martín. 2006. *Visible Identities: Race, Gender, and the Self.* Cambridge, U.K.: Oxford University Press.

Brown, Wendy. 1995. *States of Injury: Power and Freedom in Late Modernity.* Princeton, NJ: Princeton University Press.

Bulkin, Elly, Minnie Bruce Pratt, and Barbara Smith. 1998. *Yours in Struggle: Three Feminist Perspectives on Anti-Semitism and Racism.* Ithaca, NY: Firebrand Books.

Butler, Judith. 1997. *The Psychic Life of Power: Theories in Subjection.* Stanford, CA: Stanford University Press.

Cabral, Amilcar. 1973. Identity and Dignity in the Context of the National Liberation Struggle. In *Return to the Source: Selected Speeches,* 9–25. New York: Monthly Review.

Castells, Manuel. 1997. *The Power of Identity.* Vol. 2 of *The Information Age: Economy, Society, and Culture.* Malden, MA: Blackwell.

Combahee River Collective. 1979. A Black Feminist Statement. In *Capitalist Patriarchy and the Case for Socialist Feminism,* ed. Zillah R. Eisenstein, 362–372. New York: Monthly Review.

Cruz, José E. 1998. *Identity and Power: Puerto Rican Politics and the Challenge of Ethnicity.* Philadelphia: Temple University Press.

Dawson, Michael C. 1994. *Behind the Mule: Race and Class in African-American Politics.* Princeton, NJ: Princeton University Press.

Dingwaney, Anuradha, and Lawrence Needham. 1996. The Difference That Difference Makes. *Socialist Review* 26 (3–4): 5–47.

Elshtain, Jean Bethke. 1995. *Democracy on Trial.* New York: HarperCollins.

Flores, William V., and Rina Benmayor, eds. 1997. *Latino Cultural Citizenship: Claiming Identity, Space, and Rights.* Boston: Beacon.

Fox Piven, Francis. 1995. Globalizing Capitalism and the Rise of Identity Politics. *Socialist Register* 31: 102–116.

Fraser, Nancy. 1997. *Justice Interruptus: Critical Reflections on the "Postsocialist" Condition.* New York: Routledge.

Fraser, Nancy. 2000. Rethinking Recognition. *New Left Review* 3: 107–120.

Gitlin, Todd. 1995. *The Twilight of Common Dreams: Why America Is Wracked by Culture Wars.* New York: Metropolitan.

Kelley, Robin D. G. 1997. *Yo' Mama's Disfunktional! Fighting the Culture Wars in Urban America.* Boston: Beacon.

Mohanty, Satya P. 1997. *Literary Theory and the Claims of History: Postmodernism, Objectivity, Multicultural Politics.* Ithaca, NY: Cornell University Press.

Moya, Paula M. L. 2002. *Learning from Experience: Minority Identities, Multicultural Struggles.* Berkeley: University of California Press.

Schlesinger, Arthur M., Jr. 1998. *The Disuniting of America: Reflections on a Multicultural Society.* New York: Norton.

Linda Martín Alcoff

POLITICS, LATINO

The terms *Latino* and *Hispanic* are the most accepted words for a diverse population of people with linguistic, geographic, and historical similarities, but the terms are wrought more for practical convenience than descriptive clarity. The literature on Latino politics has stressed the differences between the various Latino groups since the Latino National Political Survey in 1989, the first major national survey specifically targeting Latinos. National debates over immigration policy in 1994 and 2006, however, demonstrate that despite their diversity, Latinos are a group of people distinguishable, for better or worse, by both Latinos and the electorate at-large.

LATINO ELECTORAL PARTICIPATION

The litmus test of civic participation for any group is their level of electoral turnout. David Leal, Matt A. Barreto, Jongho Lee, and Rodolfo O. de la Garza noted in "The Latino Vote in the 2004 Election" that Latino voter turnout "surged from 5.9 million in 2000 to at least 7 million in 2004" (2005, p. 41). Increasing levels of electoral participation may suggest a comparative increase in socioeconomic status, higher levels of personal interest, greater levels of civic engagement, or a greater effort on the part of the establishment to recruit Latinos. The greatest impact Latinos have had on American politics comes from speculation regarding the Latino vote, but the numbers paint a considerably different picture. Table 1 illustrates U.S. Census Bureau reports showing that registration and participation rates among Latino citizens and non-citizens have hardly changed since 1980. The increase in the raw numbers of Hispanics voting from 1980 to 2004 is attributable almost entirely to population growth, considered to be the driving force of Latino politics.

LATINOS' RELATIONSHIP WITH THE AMERICAN POLITICAL SYSTEM

In their work *The Chicano Political Experience* F. Chris Garcia and Rodolfo de la Garza illustrated four models to explain the relationship between Latinos and American society in 1977: pluralism, internal colonialism, and elitism. Rodney Hero later contributed his influential description of a two-tiered pluralistic society in 1992 with *Latinos and the U.S. Political System.*

Under the pluralist framework, groups vie with one another on a competitive field, each with their own advantages, resources, and centers of power where there are multiple access points to influence the political system. The most compelling argument for a pluralistic model is Lawrence H. Fuchs's *The American Kaleidoscope* (1990), in which he parallels the Latino immigrant experience and past immigrants who are now largely integrated into the political power structure.

By contrast, internal colonialism claims a sociopolitical system in which Latinos are dominated and exploited by other groups, even though they may have the same formal legal status of the dominant group. It emphasizes the integration of historically racist relationships between the dominant non-Latino majority and Latinos into the fabric of the political system. Distinctions from the dominant group are seen to have negative or inferior qualities, and the stereotypes of Latinos are embedded into the institutions of the social and political systems, from the electoral system to the financial and educational infrastructure.

The elitism perspective asserts that there is a privileged class of people who enjoy superior resources with racially generated attachments that serve to further appropriate the privileged class to their position at the top. The elitism model depends less on racial distinctions and more on class differences to explain the unequal distribution of power and resources that characterizes the Latino masses. Elitism is also different in that it does account for some growth in Latino influence, but Latino elites are not likely to resemble the Latino masses and are more likely to resemble their non-Latino elite cohort.

Hero argues that there is a large segment of Latinos who are structurally cut off from the opportunities that are available to the mainstream, despite the success stories. He describes a compelling perspective on Latinos' relationship with the American system, a two-tiered pluralistic society in which there is a conventional population that operates in the traditional patterns that most immigrant groups do, and a second tier that consists of a political and social subclass whose position is supported by historical and cultural inequalities that have become embedded into the fabric of the structural system. Two-tiered pluralism is a complex framework that consists of a political system that is formally unrestricting but exists within a social system that is informally constrained by negative historical relationships.

The 1994 Proposition 187 debate in California illustrates Hero's model, as Latinos were politically fully engaged, but largely helpless in their efforts to prevent Proposition 187 from passing decisively. Although Proposition 187 was deemed unconstitutional, the anti-immigration movement throughout the United States remains robust into the mid-2000s and illustrates the relationship Hero draws between Latinos and the American political and social systems. Latinos may have a legal status equal to the majority, but the continued poverty and social status of Latinos is a function of continually having to defend themselves against the mainstream, preventing them from tapping into valuable social resources.

ASSESSING LATINOS' RELATIONSHIP WITH THE AMERICAN SYSTEM

As noted above, the rate of Latino electoral participation has not changed significantly since 1980, just three years after Garcia and de la Garza outlined their models on the relationship between Latinos and the American system. After reflecting on nearly three decades of literature on Latino politics, however, de la Garza believes Latinos do indeed fit into the pluralistic model. He points out that this was not always the case and if he were to make the same assessment back in 1977, pluralism would not have been his first choice.

The empirical evidence since 1977 has swayed his opinion, suggesting that the distasteful realities of the Latino experience have indeed improved. One reason for de la Garza's initial judgment in 1977 might have been the available models at the time, which were used to explain the how, why, and whom of Latino politics. Up until 1977, the field of political behavior had largely settled into two general camps, rational actor theory and socioeconomic status theory. These theories are not exclusive, but in their stages of development before 1977, neither could sufficiently explain the position of Latinos in the American system.

The literature on Latino politics up to that point had been guided by the scholarship on African American politics and focused on grassroots movements that tended to skew the perspective toward the inequalities born out of the social and political climate of the time. These perspectives focused on the effects of socioeconomic status (SES), social capital, institutional trust, group identity, and group relations. The development of these models provides researchers with the tools to better understand the forces behind Latino politics.

Up until 1977, the strong impact that SES had on political participation was a truism in the field. The rational actor model assigned higher stakes to the socially privileged because they had a greater incentive to take an active role in a system from which they benefited. The socioeconomic status model had established the connection between participation and higher levels of SES in a variety of national and international surveys at the time. Whether it was out of civic-minded duty or rational self-interest, Latinos could hardly be seen to have had much of an incentive to participate.

Given the low SES of Latinos it was not difficult to speculate why Latinos did not participate, but the empirical models had yet to capture the depth of this dimension in Latino politics. While Latinos simply did not have the

Registration and voting of non-Hispanic whites and Hispanics in the 2004 and 1980 presidential elections

	2004			
	N/H White		Hispanic	
	Citizens only	Non-citizens included	Citizens only	Non-citizens included
Registered	75.1%	73.5%	64.0%	34.9%
Voted	67.2%	65.8%	47.2%	28.0%
	1980			
Registered	84.7%	70.3%	56.0%	36.3%
Voted	66.2%	62.8%	46.1%	29.9%

The comparison between 1980 and 2004 is an approximation because the changes in ethical and racial categories by the census does not allow true apples to apples comparison.

SOURCE: U.S. Census Bureau.

Table 1

resources to effectively participate, from a theoretical perspective one could only speculate as to how Latinos would be able to exact change on the political system.

This hole in the literature left a heavy burden on pluralism to explain the unequal distribution of resources, and the literature had hardly given much promise in Latinos' ability to traverse the social barriers that were clearly evident at the time. Elitism and internal colonialism offered the best explanation for the position of Latinos in the American system almost by default. But if the relative participation rates have not changed much since 1977, what evidence have the empirical models provided that might convince de la Garza that Latinos live in a pluralistic society?

One potential answer is that the field of Latino politics has learned that Latinos behave no differently than do non-Latinos and that ethnicity in and of itself has little direct effect on the participation rates of Latinos. Carole J. Uhlaner, Bruce E. Cain, and D. Roderick Kiewiet concluded in their 1989 article "Political Participation of Ethnic Minorities in the 1980s" that "Latino activity rates appear no lower than those of non-Hispanic whites once demographic factors and related determinants of participation are controlled" (p. 217). The behavioral models have taken a greater account of the experiences and obstacles that faced Latinos and are able to control for many of the speculative factors that had not been empirically established, such as different patterns of civic voluntarism and an underdeveloped elite-driven organizational structure necessary for effective mobilization.

More important, events since 1977 have provided many examples of Latino political success and the large Latino population has made it easier to witness a growing Latino middle class. Because of this, it is difficult to justify the internal colonialism model, and Hero's two-tiered pluralism was an attempt to rectify the internal colonialism model with the facts on the ground. Two-tiered pluralism concedes what at that point could not be argued anymore, that Latinos had indeed reached legal parity with the majority, while still relying on historical racism to explain the differences in socioeconomic status. The future may prove two-tiered pluralism to be wrong, but until then, it is still the best framework available to explain why Latinos behave the same as non-Latinos given the same characteristics, and why they do not reap identical benefits as Anglos do from the same political actions.

SEE ALSO *Behaviorism; Boricua; Caribbean, The; Citizenship; Colony, Internal; Elite Theory; Hernandez v. Texas; Immigrants, Latin American; Immigration; Indigenismo; Latino National Political Survey; Latinos; Pluralism; Stratification*

BIBLIOGRAPHY

De la Garza, Rodolfo O. 2004. Latino Politics. *Annual Review of Political Science* 7: 91–123.

Fuchs, Lawrence H. 1990. *The American Kaleidoscope: Race, Ethnicity and the Civic Culture.* Hanover, NH: Wesleyan University Press.

Garcia, F. Chris, and Rodolfo O. de la Garza. 1977. *The Chicano Political Experience: Three Perspectives.* North Scituate, MA: Duxbury.

Hero, Rodney E. 1992. *Latinos and the U.S. Political System: Two-tiered Pluralism.* Philadelphia: Temple University Press.

Leal, David L., Matt A. Barreto, Jongho Lee, and Rodolfo O. de la Garza. 2005. The Latino Vote in the 2004 Election. *PS: Political Science and Politics* 38 (1): 41–49.

Uhlaner, Carole J., Bruce E. Cain, and D. Roderick Kiewiet. 1989. Political Participation of Ethnic Minorities in the 1980s. *Political Behavior* 11 (3): 195–231.

Stephen A. Nuño

POLITICS, REPRODUCTIVE

SEE *Reproductive Politics.*

POLITICS, SOUTHERN

In politics, religion, and culture, the South is arguably the United States' most unique region. Southerners, particularly native-born white southerners, have a collective consciousness and attachment to history that exceeds that found in other regions, such as the upper Midwest, New England, and the West. A native-born Connecticut or Massachusetts resident is far less likely to identify as a "New Englander" than a native-born South Carolinian or Mississippian is to identify as a southerner. Historian David Goldfield refers to the drive among some white southerners to preserve some elements of the past as "still fighting the Civil War" in his 2002 book of the same title. While not unique to the region, several elements, including military traditions, a "culture of honor," attachment to traditional gender roles, and fundamentalist Christianity, have striking support in much of the South compared to the rest of the nation. These elements materially influence politics, and southern politics, always distinctive in the past, remains distinctive in the twenty-first century.

Which states make up the South? This question has no single agreed-upon answer, and opinions vary. Many political-science datasets include data from only the eleven former Confederate states. For the purposes of this entry, the South includes thirteen states: Virginia, North Carolina, South Carolina, Georgia, Florida, Alabama, Mississippi, Louisiana, Texas, Arkansas, Tennessee, Oklahoma, and Kentucky. The first eleven of these states were the former Confederate states—those that seceded from the Union during the Civil War. Oklahoma and Kentucky, though not former Confederate states, have cultural and political features—for example, large Southern Baptist populations—that arguably warrant their consideration as southern states as well.

CLASSIC AND CONTEMPORARY STUDIES OF SOUTHERN POLITICS

The distinctive nature of southern politics is implicitly acknowledged in the two most widely cited scholarly studies on the topic: V. O. Key's *Southern Politics in State and Nation* (1949), and Merle Black and Earl Black's *Politics and Society in the South* (1987). Key wrote when southern whites remained economically, socially, and politically dominant over blacks—as they had been since the end of slavery in 1865. Southern whites used their control over government to ensure and perpetuate racial segregation and impose rampant, official racial discrimination on wide swaths of social institutions: education, housing, employment, voting, and criminal justice, to name a few. While racial discrimination also existed in much of the North, it was more pervasive and severe, and more a product of government actions, in the South. As Key notes, most of the South was under one-party Democratic control, and most political conflict in southern states centered on factions within the Democratic Party. Factions sometimes centered on regions within states (with conflict between Delta and "hills" factions in Mississippi). In other cases, factions centered on personalities (such as the flamboyantly racist "Pitchfork Ben" Tillman of South

Carolina and Theodore Bilbo of Mississippi) or other interests, such as textile mill owners in North and South Carolina and the "big mules" of timber, iron and steel, coal, insurance, and utilities in Alabama.

Although factions sometimes splintered the Democratic Party, on racial issues there was little disagreement among southern whites at midcentury. Racial discrimination and segregation were entrenched; any (white) elected official who dared to challenge either faced severe social ostracism, economic reprisals, and certain defeat in the next election. Southern blacks had virtually no political power, and voting discrimination along with threatened and actual violence effectively deprived them of voting rights—especially in the Deep South states of Louisiana, Mississippi, Alabama, Georgia, and South Carolina. With elected officials virtually all white Democrats and with Republicans reviled by whites as the party of Lincoln, the Union, and racial equality, there was little impetus for racial change. Thus, Key concluded, "The race issue broadly defined must be considered as the number one problem on the southern agenda. Lacking a solution for it, all else fails" (1949, p. 675).

In 1987, political scientists (and twin brothers) Merle Black and Earl Black published *Politics and Society in the South.* By then, much had changed in southern politics. Federal court decisions and laws effectively guaranteed civil rights in housing, education, and employment, and the 1965 Voting Rights Act had ended various egregious practices that promoted voting discrimination and the dilution of black political power. By 1987, they wrote, the Democratic Party's monopoly in southern politics had ended, replaced by a competitive two-party system, with Republicans becoming dominant in presidential electoral votes as early as 1984, when Ronald Reagan swept every southern state. The authors also noted a decided "conservative advantage" in white public opinion: White southerners identifying as conservatives outnumbered those identifying as liberals by nearly a three-to-one margin (Black and Black 1987, p. 218, Table 10.1). This and similar findings, they argued, meant likely continued Republican gains in southern governorships, state legislatures, and delegations in the U.S. House and Senate. Black and Black's later (2002) study confirmed their suspicions, documenting strong Republican growth in the region.

The studies by Key and Black and Black are widely considered the most systematic investigations of southern politics. However, other studies also deserve note. Numan Bartley and Hugh Graham's *Southern Politics and the Second Reconstruction* (1975) was written less than ten years after the civil rights movement fundamentally reorganized race relations, and at a time when Republicans were beginning to erode the Democratic one-party

monopoly that had been entrenched from 1890 to 1950. A more recent study is journalist Peter Applebome's *Dixie Rising: How the South Is Shaping American Values, Politics and Culture* (1997). Applebome's account is rich with historical observations, economic and social data, and anecdotal evidence derived from personal observation and travels in locales such as Cobb County, Georgia; Charlotte, North Carolina; Columbia, South Carolina; and Nashville, Tennessee. Finally, some political scientists have published more focused studies of southern politics. Book-length studies in this tradition include Oran Smith's *The Rise of Baptist Republicanism* (1997), James Glaser's *Race, Campaign Politics, and the Realignment in the South* (1996), Merle Black and Earl Black's *The Rise of Southern Republicans* (2002), and Glaser's *The Hand of the Past in Contemporary Southern Politics* (2005). Clearly, the study of southern politics has matured into a well-defined subfield in political science, as much as southern history is a well-known specialty among historians.

THE CIVIL WAR, RECONSTRUCTION, DISENFRANCHISEMENT, AND JIM CROW

The Civil War (1861–1865) was a searing experience nationwide, but its physical devastation and psychological scars fell especially hard on the South. As the losing side, southerners saw their region ravaged by the Union army, with widespread destruction of and damage to homes, crops, and livelihoods. In the war's aftermath, federal troops occupied southern state capitals for over a decade—a profoundly humiliating experience for a region that already had lost a war and seen federal officials force an end to slavery, the dominant economic system of much of the region. Congress passed the Thirteenth Amendment, outlawing slavery; the Fourteenth Amendment, guaranteeing equal protection under the law, among other things; and the Fifteenth Amendment, aimed at preventing voting discrimination against blacks and freed slaves. During the Reconstruction era (1865–1877), Republicans dominated national politics and forced white southerners to accept the end of slavery, occupation by perceived federal invaders, and, sometimes, southern black elected officials. In Mississippi, Hiram Revels became the first African American to serve in the U.S. Senate (1870–1871). As Black and Black note:

> [The Democratic Party] gave southern whites something to love, honor and glorify; Republicanism gave them something to hate, despise and excoriate. Republicans were irredeemably identified with a long series of outrages against the white South—the Civil War, abolition of slavery, Reconstruction, threats of renewed fed-

eral intervention, and the exploitation of the South's vulnerable economic condition. Except in a few (mainly mountainous) areas where grassroots Republicanism persisted, public support for the party of Lincoln entailed the stigma of providing aid and comfort to the region's historical enemy. (1987, pp. 233–234)

For black southerners, Reconstruction was a brief era of relatively improved conditions. Blacks' living conditions remained difficult, but under federal control of the South, they had more freedom to pursue their destinies and faced less severe discrimination in doing so. For white southerners, Reconstruction was an uninterrupted regional nightmare. Whites' obsession was to expel the federal "invaders," end their "radical" control, and reestablish "home rule"—local control over their social, political, and economic affairs. Above all else, southern whites fought to reestablish white domination and the subjugation of southern blacks.

In 1877, the federal army withdrew from southern state capitals, bringing Reconstruction to an end. The era that followed was dubbed "Redemption" by southern whites. But for most southern blacks, "Redemption" meant the return, in different form, of the nightmarish conditions of the slavery era, including white-imposed economic exploitation through the sharecropping system. Whites sought to reestablish white Democratic control and expel the hated Republican Party and anyone friendly to it from the political system. By 1890, using a combination of terror and violence, widespread electoral fraud, racial demagoguery, and pervasive social and economic pressure on any reluctant friends, family, and neighbors, white conservative Democrats succeeded in effectively eliminating Republican competition in southern politics. The resulting virtual one-party Democratic stranglehold in southern politics lasted from 1890 to 1965.

For southern blacks, the consequences were devastating socially, politically, and economically. With a virtually unbreakable lock on political power, white Democrats imposed social, economic, and political discrimination on blacks on a colossal scale. Black southerners were shut out of political power, as whites imposed discriminatory poll taxes, literacy tests, the grandfather clause, and the white primary to perpetuate white domination and crush black opposition. These electoral tests and devices frequently were applied arbitrarily by hostile white registrars to ensure that few if any blacks could register to vote. For blacks, the result was massive disenfranchisement: the often-successful panoply of white efforts to deny voting rights to blacks. Blacks who managed to evade official voting discrimination and actually register to vote faced harassment, threats, violence, and economic retaliation. Arbitrary evictions, job terminations, and blacklisting,

ensuring that no other local employers would ever hire the person, often effectively "persuaded" blacks to avoid challenging white domination and meekly accept their lot. The costs of being an "uppity Negro" in the South—one audacious enough to challenge the racial status quo—were manifold: social ostracism, harassment and persecution by law enforcement, threats, actual violence, and possibly death by lynching. In much of the South, the only real qualification for voting was being white, though the poll tax did disenfranchise many poor whites also.

With blacks shut out of the ranks of elected officials and largely shut out of voting, the establishment of conservative white Democratic "home rule" was complete by 1890. Local and state governments passed Jim Crow laws imposing legal segregation in public schools and places, including restaurants, drinking fountains, theaters, pool halls, parks, train and bus stations, neighborhoods, and more. Blacks also faced economic discrimination; other laws prohibited blacks from holding many types of jobs, typically higher-paying, higher-status jobs. Informal customs and practices strongly reinforced these patterns. White business owners and managers commonly refused to hire blacks at all, or at best hired them only for the most menial and low-paying jobs. Southern textile mills were particularly ruthless in enforcing the color bar in employment, with black mill workers virtually nonexistent. In housing, governments forced blacks to live in segregated, usually deeply impoverished, neighborhoods, and white homeowners would, by custom, refuse to rent or sell to blacks anyway. Restaurants, theaters, libraries, and other establishments commonly refused to serve blacks altogether; colleges and universities refused to enroll them, resulting in the establishment of historically black colleges and universities, some of which still exist. Few whites dared openly sympathize with blacks or support efforts to combat segregation and discrimination. A white seen as pro-black could expect to be branded a "nigger lover" and faced the same threats, economic reprisals, and violence that "uppity Negroes" did. As Black and Black point out, even well into the twentieth century, southern whites were obsessed with maintaining "home rule"—local control over race relations:

Early in [the twentieth] century, most white southerners looked upon the rest of the nation—generally lumped together as Yankees—with abiding hostility and suspicion. Unable to forget or forgive the nightmare of war, defeat, and occupation, most whites shared the conviction that non-southerners must never again be allowed to interfere with southern racial practices. Acting almost as if it were an independent nation, the South pursued deterrence of outside intervention in race relations as the paramount objective of its "foreign" policy. (1987, p. 233)

THE CIVIL RIGHTS MOVEMENT
AND ITS POLITICAL
CONSEQUENCES

In the early twentieth century, the U.S. Supreme Court overturned some racially discriminatory voting practices. In 1915, the Court overturned the grandfather clause, and in 1944, it struck down the white primary. However, other forms of voting discrimination persisted, and until 1965, federal law did little to prevent it.

The first major federal civil rights action of the twentieth century was the Supreme Court's *Brown v. Board of Education* ruling in 1954. Overturning an 1896 legal doctrine allowing "separate but equal" public facilities, the Court ruled that racial segregation in public schools was inherently unequal. The ruling and its 1955 companion ruling (*Brown II*, ordering officials to desegregate public schools "with all deliberate speed") exploded like bombshells in the southern political landscape. Southern officials responded with outrage and unvarnished defiance. The "Massive Resistance" campaign mounted by southern officials to oppose school desegregation was intense and unrelenting. From 1959 to 1964, Prince Edward County, Virginia, closed its public schools altogether to avoid desegregation and provided money to white parents to send their children to private, whites-only schools. Meanwhile, most black children were locked out of an education for five years. In 1964, nearly 98 percent of southern black children still attended segregated schools. Only after more court orders did some districts comply with the *Brown* rulings.

During the early 1960s, efforts to integrate southern schools and universities and register blacks to vote provoked waves of violence. In 1960, sit-in demonstrators seeking integrated lunch counters faced attacks and violence. In 1961, freedom riders seeking to integrate public transportation faced more violence and beatings. In 1962, when James Meredith integrated the University of Mississippi, thousands of segregationists rioted, resulting in two deaths and mobilization of thousands of National Guard troops to restore order. In 1963, white supremacists bombed a black church in Birmingham, Alabama, killing four little girls, and NAACP leader Medgar Evers was murdered in his driveway in Jackson, Mississippi. In 1964, three civil rights workers were murdered near Philadelphia, Mississippi. In 1965, Alabama state troopers attacked unarmed voting-rights marchers with clubs, police dogs, and electric cattle prods. Searing images of these events were broadcast on national television at a time when (by 1964) 97 percent of American households had television sets. The repeated incidents of civil-rights-related violence spurred calls for concerted federal action on civil rights from the public and in Congress.

In 1964, southern members of Congress mounted ferocious opposition, including a Senate filibuster, to the 1964 Civil Rights Act. But northern Republicans and Democrats overcame the filibuster, and President Lyndon B. Johnson signed the Civil Rights Act into law in July 1964. The Civil Rights Act banned employment discrimination for most employers, and banned racial segregation in public facilities, including private businesses that serve the public such as restaurants, theaters, pool halls, hotels, and motels. In 1965, Congress passed the Voting Rights Act, which placed most of the South under federal supervision of its voting and elections laws. The Voting Rights Act banned tests or devices such as "literacy tests, educational requirements [or] good character tests" and other arbitrary actions by local registrars that promoted racial discrimination in voting. The act required covered states and districts to gain prior federal approval before implementing any changes in election laws or voting requirements. The act also banned racially discriminatory efforts to dilute black voting or political power, such as some "at large" schemes for drawing electoral districts to prevent black candidates from being elected. Finally, the Voting Rights Act allowed federal registrars to replace local registrars that continued discriminatory voting practices. The passage of the Twenty-fourth Amendment (1964) banning poll taxes lent further impetus to the drive to guarantee equal voting rights for blacks.

Overall, the Voting Rights Act was tremendously effective. In 1960, 61 percent of southern whites but only 29 percent of southern blacks were registered to vote. Racial discrimination in voting was much less rampant in Rim South states such as Tennessee and Kentucky than in the Deep South, especially Mississippi and Alabama. Although small racial disparities in voter registration and turnout remain as of 2007, differences in income and education account for most such disparities.

Politically, the civil rights movement generated shock waves that permeated southern and national politics. As political scientists Edward Carmines and James Stimson (1989) demonstrate, the civil rights movement triggered a polarization of the Democratic and Republican parties on racial issues, with Democrats moving leftward to embrace racially egalitarian policies and Republicans moving sharply rightward to oppose them. This process was already well under way during the 1964 presidential campaign. Abandoning the Republicans' historical moderation on racial issues, the 1964 Republican nominee, Senator Barry Goldwater of Arizona, openly opposed federal civil rights laws. Goldwater's position was not racist; he neither openly vilified blacks nor expressed support for negative racial stereotypes as southern segregationists had done for decades. Instead, Goldwater couched his concern in "states' rights" terms: In his view, civil rights policy was best decided by local and state governments, not the federal government. This was an enormously appealing position for white southerners, and Goldwater cracked the Democrats' monopoly on the South by winning five southern states. Goldwater's position was politically disastrous in the rest of the country, however, and President Lyndon Johnson won reelection by a landslide. After 1964, Republicans began openly pursuing a "southern strategy" of appealing to white southerners by opposing vigorous implementation of civil rights laws, embracing "law and order" campaign themes in the 1968 election, tying Democrats to unpopular groups such as Vietnam War protesters, hippies, black militants, and radical feminists, and using racially charged appeals on such issues as welfare, crime, and affirmative action to loosen white southerners' historical attachment to the Democratic Party. In 1968, Alabama governor George Wallace also ran for the presidency and won several southern states, embracing similar "law and order" and culturally conservative themes. Although he was a Democrat, Wallace's themes are often echoed in southern politics—but much more often by southern Republicans than southern Democrats.

"STATES' RIGHTS" APPEALS: ENDURING AND SELECTIVE

The states' rights appeal first introduced by Goldwater in national campaigns was nothing new in southern politics. Before 1964, southern Democrats had long declared allegiance to states' rights as a socially acceptable code for minimal federal intervention in race relations in the South—and therefore code for white supremacy. Most white southerners readily got the message. White southerners' disdain for the federal government was part and parcel of an ideology of selective minimalist government that extends to policy areas well outside race relations.

One such unmistakable impact is the region's tendency to favor a "low-tax, low-service" ethic: lower taxes, fewer government services, less regulation of business, and less government support for the disadvantaged. For example, according to the U.S. House of Representatives (2004), average 2002 monthly TANF (Temporary Assistance to Needy Families) benefits, which are set by state lawmakers, were lowest in the South. The average monthly TANF benefit was $327 nationwide; for the thirteen southern states, the average benefit was $202, and all six states with benefits less than $200 were southern states. The "low-tax, low-service" ethic also means less government regulation of business, for example, in protecting employees from workplace hazards and the environment from pollution. Southern state governors frequently encourage business executives with operations in the North to relocate to the South, touting the region's "favorable business climate": lower taxes and minimal regula-

tions on business coupled with right-to-work laws and other policies that discourage workers from joining labor unions.

The tradition of minimalist government in the South prevails on most economic and social welfare issues, but often not on social and moral issues. Southern lawmakers often prefer policies that *maximize* government activity in promoting "traditional values." Thus, gay-marriage bans have passed in twenty-seven of the twenty-eight states that have considered them, but in southern states they pass by wider margins, frequently with over 75 percent support—even 86 percent support in Mississippi (2004). Restrictive abortion laws, bans on gay adoption, and efforts to promote prayer in the public schools and Ten Commandments displays in public places are all more common in southern states. Southern elected officials' proclaimed fealty to "limited government," then, is selective. Also, conservative southern lawmakers eagerly embrace states' rights in response to liberal federal policies but not conservative federal policies. Few southern lawmakers objected to then-U.S. Attorney General John Ashcroft's effort to ensure that federal antidrug laws could overrule state laws allowing medicinal marijuana.

States' rights is a less potent symbol in southern politics than it was forty or more years ago, when it was widely understood as a desire to preserve white domination over blacks. On issues of federal versus state power, which side embraces states' rights is often predictable based on whether the federal or state government is advocating the more conservative policy.

RACIAL POLITICS IN THE SOUTH SINCE THE CIVIL RIGHTS ERA

Race remains a notable dividing line in southern politics. This is evident from examining four issues in modern southern politics and campaigns: racial appeals in campaigns (mostly covert racial appeals), Confederate flag controversies, racial redistricting, and the marked racial polarization of southern political parties.

Racial Appeals in Southern Campaigns While not limited to the South, racial appeals in southern campaigns appear with surprising regularity. Sometimes, racial appeals are less than subtle. North Carolina's Republican senator Jesse Helms was particularly famous for issuing racial appeals. In 1972, Helms, running for the U.S. Senate against a Greek American opponent, produced bumper stickers that read, "Jesse. He's one of us." In the 1984 Senate race against then-governor Jim Hunt, Helms complained about "the bloc vote," referring to North Carolina blacks, who almost universally viewed Helms as hostile to racial equality. Helms scarcely tried to burnish his image among blacks; he launched a long, eventually unsuccessful crusade against declaring a national holiday for Martin Luther King Jr. In 1990, Helms made his most famous racial appeal against Democrat and former Charlotte mayor Harvey Gantt, an African American. Late in the campaign, Gantt led Helms and appeared poised to win. The Helms campaign produced a commercial attacking Gantt on affirmative action, in which white hands were shown crumpling a job rejection letter as an announcer intoned, "You wanted that job, and you were the best qualified. But they had to give it to a minority because of a racial quota. Is that really fair?" The late Helms ad was widely credited with producing a pro-Helms surge, and Helms won reelection.

Racial appeals in southern campaigns are usually more subtle, and implicit racial issues (especially welfare) have figured prominently. In the 1991 Louisiana governor's race, Republican candidate David Duke, a former Ku Klux Klan leader, made campaign speeches to virtually all-white audiences attacking the "welfare underclass"—racial code for black welfare recipients. The same year, in Mississippi, Republican Kirk Fordice, then a political unknown, won the governor's race using an array of implicit racial appeals: opposing quotas, saying that welfare recipients should be forced to work, and attacking policies for coddling criminals. In his 2003 campaign for Mississippi's governorship, Republican Haley Barbour also raised the welfare issue (and wore Confederate-flag lapel pins on the campaign trail). Political scientists James Glaser (1996) and Tali Mendelberg (2001) provide substantial evidence of the use of implicit racial appeals, which seem particularly common in southern campaigns, where Republicans, in particular, are tempted to "play the race card" by making implicit racial appeals to white voters. Welfare, affirmative action, and crime are common issues that structure implicitly racial appeals. But as Glaser (1996) shows, others include attacking a candidate for "cozying up to" civil rights leaders such as Reverend Jesse Jackson or for not enthusiastically supporting the display of the Confederate flag.

In the 2006 U.S. Senate race in Tennessee, the Republican National Committee (RNC) sponsored a late television advertisement on behalf of Republican candidate Bob Corker against his Democratic opponent, Harold Ford Jr., who is black. The ad was widely criticized as a covert racial appeal on the issue of interracial dating and/or sex—which historically white southerners were obsessed with preventing. Between 1880 and 1950, many black men accused of dating or having sexual relations with white women were summarily lynched, in response to white assumptions that any sexual relations between white women and black men were nonconsensual, resulting from rape. The 2006 Republican ad showed a flirtatious white woman with bare shoulders and no visible other clothing, claiming "I met Harold at the Playboy

party!" The ad's conclusion showed her winking and cooing breathily, "Harold—call me!" Commenting on the Republican ad, political scientist John Geer, a leading analyst of attack advertising, said, "I've not met any observer who didn't immediately say, 'Oh my gosh! It was a race card.'" As documented by Associated Press reporter Beth Rucker (2006), Geer described the ad as "breaking new ground, and frankly, breaking new lows," and "mak[ing] the [1988] Willie Horton ad look like child's play. It is racist. That is the bottom line." Although RNC chairman Ken Mehlman denied the ad carried racial overtones, Geer and other analysts concluded otherwise. As Rucker notes, Hilary Shelton, an NAACP official, added, "In a Southern state like Tennessee, some stereotypes still exist. There's very clearly some racial subtext in an ad like that." Corker won the election, but it is unclear whether the RNC ad changed the outcome.

Confederate Flag Controversies Since 2000, three high-profile Confederate flag controversies have arisen, each over whether southern state governments should support displays of the Confederate battle flag ("stars and bars") or a state flag design containing it. For some southern whites, the Confederate flag is a symbol of heritage; for most blacks, it is a symbol of racial hatred and white domination. In Mississippi, a 2001 public referendum was held on whether to continue flying the 1894 state flag with a Confederate flag design. Voters approved keeping the Confederate flag design by a surprisingly high 65 percent to 35 percent margin. Not surprisingly, the vote was extremely racially polarized. In two 90 percent white counties, the vote ran 90 percent to 10 percent in favor of keeping the Confederate flag design. In two 80 percent black counties, the vote ran 83 percent to 17 percent in favor of replacing the Confederate design with a new one.

In Georgia in 2002, controversy over Democratic governor Roy Barnes's handling of the Confederate flag issue contributed to his upset loss to Republican Sonny Perdue in the governor's race. Confederate veterans' groups and some Republicans criticized Barnes for pushing changes to the design of Georgia's state flag to reduce the Confederate emblem's size. The Sons of Confederate Veterans and other groups argued Barnes should have put the question of redesigning the flag to a public referendum. Perdue's election put a Republican in the Georgia governor's office for the first time since Reconstruction.

In South Carolina, too, the flag issue proved electorally damaging to a Democratic governor, Jim Hodges. In 2000, Hodges approved removing the battle flag from atop the state capitol dome and moving it to a less conspicuous location on the capitol grounds. Some analysts viewed Hodges's action as contributing to his loss in South Carolina's 2002 governor's race to Republican Mark

Sanford. The Confederate flag issue, then, appears to offer a case study of the continuing importance of race in southern politics.

Racial Redistricting After the 1990 census, civil rights groups expressed concern over the underrepresentation of blacks in Congress and asked state lawmakers to redraw House districts to concentrate black voters in some mostly southern districts. The expectation was to create congressional districts with black majorities to elect more black members of Congress. In the history of congressional elections nationwide, very few majority-white districts have elected minority Congress members. After the 1990 census, some "majority-minority" districts were drawn in various southern states. Majority-minority districts are those in which a minority group (most commonly blacks) makes up a majority of the district's residents. By 1992, North Carolina, Georgia, and several other states had drawn some majority-minority districts, and these districts did elect black representatives. In 1992 in North Carolina, Melvin Watt and Eva Clayton became the first blacks elected to Congress since Reconstruction, in a state where 22 percent of the population was black. Although most majority-minority districts were intended to elect blacks, some Latino-majority districts were also drawn in Texas and Florida, both states with significant Latino populations.

Some of these racial redistricting efforts were challenged in a series of court cases. In 1996, the Supreme Court ordered the redrawing of North Carolina's majority-black First and Twelfth Districts, ruling that race was too predominant a factor, and geographical compactness an insufficiently considered factor, in drawing these districts. Melvin Watt's Twelfth District was redrawn with more compact boundaries, converting it from a majority-black district into a 47 percent black district. Watt retained his congressional seat in the redrawn district. Similarly, in Georgia, the district of Sanford Bishop, an African American, was redrawn to a 39 percent black district after another court challenge.

One impact of these and similar court challenges, then, has been to convert some previously majority-minority districts into "minority-opportunity" districts. In these, the minority group makes up less than a majority of the district's residents but enough to make it likely that a minority candidate or representative can win elections. As a general rule, in southern districts where blacks make up 45 percent or more of residents, a black candidate has a good chance to win. In districts where less than 30 percent of residents are black, a black candidate is unlikely to win. In southern districts, minority candidates or lawmakers (virtually all Democrats) are likely to win when they can combine (1) a sizable minority presence in the district—

40 percent or more is best; (2) high voter turnout from the minority group—best when minority turnout at least equals white turnout; (3) lopsided support from minority-group voters—preferably 85 percent or more; and (4) a significant share of the white vote—preferably 25 percent or more. Most white southerners identify as and vote Republican, and few minority candidates, being overwhelmingly Democrats, can expect to win more than 30 percent of the white vote.

Racial redistricting has had unintended but damaging consequences for southern Democrats. The drawing of districts to concentrate black voters has also pulled blacks out of neighboring districts, giving them larger white majorities. Since most southern whites vote Republican, these neighboring districts have more often elected Republican lawmakers. Racial redistricting, then, has resulted in the election of more Republicans and fewer Democrats to Congress from southern states. Political scientists estimate that racial redistricting has resulted in Democrats losing between seven and eleven U.S. House seats.

The impact on the numbers of southern Democratic lawmakers has not been symmetrical by race. As Earl Black (1998) shows, racial redistricting has resulted in increased representation of *black* Democrats but also sharply decreased representation of *white* Democrats holding southern congressional seats. It appears racial redistricting has contributed to sharp increases in the ranks of white Republicans holding southern U.S. House seats. Within and outside the South, the vast majority of blacks identify as Democrats and view Republicans negatively. Some southern Republicans, such as David Duke, Jesse Helms, and Trent Lott, have been openly hostile to black interests. While blacks celebrate the increases in black congressional representation that racial redistricting has produced, most also lament the loss of Democratic strength in southern congressional delegations—to which racial redistricting has also contributed.

Racial Polarization of Southern Political Parties In Congress, then, Earl Black (1998) identifies "the newest southern politics": Black Democrats have become more numerous, white Republicans have become much more numerous, and white Democrats have become much less numerous. Southern congressional delegations are increasingly polarized by race and party combined. Nowhere is this truer than in Texas. After Republicans captured the Texas legislature in the 2002 elections, they forced through a mid-decade redistricting in 2003. In January 2004, before the first election following the redistricting, Texas's U.S. House delegation consisted of sixteen Democrats and sixteen Republicans. After the 2004 election, the delegation consisted of eleven Democrats (one white, ten black or Latino) and twenty-one Republicans (twenty white, one Latino). The plan of maximizing Republican strength in Texas's U.S. House delegation had worked.

In 2006, the U.S. Supreme Court upheld the overall redistricting but overturned the drawing of some district boundaries because the Republican plan diluted Latino voting strength, in violation of the 1965 Voting Rights Act. A panel of judges redrew the boundaries to ensure a larger Latino majority in the district of the only Latino Republican, Henry Bonilla. The new district boundaries were in place for the 2006 elections, in which Bonilla lost his seat to Democrat Ciro Rodriguez, and a white Democrat, Nick Lampson, captured former House Majority Leader Tom DeLay's former seat near Houston (probably temporarily). As of 2007, racial polarization in Texas's U.S. House delegation remains nearly complete, with two white Democrats, ten black or Latino Democrats, and twenty white Republicans. In the future, both white Democrats face a strong risk of losing their seats, as they represent heavily Republican districts. Texas's U.S. House delegation may soon consist of an all-white Republican majority and an all-nonwhite Democratic minority.

In other southern states, a similar pattern holds. With few exceptions, Republican lawmakers are white (a few from Florida are Cuban American; former representative Bonilla is Mexican American; Oklahoma's former representative J. C. Watts is black). Democratic lawmakers are more racially diverse, with both white and black lawmakers and a contingent of Latino lawmakers from Texas. In state legislatures, too, Republicans are lopsidedly white while Democrats are more diverse.

In southern electorates, too, racial polarization has been striking. Especially in the Deep South, Republicans have become an overwhelmingly white party. Democrats are more racially diverse, now capturing only a minority of white votes but huge majorities (generally 85% or more) of black votes, and in Texas, sizable majorities of Latino votes. Although the degree of racial polarization of southern parties is striking, the reasons for it are not fully clear. Racial conflicts and attitudes appear to be a contributing factor in pulling southern whites out of the Democratic Party and into the Republican Party—but not the only factor. Other likely contributors include the marked social conservatism, assertive militarism, and preferences for smaller government on economic issues on which southern Republicans virtually unanimously agree. In other words, the Republican Party's attractiveness to southern whites is partly based on conservative ideology. Among southern Republicans as of 2007, politically moderate views are scarce and liberal views are nonexistent. Conversely, southern Democrats are ideologically more varied. Some (largely majority-minority) districts elect lib-eral lawmakers, but in more heavily white or conservative districts, Democrats can be moderate or even notably conservative.

As of 2007, race remains a significant factor structuring the southern party system. Political scientists Nicholas Valentino and David Sears (2005) studied the connection between white southerners' racial attitudes and Republican identification and voting. They found that racial antagonism remains higher among white southerners than white nonsoutherners, and that the association between racial antagonism and Republican voting is stronger among southern whites than nonsouthern whites. Furthermore, that association has grown stronger in recent years among southern whites, but not among nonsouthern whites. These and other findings indicate, then, that racial resentments continue to influence partisanship and voting among southern whites—to the benefit of the Republican Party.

THE CONTOURS OF MODERN SOUTHERN POLITICS

As of 2007, southern politics consists of two-party competition with highly racially polarized parties and a lopsided Republican advantage in federal elections. In state elections, Republicans dominate in some states (especially South Carolina, Georgia, Texas, and Florida), but other states, including Tennessee, Kentucky, Louisiana, and Virginia, show more partisan parity. As of 2007, Democrats have regained ground and even an edge over Republicans in North Carolina and Arkansas. Regionwide, an overwhelmingly white, and sharply and uniformly conservative, Republican Party contests elections against a racially and ideologically more diverse but generally moderate Democratic Party. The Republican Party has dominated the region in presidential elections since 1980 and in congressional elections since 1994. After the 2004 election, Democrats held only four (15%) of the region's twenty-six U.S. Senate seats and 36 percent of its House seats. The 2006 elections changed matters little; as of 2007, Democrats held 19 percent of the region's Senate seats and 40 percent of its House seats. In state elections, Democrats have become virtually irrelevant in Florida, Texas, Georgia, and South Carolina. However, Democrats have shown strength in state legislatures in Mississippi, Arkansas, North Carolina, and Alabama and won governor's races in North Carolina (2004) and Virginia (2005). In 2006, Democrats won a previously Republican-held U.S. Senate seat from Virginia and six previously Republican-held House seats in the region. However, these gains are modest, and some, especially in Texas, are probably temporary. As political scientists Philip Klinkner and Thomas Schaller (2006) demonstrate, Democratic gains in 2006 were concentrated *out-*

side the South—particularly in the Northeast and Midwest.

The 2006 elections, then, did little to change the major story of southern politics since the civil rights era: the growth of Republican support, virtually entirely among white southerners. Black and Black (1987) identified southern politics as consisting of vigorous two-party competition, with prospects for increasing Republican strength—a prediction that proved correct, as their 2002 follow-up study shows. The Republican trend among southern whites is traceable to several factors, including racial conflicts and resentments, religion and associated social conservatism, urban politics and population changes, "law and order" issues, and southern military traditions.

Racial Conflicts and Resentments As black lawmakers and activists have become more prominent among southern Democrats, it appears a racial backlash has pushed some southern whites out of the Democratic Party because of perceptions that Democrats advocate liberal policies on government social programs and are becoming too pro-black. Whites provide virtually all support for Confederate flag displays, but many southern Democratic officials fear offending blacks by supporting the flag. By emphasizing such issues as welfare and affirmative action, Republicans unmistakably have staked their claim as the home of racial conservatism, which many southern whites find appealing, partly for ideological reasons but, as Valentino and Sears's (2005) analysis indicates, partly out of continuing racial resentments as well.

Religion and Social Conservatism Like southern politics, southern religion is distinct. By numerous indicators, southerners are more religious than nonsoutherners are. Furthermore, southern religion has two major centers of gravity, according to political scientists John Green, James Guth, Lyman Kellstedt, and Corwin Smidt (2003). Among whites, they refer to the "white Protestant alliance"—especially Southern Baptist and other evangelical Christian traditions, which constitute the center of southern Republican politics. Among African Americans, black churches are an increasingly important source of support for the Democratic Party. The overall impact of these counteracting centers of political gravity is a decided conservative tilt. Southern Baptists are the largest Protestant denomination in the country, at 16.5 million members. Since 1979, the theologically fundamentalist, politically conservative faction has controlled the heavily white Southern Baptist Convention (SBC) without interruption. The SBC is a thoroughly conservative force in southern politics, and the moderate faction that contested SBC elections into the 1980s has abandoned the SBC.

Former U.S. president and lifelong Southern Baptist Jimmy Carter also renounced the SBC following its adoption of resolutions prohibiting women from serving as pastors and stipulating that wives should be "graciously submissive" to their husbands. The SBC's large numbers and lopsided Republican support easily outweigh the support that black churches can provide Democrats. Indeed, political scientist Oran Smith concluded his 1997 study *The Rise of Baptist Republicanism* by noting that the SBC and the Republican Party in the South have become virtually indistinguishable. Southern Republicans (and some Democrats), seeking political acceptance from Southern Baptists and other evangelicals, have strong incentives to take strongly conservative positions on social issues—opposing abortion, feminism, stem-cell research, pornography, gay rights, and perceived "secular humanist" influence in public life, and favoring school prayer, public Ten Commandments displays, traditional gender roles, and gay-marriage bans. Although southern religious traditions vary, the overall impact of religion in southern politics is a marked conservative (and therefore pro-Republican) influence, especially on social and moral issues, owing to the large number of Southern Baptists and other conservative Protestants in the region.

Urban Politics and Population Changes In the twentieth century, urbanization proceeded much more slowly in the South than elsewhere. But jobs and economic activity have shifted southward since World War II, and as of 2007, urban areas such as Dallas–Fort Worth, Atlanta, Charlotte, Nashville, and others are now thriving economic centers. These and similar areas have rapidly growing populations, including large numbers of migrants from nonsouthern states. These migrants were more willing to support the Republican Party than native-born white southerners were until the 1990s. In addition, those moving into southern cities were often upwardly mobile economically, making them more receptive to Republican appeals for lower taxes and less intrusive government, that is, the "low-tax, low-service" ethic. While many core cities, such as New Orleans, Richmond, Atlanta, and Memphis, have strongly Democratic black majorities, their fast-growing suburbs are heavily white and Republican. These population shifts have benefited the Republican Party, and southern "exurban" areas such as Union County, North Carolina, outside Charlotte, and suburban areas such as Cobb County, Georgia, outside Atlanta, are heavily Republican.

In some southern states, Latino populations are growing quickly. In Texas, Latinos (mostly Mexican American) make up 32 percent of the population. North Carolina and Georgia are also experiencing notable Latino immigration. Outside Florida, most Latinos migrating to southern states are Mexican American, and politically they lean Democratic. However, Latinos' political influence will probably lag behind their presence in the population because of language barriers for some and because some Latinos are not U.S. citizens, making them ineligible to vote. In Texas, Republican dominance rests on the heavily Republican tilt of the state's Anglo (white) population, and Democrats will probably climb back toward competitive status only as Latinos become more politically active and vote in greater numbers.

"Law and Order": Crime, Gun Control, and Related Issues Southerners, especially white southerners, have a pronounced conservative tilt on "law and order" issues, that is, approaches to fighting crime and drugs and punishing criminals. Most white southerners favor the death penalty, "three strikes" laws and other "get-tough" anti-crime measures, and corporal punishment in the schools, and regional policies reflect these realities. Southern states are by no means unique in allowing the death penalty; thirty-eight states, including all southern states, do. What *does* set the South apart is a greater willingness to convert death sentences to actual executions, and more numerous and frequent executions, as cultural psychologists Richard Nisbett and Dov Cohen (1996) show. Texas, in particular, far outstrips all other states in number of executions, with Virginia in second place. If Harris County, Texas (including Houston), were a state, it alone would rank third among the states in number of executions. The top four states in frequency of executions are Texas, Oklahoma, Virginia, and Florida, and southern states make up eight of the top ten states.

Southern states cluster near the top of all states in both the frequency of executions and the use of corporal punishment (spanking or paddling) to discipline school-children. Recent initiatives to extend the death penalty to multiple-offense child molesters are concentrated in southern states. Religion probably reinforces white southern support for the death penalty, corporal punishment, and other "get tough" measures. Southern Baptist and other conservative Protestant traditions typically favor literal interpretations of the Bible and endorse harsh punishment in the criminal justice system and corporal punishment in the schools, as biblically mandated. Literal interpretations of the Bible typically endorse "an eye for an eye" doctrine in criminal justice and a "spare the rod, spoil the child" doctrine in disciplining children. Popular support for state violence and aggression is a natural by-product of these realities.

On gun control, southerners more often oppose stricter gun control laws and support their relaxation. Nisbett and Cohen (1996) attribute greater southern opposition to gun control to the region's "culture of honor," which values "standing one's ground" against an attack on one's person or property, even if that results in killing the attacker. Southern laws on killing in self-defense are thus more lenient in southern than nonsouthern states, and southern gun control laws are more lenient.

Nationwide, Republican officials and candidates more often support the death penalty, the "war on drugs," mandatory-minimum sentencing, and other "get tough" measures on crime policy than their Democratic counterparts do. Likewise, opposition to gun control is concentrated in the Republican Party. As such, white southerners, who constitute the center of southern conservatism, find these positions attractive, and this probably exercises a pro-Republican pull in partisan identification and voting.

Southern Military Traditions Most historians agree that southern states are home to unusually robust military traditions, reflected in southerners' greater support for wars and willingness to fight in them. As Texas-born observer Michael Lind (2004) notes, military recruitment comes disproportionately from southern states, and southerners have been more willing to support and fight in U.S. wars overseas, including the Vietnam War, the 1991 Persian Gulf War, and the Iraq war that began in 2003. Military bases are more frequently found in southern states than elsewhere, and regional military traditions are reinforced by military academies for boys as young as ten years old. Even titles of historical studies reflect southern military traditions—for example, John Hope Franklin's *The Militant South* (2002) and John Temple Graves's *The Fighting South* (1985).

Politically, the South's militaristic bent probably strengthens Republican support, as Republicans, lacking the significant contingent of peace activists that Democrats have, tend to favor more aggressive actions overseas. As Nisbett and Cohen (1996) show, the white southern "culture of honor" reinforces strong support for defense spending and military actions overseas, as well as the use of force and violence generally (i.e., the death penalty and corporal punishment).

SOUTHERN POLITICS: CAMPAIGNS, CONTINUITY, AND CHANGE

Overall, southern politics has evolved from one-party Democratic rule to two-party competition, with a Republican advantage in federal elections and some states, but competitive party politics in other states. The movement of large numbers of white southerners from the Democratic Party into the Republican Party is the overriding story of southern politics in the twenty-first century. Equally clearly, in the South, the philosophical descendants of southern Democrats before 1960 have clearly found a new political home—not in the Democratic Party but in the Republican Party. In modern southern politics,

Republican candidates typically emphasize staunchly conservative positions on national defense, social and moral, economic, racial, and "law and order" issues—a strategy designed to gain lopsided majorities among whites. Democratic candidates walk a tightrope between emphasizing such economic issues as raising the minimum wage and opposing tax cuts (popular among blacks), while at the same time dodging charges of being "liberal" (an unpopular label among whites, especially on social and moral issues). Democrats must capture a sizable share of white votes to win, but Republicans typically write off (and sometimes try to suppress) black votes. Thus, in southern politics, as of 2007, the central social cleavage remains race. That said, southern politics evidences elements of continuity with the past, as well as significant changes. The future nature and evolution of these changes will have major implications for the course of U.S. national politics.

SEE ALSO *African Americans; Appalachia; Civil Rights Movement, U.S.; Confederate States of America; Desegregation, School; Dixiecrats; Jim Crow; Key, V. O., Jr.; Ku Klux Klan; Law and Order; Militarism; Patriotism; Politics, Black; Protest; Race; Racism; Reconstruction Era (U.S.); Secession; Segregation; Slavery; Southern Strategy; Supreme Court, U.S.; Terrorism; Voting Patterns; White Supremacy; Whiteness*

BIBLIOGRAPHY

Applebome, Peter. 1997. *Dixie Rising: How the South Is Shaping American Values, Politics and Culture.* San Diego, CA: Harcourt Brace.

Bartley, Numan V., and Hugh D. Graham. 1975. *Southern Politics and the Second Reconstruction.* Baltimore, MD: Johns Hopkins University Press.

Black, Earl. 1998. The Newest Southern Politics. *Journal of Politics* 60 (3): 591–612.

Black, Merle, and Earl Black. 1987. *Politics and Society in the South.* Cambridge, MA: Harvard University Press.

Black, Merle, and Earl Black. 2002. *The Rise of Southern Republicans.* Cambridge, MA: Harvard University Press.

Carmines, Edward G., and James A. Stimson. 1989. *Issue Evolution: Race and the Transformation of American Politics.* Princeton, NJ: Princeton University Press.

Franklin, John Hope. 2002. *The Militant South: 1800–1861.* Urbana: University of Illinois Press.

Glaser, James. 1996. *Race, Campaign Politics, and the Realignment in the South.* New Haven, CT: Yale University Press.

Glaser, James. 2005. *The Hand of the Past in Contemporary Southern Politics.* New Haven, CT: Yale University Press.

Goldfield, David R. 2002. *Still Fighting the Civil War: The American South and Southern History.* Baton Rouge: Louisiana State University Press.

Graves, John Temple. 1985. *The Fighting South.* Tuscaloosa: University of Alabama Press.

Green, John C., James Guth, Lyman Kellstedt, and Corwin Smidt. 2003. The Soul of the South: Religion and Southern Politics at the Millennium. In *The New Politics of the Old South: An Introduction to Southern Politics*, 2nd ed., ed. Charles Bullock III and Mark Rozell, 283–298. Lanham, MD: Rowman and Littlefield.

Key, V. O., Jr. 1984. *Southern Politics in State and Nation.* Rev. ed. Knoxville: University of Tennessee Press. (Orig. pub. 1949.)

Klinkner, Philip A., and Thomas F. Schaller. 2006. A Regional Analysis of the 2006 Midterms. *The Forum* 4 (3). Berkeley, CA: The Berkeley Electronic Press. http://www.bepress.com/forum/vol4/iss3/art9.

Lind, Michael. 2004. Bush's Martyrs. *The New Statesman* (UK), March 1, 2004. http://www.newamerica.net/publications/articles/2004/bushs_martyrs.

Mendelberg, Tali. 2001. *The Race Card: Campaign Strategy, Implicit Messages, and the Norm of Equality.* Princeton, NJ: Princeton University Press.

Nisbett, Richard, and Dov Cohen. 1996. *Culture of Honor: The Psychology of Violence in the South.* Boulder, CO: Westview.

Rucker, Beth. "Harold, Call Me" Ad Called Race Card. 2006. http://www.commongroundcommonsense.org/forums/index.php?showtopic=65687.

Smith, Oran P. 1997. *The Rise of Baptist Republicanism.* New York: New York University Press.

U.S. House of Representatives. 2004. Background Material and Data on the Programs within the Jurisdiction of the Committee on Ways and Means (also known as "The Green Book"). Section 7, pp. 36–37. http://waysandmeans.house.gov/media/pdf/greenbook2003/Section7.pdf.

Valentino, Nicholas A., and David O. Sears. 2005. Old Times There Are Not Forgotten: Race and Partisan Realignment in the Contemporary South. *American Journal of Political Science* 49 (3): 672–688.

Fred Slocum

POLITICS, URBAN

Urban politics draws upon many academic disciplines, particularly sociology, history, public policy, economics, demography, political science, urban planning, and public administration. The multidisciplinary nature of urban politics fosters both innovation and confusion, for there are many suggested definitions for the term. Intellectual differences aside, it is useful to characterize urban politics as the study of the institutions within and the governance of cities, suburbs, and other metropolitan areas. This article focuses on the study of urban institutions and governance in the United States.

As a field of study, urban politics is primarily concerned with urban political power. Specifically, urban scholars seek to define what urban power is, uncover who holds power in urban areas, and, more importantly, determine whether such power relationships are consonant with the ideals of American democracy. There are several theoretical approaches to studying urban power, the major tenets of which are summarized below.

ELITE THEORY OF URBAN POLITICS

Perhaps the earliest theory of urban politics is elite, or stratification theory. The elite theory of urban politics is an intellectual movement developed in the philosophies of noted political scientists and sociologists Gaetano Mosca (1858–1941), Vilfredo Pareto, Robert Michels, and Floyd Hunter, but commonly identified with C. Wright Mills and his influential book *The Power Elite* (1956). Elite theorists maintain that a few top leaders make the key decisions with little regard for popular desires. This occurs because urban areas divide naturally into distinct political classes. At the top level are the elites, most of whom are the business and financial leaders assumed to play a commanding role in urban governance. Underneath the elites is the middle class composed of the elected officials (mayors, councilmen, and the like) charged with the day-to-day

operations of the city. At the bottom level are the masses, the common citizens who have limited input and influence over their government. In defense of these social divisions, elite theorists argue that elite rule is a natural consequence of democracy and a safeguard against mob rule. A major critique against the elite theory of urban politics is that it paints a negative picture of urban democracy, for policies are made independently of public opinions, elections are perfunctory, elites are ultimately self-interested, and corruption in government is inevitable.

PLURALIST THEORY

In response to the criticisms of elite theory came the pluralist, or interest group, approach to urban politics, a scholarly tradition influenced heavily by the works of Robert Dahl, Charles Lindblom, and David Truman. Rejecting the idea that democracy is a sham, pluralists argue instead that urban governments are open and democratic, that citizens have free will, and that elections are the ultimate guarantee of democracy. Once the dominant paradigm of urban power, pluralists argue that societies consist of numerous institutions and organizations, each having diverse cultural, religious, economic, racial, and ethnic interests. Political resources divide among these different groups, and policies are made by group conflict and collective bargaining. Such group competition allows dif-

Summary of theories of urban politics

	Elite theory	Pluralist theory	Regime theory
What is power?	Resources = Power	Resources ≠ Power (power is fluid, mobile, diffuse)	Power = Multilevel Process
Who has power?	Few elites (Economic Notables)	Many elites (Interest groups)	Regimes (governmental and nongovernmental alliances)
How is power studied?	Look at reputations	Look at decisions, not reputations	Look at cooperation across institutions
Most important political division(s) in society	Elites who have the power, and the masses who do not	Multiple, competing groups that make demands on government	Leaders distinguish between their governing and electoral coalitions
Structure of power	Concentrated among a relatively small set of decision makers	Dispersed among multiple leadership groups	Varies by members of coalition
Interaction among leaders	Consensus about values and goals for society and means of achieving them	Conflict and competition over values and goals as well as means of achieving them	Strategic dependence between groups with different goals
Sources of leadership	Common backgrounds and experiences in control of institutional resources	Diversity in backgrounds and experiences and activism in organizations	Relationship between different groups pursuing shared agendas
Major institutions of power	Private organizations as well as government	Government institutions and organizations	Formal or informal institutions and organizations
Primary direction of political influence	Downward, from elites to masses	Upward, from masses to elites	Sideways across coalitions (regimes)
View of public policy	Policy benefits reflect elite preferences	Policy benefits reflect the balance of competing interest groups	Emphasizes the production rather than distribution of policy benefits
How democratic values are protected	Elite commit themselves to ensuring civic well-being	The negotiation of diverse interests ultimately benefits the common good	Through coordination, networking, and establishing relations

Table 1

ferent interests the chance to influence the outcomes of government, which ultimately furthers urban democracy. While it is an improvement over elite theory, some common critiques against pluralism are that it underestimates the strength of elites and fails to account for the interests of individuals who are systematically excluded from the political process (for example the poor, racial/ethnic minorities, and so on).

REGIME (OR COALITION) THEORY

An increasingly popular theoretical perspective is the regime (or coalition) theory of urban politics. Borrowing from the intuitions gained from the literature on foreign policy, regime theorists suggest that urban power is indirect and informal and realized through coalitions (regimes) between government and nongovernment partners. One of the more widely cited books in regime theory is Clarence N. Stone's *Regime Politics: Governing Atlanta, 1946–1988* (1989). Regime theorists contend that understanding urban governance requires examining the composition of political coalitions and the manner in which members of these coalitions are accommodated. A recurring argument among regime theorists is that power is a "social production," something that occurs when different interests unite to achieve common purposes. Decision-makers have relative autonomy, but they have to create a "capacity" to govern to be successful. To do so, leaders need to combine forces with private agencies to induce cooperation among people with access to institutional resources. Despite its widespread appeal, regime theory has its share of critics. A common argument against regime theory is that it does not adequately explain why regimes form, how they maintain themselves, or why they change.

Much of the research on American political power focuses on national trends. This is unfortunate because large-scale analyses depend on the insight gained from state, local, and municipal-level research. To borrow the phrasing of former Speaker of the House, Thomas "Tip" O'Neill (1912–1994), the study of urban politics reminds social scientists that "all politics is local."

SEE ALSO *Cities; Community Power Studies; Dahl, Robert Alan; Economics, Urban; Elite Theory; Gentrification; Hunter, Floyd; Metropolis; Mills, C. Wright; Planning; Pluralism; Political Science; Politics; Power Elite; Public Administration; Public Opinion; Public Policy; Towns; Urban Sprawl; Urban Studies; Urbanization*

BIBLIOGRAPHY

Dahl, Robert A. 1958. A Critique of the Ruling Elite Model. *American Political Science Review* 52: 463–469.

Dahl, Robert A. 1961. *Who Governs?: Democracy and Power in an American City.* New Haven, CT: Yale University Press.

Dahl, Robert A. 1971. *Polyarchy: Participation and Opposition.* New Haven, CT: Yale University Press.

Dahl, Robert A., and Charles E. Lindblom. 1976. *Politics, Economics, and Welfare: Planning and Politico-Economic Systems Resolved into Basic Social Processes.* Chicago: University of Chicago Press.

Hunter, Floyd. 1953. *Community Power Structure: A Study of Decision Makers.* Chapel Hill: University of North Carolina Press.

Judd, Dennis R., and Paul Kantor, eds. 2001. *The Politics of Urban America: A Reader.* 3rd ed. New York: Pearson Longman.

Judd, Dennis, and Todd Swanstrom. 2004. *City Politics: Private Power and Public Policy.* 4th ed. New York: Pearson Longman.

Lindblom, Charles E. 1977. *Politics and Markets: The World's Political Economic Systems.* New York: Basic Books.

Lindblom, Charles E. 1982. Another State of Mind. *American Political Science Review* 76 (1): 9–21.

Michels, Robert. 1915. *Political Parties: A Sociological Study of the Oligarchical Tendencies of Modern Democracy.* Trans. Eden and Cedar Paul. New York: Hearst's International Library.

Mills, C. Wright. 1956. *The Power Elite.* London: Oxford University Press.

Mosca, Gaetano. 1939. *The Ruling Class.* Trans. Hannah D. Kahn. New York: McGraw-Hill.

Pareto, Vilfredo. 1971. *Manual of Political Economy.* Ed. Ann S. Schwier and Alfred N. Page. Trans. Ann Schwier. New York: Kelley.

Stone, Clarence N. 1989. *Regime Politics: Governing Atlanta, 1946-1988.* Lawrence: University Press of Kansas.

Truman, David B. 1951. *The Governmental Process: Political Interests and Public Opinion.* New York: Knopf.

Ray Block Jr.

POLITICS, WOMEN AND
SEE *Women and Politics.*

POLL, EXIT
SEE *Exit Poll.*

POLL TAX

Poll taxes, also known as head taxes, soul taxes, or capitation taxes, are taxes that are levied upon individuals, rather than on income or property. Economists are divided over the efficacy of the poll tax. Some economists argue that the poll tax is a regressive tax, while others argue it is an effective mechanism for ensuring that public expenditures more closely reflect public demand. Although poll taxes are technically revenue measures, their enactment can have political implications.

Poll taxes have been part of recorded human history with Ptolemaic Egypt leaving the first records of these taxes. The poll tax has been used intermittently in European countries such as Britain, Prussia, and Russia since the Middle Ages. It was also used in some areas of the Ottoman Empire. Some European countries such as Britain and France also imposed poll taxes (also known as hut taxes) on their colonies in Africa and Asia.

In the United States poll taxes date back to its colonial era. In some jurisdictions poll taxes were linked to suffrage, while in other jurisdictions the poll tax was simply another form of revenue. In the post–Civil War era, the poll tax emerged as one of the techniques used by southern whites to disenfranchise African Americans. Along with other disenfranchising techniques, the poll tax was designed to be an instrument that could evade the reach of the Fifteenth Amendment (stating that no state may deny or abridge the right of citizens to vote on account of race, color, or previous condition of servitude; citizens may not be prevented from voting due to race) and any other federal intervention. In order to be eligible to vote, an individual had to pay a poll tax. In some cases the poll tax had to be paid almost a year in advance of the election, and in other cases the tax had to be paid for a certain period of years. In the aftermath of the political upheaval of populism (a social movement of southern and western farmers and workers) in the late 1890s, the poll tax also became a device used by the southern political elite to decrease the influence of poor whites on southern politics. By 1908, all of the southern states had enacted a poll tax. By the 1930s, as a result of the poll tax, it was estimated that white electoral participation dropped to less than a third of the total voting age population.

The administration of poll taxes varied across the states. Some states added the bill automatically to other tax bills, while other states required individuals to make a separate payment. Some states required annual payments, while others also included cumulative charges as well. These back taxes, coupled with the low cash income of many southerners, made voting an expensive proposition, thereby further depressing voter registration. Varied enforcement or non-enforcement of poll tax payments and the varied provisions across the states made the impact of poll taxes on a particular state's rate of electoral participation hard to calculate. A number of states included exemptions based on age or veteran status. What was easier to calculate was the fiscal impact of poll taxes. Although supporters of the poll tax claimed that the taxes

provided an important revenue source for local school systems, most analyses showed that only a minute fraction of school funds derived from poll tax revenues.

Although most African American leaders opposed the poll tax, leaders and organizations such as the National Association for the Advancement of Colored People (NAACP), for example, did not actively pursue poll tax reform until the 1930s. In addition to African Americans, southern women activists increasingly viewed the poll tax as a gender and class issue that undercut the promise of the Nineteenth Amendment (guaranteeing all American women the right to vote). Given the overall low incomes of white families, gender roles ensured that if a choice had to be made between paying the poll tax to ensure the right of a male to vote versus a female, the male's right to vote would invariably win out. V. O. Key Jr. (1908–1963) and his student Frederic Ogden were two of the first political scientists to systematically study the effect of the poll tax on electoral participation in the late 1940s and early 1950s. The political scientists' conclusion that the poll tax affected more whites than blacks was weakened as they did not consider the cumulative effects of the poll tax and other disenfranchising techniques on African Americans, nor did they consider the effects of this tax on the electoral participation of women.

By the late 1930s, with the support of President Franklin D. Roosevelt (1882–1945) and First Lady Eleanor Roosevelt (1884–1962), a variety of groups such as the Southern Conference on Human Welfare, the American Civil Liberties Union, and the NAACP, allied with two newly formed organizations, the National Committee to Abolish the Poll Tax and the Southern Electoral Reform League, to press for congressional enactment of a poll-tax bill. As a result of this mobilization as well as other developments, the poll tax emerged as an important national civil rights issue in the pre-*Brown v. Board of Education* (1954) era. By the end of the 1940s, the House of Representatives would ultimately pass five anti–poll tax bills, which in turn were repeatedly filibustered in the Senate by southern Democrats.

Concurrent with legislative attempts to attack the poll tax, opponents of the tax also turned to the courts where they encountered little encouragement. For example, in 1937 the Supreme Court indicated in *Breedlove v. Suttles* 302 U.S. 277 that it was not willing to see the poll tax as a suffrage test. Another important case was decided in 1941. *Pirtle v. Brown* (118 F.2d 218 [1941]) affirmed the right of states to set voter qualifications.

Despite these setbacks at the congressional and judicial level, poll tax reform achieved some success at the state level. By 1953 six out of the eleven southern states had abolished the poll tax. North Carolina abolished the tax in 1920; Louisiana in 1934; Florida in 1937; Georgia in 1947; Tennessee in 1951, and South Carolina in 1952. Of the remaining five states, two states (Alabama and Arkansas) reformed their poll taxes by decreasing the cumulative feature and the amount of the tax, and three states (Mississippi, Texas, and Virginia) failed in their attempts to repeal or amend the tax.

Nevertheless, as the civil rights movement unfolded the poll tax became less of an immediate issue. Its applicability to federal elections was prohibited in 1964 with the ratification of the Twenty-fourth Amendment, which stated: "The right of citizens of the United States to vote in any primary or other election for President or Vice President, for electors for President or Vice President, or for Senators or Representative in Congress, shall not be denied or abridged by the United States or any State by reason of failure to pay any poll tax or other tax." Despite this amendment, some states still tried to use poll taxes. A later court case, *Harper v. Virginia Board of Elections* 383 U.S. 663 (1966) extended the reach of the Twenty-fourth Amendment to state elections.

In Europe, Great Britain had enacted short-lived poll taxes in 1379 and in 1641. More recently, the British government during the administration of Prime Minister Margaret Thatcher (b. 1925) tried to enact a poll tax in 1990 as a means of controlling local government expenditures. Although initially successfully implemented in Scotland in 1989, the administration's attempt to enact a poll tax in England was met with stiff resistance by a broad range of groups. This resistance ultimately culminated in protests and riots in March 1990. The poll tax riots, as well as other factors, led to the end of the Thatcher administration. Despite the resistance, the poll tax survived under slightly different form as the Community Charge or Council Tax.

SEE ALSO *Civil Rights Movement, U.S.; Key, V. O., Jr.; Left Wing; National Association for the Advancement of Colored People (NAACP); Politics, Southern; Roosevelt, Franklin D.; Suffrage, Women's; Taxes; Thatcher, Margaret; Voting; Women and Politics*

BIBLIOGRAPHY

Key, V. O., Jr., with Alexander Heard. 1949. *Southern Politics in State and Nation.* New York: Knopf.

Kousser, J. Morgan. 1974. *The Shaping of Southern Politics: Suffrage Restriction and the Establishment of the One-Party South, 1880–1910.* New Haven, CT: Yale University Press.

Odgen, Frederic D. 1958. *The Poll Tax in the South.* Tuscaloosa, AL: University of Alabama Press

Woodard, C. Vann. 1951. *Origins of the New South, 1877–1913.* Baton Rouge: Louisiana State University.

Kimberley Johnson

POLL TAX (BRITAIN)

SEE *Thatcher, Margaret.*

POLLING

Polling involves gathering information by asking people to report their beliefs, attitudes, and behaviors. First, it is one of the most widely used techniques in social science research, of particular interest to political scientists, who use surveys such as the University of Michigan's American National Election Studies to analyze relationships between political attitudes and other attitudes, voting behavior, and participation. Second, polling has numerous applications in business through market research studies to assess customer satisfaction, identify new markets, and identify new prospective customers. Third, polling is applied in campaign politics. Party and campaign organizations frequently use tracking polls to identify candidates' standing, strengths, and weaknesses during campaigns. Fourth, polling is used in policy analysis and program evaluation. Nonprofit organizations and local, state, and national governments are often interested in their clients' opinions of their services and programs—this information is useful in program assessment and evaluation. The political scientists Barbara Bardes and Robert Oldendick (2007) provide an especially extensive discussion on the uses of opinion polls. Throughout this entry, the terms *poll* and *survey* are used interchangeably.

THE DEVELOPMENT OF SCIENTIFIC POLLING TECHNIQUES

During the twentieth century polling techniques became much more scientific, spurred in part by failed efforts by pollsters to predict presidential election results in 1936 and 1948. As noted by the political scientists Robert Erikson and Kent Tedin (2005), in 1936 a straw poll from *Literary Digest* magazine predicted that Republican candidate Alf Landon (1887–1987) would defeat Democratic president Franklin D. Roosevelt (1882–1945). The poll was off by nearly 20 percentage points, as Roosevelt won handily. Responses to this survey heavily overrepresented the wealthiest (and heavily Republican) groups of Americans. Respondents were drawn from automobile registration lists and telephone directories, but during the Great Depression, most automobile and telephone owners were wealthy. In 1948 preelection polls predicted that Republican candidate Thomas Dewey (1902–1971) would defeat Democratic president Harry S. Truman (1884–1972). However, this poll also relied on flawed sampling that overrepresented the better-off. As a result the 1948 poll overrepresented Republicans. Chastened by these polling mistakes and seeking to avoid future ones, pollsters were spurred to develop scientific polling methods.

ELEMENTS OF SCIENTIFIC POLLING

Scientific polls have several major characteristics that distinguish them from nonscientific surveys. First and foremost, scientific polls use samples of respondents that mirror the larger population under study. In a large, diverse nation like the United States, interviewing all American adults in a survey is impractical and impossible owing to prohibitive costs, resource constraints, and time limits. Thus pollsters rely on adult samples, selected randomly, such that all individuals have an equal chance of being included in the sample. This random sampling process usually yields a sample that closely reflects the characteristics of the larger population—that is, the sample is representative of the larger population. Statistically samples are most likely to be representative when random sampling methods are used and sample size—that is, the number of completed surveys—approaches or exceeds one thousand, with larger sample sizes producing better results.

Second, scientific polls use survey questions that are carefully constructed, clear and nonconfusing, and free of biased or "leading" language. Confusing language can sometimes produce major polling surprises. A 1993 Gallup Poll sponsored by the U.S. Holocaust Memorial Museum in Washington, D.C., revealed that 22 percent of Americans either were unsure of or doubted the Nazi extermination of the Jews during the Holocaust. This stunning finding was soon called into question, however. Close examination of the poll questions revealed a confusing double negative in the survey question. Follow-up polling using a revised question showed more comforting results: Only 1 percent of Americans actively doubted the Holocaust had happened, with an additional 8 percent unsure. The sociologists Howard Schuman and Stanley Presser ([1981] 1996) offer extensive evidence of the impact of question wording on survey results. Their and others' research shows that tone of wording, question ordering, question context (or lack thereof), and differences in response formats (i.e., a three-point scale versus a seven-point scale) all can significantly affect survey responses. How a question is asked, then, definitely shapes the answers received.

A third element of scientific polling is accurate and thorough reporting of results. Scientific surveys include a statement of how the poll was conducted and what the limitations of the survey are. Such a disclosure statement should include how many completed surveys there are; interviewing techniques used (in-person, telephone, or mail questionnaires); how respondents were selected (ran-

dom sampling is best); the survey's margin of error and confidence level, two numbers indicating how well results will likely extend to the general population; any additional survey techniques, such as weighting of respondents, use of variations in question wording, or interviewer characteristics; and limitations of the survey. Above all else, scientific polling means that the pollster seeks to accurately measure attitudes, opinions, and behaviors, not influence them.

Some surveys are not scientific, for varying reasons. Some news media, such as MSNBC, have Web sites where viewers can answer an online survey. These are not scientific surveys as they lack the key ingredient of random sampling. Scientific polls do not allow people to self select into completing the survey. Similarly mail-in surveys found in some magazines and call-in polls used on some television shows are unscientific. Other "surveys" sponsored by political parties, campaigns, and interest groups are unscientific because they frequently use "loaded" questions that (usually not subtly) encourage some responses over others. At best these qualify as "pseudo-polls" because their objective is not to accurately measure opinion but to arouse support for the sponsoring party or group or anger at political opponents. A 1993 *TV Guide* survey sponsored by Ross Perot contained clearly loaded questions, including "Should laws be passed to eliminate all possibilities of special interests giving huge sums of money to candidates?" Such loaded questions provide virtually no meaningful information, but they do provide examples of how some surveys fall well short of scientific standards for measuring public opinion.

POLLING IS NOT PERFECT: THE PROBLEM OF SELF-CENSORSHIP

An additional limitation of polling is that some respondents face questions they prefer not to answer, resulting in self-censorship, which can take several forms. Someone contacted by a pollster may refuse to answer some questions, refuse the entire survey, or give insincere answers. Insincere responses are especially likely on sensitive subjects, such as past drug use, sexual activity, or racial attitudes, where some respondents answer falsely to give more "socially desirable" responses. The sociologist Eduardo Bonilla-Silva (2006) studied white Americans' discourse on racial issues and found a prevalent "color blind racism" in which many whites deny holding racist attitudes, contending that racism is "a thing of the past" and that race does not impact their attitudes and behaviors. This phenomenon perpetuates white dominance by denying continuing racial discrimination, revealing negative racial stereotypes, such as attitudes that minorities (especially blacks) tend to be lazy, violent, and lacking in self-restraint and attributing racial-group differences in income, housing, education, crime, and other areas to individual choices or market forces that have nothing to do with race. The political scientist Martin Gilens (1999) found that white Americans' opposition to welfare is frequently driven by racial stereotypes that welfare recipients are usually black and that blacks are often lazy and shiftless, preferring to collect handouts rather than work.

The political scientists Jon Hurwitz and Mark Peffley (1997) found that white attitudes favoring punitive anticrime policies are often driven by stereotypes of blacks as violent and disposed to criminal acts. Similarly the political scientists Joe Soss, Laura Langbein, and Alan Metelko (2003) studied white Americans' attitudes toward the death penalty. They found that racial prejudices were by far the single strongest explanation for whites' death penalty attitudes, especially in areas where blacks comprise a larger share of the population. In all these cases, white attitudes on issues that appear non-race-related on the surface are suffused with racial stereotypes. But few whites in the early twenty-first century would admit they hold negative racial attitudes ("I'm not racist") or that those attitudes influence policy preferences. Social scientists must often use creative methods, such as unobtrusive survey questions on racial attitudes or experiments that vary question wording within surveys, to demonstrate the racial components underlying these attitudes.

THE IMPORTANCE OF POLLING IN POLITICAL SCIENCE RESEARCH

Polling has a central place in political science research. Academic survey research centers exist at major universities, such as the University of Chicago, the University of Michigan, and the University of California at Berkeley; these frequently sponsor nationwide scientific surveys. More survey research centers conduct further polling in many states. Collectively the polling conducted by these centers yields invaluable data for political scientists. For example, a researcher wishing to examine how racial stereotypes or beliefs in biblical inerrancy impact voting can use data from the University of Michigan's American National Election Studies, which measure these and many other social science variables. Statewide surveys, such as the Arkansas Poll sponsored by the University of Arkansas, or regional surveys, such as the Southern Focus Poll sponsored by the University of North Carolina at Chapel Hill, provide more data that political scientists find useful in researching attitudes in a state or region of the country. Although polling outside the United States presents many additional challenges, there is increasing demand for cross-national polling data, including that from Middle Eastern, Asian, and African nations. The World Values Survey, sponsored by multiple universities worldwide, has provided polling data from more than eighty nations since

1981. These data are opening new avenues for political scientists to better understand public opinion not just in the United States but worldwide.

SEE ALSO *Attitudes; Attitudes, Political; Attitudes, Racial; Elections; Hypothesis and Hypothesis Testing; Polls, Opinion; Psychometrics; Public Opinion; Survey; Surveys, Sample; Voting*

BIBLIOGRAPHY

Bardes, Barbara A., and Robert W. Oldendick. 2007. *Public Opinion: Measuring the American Mind.* 3rd ed. Belmont, CA: Thomson Wadsworth.

Bonilla-Silva, Eduardo. 2006. *Racism without Racists: Color-Blind Racism and the Persistence of Racial Inequality in the United States.* 2nd ed. Lanham, MD: Rowman and Littlefield.

Erikson, Robert S., and Kent L. Tedin. 2005. *American Public Opinion: Its Origins, Content, and Impact.* 7th ed. New York: Pearson Longman.

Gilens, Martin. 1999. *Why Americans Hate Welfare: Race, Media, and the Politics of Antipoverty Policy.* Chicago: University of Chicago Press.

Hurwitz, Jon, and Mark Peffley. 1997. Public Perceptions of Race and Crime: The Role of Racial Stereotypes. *American Journal of Political Science* 41 (2): 375–401.

Schuman, Howard, and Stanley Presser. [1981] 1996. *Questions and Answers in Attitude Surveys.* Thousand Oaks, CA: Sage.

Soss, Joe, Laura Langbein, and Alan R. Metelko. 2003. Why Do White Americans Support the Death Penalty? *Journal of Politics* 65 (2): 397–421.

Fred Slocum

POLLS, OPINION

Opinion polling is a method of analysis for drawing inferences about the attitudes or behaviors of a population by studying a random sample of persons from that population. Nonrandom surveys are sometimes used by social scientists for theory building, but only random samples can produce valid estimates of population traits. Since social scientists are typically interested in population traits, and since few other methods are as useful for studying population traits at the level of individuals, opinion polling with random samples has become one of the most common methods of data collection in the social sciences. Space does not allow a full treatment of this topic internationally and across the social sciences, but detailing the early adoption and continued use of opinion polls for political science research in the United States provides a useful introduction to the reasons why opinion polling remains such an important tool for the social sciences.

OPINION POLLS IN POLITICAL SCIENCE

Political scientists have long studied elections and public opinion, but before the 1940s they tended to emphasize how elections and public opinion should work in theory more than how they actually did work in practice. In part this emphasis reflected the scholarly paradigm of this period, which saw the core questions of democratic politics residing in the institutions, processes, and outcomes of political systems more than in the ways ordinary citizens made sense of them. But this emphasis was also encouraged by limitations in early methods of social analysis, which often forced scholars to speculate about factors influencing election outcomes because they lacked systematic evidence for studying many questions of interest. During this period, the best forms of voting data available to political scientists were aggregate election results that could be compared across voting districts or geographic areas, but such data had little to say about the reasons why individuals decided to participate in elections or why they supported particular candidates.

The development of random sampling surveys in the 1930s had a lasting impact on the ways that political scientists studied elections and public opinion. Nonrandom *straw polls* that included anywhere from dozens to millions of citizens had been used to predict elections and describe public opinion since the 1820s, but these proved to be invalid methods of social inquiry. Their results could not be generalized to larger populations because the people who answered such polls were not a random cross-section of society. The demise of the straw poll came in the presidential election of 1936, when the *Literary Digest* magazine incorrectly predicted a Republican win over Democratic incumbent Franklin D. Roosevelt (1882–1945). George Gallup's (1901–1984) new random sample survey correctly predicted a Roosevelt win, and he demonstrated that the Digest Poll's biased sample was the source of its inaccuracy.

The success of random sampling at predicting elections quickly encouraged its adoption by political scientists, and the 1944 publication of *The People's Choice*—the first systematic analysis of American voting behavior to use modern opinion polls—marked a major turning point in political science research. The transformation of this research tradition is widely considered to have been completed with the 1960 publication of *The American Voter*, which became a cornerstone of political behavior research in America. By this time the opinion poll—particularly the American National Election Study—had become the standard tool for political science research on mass opinion and voting behavior, as it remains a half century later.

The rapid adoption of polling came during a transitional period in political science known as the *behavioral revolution*, and stems in part from two parallel developments that were occurring at the same time. The first is the rise of *methodological individualism* as a critique of the dominant style of inquiry common to social science scholarship before the 1940s, which tended to explain any particular social phenomenon as a product of other social phenomena. For example, an election outcome might be explained as resulting from the state of the national economy. Methodological individualism held to the contrary that any social phenomenon was a collective product of individual-level behavior. For this school of thought, explaining election outcomes as a product of the economy requires understanding how economic factors influence the choices made by individual voters. Because opinion polls could measure not only political behavior but also the underlying attitudes that precede and shape such behavior, polls fit squarely with the tenets of methodological individualism and with the new paradigm of scholarship championed by behavioral researchers. The second development was the rapid growth of the science of statistics during the first half of the twentieth century. Polls not only provided information about the attitudes and behaviors of individuals, but when sampled using the new random probability methods they produced findings that could be generalized to entire populations. It was this unique combination of developments, arriving as the behavioral revolution was getting underway, that quickly transformed the opinion survey into the standard method for opinion research in the United States.

THE STATISTICAL LOGIC OF OPINION POLLING

The ability to generalize survey findings from a sample of 1,500 respondents to a population of millions comes from strict adherence to the statistical principles of random probability sampling. Researchers often want to study the attitudes or behaviors of a population, such as adults in the United States. Although they might prefer to include every member of the population in a survey, conducting a census for any but the smallest of populations is prohibitively expensive and fraught with difficulties. The solution offered by random probability sampling is a compromise. If a small subset of the population is selected at random to take the survey, then the central tendencies of that sample—such as the percentages of people holding various opinions—will tend to be quite similar to those of the population from which they were drawn. The compromise comes in how closely the sample estimates are likely to match the true characteristics of the population. Random sampling allows for a small amount of error between the mix of answers given by the sample and those that would be revealed by a census of the population, and also allows for the possibility that once in a while the sample may have quite different characteristics from the population.

Because random sampling allows researchers to accurately determine the probability that both kinds of error will occur in a given sample, they can assign a level of confidence to the likelihood that the sample results approximate the population's actual characteristics. The probability estimate for the first type of error is called the *margin of error*, defined as the range of values around a sample estimate in which the true population value is likely to be found. The size of the margin of error is determined by the number of persons included in the sample, with larger samples allowing more precise estimates. The margin of error for a sample of one thousand persons is plus or minus three percentage points, meaning that the proportion of respondents in the sample holding a particular opinion should be within three percentage points either way of the true population value. The probability estimate for the second type of error is called the *confidence level*, which is the likelihood that a population's true value falls within the range given by the sample's margin of error. Typically, random samples are drawn with a 95 percent confidence level, meaning that the population's true value should fall within the sample's margin of error ninety-five times out of one hundred.

These error estimates presume that each individual in a population has an equal and random chance of being selected, but other types of error can also influence poll results. Any violation of equal and random selection may produce *sampling errors* that can bias survey estimates away from the population's true value. *Nonresponse errors* can occur when persons selected to be in the sample are never contacted, decline to be interviewed, or refuse to answer particular questions. *Measurement errors* can be introduced by the wording of questions and the order in which they are asked. For example, answers obtained by asking respondents to select from a list of pre-determined responses—using what are called "forced-choice" questions—can produce different estimates of public opinion than answers obtained by recording the verbatim responses provided by respondents using "open-ended" questions. *Errors of conceptual validity* can occur when a question fails to adequately measure the concept of interest to survey researchers. These other types of error are not taken into account by the sample's margin of error or confidence level.

POLLS AND THE STUDY OF PUBLIC OPINION

Opinion polls are used by political scientists for four main purposes. First, polls are used to measure and predict political behavior. Pre- and postelection surveys help political scientists understand why citizens support partic-

ular candidates or parties. Election-day *exit polls* provide insights into the demographic and social characteristics of voters. Second, polls are used to chart trends in behavior and attitudes over time. *Tracking polls*, which consist of small samples taken every few days during the course of an election campaign, clarify how citizens respond in the short term to campaign activities. *Trend analyses* pose the same questions to different samples every few months or years to study long-term changes in the attitudes and behaviors of a population. Third, polls are widely used for *correlational analysis*, which examines how attitudes and behaviors are related to one another at the individual level. Fourth, polls are used to conduct general population experiments, where samples are divided into treatment and control groups to produce experimental findings. Unlike traditional laboratory experiments, the findings from survey experiments can be generalized to populations, which makes this combination of methods increasingly appealing to social scientists.

Polling has helped political scientists understand public opinion processes, but it also has changed the ways that political scientists think about public opinion. Up until the middle of the twentieth century, a sociological paradigm emphasizing the activity of organized groups informed the mainstream of opinion research in the social sciences. Before the behavioral revolution, the phenomenon of public opinion tended to be associated with action or barriers to action rather than merely with a potential to act. In contrast, newer psychological interpretations of public opinion associated with the behavioral revolution and informed by survey research have tended to view attitudes rather than actions as the primary phenomenon of interest. Likewise, while the earlier sociological conceptions of public opinion were concerned with action conducted by interested groups rather than the population as a whole, the method of random sampling has cultivated a perspective that views public opinion as an attribute of unorganized masses or entire societies. As a byproduct of this paradigm shift, the rise of polling has encouraged political scientists to neglect sociological and philosophical dimensions of public opinion research that once had been vibrant areas of social inquiry.

SEE ALSO *Exit Poll; Hypothesis and Hypothesis Testing; Methods, Quantitative; Methods, Research (in Sociology); Methods, Survey; Polling; Public Opinion; Quantification; Survey; Surveys, Sample*

BIBLIOGRAPHY

American Association for Public Opinion Research. http://www.aapor.org.

American National Election Studies. http://www.umich.edu/~nes.

Asher, Herbert. 2004. *Polling and the Public: What Every Citizen Should Know.* 6th ed. Washington, DC: CQ Press.

Campbell, Angus, Philip Converse, Warren Miller, and Donald Stokes. 1960. *The American Voter.* New York: Wiley.

Converse, Jean M. 1987. *Survey Research in the United States: Roots and Emergence, 1890–1960.* Berkeley: University of California Press.

General Social Surveys. http://www.norc.org/projects/gensoc.asp.

Gunn, J. A. W. 1995. "Public Opinion" in Modern Political Science. In *Political Science in History: Research Programs and Political Traditions*, eds. James Farr, John S. Dryzek, and Stephen T. Leonard, 99–122. New York: Cambridge University Press.

Lazarsfeld, Paul F., Bernard Berelson, and Hazel Gaudet. 1944. *The People's Choice: How the Voter Makes Up His Mind in a Presidential Campaign.* New York: Columbia University Press.

Natchez, Peter B. 1985. *Images of Voting/Visions of Democracy.* New York: Basic Books.

Price, Vincent. 1992. *Public Opinion.* Newbury Park, CA: Sage.

Scott L. Althaus

POLLSTERS

Pollsters are professionals dedicated to working with polls, which are sample surveys designed to uncover information about a defined population through questioning a representative sample. Scientific polling developed in the wake of the predictive failure of prescientific methods that used nonrepresentative samples. The most famous early pollsters began work in the 1930s and took part in government efforts to mobilize citizens in the United States during the Great Depression, the New Deal, and World War II. Soon after the war they generally emerged as heads of their own polling organizations, notably George Gallup (1901–1984), Elmo Roper, and Archibald Crossley. These names became synonymous with polling, and they not only sold clients on polling's value but also argued for and succeeded in giving polling results a prominent place in democratic politics. Gallup especially popularized polling's roll in governance, and he wrote several books on the subject, including *The Pulse of Democracy: The Public-Opinion and How It Works.* He also was a groundbreaker in the practice of regularly releasing poll results that revealed feelings about contemporary political issues. At the same time many pollsters entered academics, particularly Angus Campbell, Donald Stokes, Phillip Converse, and Warren Miller, who founded the Center for Political Studies. That group created American voting studies and the National Election Studies, a poll that offers data on voting, public opinion, and political participation and that continues in the early twenty-first century. A similar effort started later at the National Opinion Research Center, whose General Social Survey also remains in use in the early twenty-first century.

Modern pollsters play an important but somewhat underexamined social, political, and economic role in the development of information about large groups in society, especially polls directed at entire nations or states. While the number of practicing pollsters is not large, they collectively do many polls each year, often several simultaneously. Each poll can be an independent project requiring customization of two steps, creating a sample and conducting interviews. To create the sample, a population must be identified, and then chance is used to select a statistically representative subset. The interview requires developing a questionnaire with an overall theme as well as formulating specific questions. Pollsters also repeat certain questions in order to publicize specific public attitudes that have become associated with their organizations. The Gallup and Roper organizations are known, for instance, to frequently poll on citizens' approval of the U.S. president.

Pollsters tend to be budget sensitive, as they must maintain a staff that includes statisticians, interviewers, analysts, and writers as well as pay other administrative costs; thus their tasks involve satisfying clients' needs. Although they overlap, pollsters can be categorized by clientele. In broad strokes, clients are media organizations, businesses, or other private entities or academic enterprises. Media pollsters tend to work directly or indirectly with reporters and editors, generally part of the news department, to produce newsworthy tidbits about public attitudes for a wider audience. These pollsters tend to have journalistic goals and tailor efforts to supporting their organization's mission and specific projects. Increasingly media pollsters aid in the production of lifestyle pieces, like polls concerning parents' attitudes toward college.

Private pollsters work for specific clients ranging from large businesses and nonprofit organizations to political groups, including individual candidates. They use polls to uncover information clients consider valuable. Such information may help design public communication, for example, marketing a new product; assess performance by surveying customers or employees; and develop new ideas by surveying particular demographic categories. Pollsters have taken on increasing responsibility in political campaigns as well, performing similar functions but in the intense campaign environment. In assisting candidates with elections, pollsters have become central advisers, helping to assess candidates and issues, drafting advertisements, and even structuring policy proposals. In so doing pollsters play a prominent role in governance.

Within scholarly communities pollsters are spread widely in the social sciences, working for academic institutions to further knowledge about human thoughts and behavior. In addition to political science, pollsters work in sociology, communication, psychology, public health, and economics pursuing studies relevant to each discipline. The well-known studies of consumer confidence produced by pollsters at the University of Michigan, for instance, help forecast future business conditions. Likewise the Euro barometer has become widely used by scholars to compare attitudes across countries. Though most pollsters working in the early twenty-first century are nonacademics, much of their training came from universities, and academics often take advantage of data produced by nonacademic polls.

SEE ALSO *Campbell, Angus; Converse, Philip; Exit Poll; Key, V. O., Jr.; Miller, Warren; Polling; Polls, Opinion; Survey*

BIBLIOGRAPHY

Asher, Herbert B. 2004. *Polling and the Public: What Every Citizen Should Know.* Washington, DC: CQ Press.

Erikson, Robert S., and Kent L. Tedin. 2005. *American Public Opinion: Its Origin, Contents, and Impact.* 7th ed. New York: Pearson Longman.

Gallup, George, and Saul Forbes Rae. 1940. *The Pulse of Democracy: The Public-Opinion and How It Works.* New York: Simon and Shuster.

Norrander, Barbara, and Clyde Wilcox, eds. 2002. *Understanding Public Opinion.* Washington, DC: CQ.

Adam Simon

POLLUTION

Pollution is the contamination of the natural environment by one or more substances or practices. Most pollution is an externality—an unintended by-product—of the use of energy and other products that have become central to industrial society. As a consequence, pollution is very difficult to eliminate, because doing so requires change in people's use of these central products and systems. The automobile, for example, is the single most important component of the transportation systems of Western industrial economies, yet it is also a major source of air and water pollution, toxic wastes, and noise.

Pollution of vital "common resources" such as air and water is an especially challenging problem. Because these resources are owned by society as a whole and cannot be divided among individuals, their use is often regarded as being free. The benefits to the individual of using common resources (for instance, disposing of chemical wastes by dumping them in a river) are frequently tangible and immediate (in this case, avoiding the expense of proper disposal), whereas the costs of such use are typically long-term, intangible, and paid by the community as a whole (in the form of polluted water). Thus, it appears to be rational for an individual to make maximum use of common resources, even at the risk of their overuse and eventual destruction.

The single most important cause of pollution, especially in industrial societies, is the use of fossil fuels in cars, industries, and homes. Fossil fuels include petroleum, coal, natural gas, and uranium. Major forms of air pollution, such as global warming, acid rain, depletion of the stratospheric ozone layer, and airborne toxic chemicals, all result at least in part from the incomplete burning of fossil fuels. The main piece of legislation governing air pollution in the United States is the Clean Air Act Amendments (CAAA), first passed in 1970 and amended several times, most notably in 1990. The guiding principle of the CAAA was to require that industrial expansion incorporate efforts to reduce air pollution. Market-based incentives have been added to the CAAA, particularly in the 1990 acid rain title, and are considered by many economists and policymakers to be more effective and more politically palatable than the traditional command-and-control approach to pollution control.

Fossil fuels cause water pollution as well, in the form of oil spills, industrial emissions, and acid rain. Congress passed the Federal Water Pollution Control Act in 1972 to restore the integrity of U.S. waters, and the Safe Drinking Water Act in 1974, giving the Environmental Protection Agency (EPA) the power to set standards for drinking water quality, which are implemented by the states. These legislative initiatives have had demonstrable though partial success, though many aspects of water pollution control, such as the protection of wetlands, remain highly controversial and limited.

Toxic chemical wastes became an important issue in environmental policy soon after the tragedy of Love Canal, an area of Niagara Falls, New York, where the Hooker Chemical Company transferred ownership of some land to the local government for the building of a school. Hooker Chemical had previously dumped massive quantities of hazardous chemicals in the area, and families living nearby began to be alarmed by an unusually high incidence of illnesses and birth defects. The Superfund program, passed in 1980 and reauthorized in 1986, has been the most far-reaching and expensive legislative effort to clean up toxic wastes on land that has been abandoned by its owners. The program has a significant number of drawbacks, however, including the facts that a substantial amount of Superfund money has been spent on lawsuits rather than on remediation of sites, the number of sites cleaned up is a small proportion of the total proposed for cleanup, and the program has slowed almost to a standstill since the 1990s.

Another serious pollution problem stems from the use of artificial radioactivity for the development and testing of nuclear weapons as well as for the production of electrical power. Although nuclear power plants do not emit the same levels of air pollutants that coal and oil-fired power plants do, radioactive substances such as uranium and plutonium are powerful poisons. Meltdowns and near-meltdowns of nuclear plants (such as the Chernobyl disaster in 1986 in Ukraine) have sharply discouraged the use of nuclear power in the United States, as has the inability to create completely inviolable, long-term storage for nuclear wastes.

In addition, pollution problems and loss of habitats have contributed to the extinction of many species of plants and animals. The Endangered Species Act (ESA) of 1973 established a series of regulations to protect endangered and threatened species and the ecosystems on which they depend. The ESA generally has been considered to be successful; conflicts between requirements of the ESA and projects proposed by developers were effectively resolved during most of the act's existence. However, in recent years the property rights movement has taken strong exception to the continued enforcement of the ESA.

Other forms of pollution are less commonly recognized. One is indoor air pollution. As people work to bring down the high cost of heating and cooling by weatherproofing their homes, the atmosphere in these more airtight homes is more easily contaminated by pollutants such as cigarette smoke and toxins given off by carpeting, paneling, and household chemicals. Another, less commonly recognized form is light pollution: the excessive use of artificial light that brightens the dark sky, interfering with the work of amateur astronomers and harming nocturnal wildlife and other ecosystems. A third, noise pollution, refers to excessive noise levels, typically in urban and industrial areas, which not only disrupt people's lives and work but also raise blood pressure and stress levels, cause hearing loss, and interfere with the natural feeding, breeding, and migration cycles of animals.

Desertification—the encroachment of desert-like conditions into semidesert land—has been identified in large areas of Asia, Africa, and North America. The use of wood rather than oil or coal for fuel leads people in many developing nations to cut trees on a large scale; this often leads to disastrous flooding because tree roots can no longer hold topsoil in place when the rainy season comes. The burning of agricultural lands to clear dead vegetation, a common practice among farmers in many nations, can cause clouds of soot to move across neighboring nations.

Many of the most common forms of pollution have substantial economic impacts. Increases in air pollutants such as sulfur dioxide and urban ozone affect human health, causing or worsening conditions such as asthma, emphysema, and lung cancer. The resulting costs of medical treatment and shortened life expectancy affect a nation's productivity. Those who usually suffer are often the most vulnerable members of society: the elderly, the sick, the poor, and the very young. The environmental justice movement charges that the burden of pollution-caused health problems tends to fall most heavily on disadvantaged groups because these groups are least able to mobilize politically to demand pollution control. In more affluent areas, NIMBY ("not in my backyard") groups often have been successful at preventing the siting of incinerators, waste dumps, and other environmental hazards that can undermine property values in their neighborhoods.

Cleaning up pollution is very expensive as well. The EPA estimated that the provisions of the CAAA have cost $523 billion to implement between 1970 and 1990 (U.S. Environmental Protection Agency 1997). Some economists and political leaders regard this as unproductive spending, in that these expenditures do not help the businesses spending the money produce more goods. According to the 1997 EPA study, however, during this time period the application of the CAAA saved 205,000 American lives and provided between $6 and $50 trillion in economic benefits. Spending on pollution control goes in part to fund the manufacture of pollution control equipment, which adds to economic growth.

Pollution levels in the United States generally have improved as a result of the pollution-control policies of the past thirty years. Recycling and "precycling" (developing methods of manufacture that produce smaller amounts of waste) have reduced the production of solid wastes in many communities. The amount of lead (a neurotoxin) recorded in the air and in human blood samples is substantially down from 1970 levels, in large part because of the removal of lead from gasoline, due to the CAAA. Some international agreements have been effective, such as the Montreal Protocol (1987), which appears to have stabilized the problem of depletion of the stratospheric ozone layer. The improvement has been uneven, however. Urban ozone levels remain a substantial problem for most big cities in the United States. Global warming (Gore 2006) poses an extremely serious risk to the planet, and pollution problems are worsening rapidly in many industrializing nations, such as China and India.

SEE ALSO *Disaster Management; Environmental Kuznets Curves; Externality; Global Warming; Love Canal; Pollution, Air; Pollution, Noise; Pollution, Water; Regulation; Toxic Waste; Transportation Industry*

BIBLIOGRAPHY

Caldwell, Lynton K. 1996. *International Environmental Policy.* 3rd ed. Durham, NC: Duke University Press.

Gore, Al. 2006. *An Inconvenient Truth.* DVD, Paramount Home Entertainment.

Hardin, Garrett, and John Baden, eds. 1998. *Managing the Commons.* Bloomington: Indiana University Press.

Rosenbaum, Walter A. 2004. *Environmental Politics and Policy.* 6th ed. Washington, DC: CQ Press.

U.S. Environmental Protection Agency. 1997. Benefits and Costs of the Clean Air Act: Retrospective Study—1970 to 1990. Available from http://www.epa.gov/air/sect812/retro.html.

Marjorie Randon Hershey

POLLUTION, AIR

The economy extracts natural resources from the environment to be used as inputs in production processes (the *source function* of the environment). The output of these production processes may be either produced inputs for yet other production processes or final products to be directly consumed. Yet these produced inputs and final products are not the entirety of the output; there are also residual by-products of these processes (waste).

Just as the economy extracts natural resources from the environment, the economy in turn dumps many residual by-products, or waste, back into the environment (the *sink function* of the environment). There is waste at each stage of the economic process: waste from extracting and refining natural resources, waste emanating from production processes, waste in the marketing of products, and waste in the sphere of consumption. Wastes may be solid, airborne, or waterborne. Air pollution describes airborne wastes that can harm the environment and human health due to their accumulation in the atmosphere, their concentration geo-spatially, and/or their synergistic effects when combining with other wastes.

There is an interesting relationship between the total natural resources utilized and the total waste produced by the economy. That is, they are ultimately equivalent. This is due to the first law of thermodynamics, which states that matter-energy can neither be created nor destroyed; only the form of matter-energy can change. Of course, it is more complicated than a simple equality. Natural resources are frozen in the form of capital goods during the depreciation process (and capital goods from previous periods are at differing stages in the depreciation process), and there is a time element in the consumption of many final products as well. At a fundamental level, however, the equality holds.

RESOURCES AND POLLUTION

Some wastes are recyclable or reusable and others are not. The fact that all waste is not recyclable or reusable is due to the second law of thermodynamics, which states that any utilization of matter-energy decreases the total available matter-energy. In other words, some of the forms into which matter-energy is transformed can no longer be accessed. This is also known as the entropy law, and put differently means that not all the forms into which matter and energy are transformed are recyclable or reusable. That waste which is not recycled or reused is dumped into the environment.

The environment has an assimilative capacity, which is the ability of the environment to transform waste into harmless (or even beneficial) forms. This assimilative capacity, however, is not infinite. Waste at some level is not only incapable of being assimilated, but will damage or even destroy the assimilative capacity itself.

It is not simply the level of *homogeneous* waste in relation to the assimilative capacity that needs to be considered, but additionally what specific *types* of waste are being emitted. Some types of waste (e.g., mercury) are not assimilable in any quantity, and at some stock level can result in various detrimental effects, including damage to the assimilative capacity itself. In addition, it is not sufficient to simply look at each type of waste and the quantity of it emitted in isolation, one must consider also its synergistic effects. The *combinations* of different forms of waste have effects that are more damaging than the sum of the component waste products independent of one another. A classic case here is sulfur dioxide and nitric oxide resulting in acid precipitation (acid rain, fog, and snow).

The qualities and quantities of waste globally along with spatial considerations concerning the local *concentration* of wastes are crucial. And it is not simply the case that the assimilative capacity detoxifies or degrades waste instantaneously, or even within some set time period. There are *cumulation* effects that have to be dealt with. So in assessing the ability of the assimilative capacity to deal with industrial and other waste, combination effects, concentration effects, and cumulation effects all need to be carefully considered.

Furthermore, nothing guarantees that all waste that is *capable* of being recycled or reused *is* being recycled or reused. All waste, whether recyclable or not, which is dumped into the environment, may impact on the assimilative capacity. Therefore, when considering the quantities and qualities of wastes confronting the assimilative capacity, only those residuals may be exempted that are *actually* recycled. Generally speaking, the technologies do not yet exist to capture and recycle airborne emissions.

EVOLUTION OF AIR POLLUTION REGULATION

In the United States, early air pollution laws were enacted locally in Chicago and Cincinnati. These were smoke control laws that addressed only smoke emissions from coal burning. Before 1948, there was almost no real government intervention in the environment, which means that there was, by default, a market approach to natural resource use and environmental protection.

An early recorded disaster resulting from air pollution occurred in Belgium in 1930. A thermal inversion occurred in an area characterized by concentrated industry with substantial amounts of sulfur dioxide emissions and discharges of particulate matter. Air circulation, which requires horizontal or vertical air currents, is one of the keys to the dispersal of air pollution. If there is no horizontal wind movement, then vertical air currents will usually disperse the pollutants due to the fact that atmospheric temperature is inversely related to height. The temperature falls by 5.4 degrees Fahrenheit every thousand feet above the Earth's surface. So normally, the warm polluted air, being lighter, will rise and disperse into the cooler air.

However, if the temperature decrease is less than 5.4 degrees Farenheit per thousand feet, warm air, unable to rise because of the existence of even warmer air above it, hovers over the source of the pollution, trapping concentrated pollutants in the lower stratum. This phenomenon is called thermal inversion.

The thermal inversion in Belgium in 1930 resulted in sixty-three deaths and five thousand people becoming seriously ill. A similar episode occurred in Donora, Pennsylvania, a small industrial town thirty miles south of Pittsburgh, in 1948. Twenty people died and six thousand became ill. Thermal inversion combined with pollution and fog killed four thousand and caused numerous respiratory illnesses in London in 1952.

In the United States, the Donora incident led to a greater awareness of the problem of air pollution, and eventually to the Air Pollution Act of 1955. Although this act did little more than authorize and provide limited funding for research, it served as the basis for future amendments to the Act. The Clean Air Act of 1963 authorized the Public Health Service to take corrective action in addressing problems of interstate air pollution, and 1965 amendments gave the federal program the authority to curb auto emissions. The first standards for motor vehicle emissions were applied in 1968.

The Air Quality Act of 1967 strengthened the powers of state and local as well as federal authorities to set and enforce standards on a regional basis. This paved the way for the Clean Air Act of 1970, which was the first legislation to call for uniform air quality standards based on geographic regions.

The newly created Environmental Protection Agency (EPA) was given the authority to enforce two sets of standards: primary and secondary. Primary air quality standards concern the minimum air quality necessary to keep people from getting ill. These standards are based on proven harmful effects of individual pollutants. Secondary standards are intended to promote the general public welfare and prevent damage to plants, animals, and property in general. Within each geographic region, states determine how these standards are to be met.

MARKET APPROACHES TO AIR POLLUTION

Direct regulation or standards have been criticized on a number of grounds and have given rise to market approaches. Pollution taxes have been used, which it has been argued gives firms an incentive to reduce their emissions and is a lower cost method than command and control. The problem with such taxes or fees is identifying and calculating the social costs, and even if that is possible, there is no guarantee that they will reduce emissions to levels consistent with assimilative capacity.

These problems resulted in the market permits and emissions trading approach, which entails a market in pollution rights. The government makes some maximum allowable emissions standards, but then auctions off pollution permits to the highest bidders. Firms could purchase in the original market directly from the government or in secondary markets from other firms or individuals who purchased directly from the government, or in secondary markets themselves. Only after having acquired the *right to pollute* could a firm discharge polluting emissions. Here there is a tax incentive: The firm pays to reduce emissions and to seek ways of producing that pollute less, but the difference is that the total amount of pollution is fixed. In this sense, the market permit approach combines the strengths of both direct regulation and market approaches.

The market permits approach is not without its critics however. Many see the practice as government auctioning off clean air to the highest bidder. These issues are becoming particularly important as scientific evidence about problems such as global climate change becomes more reliable and available.

SEE ALSO *Externality; Global Warming; Greenhouse Effects; Pollution; Pollution, Noise; Pollution, Water*

BIBLIOGRAPHY

Baumol, William. 1972. On Taxation and the Control of Externalities. *American Economic Review.* 62 (3): 307–322.

Georgescu-Roegen, Nicholas. 1971. *The Entropy Law and the Economic Process.* Cambridge, MA: Harvard University Press.

Heilbroner, Robert. 1950. What Goes Up the Chimney. *Harper's* (January): 61–69.

Intergovernmental Panel on Climate Change (IPCC). 2007. *Climate Change 2007: The Physical Science Basis.* Geneva: WMO, IPCC Secretariat.

Kapp, Karl W. 1950. *The Social Costs of Private Enterprise.* Cambridge, MA: Harvard University Press.

Tietenberg, Thomas. 1985. *Emissions Trading: An Exercise in Reforming Pollution Policy.* Washington, DC: Resources for the Future.

Mathew Forstater

POLLUTION, NOISE

Noise pollution is undesired sound that is disruptive or dangerous and can cause harm to life, nature, and property. It is often said that noise differs from other forms of pollution in that, unlike atmospheric pollutants for example, once abated, noise leaves no residual accumulation in the environment or the human body. Noise does leave behind its effects, however, and these can deteriorate after continued exposure to harmful sounds. So it is not true, strictly speaking, that "noise ... leaves no visible evidence" (Lai 1996, p. 389).

The hazardous effects of noise depend on its intensity (loudness in decibels), duration, and frequency (high or low). High and low pitch is more damaging than middle frequencies, and *white noise* covering the entire frequency spectrum is less harmful than noise of a specific pitch. Noise may be ambient (constantly present in the background) or peak (shorter, louder sounds).

Noise-induced hearing loss (NIHL) in humans is the major, though by no means only, problem stemming from noise pollution. In 1978 the U.S. Environmental Protection Agency (EPA) Office of Noise Abatement and Control estimated that around twenty million Americans were exposed daily to noise resulting in permanent hearing loss (EPA 1978). In 1990 about thirty million people in the United States were exposed daily to occupational noise levels above 85 decibels, compared with just over 9 million people in 1981. Exposure for more than 8 hours a day to sound in excess of 85 decibels is potentially hazardous. In Germany and other developed countries, as many as four to five million people, that is, 12 to 15 percent of all employed people, are exposed to noise levels of 85 decibels or more (World Health Organization 2001).

Loud, abrupt sounds can harm the eardrum, while sustained sounds at lower volume can damage the middle ear; both types of sounds can cause psychological damage. Noise disrupts sleep and communication, and numerous studies have documented the heart-related, respiratory, neurological, and other physiological effects of noise. Stress, high blood pressure, anger and frustration, lower resistance to disease and infection, circulatory problems, ulcers, asthma, colitis, headaches, gastrointestinal disorders, and many other physiological and psychological problems have been linked directly to noise. In addition, children have been shown to suffer from slower language development and disruption of learning as a result of noise. More than five million children in the United States, ages six to nineteen, suffer from noise-induced hearing impairment (Havas 2006). In the United Kingdom, Netherlands, and Spain, exposure to noise impaired children's reading comprehension and caused a delay in reading skills development (Clark and Stansfeld 2005). In Austria, children in noisier neighborhoods were shown to suffer from increased stress and diminished motivation (Evans et al. 2001). A fetus exposed to noise may experience a change in heart rate, or it may suffer the impact of its mother's noise-related stress.

In addition, noise can harm animals and the environment, as well as physical property. Livestock and pets are harmed by noise, as are animals in the wild. Noise can also disturb wildlife feeding and breeding. Noise-related property damage includes structural damage from vibrations induced by sound waves and economic harm in the form of lower property values. The true social costs of noise pollution also must include monetary losses from sickness, absenteeism, loss of productivity and earning capacity, and much more.

Noise pollution is not new, but it has become more problematic with the developments associated with industrialization and urbanization. Between 1987 and 1997, community noise levels in the United States were estimated to have increased by 11 percent and were predicted to continue increasing at that rate or more (Staples 1997). Commercial and industrial activities, construction, aircraft, vehicular traffic (highway and off-road), and the rapid increase in the use of machines and other technologies are all associated with noise pollution. Modern household appliances and lawn and gardening equipment are increasingly common sources of noise. Like many other forms of pollution, noise appears to disproportionately affect poor and disadvantaged minority communities, and so is also an environmental justice issue.

In the United States, public policy to address noise pollution began in the early 1970s. The Noise Control Act of 1972 charged the federal government with protecting public health and welfare from noise pollution by establishing standards for noise emissions and by authorizing federal agencies to establish rules. The EPA created the Office of Noise Abatement and Control (ONAC) as a result of the Noise Control Act. The Quiet Communities Act of 1978 authorized the EPA to provide grants to state and local governments for noise abatement. In the early 1980s the Occupational Safety and Health Administration (OSHA) set standards for industrial noise exposure and criteria for hearing protection. The OSHA guidelines resulted in a reduction of noise levels and hearing loss to workers, but some hearing loss can occur even at OSHA-approved levels. In 1981 Congress agreed to the Ronald Reagan administration's proposal to cease funding for ONAC, although Congress did not repeal the Noise Control Act when it eliminated ONAC's funding.

Noise pollution can be controlled through reduction at the source, interruption of transmission paths, or protection of the receiver. Reengineering machines and simply turning down volume when possible are methods of reduction at the source. Barriers, enclosures, and other forms of soundproofing can interrupt transmission paths. The use of hearing protection is the main form of receiver protection. Experts recommend a multifaceted approach, including appropriate training on the use of equipment and on why ear protection matters, enforcement of hearing-protection regulations, and the use of new technologies that reduce noise at the source (Lusk et al. 2004). Like many other environmental problems, addressing noise pollution is complicated by issues of shared responsibility and jurisdiction, making some conventional economic approaches less effective and inviting new interdisciplinary solutions. New active noise control (ANC) technologies may assist in dealing with noise pollution in the years ahead through the use of digital processors that convert analog sounds into digital signals, allowing computer-generated "antinoise" to erase sound with sound (Alper 1991).

While market-based approaches to pollution control have become more popular in recent years, there have not yet been any emissions trading or pollution permits schemes applied to noise. It should be recalled, however, that up until the time of the first government regulation of pollution, a market-based approach was the "default" mode of pollution control.

SEE ALSO *Pollution; Pollution, Air; Pollution, Water*

BIBLIOGRAPHY

Alper, Joe. 1991. Antinoise Creates the Sounds of Silence. *Science* 252 (5005): 508–509.

Clark, Charlotte, and Stephen A. Stansfeld. 2005. The Effect of Aircraft and Road Traffic Noise on Children's Reading. *Literacy Today* 44 (9): 24–25.

Evans, Gary W., et al. 2001. Community Noise Exposure and Stress in Children. *Journal of the Acoustical Society of America* 109 (3): 1023–1027.

Havas, Valerie. 2006. Noise! The Invisible Pollution. *Current Health 2* 32 (5): 10–11.

Lai, Patrick. 1996. Noise Pollution. In *Major Environmental Issues Facing the 21st Century*, eds. Mary K. Theodore and Louis Theodore, 389–396. Upper Saddle River, NJ: Prentice Hall.

Lusk, Sally, et al. 2004. Acute Effects of Noise on Blood Pressure and Heart Rate. *Archives of Environmental Health* 59 (8): 392–399.

Staples, Susan L. 1997. Public Policy and Environmental Noise: Modeling Exposure or Understanding Effects. *American Journal of Public Health* 87 (12): 2063–2067.

U.S. Environmental Protection Agency, Office of Noise Abatement and Control. 1978. Noise: A Health Problem. http://www.nonoise.org/library/epahlth/epahlth.htm.

World Health Organization. 2001. Fact Sheet No. 258. Geneva: WHO Press. http://www.who.int/mediacentre/factsheets/fs258/en/.

Mathew Forstater

POLLUTION, WATER

Water pollution exists when water is contaminated by impurities or its quality is otherwise adversely affected, for example, by solid matter or thermal discharges. Water pollution problems have a long history that can be traced to antiquity, and the attempts of communities to control such problems have an equally long track record. The nature of water pollution problems has changed over time, and their geographic scale has steadily increased, as has the scale of institutional solutions that have been adopted to control them. This entry explores the key changes in the nature and scale of water pollution and in the institutional solutions that have been adopted as a response to it.

Pollution of water by human wastes was a key public health problem when today's developed countries urbanized in the 1800s. Urban life expectancies decreased because contaminated water supplies caused epidemics of cholera, typhoid fever, and other water-borne diseases and increased people's susceptibility to all illnesses. These problems were initially local, when wells and ground water were used for water supplies, and communities responded to them with local public health and sanitation regulations. The construction of networked water supplies and sewer systems after the mid-1800s increased the scale of water pollution. Local regulations proved powerless when sources of pollution were increasingly outside the local jurisdiction. This situation gave rise to the first state and national water pollution policies, which successfully safeguarded public health but which largely failed to improve in-stream water quality.

The nature of water pollution changed in industrialized countries around the time of World War II (1939–1945) because the war effort and postwar reconstruction resulted in the rapid growth of industrial production and increased discharge of industrial effluents. New innovations such as organic pesticides and synthetic detergents also proved potent water pollutants. The decades after the war witnessed several widely publicized environmental disasters, including mercury pollution in Minamata, Japan, that caused "Minamata disease" in the 1950s; the *Torrey Canyon* (1967) and *Amoco Cadiz* (1978) supertanker disasters in Europe; and the Santa Barbara, California, oil spill in 1969. Furthermore, there was controversy over asbestos-containing discharges from Reserve Mining into Lake Superior in Silver Bay, Minnesota, in the 1970s; the leak of toxic chemicals from the Sandoz factory in Basel, Switzerland, in 1986; and the cyanide spill from a gold mine in Baia Mare, Romania, which polluted the Tisza and Danube rivers in 2000. More recently, in November 2005, an explosion in a chemical plant in Jilin, China, polluted the Songhua River with benzene and nitrobenzene.

Water pollution continues to be a public health problem in the developing world. Worldwide, one child out of six under five years of age dies of a diarrheal disease such as cholera, typhoid fever, dysentery, and gastroenteritis, which are caused by the contamination of water by human wastes. Moreover, weak enforcement or the nonexistence of environmental and safety regulations in developing countries means that agriculture, horticulture, and mining are major sources of toxic water pollutants such as pesticides and mercury. Such pollutants have caused grave public health consequences across the developing world, but particularly in severely polluted areas such as the Aral Sea region in Central Asia. In some places, such as in Bangladesh, naturally occurring arsenic pollutes certain layers of ground water on which many communities depend for their water supply.

Most developed countries have adopted water pollution policies that have reduced conventional water pollutants from *point sources*. Conventional pollutants include biochemical oxygen demand (BOD), total suspended solids (TSS), fecal coliform, oil and grease, and pH (acidity and alkalinity). Point sources include municipal sewage treatment plants, industrial establishments, and other facilities, which only contributed about half of all conventional pollutants in the United States when the Clean Water Act of 1972, with its focus on point sources, was adopted. Water pollution originating from nonpoint sources, such as agriculture, streets and roads, and storm sewers, was not originally controlled with the same level of effectiveness. National policies have also been less successful in reducing the amount of nonconventional pollutants, such as those of toxic chemicals. More recently, market-based instruments such as fertilizer, manure, and pesticide taxes have been used in many countries for controlling water pollution from nonpoint sources. Other market-based instruments, particularly tradable effluent permits and sewerage charges, have increasingly been used also for controlling conventional water pollutants.

The incentives and capacity of states to control pollution from sources that lie outside their jurisdictions is limited, however. International environmental agreements have been negotiated to address this problem, including early agreements on the transportation of dangerous substances on the River Rhine in western Europe, which came into force between 1900 and 1902, and the Boundary Waters Treaty between the United States and Canada, which took effect in 1909. International agreements since 1970 have addressed, for example, the pollution of the marine environment by oil and dumping; the pollution of transboundary bodies of water such as the Baltic Sea, the North Sea, and the Mediterranean; the elimination of persistent organic compounds; and the international transport of hazardous materials and liability for damages caused by their transport. Some of these conventions, such as the 1992 Baltic Sea Convention, have been successful, while others have made little difference to the quality of the marine environment to date.

SEE ALSO *Pollution; Pollution, Air; Pollution, Noise*

BIBLIOGRAPHY

Andrews, Richard N. L. 2006. *Managing the Environment, Managing Ourselves: A History of American Environmental Policy.* 2nd ed. New Haven, CT: Yale University Press.

Jamison, Dean T., et al., eds. 2006. *Disease Control Priorities in Developing Countries.* 2nd ed. New York: Oxford University Press.

Kirchner, Andree, ed. 2003. *International Marine Environmental Law: Institutions, Implementation, and Innovations.* New York and The Hague, Netherlands: Kluwer.

Paavola, Jouni. 2004. Law: Water and Air Pollution. In *The Encyclopedia of World Environmental History*, Vol. 2, eds. Shepard Krech III, J. R. McNeill, and Carolyn Merchant, 778–786. London and New York: Routledge.

Tarr, Joel A. 1996. *The Search for the Ultimate Sink: Urban Pollution in Historical Perspective.* Akron, OH: Akron University Press.

Jouni Paavola

POLLUTION TAXES

SEE *Pollution, Air.*

POLYARCHY

The term *polyarchy* was introduced into the English language in the seventeenth century as a term meaning "government by many," but later fell into disuse. Robert A. Dahl and Charles E. Lindblom revived the term in *Politics, Economics, and Welfare* (1953) to refer to a process by which non-leaders control leaders. Dahl subsequently revised and developed the concept, defining it in *Polyarchy: Participation and Opposition* (1971) as a political regime that is "highly inclusive and extensively open to public contestation" (p. 8), and in *Democracy and Its Critics* (1989) as a regime in which "citizenship is extended to a relatively high proportion of adults, and the rights of citizenship include the opportunity to oppose and vote out the highest officials in government" (p. 220).

The robustness and importance of the concept are derived from three features. First, polyarchy unambiguously refers to really existing modern representative democracies that have universal suffrage. Second, it does so by focusing on two dimensions essential to these regimes, participation and contestation. Third, polyarchy specifies a limited number of institutions that together are necessary and sufficient for its existence.

Polyarchy refers to the form of government found in contemporary democracies, but it is not the same as democracy. Dahl understands democracy to be a regime completely responsive to all its citizens. As such, democracy is an ideal, and polyarchy refers to regimes at considerable distance from the ideal. The institutions of polyarchy are held to be necessary for democracy on a large scale, but not sufficient. Though usually considered a "minimalist" concept of democracy, polyarchy nonetheless constitutes a significant human achievement. No country was a full polyarchy until the 1890s when women gained the right to vote in national elections in New Zealand, and until the 1990s only a minority of the world's independent countries could qualify as polyarchies.

Polyarchy is a narrower concept than democracy in that it is comprised of just two of the many possible dimensions of democracy: political participation and contestation. Although the expansion of citizen participation in governing has been of great historical importance, in recent years universal suffrage has become widespread and most variation in polyarchy has occurred along the dimension of contestation. Polyarchy does not directly include many other dimensions often associated with democracy, such as the degree or extent of the rule of law, horizontal accountability, or actual government responsiveness to citizens, nor does it specify a level of political rights or civil liberties beyond that required for the effective presence of the institutions (listed below). Polities that qualify as polyarchies due to relatively high levels of competition and participation may vary significantly in other ways related to democracy.

Dahl has described the institutions of polyarchy, with some variation over the years. In *On Democracy* (1998) he lists them as:

1. *Elected officials.* Control over government decisions about policy is constitutionally vested in officials elected by citizens....

2. *Free, fair, and frequent elections.* Elected officials are chosen in frequent and fairly conducted elections in which coercion is comparatively uncommon.

3. *Freedom of expression.* Citizens have a right to express themselves without danger of severe punishment on political matters broadly defined....

4. *Access to alternative information.* Citizens have a right to seek out alternative and independent sources of information.... Moreover, alternative sources of information actually exist that are not under the control of the government or any other single political group....

5. *Associational autonomy....* [C]itizens also have a right to form relatively independent associations or organizations, including independent political parties and interest groups.

6. *Inclusive citizenship.* No adult permanently residing in the country and subject to its laws can be denied the rights that are available to others and are necessary to the five political institutions just listed. These include the rights to vote ... [and] to run for elective office.... (pp. 85–86)

What is important for polyarchy is that each of these institutions must be effectively present, not merely a set of nominal rights. The degree to which these institutions are effective may be measured and a scale of polyarchy established, although polyarchy is often used dichotomously, with only those polities whose institutions are effective above a certain threshold qualifying as polyarchies.

Some authors have suggested that the list of institutions of polyarchy is incomplete and have proposed additions, while others have sought to provide more concise, accurate, or inclusive operational definitions of contemporary democracy than polyarchy. That most such attempts continue to use the concept of polyarchy as their starting point is testimony to its enduring usefulness.

SEE ALSO *Associations, Voluntary; Citizenship; Dahl, Robert Alan; Democracy; Elections; Franchise; Lindblom, Charles Edward; Representation; Representative Agent*

BIBLIOGRAPHY

Dahl, Robert A. 1956. *A Preface to Democratic Theory.* Chicago: Chicago University Press.

Dahl, Robert A. 1971. *Polyarchy: Participation and Opposition.* New Haven, CT: Yale University Press.

Dahl, Robert A. 1989. *Democracy and Its Critics.* New Haven, CT: Yale University Press.

Dahl, Robert A. 1998. *On Democracy.* New Haven, CT: Yale University Press.

Dahl, Robert A., and Charles E. Lindblom. 1953. *Politics, Economics, and Welfare: Planning and Politico-Economic Systems Resolved into Basic Social Processes.* New York: Harper.

Charles D. Kenney

POLYGYNY

SEE *Dowry and Bride Price.*

POLYTHEISM

The term *polytheism*, referring to the worship of several gods, was coined in the sixteenth century. For medieval European Christians, the religious universe could be exhaustively categorized in terms of Judaism, Christianity, and paganism. This neat tripartite division was rendered obsolete by the Reformation. The first recorded use of the term *polytheism* was in a treatise against witches published in 1580 by the noted French thinker Jean Bodin (1530–1596). Significantly, Bodin also wrote an unpublished series of dialogues between "sages" who each practiced a different religion (including a Jew, a Roman Catholic, a Lutheran, a Calvinist, and a Muslim, among others) and who, unable in the end to resolve their differences, worshiped together in harmony. Bodin's dialogue suggests a moral equivalence among all these religions that might be characterized as "monotheistic," a term that would be invented slightly later.

This contrast between polytheism and monotheism appealed to secularizing Enlightenment thinkers precisely because it did not privilege Christianity. In particular, in *The Natural History of Religions* (1757), David Hume, deliberately turning his back on the biblical account, suggested that polytheism was the earliest form of human religion. It was not, he argued, born out of abstract speculation or contemplation, but rather in response to human hopes and especially fears—of illness, childbirth, war, and so on. Each such fear was governed by its own divinity, and because humans had an abundance of fears, they had a plethora of divinities. Only much later, according to Hume, did monotheism emerge as a (relatively) rational explanation of the world in terms of a single creator. In other words, polytheism was a religion of the passions, and monotheism a religion of reason. Hume was

himself pessimistic about the capacity of reason to triumph over passion, and he envisaged the past and future histories of religion in terms of oscillation between the two poles of polytheism and monotheism.

The notion that "polytheistic" religions were emotional and irrational was used by Europeans to disparage non-European peoples and their religious practices. Charles de Brosses's 1760 work *Du culte des dieux fétiches* (On the cult of the fetish gods) compared West African and ancient Egyptian religions in terms of their worship of gods who combined animal and human characteristics in a manner particularly repellent to Enlightenment criteria of rationality. Initially, late-eighteenth-century British observers of Brahmanical Hinduism characterized it as essentially monotheistic, in light of ancient texts. However, in the nineteenth century, Hindu "polytheistic" worship was evinced as evidence of the degeneration of Indian society.

Beginning in the middle of the nineteenth century, emerging anthropological theories of social evolution easily incorporated the distinction between polytheism and monotheism into their vision of human progress. Most notably, Edward Tylor's *Primitive Culture* (1871) traced the origins of religion to "animism," the belief, derived from the experience of dreams, that there existed a "soul" independent of the human body. Primitives believed that animals, plants, and even inanimate objects also had souls, making nature worship the earliest and least rational form of religion. Polytheism, involving a hierarchy of greater and lesser gods and spirits, represented an initial advance, a step in the direction of monotheism and, ultimately, "scientific" atheism. Sigmund Freud gave this perspective a psychoanalytic twist in *Moses and Monotheism* (1939), associating the plural gods of polytheism with the different urges of the id, and the God of monotheistic religions with the superego.

Beginning in the early twentieth century anthropologists challenged the broad evolutionary schemes of their predecessors, preferring to concentrate on the intensive study of small-scale societies in the field rather than on "conjectural history." Their studies were committed to demonstrating the rationality of non-European peoples and explaining their religious ideas in their own terms. They had little use for a term such as *polytheism* that, in their eyes, lumped a multitude of particular and radically different cultures and religious traditions into one broad rubric. Although the term was not the object of specific anthropological critique, anthropologists by and large avoided its use. The most conspicuous exception was E. E. Evans-Pritchard, whose influential study *Nuer Religion* (1956) described Nuer belief in and worship of a single "Spirit" (*Kwoth*) alongside a host of greater or lesser "spirits" (*kuth*). The Nuer alternatively could be described as monotheists or polytheists, a contradiction Evans-Pritchard attempted to reconcile by suggesting that lesser spirits were in fact understood as refractions of the one Spirit from the point of view of specific groups or individuals.

However, too exclusive a focus on the religious particularities of small-scale societies obscured the ways in which multiple cults of divinities could proliferate regionally, nationally, and indeed transnationally. Hinduism is an obvious example. C. J. Fuller recently argued that "fluidity—which means that one deity can become many and many deities can become one—is a supremely important characteristic of Hindu polytheism" (Fuller 1992, p. 30). Not only does this allow the cult of greater divinities such as Vishnu, Shiva, and Devi to articulate with the local worship of tutelary gods and goddesses, but it also reconciles the seemingly antithetical eighteenth- and nineteenth-century characterizations of Hinduism as monotheistic and polytheistic. Similar examples can be drawn from West Africa, such as the cults of *orishas* among the Yoruba, and the cults of their neighbors who were transported across the Atlantic by the slave trade and formed Candomble in Brazil, Vodun in Haiti, and Santeria in Cuba. As with Hindu divinities, *orishas* have multiple names if not multiple personalities, and often are associated with specific localities. The myths that relate the principal *orishas* of the Yoruba pantheon to one another exist in multiple, and sometimes contradictory, versions. It is important to point out that individual worshippers form a personal bond with one specific *orisha*. Seen in this light, polytheism is not intrinsically a fixed and overarching system, but rather a highly flexible framework that can articulate local cults within a wider regional or supraregional framework. Attempts to systematize the theology and worship of such religions, most particularly Hinduism, are modern outcomes of colonial and postcolonial situations.

SEE ALSO *Anthropology; Culture; Evans-Pritchard, E. E.; Monotheism; Religion; Sociology*

BIBLIOGRAPHY

De Brosses, Charles. [1760] 1989. *Du culte des dieux fétiches.* Paris: Fayard.

Evans-Pritchard, Edward E. 1956. *Nuer Religion.* New York and Oxford: Oxford University Press.

Fuller, Christopher J. 1992. *The Camphor Flame: Popular Hinduism and Society in India.* Princeton, NJ: Princeton University Press.

Hume, David. [1757] 1956. *The Natural History of Religion.* Ed. and intro. H. E. Root. Stanford, CA: Stanford University Press.

Matory, J. Lorand. 1994. *Sex and the Empire That Is No More: Gender and the Politics of Metaphor in Oyo Yoruba Religion.* Minneapolis: University of Minnesota Press.

Tylor, Edward B. 1871. *Primitive Culture: Researches into the Development of Mythology, Philosophy, Religion, Art, and Custom.* 2 vols. London: J. Murray.

Robert Launay

PONZI SCHEME

Ponzi scheme is the name given to any business or economic entity promising to pay a higher return to its investors than can be generated by this business's net operating income. Operations of this type are sustainable only as long as funds from new investors or lenders are available to meet outstanding payout requirements.

This phrase originated in a get-rich-quick operation devised in the early twentieth century by Charles Ponzi (Zuckoff 2005). After immigrating to the United States from Italy in 1903 and serving time in prison, Ponzi launched his scheme in Boston in mid-1919. Ponzi's operation was based on the arbitrage possibilities of the cross-border system of postal-reply coupons. In this system, people mailing documents internationally could send along coupons that enabled recipients to mail back the documents using stamps bought in the recipient's country. The system used rates fixed in 1907 that had not been adjusted for subsequent currency realignments. Ponzi and his agents took advantage of this system by converting funds into devalued currencies, using those monies to purchase postal-reply coupons, trading them (at 1907 par values) for postal coupons in countries with stronger currencies, then converting these stronger countries' coupons back into currency.

Ponzi obtained funds for his plan by offering a 100-percent return in ninety days. By July 1920 he had attracted millions of dollars to his Security Exchange Company. His scheme triggered an investment mania, and he began living luxuriously. Most of the returns paid to investors in Ponzi's schemes came from new investors' funds, not from postal-coupon investment earnings. Ponzi's scheme was exposed by the U.S. Postal Service, and federal agents raided the Securities Exchange Company in August 1920, rendering worthless the stakes of his 17,000 investors. After serving more time in prison, Ponzi was deported to Italy; he died at a charity hospital in Rio de Janeiro in 1949.

Ponzi schemes have arisen frequently, both in the past (Kindleberger 1978) and in the present. Many Ponzi schemes now operate on the Internet. Such schemes can be sustained as long as existing investors do not liquidate their positions, and as long as new investors opt in and regulators do not intervene. When a bailout is expected, it can be rational to participate in a Ponzi scheme (Bhattacharya

2003). These schemes resemble asset bubbles in that investors in both cases suspend belief and are often driven by greed; but asset bubbles arise in open markets with changing sets of investors, whereas Ponzi schemes arise via closed contracts made to well-defined sets of investors. *Pyramid schemes* are one variant of the Ponzi scheme in which the earlier in the scheme a participant signs on, the greater that person's share of excess returns.

Economists increasingly describe any situation as "Ponzi" when it involves payout obligations that can be met only through borrowing against future income. For example, in his theory of financial fragility, Hyman Minsky (1975) used the term *Ponzi finance* to denote the borrowing requirement of firms whose cash flow from current operations is insufficient to meet current liability obligations. Thomas Sowell (2003), among others, has argued that social security systems have Ponzi characteristics, in that old-age benefits liabilities are transferred across generations instead of being self-financed. Other economists, such as Stephen O'Connell and Stephen Zeldes (1988), have modeled the behavior of governments with growing fiscal deficits as Ponzi games.

SEE ALSO *Bubbles; Discounted Present Value; Discounting; Financial Instability Hypothesis; Financial Markets; Future Prices; Hedging; Leverage; Liquidity Premium; Overlending*

BIBLIOGRAPHY

Bhattacharya, Utpal. 2003. The Optimal Design of Ponzi Schemes in Finite Economies. *Journal of Financial Intermediation* 12: 2–24.

Kindleberger, Charles P. 1978. *Manias, Panics, and Crashes: A History of Financial Crises.* New York: Basic Books.

Minsky, Hyman. 1975. *John Maynard Keynes.* New York: Columbia University Press.

O'Connell, Stephen A., and Stephen P. Zeldes. 1988. Rational Ponzi Games. *International Economic Review* 29 (3): 431–451.

Sowell, Thomas. 2003. *Applied Economics: Thinking Beyond Stage One.* New York: Basic Books.

Zuckoff, Mitchell. 2005. *Ponzi's Scheme: The True Story of a Financial Legend.* New York: Random House.

Gary Dymski

POOLED TIME SERIES AND CROSS-SECTIONAL DATA

Economic datasets come in a variety of forms. The cross-sectional, time series, and panel data are the most commonly used kinds of datasets. A *cross-sectional* dataset consists of a sample of individuals, households, firms, cities, states, countries, or any other micro- or macroeconomic unit taken at a given point in time. Sometimes the data on all units do not correspond to precisely the same time period. In a pure cross-sectional analysis, such minor time differences in data collection are ignored. Figure 1 illustrates the relationship between cross-sectional data on the price of houses sold within a two-week period and the houses' size. The basic model, $y_i = c + x_i\beta + \varepsilon_i$ ($i = 1, 2, \ldots N$), where y_i is the dependent variable and x_i is a $1 \times K$ vector of explanatory variables, often has stochastic errors ε_i such that $E(\varepsilon_i/x_i) = 0$ but $V(\varepsilon_i/x_i) = \sigma_i^2$. *Ordinary least squares* (OLS) estimates that ignore heterogeneity across cross sections are unbiased but inefficient. Efficiency can be attained from *generalized least squares* (GLS) estimation. In economics, the analysis of cross-sectional data is closely associated with applied microeconomics fields such as labor economics, public finance, industrial organization, urban economics, demography, and health economics. Data on individuals, households, firms, and cities at a given point in time are important for testing microeconomic hypotheses and evaluating economic policies.

A *time series dataset* contains information on a variable or a set of variables over time. Examples of time series data include stock prices, money supply, the consumer price index, gross domestic product (GDP), annual homicide rates, and automobile sales figures. Figure 2 illustrates the time series for NASDAQ on July 7, 2006. Since past events influence the future and lags in behavior are prevalent in the social sciences, time is an important dimension in time series datasets. Unlike the arrangement of cross-sectional data, chronology is crucial in time series datasets. Time series observations are hard to analyze mainly because of the interdependency of observations over time. The basic model, $y_t = c + x_t\beta + \varepsilon_t$ ($t = 1, 2, \ldots, T$), where y_t is the dependent variable and x_t is a $1 \times K$ vector of explanatory variables, has stochastic errors ε_t such that $E(\varepsilon_t/x_t) = 0$ but $\varepsilon_t = \rho\varepsilon_{t-1} + u_t$ (u_t satisfies all classical assumptions).

Most economic data are strongly related to their recent histories. For example, information on GDP from the last quarter allows the researcher to make accurate predictions about the likely range of GDP during the current quarter, because GDP tends to remain fairly stable from one quarter to the next. OLS regression estimates that ignore the time-dependence features of time series data produce inaccurate results. Model transformation is required to produce GLS estimates that are efficient. Several modifications and embellishments to standard econometric techniques have been developed to account for and exploit the dependent nature of economic time series and to address other issues, such as the fact that some economic variables tend to display clear trends over time.

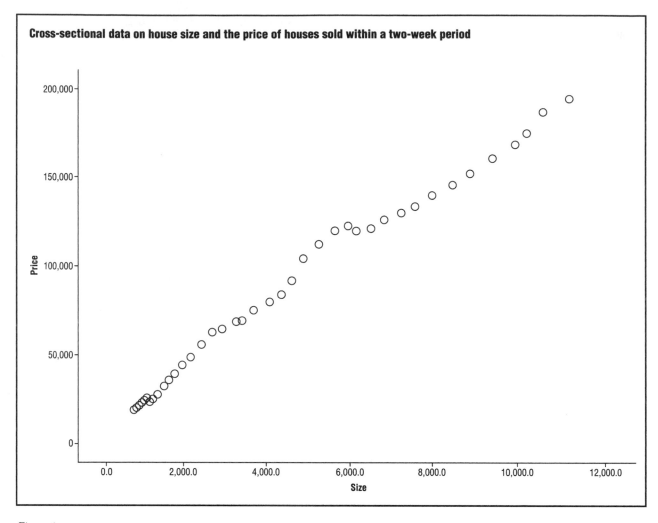

Cross-sectional data on house size and the price of houses sold within a two-week period

Figure 1

Another feature of time series data that can require special attention is the *frequency* at which the data are collected. In economics, the most common frequencies are daily, weekly, monthly, quarterly, and annually. Stock prices are recorded daily (excluding Saturday and Sunday). The money supply in the U.S. economy is reported weekly. Many macroeconomic series, such as inflation and unemployment rates, are tabulated monthly. The gross domestic product is a quarterly series. Other time series, such as the infant mortality rates in the United States, are available only on an annual basis. Many weekly, monthly, and quarterly economic data display strong seasonal patterns. For example, monthly data on crop yield differ across months simply due to changes in weather conditions. Hence, before analyzing time series data, it is important to *deseasonalize* the data or remove the seasonal trends.

A *panel* or *longitudinal dataset* varies across both time and cross-sectional units, as seen in Figure 3. This is a partial table of the entire dataset that consists of the value of

sales (*sal*), payroll (*pay*), capital expenditure (*cap*), and cost of pollution abatement (*abat*) for a set of industries followed over a three-year period. The ordering of the data by microunits first and then by time is typical of all longitudinal datasets. The number of time periods are kept constant across the cross-sectional units in *balanced panels*. Treatment for *unbalanced panels* requires further analysis.

The basic model for the *i*th cross section is $y_{it} = c_i + x_{it}\beta + u_{it}$ ($t = 1, 2, \ldots, T$), where x_{it} is a $1(K)$ matrix of explanatory variables that vary across i or t or both, c_i represents cross-sectional heterogeneity, and u_{it} is a stochastic error. The conditional mean of the disturbances is assumed to be zero. In traditional approaches, the model is *random effects* (RE) when c_i is a random variable, and *fixed effects* (FE) when c_i is a fixed parameter to be estimated (Balestra and Nerlove 1966). Yair Mundlak (1978) made a valid argument that unobserved effects c_j should be treated as random draws from the population along with y_{it} and x_{it}. In modern econometric language, in an

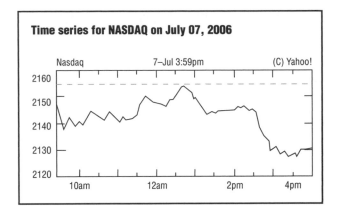

Time series for NASDAQ on July 07, 2006

Nasdaq   7–Jul 3:59pm   (C) Yahoo!

Figure 2

Industry	Time	sal	pay	cap	abat
Ind 1	1991	y_{11}	12.78	56.78	100.89
Ind 1	1992	y_{12}	10.78	48.89	x^3_{12}
Ind 1	1993	124.78	x^1_{13}	30.89	x^3_{13}
Ind 2	1991	123.67	x^1_{21}	29.56	67.89
Ind 2	1992	y_{22}	x^1_{22}	x^2_{22}	x^3_{22}
Ind 2	1993	139.99	18.89	x^2_{23}	x^3_{23}
Ind 3	1991	178.90	20.78	x^2_{31}	x^3_{31}
Ind 3	1992	y_{32}	21.22	67.89	1.28
Ind 3	1993	y_{33}	21.24	x^2_{33}	x^3_{33}

Figure 3

RE model, c_j is assumed to be uncorrelated with x_{it}, while in a FE model, arbitrary correlation between c_j and x_{it} is allowed.

Two famous studies that analyze panel datasets are the National Longitudinal Survey of Labor Market Experience (NLS) and the Michigan Panel Study of Income Dynamics (PSID). In these datasets, very large cross sections, consisting of thousands of microunits, are followed through time, but the number of time periods is often small. The PSID is a study of roughly six thousand families and fifteen thousand individuals who have been interviewed periodically from 1968 to the present. Another group of intensely studied panel datasets are those from the income tax experiments of 1970, in which thousands of families were followed for eight to thirteen quarters. For most panels, cross-sectional dependence is strong and time dependence is insignificant. Panel datasets are wide but short, and heterogeneity across units is often the central focus of the analysis. In two-way error components models, the cross-sectional heterogeneity varies across time and cross sections, that is, $y_{it} = c_{it} + x_{it}\beta + u_{it}$ or $y_{it} = c_i + \delta_t + x_{it}\beta + u_{it}$. The fundamental advantage of a panel dataset over a cross section is that it allows the researcher greater flexibility in modeling differences in behavior across individuals.

SEE ALSO *National Longitudinal Survey of Youth; Panel Study of Income Dynamics*

BIBLIOGRAPHY

Balestra, Pietro, and Marc Nerlove 1966. Pooling Cross Section and Time Series Data in the Estimation of a Dynamic Model: The Demand for Natural Gas. *Econometrica* 34 (3): 585–612.

Greene, William H. 2003. *Econometric Analysis*. 5th ed. Upper Saddle River, NJ: Prentice Hall.

Mundlak, Yair. 1978. On the Pooling of Time Series and Cross Section Data. *Econometrica* 46 (1): 69–85.

Wooldridge, Jeffrey M. 2006. *Introductory Econometrics: A Modern Approach*. 3rd ed. Mason, OH: Thomson/South-Western.

Monica Das

POOR, THE

SEE *Poverty, Urban.*

POPE, THE

SEE *Vatican, The.*

POPPER, KARL
1902–1994

Sir Karl Raimund Popper was a leading twentieth-century philosopher. His first major work, *Logik der Forschung* (The Logic of Scientific Discovery, 1935), was a methodology of the physical sciences that dispensed with induction. His second major work, in two volumes, *The Open Society and Its Enemies* (1945), was a democratic manifesto that burst out of broad yet incisive discussions of the philosophy of history, society, and politics. Slightly less influential was his slim, sober *Poverty of Historicism* (1957).

David Hume's (1711–1776) critique of induction—that universal statements of science never follow deductively from particular statements describing experience—inadvertently undermined the rationality of science. His own response to his critique was to base inductive inferences on habit rather than on rationality. Immanuel

Kant's (1724–1804) response was to base inductive inferences on the principle of induction (or of simplicity, as he called it), whose status is that of extralogical truth known with no recourse to experience: synthetic a priori knowledge. Most philosophers find Hume's response a retreat to irrationalism and Kant's response a retreat to dogmatism. They sought a different way around Hume's critique. Thus, the problem of induction, the search for a satisfactory response to Hume's critique, became a central concern of rationalist philosophy. Popper reworded the problem: how is theoretical learning from experience possible? To this, he had a new solution: learning from experience is deductive; it advances by the refutation of bold conjectures; and the bolder the better. The view of learning from experience by refutations is impervious to Hume's critique: a statement of experience conflicts with a theory. Thus, contrary to Kant, Popper viewed science as no knowledge, much less as a priori knowledge. Science then is the search for explanatory conjectures and for ways to test them. He thus shifted traditional epistemology from the positive to the negative, to *via negativa*: groping in the dark and learning from error. He likewise turned traditional positive epistemology into Socratic negative epistemology: we know that we do not know, we know the limitations of some theories. Our pursuit of knowledge engenders our best and most interesting errors.

Popper's view aimed to account for the progress of science, not for its alleged reliability. On this he made three very important comments. First, absolute reliability is impossible and conditional reliability is question-begging. Second, most applied theories and the most frequently applied ones—Galileo's (1564–1642) and Isaac Newton's (1642–1727)—are refuted. Third, current efforts to answer Hume must be hopeless and useless. In particular, reliability is not probability; to the extent that it is possible it is the elimination of some dangerous applications of science achieved by severe tests. Following probability is caution, whereas scientific thinking is bold and so are attempts to apply it. Yet because theories are hypotheses that invite critical discussion, a testable theory of induction may be welcome, but most proposed solutions of the problem of induction are untenstable and so they are pseudoscientific.

Popper's contribution to social and political philosophy accords with his negative philosophy of science. It is more significant, both politically and intellectually. He argued that any regime that safeguards the means for peaceful corrections of government errors deserves respect as a democracy. Politics invites criticism aimed at improvements, he observed, and seeking improvements is superior to—more fruitful than—the traditional theory of the sovereign that is a futile search for the best regime. This is the central message of Popper's philosophy, both theoretical and practical, regarding science, government,

and anything else worthwhile: improving is preferable to legitimating. He took particular aim at intellectuals, arguing that they had moral responsibilities commensurate with their privileges and that they had a long history of falling short. As examples, he expounded the ideas of two of his greatest intellectual heroes, Plato (427–347 BCE) and Karl Marx (1818–1883). He claimed that their devotees glossed over the defects of their philosophies, especially their illiberalism. His doctrine that great men make great mistakes from which we should learn was more challenging than his negative epistemology.

Popper deemed unscientific the doctrines of historical inevitability or historical destiny (*historicism* in his jargon) of Plato and of Marx. He said that no doctrine of this kind can be worded in a manner clear enough to be put to the test of experience, because if such a theory were to cohere with known facts, it must be vague. (Irrefutable versions of historicism are easy to invent: the simplest is the purely existential "historical destiny exists.") Ingeniously, Popper found a way to refute all reasonable versions of historicism, despite its inherent vagueness. The argument deploys two intuitive premises: future science is in principle unpredictable, and its impact on society is tremendous. Hence, no large-scale theory of the future development of society can possibly yield significant or interesting predictions.

Popper's mode of thinking leads to his greatest and most significant idea. It is his replacement of the theory of rationality that characterizes Western philosophy. Most people take for granted the idea that the best culture is their own. The first to reject this idea as too complacent were the leading ancient Greek philosophers. They deemed problematic all cultures, and what cultures espouse as true they declared to be nonbinding, conventional truths. They deemed binding only universal, absolute truths—truths by nature. Proof is required to show that an assertion is true by nature.

Popper challenged this doctrine: applying the Socratic maxims to science, he declared its rationality to rest neither on proof nor on surrogate proof but on willingness to engage in critical debate. This willingness creates a balance between tradition and science, between conservative and radical politics, between the given and the hoped for: it is a plea for reformist democracy, a view of scientific progress as an approximation to the truth and to freedom and justice, a view that applies to all walks of life, a remarkable and exciting move towards a synthesis and a challenge to push it forward. As the root of rationality is willingness to debate, reform is secondary to the replacement of both traditionalism and radicalism with the advocacy of individual autonomy.

SEE ALSO *Philosophy of Science*

BIBLIOGRAPHY

Agassi, Joseph. 1988. Sir Karl Popper in Retrospect: The Positive Power of Negative Thinking. In *The Gentle Art of Philosophical Polemics*, ed. Joseph Agassi, 479–501. LaSalle IL: Open Court.

Bunge, Mario, ed. 1964. *The Critical Approach to Science and Philosophy.* London and New York: Free Press.

Kekes, John. 1977. Popper in Perspective. *Metaphilosophy* 8: 36–61.

Levinson, Paul, ed. 1982. *In Pursuit of Truth: Essays in Honour of Karl Popper on the Occasion of his 80th Birthday.* Atlantic Highlands, NJ: Humanities Press.

Magee, Bryan. 1985. *Philosophy and the Real World: An Introduction to Karl Popper.* Chicago: Open Court.

Magee, Bryan. 1985. *Popper.* 3rd ed. London: Fontana.

Miller, David, ed. 1985. *Popper Selections.* Princeton, NJ: Princeton University Press.

O'Hear, Anthony, ed. 1995. *Karl Popper: Philosophy and Problems.* Cambridge, U.K.: Cambridge University Press.

Popper, Karl. 1945. *The Open Society and Its Enemies.* 2 vols. London: Routledge and Kegan Paul.

Popper, Karl. 1957. *The Poverty of Historicism.* London: Routledge and Kegan Paul.

Popper, Karl. [1935] 1959. *The Logic of Scientific Discovery.* London: Hutchinson. (Originally published as *Lokig der Forschung.*)

Popper, Karl. 1963. *Conjectures and Refutations: The Growth of Scientific Knowledge.* London: Routledge and Kegan Paul.

Schilpp, Paul Arthur, ed. 1974. *The Philosophy of Karl Popper.* 2 vols. La Salle, IL: Open Court.

Joseph Agassi

POPULAR CULTURE

Popular culture is the domain of cultural products created in mass quantities for a mass audience. While folk culture is the realm of face-to-face culture in small groups and high culture is the realm of cultural products produced by a few for the few, popular culture is more public than folk cultures and more easily accessible than high culture. Popular culture often appropriates ideas, forms, and formulae from both folk culture and high culture. In modern industrialized societies, popular culture appeals to the broad middle class and generally reinforces that class's views of the world.

THE ORIGINS OF POPULAR CULTURE

Although some historians argue that popular culture is very old, most scholars believe that popular culture in its present forms emerged in the nineteenth century when communication technologies (e.g., printing processes and photographic reproduction) and large-scale media organizations (newspapers, magazines, book publishers) were able to create and market messages for a large audience of consumers. Modern popular culture required the development of commodity capitalism, the stage of capitalist development when the problem of production had been solved (through technology and bureaucratic organization), leaving the problem of consumption of the goods and services produced by the society. Advertising, a form of popular culture, plays a crucial role in the creation of desire to consume the commodity goods and services produced in a capitalist society.

The role of print and electronic media (print, then film, radio, television, and Internet-based communication) in the dissemination of popular culture products leads some critics to call this realm "mass-mediated culture," and the role of markets and consumers since the latter part of the twentieth century has led some to call this realm "commodity culture." Whatever the term the key elements in identifying and analyzing popular culture are its mass production and mass consumption, often "mediated" through channels of communication that stand between the producers and consumers of the cultural products. Scholars who study popular culture believe that patterns of production, dissemination, and consumption in this realm of culture reveal much about the values and beliefs of the audience. The assumption is that if people will spend money to consume a product or an experience, then they expect that experience to satisfy some need or desire. The nature of commodity capitalism, of course, is that the satisfaction experienced by consuming popular culture products and experiences is fleeting, always bringing the audience (the customer) back for more.

Some genres of popular culture include familiar sorts of "texts," including popular fiction, magazines, advertising, film, radio programs, comic books, cartoons, television programs, recorded music, and even fast food. Other genres appear as more complex social events or experiences, such as popular music concerts, sporting events, entertainment events (e.g., professional wrestling), visits to amusement parks, leisure pastimes, or tourist experiences. In all of these cases and more, the critical element is that a mass audience pays money to consume the commodity or experience.

POP CULTURE AND SOCIAL CLASS ISSUES

Social class issues pervade discussions of popular culture. Access to the economic resources one needs to consume the products of popular culture is one of these issues, but equally important has been the issue of "taste cultures," the idea that different social classes acquire different tastes in arts and entertainment, for example. Popular culture has been dismissed by some critics as "middlebrow," a judgment that its quality is not on par with high culture, but defenders of popular culture champion it as the distinctive product of democratic societies.

Social scientists became interested in popular culture in the 1920s as Marxist scholars and others began to realize that commodity capitalism was creating a whole new realm for struggles between ideologies and centers of power. A group of intellectuals affiliated in these years with the Institute for Social Research at the University of Frankfurt am Main in Germany (known as "The Frankfurt School" of social thought and criticism) began rereading German political philosopher Karl Marx (1818–1883) and adding Sigmund Freud's (1895–1939) psychology of the unconscious, thereby developing a "critical theory" of society that saw the products of popular culture as a more effective means by which one class of people establishes hegemony in society, persuading with words and images rather than with class violence. Especially relevant to understanding popular culture is Walter Benjamin's 1936 essay, "The Work of Art in the Age of Mechanical Reproduction," which belongs to this period and school of social criticism and lays the groundwork for important inquiry into issues of authenticity, the political uses of popular art, and the possibilities of cultural change in a world of mass production and consumption.

Social scientists in the United States were a bit slower than their European colleagues to realize the importance of popular culture. In their 1929 and 1937 studies American sociologists Robert S. (1892–1970) and Helen Merrell Lynd (1896–1982) noted the importance of popular entertainments in the lives of their Middletown (Muncie, Indiana) families, but it was in the postwar years that sociologists like Paul Lazarsfeld, Kurt Lewin, Harold Laswell, Carl Iver Hovland (1912–1961), David Riesman, and C. Wright Mills (1916–1962) took mass-mediated culture seriously as the realm where middle-class ideologies of gender, race, social class, and American "exceptionalism" were exerting their power. After struggling for legitimacy in the academic world through the 1950s, the academic study of popular culture finally took hold in the 1960s. In the next decade a new cluster of ideas came from those working at the University of Birmingham Centre for Cultural Studies and elsewhere in Great Britain, again informed largely by Marxist thought. British cultural studies recognized the importance of popular culture and saw in youth cultures and in other subcultures the potential (often squandered) for resistance. As Americans and then others picked up and elaborated on the ideas offered by the Birmingham School, the study of popular (mass-mediated, commercial) culture moved to the center of these social scientists' interest in power and ideology.

PRODUCTION

Some social scientists ask and answer questions about the societal circumstances and organizations that produce popular culture. Historian and cultural studies scholar Raymond Williams, for example, led the way in creating a "sociology of culture" in the 1970s and early 1980s. His 1974 book *Television: Technology and Cultural Form* is a classic piece of cultural studies criticism, and a generation of sociologists, historians, and communications scholars has continued the examination of the ways mass media corporations organize production, create popular culture products, disseminate the products, and exert control over other organizations and realms of society. Of special interest to some scholars is the concentration of media power by certain corporations, including powerful transnational corporations, and how this affects society.

CONSUMPTION

Humanists brought to the initial media criticism of the 1950s their familiar methods from literary and art criticism, but social scientists had their own methods for understanding the meaning of texts. Content analysis of films, television shows, advertising, and other popular culture genres was a favored method of popular culture analysis for a time, and some theories of textual criticism (e.g., semiotics) provided an interdisciplinary bridge between humanistic and social scientific approaches.

The problem with most media textual criticism, whether it used humanistic or social scientific methods or a combination of these, is that the criticism appears to assume that the meanings of a popular culture text or experience are determined by the author(s) of the text. British cultural studies, especially the work by cultural theorist Stuart Hall and his colleagues, challenged that author-based model of the meaning of texts and in its place developed the position that the meanings of a popular culture text or event is a product of the active interaction between the text itself and the audience consuming the text. The creators of the popular culture may have "encoded" a series of meanings in a text or event, noted Hall, but the audience "decodes" the communication and need not accept the hegemonic reading of the text desired by the creator. Some readers or viewers might have the resources to formulate an oppositional understanding of the text, while others may adopt a more "negotiated" stance, accepting some of the creators' meanings and rejecting others.

This new view of the agency of the audience led critics to see that they would have to do fieldwork with audiences or otherwise engage in exchanges with audiences so that the critic could see how people were making their own meanings out of popular culture texts and experiences. Some social scientists use broad survey instruments for their audience response analysis. Others use interview methods with focus groups of audience members. Some put themselves in the natural settings with audiences (e.g., at Disney World) and observe how the audience interacts with and talks about the experiences.

GLOBALIZATION AND NEO-IMPERIALISM

The products of popular culture easily cross geopolitical boundaries. National film industries quickly became international, for example, but this is also true for other popular art forms, including music, literature, television, and comics. By the 1930s American films were dominating the world markets, but it was World War II (1939–1945) and the occupation of Europe and Japan by U.S. soldiers that accelerated the foreign appetite for American popular culture, in particular music, film, clothing (especially blue jeans), and comic books. By the 1950s the increasing globalization of the corporations producing popular culture was leading to what critics came to call "the Coca-Cola-ization" of the world, as it was hard to find any place in the world without that soft drink and the advertising for its consumption.

Some scholars and critics point to this international dissemination of American popular culture as a form of "neocolonialism" or "neoimperialism" by which the United States exerts ideological influence on other nations through its popular culture. Governments and nationalist social movements sometimes have resisted this American world hegemony through popular culture. Cultural studies expert Paul Gilroy and other critics see a different sort of neocolonialism in the field of cultural studies itself. Gilroy's work on the transnational movement of African people and their cultural products makes an explicit critique of the racial assumptions and of the Anglocentric and Eurocentric focus of some cultural studies scholarship.

Although American popular culture still dominates the world markets, the flow of popular culture across borders became more complicated in the turn of the twenty-first century. Japanese animated television series and films (anime) and Japanese graphic novels (manga) became very popular among American and other youth, and Korean popular culture (musical groups and television serial dramas, for example) became very popular in Japan. Scholars have mapped "world music" cultures and the movement of the music across cultural boundaries. These trends have raised speculation that there is emerging a transnational youth culture linked by communication technologies and creating a shared culture through music, dress, video games, and television.

NEW TECHNOLOGIES

Popular culture has depended on advances in technology since the nineteenth century. Technologies of mass pro-

duction and mass distribution made possible newspapers, magazines, and popular fiction (from dime novels to comic books to paperback novels). Popular music and the technologies of sound production have always been intertwined. Songwriters wrote to the time limits possible for recordings, and scholars have noted the effects of electronic amplification of music on the art of the music itself. The history of film is as much a history of technological change as of artistic change, and digital moving images may actually make film an archaic technological medium. Radio continues to evolve with the technologies, as the new satellite radio manufacturers and stations overcome the limitations of atmospheric broadcast and as increasing numbers of people listen to radio through their computers. Musicians and the companies that produce and market popular music have had to adjust to digital technological advances that make artistic and intellectual property rights difficult to enforce, as people use their computers to share music, films, and television shows. Young people seem to be "platform agnostic," as some critics call the tendency to move easily between different technologies for consuming music, film, and television. These technologies add to the globalization of popular cultural products.

The new technologies of communication are having effects on social interactions that scholars are still trying to understand. Several studies make clear the role of social class in the uses of these technologies, and several worry that the gap between rich and poor people in the world will be widened by this technology gap.

Scholars are also interested in the cognitive effects of these new technologies for disseminating and consuming popular culture. American cultural historian Walter J. Ong studied the cognitive effects of our move from primarily oral cultures to written cultures, which led him to speculate that there is a "secondary orality" emerging in electronic communication. Furthermore some scholars argue that new media entertainments, including video games and computer games, actually require increasingly complex cognitive skills, from spatial intelligence to the ability to keep track of multiple storylines and characters. The advancements in cognitive and mind sciences make it likely that those working in these natural science disciplines will collaborate even more with the social scientists studying popular culture toward understanding the social and cognitive effects of mass mediated experiences.

SEE ALSO *Capitalism; Cognition; Comic Books; Cultural Studies; Culture; Culture, Low and High; Digital Divide; Distinctions, Social and Cultural; Film Industry; Food; Frankfurt School; Freud, Sigmund; Globalization, Social and Economic Aspects of; Hall, Stuart; Humanism; Imperialism; Internet; Internet, Impact on Politics; Lasswell, Harold; Lazarsfeld, Paul*

Felix; Lewin, Kurt; Literature; Marx, Karl; Media; Mills, C. Wright; Music; Neuroscience; Property Rights, Intellectual; Radio Talk Shows; Social Science; Television; World Music

BIBLIOGRAPHY

Benjamin, Walter. 1936. The Work of Art in the Age of Mechanical Reproduction. http://www.marxists.org/reference/subject/philosophy/works/ge/benjamin.htm.

Bourdieu, Pierre. 1984. *Distinction: A Social Critique of the Judgement of Taste.* Trans. Richard Nice. Cambridge, MA: Harvard University Press.

Durham, Meenakshi Gigi, and Douglas M. Kellner, eds. 2006. *Media and Cultural Studies: Keyworks.* Rev. ed. Malden, MA: Blackwell.

Hall, Stuart, et al., eds. 1980. *Culture, Media, Language: Working Papers in Cultural Studies, 1972–1979.* London: Hutchinson.

Jenkins, Henry. 2006. *Convergence Culture: Where Old and New Media Collide.* New York: New York University Press.

Lynd, Robert Staughton, and Helen Merrell Lynd. 1929. *Middletown: A Study in American Culture.* New York: Harcourt, Brace and Company.

Lynd, Robert Staughton, and Helen Merrell Lynd. 1937. *Middletown in Transition: A Study in Cultural Conflicts.* New York: Harcourt, Brace, and Company.

Morley, David, and Kevin Robins. 1995. *Spaces of Identity: Global Media, Electronic Landscapes, and Cultural Boundaries.* London: Routledge.

Schiller, Herbert I. 1992. *Mass Communications and American Empire.* 2nd ed., updated. Boulder, CO: Westview Press.

Staiger, Janet. 2005. *Media Reception Studies.* New York: New York University Press.

Williams, Raymond. 1974. *Television: Technology and Cultural Form.* London: Fontana.

Williams, Raymond. 1982. *The Sociology of Culture.* New York: Schocken Books.

Jay Mechling

POPULAR CULTURE STUDIES

SEE *Cultural Studies.*

POPULAR MUSIC

While music that "the people" listen to has always been present, *popular music* as it is known today is a recent phenomenon dating to the late nineteenth and early twentieth centuries. Several factors are responsible for bringing about the rise of popular music. One is technological:

New technologies for the reproduction of music, such as the player piano and phonograph in the late nineteenth century and radio and sound film in the 1920s, greatly facilitated access to music, and helped prompt a proliferation of different musical styles. Another factor was the rise of consumer culture, as people increasingly came to understand themselves less through their occupations, as producers, and more through the ways that they spent their leisure time, as consumers. The growth of the modern advertising industry helped push this process along; manufacturers of player pianos and phonographs spent heavily promoting these technologies early in the twentieth century.

Yet another factor was the increased industrialization of the production of music. Modern management techniques derived from Frederick Taylor (1856–1915) and Henry Ford (1863–1947) found their way into the music business, which became increasingly rationalized, more like a business that manufactured everyday commodities.

At the same time that these developments were occurring, new musical styles were entering people's consciousness. The craze for ragtime piano music in the late nineteenth and early twentieth centuries helped fuel player piano sales. Jazz, blues, and other African American musical styles helped the American recording industry market African American performers to a broader white audience under the rubric of *race music*.

Perhaps most significant, however, was the rise of radio. Radio in the moment of its popularization, the mid-1920s, boasted greater fidelity than phonograph records and did not have the three-minute time limitation of 78 rpm recordings. And early radio was live. Listeners around the country were in thrall to dance music, which was essentially highly arranged, sanitized jazz performed by white musicians such as Paul Whiteman (1890–1967). The sensitivity of electrical microphones for radio resulted in a new style of singing called *crooning*, in which performers sang in a much more intimate way than when they sang without amplification in auditoriums. This style produced the first mass-media popular music superstars in the United States, such as Rudy Vallée (1901–1986) and Bing Crosby (1903–1977), who helped define a mode of popular musical superstardom that paved the way for later figures such as Frank Sinatra (1915–1998) and Elvis Presley (1935–1977).

After World War II (1939–1945), the invention of magnetic tape made the production of recordings much less expensive, and many small record labels sprang up to capture the sounds of African Americans who had moved from the South seeking employment. Their urban blues gave rise to rock and roll, which found a consumer base in the newly developed marketing category of teenagers in the postwar era of intensified consumption practices.

Rock and roll helped give some types of popular music, as well as musicians, greater influence and prestige than either had known before.

Today, popular music is a multinational, multibillion-dollar business dominated by American and European stars, as well as American, European, and Japanese record labels whose products are sold and traded digitally around the world. Hundreds of local styles globally are influenced by American and European sounds, some of which are picked up by labels with international connections and are marketed as *world music*.

BIBLIOGRAPHY

Frith, Simon. 1992. The Industrialization of Popular Music. In *Popular Music and Communication*, ed. James Lull, 49–74. 2nd ed. Newbury Park, CA: Sage.

Sanjek, Russell. 1988. *American Popular Music and its Business: The First Four Hundred Years*. 3 vols. New York: Oxford University Press.

Timothy D. Taylor

POPULATION CONTROL

Concern over uncontrolled population growth already existed in ancient times when scholarly discussion of population issues and evidence of efforts to control family size were recorded in Greece, China, and some other areas (Potts 2003; Zhao 2006). The advocacy for population control has grown notably since the eighteenth century, when population growth began accelerating in many parts of the world.

Population control has been promoted mainly because of the following considerations: To prevent a fall in living standards and the consequences of such a fall, population growth should not outstrip the growth of subsistence. The growth of the population needs to be contained within the biophysical carrying capacity of the earth, otherwise it will lead to overexploitation of natural resources, greatly damaging the ecosystem. In addition to such economic and environmental concerns, promotion of population control also reflects people's varying views of social reform and is regarded as an important step toward enhancing the health of women and their families, protecting people's reproductive choices, and improving sexual expression for both sexes through freedom from fear of pregnancy. In the early stages of its development, population control was also closely connected to the spread of social Darwinist ideas and the eugenics movement.

Population control can be achieved through various means, including those labeled by Thomas Malthus (1766–1834) as positive checks, such as war, famine, disease, and infanticide, that increase death rates (Malthus [1803] 1989). The most significant development in recent human history, however, has been the family-planning or birth-control movement, which is the focus of the remainder of this entry.

The family-planning movement began in Europe. Increasing use of contraception (mainly coitus interruptus and the sponge) was first observed in France in the eighteenth century. Ideas and knowledge of birth control spread in Europe (in Britain in particular) and the United States in the nineteenth century when a number of publications about family planning were widely circulated. The first family-planning clinic was established in the Netherlands in the 1880s. During the next few decades, the number of family planning clinics and organizations promoting birth control grew markedly in Europe and North America. Because of widespread family planning, fertility had already fallen to a very low level in some populations by the early twentieth century.

Significant political and socioeconomic changes took place in many countries after World War II (1939–1945). The baby boom and rapid mortality decline together led to unprecedented population growth, which further stimulated the development of the family-planning movement. Between the 1950s and 1970s, an increasing number of countries began offering family-planning services. The financial and technical assistance provided by developed countries and international organizations greatly helped family planning in less-developed countries. Modern and easy-to-use contraceptives, such as the intrauterine contraceptive device and the birth control pill, became widely available and provided women with greater choice. By the mid-1980s, family-planning programs flourished worldwide. Forty percent of national governments regarded fertility in their countries as too high, 32 percent had official policies to reduce fertility, and 86 percent directly or indirectly supported access to contraception (Tsui 2001). In the first decade of the twenty-first century, world contraceptive prevalence rates exceeded 60 percent among women of reproductive age (United Nations 2006).

It is nonetheless noteworthy that different views toward family planning and population control could be found throughout the twentieth century. For example, concern over low fertility and depopulation already existed in France and some other Western countries in the 1920s, and this concern had grown by the end of the century. In less-developed countries—especially those with relatively low population densities—environmental degradation, poverty, and many other social problems are regarded by some as the result of inequality in the distribution of power and wealth, rather than the outcome of uncontrolled population growth (Hodgson 2003). It is also argued that increasing population density could stimulate economic growth, rather than constrain it (Boserup 1965; Simon 1996).

Although family-planning programs exist in both developed and less-developed countries, there are noticeable differences between them. In most developed countries, family planning started in the nineteenth century or early twentieth century. It was largely a private and philanthropic enterprise and primarily for the purpose of granting individuals, especially women, control over their own reproduction. Programs were organized and executed mostly by voluntary family-planning associations, and governments played no part in this great social-demographic change. The early reduction of fertility was achieved largely through the use of traditional contraceptive methods. In less-developed countries, by contrast, family planning began mainly in the second half of the twentieth century. Rapid population growth in these countries was often seen as a constraint upon socioeconomic development. Family planning was adopted as an official policy to release such pressure, and was directly organized and financed by the government. In some countries, incentive and disincentive (sometimes coercive) measures were employed to induce people to regulate their reproduction. The role of modern contraceptive methods in controlling fertility was crucial in these programs.

China's family-planning program is one such example. Although family planning was promoted in some Chinese cities in the first half of the twentieth century and then again in the 1950s, China's nationwide family-planning program did not start until the early 1970s when its population reached more than 800 million. Facing this pressure, the "later-longer-fewer" policies (which encouraged people to postpone marriage and childbirth to older ages, to prolong birth intervals, and to reduce family size to one or two children) were formed and implemented through a nationwide family-planning network. Even though a great reduction in fertility was achieved between 1970 and 1978, the Chinese government further tightened its birth-control policies in 1979. In cities and advanced rural areas, couples were asked to have only one child; in other rural areas, a family could have no more than two children, although there were exceptions. These radical policies remain in effect, with minor modifications, through the use of both incentive and punitive measures, in addition to the vigorous promotion of family planning. By 2007 China's family-planning program had met its demographic goals, and the country's total fertility rate had been below replacement level for more than a decade. Despite this achievement, China's family-planning program has been accompanied by some negative developments, such as rising sex ratios at birth and an increasing number of induced abortions (similar trends have also been observed in other countries). These developments, which are related to China's long cultural tradition of son preference and the implementation of strict birth-control policies, have made the program very controversial.

At the beginning of the twenty-first century, largely due to the family-planning movement, high fertility or uncontrolled population growth was no longer an issue in many parts of the world. Many developed and some less-developed countries had experienced below-replacement fertility rates for more than a generation, and a few had even experienced a population decline. Indeed, some countries are now taking action to reverse these trends. However, fertility is still high in some countries (mainly in sub-Saharan Africa and the Middle East), where further improving family-planning services remains a major concern.

SEE ALSO *Birth Control; Demographic Transition; Demography; Family Planning; Fertility, Human; Overpopulation*

BIBLIOGRAPHY

Boserup, Ester. 1965. *The Conditions of Agricultural Growth: The Economics of Agrarian Change under Population Pressure.* Chicago: Aldine.

Hodgson, Dennis. 2003. Contemporary Population Thought. In *Encyclopedia of Population*, ed. Paul Demeny and Geoffrey McNicoll, 765–772. New York: Thomson Gale.

Malthus, Thomas Robert. [1803] 1989. *An Essay on the Principle of Population*, ed. Patricia James. Cambridge, U.K.: Cambridge University Press.

Potts, David Malcolm. 2003. History of Birth Control. In *Encyclopedia of Population*, ed. Paul Demeny and Geoffrey McNicoll, 93–98. New York: Thomson Gale.

Simon, Julian. 1996. *The Ultimate Resource.* Rev. ed. Princeton, NJ: Princeton University Press.

Tsui, Amy Ong. 2001. Population Politics, Family Planning Program, and Fertility: The Record. In *Global Fertility Transition*, ed. Rodolfo A. Bulatao and John B. Casterline, 184–204. New York: Population Council.

United Nations Department of Economic and Social Affairs, Population Division. 2006. *World Contraceptive Use 2005.* New York: Author.

Zhao, Zhongwei. 2006. Towards a Better Understanding of Past Fertility Regimes: Ideas and Practice of Controlling Family Size in Chinese History. *Continuity and Change* 21: 9–35.

Zhongwei Zhao

POPULATION GROWTH

Population growth (positive or negative) is caused exclusively by the operation of fertility, mortality, and migration. Regarding the population growth of countries and other national populations, the effect of migration is normally not as influential as the effects of fertility and mortality, usually considered to be the major factors directly causing national population growth (Hinde 1998). However, regarding the population growth of the subareas (states, provinces, counties) of national populations, migration is the single most important of the three demographic processes. Differences in birthrates and death rates in subareas of the same country are typically small compared to differences between the subareas in migration. Migration is thus the major method for redistributing the population within a country.

Fertility is a source of population growth because the number of births indicates whether a population is in a growing pattern (Hinde 1998). If a fertility rate, say the total fertility rate (TFR), is above 2.0, this indicates that on average a woman has more than two children in her lifetime. If the TFR is above 2.1, it means that the woman on average has above replacement fertility, allowing the population to grow via fertility. Mortality is also important given that the death rate determines the number of people who will no longer be able to contribute to the growth of the population. Controlling fertility, countries with high age-specific death rates in infancy and childhood are more likely to have fewer people to give birth to children and thus slower and sometimes negative rates of population growth. Constant fertility and mortality rates typically produce constant population growth rates (Hinde 1998).

The rate of population growth is not only a demographic phenomenon, it also has a broad impact on the society and people's lives. For instance, researchers have found relationships between population growth and economic growth (Barlow 1994; Blanchet 1992; Coale 1986). Robin Barlow (1994) has argued that in a relatively short period of time, an increase in fertility tends to have a negative effect on the economy, while in the long run the opposite relationship is true. Population growth can also lead to a rising demand for food. Problems of instability in food production are particularly difficult for some developing countries with high population growth rates and low technological changes in agriculture (Mellor 1982). In addition rapid population growth tends to impact the interactions between human beings and their environment. An increasing number of people in the population leads to pressures on land resources, which limits the amount of arable agricultural land and tends to worsen the situation of food supply and human reproduction (Shaw 1976). Furthermore a high rate of population growth is likely to increase population density in certain geographic areas, particularly urban settings. As a result overcrowding, unemployment, and poverty are likely to lead to social problems in some localities (Sibly and Hone 2002).

From a microperspective, the population growth rate also has significant influences on an individual's life. Researchers have found that population pressures tend to affect individuals' social reactions. They either force individuals to withdraw from social life as methods of escape or protection due to social overload (Baum and Koman 1976; Evans et al. 2000), or they provoke competition for resources, which tends to amplify people's aggressive behaviors (Calhoun 1962; Lorenz 1967). The latter reaction is often used to explain deviant social behavior in overly crowded areas (Regoeczi 2002). Residential overcrowding has also been found to have an effect on individual well-being and family relations. Children in crowded households have sometimes been observed to have difficulties in behavioral adjustment at school, to perform poorly in academic settings, and to have vulnerable relationships with their parents (Evans et al. 1998). Highly populated households have been shown to increase marital instability and result in the more frequent disciplining of children (Fuller et al. 1993). Previous research has also noted that the impacts of overcrowding on individuals often vary among different subgroups. High-density homes with mothers, children, or low-status individuals are more likely to be problematic compared to other subgroups, and they tend to report more health complaints than other subgroups (Baldassare 1981). All the above effects of high population density on individuals are considered "largely mediated by psychological stress" (Fuller et al. 1993, p. 410). Individuals, however, are not only passively affected by the condition of crowdedness, they can also be adaptive to the social context. Residential overcrowding has been considered a well-known feature of the immigrant experience in the United States, especially in Southern California. Researchers find such an overcrowding situation has been reduced due to the growth of immigrants' incomes, although patterns of decline in overcrowding vary significantly among different racial groups (Myers and Lee 1996). This phenomenon provides an example of how individuals improve the situation of overcrowdedness.

Even though psychological stress is treated as the major mediator shaping the manner in which crowding impacts individuals, other factors have been found to play a role through interaction with psychological pressures. These factors include social support for children and parents, gender, and interactions among individuals. Social support is important because individuals in crowded families are often associated with deteriorating social support structures, which may intensify an individual's psychological pressure (Evans et al. 1998). Gender is often related to the level of stress and an individual's behavior. It has been found that stress is more marked among males than among females in high-density locations (Evans et al. 1998; Freedman et al. 1972; Paulus 1988). Moreover interaction among household members tends to determine the way individuals handle psychological stress (Evans et al. 1998). Thus providing social support for crowded families, especially for males, and strengthening parent-child interaction and family members' communication may reconcile the problems in overcrowded households.

At the societal level many countries and places with rapid population growth rates and high population densities have developed a number of strategies to slow down their population growth. China, the country with the largest population in the world (almost 1.3 billion people in 2005) has made considerable efforts to reduce its fertility and control its population growth. These efforts include the "later, longer, and fewer" policy (later marriage, longer intervals between births, and fewer children) in the early 1970s (Qian 1983) and the nationwide one-birth policy announced in 1979. Consequently, along with social and economic developments, China has experienced a remarkable decline in fertility since the 1970s (Poston 2000), and this has led to considerable population control in China. These programs, however, have also raised demographic and social concerns. One of them is the unbalanced sex ratio at birth (SRB) in China. Due to the strong tradition of son preference and the policy constraints of one birth per couple, the selective abortion of female fetuses and the underreporting of female babies have led to extremely high SRBs in China since the 1980s (Zeng et al. 1993); that is, there are more boys born every year than girls. It is estimated that between the years of 2000 and 2025, there will be more than 31.6 million marriage-age Chinese males who will not be able find Chinese brides. There will not be enough Chinese women in the marriage market for them to marry. These "bare branches" may possibly result in increases in sexual crimes owing to forced marriages, girls stolen for wives, bigamy, prostitution, rape, and adultery (Poston and Zhang 2007). The surplus boys could eventually threaten national stability and international security. Thus it is crucial to strategically coordinate the population growth rate, resources, and social and economic development.

SEE ALSO *Demography; Economic Growth; Fertility, Human; Migration; Morbidity and Mortality; Population Control*

BIBLIOGRAPHY

Baldassare, Mark. 1981. The Effects of Household Density on Subgroups. *American Sociological Review* 46: 110–118.

Barlow, Robin. 1994. Population Growth and Economic Growth: Some More Correlations. *Population and Development Review* 20: 153–165.

Baum, Andrew, and Stuart Koman. 1976. Differential Response to Anticipated Crowding: Psychological Effects of Social and Spatial Density. *Journal of Personality and Social Psychology* 34: 526–536.

Blanchet, Didier. 1992. Reversal of the Effects of Population Growth on Economic Growth since the End of the 1970s: Reality or Artefact? Paper prepared for the Population Division, Department of Economic and Social Development, United Nations.

Calhoun, John B. 1962. Population Density and Social Pathology. *Scientific American* 206: 139–148.

Coale, Ansley J. 1986. Population Trends and Economic Development. In *World Population and U.S. Policy: The Choices Ahead*, ed. Jane Menken, 96–104. New York: Norton.

Evans, Gary W., Stephen J. Lepore, B. R. Shejwal, and M. N. Palsane. 1998. Chronic Residential Crowding and Children's Well-Being: An Ecological Perspective. *Child Development* 69: 1514–1523.

Evans, Gary W., Eunju Rhee, Camille Forbes, et al. 2000. The Meaning and Efficacy of Social Withdrawal as Strategy for Coping with Chronic Residential Crowding. *Journal of Environmental Psychology* 20: 335–342.

Freedman, Jonathan L., A. S. Levey, R. W. Buchanan, and J. Price. 1972. Crowding and Human Aggressiveness. *Journal of Experimental Social Psychology* 8: (6): 528–548.

Fuller, Theodore D., John N. Edwards, Sairuee Vorakitphokatorn, and Santhat Sermsri. 1993. Household Crowding and Family Relations in Bangkok. *Social Problems* 40: 410–430.

Hinde, Andrew. 1998. *Demographic Methods*. New York: Oxford University Press.

Lorenz, Konrad. 1967. *On Aggression*. Trans. Marjorie Latzke. London: Methuen.

Mellor, John W. 1982. The World Development: Food, Employment, and Growth Interactions. *American Journal of Agricultural Economics* 64: 304–311.

Myers, Dowell, and Seong Woo Lee. 1996. Immigration Cohorts and Residential Overcrowding in Southern California. *Demography* 33: 51–65.

Paulus, Paul B. 1988. *Prison Crowding: A Psychological Perspective*. New York: Springer-Verlag.

Poston, Dudley L., Jr. 2000. Social and Economic Development and Fertility Transition in Mainland China and Taiwan. *Population and Development Review* 26: 40–60.

Poston, Dudley L., Jr., and Li Zhang. 2007. How Many Extra Boys Have Been Born in China? In *Gender and Sexually Transmitted Infections in China*, eds. X. Zheng, Dudley L. Poston, and B. Gu, 50–76. Beijing: Beijing University Press.

Qian, Xinzhong. 1983. China's Population Policy: Theory and Methods. *Studies in Family Planning* 14: 295–301.

Regoeczi, Wendy C. 2002. The Impact of Density: The Importance of Nonlinearity and Selection on Flight and Fight Responses. *Social Forces* 81: 505–530.

Shaw, R. Paul. 1976. Government Perceptions of Population Growth. *Population Studies* 30: 77–86.

Sibly, Richard M., and Jim Hone. 2002. Population Growth Rate and Its Determinants: An Overview. *Philosophical Transactions: Biological Sciences* 357: 1153–1170.

Zeng, Yi, Ping Tu, Baochang Gu, et. al. 1993. Causes and Implications of the Recent Increase in the Reported Sex Ratio at Birth in China. *Population and Development Review* 19: 283–302.

Li Zhang
Dudley L. Poston Jr.

POPULATION STUDIES

Population studies is broadly defined as the scientific study of human populations. Major areas studied include broad population dynamics; fertility and family dynamics; health, aging, and mortality; and human capital and labor markets. Researchers in population studies also focus on methodology. Population studies is an interdisciplinary area of study; scholars from demography, epidemiology, sociology, economics, anthropology, and various other disciplines study populations. Various associations and centers exist throughout the United States and elsewhere. The Population Association of America, established in 1930, is a scientific, professional organization established to promote the improvement, advancement, and progress through research of problems related to human populations. Many university-based population studies centers are located throughout the United States, such as the University of Michigan's Population Studies Center and the University of North Carolina at Chapel Hill's Carolina Population Center.

POPULATION DYNAMICS

Among population researchers, demographers are concerned with the empirical study of population dynamics; that is, demographers study population determinants and consequences including size, composition, how populations change over time, and the processes influencing those changes. Demographers deal with the collection, presentation, and analysis of data relating to the basic life-cycle events and experiences of people: birth, marriage, divorce, household and family formation, migration, employment, aging, and death. They also examine compositions of populations by sex, age, race, ethnicity, occupation, education, religion, marital status, and living arrangements. Demographers further assess the distribution of populations by region, country, province or state, urban or rural area, and by neighborhood. Most demographic data come from population censuses, vital registration systems, national registers, and surveys.

Demographers use a variety of counts, rates, ratios, and other statistics to measure fertility, mortality, migration, and other population dynamics. The *crude birth rate* is the annual number of live births per thousand people;

the *general fertility rate* is the annual number of live births per thousand women of childbearing age. The *crude death rate* is the total number of deaths per thousand people; the *mortality rate* is the number of deaths in some population, scaled to the size of that population, per unit of time. The *morbidity rate* refers to the number of people who have a disease compared to the total number of people in a population. The *infant mortality rate* is the annual number of deaths of children less than one year old per thousand live births. *Life expectancy* is defined as the number of years that an individual at a given age can expect to live at present mortality levels. For example, in 2001 the average life expectancy at birth in the United States was seventy-seven years.

The crude death rate, applied to a whole population, can be misleading. For example, the number of deaths per thousand people can be higher for developed nations than for less-developed countries, despite standards of health being better in developed countries. This is because developed countries have relatively older people, who are more likely to die in a given year, so that the overall mortality rate can be higher even if the mortality rate at any given age is lower. A more complete picture of mortality and life expectancy is given by a *life table* that summarizes mortality separately at each age. A life table is a table that shows, for a given person at a given age, what the probability is that the person dies before his or her next birthday. Life tables are usually constructed separately for men and for women because of their different mortality rates. Other characteristics can also be used to distinguish different risks, such as health behaviors and socioeconomic position.

As the world population doubled from three to six billion, researchers in population studies have been examining shifts in population dynamics. The first five years of the twenty-first century saw a decline in the overall volume of population growth, with the world's population increasing at a rate of about seventy-six million people per year as of 2005. Overpopulation occurs when the population of a living species exceeds the carrying capacity of its ecological niche. At the end of the eighteenth century, economist Thomas Malthus (1766–1834) concluded that, if unchecked, populations would be subject to exponential growth. He feared that population growth would surpass growth in food production, leading to ever increasing famine and poverty. On a global scale, however, food production has grown faster than population. Moreover, contrary to Malthus's predictions, natural population growth in most developed countries has diminished to close to zero, without being held in check by famine or lack of resources. This pattern of population growth, with slow (or no) growth in preindustrial societies, followed by fast growth as the society develops and industrializes, followed by slow growth again as it becomes more affluent, is known as a *demographic transi-*

tion. Benjamin Gompertz's (1779–1865) law of mortality, a demographic model published in 1825, is a refinement of Malthus's demographic model.

Future population growth is difficult to predict. Birth rates are declining on average, but vary greatly between developed countries (where birth rates are often at or below replacement levels) and developing countries. Death rates can change unexpectedly due to disease, wars and catastrophes, or advances in medicine. *Population pyramids*, graphs that display a population's age and sex composition, are often used to provide information about future population growth or decline.

Researchers in population studies are also interested in the impact of migration on population dynamics. Migration is the geographic movement of people across a specified boundary. For instance, in the United States, suburban areas are growing more rapidly than central cities. Immigration refers to moves between countries. Immigration is one of the defining characteristics of twentieth-century America; one of the most important changes for the U.S. Census 2000 was the revision of the questions on race and Hispanic origin to better reflect the country's growing diversity.

FERTILITY AND FAMILY DYNAMICS

Population researchers are interested in various facets of family dynamics, cohabitation, marriage, childbearing, and divorce, trends in these dynamics, and differentials in fertility and family dynamics by race, ethnicity, education, and income. Fertility, the number of births for an individual or population, is distinguished from fecundity, the physiological ability of individuals or couples to have children. While the theoretical maximum is estimated to be about fifteen children per woman, even in the world's highest fertility countries the average has rarely exceeded eight. The average fertility rate for the United States in 2003 was 2.0, and the average for the world was 2.8.

Demographers are interested in how various factors influence the probability that a woman bears a child; Kingsley Davis (1908–1997) and Judith Blake (1926–1993) in the 1950s and John Bongaarts in the 1980s identified "proximate determinates of fertility." The primary trends of the second demographic transition include delays in fertility and marriage; increases in cohabitation, divorce, and nonmarital childbearing; and increases in maternal employment. Women also vary considerably in when and how many children they will have depending upon age, race, income, religion, and many other social, economic, and cultural factors.

HEALTH, AGING, AND MORTALITY

Epidemiologists, population researchers who study the distribution and determinants of disease frequency, aim to identify factors that promote health and reduce the burden of disease in human populations. A disease is broadly defined as an abnormal condition of the body or mind that causes discomfort, dysfunction, or distress to the afflicted person. Some diseases are infectious, such as influenza, and can be transmitted by a variety of mechanisms. Other diseases, such as cancer and heart disease, are noninfectious or chronic. Aging is generally characterized by the declining ability to respond to stress, increasing homeostatic imbalance, and increased risk of disease. Death is the ultimate consequence of aging. Key areas of research in aging include: demographic trends; health, disease, and disability; labor force participation and retirement; and family status.

Health researchers employ a range of study designs, often integrating molecular, cellular, medical, and social levels, with the purpose of revealing unbiased relationships between exposures such as nutrition and stress or social factors such as education to outcomes like disease, well-being, and other health indicators. Morbidity and mortality rates vary by common social categories such as age, sex, socioeconomic status, and race/ethnicity. Research on social class differentials in mortality has a long history. Higher-status individuals live healthier and longer lives than their lower-status counterparts in virtually every society. Despite improvements in public health in the last half-century, large disparities continue to persist between and within countries for a range of health indicators.

HUMAN CAPITAL AND LABOR MARKETS

Sociologists and economists in the field of population studies often examine labor markets and human capital such as education and skills. Researchers examine trends and inequalities in educational attainment. Other areas of study include labor force participation rates, how labor markets operate (including the matching of employees to jobs and differences across labor market segments), earnings differences, mobility, and inequalities by various demographic characteristics. Researchers also examine labor market trends, such as unemployment rates, as well as trends in length of employment relationships. There is a large amount of research on sex, race, and socioeconomic disparities in human capital and labor markets.

SEE ALSO *Anthropology; Demography; Economics; Family Functioning; Family Structure; Fertility, Human; Geography; Marriage; Migration; Morbidity and Mortality; Population Control; Population Growth; Sociology*

BIBLIOGRAPHY

Bongaarts, John, and Susan C. Watkins. 1996. Social Interactions and Contemporary Fertility Transitions. *Population and Development Review* 22 (4): 639–682.

Haupt, Arthur, and Thomas T. Kane. 2004. *The Population Reference Bureau's Population Handbook.* 5th ed. Washington, DC: Population Reference Bureau.

Hauser, Philip M., and Otis Dudley Duncan. 1959. The Nature of Demography. In *The Study of Population: An Inventory and Appraisal,* eds. Philip M. Hauser and Otis D. Duncan, 29–44. Chicago: University of Chicago Press.

McFalls, Joseph A., Jr. 2003. *Population: A Lively Introduction.* 4th ed. *Population Bulletin* 58 (4). Washington, DC: Population Reference Bureau.

McKeown, Thomas, and R. G. Record. 1962. Reasons for the Decline of Mortality in England and Wales during the Nineteenth Century. *Population Studies* 16 (2): 94–122.

Preston, Samuel H. 1993. The Contours of Demography: Estimates and Projections. *Demography* 30: 593–606.

Jennie E. Brand

POPULATION SURPLUS

SEE *Surplus Population.*

POPULISM

Populism, as both ideology and political movement, is nearly a universal, albeit sporadic, feature of all modern democratic political systems. One basic problem in identifying and assessing populist movements can be traced to definitional questions because their basic features are similar to those found in conventional democratic politics. For example, references to "the people" by charismatic leaders who emphasize the need for a "redeeming break" with current practice and who exploit the anger of citizens are all features of populist protest as well as staples of electoral practice. Further, the causes of populist movements are quite varied and can include a wide range of both economic and cultural issues.

In the United States after the Civil War, farmers protested against the impact of industrialization, particularly in regard to railroad rates for their crops, the cost of new machinery, and bank lending policies. These complaints coalesced into a mass movement led by the Farmers' Alliance. Populists formed their own political party in 1892 and approved a platform that expanded on these initial protests. The party later merged with the Democrats and the movement declined in part as a result of the defeat of William Jennings Bryan by William McKinley in the 1896 presidential election. Populist movements in somewhat different forms, however, continue to reemerge as a factor in American politics. While populism is possibly the only example of an indigenous radical mass movement in the United States, it is a subject of controversy among democratic theorists.

The Farmers' Alliance was a complex collection of state and local organizations, including two broad groups in the Midwest and the South, that sometimes competed with one another. Since the Southern Alliance did not admit African Americans, these farmers formed their own organization (Colored Farmers' Alliance). These groups used a variety of inventive measures to increase the price of crops. The price of cotton, for example, had declined below the cost of production. Cooperative trade agreements were made with merchants for lower prices for equipment and higher prices for produce. In some states, the alliance built its own mills for crops. Speakers and lobbyists were hired to publicize the farmers' plight. The Colored Farmers' Alliance created aid programs for needy farmers.

Differences in strategies and tactics, however, plagued the movement. Some Texas "alliancemen" favored the polices of Andrew Dunlap, who emphasized a "strictly business" approach of self-help, while others, including S. O. Dawes and Charles William Macune, sought broader goals and focused on reforming the currency system, which they had concluded was the core cause of the farmers' plight. There were also disputes between relatively economically secure farmers who could afford the "cash and carry" agreements of the cooperatives and indebted farmers who could not.

The goals of the movement began to expand in the late 1880s as the impact of these cooperative plans proved to be more limited than hoped and farmers became disenchanted with politicians who failed effectively to promote agendas that helped elect them to office. Mary Lease, a Kansas activist, allegedly urged farmers to "raise less corn and more hell." Independent candidates with alliance support ran with considerable success in midwestern states in 1890. In the South, the alliance focused upon taking over the Democratic Party. While these local efforts produced elected officials such as Tom Watson of Georgia and "Sockless" Jerry Simpson of Kansas, who would become major figures in the populist movement, the alliance leaders increasingly came to the conclusion that a national third party was the only hope for farmers.

After series of meetings in Ocala, Florida; Saint Louis, Missouri; and Cincinnati, Ohio, a national convention was held in Omaha, Nebraska, to form a new political party. The Omaha platform itself became a revered document among Populists who regarded it as a "second Declaration of Independence." The preamble, written by Ignatius Donnelly, announced that "a vast conspiracy against mankind" was about to take "possession of the world." "If not met and overthrown at once … terrible social convulsions, a destruction of civilization, or the establishment of an absolute despotism" was certain to follow. The proposals themselves were organized into three categories: finance, transportation, and land. The new party demanded the "free and unlimited coinage of silver and gold," an increase in the money supply, a graduate income tax, limits on state and federal spending, postal savings banks, public ownership of railroads, privatization of land now held by corporations "in excess of their actual needs," and reclamation of land owned by aliens. The convention also approved an "expression of sentiments," including support for a strike led by the Knights of Labor against clothing manufacturers in Rochester, New York, and urged a boycott of the firm's products. Specific endorsement of a subtreasury plan that provided for government-backed credits for farmers, which Macune had long supported, did not appear in the final document. Nor was a proposal for female suffrage included on the platform, although it had been endorsed at the Saint Louis meeting.

Delegates would likely have nominated Leonidas L. Polk, head of the National Farmers' Alliance and renowned orator, for president, but they turned instead to James B. Weaver, a former Union general, after Polk's sudden death. James G. Field, a former Confederate general, was nominated to give the ticket regional balance. Weaver campaigned widely and attempted to trace the ideology of the party back to Andrew Jackson. "The whole movement," he said, "can be summed up in one sentence: 'Equal rights for all and special privileges to none.'" The Populist Party received a million votes and twenty-two electoral votes in the 1892 presidential election. Populist candidates at the state level did quite well, although the party was unable to win control of any state government without Democratic Party support.

Several decisions proved to be crucial to the course of populism after the 1892 election. Grover Cleveland's victory as president was the result in large part of the Populist Party, which drew Republican votes, particularly in western states. The Democrats were severely weakened by the panic of 1894. Some Populists, called "fusionists," argued that they should now attempt to take control of the Democratic Party away from its conservative leaders. Others argued for a continuation of a separate third party, and others believed that a regionally based party should be the focus of the next elections. When Democrats nominated William Jennings Bryan with Populist support at the Democratic convention in Chicago in 1896, Populists feared that two presidential candidates supporting populist proposals would assure a Republican victory. Some Populists now argued that the new party should endorse Bryan rather than nominate him as their candidate. At their convention in Saint Louis, Populist delegates nominated Bryan but refused to accept his running mate, Arthur Sewall, a conservative shipbuilder, and nominated

Tom Watson instead. Populists did not anticipate that the outcome of the election would be a major national party realignment that made Republicans the dominant party for the next thirty-six years. Antifusionists claimed that Bryan's defeat was largely the result of his emphasis of monetary issues over other Populist ideas. The majority of Populists again nominated Bryan, although a faction of the party dissented and nominated their own candidates. Tom Watson ran as the presidential candidate of the Populist Party in 1904 and 1906 but received only 120,000 and 30,000 votes, respectively.

Despite the collapse of the movement, the themes of the Populist Party have sporadically remerged in American politics. Antipathy to elites, an interest in monetary plans as a fulcrum for political change, support for rural and small-town values, and acceptance of conspiratorial theories are featured in whole or in part among those who supported Senator Joe McCarthy in the 1950s and the presidential campaigns of George Wallace (1968) and Ross Perot (1992) as third-party candidates. Several presidents, including Franklin Roosevelt in 1936, Jimmy Carter in 1976, and George W. Bush in 2004, have employed some populist themes.

The "golden age of populism" in Latin America occurred later than in the United States. These movements were responses in part to the Great Depression. They grew in the context of unstable regimes, and some were more successful than their earlier North American counterparts. The exemplar was Juan Perón, who governed Argentina for two terms as president (1946–1955; 1973–74) with the support of urban workers (derisively called the "shirtless ones" by his opponents) through the promise of numerous economic benefits, the nationalization of major corporations, and the incorporation of trade unions into the government. Perón called his programs the "third way," but Peronism was in fact a volatile mixture of right- and left-wing elements. Gertúlio Vargas in Brazil and Lázaro Cárdenas in Mexico pursued some of the same policies. Vargas was an admirer of Mussolini, and Perón welcomed fascists to his country after World War II, while Cárdenas invited Leon Trotsky to Mexico after his exile. While those sympathetic to the Peronistas are still a political force and Cárdenas's regime gave birth to the Party of the Mexican Revolution, or PRM, the current rise of populism can be directly traced to reaction against the "neoliberal" policies of political leaders in the 1990s. Hugo Chavez in Venezuela and Evo Morales in Bolivia, among others, have rejected programs encouraging foreign investment and privatizing social services as policies of U.S. imperialism. Chavez's "Bolivarian Revolution" emphasizes redistributive programs based on state oil revenues, and Morales promotes the economic and cultural goals of indigenous farmers. Both frame their policies as correctives to the power of local elites and foreign economic interests.

Many scholars locate the basic features of populism in the rise of fascist regimes in Europe and thus conclude that populist appeals are a significant threat to democratic regimes. On the other hand, political leaders such as David Lloyd George in the United Kingdom and Leon Blum in France employed populist themes and programs within a democratic context. Recent populist movements reveal the same range of alternatives. Protests against immigration and economic centralization have produced populist challenges in the Netherlands, Slovakia, Austria, and France.

Scholars are divided over whether populist outbursts represent a desirable form of democratic protest against economic and political centralization or whether they pose a threat to democracy in their emphasis on the authority of the "people" and opposition to economic change.

SEE ALSO *Ballots; Chavez, Hugo; Elections; Jingoism; McCarthyism; Peronism; Personality, Cult of; Progressive Movement; Racism; Radicalism; Social Movements*

BIBLIOGRAPHY

Canovan, Margaret. 1999. "Trust the People!" Populism and the Two Faces of Democracy. *Political Studies* 47 (1): 2–16.

Goodwyn, Lawrence. 1976. *Democratic Promise: The Populist Moment in America*. New York: Oxford University Press.

Hicks, John D. 1931. *The Populist Revolt: A History of the Farmers' Alliance and the People's Party*. Minneapolis: University of Minnesota Press.

Hofstadter, Richard. 1955. *The Age of Reform: From Bryan to F.D.R.* New York: Knopf.

Kazin, Michael. 1998. *The Populist Persuasion: An American History*. Rev. ed. Ithaca, NY: Cornell University Press.

Mazzoleni, Gianpietro, Julianne Stewart, and Bruce Horsfield, eds. 2003. *The Media and Neo-Populism: A Contemporary Comparative Analysis*. Westport, CT: Praeger.

McMath, Robert C., Jr. 1993. *American Populism: A Social History, 1877–1898*. New York: Hill and Wang.

Peal, David. 1989. The Politics of Populism: Germany and the American South in the 1890s. *Comparative Studies in History and Society* 31 (2): 340–362.

Philip Abbott

PORNOGRAPHY
SEE *Obscenity*.

PORTES, ALEJANDRO
SEE *Assimilation*.

POSITIVE CRIMINOLOGY
SEE *Ortiz, Fernando*.

POSITIVE PSYCHOLOGY

During the first half of the twentieth century, psychologists who held either a behaviorist or psychoanalytic perspective were the dominant forces in American psychology. Apprehensive about what they considered the passive view of human functioning that behaviorism represented, and dissatisfied with the focus on abnormality that characterized psychoanalytic interests, a third group of psychologists called for attention to inner experience, internal processes, adaptive functioning, positive life-influences, and self-constructs. The writings of these theorists caught the attention of scholars and researchers and, during the 1950s, the humanistic movement was born. The most powerful voice in the new movement was that of Abraham Maslow (1908–1970), who proposed a dynamic theory of motivation in which internal and intrinsic motivating forces and affective processes lead to personal, social, and psychological well-being. This was a view of human functioning in which subjective experiences and positive attitudes played a prominent role.

Although widespread, the influence of humanistic psychology was erratic. The emphasis on self-processes encouraged a personal and cultural self-absorption that minimized the importance of collective well-being. Moreover, the gap from theory to practice proved difficult to breach, and many laudable but misguided efforts to nurture the self-esteem of individuals fell prey to excesses and, ultimately, ridicule. The goal of focusing on and fostering positive self-perceptions became mired in controversies over the value of self-processes in areas such as education, controversies that continue unabated to this day. Because research efforts were unsystematic and results highly inconsistent, the tenets of humanistic psychology failed to develop an empirical base. As a consequence, the humanistic movement waned during the 1980s as psychologists shifted their interest to cognitive processes and information-processing views of human functioning.

As the twenty-first century arrived, however, there was another vigorous call within the discipline for a science of psychology grounded on positive experience. This *positive psychology* has been described as the study of human strengths and optimal functioning, and one of its key aims is to foster research on the positive personal traits and dispositions that are thought to contribute to subjective well-being and psychological health. Such research stands in contrast to the traditional study of people's distress, pathology, and maladaptive functioning that continues to characterize American psychology. Moreover, although positive psychology shares with the humanistic movement the aim of advancing human fulfillment, one of positive psychology's key aims is that its methodology be firmly grounded in systematic and scientific inquiry.

The central feature of positive psychology is its dual focus on fostering wellness and preventing maladies such as depression, substance abuse, or mental disorders in individuals who are genetically vulnerable or whose problems are exacerbated by the pressures of our modern lifestyles. In education, proponents of a positive psychology call for the powerful need to prevent bullying and other school violence and to foster academic motivation.

What differentiates the approach of positive psychology from that which has characterized mainstream psychology during the last century is the abandonment of the "disease model" of human functioning in favor of a "human strengths model." The disease model, positive psychologists observe, evolved from the psychoanalytic practice of deducing normality, mental health, and well-being from the study of abnormal individuals, a method that came to dominate the discipline of psychology. In addition, psychologists have been traditionally trained to correct problems rather than prevent them. A human strengths model shifts psychologists' perspective from this focus on mental illness to one on mental health. Thus, prevention is viewed with equal import as correction, and the development of wellness is put on the same footing as the curing of illness. Positive psychologists working in clinical practice would focus on augmenting the strengths of their clients rather than simply correcting and repairing their weaknesses. Those who work in education would have it as their aim to help create healthy school and classroom climates that foster academic success and personal well-being. All professionals who practice a positive psychology would see it as their mission to make individuals stronger and more productive so that they can more easily maximize their own potential.

Because positive psychology promulgates a perspective focused on building competence, not on correcting weakness, proponents call for a focus on the human strengths that act as buffers against mental maladies. These include optimism, happiness, well-being, empathy, courage, friendship, faith, hope, love, honesty, self-determination, autonomy, insight, future mindedness, positive illusions, perseverance, physical health, wisdom, creativity, altruism, and flow. In each case, the aim of positive psychologists is to investigate how these constructs can foster positive human development. For example, those who emphasize the study of happiness are proponents of an evolutionary psychology in which improving that human quality can be accomplished by remaining in closer proximity or maintaining greater emotional close-ness to existing kin, developing deep friendships, reducing subjective distress, managing competitive mechanisms, and exploiting knowledge of evolved desires. Other psychologists suggest that human development and potential can be fostered through the cultivation of an optimistic life view in which the causes of life's events are interpreted in adaptive and beneficent ways.

The American Psychological Association (APA) has itself embraced this approach toward the study of optimal human functioning, making the first issue of the *American Psychologist* in the year 2000 a theme issue on positive psychology constructs. The APA has also joined with the John Templeton Foundation to create a new award designed to promote the advancement of the new science. The annual award provides the largest monetary prize ever given in the field of psychology.

In the area of education, researchers hope that insights available from investigations that emphasize a positive psychology will alter the present focus of drawing inferences about adaptive functioning from students who are "at-risk" or "unmotivated" to those who are resilient and resourceful. For example, positive psychology seeks to shift the emphasis from research frequently conducted on concepts such as learned helplessness and anxiety to the study of learned optimism and self-efficacy. To these ends, the new researchers urge that positive psychology constructs be integrated with those of traditional and established bodies of educational literature and lines of inquiry.

SEE ALSO *Altruism and Prosocial Behavior; Behaviorism; Creativity; Empathy; Flow; Hope; Motivation; Optimism/Pessimism; Psychoanalytic Theory; Self-Determination; Self-Efficacy; Self-Esteem*

BIBLIOGRAPHY

Aspinwall, Lisa G., and Ursula M. Staudinger. 2003. *A Psychology of Human Strengths: Fundamental Questions and Future Directions for a Positive Psychology.* Washington, DC: American Psychological Association.

Seligman, Martin E. P., and Mihaly Csikszentmihalyi, eds. 2000. Positive Psychology. Special issue. *American Psychologist* 55 (1).

Snyder, C. R., and Shane J. Lopez, eds. 2002. *Handbook of Positive Psychology.* Oxford: Oxford University Press.

Frank Pajares

POSITIVE PSYCHOLOGY CENTER

SEE *Seligman, Martin; Positive Psychology.*

POSITIVE SOCIAL SCIENCE

The words *positive, positivism, positive science,* and *positive social science* have meant many different things to many different people. In the context of French social thought, the words *positive science* were first uttered, it seems, by Madame de Staël (1766–1817), the eccentric thinker, writer, socialite, and associate of Romantic and scientific utopians of the late eighteenth and early nineteenth century (Gordon 1991, p. 271). Like others in her circle, Madame de Staël was enthusiastic about the role that scientific method could play in advancing human progress toward the goals of spiritual and material perfection. Historians of ideas typically end their trace of positive *social* science with the originators of modern sociology, that is, with Henri Saint Simon (1760–1825) and his disciple, Auguste Comte (1798–1857). Thus the linguistic turn from positive science to positive social science. There is of course some controversy over the "origins of sociology" question—for example, a case can be made for the claim that Aristotle (384–322 BCE) was the founder of sociology (and, for that matter, of economics, too)—but these claims are not a concern here.

Still, historically and methodologically speaking, positive social science is a difficult notion to define precisely. One way to define it is to name what its diverse advocates claim it is not: positive social science is not old school metaphysics, and it is not a normative branch of science, such as welfare economics or applied ethics. Against the speculative metaphysics of Plato (427–347 BCE) and Immanuel Kant (1724–1804), for example, and against the value judgments of moralists such as Jean-Jacques Rousseau (1712–1778) and Comte and the contemporary philosopher John Rawls (1921–2002), positive social scientists are united in their attempt to understand and explain the sensory world in objective, logical, factual, and value-neutral observational terms. The positive social scientist seeks a view from nowhere, or from God's eyes. He does not necessarily do the empirical, factual side of the homework on his subject; he need only claim to believe that his logic speaks to the factual and logical as ultimate arbiters of objective inquiry. Since the late nineteenth century, most adherents to positive social science have dropped the historical belief in "progress" toward "perfection" by discontinuous stages or constant evolution, the inheritance of Comte and de Staël. After the publication of *Grammar of Science* (1892) by Karl Pearson (1857–1936), and especially after the 1929 publication of *Wissenschaftliche Weltauffassung: Der Wiener Kreis* (A Scientific Conception of the World: The Vienna Circle), the manifesto of the so-called Vienna Circle, the aims of positive social science entailed a set of beliefs and an argu-

mentative style more than it did a historical explanation or perfectionist state to be aimed for.

If positive social science ever had a firm philosophical grounding, the grounding was provided not by the so-called *wertfrei* (value-free) social science of the economic sociologist Max Weber (1864–1920) but rather by a series of philosophical arguments commonly referred to as *logical positivism.* Initially a loosely knit group of philosophers, physicists, economists, sociologists, and mathematicians, the logical positivists were directly associated with or otherwise allied with the Vienna Circle. A goal of the logical positivists, early and late, was to firmly lodge the "fact/value dichotomy" into the minds of working scientists, a dichotomy first brought to the attention of philosophers by Kant and to social scientists by David Hume (1711–1776). Logical positivists tended to conflate the analytic/synthetic argument of Kant with the ought/is argument of Hume. Despite or perhaps because of their struggle to construct a "unified science," the positivists did not much quibble over their own ambiguities.

Ever since a simple faith in positivism has faded, social scientists have typically stuck to a Humean argument. Hume, many interpreters have said, suggests in Book III, Part 1, of his *Treatise of Human Nature* (1739) that one cannot derive *ought* propositions from *is* propositions. He is commonly understood to have argued that value judgments cannot be derived from factual observations. Facts and values are distinct entities, most of his interpreters have held, making a kind of fork between data and judgment. Since the 1920s the vast majority of economists, political scientists, and psychologists have taken Hume's fork as dogma. A similar influence of the fact/value dichotomy on medical and biological research has not gone unnoticed (by contrast, anthropologists and sociologists have long raised objections to it).

Logical positivists took Hume's fork to be the whole scientific meal, a belief that rapidly entered the mainstream of social scientific thought. Only scientific statements were to be accepted as "cognitively meaningful." And only axiomatic and value-neutral statements about the facts of the world would count as science. Value judgments—especially judgments of an ethical kind—were said to be the province of preachers and poets, objectively speaking, "meaningless," no guide to social or economic policy.

Often it is not obvious how one can push values entirely aside so that objective facts are the only entities revealed. Take, for example, the sentence "Iraq does not have weapons of mass destruction." At one level of reading, it is a straightforward factual claim—true, false, or uncertain. Iraq is a nation, nations engage in both self-defense and aggressive war, weapons of mass destruction have been used in war by other nations, and many nations agree on what counts as a weapon of mass destruction: these are facts. Presumably one could assemble a team of social, physical, and life scientists, trained in best-practice census tabulation, sampling theory, and experimental and analytical methods, such that—conditional on Iraqi government cooperation or military force—one could arrive at a correct answer to the central factual claim: Iraq does not have weapons of mass destruction.

But the interdependence of facts and values can be illustrated by a single change in subject-object relation. Suppose the original sentence is changed to "The United States does not have weapons of mass destruction" (a change in subject) or "Iraq does not have balloons for school decoration" (a change in object). Changing the subject from Iraq to "the United States" or the object from weapons of mass destruction to "balloons for school decoration" involves not merely a change in the facts of the subject and object, but a thorough-going change of perspective, driven not by the raw facts—however defined—but by value judgments largely or entirely embodied by the original sentence. Some officials of the U.S. government, including some high-ranking scientists, obviously do not care about, or are not troubled by, the fact that the U.S. government has weapons of mass destruction. "The United States does not have weapons of mass destruction" is not a factual statement that can elicit a similarly massive sacrifice of money, time, capital, and human lives. A change in object brings one to a similar conclusion. "Iraq does not have balloons for school decoration" is a claim that could presumably be answered by the same team of scientists, statisticians, and military personnel. But the U.S. government does not value the answer to the latter claim; it will not sacrifice many resources to discover the truth about balloons.

Fact statements and value statements are interdependent in science because human motives generate the questions and methods of science. This is not a bad thing to admit for either science or society—on the contrary, it is probably an advantage. Free and public deliberation over the values and interests of science and society is, for instance, an alternative to despotism and mass ignorance. And the expansion of free and democratic alternatives tends, social scientists agree, to increase human well-being. Opinions differ on the 2003 U.S.-led invasion of Iraq. For example, some say the loss to the world of being *wrong* about the original claim may be so large that any scientific and military investigation should receive funding until surety on the issue is achieved. But even then one is not armed with reasons sufficient to justify allegiance to the factual side of the alleged fact/value dichotomy. Different opinions on facts and values prevail over most public matters. For example, many public institutions, from elementary schooling to space exploration, persist with mass approval, despite a wide variance of professional economic opinion. To put it another way, who would spend billions of dollars trying to discover whether another nation has balloons to decorate their schools? Only a fact-crazed scientist, lacking a rhetoric of values.

At still another level of reading—as seen from the values-only side—the fact/value dichotomy remains dubious. Suppose the original sentence is changed to "According to the United States government, Iraq should not have weapons of mass destruction." The new sentence directly appeals to a value judgment. Notice it does not say exactly from whom the value judgment is coming (only "the government"). And it does not say who the speaker of the sentence is. But the word *should* has replaced the word *does*, signaling, it seems, an abandonment of facts and a decisive move over to the values side of things. But there are at least two objections one can raise to such a conclusion: (1) The author of the original sentence and her readers were never on the facts-only side of things, as the argument above suggests, in the first place; and (2) The sentence "According to the United States government, Iraq should not have weapons …", if taken in the same spirit as the supposedly facts-only claim ("Iraq does not have weapons …"), must entail a moral commitment to change the situation (that is, the situation implied by the fact that Iraq has the weapons, if they do). But if the U.S. government is to change the situation, as indeed it endeavored to do when it sought to determine factually whether Iraq had the weapons, it must commence with the same or similar scientific investigation and, perhaps, military force, as in the previous case. The decision of a scientist engaged in free inquiry is not a decision to speak about facts as against values, or positive science as against normative science; it is a decision to choose transparency over opacity. Status quo belief induces most to choose the latter. Yet by 1974 one scholar counted "two score and more of [philosopher and scientist] witnesses *against* the fact-value split" (Booth 1974, p. 207; emphasis added).

The philosopher and logician Hilary Putnam (2002) has taken the argument a step further, showing that even if one insists that *is* and *should* or *is* and *ought* are radically distinct, and that *ought* propositions cannot be derived from *is* propositions, as some scientists maintain in, for example, the case of weapons of mass destruction, there are still further "value judgments" of an aesthetic type that permeate the most factual sounding research claims. (Putnam's observation is not original, but it is nowadays rare; one can find a similar link between aesthetic qualities of science and normative judgment in Aristotle's *Rhetoric*.) Scientists value, for example, "coherence," "simplicity," and "consistency" in their models and facts (and again Putnam is hardly the first scholar to say so; cf. Burke 1950). Aesthetic values are always at play in science and are, as any scientist who has received a referee report can attest, constantly being judged by "positive" scientists.

It has been a long time since any respectable historian or philosopher of science believed that logical positivism succeeded in its goal to speak in a circumscribed, fact-and-logic only language. Today, very few philosophers adhere to the fact/value dichotomy, though, to repeat, social scientists cling to it.

POSITIVE SOCIAL SCIENCE AND NOVELTY IN ECONOMICS

Still, many novel ideas in economics have emerged despite the strange faith. Before the publication of Milton Friedman's (1912–2006) *Essays in Positive Economics* (1953), the Dutch economist Jan Tinbergen (1903–1994) and the American economist Lawrence Klein were inspired by visions of positive science to build multiequation econometric models of the Dutch and U.S. economies. The facts of these economies could be revealed through logical (that is, model-based) relations widely held by economists. Both models failed at the level of macroprediction. But for their remarkable technical achievements, both Tinbergen and Klein were awarded (in 1969 and 1980, respectively) the Nobel Prize in Economic Sciences.

Following the work on the theory of human capital by the economist and 1992 Nobel laureate Gary S. Becker, first developed in the 1950s and 1960s, positive economists and sociologists have developed new methods for examining the extent of racial and gender discrimination in labor markets. Becker has argued that competition and the pursuit of profit will drive racist and sexist employers out of business. In statistical regression analyses, researchers after Becker have attempted to show the quantitative influence of race and gender by holding constant a host of independent variables—education level, family structure, labor force attachment, and so forth—such that race and gender are the only variables left in the model to "explain" black-white, male-female, or white-male/black-female differences in wages and occupational attainment.

That an adherence to positive social science and the fact/value dichotomy is coincident with some novel ideas in social science research does not demonstrate the fact or value of positive social science, however circumscribed. Indeed, both the Tinbergen-Klein and Becker research programs have been criticized on "value-laden" grounds: new classical and rational-expectations macroeconomists object that Tinbergen's and Klein's Keynesian models of agent behavior are not "consistent" with rational choice theory (consistency being a value judgment), and a wide range of economic sociologists working in the tradition of W. E. B. Du Bois (1868–1963) and St. Clair Drake

(1911–1990) reply that Becker's independent variables are themselves the products of racial and gender discrimination (O'Connor et al. 2001), a value judgment masquerading in the econometrics as mere data.

SEE ALSO *Friedman, Milton; Methodology; Normative Social Science; Positivism; Social Science, Value Free*

BIBLIOGRAPHY

Ayer, A. J. 1936. *Language, Truth, and Logic.* London: Gollancz.

Becker, Gary S. [1957] 1971. *The Economics of Discrimination.* 2nd ed. Chicago: University of Chicago Press.

Booth, Wayne C. 1974. *Modern Dogma and the Rhetoric of Assent.* Chicago: University of Chicago Press.

Brown, Richard H. 1989. *Social Science as Civic Discourse: Essays on the Invention, Legitimation, and Uses of Social Theory.* Chicago: University of Chicago Press.

Burke, Kenneth. 1945. *A Grammar of Motives.* New York: Prentice Hall.

Burke, Kenneth. 1950. *A Rhetoric of Motives.* New York: Prentice Hall.

Friedman, Milton. 1953. *Essays in Positive Economics.* Chicago: University of Chicago Press.

Gordon, Scott. 1991. *The History and Philosophy of Social Science.* London: Routledge.

Hands, D. Wade. 2001. *Reflection without Rules: Economic Methodology and Contemporary Science Theory.* Cambridge, U.K.: Cambridge University Press.

Hirsch, Abraham, and Neil De Marchi. 1990. *Milton Friedman: Economics in Theory and Practice.* Ann Arbor: University of Michigan Press.

Kuhn, Thomas S. 1970. Postscript-1969. In *The Structure of Scientific Revolutions*, 174–210. 2nd ed. Chicago: University of Chicago Press.

O'Connor, Alice, Chris Tilly, and Lawrence Bobo, eds. 2001. *Urban Inequality: Evidence from Four Cities.* New York: Sage.

Popper, Karl R. 1959. *The Logic of Scientific Discovery.* London: Routledge.

Putnam, Hilary. 2002. *The Collapse of the Fact/Value Dichotomy, and Other Essays.* Cambridge, MA: Harvard University Press.

Shapin, Steven. 1994. *A Social History of Truth: Civility and Science in Seventeenth-Century England.* Chicago: University of Chicago Press.

Wittgenstein, Ludwig. 1922. *Tractatus Logico-Philosophicus.* Trans. D. F. Pears and B. F. McGuinness. London: Routledge.

Stephen Ziliak

POSITIVISM

There are two uses of the term *positivism* in the social sciences, one derived from sociology, the other from jurisprudence, especially international law. In sociology, positivism was a broad movement of European thought during the second half of the nineteenth century. The name derives from the fact that thinkers returned to the appreciation of positive facts so as to restore the world of nature, which idealists had reduced to a mere representation of the ego. Positivism placed greater stress on immediate experience and on the data obtained through the senses.

In jurisprudence, positivists emphasize textual analysis, in contrast to naturalists, who take treaties and other texts as a starting point for determining the guiding principles of the day. However, if there is no text and a new or revised rule of customary international law is advocated, naturalists are likely to emphasize the actual consequences of the new practice, while positivists underscore intent or motive. This is the opposite of the situation faced in textual analysis. One could imagine situations in which the claim is made that the text should be ignored in favor of a new customary principle. Where there is a conflict between positive law and customary principles, naturalists argue that the customary law claimed to exist should prevail. However, naturalists are also likely to argue that principles can be used to interpret provisions in such texts as the UN Charter, which would reduce the probability of a conflict with custom.

Positivism flourished in Latin America as nowhere else, not even in France, where it was first developed by Auguste Comte (1798–1857). It met the needs of many Latin American intellectuals who rejected Spanish and Portuguese culture and were trying to prove their independence by adopting French ideas. They considered Catholicism as a tool of Spanish imperialism, which had kept Latin America in a state of amoral, chaotic backwardness. Positivism called for progress, discipline, morality, and freedom from the tyranny of theology. The positivists rebelled against the spiritualist metaphysics shared by deists and Catholics. This rebellion turned them into agnostics and sometimes even into atheists.

ADVENT AND EVOLUTION OF SOCIOLOGICAL POSITIVISM

The sociological use of positivism emerged in France under Comte, evolving from English empiricism, which argued that experience was the only source of human knowledge. The new school of thought held that reality mechanically evolves from inferior forms until it attains consciousness in humans. According to Comte, historical observations on the process of human society show that humans have passed through three stages. First was the theological state, in which nature was mythically conceived and the individual sought the meaning of natural phenomena from supernatural beings. Second came the

metaphysical stage, in which nature was conceived of as a result of obscure forces and the individual sought to explain natural phenomena from them. Third came the positive stage, in which all abstract and obscure forces are discarded and natural phenomena are explained by their constant relationships. Comte extended the law of the three stages to include all reality.

Jurisprudential positivism emerged in the nineteenth century and gained influence in the twentieth century because of the tendency to replace customary or natural law with statutory or treaty law. In international law, positivism gained even more influence after the 1945 UN Charter. Positivists argue that the charter, and law generally, should be treated as a constitution that, following the model of H. L. A. Hart (1961), establishes "primary" rules (to make rules) and "secondary" rules based on them that establish particular policies and principles, including, but not requiring, conceptions of justice and other issues of substance. In international law, if treaties are read loosely, or principles are imputed or inflated, or customs are claimed rather than observed, positivists feel that the consent required for law to exist on the basis of explicit rules does not exist. Furthermore, in specific applications, motives matter in order to assure that the community of nations agrees. Because motives are difficult to know, the presumption of positivists is that consent for actions against prevailing interpretations of legal doctrine must be unambiguous for law to deviate from claimed fundamental principles. Opposition to what is clearly the intent of positive law as expressed in texts is normally a sign of illegality.

Sociological positivists did not follow exactly the same course in the Latin American countries. Positivism was most influential in Brazil, whose elites studied French and visited Paris, where they came to admire everything French. By the end of the nineteenth century these elites wanted to import or copy everything they associated with France. At the time, positivism became particularly important in Brazil's technical schools and military academies, where many middle-class children studied. Comte's emphasis on progress through gradual change appealed to Brazil's new elite, who saw positivism as a way of incorporating themselves into the national elite without threatening the social order on which the old elite depended. They were attracted by the idea of using military and government officials to plan economic development for progress and industrialization. They believed that by expanding economic opportunities and education, they could incorporate the disenfranchised into society without the need for widespread social or political change. Furthermore, in positivism they saw the possibility of ending foreign economic domination and colonialism in Brazil.

MAIN PHILOSOPHICAL TENETS OF JURISPRUDENTIAL POSITIVISM

Jurisprudential positivism, following a line of jurisprudence that has included the theories of Vattel, Zouche, Kelsen, and Hart, emphasizes legal rules and consent in the relations of states. Rights and obligations about rules and principles are based primarily on the words in treaties. Based on the empiricism of Locke and Hume, positivists in international law, such as Humphrey, the principal author of the Universal Declaration of Human Rights, Schachter and Henkin among lawyers and Donnelly among political scientists, have argued that rules take precedence over claimed principles or unprecedented customs of states. Without observable experience or consent, validating customs after the fact betrays self-serving, perverse incentives besides nullifying the original intent of primary rules.

Jurisprudential positivists cite three UN Charter articles that make humanitarian intervention presumptively illegal. First, Article 39 of Chapter VII limits coercion sanctioned by the United Nations Security Council (UNSC), whether by the UN or by the armies of member states, in three situations: a "threat to the peace, breach of the peace, or act of aggression." Taken literally, Article 39 (and the title of Chapter VII) does not apply to a country that is killing its own citizens but not threatening or attacking other countries. Second, positivists might also argue that unilateral humanitarian intervention would usually be illegal because of Article 2(4), except either when the UNSC finds an Article 39 situation, as indicated above, or for individual or collective self-defense to armed attack under Article 51. Article 2(4) names only three situations in which a state may not threaten or use force: (1) against the territorial integrity, or (2) political independence of any state, or (3) in any manner inconsistent with the purposes of the United Nations.

Jurisprudential positivists define a violation of territorial integrity as an armed attack on another state and a violation of political independence as a de facto partition or loss of sovereignty over part of a country. Donnelly calls for "positive non-intervention" to respect UN Charter Article 2(7)'s intervention prohibition and encourage uninhibited criticism. "Nonintervention" means only the renunciation of "intervention," in the strict sense of coercive interference. International human rights, however, are an appropriate subject for the exercise of international *influence*. Inaction in the face of human rights violations is not only morally inappropriate, it is in no way required by international law.

Some positivists, such as Schachter, would permit armed humanitarian intervention for great emergencies and with a consensus among the five permanent members of the Security Council. In commenting on UNSC Resolution 688 regarding northern Iraq, he notes that the council could invoke the Chapter VII enforcement procedures, at least if there is some threat to international peace as well. Others, such as Henkin, might be willing to forgo UNSC authorization to authorize force to stop mass murder, but not in the face of a likely veto. Positivists might be divided on whether to insist upon a consistent standard for legal humanitarian intervention or to permit it where it is politically possible. As Henkin (1991, p. 41) suggests, "The Charter does not prohibit humanitarian intervention by use of force strictly limited to what is necessary to save lives." He would presumably not accept humanitarian intervention if a UNSC consensus was absent or if a unilateral intervention were to change national boundaries or replace a government: "It has not been accepted, however that a state has a right to intervene by force to topple a government or occupy its territory even if that were necessary to terminate atrocities or to liberate detainees." Henkin also opposes using force to promote democracy, as do his ideological opposites, Franck and the Reagan administration.

SEE ALSO *Comte, Auguste; Economics; Empiricism; Friedman, Milton; Hume, David; Imperialism; Jurisprudence; Locke, John; Logic; Methodology; Naturalism; Philosophy of Science; Realist Theory; Religion; Social Science; Sociology*

BIBLIOGRAPHY

Damrosch, Lori Fisler. 1991. Commentary on Collective Military Intervention to Enforce Human Rights. In *Law and Force in the New International Order*, ed. Lori Fisler Damrosch and David J. Scheffer, 215–223. Boulder, CO: Westview.

Donnelly, Jack. 1992. Humanitarian Intervention and American Foreign Policy: Law, Morality and Politics. In *Human Rights in the World Community: Issues and Action*, ed. Richard Pierre Claude and Burns H. Weston, 307–320. Philadelphia: University of Pennsylvania Press.

Franck, Thomas M. 1992. The Emerging Right to Democratic Governance. *American Journal of International Law* 86 (1): 46–91.

Hart, H. L. A. 1961. *The Concept of Law*. Oxford: Oxford University Press.

Hawkins, Richmond Laurin. 1938. *Positivism in the United States (1853–1861)*. Cambridge, MA: Harvard University Press.

Henkin, Louis, Stanley Hoffmann, and Jeane J. Kirkpatrick. 1991. *Right v. Might: International Law and the Use of Force*. 2nd ed. New York: Council on Foreign Relations Press.

Humphrey, John P., and Ronald St. John MacDonald. 1979. *The Practice of Freedom; Canadian Essays on Human Rights and Fundamental Freedoms*. London: Butterworths.

Lenzer, Gertrude, ed. 1998. *Auguste Comte and Positivism: The Essential Readings*. New Brunswick, NJ: Transaction.

Mill, John Stuart. 1961. *Auguste Comte and Positivism.* Ann Arbor: University of Michigan Press. (Orig. pub. 1865)

Schachter, Oscar. 1991. United Nations Law in the Gulf Conflict. *American Journal of International Law* 85: 452–473.

Woodward, Ralph Lee, Jr., ed. 1971. *Positivism in Latin America, 1850–1900: Are Order and Progress Reconcilable?* Lexington, MA: Heath.

Zea, Leopoldo. 1974. *Positivism in Mexico.* Trans. Josephine H. Shulte. Austin: University of Texas Press.

Henry F. Carey

POSSESSIVE INDIVIDUALISM

SEE *Individualism.*

POSSIBILITY THEOREM

SEE *Arrow Possibility Theorem.*

POSTCOLONIALISM

Postcolonialism is a generalized term used to describe the variety of events that have arisen in the aftermath of European decolonization since the nineteenth century. Among the events included under the rubric are social change, cultural redefinition, and political upheaval on both the small and large scale. The term implies a breaking free or a breaking away from a colonizing force, but essentially the study of postcolonialism addresses issues of power, subordination, race, gender inequity, and class—and examines how these issues linger far after the colonizer has exited. It is sometimes understood that colonialism ended in the early to mid-twentieth century, but the vestiges of colonial power and influence remain in many parts of the once colonized world. These vestiges can be seen in the unequal sharing of power in government, especially when Western interests are at stake, as well as in inequities in military control, resource allocation, and economic benefits when more powerful governments and entities participate in economic exchanges with postcolonial nations.

POSTCOLONIAL THEORY

Postcolonial theory has been developed in various fields, including philosophy, literary studies, and sociology. From its beginnings in the 1960s and 1970s, with Frantz Fanon and Edward Said, postcolonial theory has addressed issues such as identity, gender, race, ethnicity, and class. It also examines how once colonized nations develop their own identities and how information among the exploited populations has been produced and used both by the colonized and the colonizers. In literary studies, postcolonial theory addresses the question of how the writing produced by the colonized and by those who colonize them responds to colonial legacies.

Postcolonial theorists can trace much of their initial discourse to Antonio Gramsci, who, in his *Prison Notebooks* ([1929–1935] 1992), examined the *subaltern*, or those who were excluded from power by virtue of their race, class, gender, ethnicity, or colonial status; this study was later taken up by Partha Chaterjee (1993), among others. Fanon, in the *Wretched of the Earth* ([1961] 1963), a work considered a landmark in colonialism studies, expressed clear anticolonialist sentiments in his discussion of the Third World. In a highly influential 1978 book, Edward Said argued that a set of attitudes he dubbed *orientalism* was a way for the West (here meaning Europe) to differentiate itself from its progenitors. Even though Europe in its modern form was essentially a product of the East, to rationalize its ascent to power it aspired to colonize the East through many means, including the physical and economic. Gayatri Spivak, another significant postcolonial theorist, has, like Chaterjee, focused on the subaltern, though as a gendered category—both in terms of those who are colonized and those who have colonized (1988). Feminist postcolonial theorists have additionally discussed sexuality, gender and diasporic communities, power and globalization, and the idea that the feminine in any capacity or context can be equated with a subaltern position.

To make the above comments more concrete, the remainder of this entry will seek to illustrate many of the issues postcolonial theorists are concerned with through a brief examination of one postcolonial country: Ireland. Ireland was a colony of the English for eight hundred years, but perhaps due to its position as a Western country, is often not understood in the same light as other colonies. Its affluence today (the 'Celtic Tiger') also makes it easy to forget that it is less than a century since that independence was gained. Since the turn of the twentieth century, Ireland has moved from being a long-term colony of England to being a postcolonial power on its own. The next section examines how Ireland became a colony, its response to colonization and the plantation system, and how it has developed its national identity in the decades following independence in 1922.

IRELAND

Ireland has been a colonized nation since the time of the Vikings in the ninth century. The Vikings were followed in 1169 by the Normans (the "Old English"), who began "civilizing" the native Irish. In more recent times, as with many colonized nations, Irish perspectives on the colonial situation varied based on the nature and closeness of economic relationships with the colonizer, and whether those relationships conferred economic advantage. During the plantation era, Anglo-Irish, who had thrown their lot in with the English, could hold lands and resources their Irish brethren were excluded by law from owning. Lower-class Irish were indentured laborers on plantations, though a few could hold small plots of land; Irish who once had held political or social power were stripped of their valuables, land, homes, and driven into exile—either to another country or into the poor counties of western Ireland.

The Reformation was brought to Ireland by Oliver Cromwell in 1649. He was not the first Englishman to arrive on Irish shores, but he was among the first to come with arms and the intent of suppressing the Irish people as a class and forcefully instituting Protestantism. In that he was very successful. A brutal military strategist, Cromwell destroyed entire towns and villages, including the walled city of Drogheda, where he burned 3,000 people alive. From then on, Ireland remained under the control of the English. Though a variety of short-lived uprisings and revolts occurred over the centuries, it was not until the Potato Famine of the mid-nineteenth century that the Irish were able to bring their plight to the attention of the rest of the Western world. Millions starved to death, millions more were forced to leave Ireland. In the space of ten years (1846–1856) Ireland's population halved from eight to four million. The 1916 Easter Uprising, led by Padraig Pearse, loosened the hold the English had over the country. Though principally limited to urban centers such as Dublin and Cork, the Uprising reverberated across the country. When the heroes of the uprising were executed or jailed in the months that followed, civil war broke out. In 1922 Ireland gained independence from England, but was partitioned—most of Ulster would remain under the English flag while the Irish Free State was inaugurated in the south.

Despite their hard-won freedom, Ireland remained closely linked with England and depended on it economically for several decades. During this time, however, following the lead of people like President Eamon de Valera, and poets and authors W. B. Yeats, Brendan Behan, and Patrick Kavanaugh, the Irish began to consciously express their own national identity through a revival of Gaelic culture. This revival, known as the Celtic Twilight, was based on a vision of Ireland as a rural idyll, in which people were closely tied to the land. With the Celtic Twilight came a revival of the Irish language, which had been on the brink of extinction, and now became part of the school curriculum. This restoration of a national language separate from that of the colonizer is a common response to decoloniza-

tion. Traditional Irish music was also revived and is now popular throughout the world. The Gaelic Athletic Association, which organizes hurling and Gaelic football and was first established in the 1880s, has steadily risen in popularity as well.

Only recently, beginning in the 1970s, has Ireland truly developed a modern national identity and become an independent economic powerhouse. Since the 1990s, Ireland has been dubbed the "Celtic Tiger," a reference to its new wealth and status. As of 2006, Ireland has the fourth strongest GDP in the world behind the United States, Norway, and Luxembourg (ESRI 2006). In July 2006 Ireland ranked second among the wealthiest nations in the world behind Japan (RTE 1, 2006).

SEE ALSO *Anticolonial Movements; Colonialism; Decolonization; Empire; Imperialism; Moral Suasion; Neocolonialism; Nkrumah, Kwame; Orientalism; Passive Resistance; Said, Edward*

BIBLIOGRAPHY

Ashcroft, Bill, Gareth Griffiths, and Helen Tiffin. 1989. *The Empire Writes Back: Theory and Practice in Postcolonial Literatures.* London: Routledge.

Chaterjee, Partha. 1993. *The Nation and Its Fragments: Colonial and Postcolonial Histories.* Princeton, NJ: Princeton University Press.

Economic and Social Research Institute, Ireland. Irish Economy Overview. Dublin: ESRI.

Fanon, Frantz. 1963. *The Wretched of the Earth.* Trans. Constance Farrington. New York: Grove. Originally published as *Les damnés de la terre* (Paris: F. Maspero, 1961).

Gramsci, Antonio. [1929–1935] 1992. *Prison Notebooks.* 2 vols. Ed. Joseph A. Buttigeig; trans. Joseph A. Buttigeg and Antonio Callari. New York: Columbia University Press.

Kiberd, Declan. 1996. *Inventing Ireland: The Literature of a Modern Nation.* London: Vintage.

Said, Edward. 1978. *Orientalism.* New York: Pantheon.

Spivak, Gayatri. 1988. "Can the Subaltern Speak?" In *Marxism and the Interpretation of Culture*, eds. Cary Nelson and Larry Grossberg, 271–313. Chicago: University of Illinois.

Kelli Ann Costa

POSTERIOR DENSITY
SEE *Bayesian Econometrics.*

POSTERIOR DISTRIBUTION
SEE *Inference, Statistical.*

POSTLETHWAYT, MALACHY
1707–1767

Malachy Postlethwayt was a prolific English writer and publicist on matters of mercantilist economics in the 1740s and 1750s. Little is known about his upbringing or formal education, although he is believed to be the brother of James Postlethwayt (d. 1761), a writer on finance and demography. Malachy Postlethwayt was elected a fellow of the Society of Antiquaries of London in 1734. His writings are claimed by Edgar Johnson to "have exerted a good deal of influence on the trend of British economic thought" (1965, p. 185).

Postlethwayt was alleged to be propagandist for the mercantilist endeavors of the Royal Africa Company, whose interests were well served by his publications *The African Trade, the Great Pillar and Supporter of the British Plantation Trade in North America* (1745) and *The National and Private Advantages of the African Trade Considered* (1746). These works supported a strategy of British commercial and manufacturing expansion through trade with Africa and the colonies, and promoted the importance of slavery for British commerce and industry.

Postlethwayt's most noted work, *The Universal Dictionary of Trade and Commerce*, appeared after he had devoted twenty years to its preparation. The first edition was published in London in installments between 1751 and 1755, and then in subsequent editions as a two-volume set in 1757, 1766, and 1774. This dictionary was a translation, with large additions and improvements, from Jacques Savary des Bruslons' *Dictionnaire universal de commerce* (1723–1730). According to Johnson, Postlethwayt's dictionary was a "huge storehouse of economic facts, laws and theory" (1965, p. 188), and his departures from the French version reflected his "greater interest in political problems; his more intense economic nationalism; and his exuberant belief in the economic usefulness of experimental philosophy" (p. 402).

In the 1757 edition of the *Universal Dictionary*, Postlethwayt outlined his vision for the establishment of a British mercantile college to benefit those who intended to work as merchants, or in gathering public revenue, or in merchandizing. He proposed that theoretical training for business should occur in formal academies and involve the study of mercantile computations, foreign exchanges and the intrinsic value of foreign coins, double-entry accounting, languages, geography, and public revenues and related laws. Postlethwayt's ideas appear to have been influential in developing the statutes and procedures of the Portuguese School of Commerce, established in Lisbon in 1759.

Postlethwayt's most important contribution to economic literature is regarded by many to be *Britain's Commercial Interest Explained and Improved* (1757), in which he outlines his concept of "physical commerce" and the policies England should follow to attain commercial parity with foreign rivals.

Whether Postlethwayt's writings were his original thoughts and words is a matter for conjecture. Johnson (1965, p. 205) notes that his *Universal Dictionary* included ideas taken from fifty other past or contemporary writers and that it had scattered throughout it practically all of Richard Cantillon's *Essai sur la nature du commerce en général* (Essay on the Nature of Commerce in General, 1755). Although Postlethwayt was alleged widely to be a plagiarist, Peter Groenewegen considers this accusation to be "greatly exaggerated" (2004, p. 1000).

Postlethwayt died suddenly on September 13, 1767, and was buried in the Old Street Churchyard, Clerkenwell, in London.

SEE ALSO *Plantation; Slave Trade; Slavery Industry*

BIBLIOGRAPHY

Groenewegen, Peter. 2004. Postlethwayt, Malachy. In *Oxford Dictionary of National Biography*, Vol. 44, ed. H. C. G. Mathew and Brian Harrison, 999–1000. New York: Oxford University Press.

Johnson, Edgar Augustus Jerome. [1937] 1965. *Predecessors of Adam Smith: The Growth of British Economic Thought*. New York: A. M. Kelley.

Postlethwayt, Malachy. 1745. *The African Trade, the Great Pillar and Supporter of the British Plantation Trade in North America*. London: printed for J. Robinson.

Postlethwayt, Malachy. 1746. *The National and Private Advantages of the African Trade Considered*. London: printed for John and Paul Knapton.

Postlethwayt, Malachy. 1747. *Considerations on the Making of Bar Iron with Pitt or Sea Coal Fire*. London: printed for J. Roberts.

Postlethwayt, Malachy. 1749. *Considerations on the Revival of the Royal-British Assiento*. London: printed for John and Paul Knapton.

Postlethwayt, Malachy. 1750. *The Merchant's Public Counting-House, or, New Mercantile Institution*. London: printed for John and Paul Knapton.

Postlethwayt, Malachy. 1751–1755. *The Universal Dictionary of Trade and Commerce*. London: printed for John and Paul Knapton.

Postlethwayt, Malachy. 1756. *A Short State of the Progress of the French Trade and Navigation*. London: printed for John Knapton.

Postlethwayt, Malachy. 1757. *Britain's Commercial Interest Explained and Improved*. London: printed for D. Browne et al.

Postlethwayt, Malachy. 1757. *Great Britain's True System*. London: printed for A. Miller et al.

Postlethwayt, Malachy. 1758. *In Honour to the Administration: The Importance of the African Expedition Considered.* London: printed by C. Say.

Rodrigues, Lúcia Lima, and Russell Craig. 2004. Mercantilist and English Influences on the Portuguese School of Commerce, 1759–1844. *Atlantic Economic Journal* 32 (4): 329–345.

Lúcia Lima Rodrigues
Russell Craig

POSTMODERNISM

Ever since its ideas first took hold in the 1980s, postmodern theory has had a significant influence on the social sciences. At the time, social theory imported certain theoretical concepts from literary criticism, including deconstruction and other discourse-based theories of textual interpretation. It is best, however, to refer to a postmodern "turn" within contemporary social science, because many academics influenced by these intellectual trends abjure the term *postmodernism*. Nevertheless, many contemporary social scientists acknowledge a debt to deconstructive methods of textual interpretation and to deconstruction's (or poststructuralism's) rejection of teleological theories (or "grand narratives") and the concept of a coherent, fixed human subject.

Judith Butler's writings on the unstable and "constructed" nature of both sex and gender identities played a crucial role in transmitting postmodern concepts into social theory and the social sciences. Yet Butler herself rejects the term *postmodernist*, claiming only to deploy deconstructive techniques to better discern the "discursive construction" of identity. Postmodern conceptions of the "hybrid," "plural," and "inconstant" nature of "identity" have had their greatest influence in the areas of cultural, gender, and postcolonial studies, though they have also influenced anthropology (e.g., James Clifford) and international relations theory (e.g., James Der Derrian).

Many people working in these areas reject behavioral, structural, and hermeneutic interpretations of the relationship between individuals, groups, and social structure, favoring instead analyses of the "decentered," "local," and "fragmented" nature of social phenomena. Postmodern social theory rejects traditional social science's goal of discerning causal relationships among social phenomena. It also rejects social science aspirations to discern superior or "parsimonious" interpretations of human behavior. In the postmodern conception, no "readerly" interpretation of a "text" can be more "truthful" than another. In fact some postmodernists refer to the concept of "truth" as "terroris-

tic," for the "truth" can only defend itself by repressive "exclusion."

Postmodernism represents both a sensibility in regard to social science research and a normative critique of modernity. According to postmodernism, the Enlightenment's search for rational understanding that could ameliorate the human condition engendered ideological or false "grand narratives" of history, which are based on "essentialist," "universal," and "fixed" conceptions of human nature. Drawing upon Jean-Francois Lyotard's analysis in *The Postmodern Condition* (1984), postmodernists reject the Enlightenment's search for "totalizing" theories that offer "universal" narratives of human motivation and experience. Building on the work of Michel Foucault, postmodern theory claims that these "grand narratives" underpinned the Enlightenment's efforts to "normalize" human beings through the bureaucratic and repressive institutions of "governance" (e.g., both state and nonstate organizations, such as the asylum and the hospital) that "categorize" human beings.

POSTMODERNISM AND DECONSTRUCTION

According to postmodernists, social theories that claim to "represent" reality fail to comprehend that humans have no unmediated access to "reality." Human conceptions of reality are, unavoidably, a product of subjective interpretation. Modern media and technology deny people the ability to discern the original author or to distinguish the original from the imitation. In 1936 Walter Benjamin argued that in an age of "mechanical reproduction" it is nearly impossible to distinguish the original from a copy. Following this lead, postmodern theorists such as Jean Baudrillard have contended that reality itself is a *simulacrum* (a copy of a copy). In a world of corporate image production and virtual realities, one cannot determine what is authentic or inauthentic, real or fake. When computers allow people to "live" in cyberspace, the very concepts of reality, time, and space are contestable and destabilized. Thus attempts to interpret the "essence" or true nature of social phenomena deny the reality that the world is a constantly shifting image.

Postmodern social theory draws heavily upon Jacques Derrida's and deconstruction's critique of structuralism. Claude Levi-Strauss's structural anthropology and Louis Althusser's structural Marxism (which investigated the structural role that class played within capitalist economics and ideology) dominated French intellectual life in the 1960s. Both of these theorists drew upon the early twentieth-century structural linguistics of Ferdinand Saussure. Saussure held that the meaning of a particular speech or language (*la parole*) is structured by the underlying structure of grammar (*la langue*, the structured relationship between signifier and signified that yields the meaning of a sign). But Derrida in *Marges de la philosophie* (1972) held that the relationship between signifier and signified is inherently unstable. For Derrida, "meaning" includes both identity (what is) and *différance* (what is not). Thus postmodernists argue that any attempt to "fix" meaning will yield repressive attempts to eliminate the ineluctable "other" of human reality.

To avoid eliminating the play of *différance*, postmodern-influenced social science rejects the "binary oppositions" that allegedly ground Western philosophy: subject-object, man-woman, reality-appearance, reason-emotion, and speech-writing. In this view, the very effort of representation and causal analysis excludes and devalues the "inferior" part of the binary term that is traditionally denigrated as being irrational or emotional. This rejection of binary oppositions as repressive and "norming" has had a profound influence on contemporary feminist and critical race theory, which warn against "essentializing" identities of gender and race. These studies of identity focus upon the "socially constructed," hybrid, and ever-shifting nature of individual and group identity.

Given the absence of a stable referential relation between subject and object, postmodernists argue that social theory should focus upon the way subjects are "constructed" by discourse itself. The postmodern conception of how the subject is a product of language and thought draws heavily upon philosophical traditions deriving from Friedrich Nietzsche. In addition, Martin Heidegger's critique of Western philosophy's ineluctable search for a fixed conception of "Being," and of its attempt to dominate nature in the name of the "human," informs postmodern analysis. Postmodern social science frequently draws upon Foucault's conception of power-knowledge discourses to examine how subjects are "produced" by discourse. While Foucault's earlier "archaeological" work on how *epistemes* (or systems of thought) "norm" and "exclude" has influenced postmodern analysis, it is his later genealogical analysis of power as "productive" and "enabling" (rather than as primarily coercive) that has most influenced postmodernism's critique of "agency." As Butler holds, the conception of a coherent, rational, human individual who exercises conscious agency ignores the reality that human identities are continually being reconfigured through performative "self-inscriptions" of dominant norms and discourses.

LACLAU AND MOUFFE AND "NEW SOCIAL MOVEMENTS"

Ernesto Laclau and Chantal Mouffe's *Hegemony and Socialist Strategy* (1985) represents a highly influential poststructuralist critique of the use of "grand narrative" in the social sciences. Rejecting a "determinist" Marxism that drew from the workers' structural position in production of the teleological necessity of a "revolutionary consciousness," Laclau and Mouffe asserted the "discursive"—and open—nature of social consciousness. In the determinist Marxist view, both social democracy and authoritarian communism believed that capitalism's interdependent division of labor would inevitably yield (whether through gradual self-organization or via a revolutionary external agent) a self-emancipating working-class movement for democratic control of the interdependent capitalist mode of production. In contrast to the Marxist tradition, Laclau and Mouffe held that one cannot—and should not—mechanistically determine a subject's "objective, true consciousness" from the subject's alleged "structural" position in society. Rather, consciousness itself is discursively produced and represents a contested arena for politics.

In this view, much of the emancipatory impulse for democracy has come from the "new" social movements of racial, gender, and sexual identity. The consciousness of these identity-based groups cannot be deduced from their "objective" social role in society. Thus social theorists had to abandon privileging the "old" movement of the working class and construct a new, plural, and democratic theory that would unite (without homogenizing) the liberatory discourses of the new social movements. Laclau and Mouffe's work has had a great influence on both social movement theory and postcolonial studies.

POSTMODERNISM AND ITS CRITICS: THE SEARCH FOR NORMS

The postmodern turn in social science has generated considerable controversy, some of it finding its way into the mass media. Most visible has been the neoconservative critique that postmodernist analysis dominates the humanities and social sciences, imparting to students a dangerous, nihilist critique of American democracy. Ironically, this critique conflates postmodernism with Marxism, despite postmodernism's hostility to macrostructural and teleological forms of social analysis, including Marxism. Some left-leaning social theorists concur with the postmodern analysis that the marketing of images and lifestyles partly supplants the production and sale of physical goods in late capitalism. But these analysts of late capitalism (such as the geographer David Harvey and the cultural theorist Frederic Jameson), in contrast to postmodernists, offer macrostructural and analytic explanations for the emergence of these phenomena. They locate the production of images-as-commodities within the global corporate conglomerates of the "infotainment," media, and publishing industries.

The postmodern rejection of the realist conception that economic and social institutions constrain the choices of individuals has occurred at a time of rapidly increasing global violence and economic and material inequality, and some critics have pointed out the ironic element in the timing of this development. Postmodernists often explain their critique of fixed, "linear" conceptions of time and space by metaphorical references to chaos theory's rejection of periodicity and to the finding of quantum mechanics that mass, force, and acceleration cannot be independently determined. This postmodernist rejection of even an "unrepresentative" realist conception of an external reality independent of theoretical interpretation helped engender the "Sokal affair." Alan Sokal, a physicist (and materialist Marxist) at New York University, submitted a paper to the postmodern journal *Social Text* in 1996. The article cleverly deployed postmodern concepts while making alleged scientific references that any physics undergraduate could readily deem to be ludicrous. After the essay was published, Sokal revealed that it was a hoax aimed at revealing postmodernism's ignorance of both science and the nature of material reality. The story made the front page of the *New York Times*.

Some leftist theorists note that the postmodern turn arose at the very moment that conservative political dominance decreased the prestige of leftist theory and practice. A crude "sociology of knowledge" of the postmodern turn might contend that, absent mass social movements contending for state power, left-wing academics retreat into the realm of pure theory. The rejoinder to this might be that postmodernism's insistence on the relevance of the particular, local, and hybrid has had a salutary effect on limiting the imperial claims of "grand narratives." Either way, analytic attempts of macrostructural and historically oriented social theorists to discern the interaction between social agency and social structure are likely to remain a major theme within social science. And the postmodern concern with the fate of marginalized groups would seem to push the discussion ethically beyond postmodernism's emphasis on the local and particular. The quasi-universal concepts of citizenship and global human rights may not have an irrefutable, a priori basis in a fixed human nature, but if human beings cannot develop shared understandings and values that bridge their differences, it is unlikely that the emancipatory, democratic project embraced by many postmodern theorists will ever be realized.

SEE ALSO *Critical Theory; Enlightenment; Ethics; Foucault, Michel; Hegemony; Knowledge; Modernism; Multiculturalism; Paradigm; Positivism; Power; Relativism; Social Constructs; Universalism*

BIBLIOGRAPHY

Best, Steven, and Douglass Kellner. 1991. *Postmodern Theory: Critical Interrogations*. New York: Guilford.

Brown, Wendy. 1995. *States of Injury: Power and Freedom in Late Modernity*. Princeton, NJ: Princeton University Press.

Butler, Judith. 1990. *Gender Trouble: Feminism and the Subversion of Identity*. New York: Routledge.

Clifford, James. 1988. *The Predicament of Culture: Twentieth-Century Ethnography, Literature, and Art*. Cambridge, MA: Harvard University Press.

Der Derian, James, and Michael J. Shapiro. 1989. *International/Intertextual Relations: Postmodern Readings of World Politics*. Lexington, MA: Lexington.

Derrida, Jacques. 1976. *Of Grammatology*. Trans. Gayatri Chakravorty Spivak. Baltimore, MD: Johns Hopkins University Press.

Foucault, Michel. 1980. *Power/Knowledge: Selected Interviews and Other Writings, 1972–1977*. New York: Pantheon.

Laclau, Ernseto, and Chantal Mouffe. 1985. *Hegemony and Socialist Strategy: Towards a Radical Democratic Politics*. London: Verso.

Lyotard, Jean-Francois. 1984. *The Postmodern Condition*. Trans. Geoff Bennington and Brian Massumi. Minneapolis: University of Minnesota Press.

Rosenau, Pauline Marie. 1992. *Post-Modernism and the Social Sciences: Insights, Inroads, and Intrusions*. Princeton, NJ: Princeton University Press.

Joseph M. Schwartz

POSTNATIONALISM

The term *postnationalism* refers to the critique of the concept of the nation as the central organizing principle of modern political identity and government. According to postnationalism, the category of the nation is no longer sufficient to describe the fundamentals of political identity or state government. In a postnational context it becomes necessary to move beyond the idea that a homogeneous national identity is the natural integrating factor of modern political community. Further, postnationalism questions the idea that the sovereign nation-state is indispensable to the order of international affairs and the functioning of the domestic rule of law.

THE CRITIQUE OF NATIONALISM

Postnationalism arose out of the critique of nationalism. It was only at the end of the eighteenth century that citizenship and national identity came together, in the figure of nationalism, for the functional purpose of providing a principle of integration that could serve to mobilize the transition from royal sovereignty to popular sovereignty. Nationalism provided the solution to the twin problems of secular legitimation and complex integration in the wake of religious schism and republican revolution.

While *citizenship* describes a purely legal relation within a political community, in modern times the tendency has been to tie it to an identity that points beyond the political sphere. Political membership based upon the principle of a unique national culture presupposes an existential difference between peoples. According to this logic, in order for a nation to be free it must remain homogenous and independent from alien influence, necessitating not only separation but also suspicion of others as corrupting forces. According to this logic, diversity becomes a threat. The concept of postnationalism seeks to break this tie between citizenship and ethnic identity or existential difference. The use of postnationalism, in this sense, is most common in debates about the future of Europe and the European Union.

THE DEMISE OF THE NATION-STATE

Postnationalism also arose from the critique of the nation-state. A large literature surrounding the topic of "globalization" has called into question the institutional capacity of the nation-state to fulfill its role as an all-encompassing form of political organization. As a result of globalization, the world's political, economic, cultural, technological, and military forces have established connections across national borders with increasing facility. Beyond the borders of the nation-state, transnational institutional authorities have emerged and become increasingly powerful. External authorities have a growing influence over the internal affairs of states, and traditional understandings of state sovereignty have been called into question by the growth of international systems of decision making, law, and security. Thus the proliferation of international decision-making bodies has tended to extend the sphere of authority beyond the nation-state. The consolidation of the World Trade Organization, for example, signifies the appearance of an international institution that claims the authority to overrule national governments. As a result, some have argued that the twenty-first century will be an era of postnationalism, in which regional organizations, such as the European Union, or international organizations, such as the United Nations, will be the principal organs of political authority, rather than the nation-state.

SEE ALSO *Borders; Globalization, Social and Economic Aspects of; Nationalism and Nationality*

BIBLIOGRAPHY

Archibugi, Daniele, David Held, and Martin Köhler, eds. 1998. *Re-imagining Political Community: Studies in Cosmopolitan Democracy*. Stanford, CA: Stanford University Press.

Habermas, Jürgen. 2001. *The Postnational Constellation: Political Essays*. Cambridge, MA: MIT Press.

Adam Lupel

POSTSTRUCTURALISM

Though often equated, poststructuralism and postmodernism are distinct intellectual phenomena. Most well-known poststructuralists, especially the French philosophers Michel Foucault (1926–1984) and Jacques Derrida (1930–2004), eschewed any association with postmodernism. Only Jean-François Lyotard (1924–1998) can be said to straddle both of these movements.

Postmodernism is as much a sensibility or cultural mood as a specific doctrine. It implies a break with modern modes of experiencing time and space, the dissolution of coherent meanings and narratives, and changes in media of communication. Politically, postmodernism is often seen as reflecting new forms of political organization such as global capitalism or new social movements that reflect cultural difference rather than unity. While aesthetic modernists often wove the fragmentary nature of modern experience into a unity, postmodernists reject the assumptions of unity as metaphysical residues of modern reason. Poststructuralism shares the postmodernist unease with totality, but it refuses to herald new forms of experience of culture, politics, or thought that would replace the modern. Rather, poststructuralism is a form (one of several) of modernity's self-criticism. Poststructuralists do not entirely reject important concepts of modernity, such as knowledge, rights, or subjectivity, but they subject these concepts to a critique that dethrones them from an imperial or originary position. They seek to avoid the totalitarian and utopian pretensions of reason and subject them to a permanent critique.

Along with Derrida, Foucault, and Lyotard, prominent poststructuralists include Gilles Deleuze (1925–1995), Roland Barthes (1915–1980), Julia Kristeva, and Jean-Luc Nancy. As the name suggests, poststructuralism arose as an intellectual movement in reaction to the shortcomings of structuralist approaches in linguistics and the social sciences. Ferdinand de Saussure (1857–1913) in linguistics and Claude Lévi-Strauss in anthropology developed theories that explained language and social action, respectively, as the product of objective structures alone. While structuralists recognized that systems of meaning were essentially arbitrary systems of linguistic difference, and not reflections of transtemporal or ultimate meaning, they were still guilty, according to critics, of a form of rationalism, in which a fixed object of meaning could be studied by objectifying procedures of social science. This explanatory strategy leads to difficulties explaining the nature of involvements of participants who had to take up and employ meanings. It cannot tell us, to use a well-known example, how a gift is given or whether it is given properly.

Poststructuralists such as Derrida argued that meaning has a performative, practical dimension not associated with an originating subjectivity. Meaning is renewed or transformed through such performances. Poststructuralists employed this practical dimension, however, to show the limits of the projects of theory not only in structuralism but in modern subjective reason as well. This critique took many forms, from Barthes' criticism of the unified literary text, to Kristeva's notion that meaning is intertextual without reference to any fixed outside order, to Deleuze's nomad thought, and to Derrida's criticism of the logocentrism of Western thought and its desire for plenitude and fullness.

Poststructuralists, hermeneutic, phenomenological, and critical approaches rely implicitly on totality and thus do not fully escape the grip of Western rationalism. The nature of the practical or performative dimension always provides resistance to fullness or totality. Derrida, for example, argued that meaning was indeterminate, that is, it was not fixed through any objective or theoretical process. Meaning is not a representation of an objective world but the disclosure of a world of meaning within which we make sense of things. However, linguistic meanings are never complete or univocal, but always fissured through ambiguity and contradiction. From another angle, Foucault argued that systems of knowledge are always formed by power interpretations, and hence are never pure or interest-free as the traditional metaphysical notion of objectivity would hold. Poststructuralism is a form of negative critique. It stresses the nonidentity between enacted performances that may always create a novel meaning and a fixed ideal sense. The indeterminacy of linguistic performance undermines the possibility of ideal meaning found in a transcendental subjectivity. In the tradition of negative critique, poststructuralists stress the nonidentity between enacting a performance and the ideal concepts of totality and practical understanding. The aim of this critique is to undermine the latent (and sometimes explicit) totalitarian assumptions of an overextended notion of reason, and thus its political thrust as well. There is no single political movement or ideology that captures all of reality, nor any utopian goal in human actions. The political is always in the particular.

Critics have equated poststructuralism with anarchic or amoral strains of postmodernism. The poststructuralist stress on the indeterminacy and internal inconsistency of thought is linked to a free-floating conceptual apparatus driven by desire and power. Poststructuralism rejects the primacy of subjectivity altogether and in contrast employs a view of social reality as fictional, without references to an outside reality. Other critics have pointed to the possible political quietism of a view that denies the viability of general or universal values. These judgments have proven to be incorrect. Poststructuralists have displaced subjectivity from its imperial role as an origin, recognizing its produced character, but they have not rejected the subject,

knowledge, or even a constructive politics. After an initial phase that placed questions of language and power at the center, poststructuralism has taken an ethical turn. Many of the major figures of poststructuralism, including Foucault, Derrida, Nancy, and Lyotard, have devoted considerable work to ethics.

There are two major strains of poststructuralist ethics. The first approach, the power-interpretive view, is associated with Foucault and Deleuze. It holds with Friedrich Nietzsche (1844–1900) that dominance is the establishment of new interpretations. The second, which is associated with Derrida, Nancy, and Lyotard, is an ethics of otherness. The ethical is equated with a nondominating otherness that is beyond being and ontology. This interpretation is heavily influenced by the work of the Lithuanian-born philosopher Emmanuel Lévinas (1906–1995).

Foucault, and for the most part Deleuze, follow Nietzsche in seeing interpretation as a form of power. In Nietzsche's view, the creation of new interpretations established what is true or false and moral or immoral. Power discloses a world of meaning. Foucault takes this formative power in an Aristotelian direction in order to view the ethical as a form of work on the self, an interpolation of self and other. Interpretative thought is not pure strategy because it draws on an expressive world-forming capacity.

The ethics of otherness draws on the poststructuralist idea of the resistance of performance to full interpretation. Against what he saw as a Hegelian notion of totality, as well as Martin Heidegger's (1889–1976) notion of homeland, Lévinas rejected the view of mutual recognition as metaphysical residue. Mutual recognition extends only to the familiar, the similar, or the identical. Such an ethics could not account for the outsider or the stranger—they can never be assimilated. Recalling another radical critic of G. W. F. Hegel (1770–1831), the outsider is a nonperson who belongs to no corporate entity. An ethics of otherness is beyond the realm of being or ontology. It can never be made explicit, but requires an attitude of openness or welcoming toward the excluded other.

Derrida, Nancy, and Lyotard all begin from Lévinas's ethics of otherness. Derrida employs what might be called a linguistic-critical approach to otherness. The limits of deconstruction are found in the notion of justice. Respect for the other is the one premise that can never be deconstructed. Derrida gives a non-Kantian account of universal justice as a reception of the other that is the precondition of any language. This leads not only to an ethics of otherness, but to a conception of democracy that is linked to the ethical demands of the other. Democracy is never fulfilled, never entirely specified, but it is always yet to be. Still, Derrida's use of otherness as a critique of ethics, politics, and philosophy denied any specific politics or doctrine. No explicit account of democracy or an ethos of otherness is possible.

In contrast, Nancy's ethical and political reflections draw on phenomenology and on Heidegger's notion of *Mitsein* (being with others) in order to develop a notion of community as incorporating otherness. Identity and difference constitute each other.

Lyotard's position is an important variation of the ethics of otherness. He begins with a notion of speech acts that gives more credence to everyday understanding than does Derrida or Nancy. Like neo-Aristotelians, Lyotard puts the faculty of judgment at the center of political reflections. Despite this similarity with interpretive approaches, Lyotard relies on Lévinas's notion of the ethical as beyond the dialogical nature of ordinary speech and action. Justice is not an ineliminable basis of his theory. Instead, justice is a political capacity that steers between the realms of action. Lyotard's conception of justice, like Hannah Arendt's (1906–1975), is drawn from Immanuel Kant's (1724–1804) critique of judgment.

Critics of poststructuralism, such as Todd May, argue that an ethics of otherness must fail. While poststructuralists correctly identify the limits of foundationalism, they often err in equating all theoretical accounts with foundationalism. Domains of inquiry that are constituted through difference or otherness are difficult to define or delimit and are inherently contradictory. Even sympathetic critics, such as Simon Critchley, find the excessive emphasis on otherness to be problematic. Critical theories that grow out of Jürgen Habermas's work have held that accountability is not just theoretical but a feature of practical activity. This postmetaphysical version of mutual recognition and mutual understanding does not, in their view, require the identity of subjects, but fosters the inclusion of the other into ethics without the need for totality.

Poststructuralism has had a significant impact on the social sciences, especially in regard to the social construction of knowledge, communication, and methodologies. Poststructuralists challenge the traditional model of objectivity, which claims to be able to represent or describe social reality. They dissent from interpretive approaches in holding that the social construction of knowledge raises an irresolvable dilemma on the nature of truth. Anthropologists, for example, have had to address questions about the adequacy of their descriptions of other cultures. They doubt whether one can represent social reality in any way. Poststructuralist anthropology often contends that anthropologists create the very phenomenon they seek to study. More recently, many social scientists have linked poststructuralism to a postpositivist perspective that overcomes the division between natural science and social science. Here, all science is a kind of

pragmatic production shaped by social motives of power and dominance.

Sociologists, while raising similar questions about the objectivity of knowledge, have employed poststructuralist perspectives to study the production of knowledge. In opposition to what they see as the interpretive theorists' emphasis on the formative power of intentional action, poststructural sociologists want to emphasize the way subjects themselves are formed by regimes of knowledge. Foucault's *The Order of Things* (1970) is an example of this type of approach, as is Bruno Latour's study of scientific practices. Latour sees science as constructed by the laboratory and its instruments, not independent of them.

In communications theory, Jean Baudrillard's influential work analyzes the way in which subjectivity is constructed as a consumer of material good and products. Charles Lemert developed a general sociological approach based on poststructuralism. Though not strictly in the camp of poststructuralism, Bent Flyvbjerg's attempt to formulate a practically oriented phronetic social science draws heavily on Foucault's linkage of power and knowledge. In addition, much of Pierre Bourdieu's (1930–2002) writing on symbolic power and the construction of social hierarchies of knowledge in universities and in "culture" was influenced by Heidegger and poststructuralism.

SEE ALSO *Other, The; Postmodernism; Subject/Self; Subjectivity: Overview*

BIBLIOGRAPHY

Barthes, Roland. 1975. *The Pleasure of the Text*. Trans. Richard Miller. New York: Hill and Wang.

Baudrillard, Jean. 1981. *For a Critique of the Political Economy of the Sign*. Trans. Charles Levin. Saint Louis, MO: Telos.

Baudrillard, Jean. 1988. *America*. Trans. Chris Turner. London: Verso.

Bourdieu, Pierre. 1977. *Outline of a Theory of Practice*. Trans. Richard Nice. Cambridge, U.K.: Cambridge University Press.

Bourdieu, Pierre. 1984. *Distinction: A Social Critique of the Judgment of Taste*. Trans. Richard Nice. Cambridge, MA: Harvard University Press.

Critchley, Simon. 1992. *The Ethics of Deconstruction: Derrida and Lévinas*. London: Blackwell.

Deleuze, Gilles. 1990. *The Logic of Sense*. Trans. Mark Lester with Charles Stivale. New York: Columbia University Press.

Deleuze, Gilles, and Felix Guattari, 1983. *Anti-Oedipus: Capitalism and Schizophrenia*. Trans. Robert Hurley, Mark Seem, and Helen R. Lane. Minneapolis: University of Minnesota Press.

Derrida, Jacques. 1976. *Of Grammatology*. Trans. Gayatri Chakravorty Spivak. Baltimore, MD: Johns Hopkins University Press.

Derrida, Jacques. 1978. *Writing and Difference*. Trans. Alan Bass. Chicago: University of Chicago Press.

Derrida, Jacques. 1994. *Specters of Marx: The State of the Debt, the Work of Mourning, and the New International.* Trans. Peggy Kamuf. New York: Routledge.

Derrida, Jacques. 1997. *The Politics of Friendship.* Trans. George Collins. London: Verso.

Dreyfus, Hubert, and Paul Rabinow. 1983. *Michel Foucault: Beyond Structuralism and Hermeneutics.* 2nd ed. Chicago: University of Chicago Press.

Flyvbjerg, Bent. 2001. *Making Social Science Matter: Why Social Inquiry Fails and How It Can Succeed Again.* Trans. Steven Sampson. Cambridge, U.K.: Cambridge University Press.

Foucault, Michel. 1970. *The Order of Things: An Archaeology of the Human Sciences.* London: Tavistock.

Foucault, Michel. 1984. *The Foucault Reader.* Ed. Paul Rabinow. New York: Pantheon.

Foucault, Michel. 1990. *The History of Sexuality.* Vol. 2: *The Uses of Pleasure.* Trans. Robert Hurley. New York: Vintage.

Gasché, Rodolphe. 1986. *The Tain of the Mirror: Derrida and the Philosophy of Reflection.* Cambridge, MA: Harvard University Press.

Hawkesworth, Mary. 2004. Political Science in New Millennium: Issues of Knowledge and Power. In *Encyclopedia of Government and Politics*, eds. Mary Hawkesworth and Maurice Kogan. 2nd ed. London: Routledge.

Kristeva, Julia. 1986. *The Kristeva Reader.* Ed. Toril Moi. New York: Columbia University Press.

Latour, Bruno. 1987. *Science in Action.* Cambridge, MA: Harvard University Press.

Lemert, Charles. 2004. *Sociology after the Crisis.* 2nd ed. Boulder, CO: Paradigm.

Lemert, Charles. 2005. *Social Things.* 3rd ed. Latham, MD: Roman and Littlefield.

Lévinas, Emmanuel. 1969. *Totality and Infinity: An Essay on Exteriority.* Trans. Alphonso Lingis. Pittsburgh, PA: Duquesne University Press.

Lévinas, Emmanuel. 1981. *Otherwise than Being: Or Beyond Essence.* Trans. Alphonso Lingis. Boston: Nijhoff.

Lyotard, Jean-François. 1984. *The Postmodern Condition: A Report on Knowledge.* Trans. Geoff Bennington and Brian Massumi. Minneapolis: University of Minnesota Press.

Lyotard, Jean-François. 1985. *Just Gaming.* Trans. Wlad Godzich. Minneapolis: University of Minnesota Press.

Lyotard, Jean-François. 1988. *The Differend: Phrases in Dispute.* Trans. Georges van den Abbeele. Minneapolis: University of Minnesota Press.

Lyotard, Jean-François. 1989. *The Lyotard Reader.* Ed. Andrew Benjamin. Oxford: Blackwell.

Marcus, George E., and Michael M. J. Fischer. 1986. *Anthropology as Cultural Critique: An Experimental Moment in the Human Sciences.* Chicago: University of Chicago Press.

May, Todd. 1997. *Reconsidering Difference: Nancy, Derrida, Lévinas, and Deleuze.* University Park: Pennsylvania State University Press.

Nancy, Jean-Luc. 1991. *The Inoperative Community.* Trans. Peter Connor, Lisa Garbus, Michael Holland, and Simona Sawhney. Minneapolis: University of Minnesota Press.

Nancy, Jean-Luc. 1992. *La Comparution* The Comparution: From the Existence of "Communism" to the Community of "Existence." Trans. Tracy B. Strong. *Political Theory* 20 (3): 371–398.

Rabinow, Paul. 1977. *Reflections on Fieldwork in Morocco.* Berkeley: University of California Press.

Rabinow, Paul. 1996. *Essays on the Anthropology of Reason.* Princeton, NJ: Princeton University Press.

Rosenau, Pauline Marie. 1992. *Post-Modernism and the Social Sciences: Insights, Inroads, and Intrusions.* Princeton, NJ: Princeton University Press.

Tyler, Stephen A. 1984. The Poetic Turn in Postmodern Anthropology: The Poetry of Paul Friedrich. *American Anthropologist* New Series 86 (2): 328–336.

White, Stephen K. 1991. *Political Theory and Postmodernism.* Cambridge, U.K.: Cambridge University Press.

Brian J. Caterino

POST-TRAUMATIC STRESS

The term *post-traumatic stress* is used to describe an individual's reaction to an experience of serious, life-threatening trauma. The trauma can come from a single event—such as a physical assault, a car accident, a natural disaster, or witnessing the death of another—or it can come through a series of events, such as chronic abuse or combat experiences. Symptoms include flashbacks, nightmares, intrusive thoughts about the event, decreased ability to concentrate, panic, memory loss, and mood changes (e.g., depression, irritability). Individuals may experience these symptoms immediately following the event, or it may be months to years before symptoms first appear. Symptoms occur in a range of intensity and longevity; for some the symptoms become debilitating.

For many individuals, post-traumatic symptoms diminish over time or with appropriate mental health services, support from friends and family, and other therapeutic or supportive interventions. Although individuals continue to feel the effects of the trauma in some form, most report that the symptoms subside or are minimal, and the effects can be managed so that the individual does not feel burdened. However, as reported by the National Center for Post-Traumatic Stress Disorder (NCPTSD), for 8 percent of men and 20 percent of women, the symptoms do not diminish and develop into post-traumatic stress disorder (PTSD). Furthermore for 30 percent of these individuals, PTSD becomes a chronic condition that persists throughout their lifetimes. PTSD is distinguished from post-traumatic stress by the intensity and duration of the symptoms and by three characteristics of symptoms: they are reexperienced, there is hyperarousal or sensitivity to stimuli, and there is avoidance of triggering stimuli.

The American Psychiatric Association (APA) outlines the PTSD diagnostic criteria in the *Diagnostic and Statistical Manual-IV-TR* (*DSM*):

A. The person has been exposed to a traumatic event in which both of the following were present: (1) The person experienced, witnessed, or was confronted with an event or events that involved actual or threatened death or serious injury, or a threat to the physical integrity of self or others; (2) The person's response involved intense fear, helplessness, or horror. Note: In children, this may be expressed instead by disorganizing or agitated behavior.

B. The traumatic event is persistently re-experienced in one (or more) of the following ways: (1) Recurrent and intrusive distressing recollections of the event, including images, thoughts, or perceptions. Note: In young children, repetitive play may occur in which themes or aspects of the trauma are expressed; (2) Recurrent distressing dreams of the event. Note: In children, there may be frightening dreams without recognizable content; (3) Acting or feeling as if the traumatic event were recurring (including a sense of reliving the experience, illusions, hallucinations, and dissociative flashback episodes, including those that occur on awakening or when intoxicated). Note: In young children, trauma-specific reenactment may occur; (4) Intense psychological distress at exposure to internal or external cues that symbolize or resemble an aspect of the traumatic event.

C. Persistent avoidance of stimuli associated with the trauma and numbing of general responsiveness (not present before the trauma), as indicated by three (or more) of the following: (1) Efforts to avoid thoughts, feelings, or conversation associated with the trauma; (2) Efforts to avoid activities, places, or people that arouse recollections of the trauma; (3) Inability to recall an important aspect of the trauma; (4) Markedly diminished interest or participation in significant activities; (5) Feeling of detachment or estrangement from others; (6) Restricted range of affect (e.g., unable to have loving feelings); (7) Sense of a foreshortened future (e.g., does not expect to have a career, marriage, children, or a normal life span).

D. Persistent symptoms of increased arousal (not present before the trauma), as indicated by two (or more) of the following: (1) Difficulty falling asleep or staying asleep; (2) Irritability or outbursts of anger; (3) Difficulty concentrating; (4) Hypervigilance; (5) Exaggerated startle response; (6) Duration of the disturbance (symptoms in Criteria B, C, and D) is more than 1 month; (7) The disturbance causes clinically significant dis-

tress or impairment in social, occupational, or other important areas of functioning.

Specify if: *Acute*: if duration of symptoms is less than 3 months; *Chronic*: if duration of symptoms is 3 months or more.

Specify if: *With Delayed Onset*: if onset of symptoms is at least 6 months after the stressor. (APA 2000, pp. 218–220)

Although these criteria are well-defined, diagnosis of PTSD is a complicated process in part because PTSD symptoms are similar to those of many other psychiatric disorders (e.g., depression), anxiety disorders, and psychotic disorders. In addition many individuals feel shamed or embarrassed by the event or their reactions and may not report the full extent of their symptoms. A multimodal approach is considered to be the most effective for accurately diagnosing PTSD. The NCPTSD suggests an approach including a clinical interview, completion of standardized assessment tools, and a physical assessment.

Statistics from the National Mental Health Association indicate that at least 5.2 million Americans (3.6 percent of U.S. adults) experience PTSD during the course of a year, and nearly 8 percent of Americans will experience PTSD at some point in their lifetimes. Researchers have shown that although PTSD can occur at any age, females develop PTSD at twice the rate of males regardless of their age.

PTSD is a relatively new term within the mental health field, having first appeared in the *DSM* in 1980. However, the concept appeared in the historical medical literature as early as during the Civil War as the term *Da Costa's Syndrome*. In World War I, World War II, and the Korean War *shell shock*, *battle fatigue*, and *war neurosis* were used to describe the troubling symptoms experienced by combat soldiers. The U.S. government did not begin systematically to focus on the origins, symptoms, and treatment of PTSD until the era following the Vietnam War. The military research on PTSD was drawn on by those working in noncombat trauma areas to better understand the impact of various forms of trauma on individuals.

If left untreated, PTSD symptoms can have an impact on all areas of a person's life and can cause both psychological and physical illnesses. Physical effects include chronic pain conditions, immune system disorders, and neurological system symptoms (i.e., memory loss, coordination of the fear response). Cognitive symptoms include distractedness and an inability to analyze events because of physical changes in the hippocampus (the brain region responsible for such processes). Emotional effects include grief, rage, sorrow, numbness, despair, and guilt, among others, as manifested in behaviors such as difficulties with interpersonal relationships and maintaining employment, addiction, isolation, and self-mutilation or self-injury. According to the NCPTSD, a majority of those with PTSD (88 percent of men and 79 percent of women) also met the criteria for a secondary psychiatric diagnosis, meaning that PTSD puts individuals at risk of other mental health disorders.

The National Child Traumatic Stress Network reports that children and adolescents are especially vulnerable to developing PTSD after experiencing a traumatic event because of their limited ability to process information, their lack of cognitive sophistication, and general issues of maturity. Children may exhibit additional symptoms, such as toileting problems, development of a disturbed sense of self, low self-esteem, academic struggles, or symptoms that interfere with a normal developmental task.

Although much remains unknown about PTSD, there are promising treatments that have been successful in treating individuals with PTSD. Some of these include prolonged exposure therapy, cognitive-behavioral therapy, family therapy, group therapy, and some drug therapies.

SEE ALSO *Anxiety; Depression, Psychological; Disease; Emotion; Memory; Mental Health; Mental Illness; Military; Mood; Panic; Psychology; Psychotherapy; Stress; Trauma; Traumatic Bonding; War*

BIBLIOGRAPHY

American Psychiatric Association. 2000. *Desk Reference to the Diagnostic Criteria from the DSM-IV-TR.* Washington, DC: Author.

Andreason, Nancy C., and Donald W. Black. 2006. *Introductory Textbook of Psychiatry.* 4th ed. Washington, DC: American Psychiatric Publishers.

Naparstek, Belleruth. 2004. *Invisible Heroes: Survivors of Trauma and How They Heal.* New York: Bantam Books.

National Center for Post-Traumatic Stress. U.S. Department of Veterans Affairs. 2006. *What Is PTSD?* http://www.ncptsd.va.gov/ncmain.

National Child Traumatic Stress Network. 2005. *The Courage to Remember: Childhood Traumatic Grief Curriculum Guide with CD-ROM.* Los Angeles: Author.

National Mental Health Association. 2006. Post-Traumatic Stress Disorder. http://www.mentalhealthamerica.net/go/ptsd.

Melissa D. Grady

POTRON, MAURICE
1872–1942

Father Maurice Potron, a French Jesuit and a graduate of France's prestigious École Polytechnique with a Ph.D. in mathematics, published major, but surprisingly little known, mathematical-economic papers between 1911 and 1941. His writings include three major findings.

First, in mathematics, he published a demonstration about the existence of solutions of nonnegative matrixes (or "linear substitutions" as he called them) as early as 1911, before Ferdinand Georg Frobenius (1849–1917) did so in 1912. In 1908 and 1909 Oskar Perron (1880–1975) and Frobenius had only demonstrated theorems related to strictly positive matrixes.

Second, in the same paper, Potron, while trying to reconcile social justice ("fair" price, "fair" wage) and economic interdependencies, was the first to apply Perron-Frobenius's theorems on a Leontief-type model, in order to find the conditions for the existence of a fair economic equilibrium, a "satisfactory economic regime" in Potron's words, allowing simultaneous adequacy between the consumption structure and that of production and work capacities, and adequacy between price and wage levels. As far as we know, nobody had used Perron-Frobenius's theorem in economics before World War II (1939–1945).

Third, in 1912 Potron laid the foundations of future input-output analysis, offering a detailed study of the expenses supported by his baker to produce a two-kilogram loaf of bread. The extension of such a study to other industries would allow precise calculation of the "effective satisfactory regime of production-consumption and prices-wages" (Potron 1912, p. 19). Indeed, he used matrixes to describe the economic interdependency between products and branches. The concept of a "technical coefficient" was used in 1912 to promote a central planning office whose mission would be to organize the economy according to social Catholic doctrine. Thus, the invention of input-output matrixes is undoubtedly due not to Wassily Leontief (1906–1999) but to Potron (1912), since Leontief's "The Balance of the Economy of the USSR" was published in 1925 and *The Structure of the American Economy*, his greatest book, in 1941. The existence of a "calculations bureau" (*bureau des calculs*) would constitute the only way to achieve a "satisfactory regime." This concern led Potron to put forward, in 1936, the use of Gauss-Lanczos's iterative method in order to help the planning office deal with the huge dimensions of the matrix, a method widely used in algorithms today.

As early as 1912, Potron introduced the number of working days per year as a relevant parameter of the viability of an economic system. He was also concerned with the possibility of demand inadequacy: in what has been called *Potron's law*, he shows how an increase in demand will raise general activity and revenue. Since he lacked academic training in economics, Potron's economic approach is mainly explained by his intellectual and social environment (Abraham-Frois and Lendjel 2004). Catholic doctrine (as expressed in 1891 in Pope Leo XIII's encyclical

Rerum Novarum on the rights and duties of capital and labor) and the network of Catholic social reformers (mainly Potron's father, Auguste Potron, as well as Henry Pupey Girard, Gustave Desbuquois, and Joseph Zamanski) led him to formulate original propositions in economics, with his own terminology and cumbersome mathematical notations. But this singularity denied him access to academia and to any audience of economists. In the last years of his life, neither his links with *X-crise*, a French association constituted between 1931 and 1939 by engineering graduates of France's École Polytechnique to deal with the global economic crisis (Fischman and Lendjel 2000), nor his membership in the Econometric Society (since 1938), nor even his participation at the eighth International Congress of Mathematics at Oslo in 1936 (probably with the help of Norwegian economist Ragnar Frisch [1895–1973]) provided him with any recognition. This has only come recently.

SEE ALSO *Input-Output Matrix; Matrix Algebra*

BIBLIOGRAPHY

Abraham-Frois, Gilbert, and Emeric Lendjel. 2001. Une première application du théorème de Perron-Frobenius à l'économie: L'Abbé Potron comme précurseur. *Revue d'economie politique* 111 (4): 639–666.

Abraham-Frois, Gilbert, and Emeric Lendjel. 2004. *Les oeuvres economiques de l'Abbé Potron*. Paris: L'Harmattan.

Abraham-Frois, Gilbert, and Emeric Lendjel. 2005. Father Potron's Early Contribution to Input-Output Analysis. Fifteenth Input-Output Conference, Beijing, June-July.

Fischman, Marianne, and Emeric Lendjel. 2000. La contribution d'X-crise à l'émergence de l'économétrie en France dans les années trente. *Revue Européenne des sciences sociales* 38 (118): 115–134.

Potron, Maurice. 1911. Application aux problèmes de la "production suffisante" et du "salaire vital" de quelques propriétés des substitutions linéaires à coefficients = 0 et leur application aux problèmes de la production et des salaires. *Comptes rendus de l'Académie des Sciences* 53: 1129–1131. Reprinted in Abraham-Frois and Lendjel (2004).

Potron, Maurice. 1912. Possibilité et détermination du juste prix et du juste salaire. *Le mouvement social* 73 (4): 289–316. Reprinted in Abraham-Frois and Lendjel (2004).

Potron, Maurice. 1913. Quelques propriétés des substitutions linéaires à coefficients ≥ 0 et leur application aux problèmes de la production et des salaires. *Annales scientifiques de l'École Normale* 30: 53–76. Reprinted in Abraham-Frois and Lendjel (2004).

Potron, Maurice. 1936. *L'aspect mathématique de certains problèmes économiques*. Paris: Author. Reprinted in Abraham-Frois and Lendjel (2004).

Gilbert Abraham-Frois
Emeric Lendjel

POULANTZAS, NICOS
1936–1979

Famous for his concept of the "relative-autonomy of the state" as well as for his debate with Ralph Miliband (1924–1994), Nicos Poulantzas was a formative neo-Marxist theorist of politics. Born into a prominent family in Greece, Poulantzas studied law at the University of Athens before moving to France, where he completed his doctoral studies in the philosophy of law. During this time, he was closely aligned with the existential Marxism of Jean-Paul Sartre (1905–1980) and Simone de Beauvoir (1908–1986), and he was a contributor to their journal *Les Temps modernes* (Modern Times). Poulantzas, however, began moving away from existentialism in 1966 and increasingly came to be influenced by the "structuralist" Marxism of Louis Althusser (1918–1990); it is largely in this context, as an Althusserian or structuralist, that Poulantzas has come to be known.

In 1969 the *New Left Review* published Poulantzas's critical review of Miliband's book *The State in Capitalist Society* (1969). This review was the first volley in what came to be known as the Miliband-Poulantzas debate. The debate largely hinged on whether the class bias of the state was a product of the class origins and affiliations of those individuals who occupied the top positions within state institutions (Miliband) or whether the class bias of the state was more a product of its structures and functions (Poulantzas). Beyond separating Marxists into what may have been an overstated divide of "instrumentalist" and "structuralist" camps, the debate highlighted a renewed Marxist interest in the theory of politics, and it foreshadowed and provoked an intense growth of research on the state, a still ongoing body of inquiry often referred to as *state theory*.

Poulantzas's most import work in this context was *Political Power and Social Classes* (1968). It is in this work that he first developed the idea of the relative autonomy of the state. According to Poulantzas, for the state to properly function as a capitalist state it must be able to go against the individual and particular interests of capitalists in order to act in their general/class interests; the state must be "relatively autonomous" from the interests and demands of capitalists. This also implied that the state could not be reduced to some reflection of economic relations or interests, as more orthodox Marxists had often done. Poulantzas argued that, as economic agents, capitalists tend to be divided and competitive. The state provides the institutional space for various factions of the capitalist class, as well as other powerful classes, to come together and form long-term strategies and alliances; this is what Poulantzas termed the *power-bloc*. At the same time, the state disorganizes the working class by dividing them into individuals/citizens, what he termed the *isolation effect*.

Poulantzas's *Fascism and Dictatorship* (1970) was an empirical case study based on his theoretical work. He examined the class foundations of fascism and understood the fascist state as an exceptional form of the capitalist state. He argued that fascism was not inevitable or some natural stage in the development of capitalism and thus that it, as a type of response to a crisis of politics, could be repeated in the future. Poulantzas applied similar ideas in one of the first Marxist studies of democratization, *The Crisis of the Dictatorships: Spain, Portugal, Greece* (1975). There he argued that the rise of democracy in each country was the outcome of a political conflict between two key factions of the capitalist class, the domestic and comprador bourgeoisie.

In Poulantzas's subsequent theoretical work, he made a key contribution to class theory when he argued against traditional "in itself" and "for itself" definitions and contended that classes do not exist outside of conflict and struggle, that classes only exist as an ensemble of practices. In *Classes in Contemporary Capitalism* (1974), he also examined the political implications of the growing transnationalization of capital (one of the first Marxist examinations of globalization), and he examined the growth of the "new" petite bourgeoisie.

In his last book, *State, Power, Socialism* (1978), he critiqued the theories of Michel Foucault (1926–1984) and Giles Deleuze (1925–1995), among many others, and refined his previous theories. Poulantzas now defined the state as a social relationship and argued that the question of its relative autonomy was a function of class struggle. Since the state was a condensation of the class struggle it was always in flux and contested; no one class had complete control, and the state always had to take the interests of the dominated classes into consideration. The degree of this relative autonomy would thus be a historical variable and would change in accordance with the content and intensity of the political struggles of the day.

Poulantzas's theoretical positions were also reflected in his political affinities and activities. His emphasis against economic determinism was an anti-Stalinist stance and reflected Poulantzas's support of democratic socialism and the radical democratic positions of Rosa Luxemburg (1870–1919), Antonio Gramsci (1891–1937), and the Eurocommunist movements of the time. Poulantzas was an active member of many leftist organizations, such as the Communist Party of the Interior in Greece and of the CFDT (Confédération française démocratique du travail; French Democratic Confederation of Labor) in France, and he often contributed to the newspapers and journals of these organizations as well as to the popular press. Given his emphasis on questions of political strategy and his support of a democratic transition to socialism (as well as the appropriation of his ideas by radical democratic currents in

France, Italy, and especially Portugal, Spain, and Greece), Poulantzas is often considered to be a key theorist of Eurocommunism. Despite his untimely death at the age of forty-three, Poulantzas's conceptual contributions and political sensibilities continue to be relevant to a wide range of concerns within contemporary social science.

BIBLIOGRAPHY

Jessop, Bob. 1985. *Nicos Poulantzas: Marxist Theory and Political Strategy.* New York: Palgrave Macmillan.

Poulantzas, Nicos. 1973. *Political Power and Social Classes.* Trans. Timothy O'Hagan. London: New Left Books.

Poulantzas, Nicos. 1978. *State, Power, Socialism.* Trans. Patrick Camiller. London: New Left Books.

Peter Bratsis

POVERTY

Poverty is among the most central problems of economics, and its alleviation is a long-standing challenge for economists and policy makers alike. The Millennium Development Goals (MDG) adopted by the United Nations in 2000 aim to lower the fraction of the world's poor by the year 2015 to half its 1990 level, where "poor" includes those subsisting on less than $1 a day. This description of poverty is close to the $1.08-per-day poverty line (in 1993 dollars) adopted by the World Bank. Defined by the $1 cut-off, in 1998 one in five people in the world (1.2 billion) were poor, and they were concentrated in South Asia (522 million), sub-Saharan Africa (291 million), and East Asia (278 million).

WORLDWIDE DISTRIBUTION OF POVERTY

Measured in terms of certain basic capabilities—health, education, political voice, credit—these regional poverty patterns persist. The 2004 Human Development Report states that sub-Saharan Africa accounts for 22 percent of the world's malnourished population and 42 percent of primary school-age children not in school. For East Asia the corresponding figures are 25 percent and 13 percent, and for South Asia, they are 37 percent and 31 percent, respectively. Thus, the $1-a-day measure seems to do a reasonable job of capturing other relevant dimensions of poverty.

How do those with less than $1 a day really live? Based on household level surveys across thirteen countries, Abhijit Banerjee and Esther Duflo (2007) give us a vivid picture: They often work multiple odd jobs (and not only in agriculture); frequently migrate temporarily for work; own few assets other than land; lack access to credit and insurance; get poor-quality health care and education (if at all); are frequently malnourished; spend much (but not all) of their income on food (50–75%), alcohol and tobacco (resisting temptations to spend more), and festivals (but few other forms of entertainment); and importantly, although they do feel the pinch of poverty, their self-reported levels of happiness and health are not particularly low. If this poverty cut-off were doubled to just $2 a day, nearly half the world's people would be deemed poor (2.8 billion)—and shockingly, they consume less in a month than what the nonpoor consume in a single day.

These figures are grim, but to gain some perspective on them and assess how realistic the MDG are, we need to measure the progress the world has made in alleviating poverty. Taking the long view, the drop in the poverty rate—from 84 percent in 1820 to 50 percent in 1950, to 24 percent in 1992—and the rise in life expectancy—from twenty-seven years to sixty-one years over the same period (Bourguignon and Morrison 2002)—is dramatic. Over a shorter period it is less so. According to the World Bank, the poverty rate worldwide has fallen from 28.7 percent in 1987 to 24.3 percent in 1998 (World Bank 2007). (These numbers are somewhat sensitive to the time period and data sources used; Angus Deaton [2002] points out that this can be explained by the use of different underlying data sources, but there is less disagreement of the pattern of changes than in levels.) Once again, there is sharp regional variation—from 26.6 percent to 15.3 percent in East Asia (mostly China) and 44 percent to 40 percent in South Asia, but stagnant around 46 percent in Africa, with an increase of 50 million in the region's poor. These sharp regional variations in poverty reduction emphasize the question of what the underlying causes of poverty are. Not surprisingly, there are multiple views on what the "right" answer.

ALLEVIATING POVERTY: IS MARKET-DRIVEN GROWTH ENOUGH?

The dominant view of the 1980s, the "Washington Consensus," still prevalent in some influential quarters (such as the International Monetary Fund), is that growth is the best answer to the poverty problem and that market-friendly policies are best suited to achieving growth. Does the data support this view? There is strong evidence of positive correlation between growth and poverty reduction—which, of course, is not the same as causation. Based on numbers from sixty countries with data for more than one year, Timothy Besley and Robin Burgess (2003) find that poverty rates are very responsive to changes in income per capita (elasticity = - 0.73 worldwide), but yet again, with large regional differences (-1.0 in East Asia versus - 0.49 in

sub-Saharan Africa). They conclude that, given historical growth rates of per capita income, growth alone is unlikely to help achieve the poverty reduction targets set in the MDG in most regions (Besley and Burgess 2003). As for evidence of market-driven growth, it is now widely agreed that the most prominent growth story of the past three decades, the "East Asian miracle," involved active government intervention in markets (Amsden 2001). Overall, support for the Washington Consensus view does exist, but it is not overwhelming. As a practical matter, many countries have had a less than favorable experience with certain aspects of "stabilization plans" based on this view—a policy package typically involving openness to trade and foreign capital markets, restrictive monetary and fiscal policies, privatization of state-owned enterprises, and deregulation of important markets. Concerted international action to tackle poverty, in the form of foreign aid, has been well below the United Nations's aid target of 0.7 percent of gross domestic product of the G7 countries (the United States, France, Germany, Italy, Japan, the United Kingdom, and Canada). But even if that aid were available, it would be only one-third of what is needed to achieve the MDG. Collectively, these realities have forced a search for alternative explanations for and solutions to the poverty problem.

THE INSTITUTIONAL APPROACH TO POVERTY REDUCTION

A shift in the thinking on poverty is also being driven by a deeper theoretical understanding of both market failure and government failure—that is, how market imperfections deny the poor a chance to make the investments needed to rise out of poverty, and why governments are not always effective in making up for this lapse. One important conclusion emerging from research in this area is the need for sound domestic institutions to promote growth and poverty reduction—more so than a country's geographical or "cultural" legacies. A natural consequence of this finding is a call—by the World Bank (World Bank 2003) and by academic economists—for a wider set of institutional reforms, including promoting democracy and other forms of political voice for the poor, the rule of law, property rights for the poor, increasing government accountability, and reducing corruption. There has been a steady trickle of evidence supporting the favorable impact of sound institutions on outcomes for the poor: for example, how property rights over land in urban areas in Peru help the poor gain access to credit, increase labor supply, and be more productive (De Soto 2000; Field 2002); how political representation for women in India results in more funds for public goods they care about (Chattopadhyay and Duflo 2004); and how a newspaper campaign concerning government accountability increased the resources reaching public schools in Uganda (Reinikka and Svensson 2001).

SERVICE DELIVERY: GETTING "TRICKLE DOWN" RIGHT

Although progress on institutional reform is crucial, it can be slow. A parallel approach is a package of policy measures that target poverty and redistribute resources to the poor through schools and health clinics, promoting small businesses, access to credit, better social safety nets, and so on. Here, theoretical research has helped to explain why certain redistribution mechanisms—for instance, in-kind rather than cash transfers—can deliver greater equity and growth when there are market imperfections. This research has shed light on the political economy of public good provision, with insights into suitable incentives for policy makers, providers, and program recipients. On the ground, the better programs have worked through effective design and implementation. For instance, Mexico's Progresa program involves cash benefits for women and their families that are conditional upon the child(ren) being sent to school and being taken for health check-ups. Microfinance—pioneered by Mohammad Yunus of the Grameen Bank—uses a combination of "peer monitoring" and group liability for borrowers, which makes possible "micro" loans to those too poor to offer collateral. One common feature of both these programs is that they channel resources to poor households through women. Such a gender-based strategy of redistribution is gaining support, given widespread evidence of women's tendency to spend more resources on children's welfare and human capital, relative to men (Haddad, Hoddinott, and Alderman 1987). It has also been recognized as a viable solution to the problem of child labor and low schooling, breaking the vicious link from current to future poverty. While there is strong evidence for the positive impact of Progresa (Schultz 2004), ongoing work is evaluating and refining the design of microfinance initiatives.

More broadly, a combination of empirical and, more recently, experimental work is helping design and systematically evaluate a host of service-delivery mechanisms, including the effect of improved child health on school attendance (Kremer-Miguel 2004); the impact of more rural bank branches on poverty (Burgess and Pande 2002); and the impact of corruption in the issuance of drivers' licenses by the government (Bertrand, Djankov, Hanna, and Mullainathan 2007).

NEW PERSPECTIVES ON POVERTY

As part of these experiments with program design and implementation, economists have sometimes found it hard to rationally explain certain choices that the poor make, be it with regard to savings, or technology adoption (Ashraf et al. 2006; Duflo et al. 2006). This gives rise to an exciting new behavioral economics approach to poverty that seeks to understand decisions of the poor from not just an economic perspective, but also a psychological one. Insight into the strengths and weaknesses of governments and markets also blurs the line between private- and public-service delivery (Besley and Ghatak 2004), giving rise to innovative approaches such as the Advanced Commitment for Vaccines initiative. Some even argue that the world's poor constitute not just an obligation for the rich, but also a vital, untapped market (Prahalad 2004).

At the international level, however, some important issues that affect poverty remain difficult to resolve. Globalization and trade have been a boon to some countries (or some areas within countries), but a bane to others, creating greater income insecurity for the poor in some developing and developed economies. International agreements on trade and immigration, intellectual property issues, and environmental pollution have not always been favorable to poor economies. These remain areas where large strides can be made toward reduction of global poverty.

SEE ALSO *Accountability; Corruption; Culture of Poverty; Development Economics; Economic Growth; Economics; Economics, Stratification; Education, USA; Government; Governmentality; Grameen Bank; Human Capital; Microfinance; Poor, The; Schooling; Stratification; Washington Consensus; World Bank, The*

BIBLIOGRAPHY

Acemoglu, Daron, Simon Johnson, and James A. Robinson. 2001. The Colonial Origins of Comparative Development: An Empirical Investigation. *American Economic Review* 91 (5): 1369–1401.

Amsden, Alice H. 2001. *The Rise of "The Rest": Challenges to the West from Late-Industrialising Economies.* New York: Oxford University Press.

Ashraf, Nava, Dean Karlan, and Wesley Yin. 2006. Tying Odysseus to the Mast: Evidence from a Commitment Savings Product in the Philippines. *Quarterly Journal of Economics* 121 (2): 673–697.

Banerjee, Abhijit, Roland Benabou, and Dilip Mookherjee. 2004. *Understanding Poverty.* Oxford: Oxford University Press.

Banerjee, Abhijit, and Esther Duflo. 2007. The Economic Lives of the Poor. *Journal of Economic Perspectives* 21 (1): 141–167.

Banerjee, Abhijit, and Andrew Newman. 1994. Poverty, Incentives, and Development. *American Economic Review* 84 (2): 211–215.

Bertrand, Marianne, Simeon Djankov, Rema Hanna, and Sendhil Mullainathan. 2006. *Does Corruption Produce Unsafe Drivers?* NBER Working Paper No. 12274.

Besley, Timothy, and Robin Burgess. 2003. Halving Global Poverty. *Journal of Economic Perspectives* 17 (3): 3–22.

Besley, Timothy, and Maitreesh Ghatak. 2004. Public Goods and Economic Development. In *Understanding Poverty*, eds. Abhijit Banerjee, Roland Benabou, and Dilip Mookherjee, 285–303. Oxford: Oxford University Press.

Bourguignon, François, and Christian Morrison. 2002. Inequality Among World Citizens, 1820–1992. *American Economic Review* 92 (4): 727–744.

Burgess, Robin, and Rohini Pande. 2005. Can Rural Banks Reduce Poverty? Evidence from the Indian Social Banking Experiment. *American Economic Review* 95 (3): 780–795.

Chattopadhyay, Raghabendra, and Esther Duflo. 2004. Women as Policy Makers: Evidence from a Randomized Policy Experiment in India. *Econometrica* 72 (5): 1409–1443.

Deaton, Angus. 2002. Is World Poverty Falling? *Finance and Development* 39 (2): 4–7. http://www.imf.org/external/pubs/ft/fandd/2002/06/deaton.htm.

De Soto, Hernando. 2000. *The Mystery of Capital*. New York: Basic Books.

Duflo, Esther, Michael Kremer, and Jonathan Robinson. 2006. Why Don't Farmers Use Fertilizer? Evidence from Field Experiments in Western Kenya. http://www-rcf.usc.edu/~hjeong/seminar/fall06/Duflo_fertilizer_BREAD_comp.pdf.

Field, Erica. 2002. Entitled to Work: Urban Property Rights and Labor Supply in Peru. http://www.economics.harvard.edu/faculty/field/papers/Field_COFOPRI.pdf.

Haddad, Laurence, John Hoddinott, and Harold Alderman, eds. 1987. *Intra-Household Resource Allocation in Developing Countries: Models, Methods, and Policy*. Baltimore, MD: Johns Hopkins University Press.

Mani, Anandi, and Sharun Mukand. 2007. Democracy, Visibility, and the Politics of Public Good Provision. *Journal of Development Economics* 83 (2): 506–529.

Miguel, Edward, and Michael Kremer. 2004. Worms: Identifying Impacts on Education and Health in the Presence of Treatment Externalities. *Econometrica* 72 (1): 159–217.

Prahalad, C. K. 2004. *Fortune at the Bottom of the Pyramid: Eradicating Poverty through Profits*. Philadelphia: Wharton School Publishing.

Reinikka, Ritva, and Lars Svensson. 2003. Local Capture: Evidence From a Central Government Transfer Program in Uganda. *Quarterly Journal of Economics* 119 (2): 679–706.

Schultz, Paul. 2004. Subsidies for the Poor: Evaluating the Mexican Progresa Poverty Program. *Journal of Development Economics* 74 (1): 199–250.

World Bank. 2003. World Development Report 2004: Making Services Work for Poor People. http://go.worldbank.org/S7MDO8EYS0.

World Bank. 2007. PovcalNet. http://iresearch.worldbank.org/PovcalNet/jsp/index.jsp.

Anandi Mani

POVERTY, INDICES OF

A poverty index measures the level of poverty in a society. In measuring the level of poverty, a poverty line or poverty threshold, usually stated in terms of income, is defined to divide the society into two separate groups. An individual is poor if that individual lives below the poverty line.

THE HEADCOUNT RATIO AND THE INCOME-GAP RATIO

The traditional poverty index is the headcount ratio, which is the proportion of people in a society who are living in poverty. If n is the total number of people in the society and m is the number of the poor, the headcount ratio is

$$H = \frac{m}{n} \text{ or } \frac{m}{n} \times 100\%$$

Another poverty index that sometimes is used is the income-gap ratio, which is the percentage of the average income shortfall of the poor to the poverty line. If μ_p is the average income of the poor and z is the poverty line, the income-gap ratio is

$$I = 1 - \frac{\mu_p}{z} \text{ or } \left(1 - \frac{\mu_p}{z}\right) \times 100\%$$

Both poverty indices, however, have serious problems in measuring the poverty level of a society adequately. For example, the headcount ratio does not consider how far a poor individual is below the poverty line; an individual just below the line and an individual far below it are treated the same in the calculation. Although the income-gap ratio does not have this problem, it does not reflect how incomes are distributed among the poor: Whether they are equally poor or some of them are desperately poor, the same level of poverty is determined. Additionally, the income-gap ratio does not deal with the number of the poor; it considers only the average income of the poor. Intuitively, for the same average income of the poor, the society should have more poverty if more people fall into poverty.

THE AXIOMATIC APPROACH

Since the publication of Amartya Sen's 1976 work on poverty measurement, the construction and evaluation of poverty indices have followed an axiomatic approach. In this approach, ideal properties for poverty measurement are formulated as axioms and a poverty index is generated to satisfy those axioms. The following are the key axioms for poverty measurement: The focus axiom states that the poverty index is not affected by a change in a nonpoor individual's income as long as that individual remains nonpoor. The restricted continuity axiom states that the poverty index is continuous in poor incomes in that a small change in a poor individual's income should not lead to a large change in the poverty level. The monotonicity axiom states that all else the same, a decrease in a poor individual's income should increase the overall level of poverty in the society. The weak transfer axiom states that all else the same, a transfer of income from a poor individual to a poorer individual should decrease the overall level of poverty. The subgroup consistency axiom states that if the society is divided into different subsocieties (such as the different states in the United States), all else the same, an increase in the poverty level of a subsociety also should increase the overall level of poverty of the society. The increasing poverty line axiom states that the poverty index should increase as the poverty line increases. Additionally, a poverty index should satisfy the unit consistency axiom: If one society (say, the United States) has more poverty than another society (say, the United Kingdom) when all incomes and the poverty line are measured in one currency unit (e.g., U.S. dollars), the conclusion should hold when another currency (e.g., British pounds) is used.

The headcount ratio does not satisfy the monotonicity axiom, the weak transfer axiom, or the increasing poverty line axiom. The income-gap ratio violates the weak transfer axiom and the increasing poverty line axiom.

Sen (1976) proposed the first axiomatic-based poverty index. Suppose all individuals' incomes are arranged in increasing order and x_i is the ith individual's income, then $x_1 \leq x_2 \leq \ldots \leq x_n$. The Sen poverty index is

$$S = \frac{2}{(m+1)nz} \sum_{i=1}^{m} (z - x_i)(m + 1 - i),$$

which also can be written as

$$S = \frac{2}{n} \sum_{i=1}^{m} \left(1 - \frac{x_i}{z}\right)\left(1 - \frac{i}{m+1}\right) = H\left[I + (1 - I)G_p \frac{m}{m+1}\right]$$

where H is the headcount ratio, I is the income-gap ratio, and G_p is the Gini coefficient of the poor incomes. The Gini coefficient is twice the area between the Lorenz curve of the poor incomes and the 45-degree diagonal line. A slightly modified version of the Sen index is the Thon poverty index:

$$T = \frac{2}{(n+1)nz} \sum_{i=1}^{m} (z - x_i)(n + 1 - i)$$

Other poverty indices include the Chakravarty poverty index:

$$C = \frac{1}{n} \sum_{i=1}^{m} \left[1 - \left(\frac{x_i}{z}\right)^{\varepsilon}\right] \text{ with } 0 < \varepsilon < 1$$

the Foster-Greer-Thorbecke poverty index:

$$FGT = \frac{1}{n} \sum_{i=1}^{m} \left(1 - \frac{x_i}{z}\right)^{\alpha} \text{ with } \alpha \geq 0$$

the Watts poverty index:

$$W = \frac{1}{n} \sum_{i=1}^{m} (\ln z - \ln x_i)$$

and the Kolm poverty index:

$$K = \frac{1}{n} \sum_{i=1}^{m} (e^{\sigma(z - x_i)} - 1) \text{ with } \sigma > 0$$

Both the Sen and Thon indices satisfy all the axioms listed above except the subgroup consistency axiom; the Chakravarty index, the Foster-Greer-Thorbecke index, and the Watts index satisfy all the axioms; and the Kolm index satisfies all the axioms except the unit consistency axiom. All these new poverty indices are referred to as distribution-sensitive indices because they satisfy the weak transfer axiom. The differences among these poverty indices lie in the ways in which the shortfall of each poor income to the poverty line is characterized and the ways in which those shortfalls across all individuals are aggregated into an overall index of poverty. For example, for the headcount ratio, each individual's shortfall is assigned a value of one if the individual is poor and zero if the individual is nonpoor, and the overall poverty level is the simple average of those shortfalls (zeros and ones). For the Sen poverty index, each individual's shortfall is recorded by $1 - \frac{x_i}{z}$ if the individual is poor and zero if the individual is nonpoor, and the overall poverty is the weighted average of those shortfalls, with the weight being $1 - \frac{i}{m+1}$, which is the relative rank of that individual among the poor. For the Watts poverty index, each individual's shortfall is recorded by $\ln z - \ln x_i$ if the individual is poor and zero if the individual is nonpoor, and the overall poverty is the simple average of those shortfalls.

CALCULATING THE POVERTY LEVEL

To calculate the poverty level of a society, one needs to define the poverty line and choose a poverty index. The definition of the poverty line varies from society to society. In the United States the official poverty line initially was developed by Mollie Orshansky of the Social Security Administration in 1963–1964 and adjusted each year thereafter for inflation. The U.S. poverty line is regarded as an absolute poverty line because it was calculated as the minimum amount of resources needed for living at a point in time and is not affected by changes in the entire income distribution. Because the minimum amount of resources needed for living depends on the specific society, the calculated absolute poverty line tends to vary from society to society. For example, an individual with an income at the U.S. poverty line would be regarded as rich in some developing countries. In poverty studies, especially in international comparisons of poverty, another type of poverty line—the relative poverty line—has been used. A relative poverty line is specified as a point in the distribution of income (e.g., one-half of the mean or median income), and the line is updated automatically over time for changes in the distribution.

Because the use of any specific poverty line, whether absolute or relative, is somewhat arbitrary, a range of poverty lines often are used to check the robustness of poverty comparisons. The resulting conditions for poverty comparisons are closely related to the conditions of stochastic dominance (Foster and Shorrocks 1988) and Lorenz dominance, which is based on comparisons of Lorenz curves. Similarly, the choice of a specific poverty index in poverty comparisons is somewhat arbitrary in light of the fact that there are multiple poverty indices that satisfy the same set of poverty axioms. If, for a specific poverty line, all poverty indices that satisfy certain axioms are used in poverty comparisons, the resulting conditions are also related to the conditions of stochastic dominance (Atkinson 1987) and Lorenz dominance.

SEE ALSO *Economics, Stratification; Gini Coefficient; Income Distribution; Inequality, Income; Poor, The; Poverty; Sen, Amartya Kumar; Social Welfare Functions; Welfare Analysis*

BIBLIOGRAPHY

Atkinson, Anthony B. 1987. On the Measurement of Poverty. *Econometrica* 55 (4): 749–764.

Foster, James E., and Anthony Shorrocks. 1988. Poverty Orderings. *Econometrica* 56 (1): 173–177.

Sen, Amartya. 1976. Poverty: An Ordinal Approach to Measurement. *Econometrica* 44 (2): 219–231.

Sen, Amartya. 1997. *On Economic Inequality.* Expanded ed. Oxford: Clarendon.

Buhong Zheng

POVERTY, URBAN

For well over a century and a half, the urban poor have been an object of intense contemplation among scholars, politicians, philanthropists, activists, and policy makers, and the topic of urban poverty has been one of the most controversial in the field of urban studies. Alternatively reviled or pitied, the urban poor tend to be characterized in academic and popular discourse as either undeserving, irrational, passive, pathological, apathetic, and in need of charity and moral reform or as deserving, resilient, exploited, and oppressed. Accordingly, explanations for the causes of urban poverty have, for the most part, vacillated between blaming the poor for their own impoverishment and explaining impoverishment in terms of urban political economy.

Research on urban poverty first gained prominence in nineteenth-century Europe and the United States as industrialization transformed the urban landscape. Its roots were primarily in early social reformism, which built on investigative journalism with survey research to make poverty visible so that it could be reckoned with by the burgeoning middle classes. In England, social reformer Charles Booth, for example, followed the earlier work of journalists Henry Mayhew and Andrew Mearns to gain widespread attention for his classificatory survey of the laboring classes, *Life and Labour of the People of London* (1902). In the United States, journalist Jacob Riis published the still famous *How the Other Half Lives* (1890). Soon thereafter, Hull House settlement founder Jane Addams spearheaded the publication of *Hull House Maps and Papers* (1895), revealing the distinctive pattern of immigration, wage inequality, and residential segregation that characterized American cities at the time.

As the first empirical studies of poverty in European and American cities, the work published by these social reformers is widely considered to be the precursor to modern social scientific poverty studies. Importantly, these studies were largely descriptive and were designed to be systematic in their classifications of the poor and in their depictions of the illicit commerce, violence, deprivation, and sloth that was sometimes present in urban neighborhoods. They were also focused squarely on the question of urban political economy, with class, wages, and employment as central categories of analysis. As the first study to establish a direct link between industrialization, the labor process, and the depreciation of living conditions in overcrowded slums, Friedrich Engels's *The Condition of the Working Class in England in 1844* became an early classic of this approach.

The rise of Chicago School sociology in the early twentieth century reoriented poverty studies away from urban political economy toward "social ecology." Less interested in class than in assimilation and social disorganization among immigrants, the Chicago approach sought to explain industrialization, commerce, and residential distribution as natural occurrences in the urban environment (Park et al. 1925). In this formulation, poverty and segregation were understood as part of a natural process of ecological succession, in which poor and segregated neighborhoods were seen as "natural areas" where new immigrants were oriented to the city, giving them a foothold before their eventual accommodation with and assimilation into the more affluent mainstream. In a series of important and highly influential field and ethnographic studies on such topics as juvenile delinquency, gangs, hobos, and slums, the Chicago School provided the social scientific basis for the understanding of urban poverty, which its protagonists tended to view as a consequence of social deviance and neighborhood disorganization. E. Franklin Frazier's *The Negro Family in Chicago* (1932) and *The Negro Family in the United States* (1939) gained wide influence in poverty studies by downplaying the importance of racial inequality, establishing a powerful connection between poverty and family structure, and arguing in particular that the matriarchal black family was "pathologically" disorganized and that it therefore perpetuated poverty. (It should be noted, however, that Frazier ultimately viewed family disorganization as temporary and that he was a strong advocate for incorporation of black men into the industrial workforce [O'Conner 2001].) In contrast, St. Clair Drake and Horace Cayton, also trained at Chicago, published *Black Metropolis* (1945). Like Du Bois's *The Philadelphia Negro* (1899) before it, they placed a stronger emphasis on the role of racial inequality in the production and reproduction of black inner-city poverty.

The influence of the Chicago School's poverty-as-cultural-pathology argument grew in the poverty scholarship and public-policy work of the 1960s and 1970s. Notably, anthropologist Oscar Lewis, best known for his widely disseminated "culture of poverty" thesis, linked behavior with the persistence of poverty (Lewis 1966). He argued that a significant faction of the poor were caught in an intergenerational quagmire of dysfunctional values and behaviors. This argument resonated with and reinforced the dominant policy positions that emerged as poverty was "rediscovered" in America in the 1960s during the War on Poverty. Famously, Lewis's influence can be seen in Daniel Patrick Moynihan's 1965 report to President Johnson, *The Negro Family: A Case for National Action*, which relied heavily on the "culture of poverty" thesis to describe black "ghetto" poverty and familial "dysfunction." Many social scientists rebutted Lewis's culturalist explanations for social "disorganization" with work showing that the consumption, labor market participation, and kinship patterns among the poor were not "dysfunctional," irrational, or self-destructive but rather survival strategies that made sense given economic constraints (see, for example, Stack 1974; Liebow 1967; Valentine 1978).

In the 1980s and 1990s, the controversy around the "culture of poverty" thesis replayed itself as the underclass debate, which focused on the poorest of the poor in cities

struggling to remake themselves under postindustrial conditions. Also centered around the behaviors of black inner-city residents, the debate this time focused on their social "isolation" and "dislocation." Pundits and policy makers on the right argued that poverty was caused by poor people's "dependency" on welfare programs (Murray 1984; Mead 1992). In rebuttal, left-liberal scholars countered the moralist formulations of the right with demographic analyses demonstrating the "structural" roots of impoverishment. William Julius Wilson (1987, 1996), among others, showed that public policies such as affirmative action, which enabled residential mobility for middle-class blacks, combined with labor market restructuring in deindustrializing cities to create an isolated underclass of chronically jobless inner-city residents. Both sides of the underclass debate were critiqued by left-leaning scholars for downplaying the persistence of racial and gender discrimination in labor markets, housing policies, and tax policies, and for perpetuating the image of the pathological poor (Goode and Maskovsky 2001; O'Conner 2001).

Recent research on urban poverty has redirected attention once again to urban political economy. In the aftermath of the 1996 welfare reform, the popularity of the poverty-as-cultural-pathology argument has abated significantly, and new policy-centered work has documented the plight of the U.S. working poor, who are not able to earn wages high enough to pull them out of poverty. More significantly, as global cities paradigms have become more influential in urban studies, the idea that urban poverty is a consequence of global shifts in economy, politics, and governance has once again taken center stage. Whereas some European Third Way scholars have shifted their focus away from poverty toward social exclusion (e.g., Giddens 1998), others have directed critical attention to the political economy of the new global inner city. In the global North, gentrification and other redevelopment strategies are displacing low-income residents from central cities (Hackworth 2007). In the global South, slums are proliferating in large measure because of new migration patterns that correspond with global shifts in industrial and agricultural production patterns (Davis 2006). Of particular interest in this work is attention to the polarizing effects of neoliberalism on cities across the world (Harvey 2005). This new work resonates with scholarship that understands poverty as fundamentally a political problem, one that is shaped dramatically by forms of activism, urban or otherwise, that either include or exclude the impoverished residents who live in cities across the globe (Maskovsky 2001; see also Piven and Cloward 1977).

SEE ALSO *Affirmative Action; Assimilation; Chicago School; Culture of Poverty; Deviance; Discrimination, Racial; Drake, St. Clair; Du Bois, W. E. B.; Frazier, E. Franklin; Immigration; Inequality, Racial; Lewis,*

Oscar; Moynihan, Daniel Patrick; Moynihan Report; Neoliberalism; Park School, The; Pathology, Social; Poverty; Racism; Slums; Underclass; Urban Renewal; Urban Sprawl; Urban Studies; Welfare

BIBLIOGRAPHY

Booth, Charles, ed. 1902. *Life and Labour of the People in London.* 17 vols. London and New York: Macmillan.

Davis, Mike. 2006. *Planet of Slums.* London: Verso.

Drake, St. Clair, and Horace R Cayton. 1945. *Black Metropolis: A Study of Negro Life in a Northern City.* New York: Harcourt, Brace.

Du Bois, W. E. B., and I. Eaton. 1899. *The Philadelphia Negro: A Social Study.* Philadelphia: Published for the University of Pennsylvania.

Engels, Friedrich. 1888. *The Condition of the Working Class in England in 1844.* Trans. Florence Kelley. London: William Reeves.

Frazier, E. Franklin. 1932. *The Negro Family in Chicago.* Chicago: University of Chicago Press.

Frazier, E. Franklin. 1939. *The Negro Family in the United States.* Chicago: University of Chicago Press.

Giddens, Anthony. 1998. *The Third Way: The Renewal of Social Democracy.* Malden, MA: Polity Press.

Goode, Judith, and Jeff Maskovsky, eds. 2001. *New Poverty Studies: The Ethnography of Power, Politics, and Impoverished People in the United States.* New York: New York University Press.

Hackworth, Jason R. 2007. *The Neoliberal City: Governance, Ideology, and Development in American Urbanism.* Ithaca, NY: Cornell University Press.

Harvey, D. 2005. *A Brief History of Neoliberalism.* Oxford: Oxford University Press.

Hull House. 1895. *Hull-House Maps and Papers: A Presentation of Nationalities and Wages in a Congested District of Chicago, Together with Comments and Essays on Problems Growing Out of the Social Conditions.* New York: T.Y. Crowell.

Katz, Michael B. 1990. *The Undeserving Poor: From the War on Poverty to the War on Welfare.* New York: Pantheon.

Lewis, Oscar. 1966. The culture of poverty. *Scientific American.* 21 5(4): 19-25.

Liebow, Elliott. 1967. *Tally's Corner: A Study of Negro Streetcorner Men.* Boston: Little, Brown.

Maskovsky, Jeff. 2001. Afterword. In *New Poverty Studies: The Ethnography of Power, Politics, and Impoverished People in the United States,* eds. Judith Goode and Jeff Maskovsky, 470–482. New York: New York University Press.

Mead, Lawrence M. 1992. *The New Politics of Poverty: The Nonworking Poor in America.* New York: Basic Books.

Murray, Charles A. 1984. *Losing Ground: American Social Policy, 1950–1980.* New York: Basic Books.

O'Connor, Alice. 2001. *Poverty Knowledge: Social Science, Social Policy, and the Poor in Twentieth-Century U.S. History.* Princeton, NJ: Princeton University Press.

Park, Robert Ezra, Ernest Watson Burgess, Roderick Duncan McKenzie, and Louis Wirth. 1925. *The City.* University of Chicago studies in urban sociology. Chicago, IL: University of Chicago Press.

Piven, Frances F., and Richard A. Cloward. 1977. *Poor People's Movements: Why They Succeed, How They Fail.* New York: Pantheon.

Riis, Jacob A. 1890. *How the Other Half Lives: Studies Among the Tenements of New York.* New York: Scribner's.

Stack, Carol B. 1974. *All Our Kin: Strategies for Survival in a Black Community.* New York: Harper & Row.

U.S. Department of Labor. 1965. *The Negro Family, the Case for National Action.* Washington, DC: U.S. Government Printing Office.

Valentine, Bettylou. 1978. *Hustling and Other Hard Work: Life Styles in the Ghetto.* New York: Free Press.

Wilson, William J. 1987. *The Truly Disadvantaged: The Inner City, the Underclass, and Public Policy.* Chicago: University of Chicago Press.

Wilson, William J. 1996. *When Work Disappears: The World of the New Urban Poor.* New York: Knopf.

Jeff Maskovsky

POWER

Power is a central concept in the social and political sciences. It is also commonplace in everyday discussions: We often refer to a political party getting into power, or to the power of governments or individuals to perform a particular action or achieve a certain result, or to someone having power over another, or to a country being a superpower. Power would appear to be self-evident. However, power is an extremely elusive concept, and there are numerous disagreements over its definition, foundation, function, and operation. Power remains, as Steven Lukes says, an "essentially contested" concept (1974, p. 26).

Power is usually associated with the bringing about of consequences. However, what these consequences are, whether or not they are intended, how they are actually brought about, who brings them about and in whose interests—are all a matter of unresolved debate across a number of different disciplines. It is not possible here to give an exhaustive list of these controversies, or to touch on all the many questions regarding the nature and exercise of power. There are, however, several major areas of contention that should be mentioned:

1. Should power be seen in terms of the actions or capacities of individual agents, or should it be seen as deriving from broader social structures?

2. Is power a resource or capacity that can lie dormant, or does it only exist when it is exercised?

3. Does power refer to the ability to achieve certain desired outcomes, or is it a relationship between agents where one exercises power over another?

4. Does power necessarily involve domination, coercion, or constraint, or can it be based on consent?

5. Is power exercised only where the consequences of a certain action are intended, or do unintended or unforeseen consequences also count as evidence of the exercise of power?

The remainder of the entry will explore a number of key theories and debates about power, which refer to several of the questions outlined above. It will also trace a certain logical development in the theorization of power from pluralist-behavioralism to structuralism to poststructuralism.

THE THREE DIMENSIONS OF POWER

The idea that power has three dimensions or "faces" comes from Lukes, who argues that the formula for power—*A has power over B to the extent that he can get B to do something that he would not otherwise do*—can be seen as operating in three distinguishable, yet interrelated, ways. The first face of power is usually associated with Robert Dahl who, along with Polsby (1963) and Wolfinger (1971), tried to show that power in the U.S. political system was distributed pluralistically. In doing so, they were opposing the "ruling elite" theorists such as Mills (1956), who believed that power was concentrated in the hands of a dominant group in society. In his study of local politics in the New Haven area of Connecticut—which he took as a microcosm of the broader distribution of power in American society—Dahl argued that there was no empirical evidence to support the idea of a ruling elite, and that, in fact, different groups were influential over different areas of policymaking (1961). Dahl's analysis contained the implicit idea that there are plural centers of power in a democratic society. More importantly, its central focus was on decision-making behavior in cases where there is an observable conflict of interests. For Dahl, power is the ability to affect another's decision-making: A exercises power over B when he can get B to make a decision that he would not have otherwise made.

However, this idea of power as decision-making was criticized for being too one-dimensional. Peter Bachrach and Morton Baratz argued that power also has a hidden or covert dimension—a "second face" (1962). Power involves not only decision-making, but also what they call *nondecision-making*. This refers to the ability of dominant elites to "set the political agenda" in such a way that certain issues are prevented from being aired, thus precluding

the very possibility of a decision being made about them. In situations of conflict, there is often a "mobilization of bias" against certain interests. The mass media would be an example of this: Whether consciously or unconsciously, it reinforces dominant values and practices, thereby delegitimizing or marginalizing opposing viewpoints and preventing *potential* issues from becoming *actual* issues. In this paradigm, power operates not necessarily by directly influencing B's decision-making, but by preventing B from raising concerns that might be detrimental to A's preferences.

Lukes, however, contends that even this understanding of power was limited, because, like the pluralist-behavioralist view, it assumed that power is only exercised in situations of observable conflict between different interests. But what if it were the case that power functioned in such a way as to prevent conflict from arising in the first place (1974)? Here Lukes points to an even more insidious dimension of power—its "third face"—where power operates not simply by A getting B to do what he does not want to do, but by shaping B's thoughts and desires in such a way that B does what A wants him to do *as if it were a free and autonomous act*. In other words, power may operate as a form of subtle thought-control or manipulation, and may cause someone to act, not according to his own interests, but in the interests of those who are exercising this power. What is being suggested here is that what we *think* we want and is in our best interests may not actually be so—our preferences may be shaped by external influences. Here we might think of the advertising industry, which sells us products that we do not necessarily need or even want, by manipulating our desires. This distinction Lukes draws between *subjective* interests and *real* interests is problematic, as discussed below, but his analysis of power is nonetheless interesting for the way it moves away from the domain of individual decision-making behavior, toward some notion of an overall structuring of the ideas and values that shape individual behavior.

STRUCTURALISM AND MARXISM

The structuralist argument is that power derives not so much from individual or even collective agents, but from their place in a broader social structure. In other words, it is the structural position of agents that allows them to exercise power over others. Marxists like Nicos Poulantzas argue, for instance, that in a relationship of class conflict, the economic and political power of the bourgeoisie—and its capacity to realize its interests—derives from its structural location within the capitalist system. In his debate with Ralph Miliband—who suggested that the class bias of the state could be explained by the privileged background and class allegiances of those who manned the state apparatus (1969)—Poulantzas argued that Miliband's view places too much emphasis on individual behavior, and neglects the effects of structural relations in the capitalist system (1973). In Poulantzas's view, power derives from the ensemble of structures that make up capitalist society, which shapes relations between classes and allows one class to dominate others.

FOUCAULT AND POSTSTRUCTURALISM

Michel Foucault further radicalizes the concept of power by taking it beyond questions of both individual behavior and structure. For Foucault, power is a *non-derivative* concept that cannot be reduced to the preferences of individual agents, economic classes, or even the structural requirements of the capitalist system. Rather, power must be studied in its own right. Here he introduces a number of important methodological innovations. Firstly, the focus must be on the "how" of power—because power only exists when it is being exercised. There is no mysterious substance called power that can lie dormant without being exercised: Indeed, Foucault goes so far as to suggest that power "as such" does not exist (1994, p. 336). Secondly, power is *relational*, rather than an individual or structural capacity: That is to say, power is a mutual relation between agents—both individual and collective. Power is a *way of acting on the actions of others*. This implies, thirdly, a certain freedom of action on the part of both agents in a power relationship. The power relationship presupposes that agents are able to act differently, that they have a range of actions open to them, and that power involves constraining or influencing these actions. Foucault argues, for instance, that slavery is not a power relationship because there is no possibility of the slave acting differently. In this sense, power is not a zero-sum game as many suggest: Rather, it involves a dynamic interplay between agents. Fourthly, then, while power is not the same as coercion, neither is it a matter of consent, as Arendt (1969) or Parsons (1969) would claim. While power constrains, there is always the possibility of there being resistance to it, even in situations of domination, where the normally free and reciprocal flow of power becomes congealed.

However, the question of resistance in Foucault's theory of power is also ambiguous and problematic (see Newman 2001; 2004). This is because Foucault sees power as being not only repressive and prohibitive, but also productive: Power *produces and incites* (1978). Unlike Lukes, who sees power as distorting the subject's "real interests," Foucault believes that this notion of "real interests" is an essentialist illusion manufactured by power itself. Power intersects with discourses and "regimes of truth" to construct the very identity of the subject. While

this avoids the dubious notion of "real interests," it would seem, at the same time, to undermine the idea of a firm ontological and normative foundation for resistance to power: The subject who resists power is at the same time constructed by it. Foucault's theory of power raises as many questions as it answers, and it should not be thought that he has revealed some elusive "fourth dimension" of power beyond which we cannot proceed any further. However, by focusing on the "how" of power, and by seeing power in terms of relationships rather than as a substance or capacity, Foucault has considerably advanced our understanding of the concept.

SEE ALSO *Arendt, Hannah; Community Power Studies; Dictatorship; Foucault, Michel; Galbraith, John Kenneth; Mills, C. Wright; Political Science; Politics; Postmodernism; Poulantzas, Nicos; Power Elite; Power, Political; Repression; Resistance; Structuralism; Wealth; Weber, Max; Zero-sum Game*

BIBLIOGRAPHY

Arendt, Hannah. 1969. *On Violence.* New York: Harcourt Brace.

Bachrach, Peter, and Morton S. Baratz. 1962. Two Faces of Power. *American Political Science Review* 56: 947–952.

Dahl, Robert A. 1961. *Who Governs? Democracy and Power in an American City.* New Haven, CT: Yale University Press.

Foucault, Michel. 1978. *Histoire de la sexualité* [The History of Sexuality]. Vol. I: *An Introduction.* Trans. Robert Hurley. New York: Pantheon.

Foucault, Michel. 1994. The Subject and Power. In *Power: Essential Works of Foucault, 1954–1984*, Vol. 3, ed. James Faubion, 326–348. Trans. Robert Hurley. London: Penguin.

Lukes, Steven. 1974. *Power: A Radical View.* London: Macmillan.

Miliband, Ralph. 1969. *The State in Capitalist Society.* New York: Basic Books.

Mills, C. Wright. 1956. *The Power Elite.* New York: Oxford University Press.

Newman, Saul. 2001. *From Bakunin to Lacan: Anti-Authoritarianism and the Dislocation of Power.* Lanham, MD: Lexington.

Newman, Saul. 2004. New Reflections on the Theory of Power: A Lacanian Perspective. *Contemporary Political Theory* 3 (2): 148–167.

Parsons, Talcott. 1969. *Politics and Social Structure.* New York: Free Press.

Polsby, Nelson W. 1963. *Community Power and Political Theory.* New Haven, CT: Yale University Press.

Poulantzas, Nicos. 1973. *Pouvoir politique et classes sociales de l'état capitaliste* [Political Power and Social Classes]. Trans. Timothy O'Hagan. London: New Left Books, 1973.

Wolfinger, Raymond E. 1971. Nondecisions and the Study of Local Politics. *American Political Science Review* 65: 1063–1080.

Saul Newman

POWER, COMMUNITY

SEE *Community Power Studies.*

POWER, MONOPOLY

SEE *Monopoly.*

POWER, POLITICAL

Political power is commonly defined as the ability or potential to influence outcomes. Yet, there are several interpretations of this definition. To some scholars, it is the ability to control outcomes or shape the behavior of others. For instance, if *A* has power over *B*, *A* can coerce *B* to do things that *B* would not otherwise do. Thus, political power is conceived of as a coercive or control mechanism. To others, political power is simply a relative and self-oriented term: *A*'s power is equal to *B*'s or *A* has more or less power than *B*, but *A* and *B* do not necessarily have a coercive power over each other. Still others conceive political power as a public good that in a democratic society is shared by everyone. The foregoing three concepts seem to be unrelated but they, as will become clear later, actually describe different levels of power at different points in time.

HISTORICAL PERSPECTIVES

Understanding the concept of political power is enhanced if analyzed with respect to different political systems. Most societies have a history of autocratic systems. Modern democracies have been established only since the advent of the Industrial Revolution. During the long history of autocratic rule, societies were governed by monarchs, warlords, and their subordinates. Political power rested upon a single person or a handful of individuals. Going back to the beginning of political history, one finds that the first leaders were probably those who had above normal social skills, ambition, and motivation. Over time, however, political power often passed to the children or families of the rulers, regardless of merit. Power was used to amass wealth, and wealth, in turn, brought more power to the ruling elites, leading to a more skewed distribution of power. The masses had little or no political or civil rights. Accession to power became a function of being a member of the royal family or the ruling elite. The conceptualization of political power as a coercive or control mechanism, *A* having power over *B*, is grounded on the experiences of autocratic rule. The Industrial Revolution, beginning in countries like England and Sweden, changed that relationship by gradually diffusing power from the ruling elites to the masses.

The concept of political power as a public good seems to be based on the experiences of ancient and modern democracies. In the classical Greek democracy, the people were both the rulers and the ruled. Political power was equally or almost equally shared among citizens. In modern democracies, political leaders are elected by the people and are considered to be representatives of the people. Political leaders are expected to make decisions that, on average, benefit the interests of their respective societies. Leaders who are unaccountable or unresponsive to the interests of the people are unlikely to be reelected. The fear of loss of office, in part, motivates leaders to excel in their job performance. In modern democracies (unlike in classical ones) citizens, for the most part, possess power in different magnitudes. For instance, although all citizens have the right to vote and are treated equally before the law, individuals do not have an equal chance of influencing public policies or winning the highest elected offices. Thus, the idea that power is a public good or is shared evenly by all in modern democracies is empirically unsupported. The thesis describes what ought to happen, not what actually happens, in modern democracies. Nevertheless, power as a public good, or the perfect equality of power, may be considered a theoretical ideal, one end of the political power continuum, and democratic societies can be judged by how far removed they are from that ideal.

DIFFUSION OF POLITICAL POWER

From Greek philosopher Aristotle to seventeenth-century thinker James Harrington to socialist Karl Marx, many have argued that the distribution of power in a given society is influenced by the distribution of wealth and education or the level of socioeconomic development. The more wealthy and educated an individual is, the more power he or she will have. Informed and affluent citizens in modern democracies have acquired greater power and fundamental political and civil rights, including the right to vote, to assemble, to run for office, to due process, and to freedom of speech.

Citizens combine their individualized power to form interest groups and political parties to make sure that their interests are protected and fostered. Accession to a position of leadership also has, for the most part, become a function of an individual's wealth, education, and, to a certain extent, personal charisma. Leaders are elected to serve the people, not necessarily to earn more power. The authority and coercive rights of leaders in democracies, unlike in autocracies, is often institutionalized, power that is impersonal and resides in the state.

POLITICAL POWER: DYNAMIC OR STATIC?

The fact that political systems have evolved from autocracies to democracies, at least in most industrial societies, may indicate that the distribution of political power is a process or a dynamic, as opposed to a static, phenomenon. The three conceptualizations of political power—power as a coercive or control mechanism, power as a relative and self-oriented term, and power as a public good—may indeed be a continuum, different points in space and time. Thus, autocracies are political systems in which the distribution of power is concentrated in the hands of a few individuals. Democracies, in contrast, are political systems in which political power, in addition to basic procedural rights such as one-person-one-vote and equality before the law, is widely diffused among individuals. Older democracies, such as those in England, evolved from autocracies only after centuries of gradual and incremental political reforms. During this long period of political change, political power of the traditional elites and the masses have been minimized and maximized, respectively. Given the presence of some asymmetry in the distribution of power, even in modern industrial democracies, and assuming that economic development will continue to grow, there is no reason to assume that democracies will fail to evolve further. Indeed, the weaknesses of the concepts of power as a coercive or control mechanism and power as a public good are, respectively, that they fail to account for the changing nature of power and the fact that power parity among individuals has not in practice been achieved in modern democracies. It is not clear that such power parity will ever be achieved. But how do researchers measure the continuous nature of political power?

Political power may be redefined as the probability of attaining the most important office in a given state, the presidency or the prime ministry. The fact that not all individuals are interested in becoming president or prime minister or the fact that only one individual can attain the highest office is not important. Rather attaining such office is important as a yardstick for calculating the level of power an individual possesses. Thus, the probabilities of winning the highest office for each individual, and hence each person's level of power, would lie between 0 and 1. The foregoing describes the concept of political power as a relative and self-oriented term: *A*'s power is equal to *B*'s or the former possesses more or less power than the latter. Given that political power is hard to quantify, however, income distribution can be a proxy for political power. Thus, the chances of each individual winning the highest office are estimated by using income levels; the higher the income of an individual, the higher the probability he or she will become a leader. The probability of winning the most important office for an individual in an ideal democracy, in which the number of adult citizens is equal to *N* and in which power is perfectly equal among individuals, would be $1/N$. However, because of inherent differences in merit among individuals, ideal democracy or a perfect equality of power will not likely be achieved. Democracies embrace individual freedom and a market economic system, which result in some citizens having more power than others. What then is the most plausible distribution of power that in the future?

Gizachew Tiruneh posits that political power in democracies will, in the long run, likely be normally distributed or take the form of a bell-curve (2004). Early-twenty-first century industrial democracies have an uneven distribution of power (and income) where the mean or average citizen is to right of center. That is, the distribution of power and income are skewed toward or in favor of the upper classes. As the level of democracy, propelled mainly by continuous socioeconomic development, increases or the level of power diffuses over time, the mean citizen will gravitate to the center of the normal curve (where the preponderant majority or the middle class is located), and, once settled at the center, will have the most decisive voice and power in democratic politics. Because those individuals to the right of the mean have, in theory, more power than those to the left of the mean and most leaders may come out of the former group, the political agendas and policies of leaders will likely be dictated by the preferences of the mean citizen. The normal distribution of power represents a democratic system whose quality or degree is likely to be optimal. In this stage of political development, the levels of democracy and power become nearly identical. Tiruneh calls this state of political evolution *normal democracy*. Assuming that power is a function of merit, the role of socioeconomic development (wealth and education) does not bring power parity among individuals per se, but erases the power bias (the skewed distribution of power) that has been created mainly by autocratic systems.

Some scholars may disagree with aspects of Tiruneh's theory of political power. For instance, they may conceive power as a static, rather than dynamic, concept. Or they may, on philosophical or moral grounds, contend that citizens ought, regardless of levels of income and rationality, possess an equal distribution of power. The validity of these contentions is unclear. Until a majority of scholars agree on a definition of political power, an understanding of the concept remains incomplete.

SEE ALSO *Autocracy; Dahl, Robert Alan; Democracy; Dictatorship; Distribution, Normal; Elections; Elite Theory; Hierarchy; Income Distribution; Inequality, Political; Monarchy; Politics; Power; Power Elite; Public Goods; Repression; Stratification; Stratification, Political; Wealth*

BIBLIOGRAPHY

Arendt, Hannah. 1970. *On Violence*. London: Penguin Press.

Dahl, Robert A. 1968. Power. In *International Encyclopedia of Social Sciences*, Vol. 12, ed. David Sills. New York: Macmillan / Free Press, 405–415.

Lasswell, Harold D., and Abraham Kaplan. 1950. *Power and Society: A Framework for Political Inquiry*. New Haven, CT: Yale University Press.

Lenski, Gerhard E. 1966. *Power and Privilege: A Theory of Social Stratification*. New York: McGraw-Hill.

Newman, Frank. 1950. Approaches to the Study of Political Power. *Political Science Quarterly* 45 (2): 161–180.

Parsons, Talcott. 1967. *Sociological Theory and Modern Society*. New York: Free Press.

Riker, William. 1964. Some Ambiguities in the Notion of Power. *American Political Science Review* 58 (2): 341–349.

Simon, Herbert A. 1953. Notes on the Observation and Measurement of Political Power. *Journal of Politics* 15 (4): 500–516.

Tiruneh, Gizachew. 2004. Towards Normal Democracy: Theory and Prediction with Special Reference to Developing Countries. *Journal of Social, Political and Economic Studies* 29 (4): 469–489.

Gizachew Tiruneh

POWER ELITE

In his 1956 work of the same name, American sociologist C. Wright Mills coined the term *power elite* to characterize a new coalition of ruling groups that rose to dominance in the post–World War II United States. Mills rejected the conventional view of a dispersed, plural, and democratic organization of power and instead saw an increasing concentration of that power in the hands of the three institutional orders that composed the power elite: the military, large corporations, and government leaders. This concentration of power was progressively more centralized and undemocratic. Public discussion and debate over policy was replaced by elite command and control. Mills argued that "within American society, major national power now resides in the socioeconomic, political and the military domains" (Mills 2000, p. 6); the family, religious, or educational arenas, dominant in other eras, have become subordinated to the *governmental-military-industrial complex*.

Much like the Frankfurt school, Mills synthesized the perspectives of Karl Marx and Max Weber. Advanced capitalist societies were characterized by increasing instrumental rationalization. Following from the dominance of means-ends and strategic rationality, bureaucratic and technological elements became the central structuring factors of social order. Political authority and social power required command and control over technologies, industrial production, the military, and in another sense the higher levels of government. Thus the new power elite derived its position from the concentration of power in large corporations and oligopolies that dominated sectors of industries, and in a strata of political leaders who directed an expanded federal state, as well as a military that dwarfed most other nations in size and had become the largest expenditure in the federal budget.

While the image of a society of small landowners with few sources of concentrated power may have been idealized, it contained an element of truth. By the end of the nineteenth century, however, the United States had become more urban and industrialized. With industrial capitalism came greater concentration of power in the large industries that dominated in the mid to late-twentieth century.

Mills opposed the pluralist school whose foremost representative was political scientist Robert Dahl. Pluralists argued that there were many centers of power in the United States, multiple interest groups that were each capable of setting agendas and checking other powerful groups through veto. Mills believed that the pluralist view was wrong. Power in the United States was highly concentrated and, in most respects, undemocratic. Only the power elite really set the agenda. The notion of a vital political public in which important issues are discussed (an idea central to John Dewey [1859–1952], another important influence on Mills) was descriptively untrue. National government was characterized by an increasing concentration of executive power and a diminution of legislative power. The pluralist outlook mistook mid-level debates on power, which may have had a plural character, for the major centers of power.

Social and political power was concentrated in a small group of interlocking elites who shared a common social world. While members of the power elite did not necessarily possess a unified class consciousness, they traveled in common social circles, followed common career paths, and formed interlocking groups.

Mills agreed with mass society theorists that the displacement of public discussion made way for the influencing, directing, and manipulating of public opinion through new media of communication. The power elites gained control of mass media but also were surrounded by a culture of celebrity in which they participated. The elites not only associated with entertainment celebrities, drawing on their cultural capital, they became celebrities themselves.

Mills's synthesis of Marx and Weber was not doctrinaire. Mills did not conceive of the power elite as *class* in Marx's sense. The three institutional orders were not united by a common relation to production, class consciousness, or simple economic interests. They constituted an elite in the sense used by Vilfredo Pareto (1843-1923) or Gaetano Mosca (1858-1941). They formed an alliance for ruling groups with interlocking membership and sociality. This alliance can shift over time and circumstance.

Mills's conception of the power elite was a major influence on the New Left, especially on its non-dogmatic appropriation of Marx and the radical tradition. It also initiated a major body of research on power structure that further challenged the pluralist argument. The most well-known proponent of power structure research is G. William Domhoff, who continued Mills's research into the social construction of elites in U.S. society.

Critics have noted that Mills may have overstated the permanent role of the military in influencing U.S. society and in forming the power elite. They point out that the nature of leading companies and industrial elite has changed rather radically since the l960s. Still recent research on the concentration of wealth and power in the United States, such as that conducted by Kevin Phillips (2003), seems to lend support to Mills's concerns.

SEE ALSO *Autocracy; Bureaucracy; Crony Capitalism; Dahl, Robert Alan; Elites; Frankfurt School; Groups; Hierarchy; Interest Groups and Interests; Leninism; Marx, Karl; Military; Military-Industrial Complex; Mills, C. Wright; Oligarchy; Pareto, Vilfredo; Pluralism; Policy Analysis; Pressure Groups; Social Influence; Stratification; Wealth; Weber, Max*

BIBLIOGRAPHY

Aronowitz, Stanley. 2003. "A Mills Revival?" *Logos* 2: 3. http://www.logosjournal.com/mills_aronowitz.pdf.

Ballard, Hoyt B., and G. William Domhoff, eds. 1968. *C. Wright Mills and the Power Elite*. Boston: Beacon Press.

Dahl, Robert. 2005. *Who Governs?: Democracy and Power in an American City*. 2nd ed. New Haven, CT: Yale University Press.

Domhoff, G. William. 2005. *Who Rules America? Power, Politics and Social Change*. 5th ed. New York: McGraw Hill.

Hayden, Tom, Richard Flacks, Stanley Aronowitz, and Charles C. Lemert. 2006. *Radical Nomad: C.Wright Mills And His Times*. Boulder, CO: Paradigm Publishers.

Lukes, Steven. 2004. *Power: A Radical View*. 2nd ed. London: Palgrave Macmillan.

Mills, C. Wright. 2000. *The Power Elite*. new ed. New York: Oxford University Press.

Phillips, Kevin. 2003. *Wealth and Democracy: A Political History of the American Rich*. New York: Broadway Books.

Brian J. Caterino

POWER POLITICS
SEE *Realism, Political.*

PRACTICE THEORY

Practice theory is generally recognized as a way to account for social life through the synthesis of societal structures and a person's individual dispositions. Pierre Bourdieu (1930–2002) is perhaps the most famous social theorist associated with this method of apprehending social life— a method that in the early 1990s he termed *genetic structuralism*. Until his death in 2002, Bourdieu held the chair of sociology at the Collège de France and directed the Centre de Sociologie Européenne.

In *Outline of a Theory of Practice* (1972), Bourdieu argued that in their attempt to account for social practice, sociologists and ethnographers must not only leave the objectivist grand theories of history and society behind, they must also abandon the unmediated subjectivism of phenomenology and existentialism. For Bourdieu, neither set of theoretical apparatuses could satisfactorily account for the social practice of everyday life. By reconstructing the dialectic between structure and agency, he hoped to reconcile the levels of abstract structures with the actions, feelings, and mental states of individual persons. It is critical to appreciate that while Bourdieu's work is situated in the ethnographic present, it works simultaneously in the world of politics and semantics of institutions, social structures, and social movements.

While Bourdieu vigorously critiqued earlier attempts to theorize social life, he also took seminal aspects of his own argument from European social theorists such as Max Weber (1864–1920), Karl Marx (1818–1883), Ludwig Wittgenstein (1889–1951), Georges Canguilhem (1904–1995), and Georges Bataille (1897–1962). In particular, his use of the concepts of domination, social class, and power reflects earlier economic and sociological theories, particularly those of Marx. In his use of personal dispositions and dynamic personal agency, Bourdieu's work reflects his rejection of Claude Lévi-Strauss's structural anthropology, which in the late 1950s and 1960s had argued that there were specific rules that governed kinship and symbolic structures in traditional society.

Instead, Bourdieu argued for an active synthesis of theory and method as tools to investigate the interactions between larger, objective structures of society and the individual. The thread that connects activism with his method is his understanding of society as a struggle of symbolic and material forces, in which the "truth" about reality is constructed both from interpretation and from structural necessity imposed by a dominant symbolic structure, which treats its particular version of reality as natural.

In order to achieve adequate analysis, he proposed a set of concepts, defined in such a way that they can be used in any ethnographic situation for the study of everyday life; in fact, it is the empirical work that actualizes this program. Bourdieu also argued that these concepts not only constitute his method of investigating social practice, they imply a theory of social structure as well. Bourdieu's basic outline for a theory of practice involves three major conceptual categories—*habitus, field,* and *capital*—as well as concepts of struggle and strategy, which evoke intentionality on the part of individuals, families, and social groups as they seek to manipulate their position in various social fields.

In brief, *habitus* refers to durable dispositions, to a sense of one's place in the social world, and it embodies our understanding of the logic of society and the place we have in it. In broader terms, it refers to social structures that operate on the person, as well as a system of models of perception and appreciation that results from our learning in the world and from our acting in the world.

Bourdieu's concept of *field* is one that reflects the space of social interaction, conflict, and competition. Fields are defined by a system of objective relations of power that lie between positions in the field. For Bourdieu, society is a system of fields that are relatively autonomous, but that nonetheless exist in relationship to one another and that collectively exist within a larger social space (defined as the overall conception of the social world). Each field is dynamic and has its own logic and its own structure and forces, which are organized around specific capitals over which individuals and groups struggle as they attempt to maintain or change their position in a field.

In using the concept of *capital,* Bourdieu rejects the purely economistic meaning of the word, and adds to it the notions of symbolic and cultural capital as ways through which class positions and power are manifested. Broadly defined, capital is a socially valued good. Symbolic capital is the most critical form of capital; Bourdieu argues that not only are precapitalist and capitalist societies organized around symbolic capital, but that capital also structures our everyday lives through the use of judgments about taste, social hierarchy, and methods of discernment. Symbolic capital is also closely connected to class privilege, and the domination of masculine ideology, which is itself related to his use of symbolic violence.

Bourdieu's work has influenced the fields of sociology, philosophy, education, and social anthropology. In particular, his work has been central in what has been called the *reproduction debate,* in which scholars investigate the reproduction of social hierarchy and the cultural production of forms of resistance, social identity, and eth-

nicity. In addition, his has been a voice in the debate on practices of authorship, reflexivity, and objectivity. Perhaps most importantly, Bourdieu has been a political voice that spoke for the dispossessed, the unheard, and those who suffered through the institutions of racism and sexism.

SEE ALSO *Bourdieu, Pierre; Habits; Habitus; Marx, Karl; Marxism*

BIBLIOGRAPHY

Bourdieu, Pierre. [1972] 1977. *Outline of a Theory of Practice.* Trans. Richard Nice. Cambridge, U.K.: Cambridge University Press.

Bourdieu, Pierre. 1979. Symbolic Power. *Critique of Anthropology* 13/14: 77–85.

Bourdieu, Pierre. 1980. *Questions de Sociologie.* Paris: Les Éditions de Minuit.

Bourdieu, Pierre. 1984. *Distinction: A Social Critique of the Judgement of Taste.* Trans. Richard Nice. Cambridge, MA: Harvard University Press.

Bourdieu, Pierre. 1985. From Rules to Strategies. *Cultural Anthropology* 1 (1): 110–120.

Bourdieu, Pierre, and Alain Accardo. 1999. *The Weight of the World: Social Suffering in Contemporary Society.* Trans. Priscilla Parkhurst Ferguson. Stanford, CA: Stanford University Press.

Bourdieu, Pierre, and Loïc J. D. Wacquant. 1992. *An Invitation to Reflexive Sociology.* Chicago: University of Chicago Press.

Cheleen Ann-Catherine Mahar

PRACTICING ANTHROPOLOGY

SEE *Anthropology, Public.*

PRAGMATISM

Pragmatism refers to the philosophical position that the test of an idea's truth is its practical consequences. Pragmatism is a reaction against abstract, romantic, and idealistic philosophies, countering instead that the truth of an idea arises from observing its consequences.

Pragmatism was in many ways a product of its era. Pragmatism's roots are in empiricism and the scientific method, and the energies and enthusiasm of late nineteenth-century American life are obvious in pragmatism. After the Civil War (1861–1865), the United States was exploding with advances in communications, transportation, and technology resulting in scientific breakthroughs and technical innovations such as immunizations, the telephone, the mechanization of industry, and the like. Thus, American pragmatism—focused on experience and consequences—was extremely different from the romanticism and idealism of much of contemporaneous European philosophy and the arts.

Pragmatism developed in discussions of the Metaphysical Club, a group of faculty and professionals meeting to discuss the issues of the day at Harvard University during the 1870s. Members of the club included the scientist Charles Sanders Peirce (1839–1914), the mathematician Chauncey Wright (1830–1875), the historian John Fiske (1842–1901), the psychologist William James (1842–1910), and lawyers such as Oliver Wendell Holmes (1841–1935), Joseph B. Warner (1848–1923), and Nicholas St. John Green (1830–1876).

Trained as a mathematician and physicist, Peirce is hailed as the father of pragmatism. He first used the term *pragmatism* in an 1878 article in *Popular Science Monthly* titled "How to Make Our Ideas Clear." Peirce's famous guide was, "Consider what effects which might conceivably have practical bearings we consider the object of our conception to have. Then our conception of these effects is the whole of our conception of the object" (Peirce 1878, p. 24). Peirce, who later renamed his pragmatism *pragmaticism*, argued that it was a powerful empirical and philosophical tool because it demanded that ideas be examined for their consequences, not for the elegance of some abstract metaphysical model. He wrote about pragmatism:

> It will serve to show that almost every proposition of ontological metaphysics is either meaningless gibberish—one word being defined by other words, and they by still others, without any real conception ever being reached—or else is downright absurd; so that all such rubbish being swept away, what will remain of philosophy will be a series of problems capable of investigation by the observational methods of the true sciences. (Peirce 1905, p. 171)

WILLIAM JAMES AND JOHN DEWEY

Certainly the best-known proponent of pragmatism was William James. Trained in medicine, he spent most of his adult life studying and teaching the new field of psychology at Harvard University. James popularized pragmatism, giving Peirce credit for its founding in a 1908 address at the University of California. In his chosen profession of psychology, James is famous for his notion of "stream of consciousness." The term is much misused today, but for James it meant that the mind is active in giving meaning to experiences that it encounters. James's pragmatism is rooted in his understanding of psychology.

James argued that the "truth" of ideas lay not in their abstract formulation but in their "cash value" as consequences in human experience. He wrote: "The whole function of philosophy ought to be to find out what definite difference it will make to you and me, at definite instants of our lives, if this world-formula or that world-formula be the true one" (James [1907] 1986, p. 50).

James applied his theories to a number of philosophical areas, including the question of religion and the supernatural. In his famous works *The Will to Believe* (1897) and *The Varieties of Religious Experience* (1902), James explored the power of the individual "will to believe." James concluded that although the materialist might wrongly conclude that religion was a fallacy, the positive effects on the life of the individual adherent (rather than the existence of God) demonstrate the "truth" of religion. He wrote: "On Pragmatic principles, if the hypothesis of God works satisfactorily in the widest sense of the word, it is true" (James [1902] 2002, p. 299).

James's contemporary, John Dewey (1859–1952), chair of the philosophy department at the University of Chicago at the turn of the century, is best known for his work on education and social issues. Dewey's guiding philosophy, *instrumentalism*, is a strand of pragmatism. Dewey was critical of abstract and theological notions of truth and reality. He defined his instrumentalism as "an attempt to constitute a precise logical theory of concepts, judgments, and inferences in their various forms, by primarily considering how thought functions in the experimental determinations of future consequences" (Dewey 1903, p. 21). Dewey's approach utilized a praxis formula for inquiry as the method for advancing knowledge. Dewey believed that through experience the mind acquires knowledge, but over time new experiences challenge the previously held beliefs. The process of inquiry, challenging staid ideas and the resulting new synthesis, is the process by which truth becomes known to the individual.

Pragmatism was applied to law by members of the Metaphysical Club, including Supreme Court justice Oliver Wendell Holmes Jr. and Nicholas St. John Green. Holmes argued that the law should be interpreted not on static historical observation of the original intent of the framers of the constitution but by considering the practical outcomes of the law or judgment in question. In other words, the cardinal rule of jurists should be the practical policy consequences of a given outcome in their deliberation. Holmes recognized that such a view of the judiciary empowers it with a dynamic and legislative function akin to that of the Congress. This practical approach to the outcomes of the law, in distinction to theories of law rooted in tradition, religion, and metaphysics, is shared among legal pragmatists.

THE PHILOSOPHY OF PRAGMATISM

In philosophical terms, pragmatism is generally considered to be nominalistic and pluralistic. Ideas are not "real" as abstract, formal categories, but change as experiences are apprehended and given meaning by the mind. The philosopher Ferdinand C. Schiller (1864–1937) wrote: "Concepts are tools slowly fashioned by the practical intelligence for the mastery of experience" (Schiller 1907, p. 64). Thus, for Schiller there is no single Truth, although there are truths that are relevant within a given context. James agreed, citing that truth was not static but "ambulatory," directly related to human experiences. Moreover, old "truths" may no longer be relevant to the contemporary setting because they no longer adequately convey meaning about the world as it is. Thus, they are no longer true.

For pragmatists, ideas are contextual and their worth derives from the utility of their consequences. This epistemology is rooted in a rejection of Western teleology and monism. For the pragmatist, there is no first cause, nor is there a single ultimate end. Rather, the world is pluralistic in that social and empirical phenomena are connected but it is the individual who gives meaning to experience, and therefore the value of a concept is in its practical consequences. James wrote: "The distinctions between thoughts and things ... the conceptions of classes with subclasses within them ... surely all these were once definite conquests made at historic dates by our ancestors in their attempts to get the chaos of their crude individual experiences into a more shareable and manageable shape" (James 1909, p. 62).

Although not exclusively an American philosophical tradition, pragmatism is usually identified with Americans such as Peirce, Holmes, Dewey, Wright, Schiller, and especially William James. However, pragmatism crossed the ocean, influencing and being influenced by others, such as the Italian authors Giovanni Papini (1881–1956) and Luigi Pirandello (1867–1936) and the French philosopher Henri Bergson (1859–1941). Other well-known pragmatists included George Herbert Mead (1863–1931), James Hayden Tufts (1862–1942), and Sidney Hook (1902–1989). Many of the assumptions of pragmatism were to influence later twentieth-century philosophical currents, particularly that of secular humanism.

SEE ALSO *Civil War; James, William*

BIBLIOGRAPHY

Dewey, John. 1903. *Studies in Logical Theory.* Chicago: University of Chicago Press.

Dickstein, Morris, ed. 1998. *The Revival of Pragmatism: New Essays on Social Thought, Law, and Culture.* Durham, NC: Duke University Press.

James, William. 1986. *Writings, 1902–1910.* New York: Library of America.

James, William. [1902] 2002. *The Varieties of Religious Experience: A Study in Human Nature.* New York: Routledge.

James, William [1907] 1986. *Pragmatism: A New Name for Some Old Ways of Thinking.* In *Writings, 1902–1910,* 112–113. New York: Library of America.

James, William. 1909. *The Meaning of Truth: A Sequel to "Pragmatism."* New York and London: Longmans, Green.

Murphy, John P. 1990. *Pragmatism: From Peirce to Davidson.* Boulder, CO: Westview.

Peirce, Charles S. 1878. How to Make Our Ideas Clear. *Popular Science Monthly* 12: 286–302.

Peirce, Charles S. 1905. What Pragmatism Is. *The Monist* 15 (2): 161–181.

Rescher, Nicholas. 2000. *Realistic Pragmatism: An Introduction to Pragmatic Philosophy.* Albany: State University of New York Press.

Schiller, Ferdinand C. 1907. *Studies in Humanism.* New York: Ayer.

Eric Patterson

PRAXIS

"Praxis," from the Latin, is the opposite of "theory." The Greek praxis and its related stem, "prassein," means "to do." It is commonly defined as "action" or "practice." Traditionally, there has been a perceived dichotomy between theory (speculation, thinking) and praxis (action, doing). However, contemporary notions of praxis, especially as the Marxists see it, reject this distinction.

There are two prevalent meanings of praxis in the modern day: one in religion and ethics, and one in social theory and political philosophy. In Catholicism, praxis refers to applying the principles and ethics drawn from religion to everyday life. It is, in a sense, applied belief. The idea is that the practice of one's religious beliefs enables one to live a just life. Hence, belief (theory) leads to a just society.

In *Phenomenology of Spirit*, German philosopher Georg Wilhelm Friedrich Hegel (1770–1831) argued for the interrelationship of thought and action, linking theory and praxis. Karl Marx (1818–1883), in a movement against idealism and metaphysics, proposed a "practical-critical" activity that combines theory with practice, where no thinking can be isolated from social practice (Marx 1845). This linkage of thinking with action marks the most sustained examination of the question of praxis in contemporary critical theory (CT).

Praxis is given a specific agenda and political program in the Frankfurt School's CT. CT erases the distinction between theory and praxis by showing how one leads to and informs the other. Praxis is theory that serves the purpose of social transformation. The social transformation sought by praxis is not only informed by critical reflection ("theory") but also by questions of justice and emancipation (social or collective action). It corresponds therefore to Marx's "practical-critical" thought.

"Theory" in CT is essentially a question about reflection as related to knowledge. As philosopher Max Horkheimer (1895–1973) understood it, CT is a form of knowledge distinguished not just by its specific object of knowledge but also by its special relation to this object. Knowledge or theory is directed at society and social relations (its object). The relation is not one of mere "interpretation" or "analysis" of this object-society. The relation to this object of study (society) is informed by the aim of emancipation. Theory is thus directed at a goal: a just society. Knowledge leads to, or at least aims for, social justice. In this sense CT is not independent of political action or program. This Marxist line, as Horkheimer elaborated, sees theory as "an element in action leading to new social forms" (Critical Theory 1972, p. 216). This emphasis on action and superior knowledge distinguishes it from traditional theory where the object of knowledge and the subject are in a passive relation. In CT, reflective theory engages with the object in such a way as to transform both itself and the object.

CT is here a program of social research, investigating social conditions of facts as well as of theory. It resists the institutional demarcation of theory and application. The philosophical (theory) and the social (praxis) come together in this formulation. It applies thought to the entirety of human existence.

CT's mode of engagement with the social can be described as "knowledge as action." It calls for active thought that continually challenges the existing state of affairs in society. The praxis of CT is in its thinking differently about the social world, where a different thinking will lead to changes in the way life is lived. CT does not offer a program of change in material experience; it offers a mode of understanding that can transform how material experience in modernity is interpreted. In CT a critique of culture may bring about changes in society because it develops new frames for interpretation, knowledge, and action.

Feminist exponents of critical ethnography express these elements most strongly in making praxis the defining moment of all investigative methodology. Such an ethnography focuses on political practice and breaks down the gap between researcher and object of research. Others, such as the education and cultural studies scholar Handel Kashope Wright, see the discipline of cultural studies as "social justice praxis work" where interpretation, or the-

ory, must be informed by a commitment to social justice. Thus, praxis is political action informed by knowledge, where knowledge itself is driven by self-reflection and the need to engage with goals of justice and emancipation.

SEE ALSO *Activism; Critical Theory; Cultural Studies; Feminism; Justice; Marx, Karl; Marxism; Science*

BIBLIOGRAPHY

Hegel, Georg Wilhelm Friedrich. 1979. *Phenomenology of Spirit.* Trans. A. V. Miller. Oxford: Clarendon Press.

Horkheimer, Max. 1972. *Critical Theory: Selected Essays.* Trans. Matthew J. O'Connell. New York: Herder and Herder.

Lather, Patti. 1991. *Getting Smart: Feminist Research and Pedagogy With/In the Postmodern.* London: Routledge.

Marx, Karl. 1977. Theses of Feuerbach. In *Karl Marx and Frederich Engels, Selected Works*, vol. 1, 13–15. Moscow: Progress Publishers.

Wright, Handel Kashope. 2003. Cultural Studies as Praxis: (Making) an Autobiographical Case. *Cultural Studies* 17 (6): 805–822.

Pramod K. Nayar

PREBISCH, RAÚL
1901–1986

Raúl Prebisch was a highly influential Argentinian economist and policymaker of the twentieth century. He is best known for proposing the idea that the world economic system consists of two connected elements—an industrialized center and an underdeveloped periphery—wherein the former dominates the latter. Contrary to the Ricardian claim that trade benefits all, Prebisch argued that trade between the center and periphery is unequal and detrimental for the periphery, and that became increasingly true as the world economy developed. His ideas were central to Latin American structuralist and dependency schools of thought. During the middle decades of the twentieth century, they led to the widespread adoption, in the periphery, of import substitution industrialization (ISI) policies that focused on "inward-directed" industrial development.

Prebisch's ideas achieved a wide dissemination and receptivity when he headed the United Nations (UN) Economic Commission for Latin America (ECLA) between 1948 and 1963. One of his central theses was that, in the long run, primary producers in the periphery faced declining terms of trade for their exports vis-à-vis manufactured goods. This view received empirical support from a 1949 UN study, *Relative Prices of Exports and Imports of Underdeveloped Countries*, which examined the period between the late nineteenth century and end of World War II. Prebisch and the ECLA pointed out that during the upswing of a trade cycle, prices of primary goods rise faster than those of industrial goods, but that they fall much more steeply during the downswing, causing an overall decline in prices by the end of the cycle. In the industrialized center, the strength of organized workers and firms causes a relatively smaller decline in the prices of industrial goods during a downswing, while the vulnerability of farmers and unorganized workers leads to sharp declines in prices in the periphery.

Prebisch's ideas were shaped by the experience of Argentina in its trade with industrialized nations such as Great Britain and the United States, both before and after the Great Depression. Another UN economist, Hans Singer, argued that income elasticity of demand for industrial goods (percentage increase in the demand for industrial goods associated with a percentage point increase in people's incomes) is higher than that for primary goods, thereby causing a decline in the benefits from trade for the periphery over the long run. Together, these ideas came to be known as the Prebisch-Singer hypothesis.

Prebisch's work has predictably attracted criticism from mainstream trade theorists. While the UN report that originally provided the empirical basis for Prebisch's theory has been largely discredited, later studies have supported the Prebisch-Singer hypothesis. International Statistics Institute (ISI) policies have been blamed for certain longstanding problems, such as unsustainable debt levels in the periphery. Notwithstanding such critiques, ISI policies have also led to substantial increases in income and the development of an industrial base in a number of developing countries.

Prebisch's insights remain important today for regions and countries in the periphery, notably Africa. Scholars continue to argue in favor of careful, "inward-directed" policies with concerted cooperation among countries in the periphery, and for the establishment of multilateral institutions that genuinely represent their interests. This vision informed the founding (in 1964) of the United Nations Conference on Trade and Development (UNCTAD), a multilateral organization that Prebisch headed for its first six years. If there was ever a need for such institutions to represent the interests of the periphery on the world stage, it is at the present critical juncture of global integration. Indeed, there is a strong and growing literature among critical development scholars on the negative effects of globalizing policies for developing countries. These scholars are arguing that existing multilateral organizations such as International Monetary Fund or World Trade Organization have not represented the interests of the periphery adequately.

SEE ALSO *Dependency Theory; Import Substitution; Industrialization; Ricardo, David; Structuralism*

BIBLIOGRAPHY

Bloch, Harry, and David Sapsford. 2000. Whither the Terms of Trade? An Elaboration of the Prebisch Singer Hypothesis. *Cambridge Journal of Economics* 24: 461–481.

Love, Joseph L. 1980. Raul Prebisch and the Origins of the Doctrine of Unequal Exchange. *Latin American Research Review* 15 (3): 45–72.

Ocampo, José Antonio. 1993. Terms of Trade and Center-Periphery Relations. In *Development from Within: Toward a Neostructuralist Approach for Latin America*, ed. Osvaldo Sunkel. Boulder, CO: Lynne Rienner.

Prebisch, Raúl. 1950. *The Economic Development of Latin America and Its Principal Problems*. New York: United Nations.

Singer, Hans. 1950. The Distribution of Gains between Investing and Borrowing Countries. *American Economic Review* 40 (2): 473–485.

Vamsi Vakulabharanam

PREBISCH-SINGER HYPOTHESIS

The classical economists believed that the terms-of-trade of primary products would show long-term improvement vis-à-vis manufactures due to the operation of the law of diminishing returns in primary production and the law of increasing returns in manufactures. The policy implication of this classical proposition is that a primary-producing country need not industrialize to enjoy the gains from technical progress taking place in manufactures; free play of international market forces will distribute the gains from the industrial countries to the primary-producing countries through the higher prices of their exports of primary products relative to the prices of their imports of manufactures (that is, the terms-of-trade will move in favor of primary-product exporting countries).

THE PREBISCH-SINGER HYPOTHESIS AND ITS POLICY IMPLICATIONS

The opposite hypothesis—the Prebisch-Singer hypothesis of long-term deterioration in the terms-of-trade of primary products—can be traced back to the early mid-twentieth-century writings of Charles Kindleberger. He thought it inexorable for the terms-of-trade to turn against primary producing countries because of the operation of Engel's law—which states the demand for goods needed for bare subsistence such as food rises less than proportionately while demand for other luxury consumption goods rises more than proportionately—in the process of world economic growth and improvements in the standard of living. It was, however, a 1945 League of Nations report prepared by Folke Hilgerdt and its subsequent follow-up by the United Nations in 1949 that is actually the origin of the Prebisch-Singer hypothesis and the related debate. It was observed in these reports that during the sixty years preceding 1938 primary product prices had fallen relative to prices of manufactures.

In the 1950s both Raúl Prebisch and Hans Singer referred to this so-called historical fact and questioned the classical proposition and its implicit support for the colonial pattern of trade. It was pointed out that productivity increased faster in the industrialized countries (constituting the North or the industrial center) than in the primary-producing countries (constituting the South or the raw-material supplying periphery), so that the terms-of-trade should have moved in favor of the South, given the factors of free trade and competition. The South could have enjoyed the fruits of technical progress taking place in industry through free trade and specialization (in primary production) without going for industrialization, as suggested in the classical writings. But this did not happen as the available evidence showed. So the primary-producing countries were advised to pursue a vigorous policy of industrialization with the suspension of the free play of international market forces.

THE EVOLUTION OF THE PREBISCH-SINGER HYPOTHESIS

In the post–World War II period, the Prebisch–Singer hypothesis provided the theoretical basis for the policy makers of the newly independent countries to adopt a path of import-substituting industrialization (ISI) through protective commercial policy. The path of ISI in basically agricultural countries required imports of machines and technology. So, in the process of industrialization these countries began to face acute balance-of-payments problems. This led many southern countries to follow the path of export-oriented industrialization. Dependence on a few primary-product exports was reduced and these began to be substituted by manufactured exports.

Meanwhile, the emphasis of the Prebisch–Singer hypothesis shifted from the relations between types of commodities to relations between types of countries. The shift of emphasis too had its origin in the writings of Kindleberger in the mid- to late 1950s. He found no conclusive evidence of deterioration in the terms-of-trade of primary products, but he did have some evidence of a decline in the terms-of-trade of the primary-producing countries (South) vis-à-vis the industrialized countries (North). In fact, both Prebisch and Singer had in mind the concept of terms-of-trade between the North and the South. But, in the absence of appropriate data, they used the series on terms-of-trade between primary products and manufactures as a proxy, with the logic that primary products dominated the then export structure of the South and manufactures dominated that of the North.

The Prebisch-Singer hypothesis generated much controversy in the academic world. In their published papers, critics such as Jacob Viner (1953), R. E. Baldwin (1955), G. M. Meier (1958), G. Haberler (1961), R. E. Lipsey (1963), Harry Johnson (1967), Paul Bairoch (1975), Ronald Findlay (1981), and many others raised different statistical questions and discarded the hypothesis. Since the 1980s, a series of studies undertaken by John Spraos (1980), David Sapsford (1985), Prabirjit Sarkar (1986a, b, 1994, 2005), Sarkar and Singer (1991), E. R. Grilli, and M.C. Yang (1988), and many others questioned the validity of the criticism and provided strong statistical support for the Prebisch–Singer hypothesis, thereby bringing it back into the limelight.

THE PREBISCH-SINGER HYPOTHESIS: DIFFERENT EXPLANATIONS

The question that logically follows is what explains the deteriorating trends in the terms-of-trade of the South? The factor highlighted by Singer is the raw-material saving and/or substituting technical progress in the North which created a demand bias against southern exports in the process of growth of northern manufactures leading to a fall in the southern terms-of-trade.

In his 1950 work Prebisch tried to explain the phenomenon in terms of the interaction of the diverse economic structures of the North and the South with different phases of business cycles. In an upswing, wages and profit, and so prices, rise more in the North than in the South due to stronger labor unions and higher monopoly power of the northern capitalists. In the downswing, northern profits and wages do not fall much due to the same reason. The burden of adjustment falls on the raw material suppliers of the South; their prices fall more than the prices of manufactures.

The diverse economic structures created an asymmetry in the mechanism of distribution of the fruits of technical progress, argued Prebisch, Singer, and Arthur Lewis in their individual works published in the 1950s. In the North, technical progress and productivity improvements led to higher wages and profit while in the South, these led to lower prices. The North-South models of Findlay (1980) and Sarkar (1997 and 2001b) supported this asymmetry. Granted this asymmetry, the terms-of-trade would turn against the interest of the South in the process of long-term growth and technical progress in both the North and the South.

In 1997 Sarkar provided another explanation in terms of product cycles. A new product is often introduced in the North. Initially there is a craze for this product and its income elasticity is very high. Owing to a lack of knowledge of its production technique, the South cannot start its production. The South produces comparatively older goods with lower income elasticity. By the time the South acquires the knowledge, the North has introduced another new product. In such a product cycle scenario, the income elasticity of southern demand for northern goods is likely to be higher than that of the northern demand for southern goods. Under these circumstances, if both the North and the South grow at the same rate (or the South tries to catch up by pressing for a higher rate of growth), the global macro balance requires a steady deterioration in the terms-of-trade of the South vis-à-vis the North.

Many other theoretical models exist to explain the Prebisch-Singer hypothesis. As it is increasingly recognized to be a fact, not a myth, many other models will be forthcoming.

SEE ALSO *Development Economics; Prebisch, Raúl; Singer, Hans; Terms of Trade; Unequal Exchange*

BIBLIOGRAPHY

Bairoch, Paul. 1975. *The Economic Development of the Third World since 1900.* London: Methuen.

Baldwin, R. E. 1955. "Secular Movements in the Terms of Trade." *American Economic Review* 45: 259–269.

Findlay, Ronald. 1980. "The Terms of Trade and Equilibrium Growth in the World Economy." *American Economic Review* 70: 291–299.

Findlay, Ronald. 1981. "The Fundamental Determinants of the Terms of Trade." In *The World Economic Order*, edited by S. Grassman and E. Lundberg. London: Macmillan: 425–457.

Grilli, E. R., and Yang, M. C. 1988. "Primary Commodity Prices, Manufactured Goods Prices and the Terms of Trade of Developing Countries: What the Long-Run Shows." *The World Bank Economic Review* 2: 1–47.

Haberler, G. 1961. "Terms of Trade and Economic Development." In *Economic Development for Latin America*, edited by H. S. Ellis. London: Macmillan: 275–297.

Johnson, Harry. 1967. *Economic Policies towards Less Developed Countries.* London: Allen & Unwin.

Kindleberger, Charles. 1943. "Planning for Foreign Investment." *American Economic Review* 33: 347–354.

Kindleberger, Charles. 1950. *The Dollar Shortage.* New York: Wiley.

Kindleberger, Charles. 1956. *The Terms of Trade: A European Case Study.* New York: Wiley.

Kindleberger, Charles. 1958. "The Terms of Trade and Economic Development." *Review of Economics and Statistics* 40: 72–85.

Kuznets, Simon. 1967. "Quantitative Aspects of the Economic Growth of Nations." *Economic Development and Cultural Change* 15: 1–140.

League of Nations. 1945. *Industrialisation and Foreign Trade.* Geneva: League of Nations.

Lewis, Arthur. 1954. "Economic Development with Unlimited Supplies of Labour." *Manchester School of Economic and Social Studies* 22: 139–191.

Lipsey, R. E. 1963. *Price and Quantity Trends in the Foreign Trade of United States.* Princeton, NJ: Princeton University Press for NBER.

Meier, G. M. 1958. "International Trade and International Inequality." *Oxford Economic Papers* 10 (New Series): 277–289.

Prebisch, Raúl. 1950. *The Economic Development of Latin America and Its Principal Problems.* New York: United Nations.

Prebisch, Raúl. 1959. "Commercial Policy in the Underdeveloped Countries." *American Economic Review* 49: 251–273.

Sapsford, David. 1985. "Some Further Evidence in the Statistical Debate on the Net Barter Terms of Trade between Primary Commodities and Manufactures." *Economic Journal* 95: 781–788.

Sarkar, Prabirjit. 1986a. "Terms of Trade Experience of Britain since the Nineteenth Century." *Journal of Development Studies* 23: 20–39.

Sarkar, Prabirjit. 1986b. "The Singer–Prebisch Hypothesis: A Statistical Evaluation." *Cambridge Journal of Economics* 10: 355–371.

Sarkar, Prabirjit. 1994. "Long-term Behaviour of Terms of Trade of Primary Products vis-à-vis Manufactures: A Critical Review of Recent Debate." *Economic and Political Weekly* 29: 1612–1614.

Sarkar, Prabirjit. 1997. "Growth and Terms of Trade: A North-South Macroeconomic Framework." *Journal of Macroeconomics* 19: 117–133.

Sarkar, Prabirjit. 2001a. "The North-South Terms of Trade: A Re-examination." *Progress in Development Studies* 1 (4): 309–327.

Sarkar, Prabirjit. 2001b. "Technical Progress and the North-South Terms of Trade." *Review of Development Economics* 5 (3): 433-443.

Sarkar, Prabirjit. 2005. "Rising Manufacture Exports and Terms of Trade: The Case Study of Korea." *Progress in Development Studies* 5 (2): 83-88.

Sarkar, Prabirjit, and Singer, Hans. 1991. "Manufactured Exports of Developing Countries and Their Terms of Trade Since 1965." *World Development* 19: 333–340.

Singer, Hans. 1950. "The Distribution of Gains between Investing and Borrowing Countries." *American Economic Review* 40: 473–485.

Spraos, John. 1980. "The Statistical Debates on the Net Barter Terms of Trade between Primary Commodities and Manufactures." *Economic Journal* 90: 107–128.

Spraos, John. 1983. *Inequalising Trade?* London: Clarendon Press.

United Nations. 1949. *Relative Prices of Exports and Imports of Under-developed Countries.* New York: United Nations.

Viner, Jacob. 1953. *International Trade and Economic Development.* Oxford: Clarendon Press.

Prabirjit Sarkar

PRECAUTIONARY MOTIVE

SEE *Money, Demand for.*

PRE-COLUMBIAN PEOPLES

The term *pre-Columbian* refers to the time before Columbus first set foot in the Americas. He sailed to find alternative routes to the East, as Asian imports had become very expensive in Europe after the Turks conquered Constantinople in 1453. Yet pre-Columbian peoples had flourishing civilizations long before the arrival of Columbus. Each society had prescribed laws and unique religions, and far from the savage cultures that history painted them to be, several societies were highly sophisticated.

Some scholars have postulated that around the time that the Israelites chose David as their king, a tribe of Asians crossed the land bridge that became the Bering Strait in search of new game. These people, called the Nadene, closely resembled modern Mongolians. About two thousand years ago, the group split into two factions—the Tlingit and Haida tribes, which went to the northwestern coast of North America—and the Athabascans, who stayed in Alaska around Lake Athabasca. But the Athabascans continued to move southward to form tribes in the Southwest.

Although this scenario is speculation, many similarities exist between the Asian peoples and Native American tribes. For instance, the mandala of the Hindus and Buddhists closely resembles the sand paintings of southwestern tribes. Early Asian calendars were also similar to those of the Aztecs. Special significance was often placed on the number four. Although no physical proof of this migration exists, signs point to its possibility. Asian tribes

may have migrated as far south as the tip of South America.

One of the oldest tribes on record lived in the Four Corners area of the southwestern United States. They were called the Pueblos, and their ancestors were the Anasazi, a tribe that existed two thousand years ago. The Anasazi are known for their elaborate apartment buildings, built on the sides of cliffs. Later, the Pueblos used adobe and wood to build their homes. Their hunter-gatherer status changed around the year 1000 BCE, when they began to plant corn, squash, and beans, and to craft fine pottery.

The people who lived in Cahokia, in what is now southwestern Illinois, are known popularly as the "mound builders" because they built large structures for underground burial, governmental, or ceremonial purposes. The society is thought to have been territorial, led by a chieftain, and possessed the most elaborate hierarchial system in its time.

In Mesoamerica, as each new culture appeared, it adapted, and often improved upon, significant elements of the civilization that had come before. The Olmecs, the original civilization, lived in wood and thatch huts in a humid area on the Gulf Coast of Mexico. They raised corn, beans, and squash, worked with fine stones, and made pottery. It is theorized that the Olmecs traveled and traded throughout the area and thereby spread their culture throughout the region.

The Zapotec capital, Monte Alban, began to flourish at about the same time as the Olmec society fell into decline. The Zapotecs may have built the first observatory, and their system of glyph writing was the first writing of any type to be used in Mesoamerica. They recorded the first calendar, although the Olmecs may have begun to develop a similar system of counting the days before them.

The Mixtecs seem to have taken over sites where Zapotecan society was failing. The Mixtecs were exquisite goldsmiths, but their most significant contribution is the written record of their history, which covered a period of almost 600 years beginning around 940 CE.

Thriving at roughly the same time was another people, whose true name is still unknown. The name *Teotihuacanos* comes from their city—Teotihuacán, named by the Aztecs long after the civilization fell. Although few written records exist, a glimpse of their culture survives in colorful frescoes, which adorn palace walls. It appears that the Teotihuacanos traded goods widely, had a class-based society with specialized jobs, and worshipped a number of gods. They were also weavers and potters and jewelers who worked in semiprecious stones. Their civilization sharply declined around 700 CE, when the city was sacked and burned, probably by barbarian tribes from the north.

The Mayan society, which first appeared around 1000 BCE, was prevalent in parts of Mexico and farther south into Central America. They refined the art of writing and the calendar to their highest forms up until that time. Mayan art developed between about 200 and 900 and is considered to be the most sophisticated and beautiful of the region. The Mayans are known for their mathematical prowess and traded in salt, cacao, and obsidian.

No society in ancient Mesoamerica was as revered as the Toltecs. Later societies credited the Toltecs with inventing astronomy, the calendar, and the arts because of the finely crafted items found in the ruined Toltec capital of Tolan; however, historical fact disproved these claims. Toltec civilization fell into decline after Tolan was burned and sacked around the year 1150, and after the city vanished, an even more sophisticated and powerful people came to revere them. They adopted Toltec music, called their artists "Totecatls," and copied Toltec artistry in sculpture, architecture, and featherwork. They even proudly claimed Toltec lineage. These people called themselves the Mexica (me-SHI-ca), but history knows them as the Aztecs.

The Aztecs were arguably the most advanced culture to have arisen in pre-Columbian times, although they are more often remembered for their ritual practice of human sacrifice. Yet the Aztecs had a well-developed military, and they enlarged their capital of Tenochtitlán, now Mexico City, through the construction of floating farm plots known as *chiampas*. The Aztecan pantheon was elaborate, their educational system substantial, and they held great esteem for the arts.

Farther into South America were the Incas, whose society developed only shortly before the arrival of Columbus in the New World. Still, they managed to expand their influence throughout western South America by the time of their demise in 1533. The Incas are most remembered for their architectural construction, such as that at the site of Machu Pichu.

In the Bahamas and the Greater Antilles Islands, which include Cuba, Puerto Rico, Haiti, the Dominican Republic, and Jamaica, the Taino culture was the dominant society before the time of Columbus, although Ciboney and Guanahatabey (western Cuba), Macorix and/or Ciguayo (Bohio), and even Carib (Lesser Antilles) were also present. They were united by Arawak, the common language. As they were island cultures, they were adept sailors, and fishing was their main occupation, but the islands also provided abundant edible fruits and they used the fauna of the land to fulfill their needs. In 1492, the Taino had a thriving civilization. As the Mesoamerican cultures had, they constructed ceremonial ballparks, and they had an elaborate hierarchy of gods. They lived in five predominant kingdoms on Hispaniola, which were led by

chieftains to whom tribute was paid. They raised crops of casaba melons, garlic, potatoes, and other fruits and vegetables, with yucca being their staple food. They had no system of writing nor a calendar, and could count only up to twenty using their hands and feet. But the Taino made exquisite handcrafted works, with pottery being the most remarkable.

Other less political societies also existed in North America before the arrival of Columbus. They were independent city-states, thriving in small groups. Their less-centralized chiefdom polities were also evident and included a central community surrounded by bordering neighbor villages. Each community had a central ruler, with a subservient underclass. When Columbus landed in the Bahamas, he was the first European to encounter the Taino. He called them "Indians" because he thought he had landed in India, and the appellation became the common term to describe all Native American peoples in the Americas.

Population estimates of pre-Columbian peoples in North American range from 8 million to more than 100 million, centered mainly in Mesoamerica and South America. However, because of incomplete evidence, the true population is difficult to determine.

SEE ALSO *Archaeology; Architecture; Columbus, Christopher; Geography; Incas; Indigenous Rights; Monarchy; Olmecs*

BIBLIOGRAPHY

Brundage, Burr Cartwright. 1963. *Empire of the Inca*. Norman: University of Oklahoma Press.

Carrasco, David. 1998. *Daily Life of the Aztecs, People of the Sun and Earth*. Westport, CT: Greenwood.

Coe, Michael D. 1996. *Mexico: From the Olmecs to the Aztecs*. New York: Thames and Hudson.

Driver, Harold E., and William C. Massey. 1957. *Comparative Studies of North American Indians*. Philadelphia: American Philosophical Society.

Henderson, John S. 1997. *The World of the Ancient Maya*. 2nd ed. Ithaca, NY: Cornell University Press.

Lamberg-Karlovsky, C. C., and Jeremy A. Sabloff. 1979. *Ancient Civilizations: The Near East and Mesoamerica*. Menlo Park, CA: Benjamin/Cummings.

Lemonick, Michael D. 1998. Before Columbus: Destroyed Almost Overnight by Spanish Invaders, the Culture of the Gentle Taino Is Finally Coming to Light. *Time* (October 19): 76(2).

Longhena, Maria. 1998. *Ancient Mexico, The History and Culture of the Maya, Aztec, and Other Pre-Columbian Peoples*. New York: Stewart, Tabori and Chang.

Patricia Cronin Marcello

PREDATOR-PREY MODELS

SEE *Predatory Pricing.*

PREDATORY PRICING

Predatory pricing is primarily a strategy of price reduction that intends to eliminate a rival firm and thus increase market power. More generally, the goal of predatory pricing may be to discipline or otherwise inhibit a competitor. Also, while price is typically the instrument used for this purpose, other actions may be taken, such as bundling, refusing to supply, or other practices that effectively raise the rival's cost of doing business. Predatory pricing is therefore just one form of predation—though arguably the most commonly practiced and studied.

Predatory pricing is a controversial issue in scholarly and legal circles alike. On one hand, price cuts can be used as a means to exclude rival firms and increase future market power. On the other, price cuts are the bread and butter of market competition. Thus it is very difficult to distinguish genuine competitive pricing from predatory (and thus anticompetitive) pricing; and even if predatory pricing has negative long run effects, in the short run it has the same positive effects of aggressive competitive pricing.

LEGAL PERSPECTIVES

Allegations of predatory behavior are as old as oligopoly competition. Starting in the nineteenth century, examples include ocean shipping, sugar, tobacco, oil, and others. For example, some historians argue that, in the late 1900s the Southern Bell Telephone Company effectively eliminated competition through a strategy of pricing below cost in response to entry.

Reviewing the evidence in one of the most prominent cases, *Standard Oil Company of New Jersey v. United States* 221 U.S. 1 (1911), economist John McGee argued that there is little support for the allegations of predatory behavior. More importantly, he argued that the concept of predatory pricing itself lacks logical consistency. Of the several reasons pointed out by McGee, one deserves special attention. McGee maintained that, in addition to the prey, the predator too suffers from predatory pricing. If the prey resists predation and remains active, then the predator eventually will give up its efforts. Anticipating this outcome, the prey is indeed better off resisting predatory efforts. Anticipating this outcome, in turn, the alleged predator is better off refraining from its predatory strategy. Even if the alleged prey were short of cash, it could always borrow from a bank with the (correct) prom-

ise that its losses are only temporary. One can hardly underestimate the influence of McGee's work, both in economics scholarship and in legal practice.

Early-twenty-first-century legal rulings in the United States illustrate a skeptical approach to the concept of predatory pricing. This is particularly apparent in two important decisions by the U.S. Supreme Court: *Matsushita Electric Industrial Co., Ltd. v. Zenith Radio Corp.*, 475 U.S. 574 (1986) and *Brooke Group Ltd. v. Brown & Williamson Tobacco Corp.*, 509 U.S. 209 (1993). Adopting the theories of McGee and his followers, the Court embraced the view that predatory pricing schemes are rarely attempted; and that, if attempted, their success is rare.

In contrast to the United States, the European Union's (EU) approach to predatory pricing (based on Article 82 of the European Community Treaty) is rather aggressive. For example, in 2003 France Telecom SA was fined for "offering its services at a loss" in the high-speed internet access market.

Broadly speaking, the U.S. and EU approaches to testing for predatory behavior are similar: They look for evidence that there is (a) a sacrifice of short-term profits; and (b) a reasonable expectation that such losses are compensated by long-term gains from greater market power. The main difference between the United States and Europe is the strength of the second requirement, which is weaker in Europe. (There is also some divergence with respect to part (a). Typically, evidence of short-term losses is gathered by comparing price to some measure of cost. The question is then what measure of cost makes the most theoretical and practical sense.)

ECONOMIC PERSPECTIVE

For a long time, McGee's analysis provided the only coherent economic theory of predatory pricing. But unlike legal practice, economic thinking has departed significantly from McGee's theory. The research suggests that there are several reasons why predatory pricing is a plausible strategy. One reason is asymmetry of information between predator and prey. By repeatedly fighting rivals with low prices, a predator increases its reputation for toughness; and thus encourages exit and discourages future entry. Alternatively, if the prey is uncertain about the predator's costs, then the latter's low prices signal that the predator's costs are low too, and so are the prey's long term prospects.

A related source of information asymmetry is between the prey and capital markets. One of the key points in McGee's case against predation is that, if the alleged prey were short of cash, banks should be willing to step in with a loan under the (correct) promise that the prey's losses are only temporary. But due to imperfect monitoring of the borrower's actions banks are forced to offer contracts where future financing is contingent on repayment of current loans. In this context, the predator may have an incentive to price below cost: While the predator loses money, so does the prey; and to the extent that lower current profitability decreases the probability of loan repayment, the predator has something to gain in the long run—the possibility that the prey, unable to secure financing, will be forced out of the market.

Finally, a third class of equilibrium models of predatory pricing is based on dynamic effects through the firms' profit functions (either through demand or through costs). Consider the case of two competitors moving down the learning curve. If the lagging firm loses the current sale, it might find itself so far behind the race that exit is the best option. Anticipating such behavior, the leader has an incentive to price aggressively, possibly below cost, thus increasing the chances of monopolizing the market. Unlike the previous theories, this one does not rely on asymmetric information between firms or between firms and capital markets. Moreover, while the learning curve provides a natural link between current sales and future profits, there are several other examples: switching costs, installed base or network effects, and so forth.

In summary, although U.S. legal doctrine is rather skeptical with respect to predatory pricing, economic theory has provided a wealth of coherent explanations of why predation is plausible.

SEE ALSO *Antitrust Regulation; Competition; Competition, Imperfect; Competition, Marxist; Game Theory; Information, Asymmetric; Monopoly; Price Setting and Price Taking; Regulation*

BIBLIOGRAPHY

Bolton, Patrick, and David S. Scharfstein. 1990. A Theory of Predation Based on Agency Problems in Financial Contracting. *American Economic Review* 80 (1): 93–106.

Cabral, Luís M. B., and Michael H. Riordan. 1994. The Learning Curve, Market Dominance and Predatory Pricing. *Econometrica* 62 (5): 1115–1140.

Kreps, David M., and Robert Wilson. 1982. Reputation and Imperfect Information. *Journal of Economic Theory* 27: 253–279.

McGee, John S. 1958. Predatory Price Cutting: the Standard Oil (N.J.) Case. *Journal of Law and Economics* 1 (October): 137–169.

Milgrom, Paul R., and John Roberts. 1982a. Predation, Reputation and Entry Deterrence. *Journal of Economic Theory* 27: 280–312.

Milgrom, Paul R., and John Roberts. 1982b. Limit Pricing and Entry under Incomplete Information: An Equilibrium Analysis. *Econometrica* 50 (2): 443–460.

Luís Cabral

PREDICTION

Prediction can be defined as "to declare in advance: foretell on the basis of observation, experience, or scientific reason" (Webster's 7th New Collegiate Dictionary). Predictions can be short-term, long-term, qualitative, quantitative, negative, positive, optimistic, or pessimistic. They can be based on hunches, guesses, folklore, astrology, palm reading, extrapolations from data, or scientific laws and theories or alleged laws of historical change. The term *prediction* overlaps with *prophecy* but has somewhat different connotations.

Not until the seventeenth and eighteenth centuries did prediction take on its modern connotations. Pierre-Simon Laplace (1749–1827), arguably its first major theorist, presented a systematic answer to the major theoretical and practical problem prediction raises: Why are we so successful in some areas of research (e.g., astronomy, physics, and chemistry) but conspicuously less successful in others, particularly human behavior? The most frequently given answers are that some phenomena are intrinsically unpredictable, or we are not using correct scientific methods, or the complexity of the phenomena rule it out, or it is due to limits of human ignorance, fallibility, and superstition. The twentieth century saw significant developments in the theory and practice of prediction, with simultaneous significant advances in predictive accuracy and a greater awareness of the limits of such accuracy.

EMPIRICAL AND PRAGMATIC SIGNIFICANCE

There are four major theories concerning the possibility of predictive success in the areas where, so far, they have been rather limited. The first is *Laplacian determinism*, named for Laplace, who asserted that an intelligence endowed with omniscience (who therefore would know the current position and velocity of all particles, as well as the laws that control their behavior) could predict every future event.

The second view, *the covering law model,* is based on the two principles involved in the Laplacian view. As developed by Karl Popper (1934), it requires that an adequate explanation be deduced from universal laws and initial conditions (a generalization of Laplace's positions and velocity). The more general and more precise the prediction, the better it is. This is because it is more testable, which in Popper's view means "falsifiable."

The third position, *probabilistic prediction,* is more modest but still in accordance with Laplace's view that our ignorance and fallibility forces us to rely on probability, not certainty, in our predictive endeavors. We can predict a 60 percent chance of rain this weekend, but not with the virtual certainty of astronomical predictions (e.g., that Venus will be in transit in 2112) or those based on

(Newtonian) laws of gravity and motion. The quantum physics uncertainty principle is often seen as the paradigm case of this type, although weather predictions and many social phenomena may be better examples, given that quantum electrodynamics has the most numerically precise, accurate predictions in the history of science.

The final theory, *pattern prediction,* originated with Warren Weaver (1894–1978), a natural scientist, but was made widely known to economists and social scientists by Friedrich von Hayek (1899–1992). This position seems furthest from Laplacian determinism. Pattern prediction downplays precise quantitative predictions, and has a weakened type of testability, due to the theory of complex phenomena adapted from Weaver. It appears to harmonize well with modern chaos theory and with probabilistic reasoning about phenomena. However, the most recent developments in the theory and practice of prediction may be making it more susceptible to quantitative precision.

Any adequate theory of prediction should allow retrodiction as a special type. If one predicts that devaluing the currency will lead to inflation, then a study of such policies in ancient Rome, Egypt, or China should find these results. This can be defined as prediction, although it concerns not the society studied but what the scholars of such societies should find.

CRITICISM OF METHODOLOGY

B. F. Skinner's behaviorism emphasized prediction and control; his position was extreme Laplacian determinism. The reason for our inability to be as successful at predicting human behavior as we are with predictions made in physics and astronomy is due to our failure to apply proper scientific method, primarily because of a lingering antiempirical belief in an inner man not subject to the laws of nature. But the history of science since Newton has postulated several unobservable entities (e.g., atoms, gravity, natural selection) with spectacular practical and empirical success.

Logical positivism (including Popper's weakened version) associated predictions with testability, meaning both verifiability and falsifiability. But it has been argued on both logical and historical grounds that a false prediction does not always disprove a theory. Nor does verification of predictions prove the theory true for purely logical reasons (the fallacy of affirming the consequent).

Popper that, in contrast to unconditional historical prophecies, scientific predictions are conditional (1963). This is based on his model described above and the laws he argues are conditional not asserting the existence of the initial conditions. But the model only works for systems that are well isolated, stationary, and recurrent (Popper 1963). This is why predictions of eclipses and the regular-

ity of the seasons can be made accurately, because the solar system is such a system. Such systems are not typical; they are special cases where scientific prediction becomes particularly impressive.

In addition, there are arguments based on the nondeterministic character of classical physics. The "three-body problem" undermines Laplacian determinism. The three-body problem arises out of the inability of physics (so far) to use Newton's laws for more than two bodies.

The twentieth-century scientist Edward Lorentz, distinguished between two types of determinism thus: "one with clear rules that apply always and everywhere" so that repetition of the same conditions makes prediction possible and another where "small variations aggregate and amplify" (Kaplan and Kaplan, 2006, p. 221) and so repetition prevents prediction. The former will result in long-run variation canceling out, with a clear pattern emerging. The latter leads to what are now called "chaotic systems," which are extremely sensitive to initial conditions.

Despite these impediments, progress has been made in improving meteorological and other types of predictions by the use of "ensemble prediction" as well as "threshold" and "pattern effects." The former involves turning predictability itself into a variable, such as temperature or rainfall. The latter combines Weaver's pattern prediction with the important idea of threshold effects, as in the second type of determinism described in the preceding paragraph. Threshold effects are best illustrated by the straw that broke the camel's back.

Developments in the last two decades are improving efforts to predict possible disasters such as earthquakes, tornadoes, epidemics, and perhaps climate change, as well as the interactions of large groups of people, their societal effects, and their impact on the environment. (Cribb, 2006). Great use has been made of modern computers, often employing simulated effects over centuries (which leaves a great margin of error due to unreliable data), possibly unjustified assumptions in constructing the models, and human fallibility, yet there are good indications of improved predictive ability with computers.

Nonetheless, we are nowhere near Laplace's omniscient intelligence, and for theoretical and practical reasons we are unlikely ever to be. The major reason is that the mathematics and data used are both so complicated (millions and millions of lines in a computer code) that no one person can master it. In addition, it relies on Baysean probability theory. The mathematics of that is not very complex, but it requires initial assignments of probability, which can then be modified by new evidence. However, there are numerous problems in deciding how to assign these so that they are not too arbitrary.

SEE ALSO *Behaviorism; Determinism; Hayek, Friedrich August von; Popper, Karl; Positivism; Probability; Skinner, B. F.*

BIBLIOGRAPHY

Cribb, Julian. 2006. Predicting the Future: It's Becoming a Science. *Cosmos* (September 20).

Kaplan, Michael, and Ellen Kaplan. 2006. *Chances Are.* New York: Viking.

Kuhn, Thomas. 1962. *The Structure of Scientific Revolutions.* Chicago: University of Chicago Press.

Popper, Karl. [1934] 1959. *The Logic of Scientific Discovery.* New York: Basic Books.

Popper, Karl. 1963. *Conjectures and Refutations.* London: Routledge.

Skinner, B. F. 1953. *Science and Human Behaviour.* New York: Macmillan.

Calvin Hayes

PREEMPTIVE STRIKE

The decision to use military force can be made in a variety of different situations and in response to numerous different triggers or actions taken by an enemy or adversary. A *preemptive strike* is a military action taken to forestall an imminent military attack or other type of threat. This type of activity is different from a *preventive action*, which is undertaken to counter a more distant threat. In this respect, a preemptive strike deals with a current threat, while preventive action deals with a potential or future threat.

Preemptive strikes are generally motivated by the fear of an impending attack or invasion. In this scenario, the leadership of a state believes its adversary is preparing for an attack or invasion. Instead of waiting for the attack to actually occur, the leadership decides to take action first—to launch a preemptive strike against the adversary.

The Israeli decision to strike against Egyptian forces on June 5, 1967, is an example of a preemptive strike. The Israelis believed that the Egyptians were poised for their own attack and that Israel could ill afford to absorb such an attack. As a result, the Israelis decided to launch a preemptive strike to forestall the imminent Egyptian attack.

A preventive action, on the other hand, would be undertaken to deal with a threat that could develop sometime in the future. With preventive action, the "threat" posed by the target is distant in nature, and in some cases a mere potentiality. The Israeli strike against the Iraqi nuclear reactor at Osiraq in June 1981 is an example of a preventive action. Israel struck the Iraqi facility in order to forestall the further development of the Iraqi nuclear program, which the Israelis viewed as a threat. This action was not really "preemptive" in nature, however, in that Iraq did not pose an imminent threat to Israel.

The distinctions between preemptive and preventive actions are important, but often confused. The 2002 *National Security Strategy of the United States of America* (NSS) describes a strategy identified as "preemptive," but in actuality it is closer to being preventive in nature. The NSS states, in the context of the threat from weapons of mass destruction, that "the greater the threat, the greater is the risk of inaction—and the more compelling the case for taking anticipatory action to defend ourselves, even if uncertainty remains as to the time and place of the enemy's attack" (p. 15). The fact that the NSS stresses that the "time and place" of the attack are unknown makes the policy preventive. However, the NSS goes on to state, "To forestall or prevent such hostile acts by our adversaries, the United States will, if necessary, act preemptively" (p. 15). While the NSS docs use the word *prevent,* it describes the policy as *preemptive.* Regardless of the terminology used to describe the policy, it fits squarely with the criteria of preventive actions. In this regard, the 2003 U.S.-led invasion of Iraq and ongoing conflict can be considered a preventive, but not preemptive, action—the threat faced was not imminent, but instead was of a more distant nature.

While preemptive strikes do involve the "first use of force," they are generally viewed to be reactive policies, or actions taken in self-defense. Preemptive strikes are usually carried out in response to some action taken by the enemy that is believed to signal preparations for an imminent attack. Preventive actions, on the other hand, are taken in response to activities that *could* develop into a specific threat at some point in time in the future.

This distinction has important implications, particularly with respect to international law. International law allows for the first-use of force in response to an imminent threat, but not in response to a distant threat. Or, in other words, preemption in response to an actual and imminent threat is OK, but preventive action is not. The line between imminent and distant threats, however, is becoming increasingly harder to distinguish in today's world. With today's modern technology, leaders no longer have the ability to see the adversary's army massing at the border in preparation for an attack.

It is also important to realize that preemptive strikes and preventive actions are not a type of war, but rather should be viewed as a "pathway to war." In other words, a preemptive strike or a preventive action may signal the beginning of a war—but they are not in and of themselves distinct types of war. Any of the numerous types of war (e.g., limited war, total war, hegemonic war) can be started through the use of a preemptive strike or a preventive action. Furthermore, since preemptive strikes or preventive actions involve the first use of force, they can only be taken *before* the outbreak of armed hostilities. Since these actions are designed to forestall an enemy attack, once such an attack has occurred, the opportunity to take preemptive or preventive action has passed.

While there are numerous arguments as to why leaders would adopt preemptive or preventive strategies, the historical record indicates that states rarely employ these types of policies. One of the possible reasons why the leadership of a state would be hesitant to launch a preemptive strike is that there are substantial political "strings" attached to these actions. The state risks being labeled the aggressor in the conflict and potentially alienating allies and friends in the process—thereby jeopardizing support that might be essential during the rest of the conflict and in later relations. Additionally, there is a great deal of uncertainty inherent in any war or armed conflict. A leader would want to be quite certain that an attack was truly imminent before he or she struck the blow that would start the war process. But, this level of certainty is rarely present, and leaders are, therefore, reluctant to utilize preemptive strikes. This does not mean that leaders never decide to launch preemptive strikes, but rather helps explain why their use is much rarer than might be otherwise expected.

SEE ALSO *Defense; Defense, National; Deterrence; War*

BIBLIOGRAPHY

Lemke, Douglas. 2003. Investigating the Preventive Motive for War. *International Interactions* 29 (4): 273–292.

President of the United States. 2002. *The National Security Strategy of the United States of America.* http://www.whitehouse.gov/nsc/nss.pdf.

Reiter, Dan. 1995. Exploding the Powder Keg Myth: Preemptive Wars Almost Never Happen. *International Security* 20 (2): 5–34.

Van Evera, Stephen. 1999. *Causes of War: Power and the Roots of Conflict.* Ithaca, NY: Cornell University Press.

Rachel Bzostek

PREFERENCE, COLOR

For most people, one of the first decisions of the day concerns color preference. College students learn that whether they are choosing an outfit for a job interview, designing a new product, or creating a Web site, the colors they choose greatly affect their final result. Psychologists report that color impression can account for 60 to 70 percent of consumer reaction. Therefore, understanding people's color preferences becomes an important learning tool.

Color preferences change as a person develops and are in part determined by a person's economic and social status. Education, environment, climate, and family heritage influence people's favorite colors. Furthermore, people have color preferences for different objects like clothing, home decorations, and cars. A person may prefer a blue shirt, yellow walls, and a red car. Babies respond more readily to bright, primary colors than to pastel colors. The favorite color of most preschool children, up to the age of five, is bright red. Young children between five and ten years old prefer bright yellow.

As people grow and mature, their color preferences change. Adults may have learned to associate red with negative things, such as blood and fire, and so their color preference changes from childhood to adulthood. Adults have been found cross-culturally to favor blue over other colors. Adult women generally prefer blue-based colors, whereas men tend to prefer yellow-based tints. Even education levels and the degree of cultural sophistication seem to affect people's color preferences. In general, highly educated and sophisticated people favor complex colors, those mixed with shades of black. In contrast, people with less education and lower income favor low-intensity, simple, or pure colors.

People respond differently to various colors depending also upon the climatic conditions in which they live. For example, Scandinavians have a preference for light yellows, bright whites, and sky blues, in contrast to their long, dark winter nights. San Franciscans, who live in an area that is often foggy and overcast, generally are not fond of gray. Conversely, cool gray is a popular color among people in Miami's sunny, hot, and humid climate.

Ethnic heritage and traditions also affect color preferences. For instance, American couples most often prefer to dress brides in white, representing purity. Chinese typically wear white to funerals and prefer black or red colors for their wedding dresses, since these colors represent joy in their culture. Americans traditionally dress their newborns in blue or pink according to gender rather than personal individual preference.

Color preferences have changed over time. In the mid-1800s, bright colors were popular, but they were replaced by more subdued tertiary colors such as muddy reds, greens, browns, blues, pinks, and ambers in the 1870s. Pastel and cream colors came back into fashion in the 1890s, and were popular during the latter part of Queen Victoria's (1819–1901) reign. But as fashions changed and furniture became more ornate, heavier, and more elaborate, room colors also became richer and darker.

Certain color preferences seem universal, such as that of "warm" and "cool" colors. People perceive red, orange, and yellow to be warm colors, reflecting the natural association with the hot sun and flames. Blue and green shades are considered cool, in relation to cool water and shady leaves. Warm colors generally include magenta, red, orange, yellow, and yellow-green. Warm colors speed up our perception of time and produce feelings that are cozy and inviting. These colors are associated with excitement, happiness, and comfort. Cool colors generally include violet, blue, and green. Emotions associated with cool colors range from calm and peace to sadness, withdrawal, and repression.

COLOR PREFERENCE AND BUSINESS

Color-preference trends help sell products. Advertisers, fashion designers, and auto manufactures know that color influences the approval of or negative response to products or services. Commercials change fashion and cultural icons—Santa Claus, for example, used to wear a blue or green suit until Coca-Cola dressed him in their trademark colors red and white. Marketers use color preferences in products and advertising based on research and market tests. Along with personal preference, the typical meanings and effects of color are factors in product development and promotion. This happens because adults habitually relate colors to emotions.

Red elevates blood pressure, respiratory rate, and appetite. Red symbolizes heat, blood, passion, love, power, excitement, vitality, and aggression. In advertising, red grabs attention and stimulates people to make quick decisions. Pink, associated with sweetness, helps sell pastries and candies.

Orange causes people to feel energetic and is often found in the décor of fast food restaurants. Yellow represents the sun and is considered a spiritual color that symbolizes deity in many religions. Because yellow is the first color human eyes process, it attracts attention in advertising.

Indian mystics favor green because they believe it to be a combination of balance and harmony. Green, a sacred color to the Egyptians, represents the promise and rejuvenation of spring. In the Middle Ages, brides wore green to represent fertility. Green helps people relax, which makes it a popular color in hospitals.

Blue, the favorite color of adults, is disliked as a color around food. Most people prefer to dine surrounded by food-related colors, such as red strawberries, green apples, yellow bananas, and brown breads. Blue is the preferred color to wear to a job interview because people associate blue with loyalty and trustfulness.

Purple became related to perceptions of royalty and richness because the color was difficult to produce in ancient times. People think of luxury when they view pur-

ple. Leonardo da Vinci (1452–1519) favored purple lighting to enhance his creativity.

Brown is favored by men more than women. Connected to the earth and wood, brown is thought to represent solidity and strength.

Black, a color preferred by many for clothing, represents power, sophistication, and formality. Black also has contrary associations with witches and criminals. Black aids advertising materials by making other colors stand out in contrast and is the preferred type color for Web sites.

White represents cleanliness and purity to many people, who prefer white for automobiles, clothing, and interior design. White automobiles show up best at night. White clothing and interior spaces feel cooler in warm climates.

Color affects people, every day of their lives, on both the conscious and subconscious levels. With a thorough understanding of the effects of color preference, businesses can make wise decisions about product development and marketing. Individuals who understand their color preferences can make wise choices when selecting clothing, home furnishings, and automobiles.

SEE ALSO *Bigotry; Colorism; Hierarchy; Prejudice; Racism; Stratification*

BIBLIOGRAPHY

Fehrman, Kenneth R., and Cherie Fehrman. 2004. *Color: The Secret Influence.* 2nd ed. Upper Saddle River, NJ: Pearson Prentice Hall.

Zentner, Marcel. 2001. Preferences for Colours and Colour-emotion Combinations in Early Childhood. In *Developmental Science* 4: 389–398.

Jeanette Fisher

PREFERENCE, GENDER

The term *gender preference* is confusing because it has a number of at best tangentially related meanings. For example, the term *gender preference* or *sexual preference* is used to describe the desire of biological parents for either a male or female child and—in the extreme—use a range of odious methods (e.g., infanticide and sex-selective abortions) to achieve that result. In patrilineal societies, the necessity for a male birth is straightforward. Less-developed societies tend to favor males for immediate utilitarian reasons and, eventually, as a primitive social security system. No such clear-cut historical and/or cultural rationales fully explain this phenomenon's occurrence in developed countries, where adoptive parents strongly prefer to adopt girls. Another use of the term *gender preference* is to describe explicit or implicit job discrimination by which women are perceived as unable to perform certain skills (e.g., tasks requiring heavy lifting and other such manual labor). Overall though, the most ubiquitous use of the terms *gender preference* and *sexual preference* is in reference to sexual orientation.

Prefer, meaning "to like better or best," is a transitive verb: It requires a direct object. Given this use of the word, *sexual orientation* is considered synonymous with *gender preference*, for most discussion of sexual orientation is about whether an individual can be labeled as homosexual, heterosexual, or bisexual—that is, whether the "direct object" is the opposite gender, the same gender, or both. Most research and theories focus on homosexuality, not heterosexuality or bisexuality. Indeed, at the heart of most explorations of sexual orientation is an attempt to determine whether homosexuality is an outcome of nature or nurture. In an effort to attain the worthwhile goal of destigmatizing homosexuality and having it successfully removed from official lists of pathologies, activists have tended to fixate on biological determinism.

Acknowledging the difficulty of parsing out the influences of nature and nurture, Mustanski, Chivers, and Bailey proposed a "thought experiment" (2002, p. 94) that would involve an ideal test of whether hormones influence sexual orientation by a prenatal, organizational action. This experiment would require sex reassignment of a random sample of newborn males reared by adoptive parents blinded to the child's natal sex. This unethical "experiment" exemplifies the extremes required to sort out these factors. Mustanski and colleagues summarized the findings of the last decade in the neurohormonal areas, including psychoneuroendrocrinology, prenatal stress, cerebral asymmetry, neuroanatomy, anthropometrics, genetics, birth order, and developmental stability. They acknowledged some consistent findings, especially regarding genetics; however, their report concludes that it remains "puzzling … how and when these biological factors act and to what degree these factors influence sexual orientation" (p. 129). They also stated, "The term biological is frequently misunderstood and misused due to it being somewhat amorphous, given that all human behaviors are enacted by the brain and thus are in some sense biological" (p. 90). Thus, they speculated, "Rather than asking if sexual orientation is biological, we believe it is more fruitful to consider whether differences in sexual orientation primarily reflect differences in social experiences, differences in biologic factors unrelated to social experiences, or both. The ultimate goal of such research will be to understand the timing and mechanism of various etiological factors that influence sexual orientation" (p. 90).

In *The Homosexual Matrix* (1975), C. A. Tripp included a section titled "The Directional Controls of Sex." Tripp stated that sexual choices made and actions taken are learned behaviors influenced by an individual experience in the context of a particular society. These learning processes are "rooted in a biological groundwork of slowly accumulating changes … over eons of mammalian evolution." Tripp followed this path from sexual activity that is "rigorously regulated by specific physiologic controls" in lower mammals where "every movement is predetermined by key responses," through primates whose "sexual patterns are neither stereotyped nor guided by specific signals; they are almost entirely dependent on individual learning," culminating in humans with an enlarged cerebral cortex. Tripp described a "progressive relaxation of specific physiologic controls over sexuality" as the cerebral cortex assumes controls of voluntary behaviors such as sexuality. "Thus, human sexuality is exceedingly variable, deriving its directionality (especially its final targeting) from what is individually learned and experienced in personal and social settings" (pp. 12–15).

John Money created a list highlighting the endlessness of teasing out the antecedents for Tripp's directionality and targeting. Describing what is required for what he labeled a lovemap, Money contended that "the variables will be genomic status; hormonal history (prenatal and postnatal); sexual brain cell functioning; history of toxic, infectious, or traumatic exposure; infantile pairbonding; juvenile troopbonding; juvenile sexual rehearsal play; sex education; adolescent sexual history; amative history in imagery, ideation, and practice; and so on" (2003, p. 238).

Ultimately, in reference to what or who leads to sexuerotic arousal and attainment of orgasm, the terms *sexual preference* and *gender preference* are oxymorons because they imply that choice is at their core. Furthermore, such terms limit the "object" that stimulates the sexuerotic arousal and its sequela to gender-based categories. Such conceptualization marginalizes the entire phenomenon of paraphilias. Any review would be negligent if it focused on the power of the attraction of gender and ignored the same power that objects such as a shoe, a goat, or a child have on some individuals. Edward Albee's realistic staging of "The Goat, or Who is Sylvia?" (2003) explores sexual orientation in a way that science has yet to attempt. Research into sexual preference needs to be broad enough to include such phenomena if it is to lead to an understanding of related conditions such as pedophilia. Use of *gender preference* as a synonym for sexual orientation limits such exploration.

SEE ALSO *Determinism, Biological; Discrimination, Wage, by Gender; Gender; Gender, Alternatives to Binary; Marriage, Same-Sex; Neuroscience;*

Psychoneuroendocrinology; Sexual Orientation, Social and Economic Consequences

BIBLIOGRAPHY

Albee, Edward. 2003. "The Goat, or Who is Sylvia?" New York: Dramatists Play Service, Inc.

Hank, Karsten, and Hans-Peter Kohler. 2000. *Gender Preferences for Children in Europe: Empirical Results from 17 FFS Countries.* Rostock, Germany: Max-Planck-Gesellschaft.

Money, John. 2003. History, Causality, Sexology. *Journal of Sex Research* 40 (3): 237–239.

Mustanski, B. S., M. L. Chivers, and J. M. Bailey. 2002. A Critical Review of Recent Biological Research on Human Sexual Orientation. *Annual Review of Sex Research* 12: 89–140.

Tripp, C. A. 1975. *The Homosexual Matrix.* New York: McGraw-Hill.

Benjamin Graber

PREFERENCES

Preferences are value judgments about the relative desirability of alternatives. In decision theory, the decision-maker's preferences are the criteria used to compare the alternatives available for choice. But preferences need not be related to choice: They may also represent how an entity values outcomes, or states of the world, that it does not choose. Depending on the setting, preferences may be objective or subjective.

In abstract, given a set X, a menu of alternatives that may be chosen or that may simply occur, an entity's preferences are a binary relation defined on X. Given two alternatives, x and y, this relation answers the question "Is x at least as good as y?" When, according to the entity, the answer is "yes," one says that the entity weakly prefers x to y (denoted $x \succsim y$).

Historically, preferences were initially treated as cardinal objects: it was postulated that to any alternative x one could attach a number $u(x)$, measuring the level of inner happiness, or utility, derived from it. Classical analyses in distributive justice and in economics during the eighteenth and nineteenth centuries, such as the utilitarianism of Jeremy Bentham (1748–1832) or the marginalism of William Stanley Jevons (1835–1882) and Carl Menger (1840–1921), required cardinal utilities. The independent contributions of Vilfredo Pareto (1848–1923) and Irving Fisher (1867–1947) in the late nineteenth century emphasized that only the ordinal information of preferences matters: That an entity prefers one alternative to another is merely a ranking. After the work of John Hicks (1904–1989) in the 1930s and Kenneth Arrow in the 1950s, it is commonly accepted that preferences are ordinal.

Suppose that a decision-maker (DM) is choosing from a menu X, and let x and y be two alternatives. It is clear that either DM likes x at least as much as y, likes y at least as much as x, is indifferent (both previous statements being true), or is unable to tell (neither statement is true). This means that $\succsim$ is a binary relation over X. If $x \succsim y$ while it is not true that $y \succsim x$, DM likes x strictly better than y; this strict preference defines a second binary relation, $\succ$, the asymmetric part of $\succsim$. A third binary relation is given by the indifference of preferences, $\sim$, the symmetric part of $\succsim$.

DM has *complete preferences* if he or she is able to compare any pair of alternatives: either $x \succsim y$ or $y \succsim x$, for any x and y. Preferences are said to be *transitive* if $x \succsim y$ and $y \succsim z$ imply $x \succsim z$. Complete and transitive preferences constitute a *complete preorder*, which is the most basic assumption on tastes of a decision-maker: DM is then said to be *rational*.

In more specific settings, additional structure allows for further properties. When X is a field over the real numbers (for example, a Euclidean space), preferences are convex if any average of alternatives is preferred to the least-preferred averaged alternative. When a definition of *more* exists for X, preferences are said to be monotonic if more implies better. When X is endowed with a topology, preferences are continuous if the at-least-as-good-as property is preserved under limits.

Preferences are representable if there exists a "utility" function, mapping X into the real line, with the property that $x \succsim y$ if, and only if, the value of the mapping at x is at least its value at y. In the 1950s Gerard Debreu (1921–2004) presented the seminal solution to the representability problem for continuous preferences. Representability does not mean that preferences have cardinal meaning: While any two functions representing given preferences contain, by construction, the same ordinal information, their cardinality may differ nontrivially. Given representable preferences, a property is ordinal if it is preserved upon increasing transformation of its representations, while cardinal properties are preserved only by affine, increasing transformations.

In economics, demand theory studies the individual choice of a bundle of commodities, at given prices and income, with preferences understood to be subjective and ordinal. In applications, a useful family of preferences delivers invariant substitution effects: The *constant elasticity of substitution* (CES) family includes *linear preferences* (perfect substitutability), *Leontieff preferences* (perfect complementarity), and *Cobb-Douglas preferences* (unitary elasticity of substitution). *Homothetic preferences* deliver demand functions that are homogeneous of degree one in income, while, with some qualification, *quasi-linear* preferences isolate all commodities but one from income effects.

When X represents an intertemporal situation, some structure is usually imposed on preferences. Suppose that $(x_0, x_1) \in X$ represents consumption in the present (x_0) and in the future (x_1). In this setting, it is usually assumed that the person is impatient to consume in the sense that $(x + \varepsilon, x - \varepsilon) \succ (x, x)$, for a small enough perturbation $\varepsilon > 0$. In this case, a simplification is usually obtained by defining an instantaneous-utility (or felicity) function v on the real line, which represents the individual's satisfaction of consumption without intertemporal considerations, and a discount factor, β, and by assuming that $\succsim$ is represented by the function $u(x_0, x_1) = v(x_0) + \beta v(x_1)$. Here, the assumptions that v is increasing and $\beta < 1$ model the hypotheses that the individual enjoys consumption and is impatient.

When the individual faces risk, the outcome of his or her choice is a random variable. In this case, X is a set of random variables (lotteries), $\succsim$ ranks these variables ex-ante (in ignorance of the outcome that they will realize), and, in general, the standard analysis of preferences applies. As in the case of intertemporal preferences, a simplification is obtained via representation by utility functions. Leonard J. Savage (1917–1971) provided axioms that guarantee the existence of an expected utility representation, as defined by Daniel Bernoulli (1700–1782) in the eighteenth century: The ex-ante utility of a lottery is measured by the mathematical expectation of the well-being that the individual would derive from the outcome of the lottery were it not subject to risk, the induced random variable $v(x)$. In this case, the felicity function has cardinal meaning: Only upon affine transformations is the representation of preferences preserved. Under expected utility, the curvature of function is used to measure individual dislike of risk. Arrow proposed two measures of risk aversion: absolute (the negative of the ratio of the second to the first derivatives of v) and relative (the absolute measure times the consumption level). An exponential representation of v exhibits constant absolute risk aversion, whereas an adaptation of the CES family yields constant relative risk aversion. Under uncertainty, completeness of preferences has been questioned: When unsure about the probabilities of different states of the world, individuals may be unable to compare all alternatives.

While research on choice often takes preferences as given, there are different theories about how humans form value judgments. In mathematical psychology, laboratory observation has led to the hypothesis that preferences (human and animal) are themselves random objects, which implies that choice itself is random (see, for example, the work of Duncan Luce and Patrick Suppes). Other prominent theories have considered the influence of experience and social interactions in the determination of preferences: While a basic view may take them as physiologically determined (so choice appears as a cognitive process), a broader view takes into account the influence of an individual's history or social context on the determination of tastes, from which choice appears as a behavioral phenomenon. These theories account for the learning processes that are embedded in sequential decision problems, for the effects of habit formation (for example, addictions) or for the influence of fashion or peer pressure on behavior (see the work of Gary Becker). Also, Amos Tversky (1937–1996) and Daniel Kahneman observed that the way in which a decision problem is framed seems to affect the choices of many individuals, which highlights the effects of perception on preferences. One more apparent anomaly of the standard theory arises in intertemporal problems, as evidence shows that often individuals choose not to delay the realization of a negative effect, which is at odds with the usual impatience postulate.

The problem of explaining how groups of individuals value alternatives has led to the definition of *social preferences*. An important difficulty in this direction was presented by Arrow in the mid-1950s: Under certain axioms, it is impossible to aggregate individual preferences into social preferences without the imposition of a "dictator" whose preferences are assumed for the whole society. Competing theories of social justice—for example, utilitarianism, Rawlsianism, or Robert Nozick's (1938–2002) libertarianism—provide prominent discussions of social preferences.

SEE ALSO *Demand; Endogenous Preferences; Lexicographic Preferences; Preferences, Interdependent; Utility Function*

BIBLIOGRAPHY

Arrow, Kenneth J. 1950. A Difficulty in the Concept of Social Welfare. *Journal of Political Economy* 58: 328–346.

Arrow, Kenneth J. 1973. Some Ordinalist-Utilitarian Notes on Rawls's Theory of Justice. *Journal of Philosophy* 70: 254–263.

Becker, Gary. 1996. *Accounting for Tastes.* Cambridge, MA: Harvard University Press.

Debreu, Gerard. 1954. Representation of a Preference Ordering by a Numerical Function. In *Decision Processes*, ed. Robert M. Thrall, C. H. Coombs, and Robert L. Davis, 159–165. New York: Wiley.

Luce, R. Duncan, and Patrick Suppes. 1965. Preference, Utility, and Subjective Probability. In *Handbook of Mathematical Psychology*, vol. 3, ed. R. Duncan Luce, Robert R. Bush, and Eugene Galanter, 252–403. New York: Wiley.

Tversky, Amos, and Daniel Kahneman. 1981. The Framing of Decisions and the Psychology of Choice. *Science* 211: 453–458.

Andrés Carvajal

PREFERENCES, INTERDEPENDENT

Interdependent preferences models rely on the basic intuition that economic agents are not always purely self-interested. This intuition may sound uncontroversial to noneconomists, but it is surprisingly so among the many economists who like parsimony and believe self-interest is a good approximation for most, or all, economic behavior.

Agent A has interdependent preferences whenever A's utility function depends on those of other agents in the reference group. Consider two agents, A and B. A's generic utility function with interdependent preferences is $U = u(x) + s(x, y, \lambda)\, v(x, y, \lambda)$, where u is the material utility component of the utility function and is a positive function of A's material consumption x; v is the interdependent utility component of the utility function and can be a function of x, is always a function of B's material consumption y, and can be a function of a vector of additional parameters λ; and s is the interdependent component weight in the utility function, is bounded between −1 and 1, and can be a function of x, y, and λ. The utility function reduces to the self-interest case if $s = 0$.

The generic utility function encompasses most interdependent preferences models (nonadditive versions are also possible):

Pure altruism where $s > 0$ and is a constant, and v is only a positive function of y (Collard 1975).

Pure envy where $s < 0$ and is a constant and v is a positive function of y and a nonpositive function of x (Clark and Oswald 1998).

Distributional models that are a function of the distribution of incomes between the players (v is a function only of x and y, with the weight s) depending on how they relate to one another (Fehr and Schmidt 1999; Bolton and Ockenfels 2000).

More complex psychological characterizations based on intentionality, as captured by the dependence on λ (Levine 1998; Falk and Fischbacher 2001; Charness and Rabin 2002).

λ could also incorporate other psychological considerations, such as group identity (Akerlof and Kranton 2000; Darity et al. 2006). There is strong empirical evidence for interdependent preferences (for reviews, see Camerer, 2003; Sobel 2005; Zizzo 2000), with distributional models outperforming pure altruism or envy (Zizzo 2003b, 2004) and intentions mattering (Falk et al. 2003).

Four limitations of interdependent preferences are their cardinality, heterogeneity, endogeneity, and context-sensitivity. *Cardinality* means that an individual's generic utility function requires strong interpersonal comparability of utility. *Heterogeneity* reflects the intuition that different people have different preferences, and the holy grail of capturing the empirical distributions of preferences is still at its early stages (see Burlando and Guala 2005 for an example). *Endogeneity* reflects the fact that environmental factors shape one's interdependent preferences, and this has policy implications (Zizzo 2003a). Most seriously, interdependent preferences are sensitive to the context of the decision problem, that is, to the way that the decision problem is perceived, with a large number of factors coming in and possibly interacting with one another (e.g., deservingness, social distance, communication, and so on) in ways that are poorly understood (Harrison and Johnson 2004; Konow 2000; Zizzo 2000, 2004). Adding dummy variables to ever more complex utility functions is hardly a solution; understanding the cognitive mechanisms underlying how agents perceive decision problems would be, but regretfully it is not a step that most economists are willing to take.

SEE ALSO *Endogenous Preferences; Evolutionary Games; Lexicographic Preferences; Preferences; Reciprocity*

BIBLIOGRAPHY

Akerlof, George, and Rachel Kranton. 2000. Economics and Identity. *Quarterly Journal of Economics* 115 (3): 715–753.

Bolton, Gary E., and Axel Ockenfels. 2000. ERC: A Theory of Equity, Reciprocity, and Competition. *American Economic Review* 90 (1): 166–193.

Burlando, Roberto, and Francesco Guala. 2005. Heterogeneous Agents in Public Goods Experiments. *Experimental Economics* 8 (1): 35–54.

Camerer, Colin, 2003. *Behavioral Game Theory: Experiments in Strategic Interaction.* Princeton, NJ: Princeton University Press.

Charness, Gary, and Matthew Rabin. 2002. Understanding Social Preferences with Simple Tests. *Quarterly Journal of Economics* 117 (3): 817–869.

Clark, Andrew E., and Andrew J. Oswald. 1998. Comparison-Concave Utility and Following Behaviour in Social and Economic Settings. *Journal of Public Economics* 70 (1): 133–155.

Collard, David. 1975. Edgeworth's Propositions on Altruism. *Economic Journal* 85: 355–360.

Cox, James C., Daniel Friedman, and Steven Gjerstad. 2004. A Tractable Model of Reciprocity and Fairness. http://www.econlab.arizona.edu/~gjerstad/papers/CFG_2005_TMRF.pdf.

Darity, William A., Patrick L. Mason, and James B. Stewart. 2006. The Economics of Identity: The Origin and Persistence of Racial Identity Norms. *Journal of Economic Behavior and Organization* 60 (3): 283–305.

Falk, Armin, and Urs Fischbacher. 2001. Distributional Consequences and Intentions in a Model of Reciprocity. *Annales d'Economie et de Statistique* 63–64: 111–129.

Falk, Armin, Ernst Fehr, and Urs Fischbacher. 2003. On the Nature of Fair Behavior. *Economic Inquiry* 41 (1): 20–26.

Fehr, Ernst, and Klaus M. Schmidt. 1999. A Theory of Fairness, Competition, and Cooperation. *Quarterly Journal of Economics* 114 (3): 817–868.

Harrison, Glenn W., and Laurie T. Johnson. 2004. Identifying Altruism in the Laboratory. http://www.altruists.org/f256.

Konow, James. 2000. Fair Shares: Accountability and Cognitive Dissonance in Allocation Decisions. *American Economic Review* 90 (4): 1072–1091.

Levine, David K. 1998. Modeling Altruism and Spitefulness in Experiment. *Review of Economic Dynamics* 1 (3): 593–622.

Sobel, Joel. 2005. Interdependent Preferences and Reciprocity. *Journal of Economic Literature* 43 (2): 392–436.

Zizzo, Daniel J. 2000. Relativity-Sensitive Behaviour in Economics. Ph.D. diss., University of Oxford, Oxford, U.K.

Zizzo, Daniel J. 2003a. Empirical Evidence on Interdependent Preferences: Nature or Nurture? *Cambridge Journal of Economics* 27 (6): 867–880.

Zizzo, Daniel J. 2003b. Money Burning and Rank Egalitarianism with Random Dictators. *Economics Letters* 81 (2): 263–266.

Zizzo, Daniel J. 2004. Inequality and Procedural Fairness in a Money Burning and Stealing Experiment. In *Research on Economic Inequality*, Vol. 11, ed. F. A. Cowell, 214–247. New York: Elsevier.

Daniel John Zizzo

PREJUDICE

Prejudice is defined as the affective or evaluative component of the tripartite attitude structure of social bias. As such, prejudice consists of the emotional reaction evoked by social group members, is informed by the cognitive component or stereotype held about the perceived social group, and predicts the discrimination or behavior exhibited toward the group members. Prejudice as a concept has interested social scientists since World War II (1939–1945). The Holocaust drove a number of Jewish psychologists from Europe to the United States, where they initiated relevant research on conformity, obedience, aggression, and prejudice.

Prejudice initially had been considered simple animosity or negative affect toward out-groups. However, beginning with Gordon Allport's *The Nature of Prejudice* (1954), social scientists began to analyze the psychological construct in a more nuanced, differentiated manner. As a result, prejudice is now viewed as more than simple animosity. Led by Allport's influential work, social psychologists in the late 1990s and early 2000s posited various intergroup emotion models to predict the types of prejudice elicited by different types of out-groups. These theories borrowed from work across the social sciences, including political science, economics, and evolutionary psychology. The gist of the models was that when we encounter an out-group member, an initial threat appraisal is based on his or her perceived social category. For instance, Susan Fiske and colleagues' Stereotype Content Model argues that the interaction of perceived warmth (good or ill intention) and competence (ability to enact the intention) predict four types of emotional prejudices evoked by the out-group member. These models therefore allow for ambivalent emotions (e.g., pity, envy) beyond a simple like-dislike (e.g., pride, contempt) dimension, and, as a result, have allowed the landscape of prejudice to become much more detailed and comprehensive.

PREJUDICE AS A DUAL-PROCESS ATTITUDE

Prejudice occupies a dual-process model of attitude processes. Attitudes comprise the evaluations of attitude-objects, and research in the 1990s unearthed the central insight that attitudes include both an explicit and implicit component. The explicit component is the easily self-reported attitude in conscious awareness. The implicit component is often hidden from our consciousness, but does inform unintentional responses to out-groups. Moreover, the implicit attitude results from learned associations picked up from social environments. Prejudice is therefore thought to have an implicit and explicit component.

A dispute followed the adoption of this dual-process framework, and the field of prejudice serves as a primary battleground. The conflict involves whether one's implicit attitude is really an attitude, and if it is, is it the same as one's explicit attitude? For instance, one may hold egalitarian beliefs about social groups and as a result, not report any prejudiced feelings toward a certain social group. However, one's implicit attitude is informed by the society one inhabits, and a stronger association between a group and negativity may lie deep in one's unconscious. Hence, even though one does not explicitly hold any prejudiced attitudes, one's implicit beliefs may contradict this position.

Nevertheless, prejudice continues to be conceived in lay terms as simple animosity—a conception that makes it a taboo topic. The advent of the civil rights movement of the 1960s changed the social norm against prejudice, and expressing overtly prejudiced attitudes slowly became unacceptable, particularly to members of minority racial and ethnic groups. This norm change did not eliminate these prejudices, however; to the contrary: Institutional imbalances alone point to continued bias. Instead, social scientists argued that prejudiced attitudes are now more often held implicitly, adding more fire to the dual-process debate.

MEASUREMENT

This antiprejudice social norm's demands persist today, preventing social science researchers from measuring prejudice simply by self-report. As a result, researchers tend to use subtle, indirect measures. For instance, instruments such as David Sears's and John McConahay's Modern Racism Scale assesses prejudiced attitudes toward black Americans via indirect questions that ask participants to make judgments about concerns related to disadvantaged minorities. The scale also has a component that measures traditional, "old-fashioned" blatant prejudice, as well as the modern, subtle component described above. This scale correlates with antiminority voting, among other behaviors.

Conceiving of prejudice in a dual-process framework also has led to the creation of implicit measures of prejudice. These measures test the strength of association between the attitude-object and negative constructs. The most popular such measure, the Implicit Association Test (IAT) developed by Anthony Greenwald and Mahzarin Banaji, uses reaction times to detect differences between the strength of prejudiced and unprejudiced associations. The test asks participants to categorize a prompt (either a word or a picture of a face) in the middle of a computer screen to either the left or the right category. In some trials one side is positive valence, the other negative, and in others, one represents a social category (black people) and the other another (white people). After several trials, valence and social category are both represented on either side (white-positive on one, black-negative on the other side) and the speed of categorization is assessed. These congruent trials are subtracted from incongruent trials where the opposite pairings are represented. A resulting faster time categorizing white-positive and black-negative pairings indicates that the association between the opposite pairings is more difficult for participants to make and thus, people show an implicit association, for example, between black and bad, white and good. The score on the IAT predicts a number of related phenomena such as nonverbal behavior in an interracial interaction, discrimination against out-groups, location on a liberal-conservative continuum, support for antidiscrimination policies such

as affirmative action, and even neural activity in brain regions associated with negative affect (disgust and fear in particular).

NEURAL COMPONENTS OF PREJUDICE

Developments in technology and in social neuroscience have illuminated the neural underpinnings of prejudice. Both white and black participants have viewed white and black faces while their neural activity was recorded using functional Magnetic Resonance Imaging (fMRI). Participants across a number of studies consistently show greater brain activity in structures associated with emotional vigilance (amygdala) and disgust (insula) when viewing unfamiliar black faces than when viewing unfamiliar white faces (although the effect is always smaller for the black participants). Further, the amount of participants' brain activity correlated with their scores on the IAT. These fMRI studies support the idea that prejudice may result in part from social learning, both because an IAT score indicates knowledge of the negative stereo-types about the social group, and because blacks also show the effect.

Social context can reduce this neural activity simply by changing the social goal of the participants. When forced to think of people as individuals, not just category members, the increased activation in the amygdala provoked by viewing black faces diminishes below significance. Converging evidence also comes from electroencephalography (EEG). This technique likewise measures brain activity, but by detecting small electrical signals produced by neural cells as they fire. These studies also demonstrate that once the social goals change, social processing changes within 200 milliseconds. Changed social goals carry over even to subsequent nonsocial tasks, as whites' efforts to appear unprejudiced cost them executive control in purely cognitive tasks.

REDUCTION OF PREJUDICE

Other than changing social goals, a few strategies reduce or eliminate prejudice, with varying degrees of success. The most successful, and ironically the most heavily debated, is the intergroup contact hypothesis proposed by Allport. According to the hypothesis, because social learning of stereotypes influences prejudice, contact with out-group members will eliminate the category-based dependence on stereotypes for information; instead, information will result from the nuanced interaction itself. The contact hypothesis utilizes potential friendship to diminish the limited, categorical perception of the out-group member based on stereotypes and replace it with a more nuanced, individuated perception. However, contact works to reduce prejudice under only certain conditions—cooperation rather than competition, equal status in the social interaction, authority endorsement, and meaningful interactions.

PREJUDICE AS AN INDIVIDUAL DIFFERENCE

Certain individual differences make one more likely to hold prejudiced attitudes than not. Political ideologies, particularly right-wing authoritarian (RWA) beliefs, predict explicit levels of prejudice. An authoritarian individual demonstrates conformity to convention, authority-sanctioned aggression against deviants, and submission to authorities. Additionally, dominance-oriented personalities also tend to be more likely to hold prejudiced beliefs because they endorse the inevitability of group hierarchy. In this view, societies minimize group conflict by promoting ideologies that endorse discrimination and the dominant social hierarchy. Essentially, social dominance orientation prefers hierarchy over equality and dominance over parity. As a result, scales that measure these two constructs have also been used as indicators of prejudice. Prejudice level therefore can be predicted by political ideologies.

BIBLIOGRAPHY

Allport, Gordon. 1954. *The Nature of Prejudice*. Reading, MA: Addison-Wesley.

Banaji, Mahzarin, and Anthony Greenwald. 1994. Implicit Stereotyping and Prejudice. In *The Psychology of Prejudice: The Ontario Symposium*, vol. 7, ed. Mark P. Zanna and James M. Olson, 55–76. Hillsdale, NJ: Lawrence Erlbaum.

Fiske, Susan T., Amy J. Cuddy, Peter Glick, and Jun Xu, Jun. 2002. A Model of (often mixed) Stereotype Content: Competence and Warmth Respectively Follow from Perceived Status and Competition. *Journal of Personality and Social Psychology* 82: 878–902.

Sears, David. 1998. Symbolic Racism. In *Eliminating Racism: Profiles in Controversy*, ed. Phyllis A. Katz and Dalmas A. Taylor, 53–84. New York: Plenum.

Tajfel, Henri. 1981. *Human Groups and Social Categories*. New York: Cambridge University Press.

Lasana T. Harris
Susan T. Fiske

PREMIUM, LIQUIDITY

SEE *Liquidity Premium*.

PRESENT ORIENTATION

SEE *Time Orientation*.

PRESIDENCY, THE

The presidency of the United States is one of the truly original creations of democratic politics. When the framers of the U.S. Constitution decided upon a democratically elected unitary executive, they did so without any contemporaneous referents. While many of the authors favored the creation of a president that was little more than chief ambassador and head bookkeeper, others had witnessed the chaos under the weak executive of the Articles of Confederation and felt that stronger leadership was necessary. The final result is an institution that represents the attempt to balance the desire for a strong leader while avoiding the pitfalls of monarchy or tyranny.

BECOMING PRESIDENT

The constitutional requirements for becoming president are relatively straightforward. All candidates for the office must be natural-born residents of the United States of at least thirty-five years of age. Rather than using a process of direct election, the authors of the Constitution opted for a process of indirect election. In this process, the voting public selects members of the Electoral College, and the Electoral College selects the president. Since the members of the Electoral College are selected by each state in a winner-take-all system, it is possible for a presidential candidate to win a majority in the Electoral College without receiving the most popular votes nationwide. This occurred in the elections of 1824, 1876, 1888, and 2000.

CONSTITUTIONAL POWERS OF THE PRESIDENT

The constitutional powers of the president fall into four general categories: military, executive, diplomatic, and legislative. Within each category, the relative lack of specificity in the language has offered presidents some measure of flexibility to expand these powers when it suited their political or institutional needs.

The president's military power resides in Article II Section 2, where the office is clearly designated as "the commander in chief of the Army and Navy of the United States." The president has consistently been assumed to be the highest-ranking military official in the nation. While presidents may choose to delegate these powers to military officials in times of conflict, the president is entrusted with the final authority in the realm of military decisions, including the use of nuclear weapons.

The presidential executive powers address the president's responsibility as the individual most responsible for overseeing the execution of federal law. Through this authority, the president oversees nearly all parts of the federal bureaucracy and is ultimately responsible for how these bureaucratic agencies apply the laws passed by

Congress. The president is also granted the authority to appoint, with the approval of the Senate, members of the cabinet, federal judges, ambassadors, and most high-ranking administrative officials.

As the head of the Executive Branch, the president has the power to execute *executive orders*. These directives inform officials in the executive branch of the president's desired policy implementation. Since the executive branch encompasses the vast majority of the federal bureaucracy, the president can use executive orders to cover a wide array of policy goals. Presidents have utilized executive orders to intern Japanese-Americans during World War II (Order 9066), prohibit employment discrimination based on race or gender (Order 11246), and to create new agencies, such as the Federal Emergency Management Agency (Order 12148). Given the strength of presidential authority, the president's power to mold policy through executive orders is clearly wide-ranging.

No formal review process exists for executive orders. Congress can pass laws that overturn executive orders, but since the president is virtually certain to veto such an act, Congress must gather enough votes to override a presidential veto in order to invalidate an executive order. Congress may also refuse to fund the section of the executive branch impacted by an executive order, though this also makes a veto more likely. Therefore, Congress rarely interferes with executive orders.

Although theoretically subject to review by the federal courts, the judiciary has overturned only two of the more than 13,000 executive orders issued by the office of the president since the Lincoln administration. Both rejections were grounded in the contention that the particular orders created new laws rather than modifying existing laws.

The power of the president in the area of foreign affairs clearly places the president at the forefront of the diplomatic apparatus. The president is specifically given the authority to receive all ambassadors and ministers from other nations. The president is also given the authority to negotiate and sign treaties with foreign nations pending Senate approval and to appoint ambassadors and other personnel to represent the interests of the United States abroad.

While the president's powers in the legislative arena are somewhat limited, those limitations are as much in the eye of the beholder as anything. The president has veto authority, which gives him the power to prevent legislation from Congress from becoming law. While Congress has the power to override presidential vetoes, the supermajority needed for a successful override gives the president a significant advantage. In addition to the power to veto legislation, the president can call Congress into special session as deemed necessary. While he is required to inform Congress about the state of the union "from time to time," he can use that event to recommend legislation to Congress that he believes to be necessary and appropriate.

THE SCOPE OF PRESIDENTIAL POWERS

In many ways, the power of the office of the presidency is shaped not by the Constitution, but by the individual. The remarkable specificity invested in the discussion of Congressional powers in Article I stands in stark contrast to the vague comments regarding presidential power in Article II (Pious 1979). While the authors of the Constitution had some general ideas of what they wanted the office to include, the relative lack of clarity has allowed occupants of the office to mold it to their own needs and desires.

The lack of clear direction regarding presidential power from the Constitution has allowed for varying interpretations of the extent of presidential authority. Throughout the nineteenth century, the assumption was that the president was limited to the powers expressly granted under the Constitution. This limited view of presidential power is generally referred to as the *Whig theory* of presidential authority. Presidents that subscribed to the Whig theory saw themselves primarily as bureaucratic administrators and ambassadors. As President James Buchanan (1791–1868) noted, "My duty is to execute the laws … and not my individual opinions" (quoted in Brinkley 1962, p.142).

Eventually, the Whig theory was deemed to be too limited and fell out of fashion at the beginning of the twentieth century. The replacement was Theodore Roosevelt's (1858–1919) much broader *stewardship theory*. Stewardship theory argues that presidential authority extends to all areas not specifically forbidden by the Constitution or statutory law. While the Whig theory saw the president as limited to the powers clearly expressed in the Constitution, stewardship theory looks for all possible outlets for presidential power and authority. Stewardship theory has remained the dominant approach to presidential authority since the presidency of Franklin Roosevelt (1882–1945).

The third theory of presidential power, the *unitary executive* theory, argues that *all* power to execute laws and manage the executive branch falls to the president. This theory, which has generated much controversy in the first decade of the twenty-first century, essentially argues that Congress passes laws but the executive branch can interpret the laws in terms of implementation. This has led to presidents issuing "signing statements" that indicate whether or not the president intends to enforce the law as Congress had it written. The unitary executive theory is seen by many critics as a violation of the separation of powers and an effort by the executive to supersede Congressional authority.

PRESIDENTIAL-CONGRESSIONAL RELATIONSHIPS

The nature of the relationship between the president and Congress is determined by several factors. The most important factor is the relative partisan control of each branch. When the majority in Congress is of the same party as the president (called *unified government*), the president is often able to work with the leadership to achieve their common policy goals. When the president and at least one chamber are controlled by opposing parties (often called *divided government*), presidents are often forced to compromise with the opposition party in order to pass legislation. The common perception is that presidents and Congress accomplish more under unified government compared to divided government, but the evidence indicates that this is likely not the case (Peterson 1990).

In addition to majority-minority status, the second major factor in determining presidential relations with Congress is the president's approval rating in the public. The more beloved the president is, the more likely Congress is to follow the president's lead. Congressional leaders realize that a popular president can campaign for or against them in any given election, and the president's popularity does have an impact on Congressional races. Conversely, an unpopular president can often find it difficult to move even small agenda items forward even under a unified government (Neustadt 1991).

In the era of broadcast media, presidents have often found it effective to use the public to generate pressure on Congress to pass a particular piece of legislation. This strategy, known as *going public*, is often used when presidents feel they need to exert external pressure on Congress to generate momentum (Kernell 2007). While these efforts do not always work, they give the president an additional, if unofficial, method to encourage Congressional action.

PRESIDENTIAL-JUDICIAL RELATIONSHIPS

As a general rule, presidents and the judicial branch do not interact on a regular basis. The most common ground they cover is actually in the process of selecting new members of the judiciary. Presidents have the authority to nominate all judges in the federal judicial system subject to the confirmation of the Senate. Presidents generally use this power to nominate judges with political beliefs similar to their own. Research shows that it is common for well over 90 percent of a president's judicial appointments to come from the same party as the president, and this becomes more relevant if the nomination involves an appellate court or the U.S. Supreme Court.

SEE ALSO *Bush, George H. W.; Bush, George W.; Carter, Jimmy; Clinton, Bill; Congress, U.S.; Constitution, U.S.; Eisenhower, Dwight D.; Elections; Electoral College; Government; Grant, Ulysses S.; Jefferson, Thomas; Johnson, Lyndon B.; Judicial Review; Judiciary; Kennedy, John F.; Lincoln, Abraham; Madison, James; Media; Nixon, Richard M.; Reagan, Ronald; Roosevelt, Franklin D.; Separation of Powers; Truman, Harry S.; Voting; Washington, George; Wilson, Woodrow*

BIBLIOGRAPHY

Bond, Jon R., and Richard Fleisher. 1990. *The President in the Legislative Arena.* Chicago: University of Chicago Press.

Brinkley, Wilfred. 1962. *President and Congress.* 3rd ed. New York: Vintage.

Corwin, Edward. 1976. *Presidential Power and the Constitution: Essays.* Ithaca, NY: Cornell University Press.

Kernell, Samuel. 2007. *Going Public: New Strategies of Presidential Leadership.* 4th ed. Washington, DC: CQ Press.

Nelson, Michael, ed. 2006. *The Presidency and the Political System.* 8th ed. Washington, DC: CQ Press.

Neustadt, Richard. 1991. *Presidential Power and the Modern Presidents: The Politics of Leadership from Roosevelt to Reagan.* New York: Free Press.

Peterson, Mark. 1990. *Legislating Together: The White House and Capitol Hill From Eisenhower to Reagan.* Cambridge, MA: Harvard University Press.

Pious, Richard. 1979. *The American Presidency.* New York: Basic Books.

Rossiter, Clinton. 1960. *The American Presidency.* 2nd ed. New York: Harcourt Brace.

Schlesinger, Arthur. 1973. *The Imperial Presidency.* Boston: Houghton Mifflin.

Geoffrey Peterson

PRESIDENT'S COMMISSION ON THE ASSASSINATION OF JOHN F. KENNEDY

SEE *Warren Report.*

PRESSURE GROUPS

Pressure groups are private organizations that attempt to influence the lawmaking process to benefit the members they represent. Though the term has been applied to corporations and nonprofit organizations engaging in advocacy, it properly refers only to organizations that represent factions of the public before government. Pressure groups form when individuals sharing some want or desire that can be realized through public policy mobilize, usually with the aide of an experienced political entrepreneur or wealthy patron. But in a highly diverse society such as the United States, it is rare that policy advancing the interests of one group can be produced without harming those of others. As lawmakers must choose between winners and losers when they divide public resources and enact regulation, pressure groups compete with each other to convince lawmakers to promote and protect their interests by offering campaign contributions and the votes of their members in elections.

The term *pressure group* is rarely used by social scientists in the early twenty-first century because how scholars view advocacy groups and lobbying has changed. It is more specific than the term *interest group* because it only conceives of groups as proactively pushing lawmakers to enact policies they desire at the expense of the electorate. This view was part of a larger belief first articulated by American behavioral scientist Arthur Bentley (1870–1957) in 1908, and which came to fruition with the behavioral revolution of the 1950s, that U.S. politics was only about competition among social factions mobilized as pressure groups. Law was simply the outcome of competition favoring the stronger group. For several reasons, however, this view declined in the late 1960s. First a major study in 1963 by Raymond Bauer and his colleagues articulated a more benign view of interest groups gaining access to lawmakers by providing services the latter required, not by pressuring them with threats of electorate reprisals. Second, in 1956 American sociologist C. Wright Mills argued that competition among advocacy groups was largely irrelevant because lawmaking was always rigged in favor of a ruling elite. Finally, in 1965 Mancur Olson demonstrated that the whole premise of many groups representing the interests of the public was untenable because the reason groups formed had little to do with any desire to influence policy.

This change from seeing groups as proactively wielding pressure also dampened an important debate among political scientists as to their importance as vehicles of representation in a democratic society. Believing the electorate to be too poorly organized and motivated to hold elected officials accountable through elections, scholars divided into two camps regarding the legitimacy of pressure groups. One, exemplified by political scientist Robert Dahl (1956), argued that groups representing minority factions were a legitimate form of representation, while the other, as described in *The Semi-Sovereign People* (1942) by E. E. Schattschneider, believed they inhibited political parties from electing slates of candidates that voters could hold responsible for the performance of government. With a decline in the belief of the real power of groups to pressure lawmakers, this debate also faded. New evidence, however, has emerged regarding how truly large and diverse the modern community of interest groups is in U.S. politics, and there is new attention in the early twenty-first century on whether groups might really be competing to shape policy. If so, it may be time to revive this debate over the role of pressure groups in democratic politics and return the term to the political lexicon.

SEE ALSO *Behaviorism; Collective Action; Dahl, Robert Alan; Interest Groups and Interests; Mills, C. Wright; Power Elite; Public Policy; Schattschneider, E. E.*

BIBLIOGRAPHY

Bauer, Raymond A., Ithiel de Sola Pool, and Lewis Anthony Dexter. 1963. *American Business and Public Policy: The Politics of Foreign Trade.* New York: Atherton Press.

Bentley, Arthur F. 1908. *The Process of Government: A Study of Social Pressures.* Chicago: University of Chicago Press.

Dahl, Robert A. 1956. *A Preface to Democratic Theory.* Chicago: University of Chicago Press.

Mills, C. Wright. 1956. *The Power Elite.* New York: Oxford University Press.

Olson, Mancur, Jr. 1965. *The Logic of Collective Action: Public Goods and the Theory of Groups.* Cambridge, MA: Harvard University Press.

Schattschneider, E. E. 1942. *Party Government.* New York: Farrar and Rinehart.

Thomas T. Holyoke

PRESTIGE

Prestige refers to a person's standing or estimation in the eyes of others. Having prestige means to be honored and respected. To understand the concept of prestige, it is useful to contrast it with other similar concepts related to the broader category of power, which refers to an individual's relative capacity to influence other people's outcomes in general.

How can prestige be differentiated from dominance, for example? Certainly, those with the power to dominate others can enjoy a kind of prestige. But definitions of prestige emphasize that we acquire prestige though our achievements, expertise, and admirable characteristics and behavior. This gives the prestigious person power, but it is usually a power to influence others through the positive emotions and attitudes elicited from them. We admire, respect, and even feel awe toward prestigious people, and these feelings are a major source of their power to influence us. In contrast, we are more likely to fear someone who is dominant.

The power inherent in the prestigious person has an earned, unforced quality. If we follow the lead of people with prestige, there is sense in which they well and truly merit their power. The honor and respect that they inspire draws us in willingly, sometimes enthusiastically. Words such as *charisma* and *hero* fit in extraordinary cases of prestige. Thus, while prestige breeds imitation and emulation, dominance creates distance and the begrudging of advantage. Prestige promotes the loving gaze; dominance, the furtive glance. Prestige produces the desire for an autograph; dominance creates resentment and unease.

Ethnographic studies show that there are also differences in how the prestigious and the dominant person behave. Despite the legitimate foundations of prestige, it does not appear to cause grandstanding and arrogance in the possessor. Rather, one sees confidence blended with self-deprecation and gratitude. Dominance, on the other had, involves swagger, implied threat at the very least, and the accentuating of superiority. Also, because prestige is earned rather than forced, the orientation of prestigious people is toward an understanding of those around them, the ones who award them prestige. Dominant people are alert to threats that forebode the taking away of their superiority and power.

All the differences between prestige and dominance hardly imply that these distinct sources of power cannot travel together. An army recruit can fear his sergeant and also respect him for the hard-earned medals. The sergeant may have no intention of striking fear in the recruit but may do so nonetheless because the capacity for punishment is inherent in the position. But that aspect of influence that flows from those hard-earned medals is different from the power that flows from holding the position itself.

It is worth emphasizing that prestige is linked to emotions, both in the person enjoying prestige and the person witnessing it in others. In evolutionary terms, these are rank-related emotions. Ranking on various characteristics is associated with access to resources that in turn lead to greater survival and reproductive success. It feels good to rank highly because one can enjoy the prestige that can come with high ranking (e.g., pride) and, correspondingly, it feels bad (e.g., shame) to have low rank. Thus, few of us are immune to the appeal of status and prestige. Most people seek the satisfactions of having prestige. And, presumably, one reason that prestigious individuals can create positive emotions in us is that they inspire us to do better ourselves.

An example of a domain in which the concept of prestige has intriguing explanatory power and where one finds considerable research focus is in marketing. This seems largely the result of the imitative, emulative poten-

tial in observing someone imbued with prestige who is also linked to products through marketing. This strategy makes good evolutionary sense, as modeling and learning from people admired for their achievements and remarkable qualities are likely to be a highly efficient way of operating. Although a typical feature of things that lead to prestige is that they are real and earned, consumer products simply linked to prestigious individuals can serve as proxies for the achievement of these features. These indicators, of course, may or may not correlate with actual characteristics in the particular case. The "status symbol" of an expensive car also driven by the rich and famous can mean actual wealth or credit card debt. The acquiring of status indicators is seductive, as it enables the apparent though often illusory achieving of prestige through short cuts. The use of the allure of prestige to affect consumers' behavior is time-honored and is the source of an oftenrepeated phrase, "conspicuous consumption," coined over a century ago by social scientist Thorstein Veblen.

It is tempting to see prestige in human groups as homologous to dominance processes in nonhumans, in which rank seems very much determined by physical power, fighting ability, and the like. However, rank in human groups is more associated with the possession of skills, expertise, and socially valued attributes. Although dominance resulting from physical power is far from irrelevant, depending on the particular culture, the ability to hold the attention of others because of earned qualities and admired attributes—the kind of things that produce prestige—is more of what leads to high rank. When Henry Kissinger noted that power is the ultimate aphrodisiac, he was not referring to the benefits, for example, of being a professional wrestler such as Gorgeous George but rather of having things relating to prestige more broadly defined. Interestingly, even Gorgeous George was a role model for Muhammad Ali, who learned some of the secrets of showmanship from this flamboyant wrestler. But Ali did not see defeating others in the boxing ring as an end in itself. He claimed that his boxing success was means to a broader goal of positive change in the world. He wanted to be a hero and inspiration for others—which indeed he was.

SEE ALSO *Ali, Muhammad (USA); Conspicuous Consumption; Culture; Distinctions, Social and Cultural; Elites; Emotion; Ethnography; Gaze, The; Hierarchy; Kissinger, Henry; Power; Shame; Social Comparison; Social Dominance Orientation; Social Influence; Veblen, Thorstein*

BIBLIOGRAPHY

Carmeli, A. Perceived External Prestige, Affective Commitment, and Citizenship Behaviors. *Organization Studies* 26 (3): 443–464.

Colarelli, S. M., and J. R. Dettmann. 2003. Intuitive Evolutionary Perspectives in Marketing Practices. *Psychology and Marketing* 20: 837–865.

Henrich, J., and F. Gil-White. 2001. The Evolution of Prestige Freely Conferred Deference as a Mechanism for Enhancing the Benefits of Cultural Transmission. *Evolution and Human Behavior* 22: 165–196.

Keltner, D., D. H. Gruenfeld, and C. Anderson. 2003. Power, Approach, and Inhibition. *Psychological Review* 110 (2): 265–284.

Solomon, M. 1999. The Value of Status and the Status of Value. In *Consumer Value: A Framework for Analysis and Research*, ed. M. B. Holbrook, 63–84. London: Routledge.

Richard Smith

PRETO

SEE *Pardo.*

PREVENTION SCIENCE

Prevention science is an area of scholarship and research in the medical and social sciences that aims to establish principles of prevention and to apply them using tested and effective prevention-intervention programs (Schinke et al. 2003). A major goal in prevention science is to identify health risks or protective factors, along with the conditions that exert beneficial or detrimental effects on health (Hawkins et al. 1992), including, for example, the factors and conditions that lead to alcohol, tobacco, or drug addiction. Thus, prevention science contributes to the design of interventions that can enhance health or reduce the risk of disease or disorders.

The concept of prevention focuses on changing naturally occurring disease-producing conditions by administering interventions early in the disease process to reduce, eliminate, or alter the events that produce diseases. Individuals or populations that experience prolonged exposure to a number of risk factors have a higher likelihood of developing a certain disease or disorder. Such individuals constitute a *high-risk group*. Strategically, interventions are implemented according to two basic approaches: (1) eliminating or reducing exposure to *risk factors*; and (2) increasing exposure to *protective factors*. The most effective prevention interventions will incorporate both strategies.

The science of prevention emphasizes rigor in the design, testing, and implementation of the most potent (or most effective) prevention interventions. The *efficacy* of an intervention refers to its potency in producing a beneficial outcome under ideal conditions. Efficacy is evaluated scientifically using randomized controlled trials. The interventions developed from such trials can be taken from laboratory to community to test the intervention's real-world effect. Randomized controlled trials examine the effect of a new intervention program when administered to an intervention group (the group that receives the improved or enhanced intervention) relative to a control group (the group that receives the standard or unimproved intervention). Under this design, researchers look for the occurrence of a greater or more beneficial posttest outcome in the intervention group as compared to the control group.

AREAS OF EMPHASIS

Prevention science focuses on the application of the principles of prevention in several areas. These areas include: (1) programs to reduce aggressive behavior in children and adolescents; (2) substance-abuse prevention programs that include teaching life skills or changing social norms; (3) community-level interventions to change laws or social ordinances to enhance public health, such as ordinances that require the use of seat belts; (4) scientific studies to test the effectiveness of prevention interventions using rigorous standards of evidence (Flay et al. 2005); and (5) various studies that generate new knowledge that adds to established principles of prevention and guides the application of these principles.

COMMUNITY PARTNERSHIPS

An important aspect of prevention science involves establishing working partnerships between prevention scientists and community members. Partners may include community members who can be described as *stakeholders*, or persons who have something to gain or lose from the implementation of a proposed community-based program. For example, a program that aims to reduce automobile accidents resulting from alcohol intoxication among adolescent drivers may encompass such stakeholders as parents, liquor-store owners, high school teachers, and other concerned individuals or groups within the community. Community partnerships, when well developed, set the stage for community input in the development of new prevention interventions. Such partnerships also promote community "buy in," or a sense of local ownership that allows a prevention program to thrive within a community.

CONTEMPORARY ISSUES

The field of prevention science faces a number of challenging issues. One important issue involves finding ways to design programs that work with greater potency, that is, programs that can increase the size of the prevention effect and the magnitude of healthy change. For example, how much can a program reduce the rate of smoking among adolescents who initiate or experiment with cigarette smoking? The more potent a program, the greater the *effect size*. Even the most effective community-based prevention programs generally exhibit only a small effect size, that is, they produce a small degree of change on specific outcome measures, such as a drop in the smoking rate among adolescents. Accordingly, one challenge facing prevention science involves increasing a prevention program's magnitude of effect.

Another issue involves the *fidelity-adaptation* controversy. Tested and effective prevention programs are generally organized into instructional manuals that provide program-delivery personnel with information and a set of activities for program sessions. Such prevention-intervention programs, when delivered exactly as prescribed within program manuals, are considered to be implemented with high *fidelity*. This approach contrasts with the challenge of program *adaptation*, which involves changing or otherwise adjusting certain aspects of a tested and effective program with specific and well-planned modifications that are necessary to make the program relevant and viable when delivered within a community (Castro et al. 2004).

Another challenge involves identifying ways in which prevention-intervention programs can be delivered broadly in several sites. A related issue involves *sustainability*, that is, identifying ways of keeping a prevention program in operation into the future by convincing a community group or coalition to adopt the program as their own and to maintain the program in operation. These prevention-science challenges serve as important areas for research and program development.

POLICY-ORIENTED ISSUES

Social policy involves the development of guidelines that govern the decision-making process used by lawmakers, administrators, civic leaders, and others as they work to solve social problems. Prevention science can inform policymakers with scientific information and evidence-based knowledge to help them make better decisions in the interest of promoting public health. Thus, prevention science can contribute to social policy by: (1) informing policymakers on theories of human behavior and on ways to prevent disease and promote health; and (2) offering tested and effective intervention techniques and programs that can improve health in specific ways.

On a larger community or regional scale, however, such principles cannot be fully implemented without the support of local policymakers. The development of legislation and local ordinances can endorse, institutionalize,

and maintain local prevention intervention programs, including, for example, ordinances prohibiting smoking in restaurants or the mandatory use of seatbelts while driving. These are examples of the contributions of prevention science to policy-related actions; in turn, social policy can aid in the implementation of prevention-science programs within diverse sectors of the community.

FUTURE ISSUES

Future challenges facing prevention science involve finding ways to design prevention programs that are more accessible, and thus more likely to be adopted and used by greater numbers of consumers. Prevention programs must also be user-friendly and widely available at an affordable cost, and they must allow consumer feedback to constantly monitor and improve the programs and keep them relevant to changing community needs. Moreover, making prevention programs more potent, whereby they produce greater and more enduring changes on targeted outcomes, remains a major challenge for prevention science. The use of new technologies and new forms of responsiveness to diverse cultural and economic consumer groups will aid in making prevention science and its interventions more socially relevant and more effective.

Prevention science is the product of ongoing research that aims to discover stable and generalizable new knowledge and intervention approaches. In the United States, this ongoing scientific endeavor aims to increase the capacity of prevention science to effectively meet the complex public health needs of growing and increasingly diverse sectors of the American population.

SEE ALSO *Addiction; Disease; Occupational Hazards; Occupational Safety; Public Health; Public Policy; Risk; Smoking*

BIBLIOGRAPHY

Castro, Felipe González, Manuel Barrera, and Charles Martinez. 2004. The Cultural Adaptation of Prevention Interventions: Resolving Tensions between Fidelity and Fit. *Prevention Science* 5: 41–45.

Collins, Linda M., Susan Murphy, and Karen L. Bierman. 2004. A Conceptual Framework for Adaptive Prevention Interventions. *Prevention Science* 5: 185–196.

Flay, Brian R., Anthony Biglan, Robert Boruch, et al. 2005. Standards of Evidence: Criteria for Efficacy, Effectiveness, and Dissemination. *Prevention Science* 6: 151–175.

Hawkins, J. David, Richard F. Catalano, and James H. Miller. 1992. Risk and Protective Factors for Alcohol and Other Drug Problems in Adolescence and Early Adulthood: Implications for Substance Abuse Prevention. *Psychological Bulletin* 112: 64–105.

Kellam, Sheppard G., and Doris J. Longevin. 2003. A Framework for Understanding "Evidence" in Prevention Research Programs. *Prevention Science* 4: 137–153.

Schinke, Stephen, Paul Brounstein, and Stephen Gardner. 2003. *Science-based Prevention Programs and Principles, 2002.* DHHS Pub No. (SMA) 03–3764. Rockville, MD: U.S. Dept. of Health and Human Services.

Felipe González Castro

PRI

SEE *Partido Revolucionario Institucional.*

PRICE, SHADOW

SEE *Shadow Prices.*

PRICE CONTROLS

SEE *Inflation.*

PRICE INDICES

In 1927 Irving Fisher provided a simple definition of price indices in his classic book on index numbers, *The Making of Index Numbers: A Study of Their Varieties, Tests, and Reliability:*

> An index number of prices, then, shows the *average percentage change* of prices from one period to another. The percentage change in the price of a *single* commodity from one time to another is, of course, found by dividing its price at the second time by its price at the first time. The ratio between these two prices is called the *price relative* of that one particular commodity in relation to those two particular times. An *index number* of the prices of a *number* of commodities is an average of their price relatives (p. 3).

To begin a discussion on price indices, some notation is important: Let $p^0 = (p_1^0, \dots, p_n^0)$ be a vector of prices for n goods in period 0. Let $p^1 = (p_1^1, \dots, p_n^1)$ be a vector of prices for the same n goods in period 1. Thus, the *price relative* of any good i is p_i^1/p_i^0. A simple way of measuring the average change in all n prices from period 0 to period

1 is to take an average of the price relatives across all of the goods. For example, the arithmetic mean of the price relatives is $P_{01} = \frac{1}{n} \sum_{i=1}^{n} (p_i^1 / p_i^0)$ and the geometric mean of them is $P_{01} = \prod_{i=1}^{n} \left(p_i^1 / p_i^0 \right)^{\frac{1}{n}}$.

As noted by E. Antony Selvanathan and D. S. Prasada Rao in their book *Index Numbers: A Stochastic Approach*, these simple measures:

> tend to consider price changes for all commodities to be equally important. However, in practice, movements of prices in essential items are considered to be more important and it is expected that any meaningful price index should accord weights to different price relatives. This principle leads to a class of weighted averages, where the weights are usually based on the value shares of each commodity (1994, pp. 19–20).

SOME WELL-KNOWN PRICE INDICES

Let $q^0 = (q_1^0, \dots, q_n^0)$ and $q^1 = (q_1^1, \dots, q_n^1)$ represent quantity vectors for the n goods in periods 0 and 1 respectively. Total expenditure in the two periods is the sum (across all n goods) of the prices multiplied by the corresponding quantities: $Y^0 = \sum_{i=1}^{n} p_i^0 q_i^0$ and $Y^1 = \sum_{i=1}^{n} p_i^1 q_i^1$. Thus, the *expenditure shares* for each good i are given by $w_i^0 = p_i^0 q_i^0 / Y^0$ and $w_i^1 = p_i^1 q_i^1 / Y^1$ for periods 0 and 1 respectively.

A *price index* is a function of the price and quantity vectors in two periods, which measures the change in the prices of the n goods between them. As in the previous section, the notation, P_{01} is used to denote a price index between periods 0 and 1. A price index can be interpreted in the same way as an individual price relative. If it is greater than one, it means that prices are increasing from period 0 to 1. If it is less than one, it means that prices are decreasing. The rate of increase or decrease of an individual price can be computed by either subtracting one from the price relative, giving the growth rate $(p_i^1/p_i^0) - 1 = (p_i^1 - p_i^0)/p_i^0$, or by taking natural logarithms of the price relative, giving $\ln(p_i^1/p_i^0) = \ln(p_i^1) - \ln(p_i^0)$. Similarly, the rate of increase or decrease in the prices of all n goods can be measured as either $(P_{01} - 1)$ or $\ln(P_{01})$.

Given a price index, P_{01}, one can always define a quantity index, Q_{01}, implicitly from the following equation: $P_{01} Q_{01} = Y^1/Y^0$, which means that the product of the price and quantity indices equals the ratio of total expenditure in the two periods.

A number of well-known price indices can be obtained by taking the weighted arithmetic or geometric means of the price relatives, where the weights depend on the expenditure shares. The *Laspeyres price index*, P_{01}^L, is obtained by taking a weighted arithmetic mean of the price relatives, where the weights are the expenditure shares for period 0. As explained by Selvanathan and Rao, the *Paasche price index*, P_{01}^P, can be obtained in a similar fashion using hypothetical expenditure shares derived from period 0 prices and period 1 quantities. Although mathematically equivalent, the Laspeyres and Paasche price indices are usually defined as follows: $P_{01}^L = \dfrac{\sum_i p_i^1 q_i^0}{\sum_i p_i^0 q_i^0}$ and $P_{01}^P = \dfrac{\sum_i p_i^1 q_i^1}{\sum_i p_i^0 q_i^1}$. *Fisher's ideal price index*, P_{01}^{FI}, is the geometric mean of the Laspeyres and Paasche price indices:

$$P_{01}^{FI} = \sqrt{P_{01}^L P_{01}^P} = \sqrt{\frac{\sum_i p_i^1 q_i^0}{\sum_i p_i^0 q_i^0} \frac{\sum_i p_i^1 q_i^1}{\sum_i p_i^0 q_i^1}}.$$

The *Tornqvist-Theil price index*, P_{01}^{TT}, is the weighted geometric mean of the price relatives with weights that are the average of the expenditure shares from the two periods: $P_{01}^{TT} = \prod_{i=1}^{n} \left(p_i^1 / p_i^0 \right)^{\frac{1}{2}(w_i^0 + w_i^1)}$. An attractive property of this index is that its natural log is a weighted sum of the natural logs of the n component price relatives:

$$ln(P_{01}^{TT}) = \sum_{i=1}^{n} \tfrac{1}{2}(w_i^0 + w_i^1) \, ln(p_i^1 / p_i^0).$$

THE TRUE COST OF LIVING INDEX AND SUBSTITUTION BIAS

In his 1992 article "Economic Theory and the BEA's Alternative Quantity and Price Indexes" Jack E. Triplett discusses the connection between a price index for a set of consumer goods and services and a cost of living index:

> a consumption price index should measure the change in the cost of maintaining a fixed, or constant, standard of living. If the price index holds the standard of living constant, then any increase in per capita consumption expenditures that exceeds the increase in the price index can be interpreted as an increase in the standard of living.... Thus, from the standard-of-living orientation, the price index measures the changing cost of a constant standard of living, and the quantity index measures increases or decreases in the standard of living (p. 49).

The *true cost of living index* was originally proposed in a 1924 paper by A. A. Konüs (an English translation was published in 1939). The true cost of living index is defined as $\dfrac{e(p^1, U(q))}{e(p^0, U(q))}$. In the definition, the *expenditure function*, $e(p, u)$, gives the minimum expenditure needed to obtain a particular standard of living, u, when prices are

p. The *utility function*, $U(q)$, in turn, gives the utility, or standard of living, associated with the quantity vector, q. Thus, the true cost of living index measures the change in the minimum expenditure needed to maintain the standard of living associated with a particular vector of quantities, q, as prices change from p^0 to p^1. (See W. E. Diewert's 1981 article, "The Economic Theory of Index Numbers: A Survey," for an extensive discussion of these concepts.)

The true cost of living index can be evaluated using any quantity vector. It could, for example, be evaluated using the quantities q^0, from period 0. In the following discussion, it will be assumed that $e(p^0, U(q^0)) = \sum_{i=1}^{n} p_i^0 q_i^0$, which means that the quantities q^0 are optimal given prices p^0. It would cost $\sum_{i=1}^{n} p_i^1 q_i^0$ to purchase the same vector of quantities in period 1 and doing so would ensure that the standard of living is unchanged. If relative prices have changed, however, it may be possible to achieve the same standard of living at a lower cost by substituting away from goods whose relative prices have increased toward goods whose relative prices have decreased. This reasoning implies that $e(p^1, U(q^0)) \le \sum_{i=1}^{n} p_i^1 q_i^0$.

It follows that the Laspeyres index provides an upper bound on the true cost of living index when the standard of living is based on the quantities from period 0, since $P_{01}^L = \dfrac{\sum_i p_i^1 q_i^0}{\sum_i p_i^0 q_i^0} \ge \dfrac{e(p^1, U(q^0))}{e(p^1, U(q^0))}$. The upward bias in the Laspeyres index, relative to the true cost of living index, is a type of *substitution bias*. The same reasoning also implies that the Paasche index provides a lower bound on the true cost of living index when the standard of living is based on the period 1 quantities, since $\dfrac{e(p^1, U(q^1))}{e(p^0, U(q^1))} \ge \dfrac{\sum_i p_i^1 q_i^1}{\sum_i p_i^0 q_i^1} = P_{01}^P$.

In general the true cost of living index depends on the choice of the quantity vector, so it would not be correct to say that the true cost of living index is bounded above and below by the Laspeyres and Paasce price indices respectively, since those upper and lower bounds are based on different quantities. A stronger result can be obtained if preferences are homothetic. As explained by Angus Deaton and John Muellbauer in their 1980 book, *Economics and Consumer Behavior*, homotheticity means that for some normalization of the utility function, doubling quantities doubles utility. Under homotheticity, it can be shown that the true cost of living index does not depend on q and is, consequently, bounded above and below by the Laspeyres and Paasche price indices respectively (see Diewert 1981). Nevertheless, homotheticity is a very strong assumption, since it implies that expenditure shares of the goods are independent of the level of total expenditure, which is contradicted by most empirical evidence (see Deaton and Muellbauer 1980).

SUPERLATIVE INDEXES

In his 1976 article, "Exact and Superlative Index Numbers," Diewert provides a strong rationale for preferring certain price and quantity indices, which he termed *superlative indexes*. The Tornqvist-Theil price index and Fisher's ideal price index are both superlative. Without going into precise technical details, essentially a price index is superlative if it can provide a good approximation to the true cost of living index even though the functional form of the expenditure function is not known (see Diewert's 1976 and 1981 articles for further discussion, including the role of homotheticity in the theory of superlative indices).

The Laspeyres and Paasche price indices are not superlative, because they just measure the change in the cost of purchasing a fixed bundle of goods and, therefore, ignore substitution. As explained by Triplett:

> Diewert showed that the Fisher Ideal index and the Tornqvist index are theoretically better measures of the cost of living than the traditional fixed-weighted Paasche or Laspeyres indexes. The superlative indexes accommodate substitution in consumer spending while holding living standards constant, something the Paasche and Laspeyres

indexes do not do. From the view of theory, the Fisher Ideal formula and the Tornqvist formula are equally good; therefore, one can choose between the two on pragmatic grounds (1992, p. 50).

In fact, there are many other superlative indices besides the two that have been discussed.

The influential 1996 Boskin Commission report, *Toward a More Accurate Measure of the Cost of Living*, concluded that the consumer price index (CPI) overstated inflation in the United States by 1.1 percent per year in 1995–1996. The report further concluded that 0.4 percent of that bias could be attributed to upper and lower level substitution. The remainder of the bias was mostly attributed to quality change and new products. Robert J. Gordon, in his 2000 paper, "The Boskin Commission Report and Its Aftermath," states:

> It is noteworthy that few if any criticisms addressed the Commission's basic recommendations that the CPI should become a COL [cost of living] index and that substitution at both the upper and lower level should be addressed within the framework of superlative index numbers (2000, p. 24).

CHAIN-WEIGHTING

Suppose there is price and quantity data for many periods denoted by p_t and q_t, where $t = 0, 1, \ldots, T$ (for example, suppose there is annual data for twenty years). One can then compute price indexes from each period to the suc-

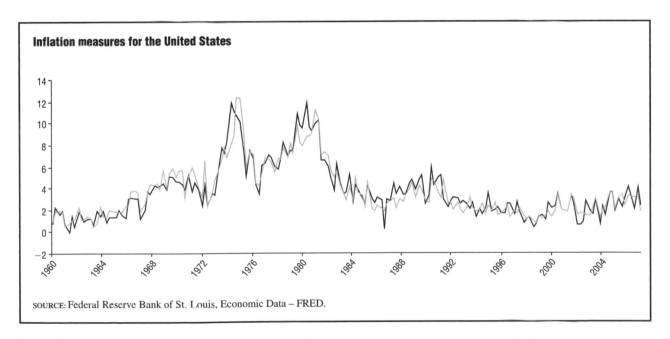

Inflation measures for the United States

SOURCE: Federal Reserve Bank of St. Louis, Economic Data – FRED.

Figure 1

cessive one, $P_{t-1,\,t}$, for all t. A time series covering more than two periods can be produced using the concept of *chain-weighting*. A chain-weighted time series can be constructed as follows: The value of the series, I_t, for any period t is the previous value of the series, I_{t-1}, multiplied by the corresponding price index for the two periods, so that $I_t = I_{t-1}P_{t-1,\,t}$ for all t. Thus, the growth rate of a chain-weighted index between adjacent periods is $(I_t - I_{t-1})/I_{t-1} = P_{t-1,\,t} - 1$. Any price index formula can be chain-weighted, although a superlative formula is preferable as previously discussed.

The Bureau of Economic Analysis (BEA) produces chain-type price indices for Personal Consumption Expenditures (PCE) and for Gross Domestic Product (GDP) for the United States, which are based on Fisher's ideal formula (see *A Guide to the National Income and Product Accounts of the United States* published by BEA in 2006). See Triplett's 1992 article, as well as Allan H. Young's "Alternative Measures of Change in Real Output and Prices, Quarterly Estimates for 1959–92" (1993) for related discussion including alternatives to chain-weighting.

EMPIRICAL ILLUSTRATION

In this section, the use of price indices to measure inflation is illustrated. Annualized quarterly percentage changes in the chain-type price indices for PCE and GDP for the United States were calculated using data from 1960Q1 to 2006Q3. These two inflation measures are graphed in Figure 1 (PCE is black and GDP is grey).

These measures indicate that inflation was relatively low and stable in the early 1960s, but was higher in the mid to late 1960s. In the 1970s inflation was higher and more volatile and, in particular, oil shocks in 1973 and 1974 and 1979 and 1980 were associated with high rates of inflation. Inflation declined in the early 1980s and has been relatively low and stable in the 1990s and beyond.

SEE ALSO *Wholesale Price Index*

BIBLIOGRAPHY

Boskin, Michael J., Ellen R. Dulberger, Robert J. Gordon, et al. 1996. *Toward a More Accurate Measure of the Cost of Living.* Final Report to the Senate Finance Committee from the Advisory Commission to Study the Consumer Price Index.

Bureau of Economic Analysis. *A Guide to the National Income and Product Accounts,* September 2006. http://bea.gov/bea/mp.htm.

Deaton, Angus, and John Muellbauer. 1980. *Economics and Consumer Behavior.* Cambridge, U.K.: Cambridge University Press.

Diewert, W. E. 1976. Exact and Superlative Index Numbers. *Journal of Econometrics* 4 (2): 115–145.

Diewert, W. E. 1981. The Economic Theory of Index Numbers: A Survey. In *Essays in the Theory and Measurement of*

Consumer Behaviour in Honour of Sir Richard Stone, ed. Angus Deaton, 163–208. Cambridge, U.K.: Cambridge University Press.

Fisher, Irving. 1927. *The Making of Index Numbers: A Study of Their Varieties, Tests, and Reliability.* Boston: Houghton Mifflin.

Gordon, Robert J. 2000. *The Boskin Commission Report and Its Aftermath.* NBER Working Paper 7759.

Konüs, A. A. 1939. The Problem of the True Cost of Living. *Econometrica* 7: 10–29.

Selvanathan, E. Antony, and D. S. Prasada Rao. 1994. *Index Numbers: A Stochastic Approach.* Ann Arbor: University of Michigan Press.

Triplett, Jack E. 1992. Economic Theory and the BEA's Alternative Quantity and Price Indexes. *Survey of Current Business* 72 (April): 48–52.

Young, Allan H. 1993. Alternative Measures of Change in Real Output and Prices, Quarterly Estimates for 1959–92. *Survey of Current Business* (March): 31–41.

Barry Jones

PRICE SETTING AND PRICE TAKING

The determination of prices in different markets is usually characterized by two opposing strategies: *price taking* and *price setting.*

PRICE-TAKING STRATEGY

In this theoretical situation, which characterizes the limiting case of "pure competition," market price is determined by the confrontation of a supply curve and a demand curve. With the usual assumption that the supply curve is increasing and the demand price is decreasing, there exists generally one intersection point. Other assumptions are that this intersection point is unique and stable, stability being warranted by adjustment processes, *tâtonnement,* which will lead to convergence on the equilibrium position. Here, the equilibrium point is unambiguously associated with the position where supply equals demand at price p^*.

The equilibrium price is determined at the intersection of the supply curve and the demand curve (see Figure 1 left); this price is "given" to the firm (see Figure 1 right), which appears as the *price taker.* The firm's production level will be determined at the intersection of this given price and its own marginal cost curve: the firm's profit is maximized at the intersection, since the marginal cost equals the marginal revenue. Producing more would be inefficient, since the marginal cost will exceed the price; producing less would mean that the marginal cost is less than the price, and profit may be increased by increasing

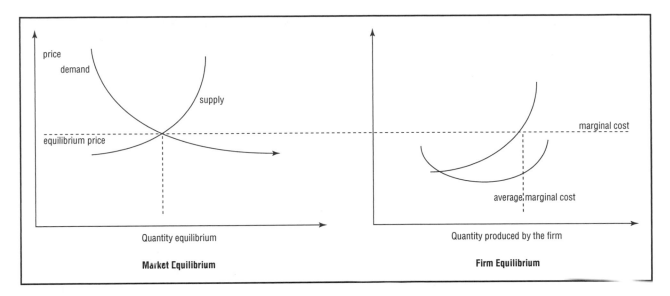

Figure 1

the production level. The individual firm makes a profit, since the price is superior to the average cost, and the total profit is obtained by multiplying the unit profit by the quantity produced.

In the conventional narrative, under long adjustment, new firms will appear in this market. The presence of positive profits induces new firms to enter. Hence, adjustment will be characterized by an increase in supply and a decrease in the market price, which will eliminate profit-making firms. Eventually, the market price level will coincide with the minimum average cost curve of the firm.

This price system plays an essential role in the information and regulation of general activity for producers and consumers. Equilibrium prices are scarcity indicators. Utility maximization implies that the market price represents the marginal value of the last dollar spent by consumers on the considered commodity. But the market equilibrium price also will represent production conditions, since the supply curve is derived from aggregation of the individual firm's marginal cost curves.

PRICE-SETTING STRATEGIES

Producers are generally able to fix, or *set*, their output price by taking into account quantities demanded by consumers.

Monopoly A monopolistic firm provides the whole product for the relevant market. The firm's demand and the market's demand are the same; hence, product demand, for which the firm is the only supplier, is a decreasing function of price. A monopoly will then maximize profit when it sets its level of output such that marginal cost is

equal to marginal revenue. Given the profit-maximizing level of output, the monopolist then uses the demand curve to find the highest price that consumers are willing and able to pay for the profit-maximizing level of output. Consequently, in this case, quantity and price are determined simultaneously.

With the assumption of linearity of average and marginal receipt, representation is simple, as indicated in Figure 2.

More complicated strategies can be taken into account. In some cases, a monopoly may try, for instance, to maximize its turnover, which will be realized when marginal revenue equals zero, determining quantity and

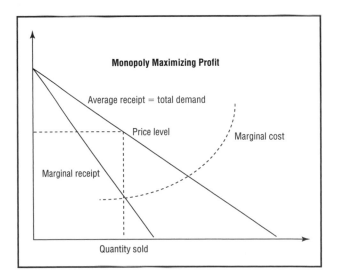

Figure 2

price. In another case, a monopoly will try to get balanced accounts—that is, zero profit—which will be realized when average cost equals average revenue. Such strategies obviously lead to more production, and can appear when a monopolist tries to avoid the "entry" of competitors.

Lastly, a monopolist may engage in *marginal cost pricing*, a strategy frequently used by publicly owned enterprises that guarantees optimal use of economic resources. The relevant level of production corresponds to equality of marginal cost and marginal revenue. Such a strategy, which appears as "optimal," may imply deficits; consequently, economists have come to "second-best" solutions. Discrimination between different types of consumers or markets also can occur. Elasticity of demand is to be taken into account in price-setting strategies.

Monopsony In the symmetrical situation of a monopsony, a large number of suppliers of a homogeneous product or service face a unique buyer. The monopsony average unit curve is represented by the supplier's curve. The monopsony's marginal cost increases with quantity, and is situated above the average cost curve. With the simplified assumption that the monopsony sells its product at a fixed price, maximization of profits will be realized when the firm buys a quantity of raw materials (or labor services), q_M, such that the value of its marginal product is equal to its marginal cost.

The purchase price paid to sellers, p_P, will correspond to this quantity on the supply curve of the product. The monopsony will set the selling price on the product market, p_S, at the point of the monopsony's average receipt corresponding to the quantity sold (in this simplified case, no transformation of the product is taken into account); the profit unit is the difference between the "purchase price," p_P and the "selling price," p_S.

Monopolistic Competition Monopolistic competition is a market structure characterized by a mixture of perfect competition and monopoly. There are a multiplicity of sellers, but each firm produces a unique product, although it is a product that is similar to those of other firms within the industrial group. So-called fast-food franchises, for example, are usually considered monopolistically competitive firms. As such, McDonald's Big Mac hamburger is considered different from, but substitutable for, Burger King's Whopper or Wendy's Single. Or, more broadly, these different burgers are also competitive substitutes for KFC's original fried chicken or Long John Silver's fish and chips. Each producer then faces a downward-sloping demand curve that is affected by the decisions of both its competitors and its consumers. An increase in the number of sellers or a decrease in attractiveness of its products mean a reduction in demand for a monopolistically competitive firm. It will sell less at all available prices. An increase in its own price means a reduction in the quantity demanded.

Similar to a monopoly, in the short run, a monopolistically competitive firm will maximize profit at the level of production such that marginal cost equals marginal revenue and the output price is consistent with consumer demand. However, if economic profits exist, this is an unstable situation; new competitors will progressively appear, which will decrease the firm's receipts. The firm's demand curve will progressively shift to the left until it is tangent to the average cost curve, a situation where the price will be set with zero profit. Further decrease in demand will lead to a new shift of the demand curve to the left, and the firm will disappear, since there is no further production level that will allow profitability.

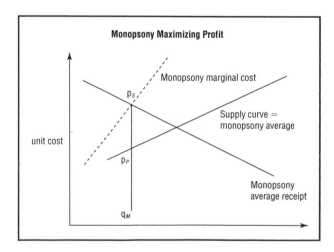

Monopsony Maximizing Profit

Figure 3

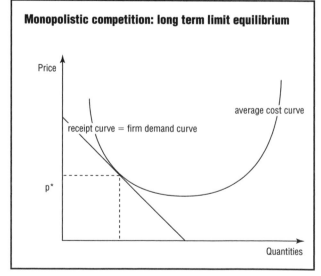

Monopolistic competition: long term limit equilibrium

Figure 4

Duopoly and Oligopoly In a duopoly or oligopoly, price setting by one competitor generally leads to price wars with fatal outcomes. Of course, it is always possible that firm *A* draws customers from firm *B* by a price decrease. But since it is also possible for *B* to do the same, the only outcome, if a price war breaks out, is perfect competition equilibrium with price being equal to marginal cost, leading to ruin for one of the competitors. So price setting is generally not the solution, except when agreements between firms lead to a situation close to a monopoly. Such situations are common, and have developed among such firms as Boeing and Airbus, Pepsi and Coca-Cola, and Ford, General Motors, and Toyota.

The only strategy left, if one excludes agreements, collusion, and various nonmarket arrangements, is a determination of quantity produced by one or more competitors, the same price being settled by all. Such a situation will be stable or unstable, according to the behavior of competitors (i.e., their aggressiveness).

It must be recognized that in many industries, firms sell very similar, nonidentical products. In such markets, it is equally easy to represent firms as price choosers or quantity choosers.

BIBLIOGRAPHY

Chamberlin, Edward H. 1962. *The Theory of Monopolistic Competition: A Re-orientation of the Theory of Value.* 8th ed. Cambridge, MA: Harvard University Press.

Cournot, A. A. [1838] 1929. *Researches into the Mathematical Principles of the Theory of Wealth.* Trans. Nathaniel T. Bacon. New York: Macmillan.

Henderson, James M., and Richard E. Quandt. 1971. *Microeconomic Theory: A Mathematical Approach.* 2nd ed. New York: McGraw-Hill.

Robinson, Joan. 1933. *The Economics of Imperfect Competition.* London: Macmillan.

Samuelson, Paul A., and William D. Nordhaus. 1998. *Economics.* 16th ed. Boston: McGraw-Hill.

Gilbert Abraham-Frois

PRICE VS. QUANTITY ADJUSTMENT

The phrase *price vs. quantity adjustment* refers to the debate over the way in which the economy adjusts over the business cycle. Neoclassical economics claims that the price mechanism (prices, wages, and interest rates) is the most important adjustment mechanism in the economy, whereas Keynesians believe that the quantity of output

and employment are the primary forces of adjustment during the business cycle, and that downward price and wage flexibility in fact tends to make things worse.

The neoclassical view claims that under conditions of perfect competition, the economy is self-correcting and therefore would not require government intervention. When labor supply exceeds labor demand, competitive pressures would compel job-seekers to accept lower wages, which would encourage firms to hire more workers, thus increasing aggregate output and employment. If the newly produced output is entirely purchased by the newly hired workers, then workers' savings would be equal to zero and the labor market would converge to full employment. However, under a more likely scenario, workers would save a portion of their income, which creates a potential problem for the self-adjusting mechanism of the market. The dual nature of saving means that on the one hand, from the workers' perspective, saving is income not spent and is therefore a benign if not a desirable decision. On the other hand, from the firms' perspective, saving is the equivalent of production not purchased. This problem, however, is dealt with in the loanable funds market. For neoclassical theory, the increased amount of savings would create an excess supply of savings relative to the demand for investment, thus driving down the interest rate due to bank competition to lend out their excess reserves. Consequently, a lower interest rate would encourage firms to borrow and invest in plant and equipment, thus continuing to hire workers up to the point where savings equal investment at full employment. The simultaneous adjustment of the labor market and loanable funds market requires price flexibility. Any obstacles to the price mechanism, such as minimum-wage laws, union bargaining wage policies, or central bank interest-rate target policies, would interfere with the self-regulating feature of the market, and are therefore undesirable.

The Keynesian view, however, was developed in the midst of the Great Depression in response to the neoclassical laissez-faire approach that dominated academic and policy circles alike. According to John Maynard Keynes (1883–1946), unemployment was not due to wage and price rigidities but rather to a lack of effective demand. Keynes rejected the loanable funds theory, which assumes that saving creates investment through interest-rate adjustments. From a macroeconomic perspective, the neoclassical model assumed that when aggregate consumption falls, aggregate saving would increase and would finance an equal amount of investment, which would keep aggregate demand high (thanks to the price mechanism). Keynes, on the other hand, showed that when the economy is in a recession or depression, consumer expectations turn negative due to unemployment and job insecurity. This leads to an aggregate reduction in consumer spending, leading to fewer sales, lower business revenues, and a downturn in business expectations about future profits. Firms will slow down production (in an attempt to reduce inventories), cancel investment spending, and eventually lay off more workers, thus leading to further deterioration in business activity.

Keynes explained that a reduction in consumer spending is likely to be accompanied by a fall in investment spending, hence an overall reduction in effective demand. It is understandable that during a recession, consumers will not go out on a shopping spree, nor will firms expand their productive capacity when they have difficulty liquidating their inventories. Therefore, the only solution to boost the economy during the recession is to increase the level of effective demand through government spending in order to compensate for low consumption and investment spending.

In Keynesian economics, the key adjustment mechanism is the level of effective demand, with aggregate investment being the engine of the economy. More investment (financed through credit rather than savings) leads to higher aggregate income, which in turn fuels more consumption and generates a residual amount of aggregate savings. The increase in consumption will, in turn, generate more revenues and stimulate positive expectations about future profits, thus helping increase the level of investment, output, and employment.

Robert W. Clower (1965) and his student Axel Leijonhufvud (1967) launched a significant attack on the neoclassical interpretation of Keynes known as the *Neoclassical-Keynesian Synthesis*, which dominated macroeconomics through the standard IS-LM model. Clower and Leijonhufvud started the so-called disequilibrium Keynesianism movement, which culminated in the creation of the famous Barro-Grossman model in 1971. The IS-LM interpretation of Keynes made the Keynesian model a special case of a neoclassical model with sticky (nonflexible) prices. Leijonhufvud, however, showed that one could understand Keynes's theoretical contribution only in the context of the rejection of the Walrasian auctioneer coordinating mechanism. Both Clower and Leijonhufvud believed that the disequilibrium situation (i.e., unemployment and effective demand failure) is the result of information and coordination deficiencies, rather than wage and price stickiness. Clower explained that when unemployed workers offer their services to firms, this does not constitute a signal of an effective demand for goods. Additionally, the change in time preference of individual economic agents—say, an increase in saving—will result in a fall in effective demand, leading to a decrease in both employment and output levels. This coordination failure results, therefore, in involuntary unemployment according to Clower and Leijonhufvud.

With the rise of the rational expectations theory, Robert Barro and Herschel Grossman abandoned the disequilibrium approach and reunited with the standard equilibrium models of New Classical economics in the late 1970s. A revival of the same (mis)interpretation of Keynes in terms of sticky prices has been echoed by New Keynesian economists since the early 1990s, claiming that in reality prices and wages are not as flexible as in the neoclassical model because of things like efficiency wages, long-term labor contracts, menu costs, credit rationing, capital market imperfection, adverse selection, and adverse incentives. New Keynesian economics is, therefore, in favor of the price adjustment approach. The Keynesian quantity adjustment approach, however, argues that downward wage and price flexibility could make things worse by adding to consumer income insecurity and business uncertainty about investment and operating costs. Therefore, downward wage rigidity and price inflexibility reduce uncertainty and provide a more stable environment for economic growth. This debate, however, continues to be one of the most important ones at the theoretical and policy level, with arguments over the usefulness of minimum-wage laws, labor unions, and discretionary fiscal policy.

SEE ALSO *Barro-Grossman Model; Business Cycles, Theories; Competition; Economics, Classical; Economics, New Classical; Economics, New Keynesian; Equilibrium in Economics; General Equilibrium; Great Depression; Sticky Prices;* Tâtonnement; *Wages*

BIBLIOGRAPHY

Barro, Robert J., and Herschel I. Grossman. 1971. A General Disequilibrium Model of Income and Employment. *American Economic Review* 61: 82–93.

Clower, Robert W. 1965. The Keynesian Counterrevolution: A Theoretical Appraisal. In *Theory of Interest Rates*, eds. F. H. Hahn and F. P. R. Berchling, 103–125. London: Macmillan.

De Long, J. Bradford, and Lawrence H. Summers. 1986. Is Increased Price Flexibility Stabilizing? *American Economic Review* 76: 1031–1044.

Fisher, Irving. 1933. The Debt-Deflation Theory of the Great Depression. *Econometrica* 1: 337–357.

Keynes, John Maynard. 1936. *The General Theory of Employment, Interest, and Money.* New York: Harcourt, Brace.

Leijonhufvud, Axel. 1967. Keynes and the Keynesians: A Suggested Interpretation. *American Economic Review* 57: 401–410.

Leijonhufvud, Axel. 1969. *Keynes and the Classics: Two Lectures on Keynes' Contribution to Economic Theory.* London: Institute of Economic Affairs.

Fadhel Kaboub

PRICE-DIVIDENDS RATIO

SEE *Market Fundamentals.*

PRICE-EARNINGS RATIO

SEE *Market Fundamentals.*

PRICE-ENHANCING RATIO

SEE *Market Fundamentals.*

PRICE-SPECIE-FLOW MECHANISM

SEE *Hume Process.*

PRICES

Prices are the rates at which goods and services are exchanged for other goods and services, or for money. In a monetized economy, the term *price* usually connotes the amount of money for which a good or service is purchased or sold. While in conventional usage, the term *price* is applied only to goods and services, in economic analysis, wages, interest rates, rents, and other money exchange rates for specialized services are also considered prices.

Prices have a critical coordinating role in a market economy. Ordinarily, an increase in a good's price conveys the information that it has become scarcer relative to the demand for it, either because its supply has fallen or because the demand for it has risen. A higher price induces existing producers to supply more of the good, and it attracts new entrants into an industry, since it tends to be associated with a higher-than-normal profit margin. Conversely, a declining price leads to reduced supply. Economists see these reactions as being exactly what is required for social efficiency, since resources should be withdrawn from uses that are less valued and drawn into uses that people value more.

Economist and social theorist Friedrich Hayek (1899–1992) argued that prices convey information about "global" (or society-wide) conditions to "local" actors (such as business owners), thereby solving a core informational problem faced by a society when it attempts to decide how best to allocate scarce resources. Hayek argued that the compactness or one-dimensionality of prices and the fact that they arise spontaneously as by-products of self-interested buying and selling activities makes them a uniquely economical way to coordinate society's resource allocation process. In the "socialist calculation debate" of the 1940s, Hayek argued that it is impossible to solve the problem of efficiently allocating resources among productive activities in an economy of specialized producers without market-generated prices. During the middle decades of the twentieth century, the apparent economic viability of the Soviet Union and like economies was sometimes viewed as contradicting that claim; yet reform-minded economists in the socialist world asserted the validity of Hayek's argument when political conditions allowed the matter to be discussed and their views ultimately prevailed.

Economic analysis distinguishes between nominal and real prices. The real price of a good is its price relative to the prices of other goods, while its nominal price is its price denominated in a currency the value of which may be changing over time. For example, if all nominal prices, including wages, were to double over a certain span of time, the real price of any given good would remain unchanged. The terminology reflects the idea that money is merely a medium of exchange without an intrinsic value of its own, and that what matters economically is therefore relative prices, including the purchasing power of people's money incomes.

In practice, changes in a country's price level can have real consequences. Inflations rarely affect all prices in perfect proportion. For this reason, and because of their asymmetric effect on, for instance, debtors versus creditors, they have significant distributional consequences. In a world of many countries and currencies, differences in rates of change in price levels affect international trade and payments. Unpredictable price changes increase risk, discouraging some investing and trading activities. Rapid price change can give rise to real costs, such as those associated with having to recalculate and reprice items frequently, the pressure to spend money as soon as it is earned, and the need to print and to carry large quantities of money.

Classical economists such as Adam Smith (1723–1790) distinguished between natural prices and market prices. While the terminology suggests that the "natural price" may have an underlying ethical quality, modern historians of economic thought generally understand the term to have been a reference to what would today be called a "long-run equilibrium price," that is, the price at which a normal or average rate of profit can be earned. This is the level toward which a good's price will adjust in the long run, through expansion or contraction of output by current producers and through exit of old and entry of new producers into the market. The "market price" is simply the price at which a good is sold at any given point in time. Since changes in supply or demand are always occurring, market prices are the prices we actually observe, while natural or long-run equilibrium prices are idealized or theoretical indicators of long-run tendencies.

Neoclassical economic theory teaches that allowing prices to be governed by the forces of supply and demand is the best way to permit them to play their role of signaling scarcity and guiding the ongoing reallocation of resources to their most valued ends. When governments intervene by setting price floors or ceilings, by taxing the sale of some goods but not others, by imposing tariffs on imports, by subsidizing some producers, or by directly determining what prices can be charged, prices become "distorted" and can no longer be counted upon to steer resource allocation toward efficient uses. In an economy in which prices are significantly distorted or controlled in these ways, it remains possible in principle to calculate what prices "should" be, that is, what they would be if market forces were permitted to determine prices freely and exclusively. The true "scarcity-reflecting" prices thus calculated are referred to by economic theorists as *shadow prices,* and they play important roles both in theoretical analysis and in some practical policy exercises.

On closer inspection, however, unregulated prices are not always the ideal, even according to neoclassical economic theory. Monopolists can push prices above levels associated with normal profit rates and efficient supply. The market prices of goods whose production destroys unpriced resources, such as clean air and water, systematically understate their true cost to society. Government interventions, such as setting a maximum price for a monopolist, breaking up monopolies so that competition will bring down prices and increase supply, or taxing polluters to force them to internalize costs they might otherwise impose on society, can at least in principle improve upon unregulated outcomes, although knowing how a government will act in practice requires an understanding of a range of political and economic factors.

Scholars who compare economic systems of different types emphasize that prices play more than a scarcity-signaling role in an economy. Prices also determine the relative incomes of different groups of economic actors. For example, higher real wages may mean lower profits and hence a smaller income gap between wage versus profit earners. A higher ratio between the wages of more-educated or skilled and less-educated or skilled workers was associated with rising income inequality in industrialized economies during the last decades of the twentieth century. In the heyday of the Soviet Union and other planned economies, planners set the wages of urban workers and the prices paid to farmers for their produce at levels consistent with the proportions of consumption versus investment desired by the political authorities. In this way, they used control over wages and prices as a method of dictating high rates of capital formation. Prices also functioned as accounting aids in the centrally planned economies. Their existence allowed economic planners to monitor the fulfillment of plan targets through a system of indicators (money flows) parallel to but distinct from indicators of physical input and output.

Their impact on the distribution of wealth, for instance between sellers and buyers, also explains why prices attract ethical attention, as epitomized by medieval European discussions of the "just price." Sellers of a resource in plentiful supply, for example unskilled labor, cannot command high prices (wages) for their service under competitive conditions, resulting in their poverty in comparison with those selling a scarce resource—perhaps access to fertile land. Companies in the oil industry earning large profits in the wake of short-run supply shortfalls attract ethical and political attention because a higher price for transportation and heating fuel means poorer consumers and wealthier company owners. Governments sometimes try to prevent such transfers by fixing a maximum price. If the supply of the commodity in question is fixed, the price ceiling will cause demand to outstrip the available supply, which will then be "rationed" by some nonprice mechanism—perhaps willingness or ability to wait in line, perhaps rules governing who can purchase on which day of the week, or perhaps government issue of coupons in limited number. In some circumstances, rationing a scarce but crucial commodity may be preferable to letting market forces operate, but in eliminating the short-run windfall that would otherwise accrue to suppliers, it can also slow the expansion of output that would reduce the commodity's scarcity in the long run.

Many governments set minimum wages, tax high incomes at steeper rates than low ones, or engage in other price-altering interventions in order to protect disadvantaged groups or moderate income inequalities. But governments face pressures from constituencies other than the poor, which also leads to price interventions. For example, tariffs preserve the profits of domestic producers at the expense of domestic consumers, and often also at the expense of forces promoting long-run competitiveness. The effect of prices on the distribution of income helps to explain a variety of government price-altering policies.

SEE ALSO *Aggregate Demand and Supply Price; Interest, Natural Rate of; Long Period Analysis; Long Run; Rent; Shadow Prices; Short Period; Short Run; Spot Market; Wages*

BIBLIOGRAPHY

Hayek, Friedrich. 1945. The Use of Knowledge in Society. *American Economic Review* 35: 519–530.

Kohler, Heinz. 1996. *Economic Systems and Human Welfare: A Global Survey.* Cincinnati, OH: South-Western College Publishing.

Mas-Colell, Andreu, Michael Whinston, and Jerry Green. 1995. *Microeconomic Theory.* New York: Oxford University Press.

Montias, John Michael, Avner Ben-Ner, and Egon Neuberger. 1994. *Comparative Economics.* Chur, Switzerland: Harwood Academic.

Varian, Hal. 1992. *Microeconomic Analysis*, 3rd ed. New York: Norton.

Louis Putterman

PRICES OF PRODUCTION
SEE *Long Run.*

PRIDE
SEE *Shame.*

PRIMACY/RECENCY EFFECTS

Is it better to go first in a debate, or second? Who has the advantage in court, the prosecutor who speaks first and can set the stage, or the defense attorney who has the final word? Do first impressions really matter? These questions and others like them have been the focus of a great deal of social psychological study since the mid-twentieth century.

Understanding when there is an advantage to going first or last could be a powerful communications tool. Not surprisingly then, determining whether or not people will attend to, remember, and be swayed by the first information they encounter (i.e., showing a *primacy effect*) or whether they will process, recall, and be convinced by the last information they encounter (i.e., demonstrating a *recency effect*) has been a major focus of research in the social psychological literature.

One of the more comprehensive approaches to the issue of primacy and recency effects has been in the persuasion literature. After World War II (1939–1945), the psychologist Carl Hovland (1912–1961) and his colleagues at Yale began to conduct research in order to understand how one could change people's attitudes, and

what contextual factors might influence the persuasive impact of a message. In their 1957 book *The Order of Presentation in Persuasion,* Hovland and his colleagues began to explore the issue of order effects. Many studies found primacy effects such that postmessage attitudes were more influenced by the first speaker or set of arguments. However, other studies found a recency effect, such that the perceivers were more influenced by the last information they encountered. Additional studies demonstrated neither primacy nor recency effects.

In 1959 members of the Yale group hypothesized that persuasion effects should work much like memory. If two messages were presented sequentially and without delay, the first message would be more persuasive because it would interfere with the processing of the second message (resulting in primacy effects). However, if the second message was presented after a sufficient delay (e.g., one week), the first message would have decayed and the second (or more recent) message would be stronger in memory, resulting in greater persuasion. Although some data supported this hypothesis, the findings were not straightforward. Interestingly, memory in and of itself was not a strong predictor of persuasion. Other research has explored how the familiarity of the issue or the types of information may influence the occurrence of primacy and recency effects.

More recent research has suggested that contextual factors, such as people's ability and motivation to process the persuasive communication, are important determinants in whether primacy or recency will occur. Duane Wegener and his colleagues have presented evidence that when people are motivated and able to process information, they will demonstrate primacy effects. However, when motivation or ability are low, recency effects will tend to occur.

Perhaps not surprisingly, given the extensive work linking persuasion and memory, a number of researchers have explored how primacy and recency effects are manifested in human and animal learning and memory. Much of the research in this area is consistent with the findings in the persuasion literature. For example, contextual factors (e.g., type or topic of information, personal responsibility for outcomes, an individual's motivation to think about the topic) have been found to moderate primacy and recency effects in human memory. Reviews of the primacy/recency literature have highlighted that both primacy and recency effects are possible depending on the context in which the information is learned.

There has also been substantial research on primacy effects in the field of impression formation (the study of how we make judgments about the people we meet). Consistent with persuasion and memory research, Phillip Tetlock and his colleagues have found that as one's motivation to be a complete information processor increases (e.g., one has personal responsibility for the decision, the outcome is perceived to be important), there is a tendency for primacy and recency effects to diminish. As motivation decreases (personal responsibility is low, people are tired), biases can occur.

Thus, the question remains: Is it better to speak first or second if you want to convince your audience? Of course, as with most psychological questions, the right answer is "it depends." Most importantly, it depends on the knowledge, ability, and motivations of the audience. The impact of this research has been felt in many domains, including communications, marketing, and political science, among others. Indeed, as long as there is the possibility of gaining an advantage in the area of communications, it will be useful to conduct research to explore how and when order effects will occur.

SEE ALSO *Persuasion; Persuasion, Message-based*

BIBLIOGRAPHY

Haugtvedt, Curtis P., and Duane T. Wegener. 1994. Message Order Effects in Persuasion: An Attitude Strength Perspective. *Journal of Consumer Research* 21: 205–218.

Hovland, Carl I., et al., eds. 1957. *The Order of Presentation in Persuasion.* New Haven, CT: Yale University Press.

Tetlock, Phillip E. 1983. Accountability and the Perseverance of First Impressions. *Social Psychology Quarterly* 46 (4): 285–292.

Steven M. Smith

PRIMARIES

Presidential and congressional primaries are intraparty election contests whereby candidates compete for the privilege of being the party's general election nominee. Direct primaries in non-southern states originated with the Progressive Era of the early twentieth century as a way to move intraparty candidate selection away from corrupt state and local political bosses and urban machines. In southern states it was seen as a way to ensure continued political domination by one party. Although first pioneered at the local level, primaries spread to state and national offices and dominated candidate selection in U.S. Senate and House races by the mid-twentieth century. At the presidential level, reforms made after the contentious 1968 Democratic National Convention placed delegate selection, and hence the selection of the party nominee, in the hands of the party rank and file and away from party elites. This led to the proliferation and dominance of primaries in the presidential selection process. Primaries are generally considered a uniquely American institution.

TYPES AND TIMING

Participation and contest rules vary by state, party, and time. There are four general types of primaries: open, semi-open, closed, and runoff. In open primaries, voters choose the party's primary in which they want to participate. Registered party members and independents who choose to participate can vote in a semi-open primary, though independents often have to change their party registration to that of party in whose primary they are participating. Only registered party members can vote in a closed primary. Primary runoffs, used especially in southern states, happen when no candidate receives a majority (more than 50%) of the vote. In a second primary or runoff, the top two vote getters face off. Runoffs may threaten a nominee's general election chances if the opposing party's candidate does not compete in a runoff. This potential disadvantage stems from the fact that one candidate has to expend resources on a second intraparty contest, while the other candidate can immediately shift focus to the interparty general election race.

A unique feature of the presidential nominating system is its extended and sequential nature. Primaries begin in New Hampshire, typically in late January or early February, and end with a slate of late states in mid-June. This serial process has given political elites and potential candidates the opportunity to move state primary dates up in the process, a procedure known as front-loading, to advantage their own political ambition or their state both politically and economically. Politically, early states have greater influence over who wins the nomination by sending signals to later voters about the viability and electability of the contenders and by helping to winnow candidates. Early states benefit economically due to increases in candidate spending, visits, mobilization efforts (including television ads), and media attention. Unfortunately, as the race progresses and it becomes clearer who the party nominee will be, the process produces disincentives for individual voter participation and reduces overall levels of voter turnout.

Congressional primaries also vary in timing and in the use of party endorsements. Some states schedule congressional primaries in early March and others as late as September of an election year. When states schedule presidential and congressional primaries on the same date, voter turnout levels increase. Some state parties attempt to influence voter choices through party endorsements. Endorsements may require candidates to meet a support threshold at the party convention to be placed on the primary ballot or may reward the top party convention vote getter with the first line of the primary ballot or with a designation as the party's candidate.

Presidential and congressional incumbents seldom encounter a viable challenge in their primary bids, and therefore these races are rarely competitive. The advantage incumbents have in fund-raising, name recognition, and perquisites of office tend to discourage competition. Strong primary challenges to incumbents are more likely to emerge when the challengers' chances of winning the nomination and general election campaigns are greater. Incumbent members of Congress who face strong primary challengers typically are those involved in a scandal, such as charges of unethical behavior, or those who stray from representing their constituents' interests. Although a surprising number of incumbents are unlikely to suffer a primary defeat amid allegations of wrongdoing, their precarious position makes them much more susceptible to a general election defeat. At the presidential level, incumbents are often challenged when their presidential approval is low. Since 1972 and the post-reform era, no presidential incumbent candidate has been defeated during the nomination campaign. In contrast, the out party contest is always competitive in presidential primaries, though this is less the case in congressional races. In open contests where there is no incumbent running, both parties generally draw a long list of nomination contenders, and the contests are more competitive.

IMPACT ON VOTERS AND PARTIES

Primaries are candidate-centered contests where candidates act strategically, directly appealing to voters. Because party identification is not a voting cue, candidate attributes figure strongly in voter decision-making. Candidate-centered contests lead to intraparty factionalization as candidates directly compete against one another for voter support. Primary factionalization, however, appears to play at best a modest role in general election outcomes. Though early research in congressional and presidential races found that the party with the more divisive primary (defined as primaries with more contentious contests and usually based on margin of victory measures) loses votes in the general election race, late-twentieth-century models demonstrate little effect once candidate quality is considered. In a presidential contest, the party appears to heal from internal divisions as the focus of the race turns to the interparty general election fight; similar factors may be at work in congressional elections. Presidential research indicates that primary supporters of losers often turn their efforts to support the party or the party nominee in the general election campaign. At the congressional level, party activists who supported a losing candidate in a divisive primary were less active on behalf of the party nominee in the short term but still expressed interest in long-term party involvement. Thus primary campaigns are a unique opportunity for new party entrants, regardless of who they supported, to become mobilized and be a

resource for general election party activity and other future party activity.

SEE ALSO *Campaigning; Political Parties; Voting*

BIBLIOGRAPHY

Atkeson, Lonna Rae. 1998. Divisive Primaries and General Election Outcomes: Another Look at Presidential Campaigns. *American Journal of Political Science* 42 (1): 256–271.

Galderisi, Peter F., Marni Ezra, and Michael Lyons, eds. 2001. *Congressional Primaries and the Politics of Representation.* Lanham, MD: Rowman and Littlefield.

Stone, Walter J., Lonna Rae Atkeson, and Ronald Rapoport. 1992. Turning on and Turning Off? Mobilization and Demobilization Effects of Participation in Presidential Nomination Campaigns. *American Journal of Political Science* 36 (3): 665–691.

Lonna Rae Atkeson
Patricia A. Jaramillo

PRIMATES

No simple set of diagnostic characteristics defines "primates." Rather, members of the order Primates share, to varying degrees, several suites of features that reflect a generally arboreal lifestyle. These attributes include:

1. Pentadactyl, prehensile hands and/or feet with nails (rather than claws) on the digits, of which the thumb and/or big toe are opposable.

2. Pronounced sensory emphasis on vision, notably through development of binocular and stereoscopic vision, as well as expansion of the visual cortex.

3. A generalized postcranial anatomy tending toward orthrograde (upright) posture.

4. A trend toward enlargement of the cerebral cortex, especially in monkeys and apes.

Primate taxonomy is debated, but 200 to 350 species are recognized. The majority are distributed in tropical and subtropical regions (roughly between the Tropics of Cancer and Capricorn) and throughout sub-Saharan Africa, south and southeast Asia, and South and Central America, although a few forms, such as the Japanese macaque, inhabit decidedly temperate habitats. Primates are chiefly rain forest and tropical forest dwellers, although many other biomes are ecologically relevant for certain groups, including savanna, woodland scrub, evergreen temperate forest, desert, and high-altitude eflinwood meadow.

Six major groups of primates are usefully distinguished:

1. Lemuriformes: the small nocturnal and larger diurnal lemurs of Madagascar.

2. Lorisiformes: the nocturnal, small-bodied lorises and bushbabies of Africa, south Asia, and island southeast Asia.

3. Tarsiiformes: the small, nocturnal tarsiers of Sumatra, Borneo, Sulawesi, and the Philippines.

4. Playtrrhini: the small- to large-bodied monkeys of Central and South America.

5. Cercopithecoidea: the medium- to large-bodied monkeys of Africa and Asia.

6. Hominoidea: the large apes of Africa and Asia, as well as humans.

The Lemuriformes and Lorisiformes form a coherent suborder, the Strepsirhini, unified by various traits, notably retention of the "rhinarium" (the naked, "wet" mammalian nose), increased reliance on olfaction, and greater seasonality of sexual behavior ("estrus"). Many strepsirhines are nocturnal. The second suborder, the Haplorhini, comprises the primates of the remaining three taxa, which exhibit predominantly diurnal habits (with the exception of tarsiers and one monkey species), enhanced vision and visual communication, and comparatively more continuous (less seasonal) sexual activity and reproduction.

DIETARY HABITS

Diversity and omnivory generally typify primate feeding strategies, rather than marked dietary specialization such as the bovid emphasis on grass. The three principal primate foods are fruits, leaves, and insects, but their relative dietary proportions vary considerably across species. Frugivory is most widely distributed: Most primates eat some fruit, and species strongly committed to frugivory are found in virtually every family. Figs (Moraceae, *Ficus* species) are an often a crucial keystone fruit source for forest primates. Because of metabolic implications of body size, folivory is more common among larger primates (greater than or equal to 13.5 pounds), such as the Old World "leaf monkeys" (Colobinae), neotropical woolly spider monkeys, and mountain gorillas. Conversely, insects are generally consumed in higher proportions by small primates (less than or equal to 3.5 pounds), such as the nocturnal strepsirhines, tarsiers, and neotropical marmosets, tamarins, and squirrel monkeys. Thus, with increasing body size, primate diets typically grade from insectivory, to insectivory-frugivory, frugivory, frugivory-folivory, and finally to folivory.

Some less common foods are nevertheless important for certain primates or in specific seasons. For example, marmosets, tamarins, and some strepsirhines rely heavily on exudates (gum), particularly seasonally. Underground storage organs (e.g., rhizomes, tubers, corms) are paramount in baboon foraging. These parts are modified stems or leaves in which the plant stores starch, minerals, and water (the potato being a well-known example utilized by humans). Nectar (for some lemurs and neotropical monkeys), grass (for gelada baboons), and seeds (for saki monkeys) are other examples. Carnivory (predation) occurs at significant rates only among baboons (*Papio* species), neotropical capuchin monkeys (*Cebus* species), and most notably chimpanzees (*Pan troglodytes*), the latter of which prey heavily upon red colobus monkeys. In contrast to the more individualistic and "opportunistic" prey capture of *Papio* and *Cebus*, chimpanzee "hunting" is performed simultaneously by multiple adult males. Researchers debate, however, whether male chimpanzees act independently of one another or coordinate their actions cooperatively through an organized division of labor (different hunting "roles") and the use of foresight and mental attribution.

The omnivorous, "generalist" feeding inclination of primates has not precluded some adaptive specializations in dentition, physiology, and behavior. One noteworthy example is the gastrointestinal tract of Colobine monkeys: In a manner directly analogous to ruminants, it contains a large, multichambered stomach with variable chemical environments facilitating fermentation by symbiotic, cellulolytic bacteria. Thus, these monkeys are able to metabolize and subsist on otherwise difficult-to-digest, mature foliage.

SOCIAL SYSTEMS AND BEHAVIOR

Perhaps the most striking features of primate biology are the diversity and complexity of social systems. Many nocturnal strepsirhines—as well as the orangutan—live in "dispersed" societies in which adult males and females inhabit individually separate home ranges wherein daily activities are independently pursued. These home ranges may partly overlap and, in some species, differ in size between the sexes. Thus, a single polygynous male may occupy and defend from other males (territoriality) a large home range encompassing several females' individual ranges. The original characterization of this arrangement as a "solitary" or "asocial" existence was understandable but inaccurate. Not only do "solitary" individuals interact at meaningful rates through indirect olfactory and vocal modalities, they may even aggregate regularly, for example, during feeding in orangutans, or at sleeping sites in some nocturnal strepsirhines. Recent mitochondrial DNA evidence from nocturnal lemurs reveals that such sleeping aggregations comprise related females, thereby suggesting a "hidden" matrilineal dimension of as yet unclear significance in these dispersed social systems.

In contrast, the diurnal lemurs and all monkeys are highly gregarious, living in permanent social groups. With few exceptions, primate societies are generally closed (interaction—particularly affiliatively—between individuals of separate groups is rare) and age-graded (immatures of multiple ages/generations are present). The size and composition of groups vary greatly, as do the nature and patterning of constituent social relationships. This variation is expressed not only between species but also often across populations of the same species.

As with mammals generally, female primates often remain in their natal area and social unit for most if not all of their lives, whereas males disperse to other groups around the age of sexual maturity. The resulting female-bonded societies are thus based on "core" affiliative networks of related females —matrilines—to which males associate in variable numbers and time periods.

For example, in some species (leaf monkeys and guenons) only one adult male lives in a group of several (typically three to ten) adult females and their offspring. Group membership is likely to confer polygynous reproductive advantages to males, although in at least some species, females copulate with other males in the population, which either live alone or in all-male "bachelor" units.

A "multimale" variant of this social system generally emerges with relatively larger female group sizes (e.g., ten to fifty). In such cases, three to fifteen adult (nonnatal) males typically reside with the females and their offspring. This social structure predominates in many of the Old World monkeys—notably the baboons and macaques—in addition to neotropical forms such as capuchin and squirrel monkeys. Relationships among females are highly differentiated, most often manifested as relatively rigid, linear dominance hierarchies organized around kinship (matrilineal relatedness). Several field and laboratory studies suggest a substantive cognitive dimension to nonhuman primate understanding of both "status" and "matrilineal kinship." Females invest heavily in activities that maintain their status, such as grooming and coalitionary support. Males similarly maintain dominance relationships that are, however, much more dynamic and unrelated to kinship.

In 10 to 15 percent of species—most notably the gibbons (Hylobatidae) and species of small neotropical monkeys—the group comprises one adult of each sex accompanied by several immature individuals of various ages. This social system was originally designated "monogamy" or the "nuclear family," but the term "social monogamy" is now preferred, particularly in light of avian

research. Individuals in over 90 percent of bird species live and breed in heterosexual pairs, but genetic data have revealed that in many species *extra-pair* paternity may be significantly high (e.g., 40 to 50%). Although not all extra-pair sexual behavior results in fertilization, it is clear that one can no longer assume that sexual or reproductive monogamy results invariably from the monogamous *social* arrangement of birds. Correspondingly, "extra-pair" copulations, pair-bond termination ("divorce"), and "nonnuclear" families do occur among socially monogamous primates, but the generality and significance of these phenomena remains less clear than is the case for birds.

A polyandrous mating system is found in some marmosets and tamarins that live in groups comprising one adult female, two adult males, and youngsters of various ages. Males, as well as young adult offspring of either sex, are primarily responsible for care of the breeding female's (fraternal) twin offspring. The reproduction of adult daughter "caretakers" may, in fact, be behaviorally or physiologically suppressed by the dominant female.

Great ape societies are characterized by comparatively attenuated female relationships. As noted, female orangutans pursue largely separate lives. Although gorillas live in unimale, multifemale groups, dispersal of females (as well as males) at sexual maturity constrains the formation of matrilineal relationships; female gorillas instead direct more social attention to the resident male. Individual female chimpanzees occupy separate home ranges, interact infrequently, and have weak dominance relationships. Females disperse at sexual maturity, whereas males remain in their natal community. Thus, the kinship element of chimpanzee society is patrilineal in nature, based on relationships among related males that collectively maintain a territory encompassing the individual home ranges of numerous "solitary" females. These males and females may join and leave temporary foraging parties that vary greatly in size and composition, dynamically undergoing "fusion" and "fission" with other foraging parties and individuals of the community over days, if not hours. Cooperation in competition is a hallmark of male social life. Hunting is one such context, as is vying for dominance and the sometimes violent territorial aggression directed against neighboring communities of related males. Although the patrilineal structure and "fusion-fission" system of social foraging also characterizes bonobos (as well as neotropical spider monkeys), bonobos are noteworthy for the much more amicable nature of their social relationships and apparent female dominance over males.

Negotiating complex relationships involving status, kinship, and affiliation over their relatively long lives is believed to have been an important impetus in the evolution of social cognition in monkeys and, especially, apes.

SEE ALSO *Alpha-male; Anthropology; Anthropology, Biological; Kinship; Kinship Selection; Social Status*

BIBLIOGRAPHY

Bergman, T. J., J. C. Beehner, D. L. Cheney, and R. M. Seyfarth. 2003. Hierarchical Classification by Rank and Kinship in Baboons. *Science* 302: 1234–1236.

Cheney, D. L., and R. M. Seyfarth. 1990. *How Monkeys See the World: Inside the Mind of Another Species*. Chicago: University of Chicago Press.

Dixson, Alan F. 1998. *Primate Sexuality: Comparative Studies of the Prosimians, Monkeys, Apes, and Human Beings*. Oxford: Oxford University Press.

Fleagle, John G. 1999. *Primate Adaptation and Evolution*. 2nd ed. San Diego, CA: Academic Press.

Kappeler, Peter M., and Michael E. Pereira, eds. 2003. *Primate Life Histories and Socioecology*. Chicago: University of Chicago Press.

Kappeler, Peter M., and Carel P. van Schaik. 2002. Evolution of Primate Social Systems. *International Journal of Primatology* 23 (4): 707–740.

Martin, Robert D. 1990. *Primate Origins and Evolution: A Phylogenetic Reconstruction*. Princeton, NJ: Princeton University Press.

Ryne A. Palombit

PRIMING

People are influenced by their immediate environment, which includes the objects, situations, and persons they encounter. Indeed, features of the environment can affect psychological experiences and behaviors so subtly that people fail to notice these influences. *Priming* refers to an unobtrusive and momentary environmental influence on an individual's psychological experiences and behaviors. The term *priming* has also been used to describe the experimental technique researchers use to study these effects in the laboratory.

How does priming work? The dominant explanation posits that environmental features temporarily activate (prime) mentally represented concepts, such as attitudes, behaviors, emotions, goals, memories, stereotypes, and traits. For example, suppose that you encounter a dog on the street. This encounter activates the concept "dog" and its associated traits, such as "furry" and "loyal." Once activated, primed concepts become more likely to influence immediate cognitions (e.g., thoughts, judgments), feelings, and behaviors. So, if immediately after encountering the dog you are asked to name a characteristic that is important in a friend, you may be temporarily more likely to say "loyalty."

Importantly, priming effects occur automatically. That is, concepts can be activated without awareness and go on to bias overt responses in ways that people do not intend and cannot control. *Supraliminal priming* describes cases in which people are aware of an environmental cue, but are not aware of its influence on them, such as in the dog example above. In *subliminal priming*, people are not even aware of an environmental cue, yet it still influences them. As an example, imagine moviegoers who are flashed a brand of drink for fractions of a second, below the radar of conscious perception, and unwittingly choose it over other beverages.

Priming effects are explained by presuming that concepts are mentally represented in an associative network. Only when associations between concepts are strong does activating one concept temporarily activate others. Because associations are strengthened through repeated and consistent pairing, environmental cues that are encountered frequently can be powerful primes. Take, for instance, relationship partners. Among students who strongly associate their mothers with the goal to work hard, subliminally priming the word *mother* will activate the goal to "work hard" and the students will persist longer and perform better on a subsequent academic test (Shah 2003). Sometimes these strong associations arise through learned sociocultural stereotypes. An individual's group membership and stereotypes related to that group can be primed and help or hinder performance, depending on the stereotype activated. For instance, if Asian American women are asked about their gender, their quantitative performance on a subsequent test will suffer, but if asked about their ethnicity, their quantitative performance will improve (Shih, Pittinsky, and Ambady 1999). Priming stereotypes can also influence members of non-stereotyped groups. Young adults exposed to words related to the elderly stereotype, including *sentimental* and *wrinkle*, will subsequently walk down a corridor more slowly (Bargh, Chen, and Burrows 1996).

The idea that behavior is not always consciously and intentionally guided raises questions about personal accountability. Suppose that a child behaves aggressively after watching violent television. To what extent is the child's aggression due to an active, intentional, conscious thought process versus a passive process that does not require conscious intention or motivation on the part of the child? The roles attributed to conscious choice versus environmental determinism in explaining aggressive behavior, and other primed behaviors, have tremendous legal and policy implications.

SEE ALSO *Collective Memory; Identity; Memory; Social Psychology; Steele, Claude; Stereotype Threat; Subliminal Suggestion*

BIBLIOGRAPHY

Bargh, John A., and Tanya L. Chartrand. 1999. The Unbearable Automaticity of Being. *American Psychologist* 54 (7): 462–479.

Bargh, John A., Mark Chen, and Lara Burrows. 1996. Automaticity of Social Behavior: Direct Effects of Trait Construct and Stereotype Activation on Action. *Journal of Personality and Social Psychology* 71 (2): 230–244.

Gladwell, Malcolm. 2005. *Blink: The Power of Thinking Without Thinking.* New York: Little, Brown and Company.

Shah, James. 2003. The Motivational Looking Glass: How Significant Others Implicitly Affect Goal Appraisals. *Journal of Personality & Social Psychology* 85 (3): 424–439.

Shih, Margaret, Todd L. Pittinsky, and Nalini Ambady. 1999. Stereotype Susceptibility: Identity Salience and Shifts in Quantitative Performance. *Psychological Science* 10 (1): 80–83.

Amy N. Dalton

PRIMITIVE ACCUMULATION

At any given time, the accumulation of capital depends on some already existing capital to invest in the production process. Therefore, it appears that the capitalist mode of production as a historical formation presupposes some "original" or "primitive" accumulation. Adam Smith (1723–1790) called this "previous accumulation" and saw it necessary for the advancement of the division of labor and therefore of what he calls the "productive powers of labour." He argues that "the accumulation of stock must, in the nature of things, be previous to the division of labour, so labour can be more and more subdivided in proportion only as stock is previously more and more accumulated" (Smith [1776] 1976). So, for example, in a market society, "a weaver cannot apply himself entirely to his peculiar business, unless there is beforehand stored up somewhere, either in his own possession or in that of some other person, a stock sufficient to maintain him, and to supply him with the materials and tools of his work, till he has not only completed but sold his web. This accumulation must, evidently, be previous to his applying his industry for so long a time to such a peculiar business" (Smith [1776] 1976).

Smith, however, grounds this claim on the ideological belief that division of labor and "stock" is somehow a feature of modern industrial societies, since "in that rude state of society in which there is no division of labour, in which exchanges are seldom made, and in which every man provides everything for himself, it is not necessary that any stock should be accumulated or stored up before-

hand, in order to carry on the business of society" (Smith [1776] 1976). This claim is in fact untrue and based on a methodological individualism typical of classical and neoclassical political economy: even in hunting and gathering societies arrows and containers are produced and "stocked" before the production of food and, typically, along a division of labor within a community of producers. By means of this ideological counterposition between a "primitive" and a modern industrial society, Smith does not need to explain the historical emergence of the peculiar form of the "previous accumulation" and of social division of labor correspondent to capitalist societies. He does address the question of how a social formation in which market relations play a marginal role in the reproduction of people's livelihoods (as in European societies up to the eighteenth century) can turn into one in which capital is accumulated in the hands of the few, while the vast majority turn into wage laborers. According to classical political economy, this previous "accumulation of stock" resulted from thrift and abstinence by a section of the population. Along this line Adam Smith, who believed capitalist market relations to be harmonious and beneficial to its participants, never confronted the historical process that originated these market relations.

Marx rendered Smith's term "previous" as "ursprünglich," which then was translated into English as "primitive" (Perleman 2000, p. 25). In Part 8 of Volume 1 of *Capital* (1867), Karl Marx (1818–1883) discusses "the so-called Primitive Accumulation." Marx adds the pejorative *so-called* to emphasize the flesh-and-blood history that formed the precondition of capitalist production. In highlighting the historical process, Marx developed a different meaning of primitive accumulation in that he linked it to the notion of capital as "class relation" rather than as "stock." Given that "the capital-relation presupposes a complete separation between the workers and the ownership of the conditions for the realization of their labour," it follows that "the process ... which creates the capital-relation can be nothing other than the process which divorces the worker from the ownership of the conditions of his own labour." By turning "the social means of subsistence and production ... into capital, and the immediate producers ... into wage-labourers," this process is therefore the basis of class formation. Thus, the "so-called primitive accumulation ... is nothing else than the historical process of divorcing the producer from the means of production" (Marx [1867] 1976, pp. 874–875).

To illustrate this process, Marx refers to English land enclosures during the sixteenth and seventeenth centuries; at times he also refers to the international dimension of primitive accumulation, such as the effect of the slave trade on Bristol and Liverpool. Furthermore, this process presupposes people's resistance and struggles either implicitly, as in the case of the "bloody legislation" (Marx

[1867] 1976, pp. 896–904), or explicitly, as in the case of the "barbarous laws against combinations of workers [that] collapsed in 1825 in the face of the threatening attitude of the proletariat" (p. 903).

There are perhaps two main interpretative frameworks of the concept of primitive accumulation within a century-long debate in Marxist literature. One framework sees primitive accumulation as a one-time/one-place phenomenon, the occurrence of which leads to the development of capitalism. The other framework instead emphasizes the continuous occurrence of primitive accumulation as an integral part of capitalism, whatever its stage of development. The first approach perhaps has its roots in Vladimir Ilyich Lenin's (1870–1924) early study, *The Development of Capitalism in Russia* (1899). In a polemic against the Populists, who believed that the absence of a developed market would prevent capitalist development in Russia, Lenin argued that the disappearance of the peasants and their communities was precisely the prerequisite for the creation of the capitalist market. Lenin saw this process as inevitable and ultimately positive, although he often underlined its contradictions.

The second interpretative framework seems to emerge from Rosa Luxemburg's (1870–1919) *The Accumulation of Capital* (1913). Her work points toward an interpretation of primitive accumulation as an integral part of capitalism and its development. Luxemburg regards Marx's schemes of expanded reproduction as a representation only of the mathematical conditions for accumulation in cases in which there are no more than two classes. In reality, she contends, capitalist production must rely on third parties (peasants, small independent producers, etc.) to be commodity buyers. Thus the enforcement of exchange relations between capitalist and noncapitalist production becomes necessary to realize surplus value. However, this exchange relation clashes with the social relations of noncapitalist production. In order to overcome the resistance to capital that arises from this clash, capital must resort to military and political violence. Here Luxemburg introduces a crucial thesis that, independently of the validity of her reasoning and interpretation of Marx's schemes of reproduction, seems to open the way to considering primitive accumulation as an inherent, continuous element of capitalism; as such it encompasses the world as a whole, and implies political and military force.

Elements of Lenin's and Luxemburg's interpretations can be found in subsequent approaches, although until the 1970s the influence of Lenin's approach seemed to be greater. For example, in his classic *Studies in the Development of Capitalism* (1963), which generated much debate on the transition from feudalism to capitalism, economist Maurice Dobb (1900–1976) used the category of primitive accumulation to denote a well-defined age of

accumulation of property rights, better known as the *mercantile age*, which predates capitalist production (p. 178). Also, in the context of the early Soviet debate on the transition to socialism, Evgenii Alexeyevich Preobrazhensky (1886–1937), in his book *The New Economics* (1926), argued for the need for a primitive socialist accumulation.

More recently, widespread opposition to global neoliberal policies of privatization and cuts in social spending linked to structural adjustment have refocused scholars' attention on the category of primitive accumulation as a continuous and integral element of capitalism, although within different interpretative frameworks. More specifically, and in relation to political-economic issues, emphasis has been put on crises of overproduction and profitability creating a need for capital to engage in primitive accumulation. Thus, George Caffentzis, for example, refers to neoliberal policies following the profitability crises of the 1970s as "New Enclosures" (1995), while more recently David Harvey refers to "accumulation by dispossession" in *The New Imperialism* (2003), situated in the contemporary crises of overproduction.

The role of social conflict and class relations in defining the continuous character of primitive accumulation is also clearly spelled out in the literature. In the essay "Separating the Doing and the Deed" (2004), Massimo De Angelis argues that in different historical phases, profit-driven capital must devise strategies of enclosures, either by promoting ex-novo areas of commodification vis-à-vis resistance, or by preserving old areas of commodification vis-à-vis ex-novo social struggles claiming "new commons." Also, and complementarily, the typology of "new enclosures" and "new commons" has been seen to include a wide range of resources, such as land, water, and knowledge, among others.

Finally, it has been argued that the current attempt by states and international institutions to control demographic rates depends on the expropriation or "enclosure" of the body, of the sexual and reproductive powers of women, for the purpose of accumulating labor power and thus promoting capital's valorization requirements. In *Caliban and the Witch* (2004), Silvia Federici shows that the witch-hunt terror in the sixteenth and seventeenth centuries opened the way for state attempts to control demographic rates and the reproduction of labor power, and she draws parallels with contemporary phenomena. In *The Invention of Capitalism* (2000), Michael Perelman has pointed out that primitive accumulation is linked to the social and sexual division of labor at least since the classical proponents of laissez-faire ideology (e.g., Adam Smith, James Steuart [1712–1780], and Edward Gibbon Wakefield [1796–1862]) were disguising a strategy for state-implemented primitive accumulation to shape the social division of labor.

464

BIBLIOGRAPHY

Bonefeld, Werner. 2001. The Permanence of Primitive Accumulation: Commodity Fetishism and Social Constitution. *The Commoner* N.2 (September). http://www.commoner.org.uk/02bonefeld.pdf.

Caffentzis, George. 1995. The Fundamental Implications of the Debt Crisis for Social Reproduction in Africa. In *Paying The Price: Women and the Politics of International Economic Strategy*, eds. Mariarosa Dalla Costa and Giovanna F. Dalla Costa, 15–41. London: Zed.

De Angelis, Massimo. 2004. Separating the Doing and the Deed: Capital and the Continuous Character of Enclosures. *Historical Materialism* 12 (2): 57–87

Dobb, Maurice. 1963. *Studies in the Development of Capitalism.* Rev. ed. London: Routledge.

Federici, Silvia. 2004. *Caliban and the Witch: Women, the Body, and Primitive Accumulation.* New York: Autonomedia.

Harvey, David. 2003. *The New Imperialism.* New York: Oxford University Press.

Lenin, Vladimir Illich. [1899] 1964. *The Development of Capitalism in Russia: The Process of the Formation of a Home Market for Large-Scale Industry.* Moscow: Progress Publishers.

Luxemburg, Rosa. [1913] 1963. *The Accumulation of Capital.* Trans. Agnes Schwarzschild. London: Routledge and Kegan Paul.

Marx, Karl. [1867] 1976. *Capital.* Vol. 1. New York: Penguin.

Mies, Maria. 1986. *Patriarchy and Accumulation on a World Scale: Women in the International Division of Labour.* London: Zed.

Perelman, Michael. 2000. *The Invention of Capitalism: Classical Political Economy and the Secret History of Primitive Accumulation.* Durham, NC: Duke University Press.

Preobrazhensky, Evgenii Alexeyevich. 1965. *The New Economics.* Oxford: Clarendon Press.

Smith, Adam. [1776] 1976. *An Inquiry into the Nature and Causes of the Wealth of Nations.* Oxford: Clarendon Press.

Massimo De Angelis

PRIMITIVISM

Definitions of the term *primitivism* have varied historically in their intellectual usage and inflection across the disciplines. In its broadest sense, primitivism is an interest in or study of societies and cultures that have an ostensibly less developed notion of technological, intellectual, or social progress. Primitive societies defined thus are those that have not progressed to a state of technological advancement and are therefore perceived as antecedent to the industrialized economies of the West. While more recent definitions of primitivism in literature, visual arts, and anthropology have emphasized the temporal relationship between primitive societies and modernity, discourses on "otherness" are discernible in the Plato's *Republic* and in Homer's description of the Cyclops in *The Odyssey*.

As an intellectual practice or school of thought, primitivism can be broken down into two main strands of inquiry—firstly, that of the empirical study of primitive societies. This approach typified nineteenth-century anthropology, in which empirical study was carried out to chronologically ascribe customs and social structures of "primitive" societies in an evolutionary relationship to Western notions of modernity. Secondly, there is the study of cultural primitivism, which can be traced to Enlightenment philosophical interests in the ideas of nature versus reason seen most notably in Jean-Jacques Rousseau's *Discours sur les sciences et les arts* (1749) [*Discourse on the Sciences and the Arts*] and his idea of the noble savage in *Discours sur l'origine et les fondements de l'inégalité parmi les hommes* (1755) and later in Denis Diderot's *Supplément au voyage au voyage de Bougainville* (1772). In French literature, René Chateaubriand's two novellas, *Atala, ou les amours des deux sauvages dans le désert* (1801) and *René* (1802) continued to explore this post-Enlightenment fascination with non-European cultures.

In the visual arts, earlier aesthetic explorations of the primitive in the work of artists Emil Nolde (1867–1956) and Paul Gauguin (1848–1903) in the nineteenth century began to develop in conjunction with new directions in the social sciences in the early twentieth century. In Europe this development was seen most clearly in the break from the disinterested intellectual focus of Victorian anthropology into the newer paradigms of cultural relativism of ethnology and ethnography that had been emerging since Franz Boas wrote *The Mind of Primitive Man* in 1911 (1983) in which he set out a new model of cultural relativism for the anthropological study of non-Western societies. This approach was taken up and developed by later cultural anthropology in Bronislaw Malinowski's *Argonauts of the Western Pacific* (1922) and *The Sexual Life of Savages in North-Western Melanesia* (1929).

The formation in 1926 of the Institut d'Ethnologie in Paris by ethnologist Marcel Mauss (1872–1950), philosopher Lucien Lévy-Bruhl (1857–1939), and ethnologist Paul Rivet (1876–1958) heralded a new era of ethnographic enquiry into the concept of the primitive in the social sciences. Large-scale interdisciplinary ethnographic projects such as the Mission Dakar Djibouti 1931–1933 brought together writers, artists, sociologists, and anthropologists to work on new conceptualizations of cultural primitivism. In Europe this development of the term *primitivism* was simultaneous with the emergence of the modernist movement in art and literature and a new aesthetic engagement with a notion of the primitive that found diverse expressions in painting, as in Pablo Picasso's *Les Demoiselles d'Avignon* (1907), inspired by his contact with African and Oceanic art in the Musée du Trocadéro. This was also found in the modernist avant-garde performances in the dadaist Cabaret Voltaire and in poetry in Blaise Cendrars's "Prose of the Trans–Siberian" (1913) and Guillaume Apollinaire's "Zone" (1913).

This renewed literary interest in primitivism was in part motivated by several texts that explored psychology, society, and religion from new intellectual and cultural perspectives: Sir James George Frazer's *The Golden Bough: A Study in Magic and Religion*, first published in 1890 (1990), the work of Sigmund Freud in *Totem and Taboo: Some Points of Agreement between the Psychic Lives of Savages and Neurotics* (2000 [1913]) and later in *Civilization and Its Discontents* (2005 [1930]). All in some way influenced some of the major works of European literary modernism such as Joseph Conrad's *Heart of Darkness* (1899), Thomas Mann's *Death in Venice* (1912), and D. H. Lawrence's *The Plumed Serpent* (1926).

Frazer's study of the primitive roots of religion was the first of its kind to examine religious practices and rituals from a cultural rather than a theological perspective, and this marked a twentieth-century movement away from simple evolutionary binary divisions between notions of "primitive" and "civilized" forms of religious practices to more culturally relativist approaches influenced by the theories of Karl Marx (1818–1883), Émile Durkheim (1858–1917), and Max Weber (1864–1920).

SEE ALSO *Anthropology; Boas, Franz; Cultural Relativism; Culture; Ethnology and Folklore; Malinowski, Bronislaw; Religion*

BIBLIOGRAPHY

Boas, Franz. 1983. *The Mind of Primitive Man*. Westport, CT: Greenwood. (Orig. pub. 1911.)

Chateaubriand, René. 1905. *Atala, ou les amours des deux sauvages dans le desert*. Boston: D. C. Heath. (Orig. pub. 1801.)

Chateaubriand, René 1970. *Réné*. Geneva: Droz. (Orig. pub. 1802.)

Clifford, James T. 1988. *The Predicament of Culture: Twentieth Century Ethnography, Literature, and Art*. Cambridge, MA: Harvard University. Press.

De Montaigne, Michel. 1979. *Des Cannibales. Essais*, ed. J. C. Chapman and Frederic Mouret. New York: Atlene.

Fabian, Johannes. 1983. *Time and the Other: How Anthropology Makes Its Objects*. New York: Columbia University Press.

Frazer, James George. 1990. *The Golden Bough: A Study in Magic and Religion*. 3rd ed. New York: St. Martin's. (Orig. pub. 1890.)

Freud, Sigmund. 2000. *Totem and Taboo: Some Points of Agreement between the Psychic Lives of Savages and Neurotics*. Amherst, NY: Prometheus. (Orig. pub. 1913.)

Freud, Sigmund. 2005. *Civilization and Its Discontents*. New York: Norton. (Orig. pub. 1930.)

Goldwater, Robert. 1986. *Primitivism in Modern Art*. Cambridge, MA: Belknap Press.

Guillaume, Apollinaire. 1972. *Zone*. Dublin: Dolmen. (Orig. pub. 1913.)

Malinowski, Bronislaw. 1922. *Argonauts of the Western Pacific*. London: G. Routledge.

Malinowski, Bronislaw. 1929. *The Sexual Life of Savages in North-Western Melanesia: An Ethnographic Account of Courtship, Marriage and Family Life among the Natives of the Trobriand Islands, British New Guinea*. London: G. Routledge.

Mauss, Marcel. 1990. *The Gift: The Form and Reason for Exchange in Archaic Societies*. London: Routledge.

Price, Sally. 2001. *Primitive Art in Civilized Places*. 2nd ed. Chicago: University of Chicago Press.

Rousseau, Jean-Jacques. 1935. *Discours sur les sciences et les arts*. Paris: E. Flammarrion. (Orig. pub. 1749.)

Rousseau, Jean-Jacques. 1954. *Discours sur l'origine et les fondements de l'inégalité parmi les hommes*. Paris: Ed. sociales. (Orig. pub. 1755.)

Rubin, William, ed. 1984. *"Primitivism" in Twentieth Century Art: Affinity of the Tribal and the Modern*. New York: Museum of Modern Art.

Stocking, George W., Jr. 1987. *Victorian Anthropology*. New York: Free Press.

Taussig, Michael. 1993. *Mimesis and Alterity: A Particular History of the Senses*. London: Routledge.

Thomas, Nicholas. 1994. *Colonialism's Culture: Anthropology, Travel and Government*. Princeton, NJ: Princeton University Press.

Torgovnick, Marianna. 1990. *Gone Primitive: Savage Intellects, Modern Lives*. Chicago: University of Chicago Press.

Carole Sweeney

PRINCIPAL COMPONENT ANALYSIS

SEE *Factor Analysis.*

PRINCIPAL COMPONENTS

Quantitative social science often involves measurements of several variables on a number of individuals. Principal components are *variates*, linear combinations of variables that have special properties in terms of variances. Variates having large variance across the population are of special interest, in that they best distinguish among individuals in it.

It is often possible to understand or interpret a set of variables through a few variates. Also, sometimes relationships are not exhibited in the observed variables but rather in combinations of them; principal components can reveal such relationships.

Variates are expressions such as 6X + 8Y or 2X + 3Y + 4Z. The sum and difference are special cases. For example, instead of a verbal *IQ, V,* and a quantitative *IQ, Q,* one might study their sum *V* + *Q* and their difference *V* − *Q.* If it is known that the sum is 260 and the difference is 20, one can see that *V* is 140 and *Q* is 120. If the original variables are replaced by the same number of variates, all the information in the original variables is retained; the original values could be recovered.

It is useful to transform to *uncorrelated* variates, containing separate information. This can be done in many ways, so the transformation can be chosen to have further desirable properties. In principal components analysis, first the variate having the largest possible variance is found. In doing this, the sizes of the coefficients (multipliers of the variables) must be controlled. For example, the variance of 6X + 8Y is 100 times that of 0.6X + 0.8Y. Only *normalized* variates, like the latter, whose coefficients have a sum of squares of one, are considered in defining principal components.

The *first principal component* is the normalized variate having maximum variance. The second principal component is the normalized variate having maximal variance among those uncorrelated with the first. The third principal component is that having maximal variance among those uncorrelated with the first two, and so on. In short, then, the principal components are uncorrelated linear combinations of maximal variance.

Principal components are computed from variances and covariances that depend upon the units of measurement, so often the data are first converted to *z-scores,* each value being replaced by the number of standard deviations above or below the mean for that variable. The resulting variables have variances equal to 1. Sometimes the original data are used, especially when the variables have the same units of measurement, for example when they are measurements of several dimensions of the same object. The operations obtaining principal components are performed on the *covariance matrix.* Use of *z* scores is equivalent to using the *correlation matrix* rather than the covariance matrix.

Principal component analysis approximates the variables using a small number of variates. In exploratory studies involving many variables, some may be dropped later if they have small coefficients in the first several principal components. To obtain a two-dimensional *scatterplot*

of a multivariate sample, the first and second principal components are used.

Principal components can be inputs to another procedure, such as *multiple regression* or *cluster analysis. Factor analysis* describes each variable as having a part that is explained by factors shared with other variables and a unique part that is not so explained; it analyzes the *shared variance* of the set of variables. Once a reduction to a smaller number of factors or principal components is made, often the pattern of coefficients leads to an interpretation of them. Here caution must be exercised. Since there are many mathematically equivalent solutions, such an interpretation is not unique; it is *an* interpretation, not *the* interpretation.

Harold Hotelling (1895–1973), an American economist and statistician, developed many of the ideas of principal components.

SEE ALSO *Cluster Analysis; Factor Analysis; Regression Analysis*

BIBLIOGRAPHY

Hotelling, Harold. 1933. Analysis of a Complex of Statistical Variables into Principal Components. *Journal of Educational Psychology* 24: 417–441, 498–520.

Stanley L. Sclove

PRINCIPAL-AGENT MODELS

Black's Law Dictionary (1999) defines a principal as someone "who authorizes another to act on his or her behalf as an agent." The principal-agent relationship appears in many contexts. An employee acts on behalf of an employer in the sense that the employer receives certain benefits from the employee's actions. Less obviously, there is a principal-agent relationship between an insurance company and an insuree, in the sense that the insurer's actions subsequent to the insurance affect the principal, in effect, via payouts.

In economics, principal-agent problems generally refer to the analysis of contracts between individuals in which the individuals have conflicting goals and where asymmetric information is present. The labor contract is a classic example. A firm, when hiring a worker, wants maximum effort from the worker, whereas in many cases the worker prefers not to perform at the maximum level. If the contract between the two provides a fixed wage independent of the effort of the worker, then the worker has no incentive to work hard. The obvious solution is to make the wage depend on the worker's effort. However, it is often the case that the relevant behavior is unobservable. While one can in principle identify the effort of an isolated worker who is producing objects, one cannot do this in more complicated environments, such as those in which many factors interact to determine output. This example illustrates some of the basic issues that exist in designing contracts in modern economies; namely, the dependence of the payoffs of the participants in a contract on the behaviors of others when these behaviors cannot be observed and can only be enforced by the terms of the contract.

This example of a principal-agent problem has focused on questions of hidden actions; that is, one agent takes an action that is unobservable to another, which affects the benefits to the contract between them. Other principal-agent models focus on the question of hidden information, in which one agent must reveal information to another in order to determine actions under the contract. The classic example of this problem concerns the writing of a contract when the disutility of a job is unknown. If the compensation a worker receives is increasing in the disutility he or she experiences, then he or she will have an incentive to claim the job is unpleasant regardless of the truth.

The analysis of principal-agent problems has led to a large number of substantive insights. For example, insurance deductibles can be understood as a way to create incentives for insurees to avoid overuse of medical care for which they are covered. These models have also been used to understand how landowners structure sharecropper contracts to elicit effort from tenants. The general problem is to structure the contract to obtain maximum expected utility for the principal subject to a constraint that the agent receives some prespecified level of utility. In their 1983 article Sanford Grossman and Oliver Hart discussed the design of optimal incentive schemes in this setting. Roy Radner demonstrated how the principal can improve design of optimal contracts by exploiting information gleaned in a repeated game setting. William Brock and Lewis Evans showed how continuous record asymptotics can be used to uncover hidden actions by agents.

Joseph Stiglitz pioneered a number of the ideas in the principal-agent literature. His Nobel Prize lecture "Information and the Change in Paradigm in Economics" (2002) is an enlightening summary of his thought. Other leading writers in this area include Grossman, Hart, Bengt Holmstrom, Paul Milgrom, James Mirrlees, Roger Myerson, Radner, and Stephen Ross; Ross's 1973 article is an early explicit use of the terms *principals* and *agents* in modern economic theory. The contemporary theory of principal-agent models is well surveyed in Andreu Mas-Collel, Michael Whinston, and Jerry Green's book *Microeconomic Theory* (1995).

SEE ALSO *Information, Asymmetric; Information, Economics of; Mechanism Design*

BIBLIOGRAPHY

Black's Law Dictionary. 1999. 7th ed. St. Paul, MN: West Group.

Brock, William, and Lewis Evans. Principal-Agent Contracts in Continuous Time Asymmetric Information Models: The Importance of Large Continuing Information Flows. *Journal of Economic Behavior and Organization* 29: 523–535.

Grossman, Sanford, and Oliver Hart. 1983. An Analysis of the Principal-Agent Problem. *Econometrica* 51: 7–45.

Mas-Collel, Andreu, Michael Whinston, and Jerry Green. 1995. *Microeconomic Theory.* New York: Oxford University Press.

Radner, Roy. 1985. Repeated Principal-Agent Games with Discounting. *Econometrica.* 53: 1173–1198.

Ross, Stephen. 1973. The Economic Theory of Agency: The Principal's Problem. *American Economic Review* 63: 134–139.

Stiglitz, Joseph. 2002. Information and the Change in Paradigm in Economics. In *Les Prix Nobel; The Nobel Prizes 2001,* ed. Tore Frangsmyr, 472–540. Stockholm: The Nobel Foundation.

William A. Brock
Steven N. Durlauf

PRIOR DISTRIBUTION
SEE *Inference, Bayesian.*

PRIORS
SEE *Bayesian Econometrics.*

PRISON INDUSTRY

Fueled by "get tough on crime" policies, incarceration rates in several developed countries have increased considerably in recent years. For instance, Australia's incarceration rate increased from 89 per 100,000 persons in 1992 to 163 per 100,000 in 2004, while Great Britain's incarceration rate grew from 90 per 100,000 in 1992 to 141 per 100,000 in 2004, according to the International Centre for Prison Studies at King's College London. The increase in incarceration rates has been most prominent in the United States; as of mid-year 2005, there were 2,186,230 inmates behind bars, with two-thirds in federal or state prisons and one-third in local jails, as cited by the U.S. Bureau of Justice Statistics (2006). Approximately 60 percent of those incarcerated in local jails have not been convicted of any crime. The United States incarceration rate in 2005 was 730 per

100,000, a rate that is higher than even the Russian Federation (at 581 per 100,000). In fact, the United States imprisons approximately 500,000 more individuals than China, which has a population five times greater than the United States. Furthermore, while the United States has 5 percent of the world's population, it holds 25 percent of the world's prison population. The United States diverts substantial economic resources to the criminal justice system. In 2003, the country spent $185 billion for police protection, corrections, and judicial activities, representing a 418 percent increase since 1982 (U.S. Department of Justice 2006). In the same year, the justice system employed nearly 2.4 million individuals.

While some believe that the recent increases in incarceration rates are related to increases in crime, most scientific studies of this issue find no such relationship. Instead, fear of crime and the demonization of criminals by the media and politicians have led to support for policies that result in more people being incarcerated, and for longer periods of time. These policies include mandatory minimum sentencing, "three strikes and you're out" laws, truth-in-sentencing legislation (which requires inmates to serve 85 percent of their sentences), and the war on drugs.

Among the major drivers and beneficiaries of these policies and the resultant incarceration binge are constituents of the prison-industrial complex. These growing incarceration rates have created a powerful coalition of vested-interest groups with stakes in keeping prisons full and building more of them. These interests include private prison companies and individuals who lobby for them; financial institutions that underwrite loans and bond issues to finance prison construction; companies involved in the construction, operation, and maintenance of correctional facilities; corporations that use prisoners as a cheap source of labor; state and local politicians with prisons in their districts, or who covet such facilities due to the presumed economic development they will stimulate; individuals employed in the criminal justice system, in particular those who serve as correctional officers in prisons; and companies that provide products and services such as food, medical, transportation, furniture, and telephone services to prisons. Under the laws of several states, prisoners can make only collect phone calls, and this situation results in considerable profit for both states and major telephone companies, with the latter charging up to six times the regular rates plus an automatic "connect fee" of $1.50 to $3.00 per inmate call. AT&T estimates that nationally, inmates place $1 billion per year in long-distance calls, and profits from contracts with MCI and GTE netted the state of California more than $16 million in 1998, while the state of New York received $21.2 million from phone-call commissions in 1997, according to Joseph T. Hallinan in his study *Going up the River: Travels in a Prison Nation* (2001). There is also a burgeoning specialty industry that sells fencing, handcuffs, drug detectors, protective vests, and other security devices to prisons.

Given the considerable profits enjoyed by corporations enriched by the booming prison industry, several communities have competed to host prisons on the assumption that prisons will generate local economic activity in the form of jobs and tax revenues. Recent research, however, casts doubt on this assumption. Prison towns often end up with a net decline in employment, notes Gregory Hooks et al. in *Social Science Quarterly* (2004). This suggests that the benefits are being reaped by distant corporations, not the local communities. This is largely because prisons hire relatively few local employees and because unpaid inmate work crews often compete with local residents for low-wage jobs.

Similar to the military-industrial complex, the prison-industrial complex has an internal logic that allows it to benefit and expand regardless of whether it is a success or failure. If the United States loses a war, it requires more spending to win the next war; if the United States wins a war, it requires more spending to ensure that it keeps on winning. In a similar fashion, if crime is increasing, we need more prisons to lower crime rates; if crime is decreasing, we need more prisons to ensure it continues to decrease (Donziger 1996).

BIBLIOGRAPHY

Bureau of Justice Statistics. 2006. Nation's Prison and Jail Population Grew 2.6 Percent during 12 Months That Ended June 30, 2005. Washington, DC: U.S. Department of Justice. http://www.ojp.usdoj.gov/bjs/pub/press/pjim05pr.htm.

Donziger, Stephen R., ed. 1996. *The Real War on Crime: The Report of the National Criminal Justice Commission.* New York: HarperPerennial.

Hallinan, Joseph T. 2001. *Going up the River: Travels in a Prison Nation.* New York: Random House.

Hooks, Gregory, Clayton Mosher, Thomas Rotolo, and Linda Lobao. 2004. The Prison Industry: Carceral Expansion and Employment in U.S. Counties, 1969–1994. *Social Science Quarterly* 85 (1): 37–57.

International Centre for Prison Studies. (n.d.) London: King's College London. http://www.kcl.ac.uk/depsta/rel/icps/world-prison-pop-seventh.pdf.

U.S. Department of Justice. 2006. Justice Expenditure and Employment in the United States, 2003. Washington, DC. http://www.ojp.gov/bjs/pub/ascii/jeeus03.txt.

Gregory Hooks
Clayton Mosher

PRISON LABOR
SEE *Servitude.*

PRISON PSYCHOLOGY

Prison psychology encompasses both clinical mental health practice within correctional settings and the study of psychological aspects of imprisonment and maladaptive behavior. As a clinical discipline, the term *correctional mental health* is often used to be more inclusive of its multiple professional disciplines and settings, which may include jails, state and federal prisons, juvenile or adult detention centers, and residential "halfway" houses, where inmates may live transitionally after leaving prison. Unlike its courtroom counterparts *forensic psychology* and *psychiatry*, which focus mainly on legal determinations related to criminal behavior, correctional mental health provides clinical assessment and treatment for incarcerated offenders.

The number of inmates in the United States increased more than fivefold between 1973 and the early twenty-first century, as a "law and order" political climate radically altered initial penal policy efforts at rehabilitation and reintegration of offenders into the community. At the same time public and private mental health resources failed to keep pace with the treatment needs of persons with mental illnesses, increasing the numbers of inmates with untreated mental illness in jails and prisons. Studies indicate that at least 8 to 19 percent of prisoners have significant psychiatric or functional disabilities, with another 15 to 20 percent requiring some form of psychiatric intervention during their incarceration. A recent history of a mental health problem (based on symptoms, diagnosis, or treatment by a mental health professional in the past year) was present in more than half of all prison and jail inmates in the United States. Since the 1970s numerous class-action lawsuits and the appearance of basic standards for correctional mental health care have prompted states to provide a system for identifying and monitoring persons with mental illness severe enough to interfere with their functioning, and for transferring at-risk inmates to treatment settings where specific types of services can be provided by trained mental health staff.

The number and credentials of mental health staff in correctional facilities vary greatly by state and locality. Some facilities have a mental health team consisting of a psychiatrist, psychologist, and social worker consulting together. Where special units for more severely ill inmates have been established, music, art, and occupational therapists, psychiatric nurses, and correctional officers may supplement the treatment team.

Prisons and jails vary greatly in mental health programs and services, as they vary in providing inmates access to the recreation, education, and vocational programs that relieve stress and boredom and can inspire a sense of mastery, positive self-concept, and the possibility (with adequate aftercare and community programs) of creating a prosocial future life. At a minimum, most correctional settings share an emphasis on preventing suicides through brief initial assessments and prompt crisis intervention. Primary treatment modalities may include psychopharmacology, group or individual psychotherapy, substance abuse treatment, and occasionally (especially for selected sex offenders) relapse prevention programs. Some facilities offer all inmates life skills training groups, including meditation and anger management, and groups such as the Houses of Healing program, which survey a range of issues commonly encountered by inmates.

Treatment needs are frequently complex. Substance abuse, homelessness, a physical or sexual abuse history, criminal recidivism, and rule violations in prison are seen more frequently in mentally ill inmates. As the inmate population has grown, so has the list of subpopulations of mentally ill inmates with special treatment needs: women, juvenile offenders, the mentally/developmentally disabled, elderly or dying inmates, sexual offenders, and those with diseases especially prevalent among inmates and the mentally ill, such as HIV and hepatitis C.

Since the 1970s the psychotherapy literature itself has changed its focus from individuals, their behavior within society, and the ways they may be rehabilitated to psychopathologies and their treatment. Critics argue that, in the pursuit of treatments for mental illness that are empirically validated or court mandated, the part of an offender that is syndromally "mad" must be distinguished from that which is morally "bad." Symptoms, diagnoses, and (especially in assessing sex offenders) actuarial data, in this view, have eclipsed the broader tasks of discovering the cause and context of offenders' maladaptive behavior and how these fractured individuals, families, and communities may be restored.

However, several factors, including the burgeoning costs of incarceration, have prompted a renewed interest in rehabilitative possibilities. Given high rates of criminal recidivism and illness recurrence when mentally ill inmates return to communities devoid of aftercare and community resources and to avoid a new round of lawsuits, several states are enhancing aftercare programs. "Prison boom" allocations relative to communities' education, job training, housing, community health care, and mental health budgets are under scrutiny. Research has shown that substance abuse treatment reduces serious crime ten times more than conventional enforcement and fifteen times more than mandatory minimum sentencing. Clear racial and economic disparities (approximately half of prison inmates are black, with an incarceration rate averaging five to seven times that of white prisoners) have prompted more discussion of culturally sensitive styles of therapy but have also raised the question of the social context producing the disparity. Women inmates, who typically have higher rates of mental illness than their male counterparts, are frequently separated from their children, who are often at increased risk of becoming the next generation of inmates with mental illness. Research has highlighted incarceration's chilling effect on marital, parenting, and other relationships as well as the marginal communities from which so many young black males have been transplanted to jails and prisons.

The landmark 1971 Stanford Prison Experiment (SPE) by the psychologist Philip Zimbardo highlights the importance of institutional environments themselves in producing maladaptive behavior. Of twenty-four young men selected as "the most normal and healthiest" following a battery of screening tests, half were randomly assigned the role of prisoner, half the role of guard. After a realistic arrest and booking, each prisoner was brought to the "prison" constructed in the basement of Stanford's Psychology Department building. Guards wore military-style uniforms and silver-reflecting sunglasses, and prisoners wore a smock with a prison ID number to enhance anonymity. Within days the "guards" were "behaving sadistically ... inflicting humiliation and pain and suffering on other young men who had the inferior status of prisoner." Signs of "emotional breakdown" caused five "inmates" to be removed from the study the first week. Zimbardo had to terminate the two-week experiment after six days, not only because of the violence and degradation by the guards but because he became aware of his own transformation into a "prison superintendent" in addition to his role as principal investigator.

Hans Toch and Kenneth Adams (2002) extended Zimbardo's "situationist" perspective within an actual prison system by documenting inmates' maladaptive behavior demographically and cross-sectionally then following each inmate's course over time. They found that disciplinary rates peak by the first six to nine months of incarceration, with the youngest inmates (especially when single, unemployed, and uneducated) having the most difficulty adapting. Where the SPE might predict progressively worsening behavior with more prolonged exposure to "prisonization," Toch and Adams found instead that inmates typically lead "compromise existences" in prison that allow for behavioral improvement for most inmates over time. Maturation with the passage of time, nonpunitive structure, and participation in even conventional activities could turn attitudes in a prosocial direction. The authors propose that the self-reform happening by chance encounters in prison might be enhanced through a problem-solving (rather than control-oriented) approach in a therapeutic community setting.

Writing in a twenty-five-year retrospective of the SPE and U.S. prison policy, Zimbardo and Craig Haney recall the era of mass incarceration that followed as "a runaway punishment train, driven by political steam and fueled by media-induced fears of crime" (Zimbardo and Haney 1998, p. 712). They conclude with a hope that the nation reconsiders its strategy of seeking and discarding "bad apples": "While a few bad apples might spoil the barrel (filled with good fruit/people), a barrel filled with vinegar will *always* transform sweet cucumber into sour pickles—regardless of the best intentions, resilience, and genetic nature of those cucumbers" (Zimbardo 2004, p. 47).

SEE ALSO *Authoritarianism; Crime and Criminology; Homelessness; Mental Health; Militarism; Prison Industry; Prisoner's Dilemma (Psychology); Prisons; Psychotherapy; Self-Concept; Zimbardo, Philip*

BIBLIOGRAPHY

Correctional Mental Health Care: Standards and Guidelines for Delivering Services. 2003. National Commission on Correctional Health Care, Chicago. http://www.ncchc.org.

Haney, Craig, and Philip Zimbardo. 1998. The Past and Future of U.S. Prison Policy: Twenty-Five Years after the Stanford Prison Experiment. *American Psychologist* 53 (7): 709–727. http://www.prisonexp.org.

Mental Health Problems of Prison and Jail Inmates. 2006. U.S. Department of Justice, Bureau of Justice Statistics. http://www.ojp.usdoj.gov.

Schwartz, Barbara K., ed. 2003. *Correctional Psychology: Practice, Programming, and Administration.* Kingston, NJ: Civic Research Institute.

Toch, Hans, and Kenneth Adams. 2002. *Acting Out: Maladaptive Behavior in Confinement.* Washington, DC: American Psychological Association.

Western, Bruce. 2006. *Punishment and Inequality in America.* New York: Russell Sage Foundation.

Zimbardo, Philip. 2004. A Situationist Perspective on the Psychology of Evil: Understanding How Good People Are Transformed into Perpetrators. In *The Social Psychology of Good and Evil*, ed. Arthur G. Miller, 21–50. New York: Guilford.

Russell J. Geoffrey

PRISONER'S DILEMMA (ECONOMICS)

The prisoner's dilemma is a classic example of an environment in which individuals rationally fail to cooperate even though cooperation would make each person better off. A standard formulation is the following: Two men commit a crime and are arrested. The following possible punishments await them. If both men confess, each will receive five years in prison. If neither man confesses, each will receive three years in prison. If one man confesses and the other does not, the confessor will receive one year in prison whereas the other receives ten.

The two men would receive the lightest sentence if both refused to confess than if neither does so. However, suppose each man is a prisoner in his own separate holding cell, so that it is impossible for the two men to coordinate their behavior. If the prisoners are acting rationally, each will confess. The reason is the following: A person convicted of a crime should confess if it reduces his prison sentence. The complication in each man's decision is that the consequence of his behavior depends on the behavior of the other man, which he does not know. However, in the prisoner's dilemma, it turns out that the rational choice for a prisoner is to confess regardless of the behavior of the other prisoner. To see this, if the other prisoner confesses, then confession brings a sentence of five years whereas not confessing brings ten years. If the other prisoner does not confess, then confession brings a sentence of one year whereas not confessing brings three. Thus, confession is a dominant strategy as it is always preferable to the alternative. The two men therefore choose strategies that, although individually rational, are collectively inferior to those they would choose if they could cooperate.

When one considers situations where individuals play a sequence of prisoner's dilemma games, rational behavior leads to very different outcomes. The reason for this is that for repeated prisoner's dilemma games, each player will be making a sequence of choices so that the decision to cooperate in one game can depend on the past behavior of the other player. This means that players can reward each other by making choices that depend on the play of their opponent. The existence of noncooperative equilibrium strategies for an infinite repeated prisoner's dilemma has been shown in many contexts; a classic formulation is explored in Drew Fudenberg and Eric Maskin's 1986 paper. It is also possible for periods of cooperation to occur in finite sequential games, as described in David Kreps et al.'s 1982 work.

The prisoner's dilemma is a basic component of any game theory textbook; a particularly insightful treatment may be found in Roger Myerson's *Game Theory* (1991). A history that places the prisoner's dilemma in the context of the development of game theory is William Poundstone's book *Prisoner's Dilemma* (1992).

BIBLIOGRAPHY

Fudenberg, Drew, and Eric Maskin. 1986. The Folk Theorem in Repeated Games with Discounting and with Incomplete Information. *Econometrica* 54: 533–554.

Kreps, David, Paul Milgrom, D. John Roberts, and Robert Wilson. 1982. Rational Cooperation in the Finitely Repeated Prisoner's Dilemma. *Journal of Economic Theory* 27: 245–252.

Myerson, Roger. 1991. *Game Theory: Analysis of Conflict.* Cambridge, MA: Harvard University Press.

Poundstone, William. 1992. *Prisoner's Dilemma.* New York: Doubleday.

William A. Brock
Steven N. Durlauf

PRISONER'S DILEMMA (PSYCHOLOGY)

The prisoner's dilemma game (PDG) is a method of indicating the results of the possible pairings of the cooperative and noncooperative choices of two players. PDG can be illustrated by either of the matrices in Figure 1. With a PDG there are two players, a column player (*A*) and a row player (*B*), each of whom has two choices, *X* or *Y*, resulting in four possible combinations of choices with each combination yielding a different set of payoffs or outcomes. Payoffs or outcomes can be thought of as rewards or as some index of player satisfaction. The usual convention is that numbers above the diagonal in each cell represent the outcomes for the column player, and numbers below the diagonal in each cell represent the outcomes for the row player. In the example matrices, the numbers, or outcomes, can be thought of as dollars.

Suppose that both players choose *X*. For the left-hand matrix this combination of choices would result in each player receiving $3. After such a combination of choices, one player, for example the column player, might be tempted to choose *Y* on the next trial. If the row player continued to choose *X*, the result would be that the column player's outcome would increase to $4, but the row player's outcome would decrease to $1. Following such a result, one can imagine that the row player would shift from *X* to *Y* on the next trial, with the result that both players would receive only $2. Such a possibility illustrates the dilemma. Each player can increase his or her outcomes by choosing *Y*, but if both players are guided by immediate self-interest, both will receive lower outcomes than could have been obtained through cooperation or mutual *X* choices.

The *X* choice is usually referred to as a *cooperative choice*, and the *Y* choice is sometimes referred to as a *competitive choice* and sometimes as a *defecting choice*. Which term is more appropriate depends on whether the *Y* choice is motivated by greed or by fear. If the *Y* choice is motivated by greed, or an interest in increasing outcomes, the choice is appropriately referred to as a competitive choice. On the other hand, if the *Y* choice is motivated by fear, or an interest in minimizing the reduction in outcome resulting from the other player's *Y* choice, the *Y*

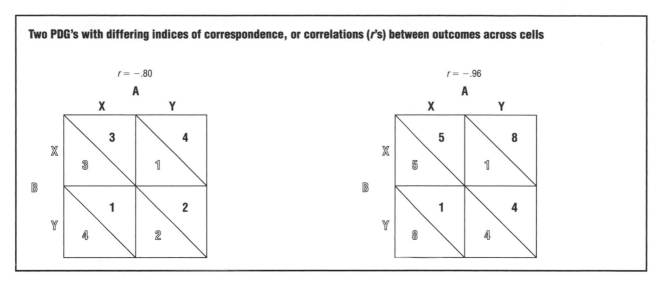

Two PDG's with differing indices of correspondence, or correlations (*r*'s) between outcomes across cells

Figure 1

choice is appropriately referred to as a defecting choice (a choice to withdraw from cooperation).

According to Matt Ridley, "broadly speaking any situation in which you are tempted to do something, but know it would be a great mistake if everybody did the same thing, is likely to be a prisoner's dilemma" (1996, pp. 55–56). An everyday example relates to being honest versus cheating. Other examples relate to overwhaling, overfishing, pollution of the air, pollution of the water, and conservation of water during a drought. These latter examples, which may involve more than two people and may provide more than two choices (e.g., how much water to save and not just whether to save or not to save water), are sometimes labeled *resource dilemmas* and sometimes labeled *commons dilemmas*. The term *commons* comes from Garrett Hardin's (1968, 1993, 1998) description of the potential "tragedy" that could result from overgrazing in a shared, but unmanaged, medieval commons or pasture. Commons dilemmas share with the PDG the assumption that the pursuit of self-interest results in collective detriment. This assumption stands in contrast to Adam Smith's (1776) marketplace model, which implies that the pursuit of self-interest results in collective benefit. One can regard many political disputes as partially flowing from disagreement regarding which model is more appropriate in a particular situation.

William Poundstone (1992, p. 123) maintains that recognition of the tension between self-interest and the common good has been widespread; he supports this assertion by citing numerous historical instances of statements similar to the "golden rule" as stated in the Bible in Matthew 7:12, "In everything, do to others what you would have them do to you." However, the conflict

between self-interest and the common good was first cast in the form of a two-by-two matrix by two mathematicians at Rand Corporation, Merrill Flood and Melvin Dresher (1952). The matrix was specifically created to provide an empirical test of mathematician John Nash's concept of an equilibrium point, developed in his 1950 dissertation at Princeton University (see Colman 1995, pp. 58–61; Nasar 1998, pp. 115–122).

For the PDG, the Nash equilibrium is the lower right-hand cell. On the assumption that each player assumes that the other player will follow his or her self-interest, the players should arrive at this mutual-*Y* cell. Such choices should, furthermore, be stable or in equilibrium, because if either player moves from this cell, he or she will receive a lower outcome. In order to test Nash's theory, Flood and Dresher had two colleagues in January 1950 play the PDG for one hundred trials. The results indicated that mutual *Y* choices, the Nash equilibrium, only occurred fourteen times. One player cooperated sixty-eight of one hundred times, and the other player cooperated seventy-eight of one hundred times. Although there was some competition, or defection, clearly the participants did not behave as Nash's theory predicted.

Subsequently, the Flood and Dresher matrix was labeled the *prisoner's dilemma game* by mathematician Albert Tucker, Nash's adviser at Princeton University. At a talk given to the Psychology Department at Stanford University in 1950, Tucker illustrated the matrix with an anecdote of two prisoners who had been arrested on suspicion of having committed a crime. Each prisoner had a choice of remaining silent (analogous to choosing *X*) or of giving evidence against the other (analogous to choosing *Y*). Either prisoner could minimize his sentence by giving evidence against the other, but when both gave evidence, the prisoners could be convicted of a more serious charge than when both remained silent.

The PDG is sometimes characterized as a matrix meeting two requirements. First, the outcomes in the four cells follow a rank order for the column player from upper right to upper left to lower right to lower left. Note from the left-hand matrix in Figure 1 that the payoffs in these cells are 4, 3, 2, 1. (For the row player, the rank order is from lower left to upper left to lower right to upper right.) Second, the average outcome for the upper-right and lower-left cells is less than the outcome in the upper-left cell. Note that 2.5, the average of 4 and 1, is less than 3. This second requirement guarantees that higher outcomes will be achieved by mutual *X* choices, rather than by alternating between the lower-left and upper-right cells.

Interdependence theory (Kelley and Thibaut 1978; Kelley et al. 2002) provides a more sophisticated perspective on the PDG. This perspective relies on four concepts that can be illustrated by the left-hand matrix in Figure 1. The first of these is labeled *actor control* (AC) by Harold Kelley and his coauthors, and reflects the direct control that each player has over his or her own outcomes. For the column player, AC is the difference in column averages (the average of 3 and 1, or 2, for the *X* column versus the average of 4 and 2, or 3, for the *Y* column). For the row player, AC is the difference in row averages. For both players, AC is 1.

The second concept is labeled *partner control* (PC) by Kelley and his associates, and reflects the direct control that the partner has over actor outcomes. For the column player, PC is the difference in row averages (the average of 3 and 4, or 3.5, for the *X* row versus the average of 1 and 2, or 1.5, for the *Y* row). For the row player, PC is the difference in column averages. For both players, PC is 2. Note that AC has a smaller absolute value than PC, and also that an increase in one player's AC results in a decrease in the partner's PC. If the column player, for example, increases AC by shifting from *X* to *Y*, the row player's PC is decreased. From the perspective of AC and PC alone, the PDG is a matrix in which a small increase in one's own outcomes results in a large loss in partner outcomes.

The third concept is labeled *joint control* (JC) by Kelley and his coauthors, and reflects the extent to which the players can maximize their outcomes by taking turns, or alternating, their *X* and *Y* choices. For both players, JC is the difference in diagonal averages (the average of 3 and 2 versus the average of 4 and 1). For both players, JC is 0; that is, there is no joint control or advantage in alternating *X* and *Y* choices. The purpose of the requirement that JC be 0 is similar to the purpose of the above requirement that the average outcome for either column or row player

for the upper-right and lower-left cells is less than the outcome in the upper-left cell.

The fourth and final interdependence theory concept is the correspondence between the two players' outcomes across the four cells. For matrices such as those in Figure 1, in which the players' outcomes are symmetric, correspondence is indexed by the correlation between the two players' outcomes across the four cells. For the PDG, the correlation is always negative; that is, in general, as one player's outcomes increase, the other player's outcomes decrease.

The correlation between the outcomes for the two players is a mathematical consequence of the AC to PC ratio. For the left-hand matrix, the ratio is 1 to 2 and the correlation is -.80. For the right-hand matrix, the ratio is 3 to 4 and the correlation is -.96. This difference illustrates the point that the PDG is not one matrix, but a family of matrices with differing AC to PC ratios. The importance of this point becomes apparent in view of the interdependence theory assumption that correspondence reflects conflict of interest. As the AC to PC ratio becomes larger, and the correlation more negative, conflict of interest increases. From the perspective of interdependence theory, some PDG situations are more likely than others to lead to conflict.

Research has indicated that when the PDG is played between two groups, each of which is required to make a consensus choice on each trial, there is frequently, but not always, more competition than there is between individuals (see Wildschut et al. [2003] for a statistical summary, or meta-analysis, of published research). This difference, which is labeled a *discontinuity effect*, has been shown to be more evident as correspondence, or the correlation between the individuals' or groups' outcomes, becomes more negative.

SEE ALSO *Common Good, The; Commons, The; Externality; Nash Equilibrium; Nash, John; Noncooperative Games*

BIBLIOGRAPHY

Colman, Andrew M. 1995. *Game Theory and Its Applications in the Social and Biological Sciences.* 2nd ed. London: Butterworth-Heinemann.

Flood, Merrill M. 1952. *Some Experimental Games, Research Memorandum Rm-789.* Santa Monica, CA: Rand Corporation.

Hardin, Garrett. 1968. The Tragedy of the Commons. *Science* 162: 1243–1248.

Hardin, Garrett. 1993. *Living within Limits: Ecology, Economics, and Population Taboos.* New York: Oxford University Press.

Hardin, Garrett. 1998. Extensions of "The Tragedy of the Commons." *Science* 280: 682–683.

Kelley, Harold H., and John W. Thibaut. 1978. *Interpersonal Relations: A Theory of Interdependence*. New York: Wiley.

Kelley, Harold H., et al. 2002. *An Atlas of Interpersonal Situations*. Cambridge, U.K.: Cambridge University Press.

Nasar, Sylvia. 1998. *A Beautiful Mind: A Biography of John Forbes Nash, Jr., Winner of the Nobel Prize in Economics, 1994*. New York: Touchstone.

Nash, John F., Jr. 1950. Non-Cooperative Games. PhD diss., Princeton University, Princeton, NJ.

Poundstone, William. 1992. *Prisoner's Dilemma*. New York: Doubleday.

Ridley, Matt. 1996. *The Origins of Virtue: Human Instincts and the Evolution of Cooperation*. London: Penguin.

Smith, Adam. [1776] 2003. *An Enquiry into the Nature and Causes of the Wealth of Nations*. London: Methuen.

Wildschut, Tim, et al. 2003. Beyond the Group Mind: A Quantitative Review of the Interindividual-Intergroup Discontinuity Effect. *Psychological Bulletin* 129: 698–722.

Chester A. Insko

PRISONS

The prison, which would become a dominant correctional strategy in Western societies, emerged in the late 1700s. Throughout its history, the prison has been used in attempts to achieve various goals of criminal sanctioning: retribution, incapacitation, general and specific deterrence, and rehabilitation. No one theory can account for the historical development and evolution of the prison. Michael Welch, a highly regarded criminologist, makes the observation that correctional ideologies, policies, and practices cannot be understood outside the political, economic, religious, and technological forces that shape them.

HISTORY OF THE PRISON

Forerunners of the more sophisticated models of the prison were *workhouses* and *houses of correction* that emerged in western Europe. In the eighteenth century, when European societies were experiencing a dramatic population shift to urban areas due to the breakdown of the feudal order and the Industrial Revolution, these institutions became a mechanism for managing the growing numbers of an urban underclass. The expressed objective of workhouses and houses of correction was to provide vocational training and to instill a work ethic among inmates. However, these institutions functioned more effectively to remove "undesirables" from the community and, most importantly, to provide a cheap source of labor to private industry.

The United States is credited with being most influential in the development and proliferation of the modern prison. A wing of the Walnut Street Jail in Philadelphia (1790–1835) was the first *penitentiary*. Influenced by the religious ideology of the Pennsylvania Quakers, the penitentiary was designed for the solitary confinement of criminal offenders, a place where they would repent for their sins without the contaminating influences of other prisoners or the community. These objectives were the foundation for the design of the Western State Penitentiary in Pittsburgh and the Eastern State Penitentiary in Philadelphia, opened in 1826 and 1829, respectively. Because it was believed that work would interfere with inmates' penitence, inmate work was not originally planned or desired by the founders of the penitentiary. However, individual handicraft work (e.g., weaving, woodcarving, leather tooling) was introduced later to ameliorate the negative consequences of solitary confinement and idleness. During the development of the Pennsylvania system, an alternative prison model, the Auburn system, emerged in New York.

The Auburn Prison opened in Auburn, New York, in 1817. The Auburn model incorporated a silent congregate work system, ostensibly through which inmates would learn vocational skills and be instilled with the work ethic. In complete silence, inmates would work in factory-like settings during the day, and return to their cells at night. The goal of the *silent system* was to prevent the spread of criminogenic values and influences among inmates. Order was maintained through a quasi-militaristic regimen, such as lockstep marching and harsh punishments for rule infractions.

The Auburn system proliferated in the United States at the same time that western European societies modeled their prisons after the Pennsylvania system. Whereas Europeans were compelled by rehabilitative ideals and what they saw as more humane treatment of inmates, the United States was motivated by the low operating costs and profits generated by cheap inmate labor sold to private industry.

Fortresslike industrial factory prisons dominated the penal landscape in the United States until the early twentieth century, when laws were passed, prompted largely by skyrocketing unemployment in the private sector during the Great Depression, restricting prison industry to the manufacture of instate public-use goods. The result of the demise of prison industry was an idle inmate population in which discipline and control, rather than production and vocational rehabilitation, became the primary objective of the prison.

A radical turn in the objectives and nature of the prison in the United States emerged following World War II (1939–1945) with the emergence and dominance of *correctional institutions*. The expressed goal of correctional institutions was the treatment and rehabilitation of inmates. Therapeutic professionals, including physicians, psychologists, educators, and social workers, were charged with diagnosing and treating inmates based on individual needs. Under indeterminate sentencing strategies, parole boards were given more discretionary power to release inmates once they were deemed to be rehabilitated.

The ideals of the correctional system began to unravel in the 1960s, in part due to overcrowding, lack of funding, and a turbulent period of unrest associated with the prisoner rights movement. Despite these systemic circumstances, a neoconservative political climate that exaggerated the failings of the rehabilitation model was successful in garnering public support for a "get tough" approach to crime. The momentum of the movement became most evident in the 1980s when the United States embarked on an "imprisonment binge." Within a decade, both the prison population and rate of incarceration more than doubled as a result of the proliferation of new federal and state prisons. This trend of expansion continued through the 1990s with the rate of incarceration reaching 491 per 100,000 U.S. citizens in 2005 compared to 139 in 1980. Longer, determinate sentences contributed to this growth, but no single factor is more responsible than the concentration on the arrest and incarceration of illegal drug offenders.

Between 1985 and 1995, over 80 percent of the increase in the federal prison population was due to illegal drug offenses. In 1985, 34 percent of prisoners were incarcerated for drug offenses; by 1995 the proportion was 60 percent. As the state prison populations tripled in the late 1900s, the proportion of inmates incarcerated for drug offenses grew from 9 percent in 1986 to 23 percent by 1995.

IMPACT ON WOMEN AND MINORITIES

The crackdown on drugs had a disproportionate impact on women and minorities, particularly African Americans. There were almost eight times as many female prisoners in 2003 as there were in 1980, and the primary reason for the growth was drug offenses.

Similarly, illegal drug offenses contributed to a much greater extent to the growth of the African American prison population in the latter twentieth century compared to the growth for whites and Hispanics. Welch points out that "African Americans represent 12 percent of the U.S. population, 13 percent of drug users, 35 percent of the arrests for drug possession, 55 percent of convictions for drug possession, and 74 percent of the prison sentences for drug convictions" (2004, p. 439).

PERSPECTIVES ON THE PRISON

The ideals and functions of the prison can be viewed from three broad and competing perspectives: conservative, liberal, and critical. From the conservative perspective, the threat of imprisonment is believed to deter would-be offenders from committing crimes (general deterrence), while the purpose of prisons is to protect society from those who are not deterred (incapacitation), and through this punishment, deter convicted offenders from repeating crimes (specific deterrence). The conservative ideology is based on a fundamental belief that criminal offenders are driven by the choice to engage in criminal behavior and that crime can be controlled through the threat of punishment and the incapacitation of those who are not deterred.

From the liberal perspective, a criminal offense is seen as a result of forces—biological, psychological, or socio-environmental—that influence the behavior. This perspective upholds the rehabilitative ideal that prisons should function to treat and rehabilitate offenders in order that they ultimately may be reintegrated into free society. Under the liberal perspective, scientific inquiry into the etiology of criminal behavior will reveal its underlying causes, and correctional rehabilitation is ideally guided by those etiological factors.

From the critical perspective, the criminal justice system is considered a means of social control that is used by the powerful class over the less powerful. Consistent with Karl Marx's (1818–1883) writings, criminal behavior is primarily the consequence of the economic order and politics in society. The criminal justice system and prisons, in particular, function to control an economically marginalized population, also defined as a surplus labor pool. Critical criminologists point to historical trends across societies in which correctional populations swell in times of abundant free-market labor and shrink in times of labor shortages. In his compelling book, *The Warehouse Prison* (2005), John Irwin adopts a critical perspective to describe the economic conditions and resulting marginalized population that spawned the prison expansion in the United States in the late twentieth century.

While the prison remains a dominant strategy aimed at controlling crime and punishing offenders in Western societies, there is a great deal of doubt among scholars that it is an effective strategy beyond retribution and incapacitation. The high recidivism rate of ex-inmates points to the general failure of imprisonment to deter or rehabilitate and, further, may promote a higher level of criminality among those released. With over 90 percent of inmates ultimately returning to free society, this is, or should be, a central concern for social reform.

Prison abolitionists advocate radical reform in the use of incarceration. Vocal prison abolitionists span both ends of the political spectrum. Pointing to the failure of the prison system to reform or deter, and to the swelling prison population, as well as to the evidence and claims that current practices are racist and classist, abolitionists promote expanded and widespread use of alternatives to incarceration for most offenses and support the decriminalization of certain behaviors, such as drug offenses. With the entrenchment of the prison as a primary means of criminal sanctioning, along with the recent privatization of prisons and of corrections, in general, the abolitionists face powerful ideological and economic barriers.

SEE ALSO *African Americans; Crime and Criminology; Davis, Angela; Deterrence; Drug Traffic; Imprisonment; Law; Punishment; Racism*

BIBLIOGRAPHY

Irwin, John. 2005. *The Warehouse Prison: Disposal of the New Dangerous Class.* Los Angeles: Roxbury.

Scalia, John. 2001. Federal Drug Offenders, 1999 with Trends 1984–99. Bureau of Justice Statistics Special Report. Washington, DC: U.S. Department of Justice, Office of Justice Programs.

Shichor, David. 2006. *The Meaning and Nature of Punishment.* Long Grove, IL: Waveland.

Welch, Michael. 2004. *Corrections: A Critical Approach.* 2nd ed. Boston: McGraw-Hill.

Douglas L. Kuck

PRIVACY

One of the main difficulties in assessing the meaning of *privacy* in the social sciences is that the term usually connotes a normative character. From the liberal defense of privacy as a right that protects individuals from state intervention and abuse, to the feminist critiques that denounce its role in disguising the oppression of women, most definitions of privacy present contrasting perspectives regarding its value or function.

Yet, when approached from the standpoint of ordinary language, privacy describes a certain domain of social practice—spatial, relational, decisional—that is generally expected to be sheltered from public scrutiny. It can be argued then, that privacy also facilitates the emergence of difference and particularity, and nourishes the development of interpersonal relations based on varying degrees of closeness and *intimacy* (Boling 1996).

The notion of privacy is closely connected to the predicate *private*, which can be ascribed to places and objects but also to practices, decisions, information, feelings, or—as critic Iris Young synthesizes—any aspect of life from which one has a right to exclude others. Control over access, then, is a central feature of privacy (Gavison 1980). Since the last decades of the twentieth century, concern over the right to privacy, its limits, and the legal measures to protect it has spanned the advances of information technologies and the incursion of the media; regulation over sexuality and the body, reproductive rights, or domestic violence; and issues of family law, such as decisions on childrearing.

In all these discussions, *privacy* designates a sphere of life that is protected from the influence of what is deemed external, be it state institutions or the public realm more generally. The history of the distinction between the private and public spheres can be traced back to the Greek philosopher Aristotle (384–322 BCE), who conceived the domain of the household and family in opposition to the *polis*, or public realm of political activity. The divide has since remained a central theoretical notion and was inherited by the social sciences, often resulting in one of the poles viewed as a residual category defined by its opposition and relative subordination to the other. Modern theories of the public sphere, for example, often relegate the private realm to a subsidiary role. Thus, Hannah Arendt (1906–1975) argues that household matters—such as the sustenance and reproduction of life—are necessary preconditions for political life but are not part of it. In a similar vein, Jürgen Habermas sees the family as functioning to prepare individuals to be rational and autonomous actors in the public realm. In both depictions the spheres are clearly distinguished by virtue of their content, the private being equated with the *domestic* realm where basic necessities of life are satisfied.

The public/private divide is one of the pillars of liberal political theory, where the private is given preeminence as the sphere of individual freedoms. Classical liberal philosophers attribute a quasi-natural quality to the private realm, which is associated to the individual in opposition to the contractual character of society. This becomes evident in John Locke's (1632–1704) natural law arguments restricting the power of the state over private property and the family, or John Stuart Mill's (1806–1873) discussion of privacy as the natural domain of liberty.

Liberalism has long considered privacy a necessary requirement for *autonomy*, as it provides the adequate milieu to develop the capacity of independent decision making that allows one to lead a self-determined or autonomous life. This argument conveys an implicit spatial understanding of privacy as isolation, or *seclusion*, straightforwardly demarcating the space of the individual from the outside. However, privacy can conversely be conceived as a condition that allows selective degrees of access and fosters intimacy and relations with others (Schoeman 1992).

Legal perspectives focus on the notion of privacy as a right, questioning if it designates a specific domain not provided for by other established rights, such as the right to property or to individual freedoms, or debating whether it is granted by the U.S. Constitution. In the American case, for example, there has been significant discussion since the late nineteenth century concerning the status of privacy as a principle of common law. Whether considered a legal right or a moral principle, however, there is an understanding of the notion of privacy as protecting individuals from unwanted contact with others and intrusion or judgment on personal decisions.

The feminist critique that emerged in the second half of the twentieth century, has consistently challenged the liberal notion that privacy benefits all equally. Through historical and theoretical elaborations, feminists have shown that the conventional distinction between the public and the private spheres is not only naturalized, but also gendered, as the domestic is considered the realm of women and thus deprived of public recognition. The defense of privacy, they argue, serves the purpose of concealing the oppression of women through the appearance of personal choice and intimacy. Feminists deny any particularity of social relationships that happen in private that inherently distinguishes them from those that take place in public, as they are all conditioned by power and hierarchy. Rather, it is the distinction between the private and the public—between a prepolitical or natural sphere and a political one—that performs the ideological role of hiding oppression. Feminist critics have moved to reject the very distinction by stating that even the personal is political (MacKinnon 1989).

Still, several scholars are reluctant to abandon the notion of privacy altogether, and propose to produce a redescription of the concept taking into account the aforementioned critiques. Political theorists like Jean Cohen or Iris Young, for example, argue that privacy does not merely obscure oppressive practices but also enables diversity by protecting from the homogenizing pressure of the public realm and facilitating differences in experience and perspectives. Moreover, the concept is useful to confront domination of women and minorities by preserving a domain of information and decision, which might involve aspects of intimacy, sexuality, the body, or other personal issues. In a similar tone to Ferdinand Schoeman's suggestions, these arguments draw away from conceiving the private and the public as clearly demarcated spaces, and view them instead as dimensions of social relations present in different spheres of life. Moving away from the normative bend, social sciences might depict privacy as a common practice emerging from and at the same time constituting a shared form of life.

BIBLIOGRAPHY

Arendt, Hannah. 1958. *The Human Condition.* Chicago: University of Chicago Press.

Boling, Patricia. 1996. *Privacy and the Politics of Intimate Life.* Ithaca, NY: Cornell University Press.

Cohen, Jean. 2001. Introduction to Section "Privacy and the State." *Social Research* 68 (1): 235–236.

Gavison, Rachel. 1980. Privacy and the Limits of Law. *Yale Law Journal* 89: 421–471.

Habermas, Jürgen. 1989. *The Structural Transformation of the Public Sphere: An Inquiry into a Category of Bourgeois Society.* Trans. Thomas Burger. Cambridge, MA: MIT Press.

Locke, John. [1690] 1980. *The Second Treatise of Government.* Ed. C. B. Macpherson. Indianapolis, IN: Hackett.

MacKinnon, Catharine. 1989. *Toward a Feminist Theory of the State.* Cambridge, MA: Harvard University Press.

Mill, John Stuart. 2002. *The Basic Writings of John Stuart Mill.* Ed. Dale E. Miller. New York: Modern Library.

Rössler, Beate. 2005. *The Value of Privacy.* Trans. R. D. V. Glasgow. Cambridge, U.K., and Malden, MA: Polity.

Schoeman, Ferdinand. 1992. *Privacy and Social Freedom.* Cambridge, U.K.: Cambridge University Press.

Young, Iris. 1990. *Justice and the Politics of Difference.* Princeton, NJ: Princeton University Press.

Valeria Procupez

PRIVATE INTERESTS

The distinction between public and private interests has deep roots in the Western political tradition, dating back to ancient times. Roman philosopher Marcus Tullius Cicero (106–43 BCE), for example, defined a "republic" as "the property of the people" and argued that the power of the state should be used only to advance the common interests of its citizens. More recently political theorists of widely varying views have argued that government power should only be used to promote the public interest rather than purely private ones.

Seventeenth-century English philosopher John Locke (1632–1704) and later theorists in the liberal social contract tradition contended that the functions of the state should be limited to those that flow from the purposes for which the people consented to be bound by the government. Should government power exceed its assigned purposes and begin to serve the narrow interests of private individuals at the expense of the general public, the latter would no longer be bound by its laws and might even have a right to rebel.

THE PUBLIC INTEREST AND AMERICAN POLITICAL THOUGHT

Distinctions between public and private interests have also played an important role in the American political tradition. Like Locke, many of the Founding Fathers believed that the powers of government should be limited to promoting the public interest, as opposed to promoting the selfish parochial interests of individuals or "factions." The Preamble of the U.S. Constitution reflects this belief, stating that the purpose of the new government is to "provide for the common defense and general welfare," a phrase repeated in the Constitution's Spending Clause, which grants Congress the power to raise taxes in order to "provide for the common Defense and General Welfare of the United States." The phrase "General Welfare" was understood to exclude the possibility of expenditures intended for the sole benefit of particular states and individuals, though there was much disagreement about where the line between "general" and local or private interests should be drawn. In the nineteenth and early twentieth centuries, American courts would periodically invalidate various economic and other regulations on the grounds that they represented "class legislation" intended to benefit narrow interest groups at the expense of the general public.

From ancient times to the present, however, advocates of differing ideologies have disagreed over the question of what interests truly count as "public" and which are merely private. The rise of the modern welfare state accentuated such divisions. Liberals and egalitarians view many redistributive programs as essential to the promotion of the public interest, while libertarians and conservatives see them as wealth transfers to narrow interest groups promoting purely private interests. The concept of the public interest maintains its hold on our imagination in part because we can each define it in a way conducive to our own preferred ideology and self-interest.

PUBLIC AND PRIVATE GOODS

Modern economic theory helps to shed light on the distinction between private and public interests through the concept of public and private goods. A public good is characterized by the fact that it is nonrivalrous and nonexclusive. Consumption of the good by one person does not prevent simultaneous consumption by others; nonexclusivity implies that, once the good is produced, it is impossible to exclude anyone in the relevant group from its benefits. A classic example is clean air. One person breathing clean air does not prevent others from enjoying it as well, and once air pollution has been eliminated in a given area, it is impossible to exclude anyone in that territory from benefiting from its removal. Standard public goods theory concludes that, absent government intervention,

public goods will tend to be underproduced by the market, since individuals will have little or no incentive to contribute to their production. Instead, many may seek to "free ride" on the efforts of others.

The distinction between public and private goods offers a possible way to draw the elusive line between public and private interests. In theory, the production of a public good is in the interests of everyone in the relevant population, yet underproduction is likely in the absence of government intervention. Thus, the provision of public goods may well be coextensive with the public interest. By contrast, private goods will usually be adequately produced by the market, and so their attempted production by government is likely to advance only private interests, transferring wealth from the general public to narrow interest groups or individual citizens.

However, the production of public goods does not fully capture the concept of the public interest as it is understood by either ordinary citizens or many political theorists. If, for example, the idea of the public interest includes some commitment to distributive justice, wealth transfers that provide only private goods may still be viewed as "public." Unemployment insurance, old age pensions, and most other welfare state programs provide benefits that economic theory would classify as private goods. Yet, an argument can be made that these programs nonetheless advance the public interest.

As a proxy for the public interest, public goods theory may be overbroad as well as underinclusive. Recent scholarship shows that traditional public goods theory may have been too quick to conclude that public goods will always be underproduced by the market. Scholars have identified several mechanisms by which an optimal level of public good production can occur even without government intervention. For example, private "planned communities" effectively produce such public goods as security and local pollution control for their residents. It may not be in the public interest for government to try to provide those public goods that are already produced in close to optimal quantities by market mechanisms.

Ultimately, the distinction between public and private interests is very difficult to define because it is more a normative concept than an empirical or theoretical one. Economics and other social sciences can help us understand whether or not a particular goal can be better achieved by the state or by the private sector. But they cannot, in and of themselves, prove that it is in the public interest.

SEE ALSO *Defense; Defense, National; Locke, John; Private Sector; Public Goods; Public Interest*

BIBLIOGRAPHY

Cicero. 1998. *The Republic and the Laws.* Trans. Niall Rudd. New York: Oxford University Press.

Locke, John. 1963. *Two Treatises of Government.* Ed. Peter Laslett. New York: Cambridge University Press.

Schmidtz, David. 1991. *The Limits of Government: An Essay on the Public Goods Argument.* Boulder, CO: Westview Press.

Schubert, Glendon A. 1982. *The Public Interest: A Critique of the Theory of a Political Concept.* Westport, CT: Greenwood Press.

Ilya Somin

PRIVATE SECTOR

The private sector is the part of a country's economy that is not controlled directly by the government; it is a term that combines households and businesses in the economy into a single group. The resources of production owned by the private sector are owned in the form of private property. The private sector includes entities such as households and individuals, for-profit enterprises, sole traders, partnerships, corporations, nonprofit-making organizations, charities, and nongovernmental organizations (NGOs). *Private sector* is contrasted with *public sector*, which is a comparable term for the governmental sector. In 2004 the private sector share of gross domestic product (GDP) in current prices in countries of the Organisation of Economic Co-operation and Development was: Australia 85.85 percent, Canada 87.72 percent, Finland 81.48 percent, France 80.73 percent, Germany 85.32 percent, Greece 87.54 percent, Italy 85.68 percent, Japan 84.38 percent, Norway 82.31 percent, Sweden 78.17 percent, the United Kingdom 83.65 percent, and the United States 89.46 percent. In contrast, in developing countries and transition economies the 2004 private sector share of GDP in current prices was lower: the Bahamas 73.29 percent, Botswana 70.50 percent, the Democratic Republic of Congo 69.07 percent, Nicaragua 76.61 percent, South Africa 75.92 percent, Bulgaria 70.36 percent, Croatia 75.36 percent, the Czech Republic 71.98 percent, Georgia 51.44 percent, and the Slovak Republic 75.69 percent (Heston, Summers, and Aten 2006). Dani Rodrik (2000) argues that the reason for the private sector's low share in developing countries is due to the fact that for governments in low-income countries, creating additional public-sector jobs is administratively easier than establishing an unemployment insurance scheme or subsidizing job security in the private sector.

The distinction between private sector and public sector reflects the two alternative methods of solving the allocation of resources in an economy: markets or government. Markets utilize private ownership of resources—thus the term *private* sector—for voluntary allocation decisions. In contrast to the public sector, the private sector—with the exception of nonprofit-making organizations, charities, and nongovernmental organizations—mainly searches for profit opportunities. Private companies and organizations produce goods and services in response to supply-and-demand forces in the market, with the final goal of making a profit for the owners and shareholders of the private enterprise.

The private sector plays a key role in accelerating economic growth in market capitalist economies. The private sector is the foundation of the market capitalist economic system. Without the private sector the capitalist market cannot exist, and vice versa. For example, the development of the private sector in transition economies was vital, and the final goal of transition was associated with the private sector being converted into the dominant sector in the economy. In all industrialized or advanced capitalist economies, the absolute and relative size of the private sector is very high. Hence, in a capitalist market economy the private sector is mostly responsible for most of the country's investments, for the generation of new job opportunities, and for the improvement of standards of living, and it is the source of most technological developments.

The government in market capitalist economies undertakes the following responsibilities to promote and support the private sector:

1. creating proper legal environment for the private sector to function, through private property rights and contract law;

2. introducing customs and tax laws that should encourage private investment;

3. often providing basic infrastructure produced by public enterprises such as water, power, land, transport and communication services, and other necessities;

4. initiating macroeconomic policies and expenditure to increase the demand for the private sector produced goods.

The private sector increases into two ways: through privatization of state-owned enterprises (SOEs) and through the creation and establishment of new firms. In this way, the share of the private sector in the economy grows. Privatization represents the transfer of state-owned assets to private ownership, alongside the creation and fostering of private businesses. Privatization is an alternative way of distributing and choosing the means of generating wealth (Marangos 2004). Consequently, it also may be considered a distribution of political and economic power in the economy. The increase of the private sector further implies the abandonment of government control over economic activity, as well as the abandonment of state monopoly in certain sectors. However, as the private sector increases, both income and wealth inequality increase, and intergenerational mobility decreases:

> It is true, however, that America was once a place of substantial intergenerational mobility: Sons often did much better than their fathers.... [However,] over the past generation upward mobility has fallen drastically. Very few children of the lower class are making their way to even moderate affluence.... In modern America, it seems, you're quite likely to stay in the social and economic class into which you were born. (Krugman 2004)

Supporters of the private sector mistrust government-initiated economic activities because they believe that the private sector is both efficient and enterprising. This further increases efficiency because of the increase in macroeconomic productivity due to the adoption of new technology. Critics of the private sector argue that the private sector does not produce public goods, that it creates private monopolies, enhances income and wealth inequality, and discourages intergenerational mobility. Public goods are commodities where the exclusion principle breaks down, and they are nonrivalrous. Such goods include, for example, lighthouses, national defense, police, fire brigades, and traffic lights. In nearly all industrialized or advanced market-capitalist economies, public goods are provided by the government and funded through the collection of state revenues.

SEE ALSO *Capitalism; Corporations; Investment; Privatization; Productivity; Property; Public Goods; Public Sector*

BIBLIOGRAPHY

Heston, Alan, Robert Summers, and Bettina Aten. 2006. Penn World Table Version 6.2. Center for International Comparisons of Production, Income, and Prices at the University of Pennsylvania, September.

Krugman, Paul. 2004. The Death of Horatio Alger. *The Nation.* January 5. http://www.thenation.com/doc/20040105/krugman.

Marangos, John. 2004. Modeling the Privatization Process in Transition Economies. *Oxford Development Studies* 32 (4): 585–604.

Rodrik, Dani. 2000. What Drives Public Employment in Developing Countries? *Review of Development Economics* 4 (3): 229–243.

Aristidis Bitzenis
John Marangos

PRIVATIZATION

Although *privatization* is an imprecise term with different meanings in different contexts, it broadly refers to loosening governmental control over public operations. The phenomenon gained prominence in the 1980s and 1990s, when governments in many advanced industrial nations reduced their stake in state-owned industries such as steel, aerospace, railroads, oil, postal services, telecommunications, electricity, gas, and water. Two decades later, the phenomenon diversified into many variants, such as outsourcing, subcontracting, "internal markets," and public-private partnerships; extends well beyond the industry sectors listed above; and is repeated in the transitional economies of the former Warsaw Pact.

CAUSES AND RATIONALE

In simple economic terms, a small number of goods and services has to be provided publicly. Their defining characteristic is that they cannot be priced and no one can therefore be excluded by price from the benefits they provide—or indeed the disbenefits, since such goods and services may be associated with public ills such as atmospheric pollution and epidemic diseases. Some significant areas of state spending are *unpriceable public goods* in this sense, including national defense and law and order. Yet there are also *policy-determined public goods*, or publicly provided private goods, such as medical care, education, pensions, and transport, which could be priced but are not. Depending on the extent to which nations subscribe to the ideals of the Keynesian welfare state, policymakers may decide to provide these goods publicly as a means to bring about greater equality among citizens. On this view, it is deemed unjust if access to (and the quality of) public services such as health care or education depends on an individual's level of income.

A further cause of the trend toward privatization was that public debt and borrowing requirements in many industrialized nations rose significantly as in the final decades of the twentieth century states found themselves having to foot the bill for burgeoning welfare provisions. Privatization was regarded as a means to cut debts by selling off state-owned assets and by transferring the responsibility for investment to private entities, the management skills and financial acumen of which were expected to create better value for the money for taxpayers.

However, while the newfound prosperity after World War II (1939–1945) led to a continuous expansion of welfare states around the world, this process came to a halt in the 1980s. This was due, first, to the up-and-coming economic paradigm of neoliberalism, which demanded that states relinquish their role in economic affairs so as to restore incentives for economic growth and efficiency. The underlying rationale was that the private sector is more efficient in providing these goods because of the disciplining effects of competition, which provides incentives to cut costs and produce goods that people want. Both productive and allocative efficiency were said to improve as a result. Furthermore, increasing processes of economic globalization put states in direct competition to each other for inward investment and provided a further rationale to cut taxes and "roll back" the state.

Finally, although the aforementioned factors triggered privatization predominantly in industrialized nations, governments in developing countries experienced an altogether different cause: the imposition of the principle of *conditionality* by institutions such as the International Monetary Fund (IMF) and the World Bank. According to the principle of conditionality, access to development aid was made conditional upon the borrower agreeing to meet specific requirements of economic liberalization, resulting in the coerced privatization (and subsequent sale to investors of mostly foreign origin) of many state-owned entities.

TYPES OF PRIVATIZATION

The term *privatization* can refer to (1) *assets*, as the sale or auctioning off of state property; (2) the *organization*, as the adaptation of organizational and legal constructs prevalent in the private sector, with the aim of creating autonomous entities unconstrained by political interference; (3) *functions*, as the abandonment of public functions in favor of market principles and actors; or a combination of the three.

The sale of assets raises problems for public policy if no real contestation from private entrepreneurs is forthcoming—for example, because the privatized entity retains its monopoly position and can therefore restrict output, raise prices, or extract excessive rents. Network utilities such as railways, water, gas, and electricity are particularly vulnerable to such scenarios, because the inherent natural monopoly means that consumers have no choice of network. As a countermeasure, policymakers tend to design complex governance schemes of regulation and deregulation aimed at preventing such exploitation.

The privatization of functions, in turn, is a policy lever that can be introduced at various junctures in the value chain, including the financing, production, provisioning, and operation stages. To use an example, a state may decide to provide publicly a good such as education or health care, but may choose to leave the financing, construction, or operation of schools or hospitals to the private sector, which then rents the finished project back to the government. The separation of production from provision has allowed many forms of such public-private partnerships (PPPs) to emerge, within which responsibilities, risks, and benefits are contractually shared between the public and private sector.

Critics of privatization argue that a private company will serve the needs of those who are most willing (and able) to pay, rather than the needs of the majority of citizens that public sector organizations would be obliged to satisfy. Furthermore, the anticipated efficiency gains, critics argue, have failed to materialize, particularly in sectors with a natural monopoly. Finally, in order to attract private investors in the first place, the sale price of many state-owned organizations awaiting privatization are claimed to have been lower than their actual value, thereby wasting taxpayers' money invested in previous decades. PPPs, in turn, are controversial because the long-run cost of paying the private sector to run the schemes are said to exceed the cost the public sector would incur to build and run them itself. The test of time will tell the extent to which PPPs provide better value for citizens.

SEE ALSO *Conditionality; Deregulation; Private Interests; Property, Private*

BIBLIOGRAPHY

Ghobadian, Abby, Nicholas O'Regan, David Gallear, and Howard Viney, eds. 2004. *Public-Private Partnerships: Policy and Experience.* New York: Palgrave MacMillan.

Newbery, David. 1999. *Privatization, Restructuring, and Regulation of Network Utilities.* Cambridge, MA: MIT Press.

Parker, David, and David Saal, eds. 2003. *The International Handbook on Privatization.* Northampton, MA: Edward Elgar.

Vickers, John, and George Yarrow. 1989. *Privatization: An Economic Analysis.* Cambridge, MA.: MIT Press.

Dirk Haubrich

PROBABILISTIC REGRESSION

Probabilistic regression, also known as "probit regression," is a statistical technique used to make predictions on a "limited" dependent variable using information from one or more other independent variables. This technique is one of several possible techniques that can be used when the presence of a "limited" dependent variable prevents the more common ordinary-least-squares regression technique from being used.

A "limited" variable here refers to both nominal-level variables and ordinal-level variables. A nominal-level variable is defined as a variable that can (1) take distinct values, but (2) those values cannot be placed in any meaningful numerical order. A variable where "yes" and "no" are the only two possible values is one common type of nominal-level variable. An ordinal-level variable is defined as a variable where (1) the variable can take several possible values and (2) these different values can be placed in some logical numerical order. A variable that measures whether a person (1) strongly agrees, (2) agrees, (3) is indifferent, (4) disagrees, or (5) strongly disagrees with some given statement is a common type of ordinal-level variable.

In order to use ordinary-least-squares regression, there must be a linear relationship between one's dependent and independent variables. One can see if this linearity requirement has been met by first making a scatterplot with the independent variable on the x-axis and the dependent variable on the y-axis, then calculating a mean for the dependent variable at each value of the independent variable and plotting this series of means on the scatterplot. If the observed series of means looks approximately like a straight line, then the linearity requirement has been met. If not, other regression techniques must be employed.

There are two main reasons why the linearity requirement of ordinary-least-squares regression is seldom met when the dependent variable of interest is nominal or ordinal. First, because there are a limited number of values that the dependent variable can take (as few as two in some cases), any straight line one would try to impose on the scatterplot could, for low and high values of the independent variable, respectively, extend far above or below the possible values that the dependent variable can take. The second reason is best described in the simple case when the dependent variable takes only two possible values. Because the scatterplot in this instance appears as a series of dots dispersed along two parallel horizontal lines, any single line one would try to impose on the scatterplot would cross each of these horizontal lines at only one point. This imposed line would not pass near many of the data points and therefore would not achieve a high degree of fit, as was originally sought. In this situation, a nonlinear function can achieve a much closer fit to the data.

When one's dependent variable fails to meet the linearity requirement of ordinary-least squares regression, one attempts to mathematically transform the dependent variable so that there is a linear relationship between the independent variable(s) and the transformed dependent variable. Common transformations include taking the natural logarithm or the square root of the dependent variable. When the dependent variable is "limited" and therefore cannot take values above a certain number or below a certain number, the mathematical function one specifies for the transformation must also not be capable of going above or below those same numbers. Probit regression uses the s-shaped cumulative distribution function of the normal distribution to meet this requirement.

Probit regression predicts the probability of seeing a given value of the dependent variable by fitting the available data to a mathematical function from which probabilities can be calculated. Specifically, this function is the inverse of the indefinite integral of the probability density function of the normal (Gaussian) distribution (also known as the "inverse cumulative density function of the normal distribution"). Formally, this function is written as $\Phi^{-1}(p) = \sqrt{2} * erf^{-1}(2p - 1)$, where erf^{-1} is the inverse error function and p is the probability of observing a particular outcome on the dependent variable.

Probit regression was first proposed by the entomologist Chester Ittner Bliss (1899–1979) in a 1934 article in *Science* titled "The Method of Probits." Noting that his dependent variable was too limited to be modeled using ordinary least-squares regression, Bliss sought to overcome this limitation by transforming his limited dependent variable into a new dependent variable that did not have the same limitations. Using a table derived from the cumulative density function of the normal distribution, Bliss converted the units of his dependent variable into what he called "probability units." Bliss then used these probability units as his new dependent variable, and fit them to the rest of his data using standard ordinary-least-squares regression. The word *probit* is simply an abbreviation of the phrase "probability unit."

Probit regression, when it was first developed, provided a powerful yet computationally simple way to model limited dependent variables. It required the use of widely available statistical tables and knowledge of the ordinary-least-squares regression technique. Yet probit regression is not the preferred method for modeling relationships between limited dependent variables and a set of independent variables in the social sciences. According to Adrian Raftery (2001), this is largely because interpreting the dependent variable when it has been transformed into probability units is not easy. Probability units have no common-sense interpretation by themselves, so they must be converted back to simple probabilities before one can effectively convey their meaning in words. A competing and more popular method, logistic regression, can handle the same types of dependent variable but has the additional advantage that the results of the procedure are more easily made interpretable in words.

In terms of binary dependent variables, there is little that distinguishes probit regression from its more popular competitor, logistic regression. Probit regression is simpler computationally than logistic regression, but this advantage is negated through the use of computer software. Ironically, however, the development of generalized linear modeling by John Nelder and R. Wedderburn beginning in 1972 and the creation of computer software for performing the technique re-created a space for probit regression. Generalized linear modeling was born out of the observation that the many different regression techniques identified at the time were more alike than they were different. Probit regression and logistic regression produced similar predictions for "limited" dependent variables *because* they were so similar on a general level. But through the process of outlining similarities between the two techniques, key differences were also highlighted. When one has an ordinal-level dependent variable and each category of the dependent variable occurs approximately an equal number of times, logistic regression is most appropriate. When middle categories of the dependent variable occur much more frequently than either low or high categories, probit regression achieves a better degree of fit. Thus, increased computing power and the development of more general statistical models helped to pinpoint a niche for probit regression.

For a more in-depth treatment of probit regression and logistic regression in a social science setting, the reader is referred to E. Scott Adler and Forrest Nelson's book *Linear Probability, Logit, and Probit Models* (1984).

SEE ALSO *Distribution, Normal; Distribution, Poisson; Distribution, Uniform; General Linear Model; Method of Moments; Nonlinear Regression; Ordinality; Pareto, Vilfredo; Probability Distributions; Regression; Regression Analysis*

BIBLIOGRAPHY

Adler, E. Scott, and Forrest D. Nelson. 1984. *Linear Probability, Logit, and Probit Models.* London: Sage.

Bliss, Chester Ittner. 1934. The Method of Probits. *Science* 79: 38–39.

Raftery, Adrian. 2001. Statistics in Sociology, 1950–2000: A Selective Review. *Sociological Methodology* 31: 1–45.

David J. Roelfs

PROBABILITY

The concern of empirical social statisticians in matters theoretical is usually limited to troubles regarding choices of random sets with repeatably observable frequencies—meant to test hypotheses that suggest some limitations on these values. (An example is the test of claims regarding discrimination.) As many statistical observations are hardly ever repeated, a huge literature discusses the question of how representative observed sets are: Is an observed distribution characteristic of the whole population, or is it due to an accidentally great deviation from it?

Diverse examinations of the likelihood of a freak accident are calculated, all made on the basis of assumptions, often reasonable but at times highly question begging. For example, social statisticians seldom notice that the calculations take empirical finds as crucial tests between hypotheses. They specify single hypotheses without troubling themselves to consider the hypotheses the calculations take as the default options. Most social statisticians are ignorant of the mathematical intricacies involved and of the fierce debates among top experts in the field as to what exactly these calculations mean. The long and the short of it is this: How representative is the sample? This question translates into a question of the sample's randomness.

Critics often suggest that randomness is wanting because the criterion of the choice of the sample introduces bias. The standard example is in biology. The use of laboratory animals introduces bias and renders some tests worse than useless. In social research it is the use of telephone books for the selection of random telephone numbers, in oblivion of the fact that in some cases the choice of people with telephones introduces bias. The best way to handle bias is to repeat the test with a new sample using different criteria. In some cases tests for the randomness of a sample may comprise random selections from the existing sample.

The most popular computer program for social statisticians, SPSS (originally Statistical Package for the Social Sciences), warns users against correlating everything in sight, because such an approach is sure to yield some useless (because unrepeatable) results. Common sense reduces such risks, but no method is foolproof. It is therefore always advisable to be wary of computer-generated numbers. To this end, it may be useful to comprehend the general ideas behind the statistics.

The term *probability* is open to different readings. Some of these may be subject to the mathematical calculus of probability (see below) and some not. Methodologists are most concerned with two of these readings, only one of which obeys this calculus. (Many insist that this need not be so.) In one sense probability, especially betting, is a matter of guesses. In another sense probability is the plausibility of a conjecture, as in the common assertion, "What you say is probable." Can different people propose competing probable views? To deny this is to dismiss without debate the views of peers who reject what seems plausible. This is inadvisable, at least in a democracy. Suppose, then, that it is possible for competing views to be probable. Since the calculus of probability ascribes to the probable the numerical value of more than one-half and considers the sum of probabilities of all alternatives to be at most unity, the probable in this sense defies this calculus.

Many methodologists deem this argument misleading. It fails for scientific ideas, they say, where such cases are a priori impossible. Not so: When two new theories compete, researchers who find both plausible seek facts that will tip the scale against one of them. In the light of such experiments, theories do gain probability in a sense that defies the mathematical theory of probability. Proof: The mathematical theory will render more probable the theory that comes closer to existing information, yet such theories are implausible. Plausibility goes to an imaginative theory that looks implausible at first and then gains support from new information. The calculus distinctly does not differentiate between information that was known before the theory was invented and the information that the theory reveals. End of proof.

Theoretical learning results from the wish to understand observed regularities. Probability is the study of luck. With no foreknowledge of the fates of individuals, we know that ensembles have a percentage of lucky members, a percentage that improves or declines with the institution of precaution or carelessness, respectively. The simplest ensemble is that of tosses of a coin. Unable to predict single outcomes, we can predict their ratio—a number between 0 and 1. We tend to assume that this ratio is one-half. Not so, because a tossed coin with one side heavier than the other will more often fall on the heavy side: It is biased or unfair. All tossed coins turn out to have a constant ratio of heads turning up; this ratio is the probability for heads. Given a coin that we have not tested, we cannot know whether the probability of heads for it is one-half, but we take it for granted that it is a fixed ratio. Moreover as most coins that we use are fair, we tend naively to assume that one that we have not tested is fair. Some gamblers misuse this naïveté regularly.

Some say that in the absence of prior information about a coin, we have to consider it fair. Of course they say this because they speak of probability in a different sense—subjective (see below). Thus even when limiting our discourse to luck, we understand probability in different ways.

The mathematical theory of probability considers in the abstract a set of items with numerical values in a manner that follows certain intuitive axioms. These are basic equations that assign to every ordered pair a and b of these items a number called p(a, b) (the *conditional probability* of a given b): p(a, b) = r $0 \leq$ r ≤ 1

The axioms of probability relate these numbers and items. Instead of going into the detail of the axioms, most textbooks, including most mathematically powerful ones, use examples, such as a series of outcomes in tosses of a coin, throws of a die, or pulls of a playing card out of a pack. These examples legitimately stand for the major theorems of the calculus, provided that the rule of equal probability that they usually exhibit is not generalized to allow for marked cards or biased or unfair coins and dice.

The troubled discussions about probability that occurred at the turn of the nineteenth century disappeared with the realization that *equiprobability* is only one possible probability distribution among many. The alternative ways to assign equiprobability seem problematic only because of erroneous methodology. Quantum theory beautifully illustrates the freedom of assigning these. The philosopher Rudolf Carnap (1891–1970), for example, tried to use one quantum probability distribution in his theory of subjective probability (1962). Deviations from traditional rules about probability are hypotheses to be tested like any other. The identification of probability with plausibility plays havoc, as tests may grant such theories plausibility. Giving up this identification dispels such troubles. The axioms of probability, then, concern measures of possibilities, and assuming any distribution is thus conjectural: The more-possible items receive a higher degree of probability, with impossibility as probability 0 and necessity as probability 1. Probability can be a measure of the possibility of success in betting, and it can be the betting success rate; it can also be more than that. This is why the axioms of probability should apply to an unspecified set of uninterpreted items.

The axioms demand, then, that every item a has a complement b, given c: if for some d, p(d, c) $\neq 1$, then p(a, c) + p(b, c) = 1. Obviously otherwise p(a, c) + p(b, c) = 2. Similarly for every a and b, there is an item c that is their conjunction: p(ab, d) = p(c, d) for every d. It turns out, as Karl Popper (1902–1994) has proved, that these rules abide by Boolean algebra (1968). The heart of probability theory is the multiplication theorem, the feel for which is central to the general feel for probability. It is intuitively obvious that probability is a monotone function: for every three items, p(ab, c) $\leq$ p(a, c); and p(ab, c) = p(a, bc) times p(b, c). For c that may be ignored (it may be understood as the universal condition, as the condition that always holds in the system under study), we may write p(a) for p(a, c). The probabilities depending on it are known as *absolute probabilities*. The multiplication law for absolute probabilities, then, is p(ab) = p(a, b) times p(b). And if p(b) $\neq 0$, then obviously p(a, b) = p(ab) divided by p(b). This makes it obvious that conditional probability is logically prior to absolute probability, since items that have zero probability appear in probability considerations of all sorts (Rényi 1970; Popper 1968).

One of the most popular reasons for the subjective view of probability is the *theory of errors*, the assumption that random errors of measurement of some given quantity cancel each other, so the most reliable hypothesis about that quantity is that it is the average of the many measurements of it. This makes probability appear as reliability (of measurements). Consider then the hypothesis that reliability of measurements follows the axioms of the theory of probability. If this reliability is measurable by the reliance that people ascribe to measurements, then this hypothesis is empirically easily refuted: People prefer impressions to averages. This is not the case with researchers, however, as they assume errors to be random. Otherwise they are ready to change their minds. Hence, the errors in question are not errors of reliability. Moreover the same formula applies to acts, such as shooting at a target, that have nothing to do with reliability. Consider the correction of a gun fixed on a gun rest, aimed at a target, and hitting the target on average at a point that is not its center. The most important aspect of this kind of exercise is that it is repeatable. Otherwise it is pointless. (The same holds for the way astronomers eliminate random errors due to atmospheric interferences.) The demand for repeatability clearly eliminates the problem of credence. Those who refuse to work on repeatable experience are invited to test it afresh. Repeatable situations with deviations are particularly important for plotting the graph of the random differences between each hit and the center of the target. These random deviations are errors in the sense of distractions, not in the sense of observers negligently making mistakes. The error graph is in the famous bell shape (achieved when the sample grows infinitely to cover all possible deviations); the smaller the errors, the thinner the bell. This is known as *dispersion*, and it is essential for the study of populations subject to diverse random deviations. In physics the expression of the wish to find sharp spectral lines is the effort to reduce random interferences in the process of radiation (heat).

Historically the strongest reason for subjective probability was provided by the Marquis de Laplace (1749–1827) and later was endorsed by Albert Einstein (1879–1955): Facts are predetermined, and probability is due to ignorance. The opposite view is that randomness is objective. The chief argument here is that the assumption of randomness is essential for almost all successful application of the calculus of probability (the exception being its application to number theory). The subjectivist view of randomness as mere ignorance leads to the defunct assumption of equiprobability. Sophisticated subjectivists admit this but take it as a challenge, relying on another, more convincing reason to view probability as subjective and randomness as ignorance. It rests on a theorem named after Thomas Bayes (1702–1761). (This is why subjectivism is often called *Bayesianism*.)

Bayes's theorem concerns inverse probabilities. It is the formula that enables the move from the value of p(*e, h*) (of empirical data given a theory) to the value of p(*h, e*) (of a theory given empirical data), from the likelihood of an effect given one of its causes to the likelihood that a given cause is responsible for the effect at hand. This formula is a theorem that is easily deducible from the multiplication law, provided all relevant probabilities are given.

This of course is an objectivist proviso; viewed subjectively, however, these provisos are convictions. This leads back to the defunct rule of equiprobability. Moreover, the most important theorem of probability theory, the law of large numbers, is not given to the subjectivist interpretation. It says that any option, however improbable, will occur in a sufficiently large collection, although the less probable the option, the less frequent it will be.

SEE ALSO *Bayes' Theorem; Bayesian Econometrics; Bayesian Statistics; Classical Statistical Analysis; Econometric Decomposition; Methods, Quantitative; Popper, Karl; Random Samples; Sampling; Science; Social Science; Statistics; Test Statistics*

BIBLIOGRAPHY

Carnap, Rudolf. 1962. *Logical Foundations of Probability.* 2nd ed. Chicago: University of Chicago Press.

Feller, William. 1967. *Introduction to Probability Theory and Its Applications.* 3rd ed. New York: Wiley.

Fisher, Ronald A. 1922. On the Mathematical Foundations of Theoretical Statistics. *Philosophical Transactions of the Royal Society of London,* ser. A, 222: 309–368.

Kolmogorov, A. N. 1956. *Foundations of the Theory of Probability.* 2nd English ed. Trans. and ed. Nathan Morrison. New York: Chelsea.

Landau, Sabine, and Brian S. Everitt. 2004. *A Handbook of Statistical Analysis Using SPSS.* 3rd ed. Boca Raton, FL: Chapman and Hall.

Leblanc, Hugh. 1989. The Autonomy of Probability Theory (Notes on Kolmogorov, Rényi, and Popper). *British Journal for the Philosophy of Science* 40: 167–181.

Levi, Isaac. 1967. *Gambling with Truth: An Essay on Induction and the Aims of Science.* New York: Knopf.

Popper, Karl. 1968. *The Logic of Scientific Discovery.* 3rd ed. London: Hutchinson.

Rényi, Alfréd. 1970. *Foundations of Probability.* San Francisco: Holden-Day.

Schrödinger, Erwin. 1989. *Statistical Thermodynamics.* New York: Dover.

Todhunter, Isaac. 1865. *A History of the Mathematical Theory of Probability from the Time of Pascal to That of Laplace.* London: Macmillan.

Joseph Agassi

PROBABILITY, LIMITS IN

The terms *limits in probability* and *probability limits* are encountered in the field of Bayesian inference and in the field of asymptotic theory; however, their meanings are applied differently in each of these two areas. In terms of popularity, probability limits as applied to Bayesian inferences seems to appear more frequently in current literature, especially in applied statistical sciences.

PROBABILITY LIMITS IN BAYESIAN STATISTICS

In Bayesian inference, or Bayesian statistics, probability limits are also referred to as "credibility limits." Probability limits are the upper and lower end-points of the probability (or credible) interval that has a specified (posterior) probability (e.g., 95% or 99%) of containing the true value of a population parameter. Probability limits are used when the parameter is considered as the realization of a random variable with given prior distribution. As the distribution is presumably assessed prior to sample evidence, such distribution is called a "prior distribution." In classical inference, the parameter is considered to be an unknown constant, and then confidence limits are applied. Both upper and lower probability limits reflect not only prior information, but also sample information; therefore they are random statistics.

Confidence limits are the upper and lower end-points of an interval around a parameter estimate, such that if an experiment were repeated an infinite number of times, in the specified percentage (usually 95% or 99%) of trials the interval generated would contain the true value of the parameter. Confidence limits may be calculated using asymptotic (normal approximation) or exact methods. Both upper and lower confidence limits are obtained (purely) from sample data, so they are also a realization of random statistics.

Bayesian inference or Bayesian statistics is based on the theory of subjective probability. A formal Bayesian analysis leads to probabilistic assessments of the object of uncertainty. For instance, a Bayesian inference might be the statement "The probability is 0.95 that the mean μ of a normal distribution lies between 5.6 to 11.3." Therefore, the 95 percent probability limits for the parameter μ are 5.6 and 11.3. The number 0.95 here represents a degree of belief, either in the sense of subjective probability coherent or subjective probability rational; it needs not correspond to any objective long-run relative frequency. By contrast, a classical inference based on the sampling theory might lead to the statement "A 0.95 confidence interval for the mean of a normal distribution is from 5.6 to 11.3." The number 0.95 in this case represents a long-run relative frequency.

Finding Bayesian Probability Limits There is some flexibility in choosing the credible limits from a given probability distribution for the parameter. Examples include:

choosing the narrowest probability interval that, for a unimodal distribution, will involve choosing those values of highest probability density (highest posterior density credible limits); choosing the probability interval where the probability of being below the interval is as likely as being above it (the interval will contain the median); and choosing the probability interval that has the mean as its central point. The following is an illustration of finding probability limits using the second method.

In a problem of making inferences about the mean λ of a Poisson distribution, the prior distribution is given as a $\Gamma(\alpha, \beta)$ distribution with known α and β. In Bayesian statistics, the parameter λ is considered to be a random variable, so a bold $\boldsymbol{\lambda}$ is used in the next sentence. Now suppose that a random sample of size n has been drawn from the underlying Poisson distribution. Let $\boldsymbol{X} = (X_1, X_2, ..., X_n)$, then the joint conditional probability density function (pdf) of $\boldsymbol{X}$, given $\boldsymbol{\lambda} = \lambda$, is

$$L(x|\lambda) = \frac{\lambda^{x_1}e^{-\lambda}}{x_1!} \cdot \frac{\lambda^{x_2}e^{-\lambda}}{x_2!} \cdots \frac{\lambda^{x_n}e^{-\lambda}}{x_n!},$$

$$x_i = 0, 1, 2, ..., i = 1, 2, ..., n.$$

The prior pdf is

$$h(\lambda) = \frac{\lambda^{\alpha-1}e^{-\lambda/\beta}}{\Gamma(\alpha)\beta^\alpha}, \quad 0 < \lambda < \infty.$$

Hence, the joint mixed continuous and discrete probability function is given by

$$L(x|\lambda)h(\lambda) = \left[\frac{\lambda^{x_1}e^{-\lambda}}{x_1!} \cdot \frac{\lambda^{x_2}e^{-\lambda}}{x_2!} \cdots \frac{\lambda^{x_n}e^{-\lambda}}{x_n!}\right]$$

$$\left[\frac{\lambda^{\alpha-1}e^{-\lambda/\beta}}{\Gamma(\alpha)\beta^\alpha}\right]$$

$$= \frac{\lambda^{\alpha-1+\Sigma x_i}e^{-\lambda(n\beta+1)/\beta}}{\Gamma(\alpha)\beta^\alpha x_1!x_2!...x_n!},$$

provided that $x_i = 0, 1, 2, ..., i = 1, 2, ..., n$ with $0 < \lambda < \infty$, and is equal to zero elsewhere. Then the marginal distribution of the sample is

$$G(x, \lambda) = \int_0^\infty \frac{\lambda^{\alpha-1+\Sigma_1^n x_i}e^{-\lambda(n\beta+1)/\beta}}{x_1!x_2!...x_n!\Gamma(\alpha)\beta^\alpha}d\lambda$$

$$= \frac{\Gamma(\alpha+\Sigma_1^n x_i)\left[\beta/(n\beta+1)\right]^{\alpha+\Sigma_1^n x_i}}{\Gamma(\alpha)\beta^\alpha x_1!x_2!...x_n!}$$

Suppose that the observations are $\boldsymbol{x} = (x_1, x_2, ..., x_n)$. Finally, the posterior pdf of λ, given $\boldsymbol{X} = \boldsymbol{x}$, is

$$k(x, \lambda) = \frac{L(x|\lambda)h(\lambda)}{G(x, \lambda)}$$

$$= \frac{\lambda^{\alpha-1+\Sigma x_1}e^{-\lambda(n\beta+1)/\beta}}{\Gamma(\alpha + \Sigma_1^n x_i)\left[\beta/(n\beta+1)\right]^{\alpha+\Sigma_1^n x_i}},$$

provided that $x_i = 0, 1, 2, \ldots, i = 1, 2, \ldots, n$ with $0 < \lambda < \infty$, and is equal to zero elsewhere. This posterior pdf is also a gamma distribution with parameters

$$\alpha^* = \alpha + \Sigma_1^n x_i, \beta^* = \beta/(n\beta + 1).$$

Notice that the posterior pdf reflects both prior information carried by (α, β) and the sample information $\Sigma_1^n x_i$.

To obtain a credible interval, note that the posterior distribution of $\frac{2(n\beta+1)}{\beta}\lambda$ is $\chi^2(2(\alpha + \sum_1^n x_i))$. Based on this, the following interval is a $(1 - \alpha)$ 100 percent credible interval for λ:

$$\left(\frac{2(n\beta+1)}{\beta}\chi^2_{1-\alpha/2}(2(\alpha + \Sigma_1^n x_i)), \right.$$
$$\left. \frac{2(n\beta+1)}{\beta}\chi^2_{\alpha/2}(2(\alpha + \Sigma_1^n x_i)) \right) \quad (1)$$

where $\chi^2_{1-\alpha/2}(2(\alpha + \Sigma_1^n x_i))$ and $\chi^2_{\alpha/2}(2(\alpha + \Sigma_1^n x_i))$ are the lower and upper quantiles of a χ^2 distribution with $2(\alpha + \Sigma_1^n x_i)$ degrees of freedom. Then, $\frac{2(n\beta+1)}{\beta}\chi^2_{1-a/2}(2(\alpha + \sum_1^n x_i))$ and $\frac{2(n\beta+1)}{\beta}\chi^2_{a/2}(2(\alpha + \sum_1^n x_i))$ are $(1 - \alpha)$ 100 percent probability limits of λ.

Relationship to Confidence Limits For the example above, the confidence limits can be obtained by applying the distribution of sample sum $\Sigma_1^n x_i$. Note that the distribution of $\Sigma_1^n x_i$ is also a Poisson distribution with $\lambda^* = n\lambda$. For the lower limit of a $(1 - \alpha)$ 100 percent confidence interval for λ can be selected so that

$$\sum_{i=\Sigma_1^n x_i}^n \frac{(n\lambda)^i e^{-(n\lambda)}}{i!} = \frac{\alpha}{2}; \quad (2)$$

and the upper limit of a $(1 - \alpha)$ 100 percent confidence interval for λ can be solved by

$$\sum_{i=0}^{\Sigma_1^n x_i} \frac{(n\lambda)^i e^{-(n\lambda)}}{i!} = \frac{\alpha}{2}. \quad (3)$$

In general, equations such as (2), and (3) above are impossible to solve algebraically. The solutions can be obtained using a search procedure on a computer.

The asymptotic confidence limits for λ may be obtained by

$$P\left(\left| \frac{\Sigma_1^n x_i - n\lambda}{\sqrt{n\lambda}} \right| \leq z_{\alpha/2} \right) = 1 - \alpha.$$

So, the $(1 - \alpha)$ 100 percent confidence limits for λ are

$$\left(\frac{2\Sigma_1^n x_i + z^2_{\alpha/2}}{2n} \right) \pm \frac{1}{n}\sqrt{\left(\frac{2\Sigma_1^n x_i + z^2_{\alpha/2}}{2} \right)^2 - (\Sigma_1^n x_i)^2}. \quad (4)$$

In addition, the further approximation for the confidence limits for λ using standard error of $\frac{1}{n}\sum_1^n x_i$ are

$$\frac{1}{n}\Sigma_1^n x_i \pm z_{\alpha/2}\sqrt{\frac{\Sigma_1^n x_i}{n}}. \quad (5)$$

Compare (1) to (4) or (5); they are quite different. Probability limits are obtained by a combination of subjective knowledge of λ and the objective information from the sample data whereas confidence limits only contain pure objective information.

There are situations in which the confidence limits and credible limits are numerically identical. For example, if μ is a location parameter of a normal distribution, and the prior for μ is uniform, then the 95 percent central confidence limits are identical to the 95 percent highest density credible limits.

PROBABILITY LIMITS IN ASYMPTOTIC THEORY

For a sequence of random variables $\{X_n\}$, if there exists a real number c such that for every small positive number ϵ the probability that the absolute difference between X_n and c is less than ϵ has the limit of 1 when $n \to \infty$, namely, $\lim_{n\to\infty} P(|X_n - c| \leq \varepsilon) = 1$, then we say that $\{X_n\}$ converges in probability to constant c, and c is called the probability limit of $\{X_n\}$ (White 1984). See Simons (1971) for how to identify probability limits.

For example, if the average of n independent, identically distributed random variables $Y_i, i = 1, \ldots, n$, with a common mean, μ, is given by $\bar{Y}_n = \frac{1}{n}\sum_{i=0}^n Y_i$, then as $n \to \infty$, $\bar{Y}_n$ converges to μ in probability. The common mean, μ, of the random variables Y_i is the probability limit of the sequence of random variables $\{\bar{Y}_n\}$. This result is known as the weak law of large numbers. In the context of estimation, we also call $\{\bar{Y}_n\}$ a (weakly) consistent sequence of estimators for μ.

More generally, convergence in probability means that a sequence of random variables $\{X_n\}$ converges to a random variable X, which is not necessarily a constant. It has not been observed that "probability limit" is used, for this general case, as a limiting random variable.

In probability theory there exist several different notions of convergence of random variables. The convergence of sequences of random variables to some limiting random variable (illustrated below) is an important concept in probability theory, and in its applications to statistics and stochastic processes. The following section presents a brief overview of the various modes of convergence of a random variable sequence, and the relationships between them (for greater detail, see Parzen 1960).

Modes of Convergence of a Random Variable Sequence
Suppose that $\{F_n\}$ is a sequence of cumulative distribution functions corresponding to random variables $\{X_n\}$, and that F is a distribution function corresponding to a random variable X. We say that the sequence $\{X_n\}$ converges to X in distribution, if $\lim_{n\to\infty} F_n(a) = F(a)$ for every real number a at which F is continuous. This is the notion of convergence used in the central limit theorem.

A sequence of random variables $\{X_n\}$ is called *convergent in probability* to a random variable X if for any $\varepsilon > 0$, $\lim_{n\to\infty} P(|X_n - X| \le \varepsilon) = 1$. Convergence in probability is the notion of convergence used in the weak law of large numbers.

A sequence of random variables $\{X_n\}$ is called *convergent in mean square* to a random variable X if $\lim_{n\to\infty} E\left[(X_n - X)^2\right] = 0$. More generally, for any $p > 0$, a sequence of random variables $\{X_n\}$ is called *convergent in p–mean* to a random variable X if $\lim_{n\to\infty} E\left[(X_n - X)^p\right] = 0$.

A sequence of random variables $\{X_n\}$ is called *convergent almost surely* to a random variable X if
$$P\left(\lim_{n\to\infty} X_n = X\right) = 1.$$

A sequence of random variables $\{X_n\}$ is called *convergent surely* to a random variable X if $\lim_{n\to\infty} X_n = X$.

Relationships between Various Modes of Convergence
There are a few important connections between these modes of convergence. Convergence in distribution is the weakest form of convergence, and is in fact sometimes called *weak convergence*. It does not, in general, imply any other mode of convergence; however, convergence in distribution is implied by all other modes of convergence mentioned herein. Convergence in probability is the second weakest form of convergence. It implies convergence in distribution, but generally does not imply any other mode of convergence. However, convergence in probability is implied by all other modes of convergence men-

tioned herein, except convergence in distribution. If $\{X_n\}$ converges in distribution to a constant c, then $\{X_n\}$ converges in probability to c. Namely, when the limit (constant) in probability exists, the convergence in probability is equivalent to the convergence in distribution. Both convergence in mean square and almost sure convergence imply convergence in both distribution and probability. However, the inverse is not commonly true; convergence in mean square does not imply almost sure convergence, and vice versa.

LEGITIMATE CRITICISMS
In order to avoid possible confusion in using the term *probability limits* in these two different contexts discussed above, we suggest using "credible limits" for Bayesian probability limits, and using "a limit that … converges to in probability" in reference to the limit of a sequence of random variables that is convergent in probability when discussing asymptotic theory.

SEE ALSO *Bayesian Econometrics; Bayesian Statistics; Econometrics; Probability Distributions; Probability Theory; Probability, Subjective; Statistics*

BIBLIOGRAPHY

Bernardo, José M., and Adrian F. M. Smith. 1994. *Bayesian Theory.* New York: Wiley.

Hogg, Robert V., Joseph W. McKean, and Allen T. Craig. 2005. *Introduction to Mathematical Statistics.* 6th ed. Toronto: Pearson Prentice Hall.

Parzen, Emanuel. 1960. *Modern Probability Theory and Its Applications.* New York: Wiley.

Simons, Gordon. 1971. Identifying Probability Limits. *Annals of Mathematical Statistics* 42 (4): 1429–1433.

White, Halbert. 1984. *Asymptotic Theory for Econometricians.* New York: Academic Press.

Xiaojian Xu

PROBABILITY, OBJECTIVE
SEE *Probability.*

PROBABILITY, SUBJECTIVE

The *subjective* or *personalist* theory of probability views probability as the likelihood that a particular individual attaches to the occurrence of an event or the truth of a proposition, rather than as the frequency with which a particular observation would occur in a long sequence of repetitions.

In his *Treatise on Probability*, published in 1921, but written as a Cambridge fellowship dissertation before World War I (1914–1918), John Maynard Keynes (1883–1946) distinguished a probability distribution over possible outcomes from an individual's degree of belief that a particular probability distribution was in fact the true probability distribution, with the degree of belief reflecting the weight of available, relevant evidence. Keynes viewed probability as an objective relation that would be perceived the same way by any rational person with the same information. Émile Borel (1871–1956) and Frank P. Ramsey (1903–1930) responded by arguing for the more subjective interpretation that a person can have any degree of belief in any given statement on any evidence, and those beliefs will still be consistent and coherent, provided only that the person's subjective probabilities attached to all possible outcomes sum to one and are bounded by zero and one, with a probability of p attached to statement or event S implying a probability of $1-p$ attached to the denial of S. (The relevant essays by Borel and Ramsey are reprinted in Kyburg and Smokler [1964]; see also Bruno de Finetti's 1937 monograph and Bernard O. Koopman's 1940 article in that volume.) In his memorial article on his friend Ramsey, Keynes accepted Ramsey's criticism on the issue of the subjectivity of degrees of belief.

Like Frank Knight's (1885–1972) *Risk, Uncertainty, and Profit* (1921), Keynes distinguished between *risk* (where outcomes are random, but the probability distribution of outcomes is known) and *uncertainty* (where the probability distribution is not known, and even a complete list of possible outcomes may not be possible). Risk is insurable, but uncertainty is not. Knight saw entrepreneurial profit as the reward for bearing uncertainty. Knight (1921, pp. 250-251) held that insurance was feasible even in situations with little objective data provided that professionals in the relevant field could make "conservative and competent" estimates (even if insurance was imperfect in such situations because of moral hazard), but that there remained some uncertainty that was "uninsurable (because unmeasurable and this because unclassifiable)," when it was not possible for businessmen to even list all the possible outcomes. According to Keynes (1921), not all degrees of belief are numerically measurable or even comparable. Writing on long-period expectations in chapter 12 of his *General Theory of Employment, Interest, and Money* (1936), Keynes invoked fundamental, uninsurable uncertainty about the prospects of another world war, technological breakthroughs, or the position of property owners in the future social order to explain the volatility of private investment spending: expectations of

the profitability of investment projects are guesses about an unknown and unknowable future, and are subject to drastic revision as scraps of new information become available. Under nonergodic conditions of true uncertainty, past observed frequencies are highly imperfect guides to future events, and a universe of discoverable regularities that can be expected to continue is a misleading analogy (Davidson 1991). Other chapters of Keynes's *General Theory*, however, proceeded as though discoverable regularities exist.

Leonard J. Savage (1917–1971) and I. J. Good developed the personalist view of probability advanced by Ramsay, de Finetti, and Koopman, and explored its implications for statistics. In this view, probability is no more than an index of a person's degree of belief in a statement (or in the occurrence of a future event), and reflects the limitations of a person's information, which may or may not reflect any inherent randomness in the world. Good and Savage emphasized Thomas Bayes's (d. 1761) theorem or rule as the way to update one's belief in the probability of statement S in light of some observed data. The probability that the data is observed and that S is true can be expressed either as the probability of the data being observed given that S is true multiplied by the prior probability that S is true, $\Pr(\text{data}|S)\Pr(S)$, or as the probability of the data being observed multiplied by the probability of S being true given that the data have been observed, $\Pr(\text{data})\Pr(S|\text{data})$. The posterior probability that S is true given that the data have been observed, $\Pr(S|\text{data})$, can be solved for as $\Pr(\text{data}|S)\Pr(S)/\Pr(\text{data})$. The approach pioneered by Good and Savage is known as Bayesianism (see Joyce 2004) and views rational behavior as the maximization of subjective expected utility (with expected utility being linear in probabilities) subject to probabilistic beliefs that have been updated according to Bayes's theorem. To the Bayesian, there is no distinction between uncertainty and risk: using available evidence in forming updated, posterior probabilities (over all possible, mutually exclusive outcomes, with "any other outcome" as one of the possibilities, so that the list is exhaustive) does not presume that a true, objective probability distribution will ever be achieved.

Various paradoxes, such as the Allais paradox and Ellsberg paradox, have been observed, in which people make choices in ways that violate Savage's axioms for rationality in the sense of maximization of expected utility given coherent and consistent beliefs about probabilities (Machina [1987] and the extensive references given there, as well as Jallais and Pradier [2005]). Experiments conducted by the psychologists Daniel Kahneman and Amos Tversky (1937–1996), for which Kahneman received the 2002 Nobel Prize in economics, revealed framing effects, in which choices made by subjects depend on how questions are put: in particular, someone may assign probability *p* to a statement (or event) *S*, yet assign some probability other than 1−*p* to not-*S*.

Daniel Ellsberg (1961) showed experimental subjects two urns, one with fifty red balls and fifty black balls and the other with one hundred balls, an unknown number red and the rest black. Offered a prize for drawing a red ball, subjects strictly preferred to draw from the first urn, yet offered a prize for drawing a black ball, they again strictly preferred to draw from the first urn, a result not consistent with any subjective probability assigned to drawing a red ball from the second urn. Several commentators have interpreted such results as displaying aversion to uncertainty or ambiguity. Savage responded to Maurice Allais's counterexample (in which Savage himself responded to twenty questions from Allais in ways that violated Savage's axioms) by reinterpreting his axioms as a normative theory, which should convince anyone to whom it was explained suitably, rather than as a positive theory of rational behavior (Jallais and Pradier 2005). Peter Fishburn, David Schmeidler, and Robert Sugden, among others, have dealt with the observed paradoxes of choices involving subjective probability by generalizing expected utility theory by dropping the standard additivity or compounding rules of probability theory (Machina 1987).

BIBLIOGRAPHY

Bayes, Thomas. 1763 An Essay Towards Solving a Problem in the Doctrine of Chances, with Richard Price's Foreword and Discussions. *Philosophical Transactions of the Royal Society of London* 53: 370–418. Reprinted with a biographical note by G. A. Barnard in *Biometrika* 45 (1958): 293–315.

Davidson, Paul. 1991. Is Probability Theory Relevant for Uncertainty? A Post Keynesian Perspective. *Journal of Economic Perspectives* 5 (1): 129–143.

Ellsberg, Daniel. 1961. Risk, Ambiguity, and the Savage Axioms. *Quarterly Journal of Economics* 75 (4): 643–669.

Jallais, Sophie, and Pierre-Charles Pradier. 2005. The Allais Paradox and Its Immediate Consequences for Expected Utility Theory. In *The Experiment in the History of Economics*, ed. Philippe Fontaine and Robert Leonard, 25–49. London and New York: Routledge.

Joyce, James M. 2004. Bayesianism. In *The Oxford Handbook of Rationality*, ed. Alfred R. Mele and Piers Rawling, 132–155. Oxford: Oxford University Press.

Keynes, John Maynard. 1921. *A Treatise on Probability*. London: Macmillan.

Keynes, John Maynard. 1936. *The General Theory of Employment, Interest, and Money*. London: Macmillan.

Knight, Frank H. 1921. *Risk, Uncertainty, and Profit*. Boston: Houghton Mifflin.

Kyburg, Henry E., Jr., and Howard E. Smokler, eds. 1964. *Studies in Subjective Probability*. New York: Wiley.

Machina, Mark J. 1987. Choice Under Uncertainty: Problems Solved and Unsolved. *Journal of Economic Perspectives* 1 (1): 121–154.

Savage, Leonard J. 1972. *The Foundations of Statistics*. 2nd ed. New York: Dover.

Robert W. Dimand

PROBABILITY DISTRIBUTIONS

The fundamental notion in statistics is that of a group (aggregate), which is usually called a *population*. This denotes a collection of objects, whether animate or inanimate, for example, a population of humans, of plants, of mistakes in reading a scale, and so on. The science of statistics deals with properties of populations, or more precisely, with the data obtained by counting or measuring properties of populations of natural phenomena. Natural phenomena include various happenings of the external world, whether human or not.

Consider a population of members each of which bears some numerical value of a variable (variate), for example, a population of men with measured height. Here the variable is the height of men. We thus have a population of variates (which can be discontinuous [discrete] or continuous). In the continuous case, the number of members possessing a variate value that falls into a given interval of the variate values is called the *frequency* in that interval. Finally, the manner in which the frequencies are distributed over the intervals is called the *frequency distribution* (or simply *distribution*).

To everything in social science there is a distribution. From the characteristics of persons and the aggregates they form—health and wealth, city size and resource endowment, happiness and social harmony—to the characteristics of myriad other entities—stock performance, volatility of money, the number of words in a language—distributions both summarize the characteristics and describe their operation.

Moreover, there are distributions for every kind of variable: continuous or discrete; defined on a support that may be any subset of numbers (positive half-line, full line, positive integers, etc.); displaying a great variety of shapes; symmetric or asymmetric; with zero, one, or many peaks; skewed to the left or the right; possessing one or several modes; and so on. As a rule, continuous distributions are specified by mathematical functions.

Functions of variables and combinations (mixtures) of variables generate new variables whose distributions show the imprint of the input distributions and their interrelations. Because approximation of a variable's distribution unlocks many doors—in theoretical analysis, where distributions are a prime tool for forecasting and prediction, and in empirical analysis, where distributions usually serve to represent the unobservables—detailed compilations of distributions are a necessary part of the social scientist's toolkit.

For introduction and comprehensive exposition, see Stuart and Ord (1994), Dwass (1970), and Tsokos (1972), and for rather encyclopedic coverage the volumes in Johnson and Kotz's series, *Distributions in Statistics*, and their revisions (e.g., Johnson, Kotz, and Balakrishnan 1994). The handbook by Evans, Hastings, and Peacock (2000) is an appropriate and valuable source for initial study.

ASSOCIATED FUNCTIONS

A variety of mathematical functions are associated with mathematically specified distributions. The most basic is the distribution function, also known as the *cumulative distribution function* (cdf). The distribution function may be defined as a mathematical expression that describes the probability that a system (consisting of several components) will take a specific numerical value or set of values (such a varying system is designated as a "random variable" and usually denoted by capital X, Y, or Z). The description of a system may involve other quantities, and the distribution function may take into account some (or all) of them. In the case of a system with one variable, the distribution function (or cumulative distribution function) is defined as the probability α ($0 < \alpha < 1$) that the variate X assumes a value less than or equal to x and is usually denoted $F_X(x)$, or simply $F(x)$:

$$F(x) = P(X \le x) \qquad (1)$$

(distinguishing, as customary, between the random variable X and its specific numerical value x). The distribution function of any random variable is a nondecreasing (usually increasing) function of x. The range of its values is [0, 1]. (Remember that the cdf is nothing else but a particular probability.)

Besides the cdf, the behavior of a random variable can be described by an "associated" function. The most common of the associated functions (and by far the most often graphed) is the probability density function (pdf), denoted $f(x)$. In the case of continuous distributions the pdf is simply the first derivative of the distribution function with respect to the value x of the corresponding variate X. (In discrete distributions it is sometimes called the "probability mass function," and is obtained by taking the difference of the consecutive values of the distribution function.) As visible from its relationship to the distribution function, the pdf, represented graphically as a curve,

possesses two main properties: (1) it is nonnegative for all values of x, $f(x) > 0$ (because the cdf is a nondecreasing function of x); (2) the total area under the curve is 1:

$$\int_{-\infty}^{\infty} f(x)\,dx = 1. \qquad (2)$$

By far the most familiar and most widely used of all (continuous) distributional shapes is the symmetric bell-shaped curve depicting the pdf of the normal (or "Gaussian") distribution. The normal distribution was popularized in the social sciences by the great Belgian scholar Lambert Adolphe Jacques Quételet (1796–1874).

Other popular associated functions used in social science are (1) the *quantile function*, which, inter alia, provides the foundation for distributional measures of inequality, such as Pen's Parade, and (2) the *hazard function*, formally defined as the ratio of the pdf to 1 minus the cdf: $f(x)/[1 - F(x)]$. The denominator, $1 - F(x)$, is also known as the "reliability function" and as the "survival function" and denoted by $S(x)$.

All the associated functions are related to each other. For example, as already noted, among continuous distributions, the probability density function is the first derivative of the distribution function with respect to x. The quantile function, variously denoted $G(\alpha)$ or $Q(\alpha)$ or $F^{-1}(\alpha)$, is the inverse of the distribution function, providing a mapping from the probability α ($0 < \alpha < 1$) to the quantile value x. Recall that the range of the values of a distribution function is (0, 1). If the distribution function rises steadily from 0 to 1 there is a unique number x_α for each α on the interval [0, 1] such that

$$F(x_\alpha) = P(X \le x_\alpha) = \alpha . \qquad (3)$$

The number x_α is a number in the set of values of X and it is the value such that the fraction α ($0 < \alpha < 1$) of the *total probability* (which is 1) is assigned to the interval $(-\infty, x_\alpha)$. This number is the αth quantile of the distribution function defined above, $F_X(x)$. (For a standard normal distribution at probability $\alpha = .5$, the value of the quantile function is 0, given that the total probability under the normal curve [which ranges from $-\infty$ to $+\infty$] up to value 0 is .5.) Important relations between the quantile and distribution functions are (Eubank 1988; Evans, Hastings, and Peacock 2000):

$$F[Q(\alpha)] = \alpha, \text{ for } F \text{ continuous}$$
$$Q[F(x)] = x, \text{ for } F \text{ continuous and} \qquad (4)$$
$$\text{strictly increasing.}$$

DISTRIBUTIONAL PARAMETERS

Quantities which appear explicitly in the expression of the distribution function are called *parameters*. Distributions usually have associated with them a number of parameters. Of these, three are regarded as basic—the location, scale, and shape parameters. The location parameter is a particular point in the variate's domain, and the scale and shape parameters govern the scale and the shape, respectively. Variates differ in the number and kind of basic parameters. For example, the normal (Gaussian) distribution has two parameters, a location parameter (the mean) and a scale parameter (the standard deviation); the Pareto distribution has a location parameter and a shape parameter; and the gamma is a three-parameter distribution (with location, scale, and shape parameters). The gamma distribution is sometimes specified as a two-parameter distribution (possessing scale and shape parameters, with the location parameter being 0).

MOMENTS, MEAN, AND VARIANCE

Borrowing from physics the idea of the moments of a function, the *mean* (or expected value) of a distribution (also referred to as *of a random variable*) is defined as the first moment about the origin (0):

$$\mu = \int_{-\infty}^{\infty} x f(x)\, dx \qquad (5)$$

(representing an ideal or a theoretical average and characterizing the central tendency). The *variance* is defined as the second moment about the mean:

$$\sigma^2 = \int_{-\infty}^{\infty} (x - \mu)^2 f(x)\, dx \qquad (6)$$

(representing dispersion of the random variable around the expected value). The square root of the variance is known as the "standard deviation" and is usually denoted σ.

SKEWNESS AND KURTOSIS

Two additional quantities are the coefficient of skewness, denoted β_1 (the positive square root of β_1 is denoted by $\gamma_1 = +\sqrt{\beta_1}$:

$$\beta_1 = \frac{\int_{-\infty}^{\infty} (x - \mu)^3 f(x)\, dx}{\sigma^3}, \qquad (7)$$

and the coefficient of kurtosis, denoted β_2:

$$\beta_2 = \frac{\int_{-\infty}^{\infty} (x - \mu)^4 f(x)\, dx}{\sigma^4}. \qquad (8)$$

The numerators of the coefficients of skewness and kurtosis are the third and fourth moments about the mean, respectively, and the denominators are the third and fourth powers, respectively, of the standard deviation. The coefficient of skewness measures the relative asymmetry and the coefficient of kurtosis measures the peakedness (and humpness) of the distribution. For the normal distribution, the kurtosis is

$$\beta_2 = 3. \qquad (9)$$

Evidently, for any symmetric distribution the skewness equals 0, given that every odd moment is zero in this case. The coefficient of kurtosis is thus sometimes defined as the expression in (8) minus 3 (usually denoted by γ_2), which may lead to ambiguity. (The Greek word κυρτόσ means "humped").

CUMULANTS

Cumulants (also known as semi-invariants) are simple functions of moments having useful theoretical properties. Unlike the moments, all the cumulants (except the first) are independent of the origin of calculations so it is unnecessary to specify the origin of calculations in giving their values.

GROUPS AND SUBGROUPS, DISTRIBUTIONS AND SUBDISTRIBUTIONS

Groups and subgroups are pivotal in social science, and the distributional operations of censoring and truncation serve to analyze subgroup structures. Using what is by now standard terminology (Gibbons 1988, p. 355), let "censoring" refer to selection of units by their ranks or percentage (or probability) points; and let "truncation" refer to selection of units by values of the variate. Thus, the truncation point is the value x separating the subdistributions; the censoring point is the percentage point α separating the subdistributions. For example, the subgroups with incomes less than \$30,000 or greater than \$90,000 each form a truncated subdistribution; the top 2 percent and the bottom 5 percent of the population each form a censored subdistribution.

There is a special link between these two kinds of subgroup structure and Blau's (1974) pioneering observation that much of human behavior can be traced to the differential operation of quantitative and qualitative characteristics. Quantitative characteristics—both cardinal characteristics (such as wealth) and ordinal characteristics (such as intelligence and beauty)—generate both truncated and censored subdistribution structures. For example, the subgroups "rich" and "poor" may be generated by reference to an amount of income or by reference to percentages of the population. However, qualitative characteristics—such as race, ethnicity, language, and religion—may be related so tightly to quantitative characteristics that the subgroups corresponding to the categories of the qualitative characteristic are nonoverlapping and thus provide the basis for generating censored subdistribution structures. For example, in caste, slavery, or segmented societies, the subdistribution structure of a quantitative characteristic may be a censored structure in which the percentages pertain to the subsets formed by a qualitative characteristic—such as "slave" and "free" or "immigrant" and "native."

SOME IMPORTANT DISTRIBUTIONS

The number of probability distributions appearing in the literature is now by a conservative estimate far more than 300, and climbing. The standard compendia highlight the basic forty or fifty distributions, and among these, the most important twenty or so appear in all textbooks and in all languages. Chronologically, the earliest distributions that were scrupulously investigated, starting from the early eighteenth century, were the normal (Gaussian) distribution and, to a lesser extent, the Cauchy distribution. The Pareto distribution was proposed by the Italian-Swiss economist and sociologist Vilfredo Pareto (1848–1923) in the late nineteenth century, and the Weibull is of more recent origin, developed by the Swedish engineer Waloddi Weibull (1887–1979) in the mid-twentieth century. Information about univariate and multivariate discrete distributions and multivariate continuous distributions is by now easily available, and these are not discussed here due to space constraints. The 2000 handbook by Evans, Hastings, and Peacock provides a lucid introduction to some forty widely used distributions. A more extensive source is the six-volume compendium by Kotz, Johnson, Balakrishnan, and Kemp under the overall title *Distributions in Statistics*, 2nd ed., 1995–2002. The *Dictionary and Classified Bibliography of Statistical Distributions in Scientific Work*, edited by Patil, Boswell, Joshi, Ratnaparkhi, and Roux, 1984, is a handy reference source.

We now present a brief description of twelve selected basic continuous univariate distributions. Table 1 reports their probability density function, mean, and variance (for a more detailed table, see e.g. Tsokos 1972, which also provides graphical display).

Uniform Distribution The uniform is a natural conception that has been in use since before printed records. Its applications include corrections for grouping, life testing, traffic-flow analyses, and round-off errors, and it provides a model for the set of relative ranks in a group or population.

Normal Distribution As indicated above, the normal (also "Gaussian," "Laplace-Gaussian," and "Gaussian-Laplace") is the most important distribution in probability theory and in mathematical as well as applied statistics. The normal's density is symmetric and bell-shaped. Values for the density, cumulative, and inverse of the standard form are extensively tabulated. The importance of the normal distribution is due to the fact that under general conditions, the sum of many independent variables tends, as the number of variables increases, to the normal. The relevant conditions are provided in the central limit theorem.

Lognormal Distribution The lognormal distribution is defined on the positive support; it is unimodal with a long right tail. Its name refers to the fact that the logarithm of a lognormal variate has a normal distribution. The lognormal is widely used in the biological, physical, and sociobehavioral sciences, including economics, and even in philology. It serves as a model for income, physician's consulting time, sickness absence, number of persons in a census occupational category, height and weight, automobile insurance claims payments, and size of oil and gas deposits.

Exponential Distribution The exponential (more precisely, the "negative exponential") has a mode at the origin ($x = 0$) and a long right tail. It is widely used in studies of lifetimes, life testing, and life characteristics, producing usable approximate solutions to difficult distributional problems. It also provides the model for social status in the case where status arises from one (or several perfectly positively related) personal characteristic(s). Its mirror image, the positive exponential, has a mode at its upper bound and a long left tail. Justice processes generate both negative exponential and positive exponential distributions. Recent extensions by Jasso and Kotz (2007) are geared towards applications in the social sciences (see below).

Weibull Distribution The Weibull is an asymmetric single-peaked distribution defined on the positive support. It is widely used in analyses of reliability problems, the theory of sound, health phenomena, human performance, duration of industrial stoppages, and migratory systems.

Gamma Distribution The gamma is defined on the positive support; it is unimodal and asymmetric and has a

Probability Density Function, Mean, and Variance of Some Important Continuous Univariate Distributions

Variate	Probability Density Function	Mean	Variance
Uniform (Rectangular) $a < x < b$	$\dfrac{1}{b-a}$	$\dfrac{a+b}{2}$	$\dfrac{(b-a)^2}{12}$
Uniform standard form $0 < x < 1$	1	$\dfrac{1}{2}$	$\dfrac{1}{12}$
Normal (Gaussian) $-\infty < x < \infty$	$\dfrac{1}{\sigma\sqrt{2\pi}}\exp\left\{\dfrac{-(x-\mu)^2}{2\sigma^2}\right\}$	μ	σ^2
Normal standard form $-\infty < x < \infty$	$\dfrac{1}{\sqrt{2\pi}}\exp\left\{\dfrac{-x^2}{2}\right\}$	0	1
Lognormal $x > 0, c > 0$	$\dfrac{1}{xc\sqrt{2\pi}}\exp\left\{-\dfrac{\left(\dfrac{c^2}{2}+\ln\dfrac{x}{\mu}\right)^2}{2c^2}\right\}$	μ	$\mu^2\left\{\left[\exp\left(c^2\right)\right]-1\right\}$
Weibull $x > 0, \lambda > 0, k > 0$	$\dfrac{k}{\lambda}\left(\dfrac{x}{\lambda}\right)^{k-1}\exp-(x/\lambda)^k$	$\lambda\Gamma\left(1+\dfrac{1}{k}\right)$	$\lambda^2\Gamma\left(1+\dfrac{2}{k}\right)-\left[\Gamma\left(1+\dfrac{1}{k}\right)\right]^2$
Weibull standard form $x > 0, k > 0$	$kx^{k-1}\exp(-x^k)$	$\Gamma\left(1+\dfrac{1}{k}\right)$	$\Gamma\left(1+\dfrac{2}{k}\right)-\left[\Gamma\left(1+\dfrac{1}{k}\right)\right]^2$
Exponential $x > 0, \lambda > 0$	$\lambda\exp(-\lambda x)$	$\dfrac{1}{\lambda}$	$\dfrac{1}{\lambda^2}$
Exponential standard form $x > 0$	$\exp(-x)$	1	1
Gamma (2-parameter) $x > 0, \lambda > 0, c > 0$	$\dfrac{(\lambda x)^{c-1}\lambda\left[\exp(-\lambda x)\right]}{\Gamma(c)}$	$\dfrac{c}{\lambda}$	$\dfrac{c}{\lambda^2}$
Gamma standard form $x > 0, c > 0$	$\dfrac{x^{c-1}e^{-x}}{\Gamma(c)}$	c	c
Pareto $x > \dfrac{\mu(c-1)}{c}, c > 1$	$\left[\dfrac{\mu(c-1)}{c}\right]^c cx^{-c-1}$	μ	$\dfrac{\mu^2}{c(c-2)}, c > 2$
Pareto standard form $x > 1, c > 1$	cx^{-c-1}	$\dfrac{c}{c-1}$	$\dfrac{c}{(c-1)^2(c-2)}, c > 2$

Notes: In the formula for the beta distribution, "B" denotes the beta function, and $\Gamma(\cdot)$ appearing in formulas for the gamma and Weibull distributions denotes the gamma function.

(CONTINUED)

Probability Density Function, Mean, and Variance of Some Important Continuous Univariate Distributions

Variate	Probability Density Function	Mean	Variance
Laplace (double-exponential) $-\infty < x < \infty, b > 0$	$\dfrac{1}{2b} \exp\left\{ -\dfrac{\|x - \mu\|}{b} \right\}$	μ	$2b^2$
Laplace standard form $-\infty < x < \infty$	$\dfrac{e^{-\|x\|}}{2}$	0	2
Beta $a < x < b$ $p > 0, q > 0$	$\dfrac{(x - a)^{p-1}(b - x)^{q-1}}{\left[B(p,q)\right]\left[(b-a)^{p+q-1}\right]}$	$a + \left(\dfrac{p}{p+q}\right)(b-a)$	$\dfrac{(pq)(b-a)^2}{(p+q)^2(p+q+1)}$
Beta standard form $0 < x < 1$ $p > 0, q > 0$	$\dfrac{x^{p-1}(1-x)^{q-1}}{B(p,q)}$	$\dfrac{p}{p+q}$	$\dfrac{pq}{(p+q)^2(p+q+1)}$
Logistic $-\infty < x < \infty, b > 0$	$\dfrac{\exp\left[-(x-\mu)/b\right]}{b\left\{1 + \exp\left[-(x-\mu)/b\right]\right\}^2}$	μ	$\dfrac{\pi^2 b^2}{3}$
Logistic standard form $-\infty < x < \infty$	$\dfrac{e^x}{(1+e^x)^2}$	0	$\dfrac{\pi^2}{3}$
Cauchy $-\infty < x < \infty, b > 0$	$(\pi b)^{-1}\left\{1 + \left[(x-a)/b\right]^2\right\}^{-1}$	—	—
Cauchy standard form $-\infty < x < \infty$	$\pi^{-1}(1+x^2)^{-1}$	—	—
Power-Function $0 < x < \dfrac{\mu(c+1)}{c}, c > 0$	$\left[\dfrac{c}{\mu(c+1)}\right]^c cx^{c-1}$	μ	$\dfrac{\mu^2}{c(c+2)}$
Power-Function standard form $0 < x < 1, c > 0$	cx^{c-1}	$\dfrac{c}{c+1}$	$\dfrac{c}{(c+1)^2(c+2)}$
Equal (Dirac delta)	—	μ	0

Notes: In the formula for the beta distribution, "B" denotes the beta function, and $\Gamma(\cdot)$ appearing in formulas for the gamma and Weibull distributions denotes the gamma function.

long right tail. It includes as special cases the exponential, whose mode is at the origin, and the Erlang distribution, whose shape parameter c is an integer. The gamma is used to represent lifetimes and personal income, as well as daily demand for electrical power and the distribution of single-species abundances at equilibrium. It arises also in the study of social status, where it provides a model of the case where status is generated by two or more independent characteristics, and in the study of justice, where it provides a model of the case where the justice evaluation is generated by two or more independent ordinal characteristics.

Pareto Distribution The Pareto has a mode at its positive origin and a very long right tail. It is used to model personal income, firm size, city size, and occurrence of natural resources. Because the Pareto has a positive infimum, it is ideal for modeling income distributions that have a "safety net." Recently it has been used in connection with the random walk hypothesis of common stock prices.

Laplace Distribution (Double Exponential) The Laplace is a symmetric distribution with a sharp point at its mode—it arises, inter alia, from the difference between two identical exponential distributions. It is similar to the normal, but the smooth top of the bell is replaced by a needle peak. It is the "prior distribution" in Bayesian statistical analysis. It is used as a substitute for the normal in robust statistics analysis, and provides a model for demand during lead time for slow-moving items. It also arises in the study of justice, in the case where both actual incomes and personal ideas of just incomes are independently and identically Pareto distributed; the asymmetrical Laplace form arises in the case where actual incomes and personal ideas of just incomes are independently and nonidentically Pareto distributed.

Beta Distribution The beta is a very flexible family, being a generalization of the uniform distribution. It provides the prior distribution for binomial proportions and serves in models and analyses of hydrologic variables, project planning/control systems (such as PERT), tool wear, construction duration, transmission of HIV virus, traffic flow, and risk analysis for strategic planning. Via its special case, the power-function distribution, it also is used to model the income distribution.

Logistic Distribution The logistic is a symmetric unimodal distribution defined on the real line. It is used in analyses of growth (including the growth of human populations), quantal response data, psychological issues, weight gain, and physiochemical phenomena. It also is sometimes used as a substitute for the normal.

Cauchy Distribution The Cauchy is a symmetric unimodal distribution defined on the real line. Its density is similar to the normal's but with thicker tails. It has the interesting (and restrictive in applications) property that moments (including the expected value) are not defined. Advances in computational procedures diminish the effect of the absence of moments, and the Cauchy distribution is nowadays often used (in particular in financial applications) as an alternative to the normal distribution.

Power-Function Distribution The power-function, a special case of the beta, is defined on the positive support; it can have a left tail or a right tail, depending on whether its shape parameter is larger or smaller than 1. When the shape parameter is 1, the power-function becomes the uniform distribution. Because the power-function has a supremum, it is appropriate for modeling situations marked by scarcity.

To summarize, the normal, Cauchy, Laplace, and logistic distributions are defined for all real values; the exponential, Weibull, gamma, and lognormal distributions are defined for all positive values; the Pareto distribution is defined for all positive values larger than a

specified number; the beta distribution (and the continuous uniform distribution) are defined for an interval of a specified length.

Some of the distributions in the list are rivals for modeling some phenomena. For example, the gamma and lognormal are competitors for modeling size distributions, and the exponential and Weibull are competitors for modeling reliability. Many other distributions are used in social science to model sociobehavioral phenomena, and still more distributions arise from sociobehavioral operations. For example, status processes generate, besides the Erlang, a general Erlang and new variates called *ring-exponential* and *mirror-exponential distributions* (Jasso and Kotz 2007). Further, in addition to the pivotal normal, other distributions used in mathematical and applied statistics include the chi-squared, Student's *t*, and the *F* distribution (central and noncentral).

Finally, special mention must be made of the equal distribution (sometimes called "degenerate" when defined as discrete, and "Dirac's delta" when defined as continuous), which provides a model for a perfectly equal distribution and thus serves as a benchmark in analyses of social inequality (Jasso 1980; Jasso and Kotz 2007).

SEE ALSO *Bayesian Econometrics; Bayesian Statistics; Central Limit Theorem; Distribution, Normal; Distribution, Poisson; Distribution, Uniform; Method of Moments; Pareto, Vilfredo; Probabilistic Regression*

BIBLIOGRAPHY

Blau, Peter M. 1974. Presidential Address: Parameters of Social Structure. *American Sociological Review* 39: 615–635.

Dwass, Meyer. 1970. *Probability: Theory and Applications*. New York: W. A. Benjamin.

Eubank, Randall L. 1988. Quantiles. In *Encyclopedia of Statistical Sciences*, Vol. 7, eds. Samuel Kotz, Norman L. Johnson, and Campbell B. Read, 424–432. New York: Wiley.

Evans, Merran, Nicholas Hastings, and Brian Peacock. 2000. *Statistical Distributions*. 3rd ed. New York: Wiley.

Gibbons, Jean Dickinson. 1988. Truncated Data. In *Encyclopedia of Statistical Sciences*, Vol. 9, eds. Samuel Kotz, Norman L. Johnson, and Campbell B. Read, 355. New York: Wiley.

Jasso, Guillermina. 1980. A New Theory of Distributive Justice. *American Sociological Review* 45: 3–32.

Jasso, Guillermina, and Samuel Kotz. 2007. A New Continuous Distribution and Two New Families of Distributions Based on the Exponential. *Statistica Neerlandica* 61(3): 305–328.

Johnson, Norman L., Samuel Kotz, and N. Balakrishnan. 1994. *Continuous Univariate Distributions*, Vol. 1. 2nd ed. New York: Wiley.

Patil, Ganapati P. 1984. *Dictionary and Classified Bibliography of Statistical Distributions in Scientific Work*. Vols. 1-3. Burtonsville, MD: International Cooperative Publishing House.

Stuart, Alan, and J. Keith Ord. 1994. *Distribution Theory*. Vol. 1 of *Kendall's Advanced Theory of Statistics*, 6th ed. London: Edward Arnold.

Tsokos, Chris P. 1972. *Probability Distributions: An Introduction to Probability Theory with Applications*. Belmont, CA: Duxbury Press.

Guillermina Jasso
Samuel Kotz

PROBABILITY THEORY

With the identification of Huygens's 1657 book *Ratiociniis in aleae ludu* as its first text, Ian Hacking characterizes the decade around 1660 as *the* decade of the birth of probability. He chooses to bring the story of its emergence to an end with the year of publication of Jacques Bernoulli's *Ars Conjectandi* in 1713:

> In that year probability came before the public with a brilliant portent of all the things we know about it now: its mathematical profundity, its unbounded practical applications, its squirming duality, and its constant invitation for philosophizing (Hacking 1975, p. 143).

Hacking structures his prehistory, a "prehistory … more important than the history," around the dual notions of the aleatory versus the epistemic: "the degree of belief warranted by evidence" versus the "tendency displayed by some chance devices to produce stable relative frequencies" (1975, p. 1).

Augustin Cournot (1843) and Francis Edgeworth (1884, 1922), and following them in the second quarter of the twentieth century, John Maynard Keynes and Frank P. Ramsey, distinguished students of economy and society, all had a deep and abiding interest in probability theory, but struggled with the definition of their (instrumental) subject. Edgeworth, in particular, settled in his 1884 paper on the description of probability as "importing partial incomplete belief," but was unsure about "how far the gradations of belief are a subject of science" (p. 223). Returning to the term, and to the "philosophy of chance" forty years later, he flatly stated that "probability seems not to admit of definition" (Edgeworth 1922, p. 257). Already, his 1911 entry on *probability and expectation* for the *Encyclopedia Britannica* had opened with the following demurral:

> As in other mathematical sciences, so in probabilities, or even more so, the philosophical foundations are less clear than the calculations based thereon. On this obscure and controversial topic, absolute uniformity is not to be expected (p. 376).

In his biographical essay on Ramsey, Keynes responded to Ramsey's (1922, 1926) critique of his "objective theory of probability" with a wary ambivalence:

> The calculus of probabilities belongs to formal logic. But the basis of our degrees of belief—or the *a priori* probabilities, as they used to be called—is part of our human outfit, perhaps given us merely by natural selection, analogous to our perceptions and our memories rather than to formal logic. So far I yield to Ramsey—I think he is right. But in attempting to distinguish "rational" degrees of belief from belief in general he was not yet I think quite successful (Keynes 1933, pp. 338–339).

In her discussion of the "subjective theory of probability," Maria Galavotti alluded to Ramsey's scepticism concerning a single notion of probability equally applicable "in logic and in physics," and quoted Bruno de Finetti's bald antirealist claim that "probability does not exist" (Galavotti 1991, pp. 241, 246). Colin Howson's (1995) conclusion then that the foundations of probability have not yet entered a "final stable phase" was only fitting.

Whatever the final phase and the precise definition, *equipossibility* and *asymptotics* are identified as foundational in any application of the subject. In his endorsement of the equal-treatment property, and of the "utilitarian who thinks it 'fair' to treat as equals those between whom no material difference is discerned, … [to] treat as equals things which are not known to be unequal," Edgeworth relied on the standard of statistical uniformity to consider John Venn's claim that "whereas full belief about an event is either verified or disproved by the event, fractional belief can only be verified or disproved by a series of events" (Edgeworth 1884, pp. 234, 225). It is of interest to trace the evolution of this Laplacian idea to the role it plays as a principle of indifference in Keynes's objective theory, and to the assignment of equal initial degrees of confirmation in Rudolf Carnap's system of inductive logic based on "logical probability"; (see Gillies 2000, chapters 2 and 3; Ayer 1963, chapters 7 and 8; and Ayer 1972, chapter 2). Hacking, too, devotes discussion to "equally possible cases," before moving on to the "first limit theorem" (Hacking 1975, chapters 14 and 17). In his history of the subject in the nineteenth century, he observes an attitude, especially among the French.

> When there are enough events they display regularities. This law passed beyond a mere fact of experience. It was not something to be checked against experience; it was the way things had to be. The law of large numbers became a metaphysical truth (Hacking 1990, p. 104).

By the middle of the twentieth century, however, the logical and mathematical presuppositions of such a law were well-understood (see Ayer 1972, section 2.D).

It is now conventional to see Andrei Kolmogorov (1933) as having laid the mathematical foundation of the subject in the theory of measure, and in having brought probability into the mathematical mainstream by providing a rigorous framework for the study of an infinite sequence of coin tosses, and even for an uncountably indexed set of trials. Authoritative texts abound for the mathematics of probability, and the tables of contents in Jeffrey Rosenthal's *A First Look at Rigorous Probability Theory* (2000) or in A. V. Skorokhod's *Basic Principles and Applications of Probability Theory* (2004), for example, bring out what is now considered to be the standard subject matter. What is important is that rather than attempting probability on the same rigorous basis as the rest of mathematics, after Kolomogorov, the question turns to the insights that probability can give rather than take from the rest of mathematics: from analysis, dynamical systems, optimization, and even number theory and geometry (see Lasota and Mackey 1994; de Melo and van Strein 1993; Steele 1997; and Dajani and Kraaikamp 2002 and their references). The subject has attained a maturity that it can be studied solely through counterexamples, as in Jordan Stoyanav (1987), but as Joseph Doob (1994a) documents, this mathematical coming-of-age has resulted in some tension between probabilists and measure-theorists. Indeed the issue—a mini-issue really— reduces to the essential difference between a measure and a probability, a difference encapsulated in the concept of independence and in a bounded rather than an unbounded measure: For the former, Mark Kac's (1964, 1985) elegant emphasis is unparalleled, and for the latter, one can hardly do better than begin with a comparison of Walter Rudin (1987) and Doob (1994b).

A subsidiary question then arises as to the evolution and the autonomy of the subject of *statistics* as distinct from that of *probability*. If the notion of *independence* is a synecdoche for one, is the notion of *sufficiency* that for the other? If Hacking (1975) is devoted to one, is Hacking (1990) devoted to the other? It is interesting that Ramsey, de Finetti, and Leonard Savage do not make it to the index of Hacking's investigation of "statistical fatalism," and how "an avalanche of numbers turned rational moral science into empirical moral science" (1990, pp. x, viii). However, if the distinction between the theories of probability and measure is a mini-issue, the distinction between probability and statistics is almost surely a nonissue, and it would be a naive anthropology indeed that uses professional societies and journals to refute the fact of one community finding its true identity in the other (see Khan 1993 in this direction). In any case, current conventions see Savage (1954, 1962) as consolidating the earlier insights into a strongly contending, if not dominant, framework for statistical decision theory, one in which utility and (finitely additive as opposed to countably additive) probability are intertwined (see Hacking 1965, chapter 13 for evaluation and possible synthesis).

Savage (1954) is also seen as bringing to culmination the original ideas of Ramsey and de Finetti and providing a founding text for individual decision making. His text thus fulfills Edgeworth's promise of a "mixed science of probability and utility: of what Laplace (1814) calls *espèrance*, the product of probability and utility; that quantity which to maximize is the main problem of the Art of Measurement—of the art proper" (Edgeworth 1884, p. 235). The modern twist lies in the use, nothing if not dramatic, of the theory of expected utility to depart from the notion of expectation as Laplace defined it, and to construct a theory of nonexpected utility. After an identification of Kreps (1988), Karni and Schmeidler (1991) and Machina and Schmeidler (1992) as the relevant texts, I move on.

With the wholesale importation of the idea of a continuum of agents into more applied areas of economics— macroeconomics certainly, but also the economics of labor and industry, albeit in a framework of identical agents buffeted by independent exogenous shocks—a law of large numbers for a continuum of random variables became an instrumental necessity. The models were geared to exploit the plausible intuition that aggregation removed idiosyncratic uncertainty, and it was difficult to see how the averaging operation of Laplace could not cancel out errors without a tilt or a dependence to them, not only asymptotically but also for a suitably idealized limit. In other words, there was a demand for a framework that was hospitable to the averaging of an independent continuum, and could thereby execute what the Lebesgue probability measure could not, and cannot, do (on this, see Doob 1994a; Khan and Sun 1999; and Sun 2006). In a landmark paper, Peter Loeb (1975) offered such a framework, and Yeneng Sun exploited it to deliver not only a law of large numbers, but also a variety of novel probabilistic patterns and dualities concerning independence and exchangeability (see Sun 1998ab). R. J. Aumann's limitation on the diversity of agent characteristics through the assumption of a finite number of commodities is now translated into a possibly analogous limitation that requires the order of averaging over names and states of nature not to matter, a limitation that yokes Fubini to an event space richer than the one conventionally constructed for products (see Hammond and Sun 2003a, 2003b, 2006a, 2006b). Thus, in its needs and demands for a limit law of great numbers, probability theory was led to supply new adjectives for a probability measure, and thereby surely to go beyond the original Kolmogorov axioms (in addition to Fajardo's 1999 overview, see Khan and Sun 2002 and Sun 2006).

Stochastic dynamics, and a surge of interest in functional analysis, had already led probability theory to a study of function-valued and vector-valued random variables, as in Joseph Diestel and Jerry Uhl (1977); after Aumann's formalization of Edgeworth's conjecture (see Anderson 1991 for details and references), economic theory led it to a study of set-valued random variables. Laplace's *espèrance* was correspondingly generalized to sets, as was the induced law of a random variable and the law of large numbers; once random sets are made tractable, it is a small step to the consideration of random preferences, random economies, set-valued martingales, and a variety of other set-valued notions. (In addition to Khan and Sun 2002, see Sun 1999, Majumdar and Rotar 2000, and Bhattacharya and Majumdar 2004.)

We conclude this entry by pointing out that its narrower compass has forced a neglect of the economics of information and the affiliated fields of game theory and finance, let alone the manifold applications to sociology, behavioral psychology, quantum mechanics, and evidence-based bio-medical sciences. But even a briefly adequate view of these other applications surely requires another entry.

SEE ALSO *Classical Statistical Analysis; Keynes, John Maynard; Probability; Probability Distributions; Risk; Statistics; Statistics in the Social Sciences; Uncertainty*

BIBLIOGRAPHY

Anderson, Robert M. 1991. Non-Standard Analysis with Applications to Economics. In *Handbook of Mathematical Economics*, Vol. 4, eds. Werner Hildenbrand and Hugo Sonnenschein, 2145–2208. New York: North-Holland.

Artstein, Zvi. 1983. Distributions of Random Sets and Random Selections. *Israel Journal of Mathematics* 46: 313–324.

Aumann, R. J. 1965. Integrals of Set-Valued Functions. *Journal of Mathematical Analysis and Applications* 12: 1–12.

Ayer, Alfred J. 1963. *The Concept of a Person*. New York: St. Martin's Press.

Ayer, Alfred J. 1972. *Probablity and Evidence*. New York: Columbia University Press.

Bhattacharya, Rabi, and Mukul Majumdar. 2004. Dynamical Systems Subject to Random Shocks: An Introduction. *Economic Theory* 23: 1–12.

Cournot, Augustin A. [1843] 1984. Exposition de la Théorie des Chances et des Probabilités. *Oeuvres de Cournot*, Vol. 1. Paris: J. Vrin.

Dajani, Karma, and Cor Kraaikamp. 2002. *Ergodic Theory of Numbers*. Washington, DC: Mathematical Association of America.

Debreu, Gérard. 1967. Integration of Correspondences. In *Proceedings of the Fifth Berkeley Symposium on Mathematical Statistics and Probability* 1 (2): 351–372. Berkeley: University of California Press.

De Finetti, Bruno. [1937] 1964. La Prévision: ses lois logique, ses sources subjectives (Foresight: Its Logical Laws, Its Subjective Sources). In *Studies in Subjective Probability*, eds. Henry E. Kyberg and Howard E. Smokler, 93–158. New York: John Wiley.

De Finetti, Bruno. [1938] 1985. Probabilisti di Cambridge (Cambridge Probability Theorists). *Manchester School of Economic and Social Studies* 53: 348–363.

De Melo, Wellington, and Sebastian van Strein. 1993. *One-Dimensional Dynamics*. Berlin: Springer-Verlag.

Diestel, Joseph, and Jerry J. Uhl Jr. 1977. *Vector Measures*. Providence, RI: American Mathematical Society.

Doob, Joseph L. 1994a. The Development of Rigor in Mathematical Probability, (1900–1950). In *Development of Mathematics, 1900–1950*, ed. Jean-Paul Pier, 157–169. Berlin: Berkhauser-Verlag.

Doob, Joseph L. 1994b. *Measure Theory*. Berlin: Springer-Verlag.

Edgeworth, Francis Y. 1884. The Philosophy of Chance. *Mind* 9: 223–235.

Edgeworth, Francis Y. 1922. The Philosophy of Chance. *Mind* 31: 257–283.

Fajardo, Sergio. 1999. Nonstandard Analysis and a Classification of Probability Spaces. In *Language, Quantum, Music*, eds. Maria L. Dalla Chiara, Roberto Guintini, and Federico Laudisa, 61–71. Dordrecht, Germany: Kluwer Academic.

Galavotti, Maria C. 1991. The Notion of Subjective Probability in the Work of Ramsey and de Finetti. *Theoria* 67: 239–259.

Gillies, Donald. 2000. *Philosophical Theories of Probability*. London: Routledge.

Hacking, Ian. 1965. *Logic of Statistical Inference*. Cambridge, U.K.: Cambridge University Press.

Hacking, Ian. 1975. *The Emergence of Probability*. Cambridge, U.K.: Cambridge University Press.

Hacking, Ian. 1990. *The Taming of Chance*. Cambridge, U.K.: Cambridge University Press.

Hammond, Peter J., and Yeneng Sun. 2003a. Monte Carlo Simulation of Macroeconomic Risk with a Continuum of Agents: The Symmetric Case. *Economic Theory* 21: 743–766.

Hammond, Peter J., and Yeneng Sun. 2003b. Monte Carlo Simulation of Macroeconomic Risk with a Continuum of Agents: The Symmetric Case. *Economic Theory* 21 (2): 743–746.

Hammond, Peter J., and Yeneng Sun. 2006a. The Essential Equivalence of Pairwise and Mutual Conditional Independence. *Probability Theory and Related Fields* 135: 415–427.

Hammond, Peter J., and Yeneng Sun. 2006b. Joint Measurability and the One-Way Fubini Property for a Continuum of Random Variables. *Proceedings of the American Mathematical Society* 134: 737–747.

Howson, Colin. 1995. Theories of Probability. *British Journal of the Philosophy of Science* 46: 1–32.

Kac, Mark. 1964. *Statistical Independence in Probability, Analysis, and Number Theory*. Washington, DC: Mathematical Association of America.

Kac, Mark. 1985. *Enigmas of Chance.* New York: Harper and Row.

Karni, Edi, and David Schmeidler. 1991. Utility Theory with Uncertainty. In *Handbook of Mathematical Economics,* Vol. 4, eds. Werner Hildenbrand and Hugo Sonnenschein, 1763–1831. New York: North-Holland.

Keynes, John M. [1921] 1963. A Treatise on Probability. In *The Collected Writings of John Maynard Keynes,* Vol. 8. London: Macmillan.

Keynes, John M. [1933] 1985. Essays in Biography. Expanded version in *The Collected Writings of John Maynard Keynes,* Vol. 10. London: Macmillan.

Khan, M. Ali. 1985. On the Integration of Set-Valued Mappings in a Non-Reflexive Banach Space, II. *Simon Stevin* 59: 257–267.

Khan, M. Ali. 1987. Correspondence. In *The New Palgrave: A Dictionary of Economics,* Vol. 1, eds. John Eatwell, Peter K. Newman, and Murray Milgate, 679–681. London: Macmillan.

Khan, M. Ali 1993. On the Irony in/of Economic Theory. *Modern Language Notes* 108: 759–803.

Khan, M. Ali, and Yeneng N. Sun. 1999. Weak Measurability and Characterizations of Risk. *Economic Theory* 13: 541–560.

Khan, M. Ali, and Yeneng N. Sun. 2002. Non-Cooperative Games with Many Players. In *Handbook of Game Theory with Economic Applications III,* eds. Robert J. Aumann and Sergiu Hart, 1761–1808. Amsterdam: Elsevier Science.

Kolmogorov, Andrei N. [1933] 1956. *Foundations of the Theory of Probability.* Trans. Nathan Morrison. New York: Chelsea.

Kreps, David M. 1988. *Notes on the Theory of Choice.* Boulder, CO: Westview Press.

Laplace, Pierre-Simon. [1814] 1951. *Essai philosophique sur les probabilités (Philosophical Essay on Probabilities).* New York: Dover.

Lasota, Andrzej, and Michael C. Mackey. 1994. *Chaos, Fractals, and Noise: Stochastic Aspects of Dynamics.* New York: Springer-Verlag.

Loeb, Peter A. 1975. Conversion from Nonstandard to Standard Measure Spaces and Applications in Probability Theory. *Transactions of the American Mathematical Society* 211: 113–122.

Machina, Mark, and David Schmeidler. 1992. A More Robust Definition of Subjective Probability. *Econometrica* 60: 745–780.

Majumdar, Mukul, and Vladimir Rotar. 2000. Equilibrium Prices in a Random Exchange Economy with Dependent Agents. *Economic Theory* 15: 531–550.

Ramsey, Frank P. 1922. Mr. Keynes on Probability. *Cambridge Magazine* 11: 3–5.

Ramsey, Frank P. [1926] 1931. Truth and Probability. In *The Foundations of Mathematics and Other Logical Essays,* 156–198. London: Routledge and Kegan Paul.

Rosenthal, Jeffrey S. 2000. *A First Look at Rigorous Probability Theory.* Singapore: World Scientific.

Rudin, Walter. 1987. *Real and Complex Analysis.* 3rd ed. New York: McGraw-Hill.

Savage, Leonard J. 1954. *The Foundations of Statistics.* New York: John Wiley.

Savage, Leonard J. 1962. *The Foundations of Statistical Inference: A Discussion.* Updated ed., 1970. London: Methuen.

Skorokhod, A. V. [1989] 2004. *Basic Principles and Applications of Probability Theory.* Berlin: Springer-Verlag.

Steele, J. Michael. 1997. *Probability Theory and Combinatorial Optimization.* Philadelphia: Society for Industrial and Applied Mathematics.

Stoyanov, Jordan M. 1987. *Counterexamples in Probability.* 2nd ed. New York: John Wiley and Sons.

Sun, Yeneng N. 1998a. A Theory of Hyperfinite Processes: The Complete Removal of Individual Uncertainty via Exact LLN. *Journal of Mathematical Economics* 29: 419–503.

Sun, Yeneng N. 1998b. The Almost Equivalence of Pairwise and Mutual Independence and the Duality with Exchangeability. *Probability Theory and Related Fields* 112: 425–456.

Sun, Yeneng N. 1999. The Complete Removal of Individual Uncertainty: Multiple Optimal Choices and Random Economies. *Economic Theory* 14: 507–544.

Sun, Yeneng N. 2006. The Exact Law of Large Numbers via Fubini Extension and the Characterization of Insurable Risks. *Journal of Economic Theory* 126: 31–69.

M. Ali Khan

PROBIT REGRESSION
SEE *Probabilistic Regression.*

PRO-CHOICE/PRO-LIFE

The abortion debate in the United States connects to wide-ranging cultural arguments about civil liberties and gender. Legal abortion raises questions concerning the role of women in society, the place of motherhood in meanings of womanhood and family, the biological and social status of the fetus, the separation of church and state, and the legal understanding of privacy. Diverse views on these issues have come to be polarized into absolutist positions named *pro-choice* (supporting legal elective abortion) and *pro-life* (opposing legal abortion), politicized terms that do little to characterize the complex experiences of women who face inopportune or otherwise compromised pregnancies.

In the nineteenth century, American women of all social classes could legally procure an abortion, which often entailed using herbal abortifacients. However, as "regular" physicians distinguished themselves from midwives and homeopaths, many lobbied state legislatures to criminalize induced abortion. Shortly after its formation in 1847, the American Medical Association (AMA) declared human life to begin at conception and not, as midwives and lay women held, at "quickening," midway through gestation when a woman first feels fetal movement in the womb. In taking an anti-abortion stance, physicians professionalized and also moralized their practice through association with saving lives. By the end of the century, abortion was defined as a medical issue and was criminalized at the state level throughout the United States.

Following legislation in several states relaxing abortion restrictions, the U.S. Supreme Court's 1973 ruling in *Roe v. Wade* decriminalized elective abortion in the first trimester of pregnancy, allowing abortion in the second trimester given cause that "reasonably relates to the preservation and protection of maternal health," and in the third "when it is necessary to preserve the life or health of the mother." In *Roe* the court interpreted women's right to terminate pregnancies and physicians' right to perform abortions as within constitutional rights to privacy; abortion in the United States is thus framed as a "negative" right to act without government interference, rather than an "affirmative" right guaranteed by the state. It is an historic irony that abortion was medicalized in order to restrict its practice, only to be legalized a century later based on its status *as* medical procedure, a private matter between patient and doctor.

Supporters of *Roe* argue that legal abortion is necessary to protect women from unsafe pregnancies and nonmedical abortions. For feminists, women's "right to choose" abortion in the first trimester symbolizes liberation from patriarchal control over women's sexual and reproductive lives. It also reinforces a more expansive view of adult womanhood than one rooted in a biological capacity to reproduce. For the 1970s feminist movement, the "right to choose" abortion became synonymous with a woman's right to choose whether, when, and how often to become a mother.

The American pro-life movement was galvanized by the *Roe* decision. Grassroots organizing built up a single-issue voting block of Catholics, Evangelical Protestants, and political conservatives. Pro-lifers argue that abortion is a sin and therefore criminal. Many also condemn legal abortion for eroding traditional gender roles and what is taken to be women's special moral standing based on the capacity to bear children. Pro-life activists redefined the question of "life" in the American abortion controversy as a matter of fetal, rather than maternal, right to life. Ultrasound images of free-floating fetuses are used in propagandistic displays to portray fetal life not only as viable but autonomous, suggestive of personhood—a requisite for having rights. Pro-life campaigns project images of intact, well-developed fetuses despite the fact that 90 percent of abortions in the United States occur during the first trimester, while late term abortions are generally performed only in cases of fetal abnormality. Radical pro-lifers view abortion as a holocaust, a symbol of America's moral degeneracy. During the late 1980s and 1990s, several abortion providers were murdered by extremists who championed a vision of a Christian nation currently in millenarian "end times," during which God's law prevails over human law.

Although pro-choice rhetoric is consistent with American values of self-determination, "choice" may be a limited symbol for reproductive rights; many women experience abortion not as desirable, but as an unfortunate necessity following failed contraception, forced intercourse, or a diagnosis of fetal abnormality. In the 1990s, reproductive rights groups ran into conflict with disability rights activists over the possible eugenic use of elective abortion to limit the range of acceptable human life following prenatal screening, such as for Down's syndrome. Further, women's ability to "choose" an abortion in the United States remains subject to federal and state-level legislative restrictions. The 1976 Hyde Amendment restricts government-funded elective abortions (through Medicaid). In 2000, 87 percent of U.S. counties lacked abortion providers.

Following the George W. Bush administration's 2001 signing into effect of the Mexico City Policy (called the "Global Gag Rule" by reproductive rights advocates), developing countries have felt the effects of American abortion controversies. This policy, cutting off U.S. international aid money to organizations directly or indirectly engaged in abortion-related services, including referral, has also hampered the promotion of contraceptives and HIV-awareness. Illegal abortions continue to be a significant cause of morbidity and mortality among women of reproductive age throughout the nonindustrialized world.

Pro-choice and *pro-life* are not universally meaningful terms. Worldwide, the legal status and availability of abortion is often determined by government interest in population control, rather than religious or moral concern for life and family. The People's Republic of China has implemented its one-child policy in part through mandatory abortions; Nicolae Ceauçescu's regime in Romania, on the other hand, attempted to accelerate population growth by banning abortion and contraception. Under state socialism, reproduction has been considered a form of production subject to government regulation. The Soviet Union provided workers with medical abortion as routine birth control; in impoverished 1990s Russia abortions outnumbered live births two-to-one.

Japan legalized abortion in 1948 when families and the government shared interests in reducing family size. Women in Japan, as in southern Europe, turned to abortion during World War II to cope with wartime poverty.

Initially used by mothers to limit family size but now practiced by women of all ages, abortion in countries like Japan, Greece, and Russia is not regarded as posing a symbolic threat to motherhood. In these countries, economic considerations are said to trump religious belief in guiding decisions to terminate pregnancies. Historic memory of the war and political expectations of the European Union help explain why Italians support legal elective abortion (available since 1978), even as abortion remains highly restricted in Roman Catholic Latin America.

Where abortion is medicalized as routine birth control, a backup to nonmedical contraceptive methods, it is medical contraception rather than abortion that symbolizes women's liberation. In countries with high abortion rates, family planning workers, frequently trained in the United States or Britain, work to dissuade women from relying on abortion to control births, often by emphasizing potential physical, psychological, and even moral hazards of the procedure. In countries with declining population growth rates, as in Southern Europe, "pro-life" campaign materials imported from the United States are combined with nationalist pro-natal rhetoric.

When influenced by patriarchal, religious, and nationalist beliefs, legalization can restrict women's access to abortion. Turkey's 1983 Population Planning Law allows elective abortion through ten weeks of pregnancy, but a married woman's husband must consent. Germany, cognizant of the Nazi history of eugenic applications of abortion, requires counseling and a three-day waiting period before granting medically approved abortion.

SEE ALSO *Abortion; Abortion Rights;* Roe v. Wade

BIBLIOGRAPHY

Ginsburg, Faye D. 1989. *Contested Lives: The Abortion Debate in an American Community.* Berkeley: University of California Press.

Luker, Kristin. 1984. *Abortion and the Politics of Motherhood.* Berkeley: University of California Press.

Paxson, Heather. 2004. *Making Modern Mothers: Ethics and Family Planning in Urban Greece.* Berkeley: University of California Press.

Solinger, Rickie, ed. 1998. *Abortion Wars: A Half Century of Struggle, 1950–2000.* Berkeley: University of California Press.

Heather Paxson

PRODUCER SURPLUS

Market transactions typically increase the well-being of the participants. Consumers, sellers, and input providers may all enjoy a surplus from production and exchange.

Producer surplus (introduced by English economist Alfred Marshall [1842–1924]) is the benefit on the production side from voluntarily participating in market transactions. The concepts of consumer surplus and producer surplus are widely used for evaluating policy changes: cost-benefit analysis recognizes that benefits accrue as surplus and so are not always measured in market transactions. Producer surplus consists of gross profits accruing to firms and economic rents accruing to input owners (in special cases, it consists only of one or the other). It is often depicted as the area to the left of the supply curve and below the horizontal line representing price.

A firm's supply curve is determined by its cost. Two cases are commonly considered. In the first, the quantity supplied increases continuously from zero as the price rises (corresponding to increasing average avoidable costs). Then, the firm's supply curve is its marginal cost curve. Any point on it characterizes a price and output whose product is the firm's revenue. The area below the curve is the avoidable cost at that quantity, and hence the area to its left and below the price is this producer's surplus. The second case covers the standard U-shaped average cost curve. For prices below a threshold level (the minimum average avoidable cost) the firm produces nothing, but at or above this threshold the firm is willing to supply a strictly positive output. Then, the firm's supply curve is its marginal cost curve above average avoidable cost. The area to the left of the supply curve and below the price is this producer's surplus. To see this, note that this surplus is zero at the threshold price since the firm is indifferent between producing and not producing. If price increases, the quantity supplied rises and the revenue rectangle expands. The area below the supply curve represents the increase in costs, so the difference is this producer's surplus. In either case, a firm's profit equals its producer surplus minus sunk (unavoidable) costs.

If all inputs are supplied to the industry perfectly elastically, input prices are constant. In the long run, the market supply curve is perfectly elastic, reflecting zero profit and zero producer surplus. If the number of firms is fixed (as in the short run), the market supply is the horizontal sum of individual supplies, and producer surplus is the sum of the individual firms' producer surpluses. All producer surplus accrues to firms since inputs earn no rents.

Now suppose instead that at least one input supply curve slopes upward. This gives rise to an upward-sloping market supply curve because increased industry output bids up the prices of those inputs with upward-sloping supply curves. In the long run, free entry ensures zero profits, and the supply-side benefits from the market accrue only to the owners of inputs whose prices are bid up. The area below the price and left of the supply curve measures the economic rents received by input owners.

With a fixed number of firms, the market supply curve is more inelastic than the horizontal sum of the individual firms' supply curves: firms take input prices as given, but these are bid up as industry output expands. Then, the area between the market supply curve and the horizontal sum represents the rents accruing to input owners.

SEE ALSO *Consumer Surplus*

BIBLIOGRAPHY

Marshall, Alfred. [1890] 1920. *Principles of Economics.* 8th ed. New York and London: Macmillan.

Mishan, E. J. 1968. What Is Producer's Surplus? *American Economic Review* 58: 1269–1279.

Simon P. Anderson
Maxim Engers

PRODUCT DIFFERENTIATION
SEE *Competition, Imperfect.*

PRODUCT QUALITY
SEE *Quality, Product.*

PRODUCTION

In political economy the term *production* refers not merely to technical processes but also to the motives and the way human actions are organized to bring the output to existence. Consequently, production is a social process, and a theory of production can be linked to a theory of social development and change. One of the characteristics of production is that it takes time. The Austrian capital theory, and specifically the work of Eugen von Böhm-Bawerk (1889), emphasized the time character of production stemming from the division of labor. Karl Marx emphasized the so-called "realization" problem in his critique of the Say's Law. John Maynard Keynes extended this problem to the role of uncertainty and expectations in monetary production economy.

The idea that production takes time was common for the Physiocrats, but after Adam Smith (1776) put forward the importance of the division of labor for explaining industrial growth, this concept became central for the argument of roundaboutness of production. Increasing division of labor requires more capital goods, and the pro-

duction of these lengthens the production process. John Rae (1834) argued that increased division of labor goes together with increased durability of capital and hence longer periods of time required for production. Böhm-Bawerk (1889) conceptualized a "production function" in which he made the level of output obtained per unit of capital a function of the degree of roundaboutness of the production method. He argued that more roundabout methods of production are more capital intensive and therefore more productive. Maxine Berg (1980) connected the shift from concern with the division of labor to fixed capital formation to the social conflict in the early 1830s, which was prompted by technological development and by the so-called "machinery question"—the consequences of implementing radically new techniques and forces of production at the beginning of the nineteenth century.

SCOPE OF PRODUCTION THEORY

With the emergence of the marginalist approach in economics in the nineteenth century, relative prices were put forward as the driving force for change, and the scope of production theory in this tradition became conflated with a theory of exchange. As a contrast, Marx, Thorstein Veblen, Keynes, and Dudley Dillard, among others, focused on "monetary production," where money is not merely "the great wheel of circulation," as Adam Smith characterized it.

Marx viewed the relations of exchange as a manifestation of the relations in production, which determine the social, political, and spiritual aspects of life (Marx 1859, p. 100). Although it appears as if exchange, or circulation of commodities, dominates production in capitalist economies, production is the causal force in classical political economy. This is not to say that there is no interaction between exchange and production. As Smith argued in the *Wealth of Nations* (1776), the division of labor, or production, is limited by the extent of the market (or expanding possibilities for exchange). The point is that the consequence of reducing production relations to the exchange and circulation of commodities explains away the contradictions and conflicts of capitalist production. Marx in *Capital*, Volume I, made this argument in his critique of Say's Law (which holds that supply creates its own demand, and there is no possibility of the economy functioning below full employment), and referred to this tradition in economic analysis as "apologetic economy" (p. 114). Not only was production reduced to relations of circulation in this approach, but also circulation was explained as merely the barter of commodities, which is not characteristic for capitalist economies.

In his 1933 article "Monetary Theory of Production" and in the *General Theory* (1936) Keynes added a distinct component to the circuit theory of capitalist production—production of money by means of money. That component was liquidity preference. Keynes argued that money, with its special properties (low or zero elasticity of production and substitution) is crucial for understanding the changes and direction of output and employment at the macroeconomic level. Thus, he reaffirmed the importance of Marx's realization problem for understanding a capitalist system.

Keynes recognized that because the decisions to undertake investment had to be made before the results were known, and because the future returns from capital assets would be uncertain, the confidence of expectations in the occurrence of future events becomes important for the occurrence of current investment. As a measure for this confidence Keynes proposed the concept of "liquidity preference" to replace the traditional quantity theory where the rate of interest is determined by "real" factors such as the productivity of capital and thriftiness. As a measure of investors' confidence in their expectations for the occurrence of future events, liquidity preference determines the price that will be paid to possess money today.

MONETARY THEORY OF PRODUCTION

In a monetary production economy the "return" from holding money comes from its liquidity premium (Keynes [1936] 1964, p. 227). Each asset has an expected total return (an own-rate of interest) composed of $q - c + l + a$, where q is the expected income from employing the asset in production; c is the carrying cost; l is the liquidity premium; and a is the expected capital gains (appreciation or depreciation). Physical capital will have a return comprised mainly of the yield it is expected to generate from employing it in production. Carrying costs are insignificant for liquid assets, but they would be large for physical capital that depreciates over time. The liquidity premium has two roles: first, protection from future uncertain conditions (expressed through increased liquidity preference); and second, opportunity for profiting from future uncertain conditions (expressed through animal spirits). Expectations about the returns from new investment are compared to those of existing capital, financial assets, and money. The interest rate on money competes with the expected return from employing capital in production—that is, with the marginal efficiency of capital. A situation in which the expected returns of assets are equal, so "that there is nothing to choose in the way of advantage between the alternative" (Keynes [1936] 1964, p. 228), is defined in Keynes's analysis as equilibrium—a state of rest, not market clearing. In equilibrium the interest rate on money would be equal to the marginal efficiency of capital. But Keynes notes that this does not indicate at what level the equality

will be effective. The expected return from holding money as a store of value could be in "equilibrium" (state of rest) with the expected returns from all existing assets at an income below full employment.

Because money is something that cannot be produced, and demand for it cannot be readily choked off, Keynes came to the conclusion that unemployment develops "because people want the moon"—the object of their desire, money, cannot be produced (Keynes [1936] 1964, p. 235). Thus, Keynes's monetary theory of production explains unemployment not merely through a realization problem (as other economists employing the concept of the circuit do) but through the nature of money and its relation to production and distribution. In the tradition of classical political economy, Keynes's monetary theory of production emphasized conflict. However, the marginalist schools based on "real-wage" systems demonstrated a harmony of cooperative exchange and equal status of the various revenue shares in production. This is due to the construction of functional relations between quantity consumed and utility on the demand side, and between quantity produced and cost on the supply side, and the resulting symmetry between consumption and production in the marginalist theory (Bharadwaj 1984).

The proposition that capitalists and workers have symmetrical roles in production was put forward by means of conceptualizing their payments as remuneration for their "services" and contribution to production. Profits are viewed as symmetrical to wages as remuneration for the sacrifices of capitalists and as reward for their "waiting," in the same manner that wages reward labor efforts. Consequently, the distinction between wages and profits is blurred as these are merely returns for homogeneous "factors of production." The revenue shares are not qualitatively different, as the distinction between the various factors is also obscured. Overall, the shift toward the centrality of individuals' self-interest and its role in determining relative prices of commodities put forward a conception of an inherently just, value-free mechanism of distribution and production decisions.

MARGINALIST THEORY AND ITS CRITICS

The analytical construct of supply and demand as an explanation of production and distribution was a departure from classical political economy, and it refocused economic theory onto exchange under competition. Increasing returns created problems for the assumption of competition in the neoclassical system, which was pointed out by Piero Sraffa (1926). The possibility for decreasing overhead fixed costs when output increases provides the theoretical possibility for a monopoly, which violates the assumption of competition. The theory of monopolistic competition emerged as an attempt to solve this problem. The theory of diminishing returns is grounded in the supposed technical fact that there is a decreasing productivity of the successive portions of a constant factor of production. The understanding that if more and more inputs are applied to a given piece of land the average output inevitably diminishes has been extended to other factors of production, as well as to the theory of consumption in the form of diminishing marginal utility. The latter is explained by "human nature" rather than technical conditions. Indeed, Sraffa (1926) argued that the same is also valid for diminishing returns, as the producer is the one who ranks the alternative combinations of resources according to their returns. If decreasing returns are not a technical fact, then the producer's technical choices would not be ranked independently of distribution.

Sraffa critiqued the marginalist theory of production in *Production of Commodities by Means of Commodities* (1960) on the grounds that diminishing returns to a variable factor presupposes a possibility of substitution, which is problematic when there is heterogeneity of inputs that are also produced. Joan Robinson in "The Production Function and the Theory of Capital" (1953) also pointed out that substitution between capital and labor inputs does not take place within the production process in the way that marginalist theory suggests. Capital inputs are not simply added to or subtracted from other inputs used in production following changes of relative prices. In the marginalist tradition, relative prices then are interpreted as indicative of relative scarcities, instead of being linked to the production process (Roncaglia 1978, p. 92).

A production schema depicts the principal flows of produced goods in the technically required sequence. Such schema has a corresponding quantity model that refers to a precise system of production equations where the level of final demand determines the level of output, intermediate inputs, and labor inputs. The production schema, together with the quantity schema and the pricing model—referring to a precise system of pricing equations—form the price-quantity monetary production model of the economy as a whole (Leontief 1951; Lowe 1976; Pasinetti 1977; Lee 1998).

In the marginalist tradition the profit, often conflated with the interest rate, is presented as the price of a particular commodity—capital, which is subject to the functioning of the supply and demand mechanism. Thus, an increase in the price of capital would bring about an increase in the supply, and a decrease in the demand for this "commodity." The problem that Sraffa identified and Robinson discussed is that this reasoning presupposes a measure of capital that does not depend on the distribution of income between wages and profits. Sraffa (1960) showed that such a measure cannot exist. Consequently,

the linking of variations in output to variations in the quantity of capital and labor utilized in production is undermined. Under these circumstances, profit and wage rates cannot be determined on marginalist principles. Consequently, this critique of capital disputes the harmonious vision of production and distribution characteristic of the neoclassical exchange-based approach, and brings back the issue of conflict within the monetary theory of production.

SEE ALSO *Capital; Economics, Keynesian; Economics, Neoclassical; Economics, Post Keynesian; Expectations; Keynes, John Maynard; Labor; Marginalism; Marx, Karl; Profitability; Robinson, Joan; Sraffa, Piero; Technological Progress, Economic Growth; Veblen, Thorstein*

BIBLIOGRAPHY

Berg, Maxine. 1980. *The Machinery Question and the Making of Political Economy, 1815–1848*. Cambridge, U.K.: Cambridge University Press.

Bharadwaj, Krishna. 1986. *Classical Political Economy and Rise to Dominance of Supply and Demand Theories*. Andhra Pradesh: Universities Press, India.

Böhm-Bawerk, Eugen von. [1889] 1891. *The Positive Theory of Capital*. London: Macmillan.

Dillard, Dudley. 1980. A Monetary Theory of Production. *Journal of Economic Issues* 16 (2): 255–275.

Keynes, John Maynard. [1933] 1973. A Monetary Theory of Production. *The Collected Writings*, vol. 7. London and Basingstoke, U.K.: Macmillan.

Keynes, John Maynard. [1936] 1964. *The General Theory of Employment, Interest, and Money*. New York: Harcourt, Brace, Jovanovich.

Lee, Fred. 1998. *Post Keynesian Price Theory*. Cambridge, U.K.: Cambridge University Press.

Leontief, Wassily. 1951. *The Structure of American Economy, 1919–1939*. White Plains, NY: International Arts and Sciences Press.

Lowe, Adolf. 1976. *The Path of Economic Growth*. Cambridge, U.K.: Cambridge University Press.

Marx, Karl. [1859] 1999. *A Contribution to the Critique of Political Economy*, ed. Maurice Dobb. New York: International Publishers.

Marx, Karl. [1867] 1977. *Capital*. New York: Vintage Books.

Pasinetti, Luigi. 1977. *Lectures on the Theory of Production*. New York: Columbia University Press.

Rae, John. 1834. *Statement of Some New Principles on the Subject of Political Economy*. Boston: Hilliard Gray and Company.

Robinson, Joan. 1953. The Production Function and the Theory of Capital. *Review of Economic Studies* 21: 81–106.

Roncaglia, Alessandro. 1978. The Sraffian Contribution. In *A Guide to Post-Keynesian Economics*, ed. Alfred Eichner, 87–99. White Plains, NY: M. E. Sharpe.

Smith, Adam. [1776] 1976. *An Inquiry into the Nature and Causes of the Wealth of Nations.* Oxford: Clarendon Press.

Sraffa, Piero. 1926. Increasing Returns and the Representative Firm. *Economic Journal* 36 (144): 535–550.

Sraffa, Piero. 1960. *Production of Commodities by Means of Commodities.* Cambridge, U.K.: Cambridge University Press.

Veblen, Thorstein. 1904. *The Theory of Business Enterprise.* New York: Scribner's.

Zdravka Todorova

PRODUCTION FRONTIER

In economic theory a production frontier is a mathematical relationship describing the maximum quantity of output that an organization can obtain from a given collection of resources given the technology in use. An equivalent definition specifies the minimum resources an organization requires to produce a given quantity of output, again given the technology in place. A production frontier is thus the economist's distillation of the detailed information contained in the engineer's blueprints that describe what is possible. Organizations operating on the production frontier avoid waste and are technically efficient. Organizations operating beneath the production frontier waste resources and are technically inefficient. The degree of technical inefficiency increases with the distance to the production frontier.

A cost frontier is a dual mathematical relationship that describes the minimum expenditure an organization requires to produce some quantity of output given the prices it pays for the resources it employs in the production process and given the technology in place. Technical efficiency is necessary but not sufficient for operation on the cost frontier. A second requirement is that resources be allocated efficiently in light of the resource prices paid by producers. Organizations achieving both technical and allocative efficiency operate on the cost frontier and are cost efficient. However, if waste in the organization causes actual output to fall short of maximum possible output or if resources are misallocated in light of their respective prices, then actual cost exceeds minimum feasible cost. Organizations failing to fulfill both efficiency conditions operate above the cost frontier and are cost inefficient. The degree of cost-inefficiency increases with the distance to the cost frontier.

Over a short period of time the assumption of a given technology underlying a fixed frontier is reasonable. Over a longer period of time existing technology diffuses and new technologies are introduced. Technical progress shifts the production frontier up, increasing the maximum output that can be obtained from a given collection of resources, or reduces resource requirements for a given amount of output. Consequently, technical progress shifts the cost frontier down, reducing the minimum cost that must be incurred to produce a given quantity of output.

Just as it is not possible to know how fast a human can run one hundred meters, the production frontier and the cost frontier of economic theory are unknown. However, it is possible to identify faster runners and slower runners and to observe improvements in best practice through time. It is also possible to identify best-practice organizations and less efficient organizations and to track their performance through time. Thus, theoretical production and cost frontiers are approximated by best-practice production and cost frontiers.

Approximation requires an empirical technique. In 1957 Michael James Farrell used primitive linear programming techniques to construct a best-practice production frontier. However, his contribution remained largely overlooked for twenty years. In 1977 the team of Dennis J. Aigner, C. A. Knox Lovell, and Peter Schmidt and the team of Wim Meeusen and Julien van den Broeck used statistical techniques to develop a best-practice production frontier concept now known as stochastic frontier analysis. A year later the team of Abraham Charnes, William W. Cooper, and Edwardo Rhodes refined Farrell's linear programming techniques to construct an alternative best-practice production frontier concept known as data envelopment analysis. Both approaches to the construction of best-practice production frontiers have been used to provide empirical measures of relative technical efficiency. Both approaches have been extended to the construction of best-practice cost frontiers and to the empirical measurement of relative cost efficiency.

Best-practice production and cost frontiers have been used to test a variety of hypotheses having a direct bearing on public policy. Perhaps the most significant hypothesis is that market structure matters. A highly competitive marketplace rewards organizations operating at or near best practice with growing market share and penalizes inefficient organizations with shrinking market share, often to extinction. A less competitive marketplace can shelter inefficient organizations. A popular example is provided by trade liberalization, which subjects domestic producers to increased foreign competition. A common empirical finding is that trade liberalization brings aggregate performance gains attributable among other factors to improvements in the efficiency of continuing domestic firms, to entry of relatively efficient foreign firms, and to exit of relatively inefficient domestic firms.

A second popular hypothesis is that ownership matters. Private organizations have different incentives and face different constraints than public organizations. When the two operate in the same marketplace, one group may operate closer to best practice than the other. Education and health care are two sectors in which numerous public/private performance comparisons have been conducted, with the empirical evidence being mixed.

A third hypothesis asserts that regulation matters. Ill-designed regulatory frameworks inhibit best practice by diverting resources away from production toward compliance. Thoughtfully designed regulatory frameworks can enhance best practice by providing incentives for organizations to operate efficiently and to improve their efficiency through time. One regulatory context in which theoretical predictions have been quantified by empirical investigation concerns the impact of alternative forms of environmental control on organizational performance. In this context, however, the private cost of reduced efficiency must be balanced against the social benefits of environmental protection.

The theoretical concept of production and cost frontiers is universally accepted. However, the empirical implementation of best-practice frontiers and their use in the policy arena has attracted some criticism. One criticism asserts that the mathematical framework is necessarily incomplete and fails to incorporate the objectives of and constraints faced by the organization and its stakeholders. In 1976 George J. Stigler claimed that "waste is not a useful economic concept. Waste is error within the framework of modern economic analysis" (p. 216). A second criticism asserts that the empirical implementation fails to control adequately for variation in the operating environment, thereby confusing variation in operating efficiency with variation in factors beyond the control of management. This concern has inhibited the use of best-practice frontiers in evaluating the relative performance of educational institutions, health care providers, and regulated utilities.

SEE ALSO *Fixed Coefficients Production Function; Production; Production Function*

BIBLIOGRAPHY

Aigner, Dennis J., C. A. Knox Lovell, and Peter Schmidt. 1977. Formulation and Estimation of Stochastic Frontier Production Function Models. *Journal of Econometrics* 6 (1): 21–37.

Charnes, Abraham, William W. Cooper, and Edwardo Rhodes. 1978. Measuring the Efficiency of Decision-Making Units. *European Journal of Operational Research* 2 (6): 429–444.

Farrell, Michael James. 1957. The Measurement of Productive Efficiency. *Journal of the Royal Statistical Society, Series A, General* 120 (3): 253–281.

Meeusen, Wim, and Julien van den Broeck. 1977. Efficiency Estimation from Cobb-Douglas Production Functions with Composed Error. *International Economic Review* 18 (2): 435–444.

Stigler, George J. 1976. The Xistence of X-Efficiency. *American Economic Review* 66 (1): 213–216.

C. A. Knox Lovell

PRODUCTION FUNCTION

The principal activity of a firm is to produce a good or provide a service, that is, to turn inputs into output. To represent this process, economists use an abstract model of production. The central concept in this model is the *production function*. A production function is a mathematical description of the various technical production possibilities faced by a firm. Algebraically, it is written as

$$q = f(x_1, x_2, \ldots x_n) \qquad (1)$$

where q represents the flow of output produced and $x_1, \ldots, x_n$ are the flows of inputs, each measured in physical quantities—for example, the number of bushels of corn produced and the number of tractors and workers utilized. Often, production functions appear in textbooks written with two inputs as $q = f(k, l)$, where k denotes the amount of capital and l denotes the amount of labor. To simplify, we will use this production function in the remainder of the entry. Equation (1) is assumed to provide, for any conceivable set of inputs, the engineer's solution to the problem of how to best (most efficiently) combine different quantities of those inputs to get the output. Therefore, a production function can be understood as a constraint on the activities of producers that is imposed by the existing technology.

It is important to stress that, as noted above, equation (1) is essentially an *engineering* relationship. As such, it allows for no testing of economic hypotheses. Actual observed data are the results of economic decisions in which the production function is but one constraint. However, the key question from an *economic* point of view is how the levels of output and inputs are chosen by profit-maximizing firms. Thus, economists use production functions in conjunction with marginal productivity theory (see below) to provide explanations of factor prices and the levels of factor utilization. Whereas the engineering production function captures the maximum level of output that can be achieved if the given inputs are efficiently employed, the economic production function reflects the "best-practice" use of the available input and output combinations.

PROPERTIES OF THE PRODUCTION FUNCTION

The *marginal physical product* of an input is the additional output that can be produced by employing one more unit of that input while holding all other inputs constant. Algebraically, $\frac{\partial q}{\partial k}$ is the marginal physical product of capital, and $\frac{\partial q}{\partial \ell}$ is the marginal physical product of labor. It is assumed that both marginal products are positive, that is, $\frac{\partial q}{\partial k} > 0$ and $\frac{\partial q}{\partial \ell} > 0$ (a negative marginal product means that using more of the input in question results in less output being produced). It is also usually assumed that the production process exhibits diminishing marginal productivity. This means that successive additions of one factor while keeping the other one constant yields smaller and smaller increases of output, that is, $\frac{\partial^2 q}{\partial k^2} < 0$ and $\frac{\partial^2 q}{\partial \ell^2} < 0$.

Factor elasticity (ε) is the percentage change in output in response to an infinitesimal percentage change in a factor given that all other factors are held fixed, that is, $\varepsilon_\ell = \frac{\partial q}{\partial \ell} \frac{\ell}{q}$ and $\varepsilon_k = \frac{\partial q}{\partial k} \frac{k}{q}$.

The *marginal rate of technical substitution* (*MRTS*) shows the rate at which labor can be substituted for capital while holding output constant at the level q_0, that is, $MRTS$ (ℓ for k) $= -\frac{dk}{d\ell}\Big|_{q=q_0}$. It can also be shown that the *MRTS* equals the negative of the ratio of marginal productivities, that is, $MRTS$ (ℓ for k) $= -\frac{dk}{d\ell}\Big|_{q=q_0} = -\frac{\partial q}{\partial \ell} / \frac{\partial q}{\partial k}$. This expression indicates that the gain in output from increasing *l* slightly is exactly balanced by the loss of output from suitably decreasing *k* (so as to keep output constant at the level q_0). It is important to note that for large ratios of *k* to *l*, the *MRTS* is a large positive number, indicating that a large amount of capital can be given up if one more unit of labor becomes available. On the other hand, when a large amount of labor is already in use, the *MRTS* is low, indicating that only a small amount of capital can be exchanged for an additional unit of labor if output is to be held constant. This is the so-called property of *diminishing MRTS*, which states that progressively reducing the amount of one input while maintaining a constant output level will require progressively large increases of the other input. Diminishing *MRTS* requires both positive and diminishing marginal productivities and $\frac{(\partial q / \partial \ell)}{\partial k} > 0$, that is, that an increase in capital leads to a higher marginal productivity of labor.

If the production function is given by $q = f(k,l)$ and all inputs are multiplied by the same positive constant $t > 1$, the degree of *returns to scale* can be classified as follows: (1) constant if $f(tk,tl) = tf(k,l) = tq$; (2) increasing if $f(tk,tl) > tf(k,l) = tq$; and (3) decreasing if $f(tk,tl) < tf(k,l) = tq$.

The *MRTS* is a useful measure of substitutability of one factor for another, given output. However, it depends on the units in which both labor and capital are measured. An alternative measure, independent of the units of measurement, is the *elasticity of substitution* (σ). It measures the percentage change in the relative amount of the factors employed resulting from a given percentage change in the relative marginal products (that is, the *MRTS*). Assuming there are only two factors of production: $\sigma = \frac{d(k/l)}{(k/l)} / \frac{d(MRTS)}{MRTS}$. Given that k/l and *MRTS* move in the same direction, $\sigma > 0$. However, this is not true in the case of a production function with more than two inputs, in which case there are different definitions of the elasticity of substitution (see Chambers 1994, pp. 27–36). A high σ means that the *MRTS* does not change much relative to k/l. In the extreme $\sigma = \infty$, the two inputs are said to be perfect substitutes. On the other hand, a low σ means that the *MRTS* will change by a substantial amount as k/l varies. For example, if $\sigma = 0$, the inputs are used in fixed proportions and substitution is not possible.

MOST COMMON PRODUCTION FUNCTIONS

Fixed proportions (or Leontief): $q = min(\alpha_1 k, \alpha_2 l)$, α_1, $\alpha_2 > 0$. This production function is characterized by $\sigma = 0$, as the marginal products are not defined. In this case, capital and labor must be used in fixed proportions. This production function offers a good approximation to many real-world industrial processes.

Cobb-Douglas: $q = Ak^{\alpha_1} l^{\alpha_2}$. This is the most ubiquitous form in empirical analyses at the macroeconomic level. The marginal product of capital equals $\frac{\partial q}{\partial k} = \alpha_1 (q/k) > 0$ (and $\frac{\partial^2 q}{\partial k^2} = \alpha_1 (\alpha_1 - 1)(q/k^2) < 0$ provided $0 < \alpha_1 < 1$); and that of labor equals $\frac{\partial q}{\partial \ell} = \alpha_2 (q/\ell) > 0$ (and $\frac{\partial^2 q}{\partial \ell^2} = \alpha_2 (\alpha_2 - 1)(q/\ell^2) < 0$ provided $0 < \alpha_2 < 1$). This production function can exhibit any degree of returns to scale, as $A(tk)^{\alpha_1}(tl)^{\alpha_2} = At^{\alpha_1 + \alpha_2} k^{\alpha_1} l^{\alpha_2} = t^{\alpha_1 + \alpha_2} q$. In this production function, $\sigma = 1$, that is, the elasticity of substitution does not vary with the combination of factors used.

CES: $q = \gamma [\delta k^{-\rho} + (1 - \delta) l^{-\rho}]^{-(\varepsilon/\rho)}$, where $\gamma > 0$ is an efficiency parameter; $0 \leq \delta \leq 1$ is a distribution parameter;

$\rho \leq 1$ is the substitution parameter; and $\varepsilon \geq 0$ denotes the degree of returns to scale. For this production function, $f(tk, tl) = t^\varepsilon q$, and ρ is the substitution parameter, which equals $\rho = \dfrac{\sigma - 1}{\sigma}$. This implies that the elasticity of substitution is $\sigma = 1/(1 - \rho)$.

Translog. $logq = \beta_0 + \beta_k logk + \beta_l logl + \beta_{kk}(logk)^2 + \beta_{ll}(logl)^2 + \beta_{lk}(logk)(logl)$. Mathematically, this is a second-order expansion, which is easy to implement empirically. In this case, estimates of marginal products and the elasticity of substitution are functions of the coefficients and the input levels. This form is flexible in that it imposes no assumptions on the elasticity of substitution. Other widely used flexible forms include the quadratic and the square root production functions (Beattie and Taylor 1985; Chambers 1994).

DUALITY

A major development since the late 1960s has been the dual formulation of production theory. This approach consists in recovering through the profit or cost functions the properties of the underlying production function. The cost function $TC(q, w, r)$ represents the minimum cost of producing output for any set of input costs (see Beattie and Taylor 1985, chap. 6, and Chambers 1994). The dual approach is very convenient in applied work because it deals directly with observed economic data generated by markets (that is, factor prices and output). For example, the Cobb-Douglas cost function dual of the production function $q = Ak^{\alpha_1}l^{\alpha_2}$ is given by the expression $TC = kq^{1/\nu} r^{\alpha_1/\nu} w^{\alpha_2/\nu}$, where k is a constant, r is the user cost of capital, w is the wage rate, and $\nu = \alpha_1 + \alpha_2$ is the degree of returns to scale.

TECHNICAL PROGRESS

Technical progress in economics refers to the impact of the adoption of new techniques on production (or cost). Analytically, the simplest way to represent technical progress is through a shift in the production function over time, that is, $q = f(k, l, t)$, where t is an index of the level of technology. In the analysis of time series data (one economic unit observed over time), time is used as a proxy for t. Technical progress is measured by how output changes as time elapses with the input bundle held constant. The rate of technical progress is defined as $T(k, l, t) = \dfrac{\partial \ln f(k, l, t)}{\partial t}$. The representation of technical progress this way, though convenient, is very unrealistic, for it assumes that technical progress does not require new inputs and, further, that the production function maintains the same form as time elapses (see Chambers 1994, chap. 6).

PRODUCTION FUNCTIONS IN APPLIED WORK

In this section, first, we provide some useful references for the reader interested in estimating production functions empirically; second, we provide examples of applications in microeconomics; and finally, examples of applications at the macroeconomic level.

Hands On: Estimating Production Functions Given the availability of computers and sophisticated software packages, estimation of production functions (that is, the use of statistical methods applied to real data in order to obtain values of the relevant parameters, such as the factor elasticities, the elasticity of substitution, or the degree of returns to scale) does not present serious problems from the technical and data points of view. Kenneth Wallis (1979, chap. 2) offers a classical and very accessible introduction to the estimation process. Ernst Berndt (1991, chap. 9) also offers a hands-on approach. R. L. Thomas (1993, chap. 11) offers a modern treatment with discussion of recent advances in time-series econometrics, such as unit roots and cointegration analyses. Estimation of engineering production functions requires the availability of data in physical terms for output and inputs. See Sören Wibe (1984) for a survey of estimation of engineering production functions. At aggregate levels (sectors or total economy), there are now many databases that contain series of output and inputs.

As noted above, economists use production functions in conjunction with marginal productivity theory to provide explanations of factor prices and the levels of factors utilization. Observed prices, output, and inputs are generated by a set of simultaneous relationships, and so it is inappropriate to estimate the production function as a single equation treating capital and labor as exogenous variables. In the simplest case, assuming perfect competition in product and factor markets, the prices of output, capital, and labor are exogenous. In the case of the Cobb-Douglas production function, the marginal productivity conditions are given by the equality of the factor prices to the marginal productivities, that is $\dfrac{\partial q}{\partial k} = \alpha_1(q/k) = r$ and $\dfrac{\partial q}{\partial \ell} = \alpha_2(q/\ell) = w$, where r denotes the price of capital (that is, the user cost of capital) and w denotes the price of labor (that is, the wage rate). The firm's optimal output and input levels result from jointly estimating these two equations together with the production function $q = Ak^{\alpha_1}l^{\alpha_2}$.

Examples of Applications in Microeconomics Efficient production decisions require that the marginal productivity of an input equals its market price. Therefore, comparing the marginal productivity with input prices permits the analyst to test whether inputs are allocated efficiently. Pranab Bardhan's "Size, Productivity, and Returns to Scale" (1973) is a seminal paper in the literature. Bardhan estimated farm production functions to test the efficiency of land and labor allocations in rural areas of developing economies. Likewise, Hanan Jacoby (1993) illustrates how such tests can be refined and the difficulties in estimating marginal labor productivities.

The degree of returns to scale displayed is of great interest to market regulators. Mergers between rival companies reduce costs and potentially enhance welfare if they are in processes that are subject to increasing returns to scale. Similarly, the argument for granting exclusive franchises to operators providing certain public services (most notably public utilities) hinges upon the assumption that the activity displays increasing returns to scale over the relevant range of output (see Train 1991).

Elasticities of substitution are important for understanding how changes in the price of one input impact the demand for others. Ernst Berndt and David Wood (1975), in the aftermath of the first oil shock, showed that capital and energy were complements in U.S. manufacturing. This implies that fiscal incentives to stimulate investment would promote greater energy use.

Examples of Applications in Macroeconomics In broad terms, aggregate production functions are estimated empirically in macroeconomic work for the following purposes: (1) to obtain measures of the elasticity of substitution between the factors, and the factor-demand price elasticities; such measures are used for predicting the effects upon the distribution of the national income of changes in technology or factor supplies; (2) to apportion total growth into the accumulation of factors of production and technical change between two periods; (3) to test theories and quantify their predictions; and (4) to assess the likely effects of macroeconomic policies. Likewise, much work in international trade and labor economics uses the production function as one of their main pillars.

However, the most important application of production functions in macroeconomics is in the field of growth theory. Since the 1980s, the field of growth theory has mushroomed with the development of the so-called endogenous growth models (see, for example, Barro and Sala-i-Martin 1995; Aghion and Howitt 1998; and Valdés 1999). These models posit production functions with increasing returns to scale, an elasticity of capital of unity, externalities, or some combination of these. In order to assess the importance of these assumptions, economists have estimated aggregate production functions for entire economies, for the manufacturing sector, or for more narrowly defined industry aggregates with a view to testing if the real world is characterized by such phenomena. Paul

Romer (1987), Robert Hall (1990), Ricardo Caballero and Richard Lyons (1992), N. Gregory Mankiw et al. (1992), David Backus et al. (1992), Susanto Basu and John Fernald (1995, 1997), Craig Burnside (1996), and others have attempted to document the empirical importance of the phenomena of increasing returns and externalities hypothesized by the new growth models.

The other important application of production theory in the area of growth is referred to as *growth accounting*. Here the purpose is to decompose overall output growth into the contributions of factor accumulation and technological progress. In this case, the factor elasticities are not estimated econometrically but assumed to be equal to the factor shares (under profit maximization and competitive markets), which can be obtained from the national accounts. In fact, the purpose of growth accounting is to estimate residually the contribution of technical progress (the shift in the production function) to overall growth. In growth rates, the production function $q = f(k, l, t)$ can be written as $\hat{q} = \varepsilon_k \hat{k} + \varepsilon_l \hat{l} + T$ where ε_k and ε_l are the factor elasticities. The only unknown here is T, the rate of technical progress, which can be obtained as $T = \hat{q} - \varepsilon_k \hat{k} - \varepsilon_l \hat{l}$.

THE AGGREGATION PROBLEM

Macroeconomic work assumes that the economy produces a single homogenous output with "quantities" of homogenous inputs. In most applied work, this assumption is not even discussed, and applied economists use published (aggregate) data from the national accounts, for example. However, at the aggregate level, output and inputs are not physical quantities. The output of a nation (GDP) must be expressed in monetary units. Capital is not measured as a collection of machines, but as the result of a series of investments (thus also expressed in monetary units) added up through the perpetual inventory method and assuming some rate of depreciation. In other words, in aggregate work, economists actually estimate $V = F(J, L)$, and not $q = f(k, l)$, where V is real aggregate value added, L is total employment, and J is the deflated or constant-price value of the stock of capital. When these variables are used as arguments in a production function, they present a serious problem. This is that aggregate production functions cannot be, in general, derived theoretically. If one asks for the conditions under which a series of microproduction functions can be properly aggregated so as to yield an aggregate production function, such conditions are so stringent that it is difficult to believe that actual economies can satisfy them. In other words, for practical purposes, aggregate production functions do not exist (Felipe and Fisher 2003, 2006).

This led a number of economists to ask the following question: If aggregate production functions do not exist, what do applied economists find when they get aggregate data and estimate a regression? The answer is that all they do is approximate the accounting identity that relates definitionally the value of total output to the sum of the value of total inputs, that is, $V_t \equiv W_t + \Pi_t \equiv w_t L_t + r_t J_t$, where V is real value added, W is the total wage bill in real terms, Π denotes total profits (*operating surplus* in the NIPA [National Income and Product Accounts] terminology) also in real terms, w is the average real wage rate, L is employment, r is the average ex-post real profit rate, and J is the deflated or constant-price value of the stock of capital. The symbol $\equiv$ indicates that the expression above is an accounting identity. In a series of papers, Jesus Felipe (2001), Felipe and F. Gerard Adams (2005), and Felipe and John S. L. McCombie (2001, 2003) have shown that this identity can be rewritten as $V = F(J, L)$. This argument explains why aggregate production functions, despite the fact that they do not exist, tend to "work" (that is, the fit is high when estimated econometrically and, at least at times, the factor elasticities approximate the factor shares), and why it deprives most applied work with aggregate production functions of any meaning and significance.

SEE ALSO *Cambridge Capital Controversy; Physical Capital; Production; Smith, Vernon L.*

BIBLIOGRAPHY

Aghion, Philippe, and Peter Howitt. 1998. *Endogenous Growth Theory*. Cambridge, MA: MIT Press.

Backus, David, Patrick J. Kehoe, and Timothy J. Kehoe. 1992. In Search of Scale Effects in Trade and Growth. *Journal of Economic Theory* 58 (2): 377–409.

Bardhan, Pranab. 1973. Size, Productivity, and Returns to Scale: An Analysis of Farm-Level Data in Indian Agriculture. *Journal of Political Economy* 81 (6): 1370–1386.

Barro, Robert, and Xavier Sala-i-Martin. 1995. *Economic Growth*. New York: McGraw-Hill. 2nd ed., 2004, Cambridge, MA: MIT Press.

Basu Susanto, and John G. Fernald. 1995. Are Apparent Spillovers a Figment of Specification Error? *Journal of Monetary Economics* 36 (1): 165–188.

Basu Susanto, John G. Fernald. 1997. Returns to Scale in U.S. Production: Estimates and Implications. *Journal of Political Economy* 105 (2): 249–283.

Beattie, Bruce R., and C. Robert Taylor. 1985. *The Economics of Production*. New York: Wiley.

Berndt, Ernst. 1991. *The Practice of Econometrics: Classic and Contemporary*. Reading, MA: Addison-Wesley.

Berndt, Ernst, and David O. Wood. 1975. Technology, Prices, and the Derived Demand for Energy. *Review of Economics and Statistics* 57 (3): 259–268.

Burnside, Craig. 1996. Production Function Regressions, Returns to Scale, and Externalities. *Journal of Monetary Economics* 37 (2): 177–201.

Caballero, Ricardo J., and Richard K. Lyons. 1992. External Effects in U.S. Procyclical Productivity. *Journal of Monetary Economics* 29 (2): 209–225.

Chambers, Robert G. 1988. *Applied Production Analysis: A Dual Approach*. Cambridge, U.K.: Cambridge University Press.

Felipe, Jesus. 2001. Endogenous Growth, Increasing Returns, and Externalities: An Alternative Interpretation of the Evidence. *Metroeconomica* 52 (4): 391–427.

Felipe, Jesus, and F. Gerard Adams. 2005. 'A Theory of Production': The Estimation of the Cobb-Douglas Function, a Retrospective View. *Eastern Economic Journal* 31 (3): 427–446.

Felipe, Jesus, and Franklin M. Fisher. 2003. Aggregation in Production Functions: What Applied Economists Should Know. *Metroeconomica* 54 (2–3): 208–262.

Felipe, Jesus, and Franklin M. Fisher. 2006. Aggregate Production Functions, Neoclassical Growth Models, and the Aggregation Problem. *Estudios de Economia Aplicada* 24 (1): 127–163.

Felipe, Jesus, and J. S. L. McCombie. 2001. The CES Production Function, the Accounting Identity, and Occam's Razor. *Applied Economics* 33 (10): 1221–1232.

Felipe, Jesus, and J. S. L. McCombie. 2003. Some Methodological Problems with the Neoclassical Analysis of the East Asian Miracle. *Cambridge Journal of Economics* 54 (5): 695–721.

Hall, Robert E. 1990. Invariance Properties of Solow's Productivity Residual. In *Growth/Productivity/Employment: Essays to Celebrate Bob Solow's Birthday*, ed. Peter Diamond, 71–112. Cambridge, MA: MIT Press.

Jacoby, Hanan. 1993. Shadow Wages and Peasant Family Labor Supply: An Econometric Application to the Peruvian Sierra. *Review of Economic Studies* 60: 903–921.

Mankiw, N. Gregory, David Romer, and David N. Weil. 1992. A Contribution to the Empirics of Economic Growth. *Quarterly Journal of Economics* 107 (2): 407–437.

Romer, Paul. 1987. Crazy Explanations for the Productivity Slowdown. In *National Bureau of Economic Research Macroeconomics Annual 1987*, 163–202. Cambridge, MA: MIT Press.

Thomas, R. L. 1993. *Introductory Econometrics*. 2nd ed. London and New York: Longman.

Train, Kenneth. 1991. *Optimal Regulation: The Economic Theory of Natural Monopoly*. Cambridge, MA: MIT Press.

Valdés, Benigno. 1999. *Economic Growth: Theory, Empirics, and Policy*. Northampton, MA: Edward Elgar.

Wallis, Kenneth F. 1979. *Topics in Applied Econometrics*. 2nd ed. Minneapolis: University of Minnesota Press.

Wibe, Sören. 1984. Engineering Production Functions: A Survey. *Economica* 51: 55–64.

Jesus Felipe
Aashish Mehta

PRODUCTIVE CLASS
SEE *Physiocracy.*

PRODUCTIVITY

Productivity is a measure of output relative to input. It can be calculated in a number of different ways, and in a variety of different situations, both over time and within sets of firms, industries, countries, or other organizations.

The two principal measures are labor productivity and total factor productivity (TFP, sometimes loosely called the Solow residual). For the former, it is typical to take the ratio of output to the quantity of labor input, for example, the number of automobiles produced per production worker or the number of automobiles per hour of production worker time. For the latter, it is typical to take the ratio of output to the weighted sum of a broader set of inputs (sometimes labor and capital together; sometimes labor, capital and intermediate inputs, taken together). While labor productivity is easier to measure, TFP is often preferred as a measure of productivity since TFP growth represents output growth not accounted for by the growth of inputs, whereas labor productivity growth reflects both TFP growth and changes in the capital to labor ratio.

Although a single productivity number is of some interest, it is often better to have time-series productivity data for a particular unit or a cross-section of productivity data for a range of similar units. Furthermore, the definitions of labor productivity and total factor productivity are straightforward, but there are a large number of potential problems of measurement when it comes to defining just what is meant by output and by the various inputs. For example, in the case of the quality of inputs, should labor inputs be adjusted for the skills of workers and, if so, how? There are also a large number of problems in aggregating various outputs and inputs together. For example, in the case of TFP it is usual to weight labor and capital by their shares in value-added, which makes certain assumptions about the nature of the production function.

Empirically, the majority of work on national productivity growth has been conducted for the United States, which has presented a number of interesting features. First, there was a marked slowdown in productivity growth in the 1970s associated with the economic turbulence of that decade (oil shocks, stagflation, and so on) as well as structural changes (the rise of the service sector which historically has had slower productivity growth than manufacturing, as well as being harder to measure). Second, there has been a marked speedup (especially relative to European productivity growth rates) since 1995, associated with the spread of information and communication technologies throughout the U.S. economy, but

most particularly in the financial, wholesale, and retail industries.

International comparisons of productivity are particularly difficult because of problems with exchange rates and differences in industrial structure. The United States enjoys a substantial advantage in terms of output per worker over every other major economy in the world—14 percent higher in 2004 than the G7 average. This is driven by a higher ratio of capital per worker, high labor utilization, and high levels of technology. The relative position of the United States is somewhat less advantageous in terms of output per worker hour. According to data from the Organization for Economic Cooperation and Development (OECD), if the United States in 2004 is taken to have a productivity level (output per hour) of 100, the Eurozone has a level of 87, with the United Kingdom at 86, Germany at 91, and France at 103. Substantially larger gaps remain with other OECD members, with Japan at 70, Czech Republic at 45, and Mexico at 29. The excellent performance of France is often seen as a result of high capital intensity and a labor market that tends to favor employment of skilled rather than unskilled workers.

Finally, the level of productivity is an important determinant of the standard of living, which is often measured by the gross domestic product (GDP) per person. However, higher productivity does not necessarily imply a higher standard of living. In addition to productivity per worker hour, GDP per person also depends on hours worked per worker and the employment rate (employment per person) and these latter two factors are affected by national and local labor market institutions. Based on data from the OECD survey of the Euro area, GDP per person in the Euro area was 30 percent lower than that of the United States in 2002, with just over two-thirds of that shortfall due to lower labor resource utilization and the other one-third due to lower labor productivity.

SEE ALSO *Cambridge Capital Controversy; Economic Growth; Marginal Productivity; Physical Capital; Production Function; Savings Rate*

BIBLIOGRAPHY

Durlauf, S., and J. Temple. 2005. Growth Econometrics. In *Handbook of Economic Growth*, ed. P. Aghion and S. Durlauf, Vol. 1A, 555–663. Amsterdam: North-Holland.

Jorgenson, D., Mun S. Ho, and Kevin J. Stiroh. 2005. *Information Technology and the American Growth Resurgence.* Vol. 3 of *Productivity.* Cambridge, MA: MIT Press.

Gavin Cameron

PROFANITY

Most media and social science treatments of profanity fail to grasp the significance of its underlying neurological, psychological, and sociocultural functions. The term *profanity* generally describes forms of offensive or vulgar speech that are scatological, irreligious, or sexual (e.g., *shit, hell,* and *fuck*). The *American Heritage Dictionary* (2000) definition refers to "abusive, vulgar, or irreverent language." The concept of profanity in most cultures also extends to offensive gestures, such as the middle-finger gesture; behaviors, such as pelvic thrusting; and forms of art, for example, sexual content in the motion picture *The Last Temptation of Christ* or modern artwork such as *Piss Christ* by Andres Serrano.

The preceding works of art are offensive because they affront religion, which is in line with the original usage of the term *profanity*. From the fifteenth through the nineteenth century profanity had a more precise meaning, referring specifically to irreligious speech or behavior and not merely vulgarity. Biblical taboos restricted sacrilegious speech, as defined by religious authorities, for example the commandment not to use the Lord's name in vain.

The word *profane,* according to the *Oxford English Dictionary* (1989), can be traced in writing to 1483. It literally meant outside of the church, secular, not concerned with religion or religious purposes, and by extension not holy, impure or defiled; as a verb it described treating something sacred with abuse, irreverence, or contempt. This definition of profanity is similar to that for *blasphemy,* which refers to an act of insulting or showing contempt or lack of reverence for God. Blasphemy is currently understood as a pointed attack on religion and religious figures, as opposed to merely showing irreverence. For example, Salman Rushdie's *The Satanic Verses* (1988) was considered by Muslims to be blasphemous toward Islam because of its insulting references to Muhammad.

The concepts of profanity and blasphemy form an integral part of European law regarding obscenity. British obscenity laws, which formed the foundation of American obscenity law, were adapted by the American colonies in the 1600s. They were predicated on the idea that offensive speech has the power to corrupt and deprave people, especially women and children. Early obscenity decisions in both England and the United States dealt with profanity and blasphemy, that is, speech offensive to religion and religious figures. In the late 1800s there was a shift from religion to sexuality as the basis of obscenity. Around the time of the U.S. Civil War (1861–1865) the postal service broadened its censorship of irreligious material to include materials of a sexual nature (e.g., photographs or post cards mailed to soldiers). A historical analysis by Stuart Flexner (1976) indicated that the power of profan-

ity to offend declined throughout the nineteenth century, being supplanted by sexual words and phrases in the United States and other English speaking countries. Since the early 1900s, obscenity cases in the United States have dealt exclusively with sexual materials and their effects on adults and children.

Educators regard the use of profanity as a problem of style more than an affront to religion. In most modern cultures profanity is regarded as substandard speech and inappropriate in formal communication, for example at school. The changing acceptability of profanity in U.S. society is mirrored in motion picture language restrictions. In the early 1900s, U.S. film censorship boards were highly influenced by the church, and religious profanities were explicitly forbidden. The 1939 American classic *Gone with the Wind* made history when Clark Gable uttered one of cinema's most famous lines, "Frankly, my dear, I don't give a damn," resulting in a $5,000 fine. Jay (1992) reported how language in film was heavily censored in the United States prior to the evolution of the rating system used by the film industry since 1968, which permits hundreds of profanities and obscenities in a film for adults, and fewer in films for teenagers and young children. Offensive language is restricted in almost all media around the world (the Internet and satellite radio being exceptions in most countries); censorship occurs in television, radio, newspaper, billboard, magazine, and advertising content. Profanity is heard more frequently in media than obscenity, but that trend could change.

In the United States, the Federal Communications Commission (FCC) has always regulated obscenity on the airwaves, and following the 1978 Supreme Court ruling in *FCC v. Pacifica Foundation,* expanded its scope to include "indecent" speech, defined as patently offensive references to sexual and excretory functions. *Pacifica* was based on a complaint by John Douglas, a member of the Planning Board of Morality in Media, about a radio station's afternoon broadcast of George Carlin's comedy routine "Filthy Words," which featured seven words not allowed on television. In the early 2000s, conservative political action committees in the United States (e.g., Parents Television Council, Morality in Media) pressured the Federal Communications Commission (FCC) to ban religious profanity from television and radio. Since 2003, the FCC has vacillated on whether "fuck" is universally obscene or not, depending on the context. The FCC originally ruled that "fuck" was not obscene when pop singer Bono uttered the word at the 2003 Golden Globe Awards. The commission reversed itself in 2004, ruling that it was obscene. When ABC broadcast the World War II film *Saving Private Ryan* in 2005, the FCC allowed the offensive speech because soldiers naturally used profanity and obscenity in the heat of battle.

As profanity came to be seen as less offensive than sexual obscenity, profanity became more common in public places, on television, on radio, and in newspapers. Timothy Jay (1992, 2000) published data indicating that profanities are among the most frequently spoken swear words; they are learned in early childhood and persist into old age. People's feelings about profanity often depend on their view of religion. Religious people are less likely to use profanity than non-religious people, and religious people are more offended by profanity in the media than are non-religious people. Some religious people are more offended by profanity than by obscenity; for example, Jay (2005) documented how religious working-class women will frequently use obscenities at work but are reluctant to use profanities. Restrictive attitudes toward profanity have led to complaints about profanity in popular media. Although religion-based complaints are predicated on the notion that children will be harmed by profanity, there is no social science data to indicate that profanities are psychologically harmful to listeners.

It is normal for people to use profanity, but its use depends critically on the social context. Brain damaged patients may have difficulty suppressing profanity. Jay (2000) has demonstrated both the universality of profane speech and behavior and the culturally determined nature of profanity by observing the behavior of Tourette's syndrome patients. Tourette's syndrome (TS) is a motor disorder characterized by uncontrollable movements (e.g., grimacing, head turning, or arm flailing) and vocalizations (e.g., yelling, grunting, or swearing). Uncontrollable obscene gestures and movements (copropraxia) and speech (coprolalia) occur in 25 to 30 percent of Touretters, and tend to feature the most socially inappropriate behaviors in a given culture. What a Touretter produces during a seizure depends on cultural and developmental context. English-speaking Touretters might utter obscenities such as *fuck, cunt*, and *motherfucker*, brandish the middle finger, or act out vulgar behaviors such as simulated masturbation. A young woman with TS in Kuwait is more prone to expose a naked leg, a gesture forbidden in her culture. Japanese and Chinese TS patients are more likely than English speakers to utter insults based on ancestral allusions (e.g., *aunt fucker*). Touretters in countries where religion is dominant are more likely to use profanities (e.g., *holy mother*) than Touretters from more secular countries. Coprolalia in the form of sign language also occurs among members of the deaf community with TS.

Originally meant to denote an offense toward religion, the term *profanity* now refers to a broader range of offensive speech and behavior, which is regarded by many people as too coarse for public use. Context-sensitive social science interpretations of profanity support a less restrictive view of profanity.

SEE ALSO *Norms*

BIBLIOGRAPHY

Flexner, Stuart Berg. 1976. *I Hear America Talking: An Illustrated Treasury of American Words and Phrases.* New York: Van Nostrand Reinhold.

Jay, Timothy B. 1992. *Cursing in America: A Psycholinguistic Study of Dirty Language in the Courts, in the Movies, in the Schoolyards, and on the Streets.* Philadelphia: John Benjamins.

Jay, Timothy B. 2000. *Why We Curse: A Neuro-Psycho-Social Theory of Speech.* Philadelphia: John Benjamins.

Jay, Timothy B. 2005. American Women: Their Cursing Habits and Religiosity. In *Gender and the Language of Religion,* ed. Allyson Jule, 63–84. New York: Palgrave Macmillan.

Timothy B. Jay

PROFESSIONALIZATION

Several attributes set *professionals* apart from *nonprofessionals*: (1) establishing formal means of recruiting and training members for the occupation; (2) creating associations to disseminate knowledge in the field, represent and promote the interests of its practitioners, and regulate and standardize its practices; (3) establishing stringent membership requirements and standards in practice; (4) getting official recognition; and (5) developing a code of ethics to make exclusive claims on qualifications, expertise, and jurisdiction. Taken together, these elements are critical in the making of a profession.

Formal education has gatekeeping as well as status-claiming functions. Requiring someone to receive formal training in a field, via university education, is the first step toward securing monopoly control of specialized knowledge. Formalizing the training process serves to invalidate the claims made by those who have obtained such knowledge solely through experience. Implementing this process would potentially limit the number of people acquiring formal education in the field and, in turn, gain control over who might enter the profession. Having everyone undergo similar training would also standardize the socialization process for all practitioners in the field.

Besides requiring formal training at schools, establishing professional organizations contributes to professionalization. Stringent membership criteria underscore the overall strength of a professional organization, which could be a unifying force for its practitioners. If the practitioners could agree on a set of universal standards to clearly define themselves, they could restrict membership to those who can meet the stringent requirements for full memberships and, more important, set the stage for a full closure in the profession (i.e., collective control over entry into the profession). Thus, nurturing unity and maintaining a strong spirit of professionalism would enhance the professional standing of its practitioners. Conversely, changing or lowering membership requirements reflect practitioners' loose attachment to the profession and a lack of closure.

The process of securing closure is incomplete without legal backing from the state. Licensure allows practitioners to ward off competition from outsiders. Aside from restricting entry, state laws give all practitioners the exclusive right to perform certain tasks or to provide services in the market. State licensure constitutes the "grand prize" in securing control over one's work. For example, certification by degree and examinations allows medical doctors and lawyers to eliminate potential competitors from related fields. In these professions, experience cannot be substituted for certification.

Developing and accepting a code of conduct is vital for the development of a profession. A professional society sets clear boundaries of acceptable professional values and conduct for its practitioners. Adopting an ethics code also signifies members' commitment to the interest of the public (or clients) rather than to a third party. To gain and maintain the public's confidence in practitioners' integrity, skills, and performance, practitioners are expected to live up to the code of ethics. Developing professional guidelines can be construed as the final stage of securing jurisdiction control. A set of professional ethics for, by, and of the practitioners preserves their professional standing as well as autonomy. It is a means of maintaining internal control as much as a measure of minimizing external interference.

The code of ethics for professionals first and foremost proclaims members' commitment to the public and their dedication to the values of the profession. The profession requires members to have a strong sense of dedication and commitment to the profession. The code also spells out the obligations and responsibilities of the practitioners to the profession and to their peers: being loyal, trustworthy, and honest; using discretion and exercising good judgment; and holding one's and others' actions to the highest standards.

Being a professional is a tall order. The code of ethics for a profession not only unifies practitioners, it implies that the practitioners themselves have the desire, ability, and obligation to monitor their own professional behavior. The penalties for those who fail to live up to the pledge would be reprimand, suspension, or termination of licensure. This code of conduct is developed to fulfill a sense of professionalism among practitioners. It is also a self-declaration of the profession's autonomy, high status, commitment, and self-policing.

The *career model* of professional development postulates that professionalization is sequential in that there is a fixed pattern of development, evolution, and internal differentiation. Each of the elements noted earlier constitutes a chronology of events in professionalization. Social scientists have used the career model to make sense of the developmental process for established fields (e.g., medicine, law, theology) and new occupations (e.g., computer science, engineering).

Practitioners in "new" professions are organized differently from those in "old" professions. For instance, medical doctors have kept jurisdiction control firmly in their hands through formal training and mandatory licensing. They strive for autonomy, status, and recognition in the society, rather than aspiring to be entrepreneurs.

The *functional model* pays attention to how and to what extent these activities foster professional development. The sequencing of these functions is closely linked to professionalization. Practitioners first call for exclusion, followed by the establishment of jurisdiction, internal controls, and external relations. Professional development is seen as an outcome of different stages of securing control over jurisdiction in a field.

The *professional model* focuses on the characteristics shared by professions, rather than on the processes of professional development. All professions share several commonalities. A profession is an occupational group with an abstract, theoretical knowledge base, acquired primarily through extensive formal training. A profession is an activity based on formal training and higher learning. Its practitioners are agents of formal knowledge. Professions enjoy the autonomy to establish their own standards of assessment and control. Hence, self-policing members' behavior and practices becomes an obligation of a profession. Its practitioners see their vocation as a "calling" rather than simply a job. Members of a profession are expected to have a lifetime commitment to their careers and to develop a strong sense of professional identity and dedication to their work.

There are differences among the three models of professional development in their emphasis on sequence of events, functions, or properties. To set themselves apart from nonprofessionals, professionals ought to have ways and means of defining and maintaining their monopoly power. This common theme highlights the ideological and organizational aspects of professionalism. All three models share a common theme that, due to their unique knowledge bases, professions have the desire for authority and freedom, though in varying degrees, to set their own boundaries of expertise, internal and external control, and activities.

Not all professions are truly "free" professions. Medicine, law, and dentistry come close to having all of the characteristics of a profession. Doctors and lawyers have been able to maintain control over their jurisdiction. Dentists also enjoy a high degree of professional autonomy compared to their counterparts in accounting. Entry to medicine, law, and dentistry is regulated by academic and nonacademic requirements. Only licensed doctors, lawyers, and dentists can practice in the United States. These gatekeeping techniques are so effective that even foreign nationals with similar credentials or experience from abroad cannot practice in the United States unless they satisfy the U.S. licensing requirements.

In contrast, there are fewer restrictions to move into other professions. Engineering will never come close to being a truly autonomous profession. It is a semiprofession in that it has a body of specialized knowledge and requires extended training. However, in the absence of mandatory licensing for all entrants, it cannot effectively block anyone without a college degree from becoming an engineer. Engineers do not enjoy legitimate protection from competition in the labor markets. Contemporary engineering can be considered a bureaucratic profession. Due to the organization and nature of engineering work, it is impossible for its practitioners, including the self-employed, to insulate themselves from business and industrial influence. Not only do engineers not have the means to be completely independent from the patrons of their services, they may not have the desire to be independent. Engineers tend to seek power, status, and mobility within an organization. A strong orientation to their profession may be counterproductive to career advancement in bureaucratic institutions.

Experience can substitute for formal education in computer work. Employers can promote an experienced worker without an advanced degree in management to head a division of young, college-educated workers. Degrees in social work are required for some but not all social workers. The military is different from other professions in that extensive training is required for all participants. Compared to their counterparts in civilian employment, workers in this "total institution" do not enjoy a high degree of professional independence. However, one can make the argument that the rites of passage into the military may induce a relatively strong sense of professional commitment. Advanced degrees in one's field, such as a doctorate, are usually required for teaching in higher education. Yet, a medical degree is not required for teaching in medical schools. None of these professions in the civilian sector has a monopoly of jurisdiction control. The good news is that outsiders enjoy greater access to these professions than to the legal or dental professions. On the other hand, talented individuals may be more

attracted to professions with tighter gatekeeping for social status, autonomy, and earnings.

Administrative and managerial positions have been classified as "professional occupations" in the U.S. Census and in scholarly research. Those who perform primarily administrative or managerial tasks may have received formal (e.g., a master's degree in business administration) and ongoing professional or organizational training. There are professional associations (e.g., the American Management Association) for managers to advance members' career interests. However, administrators may not possess as much professional autonomy as do doctors or dentists. Like scientists or engineers, managers are semi-professionals.

BIBLIOGRAPHY

Abbott, Andrew. 1988. *The System of Professions: An Essay on the Division of Expert Labor.* Chicago: University of Chicago Press.

Bell, Daniel. 1973. *The Coming of Post-Industrial Society: A Venture in Social Forecasting.* New York: Basic Books.

Tang, Joyce, and Earl Smith, eds. 1996. *Women and Minorities in American Professions.* Albany: State University of New York Press.

Trice, Harrison M. 1993. *Occupational Subcultures in the Workplace.* Ithaca, NY: ILR Press.

Wilensky, Harold L. 1964. The Professionalization of Everyone? *American Journal of Sociology* 70: 137–158.

Joyce Tang

PROFESSIONAL-MANAGERIAL CLASS
SEE *Managerial Class; New Class, The.*

PROFESSORIATE

The professoriate comprises faculty in postsecondary institutions who have specialized expertise in one of the many academic disciplines or professional fields and who teach and to varying degrees engage in research, institutional governance, and service (for example, provide medical care). In the early twenty-first century the professoriate includes approximately 3.5 million professionals teaching more than 80 million students worldwide (Task Force on Higher Education and Society 2000).

The evolution of the academic profession has been inextricably linked to changes in fields of study, colleges and universities, and national systems of higher education. The kaleidoscope of organizational structures and operations that characterize postsecondary institutions are associated with an array of faculty employment and career patterns as well as differences in the nature of academic work. The teaching and research of a psychologist differ from a chemist's, and the career path of a professor in a German university only slightly resembles that of a professor in a small American liberal arts college. Hence treating the professoriate as a single professional group is often difficult.

Despite the differences, there are some core features of the profession that can be attributed to the common origins of most contemporary universities in the medieval European universities. Specifically, a history of the professoriate should take into account the nature of academic work, professors' autonomy, and their roles in institutional governance.

HISTORY OF THE ACADEMIC PROFESSION

A fundamental difference in the overall governance of higher education distinguishes the United States from other nations. Whereas in most countries there is a national system of public higher education with government bodies that set policies for all institutions under their jurisdictions, this is not the case in the United States. In the United States control of higher education is decentralized, and responsibility for funding and governance is delegated to individual states. States in turn have given individual universities leeway to establish their own faculty employment practices. Consequently, variations among campuses are greater in the decentralized U.S. higher education "system" than is the case in a centralized one, where conditions of employment are determined by national policies. For a variety of reasons, countries with centralized national systems are looking to the United States as an example of how professorial roles might be restructured. Hence it is instructive to consider the history of the U.S. professoriate in some detail.

The Professoriate in the Decentralized U.S. System The earliest colleges, founded in British colonies, were modeled after Oxford and Cambridge, and their mission was to prepare children of means for public life and further study in medicine, law, or theology. Education was for the privileged class—the elite—and the classical curriculum varied little from that found in the Middle Ages: ethics, metaphysics, and natural philosophy. The language of instruction was Latin.

From the opening of Harvard College in 1636 until the early 1800s, tutors predominated in the professoriate. Recruited from among recent graduates, tutors were considered qualified to teach all subjects. The curriculum was set, and campus governance was the responsibility of a lay board and a strong president.

In the 1720s Harvard made the first "permanent" faculty appointments: endowed professorships in divinity, mathematics, and natural philosophy. Professors differed from tutors in that they usually had some advanced professional training, were appointed to and taught almost exclusively in one subject area, and remained in their positions longer. By 1795 approximately 105 professors were distributed across nineteen colleges. However, the faculty career was not financially viable, so most professors also earned incomes as clergymen, lawyers, and physicians. In the early 1800s the work of Enlightenment scholars, emphasizing scientific reasoning and truth, edged into undergraduate curricula. New areas of academic knowledge with new modes of research emerged, bringing opportunities for postbaccalaureate education outside the traditional professions. The German university, with its ideals of unfettered inquiry and faculty simultaneously engaged in teaching and research, became the model to which the United States aspired, and Americans went abroad for advanced education.

The late 1800s brought specialized colleges for women and blacks and land-grant institutions devoted to utilitarian education. Disciplinary associations (for example, the American Chemical Society) were established, providing avenues for faculty publication that brought national recognition to scholars and their universities. American doctoral education began in earnest. Yale granted the first PhD in 1861, and in 1876 the first exclusively graduate school was founded—Johns Hopkins University.

Further differentiation of postsecondary institutions occurred as the American graduate university began to take shape alongside the liberal arts, specialized, and land-grant institutions. Its core was a four-year undergraduate college organized into disciplinary departments, with graduate and professional programs arrayed around it. These universities exerted profound influences on the definition of academic knowledge and on the professional norms and values of the professoriate. In 1913 faculty in the leading graduate universities called a meeting to set professional standards for university-based scholars, paving the way for the founding of the American Association of University Professors (AAUP) in 1915.

The late 1800s and early 1900s were pivotal years for the academic profession. The earned PhD was becoming a requirement for entry. Growing numbers of individuals moved directly from doctoral study to faculty positions. The ranks of instructor, assistant professor, and professor were forged into a distinguishable career. Individuals were appointed in departments representing specialized disciplinary areas. Structural changes in universities enhanced professors' work autonomy and their authority in academic personnel matters. Primary responsibility for academic decisions such as curriculum and faculty hiring migrated to professors.

Between 1921 and 1945 state and federal governments recruited faculty to help solve societal problems, increasing the visibility and stature of the professoriate. The prestige of graduate universities became calibrated in terms of student quality and achievement and faculty prominence and research accomplishments. Between 1920 and 1940 the annual production of doctorates increased from 620 to about 3,300. At the same time new institutions—two-year colleges and normal schools with qualitatively different programs—were created to meet the needs of immigrants and part-time students interested in technical and semiprofessional occupations. Nationally, institutional differentiation and enrollments increased. Student and faculty profiles changed as access to higher education widened and the "massification" of higher education progressed.

Although the professoriate grew in stature and assumed primary responsibility for academic matters, faculty served at the pleasure of institutional governing boards and presidents. Faculty did not enjoy the economic security or due process that characterized other professions, and they chafed at restrictions on their academic freedom. The AAUP, with the American Association of Colleges, crafted professional guidelines to address these problems and in 1940 produced the Statement of Principles on Academic Freedom and Tenure. The statement articulated the concept of continuous tenure, meaning that an individual could not be fired without a judicial hearing, and provided guidelines for awarding tenure. The authors proffered tenure as a means to protect academic freedom and ensure "a sufficient degree of economic security to make the profession attractive to men and women of ability" (American Association of University Professors). Another AAUP report on faculty governance from this period asserted that professors were not employees to be managed by administrators but professionals to be consulted on institutional decisions—in particular faculty appointments and promotions and educational matters.

After World War II, as a result of federal legislation such as the GI Bill, enrollments tripled, as did the need for professors. Established graduate education programs grew, and new ones were created. Government funding for research burgeoned. The confluence of these events in the 1950s further expanded the influence of graduate universities, diffusing the research ethos throughout academe. The specialized scholar came to epitomize the academic professional.

In the 1960s faculty enjoyed ready employment, funding for research, career advancement, and geographic mobility. Faculty autonomy strengthened as departments assumed primary responsibility for academic decisions and faculty personnel matters. The standards for faculty promotion and tenure heightened. Economic conditions worsened in the 1970s, and undergraduate enrollment declined. Professors were criticized for valuing esoteric research, being inattentive to undergraduates, and failing to diversify by hiring and promoting women and minorities. Beginning in the 1980s the nation's economic policies shifted greater responsibility for funding their education to students and encouraged greater cooperation between postsecondary institutions and business. State and federal governments called for greater fiscal and educational accountability.

Beginning in the 1990s and continuing into the early twenty-first century reduced campus budgets, attributed to lost tax dollars and diminished tuition revenue, and the need for instructional flexibility were reasons given for significant changes in personnel practices. Faculty appointments were changed from tenure track, with its assumption of continuous employment, to term appointments that specify a fixed period at the end of which a person is released or the contract is extended. The proportion of the U.S. professoriate employed full-time dropped from 78 percent to 56 percent between 1970 and 2001, and the majority of full-time appointments in the 1990s were off the tenure track—about 53 percent in 1997 (Finkelstein and Schuster 2001). Unionization of nontenure-track faculty has increased, providing an alternative to traditional forms of shared governance on some campuses.

The Professoriate in Centralized Higher Education Systems Certain factors have had pervasive and similar effects on the professoriate in both the United States and other countries. For example, new modes of inquiry as well as calls for more utilitarian programs of study have altered postsecondary institutions and the nature of academic work worldwide. However, different national contexts and cultural traditions have led to variations in employment conditions and career structures within the professoriate. For example, in the former Soviet republics, the requirements for different programs of study and rigid workload guidelines are set by the national government and constrain faculty autonomy in their teaching. In western Europe professors participate in and greatly influence decisions about academic matters, but nonprofessors have little to no power. Some nations maintain separate organizational structures for professors' teaching and research, such as the research institutes and academies of science found in Germany and throughout eastern Europe. Yet Britain has created an institutional ranking system in which placement depends heavily on the research productivity of the university's faculty. In certain nations—

France, Germany, and Italy, for example—professors are civil servants and enjoy a form of tenure based on their status within the public-service sector. In contrast, the British government removed faculty from the civil service ranks, and now all faculty hold fixed-term appointments. Professors in Latin America must compete periodically with a national pool of applicants for the positions they hold. Some countries—China, for example—are implementing policies that will require faculty to fund parts of their full-time positions with money obtained through research grants.

Such examples highlight variations in the professoriate across centralized higher education systems. Academic work continues to be shaped by changes outside as well as within academe, and it appears that several professional features of the professoriate—autonomy and career stability in particular—are being eroded.

PROFESSIONAL REQUIREMENTS

The configuration of faculty activities and the credentials of professors vary by field, institutional mission, and national context. In the United States, for example, a research university professor with graduate and undergraduate students and a research laboratory distributes her or his time differently than does a community college professor who teaches five or more undergraduate courses. In France the credentials to teach lower division university courses are the same as those required to teach in the elite university preparatory schools.

U.S. colleges set their own personnel policies and practices, but typically, when they seek tenure track faculty, they announce openings in national venues. Search committees made up primarily of faculty screen applicants, interview candidates, and ultimately recommend preferred candidates to administrators. Selection is based on merit criteria, such as academic credentials, publication quality, and peer recommendations. Fixed-term appointments are handled differently, especially if the employment period is brief. In countries with national systems, traditions differ, but typically a government body establishes personnel policies and practices for all postsecondary institutions.

The U.S. tenure track has three ranks: assistant professor, associate professor, and professor. After a probationary period, assistant professors are evaluated and are either promoted to associate professor and awarded tenure or dismissed. Reappointments and promotions of fixed-term faculty are also based on performance evaluations. Faculty may be dismissed from their tenured or nontenured positions because of misconduct, financial exigencies, or post-tenure reviews that document inadequate performance.

In other countries the sequence of positions held by nonprofessors varies greatly, as do national policies regarding whether a person can earn promotion in the university where he or she is currently employed. In contrast with the United States, where faculty can be promoted through the ranks in a single institution, the careers of academics unfold within national systems. Faculty must often migrate from one institution to another to advance their careers. The Humboldtian university chair system, in which each discipline (department) has one professor—the chair—was copied widely and has significantly influenced faculty careers in many nations. A professor enjoys permanent employment, but nonprofessors are on fixed-term contracts, and to be promoted, they must successfully compete for a position at another university. Nonprofessors must complete a "second doctorate" (the *Habilitation*) to be eligible for a professorial appointment. While they complete the *Habilitation*, these nonprofessors hold either paid or unpaid university teaching and research appointments. Unlike in the United States, where junior faculty and professors participate in decision-making with respect to a range of academic issues, in Germany a significant gap in authority exists between these two groups.

SOCIETAL PERCEPTIONS

Throughout the 1950s and 1960s, public views of the academic profession were positive, and occupational prestige was high. However, public perceptions began to change in the 1970s. Criticism of the professoriate appeared regularly in the popular press, students rioted in some countries, and there were general calls for accountability. Faculty productivity, instructional quality, research relevance, and tenure were all questioned in the last thirty years of the twentieth century. The political beliefs of faculty, particularly in the social sciences and humanities, have also drawn criticism. As guaranteed employment and pay in other professions declined, disapproval of U.S. institutional tenure and presumed tenure of professors who are civil servants intensified. However, sociological studies suggest the occupation has remained among the highest in prestige.

CHALLENGES

The academic profession faces multiple challenges. Here are a few:

- One challenge results from government pressures for accountability and structural changes in faculty roles. Proponents of increased efficiency and those who want to change the balance of power among faculty, administrators, and government bodies argue that tenure (both as defined in the United

States and in national civil service careers) is outmoded and advocate fixed-term faculty appointments as an alternative. Critics of such appointments believe they diminish the quality of the professoriate and the conditions of academic work that have made higher education successful: professional autonomy, academic freedom, and economic security. These divergent views of the professoriate are a source of tension among government officials, university administrators, and faculty.

- Since the nineteenth century, teaching and learning through simultaneous engagement in scholarship and instruction has been a cornerstone of the strongest higher education systems in the world. Critics of personnel policies that prioritize fixed-term positions with heavy teaching loads challenge what they believe is a failure to recognize the impact on the advancement of knowledge that has resulted in countries that have adopted such practices.

- Yet another challenge for the professoriate is changes in government and foundation research support. Funding for research in some areas is abundant. In others, especially the arts and humanities, monies are scarce. The attractiveness of fields and the availability of future scholars may be affected by this situation.

SEE ALSO *Cambridge University; Education, USA; Intellectualism, Anti-; New Class, The; University of Oxford; University, The*

BIBLIOGRAPHY

American Association of University Professors. 1940 Statement of Principles on Academic Freedom and Tenure. http://www.aaup.org/AAUP/pubsres/policydocs/1940stateme nt.htm?wbc_purpose=Basic&WBCMODE=PresentationUnp ublished.

Baldwin, R. G., and J. L. Chronister. 2002. What Happened to the Tenure Track? In *The Question of Tenure*, ed. Richard P. Chait, 125–159. Cambridge, MA: Harvard University Press, 2002.

Blackburn, Robert T., and Janet H. Lawrence. 1995. *Faculty at Work: Motivation, Expectation, Satisfaction*. Baltimore, MD: Johns Hopkins University Press.

Fairweather, James S. 1996. *Faculty Work and Public Trust: Restoring the Value of Teaching and Public Service in American Academic Life*. Boston: Allyn and Bacon.

Finkelstein, Martin J. 1984. *The American Academic Profession: A Synthesis of Social Scientific Inquiry since World War II*. Columbus: Ohio State University Press.

Finkelstein, Martin J., and Jack H. Schuster. 2001. Assessing the Silent Revolution: How Changing Demographics Are Reshaping the Academic Profession. *American Association for Higher Education Bulletin* 54 (2): 3–7.

Institute of Education Sciences, U.S. Department of Education. 2004. Digest of Education Statistics, Chapter 3. Postsecondary Education. National Center for Educational Statistics. http://nces.ed.gov/programs/digest/d04/ch_3.asp

Rudolph, F. 1962. *The American College and University: A History*. Athens: University of Georgia Press.

Task Force on Higher Education and Society. 2000. *Higher Education in Developing Countries: Peril and Promise*. Washington, DC: The World Bank.

Janet H. Lawrence

PROFILING, RACIAL
SEE *Policing, Biased.*

PROFITABILITY

At first sight profit appears to be a simple concept that is defined as the residual of revenues from the cost of production; the related concept of profitability is defined as the ratio of profits to some basis, with the most commonly employed basis being invested capital. The simple concept of profitability is of great significance for understanding the motion of the capitalist system because the desire for and promise of profit motivate entrepreneurs to initiate productive activity and because the level of profitability is the measure of the success or failure of an endeavor. Consequently, measuring current and past profitability as well as projecting future profitability is crucial for entrepreneurial decisions with regard to the expansion or contraction of investment in the current activity or alternative activities, the possibility of takeovers, and the like.

DEFINITIONS OF COSTS AND PROFITS

In spite of the fact that profitability appears to be easy to define, a closer examination reveals that in reality costs, which are crucial for the determination of profits, are difficult to define in a generally accepted way. The usual textbook discussion of costs refers to the definitions of costs by accountants and economists. Definitions by accountants record only explicit costs, that is, all monetary expenses incurred in the production and sale of goods and services, whereas those by economists include additional costs called the implicit or opportunity cost: the compensation for not exploiting the best alternative opportunity. Clearly, the notion of profits of the economist includes that of the accountant, and this implies that profits in the economist's sense exist if the revenues from sales exceed both the explicit and the implicit costs. Economic profit sometimes is referred to as supernormal or excess profit, and the normal profit (rate) is the part of the cost that usually is identified with the interest (rate).

In light of these distinctions, it is clear that there is no single definition of profitability even for accountants because costs and therefore profits depend on various accounting practices and the purposes they serve. For example, accountants usually convey different pictures of a firm's profitability to the government and to the stockholders. Similarly, economists use different measures of profitability, such as profits over invested capital and profits over equity, among a host of others. However, the Cambridge capital controversies show that it is difficult to deal with profitability because it involves the evaluation of capital goods, which requires the prior knowledge of equilibrium prices. Those prices can be estimated only if one knows the average rate of profit of the economy. That estimation, however, requires the evaluation of invested capital, among other things, creating a vicious cycle from which there seems to be no exit.

MEASUREMENTS OF PROFITABILITY

Thus, economists have further difficulties in the estimation of the proper notion of profitability, which usually is identified with the internal rate of return (IRR): the discount rate that equalizes the value of the investment project with the present value of the future stream of expected profits that will result from the lifetime of the investment project. The IRR concept has certain limitations that, among other things, have to do with the idea that only the short-term horizon is relevant for investment decisions. This is why economists make use of the economic rate of return (ERR), which is the IRR over a specific, much shorter period of the firm's life. Even this notion of profitability, however, is hard to measure with actual data, and so economists revert to the accounting rate of profit (ARP): the ratio of the value of a flow of profit in a specific period to the value of the stock of capital.

It is true that in any particular instance the ARP for firms and industries will be different from the respective ERR. More specifically, in 1983 Fisher and McGowan showed that as a result of depreciation methods, the projected cash profiles over time and the growth rate of a firm make ARPs fall short of a good approximation to the ERP. The problem with these experiments is that they were performed with numerical examples, not with actual data. By contrast, in 1990 Duménil and Lévy, using actual data from the U.S. economy over a long period, contended that for all practical purposes and under certain conditions and for certain types of economic problems the ARP can serve as a reliable approximation of the ERR.

In spite of criticisms economists use the notion of the ARP in many applications, such as industrial organization studies; if a particular industry makes an ARP above the economy's average ARP for a considerable period, economists say that this may be evidence of economic (sometimes called excess or even supernormal) profit that accrues to a firm or an industry. This may be due to the exercise of monopoly power or the presence of barriers to entry, which prevent new firms from seizing such profit opportunities. Economic profit is viewed as a departure from the ideal of perfect competition, and the government must take action to correct the situation in its effort to make economic life look more like the perfectly competitive model, in which economic profit in the long run is zero. Furthermore, the ARP has been used, along with other variables, in econometric specifications as a determinant of investment behavior and capital accumulation. The idea is that excess profits attract investment, and therefore capital accumulation accelerates to the point where excess profits are competed away; the opposite is true in the cases of losses.

ARP also has been used in historical studies as an indicator of the expansion or contraction of an economy. In fact, it has been shown that the contraction phase of an economy is associated with a protracted falling ARP that leads to stagnant or even falling total real profits, giving rise to pessimistic expectations and thus discouraging aggregate investment and increasing the rate of unemployment. The opposite is true with a rising rate of profit, which creates an atmosphere of optimism, encouraging investment spending, lowering unemployment, and setting the stage for prosperity.

SEE ALSO *Average and Marginal Cost; Cambridge Capital Controversy; Capital; Profits; Rate of Profit; Revenue*

BIBLIOGRAPHY

Duménil, Gérard, and Dominique Lévy. 1990. Post Depression Trends in the Economic Rate of Return for U.S. Manufacturing. *Review of Economics and Statistics* 72 (3): 406–413.

Fisher, Franklin M., and John J. McGowan. 1983. On the Misuse of Accounting Rates of Return to Infer Monopoly Profits. *American Economic Review* 73: 82–97.

Lefteris Tsoulfidis

PROFITS

Any discussion of profits must carefully distinguish between profits at the microeconomic level of the firm and profits at the macroeconomic or aggregate level, that is, in the economy as a whole. In mainstream economics, the existence of profits at the microeconomic level is not a complicated issue: An individual firm can make profits or losses in the short run based on its sales and the price at which its good or service is sold. In other words, as long as total revenue is greater than total costs, gross profits are realized. In perfect competition, given the nonexistence of barriers to entry, economic profits are necessarily nil in the long run—a condition of equilibrium analysis, where marginal cost must be equal to marginal revenue.

At the macroeconomic level, orthodox or mainstream economists associate the existence of profits to market imperfections: As stated above, profits do not exist in perfect competition. Yet, by allowing for some imperfections, profits will exist in less than perfectly competitive markets, such as in oligopolistic markets and under monopolistic competition, to name a few. At both levels, profits are always maximized by firms.

A second explanation of profits in neoclassical theory sees them not so much as a surplus value where a firm's revenues are greater than its costs. Instead, we can also see profits as a reward: If an individual has savings, he can choose to consume today or postpone his consumption to a later date and lend his savings to someone who is willing to borrow them. In this sense, the lender is reimbursed his initial loan plus interest, which is his reward for sacrificing consumption today for consumption tomorrow.

For heterodox economists, however, the existence of monetary profits at the macroeconomic (aggregate) level has always been a conundrum. In fact, as we will see, they do not exist—that is, at the macroeconomic level, profits are necessarily nil in theory. This conclusion poses a number of challenges that are tied to the way in which production is financed and the way money is created by bank credit. Yet, profits must exist so that at the macroeconomic level, firms as a whole are able to cover not only their costs of production but also the interest on their bank debt. So where does the extra money come from? To borrow a popular expression from Karl Marx (1818–1883), how does *M* become *M'*?

PRODUCTION FINANCE AND THE ENDOGENEITY OF MONEY

For heterodox economists, firms do not finance production or purchase capital goods with prior savings. Indeed, unlike in neoclassical or mainstream theory, savings only play a passive role in the production process. This is but the first of the *reversed causalities* within heterodox economics. Rather, since the economy is seen as a logical sequence of irreversible events that operate in historical time within a monetary economy, savings arise from income that logically follows a prior investment. Two

questions arise. First, if investment is not financed by savings, how is it financed? Second, will this have any implications for the generation of profits?

Overall, heterodox economists see the economy as a dynamic interactive process between various social groups, such as wage earners, firms, and banks. Such a class-based approach is at the heart of the explanation of macroeconomic profits.

In a monetary economy of production, as advocated by John Maynard Keynes (1883–1946), this circuit of irreversible events begins with the determination of production plans by firms (planned production)—that is, wages are set and production levels are determined, as are other costs of production, such as the rate of interest, exogenously determined by the central bank according to its policy objectives. At this stage, therefore, firms are able to properly determine their financing needs for the production process to begin. In the aggregate, we can argue that firms need to borrow *M*.

As Keynes pointed out, "banks are special," in the sense that they are entrusted with the role of financing the production process: They "hold the key." Banks are therefore an important part of not only the production process but also the realization of profits, as we will see below.

Once firms approach a bank for the financing of their production plans, banks will then evaluate the creditworthiness of the potential borrowers. Provided firms have the sufficient collateral to secure a loan, or provided they otherwise meet the strict lending criteria of the banks—such as the firm's ability to generate profits, the firm's net worth, the firm's ability to withstand transitory shocks, and certain key financial ratios, such as cash flows and debt/equity—they will receive the funds to cover their production costs, which may be called the *initial finance* phase. Of course, some firms will not be able to secure credit, thereby jeopardizing production and output (Graziani 2003).

Once credit has been secured and a loan is made, usually as a line of credit, firms will draw on their line of credit to pay wages and purchase other inputs of production. As they pay wages, bank accounts of wage earners will increase; money is created. In this sense, the creation of money is parallel to the creation of incomes.

Once incomes are created, wage earners will carry out their consumption and saving plans according to their needs. As they consume, money flows back to firms as revenue as they sell their goods and services to consumers. In this sense, firms are able to capture a portion of their initial outlays from the direct consumption by wage earners in the overall economy. Firms will use these funds to extinguish their existing debt toward the bank, which in the process will also destroy money.

Once their consumption plans are carried out, wage earners will assign the remaining component of their wages to savings. We can identify two types of savings: *financial* savings, which are used to purchase obligations on financial markets, and *hoarded* savings, which then remain in the wage earners' bank account, which consists of the demand for money balances.

Although both types of savings may appear similar, they are in fact very different and play very different roles. In the first instance, when households purchase financial obligations, these funds flow back to firms. Firms will then use these funds to reimburse their debt toward the banking system. In this sense, as Keynes once argued, there is no difference between consumption and financial saving, as they both play the same role. Both are, in fact, part of *final financing*. This is the reflux phase of the circuit of production. It is the phase of the destruction of money.

From the above discussion of the economy as a monetary circuit, two fundamental conclusions about the heterodox approach can be drawn. First, the money supply is endogenous and responds to the needs of production (Lavoie 1992; Moore 1988; Rochon 1999). Credit creates money, which is another reverse causality inherent in the heterodox approach. Money endogeneity suggests therefore that there is no excess money. The money supply always adapts to the requirements of the economy; such is the characteristic of a monetary economy of production.

Unlike neoclassical theory, where the money supply is an exogenous stock imposed by the central bank, heterodox economists consider the flow nature of credit and money as a fundamental characteristic of production economies. In this sense, the banking system is at the heart of the production process and of the endogeneity of money. The existence of money therefore is the result of debt between firms and banks. Heterodox economists therefore argue that the money supply is credit-led and demand-determined.

The second conclusion, however, is even more important. Indeed, if firms borrow M, how can they make any profits if, at best, they succeed in capturing only M, assuming no savings? Even more importantly, how can firms in the aggregate generate revenues to even pay the interest on their bank loan?

Granted, the above example is a simplified model, but even if we were to complicate the model by adding a government, the open economy, or additional realistic characteristics of a production economy, it would not change the fundamental conclusion that, at best, firms can only succeed in capturing what they injected into circulation at the beginning of the circuit. The question, therefore, is simple: If profits exist at the macroeconomic level, how can we explain the transformation of M into M'?

Heterodox economists have proposed a number of possible solutions to this conundrum. For instance, some have suggested that profits can be accounted for, provided we assume several circuits that overlap with each other. In other words, in the real world, production periods are staggered in the sense that firms or sectors do not borrow and reimburse their debt all at the same time. As such, several sources of monetary outlays would exist simultaneously, thereby providing firms with more than M at any one time.

Another possible solution consists in considering the existence of the state or an open economy. Under each of these conditions, there is an additional injection of outlays coming from the state and from other countries. In this sense, when the government undertakes fiscal expenditures, they increase aggregate demand and translate into additional revenues for firms. Yet, the problem with this solution is that while expenditures are revenues for firms, taxes are a drain on the circuit. As such, for this solution to be a viable and general solution, it requires that governments consistently incur fiscal deficits.

In an open economy, of course, countries are increasing their exports, which increase the proceeds of domestic firms, with which they can extinguish their debt toward the banking system and show some profits. This additional influx of revenue would account for the transformation of M into M'. Yet, as in the above example, this solution remains a limiting case, and not a general solution: While exports represent an influx of additional revenues, imports are the opposite. In this sense, this solution only applies in situations of net exports (trade surplus).

There is no doubt that all the above suggestions contribute in some way to the existence of macroeconomic profits. Yet, they all consist of ultracircuit explanations, in the sense that they all require that we amend the basic circuit by allowing some external explanation, such as the state, the rest of the world, or additional, overlapping circuits. What is required is a general theory of macroeconomic profits that applies in all circumstances.

For Marxists, since the value of goods reflect the labor hours used in their production (the labor theory of value), profits can be explained because capitalists are able to extract from labor a greater value out of their work or labor power. In other words, capitalists, as owners of the means of capital, are able to exploit workers: Capitalists are thus able to extract "surplus value" from the workers and enjoy profits.

A GENERAL THEORY OF PROFITS

How can we therefore account for profits within a single period of production without relying on external solutions? Recall that until now, this entry has said nothing about the financing of investment. Yet, just like production, investment must be financed. Assume therefore that like wages, investment is financed with the use of bank credit. Yet, unlike wages that are financed with short-term credit that needs to be reimbursed at the end of the production circuit, investments are long-term credit: Firms do not reimburse the whole value of investment within the same period, but rather typically reimburse investment over several periods. In that way, while firms in the aggregate borrow to cover wages (and other costs of production) and the purchase of investment goods, they only reimburse a fraction of that total value, which accounts for the existence of profits at the macroeconomic level.

SEE ALSO *Capitalism; Capitalist Mode of Production; Economics; Economics, Marxian; Economics, Neoclassical; Economics, Neo-Ricardian; Economics, Post Keynesian; Entrepreneurship; Long Period Analysis; Marginalism; Markup Pricing; Profitability; Rate of Profit; Surplus; Surplus Value*

BIBLIOGRAPHY

Graziani, Augusto. 2003. *The Monetary Theory of Production.* Cambridge, U.K.: Cambridge University Press.

Lavoie, Marc. 1992. *Foundations of Post-Keynesian Economic Analysis.* Aldershot, U.K.: Edward Elgar.

Moore, Basil J. 1988. *Horizontalists and Verticalists: The Macroeconomics of Credit–Money.* Cambridge, U.K.: Cambridge University Press.

Rochon, Louis-Philippe. 1999. *Credit, Money and Production: An Alternative Post-Keynesian Approach.* Cheltenham, U.K.: Edward Elgar.

Louis-Philippe Rochon

PROGRAMMED RETARDATION

The concept of "programmed retardation" comprises policies, programs, and instructional practices designed to guarantee educational failure for students. Significantly, following the U.S. Supreme Court's momentous *Brown v. Board of Education* decision of 1954, education strategies originally implemented to deny quality education to many black students began an overall decline of America's public schools in both urban and suburban areas. This trend has led writers of dramatically different viewpoints to comment on America's declining educational competitiveness in the world (e.g., Berman 2006; Friedman 2006).

In April 1983, the National Commission on Excellence in Education, which is part of the U.S. Department of Education, issued a report that stated unambigu-

ously that "the educational foundations of our society are presently being eroded by a rising tide of mediocrity that threatens our very future as a Nation and a people." The report, titled *A Nation at Risk*, likened the devastation of public education to "an act of war." "We have in effect," the report warned, "been committing an act of unthinking, unilateral educational disarmament." Many Americans seemed shocked by the report's findings, though they were not a new discovery.

The source of the crisis in public education in many of America's cities can be traced back to the late 1950s and 1960s. The *Brown* decision ended state-sanctioned racial apartheid in America's public schools; but the reasoning that all black schools were inherently inferior was incorrect. In a deliberate attempt to distort and evade the Court's decision, many urban school systems outside of the South installed a pupil assignment policy known as "tracking," which effectively resegregated many schools by channeling the majority of black students into the lowest "track" early in their educational careers.

Interpreting the *Brown* ruling as an opportunity to improve their children's education, black residents in many cities across America fought the policy of tracking. In 1969 the community activist Jewell Mazique labeled the policy "programmed retardation," declaring that tracking was more harmful than the conservative practice of racist segregation in the Old South.

Reasoning that poor education would ultimately hurt black and white working-class children in the nation's capitol, community leaders called for neither racial integration nor segregation. Instead, they demanded quality education. Mazique and other Washington, D.C., community activists defined this educational goal unambiguously, calling for: (1) the distribution and mastery of the fundamental tools of learning—namely reading, writing, computational skills, and thinking; (2) academic motivation; and (3) positive character development (Mazique 2000).

As in so many other urban areas, Washington, D.C.'s black community lost the political struggle for quality education. In 1967, the celebrated *Hobson v. Hansen* case terminated the school system's tracking policy, but the court claimed that racial integration automatically improved the educational performance of black students. Liberal civil rights leaders and educational managerial elites won the day and began to implement various racial integration policies. By the 1970s, many schools system adopted the policy of racial-balance busing, which transported a percentage of black students (and later Latino students) from their neighborhood schools to white schools in order to achieve racial balance. Magnet school programs and other education experiments also were implemented in order to bring about racial integration.

Because integration is not an end in itself but only a means to an end, the contradictions and dilemmas of this approach quickly became apparent. Authentic racial integration, however, could not be realized with policy strategies that focused mainly on the well-being of white students and their schools. Therefore, as many black students were drawn away from their local schools and communities, these schools and other community institutions continued to decline as a result of neglect and economic impoverishment.

Yet educational managers and civil rights elites put forward racial integration as the singular goal of education, demanding that it be imposed on public schools at all costs. However, the implementation of various racial integration policies did not result in educational equality for black students. This was the case because educational professionals and civil rights elites overlooked the issue of quality education. As a result, good classroom teaching declined, the fundamental tools of knowledge were abandoned, and positive character building was perverted. Beginning in the 1970s, many school systems turned away from teaching students important values, such as respect for others and self-restraint, which severely distorted the acculturation and socialization functions of schooling.

Moreover, as white flight, and later middle-class black flight, from cities to suburbs accelerated in the late 1960s and 1970s, America allowed its urban areas and their schools to decay and deteriorate. In the process, school regimes bused African American and Latino children to an expanding system of largely white and affluent suburban schools in order to achieve "racial balance." This tactic helped to destroy the sense of community in many urban areas, and inner-city life became increasingly characterized by economic impoverishment, political disenfranchisement, and cultural despair. The consequences of this course of events became evident with the collapse of public education in urban areas across the nation. Ironically, school budgets have continued to rise, along with a growing ossification and inefficiency in urban school bureaucracies.

Adding insult to injury, liberal members of the educational managerial elite rationalized the denial of quality education to black students by applying various theories of cultural deprivation. To observers like Mazique, categorizing African-descended Americans as "culturally deprived" or "culturally disadvantaged" has merely compounded and continued the legacy of cultural domination and the denial of black human dignity that began during the Atlantic slave trade. It is a strategy for keeping the oppressed in a condition of oppression.

These unfortunate educational trends and developments characterized urban and less affluent public school systems in the 1960s and 1970s. Since then, however, even many suburban and more affluent public school systems have experienced an educational crisis. They confront a growing rate of complex problems, including functional illiteracy, violence, increased dropout (and "pushout") rates, discipline problems, drug use, teenage pregnancy, gang activity, and teacher burnout. As a result, generations of young people are being educationally sabotaged in many public schools across America. In his book *Retarding America: The Imprisonment of Potential* (1993), Michael Brunner demonstrates that programmed retardation, and especially the failure to teach young people to read, results in increasing juvenile crime and incarceration.

In the current stage of American postindustrial development, the collapse of public schooling is frightening. Continued public school experimentation—including privatizing strategies or policies supposedly designed to "leave no child behind"—has not proved successful in big-city school systems. Yet in the emerging society, knowledge and the management of people are supplanting money and manufacturing as the only sources of political and economic power. Resisting the professional-managerial class' cultural domination and intellectual imperialism requires that people come to view knowledge and its utilization as sources of power. Learning, therefore, needs to be understood as a lifelong project and an indispensable investment for social development. Educational credentials will more and more be the key to a person's role in society. However, more than the possession of certificates and diplomas will be required to put one's knowledge into practice. Knowledge-based performance and decision making will be the necessary attributes of the educated person.

To many observers, a generation or more of urban African American and Latino students have been betrayed by the U.S. educational system, and their educational underdevelopment is undercutting their ability to survive and develop in a postindustrial society grown cynically indifferent to social suffering. To overcome a looming educational crisis, America will need to devise and implement a national educational strategy, guided by the principle that in the new age of knowledge, science, and technology, investment in quality educational advancement is the very foundation of national development and competitiveness.

SEE ALSO Brown v. Board of Education, *1954; Desegregation, School; Education, Unequal; Educational Quality; Race and Education; Resegregation of Schools; Segregation, School; Tracking in Schools*

BIBLIOGRAPHY

Berman, Morris. 2006. *Dark Ages America: The Final Phase of Empire*. New York: W. W. Norton.

Brunner, Michael S. 1993. *Retarding America: The Imprisonment of Potential.* Portland, OR: Halcyon House.

Friedman, Thomas L. 2006. *The World Is Flat: A Brief History of the Twenty-First Century.* Updated ed. New York: Farrar, Straus and Giroux.

Hayes, Floyd W., III. 1990. Race, Urban Politics, and Educational Policy-Making in Washington, D.C.: A Community's Struggle for Quality Education. *Urban Education* 25 (3): 237–257.

Mazique, Jewell R. C. 2000. Betrayal in the Schools. In *A Turbulent Voyage: Readings in African American Studies*, 3rd ed. Ed. Floyd W. Hayes III, 392–398. San Diego, CA: Collegiate Press.

Floyd W. Hayes III

PROGRAMMING, LINEAR AND NONLINEAR

The need for extremal values (maxima or minima) of a function whose variables might have to satisfy certain constraints leads to a problem of *optimization*. In its most general form, an optimization problem is ordinarily expressed as maximize $F(x)$ subject to $x \in X$, the symbol $\in$ standing for "is an element of." Posing the problem in terms of maximization is not restrictive since $\min_{x \in X} F(x) = -\max_{x \in X}\{-F(x)\}$.

Such extremal problems are classified according to the mathematical properties of the *objective function F* and the *feasible region X*. The optimization problem is said to be *feasible* if and only if its feasible region is nonempty. This entry will restrict attention to the case where X is a subset of a finite-dimensional vector space, say Euclidean n-space, E^n so that $x = (x_1, x_2, ..., x_n)$ denotes a vector of n variables. Problems of this sort are also called *mathematical programs*, and their study is called *mathematical programming*. When $X = E^n$, the problem is said to be *unconstrained*. Finding relative minima and maxima in elementary differential calculus ordinarily deals with unconstrained optimization problems on the real line. In advanced calculus, one encounters multivariate unconstrained optimization. A related problem class is that in which X is the solution set of a system of equations $g_i(x) = 0$, $i = 1$, m. Symbolically, $X = \{x: g_i(x) = 0, i = 1, ..., m\}$. When suitable differentiability and linear independence conditions hold, optimization problems of this form can be handled by the *method of Lagrange multipliers*, an approach dating back to the eighteenth century (long before the term *programming* was used).

LINEAR PROGRAMMING

Among constrained optimization problems, the linear programming problem is the leading representative. *Linear programming* (LP) can be described as the problem of maximizing a linear function F over a polyhedron X. This means that the objective function has the form $F(x) = c_1x_1 + ... + c_nx_n$, where $c_1, ..., c_n$ are given constants, and the *polyhedron X* is the set of solutions of a system of *linear inequalities*, say:

$$a_{i1}x_1 + ... + a_{in}x_n \leq b_i, \quad i \in \mathcal{I}_1 = \{1, ..., m\}. \tag{1}$$

In many practical applications, the variables x_j are required to satisfy $x_j \geq 0$. Such a nonnegativity constraint is equivalent to $-x_j \leq 0$, a special case of (1).

Economics is the foremost social science field of application for LP (and nonlinear programming as well). The optimal allocation of scarce resources is a typical example. For instance, suppose a firm manufactures n products from m resources. Each unit of product j consumes a_{ij} units of resource i, of which there are b_i units available. It is assumed that the consumption of the resources by product j is proportional to the level x_j of the corresponding production activity; it is assumed further that the consumption effects are additive. In that case, the total amount of resource i consumed by the n production levels $x_1, x_2, ..., x_n$, is $a_{i1}x_1 + a_{i2}x_2 + ... + a_{in}x_n$, and each of these sums must not exceed the amount available, namely b_i. The unknown production levels x_j are naturally nonnegative. Finally, it is assumed that the aim is to maximize the profit resulting from the production and that it is of the form $p_1x_1 + p_2x_2 + ... + p_nx_n$. Thus, the optimization problem is:

$$
\begin{aligned}
\text{maximize} \quad & p_1x_1 + p_2x_2 + ... + p_nx_n \\
\text{subject to} \quad & a_{11}x_1 + a_{12}x_2 + ... + a_{1n}x_n \leq b_1 \\
& a_{21}x_1 + a_{22}x_2 + ... + a_{2n}x_n \leq b_2 \\
& \qquad\qquad \vdots \qquad\qquad\qquad \vdots \\
& a_{m1}x_1 + a_{m2}x_2 + ... + a_{mn}x_n \leq b_m \\
& x_j \geq 0, \quad j = 1, 2, ..., n
\end{aligned} \tag{2}
$$

In some instances, it is appropriate to introduce other linear constraints in (2). These could be *output requirements* $a_{i1}x_1 + a_{i2}x_2 + ... + a_{in}x_n \geq b_i$, $i \in I_2$, or *material balance equations* $a_{i1}x_1 + a_{i2}x_2 + ... + a_{in}x_n = b_i$, $i \in I_3$. What results is still a linear programming problem.

Two historically important cost-minimization problems illustrate further applications of linear programming in economics and planning. The first of these is called the *diet problem*, which calls for a plan whereby a given set of nutritional requirements can be met from a given set of ingredients at minimum cost. In this case, one has nutritional requirements $r_1, r_2, ..., r_m$ for vitamins, minerals, calories, and so on. These requirements are to be met by combining appropriate amounts of n ingredients $j = 1, \ldots,$ n having unit costs $c_1, \ldots, c_n$, respectively. Each unit of ingredient j contributes a_{ij} units of nutrient i. The proportionality and additivity of these contributions is assumed. Thereby, the problem can be stated as:

$$
\begin{aligned}
\text{minimize} \quad & c_1 x_1 + c_2 x_2 + \ldots + c_n x_n \\
\text{subject to} \quad & a_{11} x_1 + a_{12} x_2 + \ldots + a_{1n} x_n \geq r_1 \\
& a_{21} x_1 + a_{22} x_2 + \ldots + a_{2n} x_n \geq r_2 \\
& \qquad \vdots \qquad\qquad\qquad \vdots \\
& a_{m1} x_1 + a_{m2} x_2 + \ldots + a_{mn} x_n \geq r_m \\
& x_j \geq 0, \quad j = 1, 2, \ldots, n
\end{aligned}
$$

The formulation can be modified by including constraints such as upper bounds on the amounts of individual ingredients. This model is widely applied in making animal feed.

The second of these applications is called the *transportation problem:*

$$
\begin{aligned}
\text{minimize} \quad & c_{11} x_{11} + \ldots + c_{mn} x_{mn} \\
\text{subject to} \quad & x_{i1} + \ldots + x_{in} \leq a_i, \quad i = 1, \ldots, m \\
& x_{1j} + \ldots + x_{mj} = d_j, \quad j = 1, \ldots, n \\
& x_{ij} \geq 0, \quad i = 1, \ldots, m, \quad j = 1, \ldots, n
\end{aligned}
$$

which arises in the context of shipping but, in fact, finds use in other areas as well. In this case, a single commodity is to be "shipped" from m "origins" to n "destinations." At origin $i = 1, \ldots, m$, there is a supply of a_i units of the commodity. At destination $j = 1, \ldots, n$, there is a demand for d_j units of the commodity. To meet the demands from the supplies it is necessary that $a_1 + \ldots + a_m \geq d_1 + \ldots + d_n$. The cost of shipping a unit of the commodity from i to j is denoted c_{ij}. Under the assumption of linearity, the cost of shipping x_{ij} units of the commodity from origin i to destination j will be $c_{ij} x_{ij}$. The total cost is $c_{11} x_{11} + \ldots + c_{mn} x_{mn}$. The *assignment problem* is a special case of the transportation problem in which $m = n$ and $a_i = d_j = 1$ for all i and j. Feasibility considerations then force the "≤" inequalities to hold as equations. The assignment problem arises in both minimization and maximization situations.

In addition to the aforementioned applications, one finds the computation of optimal mixed strategies in finite, two-person, zero-sum (matrix) games, problems of optimal blending, electric power dispatch, manpower planning, investment planning, and many more. Such topics are covered in George B. Dantzig's *Linear Programming and Extensions* (1963).

Standard Form For computational purposes, the constraints of a linear program are usually expressed as a sys-

tem of linear equations in nonnegative variables. This is called *standard form*. Any legitimate linear program can easily be brought to standard form. Thus $a_{i1} x_1 + \ldots + a_{in} x_n \leq b_i$ becomes $a_{i1} x_1 + \ldots + a_{in} x_n + s_i = b_i$, with $s_i \geq 0$, and $a_{i1} x_1 + \ldots + a_{in} x_n \geq b_i$ becomes $a_{i1} x_1 + \ldots + a_{in} x_n - s_i = b_i$, with $s_i \geq 0$. Any variable x_j that is not sign-restricted can be replaced by the difference of two nonnegative variables: $x_j = x'_j - x''_j$. A variable x_j constrained to be nonpositive can be replaced by $x_j^- = -x_j$.

Duality To every linear programming problem there corresponds a *dual problem* constructed from the same data used in a different way. The dual problem is again a linear program whose form depends on that of the given problem, which in this relationship is called the *primal problem*. Thus, if the primal problem is (2), the dual problem is:

$$
\begin{aligned}
\text{minimize} \quad & b_1 y_1 + b_2 y_2 + \ldots + b_m y_m \\
\text{subject to} \quad & a_{11} y_1 + a_{21} y_2 + \ldots + a_{m1} y_m \geq p_1 \\
& a_{12} y_1 + a_{22} y_2 + \ldots + a_{m2} y_m \geq p_2 \\
& \qquad \vdots \qquad\qquad\qquad \vdots \qquad\qquad (3) \\
& a_{1m} y_1 + a_{2m} v_2 + \ldots + a_{mn} y_m \geq p_n \\
& y_i \geq 0, \quad i = 1, 2, \ldots, m
\end{aligned}
$$

The dual of a linear program in standard form is like (3) except for the fact that its variables y_i are *free* (not sign-restricted).

These (and other) pairs of primal and dual linear programs are intimately linked in the following way.

Duality Theorem of Linear Programming Let X and Y denote the feasible regions of (2) and (3), respectively. Then

$$
p_1 x_1 + \ldots + p_n x_n \leq b_1 y_1 + \ldots + b_m y_m \qquad (4)
$$

for any $x \in X$ and any $y \in Y$. If equality holds in (4), then x and y are optimal solutions of their respective programs. Moreover, the primal problem has an optimal solution $\bar{x}$ if and only if the dual problem has an optimal solution $\bar{y}$; when this is the case, equality holds in (4). If the feasible regions X and Y are both nonempty, then both problems have optimal solutions. If only one of the two problems is feasible, then the objective function of that problem is unbounded in the direction of extremization.

Simplex Method The general formulation of the linear programming problem and the *simplex method* for its solution were advanced by the American mathematician George B. Dantzig (1914–2005) in 1947. This method continues to be the main algorithm for solving problems of this class.

The simplex method works with linear programs in standard form and takes advantage of the fact that in order to find an optimal solution, it suffices to confine attention to the vertices of the polyhedral feasible region, X. Starting from a known vertex of X, the method generates a path along the edges of X as it moves from one vertex to an adjacent vertex. As long as "cycling" does not occur, the process is guaranteed to terminate after visiting finitely many vertices. When the algorithm finds an optimal solution of the primal problem, it reveals an optimal solution of the dual problem as well. However, it may happen that a vertex of X is not known in advance and will have to be found. Techniques are available for finding a vertex of X (if one exists) and for preventing cycling.

Sensitivity Analysis The optimal value of the objective function of an LP, say (2), depends on the input-output coefficients a_{ij}, the right-hand side constants b_i, and the objective function coefficients p_j. The study of how changes in these parameters affect the optimal value is called *sensitivity analysis* or *postoptimality analysis*. The most frequently used fact emerging from this kind of analysis is that (in the nondegenerate case) the rate of change of the optimal value z with respect to a change in the ith right-hand side parameter b_i equals the dual variable y_i corresponding to the ith constraint; in symbols $\partial z / \partial b_i = y_i$.

Large-scale Linear Programming Many practical applications engender very large-scale models, often running to tens or hundreds of thousands of equations and a million or more variables. Solving large-scale problems requires powerful computers and specialized algorithms that often exploit the structure of the coefficient matrix corresponding to the constraints. The decomposition principle of Dantzig and Philip Wolfe (1960) is of this type. It is intended for problems with block-angular structure in which there are many organizational units whose corresponding variables appear in a relatively small number of coupling constraints that represent the central administration and otherwise only in constraints that pertain to that unit.

NONLINEAR PROGRAMMING

An optimization model with an objective function or at least one constraint function that is not linear is called a *nonlinear programming problem* (NLP).

Nonlinearity can arise in many ways, thereby yielding diverse types of NLPs. The oldest and easiest to comprehend are *quadratic programming* problems, wherein the constraints are just like those of an LP but the objective

function is quadratic (rather than linear). The first to identify (and name) this problem class was the economist Robert Dorfman (1916–2002) in his monograph *Application of Linear Programming to the Theory of the Firm* (1951). In analyzing production scheduling for monopolized products, the assumption of constant marginal production costs may not hold. As the monopolist's production increases, it may begin to saturate the market, thereby lowering the price at which products can be sold. Alternatively, the monopolist can restrict production in order to uphold the price of the product. Dorfman's model covers those cases where the firm produces m monopolized products jointly and where it faces linearly decreasing marginal revenues. When the prices at which the products can be sold are decreasing linear functions of the outputs y_i such as $p_i(y_i) = f_i - g_i y_i$, where f_i and g_i are positive constants, the revenue from the sale of the output vector $y = (y_1, \ldots, y_m)$ is $\sum_{i=1}^{m} f_i y_i - g_i y_i^2 = (f_1 y_1 - g_1 y_1^2) + \ldots + (f_m y_m - g_m y_m^2)$.

The inputs to the n production processes are assumed to be $x_1, \ldots, x_n$ measured in monetary units. The input-output relations are assumed to be given by the linear equations $y_i = \sum_{j=1}^{n} h_{ij} x_j$, $i = 1, \ldots, m$. The sum of the x_j represents the cost of the production, so that $\sum_{i=1}^{m} (f_i y_i - g_i y_i^2) - \sum_{j=1}^{n} x_j$ is the profit resulting from an expenditure of $\sum_{j=1}^{n} x_j$ on the production. The equations $y_i = \sum_{j=1}^{n} h_{ij} x_j$ permit one to substitute for the y_i thereby obtaining the objective function in terms of the x_j alone. The x_j might need to satisfy linear constraints, such as (2). The result is then a linearly constrained maximization problem with a quadratic objective function, that is, a quadratic program.

Sometimes optimization problems arise in purely technical settings. For instance, it is often necessary to minimize the *distance* from a point $\bar{x}$ to a set X. When the measure of distance is the Euclidean metric and the set in question is defined through a system of linear inequalities, the resulting problem is a quadratic program with objective function:

$$\sum_{j=1}^{n} (x_j - \bar{x}_j)^2. \tag{5}$$

Convexity and Convex Programming One of the most important concepts in linear and nonlinear programming is that of *convexity*. A set X is said to be *convex* if it contains the entire line segment between any two of its points. The *line segment* between the points u and v in a real vector space is $\{x : x = \lambda u + (1 - \lambda)v, \text{ for all } 0 \leq \lambda \leq 1\}$. All polyhedral sets (1) are easily seen to be convex. A function f defined on a convex set X is said to be convex there if the inequality $f(\lambda u + (1 - \lambda)v) \leq \lambda f(u) + (1 - \lambda)f(v)$ holds for all vectors $u, v \in X$ and all scalars λ satisfying $0 \leq \lambda \leq 1$.

All linear functions are convex. A notable example of a nonlinear convex function is the quadratic function given in (5). The nonnegatively weighted sum of a finite number of convex functions is again convex. A *concave function* is one whose negative is convex. In minimization problems, it is desirable to have a convex minimand defined on a convex set, in which case the problem is called a *convex program*. (In the case of maximization problems, one would analogously prefer a concave maximand defined on a convex set. Such problems are called *concave programs*.) The main reason for this is that local minima (maxima) in convex (concave) programs are global minima (maxima). This property need not hold in so-called *nonconvex programs*.

FIRST-ORDER OPTIMALITY CONDITIONS

In all optimization problems, it is essential to have a clear, testable definition of what is meant by the (local) optimality of a candidate solution to the problem. Since LPs and NLPs normally have infinitely many feasible solutions, it is important to know what extra conditions must be satisfied by those that are (locally) optimal. In the case of linear programming—where the simplex method is used—one essentially has information that reveals whether passage from a particular vertex to any adjacent vertex will improve the objective function value. If not, the vertex yields an optimal solution. This information is obtained by checking the signs of certain numbers in the algebraic representation of the problem.

In nonlinear programming, the matter is far less simple. A major tool used for finding a local minimum is the following result.

Theorem (Karush-Kuhn-Tucker Theorem) Suppose $\bar{x} = (\bar{x}_1, \ldots, \bar{x}_n)$ is a local maximum for the nonlinear program

maximize $\qquad F(x_1, \ldots, x_n)$

subject to $\qquad g_i(x_1, \ldots, x_n) \leq 0, \quad i = 1, \ldots m$ $\qquad$ (6)

and that the functions $F, g_1, \ldots, g_m$ are differentiable at $\bar{x}$. If the gradients $\nabla g_i(\bar{x})$ of the constraint functions at $\bar{x}$ satisfy a suitable regularity condition (one such being linear independence of the gradients), then there exist multipliers $y_1, \ldots, y_m \geq 0$ such that

$$\nabla F(\bar{x}) = y_1 \nabla g_1(\bar{x}) + \ldots + y_m \nabla g_m(\bar{x}) \qquad (7)$$

$$y_i g_i(\bar{x}) = 0, \quad i = 1, \ldots, m \qquad (8)$$

Collectively, (7) and (8) are called the *Karush-Kuhn-Tucker (KKT) conditions*. Because $g_i(\bar{x}) \leq 0 \leq y_i$ for each i, the conditions (8) imply that at least one of y_i and $g_i(\bar{x})$ must be zero. Accordingly, these are called *complementary slackness conditions*. The *stationarity condition* (7) then says

that, at a local maximum, the gradient of the objective function is a linear combination of the gradients of the constraints for which $g_i(\bar{x}) = 0$; the corresponding y_i are called *generalized Lagrange multipliers*.

It bears repeating that when the assumptions of the KKT theorem hold, conditions (7) and (8) necessarily hold. Since these assumptions do hold in most instances, the KKT theorem provides a mechanism for seeking candidate local maxima. In the absence of further hypotheses, it is not guaranteed that a solution of the KKT conditions will be a local maximum of the NLP. However, when the objective function and the constraint functions are all concave, a solution of the KKT conditions must be a global maximum of the optimization problem. In this instance, the KKT conditions are necessary and sufficient for the global optimality of $\bar{x}$. Beyond the first-order optimality conditions given above, there exist second-order optimality conditions, but the discussion of such matters exceeds the scope of this entry.

Lagrangian Duality Relative to (6) with feasible region X, there is the corresponding Lagrangian function $L(x, y) = F(x) - \sum_{i=1}^{m} y_i g_i(x)$.

From the Lagrangian function, one defines the *Lagrangian dual problem*, which calls for minimizing the function $\varphi(y) = \sup_{x \in X} L(x, y)$. An immediate consequence of this definition is $\sup_{x \in X} F(x) \leq \inf_{y \geq 0} \varphi(y)$. If $F(x) = \varphi(y)$ where $x \in X$ and $y \geq 0$, then x and y are optimal for their respective programs. R. Tyrrell Rockafellar's *Convex Analysis* (1970) gives a comprehensive theory of duality for convex programming.

Nonlinear Programming Algorithms Nonlinear programs can differ greatly in the mathematical properties possessed (or lacked) by the functions through which they are defined. Examples of such properties include convexity and differentiability. NLPs whose constraint functions are *affine*, that is, of the form $a_{i1}x_1 + \ldots + a_{in}x_n - b_i$ for $i = 1, \ldots, m$, constitute a special class of which the quadratic programming problem is a notable member. Another property is that of problem structure: Some are very large and "sparse"; others are small and "dense." A dense problem is one in which each of the functions actually depends on a high percentage of the total set of variables. Some nonlinear programs include (linear or nonlinear) equations among the constraints. The methods used to solve NLPs tend to take advantage of problem characteristics, and for this reason, differ greatly from one another. Even so, they share some common properties.

A common feature of mathematical programming algorithms is their iterative nature. Starting from a trial solution x^0, a sequence of trial solutions $x^1, x^2, \ldots$ is generated until one of them, say x^k satisfies a specified criterion indicating that it is an (approximately) optimal solution or that some other reason for halting the process holds. The steps of the algorithm constitute the process by which one passes from a given iterate to its successor. In some cases, this may entail the solution of one or more optimization subproblems. For linear programming and certain instances of quadratic programming, there are algorithms that generate a *finite* sequence of trial solutions ending with an optimal solution or evidence that none exists. Algorithms for nonlinear programming are more often *convergent* than finite. When the KKT theorem is applicable, the matter of finding a solution boils down to solving a system of equations (for which numerical methods are available). But before this can be done, it is necessary to try to identify exactly which equations need to be solved. The optimality conditions, and especially the information provided by Lagrange multipliers, play a large part in algorithmic strategies.

SEE ALSO *Hamilton's Rule; Linear Systems; Manifolds; Matrix Algebra; Maximin Principle; Maximization; Minimization; Nonlinear Systems; Objective Function; Optimizing Behavior*

BIBLIOGRAPHY

Dantzig, George B. 1963. *Linear Programming and Extensions.* Princeton, NJ: Princeton University Press.

Dantzig, George B., and Mukund N. Thapa. 1997. *Linear Programming 1: Introduction.* New York: Springer.

Dantzig, George B., and Philip Wolfe. 1960. Decomposition Principle for Linear Programs. *Operations Research* 8: 101–111.

Dorfman, Robert. 1951. *Application of Linear Programming to the Theory of the Firm.* Berkeley: University of California Press.

Fiacco, Anthony V. 2001. Nonlinear Programming. In *Encyclopedia of Operations Research and Management Science,* 2nd ed., eds. Saul I. Gass and Carl M. Harris, 572–580. Boston: Kluwer.

Gill, Philip E., Walter Murray, and Margaret H. Wright. 1981. *Practical Optimization.* London: Academic Press.

Hillier, Frederick S., and Gerald J. Lieberman. 2005. *Introduction to Operations Research.* 8th ed. Boston: McGraw-Hill.

Nemhauser, George L., Alexander Rinnooy Kan, and Michael J. Todd, eds. 1989. *Optimization.* Amsterdam: North-Holland.

Nocedal, Jorge, and Stephen J. Wright. 1999. *Numerical Optimization.* New York: Springer.

Rockafellar, R. Tyrrell. 1970. *Convex Analysis.* Princeton, NJ: Princeton University Press.

Richard W. Cottle

PROGRESS

Social scientists have historically concerned themselves with identifying patterns in the way people interact with their environment in order to account for factors that enhance both stability and change in society. This concern with the conditions that underlie the preservation and improvement of the human condition made the concept of *progress*—from the Latin *progredior,* meaning "a going-forward" or "advance"—an attractive analytical construct to the nascent social sciences in the nineteenth century.

While some scholars have traced *progress* back to classical Greece and Rome, most agree that, as an organizing concept in the social sciences, the concept derives its full meaning from specific developments in modern Europe. These included the growth of the physical sciences and theories of knowledge since the seventeenth century; the concern of eighteenth-century social philosophers with political, economic, and social reforms; and the influence of the biological model of evolution and a secular philosophy of history in the nineteenth century.

As early as the eighteenth century, the idea of progress marked a growing confidence in what many then believed to be the unlimited potential of science and human reason to create favorable conditions for improved human life. Following Auguste Comte's *positivism,* which sought to extend the empirical method of the natural sciences to the study of social processes, *progress* came to epitomize the conviction that, as in nature, developments in society were regulated by innate laws. Through a scientific study of society, these laws could be deduced and their interactions with other social phenomena could be modified to ensure a desired social outcome. On the one hand, this meant that civilization was moving through cumulative stages of improvement so that even catastrophes like wars, epidemics, and earthquakes came to be viewed as temporary reversals, even necessary evils, in a movement to a happy ending. On the other hand, it implied that human beings, equipped with scientific knowledge, could alter this movement to influence the quality or quantity of the end product. Social institutions such as schools, prisons, and hospitals serve this purpose of complimenting natural laws to enhance the knowledge, morality, and health of members of society. In his *The Idea of Progress: An Inquiry into Its Origin and Growth,* Irish historian John Bagnell Bury (1861–1927) famously captured the optimism of this view by defining *progress* as the belief that "civilization has moved, is moving, and will move in a desirable direction" (1920, p. 2).

Most importantly, *progress* provided the social sciences with a rational solution to the old problem concerning the causes, mechanisms, and ends of social change. Where in earlier times change was generally dreaded and attributed to chance or supernatural intervention, it would thenceforth be viewed positively as the outcome of processes that could both be predicted and objectively verified. There were ideological differences among social scientists concerning the mechanisms of social change. For social conservatives like Auguste Comte (1798–1857), change proceeded in an orderly manner through rational interventions by an elite class of social engineers, while for radicals like Karl Marx (1818–1883), change was attributed to class conflicts. This general understanding of *progress* as both law-governed and subject to human manipulation remained central in the social sciences up to the twentieth century.

Contrary to the atmosphere of optimism that attended the birth of modern social institutions, however, world events in the twentieth century gave rise to strong doubts about the desirability of the direction of human civilization. Two world wars, particularly the atrocities in Nazi Germany, and a succession of liberation wars in European colonies led to such intellectual and political criticism of *progress* that by the middle of the century the concept had lost its earlier luster. Thus, while in the 1930s sociology textbook series in the United States still included a volume on *progress*, by the late 1940s the historian Sidney Fay (1876–1967), in his article "The Idea of Progress," would declare the concept "logically meaningless" (1947, p. 231). Even the first edition of the *International Encyclopedia of the Social Sciences* (1968) did not include *progress* as a separate entry.

Ironically, reconstruction efforts in the wake of the very events that led to the decline of *progress* invested a new set of concepts with some of the basic assumptions that the obsolescent *progress* had generated. The decolonization movements in the 1960s and 1970s fuelled internal hopes for economic growth, self-determination, and social justice in the former European colonies. In this context, progress meant catching up with former colonizing countries by improving conditions of living through mass education and expanded social service. The economic plight that soon besieged these newly independent countries led to increasing interventions by international financial institutions like the World Bank, with the goal of encouraging growth-focused economic policies. New concepts like *development*, *modernization*, and *structural adjustment* moved in to fill the conceptual space vacated by *progress*.

CONCLUSION: WHAT WENT WRONG WITH PROGRESS?

Criticisms of *progress* both predated and outlived the calamities of the twentieth century mentioned above. They ranged from theoretical challenges of its analytical purchase to political denunciation of the social implications of some of the assumptions it had generated. One of

these assumptions was aptly expressed by the Marquis de Condorcet (1743–1794), who declared in his *Sketch for a Historical Picture of the Progress of the Human Mind* that "the perfectibility of man is truly indefinite" (1793, p. 211). In itself, the notion that human beings can improve is not controversial. It is the idea behind educational institutions. However, the uncritical extension of scientific methods to the study of social life effectively reduced the diffuse and fluid interactions of everyday life to patterned behavior. If human behavior follows a determinant blueprint whose laws can be identified, does this mean we can socially engineer people to behave in certain ways and not others? In the context of fascist regimes and other forms of dictatorships in the twentieth century, the question was more than merely rhetorical.

Some philosophers and historians of science have also pointed out that science and reason are themselves not disinterested tools of knowledge but they can be used to perpetrate prejudice and domination. In the wake of Nazi theories of racial superiority, for instance, the earlier suggestion by the eugenicist Francis Galton (1822–1911) that social conditions could be created to ensure improved racial characteristics in future generations created fears of racial genetic profiling and contributed to the decline of eugenics as a science.

Cultural evolution, or the idea that whole cultures develop along a line of progressive improvement from barbarism to modern civilization generated the assumption that European cultures were at the apex of this cultural progress. On the basis of this assumption, European colonization of other people was often justified as a humanitarian mission to accelerate or guide their civilization. The idea, central to *progress*, of a universal history or of history as driven by a single universal norm also generated the assumption that people in other parts of the world existed outside history until the arrival of Europeans on their shores.

Another important aspect of *progress* was the emphasis on rationality and scientific thought, which put human beings at the center of social progress as its rational movers. Earlier critics of this humanist assumption had attributed social progress to nonhuman forces, such as the structured relations of social classes for Marx and the social division of labor for Émile Durkheim (1858–1917). In art, literature, philosophy, and social sciences, other critics have portrayed the human being as alienated, insecure, fragile, brutal, emotional, and as just one part of a complexly structured reality. *Progress* as an analytical concept developed in an environment in which men were generally assumed to be the standard bearers of the human species. Feminist critics have highlighted the fact that ideas about the "unity of humankind" and "perfectibility of human beings" were held contemporaneously with practices and beliefs that denied political rights to women.

While *progress* generated some questionable assumptions, it also highlighted our collective capacity to improve the conditions of our lives. Among its advocates were people like the American philosopher and educator John Dewey (1859–1952), who emphasized that progress meant improving the efficiency of social institutions that are set up to meet the needs of all members of society.

SEE ALSO *Development; Modernization; Positivism*

BIBLIOGRAPHY

Bury, John Bagnell. 1920. *The Idea of Progress: An Inquiry into Its Origin and Growth.* London: Macmillan.

Comte, Auguste. 1974. *The Essential Comte: Selected from* Cours de Philosophie Positive. Ed. Stanislav Andreski. Tran. Margaret Clarke. New York: Barnes and Noble.

Fay, Sidney. 1947. The Idea of Progress. *American Historical Review* 52 (2): 231–246.

Lasch, Christopher. 1991. *The True and Only Heaven: Progress and Its Critics.* New York: Norton.

Zolani Ngwane

PROGRESSIVE MOVEMENT

The Progressive movement is a broad label for the various economic, social, and political reform movements that took place in the United States between 1900 and 1914. Given the diversity among the reform efforts proposed or undertaken during this period, many scholars have disputed whether in fact this period should be treated as one common movement. It is true that many progressive Americans at the turn of the century supported a wide variety of reforms with different and sometimes irreconcilable goals. Nevertheless, the tendency to regard this period as a common whole is generally justified by the fact that the majority of reformers identified the same problems in America despite the wide variety of solutions they proposed. Throughout the Progressive Era, a common concern sets the tone for nearly every discussion of economic, social, and political policy: an uneasiness in the population brought about by the dramatic development of modern industry and the material and social changes it wrought in the lives of average citizens. Because of the substantial changes incurred from the emergence of large-scale mass production, the centralization of industry, the demand for greater specialization in labor, and the rise of new modes of transportation and communication, the landscape of the nation seemed suddenly transformed from a simple country of small, tightly knit communities into a complex giant of interspersed economic activities. In this new environment, the relationship of the individual to the broader economic, social, and political community took on an entirely new form.

As the United States entered the twentieth century, many progressives argued that the nation's institutions and fundamental beliefs about the nature of government lagged behind the country's dynamic economic and social growth. Railroad development had extended to nearly 200,000 miles and engulfed the nation in a dense network of trunk lines that had transformed its relatively autonomous communities and states into a single body of fluid commerce. According to many progressives, democracy had not kept pace with the national economic development of the industrial era due to its outdated understanding of federalism and the system of constitutional checks and balances. Many progressives thought that doctrines such as federalism, property rights, and separation of powers had rendered governments so inept that when state legislatures did pass regulations they proved harmful to both customers and the efficiency of business and industry, particularly railroad operations. Federal land grants to railroads and farmers during the late 1800s, made with very few contingencies out of deference to federalism, had led to reckless speculation by farmers and land owners, leaving the natural resources of the country in disarray. The rise of mass production in the steel, lumber, flour, textile, and meat industries had a major economic impact on the services provided by artisans, local mills, and jobbers, demanding an entirely new breed of legislation and regulation to handle the complex arrangements of modern industry.

The difficulty in regulating these corporations was most dramatically expressed in the case of *United States v. E. C. Knight Co.* (1895). Although E. C. Knight, a Philadelphia-based sugar-refining company, had consolidated nearly 98 percent of the nation's sugar production, the U.S. Supreme Court held that refining was manufacture, not commerce, and thus could not be regulated under the interstate commerce clause of the U.S. Constitution. Distinctive to the Progressive Era was the belief that these obstacles to reform were not the result of temporary misjudgments by legislators or judges, but permanent defects in the institutional arrangements of American government.

From the political dilemma of government in a postindustrial age, progressivism developed along two lines: reformers bent on accomplishing concrete changes in the American system of government on the local, state, and federal levels, and intellectuals concerned with providing a revised notion of political life based on a new conception of human nature. As an intellectual movement, the Progressive Era was an intensely active period of new ideas among a diverse body of thinkers from many fields of expertise. Despite their differences, almost all of these intellectuals raised doubts about the fundamental tenets of American political thought. In contrast to the fixed principles of human nature—the self-evident truths of equality and rights articulated in the Declaration of Independence—the progressives believed that a basic understanding of human nature involved a more fluid conceptual framework, such as the concepts implied in Charles Darwin's (1809–1882) theory of evolution.

The impact of Darwin's *Origin of Species* (1859) in social theory had raised serious questions about whether human beings were indeed created equal and endowed from birth with certain "unalienable rights." Social Darwinists, as they came to be known, denied that human nature could be understood from such axiomatic principles, and some even challenged the fundamental political maxim that followed: governments derive their just powers from the consent of the governed. Enamored of the concept of natural selection and "survival of the fittest," a new generation of scholars following the seminal work of William Graham Sumner (1840–1910) argued that political life ought to be geared toward the elevation of more talented individuals over less gifted or educated members of society, regardless of individual consent. Thinkers like the economist Irving Fisher (1867–1947), Sumner's doctoral student at Yale, had even made the case for eugenics and the sterilization of the mentally infirm. Others, like John Dewey (1859–1952), while concurring with the basic premise of social Darwinism, contended that survival depended not on the elevation of certain individuals, but on a collective effort by all to overcome threats posed to the collective interests of the whole.

This theoretical debate over human nature had implications for the political direction of the reform movements. While some progressive intellectuals believed that the emergence of powerful corporations constituted a positive development, in which more-efficient entities capitalized on their superior capability over less-efficient organizations and modes of production, others argued that these corporations presented a challenge to the common welfare. Such a challenge could only be met by reforms in law and the country's institutions of government.

THE ACHIEVEMENTS OF PROGRESSIVISM

While it is true that progressives never achieved the passage of constitutional amendments that equaled the breadth of their criticism, the movement did manage to spur a number of significant reforms at the local, state, and national levels of government. Such reforms sought to bring American government to a level of parity with the modernization that had taken place within civil society.

Municipal Reforms Progressivism was initially most successful at the level of municipal reform. Many American cities during the early twentieth century suffered from mismanagement and corruption. Under the control of party bosses and public utility magnates, city aldermen were often the stooges of special privilege rather than the guardians of urban health and safety. Through a series of reform efforts, urban dwellers managed to eliminate the most obtrusive corruption in their cities. Citing partisan politics as the main obstacle to triumph over corruption, many municipalities introduced such progressive reforms as the initiative, the referendum, and the Australian ballot to encourage greater civic participation and weaken the strong arm of political bosses. Other cities, however, took more dramatic steps during this period by replacing potentially corruptible politicians in city government with so-called nonpartisan experts in urban management.

These two approaches to municipal reform illustrate how the movement's diverse and even contradictory efforts aimed at solving the same problems. Some progressives hoped to eliminate corruption through increased democratic methods, such as the initiative. Others embraced the new methods of scientific management codified by Frederick W. Taylor (1856–1915), author of *The Principles of Scientific Management* (1911), a work that spurred a movement for greater efficiency and expertise in all aspects of American life, including politics, as illustrated in such municipal reforms as the adoption of the post of city manager. While the above proposals differed, they shared the common view that democratic politics as traditionally practiced in the United States had led to corruption under the new demands of modern industrialism.

State Reforms Though less successful than municipal reformers, progressives at the state level could boast of major accomplishments in a number of states. As Wisconsin governor from 1901 to 1906, Robert M. La Follette (1855–1925) was probably the nation's most ambitious progressive reformer, championing such state causes as railroad rate reform, procedural reforms in the legislature, progressive taxation, the open primary system, and the direct election of U.S. senators. William S. U'Ren (1859–1949) pioneered the use of the initiative, recall, and referendum in Oregon, while Hiram Johnson (1866–1945) in California successfully campaigned for the popular election for U.S. senators and to permit candidates to register with more than one political party. Other states achieved numerous reforms aimed at greater efficiency in the administration of state governments, particularly in the area of executive and bureaucratic reorganization. By adopting higher standards for admission to civil service positions and organizing administrative offices in state government to attract greater expertise, many states were able to reduce waste and corruption, which had been an obstacle to the effective regulation of their economies.

Federal Reforms While progressivism did not produce the realignment in national politics that many political leaders had hoped for, the period did compile an impressive record of legislation at the federal level. These reforms would redefine relations between the national government and the country's economy.

One of the most notable transformations in the role of the government in the nation's economy began in 1902 as Theodore Roosevelt's (1858–1919) administration pioneered the federal conservation reform movement under the Newlands Restoration Act (1902), which empowered the federal government to regulate the country's natural resources with the help of experts in resource management. Like many progressive reforms, proponents of these changes also hoped to use the conservation movement as a means of introducing nonpartisan scientific expertise into the government's management of the economy. Under Roosevelt, and later even more vigorously under Howard Taft (1857–1930), the trusts that had for years operated in violation of the antimonopoly provisions of the Sherman Antitrust Act (1890) were prosecuted by the federal government. By 1914 the Sherman Antitrust Act was strengthened by the passage of the Clayton Antitrust Act (1914), which prohibited discriminatory pricing, conditional sales intended to dilute competition, mergers and acquisitions that inhibit competition, and interlocking directorates. Like the reforms in conservation, the Clayton Antitrust Act was designed to incorporate nonpartisan expertise into the government's regulation of the economy. To enforce the provisions of the Clayton Antitrust Act, Congress created the Federal Trade Commission (FTC) in 1914. The FTC would be staffed with five commissioners appointed by the president, with the advice and confirmation of the Senate. Rather than specifying the type of anticompetitive activities that would be prohibited, as the Sherman Antitrust Act had done, the FTC was granted the power to determine what kind of activity was harmful to the interests of the national economy, and could regulate accordingly.

Between 1903 and 1906 the federal government also made progress toward mitigating concerns over the power of the railroads and their discriminatory practices in favor of big business. In 1903 Congress passed the Elkins Act, which prohibited rebate schemes responsible for discriminatory shipping prices that angered economically disadvantaged farmers. In 1906 Theodore Roosevelt

successfully negotiated the passage of the Hepburn Bill, which gave the Interstate Commerce Commission power to set maximum railroad rates. Besides remedial legislation addressing economic inequalities among the public, the federal government also began protecting the health and safety of consumers. Congress passed the Meat Inspection Act (1906), which required health inspections for food-processing plants, and the first Food and Drug Act (1913), which required companies to clearly label the ingredients and contents of their products.

Not only did government expand its reach within civil society during this period, it also released its grip on foreign trade, in contrast to previous regulations that had worked to the disadvantage of consumers. Under the administration of Woodrow Wilson (1856–1924), Congress repealed much of the tariff support for American industries with the passage of the Underwood Tariff (1913), which stripped many industries of the economic advantages they enjoyed under the former system.

Although constitutional reforms fell far short of progressive aspirations, two important amendments were passed during this period. Both the Sixteenth Amendment establishing Congress's power to legislate for an income tax and the Seventeenth Amendment for the direct election of U.S. senators were ratified in 1913. Establishing a progressive income tax fit the long-term reform goal of equalizing the burden of federal revenue and easing the sectional antipathy that had arisen from debates over the tariff. The direct election of senators satisfied the more democratic strain of progressivism, which aimed at introducing greater democratic participation into the choosing of the nation's elected officials; reformers hoped that politicians who were beholden to party machines in state legislatures would be removed from office.

Despite its achievements, progressivism ultimately waned as a movement in the United States when the public's attention shifted to the international concerns of World War I (1914–1918). Another explanation for the demise of the movement may have been its breadth as an umbrella for many different types of reform. Unable to identify a coherent purpose among the many ideas for political reform in the age of industrial modernization, progressives could not sustain the public attention necessary to effectuate a major realignment in American politics.

SEE ALSO *Antitrust; Antitrust Regulation; Eugenics; Fisher, Irving; Inequality, Wealth; Labor Union; Modernization; Monopoly; Populism; Progressives; Public Health; Railway Industry; Regulation; Sanitation; Social Movements; Suffrage, Women's; Taylorism; Urbanization; Wilson, Woodrow*

BIBLIOGRAPHY

Buenker, John D. 1973. *Urban Liberalism and Progressive Reform.* New York: Scribner.

Crunden, Robert Morse. 1982. *Ministers of Reform: The Progressives' Achievement in American Civilization, 1889–1920.* New York: Basic Books.

Dewey, John. 1935. *Liberalism and Social Action.* New York: Putnam.

Eisenach, Eldon J. 1994. *The Lost Promise of Progressivism.* Lawrence: University Press of Kansas.

Ekirch, Arthur Alphonse. 1974. *Progressivism in America: A Study of the Era from Theodore Roosevelt to Woodrow Wilson.* New York: New Viewpoints.

Forcey, Charles. 1961. *The Crossroads of Liberalism: Croly, Weyl, Lippmann, and the Progressive Era, 1900–1925.* New York: Oxford University Press.

Hays, Samuel P. 1995. *The Response to Industrialism, 1885–1914.* 2nd ed. Chicago: University of Chicago Press.

Hofstadter, Richard. 1944. *Social Darwinism in American Thought, 1860–1915.* Philadelphia: University of Pennsylvania Press.

Hofstadter, Richard. 1955. *The Age of Reform: From Bryan to F. D. R.* New York: Knopf.

Kloppenberg, James T. 1986. *Uncertain Victory: Social Democracy and Progressivism in European and American Thought, 1870–1920.* New York: Oxford University Press.

Noble, David W. 1981. *The Progressive Mind, 1890–1917.* Rev. ed. Minneapolis, MN: Burgess.

Sklar, Martin J. 1988. *The Corporate Reconstruction of American Capitalism, 1890–1916: The Market, the Law, and Politics.* New York: Cambridge University Press.

Wiebe, Robert H. 1967. *The Search for Order, 1877–1920.* New York: Hill and Wang.

J. David Alvis

PROGRESSIVE TAXES

SEE *Taxes, Progressive.*

PROGRESSIVES

Progressives are people who strive to make government and society better—more democratic, more inclusive, and fairer. Toward this end, progressives engage in a broad range of activities aimed at reforming economic, social, and political institutions and processes. The term *progressive* encompasses a diverse and difficult–to–characterize variety of groups and ideologies. In general, progressives are activists who thrived during two periods in American history: The first progressive period ran from the 1890s to the 1920s; the second ongoing progressive period began in the 1960s.

THE PROGRESSIVE ERA

America's first period of progressivism, known as the Progressive Era, came at the height of industrialization and urbanization in the United States. Although the goals and the types of reforms that progressives sought during this period differed, perhaps nothing characterizes the Progressive Era better than the impulse to reform. At the time, the United States was characterized by the increasing dominance of large corporations and political party machines, which progressives perceived as a threat to the American ideals of democracy and individual freedom. Corporate dominance inhibited the capacities of the vast majority of Americans to achieve social mobility, and urban-based political party machines were seen as corrupting the democratic process.

In response, progressives challenged laissez-faire ideology by arguing that good government could help solve problems. Progressives promoted, often successfully, a long list of reform legislation at all levels of government, including regulation of railroads, public utilities, and banks; laws protecting women and child laborers; and the passage of workers' compensation and minimum-wage legislation. Progressives also worked for a progressive income tax; relief for the poor; a host of electoral reforms, including the direct election of senators, direct primaries, referendums, and recalls; voting rights for women; nonpartisan election systems; civil service; and commission-manager and council-manager forms of local government. Such reforms aimed at strengthening popular sovereignty and produced significant and lasting results, even if some reforms did not lead to intended outcomes.

Progressivism had its roots in the populist movement of the late nineteenth century, as well as the struggles for equality for women and better living conditions for workers. Similar to the response of radical agrarian and working-class groups during the Gilded Age, progressives targeted many of the same problems wrought by industrialization, urbanization, and immigration: the spread of poverty, rapid financial and industrial concentration, and the oligarchic character of the political parties.

As the power of corporations expanded and social strife spread, middle-class social workers established settlement houses and other programs to ameliorate human degradation in city slums. Muckrakers, or investigative journalists, illuminated the corruption of corporate influence in politics and society. Religious groups promoted a social gospel that raised concerns about poverty, corruption, and the concentration of economic power and called on the moral conscience of the nation. Labor unions and workers organized to improve wages and working conditions, and to make business more responsible through regulation. Women organized against child labor, in support of a minimum wage and a maximum number of working hours, and in favor of temperance. Even businessmen joined progressives in attacking political machines and promoting reform regimes. Thus, progressivism included professionals who undermined the foundations of laissez-faire ideology and promoted an ideal of public interest.

Yet progressivism was an uneasy coalition and not a cohesive movement. Progressivism during this period actually encompassed numerous movements for reform on the local, state, and national levels. These movements were diverse and sometimes even mutually antagonistic. Some progressives, such as socialists, sought fundamental change and structural reform to achieve social justice. Other progressives, such as middle-class professionals, strove for social order and more modest reform. Similarly, Protestant patrician reformers differed in their goals, approach, and sensibilities from Catholic, immigrant, and urban liberal progressives. There were also overtly reactionary groups involved in Progressive Era reform efforts, including eugenicists and antiblack and anti-immigrant groups. Thus, the Progressive Era was an ideologically fluid period where particular groups focused on different issues, and shifting coalitions competed to reshape American society. Despite their varying agendas, shared ideals of antimonopolism, efficiency, and social justice propelled and sustained the diverse progressive reform coalitions.

For example, new types of professionals members of an emerging middle class, and members of religious organizations and business groups—pressed for reforms that focused in particular on urban America. These progressives strove to undermine big-city political machines, which had in many cities retained the loyalty of immigrant working-class voters. Middle-class reformers regarded political machines as inefficient and corrupt, and they attacked the use of government resources as patronage—whether in the form of jobs for loyal party workers and supporters, or the distribution of municipal franchises, licenses, and contracts to favored businesses, sometimes in exchange for graft. Protestants attacked the tolerance of urban politicians for gambling, prostitution, and liquor, vices that offended middle-class sensibilities. The faith of progressives in scientific organizational principals led them to propose independent governmental institutions staffed by nonpartisan experts.

Labor and radical socialist groups attacked political machines for other reasons, such as the practices of allowing business groups to dominate economic policymaking and using police forces to break strikes. These socialist progressives fought to rein in corporate power and broaden government authority to improve education,

expand social and municipal services, and advance social justice.

More often, however, progressive reform outcomes represented the interests of middle- and upper-class Americans. Middle-class reformers undermined working-class political power by backing the creation of independent commissions and boards that eliminated important powers from city councils and aldermen (city council members). These reformers also advocated the election of officials from neighborhood-based wards and the establishing of at-large schemes of political representation. Middle- and upper-class progressives also revised city charters and promoted new forms of government that shifted power to higher levels that they could more easily influence. Such reforms included implementing a commission form of government and a city-manager system. Some reform efforts during this period also reflected middle-class bigotry. Anti-immigrant groups, for example, were responsible for drastically reducing the flow of newcomers that could enter the United States and restricting the proportion of non–Western European immigrants allowed to enter. Advocates of eugenics employed pseudo-scientific methods in their reform efforts.

Despite the antibusiness stance of most progressives, they rarely questioned the basic structure of capitalist principals as vigorously as working and radical groups did. On the contrary, when the expansion of the public interest implied extending democracy to social as well as economic life, many progressives were ambivalent. Worker- and socialist-led movements, however, pushed the progressive critique further.

Politically, progressives allied themselves with particular factions of both the Democratic and Republican parties. Some progressive activists also mounted independent and third-party challenges. At the national level, progressives rallied behind Teddy Roosevelt (1858–1919) in 1912 as he ran for a second full term as president, this time as an independent under the Progressive Party ("Bull Moose") banner. During his campaign, Roosevelt championed greater regulation of capitalism. In 1924 Robert M. La Follette Sr. (1855–1925), a U.S. senator from Wisconsin, ran for president as the Progressive Party candidate. La Follette, whose politics were more left wing, called for public ownership of the railroads during his campaign. Overall, progressives were more successful at the state and local levels, where they succeeded in electing members of the U.S. Congress, including Moses P. Kinkaid of Nebraska and Hiram W. Johnson of California, as well as scores of state legislators, and city officials.

The Progressive Era left an enduring legacy. Progressives promoted an ethos for harnessing government power to promote the public interest, which laid the foundation for the active participation of government in solving social problems that would emerge during the 1930s and 1940s in the New Deal of Franklin D. Roosevelt (1882–1945). Many of the changes to law and government structures born during the Progressive Era remain in force at the beginning of the twenty-first century.

CONTEMPORARY PROGRESSIVES

Like their historical counterparts, the progressives who emerged during and after the 1960s criticize the concentration of economic and political power and engage in a broad range of activities aimed at making the economy more democratic and government more representative, responsive, and accountable. To achieve these goals, progressives fight against inequality and for social justice, and seek to foster ways ordinary citizens can more directly participate in decision making and self rule at all levels.

Contemporary progressives are associated with the social movements of 1960s, including the civil rights, Black Power, antiwar, youth, and countercultural movements, as well as later movements centered on women's rights, labor, the environment, immigrant and human rights, gay and lesbian rights, antiglobalization and global justice, and peace. Contemporary progressives often try to form connections among the various struggles, an orientation embodied in a popular slogan: "think globally, act locally."

Many progressives embrace left-wing or radical ideologies, including Marxism and anarchism. Many contemporary American radicals prefer the term *progressive* because it is safer and more palatable than *socialist* and *communist*. Contemporary progressives contend that a better future is possible, and they strive to create a radically egalitarian, community-controlled world that meets human needs through environmentally sustainable development. They target multinational corporations and international institutions, such as Wal-Mart and the World Trade Organization (WTO), and they engage in a variety of tactics to achieve their goals, from lobbying and nonviolent civil disobedience to militant protest and outright rebellion. Their efforts often incorporate new communications technology, and they have developed innovative strategies and political savvy.

In many ways, these contemporary progressive organizations model a progressivist vision in that they are comprised of many participants with few leaders. In addition, progressive coalitions embody groups that have not always seen eye to eye, including labor union members, immigrants, civil rights leaders, anti-sweatshop activists, environmentalists, human rights advocates, socialists and anarchists, and middle-class professionals. Progressives have spearheaded campaigns to achieve living-wage laws, advance public health, provide affordable housing, and

protect the public sector and space. Contemporary progressives cross borders and continents, and are made up of participants from both the developing and developed worlds. They criticize the prevailing philosophy that governments should make way for the free market's invisible hand, arguing that free trade is not always fair trade. In short, progressives attempt to think—and more importantly, act—beyond present-day predicaments, and they strive for a stronger democracy with greater citizen involvement in problem solving. Only then, they believe, will real equality and social justice be achieved.

Politically, American progressives have formed or allied themselves with various third political parties, including the Green Party, the Reform Party, and the Labor Party. These groups have supported such independent-minded candidates as Ralph Nader, Bernard Sanders, Paul Wellstone, Barbara Boxer, and Dennis Kucinich.

SEE ALSO *Gilded Age; Populism; Progressive Movement*

BIBLIOGRAPHY

Alinsky, Saul David. 1946. *Reveille for Radicals.* Chicago: University of Chicago Press.

Berg, John C. 2002. *Teamsters and Turtles? U.S. Progressive Political Movements in the 21st Century.* Lanham, MD: Rowman and Littlefield.

Brecher, Jeremy, Tim Costello, and Brendan Smith. 2000. *Globalization from Below: The Power of Solidarity.* Boston: South End.

Fink, Leon, ed. 2001. *Major Problems in the Gilded Age and the Progressive Era: Documents and Essays,* 2nd ed. Boston: Houghton Mifflin.

Freeman, Jo, and Victoria Johnson, eds. 1999. *Waves of Protest: Social Movements Since the Sixties.* Lanham, MD: Rowman and Littlefield.

Hofstadter, Richard, ed. 1963. *The Progressive Movement: 1900–1915.* Englewood Cliffs, NJ: Prentice-Hall.

McGerr, Michael. 2003. *A Fierce Discontent: The Rise and Fall of the Progressive Movement in America.* New York: Free Press.

Shepard, Benjamin, and Ronald Hayduk. 2002. *From ACT UP to the WTO: Urban Protest and Community Building in the Era of Globalization.* New York: Verso.

Weibe, Robert. 1962. *Businessmen and Reform: A Study of the Progressive Movement.* Cambridge, MA: Harvard University Press.

Ronald Hayduk

PROLETARIAT

The English word *proletariat* is derived from the Latin *proletarius*, first used in the sixth century BCE to designate a census category encompassing those without property, who it was supposed could only contribute their sons to the state (proles=offspring). The Latin term (and its equivalents in other languages) came to refer to the poorest class of nonslaves and to paupers. In the early nineteenth century, however, proletariat began to acquire a more precise meaning, and by the 1830s it was often used to refer to the newly emerging class of wage laborers in capitalist societies, formed by the expulsion of much of the peasantry from the land.

MARX'S THEORY

It is in this more precise sense of those who do not possess their own means of production, and who must therefore labor for others for a wage in order to make a living, that political philosopher Karl Marx (1818–1883) began to use the term in the 1840s. Marx saw the proletariat as a "universal class," in the sense that its social position drives it toward the overthrow of capitalist relations of production, which he believed would bring about the end of all forms of exploitation and oppression, and thus universal human emancipation.

Marx wrote in the Communist Manifesto, "Society as a whole is more and more splitting up into two great hostile camps, into two great classes directly facing each other: bourgeoisie and proletariat" (Gasper 2005, p. 40). The bourgeoisie, or capitalist class, consists of the relatively small number of people who own or control the means of creating wealth—including land and raw materials; mines, factories, and offices; machinery and technology—and who can employ wage laborers to work for them. Proletarians perform most of the work in capitalist economies, but they have little or no control over their work-lives or over the wealth that they produce. The relationship between the bourgeoisie and the proletariat is an exploitative one because the latter is paid less than the value that its labor creates, with the surplus being kept by the bourgeoisie. While wages may rise if workers are well organized and during periods of economic growth, competition between capitalists compels employers to reduce labor costs as much as possible, particularly during recurring periods of capitalist economic crisis.

During Marx's lifetime, wage laborers constituted a majority of the working population only in Great Britain, some other parts of northern Europe, and the northeastern seaboard of the United States, with the vast majority of the world workforce still peasants engaged in small-scale rural production. Today, by some estimates, wage laborers are a majority of the world's population. However, it was less its size than its structural and strategic location that made the proletariat important for Marx. Marx believed that antagonism with the bourgeoisie leads proletarians to organize themselves into trade unions and other forms of association. Because workers in modern

capitalism are concentrated in urban centers and in large workplaces, they have enormous social and economic power when organized, exhibited in their ability to bring whole economies to a halt through the weapon of the mass strike. By contrast, what Marx called the lumpenproletariat (literally the proletariat in rags, i.e., those sections of the population permanently or near-permanently excluded from the workforce), lacks this power and is therefore not a revolutionary class, although it is more oppressed than the proletariat. Even where wage laborers are a minority, their structural position gives them the ability to draw wider social circles into struggle under their leadership, including the majority of the peasantry.

In the course of the struggle to protect their interests, proletarians are repeatedly led to challenge bourgeois institutions (for instance, by ignoring legal restrictions on strike action) and to question the general framework of bourgeois ideas that confers legitimacy on the status quo. As the movement develops, Marxist theory contends that class-consciousness increases among workers and narrow economic demands give way to broader political ones. At the same time, divisions within the class—based on sectional interests, nationality, race, ethnicity, and so on—will tend to be overcome. If carried to a successful conclusion, this process will culminate in the revolutionary overthrow of the bourgeoisie. The proletariat will replace the bourgeoisie as society's ruling class and begin instituting changes that will gradually lead to the elimination of class divisions entirely.

CRITICISMS OF MARX AND THE PROLETARIAT TODAY

Critics generally raise two kinds of objection to Marx's account of the proletariat. One is that the proletariat in Marx's sense has declined in importance as capitalism has developed. It is certainly true that the structure of the workforce in developed capitalist countries has changed dramatically since the mid-nineteenth century, and the proportion of factory and manufacturing workers has been declining for decades. But while Marx often emphasized the role of the industrial proletariat, this is only one segment of the capitalist working class, and as its relative size has shrunk, the size of other segments has grown. Moreover, segments of the workforce that had not previously been regarded as parts of the working class (such as teachers and office workers), have found their work increasingly routinized and controlled by their employers, and have often unionized in response. It should also be noted that on a global scale the number of industrial workers is greater than ever, and that even in developed countries they may continue to play a disproportionately important role in the working-class movement.

The second objection is that wage laborers, at least in the advanced capitalist world, have benefited enormously from economic growth, and—even if still technically exploited—no longer have an interest in the revolutionary overthrow of capitalism, if they ever did. Contemporary Marxists acknowledge the large rise in living standards, although they are likely to emphasize the role of class struggle in achieving them and the fact that they are far from evenly distributed. More importantly, they argue that the gains should not be regarded as permanent, that capitalism is inherently unstable, and that its continued turbulence will bring about new economic, social, and environmental crises. On this view, it is because such crises are unavoidable, and because they will make life for the majority of wageworkers unacceptable, that the proletariat retains its revolutionary potential.

SEE ALSO *Capitalism; Lumpenproletariat; Marx, Karl; Marx, Karl: Impact on Economics; Marxism; Revolution; Surplus; Unions; Wages; Working Class*

BIBLIOGRAPHY

Braverman, Harry. 1974. *Labor and Monopoly Capital*. New York: Monthly Review Press.

Draper, Hal. 1978. *Karl Marx's Theory of Revolution, Vol. II: The Politics of Social Classes*. New York: Monthly Review Press.

Gasper, Phil, ed. 2005. *The Communist Manifesto: A Road Map to History's Most Important Political Document*. Chicago: Haymarket Books.

Philip Gasper

PROLIFERATION, NUCLEAR

Although recent events pose serious challenges to international efforts to limit the global spread of nuclear weapons, the nonproliferation regime is by many measures a great success. Despite pessimistic past projections that the world would by now contain twenty, thirty, or more nuclear weapons states, only three countries have joined the five nuclear weapons states acknowledged by the nuclear Non-Proliferation Treaty (NPT) in 1968 in openly declaring their status. As the cornerstone of international efforts to limit the spread of nuclear weapons, the NPT is unusual in two respects. First, in contrast to virtually all international treaties, it is discriminatory by design. The treaty recognizes and locks in inequality by regulating access to powerful weapons. Second, despite inequalities in rights and obligation, membership has grown to make the NPT the most widely ratified arms-control agreement in history, with 187 parties. In 2006,

the only countries in the world remaining outside the treaty were India, Israel, and Pakistan (although North Korea declared its withdrawal in 2003). However, in recent years the regime has faced its greatest challenges, ranging from the potential emergence of new nuclear weapons powers to the apparent disinterest of the United States in the NPT.

THE NUCLEAR NON-PROLIFERATION REGIME

The impetus for the NPT grew out of dissatisfaction with the "Atoms for Peace" policies promoted by U.S. president Dwight D. Eisenhower's administration during the 1950s. Under this program the United States offered unrestricted access to nuclear fuel in exchange for the promise that it be used only for peaceful purposes. The Atoms for Peace framework established the core bargain that would underpin the NPT: Countries that give up the military potential of the atom should be able to enjoy the full peaceful benefits of it. Oversight tasks were vested in a United Nations (UN) agency created to monitor Atoms for Peace transfers: the International Atomic Energy Agency (IAEA).

However, shortcomings in the Atoms for Peace/IAEA framework soon became apparent. By focusing only on nuclear materials transferred explicitly under specific agreements, the arrangement neglected to regulate technology, material, and knowledge developed indigenously (or copied from transferred material). At the initiative of the United States, Soviet Union, and United Kingdom, a new framework designed to monitor and regulate all nuclear material was negotiated. This became the nuclear Non-Proliferation Treaty, which opened for signatures in 1968 and entered into force in 1970. A grand bargain forms the core of the NPT: In exchange for forgoing nuclear weapons, nonnuclear weapons states gained access to technology necessary for nuclear energy and secured a commitment from the nuclear weapons states "to pursue negotiations in good faith" aimed at nuclear disarmament. The treaty thus strives to stem both horizontal proliferation (the spread of weapons beyond the five nuclear weapons states acknowledged by the treaty: the United States, Soviet Union, United Kingdom, France, and China) and vertical proliferation (by reducing the arsenals of these five). Article X of the treaty allows a party to withdraw from the treaty if "extraordinary events" jeopardize the "supreme interests of its country." All other parties of the treaty and the UN Security Council must be notified three months prior to withdrawal. The NPT has a supply-side orientation aimed at regulating the use of nuclear technology, with relatively little concern for reducing the demand for nuclear weapons. To the extent that states desire nuclear weapons to gain security and prestige, the NPT does relatively little.

SAFEGUARDS AND EXTENSION OF THE TREATY

The NPT established a set of international safeguards to obstruct the diversion of nuclear material and technology from energy to weapons programs. Administered by the IAEA, safeguards entail the monitoring and inspection of material and facilities declared by the signatory state. Iraq exposed the loophole in this arrangement by limiting its weapons-related activity to clandestine, undeclared facilities that remained outside the IAEA's inspection regime. To close this loophole, the IAEA obtained an expanded legal mandate in the form of an additional protocol providing inspectors with the authority to visit any and all facilities, declared or not. First available for signature in 1997, the Additional Protocol remains voluntary; members are encouraged, but not required, to sign. As of 2006, 78 Additional Protocol agreements are in force, and 110 states have signed them.

Although central to the treaty, safeguard arrangements are not backed by an effective enforcement mechanism. The IAEA itself can only suspend technical assistance to a country in violation of its safeguard agreements. To pursue stricter measures, the IAEA must refer a noncomplying country to the UN Security Council, which can choose to impose further sanctions. These range up to and include military intervention if action is taken under Chapter VII of the UN charter, which permits military intervention by other states in the face of a threat to international peace and security. However, the difficulty of achieving consensus in the Security Council—where each of the five nuclear weapons states (NWS) holds a veto—makes vigorous enforcement unlikely.

India's "peaceful nuclear explosion" in 1974 exposed another weakness in the NPT-based nonproliferation regime by demonstrating that nuclear technology transferred for peaceful uses could easily be misused. In response the United States proposed forming the Nuclear Suppliers Group (NSG), a group of nuclear technology exporters that seeks to control the export of nuclear materials, equipment, and technology. Growing from an initial membership of seven in 1975 to forty-five in 2006, the NSG had the advantage of including countries not party to the NPT (at the time of its origin including France, who, along with China was given NWS status but had refused to sign until 1992) and regulating exports to all countries. However, Pakistan's nuclear weapons program revealed two shortcomings in the NSG: National exports were weak at blocking transfer of subcomponents, and

countries varied widely in the vigor with which they regulated exports.

In 1995 after month-long negotiations, the NPT extension conference adopted a motion to extend the treaty indefinitely. Although successful, the negotiations revealed divisions among members, most notably dissatisfaction among many non-nuclear powers at the limited progress of the NWS in reducing their own arsenals. Responding to these concerns, the conference adopted a "Principles and Objectives" calling for the completion of a Comprehensive Test Ban Treaty, the conclusion of a fissile material cut-off treaty, and the "determined pursuit" by the NWS of efforts to reduce nuclear arsenals. The extension conference also established a strengthened review process in which conferences to promote full implementation are held at five-year intervals. The first review conference in 2000 called once again for the "unequivocal undertaking" by the NWS of steps toward reducing their nuclear arsenals. Divisions among members had grown so great by the time of the 2005 review conference that members were unable even to agree on an agenda.

POST–COLD WAR CHALLENGES

The immediate aftermath of the cold war brought both peril and promise in terms of the spread of nuclear weapons. The collapse of the Soviet Union created three new nuclear powers overnight in 1991, as Belarus, Kazakhstan, and Ukraine inherited the nuclear weapons that had been stationed in their territories. Moreover, many scholars believed that the combination of security guarantees and restraint provided to their allies by the United States and the Soviet Union during the cold war had limited the spread of nuclear weapons. Removal of these guarantees and restraints, it was feared, might increase the demand for nuclear weapons. Finally, economic distress, rampant crime, and widespread corruption in Russia fed fears that some of its 27,000 nuclear weapons and large stock of weapons-grade uranium and plutonium would find their way to either terrorists or non-nuclear states.

Yet in the first years after the cold war, the promise seemed to outweigh peril. Belarus, Kazakhstan, and Ukraine all returned their weapons to Russia and joined the NPT. South Africa, which had accumulated a small nuclear arsenal, renounced its weapons and joined as well. France and China joined in 1992. And in response to the revelations of Iraq's circumvention of the safeguard regime, NPT members strengthened inspections, established the Additional Protocol, and extended the treaty indefinitely. Finally, North Korea's attempt to leave the NPT and acquire nuclear weapons appeared defused by the 1994 Agreed Framework accord with the United

States. Contrary to most expectations, by the mid-1990s there were still only five overt nuclear powers (although Israel, India, and Pakistan had unacknowledged weapons capabilities), the number of countries pursuing weapons was falling, and the NPT had become nearly universal.

CURRENT PROSPECTS

Recent years have seen new challenges emerge, exposing weaknesses in the nonproliferation regime. The decision of India and Pakistan to test nuclear weapons in 1998 heightened concerns about the three nuclear weapons powers that remain outside the NPT (although Israel does not publicly declare its nuclear weapons status, its nuclear capabilities are widely acknowledged). The three non-NPT nuclear powers are problematic because many countries joined the NPT on the belief that no other countries would openly declare nuclear status. If states successfully retain nuclear weapons outside the treaty, the incentives for members to exercise restraint become ineffective.

The apparent efforts of Iran and North Korea to pursue nuclear weapons from within the treaty pose an even more serious challenge. North Korea detonated a nuclear device in October 2006, and Iran is widely believed to be pursuing nuclear weapons. Both appear to be taking advantage of a key feature of the NPT: Countries can master the nuclear fuel cycle within the treaty and then withdraw to take the final steps in developing nuclear weapons. Obtaining weapons-grade fissile material—highly enriched uranium-235 or plutonium-239—is the only really serious obstacle to developing nuclear weapons. Yet the treaty facilitates mastery of the skills and technology necessary to enrich uranium and to separate plutonium from spent fuel. Once these tasks have been mastered, it is a short step from peaceful activities to producing weapons-grade material. The treaty thus bars countries from making nuclear weapons while providing them with much of the means to do so. Although this tension has long been recognized, no state appears to have pursued this path except North Korea and, perhaps, Iran. If North Korea and Iran acquire an open nuclear weapons capability, it may spur other countries to leave the NPT and also pursue weapons; Japan, South Korea, Saudi Arabia, and Egypt are frequently suggested as possibilities.

The revelation in 2003 that Pakistani nuclear scientist A. Q. Khan, who headed Pakistan's nuclear program for almost twenty-five years, had been running a private proliferation network for the export of nuclear technology exposed further weaknesses in the nonproliferation regime. Most of the efforts to control the spread of nuclear technology, such as the Nuclear Suppliers Group, focus on stopping exports from the most technologically advanced countries. Yet the revelations that Khan ran a network selling everything from centrifuges for enriching

uranium to bomb designs to Iran, Libya, North Korea, and perhaps a fourth country, raised fears that countries in the developing world with diverse capabilities could trade among themselves to bolster their nuclear programs, bypassing export controls. These fears prompted responses from both the United States and the United Nations. The United States announced the Proliferation Security Initiative (PSI), in which participating nations agree to forbid suspect shipments. With more than 70 countries participating by 2007, the PSI, unlike other controls, addresses technology transfer among developing countries. And in 2004 the UN Security Council passed Resolution 1540, which requires all members to establish export and transshipment controls over technology relevant to the development of nuclear, chemical, or biological weapons.

Discovery of the Khan network also heightened fears that nuclear weapons might fall into the hands of terrorist organizations. Similar private sector networks, poorly secured weapons and material in Russia, and North Korea are the most frequently cited possibilities as sources of atomic bombs for terrorists. Analysts are divided on the magnitude of this threat. Although nuclear devices would not help most terrorist organizations achieve their goals, terrorists with apocalyptic beliefs or those bent on meting out severe punishment to enemies may find them attractive, and evidence does suggest that Al Qaeda has a persistent interest (of debatable intensity) in weapons of mass destruction.

Although many of the challenges facing the nonproliferation regime suggest the necessity of revising the NPT, current policies of key states make that task difficult. Many see recent U.S. policies as retreats from commitments made at the 1995 review conference; these policies include the failure to ratify the Comprehensive Test Ban Treaty, the abandonment of the qualified no-first use pledge made by U.S. president Jimmy Carter's administration to NPT members, and the persistent interest in new nuclear weapons designs. In addition, the U.S. invasion of Iraq is widely believed to have spurred proliferation by enhancing the appeal of nuclear weapons in the eyes of insecure regimes. Any bargain to reinvigorate the NPT would require commitment by the United States and the other four NWS to move forward on their commitments to disarmament, and most likely require some kind of agreement on the status of the three nuclear weapons states that remain outside the treaty. Given current policies, achieving agreement on reforms appears difficult, if not impossible.

SEE ALSO *Al-Qaeda; Cold War; Deterrence, Mutual; Terrorism; Weaponry, Nuclear; Weapons of Mass Destruction*

BIBLIOGRAPHY

Braun, Chaim, and Christopher F. Chyba. 2004. Proliferation Rings: New Challenges to the Nuclear Nonproliferation Regime. *International Security* 29 (2): 5–49.

Manning, Robert A., and Zachary S. Davis. 1998. Nonproliferation and Denuclearization. In *The Absolute Weapon Revisited*, ed. T. V. Paul, Richard J. Harknett, and James J. Wirtz, 263–297. Ann Arbor: University of Michigan Press.

Paul, T. V. 2003. Systemic Conditions and Security Cooperation: Explaining the Persistence of the Nuclear Non-Proliferation Regime. *Cambridge Review of International Affairs* 16 (1): 135–155.

Sagan, Scott D. 2000. Rethinking the Causes of Nuclear Proliferation: Three Models in Search of a Bomb. In *The Coming Crisis*, ed. Victor A. Utgoff, 17–50. Cambridge, MA: MIT Press.

Singh, Sonali, and Christopher R. Way. 2004. The Correlates of Nuclear Proliferation. *Journal of Conflict Resolution* 48 (6): 859–885.

Smith, Roger K. 1987. Explaining the Non-Proliferation Regime: Anomalies for Contemporary International Relations Theory. *International Organization* 41 (2): 253–281.

Christopher Way

PROMOTION, EXPORT

SEE *Export Promotion.*

PROMOTION, IMPORT

SEE *Import Promotion.*

PROPAGANDA

Propaganda refers to the use of communication techniques to affect people's thinking and behavior. Any technique or action that attempts to influence the emotions, attitudes, values, beliefs, or actions of a group can be described as propaganda. Typically, propaganda benefits the sponsor and puts the interests of the sponsor above those of the recipient. As an instrument of persuasion and psychological coercion, it seeks to compel the recipient to submit to the will of the sponsor. Propaganda is thus different from education, which seeks to develop independent thinking, and from information, which is based on objective facts.

Many practitioners of propaganda have insisted that they merely transmit "education" and "information." Other euphemisms they use to describe their trade include "public relations," "public affairs," "public communication," "public information," "public diplomacy," "psychological warfare," "psychological operations" (or "psyops"), and "communication." At the end of the twentieth century the word *spin* became a popular and somewhat derogatory euphemism for propaganda.

Propaganda does not necessarily include lies, as many people believe. Often, propaganda involves truthful statements that are presented, or twisted, to serve the interests of the sponsor. In addition, propaganda is not always verbal: Although speeches, articles, leaflets, books, and rhetorical ploys are common forms of propaganda, so too are photographs, films, music, monuments, currency, flags, parades, and symbols. Propaganda also can include deeds—actions calculated to have an impact on the perceptions of others.

Today the word *propaganda* has a negative connotation, but originally it was a Latin term referring to the reproduction of plants and animals. It developed a positive religious association in the seventeenth century, when Pope Gregory XIII created a commission of cardinals (*de propaganda fide*) to spread the Catholic faith in foreign lands. In the next century some English speakers began to use *propaganda* to refer to the spread of political ideals, though not necessarily in a negative way. Many people continue to use the word *propaganda* in a political context, but propaganda need not be a product of a government or political organization. The advertising and public relations industries, for example, conduct propaganda on behalf of businesses and other nongovernmental organizations.

As a technique of persuasion, propaganda has been a feature of human life since the first civilizations were founded. The scope and intensity of propaganda, however, increased dramatically in twentieth century. As the communication and information revolutions gathered steam, governments, businesses, interest groups, and revolutionaries turned increasingly to propaganda to advance their agendas in a crowded marketplace of ideas. At the turn of the twentieth century many elite observers expressly advocated the use of propaganda as an instrument of social control. Theorists such as Gustave LeBon (1841–1931) and Walter Lippmann (1889–1974) issued alarmist warnings of a coming age of "mass society." Fearing that an uninformed public (which they called the "herd") would undo the social fabric of society, they suggested that elites should manipulate images and symbols to control the masses.

World War I marked an especially notable turning point in the history of propaganda. It was widely perceived as a "total war": an all-encompassing battle for national survival that demanded the mobilization of all the nation's resources. All the major governments involved in the conflict developed propaganda bureaus to mobilize their publics for total war. The armies of the belligerents also developed sophisticated techniques of psychological warfare to demoralize enemy soldiers. Much of the war's propaganda consisted of wild exaggerations, crude images, and stories of atrocities. Warring governments played up nationalistic and patriotic sentiments while at the same time demonizing their enemies as barbaric savages. One of the most famous propaganda episodes of the war was a fabricated story circulated by British agents claiming that Germans were using human corpses to make soap. When the United States joined the war on the side of the Allies in 1917, President Woodrow Wilson added a peculiarly idealistic character to the propaganda by selling the war as a fight for democracy that would end all wars.

In the aftermath of World War I popular suspicion of propaganda as a technique increased, and many ordinary people came to use the word *propaganda* as a synonym for *lies*. The negative connotation was furthered by the conspicuous use of propaganda by totalitarian and fascist regimes in the 1920s and 1930s. The communist government in the Soviet Union, the fascist government in Italy, and the National Socialist regime in Germany all relied on propaganda techniques to come to power, to legitimize their rule, and to facilitate expansionist ventures abroad.

World War I also helped to stimulate the professionalization of propaganda techniques in democracies. The public relations and advertising professions ballooned into massive independent industries in the 1920s and 1930s. Most of the leaders in these fields developed their expertise working for government propaganda bureaus during the war. Additionally, more and more academic researchers began conducting serious social science investigations into the management of public opinion. World War II and the Cold War accelerated this trend by funneling money into the scholarly field of communication which emerged, in large part, from government-sponsored research into public opinion management.

Perhaps the most famous propagandist in history was Joseph Goebbels (1897–1945), who disseminated Adolf Hitler's doctrine of racial supremacy in Nazi Germany. But probably the most *influential* propagandist was an American: Edward Bernays (1891–1995), the so-called "father of public relations." By his example and through his many writings—including the still-consulted *Crystallizing Public Opinion* (1923) and *Propaganda* (1928)—Bernays established the core principles that continue to be used in propaganda and public relations to this day.

Although the development of propaganda in the twentieth century was tied instrumentally to warfare and national security causes, propaganda techniques have become a reality of modern life. Few political leaders, celebrities, interest groups, businesses, and organizations

go without an image advisor, public relations counselor, or spokesperson—all effectively "propagandists" working to advance the causes of their sponsors.

SEE ALSO *Advertising; Persuasion; Persuasion, Message-based; Politics*

BIBLIOGRAPHY

Bernays, Edward. 1923. *Crystallizing Public Opinion.* New York: Boni and Liveright.

Bernays, Edward. 1928. *Propaganda.* New York: Horace Liveright.

Ewen, Stuart. 1996. *PR!: A Social History of Spin.* New York: Basic Books.

Taylor, Philip M. 1990. *Munitions of the Mind: War Propaganda from the Ancient World to the Nuclear Age.* Glasgow, Scotland, U.K.: William Collins Sons and Company.

Thomson, Oliver. 1999. *Easily Led: A History of Propaganda.* Thrupp, Stroud, U.K.: Sutton.

Kenneth Osgood

PROPENSITY TO CONSUME, MARGINAL

A marginal propensity to consume is, in economics, a change in consumption associated with a change in a factor that determines consumption. The most common use of the term is with respect to income. The concept stems from John Maynard Keynes's (1883–1946) *General Theory of Employment, Interest, and Money* (1936), Book III of which is titled "The Propensity to Consume." Keynes defines the marginal propensity to consume as the change in consumption associated with a change in income (p. 115); later usage has differentiated a number of these propensities.

In elementary Keynesian models of the aggregate economy, the marginal propensity to consume from income determines the *expenditure multiplier*, the amount that total output will increase from an increase in autonomous spending (Keynes emphasizes this point in the *General Theory* immediately below his introduction of the term). If the marginal propensity to consume from income is nine-tenths, a one-dollar increase in autonomous spending will induce an initial increase of ninety cents in consumer spending and income; this ninety-cent increase in income will then induce a further increase of eighty-one cents in consumer spending and income, and so on. The sum of the increases in income will be ten dollars, or the product of the one dollar injection of autonomous spending and the inverse of one minus the marginal propensity to consume from income. Models developed since the *General Theory* have attenuated the value of the multiplier from the very large ones suggested in the early analysis (in full employment models the multiplier will be zero); however, it is still the case that there will be a positive relationship between the multiplier and the marginal propensity to consume from income.

Given the central role of the marginal propensity to consume from income in Keynesian analysis, empirical work on measuring this variable started shortly after the *General Theory* appeared. Early examination of U.S. data, most notably those compiled by Simon Kuznets (1901–1985), suggested that the marginal propensity to consume from income in the short run was substantially less than in the long run. From the 1940s through the 1960s, three broad models of consumer behavior were proposed to explain this divergence. (1) The relative income hypothesis, proposed by James Duesenberry, argued that consumers are reluctant to change their living standards upon experiencing changes in income. Duesenberry maintained that consumption is partly affected by previous peak levels of income. Hence, the marginal propensity to consume out of income will be lower in the short run than in the long run. (2) The permanent income model of Milton Friedman argued that consumers recognize that a very large portion of income changes will be short-lived, or transitory, and will only change spending for those movements that are viewed to be permanent. In the long run, a higher share of income changes will be permanent. (3) The life-cycle model associated with Franco Modigliani (1918–2003) accepted the logic of the permanent income model but modified it to propose that the aggregate marginal propensity to consume out of permanent income would be affected by the distribution of income changes across age groups.

The distinction between the marginal propensities to consume out of permanent and transitory income became of significant policy interest in the United States in the 1960s and 1970s when a number of explicitly "temporary" changes in income taxes were enacted, and others proposed. Research suggests that the consumer spending impact from the enacted temporary tax changes was smaller than from "permanent" tax changes, in line with the idea that the marginal propensity to consume from transitory income is lower than that from permanent income.

More recent studies have noted the anomaly that the propensity to consume from temporary tax changes, while lower than from permanent changes, is considerably higher than theory would suggest. "Liquidity constraints" (the recognition that many consumers are unable to make the costless borrowing adjustments required for the strict permanent income theory to hold) are one plausible explanation for the high propensity. Other research has

emphasized how precautionary saving motives—the need for many households to accumulate financial assets to insure against income losses—can affect the propensity to consume from income changes. The spending of households that need to accumulate precautionary savings will, in general, be more sensitive to purely transitory income changes than theory suggests, thus blurring the distinction between the propensities to consume from permanent and transitory income.

PROPENSITY TO CONSUME FROM WEALTH

The marginal propensity to consume from wealth is the partial derivative of consumer spending with respect to household wealth. The life-cycle model highlights the importance of wealth accumulation for retirement in the household spending and saving decision. This emphasis brought the wealth propensity to prominence. Movements in the value of wealth are, in principle, one-time events that will affect spending through the remainder of a consumer's life. Hence, the marginal propensity to consume from wealth is much smaller than that from income (less than one-tenth from wealth, seven-tenths or higher from permanent income), but given the enormous magnitude of changes in the value of aggregate wealth, even a small number raises the likelihood that major shifts in aggregate consumption could be generated.

The precise size of the aggregate marginal propensity to consume from wealth has been an active issue in the United States since the middle of the 1990s, given the increase in household wealth relative to income and the very large swings in market values. One line of research has emphasized that typically, a disproportionate share of changes in observed wealth (even some movements in wealth persisting for several years) are likely transitory. In other words, a large share of changes in observed aggregate wealth may not factor into consumer spending because households may not believe they will persist indefinitely. In particular, wealth movements that appear inconsistent with other economic developments, such as changes in income or productivity, could be regarded as transitory. Analysts and forecasters should not be assumed to have any special insight into the permanence of currently observed changes in the value of wealth. It follows that applying any estimate based on past experience of the aggregate marginal propensity to consume from wealth to project the spending impact of an observed movement in wealth may be problematic.

SEE ALSO *Absolute Income Hypothesis; Consumption; Economics, Keynesian; Keynes, John Maynard; Multiplier, The; Propensity to Import, Marginal; Propensity to Save, Marginal*

BIBLIOGRAPHY

Friedman, Milton. 1957. *A Theory of the Consumption Function.* Princeton, NJ: Princeton University Press.

Keynes, John Maynard. 1936. *The General Theory of Employment Interest and Money.* New York: Harcourt, Brace.

Ludvigson, Sydney, and Charles Steindel. 1999. How Important Is the Stock Market Effect on Consumption? *Federal Reserve Bank of New York Economic Policy Review* 5 (2): 29–51.

Charles Steindel
Any comments or statements in this entry represent the views of the author only and not necessarily those of the Federal Reserve Bank of New York or the Federal Reserve System.

PROPENSITY TO IMPORT, MARGINAL

The marginal propensity to import is the increase in imports that is caused by a certain increase in income. This concept expresses the idea that as income of economic agents (firms and households) increases, so does their demand for intermediate and consumption goods imported from abroad. Since this relation also holds for the whole economy, at the aggregate level the marginal propensity to import can be calculated as the ratio between the increase in total imports of an economy and the increase in its output. In mathematically formalized economic models, the marginal propensity to import is equal to the partial derivative with respect to output in an import function. If imports are assumed to be a linear function of output, the marginal propensity to import is equal to the slope of the resulting straight line. The concept of the marginal propensity to import is related to the concept of the average propensity to import, which is equal to the ratio of total import to total income.

The marginal propensity to import plays a role in determining the size of the Keynesian multiplier (Blanchard 1997, pp. 232–235). In the Keynesian multiplier model extended to an open economy, some of the increased demand caused by a domestic expansion falls not on domestic goods but on foreign goods. This effect will be bigger, the higher is the marginal propensity to import of the domestic country. In the extreme case in which the additional domestic demand falls completely on imported goods (when the marginal propensity to import is equal to one), the multiplier is equal to one. Empirically, however, the marginal propensity to import is likely to fall between zero and one, which implies a multiplier larger than one even in an open economy. Since imports tend to be equal to a larger share of the economy for smaller countries, the magnitude of the leakage effect

of domestic demand expansions into imports is likely to be inversely related to the country size.

An attractive empirical feature of the concept of marginal propensity to import is that it is easily measurable and can be used to forecast the change in imports stemming from a certain expected change in output. For example, if total domestic output in country *A* increases by 1,000 in a given year, and imports increase by 200 in the same year, the marginal propensity to import is equal to 200/1,000 = 0.2. Assuming that the government expects output to increase by 2,000 in the following year, the projected increase in imports calculated on the basis of the marginal propensity to import is 0.2 × 2,000 = 400. This methodology is obviously based on the assumption that the marginal propensity to import remains constant. This might be a reasonable assumption in the short run. However, the size of the marginal propensity to import is affected by changes in the relative prices of domestic and foreign goods and could therefore change in the long run, or if the economy is hit by a significant exchange rate shock.

SEE ALSO *Balance of Trade; Imports; Multiplier, The; Propensity to Consume, Marginal; Propensity to Save, Marginal; Trade*

BIBLIOGRAPHY

Blanchard, Olivier. 2005. *Macroeconomics*, 4th edition. Upper Saddle River, NJ: Prentice Hall.

Giovanni Ganelli
The opinions expressed are personal and should not be interpreted as reflecting any view of the International Monetary Fund.

PROPENSITY TO SAVE, MARGINAL

In economics, a marginal propensity to save is the additional savings associated with a change in a factor that determines saving. Since saving is the difference between income and consumption, a marginal propensity to save is related to a marginal propensity to consume in a simple fashion. For example, the marginal propensity to save from household income is one minus the marginal propensity to consume from household income, and the marginal propensity to save from wealth is the negative of the marginal propensity to consume from wealth.

Any analytical result regarding marginal propensities to consume can be readily expressed in terms of marginal propensities to save. For example, in simple Keynesian analysis the autonomous expenditure multiplier is equivalently the inverse of one minus the marginal propensity to consume from income and the inverse of the marginal propensity to save from income.

In policy discussions and proposals, distinctions between national and personal saving should be kept in mind in applications of estimates of the marginal propensity to save and other arguments of the saving or consumption function. Numerous proposals have been offered to increase personal saving in the United States through tax or other fiscal incentives increasing the after-tax rate of return available to households. Discussions of these proposals often involve estimates of the responsiveness of household or personal saving to changes in the rate of interest, which is connected to the marginal propensity to save with respect to the rate of return. What is sometimes not emphasized is that a full analysis of these policies likely requires looking beyond the personal propensity to save with respect to the rate of return. For instance, such policies would likely increase after-tax personal income, and the marginal propensity of personal saving with respect to after-tax personal income is surely positive. This effect would add to saving generated through a positive rate of return propensity, or offset a decline in saving generated through a negative rate of return propensity. However, these policies (unless negated by other changes), will also increase government outlays or reduce tax revenue, thus reducing government saving. Hence, the effect on national saving of these policies would be problematic even if personal saving increased.

In sum, knowledge of the marginal propensity of personal saving with respect to the rate of return does not provide complete information about the effect on national saving of policies of this type. If the aim of such policies is to encourage saving by certain groups of people, or the policies are financed from tax revenues or cuts in government outlays, analysis of individual household responses would be adequate. But if the aim is to increase national saving and capital formation, and the policies are financed through increased borrowing, broader analysis would appear to be warranted. The parameters of interest will then be marginal propensities of national, not personal, saving with respect to its arguments.

SEE ALSO *Economics, Keynesian; Propensity to Consume, Marginal*

BIBLIOGRAPHY

Steindel, Charles. 1981. The Determinants of Private Saving. In *Public Policy and Capital Formation*. Washington, DC: Board of Governors of the Federal Reserve System.

Charles Steindel

Any comments or statements in this entry represent the views of the author only and not necessarily those of the Federal Reserve Bank of New York or the Federal Reserve System.

PROPERTIES OF ESTIMATORS (ASYMPTOTIC AND EXACT)

Economic models are useful in making statistical predictions and policy evaluations. These models include statistical mean models, regression models, simultaneous equations models, limited dependent variable models, and panel and spatial models, among others. Based on the sample data, econometric methods are used to estimate these models, and then the testing of relevant economic hypotheses can be conducted. The commonly used estimators are least squares or generalized least squares, maximum likelihood, generalized method of moments, and empirical likelihood. The hypothesis-testing procedures are Wald's, Rao's score, and likelihood ratio methods. Since all these methods are based on sample information, the statistical properties of these procedures are of great interest for both small and large samples. The properties include studying the distribution; unbiasedness, which implies the average value of the difference between a sample estimator and the corresponding population parametric is zero; and efficiency, which means a smaller variability. For large samples, the estimators are consistent if they converge to their true parameter values. In the context of hypothesis testing, a test having a correct size and high power implies the probability of rejecting an assumed economic model when the model is true and not true, respectively. All these have led to the development of *asymptotic theory econometrics* (White 2001) and *finite sample econometrics* (Ullah 2004).

Asymptotic theory provides the properties of estimators and test statistics for large samples. The statistical methods used to develop such properties are the *law of large numbers* and *central limit theorems* (see Chung 2001). There is extensive literature on the asymptotic properties of econometric estimators and test statistics (see White [2001] for linear models; Jennrich [1969] and Gallant [1987] for nonlinear models).

Finite sample econometrics deals with the exact and approximate properties of estimators and test statistics. The exact properties are valid for any size of the sample; however, the derivation of the exact analytical properties is often difficult, especially for the large class of applied economic models that can be nonlinear, nonnormal, or dynamic. Furthermore, even when the analytical exact results are obtained, they are usually expressed in terms of complicated multivariate integrals or infinite series, and they do not provide meaningful interpretations and conclusions (see Ullah 2004). In view of these problems, a vast amount of literature has developed on the approximate analytical properties of estimators and test statistics using the procedures developed by Francis Edgeworth (1896) for distributions and Anirudh Nagar (1959) for moments. The simulation-based approximate properties have also been extensively analyzed, especially using bootstrapping procedures (see Hall 1992; Horowitz 2001). The analytical and simulation-based approximate results can tell us how much we lose by using asymptotic theory results and how far we are from the known exact results.

It is well known that large sample properties may not imply finite sample behavior of econometric estimators and test statistics, and this can give misleading results for small or even moderately large samples. For example, an estimator can be biased for the finite sample but unbiased asymptotically. Also, two estimators may be asymptotically unbiased and have the same variances and asymptotic distributions, but, in the finite sample case, these two estimators may have different biases, variances, and distributions. Thus the statistical inference for the asymptotic case can be quite different compared to the finite sample case. Also, if the asymptotic results are used for small samples, then the conclusions or interpretations of the econometric analysis may be misleading.

R. A. Fisher (1921, 1922) and Harald Cramér (1946) laid the foundations of statistical finite sample theory on the exact distributions and moments. This exact theory on distributions and moments was brought into econometrics by the seminal work of Trygve Haavelmo (1947), T. W. Anderson and Herman Rubin (1949), Leonid Hurwicz (1950), R. L. Basmann (1961), and Peter C. B. Phillips (1983), among others. Another major development took place through Nagar's work (1959) on obtaining the approximate moments of econometric estimators. This was followed by research by J. D. Sargan (1975) and Phillips (1980), who rigorously developed the theory and applications of the Edgeworth expansions to derive the approximate distribution functions of econometric estimators. Most of the contributions, however, were confined to the analytical derivation of the moments and distributions of the econometric statistics with independent and identically distributed (i.i.d.) normal observations. These also included the finite sample results using the Monte Carlo methodology (Hendry 1984) and advances in bootstrapping (resampling) procedures (Hall 1992). The analytical and bootstrap results for models that are nonlinear with nonnormal and non-i.i.d. observations remain a challenging task for future development. Some development has begun to take place for approximate analytical results (see Ullah 2004; Bao and Ullah 2006). Similarly, there are developments in the bootstrapping procedures for studying the properties of estimators with i.i.d. as well as dependent and nonstationary observations (see Horowitz 2001).

The study of asymptotic and finite sample properties is a fundamental issue of statistical inference, since the quality of data-based inference depends on the properties of estimators and test statistics used in the inference. The developments described provide analytical and simulation-based procedures for the properties of estimators and test statistics. The frontier of this research area has moved forward over the years, but some challenging issues remain. With advances in computer technology, this subject will further develop in both the analytical and the bootstrapping domains.

BIBLIOGRAPHY

Anderson, T. W., and Herman Rubin. 1949. Estimation of the Parameters of a Single Equation in a Complete System of Stochastic Equations. *Annals of Mathematical Statistics* 20 (1): 46–63.

Bao, Yong, and Aman Ullah. 2006. The Second-order Bias and Mean Squared Error of Nonlinear Estimators in Time Series. Unpublished Manuscript. University of California, Riverside, 2006.

Basmann, R. L. 1961. Note on the Exact Finite Sample Frequency Functions of Generalized Classical Linear Estimators in Two Leading Overidentified Cases. *Journal of the American Statistical Association* 56: 619–636.

Chung, Kai Lai. 2001. *A Course in Probability Theory.* 3rd ed. San Diego, CA: Academic Press.

Cramér, Harald. 1946. *Mathematical Methods of Statistics.* Princeton, NJ: Princeton University Press.

Edgeworth, Francis Y. 1896. The Asymmetrical Probability Curve. *Philosophical Magazine* 41: 90–99.

Efron, Bradley. 1979. Bootstrap Methods: Another Look at the Jackknife. *Annals of Statistics* 7: 1–26.

Fisher, R. A. 1921. On the "Probable Error" of a Coefficient of Correlation Deduced from a Small Sample. *Metron* 1: 1–32.

Fisher, R. A. 1922. The Goodness of Fit of Regression Formulae, and the Distribution of Regression Coefficients. *Journal of the Royal Statistical Society* 85 (4): 597–612.

Gallant, A. Ronald. 1987. *Nonlinear Statistical Models.* New York: Wiley.

Haavelmo, Trygve. 1947. Methods of Measuring the Marginal Propensity to Consume. *Journal of the American Statistical Association* 42 (237): 105–122.

Hall, Peter. 1992. *The Bootstrap and Edgeworth Expansion.* New York: Springer-Verlag.

Hendry, David F. 1984. Monte Carlo Experimentation in Econometrics. In *Handbook of Econometrics,* vol. 2, eds. Michael Intriligator and Zvi Griliches, 934–976. Amsterdam: North-Holland.

Horowitz, Joel L. 2001. The Bootstrap in Econometrics. In *Handbook of Econometrics,* vol. 5, eds. James Heckman and Edward Leamer, 3160–3228. Amsterdam: North-Holland.

Hurwicz, Leonid. 1950. Least Square Bias in Time Series. In *Statistical Inference in Dynamic Economic Models,* ed. Tjalling C. Koopmans. New York: Wiley.

Jennrich, R. I. 1969. Asymptotic Properties of Nonlinear Least Squares Estimators. *Annals of Mathematical Statistics* 40: 633–643.

Nagar, Anirudh. L. 1959. The Bias and Moment Matrix of the General k-Class Estimators of the Parameters in Simultaneous Equations. *Econometrica* 27 (4): 575–595.

Phillips, Peter C. B. 1980. Finite Sample Theory and the Distributions of Alternative Estimators of the Marginal Propensity to Consume. *Review of Economic Studies* 47 (1): 183–224.

Phillips, Peter C. B. 1983. Exact Small Sample Theory in the Simultaneous Equations Model. In *Handbook of Econometrics*, vol. 1, eds. Michael Intriligator and Zvi Griliches, 449–516. Amsterdam: North-Holland.

Sargan, J. D. 1975. Gram-Charlier Approximations Applied to t Ratios of k-class Estimators. *Econometrica* 43 (2): 327–346.

Ullah, Aman. 2004. *Finite Sample Econometrics.* New York: Oxford University Press.

White, Halbert. 2001. *Asymptotic Theory for Econometricians.* Rev. ed. San Diego, CA: Academic Press.

Aman Ullah

PROPERTY

In the social sciences the concept of property or property rights refers to social mechanisms that control the use of valuable resources and create opportunities and incentives for private and public actors. Those mechanisms have profound consequences for social outcomes and over time are shaped by social outcomes. Many scholars, such as Douglass C. North in his 1990 *Institutions, Institutional Change, and Economic Performance,* use the terms *institutions* and *property* virtually synonymously. Modern social science has borrowed the concept from law but typically refers to real or de facto control of resources rather than formal legal or de jure control, which is the usual legal connotation. Law, moreover, gives property a narrower interpretation than does social science. In law, property is only one of several legal control mechanisms, which include tort law, criminal law, antitrust law, and constitutional law. In social science, property (or institutions) refers to all formal control mechanisms (rules and their enforcement) as well as informal ones such as social norms and ideologies.

THE VARIETY OF PROPERTY RIGHTS

A scarce resource or asset usually has mutually exclusive uses as well as compatible uses. A pasture cannot be used simultaneously as a shopping center, although various other uses are not excluded automatically. The grazing function of pastures often is not affected when aircraft use the airspace above, transportation tunnels are dug below, hikers cross the area on foot, and passing trains emit noise and vibrations. Property rights to a resource can be unified or partitioned by use.

A fundamental problem arises when a specific use of resource A interferes with the use of resource B by creating unwanted costs for the owner of B. Airplanes and automobiles often disturb the peace of homeowners, and factories pollute their surroundings. Uncompensated physical impact (known as negative or positive spillover or external effects) in principle is due to weak or absent property rights. Homeowners, for instance, have incomplete control (property rights) of the air they breathe and the sound waves that penetrate their residences.

Property consists of bundles of rights. In 1996 Elinor Ostrom and Edella Schlager identified five elements of rights to natural resources that appear in various bundles: access, rights to hike or canoe, for instance, but excluding rights to withdraw resource units; withdrawal, such as the right to catch fish or divert water; management, the right to maintain, improve, and transform a resource; exclusion, the right to decide who has access and withdrawal rights and how those rights are transferred; and alienation, the right to lease or sell exclusion and management rights.

Property systems vary with the ways in which categories of rights are divided and users and/or controllers are organized. The concept of public property has little meaning unless one identifies the exact bundle of rights, those who actually control the various elements, and the controllers' incentives and opportunities. Similarly, by itself the term *private property* has little empirical content. Private property rights often are shared among independent private parties and delimited and restricted by the state. In law a privately owned corporation is classified as a legal individual, but the behavior of such entities depends on their internal organization and external constraints. Although their views are contested, as early as 1933 Adolf Berle and Gardiner Means in *The Modern Corporation and Private Property* drew attention to the possibility that shareholders, the formal owners, have limited control over their managers. Similar agency problems arise in public organizations that range from representative parliaments to nationalized industries.

The literature often confuses two distinct concepts: common or communal property and public domain or open access. Common or communal property involves arrangements by which a group of individuals jointly control access, withdrawal, and management rights to a resource such as a water system or pastureland. The usual defining characteristic of common or communal property is that the group lacks authority to alienate the resource to outsiders. Under appropriate circumstances common or communal property can be an efficient arrangement, as Elinor Ostrom showed in 1990 in *Governing the Commons: The Evolution of Institutions for Collective Action*. Property is absent, however, when a resource is in the public domain with no limits on withdrawal rights. This condition, which also is called open access, implies that no user has the incentive to maintain or improve the resource and invest in sustainable utilization. Lack of maintenance and unconstrained use eventually will dissipate the resource rent, as is happening in many high-sea fisheries. Open access conditions sometimes emerge in de jure property systems when the enforcement of private, public, or communal rights is weak.

EFFECTIVE PROPERTY RIGHTS

Property rights are said to be effective or efficient only with reference to specific goals. If the goal is to maximize the joint value of assets that belong to a social group (maximize wealth per capita), the community must minimize the sum of three cost categories: the costs of traditional production (transformation), exclusion, and internal governance. High exclusion cost sometimes rules out the option of dividing a resource such as the atmosphere, fish stocks in the ocean, or knowledge among individual owners and enforce exclusive ownership. Eventually new technologies and new types of organization may enable exclusion and, for instance, make possible exclusive ownership of individual fish in the oceans.

It is often efficient for independent actors to cooperate in utilizing a resource and share property rights if they can solve the problem of internal governance. The governance problem arises because opportunistic actors have a propensity to follow their self-interest and exploit their co-owner, for instance, by withdrawing more than their allocated share of units from a fishery or an orchard or failing to cooperate in doing maintenance work. Incentive schemes and direct monitoring are used to contain internal governance problems. High internal governance costs limit joint ownership, but new technologies and new forms of organization can lower those costs.

THE EVOLUTION OF PROPERTY RIGHTS

Recent studies indicate that the structure of property rights (institutions) is the fundamental explanation for long-term economic growth. In 2004 Dani Rodrik and coauthors provided empirical evidence for this proposition in "Institutions Rule: The Primacy of Institutions over Geography and Integration in Economic Development." The importance of property rights for economic progress raises two related questions: How do property rights evolve over time? Why do societies tolerate systems of property rights that cause economic decline?

Social science provides at least two perspectives on the evolution of property rights: the notion of unplanned or spontaneous evolution, which often is associated with the work of Friedrich Hayek, and planned or administered change, such as recent attempts at transition in Eastern Europe and in developing countries. Spontaneous evolution and administered change, however, need not be mutually exclusive. The history of the Soviet Union suggests that the general direction of change in property systems, for instance, away from or toward markets, often is administered centrally whereas the details and actual outcomes depend on spontaneous, decentralized interactions.

The state is the ultimate guarantor or destroyer of secure property rights. To finance projects such as warfare, powerful rulers and their cohorts throughout history have created uncertainty about investment projects by appropriating the wealth of their subjects. Stable property rights have emerged only when the balance of power has shifted against the rulers; that has occurred when social developments have increased the de facto power of groups such as feudal barons or a new middle class. Those groups sometimes have used their new strength to constrain the de jure power of the state, tie the hands of the ruler, and create limited government. These autonomous and path-dependent developments often are fostered by historical accidents. Dutch primacy in world trade and the Industrial Revolution in England were fundamentally not planned or administered events.

If flaws in the system of property rights are the root cause of economic decline, why do potential investors and producers not persuade their rulers to reform the system, expand the tax base, and share the fruits of growth? Failure to cooperate is caused by uncertainty about exactly who will gain materially from reforms, how reforms will affect future power relationships, and the high costs of making credible promises. When the state is not bound by strong judicial or other mechanisms, agreements between social groups and current or future rulers lack credibility. Political bargaining about property rules requires a balance of power and credible constraints. In addition to power relationships, social norms and ideology appear to play a role in the evolution of limited government.

PROPERTY IN THE NEW ECONOMY

A system of property rights is of great practical importance when the system fails to support advanced production technologies and wastes resources on a large scale. Large-scale failures are prevalent in developing countries and occur universally in the use of certain natural resources, such as the atmosphere. In a high-income country rapid technological change can undermine a previously effective property system and retard the country's future development unless appropriate adjustments are made.

The new economy with its network industries and knowledge-based firms presents this type of challenge. Knowledge or intellectual property has replaced the plants and equipment of the Industrial Revolution as the engine of growth. Once they are made available, knowledge products have characteristics of public goods in that knowledge cannot be used up. In the new economy property regimes must balance two conflicting goals: giving scientists and technicians strong incentives to discover new knowledge and innovate and creating competition in the distribution of knowledge goods with output prices near the marginal cost, which often is close to zero.

The solution requires a difficult compromise. The initial creation of knowledge goods such as computer software and medicinal drugs entails high fixed costs, whereas the marginal cost of reproducing existing goods is often close to zero. Efficient intellectual property regimes must stimulate the supply of innovations by giving innovators an opportunity to cover their fixed costs while not allowing them to raise their prices so high that they limit the distribution of valuable products such as drugs. Various devices are used to create intellectual property, including patents, copyrights, trademarks, and trade secrets. In recent years the scope of patents has expanded, for instance, to include basic research in university laboratories. Some critics maintain that the use of patents and copyrights has exceeded sensible limits. Digitalization of knowledge and the rise of the Internet have worked in the opposite direction and undermined intellectual property rights, for instance, by lowering the cost of copying and distributing music and the contents of books.

For high-income as well as developing countries the lesson is the same: Economic progress depends on how each community adjusts its property rights to new technologies and new opportunities. The adjustment is determined in interactions between the state and powerful social groups, with the uncertain results depending on the balance of power, the structure of the political system, ideological beliefs, and available knowledge.

SEE ALSO *Coase Theorem; Common Land; Computers: Science and Society; Corporations; Cyberspace; Externality; Franchise; Governmentality; Institutionalism; Internet; Knowledge Society; Land Claims; North, Douglass; Overfishing; Property Rights; Resources; Social Science; Tragedy of the Commons; Transaction Cost*

BIBLIOGRAPHY

Acemoglu, Daron, and James A. Robinson. 2006. *Economic Origins of Dictatorship and Democracy.* Cambridge, U.K., and New York: Cambridge University Press.

Barzel, Yoram. 1997. *Economic Analysis of Property Rights.* 2nd ed. Cambridge, U.K., and New York: Cambridge University Press.

Berle, Adolf A., and Gardiner C. Means. 1933. *The Modern Corporation and Private Property.* New York: Macmillan.

Coase, R. H. 1960. The Problem of Social Cost. *Journal of Law and Economics* 3 (1): 1–44.

Eggertsson, Thráinn. 2005. *Imperfect Institutions: Possibilities and Limits of Reform.* Ann Arbor: University of Michigan Press.

North, Douglass C. 1990. *Institutions, Institutional Change, and Economic Performance.* Cambridge, U.K., and New York: Cambridge University Press.

Ostrom, Elinor. 1990. *Governing the Commons: The Evolution of Institutions for Collective Action.* Cambridge, U.K., and New York: Cambridge University Press.

Ostrom, Elinor, and Edella Schlager. 1996. The Formation of Property Rights. In *Rights to Nature: Ecological, Economic, and Political Principles of Institutions for the Environment,* eds. Susan Hanna, Carl Folke, and Karl-Göran Mäler, 127–156. Washington, DC: Island Press.

Posner, Richard A. 2005. Intellectual Property: The Law and Economics Approach. *Journal of Economic Perspectives* (19) 2: 57–73.

Rodrik, Dani, Arvind Subramanian, and Francesco Trebbi. 2004. Institutions Rule: The Primacy of Institutions over Geography and Integration in Economic Development. *Journal of Economic Growth* 9 (2): 131–165.

Thráinn Eggertsson

PROPERTY, PRIVATE

The institution of private property is one of humankind's principal social arrangements. By defining and assigning legal ownership, property tends to promote the production, exchange, and accumulation of wealth. Property is especially lauded for the protection it is thought to provide against overbearing, arbitrary, and capricious government action. The institution, however, is more complicated than that laudatory view might lead one to believe.

Numerous theories of property have been formulated over the centuries. These are theories of the origin of property, the justification of property, the nature of property qua property, the evolution of property, the operation of the institution of property, and, among other things, how property interacts with other institutions. Some or many of these theories share a preoccupation with or defense of the received details of the institution. The typical argument is that the defense of a detail is instrumental to the defense of the institution as a whole. But these theories tend to be applied to different instantiations of property. If a proposed change in the law of property be designated *B*, then it is likely to be opposed insofar as it would change property provision *A*; then, after *B* is adopted, and another change, *C*, is proposed that will alter *B*, *B* is defended in much the same terms as *A* was defended. The argument is to conserve existing rights. The same is true of multiple jurisdictions, the details of whose respective property institutions vary between them. The arguments used in defense of different existing sets of details are likely to be the same. To be in favor of property, therefore, is to be in favor of the results that the institution likely will promote. Whether a particular system of property is to include some detail is quite another matter.

One important implication of the foregoing is that different instantiations of property will yield different results. Putting it again formally, rights structure *I* will generate market structure *I* and demand-and-supply structure *I*, and these in turn will result in resource allocation structure *I* and distribution (of opportunity, income, and wealth) structure *I*; and similarly with rights structure *II* ultimately resulting in distribution structure *II*. That is to say, there is no unique result, only results specific to the initial structure of rights, and so on.

One group of theories of property presumes that property is, or is derived from, the natural order of things. This presumption commits the naturalistic fallacy, namely, to intuit that because something exists it does so because it is either natural or derived from nature. This is fallacious in part because of the multiplicity of property systems and in part, indeed especially, because every property system is socially constructed, a product of human collective action, and not given by nature.

The institution of property is, for most practical purposes, the law of property, and the law of property is generated by government. Property is a mode of protecting interests, and any actual property system protects certain interests and not others. If *A* and *B* are in the same field of action and have conflicting interests, protecting *A*'s interest by law is substantively different from, but the analytical equivalent of, protecting *B*'s interest. To see that property is a mode of protecting interests enables one to see other aspects of property. One aspect is that property is not protected because it is property; property is property because it is protected. Another aspect is that litigation and lobbying are the means of promoting one's interests to be protected as property by either changing or not changing the law. A corollary is that the right to petition government about its protection of one's interests is a very important right; where one group has such access and another does not, it is more than likely that the former group will more largely and more effectively get its interests protected as property than the latter group. Another aspect of property has to do with regulation. If property is defined as antecedent to government (as in saying it

derives from nature), then any regulation by government is a taking of part of that property. If property is defined as a product of government, then no such taking occurs: government is only changing the interest to which it is giving its protection. Thus, as a corollary, regulation may be formally identified as the protection of *A*'s interest against *B*; in which case, so-called deregulation does not mean that government is no longer regulating. Rather it means that *A*'s interest is no longer protected against *B*, and that government is now protecting *B*'s interest rather than *A*'s. Such regulation (or deregulation) is a principal mode through which the law of property and therefore the institution of property changes.

Not all government protection of interests is designated property. What makes the institution of property so special is that a higher level of protection is generally thought to be given to interests protected as property than to interests not so protected, that is, protected as ordinary rights. For example, the right to be paid by one's employer in lawful money, or to have so many restrooms per hundred workers, or to have clean air at work (no more than a certain maximum of impurities and toxic elements) are rights that government can withdraw or change much more easily than it can change the property right to pollute; this is so even though the three specified rights may be seen as checks on property rights.

This latter point underscores another aspect of property: while the institution of property provides some measure of protection against government, that is, providing a check on the power of government, the government is itself a check on the power of property. This conflict is central to the institution of property and its evolution; what is important is what people are led to believe concerning which power should be checked. Moreover, determining which power needs to be checked by the other, and how, is largely a matter that is worked out by government, typically the courts. But such is only largely the case, inasmuch as voting for senators, representatives, and judges is in part a matter of providing citizen input into the process of whether *A*'s interest or *B*'s interest is to be protected or whether in a particular situation property owners or government itself is to be held in check.

Property, it is important to see, is relativist and is so in several ways. First, property rights are relative to the actions of the government that generates them. Second, property rights are relative to each other. And third, property rights are relative to the situation in which they exist. The economic significance of a right, therefore, is a function of: (1) the law that protects it relative to other protected interests; (2) others' rights; and (3) the buying and selling activities, macroeconomic conditions, and other variables that comprise the economy. Competition itself is a way of destroying the value of others' property insofar as one competes to attract their customers to you.

The institution of property is so important not merely because of its status among other institutions, nor its function in promoting production and material well-being, and so on, but because of the decision making that goes into making and adjusting the rights that constitute property. Property is sometimes described through the analogy of a bundle of sticks. Each stick constitutes a potential ability to act or to be immunized against the consequences of others' actions. This decision making is about who can do what to whom and has several dimensions. These are evident in the transformation of the economic system from one in which landed property had both economic significance and governance authority, to one in which both landed and nonlanded property, as well nonpropertied persons, participate in economic and political decision making. Apropos of the conflict between continuity and change, both small and large, or systemic, changes in property systems have taken place. Apropos of the conflict between freedom and control, the most fundamental changes are those that involve changes in the decision-making or power structure of the economy.

Also evident is the legal-economic nexus in which polity and economy do not simply interact but mutually help form each other. At the heart of both the transformation and the nexus is property and other rights as both cause and consequence. The total structure of rights constitutes the structure of decision making in markets and in government. Although rooted in the past, with decision making over changes in property keeping a selective eye on past legal precedents, seeking justice through continuity, the institution's social function is oriented toward the future, in the encouragement it provides for economic activity and the structure given to that encouragement, as well as to the path to be taken by legal, social, political, and economic change. Not all sources of property need be normatively equal, nor are all property and other rights substantively equal.

SEE ALSO *Private Interests; Private Sector*

BIBLIOGRAPHY

Auerbach, Carl A., Lloyd K. Garrison, Willard Hurst, and Samuel Mermin. 1961. *The Legal Process: An Introduction to Decision-Making by Judicial, Legislative, Executive, and Administrative Agencies*. San Francisco, CA: Chandler.

Commons, John R. 1924. *Legal Foundations of Capitalism*. New York: Macmillan.

Hamilton, Alexander, James Madison, and John Jay. 1961. *The Federalist*. Ed. Benjamin Fletcher Wright. New York: MetroBooks.

Lindblom, Charles E. 1977. *Politics and Markets: The World's Political Economic Systems*. New York: Basic Books.

Mercuro, Nicholas, and Warren J. Samuels, eds. 1999. *The Fundamental Interrelationships between Government and Property*. Stamford, CT: JAI.

Samuels, Warren J. 2007. *The Legal-Economic Nexus: Fundamental Processes*. New York: Routledge.

Schmid, A. Allan. 1987. *Property, Power, and Public Choice: An Inquiry into Law and Economics*. 2nd ed. New York: Praeger.

Warren J. Samuels

PROPERTY RIGHTS

Property rights consist of a person's ability to own, transfer, and use that which a person owns without government coercion. Property rights and economic freedom are interrelated in that a person cannot engage in economic activity if the state does not recognize and defend that person's right to own property, and because it is meaningless to have the ability to speak and act freely if one lacks the ability to monetize one's words and actions.

The way in which property rights are defined depends on which of two premises is taken as the starting point. Rights of ownership either originate with society as a whole and are bestowed by society on individuals from time to time or originate with individuals and are bestowed by individuals on society from time to time. The former is the position of socialist philosophers; the latter, that of classical liberal philosophers.

THE CLASSICAL LIBERAL POSITION

Classical liberalism begins with the premise that an individual's life belongs to that individual. This ownership of self, classical liberals believe, is not something that is bestowed by human-made law but is a natural right that arises by virtue of an individual's status as a human being. Starting from the assumption that individuals own their own lives, classical liberals argue that it logically follows that individuals own their own labor because labor is the action of the self and individuals own themselves as a matter of natural law. Because individuals own their own labor, they also own the wages they earn from that labor because the wages are what they receive in exchange for the labor they own. Similarly, an individual owns the things that individual buys with his or her wages because those things are traded for the wages that were traded for labor that is the result of action by the self that the individual naturally owns. Thus, classical liberals maintain that property rights are sacrosanct as a matter of natural law.

The principle of natural law is invoked in the U.S. Bill of Rights, which speaks of "inalienable rights": rights that exist as a matter of people's state as humans and that can be neither established nor revoked by government action. Although the individual may choose to give up some property rights to society for the common good or in exchange for protections granted by society, classical liberals maintain that those rights are the individual's to give up, not society's to take.

THE SOCIALIST POSITION

Socialism begins with the position that it is the responsibility of society to ensure an equitable distribution of ownership. That obligation falls to society because, socialists believe, when individuals are left to their own devices, political and economic power become concentrated in the hands of the strong, who then exploit the weak. Thus, because it is the responsibility of society to protect all its members, property rights must belong to society as a whole. In the socialist framework the society bestows property rights on individuals to maintain equality of income and wealth.

The socialist position was greatly influenced by the exploitation of western workers in the late nineteenth century. The German philosopher Karl Marx maintained that workers had a right to the value of their labor and that a system that allowed employers to profit from the fruits of workers' labors is destined to bring about the exploitation of those workers. Marxist socialists maintain that the way to avoid this exploitation of labor is for the state to own the means of production. Removing private ownership means that the government must decide how the means of production are to be used. This is accomplished by a central planning board that decides how much output industries will produce, what prices they will charge, and how much they will pay their workers.

Communism is regarded as the next evolutionary step beyond socialism. In the socialist system, the government owns the means of production only. Individuals still maintain ownership of their personal property. In the Communist system, the government keeps all property rights to itself and the individual owns nothing. In the Communist system, people work for no wage and receive everything they need from the government at no cost. What is common to the socialist and Communist frameworks is that property rights originate with society, not with the individual. Despite the use of the term, no modern country has ever achieved a Communist framework. Even those that have come closest, Russia, China, and North Korea, have not succeeded in attaining government control of all property. Modern examples of Communist systems are seen in religious communities whose members take vows of poverty. In these communities, the individual owns nothing but is granted use of property owned by the community.

EXTERNALITIES AND THE TRAGEDY OF THE COMMONS

Economists argue that it is important that property rights be well defined. When they are not, there is a disconnect between individuals who make decisions and individuals who must live with the consequences of those decisions. This situation is known as externalities and the tragedy of the commons.

In the case of externalities one individual imposes a cost on another that would necessitate compensation for the second individual if property rights were well defined. For example, a factory that pollutes the air imposes a cost on people who breathe the air. Because the factory does not bear the cost of pollution, it has an incentive to pollute more than it would otherwise. If property rights are defined so that those people own the air, the factory is forced to compensate them for the air it pollutes. The result is that the factory pollutes less. If property rights are defined so that the factory owns the air, people must pay the factory to pollute less so that the air will be breathable. Again, less pollution is created. Thus, when property rights are poorly defined, the economy produces more of the good than is socially optimal. When property rights are well defined, regardless of whom the rights are assigned to, the economy produces the socially optimal quantity of product.

The economic problem of the tragedy of the commons also results from poorly defined property rights. For example, if everyone in a village together owns a plot of pastureland (a commons), each person is free to graze his or her cattle on the land. However, because the ownership is spread over so many people, no single person has an incentive to maintain the land. The result is that the land will be overgrazed. However, if one person owned the land, that person would have the ability to profit from owning the land and therefore would have an incentive to maintain it.

A contemporary example of the tragedy of the commons is the treatment of endangered species. In countries that have outlawed the killing of elephants the elephant population dwindles because poachers have an incentive to evade the law and no one has an incentive to protect the elephants. Conversely, in the few countries in which killing elephants is legal, the elephant population is flourishing because people have an incentive to help the elephants thrive so that they can be harvested at a profit. As an extension of this example, cows are not endangered in the United States despite the fact that Americans consume millions of tons of beef annually. Because it is legal to own cows, farmers have an incentive to maintain herds and cull them at a profit. The decimation of the American buffalo, in contrast, occurred because cattlemen came to the plains before the rule of law was established. Without law to enforce property rights, the buffalo were a common resource and so were hunted to near extinction.

SEE ALSO *Bill of Rights, U.S.; Capitalism; Coase Theorem; Communism; Externality; Freedom; Government; Individualism; Liberalism; Market Economy; Natural Rights; Property; Socialism; State, The; Tragedy of the Commons*

BIBLIOGRAPHY

Bastiat, Federic. 1850. *Economic Harmonies.* Ed. George B. de Huszar, trans. W. Hayden Boyers. Irvington-on-Hudson, NY: Foundation for Economic Education, 1996.

Hoppe, Hans-Hermann. 1989. *A Theory of Socialism and Capitalism.* Boston: Kluwer Academic Publishers.

Marx, Karl. 1867. *Capital.* Trans. and ed. S. Levitsky. Washington, DC: Regnery, 2000.

Von Mises, Ludwig. 1979. *Economic Policy: Thoughts for Today and Tomorrow.* South Bend, IN: Regnery/Gateway.

Antony Davies

PROPERTY RIGHTS, INTELLECTUAL

Intellectual property rights (IPR, or IPRs) are the rights of artists and inventors to get legal protection against unauthorized copying of their work. There are three main subtypes of IPRs: copyrights, trademarks, and patents. Copyrights apply to literary and artistic works, such as books, music, and computer programs; trademarks cover brand names, such as Coca-Cola®; and patents are awarded for new and useful inventions, such as the active ingredient of the molecule of a new antihypertension drug. In advanced industrial countries, IPRs account for an increasingly larger proportion of gross domestic product (GDP). In less developed countries, however, very little indigenous copyright-, trademark-, and patent-protected goods are produced.

Genuine IPR goods are often prohibitively expensive for citizens of the developing world. For example, in many countries in Asia and Africa, the cost of a computer software program is equal to the average per capita income. Thus, global income inequalities have given rise to a situation in which developing countries produce and consume illegitimate copies of IPR-protected goods. Usually, these goods are referred to as either pirated goods (for copyright-protected goods, such as software, books, and music) or counterfeit goods (for trademark- and patent-protected goods). The severity of piracy and counterfeiting varies, depending on the type of goods, the historical period, and the geographical location of goods. For exam-

ple, the United States was notorious for not protecting foreign copyrights well into the twentieth century. Similarly, many African and Asian countries do not provide patent protection for pharmaceuticals. At the turn of the twenty-first century, software piracy and trademark counterfeiting are the best-known examples. According to estimates of the Business Software Alliance (BSA), in 2005 alone, $34 billion worth of business software was pirated worldwide. While copyright piracy poses no threat to consumers, some trademark and patent counterfeiting can have harmful effects on consumer health and safety. For example, fake (counterfeit) foods and medicines can lead to human death, while fake automobile parts have been linked to traffic deaths (Phillips 2005). One example of a counterfeit food is the "Sars" candy bar appearing in 2003, which is a counterfeit of the Mars candy bar.

How can IPR counterfeiting be eliminated? IPRs are protected both by national legislation and by various types of international treaties. In the United States, the 1976 Copyright Act, the 1946 Trademark Act ("Lanham Act"), and the 1985 Patent Act provide guarantees for the holders of IPRs. Most countries around the world have national laws protecting at least some types of IPRs. In addition, there are several dozen international IPR treaties. The main IPR treaties are the 1886 Berne Convention for the Protection of Literary and Artistic Works (for copyrights) and the 1883 Paris Convention for the Protection of Industrial Property (for trademarks and patents). The World Intellectual Property Organization (WIPO) in Geneva administers the Berne and Paris Convention, in addition to twenty-two other treaties covering the entire panoply of IPRs. Currently, WIPO has 183 member countries. Separately from WIPO, the World Trade Organization (WTO) administers the Agreement on Trade-Related Aspects of Intellectual Property Rights (TRIPS), which has been ratified by 149 countries. Despite the wealth of international agreements, however, there have not been radical improvements in the protection of IPRs in individual countries, and piracy and counterfeiting continue to exist around the world. This situation exists because international agreements are not self-enforcing and cannot be implemented without the will of individual national governments.

There are two mechanisms through which developed countries can compel developing countries to enforce international IPR agreements. The first one is the threat of trade sanctions. In the United States, the Omnibus Trade and Competitiveness Act of 1988 allows the U.S. Trade Representative to impose trade sanctions against countries that do not provide adequate IPR protection. Although virtually never imposed, the threat of trade sanctions can help sensitize some countries about the need to enforce IPR laws. This is a particularly powerful instrument against small states (e.g., Thailand) that are heavily dependent on trade with the United States. For bigger states, however, the threat of trade sanctions is not an effective mechanism for bringing about meaningful improvements in IPR enforcement. In such countries, the threat of withdrawing foreign direct investment (FDI) has proven to be a more successful strategy. For example, in China, the Quality Brands Protection Council (QBPC), representing more than 100 foreign companies with over $20 billion of investment in China, has been remarkably successful in lobbying the Chinese government to enhance IPR enforcement (Dimitrov 2004). Developing countries that invest in IPR, especially the development of indigenous patented technology, can be more competitive in the global economy.

In conclusion, IPRs protect valuable, yet often pirated products. Although multiple international IPR treaties exist, good enforcement depends on the will of domestic governments to implement them. When properly applied, foreign pressure can help sensitize the governments of developing countries to the benefits of providing stronger IPR protection.

SEE ALSO *European Union; World Trade Organization*

BIBLIOGRAPHY

Business Software Alliance. 2006. Third Annual BSA and IDC Global Software Piracy Study. http://www.bsa.org/globalstudy/upload/2005-2006%20Global%20Piracy%20Study.pdf.

Dimitrov, Martin. 2004. Administrative Decentralization, Legal Fragmentation, and the Rule of Law in Transitional Economies: The Enforcement of Intellectual Property Rights Laws in China, Russia, Taiwan, and the Czech Republic. PhD diss., Stanford University.

Phillips, Tim. 2005. *Knockoff: The Deadly Trade in Counterfeit Goods: The True Story of the World's Fastest Growing Crime Wave*. London: Kogan Page.

Sell, Susan. 2003. *Private Power, Public Law: The Globalization of Intellectual Property Rights*. New York: Cambridge University Press.

Martin Dimitrov

PROPOSITION 2 (MICHIGAN)

SEE *California Civil Rights Initiative.*

PROPOSITION 209 (CALIFORNIA)

SEE *California Civil Rights Initiative.*

PROPRIETARY CLASS

SEE *Physiocracy.*

PROSLAVERY ARGUMENTS

SEE *Slavery.*

PROSOCIAL BEHAVIOR

SEE *Altruism.*

PROSPECT THEORY

Prospect theory is a psychologically-based framework that describes the mental processes involved when an individual makes a choice among uncertain prospects. In the 1970s Israeli-born psychologists Daniel Kahneman and Amos Tversky (1937–1996) developed prospect theory along with a body of work that came to be known as *heuristics and biases*. The Nobel Prize committee singled out prospect theory when they awarded Kahneman the 2002 Nobel Prize in Economics, which he shared with economist Vernon Smith.

Prospect theory holds that people's psychological makeup induces them to value the outcomes of decision tasks as either *gains* or *losses* relative to some reference point. Moreover, people tend to become less sensitive to incremental gains or losses, meaning that the additional sensation associated with either an incremental gain or loss is less than the previous comparable increment. In addition, losses are experienced more acutely than gains, a feature that Kahneman and Tversky called *loss aversion*. Taken together, the features just described give rise to a value function over gains and losses that is S-shaped—concave in gains and convex in losses. Moreover, the function features a kink at the origin, and is more steeply sloped for losses than for gains.

Prospect theory also holds that psychologically people overweight low probabilities and underweight probabilities whose magnitudes are moderate or high. According to prospect theory, a person facing a decision task evaluates each possible decision in the decision menu using a rating function. The rating function is a sum of products, where each product combines a value and an uncertainty weight. The decision that receives the highest rating is the one the decision maker chooses.

The S-shaped value function typically induces people to behave in a risk-averse fashion when the potential outcomes involve only gains, and to behave in a risk-seeking fashion when the potential outcomes involve only losses. However, because of the weighting function, this pattern can be reversed when low probabilities are involved. Specifically, the weighting function can induce people to behave in a risk-seeking fashion when the potential outcomes involve only gains, and in a risk-averse fashion when the potential outcomes involve only losses.

When prospects involve a mixture of potential gains and losses, loss aversion will tend to induce people to act as if they are averse to risk. In particular, the kink at the origin of the value function leads people to exhibit a strong preference for certain outcomes over uncertain outcomes.

The manner in which a decision task is framed is known as *framing*. When people frame their decision tasks they are said to engage in *editing*. Prospect theory explains why people often frame complex decision tasks as sequences of simpler decision tasks, and then make decisions by applying value functions and weighting functions to each of the subtasks. In doing so, they might overlook connections among subtasks, and as a result choose inferior decisions, behaving as if they were throwing away money.

Prospect theory has had a profound influence on economic scholarship. It has been used to explain investors' disposition to sell their winners too early and hold their losers too long; corporate managers' reluctance to terminate losing projects; the equity premium puzzle about why the difference between the return to stocks and the return to bonds is puzzlingly high; why certain types of investors find cash dividends attractive; and why corporate managers appear willing to leave money on the table when their firms participate in initial public offerings. Prospect theory, especially the concept of loss aversion, has also had an impact on psychological research.

Prospect theory is a descriptive theory, unlike *expected utility theory*, which is the normative framework most commonly used in economic modeling. A comprehensive treatment of expected utility theory can be found in the *Handbook of Utility Theory* (1998). Whereas expected utility theory assumes that final wealth is the carrier of value, prospect theory assumes that change in wealth is the carrier of value. Whereas expected utility theory assumes that people are immune to framing effects, prospect theory assumes that framing has an effect on people's choices. Whereas expected utility theory assumes that people do not distort probability values, prospect theory assumes that people overweight low probabilities and underweight moderate to high probabilities. Whereas expected utility theory assumes that people are uniform in their attitude toward risk, prospect theory assumes that people's attitude toward risk is situation specific. Whereas

the axioms that underlie expected utility are normatively desirable, experimental evidence suggests that in practice, people tend to violate some of these axioms, and instead behave more in accordance with prospect theory.

SEE ALSO *Decision-making; Expected Utility Theory; Uncertainty*

BIBLIOGRAPHY

Hammond, Peter, Christian Seidl, and Salvador Barberà, eds. 1998. *Handbook of Utility Theory*. Boston and Dordrecht, Netherlands: Kluwer Academic.

Kahneman, Daniel, and Amos Tversky. 1979. Prospect Theory: An Analysis of Decision Under Risk. *Econometrica* 47 (2): 263–292.

Tversky, Amos, and Daniel Kahneman. 1992. Advances in Prospect Theory: Cumulative Representation of Uncertainty. *Journal of Risk and Uncertainty* 5: 297–323.

Hersh Shefrin

PROSTITUTION

Prostitution involves the exchange of sex for money or other material compensation. The most common type of prostitution involves women who provide sex to male customers.

Prostitution has a long history, and is sometimes called "the oldest profession." It has not always been condemned and stigmatized. In ancient times, some forms of prostitution were viewed positively. *Sacred prostitution*, where a temple priestess had sex with men, was a way of worshiping the deity. In ancient Greece, prostitution was an accepted part of life. The highest-status prostitutes, the *hetaerae*, were valued for their intellect and companionship, and at their salons they entertained politicians, artists, and scholars. The *hetaerae* enjoyed much more freedom and mobility than other Greek women of the time.

PROSTITUTION AND GENDER RELATIONS

For most of history, however, prostitution has been condemned, and gender bias has been marked: Prostitutes have been blamed for a large number of social problems, but male customers and profiteers were rarely chastised. This double standard continues to this day.

Prostitution reflects larger, traditional gender relations between men and women. First, for the most part, it is men, not women, who typically pay for sex, which is an outgrowth of the broader worldwide pattern of objectification of women. Customers' motives for buying sex differ, including satisfying a "need" for sex, inability to find a conventional partner, desire for a certain type of sex or sex with a certain type of woman, fulfilling a fantasy, or engaging in risky behavior (Monto 2004). Second, reflecting women's subordinate status in society, gender inequality is pervasive in prostitution. Female prostitutes are paid for their services, but often not under conditions of their choosing. For those who have male managers (pimps, brothel owners, etc.), the women have little if any control over their working conditions and are subject to significant economic exploitation.

Third, prostitutes are vulnerable to victimization, and this victimization is gendered. Male customers, pimps, and other men sometimes engage in violence and other types of abuse. A significant number of prostitutes report that they have been robbed, raped, or assaulted at some time in their career, and serial killers prey on streetwalkers. Because no study of sex workers is based on a representative sample, it is impossible to tell how frequently they experience violence, but it is clearly an occupational hazard. Customers are sometimes robbed and assaulted as well, but most of the victimization is directed at female prostitutes. Fourth, gender inequality is also the norm in the criminal justice system's treatment of prostitution. Where prostitution is illegal, prostitutes continue to be arrested much more often than their male customers. Unequal justice is less pronounced in some cities than in others, and some cities periodically target customers but, overall, the police tend to focus on prostitutes (Weitzer 1999). Fifth, gender bias is apparent in portrayals of prostitution in the mass media. Films, television shows, popular music, and literature usually depict prostitution negatively, although it is occasionally romanticized. There are, of course, some realistic or sympathetic portrayals in popular culture, such as Sting's 1999 song, "Tomorrow We'll See," but such depictions are rare exceptions to the rule.

INDOOR PROSTITUTION, STREET PROSTITUTION, AND MALE PROSTITUTION

There are exceptions to this general pattern of gender inequality. Not all prostitutes are exploited or victimized. *Indoor workers* who sell sex in brothels and massage parlors, as independent call girls, or as employees of escort agencies are less likely to be abused by customers than *street prostitutes*, and the indoor workers are also less economically exploited, express greater job satisfaction, and have higher self-esteem than their street-level counterparts (Vanwesenbeeck 2001; Weitzer 2005). Research shows that some indoor workers have quasi-romantic encounters with customers—not limited to sex but including conversation, cuddling, emotional support, and intimacy (Lever and Dolnick 2000). Indoor prostitutes are also less likely

than streetwalkers to use addictive drugs and are at significantly lower risk of sexually transmitted diseases (Plumridge and Abel 2001). There is one important exception to this portrait of indoor prostitution: Women who are recruited by force or fraud and trafficked to work in brothels are at high risk for subsequent exploitation and victimization.

Gender inequality is absent in the case of male prostitutes, who sell sex to other men, who comprise a significant minority of the sex trade. Male prostitutes may be sexually objectified in the same way as female prostitutes, but compared to female streetwalkers, male prostitutes have greater control over their working conditions (few males have pimps); are less likely to have been abused as children, to be forced into prostitution, and to experience violence from customers; are more likely to enjoy their work overall and to derive sexual gratification from it; and are less susceptible to arrest or harassment by the police (Aggleton 1999; West 1993).

In sum, workers in different sectors of the sex trade, as well as male and female workers, experience different kinds of working conditions and varying degrees of victimization, exploitation, freedom, and job satisfaction. The type of prostitution is extremely important.

TRENDS

Today, the sex trade is a huge business worldwide, with numerous providers, customers, and third-party profiteers. Since prostitution is illegal in many places and stigmatized everywhere, it is impossible to determine exactly how prevalent it is or whether it is increasing, but a significant number of men admit to having bought sex from a prostitute. According to a 2000 survey, 17 percent of American men have paid for sex at some time in their lives, compared to 16 percent of Australian men (in 2001) and 9 percent of British men (in 2000). The real numbers are likely higher, given the tendency to underreport disreputable activity.

The Internet offers unprecedented new opportunities for sex workers to communicate with clients and set up appointments. Several major Web sites contain message boards that offer a wealth of information for customers: what to expect in terms of services and prices; "reviews" of a certain worker's appearance, demeanor, and performance; and the offerings of specific establishments (e.g., a massage parlor, an escort agency). Customers' chat rooms and message boards provide a fascinating window into the reasons why men buy sex, what they are looking for in a provider, norms regarding appropriate treatment of workers, and clients' general views about paid sex and the sex industry.

Another trend is the growing internationalization of the sex trade. *Sex tourism* involves persons who travel from one country to another for the purpose of having sex with a prostitute in the destination country. Most sex tourists are men, but a small number of female tourists buy sex from local men in the Caribbean and elsewhere. Travel companies around the world promote sex tourism, providing information to prospective customers and offering package tours.

In some places, such as Holland, sex tourism accounts for a significant share of the country's tourism revenues. One study found that the sex industry accounted for between 2 and 14 percent of the gross domestic product in Thailand, Indonesia, Malaysia, and the Philippines (Lim 1998). Customers pump a substantial amount of foreign currency into these economies, which explains why these governments tacitly support the sex trade. In Thailand alone, prostitution earned $23 to $27 billion from 1993 to 1995 (Lim 1998).

Among the reasons why international travel for sex is seen as attractive, compared to buying sex in one's own country, are anonymity and low risk of detection, low prices, and a desire to have sex with a member of a particular racial or ethnic group. In Thailand, for example, most of the foreign customers are affluent and come from Australia, Germany, the United States, and Japan, and most of the workers are Thai or Filipino women, many of whom originally came from poor rural areas and sell sex to support their families back home. There is, therefore, a striking class disparity between most workers and most foreign customers.

Some sex tourists travel to other countries with the specific purpose of having sex with minors. Doing so in certain foreign countries is seen as far less risky than engaging in such conduct in a customer's home country. Some nations, including the United States and Canada, have passed laws prohibiting their citizens from buying sex from minors outside the home country, though these laws are difficult to enforce.

SEE ALSO *Patriarchy; Pimps*

BIBLIOGRAPHY

Aggleton, Peter, ed. 1999. *Men Who Sell Sex: International Perspectives on Male Prostitution and HIV/AIDS*. Philadelphia: Temple University Press.

Lever, Janet, and Deanne Dolnick. 2000. Clients and Call Girls: Seeking Sex and Intimacy. In *Sex for Sale: Prostitution, Pornography, and the Sex Industry*, ed. Ronald Weitzer, 85–100. New York: Routledge.

Lim, Lin Lean. 1998. *The Sex Sector: The Economic and Social Bases of Prostitution in Southeast Asia*. Geneva: International Labor Office.

Monto, Martin. 2004. Female Prostitution, Customers, and Violence. *Violence Against Women* 10: 160–168.

Plumridge, Libby, and Gillian Abel. 2001. A Segmented Sex Industry in New Zealand: Sexual and Personal Safety of Female Sex Workers. *Australian and New Zealand Journal of Public Health* 25: 78–83.

Vanwesenbeeck, Ine. 2001. Another Decade of Social Scientific Work on Prostitution. *Annual Review of Sex Research* 12: 242–289.

Weitzer, Ronald. 1999. Prostitution Control in America: Rethinking Public Policy. *Crime, Law, and Social Change* 32: 83–102.

Weitzer, Ronald. 2005. New Directions in Research on Prostitution. *Crime, Law, and Social Change* 43: 211–235.

West, Donald. 1993. *Male Prostitution*. Binghamton, NY: Haworth.

Ronald Weitzer

PROTECTED MARKETS

A protected market is defined as one shielded from competition. The analytical concept dates back at least to Adam Smith, David Ricardo, Alfred Marshall, and other economists who analyzed the implications of imperfect competition, trade restrictions, and market power. Market protections may be natural or man-made, private or public, and welfare enhancing or depleting.

Some markets are naturally protected from competition by high costs of transportation because of distance, bulk, or terrain. A market isolated by high transport costs and characterized by economies of size so that only one firm can operate at low unit cost is called a natural monopoly. A cooperative form of business organization owned by patrons or government regulation of pricing has been used to avoid exploitation of producers and consumers in such naturally protected markets.

Naturally protected markets are the exception; protected markets more frequently emerge from deliberate action by firms, organizations, and government. Firms engage in exclusionary, predatory, and price-fixing behavior to create or exploit protected markets (Black 2002). Most nations have antitrust laws to avoid or countervail such exercise of market power. In the modern age of sophisticated science, technology, and information systems, firms turn to other strategies to protect markets. For example, a firm may protect its market by encouraging excessive standards (suited to the firm in question but not to other firms), by aggressive advertising, by exploitation of public ignorance (e.g., fear of chemicals or pathogens in tap water or in conventionally produced food), and by market power to expand shelf space in supermarkets.

In the case of organizations, workers form unions to protect their labor market from competition and so enable collective bargaining to raise wages and improve working conditions. Workers in some countries have lobbied successfully for laws requiring large severance payments, high minimum wages and unemployment compensation, long vacations, short workweeks, and strict work rules. A consequence, illustrated by France, is high overall labor costs that discourage employment, especially of young, inexperienced workers. These factors coupled with racism and discrimination in French labor markets brought long-term unemployment rates of 20 percent or more among Muslim youth in the *banlieue* neighborhoods across France, sparking massive social unrest in 2005.

Turning to markets protected by government, border controls attempt to protect domestic workers from immigrant laborers willing to work for low wages and benefits. The result is salutary for domestic workers but hurts would-be migrant workers. Thus, policies to protect labor and industry can be divisive, creating a dual labor market of cosseted job-secure workers with generous benefit packages on one hand and poor unemployed and underemployed workers with limited future prospects on the other.

Governments of some countries pursue an infant industry policy or industrial policy by protecting selected domestic firms through tariffs, quotas, and regulation of competing imports while also promoting the firms with subsidies in the form of cheap credit, low taxes, and concessional access to public research and educational benefits. Such market protection is intended to help new firms until they attain the critical mass necessary to compete in international markets without assistance. A problem is that governments are not very adept at picking industrial winners. Target industries and firms are likely to be favored for political rather than sound economic reasons. Partly because market protection invites complacency in industry, favored treatment tends to be institutionalized and continued even after the favored industry was expected to mature.

Instruments such as tariffs, licenses, and regulations used to protect markets create economic rents—the stream of income generated over time by such instruments. Individuals, firms, and organizations have reason to engage in unethical practices, lobbying and bribing politicians and bureaucrats to create or remove such instruments. The consequence is corruption in government.

However, some market protections are justified and raise real national income. Firms that protect their market by being a first mover or by innovating faster than competitors serve consumers and raise national income. Market protection is useful in supplying public goods. In a laissez-faire competitive market, firms can recover only the marginal cost of their products. Hence, a firm is dissuaded from developing a new soybean variety, for exam-

ple, because it cannot recover the millions of dollars spent to develop the seed. Governments award patents, copyrights, and trademarks so that firms can protect their intellectual property. Thus, firms can exercise market power to charge prices above marginal costs and pay for research and development.

Charging above marginal cost is a second-best policy. The first-best "textbook" policy in such cases is to rely on the public rather than the private sector to develop and pay for such technology. But governments do not have a favorable record, suffering from a dearth of funding and a surfeit of political misdirection in providing such public goods.

Society benefits from grades, standards, and sanitary and phytosanitary regulations that improve private market performance. Unfortunately, these and other market protections sometimes are employed to the detriment of society. The World Bank (Anderson et al., pp. 346, 351, 352) estimates that elimination of 2006 barriers (tariff and nontariff impediments not justified by sound science) to international trade in goods would add $278 billion to world income each year by 2015 and beyond—nearly half of that accruing to developing countries.

Public protection of markets often is justified to serve the environment (Southgate et al. 2007, pp. 103–123). Natural resources such as oceans, the atmosphere, and land are frequently open-access property inviting overuse. The consequent overexploitation of open-access property is called the tragedy of the commons. Uncontrolled access leads users to exploit resources "before the hoarders get them." In 1960 Nobel laureate Ronald Coase pointed out that creation of property rights to such resources can align private with social incentives to achieve efficient resource use.

An example is the "cap and trade" market employed successfully to reduce sulfur dioxide emissions at low economic cost in the United States. The system begins with emission permits issued to each firm. The permits, which can be sold to firms or given to firms (reduced appropriately from historic emission levels), are negotiable. Firms that can reduce emissions at low cost sell their permits to firms expanding emissions to produce highly valued products.

In conclusion, prudent public policy to privatize, deregulate, and open markets at home and abroad has the potential to improve the quality of life around the world. In some cases that means opening markets, as in international trade. In other cases that means protecting markets, as in cap and trade systems for effluents or in patents for intellectual property.

SEE ALSO *Coase Theorem; Coase, Ronald; Competition; Infant Industry; Marshall, Alfred; Monopoly; Pollution; Predatory Pricing; Regulation; Returns,*

Increasing; Ricardo, David; Smith, Adam; Theory of Second Best; Tragedy of the Commons

BIBLIOGRAPHY

Anderson, Kym, Will Martin, and Dominique van der Mensbrugghe. 2006. Market and Welfare Implications of Doha Reform Scenarios. In *Agricultural Trade Reform and the Doha Development Agenda.* Eds. Kym Anderson and Will Martin, Report No. 34206. New York: Palgrave Macmillan, and Washington, DC: World Bank. Chapter 12.

Black, John. 2002. Barriers to Entry. *A Dictionary of Economics.* Oxford University Press. Oxford Reference Online. http://www.oxfordreference.com/views/ENTRY.html.

Coase, Ronald. 1960. "The Problem of Social Cost." *Journal of Law and Economics* 3 (1): 1–44. Reprinted in *Economics of the Environment: Selected Readings.* 4th ed. Ed. Robert Stavins. New York: Norton, 2000.

Southgate, Douglas, Douglas Graham, and Luther Tweeten. 2007. *The World Food Economy.* Malden, MA: Blackwell.

Luther Tweeten

PROTECTION, EQUAL

SEE *Equal Protection; Equality.*

PROTECTIONISM

Protectionism includes a broad range of obstacles created by governments to change the flows of international trade. A variety of policy instruments for trade barriers, including tariffs, quotas, and subsidies, has historically been used to protect domestic import-competing industries and to encourage exports. Occasionally, extreme measures such as a total prohibition of certain imports (bans) and sanctions are employed for economic or political reasons. Also, to avoid retaliation, or a "trade war," strategies such as voluntary export restraints may occasionally be used. Broader restrictive measures that may be regarded as policies aimed at shaping the pattern of trade include: exchange-rate controls; the creation of monopoly power by establishing cartels, such as the Organization of Petroleum Exporting Countries (OPEC), to stabilize prices of raw materials; free trade areas, such as custom unions; most-favored-nations principles; relaxed property-rights protection; environmental standards; and imports certificates.

The effect of trade barriers on individual countries depends upon market structure in the world and the type of policy tools used. Protectionism in principle alters the allocation of resources, creating distortions and inefficiencies in production. While free trade as the rule of thumb is best, there are exceptions. For example, it has been argued that some trade strategies, such as temporary and targeted protection of key infant industries, may benefit the domestic economy in the long run, though the effects on the global economy are unclear. In fact, some of today's industrial powers have benefited from such protectionist policies in the past. Similarly, the optimum tariff concept suggests that limited tariffs on imports may be advantageous to a nation, though world efficiency would diminish.

ANCIENT HISTORY

In ancient times, trade routes such as the Silk Road, the Spice Route, and the Incense Road were created and supported by governments to facilitate the exchange of goods between civilization centers in China, the Mediterranean, and Europe. During this period, raising revenue, rather than protection of domestic producers, was the primary objective of tariffs. For example, revenues from tariffs were used to build and maintain bridges and roads to make trade possible. However, China, between the late tenth and thirteenth centuries, maintained strict control over maritime trade by monopolizing exports, restricting trade to a few ports, imposing tariffs on imports, and regulating the purchase of traded Chinese goods. Trade was also a persistent issue in the relationship between Europe and the East. For example, the Crusaders banned trade with their Mediterranean foes, and only after conquering the eastern Mediterranean did they open it to European shipping.

In the sixteenth century, with the rise of nation-states, mercantilists introduced a formal analysis of winners and losers in trade and exercised protectionist policies lasting through the eighteenth century to accumulate gold and silver for armies. The mercantilists maintained that precious metals were the only things of value. In France, Jean Baptiste Colbert (1619–1683) brought all aspects of production under state control, including luxury goods, in order to improve industry in the colonial empire. To stimulate trade, the French government established an alliance with business by building and repairing canals and even subsidizing shipbuilders and shippers. Also, to defend French industry against foreign competition, Colbert imposed tariffs on imported cloth and subsidized the settlement of Dutch weavers into France. To discourage domestic consumption of exportable luxury goods, excise taxes known as *sumptuary taxes* were imposed. However, the extreme protectionist policies of Colbert did not bring prosperity to the French economy because the costs of such intervention exceeded the value of the benefits.

The protective trade policies of the mercantilists in Britain and Germany, on the other hand, were shaped by interest groups, wars, and recessions. For example, in

Britain, Thomas Mun (1571–1641), director of the East Indian Company, maintained a state-supported monopoly over trade with India because of his lobbying power and influence in the Parliament.

MODERN HISTORY

At the start of the Industrial Revolution in the late eighteenth century, as belief in the protectionist policies of the mercantilists was dwindling, the views of physiocrats gained popularity. The physiocrats believed that land is the source of value and were the first to articulate free trade under their laissez-faire policy, according to which there should be no tariffs on the export of agricultural goods. Later, the English classical economists Adam Smith (1723–1790) and David Ricardo (1772–1823) rebelled against the mercantilists' protectionist doctrine. Using the comparative advantage argument, Ricardo advocated free trade and attacked the corn laws, which limited the import of grain into England to protect domestic farmers. Assuming what was called later *perfect competition*, Smith viewed unconstrained expansion of markets through free international trade as a powerful force providing additional opportunities for specialization and the division of labor.

Although liberal trade policies gained prominence in the nineteenth century, some economists on both sides of the Atlantic questioned the assumptions of these free trade theories. They argued that in the presence of positive externalities and dynamic economies of scale, government must pursue activist national policies to promote economic development and industrialization. Among these economists, Friedrich List (1789–1846) of Germany is notable for the power of his argument and his historical exemplars—demonstrating how, alternatively, free trade or protectionism is useful, depending on the stage of economic development. In the nineteenth century, Hamburg was a major trading center benefiting from free trade, even as the largely agricultural economy of Germany was becoming overwhelmed by the industrial supremacy of Great Britain. List linked economic development and industrial growth to the national interest and security of Germany, and he called for elimination of internal tariffs among states and for the expansion of the custom union (*Zollverein*). He also pleaded for protection of infant industries with tariffs as a part of a broader development strategy that included other policies, such as the creation of a national railway network. List did not suggest a return to mercantilist policies; rather, he believed in the importance of manufacturing to the national economy. Living in the United States in the 1830s, List was influenced by the views of Alexander Hamilton (1755/57–1804), who, like List, was critical of protectionist policies such as corn laws and agreed with Adam Smith on national defense as

a justification for protectionism. The infant industry argument was also supported by prominent contemporary economists, such as John Stuart Mill (1806–1873) and Alfred Marshall (1908–1993).

Historically, changes in economic theories seem to have motivated changes in government trade policies, though the direction of causation is not always clear. With the new ideological tool of laissez-faire, government policies moved toward more free trade during the nineteenth century. In the late nineteenth century, a revolution in shipping and an expansion of railways contributed to falling transportation costs, offsetting rising tariffs. The use of trade barriers rose during the twentieth century's two world wars. However, after World War II (1939–1945), international organizations, such as the General Agreements on Tariffs and Trade (GATT), brought order to world trade by allowing a multilateral system of rules for government trade policies. During the oil and financial crises of the 1970s, protectionism tended to expand again in world trade. However, the Uruguay Round of the GATT trade negotiations led in 1995 to the formation of the World Trade Organization (WTO), which provides a forum for trade negotiations and dispute resolution among member states. The WTO has experienced some success in reducing trade barriers and reaching agreements in the areas of financial services, telecommunications, and information technology. In agriculture, however, reducing subsidies among developed countries has remained a challenge for the WTO.

PHILOSOPHIES OF PROTECTIONISM

While the old protectionism philosophy was concerned with attracting and retaining precious metals, modern protectionism theories are interested in the production benefits of restricted trade policies. Some of the new theories of international trade consider the consequences of economies of scale and relax the assumption of perfect competition. These theories question comparative advantage as the explanation for trade, and renew support for protectionism for national interests.

The historical pattern of government policy on international trade appears to exhibit cyclical movements between free trade and protectionism. The apparent systemic shifts between openness and protectionism are caused by a variety of factors, such as hegemonic stability emphasizing the importance of leadership. For example, in the second half of the nineteenth century, after Britain became the world economic and political power, it pursued an open economic system. U.S. leadership after World War II and the dominance of capitalism led to a worldwide reduction in tariffs by GATT. Other causes of changes in international trade policies include excess industrial capacity and overproduction or a glut of agricultural products leading to high unemployment, declining profitability, and eventually protectionism, and developments of new economic theories, such as those by Smith and Ricardo. It is even argued that patriotic sentiments help shape protectionist beliefs.

EMPIRICAL EVIDENCE

Numerous studies since the 1980s examine various protectionist policies and their effects. For example, some studies have shown that the greatest growth in the world has been associated with the most liberal trade policies (Capie 1994; Baldwin 1986). However, since the late 1950s, some of the empirical evidence and casual observations have not been fully consistent with the simple theory of comparative advantage. In some cases, endogenous technological change, economies of scale, and imperfect competition have explained patterns of international trade better than the simple law of comparative advantage and have provided justification for government intervention. Strategic trade policies of export subsidies and import restrictions, targeting sensitive industries with increasing return and imperfect competition, have been successful in some countries in creating sustainable comparative advantage. However, economists such as Paul Krugman (1995) argue that the influence of interest groups on governments can lead to excessive and misguided interventions that are likely to raise national income but benefit only a small group of people. In other words, real world politics is as imperfect as markets. Typically, a small group of stakeholders in the protected industry benefit from protectionist policies, whereas the costs are distributed among a large number of consumers. Therefore, as Jong-Wha Lee and Phillip Swagel (1997) argue, while protectionism is inefficient economically, it may be efficient politically.

Gene Grossman and Elhanan Helpman (1994) produce a more rigorous analysis of protectionism and the role of interest groups. In their model, the structure of protectionism is determined by the elasticity of import demand, which determines the degree of welfare distortion and the ratio of imports to domestic output, showing the political significance of the domestic industry. Daniel Trefler (1993) carries this argument further by demonstrating that the level of trade protectionism is endogenously determined. According to the theory of endogenous protectionism, as import penetration rises in an industry, lobbying activities by interest groups intensify, leading to greater protection.

Investigating the determinants of trade barriers, Edward Ray (1981a) finds that tariff and nontariff barriers are the result of both economic and political factors. Ray's cross-sectional study of U.S. trade finds that both the existence and intensity of nontariff barriers affect

exports, though the profitability of protectionism depends on industry characteristics. Elsewhere, Ray (1981b) finds that industries with an apparent comparative advantage and with larger consumer losses tend to receive more protection in the United States. While tariffs are positively related to labor intensity, they are inversely related to the capital/labor ratio. Interestingly, the opposite is true for nontariff barriers. Furthermore, nontariff barriers are negatively related to seller concentration and geographical concentration, but tariffs are positively related to seller concentration and geographical concentration. Lee and Swagel (1997) accounted for country and industry characteristics and found that weak, declining, and politically important industries tend to receive more protection than exporting industries.

SEE ALSO *Absolute and Comparative Advantage; Quotas, Trade; Tariffs; Trade, Bilateral*

BIBLIOGRAPHY

Baldwin, Robert E. 1986. The New Protectionism: A Response to Shifts in National Economic Power. NBER Working Papers Series 1823. Cambridge, MA: National Bureau of Economic Research.

Bhagwati, Jagdish N. 1988. *Protectionism*. Cambridge, MA: MIT Press.

Canterbery, E. Ray. 2003. *The Making of Economics*. 4th ed. River Edge, NJ: World Scientific.

Capie, Forrest. 1994. *Tariffs and Growth: Some Illustrations from the World Economy, 1850–1940*. Manchester, U.K.: Manchester University Press.

Grossman, Gene M., and Elhanan Helpman. 1994. Protection for Sale. *American Economic Review* 84 (4): 833–850.

Krugman, Paul. 1995. *Development, Geography, and Economic Theory*. Cambridge, MA: MIT Press.

Lee, Jong-Wha, and Phillip Swagel. 1997. Trade Barriers and Trade Flows Across Countries and Industries. *Review of Economics and Statistics* 79 (3): 372–382.

Ray, Edward John. 1981a. The Determinants of Tariff and Nontariff Trade Restrictions in the United States. *Journal of Political Economy* 89 (1): 105–121.

Ray, Edward John. 1981b. Tariff and Nontariff Barriers to Trade in the United States and Abroad. *Review of Economics and Statistics* 68 (2): 161–168.

So, Billy K. L. 2000. *Prosperity, Region, and Institutions in Maritime China: The South Fukien Pattern, 946–1368*. Cambridge, MA: Harvard University Press.

Trefler, Daniel. 1993. Trade Liberalization and the Theory of Endogenous Protectionism: An Econometric Study of U.S. Import Policy. *Journal of Political Economy* 101 (1): 138–160.

Akbar Marvasti

PROTEIN GAP
SEE *Malnutrition.*

PROTEST

Social protest is collective action that uses unconventional means to press claims on institutional authorities to alter conditions and address collective grievances. From suicide bombings, to peaceful street marches, to religious ceremonies ordaining women as Catholic priests or acts of sabotage and passive resistance, social protests make claims on the state and other institutional authorities to correct perceived injustices, alter practices and understandings, and redistribute access to social goods. In the process, these protests also construct new collective identities and forge new meanings that inform politics and everyday life and bring about changes in popular culture, social practices, and institutional structures. While all protests are political in the minimal sense that securing desired changes typically requires gaining the cooperation and approval of political authorities, many protests are explicitly political in that they attempt to change public policies, the personnel in the government, and the structure of the state.

Protests vary in their visibility and methods. Everyday *resistance* is the most covert, involving acts of noncooperation, such as military desertion and foot-dragging by peasants, to more proactive acts, such as using symbols and gestures of authority to highlight discrepancies between how authorities act and their claims about what is fair and equitable (Scott 1985). Popular songs about exploitative bosses, as well as poetry highlighting the evils of landlords and heralding the heroism of the common people, put authority into question and prepare the way for more concerted protests. In Poland during the 1980s, for example, workers, artists, and intellectuals used the symbolism of the socialist state to question the extent to which the state actually represented worker interests, thereby paving the way for the demonstrations, vigils, and marches of the Solidarity movement (Osa 2003).

By questioning authority, everyday resistance may open the way to *institutional protests* that are overt, entail collective mobilization, and are legal or at least recognized by authorities as a legitimate form of expression. Initially, these protests are often illegal, but, through a process of accommodation with authorities and public acceptance, they become legitimized. By "striking their sails," eighteenth-century sailors forced ship captains to pay back wages, distribute the "grog ration," or put into shore. Later, the *strike* became a legally regulated form of protest, with government agencies responsible for certifying strikes and court regulation of picketing, marches, and the use of strike funds. In the 1770s early American colonists burned effigies and dumped tea into Boston Harbor, and organized widespread boycotts by refusing to pay new taxes imposed by the British Crown. Later, boycotts became legally regulated, and were split into *primary boycotts* (directed against the primary target) and *secondary boycotts* (directed against a third party, such as a grocery store that sells boycotted products).

Historically, forms of institutional protest were forged by excluded groups, such as industrial workers and racial minorities, who turned to protest when the conventional politics of voting and lobbying were unavailable or ineffective. Francis Piven and Richard Cloward (1977) argue that protests retain their leverage so long as they are illegitimate, but lose potency as they become regulated. In contemporary Western democracies, protest marches and demonstrations are mobilized by all types of groups, including corporations, churches, professional societies, and trade associations. Such protests have become legally regulated events, leading to the conclusion that Western democracies have become social movement societies (Meyer and Tarrow 1998). Sidney Tarrow (1998) argues that, by the early twentieth century, such institutional protests had become "modular" in that they are readily understood and available for most literate and media-conscious populations as a vehicle for expressing their interests.

Illegal or illegitimate protests that violate institutional rules and understandings are more disruptive and require more commitment. In such cases, protestors directly disrupt ongoing institutions by blocking access to them or impeding their routine operation and by directly defying authority. Nonviolent resistance or civil disobedience is one form of this category of protest. Drawing on Mohandas Gandhi's (1869–1948) theory of passive resistance (Sharp 1973), in the early 1960s black college students organized lunch counter sit-ins across the American South, refusing to move until they were served and challenging authorities to arrest them until their demands for racial desegregation were recognized (Orum 1972; McAdam 1999). In the early 1970s in Northern Ireland, Irish Republican Army supporters staged hunger strikes in the prisons, refusing to cooperate with authorities and ultimately bringing into question the legitimacy of British policies and rule in the region (White 1993). Nonviolent resistance is typically framed in terms of a universal moral claim, such as "God's law" or the "natural order," that supersedes existing institutions.

All these forms of protest attempt to exert influence directly by imposing negative sanctions and creating uncertainty in the eyes of targets, and indirectly by mobilizing third-party bystanders to support demands for change. Protestors engaging in *collective violence* attempt to exert influence by imposing physical injury or harm on targets, forcing targets to comply or destroying their will to resist change. Violence creates clarity and polarization by forcing potential allies and bystanders to choose sides. This makes violence a risky strategy, especially for weak and poorly organized groups. Violent protest is almost certain to provoke repression or counterviolence as authorities claim the need to protect "law and order," leading to arrests or destruction. Except where the state is already weak or has already collapsed, political authorities typically hold the advantage and respond with police and military force, as well as less obtrusive forms of social control (Davenport 2005). Groups that resort to violence typically have to go underground, using "safe houses" and secret codes, imposing iron discipline on their members, and resocializing activists to become "true believers" whose world is reduced to a single cultlike movement or group.

Protest has multiple causes. First are *collective grievances*, typically stemming from abrupt and widely experienced social strains or discontinuities that disrupt everyday life. Mass unemployment, political flight due to war and civil violence, and widespread hunger due to famine and political chaos are often critical. Second are *resources*, especially leadership and collective organization, that facilitate mobilization. More-cohesive groups that share collective identities and networks of solidarity, as well as experienced local leaders, are much more likely to protest. Black ministers and church leaders in the United States, for example, were central to organizing many of the civil rights protests of the 1950s and 1960s (Morris 1984). Third are *cultural resources* in terms of collective identities and understandings that can be used to frame and justify protest. Framing defines conditions as unjust and subject to change, thereby allowing groups to protest (Snow and Benford 1988). Fourth are *political opportunities*, that is, "the probability that social protest actions will lead to success in achieving a desired outcome" (Goldstone and Tilly 2001, p. 182). Electoral candidates faced with closely divided government and close elections make appeals to political outsiders in the hope that these groups might provide the votes needed for victory. In the United States, the closely fought national elections in the late 1950s and early 1960s made the black vote an appealing resource for both Republicans and Democrats, which encouraged civil rights protests by creating signals of governmental responsiveness (McAdam 1999). Similarly, these electoral contests helped trigger the farmworker movement of the 1960s, as well as a wave of student, women's, disabled, and other minority protests (Jenkins 1985).

Does protest create social change? Most protests fail in their broader objectives, especially as envisioned by critical intellectuals and activists (Rochon 1998). But protests nonetheless set in motion processes that often result in improvements for aggrieved groups. The labor protests of the 1930s helped create industrial unions, which became an important device for providing better wages, benefits, and job security for workers. Civil rights protests helped abolish Jim Crow laws and legal racial segregation, which characterized the United States through the 1960s, paving the way for black elected officials to introduce improved urban services in many southern communities (Button 1989). Anti–Vietnam War protests, especially the more violent and disruptive protests, helped push the U.S. Congress to adopt legislation limiting the war effort and eventually contributed to a reversal of U.S. foreign policy (Burstein and Freudenberg 1978; McAdam and Su 2002). These changes were not due simply to protests, but protests contributed to a broader set of political processes that have often generated policy and broader institutional and cultural changes. By initiating and stimulating these changes, protest can be seen as a rational and effective method of gaining political and social influence.

SEE ALSO *Activism; Anticolonial Movements; Authority; Civil Disobedience; Civil Rights Movement, U.S.; Jim Crow; Mau Mau; Participation, Political; Passive Resistance; Resistance; Social Movements; Vietnam War; Violence*

BIBLIOGRAPHY

Burstein, Paul, and William Freudenberg. 1978. Changing Public Policy: The Impact of Public Opinion, Anti-War Demonstrations, and War Costs on Senate Voting on Vietnam War Motions. *American Journal of Sociology* 84: 99–122.

Button, James. 1989. *Blacks and Social Change: Impact of the Civil Rights Movement in Southern Communities*. Princeton, NJ: Princeton University Press.

Davenport, Christian. 2005. Introduction: Repression and Mobilization. In *Repression and Mobilization*, ed. Christian Davenport, Hank Johnston, and Carol Mueller, vii–xii. Minneapolis: University of Minnesota Press.

Goldstone, Jack A., and Charles Tilly. 2001. Threat (and Opportunity). In *Silence and Voice in the Study of Contentious Politics*, ed. Ronald Aminzade, Jack Goldstone, Doug McAdam, et al., 179–194. New York: Cambridge University Press.

Jenkins, J. Craig. 1985. *The Politics of Insurgency: The Farm Worker Movement of the 1960s*. New York: Columbia University Press.

McAdam, Doug. 1999. *Political Process and the Development of Black Insurgency, 1930–1970*. 2nd ed. Chicago: University of Chicago Press.

McAdam, Doug, and Yang Su. 2002. The War at Home: Antiwar Protests and Congressional Voting, 1965 to 1973. *American Sociological Review* 67: 696–721.

Meyer, David, and Sidney Tarrow, eds. 1998. *The Social Movement Society: Contentious Politics for a New Century.* Lanham, MD: Rowman and Littlefield.

Morris, Aldon. 1984. *The Origins of the Civil Rights Movement: Black Communities Organizing for Change.* New York: Free Press.

Orum, Anthony. 1972. *Black Students in Protest: A Study of the Origins of the Black Student Movement.* Washington, DC: American Sociological Association.

Osa, Maryjane. 2003. *Solidarity and Contention: Networks of Polish Opposition.* Minneapolis: University of Minnesota Press.

Piven, Frances, and Richard Cloward. 1977. *Poor People's Movements: Why They Succeed, How They Fail.* New York: Pantheon.

Rochon, Thomas R. 1998. *Culture Moves: Ideas, Activism, and Changing Values.* Princeton, NJ: Princeton University Press.

Scott, James. 1985. *Weapons of the Weak: Everyday Forms of Peasant Resistance.* New Haven, CT: Yale University Press.

Sharp, Gene. 1973. *The Politics of Nonviolent Action.* Boston: Sargent.

Snow, David E., and Robert Benford. 1988. Ideology, Frame Resonance, and Participant Mobilization. In *International Social Movement Research*, ed. Bert Klandermans, Hanspeter Kriesi, and Sidney Tarrow, 197–217. Greenwich, CT: JAI.

Tarrow, Sidney. 1998. *Power in Movement: Social Movements and Contentious Politics.* 2nd ed. Cambridge, U.K., and New York: Cambridge University Press.

White, Robert W. 1993. *Provisional Irish Republicans: An Oral and Interpretive History.* Westport, CT: Greenwood.

J. Craig Jenkins

PROTEST MOVEMENTS

SEE *Social Movements.*

PROTESTANT ETHIC, THE

Published originally as two long articles in 1904 and 1905, Max Weber's classic *The Protestant Ethic and the Spirit of Capitalism* (1920) is one of the most enduring and widely read volumes in modern social science. On its publication it immediately set off a heated debate and, remarkably, to this day the controversy has continued almost undiminished.

The Protestant Ethic investigated whether the "Protestant ethic" found among seventeenth-century Puritans (mainly Calvinists, Methodists, Baptists, and Quakers) "coparticipated" in giving birth to a driving force Weber (1864–1920) saw as contributing to the rise

of the industrial west: a secular "spirit of capitalism." Adherents of this "modern economic ethic," he argued, viewed work as a vocational calling (*Beruf*). Characteristic was a rigorous—an ascetic—organization of occupational life according to a set of values, a methodical and dutiful striving for profit and wealth, and a systematic reinvestment of money rather than its enjoyment.

THE DOCTRINE OF PREDESTINATION

The doctrine of predestination anchors Weber's argument in *The Protestant Ethic.* According to the French theologian John Calvin (1509–1564), an inscrutable Old Testament God, omniscient and omnipotent, has determined that only a chosen few will be reborn into heaven. Good works or ethical behavior can never influence His decisions. Unbearable anxiety and fatalism were the consequence of this doctrine for the faithful, Weber noted. However, revisions were undertaken in the late sixteenth and early seventeenth centuries by the "Puritan Divines," a group of Methodist, Calvinist, Quaker, and Baptist ministers, theologians, and lay believers in England. Herein lies the source of the Protestant ethic, Weber maintained.

Weber's analysis at this point can be seen to divide into two stages. First, the Puritans elevated to the forefront methodical work and wealth. The purpose of life itself involved labor, they argued; work in a calling is "commanded to all" by God, and He is gratified by the active execution of His will by believers. Moreover, by taming base wants and desires, systematic labor assists concentration upon God and His plan; it also dispels the overwhelming doubt, anxiety, and sense of moral unworthiness caused by the doctrine of predestination. A parallel sanctification took place in respect to wealth. The creation of God's kingdom constituted the purpose of this short life, according to the Puritans, and an earthly cosmos of wealth and abundance would surely serve His glory. Methodical work—a crucial means toward this noble end—thereby acquired a further special dignity. In sum, this ascetic Protestantism bestowed clear "psychological premiums" upon constant labor and the search for riches. Both activities lost their exclusively mundane meaning and became providential.

Although influential, this sanctification failed to overcome fully the long-standing ethos anchored in medieval Catholicism. Labor, according to this "traditional economic ethic," was understood as a necessary evil, and profit was seldom earned honestly. If this "frame of mind" was to be banished, work and wealth had to acquire an even more comprehensive sanctification, *The Protestant Ethic* held. Furthermore, the all-important question to anxious believers—"am I among the saved?"—had not yet been answered adequately. In this regard, the second stage of Weber's analysis proves crucial.

Despite the predestination decree, the Puritan Divines concluded that *signs* from God of the believer's salvation status could be discovered. Above all, the deity's favor seemed apparent if the devout demonstrated a capacity, as required by their vocational calling, either to labor systematically or to remain focused upon the onerous task of acquiring wealth. Indeed, the faithful convinced themselves that their strength and discipline to do so, as well as their intense devotion and righteous conduct, came from God: His energy was "operating within." And surely this majestic divinity would bestow His powers only upon the predestined elect. Methodical work and great wealth now became "evidence" of one's favorable salvation status.

FROM "SPIRITUAL FOUNDATION" TO "MECHANICAL FOUNDATION"

Now awarded psychological premiums in an even more thorough manner, constant labor and the possession of riches became viewed by believers as testifying to their salvation. They offered literal proof (*Bewährung*) to the devout of redemption. As anxiety declined, the depressed and bleak Puritan became transformed into the disciplined "tool" of God's will, proudly engaged in the task of building His glorious kingdom on earth.

According to Weber, this methodical-rational organization of life and inner-worldly asceticism—a "Protestant ethic"—distinguished the "Puritan style of life." The faithful focused their energies and conduct in a comprehensive manner upon God's will, restricted consumption, reinvested profits, banished the traditional economic ethic, and placed work at the center of life. Extreme loyalty to His grand design marked the devout, as did cognizance that riches emanated from the hand of this omnipotent deity and thus belonged exclusively to Him and His kingdom. Wealth *must* be, on His behalf and for His community, invested instead of enjoyed. Simultaneously, the image of those engaged in business and oriented to profit changed: Rather than viewed as calculating, greedy, and self-interested, as had been the case since antiquity, capitalists were now perceived as honest employers engaged in a noble project given by God. The halo of religion—a "spiritual foundation"—surrounded their activities, and hence the understanding of the production and exchange of goods as involving exclusively utilitarian calculations and clever business procedures must be abandoned, Weber contended. Specialists in vocations—a new "type of person" (*Menschentyp*)—now embarked upon the stage of western history. They "coparticipated" in the formation of the spirit of capitalism and constituted one of its major "social carriers."

Weber saw this "modern economic ethic," which is represented in *The Protestant Ethic* by Benjamin Franklin (1706–1790), as providing an underlying psychological thrust and legitimation to modern capitalism's early development in the eighteenth and nineteenth centuries. However, its value-oriented roots gradually died out as industrialization and urbanization proceeded over the last two centuries, and today capitalism unfolds exclusively on a purely "mechanical foundation." Impersonal exchange relationships, pragmatic necessities, and manifold external constraint—a "steel-hard casing" (*stahlhartes Gehäuse*)—now predominate. "The Puritan," Weber maintained, "*wanted* to be a person with a vocational calling; we *must* be" ([1920] 2008, p. 123).

CRITICISMS OF WEBER

Controversy surrounded *The Protestant Ethic* immediately after its publication. Generations of critics and defenders have debated vehemently "the Weber thesis." Arguably, no other volume in the social sciences in the English-speaking world has generated a more intense and long-term discussion. Four of the major lines of criticism are adumbrated here.

First, commentators have frequently viewed *The Protestant Ethic* as proposing that ascetic Protestantism caused, in a linear manner, modern capitalism. Innumerable critics then insisted that beliefs never explain historical change. Some maintained that new technologies introduced industrial capitalism (e.g., the cotton gin, the steam engine); others perceived the heroism and greed of great capitalists (e.g., Rockefeller, Carnegie, Vanderbilt) as pivotal; still others insisted that sheer business astuteness or the economic and political power and interests of a dominant class were central—and then argued that a systematic work ethos developed out of power and interests alone. All then dismissed *The Protestant Ethic* as naively trumpeting the power of ideas to change history. This criticism—"Weber is an idealist"—misses the mark, however. *The Protestant Ethic* acknowledged the necessity for a complex and multidimensional analysis ([1920] 2008, p. 125), yet Weber focused intentionally in this volume upon only "one side" of the causal configuration. He did so in order forcefully to bring a heretofore neglected cultural factor into an ongoing debate. Moreover, as noted, he sought to explain the origin of the spirit of capitalism rather than of modern capitalism.

Weber held in *The Protestant Ethic* that subsequent research must address the large question of whether the spirit of capitalism played a significant part in calling forth industrial capitalism. In fact, this broad theme—the unique development of the modern west out of arrays of "ideas and interests"—directly captured his attention in an ambitious series of comparative studies almost entirely neglected by his critics. He asked, what constellations of interacting social, economic, political, technological, legal, and religious activities explain the particular historical pathway taken in the west? How can sociologists oriented to multiple causes analyze the specific direction and outcome of western history? *The Protestant Ethic*'s exploration of the *religious* sources behind the secular spirit of capitalism must be understood as Weber's first step toward fulfilling this broad-ranging agenda.

Second, theologians in particular have been critical of Weber's discussions of Catholic, Lutheran, and ascetic Protestant doctrines. Many have dissected Calvin's teachings and failed to discover an emphasis upon work in a vocation. However, these scholars have neglected to note Weber's distinction between Calvin's doctrines and the ascetic Protestantism of the sixteenth and seventeenth centuries. He locates the source of the Protestant ethic in the Puritanism of this latter period rather than in Calvin's teachings, and emphasizes the many revisions of Calvin's thought introduced by the Puritan Divines.

Third, commentators frequently insisted that capitalism predated Puritanism. They discovered it to be significantly widespread in the ancient and medieval worlds in the west and Middle East, as well as in China and India. Although Weber maintained that his main concern in *The Protestant Ethic* involved the origins of a Protestant ethic and the extent of its influence upon a spirit of capitalism, capitalism's general origins were also of interest to him. His discussion of this theme, however, distinguished sharply between modern industrial capitalism on the one hand and "political," or "adventure," capitalism on the other hand. Whereas the former—his interest—arose only in the modern west, the latter appeared universally, he held.

Fourth, a long list of critics argued that two Renaissance figures, the great entrepreneur Jacob Fugger (1459–1525) and the urban architect and aesthetician Leon Battista Alberti (1404–1472), possessed a spirit of capitalism essentially similar to Benjamin Franklin's. These commentators further maintained that the spirit of capitalism blossomed forth exclusively out of practical interests and utilitarian business astuteness. A religious source must be seen as both superfluous and historically inaccurate, they insisted.

Weber countered this attack in endnotes added in 1919 and 1920 to *The Protestant Ethic* by repeating and elaborating upon his defense against these "relativizing" critics. While noting that Alberti and Fugger had accommodated to, rather than changed, the economic conditions of their time, Weber contended that the central issue here involves a distinction—pivotal for him yet unacknowledged by the critics—between utilitarian activity on the one hand and value-oriented activity on the other

hand. Motives vary, he emphasized, and the "practical-rational" approach to life is not dominant in all groupings in all historical epochs. This commentary, he maintained, neglected the ways in which values may independently motivate action. Indeed, a *methodical* aspect—an element indispensable for the birth of the spirit of capitalism and the shattering of the traditional economic ethic—was alone introduced by action oriented to values, according to Weber.

In sum, Weber often has been misunderstood by his many critics. A dynamic tapestry characterizes *The Protestant Ethic* analysis. Despite regular indictments, the Weber thesis survives to this day and must be confronted by scholars seeking to understand the rise of modern capitalism. By calling attention to the important historical roles played by both a Protestant ethic and a spirit of capitalism, *The Protestant Ethic* questions all those theories that explain the origin of the modern world exclusively by reference to utilitarian activity (for example, rational choice theory) or structural transformations (whether of Marxian or Durkheimian lineage). The varying *subjective meaning* of persons in demarcated groups proved central to Weber, as did the other-worldly, value-oriented ancestry of the modern world. The Puritan's asceticism originated from his life "in but not of" the world.

The Protestant Ethic must be comprehended as the father of all schools of sociological thought that, in seeking to explain long-range social change, explicitly attend to cultural forces. It must be further understood as declaring emphatically that the past is interwoven with, and influences, the present. Finally, in an age of universalizing globalization, *The Protestant Ethic* conveys the causal significance of the indigenous cultural make-up inevitably manifest when a nation embarks upon an economic modernization course. He admonished social scientists generally to take account of religion-based background contexts for social change.

SEE ALSO *Culture; Norms; Values*

BIBLIOGRAPHY

Chalcraft, David J., and Austin Harrington, eds. 2001. *The "Protestant Ethic" Debate: Max Weber's Replies to His Critics, 1907–1910*. Liverpool, U.K.: Liverpool University Press.

Kalberg, Stephen. 2003. Max Weber. In *The Blackwell Companion to Major Social Theorists*, ed. George Ritzer, 132–192. Oxford: Blackwell.

Kalberg, Stephen, ed. 2005. *Max Weber: Readings and Commentary on Modernity*. Oxford: Blackwell.

Lehmann, Hartmut, and Guenther Roth, eds. 1993. *Weber's "Protestant Ethic": Origins, Evidence, Contexts*. New York: Cambridge University Press.

Swados, William H., and Lutz Kaelber, eds. 2005. *The "Protestant Ethic" Turns 100*. Boulder, CO: Paradigm.

Weber, Max. [1920] 2008. *The Protestant Ethic and the Spirit of Capitalism and Other Writings on the Rise of the West.* Trans. Stephen Kalberg. New York: Oxford University Press.

Stephen Kalberg

PROTESTANTISM

Protestantism is generally thought of as being one of the three major branches of the Christian faith (the other two being Roman Catholicism and Eastern Orthodoxy). Protestantism is a broad category. It includes, for example, Anglicans, Baptists, Campbellites, Congregationalists, Lutherans, Methodists, Mennonites, Nazarenes, Presbyterians, Quakers, Seventh-Day Adventists, and Unitarians. Texts that are generally taken to embody the spirit of Protestantism include Martin Luther's translation of the Bible into the German language, John Calvin's *Institutes of the Christian Religion*, the Anglican *Book of Common Prayer*, John Milton's *Paradise Lost*, Isaac Watts's *Hymns and Spiritual Songs*, John Woolman's *Journal*, George Eliot's *The Mill on the Floss*, Søren Kierkegaard's *The Sickness unto Death*, the *Barmen Declaration*, and the Rev. Dr. Martin Luther King Jr.'s *Letter from Birmingham Jail*.

HISTORY AND GEOGRAPHY

Protestantism arose in Western Europe in the sixteenth and seventeenth centuries. It came into being as the result of the efforts of men such as John Calvin, John Knox, Martin Luther, Menno Simons, and Huldrych Zwingli to "reform" what they saw as the "errors" of the Roman Catholic Church. The drive to "correct" these "mistakes" ended up profoundly transforming the political, as well as the religious, institutions of Western Europe. Indeed, scholars have claimed that the Protestant Reformation played a crucial role in creating the religious, political, social, economic, and cultural formations that came to embody "modernity."

There is no scholarly consensus on the number of Protestants in the world. If one adopts a quite broad definition and counts people who are only nominally Christian as well as those who are quite devout, then one might argue that the total is over 800 million. Although Protestantism was created in Western Europe, it has spread throughout much of the world. Protestant beliefs and practices are quite common, of course, in Australia and North America, and have a strong foothold in some Asian countries—South Korea and the Philippines, for instance. Protestants make up sizable minorities in Latin American nations such as Brazil, Costa Rica, El Salvador, and Guatemala. In a number of African countries (Lesotho, Liberia, Malawi, Namibia, South Africa, and Swaziland, for instance), Protestants constitute a large proportion of the citizens. Indeed, some scholars have argued that Protestantism's future may lie in Africa and Latin America rather than in Europe or North America. Certainly, it now seems to be far more vital in Africa and Latin America than in some of the nations of Western Europe.

PRACTICES

From the sixteenth century to the present, Protestants have consistently claimed to be highly suspicious of "empty ritualism." Such suspicions notwithstanding, over the centuries Protestants have developed a set of powerful religious practices that vivify the doctrines and symbols of the Christian faith. Some Protestants (Lutherans and Anglicans especially) have maintained carefully crafted formal liturgies. The roots of those liturgies stretch back to—indeed reach back beyond—the sixteenth century, and have much in common with Catholic and Orthodox liturgies. Other Protestants, often referred to as Evangelicals, have created revival services intended to convert nonbelievers into devout Christians. And since the beginning of the twentieth century, a group of Protestants who are often labeled Pentecostals or Charismatics have held services that focus on the "gift of tongues." This gift—which often results in a kind of ecstatic speech that is not intelligible to hearers—is thought of as a sign of the power of the Holy Spirit.

As a general rule, Protestants tend to display a strong love for singing hymns and gospel songs. Accordingly, a good portion of many Protestant worship services is devoted to choral and congregational singing. Protestant worship services also tend to devote a good deal of time to listening to homilies and sermons. These sermons, which are sometimes filled with emotion and sometimes quite erudite, are intended to help the people who hear them comprehend the truths of the Christian faith as those truths are set forth in the Christian scriptures.

Indeed, the importance of the Christian scriptures in shaping Protestant practice and belief is difficult to exaggerate. Reading the scriptures aloud is one of the high points of many Protestant worship services, and the hymns Protestants sing are often based on passages from the Bible. (Martin Luther's "A Mighty Fortress is Our God" is, for example, based on Psalm 46.) The scriptures also play a large role in the private devotional practices of most Protestants. And Protestants greatly value Bible study groups and Sunday School classes in which small groups meet together to ascertain the meaning of passages from the Bible.

It is no accident that many Protestant devotional practices focus on the Christian scriptures, for Protestants have tended to see the Bible—rather than the traditions of the church—as the surest guide to understanding the nature of reality and of God. Protestants have often expressed a certain distrust of human reason or of observations of nature as a way to grasp the truth. If given a choice between relying on observations of nature, reason, tradition, or the Bible as a way to understand the nature of God and the universe, many Protestants would say, without hesitation, that their choice would be the Bible.

In part because they tend to put great confidence in the power of the Christian scriptures, correctly comprehended, to disclose the nature of ultimate reality, Protestants sometimes have acted in ways that have seemed to smack of hubris. In its most extreme form, this apparent hubris has resulted in some Protestant leaders coming close to asserting that the Bible is infallible and that they themselves have fully and correctly comprehended the truths that are taught therein. Critics have sometimes argued that this self-confident scripturalism is one of the hallmarks of Protestantism and that its predilection for that kind of scripturalism makes Protestantism a particularly dangerous form of religion. Such arguments are not without merit.

It should also be noted, however, that Protestants (like many other religious human beings) have sometimes been keenly aware of human finitude. This has sometimes led Protestants to fiercely critique all human attempts to speak for God and all human claims to have fully understood God's nature and desires. Some Protestants have gone so far as to say that all human ideas and beliefs—including all Protestant ideas and beliefs—are very far from the mind of God. Under some conditions, the Protestant view of the world can, therefore, inculcate a good deal of humility within the people who adhere to it.

SOCIAL TEACHINGS

The Protestant tendency to see all human institutions as imperfect has sometimes been connected with a wide-ranging set of emancipatory impulses. Protestant beliefs and practices played an important role, for instance, in the abolitionist movements of the eighteenth and nineteenth centuries. Those beliefs and practices have sometimes been linked, too, with anticolonial and feminist movements. Many Protestants have, on occasion, fiercely critiqued the behavior of the nation-states in whose borders they resided. Created in part in reaction to what sixteenth- and seventeenth-century reformers saw as an overly rigid and overly powerful set of ecclesiastical institutions, Protestantism has sometimes tended to value "freedom" over "tradition" and "conscience" over the "laws of men."

Protestantism has also, many scholars would assert, served to naturalize a wide range of inegalitarian social relationships. In the eighteenth and nineteenth centuries, for example, Protestants wrote and preached countless defenses of the institution of chattel slavery. In the twentieth century, many white Protestants living in the United States (especially those living in the former slave states) advanced theological defenses of white supremacy. Indeed, pious Protestants often played crucial roles in Southern campaigns to defeat the civil rights movements of the 1950s and 1960s.

Patriarchal social relations have also often been naturalized by Protestant beliefs and practices. Protestants have generally thought of God as masculine and referred to God with masculine pronouns. Protestant churches have generally believed that to obtain salvation a woman must submit herself to the authority of this masculine Lord. Historically, women have been taught that it was "natural" for them to defer to men. Protestant churches have also tended to see persons who have sex with someone to whom they are not married as rebelling against God's laws. Protestant churches have taught that women who have sex with other women and (especially) men who have sex with other men are violating God's fundamental laws, and these sorts of violations have been regarded as particularly unnatural and repugnant. In general, Protestant churches have tended to be organizations in which heterosexual norms have been enforced quite strictly.

Scholars do not agree on the precise nature of the relationship between Protestantism and capitalism. Some scholarly analyses of that relationship (Max Weber's, for instance) emphasize Protestantism's role in creating circumstances in which modern capitalism could arise and flourish; other scholarly analyses (R. H. Tawney's, for example) focus on ways in which the rise of capitalism decisively influenced Protestants' assumptions and habits. Most scholars would, however, assert that Protestant churches have tended to naturalize the authority of capitalist institutions. Protestant churches have often seen commercial success as a sign of Godly favor and they have often acted as though it was natural for businessmen to play a large role in running church affairs. Protestant churches have eagerly adopted techniques and methods developed by businessmen. Indeed, many have been run in ways strikingly similar to those of for-profit corporations.

The "peace churches" (Mennonites, for example) have sometimes raised pointed questions about whether the violence employed by nation-states can be reconciled with the life and teachings of Jesus. But for the most part, however, Protestants have tended to see nation-states and nationalism as natural, even as ordained by God. They have been reluctant to challenge state authority even when it conflicts with Christian beliefs.

SEE ALSO *Fundamentalism, Christian; Protestant Ethic; Weber, Max*

BIBLIOGRAPHY

Comaroff, Jean, and John Comaroff. 1991. *Of Revelation and Revolution: Christianity, Colonialism, and Consciousness in South Africa.* 2 vols. Chicago: University of Chicago Press.

Dillenberger, John, and Claude Welch. 1954. *Protestant Christianity Interpreted through Its Development.* New York: Scribner.

Hillerbrand, Hans Joachim, ed. 2004. *The Encyclopedia of Protestantism.* New York: Routledge.

McGrath, Alister E., and Darren C. Marks, eds. 2004. *The Blackwell Companion to Protestantism.* Malden, MA: Blackwell.

Melton, J. Gordon. 2005. *Encyclopedia of Protestantism.* New York: Facts on File.

Stoll, David. 1990. *Is Latin America Turning Protestant?: The Politics of Evangelical Growth.* Berkeley: University of California Press.

Tawney, R. H. 1926. *Religion and the Rise of Capitalism.* London: John Murray.

Watt, David Harrington. 2002. *Bible-Carrying Christians: Conservative Protestants and Social Power.* New York: Oxford University Press.

Weber, Max. 1905. *The Protestant Ethic and the Spirit of Capitalism.* Trans. and ed. Peter Baehr and Gordon C. Wells. New York: Penguin, 2002.

David Harrington Watt

PROTOTYPES

A *prototype* is a cognitive representation that exemplifies the essential features of a category or concept. Specifically, a prototypical representation reflects the central tendency or the average or typical attributes of the members of a category. For example, the prototype of *table* consists of the knowledge that a table has four legs propping up a flat surface. People store prototypical knowledge of social groups (e.g., librarians), objects (e.g., tables), events (e.g., dining out), and ideas (e.g., the perfect date). These prototypical representations facilitate people's ability to encode, organize, and retrieve information about everyday stimuli.

An early pioneer of prototype research was psychologist Eleanor Rosch, whose work during the 1960s and 1970s was inspired by the Aristotelian assumption that categories are logical entities whose membership is defined by an item's possession of simple matching features. Rosch argued that not all items within a category have an equal degree of membership—that is, that potential category members vary in their distance from prototypical exemplars. In short, category membership is not absolute but a matter of degree, and these differing degrees of membership have important implications for

information processing. For example, people are quicker to agree with the statement "a robin is a bird" than to the statement "a turkey is a bird." Moreover, people are more likely to remember statements that are conceptually prototypical (e.g., "the boulder fell down the mountain") than those that are conceptually nonprototypical ("the lettuce fell down the mountain").

During the 1970s and 1980s, Nancy Cantor and Walter Mischel extended Rosch's work on prototypes to the realm of social perception and social categories. According to Cantor and Mischel, there exist basic personality categories that social perceivers use to facilitate information processing about other people. This research was important in showing that people do not simply store specific, concrete items of information about others, but they routinely form abstract, prototypical representations. For example, when given traits about a person suggesting extroversion (e.g., friendly), people will later erroneously recall that they were given other traits (e.g., energetic) that fit the prototype of extroversion. These findings suggest that people are economical in their mental storage of information about others, relying on prototypes to influence the interpretation and accurate memory of specific personality trait information.

A concept in psychology that is related to the notion of prototype is *schema*. These two terms are often used interchangeably, but there are subtle differences. *Prototype* refers to a specific ideal image of a category member, with all known attributes filled in. For example, the prototypic "apple" may engender a representation of red, round fruit, even if actual category members vary so much on these characteristic dimensions that the prototype becomes meaningless for identifying them (e.g., some apples are green). An alternative to the prototype view of categorical knowledge is the concept of schema, which suggests that particular attributes can be ignored. For example, although we may associate "red" with apple, the schema concept allows for some features to remain unspecified. This greater flexibility with the schema concept may explain the wider use of the term *schema*, rather than *prototype*, in the social psychology literature.

Eliot Smith (1998) has argued that the distinction between schemas and prototypes is largely inconsequential and that four general points can be made about schema and prototype-based processing. First, schemas and prototypes are preexisting knowledge structures that are learned from other people or from experience. Second, the effects of schemas and prototypes on free recall tasks result from two sources: information processing that occurs at the time the stimulus information is first learned, and information processing that occurs when the information is later retrieved or reconstructed. Third, schemas and prototypes can be primed, thus influencing interpretations of information presented later. Finally, separate processes may govern our recall of specific traits and our overall evaluations of a person, rendering prototypes just part of the process of knowing others.

As Smith also has noted, psychologists in the twenty-first century have moved away from models of mental representations that portray knowledge units as static or stored in memory. In contrast, contemporary cognitive models view knowledge representations as active, interactive, flexible, and sensitive to context. The relatively new field of cognitive science, with its ties to computer modeling and neuroscience, promises to shed significant future light on the more dynamic role of prototypes in influencing phenomena at multiple levels of analysis, including neural, mental, and social.

SEE ALSO *Central Tendencies, Measures of; Priming; Psychology; Schemas; Social Psychology*

BIBLIOGRAPHY

Cantor, Nancy, and Walter Mischel. 1979. Prototypes in Person Perception. In *Advances in Experimental Social Psychology*, ed. Leonard Berkowitz, Vol. 12, 3–52. New York: Academic Press.

Rosch, Eleanor. 1978. Principles of Categorization. In *Cognition and Categorization*, ed. Eleanor Rosch and Barbara B. Lloyd, 47–83. Hillsdale, NJ: Erlbaum.

Smith, Eliot R. 1998. Mental Representations and Memory. In *The Handbook of Social Psychology*, ed. Daniel Gilbert, Susan Fiske, and Gardner Lindzey, Vol. 1, 391–445. 4th ed. New York: McGraw-Hill.

Scott T. Allison
James K. Beggan

PROUDHON, PIERRE-JOSEPH

SEE *Anarchism.*

PSEUDOPANEL DATA

SEE *Data, Pseudopanel.*

PSYCHIATRIC DISORDERS

The 2000 version of the American Psychiatric Association's diagnostic manual, the *Diagnostic and Statistical Manual of Mental Disorders*, 4th edition (termed *DSM*-IV for short), contains nearly 400 mental disorders,

distributed across seventeen broad categories. These categories include childhood disorders, schizophrenia and psychotic disorders, mood disorders, substance-related disorders, anxiety disorders, eating disorders, sleep disorders, personality disorders, sexual- and gender-identity disorders, and impulse-control disorders. The number of mental disorders has ballooned from the first *DSM* edition in 1952 to the present, reflecting an increased "splitting" of broad mental illness categories into narrower ones.

DSM-IV AND MULTIAXIAL FORMULATION

DSM-IV describes individuals along five axes, or dimensions of functioning, the first two of which focus on what is conventionally regarded as mental illness. By providing users with a multiaxial formulation, *DSM*-IV aims to paint a reasonably comprehensive picture of each individual.

Axis I lists most major mental disorders, such as schizophrenia, mood disorders, and anxiety disorders. In general, researchers view these disorders as acute problems that are superimposed on individuals' preexisting functioning.

Axis II lists personality disorders and mental retardation, which ostensibly differ from Axis I disorders in their greater persistence over time. Personality disorders are extremes of personality traits, such as impulsivity, dependency, and anxiety, that are inflexible, maladaptive, or both. Mental retardation is characterized by an IQ (intelligence quotient) of approximately 70 or below, severe deficits in adaptive functioning (e.g., inability to cook or dress oneself), and onset prior to adulthood.

Axis III lists medical conditions that can be relevant to individuals' psychological functioning. Medical conditions can adversely affect the prognosis of many mental disorders and mimic the symptoms of many others. For example, hypothyroidism and stroke can produce the full clinical picture of major depression, a condition characterized by extreme sadness and loss of pleasure, along with such features as extreme guilt, sleeping and eating difficulties, and suicidal thinking.

Axis IV lists recent life stressors, such as death of a relationship partner or friend, and environmental problems, such as housing difficulties, extreme poverty, or inadequate access to mental health services. These psychological factors can precipitate or maintain mental illnesses. For example, research indicates that certain negative life events, especially those involving losses of loved ones, can trigger major depression in predisposed individuals. Evidence also suggests that schizophrenia, a condition marked by unusual thinking, delusions (fixed false beliefs), and hallucinations (perceptions occurring in the absence of any stimulus), can be triggered in some predisposed individuals by the stresses associated with poverty. Nevertheless, evidence suggests that causality also operates in the reverse direction because, for example, the deteriorating job skills associated with schizophrenia can lead to poverty.

Axis V describes the individual's overall level of daily functioning. The inclusion of this axis acknowledges that people with the same psychiatric disorder differ markedly in their levels of adaptation to the environment. For example, some people with major depression are almost constantly bedridden, suicidal, or both, whereas others manage to perform surprisingly well in their occupational and family lives despite intense psychological pain.

DEFINING PSYCHIATRIC DISORDER

Theoreticians have long struggled with the question of what, if anything, all disorders of psychological functioning have in common. Although they have proposed numerous definitions of psychiatric disorder, all of these definitions have their shortcomings.

A subjective distress model posits that all mental disorders are marked by inner turmoil. Although many mental disorders, such as panic disorder (a condition marked by sudden surges of intense anxiety), are associated with subjective distress, some others, such as antisocial personality disorder (a condition marked by a long-standing history of illegal and irresponsible behavior) are associated with minimal subjective distress.

A statistical model posits that mental disorders are marked by statistical rarity. Although many mental disorders, such as infantile autism (a condition originating in infancy that is associated with serious deficits in language, social bonding, and imagination), are relatively rare in the population, others, such as major depression, are fairly common.

An evolutionary model posits that all mental disorders generate biological disadvantage, such as reduced life span or reduced ability to reproduce. Although some mental disorders, such as major depression, are associated with increased rates of suicide and therefore clear-cut biological disadvantage, others, such as specific phobia (an intense and irrational fear of an object, place, or situation), are not associated with any apparent reduction in lifespan or reproductive capacity.

In the 1990s Jerome Wakefield attempted to remedy these shortcomings by proposing that all mental disorders are harmful dysfunctions. According to Wakefield, all mental disorders (1) produce undesirable consequences for the affected individual, society, or both (harm); and (2) are characterized by the failure of a psychological system to perform its evolved function (dysfunction). For example, according to Wakefield, paranoia ("delusional disorder" in DSM-IV) is a mental disorder because (1) people with paranoia frequently experience marked distress, and (2) paranoia reflects a failure of the human threat system to operate properly. Specifically, in paranoia the threat detection system either reacts to nonexistent dangers or overreacts to mild ones. Yet the harmful dysfunction formulation has its limitations. In particular, some conditions, such as anxiety disorders, do not appear to stem from dysfunctions. Instead, in most cases these conditions seem to result from evolved systems reacting in adaptive ways to subjectively perceived threats.

In light of the problems with previous attempts to define disorder, some authors have proposed that psychiatric disorders are best conceptualized in terms of a family resemblance model. Just as brothers and sisters within a large family tend to look similar but do not share any single facial characteristic, mental disorders typically share a loosely covarying set of features. These features include subjective distress, statistical rarity, biological dysfunction, impairment, societal disapproval, irrationality, and loss of control over one's behavior. From this perspective, there is no "bright line" demarcating abnormality from normality, but rather a constellation of partly overlapping attributes that set most psychiatric disorders apart from healthy functioning.

LABELING THEORY AND RESPONSES TO IT

The mental illness concept has long had its harsh critics. Advocates of labeling theory, such as Thomas Szasz (b. 1920), have argued that diagnoses of mental illness are merely pejorative names that society attaches to behavior that it finds objectionable. In a 1961 book Szasz referred famously to mental illness as a myth, contending that what the mental health profession calls psychological disorders are actually "problems in living," that is, difficulties in adjusting one's behavior to societal demands. Many labeling theorists further contend that psychiatric diagnoses are culturally relative, because the behaviors that societies deem abnormal vary markedly across place and time.

Labeling theory has served a valuable function by reminding psychologists and psychiatrists that diagnoses are readily abused. Many nonscientific "diagnoses" in the popular psychology literature, such as sexual addiction, codependency, and road-rage disorder, are scant more than descriptive labels for undesirable behaviors. These labels yield little new information. For example, labeling an aggressive driver with road-rage disorder informs us only that this person frequently loses his or her temper while driving, a fact of which we were already aware.

Nevertheless, labeling theory's critique of psychiatric diagnostic systems and the concept of mental illness falls short on at least three grounds. First, many devalued behaviors, such as laziness, slovenliness, rudeness, and racism, are not mental disorders. Therefore, there is more to psychiatric disorder than social undesirability.

Second, many labeling theorists have overstated the cultural relativity of mental disorders. Admittedly, some mental disorders are specific to certain cultures. For example, koro, a condition characterized by a pathological fear that one's genitals are disappearing, is localized largely to parts of Southeast Asia. Nevertheless, many major psychological disorders appear to be present across most, if not all, cultures. In 1976 Jane Murphy conducted a significant study of two societies that had experienced essentially no contact with Euro-American culture—a group of Yorubas in Nigeria and a group of Eskimos near the Bering Strait. These cultures had terms for disorders that were strikingly similar to several Euro-American disorders, including alcoholism, schizophrenia, and psychopathic personality, a condition marked by dishonesty, callousness, guiltlessness, and lack of empathy.

Third, many psychological diagnoses do more than describe already known behaviors. As Eli Robins and Samuel Guze observed in a classic 1970 article, valid psychological diagnoses provide us with novel information. For example, if we accurately diagnose an individual with bipolar disorder, formerly known as manic depression, we will learn several things about that individual that we did not know previously. Among other things, we will learn that this individual (1) experiences relatively sudden episodes of both mania (a condition marked by dramatically elated mood, energy, and self-esteem, along with poor judgment and impulsivity) and depression, typically punctuated by periods of essentially normal functioning; (2) is more likely than nonaffected individuals to have one or more biological relatives with mood disorders; (3) is at heightened risk for other psychological difficulties, including substance abuse and suicide; and (4) will probably respond positively to certain medications, such as lithium carbonate and antiseizure agents.

PREVALENCE OF MENTAL DISORDERS

Several large survey studies conducted in the 1980s, 1990s, and early twenty-first century have yielded valuable knowledge regarding the prevalence of major mental disorders in the general population. A 2005 study by Ronald Kessler and his colleagues revealed that between 25 percent and 30 percent of Americans suffer from anxiety disorders such as phobias, about 20 percent suffer from mood disorders such as depression and bipolar disorder, and about 15 percent suffer from substance-abuse disorders such as alcoholism. A surprisingly large proportion of Americans, perhaps 25 percent, also suffer from

impulse-control disorders such as kleptomania (marked by recurrent stealing) and pathological gambling. On a lifetime basis, the most prevalent single disorder appears to be major depression, which afflicts about 17 percent of Americans at some point in their lives.

Survey studies also reveal important gender differences in the prevalence of some mental disorders. For example, in most populations major depression is about twice as common in women than in men. Antisocial personality disorder, in contrast, is about three times as common in men as in women. The reasons for these gender differences are unknown, but remain an active area of research investigation.

Race differences in the prevalence of psychopathology tend to be less pronounced than gender differences, although there are notable exceptions. For example, post-traumatic stress disorder, a condition marked by severe anxiety and avoidance reactions following a traumatic event (e.g., a rape, shooting, or motor vehicle accident), appears to be more prevalent in African Americans than in whites, perhaps because individuals in poor, inner-city areas, including many African Americans, often witness and experience traumatic events. Alcoholism is more prevalent in Native Americans than in other individuals, probably for a mixture of genetic and environmental reasons, the latter including poverty and alienation from the broader American society.

CAUSES OF MENTAL ILLNESS

The past several centuries have witnessed a variety of approaches to the etiology, or causation, of psychiatric illnesses. Etiological models of psychological disorder have shifted over time in accord with prevailing societal conceptions.

During the Middle Ages many people embraced a demonic model, which viewed mental illnesses largely as the product of evil spirits infecting the mind. Not surprisingly, exorcism was often the preferred "treatment" of the day. In succeeding centuries, conceptions of the causes of mental disorder became progressively more rooted in naturalistic as opposed to spiritual explanations.

Psychodynamic approaches, originated by Sigmund Freud (1856–1939) and his followers, place substantial emphasis on the role of early life experiences, unconscious influences, and psychological conflict in the genesis of mental disorder. For example, psychodynamic theorists might view obsessive-compulsive disorder, an anxiety disorder characterized by repeated intrusive thoughts (e.g., fears of contamination) and by unsuccessful efforts to neutralize them (e.g., frantic cleaning), as an unconscious psychological defense against deep-seated fears of loss of emotional control. These fears, in turn, may trace their roots to aversive childhood experiences, such as physical or sexual trauma. Despite their value in generating hypotheses concerning the causes of mental illness, psychodynamic theories have proven difficult to test.

Behavioral approaches, influenced by the work of John B. Watson (1878–1958), B. F. Skinner (1904–1990), Joseph Wolpe (1915–1997), and others, conceive of mental disorder as maladaptive learned habits. For behaviorists, atypical and disturbed behaviors are governed by the same learning processes as other behaviors. For example, behaviorists might attempt to explain a phobia of dogs in terms of an early unpleasant experience with a dog in conjunction with subsequent avoidance behavior. By avoiding dogs whenever they are within sight, the victim of a dog bite experiences short-term relief. Yet this person also forfeits the opportunity to learn that most dogs are not as dangerous as he or she fears.

Cognitive approaches, pioneered by Albert Ellis (b. 1913), Aaron Beck (b. 1921), and others, posit that psychological disorders derive from irrational patterns of thinking. Cognitive theorists emphasize that an individual's interpretations of events, rather than events themselves, are the principal determinants of behavior. They regard unfounded beliefs about oneself, the world, and the future—such as the belief that "I must be perfect" or that "I must be liked by everyone to be a worthwhile person"—to be risk factors for depression and other disorders.

Biological approaches focus on physiological factors, such as genetic influences, early damage to the central nervous system, and hormonal abnormalities, as predisposing factors in mental illness. There is compelling evidence from twin and adoption studies—which permit researchers to disentangle the roles of genes and environment—that genetic factors play a substantial role in a wide array of psychiatric disorders, including schizophrenia, mood disorders, and anxiety disorders. There is also preliminary but growing evidence that viral infections prior to birth may set the stage for subsequent schizophrenia.

The advent of sophisticated neuroimaging techniques such as PET (positive emission tomography) and fMRI (functional magnetic resonance imaging) has been a substantial boon to biological approaches, as these techniques have allowed researchers to discover which brain areas are underactive or overactive during certain tasks. For example, many individuals with schizophrenia exhibit decreased activity in their frontal lobes, which is consistent with the poor judgment, inadequate planning, and memory deficits often observed in this condition. The human genome project also promises to add to our understanding of the biological underpinnings of mental disorder, because it is permitting researchers to identify genes linked to specific psychological disorders.

Proponents of differing etiological models have often sorted themselves into highly partisan camps, separated as much by ideology as evidence. Yet, few if any of these etiological approaches are mutually exclusive. Moreover, most researchers and theorists agree that the causes of mental disorders are likely to be multifactorial, that is, produced by many variables rather than one. In some cases, these causal variables may interact. For example, several studies indicate that a genetic abnormality that affects serotonin, a chemical messenger in the brain, may combine with life stressors to trigger depression. As a consequence, the most fruitful approaches to understanding mental disorder will probably involve multidisciplinary collaborations among researchers from diverse theoretical perspectives.

SEE ALSO *Alcoholism; Anxiety; Behaviorism; Cognition; Cultural Relativism; Depression, Psychological; Freud, Sigmund; Madness; Manic Depression; Mental Health; Mental Illness; Mental Retardation; Mood; Nature vs. Nurture; Neuroticism; Obsessive-Compulsive Disorder; Panic; Personality; Post-Traumatic Stress; Psychopathology; Psychotherapy; Schizophrenia; Stress*

BIBLIOGRAPHY

American Psychiatric Association. 2000. *Diagnostic and Statistical Manual of Mental Disorders*. 5th ed., text rev. Washington, DC: American Psychiatric Association.

Breslau, J., K. S. Kendler, M. Su, S. Gaxiola-Aguilar, and R. C. Kessler. 2005. Lifetime Risk and Persistence of Psychiatric Disorders across Ethnic Groups in the United States. *Psychological Medicine* 35: 317–327.

Goodwin, Donald W., and Samuel B. Guze. 1996. *Psychiatric Diagnosis*. 5th ed. New York: Oxford University Press.

Gorenstein, Ethan E. 1992. *The Science of Mental Illness*. San Diego, CA: Academic Press.

Kendell, Robert E. 1975. The Concept of Disease and Its Implications for Psychiatry. *British Journal of Psychiatry* 127: 305–315.

Kessler, Ronald C., Wai T. Chui, Olga Demler, and Elaine E. Walters. 2005. Prevalence, Severity, and Comorbidity of 12-Month DSM-IV Disorders in the National Comorbidity Survey Replication. *Archives of General Psychiatry* 62: 617–627.

McHugh, Paul R., and Phillip R. Slavney. 1998. *The Perspectives of Psychiatry*. 2nd ed. Baltimore, MD: Johns Hopkins University Press.

Meehl, Paul E. 1973. *Psychodiagnosis: Selected Papers*. Minneapolis: University of Minnesota Press.

Murphy, Jane. 1976. Psychiatric Labeling in Cross-Cultural Perspective. *Science* 191: 1019–1028.

Nathan, Peter E., and Jack M. Gorman, eds. 2002. *A Guide to Treatments That Work*. 2nd ed. New York: Oxford University Press.

Robins, Eli, and Samuel B. Guze. 1970. Establishment of Diagnostic Validity in Psychiatric Illness: Its Application to Schizophrenia. *American Journal of Psychiatry* 126: 983–987.

Szasz, Thomas. 1960. The Myth of Mental Illness. *American Psychologist* 15: 113–118.

Wakefield, Jerome C. 1992. The Concept of Mental Disorder: On the Boundary between Biological Facts and Social Values. *American Psychologist* 47: 373–388.

Scott O. Lilienfeld
Kristin Landfield

PSYCHIATRY

SEE *Mental Health; Psychotherapy; Psychotropic Drugs.*

PSYCHOANALYTIC THEORY

Founded by the Austrian neurologist and physician Sigmund Freud (1856–1939), psychoanalytic theory is a framework for understanding the impact of the unconscious on thoughts, feelings, and behavior. Freud posited that most of what motivates individuals lies outside of their immediate awareness. Borne out of Freud's treatment of patients with neurological disorders, psychoanalytic theory describes both normal and abnormal human experience and emphasizes the lasting impact of early childhood events on adult personality and psychological development. Psychoanalysis, the clinical application of Freud's theory, is a tool that explores the unconscious mind in order to relieve painful emotional symptoms and increase self-awareness. Psychoanalysis is the forerunner of most forms of modern psychotherapeutic techniques. To this day, psychoanalytic theory and the practice of psychoanalysis continue to evolve in ways that support, discard, and expand some of Freud's original principles.

At the heart of Freud's ideas was his seminal work *The Interpretation of Dreams* (1900), which describes dreams as unconscious wish fulfillments. Freud contended that there are core sexual and aggressive wishes that the conscious mind finds unacceptable and represses. These wishes are symbolically expressed in dreams. The surface details and narrative structure of the dream—what we remember—are referred to as the *manifest content*. The *latent content* of the dream represents its unconscious hidden meaning and can only be discovered through the process of interpretation.

Freud described other ways in which the unconscious is revealed in everyday life. For example, what Freud called a *parapraxis*, known today as a "Freudian slip" or "slip of the tongue," is popularly understood to describe the occurrence of an unconscious wish "accidentally" being revealed in an individual's speech or writing. For instance, a man who calls his wife "mom" may unconsciously reveal repressed thoughts or feelings that he has about either woman. Freud also argued that jokes can be derivative expressions of unconscious sexual or aggressive feelings disguised as humor.

Freud's explication of dreams and the unconscious led him to develop a more comprehensive theory of the mind. His *topographical model* posited conscious, unconscious, and preconscious parts of the mind. The *unconscious* contains all that is outside of immediate awareness, whereas the *conscious* contains those parts of which individuals are immediately aware. Information that is not in immediate awareness but is easily retrievable is called *preconscious*. Freud used the analogy of an iceberg to describe this model: Only a small tip of a much larger iceberg is visible above water, much like only a small fraction of the mind is conscious. Most of the mind lies in the unconscious, below the level of awareness.

Complementing the topographical model, Freud also proposed a structural model of the mind that includes three parts: *id, ego,* and *superego.* The id is unconscious and active at birth, and encompasses all of the instinctual and bodily wishes. It operates according to the *pleasure principle*, which has as its sole goal the immediate gratification of all urges. The ego operates mostly out of the *reality principle*, which accounts for reality factors and social norms that prohibit instinctual urges from being immediately gratified. The ego helps to regulate the frustration from ungratified id drives. The superego is the moral part of the mind that represents an individual's internalized sense of parental and societal values. Freud compared the conflict between the id and the ego to that between an unruly horse and its rider; the rider (ego) has to direct the unbridled energy of the horse (id) in a way that is neither too permitting nor too restrictive. These conflicts are at the heart of both classic and modern psychoanalytic theories' understanding of symptoms, psychopathology, and defense mechanisms.

When unacceptable and unconscious id drives approach conscious awareness, a sense of danger and anxiety develops. Defense mechanisms are employed by the ego to defend against this anxiety. In a *compromise formation*, the ego attempts to express these id impulses in socially appropriate ways while accounting for the moral and societal values of the superego; there is a compromise between the original wish and the anxiety against the wish. Some examples of defense mechanisms are *projection, displacement, reaction formation,* and *sublimation.*

Projection occurs when an individual's own unacceptable impulses are attributed to another person. The boy who, before dinner, asks his mother if she wants a cookie projects his own desire onto her because he may feel ashamed by his wanting something that has been prohibited in the past. Displacement is the transferring of unacceptable thoughts or feelings one might have towards an object onto a more acceptable target object: A man who is mad at his wife "displaces" his dangerous angry feelings when he comes home and kicks the dog. Reaction formation involves the blocking of an unacceptable impulse by acting in an exaggerated and opposite way. For example, a new mother's friend may shower the mother with gifts and praise to conceal her own feelings of jealousy at not having a baby. Sublimation is considered one of the more mature defense mechanisms, and involves the redirection of unacceptable impulses into constructive, healthier endeavors. A successful surgeon sublimates unconscious aggressive impulses through the helpful act of surgery. The use of defense mechanisms is a natural function of living that helps individuals manage overwhelming thoughts and feelings. The rigid and pervasive adherence to particular defense mechanisms and styles of coping, however, may become maladaptive, often causing more psychological and emotional turmoil than it resolves.

Psychoanalytic theory encompasses views on human development and personality. According to Freud's theory there are five stages of psychosexual development that children must negotiate. At each stage id energies, called *libido*, are focused on various parts of the body called *erogenous zones*. The stages are: oral, anal, phallic, latent, and genital. During each stage a child must negotiate fulfilling those pleasures in the context of growing social rules and norms. The pleasure area during the oral phase is the mouth, and actions such as sucking, teething, and biting are prominent. During the anal phase children must reconcile the pleasures of retaining and eliminating feces (and urine) and the socially imposed responsibility of toilet training. During the phallic phase bodily pleasures are obtained from self-stimulation of the genitals. It is during this phase that the challenge of the *Oedipal complex* is confronted. Fond of antiquity and the classics, Freud named this complex to invoke the themes of Sophocles's Greek tragedy *Oedipus Rex*, a tragedy in which the character Oedipus unknowingly kills his father and marries his mother. Freud argued that in this complex, children feel repressed sexual attraction towards the parent of the opposite sex and aggressive hatred of the same-sex parent. During the next phase, the latency phase, libidinal instincts are repressed, only to reemerge at the start of puberty and the genital phase. At this time the focus is on genital pleasures with another person, leading toward the development of adult sexuality. When individuals have difficulty resolving the conflicts that each particular stage

presents, they may become fixated, which affects adult personality.

These stages are important ideas in the history of psychoanalytic theory, but they are not distinct and precise developmental events. Rather, they are theoretical conceptualizations of some of the important challenges of psychological maturation. Nonetheless, they live on in modern parlance. Someone who is "orally fixated," for example, may have been overly indulged during the oral phase of psychosexual development and later, as an adult, develop an oral symptom such as excessive drinking or cigarette smoking. An adult described as "anal" may be excessively concerned with orderliness, timeliness, and control, much as a toddler in the anal phase must negotiate the pleasures and challenges of bowel control.

Encompassed in psychoanalytic theory of all types are the ideas of cure and personal growth. Psychoanalysis represents the clinical application of psychoanalytic theory to the issues of psychopathology, neurosis, psychosis, and dysfunctional patterns of living. It is an intense form of psychological treatment that involves four to five sessions per week with a trained psychoanalyst (usually a psychiatrist, psychologist, or social worker) and lasts several years. Patients lie on a couch and are asked to speak as freely as they can about whatever comes to their minds, a process called *free association*. As with dream interpretation, the theory holds that free associations, no matter how irrelevant, obscure, or trivial they may seem, exhibit an internal logic that, through the process of interpretation, reveals conflicts of the unconscious that can be worked through to bring about symptom relief. Integral to this intense form of treatment is the development of *transference*, which occurs when a patient unconsciously transfers onto the psychoanalyst the thoughts, feelings, and conflicts that they have toward early caregivers. Working through the transferred conflicts in the unique interpersonal relationship with the psychoanalyst is a key component of the psychoanalytic theory of cure. Psychoanalytically informed psychotherapy, though similar in guiding principles, differs from psychoanalysis in that an analytic couch is not typically used, sessions are less frequent, and transference issues, though present, are not as fully integrated in the curative process.

As a prolific theorist, writer, and practitioner, Freud had many followers, some of whom broke ranks with aspects of his theory. Carl Gustav Jung (1875–1968), for example, was the heir apparent to the psychoanalytic movement until theoretical differences ended his professional relationship with Freud. Jung emphasized religion, archetypes, and what he called the *collective unconscious*, a culturally shared set of unconscious symbols. Alfred Adler's (1870–1937) emphasis on individual striving for superiority and Karen Horney's (1885–1962) integration of feministic views of psychological development and functioning—something Freud is often criticized for ignoring—represent some of the earliest expansions of psychoanalytic theory.

Modern additions to psychoanalytic theory, such as object-relations theory, move away from strict drive- and conflict-motivated models to more relational and interpersonal ones. That is, interpersonal relationships, in addition to internal bodily drives and instincts, play an increasingly important role in individuals' conscious and unconscious notions of self and other. As such, these issues are often played out in rich and meaningful ways in psychoanalytic treatment, which most modern psychoanalytic practitioners view as inherently more relational than Freud's original conception.

The ever-evolving system of psychoanalytic theory that exists today is arguably one of the most far-reaching and pervasive theories of the last one hundred years. One can hardly escape the influence of Freud's unique system of thought. As a theory of symbolic and hidden meanings, psychoanalytic theory is often applied to the critical understanding of literature, poetry, cinema, and the visual arts. Anthropologists have used psychoanalytic ideas to explore and understand the relationship between individuals and their cultures. Modern neuroscience has even paved the way for the emerging field of neuropsychoanalysis, which aims to integrate psychoanalytic ideas with physically observable brain structures, neural pathways, and brain chemistry. Psychoanalytic theory has often been criticized as being the unscientific, dogmatic, chauvinistic, illogical, and narcissistically insular theory of one man, Freud. Fair though aspects of these criticisms may be, the psychoanalytic theory of today offers a comprehensive and cogent account of the human condition.

SEE ALSO *Consciousness; Dreaming; Freud, Sigmund; Jung, Carl; Oedipus Complex; Psychology; Psychotherapy; Sublimate; Subliminal Suggestion*

BIBLIOGRAPHY

Crews, Frederick C., ed. 1998. *Unauthorized Freud: Doubters Confront a Legend.* New York: Viking.

Ellenberger, Henri F. 1970. *The Discovery of the Unconscious: The History and Evolution of Dynamic Psychiatry.* New York: Basic Books.

Freud, Sigmund. [1900] 1965. *Interpretation of Dreams.* Trans. James Strachey. New York: Avon Books.

Gay, Peter. 1998. *Freud: A Life for Our Time.* New York: W. W. Norton.

Mitchell, Stephen A., and Margaret J. Black. 1995. *Freud and Beyond: A History of Modern Psychoanalytic Thought.* New York: Basic Books.

Psychodynamic Diagnostic Manual Task Force. 2006. *Psychodynamic Diagnostic Manual.* Silver Spring, MD: Alliance of Psychoanalytic Organizations.

Steven J. Hanley

PSYCHODYNAMIC THEORY

SEE *Equilibrium in Psychology; Freud, Sigmund.*

PSYCHOLINGUISTICS

Psycholinguistics studies the way in which operations of the mind make language possible. It is a cross-disciplinary field, drawing upon ideas and findings from areas such as cognitive psychology, theoretical linguistics, phonetics, neurology, discourse analysis, computer science, semantics, and education. It is especially indebted to the first of these, which provides many of its basic tenets and its research methods.

Specifically, the field explores the cognitive processes that underlie the use, storage, and acquisition of language. Affective and contextual factors are a concern only as far as they impact upon performance. Although psycholinguists recognize that language users are individuals possessing different linguistic repertoires, their main goal is to identify general patterns of behavior across users. Those patterns might reflect the capabilities and biases of the human brain or the processing requirements of the language under investigation.

Psycholinguistics has a relatively recent history. It did not come into its own as a subject until the early 1960s, when behaviorist approaches to the study of the mind lost favor. However, interest in related topics can be traced back to eighteenth-century diaries recording the language development of children, to nineteenth-century research on the location of language in the brain, to the introspective methods of Wilhelm Wundt's psychology laboratory (established 1879), and to Francis Galton's work on word associations.

LANGUAGE PROCESSING

Those who work in the field of language processing seek to identify the processes, often highly automatic, that underlie the two productive skills (speaking and writing) and the two receptive ones (listening and reading). Starting with the generation of ideas, accounts of language production allow for macro-planning at discourse level and local micro-planning in relation to the utterance about to be produced. The resulting plan is given linguistic form, which is stored in what is termed a mental buffer while the utterance is being produced.

Accounts of language reception recognize two stages. In decoding, the user identifies units of language within the input and builds smaller ones into larger. Current models represent the listener or reader as seeking potential matches at many different levels of representation (sound, letter, syllable, word) as well as relying on external cues provided by sources such as world knowledge or speaker knowledge. There were early suggestions that skilled readers and listeners spared themselves decoding effort by relying upon contextual cues. However, the key to skilled performance has been shown to lie in efficient decoding, which releases memory capacity and enables the reader or listener to give adequate attention to higher-level meaning.

Meaning construction is heavily dependent upon a process of interpretation. It requires the reader or listener to expand on the literal significance of the input by adding in what the writer or speaker appears to have left unexpressed. The user also decides on the relative importance of the new information, adds it to the meaning representation built up so far in the discourse, and checks for consistency.

Some language processing research relies upon observational data or upon introspective methods such as verbal report. However, the most favored approach is experimental. Importance is accorded to methods that tap in to processes on line, in other words, as they are occurring. There is a preference for parametric data in the form of, for example, the reaction times involved in carrying out a small-scale task such as distinguishing actual words from non-words.

LANGUAGE STORAGE

A long-term area of interest has been the way in which vocabulary is stored in the language user's mental lexicon. A word's lexical entry specifies its spoken and written forms, its word class, its senses, and the way it participates in larger linguistic structures. There is uncertainty as to whether word-forming prefixes and suffixes such as *un–* or *–less* have their own entries. Current theory represents entries as interconnected within the mind of a user, with much stronger connections between those that frequently co-occur.

More recently, interest in storage has been extended to the ways in which sounds and grammar are represented in the mind. In conventional accounts, it tends to be assumed that sounds are stored as templates or prototypes against which variations can be matched, while grammar takes the form of abstract, internalized rules. However, growing evidence of the enormous storage capacity of the mind suggests that language users may retain precise records of the many utterances they encounter throughout their lives. Their ability to recognize sounds, words, and even patterns of grammar consequently derives not from generalizations but from millions of accumulated examples. On this analysis, the frequency with which strings of sounds and words are encountered is an important factor in the ease with which an individual retrieves them when they are needed. The premise is supported by evidence from computer modeling on connectionist principles, which has shown (so far in a limited way) that it is possible for a program to acquire a set of grammatical rules and exceptions by dint of exposure to repeated examples.

LANGUAGE ACQUISITION (OR DEVELOPMENTAL PSYCHOLINGUISTICS)

Any discussion of how children acquire language is influenced by the long-running debate as to whether language is innate and genetically transmitted (a nativist view) or whether it is acquired wholly or mainly through exposure to the language of adult caregivers (an empiricist view). Early comments by the American linguist Noam Chomsky (b. 1928) about the poverty of the stimulus (the uninformative nature of the speech samples provided to the child) have been challenged by analyses of child directed speech (CDS). Many child language researchers therefore adopt a neutral position or propose that language may be partly innate.

Research in this area falls into two broad traditions. One is theory-driven and adopts the assumption that linguistic descriptions of grammar correspond to actual mental processes. Drawing especially on Chomskyan accounts, this line of enquiry seeks evidence in children's speech of universals of language, of common default values for certain features and of the adjustment of those values to match the target language.

A second branch is data-driven. It studies samples of child language, using the analytical tools provided by mainstream linguistics and discourse analysis. Researchers have formed conclusions about the way in which a child develops a phonological system, although the precise relationship between hearing and producing spoken words remains unclear. Vocabulary has been studied in relation to the words that are acquired earliest and to the rate at which the child's knowledge increases. Especially important have been studies of how the child manages to construct conceptual categories such as *flower* or *bird* from discrete examples of the category. Studies of grammar have monitored the gradual increase in length of utterance and in the complexity of the syntax used and the concepts expressed.

The research method most favored in language acquisition studies consists of longitudinal observation based upon diaries or recordings. One outcome has been the assembly of a large international corpus of child language known as the Child Language Data Exchange System, or CHILDES. Researchers sometimes employ interviews with children to elicit specific linguistic items. Experimental methods have also been devised that enable a researcher to track the shifts of attention of a prelinguistic infant and thus to assess the infant's ability to discriminate between different signals.

A very different area of acquisition research investigates the way in which learners master a foreign language. Psycholinguistic theory provides a framework for studying both the cognitive processes that lead to expertise in the target language and the additional cognitive demands imposed upon the second language (L2) user by unfamiliar phonology, lexis, and syntax. The concepts of attention, working memory, and automaticity have proved especially useful; and an understanding of L2 fluency has been enhanced by first-language evidence of how speech is assembled.

TECHNOLOGICAL ADVANCES

In recent years, all these areas of psycholinguistics have been assisted by technological advances, especially the advent of brain imaging equipment. Researchers can now monitor brain activity while a subject is undertaking a language processing task; the purpose being to discover which parts of the brain are engaged and at which stages. They can identify where different types of linguistic information are located within the brain. They can even track the processing taking place in the brains of prelinguistic children.

Recent neurolinguistic findings build upon a long tradition of research on language in the brain, going back to the nineteenth century. It was assumed then that language was lateralized to the left hemisphere for most language users and stored in two small areas, named after the researchers Paul Broca (1824–1880) and Carl Wernicke (1848–1905). However, modern technology has demonstrated that the right hemisphere also plays its part, handling larger-scale constructs such as intonation and discourse structure. It has also shown that language is widely distributed throughout the brain, relying upon massive neural connections for rapid transmission.

Loosely associated with the study of language in the brain are a number of other areas of enquiry. One explores the question of whether language is a form of communication peculiar to human beings; another, the question of how language evolved. Both consider the possibility that language owes its existence to the unique configuration of the human brain in addition to the evolution of the human vocal apparatus.

A final area worth noting is the contribution that psycholinguistics makes to an understanding of language impairment—both developmental impairment (manifested from infancy) and impairment that is acquired as the result of accident or illness. Psycholinguists concern themselves with the processes that contribute to dyslexia and dysgraphia, with aphasic symptoms produced by strokes, and with disorders of speech. Besides contributing to the work of clinicians, this research helps to shed contrastive light on normal language processing. Similarly, work on the relationship between language and other cognitive skills in conditions such as Down syndrome or autism provides insights into whether language is part of general cognition or develops independently of it.

SEE ALSO *Anthropology; Child Development; Chomsky, Noam; Cognition; Communication; Disease; Neuroscience; Psychology; Rhetoric; Signals; Symbols; Theory of Mind*

BIBLIOGRAPHY

Aitchison, Jean. 1998. *The Articulate Mammal: An Introduction to Psycholinguistics.* 4th ed. London: Routledge.

Aitchison, Jean. 2003. *Words in the Mind: An Introduction to the Mental Lexicon.* 3rd ed. Malden, MA: Blackwell.

Brown, Colin M., and Peter Hagoort, eds. 1999. *The Neurocognition of Language.* Oxford: Oxford University Press.

Crystal, David, and Rosemary Varley. 1998. *Introduction to Language Pathology.* London: Whurr Publishers.

Deacon, Terrence W. 1997. *The Symbolic Species: The Co-evolution of Language and the Brain.* New York: W.W. Norton.

Field, John. 2004. *Psycholinguistics: The Key Concepts.* London: Routledge.

Foster, Susan H. 1990. *The Communicative Competence of Young Children: A Modular Approach.* London; New York: Longman.

Harley, Trevor. 2001. *The Psychology of Language: From Data to Theory.* Hove, U.K.: Psychology Press.

Lust, Barbara C., and Claire Foley, eds. 2004. *First Language Acquisition: The Essential Readings.* Malden, MA: Blackwell.

Obler, Loraine K., and Kris Gjerlow. 1999. *Language and the Brain.* Cambridge, U.K.: Cambridge University Press.

John Field

PSYCHOLOGICAL CAPITAL

Conventional microeconomics assumes that individuals seek to maximize their happiness, often called utility, by consuming goods and services while being constrained by their earnings. Tibor Scitovsky (1976) in his seminal work on consumer behavior suggested that psychological factors such as arousal, status, and sense of control over life events may influence happiness. In addition, Art Goldsmith, Jonathan Veum, and William Darity Jr. (1997b) assert that psychological elements affect workplace performance and, hence, earnings. Thus, psychological factors must be accounted for to attain a rich understanding of consumer behavior. Behavioral economics is the subfield of economics that integrates insights from economics and psychology into the study of economic and social behavior. "Psychological capital" refers to the collection of values, norms, perceptions, cognitive elements, and affective or emotional factors embedded in a person that can be expected to influence happiness and earnings. This essay provides an overview of how the concept of psychological capital has been integrated into social science research.

PSYCHOLOGICAL CAPITAL, HAPPINESS, AND EARNINGS

The roots of behavioral economics, and hence the importance of psychological capital, can be found in the discovery by economists that economic motives are often at odds with actions and that in many instances psychological elements appear to shape behavior. For instance, conventional economists adopt the assumption that individuals are rational decision makers who compare the additional benefits and costs of an action and engage in those activities offering a net gain. This perspective, however, is difficult to square with many commonly observed behaviors including customers tipping at a restaurant they will never again frequent because it is so far from their home. Psychologists explain this behavior as evidence that actions are guided by values, such as fairness, and cultural norms learned through socialization. There is also reason to believe that perceptions regarding safety and economic security are important determinants of happiness. Joblessness, especially unemployment, creates a sense of economic vulnerability. Goldsmith, Veum, and Darity (1997a) draw a connection from unemployment to poorer psychological well-being in several distinct but interrelated ways: as a consequence of lower self-esteem; as a result of a feeling that life is not under one's control, leading to helplessness and depression; and as a loss of the social byproducts of participation in a work environment.

Psychological elements are expected to affect a person's wage, which in turn influences his or her level of consumption and happiness. A standard argument in economics is that a person's wage is tied to his or her workplace performance or productivity, which is largely governed by his or her level of skills, called human capital. Of course, effort on the job is also expected to influence productivity and wages. Carl Shapiro and Joseph Stiglitz

reported in 1984 that economists claim that workplace effort is promoted by fear of joblessness or, according to George Akerlof in 1982, to reflect gratitude for favorable treatment by the firm. Expectancy theory is the most widely accepted and empirically supported theory of motivation or effort among psychologists. According to expectancy theory the strength of a person's motivation depends on the extent to which he or she believes that exertion, performance, and reward are linked tightly. Attribution theorists have proposed that an aspect of personality—locus of control—governs a person's perception of the strength of the connection between exertion, performance, and reward. Julian Rotter in 1966 classified individuals who believe they are masters of their own fate, and hence bear personal responsibility for what happens to them, as internalizers. Externalizers are those who believe they have little, if any, influence on the events that influence their lives. Expectancy theory predicts that a person with a more internal locus of control will be more motivated than a comparable individual whose locus of control is external.

MEASURING PSYCHOLOGICAL CAPITAL

Psychological capital is a broad term used to encompass various features of an individual's mind-set and personality, including motivation and emotional wellbeing. The convention in psychology is to use a battery of questions, called an inventory, to obtain a scale that gauges the psychological construct to be measured, such as motivation—locus of control—or self-esteem. Morris Rosenberg developed a survey instrument in 1965 to measure self-esteem because opinions about "self" are virtually the most treasured of our opinions and a crucial aspect of personality. He conceives of self-esteem as multidimensional, comprising notions of worth, goodness, health, appearance, skills, and social competence. Rosenberg uses a series of questions, each answered on a two point (0,1) basis. His measure of self-esteem may range in value from 0–6, with a higher value representing a greater level of self-esteem. Herb Lefcourt used a similar methodology in 1982 to measure locus of control, with larger values reflecting a more internal orientation, and hence a higher level of motivation.

Many economists are skeptical that elements of a person's psychological capital, such as locus of control, can be measured accurately by scales constructed from self-reported evaluations collected in the form of responses to survey questions. Their concerns are twofold. First, that it is difficult to compare responses across individuals because their replies are not anchored to a common baseline. Consider a question aimed at assessing a person's mental health that asks how often they have feelings of anxiety, with response options including; 1 equating to never, 2 for occasionally, 3 representing often, and 4 meaning all of the time. Two different persons who have similar bouts of exposure to depression may answer this question differently, one reporting *occasionally* and the other *often*, resulting in misclassification error because their frame of reference is different—there is no common baseline. To reduce this problem investigators transform responses to a two-point scale such as *never* versus *not never*, which reduces misclassification error.

The second concern is that subjective responses may differ widely from objective evaluations. A person may report feeling anxious while a professional evaluation of the individual conducted by a physician or clinical psychologists may lead them to conclude that the person is not suffering from anxiety. Research by Anne Case, however, offers evidence that a person's subjective responses to health questions about his or her children are virtually identical to independent assessments conducted by a physician. Thus, social scientists now conduct empirical studies of the link between psychological capital and economic outcomes. For instance, as reported by Goldsmith, Veum, and Darity in 2000, they find that persons who are more internal in their outlook—those more motivated—earn higher wages, and that unemployment leads to lower self-esteem and a more external perspective (1997a). The mental health consequences of adverse developments, however, will be less severe for persons with an external outlook because they do not blame themselves for the situation. Thus, high status individuals with an internal locus of control are particularly vulnerable in terms of emotional well-being to negative occurrences that arise at the workplace or in the family. Minorities often hold an external locus of control both as a result of past discrimination and as a defense mechanism to avoid self blame for undesirable outcomes that are beyond their control. Thus, members of minority groups may experience less harm to their mental health due to adverse social and economic developments.

SEE ALSO *Economics, Labor; Locus of Control; Mental Health; Rosenberg's Self-Esteem Scale; Rotter's Internal-External Locus of Control Scale; Self-Esteem*

BIBLIOGRAPHY

Akerlof, George A. 1982. Labor Contracts as a Partial Gift Exchange. *Quarterly Journal of Economics* 97: 543–569.

Case, Anne. 2002. Economic Status and Health in Childhood: The Origins of the Gradient. *American Economic Review* 92 (5): 1308–1334.

Goldsmith, Arthur H., Jonathan R. Veum, and William Darity Jr. 1997a. Unemployment, Joblessness, Psychological Well-Being and Self-Esteem: Theory and Evidence. *Journal of SocioEconomics* 26 (2): 133–158.

Goldsmith, Arthur H., Jonathan R. Veum, and William Darity Jr. 1997b. The Impact of Psychological and Human Capital on Wages. *Economic Inquiry* 35 (4): 815–829.

Goldsmith, Arthur H., Jonathan R. Veum, and William Darity Jr. 2000. Motivation and Labor Market Outcomes. *Research in Labor Economics* 19: 109–146.

Lefcourt, Herb. 1982. *Locus of Control: Current Trends in Theory and Research*. 2nd ed. Hillsdale, NJ: L. Erlbaum Associates.

Rosenberg, Morris. 1965. *Society and the Adolescent Self-Image*. Princeton, NJ: Princeton University Press.

Rotter, Julian B. 1966. Generalized Expectancies for Internal Versus External Control of Reinforcement. *Psychological Monographs* 80: 609.

Scitovsky, Tibor. 1976. *The Joyless Economy: An Inquiry into Human Satisfaction and Consumer Dissatisfaction*. New York: Oxford University Press.

Shapiro, Carl, and Joseph E. Stiglitz. 1984. Equilibrium Unemployment as a Worker Discipline Device. *American Economic Review* 74 (3): 433–444.

Arthur H. Goldsmith

PSYCHOLOGICAL DEFENSE

SEE *Napoleon Complex*.

PSYCHOLOGY

The term *psychology* has been used to refer to the study of the soul, consciousness, behavior, the mind, or the brain, depending on the era and cultural context investigated. In the nineteenth century German philosopher-psychologist Friedrich Eduard Beneke (1798–1854) defined his new psychology as the natural science of inner experience and suggested that the subject matter of psychology was what one finds in oneself. His countryman Wilhelm Wundt (1832–1920), who is often considered one of the central figures in the creation of modern psychology, defined the subject matter of psychology as the total content of experience in its immediate character. William James (1842–1910), one of the pioneers of American psychology, defined psychology as the science of mental life, both of its phenomena and of its conditions.

In a 1989 study, Tracy B. Henley and his colleagues showed that in the first third of the twentieth century psychology was defined the majority of the time as including concepts of *mind, consciousness,* or *mental activity.* Between 1930 and 1969, the prime time of behaviorism, these terms were barely mentioned in North American psychology, although with the coming of the *cognitive rev-*

olution they became widely used again. Use of the term *behavior* increased throughout the twentieth century, with later definitions including both behavior and mental activity. Definitions of psychology reflect the dominant research programs in a particular context.

PSYCHOLOGICAL TOPICS

Psychology did not exist as an independent discipline before the nineteenth century, although psychological topics were studied long before then. The study of the soul (*psyche*) goes back to Greek philosopher Aristotle (384–322 BCE) who wrote a pioneering work entitled, in Latin, *De anima* (On the soul). Aristotle discussed the five senses as well as perception, thinking, and imagination. He also discussed memory and dreaming. He did not study intelligence quotient (IQ), motivation, or prejudice, however, which are all later psychological constructions.

In the eighteenth century German philosopher and mathematician Christian Wolff (1679–1754) divided the study of the soul into two parts: *rational psychology* and *empirical psychology*. *Rational psychology* depicted what the human soul was capable of. He discussed the soul's substantiality, simplicity, immateriality, immortality, as well as the mind-body problem, and provided logical proofs that the soul was immaterial. *Empirical psychology* aimed to identify psychological principles on the basis of concrete experiences of what actually happened in the human soul. *Empirical* referred to something that could be determined through experiences rather than reason. Wolff's empirical psychology addressed the ability of the soul to know and to desire, the interaction of the soul and the body, and the *faculties* of the soul. Psychology concerned the study of the soul until the mid-nineteenth century, when German philosopher Friedrich Albert Lange (1828–1875) proclaimed a psychology without a soul.

Present-day psychology covers a wide range of topics such as biological bases of behavior, sensation, perception, memory, cognition, emotion, motivation, learning, language, dreaming, social interaction, prejudice, development, aging, intelligence, personality, stress, psychopathology, and psychotherapy. In psychology each concept is subdivided and studied in its parts: For example, memory is subdivided into short-term memory, long-term memory, working memory, explicit memory, and implicit memory, among others. Memory can be researched from a developmental, social, or biological perspective, each of which provides a variety of theoretical frameworks.

PSYCHOLOGY AS A DISCIPLINE

In the sixteenth century the word *psychologia* (psychology) first appeared in a book title, although some research does indicate earlier usage of the term. In 1590 Rudolf

Goclenius (1547–1628), a German professor of physics, mathematics, logic, and ethics used the term.

Some historians suggest that the acceptance of psychology as an institution of research and teaching at universities first occurred during the first half of the nineteenth century during a period of transformation for German universities. With the establishment of state-funded and state-controlled classical high schools, professors of philosophy were asked to teach courses on psychology and pedagogy for classical high school teachers-in-training. Because psychology was understood as the scientific basis for pedagogy, teacher candidates were required to take exams in the discipline of psychology. Horst Gundlach (2004) offers 1824, the year in which Prussia established psychology as an examinable discipline at its universities, as the origin of the discipline of psychology. Most books on the history of psychology, however, list its inception from 1879, the year in which Wundt began to conduct psychological experiments in his new psychological laboratory at Leipzig, Germany. From a critical perspective it is difficult to attribute the birth of a discipline to a single event. The institutionalization of psychology—the establishment of an academic discipline that followed university rules—occurred at different times in different geographical or national contexts.

PSYCHOLOGY AS A PROFESSION

Psychology as a profession or an expert occupation became a reality in the twentieth century. The professionalization of psychology can be linked to the development of other institutions in European and North American culture. The transformation of the legal system required experts, for example, regarding the validity of testimony and the reliability of memory; the health system needed experts in dealing with the mental health problems of patients; the prison system sought professionals who could provide information on the progress of rehabilitation and the likelihood of re-offending; the school system needed expertise in order to determine which children would need special education; and industry and corporations needed experts on personnel selection, the improvement of productivity, and advertising. In all of these applied fields psychologists emerged and claimed scientific knowledge.

In addition, public demand for psychological expertise increased; for example, regarding the parenting of children, people sought advice on the adequate amount of emotional contact, sensory stimulation, potty training, masturbation, and the appropriate extent of parental control at different ages. The search for expertise on how to have fulfilling romantic relationships, to be successful, and even live life led to the birth of *pop psychology*. Prominent examples of pop psychologists include former academic John B. Watson (1878–1958), whose book *Psychological Care of Infant and Child* (1928) contained historically contingent ideas such as that one should never hug or kiss a child, and Dr. Phil McGraw, whose media-magnified psychological activities are largely rejected by academic psychologists. There were a number of troubling manifestations of the professionalization of psychology as well: German psychology expanded in the context of the militarization of the *fatherland* at the beginning of the twentieth century; and U.S. psychologists, using IQ tests, labeled populations from Eastern and Southern Europe and non-European *races* mentally inferior during the great immigrations of the same time period.

PSYCHOLOGY'S RISE

According to Steven Ward, psychology's integration with other institutions has made it a uniquely successful field. Psychology flourished in the twentieth century in terms of its intellectual and social expansion. Psychology is one of the most popular undergraduate majors in North America and many European countries. The American Psychological Association (APA), the largest association of psychologists worldwide, has 150,000 members. The APA has more than fifty divisions that cover traditional experimental, social, developmental, or clinical psychology; the psychological study of lesbian, gay, and bisexual issues; peace psychology; and the advancement of pharmacotherapy, among many other diverse topics.

There are several thousand journals dedicated to psychology, and the APA's *Publication Manual* (2001), a style guide, has been adopted by most psychologists and by professionals in other disciplines as well. As a profession psychology pervades popular consciousness in the twenty-first century. The increasing global dominance of American psychology after 1945 reflects the economic power of the United States. But psychology did not only succeed as an institution; it also thrived in the *psychologization* of human life. The public and many expert cultures explain human and social events in psychological terms: Individual decisions, the arts, political crises, economic problems, history, and terrorism are all explained with the help of psychological categories.

CONTROVERSIES IN PSYCHOLOGY

The importance of psychology as a scientific discipline and in everyday life is clear. However controversies regarding basic precepts continue among psychologists.

The Dualism of Psychology Psychology can comprise understanding or explaining psychological objects and events. For example, one can explain the physiological mechanisms of memory or one can understand the specific content of a person's memory that is formed within

meaningful life experiences. Psychologists with a *natural-scientific* orientation emphasize the explanation, prediction, and control of behavior or cognition, while psychologists with a *human-scientific* perspective focus on thinking, feeling, and willing based on the assumption that reflection, intention, and action are meaningful processes. German philosopher Wilhelm Dilthey (1833–1911) provided a systematic foundation for two types of psychology when he divided the discipline into *descriptive* (human-scientific) and *analytical* explanatory (natural-scientific) parts. He argued that psychology's subject matter was human experience and thus its method must be understanding. German experimental psychologist Hermann Ebbinghaus (1850–1909) endorsed psychology as a natural science that did not need the method of understanding and should rely on natural-scientific explanation and experimental methods. Wundt, who many see as the father of German experimental psychology, divided the science into an experimental branch that focused on precise analysis of the basic processes of consciousness, and an observational *Völkerpsychologie* (cultural psychology) that covered complex psychological processes that accompany the development of human communities and mental products in the context of values, customs, and language.

In the North American tradition Gordon Allport observed an increasing *nomothetic*, natural-scientific commitment of psychology, but he petitioned for the inclusion of an *idiographic* approach in scientific psychology. Human-scientific approaches (hermeneutic, existential, humanistic psychologies) generally have been marginalized since the twentieth century, although they have never been totally abandoned, especially in clinical contexts. The impact of the natural-scientific approach was so powerful that even Sigmund Freud considered his method of psychoanalysis to be natural-scientific. The dualism of psychology is surfacing again in discussions surrounding *quantitative* versus *qualitative* methods, with the latter gaining more acceptance in the early twenty-first century.

Unification Dualism is one facet in an ongoing discourse regarding unification. Since the end of the nineteenth century, theoretical psychologists and later Russian psychologist Lev Semyonovich Vygotsky (1896–1934) have critiqued the missing unity of psychology. In the first half of the twentieth century the focus was on the unification of large research programs such as psychoanalysis, behaviorism, Gestalt psychology, and structuralism, and later unification was demanded regarding the multiplicity of theories, approaches, and empirical results that were often contradictory. Psychology as it exists in the early-twenty-first century is so diverse in its conceptual and theoretical positions and so fragmented in its identity that multiple psychologies rather than a unitary psychology have prevailed.

Solutions to the unification problem in the past have largely been based on a conceptual reductionism in promoting a single program such as behaviorism. Some have called for unifying theories of unification before any unification of the discipline could succeed. Proponents of unification demand unification for theoretical reasons. For example, the increasing demand for interdisciplinary work must remain fragmented if it is not clear what the discipline of psychology stands for. Opponents of unification suggest that the lack of unity makes psychology an extremely adaptive discipline that is able to work with other fields in academic and applied settings. The factual lack of theoretical unity has led to the phenomenon that mainstream psychology identifies itself by the commitment to a specific methodology, namely an experimental-statistical point of view.

Dichotomies Psychology throughout its history has struggled with conceptualizing the relationship between society and the individual, nature and nurture, and mind and body. The lack of an adequate conceptualization of the individual and society has led to criticisms that psychology is too individualistic in its theories and practices. For example, a person's psychological distress regarding homelessness cannot solely be explained, understood, and solved on an individual level. Even social psychology, which by definition should take the social context into account, does not provide ecological relevance because many studies use undergraduate students in laboratories as subjects. Klaus Holzkamp (1972) argues that in the real world there are many more variables that influence behavior and cannot be included in their complexity in an experiment.

The mind-body problem has been addressed in behaviorism in a reductionist way by denying or neglecting the reality of a mind. Neuropsychological researchers have developed more sophisticated theories since the late twentieth century. The largest political impact derives from an inadequate conceptualization of the nature-nurture debate. This dichotomy is most prominent in IQ controversies but also surrounds the heritability of pathologies, personality, and other psychological characteristics. The lack of an adequate understanding of nature-nurture has led psychologists to make premature judgments about alleged inborn intelligence. The heritability of intelligence received widespread public attention in the context of British educational psychologist Cyril Burt's (1883–1971) fraudulent data on twins and in connection with the issue of "race." As Stephen Jay Gould and others have pointed out many interpretations were unsupported by data but these interpretations were presented as factual knowledge. Many of the premature conclusions should be labeled *epistemological violence* (Teo 2005).

Natural Kinds versus Social Kinds More recently there has been a debate regarding whether psychological concepts are *natural kinds* or *social kinds*. Kurt Danziger (1997) suggests that many psychological concepts are social constructions that have become social reality. This idea has had an impact on research and practice and means that psychological concepts are bound to culture not to nature. Thus American or European psychology, indigenous psychologies themselves, cannot be exported straightforwardly to another cultural context. Many psychologists are often unaware that in believing their concepts can be used globally, they display misplaced ethnocentricity.

Professionalization The professionalization of psychology itself is a debated topic in academia. There have always been proponents and opponents, and this struggle has continued into the twenty-first century. For example, in the United States an American Psychological Society was founded in 1988 as a response to APA, which was perceived as catering to the interests of applied psychologists but not academics. One of the recent topics discussed in the context of the profession are prescription privileges for psychologists in some U.S. states. This topic is significant because it connotes a shift from a psychological to a medical model of mental illness. From the perspective of health insurers, allowing psychologists to prescribe drugs means cost reduction. However, giving such rights to psychologists challenges a long-standing privilege reserved to medical doctors, with probable economic consequences for that profession.

SEE ALSO *Achievement; Allport, Gordon; American Psychological Association; Anxiety; Attention-Deficit/Hyperactivity Disorder; Attitudes, Behavioral; Autokinetic Effect; Behavior, Self-Constrained; Behaviorism; Bettelheim, Bruno; Body Image; Brazelton, T. Berry; Child Behavior Checklist; Child Development; Cognition; Cognitive Dissonance; Consciousness; Contempt; Coping; Dementia; Depression, Psychological; Diathesis-Stress Model; Erikson, Erik; Family Functioning; Festinger, Leon; Foucault, Michel; Freud, Sigmund; Fromm, Erich; Gender; Gilligan, Carol; Goffman, Erving; Guttman Scale; Hite, Shere; Infidelity; Ingratiation; IQ Controversy; James, William; Jones, Edward Ellsworth; Jung, Carl; Kinsey, Alfred; Locus of Control; Maccoby, Eleanor; Manic Depression; Marital Conflict; Mechanism Design; Memory in Psychology; Mental Health; Mental Illness; Mental Retardation; Milgram, Stanley; Nature vs. Nurture; Neuroscience; Oedipus Complex; Operant Conditioning; Optimism/Pessimism; Overachievers; Overeating; Pavlov, Ivan; Post-Traumatic Stress; Priming;*

Professionalization; Psychoanalytic Theory; Psycholinguistics; Psychometrics; Psychosomatics, Social; Psychotherapy; Pygmalion Effects; Race; Racism; Realism; Realism, Experimental; Rotter's Internal-External Locus of Control Scale; Scarr, Sandra Wood; Self-Control; Self-Esteem; Sexuality; Sherif, Muzafer; Skinner Box; Skinner, B. F.; Social Psychology; Spock, Benjamin; Steele, Claude M.; Stereotype Threat; Strategies, Self-Handicapping; Stress; Stress-Buffering Model; Underachievers; Undereating; Zimbardo, Philip

BIBLIOGRAPHY

American Psychological Association. 2001. *Publication Manual of the American Psychological Association.* 5th ed. Washington, DC: Author.

Danziger, Kurt. 1997. *Naming the Mind: How Psychology Found Its Language.* London: Sage.

Gould, Stephen Jay. 1996. *The Mismeasure of Man*, revised and expanded. New York: Norton.

Gundlach, Horst. 2004. Reine Psychologie, Angewandte Psychologie und die Institutionalisierung der Psychologie [Pure psychology, applied psychology, and the institutionalization of psychology]. *Zeitschrift fuer Psychologie* 212 (4): 183–199.

Henley, Tracy B., Michael G. Johnson, Elizabeth M. Jones, and Harold A. Herzog. 1989. Definitions of Psychology. *Psychological Record* 39 (1): 143–152.

Holzkamp, Klaus. 1972. *Kritische Psychologie: Vorbereitende Arbeiten* [Critical psychology: Preparatory works]. Frankfurt am Main: Fischer.

Smith, Roger. 2005. The History of Psychological Categories. *Studies in History and Philosophy of Biological and Biomedical Sciences* 36: 55–94.

Teo, Thomas. 2005. *The Critique of Psychology: From Kant to Postcolonial Theory.* New York: Springer.

Vygotsky, Lev Semyonovich. 1997. The Historical Meaning of the Crisis in Psychology: A Methodological Investigation. In *Problems of the Theory and History of Psychology.* Vol. 3 of *The Collected Works of L. S. Vygotsky*, eds. Robert W. Rieber and Jeffrey Wollock, 233–343. New York: Plenum.

Ward, Steven C. 2002. *Modernizing the Mind: Psychological Knowledge and the Remaking of Society.* Westport, CT: Praeger.

Thomas Teo

PSYCHOLOGY, ADOLESCENT

SEE *Adolescent Psychology.*

PSYCHOLOGY, AGENCY IN

The concept of *agency* as a psychological dimension refers to the process of behaving with intentionality. Human beings exercise agency when they intentionally influence their own functioning, environments, life circumstances, and destiny. To posit that human beings have agency is to contend that they are self-organizing, proactive, self-regulating, and self-reflecting rather than reactively shaped by environmental forces or driven by concealed inner impulses. This is not to say that people always behave agentically. A driver who inadvertently runs a stop sign would not be considered the agent of that event because he did not intend to commit the infraction. An intention is a mental representation of a future course of action to be performed. It represents a proactive commitment to act.

Human agency has four core properties. The first is *intentionality*. People create and engage plans and strategies with which they realize their predetermined intentions to act in a certain manner. The second property is *forethought*, which addresses the temporal dimension of human agency. People make plans, set goals, and anticipate the likely outcomes of their prospective actions. To set plans in motion so as to bring about the desired outcomes, people must self-regulate their thinking and behavior. Thus, the third property of human agency is *self-reactiveness*, a process through which individuals not only make plans and choices but also construct the appropriate courses of action and regulate their execution. Because actions must be examined in order to be corrected, the fourth agentic property is *self-reflectiveness*. Through proactive self-awareness, people can reflect on their capabilities, the soundness of their thoughts and actions, and the meaning of their pursuits. As a consequence, they can make needed adjustments.

In addition to possessing four properties, agency operates through three modes: *individual, proxy,* and *collective.* When agency is exercised individually, one brings one's own personal influence to bear on one's own functioning and on the environmental events that comprise one's life. When people cannot exercise their personal influence, however, they must seek their well-being and obtain the outcomes they desire through the exercise of proxy agency. In this mode, people appeal to others who can secure these benefits for them. Thus, children turn to parents, students to teachers, and citizens to elected officials. Finally, people must often work together to obtain the things they need. Thus, they must pool their knowledge, skills, and resources, form alliances to advance common interests, and work collectively to obtain those things that they cannot obtain on their own.

To exercise human agency, people must believe in their capability to attain given ends. These *self-efficacy* beliefs are the foundation of human motivation, well-being, and accomplishment. Whatever other factors serve as guides and motivators, they are rooted in the core belief that one has the power to effect changes by one's actions, that one's locus of control is internal rather than external. This is because unless people believe that their actions can produce the outcomes they desire, they have little incentive to act or to persevere in the face of difficulties.

SEE ALSO *Self-Determination Theory*

BIBLIOGRAPHY

Bandura, Albert. 1982. Self-Efficacy Mechanism in Human Agency. *American Psychologist* 37: 122–147.

Bandura, Albert. 1989. Human Agency in Social Cognitive Theory. *American Psychologist* 44: 1175–1184.

Elder, Glen H., Jr. 1994. Time, Human Agency, and Social Change: Perspectives on the Life Course. *Social Psychology Quarterly* 57: 4–15.

Markus, Hazel R., and Shinobu Kitayama. 1991. Culture and the Self: Implications for Cognition, Emotion, and Motivation. *Psychological Review* 98: 224–253.

Frank Pajares

PSYCHOLOGY, DEVELOPMENTAL

SEE *Stages of Development.*

PSYCHOLOGY, FLOW

SEE *Flow.*

PSYCHOLOGY, POLITICAL

SEE *Political Psychology.*

PSYCHOLOGY, PRISON

SEE *Prison Psychology.*

PSYCHOLOGY OF TEACHING

SEE *Teachers.*

PSYCHOMETRICS

Psychometrics literally means "psychological measurement." It is the methodology that deals with designs, administrations, and interpretations of measurement on individuals' constructs such as abilities, attitudes, personality, knowledge, quality of life, and so on. There are several major components in psychometric theory, including classical test theory, item response theory, factor analysis, structure equation modeling, and statistical methods and computing. A *psychometrician* is an expert who practices psychometrics. He or she usually holds a postgraduate degree in either educational measurement or quantitative psychology.

CLASSICAL TEST THEORY

Reliability is a major concern for any kind of measurement, which copes with issues in measurement consistency. Classical test theory (CTT) views the score of an individual as a random variable X that can be decomposed by a fixed true score T plus an error: $X = T + E$, where the expected value of X is T, that is, $E[X] = T$ and $E[E] = 0$. Moreover, for a given population, $\sigma_x^2 = \sigma_T^2 + \sigma_E^2$. If $\sigma_E^2 = 0$, then the measurement X is perfectly reliable. Thus, the reliability of a test, often denoted as $\rho_{XX'}$, can be defined as

$$\rho_{XX'} = \frac{\sigma_T^2}{\sigma_X^2} = \frac{\sigma_T^2}{\sigma_T^2 + \sigma_E^2}.$$

According to the above, $\sigma_E = \sigma_X\sqrt{1 - \rho_{XX'}}$. Therefore, for a student who received score X, a 68 percent confidence interval for his or her true score is $X \pm 1(\sigma_E)$. Adequately quantifying indices to measure reliability is at the core of CTT. Let ρ_{XT} be the correlation coefficient between X and T. It can be proved $\rho_{XT}^2 = \rho_{XX'}$, where ρ_{XT} is the Pearson correlation between X and T. In statistics ρ_{XT}^2 is interpreted as the proportion of variation in T that is related to the variation in X. Thus, the larger the value of ρ_{XT}, the more reliable the measurement. Because T is unobservable, methods were proposed to estimate ρ_{XT}^2. For example, if two parallel forms of a test are administered simultaneously to the same population, it can be proved $\rho_{XX'} = \rho_{XT}^2$, where X and X' are scores of the two tests and $\rho_{XX'}$ is the correlation. This implies that reliability can be estimated from two parallel tests. When there is only one single test available, the correlation between its odd and even items, say $\rho_{YY'}$, measures the internal consistency between the half-tests and is called the "split-half reliability coefficient." According to the Spearman-Brown formula, the reliability for the entire test can be obtained from that in half-test:

$$\rho_{XX'} = \frac{2\rho_{YY'}}{1 + \rho_{YY'}}.$$

In the early days of psychometric research, numerous methods were proposed to estimate reliability indices, including Cronbach's coefficient-α, Kuder-Richardson's KR-20, and so on.

Another important concept in psychometrics is *validity*, which concerns the purpose of measurement; a measure is valid if it measures what it purports to measure. A pivotal task in psychometric research is to search for adequate methods to assess all kinds of validities, such as *content validity*, *criterion related validity*, and *construct validity*. Though they all were created to gauge the correlation between a measure and its purpose, each one plays a unique role. *Criterion related validity* is used to demonstrate the accuracy of a measure with respect to a criterion that has been demonstrated to be valid. For example, a job-screening test was shown to be an accurate test for job performance. Let X be the job-screening test score collected last year and Y be the job-performance rating of this year, where X can be called a predictor score and Y is called a criterion score. A straightforward quantity to assess the validity by using X to predict Y is the Pearson correlation between X and Y, ρ_{XY}. The larger the value of ρ_{XY} is, the more valid it is to use test score X to predict Y. Y can be predicted by least-squares linear regression

$$\hat{Y} = \rho_{XY} \frac{\sigma_Y}{\sigma_X} (X - \bar{X}) + \bar{Y},$$

where $\hat{Y}$ is the predicted criterion score, $\bar{X}$ and $\bar{Y}$ are the sample means, and σ_Y and σ_X are sample standard deviations.

Construct validity is a relatively newly developed form of validity. It refers to the degree to which the measure associates the construct that it was designed to measure. According to Mary Allen and Wendy Yen (1979), establishing construct validity is an ongoing process that involves the verification of predictions made about the test scores. Suppose a new test is proposed to measure a construct; according to theory, male and female should perform similarly if they are all at the same construct level. This hypothesis needs to be tested. If the testing is supported by the data analysis, the construct validity is enhanced.

FACTOR ANALYSIS

Factor analysis (FA) is another important component in psychometric theory. It has been commonly used to examine the structure of correlations among a set of observed scores. These scores can be either subscores of a test or the scores of several different tests. When FA is conducted, tests that are influenced by the same factor are shown to have high factor loadings on such factor. By conducting FA, researchers can identify factors that explain a variety of results among subtests or different tests. For example, a potential research question could be "How many traits are these tests measuring?" There have been immense applications and generalizations, including both confirmatory factor analysis and exploratory factor analysis. FA was originally developed within psychometrics for studying human intelligence testing, but it has become a frequently used methodology in many areas of psychology, social sciences, business, economics, engineering, and biology.

ITEM RESPONSE THEORY

Item response theory (IRT) is a relatively new methodology in psychometric theory. It is also referred to as "latent trait theory." In CTT the true score of an examinee, which can be interpreted as the examinee's ability level, is test dependent. When the test is easy, the examinee tends to have high true score; when the test is difficult, the examinee tends to have lower true score. The difficulty level for either an item or a test is population dependent. In order to overcome the shortcomings of CTT, IRT was created in an attempt to incorporate certain desirable features, such as examinee ability estimates, which are not test dependent, and item characteristics, which are not group dependent. IRT is based on certain fundamental assumptions: (1) For a dichotomously scored item, the performance of an examinee on the item can be predicted by knowing his or her latent trait (or set of latent traits); and (2) the relationship between examinees' item performance and the required latent trait (or traits) to perform on the item can be described by a response function (see, e.g., Hambleton, Swaminathan and Rogers 1991). As for a polytomously scored item, a set of response functions are needed.

Different models were proposed. The most commonly used model for dichotomously scored items is a three-parameter logistic model. Let X_j be the score for a randomly selected examinee on the jth item; $X_j = 1$ if the answer is correct and $X_j = 0$ if incorrect, and let $X_j = 1$ with probability $P_j(\theta)$ and $X_j = 0$ with probability $1 - P_j(\theta)$ where $P_j(\theta)$ denotes the probability of a correct response for a randomly chosen examinee of latent trait θ; that is, $P_j(\theta) = P\{X_j = 1|\theta\}$, where θ is unknown and has the domain $(-\infty, \infty)$ or some subinterval on $(-\infty, \infty)$. When the three-parameter logistic model (3PL) is used, the probability becomes

$$P_j(\theta) = c_j + (1 - c_j) \frac{1}{1 + e^{-a_j(\theta - b_j)}},$$

where a_j is the item discrimination parameter, b_j is the difficulty parameter, c_j is the guessing parameter.

Polytomous IRT modeling is another important application in IRT. Assume that the response of an examinee to the j-th item can be categorized into one of a set of $m + 1$ categories; that is,

$$P_{jk}(\theta) \equiv \text{Prob}\{X_j = u_{jk}|\theta\}.$$

In other words,

$$X_j = \begin{cases} u_{j0}, & \text{with probability } P_{j0}(\theta), \\ u_{j1}, & \text{with probability } P_{j0}(\theta), \\ \vdots & \vdots \\ u_{jm}, & \text{with probability } P_{j0}(\theta), \end{cases}$$

where $\sum_{k=0}^{m} P_{jk}(\theta) = 1$, and $P_{jk}(\theta)$ is referred to as the item category response function. When the category sequence is an increasing order $u_{j0} < u_{j1} < \ldots < u_{jm}$, the model is referred to as an "ordered polytomous model." There are numerous IRT models, such as the graded response, partial credit, and nominal models.

Popular applications of IRT include latent trait estimation, item parameter calibration, modeling and detection of differential item functioning (DIF), linking and equating, and computerized adaptive testing.

NEW DEVELOPMENTS IN PSYCHOMETRIC THEORY

Perhaps one of the biggest challenges for psychometricians today is how to keep abreast of the rapid developments in technology. Computerized Adaptive Testing (CAT) and Internet-Based Testing (IBT) are undergoing rapid growth. Although the implementation of new technologies has led to many advantages, such as new question formats, new types of skills that can be measured, easier and faster data analysis, faster score reporting, and continuous testing, many research questions remain unanswered. For example, how does one improve CAT test security without sacrificing estimation efficiency? How does one detect cheating behavior from an examinee's response pattern? How does one automatically grade examinees' performance in a large scale performance based assessment? How does one use test scores to make inferences about examinees' cognitions? Another big challenge stems from the fact that an unprecedented number of people are taking tests daily, from K-12 educational assessments, college admissions tests, job application and placement tests, professional licensing exams, survey research, psychiatric evaluations, and medical diagnostic tests. As such, the need for new methods is apparent in many aspects of psychometric development. Examples of some new developments are discussed below.

Large-Scale Automated Test Assembly Large-scale application of computer-based achievement tests and credentialing exams has generated many challenges to test development. One of these challenges, maintaining content representation in multiple forms, is central to test defensibility and validity. Manually assembling parallel test forms is not only time consuming, but also infeasible when a great number of forms are needed. Utilizing auto-

mated test-assembly (ATA) procedures reduces the workload of test developers and ensures the quality of the assembled test forms. ATA methods can be achieved by *constrained combinatorial optimization*, which involves how to best arrange the controllable elements in large complex systems in order to achieve a specified goal. A typical test-assembly problem can be treated by selecting items so that the assembled test satisfies a certain reliability index (objective function) subject to constraints such as test length and content coverage. Several methods were proposed. According to Wim van der Linden (2005), binary linear programming seems to be a popular method for test assembly due to two reasons: (1) the techniques are well developed within the field of operations research, and (2) some commercial software packages are readily available and user-friendly. Other promising ATA methods include sampling and stratification, weighted deviation, network flow, and optimization methods.

Automatically Scoring Performance-Based Assessment A new trend in large-scale assessment is to increase the portion of performance-based tasks in standardized testing. With the rapid development in computer technologies, more and more computer-based tests (CBT) for a variety of innovative constructed-response tasks have become available. Examples of such tasks include writing an essay or diagnosing a computer-simulated patient. However, grading on these complex tasks demands tremendous effort. Due to the subjectivity in human readers' scoring process, each task requires two or more content experts to review, which is very time consuming and pricey. Moreover, oftentimes there are several thousand or more students taking a given exam. How do we grade such examinations? Can we use automated scoring systems to address the cost issues and make the scoring more consistent? One of the most innovative developments in psychometrics for the last decade is automated scoring of complex tasks.

The Electronic Essay Rater (E-rater) is a technology developed by the Educational Testing Service (ETS) to score essays automatically based on holistic scoring guide criteria (see Burstein et al. 1998). The E-rater is designed to provide a distinct scoring model for each new essay topic. In the first step, a few hundred essays on the same topic were randomly sampled as a "training sample" and then scored by well trained human raters. The human scores are treated as the values of a dependent variable Y. Second, a set of variables are derived statistically from the learning sample, either through Natural Language Processing (NLP) techniques or by simple "counting" procedures. These feature variables, say $X_1, \ldots, X_n$, are treated as a set of "independent variables" and a linear regression model is established

$$Y = B_0 + B_1 X_1 +, \ldots, + B_n X_n + \varepsilon.$$

Third, a stepwise linear regression analysis is performed on the feature variable $X_1, \ldots, X_n$ extracted from the training dataset to identify a subset of features that parsimoniously explains observed variation in the consensus scores. Lastly, the final score prediction for cross-validation sets is performed using these estimated equations. Once the scoring model is established, the scores of the examinees outside the learning sample can be "predicted" by the linear model. Several million essays have been scored by E-rater since it was adopted for scoring the GMAT in 1999, and the technology is being considered for use with the Graduate Record Examination, for graduate school admissions, and the Test of English as a Foreign Language, which assesses the English proficiency of foreign students entering U.S. schools (Mathews 2004).

Measuring Patient-Reported Outcomes Conventional clinical measures of disease such as x-rays and lab results do not fully capture information about chronic diseases and how treatments affect patients. In order to get remedial measure, self-completed questionnaires are often administered to patients to assess their subjective experiences such as symptom severity, social well-being, and perceived level of health. Such measurement of patient-reported outcomes (PROs) is important for disease intervention. Many psychometric approaches can be used to meet the needs of clinical researchers across a wide variety of chronic disorders and diseases.

In particular, the CAT technology developed in educational testing can be used innovatively in health-related quality-of-life (HQOL) measures, in which a next item is selected based on the response the patient has given to the previous question. According to Frederic Lord (1971), an examinee is measured most effectively when test items are neither too "difficult" nor too "easy." Heuristically, if the examinee answers an item correctly, the next item selected should be more difficult; if the answer is incorrect, the next item should be easier. Note that in HQOL applications, the term *difficulty* is analogous to *severity*. For example, asking a patient if it is difficult to climb the stairs might measure a lower level of severity than asking if it is difficult to walk 1 mile. Thus, items are tailored to the individual with greater estimation precision and content validity. According to the National Institutes of Health (2003), such a CAT HQOL system would be useful in clinical practice to assess response to interventions and to inform modification of treatment plans.

Psychometric application in HQOL shares many similarities with its use in educational testing, with, for example, reliability and validity being the highest priorities for both. However, different perspectives do exist. For example, the length of the assessment for a particular

domain in HQOL is a much greater concern, especially when many domains must be assessed in a population of patients with a chronic disease, because patient burden must be carefully considered. The need for more psychometric research in developing, evaluating, and applying HQOL measures is growing, and undoubtedly, this will advance the field of psychometrics.

SEE ALSO *Cliometrics; Eugenics; Factor Analysis; Galton, Francis; Intelligence; Measurement; Pearson, Karl; Probability; Psychology; Reliability, Statistical; Scales; Spearman Rank Correlation Coefficient; Statistics; Statistics in the Social Sciences; Structural Equation Models; Validity, Statistical*

BIBLIOGRAPHY

Allen, Mary J., and Wendy Yen. 1979. *Introduction to Measurement Theory*. Monterey, CA: Brooks Cole.

Burstein, Jill, Lisa Braden-Harder, Martin Chodorow, et al. 1998. Computer Analysis of Essay Content for Automated Score Prediction: A Prototype Automated Scoring System for GMAT Analytical Writing Assessment Essays. ETS Research Report 98–15. http://www.ets.org/research/researcher/RR-98-15.html.

Hambleton, Ronald K., Hariharan Swaminathan, and H. Jane Rogers. 1991. *Fundamentals of Item Response Theory*. Newbury Park, CA: Sage.

Lord, Frederic. 1971. Robbons-Monro Procedure for Testing. *Educational and Psychological Measurement* 31: 3–31.

Mathews, Jay. 2004. Computer Weighing in on the Elements of Essay. *Washington Post*, August 1.

National Institutes of Health. 2003. Dynamic Assessment of Patient-Reported Chronic Disease Outcomes. RFA-RM-04-011. http://grants.nih.gov/grants/guide/rfa-files/RFA-RM-04-011.html.

Van der Linden, Wim J. 2005. *Linear Models for Optimal Test Design*. New York: Springer.

Hua-Hua Chang

PSYCHONEURO-ENDOCRINOLOGY

Psychoneuroendocrinology (PNE) is the study of the dynamic interaction of hormones with the central and peripheral nervous systems, toward the manifestation of behavior, cellular activity, systems-level functionality, and body processes, as well as their clinical applications. PNE is rooted in philosophy and the search for an understanding of the duality or unified nature of the "mind" and "body." Philosophers wrote copiously about the influence of cognitive and affective processes on physiology, and vice versa, and established the intellectual foundation for the development of PNE as a scientific discipline.

Throughout the nineteenth and twentieth centuries, many advances in medicine and science were guided by the pursuit of an understanding of the relationship of the "mind" to the "body." Many philosophers, physicians, psychologists, and others argued for duality and that the entities were separate and disintegrated. A vocal group of equally qualified and proliferative writers adamantly made a case for integration of the "mind" and "body" and ultimately yielded a coherent and well-articulated philosophy that posited a functional interaction of behavior, the nervous system, and hormones.

PNE evolved from an effort to understand the complex factors that influence human behavior and the development of normality and pathology. This evolution of the development of PNE was not unlike the occurrences that marked the development of many other areas of study (psychoneuroimmunology, psychophysiology, etc.) from a common philosophy of "integration," resulting in many similarities between disciplines.

Psychoneuroendocrinology can be viewed as extremely similar to psychoneuroimmunology (PNI). Both study the influence of psychological and neurological processes on the manifestation of behavior and disease. However, PNE focuses on endocrine pathways, whereas PNI focuses on immune pathways. Clearly, there is an intimate relationship between hormones and immunity, and it is functionally impossible to discuss the influence of one without discussing the impact on the other. PNE, however, is most often distinguished from other disciplines by a focus on a primary mechanism of action, *hormones*, on affected cells, tissues, organs, systems, and the body.

Many of the activities of researchers and clinicians from diverse disciplines such as psychiatry, psychology, neurology, endocrinology, molecular and behavioral genetics, and behavioral medicine are often broadly covered under the umbrella of activities that are considered PNE. Topics that are increasingly studied by psychoneuroendocrinologists include but are not limited to glycemic control, chronic pain, infertility and contraception, autoimmunity, Alzheimer's Disease and other dementias, addiction and compulsive disorders, exercise physiology, cancer, language acquisition and pervasive developmental disorders, marriage and mate selection, reactions to physical and psychological trauma, and racism, inequity, and discrimination.

In 1969 the International Society of Psychoneuroendocrinology was founded in Milan, Italy. Today, this organization represents PNEs across the world and has grown in size and scope. The organization represents the interest of approximately 450 researchers and clinicians toward the goal of promoting, initiating, facilitating,

and disseminating into public and clinical forums, basic, clinical, and applied interdisciplinary research in psychoneuroendocrinology.

SEE ALSO *Alzheimer's Disease; Marriage; Mental Illness; Pathology, Social; Philosophy; Psychopathology; Racism; Stress*

BIBLIOGRAPHY

France, C. R., F. J. Keefe, C. F. Emery, et al. 2004. Laboratory Pain Perception and Clinical Pain in Post-Menopausal Women and Age-Matched Men with Osteoarthritis: Relationship to Pain Coping and Hormonal Status. *Pain* 112: 274–281.

International Society of Psychoneuroendocrinology. http://www.ispne.org.

Kajantie, E. and D. I.W. Phillips. 2006. The Effects of Sex and Hormonal Status on the Physiological Response to Acute Psychosocial Stress. *Psychoneuroendocrinology* 31(2): 151–178.

Surwit, R. S., M. Van Tilburg, N. Zucker, et al. 2002. Stress Management Improves Long-Term Glycemic Control in Type 2 Diabetes Mellitus. *Diabetes Care* 25: 30–34.

Uhart, M., R. Y. Chong, L. Oswald, et al. 2006. Gender Differences in Hypothalamic-Pituitary-Adrenal (HPA) Axis Reactivity. *Psychoneuroendocrinology* 31(5): 642-652.

Christopher L. Edwards

PSYCHONEURO-IMMUNOLOGY

Psychoneuroimmunology (PNI) is the study of interactions between the mind, the nervous system, and the immune system. The mind involves thoughts, emotions, and experiences; the nervous system involves the brain, the spinal cord, and nerves; and the immune system involves cells and organs protecting the body from invaders. The mind and the immune system communicate through the peripheral nervous system and through hormones and cytokines, and this communication enables the immune system to be responsive to psychosocial factors and to signal the brain.

The field of PNI is interdisciplinary and has over the years contributed to the contemporary trend toward viewing health and disease as multifactorial. During the 1960s and 1970s, evidence began to accumulate indicating that the immune system could be influenced by psychological phenomena. In 1964 George F. Solomon and Rudolf Moos proposed that the development of rheumatoid arthritis was related to personality factors, advancing the possibility of psychoneuroimmunological phenomena, and Robert Ader and Nicholas Cohen demonstrated in 1975 that conditioning could affect the immune response by pairing taste with an immunosuppressive drug. Today, there is little doubt that a number of factors—biological, environmental, behavioral, and psychological—can interact to impact the progress and course of many illnesses.

Psychoneuroimmunology research strives to expand the understanding of how psychosocial factors can influence people's health, either positively or negatively. Research on the influences of psychological factors on the endocrine and immune systems involve examinations of the effects of stressors on these systems, and evidence clearly indicates that psychological and physical stressor exposure can affect the immune system. Stressor exposure also influences the endocrine response, changing levels of hormones such as cortisol. The effects of stressor exposure depend critically on the characteristics of the stressor. Acute stressors that last only minutes can be adaptive as part of a fight or flight response, whereas longer term stressors have less potentially beneficial effects. For example, chronic stressors, such as having a spouse with dementia, have been found to decrease both the cytotoxic and antibody-producing functions of immune cells. Adverse changes in immune functioning have also been associated with divorce, bereavement, unemployment, and other stressful episodes. Research has also demonstrated the importance of healthy social relationships and individual differences that buffer the psychological effects of stress, such as optimism, to better immune function.

Individual differences may not only confer an adaptive impact on the immune system, however. Studies on repression, which is characterized by low self-report of anxiety and avoidance of anxiety-provoking stimuli, but also by high defensiveness, have found associations between repression and poorer cellular immunity. Also, cynical hostility, which reflects suspiciousness, mistrust, and anger, appears to increase the physiological response to stressors involving social interactions and has been associated with increased susceptibility to illness. Clearly, individual differences can impact the immune system in a number of ways.

Studies have shown that stressful experiences can alter elements of the immune response, as well as impact health and disease onset. However, research has not yet convincingly linked these findings together to conclude that alterations in the immune system are in fact the mechanisms through which stressor exposure augments vulnerability to disease.

SEE ALSO *Optimism/Pessimism; Stress*

BIBLIOGRAPHY

Ader, Robert, and Nicholas Cohen. 1975. Behaviorally Conditioned Immunosuppression. *Psychosomatic Medicine* 37 (4): 333–340.

Ader, Robert, David L. Felten, and Nicholas Cohen. 2001. *Psychoneuroimmunology.* Vol. 2. 3rd ed. San Diego, CA.: Academic Press.

Segerstrom, Suzanne C. 2000. Personality and the Immune System: Models, Methods, and Mechanisms. *Annals of Behavioral Medicine* 22: 180–190.

Segerstrom, Suzanne C., and Gregory E. Miller. 2004. Psychological Stress and the Human Immune System: A Meta-analytic Study of 30 Years of Inquiry. *Psychological Bulletin* 130 (4): 601–630.

Solomon, George F., and Rudolf Moos. 1964. Emotions, Immunity, and Disease: A Speculative Theoretical Integration. *Archives of General Psychiatry* 11: 657–674.

Lise Solberg Nes

PSYCHOPATHOLOGY

Psychopathology, also referred to as mental disorder, is considered present when a behavior pattern or emotional state causes an individual clinically significant distress, dysfunction, or impairment in social, occupational, or other important areas of functioning or is widely deviant from social or cultural norms. This conceptual definition is somewhat subjective and might be difficult to apply in specific cases, in part because behavior patterns found to be acceptable according to the norms of one group or culture might be seen as abnormal or deviant in another. For example, self-mutilation is seen as an expression of piety in some cultures and as a sign of pathology in others.

An alternative means of defining psychopathology is to follow a more objective guide to psychiatric diagnosis in which specific symptom criteria are assessed for a standard set of mental disorders. Two related diagnostic protocols contain these specific criteria: *The Diagnostic and Statistical Manual of Mental Disorders* (DSM, American Psychiatric Association), and *International Classification of Diseases* (ICD, World Health Organization). Table 1 displays DSM criteria for the diagnosis of schizophrenia.

Diagnostic criteria for schizophrenia

A. Characteristic symptoms (two or more)
    a. Delusions
    b. Hallucinations
    c. Disorganized speech
    d. Grossly disorganized or catatonic behavior
    e. Negative symptoms (flat affect, avolition)
B. Social or occupational dysfunction in work, self-care, or social relations
C. The duration of the disturbance is at least six months
D. Symptoms not due to ingestion of medicine or drugs or due to other mental or medical disorders

SOURCE: American Psychiatric Association 1994.

Table 1

CATEGORIES OF MENTAL DISORDER

There are several broad categories of mental disorder representing differences in severity or degree of maladaptiveness. *Psychotic* disorders are among the most severe in that such patients are said to be out of touch with reality. For example, people suffering from schizophrenia often experience *hallucinations*, aberrant perceptions, such as hearing voices that others do not hear or seeing things others do not see while believing them to be actually occurring. They might also experience *delusions*, false beliefs, such as that they are being pursued by aliens because they hold some secret of the universe. Another defining characteristic of schizophrenia is the presence of *thought disorder*, in which patients are unable to maintain a coherent train of thought as their minds jump from topic to topic without apparent awareness that they are doing so.

Bipolar disorder (formerly known as manic depression) involves alternating episodes of *mania* in which patients are hyperactive, feel elated, and need little sleep. They might also experience delusions consistent with their mood, such as believing that they are invincible, brilliant, or have a theory that will save the world. Ultimately, they lapse into severe depression and may be unable to function at all while experiencing delusional beliefs, such as that they are dead or that their bodies are hollow.

Neurotic disorders are of a lesser degree of severity than the psychotic disorders yet cause significant distress and dysfunction to millions of people. Among the most prevalent of these are the *anxiety disorders*, which include the phobias, panic disorder, obsessive-compulsive disorder, and post-traumatic stress disorder. *Mood disorders*, such as *major depression*, are also quite common and can be episodic or continuous if not treated.

Organic mental disorders occur as a result of brain injury or disease, including *dementia* due to Alzheimer's disease, head injury, Parkinson's disease, or ingestion of toxic substances such as alcohol or inhalants. The primary areas of dysfunction in organic mental disorders include impaired abstract reasoning, lack of judgment, and impulsivity. In dementia in particular, memory deficit for new material is pronounced, and in more advanced stages entails loss of recall of previously familiar information, including recognition of family members and friends. Organic mental disorders can also involve delusions and depressive symptoms.

One in four American adults age eighteen and older has a DSM-diagnosable mental disorder within any given year. However, only one in seventeen (6 percent), suffers from serious mental disorder, such as schizophrenia or bipolar disorder. Table 2 displays prevalence figures for several of the more common mental disorders in the adult U.S. population. Approximately 20 percent of children are

Prevalence of selected mental disorders in U.S. adults

Diagnostic category	Prevalence (percentage) in a given year
Phobias	15.2
Major depressive disorder	5.3
Post-traumatic stress disorder	3.6
Antisocial personality disorder	2.1
Bipolar disorder	1.7
Panic disorder	1.6
Schizophrenia	1.3
Anorexia nervosa	0.1

SOURCE: National Institute of Mental Health 2007.

Table 2

also estimated to have a diagnosable mental disorder, but less than 9 percent are considered serious. These prevalence figures are only general averages that vary by gender, by culture and ethnicity, and from rural to urban areas. Some mental disorders found only in certain cultures are said to be *culture bound*, such as "running amok" in Malaysia.

THE ROLE OF GENES

Family and twin research demonstrates that there are genetic components that predispose some people to mental disorders. The closer one's relationship to a family member with schizophrenia, for example, the more likely that person will develop the disorder. Children born of two schizophrenic parents have a 46 percent chance of developing schizophrenia at some time in their lives. Similarly, if one member of an identical twin pair becomes schizophrenic, in 48 percent of cases the co-twin will also become schizophrenic. The fact that all such identical co-twins do not become schizophrenic indicates that more than genetics is involved in developing the illness. Various environmental factors hypothesized to be involved along with the genetic predisposition in determining who becomes mentally disordered include family and life stresses, early traumatic events, and maternal illnesses at critical periods during gestation. Some anxiety, depression, and substance abuse disorders also have genetic liabilities, although the genetic contributions in most cases are not as strong as for schizophrenia and bipolar.

ASSESSING MENTAL DISORDERS

Psychological assessment is the process of examining a patient to understand the range of possible problems or symptoms that can then lead to a diagnosis and treatment plan. One common assessment process is administration of a *mental status examination*, which is a semi-structured sur-

Mental status examination

Area Assessed	Sample questions or observations
• Orientation in time, place, and person	"Where are you? What year is it?
• Physical appearance	Is patient appropriately groomed and dressed?
• Mood and affect	"How do you feel today?"
• Thought processes	Is train of thought coherent, disconnected?
• Thought content	Does patient have delusions?
• Memory	Can patient recall three items after five minutes?
• Judgment	"What should you do if you find a lost wallet?"
• Abstract reasoning	"How are a peach and a banana alike?"
• Attention	"Count backwards from 50 by 3s"

SOURCE: University of California, San Diego, School of Medicine 2006.

Table 3

vey of a patient's mental, emotional, cognitive, and behavioral functioning. Sample questions are shown in Table 3.

Personality tests, such as the Minnesota Multiphasic Personality Inventory (MMPI), are self-administered questionnaires in which patients respond to a series of statements by indicating "true" or "false." Examples include "I am sure that many people are out to get me" and "My head aches all over." Patterns of responding to some 567 statements are statistically compared with patterns from samples of the normal population and of patients with various psychiatric disorders.

Brain scans represent an advance in technological assessments. X-ray and digital imaging of brain structure and function can highlight brain abnormalities associated with some mental disorders, particularly the dementias and schizophrenia.

CONSEQUENCES OF MENTAL DISORDERS

The consequences of being mentally ill are great both for the individual and for society. For the individual, there is a strong social stigma attached to mental illness that may manifest itself in many ways, such as employment discrimination, which is greater for the mentally disabled than for the physically disabled. Fully half of employers are reluctant to hire someone with a psychiatric history or someone currently taking medication for depression.

The economic consequences for society are great as well. The World Health Organization estimates that mental illness accounts for 15 percent of the burden of disease (years lost as a result of premature death and disability) in developed countries—more than the burden caused by all types of cancers. For women, depression causes more disease burden than any other illness. In fact major depres-

sion is the leading cause of disability worldwide among individuals five years of age and older.

TREATMENTS

Numerous treatments for mental disorders have emerged, varying according to the state of medical science at any given time. When mental disorder was thought to be caused by malevolent spirits infesting the brain, treatment consisted of chipping holes in the skull (trephining) to let the evil spirits out. When overcharged blood vessels were thought to be the cause, bloodletting was prescribed to reduce pressure on the brain and to bring patients back to their senses. Although these forms of treatment are no longer used in European and North American medicine, the focus remains on the brain. Brain processes are targeted to be changed through social, psychological, or biochemical means; the bloodstream transports chemicals to the neuroreceptors in the brain to effect therapeutic emotional, behavioral, and cognitive changes.

In the late nineteenth century Sigmund Freud pioneered the use of psychological processes to effect change in mental and emotional states. His original procedures have become the subject of much debate in the fields of psychology and psychiatry, but research demonstrates that other psychological treatment procedures are quite effective in treating a number of highly prevalent mental disorders. One group of treatments, referred to as *cognitive behavioral therapy*, focuses on assisting patients to systematically alter their thinking processes and their behaviors in ways that effect changes in the emotions and behaviors that led to and perpetuate their dysfunction. These procedures have been particularly successful in treating anxiety disorders and depression and are as effective as medications for treating these conditions.

Psychotropic drugs are perhaps the most widely used treatments for mental disorders in the early twenty-first century. *Antianxiety* medications, such as the benzodiazepines (e.g., Xanax, Valium, Atavan), effectively reduce felt anxiety but have a drawback in that they are potentially addictive. These antianxiety drugs work with the GABA system of neurotransmitters, which work to inhibit nerve transmission in areas of the brain that relate to anxiety.

A widely used class of *antidepressants*, some of which also have antianxiety properties, are the selective serotonin reuptake inhibitors (e.g., Prozac, Zoloft, Paxil). These drugs increase the availability of the neurotransmitter serotonin in the brain and relieve depression and some anxiety.

Psychotic conditions, such as schizophrenia, are treated with several types of *antipsychotic* drugs (e.g., Thorazine, Haldol, Clozaril, Risperidol). These medications tend to block the neurotransmitter *dopamine*, which is thought to underlie schizophrenia symptoms and related psychotic states. Bipolar disorder, mania, is now treated with drugs, such as Geodon and Seroquel, that tend to reduce the hyperactive manic state and associated psychotic delusions. Although they are largely successful in reducing psychotic symptoms, prolonged use of these drugs can lead to severe movement disorders, such as Parkinsonism and tardive dyskinesia.

Psychosurgery, brain surgery to affect changes in mental or emotional states, was widely used until the advent of antipsychotic drugs in the mid-twentieth century. Since then it has been used rarely, only in cases unresponsive to standard therapies. *Electroconvulsive therapy* continues to be used in severe cases of depression, in which patients are unresponsive to psychotherapy or antidepressant medications. *Transcranial magnetic stimulation* is a promising new experimental procedure for treating severe depression and involves applying powerful electromagnets directly to the skull.

SEE ALSO *Deviance; Madness; Manic Depression; Mental Illness; Neuroticism; Psychotherapy; Schizophrenia*

BIBLIOGRAPHY

American Psychiatric Association. 1994. *Diagnostic and Statistical Manual of Mental Disorders.* 4th ed. Washington, DC: Author.

Davidson, Gerald C., John M. Neale, and Ann M. Kring. 2004. *Abnormal Psychology.* 9th ed. Hoboken, NJ: Wiley.

Gaw, Albert C., ed. 1993. *Culture, Ethnicity, and Mental Illness.* Washington, DC: American Psychiatric Press.

Gottesman, Irving I. 1991. *Schizophrenia Genesis: The Origins of Madness.* New York: Freeman.

National Institute of Mental Health. 2006. Publications. http://www.nimh.nih.gov/publicat.

National Institute of Mental Health. 2007. Statistics. http://www.nimh.nih.gov/healthinformation/ statisticsmenu.cfm.

University of California, San Diego, School of Medicine. 2006. A Practical Guide to Clinical Health. The Mental Status Exam (MSE). http://medicine.ucsd.edu/clinicalmed/mental.htm.

Ronald A. Kleinknecht

PSYCHO-PHARMOGENOMICS

SEE *Psychotropic Drugs.*

PSYCHOSEXUAL DEVELOPMENT

SEE *Psychoanalytic Theory.*

PSYCHOSOMATICS

The term *psychosomatic* relates primarily to a physical concern, symptom, or illness of the body originating from emotional and thinking processes. The *psychosomatic* is born from an appreciation that the mind influences the body and the body influences the mind, and that pathology is the multifactoral product of biological, psychological, and social processes.

Historically, *psychosomatic* referred to the adverse impact that psychic and hysterical struggles exerted onto physical functioning and illness. Many illnesses (asthma, tuberculosis, allergies, chronic headaches, epilepsy, fibromyalgia, hypertension, interstitial cystitis, irritable bowel syndrome, etc.) were initially, in a pejorative manner consistent with the zeitgeist of the times, conceptualized and evaluated as being hysterical reactions to psychic disturbances. In this mostly psychodynamic context promoted by Josef Breuer (1842–1925), Sigmund Freud (1856–1939), and other theorists, the term *psychosomatic illness* was used to describe physical symptoms and diseases whose primary etiologies were emotional and mental processes.

More recently, a psychosomatic illness is conceptualized as one whose etiology cannot be described by physical or organic causes or whose etiology is idiopathic. In cases of unknown or ambiguous onset, anger, hostility, repressed sexual tension, and guilt are often ascribed as etiological precipitants of disease. In other cases, even when significant biological factors clearly influence the onset and course of illness but psychic disturbance is saliently present (depression, anxiety, hostility, etc.), the term *psychosomatic* is also used to reference the interaction of psychiatric and biological processes on symptom and disease manifestation.

Consequently, psychosomatic illnesses refer to symptoms or diseases that have psychic onset or psychic influences on the course, duration, or resolution of symptoms. Notably, psychosomatic illnesses have *real* symptoms and are diseases with *real* physical manifestations. This distinction is important in comparison to disorders where motivational and conscious factors characteristic of the patient influence the reporting of feigned diseases. For example, as a psychosomatic manifestation, the gastrointestinal symptoms associated with irritable bowel syndrome (diarrhea, constipation, or abdominal pain and cramping) may increase during periods of prolonged or intense emotional stress. Similarly, the magnitude of an asthmatic onset may be reduced with relaxation, focused deep breathing, or other behavioral techniques that alter physiology.

As in the previous example, psychosomatic illnesses have brought about a focus on interventions that exploit the known relationship between the mind and body. The study of such interventions is known as *psychosomatic medicine*, and the journal that is most aligned with this pursuit is *Psychosomatic Medicine*, the official journal of the American Psychosomatic Society. In its basic conceptualization, psychosomatic medicine is the science of treating the mind and body toward the reduction of morbidity and mortality.

The methodology of inquiry, as well as the topics explored by clinicians and researchers who practice and study psychosomatic medicine, have evolved over many years. Most often, the scientific inquiry and reviewers' and editors' choices for published articles have been reflective of scientific and societal priorities at the time.

One of the best discussions of this evolution in methodologies and priorities for clinicians and researchers appears in a review article in *Psychosomatic Medicine* of papers published in the journal on the topic of pain from 1940 to the end of the 1990s (Keefe et al. 2002). The authors found that in the 1940s "case studies" were one of the major methodologies published on the topic. However, by the 1950s the number of such publications had decreased by more than 50 percent, and by the 1970s case studies were rarely published in the journal. In contrast, the number of published studies exploring the role of personality traits and individual differences on pain was relatively small in the 1940s, but it had increased more than 400 percent by the end of the 1990s.

More reflective of deeply rooted societal beliefs about race and ethnicity, there were no studies published on the impact of race, ethnicity, and culture on pain in the 1940s, 1950s, or 1960s in *Psychosomatic Medicine*. Two such studies appeared in the journal in the 1970s, and only one was published in the 1980s. Only four articles were published on racial and ethnic influences on pain in the 1990s, for a total of seven across sixty years. This lack of published studies is interpreted as demonstrative of the infancy of general interest, knowledge, and understanding of racial and ethnic influences on medical outcomes in society, medicine, and psychosomatic medicine.

Issues of gender differences in psychosomatic illnesses have a much more robust and long history within psychosomatic medicine. The first studies of gender on the prevalence and experiences of pain appeared in *Psychosomatic Medicine* in the 1950s. There was a steady number of publications on this topic throughout the 1950s, 1960s, and 1970s, with a rise in the 1980s and a fourfold increase in the 1990s. A similar pattern in the number of published articles after 1980 can be seen for pain induction studies and pain treatment studies.

The current state of psychosomatic medicine seems embedded in the historical roots of the discipline and is focused on such issues as coping and the impact of psychological constructs like depression and anxiety on biological, neurological, endocrine, and other symptom and disease-related outcomes. Although the horizon is bright with an increased number of studies that focus on individual differences and the impact of demographic factors like race, ethnicity, age, and geographic region on disease-related outcomes, there is still much work to be done.

As evidence of a new global environment and a terrorism-conscious world, experts in psychosomatic medicine are increasingly involved in the development of health policies and are advocates for the collaboration between medical practitioners and public health officials toward more effective responses to international and local threats. Many government officials have begun to recognize the unique skill sets that experts in the field possess and are utilizing these skills to more effectively implement public health policy. The use of advanced statistical methodologies by researchers in psychosomatic medicine allows for the development of more ecologically valid predictive models of human health and behavior. Journals such as *Psychosomatic Medicine* and *Psychosomatics* highlight the zeitgeist of the discipline and provide a forum for scientific communication among researchers.

SEE ALSO *Disease; Medicine; Pathology, Social; Personality; Psychology; Psychopathology; Psychosomatics, Social; Psychotherapy; Public Health*

BIBLIOGRAPHY

Blumenfield, Michael, and James J. Strain. 2006. *Psychosomatic Medicine*. Philadelphia: Lippincott.

Keefe, Francis J., Mark A. Lumley, Angela Buffington, et al. 2002. The Changing Face of Pain: Evolution of Pain Research in *Psychosomatic Medicine*. *Psychosomatic Medicine* 64: 921–938.

Kubo, Chiaru, and Tomifusa Kubok, eds. 2006. *Psychosomatic Medicine: Proceedings of the 18th World Congress on Psychosomatic Medicine*. New York: Elsevier.

Van Tilburg, Miranda, Cynthia C. McCaskill, James D. Lane, et al. 2001. Depressed Mood Is a Factor in Glycemic Control in Type 1 Diabetes. *Psychosomatic Medicine* 63: 551–555.

Christopher L. Edwards
Camela McDougald

PSYCHOSOMATICS, SOCIAL

Social psychosomatics attempts to explain how social psychological processes—thoughts, feelings, and emotions—influence bodily changes. More generally, the field of social psychosomatics seeks to explore the links between social processes and physical illness. This field of study is principally concerned with the influence of emotional stimuli on physiologic changes. This relationship is bidirectional, with emotions influencing biological changes and physical health influencing emotion. Indeed, numerous studies have shown that overall health is the best predictor of happiness in adults.

Interest in the relationship between emotions and bodily processes extends as far back as Socrates and Hippocrates, who believed that emotion was a critical influence on health and disease. Modern day social psychosomatics is an interdisciplinary field that combines research from the fields of psychology, sociology, anthropology, medicine, and many others. The "fight or flight" response is well known throughout both the social and medical fields. Like other animals, our bodies release adrenaline in preparation to either face or flee from an environmental stressor. While this was at one point evolutionarily adaptive, and remains so in situations requiring split-second decisions, long-term activation of this stress response may have detrimental health consequences.

PSYCHONEUROIMMUNOLOGY

One particular branch of social psychosomatics that has been particularly influential in recent years is psychoneuroimmunology. This term describes the influence of psychological processes on immune system functioning. In particular this field of study examines the influence of stress on the susceptibility to infectious disease processes, such as the common cold. According to a 1991 study by Sheldon Cohen, David A. J. Tyrrell, and Andrew P. Smith, one illustration of this approach is known as a "viral challenge." In such a study participants are quarantined in a laboratory setting for a particular period of time. During this time participants undergo medical exams, complete questionnaires assessing their physical and mental health as well as health behaviors, and respond to psychosocial measures that describe various aspects of their personality and the amount of stress they are currently experiencing. Following this initial assessment, participants are given nasal drops containing a strain of a virus or a placebo. For the next few days, participants undergo daily examinations to assess for the presence of viral symptoms and the number of tissues used are counted and weighed. The "viral challenge" technique allows the impact of stress on susceptibility to the common cold to be analyzed, while controlling for exposure to the illness. The paradigm also enables the study of other factors thought to influence susceptibility to illness, including personality variables.

Another means of exploring the influence of stress on health is to examine viruses that are usually held latent by active immune systems, but that may return when the person is exposed to high levels of stress, such as a major life event. One virus that illustrates this scenario is the herpes virus, thought to be responsible for diseases such as cold sores, genital lesions, and mononucleosis. While the virus is typically suppressed by a strong immune system, it will flare, and studies have supported the idea that there is a relationship between negative emotional states, such as stress, and flare-ups.

HOW PERSONALITY MAY AFFECT HEALTH

Another indication of the impact of mind states on the body are diseases that seem to be strongly connected to certain personality types. For example, people who display high levels of aggression, hostility, or anger seem to be more likely to develop cardiovascular problems, while those people who are shy or socially isolated seem to be more likely to develop immune and metabolic illnesses.

While most research has focused on the negative repercussions certain emotions or life events may have on physical health, other research has focused on positive emotions that can foster health and well-being. Indeed studies have shown that factors such as high self-esteem, a strong sense of self-efficacy, and resilience predict positive changes in mental and physical health. Other positive factors that have been studied are hope, optimism, social support, and positive interpersonal relationships. Indeed studies have shown that these positive qualities can hasten recovery from serious injury or illness, while people who do not have these qualities are at greater risk for developing illnesses such as heart disease and cancer. A 2006 review by Sheldon Cohen and Sarah D. Pressman demonstrated an ongoing association between positive affect and lower rates of morbidity, illness, pain, and increased longevity, while John C. Barefoot and colleagues in their 2005 study found that people with heart disease who had larger and more diverse social networks had better outcomes.

In summary the field of social psychosomatics explores the connection between social processes and physical health, seeking to discover both the consequences and benefits of the link between our social world and our physical beings, as well as examining potential factors that may reduce or exacerbate the link.

SEE ALSO *Emotion; Morbidity and Mortality; Psychology; Psychoneuroimmunology; Psychosomatics; Stress; Stress-Buffering Model*

BIBLIOGRAPHY

Barefoot, John C., Morten Grobaek, Gorm Jensen, et al. 2005. Social Network Diversity and Risks of Ischemic Heart Disease and Total Mortality: Findings from the Copenhagen City Heart Study. *American Journal of Epidemiology* 161 (10): 960–967.

Cohen, Sheldon, David A. J. Tyrrell, and Andrew P. Smith. 1991. Psychological Stress and Susceptibility to the Common Cold. *New England Journal of Medicine* 325 (9): 606–612.

Cohen, Sheldon, and Tracy B. Herbert. 1996. Health Psychology: Psychological Factors and Physical Disease from the Perspective of Human Psychoneuroimmunology. *Annual Review of Psychology* 47: 113–142.

Cohen, Sheldon, and Sarah D. Pressman. 2006. Positive Affect and Health. *Current Directions in Psychological Science* 15 (3): 122–125.

Everson, Susan A., Debbie E. Goldberg, George A. Kaplan, et al. 1996. Hopelessness and Risk of Mortality and Incidence of Myocardial Infarction and Cancer. *Psychosomatic Medicine* 58 (2): 113–121.

Maunder, Robert G., and Jonathan J. Hunter. 2001. Attachment and Psychosomatic Medicine: Developmental Contributions to Stress and Disease. *Psychosomatic Medicine.* 63 (4): 556–567.

Victoria W. Willard

PSYCHOSURGERY

SEE *Lobotomy.*

PSYCHOTHERAPY

Psychotherapy is the treatment of mental illness, emotional difficulties, or behavioral problems through usually non-invasive psychological means. It is based on the premise that human psychological suffering can be alleviated by speaking and listening. At its core, psychotherapy involves the interpersonal interaction between a trained professional and a suffering individual. Collectively, the varied forms of psychotherapy are often referred to as "talking therapies." The specific techniques used in any psychotherapy depend largely on the theoretical orientation of the psychotherapist. Most approaches to psychotherapy can be traced in origin to one of the following schools: psychoanalytic, behavioral, cognitive, or humanistic. In practice, however, much of what is called psychotherapy today involves an evolving, fluid, and personalized use of techniques that depend on the specific problem, the professional's training, and the sufferer's needs. The goals of all types of psychotherapy typically involve the reduction of symptoms (e.g., depression, anxiety), altering maladaptive patterns of living (e.g., alcohol abuse, compulsive gambling), and/or improvement in specific areas of life functioning (e.g., increased capacity for work, creativity, or relationships).

The advent of modern psychotherapy can arguably be attributed to the work of Franz Anton Mesmer (1734–1815). Though few, if any, of his ideas would be recognized today as sound practice, his work marked an important shift from religious theories and explanations of healing (i.e., exorcisms) to theories based on scientific understandings of the time. The trance-like state Mesmer induced in individuals (still known colloquially today as being "mesmerized") was the precursor to hypnosis, a practice that French neurologist Jean-Martin Charcot (1825–1893) began using more specifically to treat patients with psychological difficulties. As a student of Charcot's, Sigmund Freud (1856–1939) first began using hypnosis to treat patients before he abandoned it for what would later become his revolutionary method of psychoanalysis. Decades of theoretical evolution of psychoanalytic theory has spawned a vast array of psychotherapies.

Though a contemporary of Freud's, Ivan Pavlov's (1849–1936) work represents a different yet important developmental line in the understanding of human behavior and learning. Known for his work studying the reflexive behavior of dogs, Pavlov discovered how certain behavioral responses could be experimentally brought about, or "conditioned," by pairing specific stimuli with other naturally occurring behaviors. This principle was used by American psychologists John B. Watson (1878–1958) and B. F. Skinner (1904–1990) in the clinical application of behaviorism, behavior therapy, and then to cognitive and cognitive-behavioral therapy. Historically, behavioral and cognitive psychotherapies have been viewed as an important counterargument to the earliest psychoanalytic ideas and techniques. In fact, the trailblazers of the behavior and cognitive psychotherapy movement, Albert Ellis (b. 1913) and Aaron Beck (b. 1921), both had early psychoanalytic training and interests.

PSYCHOANALYSIS

Developed by Sigmund Freud, psychoanalysis is often recognized as the first modern form of psychotherapy. It is based on the assumption that psychological symptoms are caused by unconscious conflict often rooted in one's early childhood experience. The aim of psychoanalysis is to bring unconscious conflicts into conscious awareness through the processes of introspection, insight, and interpretation. In a collaborative effort, the patient and therapist examine and try to resolve these conflicts, freeing the patient to live a more adaptive, healthy, and fulfilling life.

Freud discovered that examining the unconscious required some special tools. Foremost of these was the process of "free association," the uncensored report of all thoughts and fantasies, regardless of content. What seemed potentially irrelevant, tangential, or embarrassing to the patient was seen by Freud to have disguised connections and meanings that once understood would help reveal unconscious conflicts and reduce suffering. To promote free association, an analytic couch was often used, with the analyst sitting behind the couch and listening to the patient. Freud also viewed dreams as disguised and symbolic representations of unconscious conflicts, which could be useful in the psychoanalytic process. The interpretation of these conflicts brought about change, according to Freud.

As Freud's understanding of psychoanalytic theory evolved he began incorporating such ideas as transference, resistance, and defensive mechanisms into his theory of cure. The practice of psychoanalysis continues to evolve today in ways that maintain, reject, and expand some of Freud's original principles. Although traditional psychoanalysis (usually four to five appointments per week for several years) is not as popular as it was in the first half of the twentieth century, at the beginning of the twenty-first century it remains a sought-after treatment modality for some people. A more popular variant of psychoanalysis is face-to-face psychoanalytic psychotherapy, which uses many of the same principles as psychoanalysis but is less frequent (usually one to two appointments per week). In the psychoanalytic community, psychoanalysis is viewed as the treatment of choice for a wide range of psychological difficulties, including depression, anxiety, and personality disorders. Though the cost and length of treatment has been criticized as being prohibitive for many individuals, proponents of psychoanalysis and psychoanalytic psychotherapy argue that benefits are more comprehensive and longer lasting than other forms of treatment.

BEHAVIORAL THERAPY

Behavior therapy emphasizes the scientific understanding of observable behaviors, rejecting the importance of self-awareness, insight, and the unconscious as valued in psychoanalytic techniques. The goal of most forms of behavior therapy is to increase desired behaviors and decrease undesired ones. It is a collective group of therapeutic techniques based on systematically researched theories of learning and behavior. For example, Pavlov's discovery of "classical conditioning," or Pavlovian conditioning, led to an increased understanding of how certain behaviors could be learned. In his experiments with dogs, Pavlov found that the repeated pairing of a bell immediately proceeding the presentation of meat powder would eventually "condition" the dogs to salivate when the bell was later presented alone (without the meat powder). John B. Watson's (1878–1958) famous "Little Albert" experiment demonstrated how fear of a non fear-inducing white rat could be conditioned in a toddler boy by the repeated pairing of a loud noise with a the presentation of the rat. While the increase of salivation in dogs or the induction of fear in infants are hardly desired outcomes of modern psychotherapeutic techniques, these principles of classical conditioning have had a far reaching influence on subsequent developments of different forms of behavior therapy.

"Systematic desensitization," for example, is a behavioral therapy technique that uses principles of classical conditioning to help gradually alleviate specific phobias (e.g., fear of flying) or reduce the symptoms of certain anxiety disorders. "Flooding" (also called exposure therapy) is another form of behavior therapy used to help reduce anxiety by exposing an individual to a feared stimulus until the anxiety is extinguished. Though not commonly used in modern day, "aversion therapy" is a controversial behavior therapy technique that pairs unwanted behaviors with unpleasant results in order to reduce the behavior (e.g., pairing alcoholic beverages with a chemical substance that causes nausea). Other behavioral approaches involve principles of "operant conditioning" that Skinner was most noted for. Operant conditioning relies heavily on ideas of reinforcement and punishment in the service of increasing desired behaviors and decreasing unwanted behaviors.

Behavior psychotherapies tend to be directive, specific, and symptom focused. They are most popularly associated with the treatment of specific phobias, various anxiety disorders, or maladaptive behaviors (e.g., addictions, pedophilia). While research suggests that these techniques can be highly effective, especially in the short term, there is some debate as to how lasting the effects can be. A criticism of a strict behavioral approach to treatment is that it does not address underlying causes of the behaviors. The principles of behaviorism and behavioral psychotherapy are often used most successfully in conjunction with other theoretical approaches.

COGNITIVE THERAPY

Since the 1960s cognitive psychotherapy has been the predominant force in the treatment of many psychological difficulties. The basic assumption of all forms of cognitive therapy is that thinking impacts feeling. For example, cognitive therapists posit that an individual may be feeling depressed because of certain thoughts the person has (e.g., "I am not good enough"). In contrast to behaviorism's focus on observable behaviors, the aim of cognitive therapy is to address, challenge, and alter maladaptive thoughts and cognitions. This can be done in many ways.

Developed by Ellis, Rational Emotive Therapy, also known as Rational Emotive Behavior Therapy, is a confrontational form of cognitive therapy that involves active and direct confrontation of an individual's irrational beliefs. This type of intervention was intended by Ellis to be somewhat jarring to patients so as to highlight how individuals' thoughts and beliefs were irrational appraisals of events that led to self-imposed suffering (e.g., depression, anxiety). As such, alleviation of symptoms came about by attacking these irrational thoughts directly.

Beck is known for developing a less confrontational, gentler approach to cognitive psychotherapy. Beck's work, and many approaches that follow, focuses on correcting errors of reasoning called "cognitive distortions." These distortions are said to create and maintain negative feelings such as anxiety or depression. For example, a young man engages in the cognitive distortion of catastrophizing (e.g., assuming the worst case scenario) when he believes that his public speaking will provoke unbearable anxiety and illicit embarrassing ridicule. In reality, however, the experience may just be uncomfortable. A cognitive therapist would address with this young man the distortions of his thinking. Other cognitive distortions include "overgeneralization," "all-or-nothing thinking," and "jumping to conclusions." All of these distortions are automatic in nature and the process of cognitive psychotherapy works to reprogram these thoughts into more adaptive ones. Technically, cognitive psychotherapy tends to be directive with an emphasis on self-monitoring, problem solving skills, behavioral experiments, and improved decision making. Many cognitive therapists utilize homework assignments to encourage patients to continue monitoring their thoughts and feelings when outside the consulting room.

The term cognitive-behavioral psychotherapy is often used to describe the natural and practical mix of many of the cognitive and behavioral techniques described. In general, cognitive and cognitive-behavioral therapy utilize a much more structured and guided approach. It has proven to be a highly effective, efficient, and often time-limited treatment of many psychological disorders. Its structure also lends itself well to empirical investigation. Cognitive and cognitive-behavioral psychotherapy is the predominate form of psychotherapy being practiced in the United States today.

HUMANISTIC THERAPY

Having its roots in existential philosophy, humanistic psychotherapy is based on the ideas and practice of Abraham Maslow (1908–1970) and Carl Rogers (1902–1987). Often referred to as a "third force" of modern psychology and psychotherapeutic technique, humanistic psychotherapy represents an alternative to the larger psychoanalytic and cognitive-behavioral approaches. Both Maslow and Rogers focused on the ideas of psychological growth and deemphasized the notion of mental illness. Developed in the 1960s, humanistic psychotherapy posits that humans have an innate desire to maximizing personal growth and fulfillment, a goal termed by humanistic thinkers as "self-actualization." The blocking of self-actualization is viewed by humanistic therapists as the source of psychological suffering.

Perhaps more than any other clinician, Rogers's person-centered therapy illuminated the more universally practical components of psychotherapy, regardless of orientation. His focus on a genuine, empathic, and honest relationship between therapist and sufferer has been viewed as instrumental across many therapeutic disciplines. Humanistic psychotherapy tends to be non-directive. The humanistic psychotherapist focuses on the patient's current feelings and experiences. The goal of Rogers's type of psychotherapy is to listen in an empathic way that allows the patient to feel heard and understood. It was this understanding, Rogers believed, that helped patients navigate personal roadblocks and live more fulfilled and meaningful lives. Other important variants of humanistic psychotherapy were practiced by Rollo May (1909–1994), Victor Frankl (1905–1997) and James Bugental (b. 1915).

OTHER PSYCHOTHERAPIES

The various practices described share in common the most traditionally recognized form of psychotherapy: one trained professional listening and speaking with a suffering individual. There are, however, other forms of psychotherapy that deserve mention. As early as the 1940s, psychotherapy in a group setting was an accepted form of treatment.

The unique benefits of the interpersonal experience coupled with the increased patient-to-therapist ratio maintains group psychotherapy as a popular alternative to individual psychotherapy. Support groups led by lay persons or fellow suffers, such as Alcoholics Anonymous, remain a popular treatment choice for individuals. Specific psychotherapies have been designed to work with families, couples, or even in industrial settings. Play therapy is often a method used by practitioners working with children. There are also different forms of psychotherapy that involve the use of music or art. The variety of problems, populations, theoretical orientations, and modalities, coupled with each psychotherapist's individual style, makes the number of different types of psychotherapy virtually endless.

BIOLOGICAL CONSIDERATIONS AND RESEARCH

The biological treatment of psychological distress has become inextricably linked to current ideas about psychotherapy. The 1950s marked an explosion of scientific research that led to new understandings about the connection between brain chemistry and psychological disorders. Most notably, the advent of psychotropic medication demonstrated that medicines could influence individuals' thinking, feelings, and behaviors in ways that brought about relief of symptoms. This development has drastically changed the way people suffering from mental health issues receive treatment. Though it has not supplanted psychotherapy as a treatment modality, psychopharmacology has proven to be an important aspect of treating many disorders. Findings suggest that for most mental health issues, a combination of psychotherapy and medication is often more effective than either alone or none at all.

Critics of the biological approach often state that medication alone treats only symptoms and does not address underlying, more psychological causes, often leaving individuals dependent on medications to maintain a sense of mental health. The effectiveness and efficiency of symptom relief that some medication has demonstrated, however, solidifies the medical treatment of mental illness as an important modality that is here to stay. That said, new developments in neuroscience, brain imaging, and research techniques are beginning to demonstrate how psychotherapy alone can alter brain chemistry. This nascent line of research has begun focusing the historically fuzzy distinction between mind and body that has puzzled philosophers and scientists for thousands of years.

Psychiatry itself is a biologically oriented field. As compared to other mental health fields such as clinical psychology, counseling psychology, and social work, modern psychiatric training involves relatively little instruction or experience in the practice of psychotherapy. This has not always been the case. At the height of its popularity in the United States, psychoanalysis was practiced almost exclusively by psychiatrists. It was only in the late 1980s that psychologists, social workers, and counselors were first accepted into American psychoanalytic training institutes. Although some psychiatrists practice various types of psychotherapy as part of their profession, most do not and the balance of psychotherapy practice has shifted to non-medically trained professionals. As a medical profession with prescription privileges, however, psychiatrists are the most knowledgeable and well-trained in the area of psychotropic medication and the biological treatment of mental illness.

In the study of mental health treatment there is a growing call for the introduction and dissemination of psychotherapy approaches to be scientifically sound and have evidence-based proof of effectiveness. This comes from a social value of consumer protection as well as the financial pressures inherent in increasing health care costs. The structured nature of cognitive and behavioral psychotherapy techniques have made these forms of treatment better suited to traditional experimental designs and standardization, whereas the less structured and more individualized psychoanalytic and humanistic treatments present more complicated research challenges. This makes comparing the effectiveness of one type of therapy versus another understandably problematic. What constitutes proof is also a matter of debate among researchers, practitioners, and patients alike. While the scientific study of psychotherapy process and outcome likely will continue to illuminate and inform the public about treatment options, it is important to always consider the limitations of such research.

Debates between theoretical camps of psychotherapy have had a history of contention, each, at times, extolling the virtues of their own techniques and criticizing the deficits of the others. This debate has also been informative, propelling the understanding of what helps troubled people feel better. In some ways the debate is like the fable of the six blind men asked to describe an elephant to one another. Having only the sense of touch, one man described the smooth coolness of the ivory tusk, another the furrowed curve of the trunk; a third the wispy tuft of the tail, and so on. Each man could hardly believe that he was describing the same thing as the other.

SEE ALSO *Anxiety; Classical Conditioning; Depression, Psychological; Emotion; Existentialism; Freud, Sigmund; Maslow, Abraham; Medicine; Mental Illness; Operant Conditioning; Pavlov, Ivan; Psychoanalytic Theory; Psychology; Psychoneuroendocrinology; Skinner, B. F.*

BIBLIOGRAPHY

Beck, Aaron T. *Cognitive Therapy and the Emotional Disorders.* 1976. New York: International Universities Press.

Beck, Judith S. *Cognitive Therapy: Basics and Beyond.* 1995. New York: Guilford Press.

Frank, Jerome D., and Julia B. Frank. *Persuasion and Healing: A Comparative Study of Psychotherapy*, 3rd ed. 1993. Baltimore, MD: Johns Hopkins University Press.

Freud, Sigmund. *New Introductory Lectures on Psycho-Analysis.* 1933. New York: W. W. Norton.

McWilliams, Nancy. *Psychoanalytic Psychotherapy: A Practitioner's Guide.* 2004. New York: Guilford Press.

Prochaska, James O., and John C. Norcross. 2006. *Systems of Psychotherapy: A Transtheoretical Analysis*, 6th ed. Pacifica Grove, CA: Thomson Brooks/Cole.

Rogers, Carl. *On Becoming a Person.* 1961. Boston: Houghton Mifflin.

Skinner, B. F. *Science and Human Behavior.* 1953. New York: Macmillan.

Yalom, Irivin D., and Molyn Leszcz. 2005. *The Theory and Practice of Group Psychotherapy*, 5th ed. New York: Basic Books.

Steven J. Hanley

PSYCHOTROPIC DRUGS

Psychotropic drugs are substances prescribed to affect one's behavior, emotions, or cognition. They can be categorized into the following drug classes: antipsychotics, antidepressants, anxiolytics, mood stabilizers, and stimulants. Psychotropic drugs are routinely used to treat various mental disorders, and their efficacy is determined by how well the drug decreases the presenting symptoms of a disorder, as well as the presence or absence of side effects.

PSYCHOTROPIC DRUG CLASSES

Antipsychotics are prescribed primarily to manage the symptoms associated with schizophrenia, autism, and other developmental disabilities. On occasion, they are used in combination with other drugs to treat depression and bipolar disorder. There are two classes of antipsychotic drugs: typical and atypical. The difference between these two groups lies in their mechanism of action. Typical antipsychotics are highly selective for dopamine receptors, specifically D2 receptors. Unfortunately, because of this selectivity, movement disorders (e.g., tardive dyskinesia) are a side effect of the typical antipsychotics. Given this undesirable side effect, atypical antipsychotics were developed. They differ from the typical antipsychotics in that they have a lower affinity for D2 receptors, and affect other neurotransmitter systems such as serotonin. Atypical antipsychotics have significantly fewer motor side effects; however, weight gain is an issue.

Antidepressants are used in the treatment of depression, post-traumatic stress disorder, anxiety, and obsessive compulsive disorder. There are three major classes of antidepressants prescribed: monoamine oxidase inhibitors (MAOIs), tricyclic antidepressants (TCAs), and selective serotonin reuptake inhibitors (SSRIs). The best known of these is the SSRI. SSRIs exert their effect by blocking the reuptake of serotonin from the synapse into the presynaptic neuron, thus increasing its availability postsynaptically. Physiological side effects associated with SSRIs are usually minimal and transient, with the exception of sexual dysfunction. Increases in suicide ideation in adolescents treated with SSRIs have been reported, and thus SSRIs are not generally recommended for use with this population. Despite their popularity, SSRIs have not been found to be any more effective at treating depression than any other antidepressant.

Anxiolytics are prescribed to treat anxiety and sleep disorders. There are two classes of anxiolytics, benzodiazepines and non-benzodiazepines. Benzodiazepines exert their effects by increasing the efficiency of gamma-aminobutyric acid (GABA), an inhibiting neurotransmitter. These drugs are fast-acting, and side effects include the potential for physiological addiction. Non-benzodiazepines include buspirone, which exerts its effect via activity at serotonin receptors. The potential for abuse with non-benzodiazepines is less than with benzodiazepines, but they also appear to be less effective at treating anxiety disorders than benzodiazepines.

Although lithium is the only drug used specifically for the treatment of bipolar disorder, anticonvulsants such as lamotrigine also have been demonstrated to have mood-stabilizing properties. At the present time, the neuropharmacology of these drugs in the treatment of mood disorders is not understood, and both lithium and certain anticonvulsants require routine blood monitoring to guard against toxicity.

Finally, stimulants are prescribed to treat attention disorders such as attention deficit/hyperactivity disorder (ADHD). These drugs operate by increasing the availability of dopamine, epinephrine, norepinephrine, and/or serotonin. Side effects associated with stimulants are decreased appetite and difficulty sleeping.

EFFICACIOUS USE OF PSYCHOTROPIC DRUGS

Prior to the advent of psychotropic drugs in the late 1940s, treatment of psychiatric disorders included admittance to asylums, physical restraints, and psychoanalysis. Consistent and effective results of treatment were often elusive. Advances in technology and the convergence between the fields of psychiatry, neurology, genetics, and neuroscience have made it possible to evaluate the therapeutic effects of psychotropic drug use, and to make predictions about who will respond well to their use. The application of neuroimaging techniques such as functional magnetic resonance imaging (fMRI) to drug evaluation allows assessment of changes in cerebral blood flow, volume, and oxygenation as a function of psychotropic drug use that may provide an indication of the efficaciousness of psychotropic treatment in disorders such as schizophrenia and depression (Tracey and Wise 2001). Psychopharmacogenomics is another approach that attempts to predict efficacious drug treatment (Malhotra, Murphy and Kennedy 2004). The goal is to identify polymorphisms or mutations of genes involved in receptor function, pharmacokinetics, and pharmacodynamics, to determine who is at an increased risk for experiencing side effects of psychotropic drugs. With each of these technological advances, the aim is to improve prescribing practices and provide individualized, effective treatment while ensuring quality of life.

SEE ALSO *Adolescent Psychology; Cognition; Emotion; Genomics; Mental Health; Mental Illness; Neuroscience; Psychoanalytic Theory; Psychology; Psychoneuroendocrinology; Psychoneuroimmunology; Psychotherapy; Suicide*

BIBLIOGRAPHY

Malhotra, Anil K., Greer M. Murphy, and James L. Kennedy. 2004. Pharmacogenetics of Psychotropic Drug Response. *American Journal of Psychiatry* 161 (5): 780–796.

Stahl, Stephen M. 2000. *Essential Psychopharmacology: Neuroscientific Basis and Practical Applications.* 2nd ed. Cambridge, U.K.: Cambridge University Press.

Tracey, Irene, and Richard G. Wise. 2001. Pharmacological fMRI: A New Tool for Drug Development in Humans. *Journal of Pharmacy Practice* 14 (5): 368–375.

Maria G. Valdovinos

PUBLIC ADMINISTRATION

Public administration is a practice of government, an academic study, and a political reform movement. While public policy is the study of the process of making laws and government programs, public administration implements these policies and studies and seeks to improve this implementation.

The administration of King Frederick William I of Prussia (1688–1740) in the eighteenth century and an 1887 journal article by political scientist and future U.S. president Woodrow Wilson (1887) emphasized the need to create and use a nonpolitical, career civil service in order to implement policies more honestly and efficiently. With the rapid increase in industrialization and urbanization in the United States during the late nineteenth and early twentieth centuries, public administration developed further as an academic study at major universities and as a political reform movement within federal, state, and local governments. In particular, the public administration movement wanted to transform most entry-level government jobs from politically appointed positions to merit-based civil service positions determined by standardized tests and protected from improper political influence. The Pendleton Act of 1883 began merit-based testing and hiring for federal jobs, and state and local governments gradually adopted similar reforms.

During the twentieth century, public administration also wanted to apply the methods, organizations, and values of business administration to government. In particular, people who wanted to "run government like a business" wanted public administration, especially in local government, to be as cost efficient, productive, and professional as corporations in managing personnel, providing goods and services, and spending funds. This perspective and objective are especially evident in the city manager form of government. This is a type of government in which a city or town council hires a city manager to exercise the administrative, personnel, and budgetary powers typically exercised by elected mayors in other forms of local government. The Budget and Accounting Act of 1921, the recommendations of the Brownlow and Hoover commissions, and the Civil Service Reform Act of 1978 reflected similar business-like practices and values in personnel and budgetary management as they applied to the federal government. According to the book *Democracy and the Public Service* by Frederick C. Mosher (1968), the Brownlow commission of 1937, chaired by political scientist Louis Brownlow, and the Hoover commissions of 1949 and 1955, chaired by former president Herbert C. Hoover (1874–1964), respectively recommended the creation of the Executive Office of the President (EOP) in order to assist the president's administration of the federal bureaucracy and an improvement of the relationship between political appointees and top civil servants within the executive branch.

During the 1990s, the widely read and influential book by Vice President Al Gore (b. 1948) called *Reinventing Government* (1993), about his work with the National Performance Review (NPR), explained and advocated the "Third Way" of experimenting with the greater use of nonprofit organizations to provide some public services as an alternative to the extremes of probusiness conservatism and progovernment liberalism. Following the terrorist attacks of September 11, 2001, the federal bureaucracy was expanded to include the Department of Homeland Security and reformed to facilitate greater communication and coordination among federal agencies and between the federal and state governments regarding terrorist-related national security, surveillance, immigration, and transportation safety issues.

SEE ALSO *Administrative Law; Bureaucracy; Government; National Security; September 11, 2001*

BIBLIOGRAPHY

Gore, Al. 1993. *Creating a Government That Works Better and Costs Less: The Gore Report on Reinventing Government.* New York: Random House.

Johnson, William C. 1992. *Public Administration: Policy, Politics, and Practice.* Guilford, CT: Dushkin Publishing Group.

Mosher, Frederick C. 1968. *Democracy and the Public Service.* New York: Oxford University Press.

Osborne, David, and Ted Gaebler. 1992. *Reinventing Government: How the Entrepreneurial Spirit Is Transforming the Public Sector.* New York: Plume.

Wilson, Woodrow. 1887. The Study of Public Administration. *Political Science Quarterly* 2 (June): 197–222.

Sean J. Savage

PUBLIC ASSISTANCE

At any point in time, some members of an affluent or poor society may be unable to fully support themselves due to a variety of circumstances, including adverse economic conditions (e.g., unemployment), health problems (physical or mental infirmity), changes in family circumstances (e.g., births, deaths, divorce), age factors (e.g., youth, advanced age), and natural disasters. In these situations, the government, in fulfilling its role as enhancer of the well-being of its citizens, may intervene by providing assistance to the affected individuals or families. For the sake of long-term viability, however, it is important to design a system that encourages able-bodied adult public assistance beneficiaries to become self-supporting again. Because public assistance programs seek to provide an economic or social safety net to the disadvantaged or vulnerable members of society, it is not surprising that such programs are subjects of extensive public policy debates in democratic societies. These debates focus on the long-run viability of specific public assistance programs, on distributional impacts, on whether public assistance encourages or discourages job-seeking and childbearing, and on whether or not programs help beneficiaries escape from poverty and welfare dependence, as well as the extent to which governments should be providing such programs.

The governments of the United States, Canada, Japan, and other industrialized countries have developed comprehensive public assistance programs over the years to assist the poor and needy financially or through medical care, employment training, and a variety of other programs. Because of their comprehensive public assistance programs, these countries are labeled *welfare states*. The sociologists James Rice, Robert Goodin, and Antti Parpo (2006) have articulated some ways in which welfare states contribute to people's well-being.

THE MEANING OF PUBLIC ASSISTANCE

To many people, public assistance is synonymous with welfare benefits (and because the latter is often perceived negatively, so too is the former). Strictly speaking, public assistance is broader than welfare; it includes cash benefits (e.g., social assistance), direct "in-kind" provision of goods and services (e.g., food stamps, child care services), and tax breaks (e.g., tax credits for families with dependent children). The designation *public* arises from the fact that some level of government (central, state, or local) controls the relevant financial flows; thus, benefits provided by private charities are not considered public assistance, except in cases where public expenditures are channeled through private charities. Three salient aspects of public assistance programs follow from the above definition. First, the assistance is intended to be provided for the direct benefit of needy individuals or families. Second, because some level of government controls the relevant financial flows, the governments in power influence such expenditures. Third, the benefits, which can be cash, in kind, or in the form of tax breaks, must address some social or economic goal.

Since the 1930s many specialized public assistance programs for low-income households, seniors, youth, the sick and handicapped, and the unemployed have been launched in the United States, in response to changing economic and social conditions. A partial list of such programs includes the Food Stamp Program (FSP), Medicaid, Supplemental Security Income (SSI), Aid to Families with Dependent Children (AFDC), Temporary Assistance to Needy Families (TANF), General Assistance (GA), Job Opportunities and Basic Skills (JOBS), Earned Income Tax Credit (EITC), and the Low Income Home Energy Assistance Plan (LIHEAP). TANF (which replaced AFDC) is what is commonly referred to as *welfare*; it assists needy families with dependent children, whereas SSI is designed to assist the blind, aged, and disabled. Most of these programs are means-tested (or income-tested)—that is, benefit eligibility is restricted to individuals or households whose income and/or assets are valued below some threshold level. For example, Medicaid provides medical assistance for only certain low-income individuals and households, and FSP ensures provision of adequate nutrition to low-income individuals and households by supplementing their food budget.

According to statistics provided by the U.S. Social Security Administration (2006), in 2002 there were 49.754 million recipients of Medicaid, at a total cost of $213.491 billion; an average of 5.058 million recipients of TANF/AFDC per month, at a total cost of $9.717 billion; an average of 19.094 million recipients of food stamps, at a total cost of $18.257 billion; and 6.940 million recipients of SSI in December 2002, at a cost of $34.567 billion.

ECONOMIC IMPACT OF PUBLIC ASSISTANCE

Public assistance programs are designed to achieve economic and social goals. Two such goals are noteworthy. First, the provision of public assistance is a step toward creating an egalitarian society in which all citizens enjoy a reasonably decent standard of living. Second, public assistance spending may serve as a tool for regulating demand, structuring the labor market, and stabilizing the economy.

Opponents of public assistance programs claim, among other things, that such programs provide disincentives to work and incentives to bear children. These programs also, they assert, divert scarce resources away from productive uses (e.g., investment) to unproductive social services and contribute toward creating a large number of poor and welfare-dependent individuals and families. These viewpoints have motivated extensive empirical research on the economic and social impacts of specific U.S. public assistance programs. The conclusions of this research have been mixed: For example, case study research by the economist Barbara Wolfe (2002) found that work-effort disincentives exist in both TANF and AFDC. The economists Dean Jolliffe, Craig Gundersen, Laura Tiehen, and Joshua Winicki (2005) examined the impact of FSP on child poverty and found that food stamp benefits lead to large reductions in the poverty gap. The sociologists Taryn Lindhorst and Ronald Mancoske (2006) tracked TANF recipients who were involuntarily removed from welfare rolls, as a result of the increased use of sanctions and time limits on welfare, and identified several negative social and economic effects.

THE U.S. PUBLIC ASSISTANCE RECORD

How does the United States fare relative to other industrialized Organization for Economic Cooperation and Development (OECD) countries in terms of commitment to supporting the standard of living of poor and needy individuals and families? Ideally, comparison should be made on the basis of an examination of the gross (before-tax) total public expenditures on each public assistance program as a ratio of the size of the economy as measured by gross domestic product (GDP), with higher values indicating greater commitment. Although public assistance programs in different countries share the common goal of assisting the poor and needy, there are significant cross-country variations in program design, which makes international comparison problematical. To deal with this problem, the OECD has attempted to create a comprehensive database of internationally comparable data on public social expenditures, which include expenditures on public assistance programs, in the OECD countries. The database focuses on nine social policy areas: namely, *old age*, *survivors*, *incapacity-related benefits*, *health*, *family*, *active labor market policies*, *unemployment*, *housing*, and *other social policy areas*. Because most public assistance programs are means-tested, public expenditures on means-tested programs as percentages of GDP provide a good sense of how levels of public assistance, in particular, compare.

Table 1 shows the gross (before-tax) total public social expenditures and total expenditures on means-tested programs as percentages of GDP for several OECD

Table 1: Total Public Social Expenditure and Total Expenditure on Means-Tested Programs as a Percentage of GDP for Selected OECD Countries (2003)

Country	Public Social (% GDP)	Means-tested (% GDP)
Australia	17.9	7.3
Austria	26.1	1.2
Belgium	26.5	0.9
Canada	17.3	3.5
Denmark	27.6	1.0
Finland	22.5	2.9
France	28.7	1.4
Germany	27.6	1.1
Greece	21.3	1.4
Iceland	18.7	1.2
Ireland	15.9	2.6
Italy	24.2	0.7
Japan	17.7	0.4
Luxembourg	22.2	0.9
Netherlands	20.7	1.1
New Zealand	18.0	3.4
Norway	25.1	1.1
Portugal	23.5	0.0
Spain	20.3	1.5
Sweden	31.3	0.7
Switzerland	20.5	1.7
United Kingdom	20.1	2.2
United States	16.2	1.3
OECD Average	20.7	1.5

SOURCE: OECD (2007).

Table 1

countries, as reported by OECD (2007). It is apparent from the table that the United States fares poorly in relation to most industrialized OECD countries, especially the Nordic countries, when gross public social expenditures are considered. In fact, the United States falls below the OECD average for every year between 1990 and 2003. Sweden's total public social expenditure as a percentage of GDP, which is the highest among the OECD countries for every year between 1990 and 2003, is about twice that of the United States. Another interesting feature of the table is that the total U.S. public social expenditure is very comparable to that of Japan, with both falling below the OECD average. A slightly different story emerges when means-tested programs, which are characteristic of most public assistance programs, are considered. For means-tested programs, the United States and Japan also fall below the OECD average and both countries fare much worse than Australia, Canada, New Zealand, Finland, Ireland, and the United Kingdom.

SEE ALSO *Compensation, Unemployment; Medicaid; Medicare; National Health Insurance; Poverty; Public Health; Social Welfare System; Transfer Payments; Welfare State*

BIBLIOGRAPHY

Jolliffe, Dean, Craig Gundersen, Laura Tiehen, and Joshua Winicki. 2005. Food Stamp Benefits and Child Poverty. *American Journal of Agricultural Economics* 87 (3): 569–581.

Lindhorst, Taryn, and Ronald J. Mancoske. 2006. The Social and Economic Impact of Sanctions and Time Limits on Recipients of Temporary Assistance to Needy Families. *Journal of Sociology and Social Welfare* 33 (1): 93–114.

Midgley, James. 2001. The United States: Welfare, Work, and Development. *International Journal of Social Welfare* 10 (4): 284–293.

Organization for Economic Cooperation and Development. 2007. *OECD Social Expenditure Database (SOCX2007), 1980–2003.* http:// www.oecd.org/statistics/social/.

Ozawa, Martha N. 2004. Social Welfare Spending on Family Benefits in the United States and Sweden: A Comparative Study. *Family Relations* 53 (3): 301–309.

Rice, James Mahmud, Robert E. Goodin, and Antti Parpo. 2006. The Temporal Welfare State: A Crossnational Comparison. *Journal of Public Policy* 26 (3): 195–228.

U.S. Social Security Administration. 2006. Annual Statistical Supplement 2005. http://www.ssa.gov/policy/docs/statcomps/supplement/2005/.

Wolfe, Barbara L. 2002. Incentives, Challenges, and Dilemmas of TANF: A Case Study. *Journal of Policy Analysis and Management* 21 (4): 577–586.

Tomson Ogwang

PUBLIC BROADCASTING SYSTEM
SEE *Television.*

PUBLIC CHOICE THEORY

Public choice theory is a positive theory of interest group politics that applies the microeconomic perspectives of market exchange to political and policy problems. Borrowing from Anthony Downs's approach of policy selection (1957), wherein governments select policies to appeal to a winning coalition of voters, public choice theory considers the ways in which interest groups' policy preferences and relative bargaining power will affect government policies. The theory assumes a logic in which the government awards policy goods to those groups best able to lobby for their interests. Although the public choice method borrows from economics, its principal uses have been in the analysis of political questions. Public choice theory and interest group politics have generally been used in a variety of political contexts, such as tax policy (Becker 1983), trade protection (Schattschneider 1935; Eichengreen 1989), public good provision (Olson 1965), and economic sanctions (Kaempfer and Lowenberg 1992).

According to public choice theory, although a market analogy is a useful way to conceive of policy selection, there remain significant differences between economic exchange markets and political exchange markets. For example, economic market exchanges are generally believed to: (1) be undertaken voluntarily, (2) benefit all those involved, and (3) be Pareto optimal. Political markets, on the other hand, tend to favor one group over others, and are thus distributional and inherently conflictual. Thus, the political market is characterized by competition between opposed interest groups that expend their political capital to secure their preferred policies.

Through this competition over policies between opposed interests, the policy goods ultimately awarded by a government will reflect the influence-weighted preferences of the opposed interest groups. More formally, the political market will equilibrate when the influence-weighted utilities of the stronger groups are equal to the influence-weighted disutilities of their weaker opponents. Furthermore, policy changes will result from shifts in either the underlying distribution of the power of opposed groups or as a result of shifts in the relative salience that groups hold for issues of concern. These shifts will, in turn, influence decisions on where these groups expend their scarce political capital.

Public choice theory has two principal variants: the "Chicago School," which considers the awarding of policy goods through a political market as relatively benign; and the "Virginia School" (based at George Mason University), which is concerned about how competition over government largess undermines social welfare through deadweight costs and inefficiencies. Members of the Chicago School, such as Gary Becker, argue that these social deadweight costs will be minimized for two reasons. First, because the utility of policy goods increases at a diminishing rate (as market distortion and deadweight costs accumulate), winner groups will become decreasingly inclined to lobby for further rents, while loser groups will become increasingly inclined to lobby for relief and a rationalization of the political economy. Secondly, because loser groups lobby to ensure that they suffer the minimum disutilities possible, they will reduce deadweight costs further. As a result, the competition between opposed groups will reduce social costs to a minimum.

On the other hand, members of the Virginia School point out that, because of their political nature, rent transfers are often highly inefficient in order to disguise the extent of the pilfering from the community chest undertaken by beneficiary groups. Worse, when rents are highly concentrated and their costs are widely defused, narrow rent-seeking interests may be able to exploit collective action problems on behalf of the larger body politic for their own benefit, resulting in further net social and economic inefficiencies. For example, the economist Gordon Tullock notes that farm support is often given through inefficient market manipulation, as opposed to more efficient cash subsidies, in order to conceal the real scope of the super-normal returns to farming interests through the political process (1989). Thus, due to their concern with the interaction between interest group pressures and rent-seeking and governments' proclivity for overregulation, the Virginia School is pessimistic with respect to interest groups' normative impact on policy outcomes.

Although public choice theory and interest group politics have been used with some success in the political economy and economics literatures, critics have noted two potentially significant problems with this body of work. First, public choice theory may give short shrift to the key role that domestic institutions play in determining policy outcomes, because the groups of interest are often modeled as if they were operating in an institutionally unconstrained policy market. Yet while work in the public choice tradition often does not explicitly address institutions, they can still be incorporated into such a framework. As politically determined rule- and agenda-

setting mechanisms, institutions are amenable to the same lobbying and bargaining processes described above. That is, by thinking of institutions as meta-policies, public choice tools can be used to endogenously analyze institutions' creation and downstream effects.

Second, critics allege that public choice theory, which was developed primarily within the American political context, is unsuited to nondemocratic countries in which the capacity of opposition groups to lobby for their policy preferences is repressed. It is important to note that the metaphor of "lobbying" need not be taken literally, however. As conceived of in public choice theory, lobbying can refer to any kind of influence. Regardless of the type of regime, political bargaining always takes place, even if it is only implicit. Although the preferences of excluded groups in nondemocratic countries may not affect the political process directly, they may do so indirectly, since disenfranchised groups can signal their policy preferences by engaging in acts of political resistance such as fomenting armed rebellion. This resistance, or the threat of it, effectively acts as a tax on the ruling group's willingness and ability to unilaterally set policy because it raises the costs of enforcement and administration. Thus, even in nondemocratic states, policies will be determined through a bargaining process between opposed groups, although ruling groups in authoritarian regimes are, of course, likely to enjoy policies far closer to their preferences. In these regimes there is an extreme concentration of political capital, in contrast to its relative diffusion within democratic regimes.

BIBLIOGRAPHY

Becker, Gary S. 1983. A Theory of Competition Among Pressure Groups for Political Influence. *Quarterly Journal of Economics* 98 (3): 371–400.

Downs, Anthony. 1957. *An Economic Theory of Democracy.* New York: Harper.

Eichengreen, Barry. 1989. The Political Economy of the Smoot-Hawley Tariff. *Research in Economic History* 12: 1–43.

Kaempfer, William, and Anton Lowenberg. 1992. *International Economic Sanctions: A Public Choice Perspective.* Boulder, CO: Westview Press.

Major, Solomon, and Anthony J. McGann. 2005. Caught in the Crossfire: "Innocent Bystanders" as Optimal Targets of Economic Sanction. *Journal of Conflict Resolution* 49 (3): 337–359.

Mueller, Dennis C. 2003. *Public Choice III.* New York: Cambridge University Press.

Olson, Mancur. 1965. *The Logic of Collective Action.* Cambridge, MA: Harvard University Press.

Tullock, Gordon. 1989. *The Economics of Special Privilege and Rent Seeking.* Boston: Kluwer Academic.

Solomon Major

PUBLIC GOODS

Public goods such as law enforcement, national defense, highways, and environmental regulation are typically provided by governments rather than the private sector, although this is not a requirement. Governments provide these because public goods share two properties that make their provision by private firms difficult. The first is that there is no rivalry in their consumption: Use of a public good by one individual does not decrease its value to others. The second is that the benefits are freely accessible to all, so no individual can be excluded from the use of these goods.

The first condition implies that financing production by charging a price for access to the good would inefficiently restrict access to the good. The second condition of non-excludability implies that charging a price is also infeasible from a practical standpoint (Figure 1). As a result, private firms will generally have little incentive to produce public goods: Provision requires collective action among those parties desiring the good (Olson 1965). Insufficient financing for production is likely to result from voluntary contributions, however, since individuals need not pay a price to enjoy an open-access public good. This has been called the *free-rider problem*. As a result, provision of public goods generally falls to governments, which have the coercive power necessary to levy the taxes required to pay for the goods.

A difficulty arises, however, in establishing both equity and the preferred level of a public good. To provide the sufficient level of a public good, governments must know how much individuals benefit from it. Optimally, an individual's tax assessment would then reflect his or her own valuation of the public good. In practice, however, when individuals know they cannot be denied access to

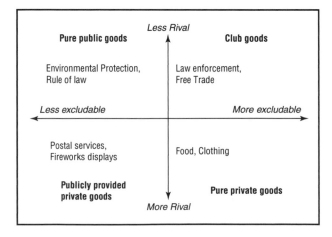

Figure 1: Non-rivalry of Benefits (Desirability) vs. Excludability (Feasibility)

the good and will be assessed taxes in proportion to their announced valuation, they have no incentive to reveal their true preferences (the free-rider problem again). Economists have studied various means by which governments can induce individuals to provide information about their preferences. The key to these revelation mechanisms is that the taxes levied on the individual to finance the good must be set independently of their announced valuation.

This fact, combined with the fixed costs of designing a tax system, provides one explanation for the observation that countries typically organize so that a single government provides multiple public goods, rather than having a system of overlapping jurisdictions each responsible for a single public good. Not all public goods are most efficiently provided by a single centralized authority, however, and a hierarchy of jurisdictions and subjurisdictions may exist for providing public goods. One example is the U.S. system of federal, state, and local governments, in which the federal government provides military defense, regulates commerce, and designs social welfare programs to achieve equity goals, while state governments set regulations on social behavior and local governments provide a range of services from education to street cleaning. Another example is the hierarchy between public goods provided within sovereign nation-states and global public goods that must be provided through collective action among a group of nation-states, such as peacekeeping, international regulation of civil aviation and commerce, exchange rate management, and efforts to combat global warming.

Analytically, the key distinction between global, national, and state or local public goods rests on two dimensions: the sovereignty of the nation-state and the mobility of the citizenry. The free-rider problem can be overcome in providing public goods at the level of the nation-state and its subjurisdictions through the coercive power of governments to enforce tax and regulatory policies, but no similar mechanism exists for the provision of global public goods. Similarly, within the nation-state, citizens are typically free to live in the subjurisdiction that offers their preferred combination of public-good provision and tax burden. As a result, efficient provision can be achieved by citizens "voting with their feet" (Tiebout 1956). Migration between nation-states is more difficult, however, and between planets impossible, so the political process by which national and global public goods are determined is crucial.

Ideally, responsibility for public goods should be allocated among the hierarchy of governments using several criteria: (1) the extent of nonrivalry (including both the proportion of fixed costs relative to variable costs and the geographic scope of the benefits); (2) the uniformity of

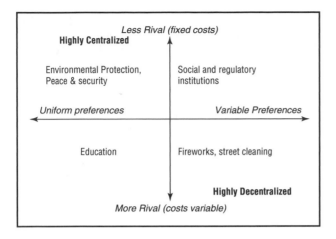

Less Rival (fixed costs)

Highly Centralized

Environmental Protection, Peace & security

Social and regulatory institutions

Uniform preferences   *Variable Preferences*

Education

Fireworks, street cleaning

Highly Decentralized

More Rival (costs variable)

Figure 2: Optimal Centralization of Public Good Provision

opinion regarding the preferred nature of the public good; and (3) problems of adverse selection. Public goods that entail relatively high fixed costs and have widespread benefits, such as maintaining peace and security through law enforcement and the military, or maintaining clean air and water and a stable climate through environmental protection, should optimally be provided at a centralized level (Figure 2). Where preferences over the size, quality, or nature of the public good vary widely, however, more decentralized provision may be preferable. This is particularly true for goods that have more limited geographic benefits, and thus a higher degree of rivalry, such as public education and community social activities. Wallace Oates (1972) argues further that policies designed to achieve distributional equity goals are also best provided at a federal level to avoid the adverse budgetary effects that might arise with poorer families selecting to live in, and richer families selecting to live outside of, those state and local jurisdictions with more progressive policies.

It is worth noting that not all publicly provided goods are pure public goods by the conventional definition employed in this entry. Information, for instance, is nonrival in consumption but certainly potentially excludable. Legal rights and the rule of law are potentially excludable as well, as history has demonstrated to many disenfranchised communities. Common property resources like fish, on the other hand, are nonexcludable, but their consumption is rival. In each case government regulation of the provision process—whether through patent law, civil rights legislation, or fishery management—can in principle be desirable. In weak and failed states, however, regulation of resources may generate incentives for corruption, as officials "sell" licenses and grant access for personal profit. In other cases, governments have opted to provide private goods, such as education, health care, or postal services, all of which are both rival and excludable, in order to capitalize on fixed costs, achieve beneficial externalities, or to adopt certain standards (the benefits of which are both nonrival and nonexcludable).

SEE ALSO *Collective Action; Institutionalism*

BIBLIOGRAPHY

Oates, Wallace E. 1972. *Fiscal Federalism.* New York: Harcourt Brace.

Olson, Mancur. 1965. *The Logic of Collective Action: Public Goods and the Theory of Groups.* Cambridge, MA: Harvard University Press.

Samuelson, Paul A. 1954. A Pure Theory of Public Expenditure. *Review of Economics and Statistics* 36 (4): 387–389.

Tiebout, Charles M. 1956. A Pure Theory of Local Expenditures. *Journal of Political Economy* 64 (5): 416–424.

Mark R. Hopkins

PUBLIC HEALTH

Public health is a branch of the social and health sciences, as well as a field of social and health endeavor, that aims at collective action for the prevention of disease and the promotion of health. The U.S. Institute of Medicine offers this definition: "public health is what we, as a society, do collectively to assure the conditions in which people can be healthy" (K. Gebbie, L. Rosenstock, and L. M. Hernandez 2003). Depending on the political philosophy of governance and the role of the state, this aim and its operational applications have taken different shapes in different contexts. In some contexts, "public health" refers to public-sector health; in other contexts, the term refers to the public's health.

Public health is as old as history itself. Most holy texts (including the Bible, Torah, and Qur'an) contain instructions regulating sanitary behavior. Other belief systems, such as the Indian Ayurveda (from the Sanskrit *ayu*—life and *veda*—knowledge of), have formulated prescriptions for leading healthy lives. The Hippocratic writings have been highly influential in Western conceptualizations of health and illness. Although the ancient Greek physician Hippocrates (c. 460–377 BCE) and his school are found to be the fathers (and mothers) of modern medicine, their instructions for healthy housing are the direct forebears of current perspectives on environmental health.

The rise of modern public health occurred in the mid-nineteenth century. With the advance of statistics and empirically-based science, health advocates (later known as the *hygienists*) in France, Germany, England, and the United States endeavored to link disease patterns to environmental conditions. These hygienists had roots in engineering, law, and charity, and to a lesser extent in emerging scientific—allopathic—medicine. British royal anesthesiologist John Snow (1813–1858) made a breakthrough in 1854. Using an ancestor of what is known as a geographic information system, Snow was able to attribute cholera outbreaks in Victorian London to the quality of water coming from the city's Broad Street pump.

Although public health *science* had certainly made its mark with the work of early epidemiologists, public health *action* was relatively slow to follow, mostly because the proposed interventions met with considerable political resistance. The idea that large infrastructural works (sewage systems, garbage collection, piped water) had to be put in place for the public good was persistently countered with arguments that the delivery of appropriate individual health care services, and emphasis on the responsibilities of individuals for their lifestyles, would yield better results. Ultimately, though, the political argument that the workforce was withering as a result of lack of public action won over the critics.

Formal public health training in this tradition started at the Massachusetts Institute of Technology in 1889 and at the London School of Hygiene and Tropical Medicine in 1899. A pressing debate emerged in the United States around the question of whether public health was a branch of medicine and should thus be taught in medical schools. The Flexner Report (1910), sponsored by the Carnegie Foundation, found that schools of public health should be separate entities. In Europe, however, there was a commonly shared belief that public health was an integral part of the medical realm. Outside the United States, the Rockefeller Foundation eventually sponsored schools of public health that were closely allied with medicine (in Zagreb, Beijing, and London). Public health in Europe became known as *social medicine* or (in the United Kingdom) as *public health medicine.*

The breakthrough stature that the field had acquired in the second half of the nineteenth century withered, regrettably, as a consequence of advances in vaccine development and immunology. The dominant idea became that most, if not all, disease could be treated or prevented through immunological interventions. Public health could contribute to this notion by developing population-based vaccination campaigns. The social and political aspects of public health science and action lost prominence, even in those realms where the political dimensions of health issues were blatantly obvious. Governments had been engaging, since a failed first meeting in Paris in 1851, in a series of "sanitary conferences" aimed at regulating the transmission of disease between nation-states through measures such as quarantine. Such efforts would clearly have had an impact on trade, which was why most of these conferences had limited success.

In the era of globalization, little has changed in the public health landscape. Trade and mobility are profound drivers of the potentially rapid spread of infectious diseases such as avian influenza or SARS (severe acute respiratory syndrome)—the 2003 SARS outbreak in China led to a World Health Organization (WHO) travel warning for Toronto—and tensions between individual foci on the promotion of health and community-based orientations have not been resolved.

One would, for instance, expect that modern public health knowledge and practices would have been able to prevent the Black Death (or "pestilence") that ravaged Europe in the mid-fourteenth century. At the time, witchcraft, ethnicity (arguments reminiscent of those voiced in the twentieth century on the HIV/AIDS epidemic by some religious groups), and seasonal bad airs were blamed for the pandemic. Current scientific knowledge of the disease pathogen and its vectors would, supposedly, account for more effective interventions, reducing overall mortality. This supposition is only partly true. Bubonic plague is still endemic in many nations. Similarly, the global community has not been able to fully contain or control contemporary cholera pandemics, nor will it be able to fully prevent annual influenza outbreaks, including those caused by particularly virulent pathogens such as the H1N5 avian influenza virus. It must be recognized that pathogens are an inseparable element of the global ecosystem, and global public health surveillance and control systems—partly due to political indolence, sometimes referred to as a "betrayal of trust"—have only a limited capacity to proactively engage in their complete prevention.

Many international organizations include health in their considerations: for example, the International Labor Organization (ILO) deals with workplace health, UNICEF with maternal and child health, the UN-Habitat with urban health, and UNESCO with education for health in schools. The United Nations technical agency responsible for health matters since its inception in 1948 (its establishment urged by Brazil and China at the UN founding conference in San Francisco in 1945) is the WHO.

The WHO is the only UN technical agency that, apart from a global headquarters and national liaison offices, has six Regional Offices (in Europe, the eastern Mediterranean, Africa, Southeast Asia, the Western Pacific, and the Americas). These offices formulate "regional" policies following directions from the global World Health Assembly. The programs of the WHO in its first decades focused on infectious disease. The greatest accomplishment of this era is the first and only eradication of a major human disease, smallpox (1967–1977). This accomplishment also signaled, however, the end of the infectious disease paradigm. From the launch of the "primary health care" approach following an international meeting in Alma Ata (Almaty), Kazakhstan, in 1978, the community and social aspects of health promotion and the management and delivery of care became more important than biomedical intervention considerations. In this shift, the WHO has experienced great successes and failures. Under the visionary leadership of Halfdan Mahler (1973–1988), the WHO positioned itself as a powerful broker for health between professionals, governments, and communities. The WHO's next director-general, Hiroshi Nakajima (1988–1998), was accused of letting the organization fall victim to corruption, a pawn of (pharmaceutical) industries, with an ineffective bureaucracy not responsive to such global threats as HIV/AIDS nor the call for evidence-based medicine and public health. His successor, Gro Harlem Brundtland (1998–2003), was elected to take charge and reposition the organization. One of her most visible accomplishments was the commissioning of a series of studies into macroeconomics and health chaired by the American economist Jeffrey Sachs. Lee Jong-Wook (1945–2006), who became WHO director-general in 2003, further advanced the social science angle of the organization by appointing in 2005 a prestigious Commission on Social Determinants of Health. This commission is to report on early child development, health systems, employment, globalization, urban settings, and gender in public health, among other issues. This range of topics again emphasizes the intrinsically political nature of public health.

In the 1990s, the WHO established a list of essential functions to which public health agencies should strive to conform:

- Prevention, surveillance, and control of communicable and noncommunicable diseases
- Monitoring of health situations
- Health promotion
- Occupational health
- Protection of the environment
- Public health legislation and regulations
- Public health management
- Specific public health services
- Personal health care for vulnerable and high-risk populations

The list reflects the ideal that public health must embrace insights from the social and natural sciences. These would range, for instance, from molecular medicine to empowerment and community development, toxicology, and political science. Some disciplines, such as epidemiology and health services research, are uniquely aligned to the public health realm. Others have specialized

branches related to public health, notably biostatistics, health economics, sociology, anthropology, psychology, and environmental health. In many universities, schools of public health provide a critical link between faculties. However, the domain is also rich in contention, particularly where the survival or growth of "established" disciplines is concerned. A pivotal review by the U.S. Institute of Medicine, for instance, demonstrated the enormous untapped potential for insights from the social and behavioral sciences in the promotion of health. These insights, for reasons linked to "disciplinary exclusiveness," have not yet pervaded "traditional" public health research and teaching.

Another level of rivalry has developed around the application of public health expertise. On a scale, two extremes are found. One, predominantly carried by laboratory-based public health sciences, poses that clinical expertise determines courses of action. This would, for instance, relate to the legitimacy to implement population-wide vaccination or risk-behavior-change campaigns (top-down). Others, notably the radical social sciences, start from the position that health is an inherently social condition and that community-driven action is most appropriate (bottom-up). Agreement is difficult to reach, and a "mixed-scanning" approach is often advocated by the WHO and many local public health agencies.

An organization strongly committed to the bottom-up approach is the global People's Health Assembly (PHA), an alliance of academics, communities, and nongovernmental organizations. The PHA endeavors to balance the expert-driven globalized stance with a community-based local ("glocal") approach. A major imbalance with which both the PHA and the WHO struggle is the "ninety/ten divide": 90 percent of the global public health research effort is spent on only 10 percent of the global health burden. Important players in this arena, apart from the WHO, are private sector entities. These include pharmaceutical industries and charitable organizations such as the Bill and Melinda Gates Foundation (the largest single donor to public health efforts—over $5 billion—in 2005).

The nexus between globalization and health is an important research challenge. Like the unresolved ninety/ten divide, most public health research resources are devoted to issues in industrialized nations. These include such matters as access to and the efficiency of health services—for example, medical technology assessment and health services financing schemes (often mirroring, again, the difference between public sector or the public's health). A critical issue in these analyses is the inequitable distribution of access, as well as disease burden, within and not between nations. Research into equity and inequalities in health top many European agendas; in other countries, such terms have been deemed politically taboo, which has not prevented research into areas that are alternatively labeled with less value-laden terms, such as *social exclusion* or *diversity and health*. Ethnicity, socioeconomic status, heredity, and gender issues thus remain at the core of many public health controversies.

SEE ALSO *Disease; Health Economics; National Health Insurance; World Health Organization*

BIBLIOGRAPHY

Breslow, Lester, ed. 2002. *Encyclopedia of Public Health*. 4 vols. New York: Macmillan Reference/Gale Group.

Gebbie, K., L. Rosenstock, and L. M. Hernandez, eds. 2003. *Who Will Keep the Public Healthy? Educating Public Health Professionals for the 21st Century*. Washington, DC: National Academies Press.

Winslow, C.-E. A. 1920. The Untilled Fields of Public Health. *Science* 51 (3106): 23–33.

World Health Organization. Commission on Social Determinants of Health. http://www.who.int/social_determinants/en/.

Evelyne de Leeuw

PUBLIC INTELLECTUALS

SEE *Intellectuals, Public.*

PUBLIC INTEREST

While there is no one public interest, most political philosophers credit some notion of collective welfare. Examples include French philosopher Jean-Jacques Rousseau's "general will," U.S. president James Madison's "collective good," or English philosopher Jeremy Bentham's "greatest good for the greatest number." In debate, public interest is often invoked when a faction's influence harms the larger group. As James Madison defined it in Federalist Paper number 10, the tenth Federalist Paper in a series of published articles arguing for the ratification of the U.S. Constitution:

> By a faction, I understand a number of citizens, whether amounting to a majority or a minority...united and actuated by some common impulse of passion, or of interest, adversed to the rights of other citizens, or to the permanent and aggregate interests of the community.

There are two core conceptions of the public interest, *organic/republican* and *utilitarian/liberal*. In Western philosophy, "republican" societies regard the state or society as a collective entity, possessing virtues and commanding citizen obligations that dominate individual or self-interested objectives. "Liberal" conceptions of public interest focus on individual welfare or value, and invoke some assumption justifying interpersonal comparisons of value or satisfaction.

Political theorists couple normative conceptions of public interest with claims about institutional design. One extreme is the Rousseau-Marx approach (named after Rousseau and German political philosopher Karl Marx), which suggests an objective underlying definition of the good or virtuous society. According to this approach, any action or policy that violates this objective "public interest" is a mistake, or even a crime against citizens.

Near the other extreme are conceptions of the public interest that credit consensus, appealing not to objective values but to deliberation. In varying degrees this view is embodied in the writings of John Rawls, Jürgen Habermas, and James Fishkin. This approach claims that reasonable people can achieve consensus (or near consensus) on public policy problems through deliberation.

But some would go further. "Agonistic pluralists," such as Chantal Mouffe, require only that citizens disagree peacefully. Policy debates, in this view, are value-laden and emotional, so requiring consensus causes violence. The democratic process is the alternative to violence, an arena in which fundamental differences can be aired and discussed, preventing difference from hardening into enmity and violence. In this regard, it is participation and democratic engagement, *in and of itself*, that is the public interest.

RATIONAL CHOICE THEORY

Another approach, rational choice theory, is consequentialist and utilitarian. The public interest can only be defined, in this tradition, in terms of the Pareto criterion. The Pareto principle is essentially unanimity: Given a status quo policy A, new policy B serves the public interest if, but only if, all members of the society prefer B to A. A weaker comparison would allow that many citizens are indifferent between A and B, but at least one prefers B to A, and none prefer A to B.

Other proponents might extend valid public interest arguments to include the work of welfare economists John Hicks and Nicholas Kaldor. Their "compensation," or "potential Pareto" principle, defines the public interest in terms of monetized gains and losses. If some citizens prefer new policy B to status quo A, but others prefer A to B, then the Pareto criterion does not apply. But the policy authority can still discover the public interest, adding up the gains (how much would those who prefer B sacrifice to effect the change?) and the losses (how much would those who prefer the status quo offer to block the change?). If the summed gains exceed the summed losses, then the gainers can compensate the losers and still leave some surplus. Disagreement becomes unanimity.

Cost-benefit analysis uses this reasoning to derive the public interest. So does the use of eminent domain, which governments use to take private property in the public interest. The difference is that compensation must be paid in the case of eminent domain, where no compensation is needed in a cost-benefit analysis. Both procedures are as close as we can get to implementing Bentham's "greatest good for the greatest number."

PUBLIC CHOICE THEORY

Public choice theory is a strand of rational choice that makes two more assumptions about the formulation of the public interest. First, the public interest is defined in utilitarian terms. Second, all participants, including public officials, pursue their perception of their private interest. But the public officials respond to incentives created by institutions.

For example elected officials must seek reelection, and therefore serve voters, though out of self-interest, not love for the voters. Institutional design is the key to creating this coincidence of public interest and private action of officials. In Federalist Paper number 51 the authors wrote, "Ambition must be made to counteract ambition." A federal system, with separation of powers, reasoned Madison and coauthor Alexander Hamilton in this essay, transforms private interest to coincide with the public interest.

Kenneth Arrow's famous "Impossibility Theorem," introduced in his 1963 book *Social Choice and Individual Values* illustrates a problem with any specification of public interest in terms of individual preference "lists." Arrow's result, which shows that only dictatorship satisfies the other normative criteria he specifies for ethically defensible government, raises important questions about the coherence of democracy as a means of discovering the public interest. But since the Arrow argument affects only disaggregated utilitarian conceptions of the public interest, organic conceptions might still be defended on some other grounds.

An alternative approach to public choice theory is to begin with the psychological determinants of citizen conceptions of the public good, and to build upon this foundation a more psychologically oriented theory of the actions of public officials based on conceptions of community and the obligations of health professionals to serve the public interest. This view can be found in a large number of different public health disciplines, but it is most coherently developed in community psychology, as outlined in Julian Rappaport's 1977 book *Community Psychology: Values, Research, and Action*. Some psychologists practicing "critical community psychology" argue that much preventable human suffering can be traced to policies and institutions that violate and suppress the public interest. Treating individual psychopathologies, in this view, is a red herring. The only effective "treatment" is to work for social justice, ameliorating disparities and transforming institutions to make such disparities less likely to reappear. Thus, knowledge of the public interest imposes an obligation on health professionals to work outside of their narrow specialties toward social change.

How might one tell if a policy serves the public interest, an official's private interest, an organized group's interest, or something else? The answer is contingent on many things, as Arthur Denzau and Michael Munger showed in their 1986 article "Legislators and Interest Groups: How Unorganized Interests Get Represented." The essential responsiveness of a political system to the public interest depends on legislator goals, agency professionalism, the private influence of organized groups, and the competitiveness of the electoral system. But public interest also is contingent on citizens' sophistication. If citizens know their private interests, and understand how policies affect those interests, then competitive elections push policy close to the public interest, at least in utilitarian terms. But if citizens do not understand their private interests, or if complex policies are misunderstood or misrepresented in public discourse, or even if elections are not competitive due to campaign finance or party organization barriers, public policy will diverge sharply from the public interest in favor of policies favored by narrow special interests.

SEE ALSO *Arrow Possibility Theorem; Bentham, Jeremy; Cost-Benefit Analysis; Habermas, Jürgen; Interest Groups and Interests; Pareto Optimum; Philosophy, Political; Preferences; Psychology; Public Interest Advocacy; Public Policy; Public Sector; Public Welfare; Rational Choice Theory; Rawls, John; Rousseau, Jean-Jacques; Utilitarianism; Welfare Economics*

BIBLIOGRAPHY

Arrow, Kenneth. 1963. *Social Choice and Individual Values.* 2nd ed. New York: Wiley.

Denzau, Arthur, and Michael Munger. 1986. Legislators and Interest Groups: How Unorganized Interests Get Represented. *American Political Science Review* 80: 89–106.

Fishkin, James. 1993. *Democracy and Deliberation: New Directions for Democratic Reform.* New Haven, CT: Yale University Press.

Habermas, Jürgen. 1996. *Between Facts and Norms: Contributions to a Discourse Theory of Law and Democracy.* Trans. William Rehg. Cambridge, MA: MIT Press.

Jay, John, Alexander Hamilton, and James Madison. 1787. The Federalist #10: The Union as a Safeguard against Domestic Faction and Insurrection. *The New York Packet*, November 23.

Jay, John, Alexander Hamilton, and James Madison. 1788. The Federalist #51: The Structure of the Government Must Furnish the Proper Checks and Balances between the Different Departments. *The New York Packet*, February 8.

Kaldor, Nicholas. 1939. Welfare Propositions in Economics. *Economic Journal* 69: 549–552.

Mouffe, Chantal. 2000. *The Democratic Paradox.* New York: Verso.

Rappaport, Julian. 1977. *Community Psychology: Values, Research, and Action.* New York: Holt, Rinehart, and Wilson.

Rawls, John. 1971. *A Theory of Justice.* Cambridge, MA: Belknap Press of Harvard University Press.

Rousseau, Jean-Jacques. 1947. *The Social Contract.* New York: Hafner. (Orig. published in 1762.)

Michael Munger

PUBLIC INTEREST ADVOCACY

Public interest advocacy is performed by organizations that exist primarily to promote a common good that extends beyond the narrow economic or sectarian goals of their members or supporters. Organizations in this domain typically address such issues as consumer protection, free markets, the environment, taxation, peace, fiscal responsibility, campaign finance reform, civil rights, and social welfare. Prominent examples include the American Civil Liberties Union, the Center for Science in the Public Interest, Common Cause, the National Taxpayers Union, the Natural Resources Defense Council, Peace Action, and Public Citizen. Public interest advocacy groups make up less than 5 percent of the total interest-group universe in Washington, D.C., which is heavily dominated by corporations, business associations, and occupational groups. Public interest groups are disproportionately visible, however, allowing them to draw more attention from the media and spots at congressional hearings than their numbers alone would suggest.

A precise delineation of which organizations are engaged in public interest advocacy is difficult to establish. First, the term "public interest" is fundamentally ambiguous. One person's public interest may be another person's special interest, and vice versa. All organizations have an incentive to frame their concerns in terms of the public interest, even if they are motivated principally by private interests. Second, economic interests are increasingly using the facade of public interest advocacy to conceal their private political agendas from the public. For example, in the late 1990s, the pharmaceutical industry established "Citizens for Better Medicare" as a front organization to stop the enactment of prescription drug legislation that would have been adverse to its economic interests. Third, many traditional public interest advocacy organizations are assembling portfolios and boards of directors that bear closer resemblance to the for-profit sector than to the not-for-profit sector. As a result, classifying a group as a public interest advocacy organization requires probing beneath the surface of its stated mission and goals to discover its sources of financial and political support.

Ambiguities of classification aside, public interest advocacy organizations play a major role in representing otherwise neglected constituencies. They are often able to overcome the free-rider problems inherent in the provision of collective goods by offering selective incentives for individuals to contribute to their organizations, by using informal pressures distributed through decentralized social networks, by attracting generous patrons, and by latching on to new areas of government involvement. Their tactics include lobbying, testifying at congressional hearings, submitting regulatory comments, mobilizing grassroots constituents with public rallies and letter-writing campaigns, buying media advertising, filing amicus curiae briefs with appellate courts, and sponsoring class-action or other lawsuits. They most readily influence public policy when they raise new issues on the public agenda, establish reputations as experts on policy issues, demonstrate the ability to reliably mobilize constituencies important to politicians, become connected as key brokers within issue networks, or reframe issues to change a debate in favor of their concerns.

Public interest advocacy has had a major impact on the formulation of environmental legislation, such as the Clean Air Act Amendments of 1970, which made uniform national emissions standards a goal of national public policy. More recently, public interest advocacy was instrumental in passing the Bipartisan Campaign Reform Act of 2002, which banned unlimited "soft money" contributions to national political parties. These campaigns benefited from the charismatic leadership of political entrepreneurs such as Ralph Nader, who founded (or helped to found) more than a dozen public interest advocacy organizations (such as Public Citizen and the Public Interest Research Groups) over the course of his lifetime.

The dramatic rise of public interest advocacy organizations, following largely from the mass social movements of the 1960s and 1970s, has significant implications for the nature of civil society in the United States. First, their rise reflects, and helps to drive, a shift in advocacy away from material concerns (such as rising wages) toward post-material concerns (such as environmentalism). Second, their growth leads to a shift away from organizations based on the active participation of their members and toward organizations that rely on their members only to pay dues or provide financial support ("checkbook" members). Because these organizations are generally managed by paid, middle-class professionals rather than by citizen-activists, they may mute efforts toward genuine civic engagement.

Political pressures sometimes undermine the willingness of organizations to engage in public interest advocacy. Not-for-profit organizations are often discouraged from undertaking advocacy efforts because of concerns about losing their tax-exempt status under federal law. Not-for-profit organizations are permitted to engage in lobbying if it is not a "substantial" part of their activities. However, lack of clarity about how much activity meets the substantial threshold leads many not-for-profit executives to worry that the Internal Revenue Service could construe any level of political activity as a violation of the law. As a result, the not-for-profit sector as a whole pursues less public interest advocacy than is permissible under current law.

The range of public interest advocacy is limited not only by the external political pressures on an organization but also by its internal political dynamics. Advocacy organizations frequently do not represent all the constituencies within their purview equally. Leaders are more likely to direct their attention to the concerns of advantaged subgroups within their memberships in lieu of working on issues important to disadvantaged subgroups. When working on advantaged-subgroup issues, leaders tend to frame the issues as if they affect the majority of the organization's constituents, even if the advantaged subgroup in fact is a minority. Conversely, when talking about disadvantaged-subgroup issues, leaders tend to frame the issues as if they affect a minority within the organization, no matter how large the actual population. The consequence of these tendencies is that groups that are intersectionally marginalized—that is, they have more than one marginalized status, such as black women—are the least represented by public interest advocacy organizations.

The increasingly partisan nature of American politics leaves the future of public interest advocacy organizations in question. The more that all advocacy is viewed as following from predetermined partisan or ideological points of view, the harder it is for some observers to accept that any organization legitimately advocates for an unbiased public interest. While the number of public interest advocacy organizations continues to grow robustly, the general political environment surrounding them threatens to reduce their relevance.

SEE ALSO *Campaigning; Collective Action; Collectivism; Free Rider; Interest Groups and Interests; Politics; Private Sector; Public Interest; Public Sector; Social Welfare Functions*

BIBLIOGRAPHY

Berry, Jeffrey M. 1977. *Lobbying for the People: The Political Behavior of Public Interest Groups.* Princeton, NJ: Princeton University Press.

Berry, Jeffrey M. 1999. *The New Liberalism: The Rising Power of Citizen Groups.* Washington, DC: Brookings Institution Press.

Berry, Jeffrey M., with David F. Arons. 2003. *A Voice for Nonprofits.* Washington, DC: Brookings Institution Press.

Esterling, Kevin M. 2004. *The Political Economy of Expertise.* Ann Arbor: University of Michigan Press.

Heaney, Michael T. 2006. Brokering Health Policy: Coalitions, Parties, and Interest Group Influence. *Journal of Health Politics, Policy and Law* 31 (5): 887–944.

Jones, Charles O. 1975. *Clean Air: The Policies and Politics of Pollution Control.* Pittsburgh, PA: University of Pittsburgh Press.

Leech, Beth L., Frank R. Baumgartner, Timothy La Pira, and Nicholas A. Semanko. 2005. Drawing Lobbyists to Washington: Government Activity and the Demand for Advocacy. *Political Research Quarterly* 58 (1): 19–30.

Olson, Mancur. 1965. *The Logic of Collective Action: Public Goods and the Theory of Groups.* Cambridge, MA: Harvard University Press.

Schattschneider, E. E. 1960. *The Semisovereign People.* New York: Holt, Rinehart and Winston.

Skocpol, Theda. 2003. *Diminished Democracy: From Membership to Management in American Civic Life.* Norman: University of Oklahoma Press.

Strolovitch, Dara Z. 2006. Do Interest Groups Represent the Disadvantaged? Advocacy at the Intersection of Race, Class, and Gender. *Journal of Politics* 68 (4): 894–910.

Michael T. Heaney

PUBLIC INTEREST ANTHROPOLOGY

SEE *Anthropology, Public.*

PUBLIC OPINION

In democratic societies, governments are widely expected to respond to citizens' preferences. This implies that an accurate process for measuring these preferences exists. However, the capacity to measure public opinion scientifically was not developed until the twentieth century. Modern polling techniques have greatly expanded the ability of government officials to measure public opinion, including opinions of subgroups in society, and to act accordingly in their decision making. Public opinion is frequently measured today, and it has wide-ranging applications in business, academic settings, politics, and policy-making.

DEFINITION AND SCOPE OF PUBLIC OPINION

The political scientists Robert Erikson and Kent Tedin define public opinion as "the preferences of the adult population on matters of relevance to government" (2005, p. 6). However, in early American history, public officials conceived of public opinion primarily as the attitudes of the most educated, affluent subgroup of white males, who were also in the best position to convey their views to officials. The expansion of voting rights nationwide—first to white males who did not own property, (1830s), and then to women (1920), to African Americans (1965) and finally to those from eighteen to twenty-one years of age (1971)—forced public officials to broaden their conception of whose opinions deserved their attention. In addition, the United States' population continues to grow, with much of this growth coming from immigration.

These developments mean that pollsters face the mounting challenge of measuring opinions from a sample that accurately reflects an ever-growing, ever-changing population. The influx of immigrants sometimes raises language barriers to pollsters (although some pollsters use Spanish-speaking interviewers), and new technologies (such as answering machines, "caller ID" boxes, and cellular phones) are creating new barriers to pollsters' reaching survey respondents by telephone, the preferred method.

THE HISTORY OF THE MEASUREMENT OF PUBLIC OPINION

Before and during the nineteenth century, there were very few systematic methods for measuring public opinion. The best nineteenth-century method available, the straw poll, was conducted by magazines and newspapers, which asked readers to send in a response ballot. Most straw polls centered on predicting presidential elections. For example, in 1896 the *Chicago Record* conducted an elaborate and expensive straw poll to predict the outcome of the hard-fought presidential election between William McKinley and William Jennings Bryan. However, some straw polls sought to measure issue preferences, especially in the 1920s, when they were used to measure attitudes about the emotional issue of Prohibition.

Straw polling was necessarily haphazard and informal, only capturing opinions of those who read such publications—generally the most affluent and educated. They were of very limited use, then, in gauging opinions of American adults generally. The upper-class bias in straw polls had serious consequences during the 1936 presidential election between Franklin D. Roosevelt and Alf Landon. That year, *Literary Digest* magazine sponsored a nationwide straw poll using respondents whose names were drawn from telephone directories and automobile registration lists. The *Literary Digest* poll predicted that Landon, the Rebublican candidate, would win the presidential election, 57 percent to 43 percent. Instead, Roosevelt swept to a landslide re-election, winning 62.5 percent of the popular vote. The fatal flaw of the *Literary Digest* poll was that its respondents were on average much more wealthy than the average American. During the Great Depression, the affluent were heavily Republican, but they were greatly outnumbered by the less affluent, who voted resoundingly Democratic, thus ensuring Roosevelt's victory. The *Literary Digest* polling fiasco was a major contributor to the magazine's bankruptcy in 1938.

THE DEVELOPMENT OF SCIENTIFIC OPINION POLLING

While 1936 sounded the death knell for straw polling, it also marked the advent of a new era of scientific polling. In 1936, three younger pollsters with market-research backgrounds, Archibald Crossley, Elmo Roper, and George Gallup, also conducted polls to predict the presidential election. Though still 7 percent off the mark, they fared far better, predicting that Roosevelt would win 56 percent of the popular vote. All three pollsters would go on to found their own polling organizations, with the Gallup Poll the most famous of them. Gallup introduced important new methods in polling, including use of in-person interviews and adopting "quotas" to ensure that samples of respondents reflected social and economic characteristics of the larger population. For example, if the national population were 49 percent male, 17 percent African American, 68 percent Protestant, and so on, Gallup would strive to ensure that his respondent pools reflected similar proportions.

This "quota sampling" technique would soon prove problematic itself, however. In 1940 and 1944, Gallup's polls accurately predicted presidential election results, but each time they overestimated the Republican vote. In 1948 the Gallup Poll predicted that the Republican candidate for president, Governor Thomas Dewey of New York, would defeat the incumbent, President Harry S. Truman, by a margin of 49.5 percent to 44.5 percent. The Crossley and Roper polls also predicted Truman's defeat, by even wider margins. But after a surge in support during the campaign's final week, Truman emerged victorious. Analyses of the failings of the 1948 polls centered on the use of quota sampling, which under-represented social and economic groups more likely to favor Democrats. After 1948, pollsters abandoned quota sampling in favor of probability sampling, which uses random sampling techniques to select communities, neighborhoods, households, and eventually adult individuals, such that all have equal probabilities of being contacted by the pollster. Although not perfect, probability sampling remains the best method pollsters have of generating samples of poll respondents that accurately reflect the larger population of American adults.

THE ADVENT AND GROWTH OF ACADEMIC POLLING

George Gallup and his contemporaries Roper and Crossley were commercial pollsters, concerned with profitability. During the 1940s, academic researchers, especially social scientists, realized the importance of polling for research purposes as well. In 1941 the National Opinion Research Center (NORC) was founded at the University of Chicago, and in 1946 a group of scholars founded the Survey Research Center (SRC) at the University of Michigan. Authors affiliated with both the NORC and SRC would soon produce major studies using nationwide surveys conducted by these organizations. The most important of these was *The American Voter* (1960), a prolific study of American public opinion and voting by the political scientists Angus Campbell, Philip Converse, Warren Miller, and Donald Stokes. Both NORC and SRC continue to sponsor large nationwide surveys every election year, and the results of these surveys are widely used by pollsters, government officials, journalists, and political scientists. The SRC, along with the University of Michigan's Center for Political Studies, has conducted the American National Election Studies (ANES) every even-numbered year since 1948. Other important academic-based surveys include the NORC-sponsored General Social Survey (GSS), which has occurred annually or biannually since 1971.

Both the ANES and GSS rely on in-person interviewing, which is extremely expensive. The ANES typically interviews respondents both before and after presidential elections, asking hundreds of questions, with total interviewing times of three hours or more. Academic polls typically devote considerable time and resources to accurate sampling, clear question wording, and thorough reporting of results. Most poll questions yield closed-ended, fixed-format responses (such as agree/disagree, a 7-point scale, or even a 100-point scale), which produce results that can be expressed in numbers and subjected to statistical analysis. This emphasis on quantification is virtually universal

in academic polling today, and it is also common in commercial polling, including the market research studies businesses commonly use to identify new markets or measure customer satisfaction, among other things.

The mass media, too, are now heavily involved in polling. Because of the fast pace of politics, media organizations frequently sponsor surveys to measure opinions on important issues of the day. During election campaigns, media-sponsored tracking polls ("if the election were held today, who would you vote for?") are common also. Major media organizations that often commission nationwide surveys include the *New York Times*, which often partners with CBS News, and the *Washington Post*, which often partners with ABC News. Most media-sponsored surveys are conducted by telephone because of the high costs and large investments of time that in-person interviews require.

THE INTERNATIONAL SCOPE OF PUBLIC OPINION RESEARCH

Public opinion polling is not uniquely American, though many modern polling techniques were introduced and refined by Americans. Polling is big business worldwide, with both commercial and academic polling organizations easy to find in industrialized democracies. In less developed nations, polling organizations are less common, though citizens in Asia, Africa, and Latin America are increasingly sought after by pollsters. For example, the University of Iowa political scientists Arthur Miller and Vicki Hesli have directed surveys measuring Russian citizens' attitudes toward democracy, and their findings have been published in major political science journals. Although there is increasing interest in conducting surveys outside of industrialized nations, doing so entails considerable additional costs and challenges. Native speakers in the local language, such as Swahili, Japanese, or Uzbek, are mandatory, and careful and accurate translation of the survey is essential. Cultural differences may also create unexpected challenges for the pollster, and the usual limitations of probability sampling almost certainly are magnified in cross-national survey research. According to the 2000 U.S. Census, 97.6 percent of American households have telephones; in some other nations, however, far fewer households have them. This reality may require in-person interviews for some cross-national surveys, with the attendant expenses for travel, hiring and retaining interviewers, and other challenges.

PUBLIC OPINION AND GOVERNMENT RESPONSIVENESS

Political scientists have identified two major orientations adopted by government officials in response to public opinion: the delegate and the trustee orientations. The "delegate" attends closely to, and follows, public opinion. Consider a lawmaker who favors stricter gun control laws, but whose district has a majority opposed to them. This lawmaker would act as a delegate by setting aside her own views and voting consistent with the majority in her district. The "trustee" often takes public opinion into account, but is more willing to vote based on personal views, or on the perception of what is best for the district. For trustees, then, lawmaking is more often independent of public opinion. In the example above, the trustee might vote in favor of tightening gun control laws, motivated by personal convictions. In general, delegates are more likely to follow public opinion, while trustees are more likely to act independently of public opinion and try to lead it, which would include educating constituents on "why I voted this way."

Both the delegate and trustee orientations can pose problems for lawmakers. For delegates, following public opinion can be difficult if decisions need to be made on issues that pollsters have not included in their surveys. Furthermore, some thinkers, like the journalist Walter Lippman, have argued that many people lack knowledge of or interest in political issues, and thus are susceptible to manipulation by propaganda from political elites. Similarly, the political scientist John Zaller has analyzed survey responses, finding that some respondents "fabricate" survey responses on the spot when poll questions center on topics they know little about. These "nonattitudes," Zaller contends, are a growing problem for survey researchers, given that Americans' knowledge of and interest in politics have declined. For trustees, ignoring public opinion to cast votes based on personal convictions can have electoral consequences. An official who often votes against the views of a majority of constituents, especially on high-profile issues, risks electoral defeat.

Although the evidence does not always demonstrate a causal relationship, it is likely that public opinion influences policy more often than not. The political scientist Alan Monroe found in 1979 that when public opinion favors a policy change, that change occurs 59 percent of the time. Likewise, when opinion favors maintaining the status quo, the policy change occurs only 24 percent of the time. Similarly, the political scientists Robert Erikson, Gerald Wright, and John McIver found in 1994 that states with conservative opinions produce conservative policies, while states with liberal opinions produce liberal policies. Public opinion, then, appears to have policy consequences, and government officials do respond to public opinion more often than not. More generally, understanding public opinion is valuable in the realms of business (through market research), the media (through tracking and other media-sponsored polls), academia, and government.

SEE ALSO *Ideology; Measurement Error; Random Samples; Selection Bias; Statistics; Survey*

BIBLIOGRAPHY

Campbell, Angus, Philip E. Converse, Warren E. Miller and Donald E. Stokes. 1960. *The American Voter*. New York: Wiley.

Erikson, Robert S., and Kent L. Tedin. 2005. *American Public Opinion: Its Origins, Content and Impact*. 7th ed. New York: Pearson Longman.

Erikson, Robert S., Gerald C. Wright, and John P. McIver. 1993. *Statehouse Democracy: Public Opinion and Policy in the American States*. New York: Cambridge University Press.

Lippmann, Walter. 1922. *Public Opinion*. New York: Harcourt, Brace.

Monroe, Alan D. 1979. Consistency between Public Preferences and National Policy Decisions. *American Politics Quarterly* 7 (1): 3–21.

Zaller, John. 1992. *The Nature and Origins of Mass Opinion*. Cambridge, U.K.: Cambridge University Press.

Fred Slocum

PUBLIC POLICY

Public policy refers to a set of interrelated decisions governments make to select goals where the market is not working. Governmental officials establish laws and institutions to correct the perceived problems in a continual process that involves elected officials, governmental employees, lobbyists, and public-policy experts. As social scientists developed more methods and tools, both law and public-policy analysis, originally conceived of as a branch of political science, expanded to include all social scientists, but in the twenty-first century public-policy analysis is dominated by lawyers and economists.

Public policy is the making of governmental rules and regulations to benefit not one individual but society as a whole. It asks, what is the best way to conceive and evaluate policies aimed at the public as a whole and its various subgroups? Who benefits? How much does it cost? It runs through a political process, but economic, social, legal, and psychological influences help determine the possible choices and measured impacts. Often, the results of a public-policy choice are measured in statistical terms so as to seem as objective as possible.

According to Thomas A. Birkland (2005), consensus is lacking on a more precise definition of public policy. Birkland outlines several possible definitions of public policy, always starting with the actions of government and the laws and appropriations that determine those actions. Birkland then indicates that the elements common to all definitions of public policy are: (1) It is made in the name of the "public"; (2) it is generally made or initiated by government; (3) it is interpreted and implemented by public and private players from corporations and nonprofit institutions; and (4) it also includes what the government chooses not to do.

While the study of politics has a long history, the systematic study of public policy, on the other hand, can be said to be a twentieth-century creation. It dates to the Progressive Era, when early social scientists began to recommend and rank possibilities for solving public problems. Then public policy included policies having to do with crime, poverty, health, education, and foreign affairs. Later it expanded as problems changed, and by the close of the twentieth century also included policies bearing on energy, the environment, defense, sex (e.g. same-sex marriages, sexual education and the like), and other social welfare issues. It is difficult to conceive of a united "department of public policy" because it is interdisciplinary by its very nature. It also expands beyond social science to the formation of policy objectives that are value laden. Scholars and researchers from a wide range of disciplines use different tools and methods. It takes a skilled social scientist to explain clearly a complex program such as Medicare to decision makers and other parties in the public-policy debates.

Marilyn Moon (2006), though, offers one of the best such explanations by explicitly, systematically, and logically describing and analyzing a public-policy program that offers what the market fails to do: health insurance for an aging and disabled public. Policy makers are wholly confused about how the program works and what alternatives are available to them. Moon's book creates a primer by translating social science research into public policy. She is an applied economist who understands perhaps the most complex public-policy program in the United States, both as a matter of law and governmental practice. Her interdisciplinary analysis examines the alternatives of a national program that must work through the states and reach people on the local level. She clearly lays out criteria for evaluating the current Medicare program and how well it is working.

Since the biggest United States public programs are defense, Medicare and Medicaid, crime prevention, and education, she sets a high standard for describing and analyzing these other billion-dollar allocations. For example, nearly every nation-state has an organization to defend itself from foreign threat. But how best is this organized? Most nation-states, and even some subgroups, have an army and air force. But how should these forces be paid for (economics), organized from members of the population (sociology), positioned (geography), related to the legal system (law), dealt with in terms of individuals of the

nation or subgroup (psychology), and best measured as to its effectiveness (statistics)?

Yet because the subject matter that fits into the category of social sciences evolves in parallel with societal changes, new fields of study, issues, and concepts will be added, such as the ethics of censorship, the value of income distribution, proper support of the arts, public sanction of same-sex marriage, and the psychological and economic aspects of helping people age with dignity. But all vexing policy problems require more than social sciences can deliver. They involve value judgments.

Usually the different avenues contemporary public policy takes are determined by the problems of the day. For example, as the late twentieth century spawned a whole new batch of medicines, nation-states and subgroups had to figure out how to handle health care in different ways. One can have a national system of health care delivered and paid for in any number of ways. These usually range from each person who is a member of the nation paying for his or her own care to insurance by corporations to governmental units handling the needed tasks. Most often it is some mixture of systems in flux.

How do social scientists communicate new approaches to public policy? There are the usual books and journals. But key are conferences that bring scholars of different social sciences together. A conference on aging issues might include not only social scientists but also medical researchers, operators of assisted-living facilities, and a plethora of experts to discuss ways to coordinate research efforts on policy opportunities and reform agendas.

These conferences might be funded by the National Institutes of Health and other national agencies, state agencies on crime prevention, or local schoolteachers and administrators. Public-policy agencies on a national or international level can offer and pay for conferences that no single group can afford. So, for example, all nation-states want the best tools to prevent disease. In the United States, this is done by the federal government's National Institutes of Health, or NIH. It does some of its own research on a campus in Bethesda, Maryland (just outside Washington, D.C.), and by making grants of money to university researchers. Profit-seeking corporations usually do little of this basic research because it is not a profitable investment.

We can rank public-policy commitments by the amounts of money spent. In advanced capitalist nations, these commitments prominently include defense, social insurance, health care, and education. Defense and social insurance are usually provided collectively by the nation, while education is far more fragmented, usually at the local and state level in the United States. Health care is an issue everywhere, for it is evolving as the possibilities of cures and prevention increase.

The policy process (and the input of public-policy experts) depends of the degree of democracy of the nation-state. If some form of democracy is in play, then lawmakers at the federal, state, and local levels are voted into office and asked to make public policy that is best for their constituencies. But in more autocratic nations, the decisions are simply made at the top and implemented. At the beginning, this seems easy because basic needs for the whole are paramount. But as these policies are translated into practice, it becomes far more difficult because special interests lobby for laws and policies they claim are best for the whole but also (less articulated) best for them as a group.

In the twentieth century schools and departments of public policy in universities have developed. They usually take the form of an interdisciplinary center for social science applications to government, education, health, social welfare, and the like. Most major research universities have a school of public policy. It usually contains a core of tenured faculty, but the majority of the faculty is drawn from allied departments such as economics, sociology, psychology, and political science, as well as from medical and law schools. Many public-policy analysts earn a Master of Public Policy (or a Master of Public Administration) in such programs, while others earn specialized degrees, such as an MEd for specializing in educational policy or an MSW for specializing in social welfare policy.

Trained graduates can go to work for governments, lobby organizations (such as AARP's Public Policy Institute, headquartered in the nation's capital), advocacy groups (such as the Medicare Rights Center in New York City), or think tanks such as the Brookings Institution and the RAND Corporation. Later, usually with experience, they can return to teach at universities such as Harvard, Michigan, Wisconsin, and the University of California at Berkeley, to name but four of the more notable and sizable public-policy programs.

SEE ALSO *Decision-making; Government; Nation-State; Nondecision-making; Political Science; Politics; Public Administration; Public Choice Theory; Public Goods; Public Interest; Public Sector; Public Sphere; Regulation; Research, Trans-disciplinary; Social Science; State, The; University, The; Values; Welfare Economics*

BIBLIOGRAPHY

Birkland, Thomas A. 2005. *An Introduction to the Policy Process: Theories, Concepts, And Models of Public Policy Making*, 2nd ed. Armonk, NY: M. E. Sharpe.

Dunn, William N. 2003. *Public Policy Analysis: An Introduction*, 3rd ed. Upper Saddle River, NJ: Pearson Prentice Hall.

McCool, Daniel C., ed. 1995. *Public Policy Theories, Models, and Concepts: An Anthology.* Englewood Cliffs, NJ: Prentice Hall.

Moon, Marilyn. 2006. *Medicare: A Policy Primer.* Washington, DC: Urban Institute Press.

Moran, Michael, Martin Rein, and Robert E. Goodin. 2006. *The Oxford Handbook of Public Policy.* New York: Oxford University Press.

Douglas Gomery

PUBLIC RIGHTS

Within the domain of thinking about rights, the preponderant nineteenth-century typologies distinguished between natural, political, civil, and social rights, with varying accounts of the relationship among them. In the 1860s, however, as political activists and legal thinkers grappled with the question of the scope and meaning of freedom for those who had previously been held as slaves, the concept of *public rights* was introduced into debate as a means of articulating resistance to inequalities associated with castelike systems of privilege.

Capturing the element of dignity and honor at stake in the treatment of citizens in public places, public rights encompassed what is now termed equal access to public accommodations and public transportation, and could be extended to prohibit segregation in public schools. The concept and content of public rights, however, were strongly opposed by conservatives, who associated its claims with what they called "social equality"—a derogatory term they used to evoke images of forced physical intimacy across racial lines, particularly the proximity of black men to white women. Although the term *public rights* was lost to jurisprudence in the United States by the late 1870s, much of its content would subsequently be incorporated into the expanded notion of civil rights that underlay the twentieth-century movement for justice for African Americans.

The formal category of public rights seems first to have been proposed in the 1830s by an Italian jurist, Pellegrino Rossi, who held the chair of Constitutional Law at the Collège de France in Paris. True to the constitutional monarchy under which he had been appointed, Rossi believed that the state could limit political rights, arguing that access to suffrage should depend on capacity, which he assumed to vary among different groups of citizens. In keeping with the anti-aristocratic spirit of the earlier French Declaration of the Rights of Man and of the Citizen, however, Rossi endorsed universal public rights, within which he included rights of assembly, conscience, and free expression. These, he argued, were fundamental rights of humans as social beings and should not be restricted on the basis of privileges of birth or presumed capacity.

The phrase *public rights* was introduced and given an expanded meaning in the United States as the end of slavery and the debates over the Fourteenth Amendment to the Constitution made it clear that men and women who had been considered property would now become the bearers of rights. Everything turned on the question: Which rights? Moderates contended that former slaves and other persons of African descent might henceforth hold certain civil and political rights, but that social rights fell outside the proper scope of legislation. This formula could leave broad areas of public life—including education, public transport, and public accommodation—outside the action of equal-rights lawmaking.

In 1867 and 1868, a group of radical delegates to Louisiana's Constitutional Convention proposed an alternate schema: The state should guarantee to all its citizens "the same civil, political, and public rights and privileges." This construct, advanced by members of an alliance of long-free men of color, local and northern-born white radicals, and former slaves, allowed the delegates to avoid the word *social,* which their enemies had used to accuse them of seeking an unearned "social equality." The radicals won, and the 1868 Louisiana Constitution mandated equal access, independent of color, to public transportation, public accommodations, and places of public entertainment, including saloons and restaurants. For a decade, this document provided a framework for racially integrated schools and permitted victims of discrimination in the public sphere to sue for damages.

A commitment to equal public rights for all citizens subsequently appeared in the platform of the national Republican Party in 1872 and again in 1876. With the reversal of Reconstruction in the late 1870s, however, the concept almost vanished. Newly ascendant white-supremacist Democrats expunged it from the 1879 state constitution in Louisiana, and national Republicans dropped it from their platform.

Among some equal-rights activists, however, a variant of the concept remained alive and well. As southern Democrats pushed forward with the political project of white supremacy in the 1880s and 1890s, restricting suffrage and imposing state-mandated segregation, the lost language of the 1868 Louisiana Constitution became a touchstone for such figures as Rodolphe Desdunes, a cigar seller who helped mount the challenge to segregation on the railroads that led to the U.S. Supreme Court case *Plessy v. Ferguson.* The Citizens' Committee that arranged Homer Plessy's test case drew on a broad base of urban and rural activists, including artisans, schoolteachers, and even some Cuban émigré cigar workers, one of whose leaders framed his support explicitly in the language of "public rights" (Scott 2005, pp. 88–93, 151).

When the case reached the Supreme Court, Plessy's attorneys invoked broad anticaste principles rooted in an expansive concept of national citizenship. Their arguments went down to defeat before the Court, whose majority accepted the white supremacists' sleight-of-hand that portrayed Plessy's opposition to caste distinctions as a presumption to "social equality" that no law could impose. The language of the briefs drafted for Plessy was nonetheless echoed in Justice John Marshall Harlan's memorable dissent, in which he held "caste" to be antithetical to the principles of the nation.

In its time, the concept of equal public rights provided a coherent basis for claiming formal respect in the public sphere. Its use rested on a coalition and a movement that did not prevail, but it left a conceptual legacy for those who would subsequently renew the struggle under the name of civil rights.

SEE ALSO *Caste; Civil Rights; Civil Rights Movement, U.S.; Constitution, U.S.; Human Rights; Justice; Natural Rights; Reconstruction Era (U.S.); Segregation; Separate-but-Equal; Slavery; White Supremacy*

BIBLIOGRAPHY

Official Journal of the Proceedings of the Convention for Framing a Constitution for the State of Louisiana, 1867–1868. New Orleans, LA: J. B. Roudanez.

Primus, Richard. 1999. *The American Language of Rights.* Cambridge, U.K.: Cambridge University Press.

Rossi, Pellegrino. 1835–1837. *Cours de droit constitutionnel professé à la Faculté de Droit de Paris.* Vol. 1. Paris: Librairie de Guillaumin et Cie., 1866.

Scott, Rebecca. 2005. *Degrees of Freedom: Louisiana and Cuba after Slavery.* Cambridge, MA: Harvard University Press.

Rebecca J. Scott

PUBLIC SECTOR

The term *public* refers either to the people affected by some property or activity or to government property and activities. The *public sector* is the governmental sphere of an economy. Economists classify four basic functions of the public sector: the provision of collective goods and services, the redistribution of income and wealth, the promotion of stabilization and growth, and the prevention of social costs and market failures from crime, pollution, congestion, and monopoly.

The word *public* refers to the public sector in the following terms: public administration, public debt, public economics, public employment, public finance (and revenues and expenditures), public insurance, public libraries, public office, public ownership, public policy, public schools, public servant, and public works. The word *public* refers to people in the following terms: public corporation, public goods, public health, publicly held, public offering, public opinion, and public relations. Some terms, such as public domain, public service, public utilities, and public welfare, can refer to either serving the people or to government operations. Companies can be nominally private but under so much control by government that in effect the operation is in the public sector.

The branch of economics that studies collective decisions and decisions that affect the public is called *public choice*. The field includes voting, bureaucracy, and the policies enacted by elected officials. Public finance, a much older branch of economics, examines actual and optimal taxes and incentives as well as the economic impact of fiscal policy. A key concept in public choice is *rent seeking*, the influence of various interests that seek to transfer wealth (unearned rents) to themselves at the expense of the public. But also the median voter theorem states that policy makers cater to the voters in the middle of a policy spectrum. Thus the policy outcome can vary. Public choice as a field of study does not imply any particular policy outcome or normative viewpoint.

THE GROWTH OF THE PUBLIC SECTOR

In ancient Greece *public* referred to politics and government, the private sphere being the family and nongovernmental enterprises, such as farming and trade. Until the 1800s public sectors were mainly concerned with the military, taxation, legislation, relief for the indigent, administration of state land, maintenance of royalty, public works, and control of trade. During the 1800s the public sector expanded into municipal police and governmental schooling. In the latter 1800s, responding to socialist movements, Germany, followed by Great Britain and other countries, expanded the public sector to include social security and other welfare programs on a national scale. In the early 1900s central banking extended government further into money and banking, especially after countries switched from commodity money to fiat money. Russia in 1917 established the Union of Soviet Socialist Republics, which put its whole economy in the public sector.

The income tax as well as the value-added taxes established in Europe and other countries facilitated a great expansion of the public sector. In the United States there was a large expansion of government under the New Deal of President Franklin Roosevelt, including the establishment of Social Security. The public sector expanded again during the 1960s with the introduction of Medicare and Medicaid. In the late twentieth century the public sector became more involved in protecting the natural environment.

Wagner's Law, named after Adolph Wagner, states that economic growth is accompanied by an increased gross domestic product (GDP) share of the public sector. The public may demand greater collective services, such as better education, as wealth increases, but some theorists propose that much of the expansion is in response to previous interventions that create distortions. For example, a city policy that limits development can result in higher rentals, which then induce the city to respond with rent control. Governments have also increased their role in economic development by providing education, research, and infrastructure. Many government programs, such as medical care and housing subsidies, are in response to poverty and economic insecurity. War has also ratcheted up the public sector, as the size of government rises during wartime but then does not return to its prewar level. Governments now commonly seek to promote economic growth with investments in infrastructure and by the expansion of money and credit. Governments also finance activities such as basic research when markets are perceived as failing to provide sufficient amounts, as the benefits apply to the economy as a whole.

PUBLIC SECTOR PROVISION

The government can directly produce goods and services such as the military, postal service, schools, streets, highways, parks, police, and fire protection or contract out the production to private enterprise. Much of governmental expenditure consists of transfer payments. By imposing costs, government regulations can have the effect of taxation. For example, if firms are required to provide medical insurance to employees, that has a similar effect to taxing the firms and using the funds to subsidize the insurance.

Taxation has a social cost beyond the funds paid to government, an "excess burden" or "deadweight loss" caused by the reduction of output and investment caused by taxes. The amount of deadweight loss depends on the amount of the tax and the elasticity of the item taxed, that is, how its quantity responds to a change in price. Since land has a fixed supply, taxes on land value have no deadweight loss. There is also no excess burden if the tax, such as a pollution levy, also reduces social costs by a greater amount. User fees, based on benefits, also have no excess burden.

The effects of government borrowing depend on how the funds are borrowed, how the funds are spent, whether the spending stimulates the use of untapped resources, and the extent to which various financial investments substitute for one another. In some cases, government borrowing can raise interest rates and crowd out private investing, but in other cases, especially if there is high unemployment, if funds are borrowed from abroad, if the borrowing is for productive investments complementary to private investment, if private savings rise to offset government borrowing, or as noted by Benjamin M. Friedman (1978), if the borrowing uses short-term bonds that substitute for money, government borrowing can result in "crowding in" or a stimulus to private investment. Many economists think that optimally government should borrow money only for productive investments, including enhancements to human capital, and use current revenues for its collective consumption, such as military operations.

The size of the public sector can be measured by the total amount of spending, the share of GDP, workers employed, and public sector assets and liabilities. The U.S. federal government spent $2.5 trillion in 2005, 20 percent of GDP. State and local governments spent from their own sources $1.4 trillion, 11 percent of GDP. The relative size of government for the members of the Organization for Economic Cooperation and Development with developed economies grew from 27 percent in 1960 to 48 percent in 1996. Government outlays as a percentage of GDP in 1996 were 44 percent in the United Kingdom, and Denmark was the highest at 61 percent.

MACROECONOMIC ACTIVITY AND INTERNATIONAL TRADE

A large public sector can increase the trade deficit to the extent that taxation makes exports more expensive and to the extent that government spends its funds abroad, as in the case of a war. Governments mostly affect international trade with tariffs and restrictions, such as quotas, and with policies that affect foreign-currency exchange rates.

LABOR AND THE ENVIRONMENT

In most developed economies, public sector labor is about 15 percent of employment. Several studies have concluded that workers in the public sector tend to be better paid than those in the private sector. Government workers typically are under a civil service system by which it is difficult to fire an unproductive worker. A more fundamental element of the cost of labor in the public sector is Baumol's cost disease, put forth by William J. Baumol and William G. Bowen (1966), who argued that productivity in services such as an orchestra or education has changed little compared to that in manufacturing, which explains the increase in relative costs in the service-intensive public sector.

With global warming recognized as an urgent issue, people increasingly seek remedies in government policy. The taxation of pollution is more efficient than regulations, as the former permits firms and households to

adjust according to their individual costs and benefits. Pollution permits that trade in a market are also used to increase the cost to business of polluting more. Environmentalists have proposed a "green tax shift" that increases pollution charges while reducing taxes that have an excess burden, a policy that would minimize the economic costs of reducing pollution.

Advancing technology has meanwhile reduced the rationale for some large-scale government involvement, as knowledge becomes more easily accessible and the private sector becomes more capable of providing infrastructure, such as tolled highways and decentralized utilities. Nevertheless, conflict tends to expand the public sector, so the future role of the public sector depends on the interplay of advancing technology, threats to security and the environment, and the influence of theoretical knowledge and real-world experience in shaping public opinion.

SEE ALSO *Capitalism; Economics, Public; Government; Planning; Policy, Fiscal; Policy, Monetary; Private Sector; Public Choice; Public Goods; Public Utilities; Socialism; State Enterprise; Taxes*

BIBLIOGRAPHY

Baumol, William J., and William G. Bowen. 1966. *Performing Arts: The Economic Dilemma.* New York: Twentieth Century Fund.

Edwards, Chris. 2005. *Downsizing the Federal Government.* Washington, DC: Cato Institute.

Friedman, Benjamin M. 1978. Crowding Out or Crowding In? Economic Consequences of Financing Government Deficits. *Brookings Papers on Economic Activity* 1978 (3): 593–641.

Gwartney, James, Randall Holcombe, and Robert Lawson. 1998. *The Size and Functions of Government and Economic Growth.* Washington, DC: Joint Economic Committee Study.

Harrison, Fred, ed. 1998. *The Losses of Nations: Deadweight Politics versus Public Rent Dividends.* London: Othila.

Papadimitriou, Dimitri, ed. 2006. *The Distributional Effects of Government Spending and Taxation.* New York: Palgrave Macmillan.

Fred Foldvary

PUBLIC SPHERE

Discourse on the public sphere derives from the work of the German social theorist Jürgen Habermas, particularly with his first major work, *The Structural Transformation of the Public Sphere,* which first appeared in Germany in 1962, and in what some consider to be his magnum opus, *The Theory of Communicative Action* (1981). In these and other works, Habermas has been concerned with explicating the historical and social structural factors that have served to inhibit or advance democracy. Given the centrality of free and open dialogue for the functioning of democracy, of particular concern to Habermas is identifying where such discussions take place and under what conditions. His guiding question has been: Where is the space in which democracy is nurtured? Habermas refers to this space as the *public sphere*, a term related to *civil society*, which refers to a realm of social life distinct from both the state and the market, where participation in public life occurs with a spirit of cooperation and a norm of reciprocity. Seen in this light, Habermas construes the public sphere as a space within civil society. By claiming that a prerequisite of a democratic polity is an autonomous public sphere, Habermas can be seen as building on the work of Max Weber (1864–1920) and Seymour Martin Lipset (1922–2006) in attempting to identify the most important social structural conditions underpinning democratic societies.

What Habermas refers to as the "bourgeois public sphere" came into its own in the nineteenth century, most fully in Britain, as a result of the triumph of capitalism and the establishment of a laissez-faire state. In contrast to the feudal era, in which the economy and polity were intimately linked, in the earliest phase of the capitalist industrial era this linkage was uncoupled. The public sphere can be visualized as being carved out between the economy and the state, being separate and distinct from them. It is an arena that is accessible to all citizens on the basis of equality and thus is not dominated or controlled by powerful economic actors or by state officials. His perspective on this sphere has been depicted as a theater where political discourse occurs.

The public sphere requires the existence of independent voluntary associations of citizens and an institutionalized apparatus that permits the unrestricted dissemination of information and ideas. Thus the panoply of organizations—ranging from local parent-teacher associations and neighborhood clubs to labor unions, human rights organizations, environmental organizations, and so on—is part and parcel of this arena. In addition, so are media committed to ensuring that citizens are informed about the vital issues of the day and to providing outlets for articulating an array of stances on issues and forums for debate and dissent.

Critics of Habermas contend that he tends to romanticize the public sphere during its earlier years, confusing his ideal vision about how it should have functioned with the reality of the historical situation, which involved from its inception persistent intrusions of powerful economic interests and the repressive tactics of the state. The result was that the public sphere never managed to be as autonomous as he seems to think. This may be a somewhat unfair characterization of Habermas's position because he provides ample evidence of being aware of the

limitations of actual existing public spheres in the past. He does think, however, that public spheres in the past exhibited greater autonomy than their contemporary versions.

At the same time Habermas leaves himself open to charges of utopian thinking, especially when he develops the ideal of a state of undistorted communication, free from coercion and restraint. In his view, democratic decisions arise dialogically. In an ideal speech situation, people talk to others to come to an understanding of which ideas and values are best, not to manipulate others to get one's way. In other words, he assumes a willingness on the part of citizens to freely embrace the better argument. There are examples of situations in which this ideal seems to have been more or less realized, such as old New England town meetings and Quaker meetings. The participants in these examples can be fairly depicted as being cooperative, tolerant, critical, self-reflective, and rational, whereas the differences among them in terms of both economic status and levels of human capital are not great.

Two other criticisms have been leveled at Habermas's portrait of the public sphere. First, some feminists contend that he is insufficiently attentive to the relationship between the private and public spheres and its implication for gender relations. Second, he has been accused of operating with an overly rationalistic and overly civilized view of human nature.

Habermas has expressed concern that the public sphere in what he describes as "late capitalism" is threatened by what he calls "refeudalization." What he refers to is the tendency to link or integrate the economy and the polity in a way quite at odds with their separation in the earlier period of capitalist development. Given his focus on communication, it is not surprising that he is particularly apprehensive about the concentration of media power in the hands of political and economic elites. Large media conglomerates have arisen to choke dissident voices out of the market, and these corporations, far from being independent of political power, serve as apologists for it. The result is that genuine public debate has given way to propaganda and increasingly sophisticated public relations.

Although the portrait he paints might lead to despair regarding the future of democracy, Habermas presents a cautious optimism. In particular he sees in the new social movements—environmental, antinuclear, peace, feminist, and so forth—potential for change. These movements have abandoned any belief in the possibility of revolutionary change, opting instead for radical reforms and a commitment to nonviolent change. Underlying his tempered hope for the future is a particular understanding of human nature. It presupposes that people are by nature political and thus concerned about and willing to participate in issues related to the well-being of society as a whole.

SEE ALSO *Associations, Voluntary; Civil Society; Feminism; Government; Habermas, Jürgen; Persuasion; Public Sector; Rationality; Utopianism; Volunteerism; Weber, Max*

BIBLIOGRAPHY

Calhoun, Craig, ed. 1992. *Habermas and the Public Sphere.* Cambridge, MA: MIT Press.

Habermas, Jürgen. [1962] 1989. *The Structural Transformation of the Public Sphere: An Inquiry into a Category of Bourgeois Society.* Trans. Thomas Burger. Cambridge, MA: MIT Press.

Habermas, Jürgen. 1979. *Communication and the Evolution of Society.* Trans. Thomas McCarthy. Boston: Beacon.

Habermas, Jürgen. [1981] 1984–1987. *The Theory of Communicative Action.* 2 vols. Trans. Thomas McCarthy. Boston: Beacon.

Habermas, Jürgen. 1996. *Between Facts and Norms: Contributions to a Discourse Theory of Law and Democracy.* Trans. William Rehg. Cambridge, MA: MIT Press.

Zaret, David. 2000. *Origins of Democratic Culture: Printing, Petitions, and the Public Sphere in Early-Modern England.* Princeton, NJ: Princeton University Press.

Peter Kivisto

PUBLIC UTILITIES

Public utilities are firms that are sometimes synonymous with natural monopolies. Some examples of public utilities include the Tennessee Valley Authority and Illinois Power.

These organizations are generally so called because there is structurally no room for market competition—one firm can "naturally" produce at lower costs than competitors who are eventually priced out of the market. Thus, natural monopolies tend to be regulated by governments in the public interest. However, being a natural monopoly is not a necessary prerequisite for government regulation. Industries that are not natural monopolies may be regulated for a number of reasons, including service reliability, universal access, and national security.

Public utilities generally supply goods or services that are essential, like water, electricity, telephone, and natural gas. For example, the transmission lines for the transportation of electricity or natural gas pipelines have natural monopoly characteristics in that once these lines are laid by one utility, duplication of such effort by other firms is wasteful. In other words, these industries are characterized by economies of scale in production.

Left to themselves, private utility companies would make decisions that are most profitable for them. Such decisions generally involve too high prices and relatively little service compared to competitive conditions. These decisions may or may not be in the best interests of the society. The government or the society would like to see these services being economically accessible to all or most of the population.

Not all utility companies are in the private sector. In many countries, utilities are owned by the government. Generally, in these cases, the government creates autonomous bodies for government utilities to prevent them from day-to-day political interference. In such instances, the government utilities' goals are better aligned with societal goals; however, they tend to be less efficient than their private sector counterparts.

Two main issues facing public utilities are coverage of service area and pricing. Alternately stated, the regulators try to balance the competing aims of economic efficiency and social equity. Economic efficiency generally requires that markets be left to work by themselves with little intervention. Such instances are usually not equitable or fair (some consumers might be priced out of the market). Equity issues demand that everyone gets the service at a "just" price. However, these instances can turn out to be inefficient (think about the cost to an electric utility of having to run cables a number of miles especially to serve one or two remote fishing cabins that are used sparingly).

In general, the pricing of the services of public utilities is problematic. As mentioned above most public utilities are structural monopolies, implying that there is no room for competition in the market for services they provide. However, if they are left alone to price like monopolies, the resulting price is too high and a large part of the market area may not be served. While the utility companies have no complaints about such arrangements, given the essential nature of the services they provide, the society would like to provide such services to all or most of the population. Think, for instance, about the undesirability of denying heat to someone in the winter. Hence, their pricing actions are regulated.

However, these decisions are somewhat problematic. If these utilities are mandated to set prices at the low competitive levels, they generally end up making losses. So there continues to be an ongoing tussle between regulators and the utility companies regarding a "fair" price between the monopoly and competitive levels.

Common alternate pricing actions include (1) setting prices equal to average production costs and serving the maximum area possible; (2) rate of return regulation; and (3) price cap regulation. Under average cost pricing, the utility is assured of breaking even, since the prices equal average costs. The equity aspects are somewhat met since most of the market is being served. However, the regulated firm lacks incentives to minimize costs. Under rate of return regulation, the regulators let the firms charge any price, provided the rate of return on invested capital does not exceed a specified rate. Whereas such regulation is flexible in allowing pricing freedom and frees the regulators from monitoring prices, a key drawback is that such regulation can lead to overcapitalization. In other words, when the rate of return is fixed at 5 percent, then the firm can charge higher prices by investing more in capital than it would otherwise (i.e., 5% of $10 million is greater than 5% of $6 million). Price cap regulation directly sets a limit on the maximum price charged by regulated firms. This type of regulation can result in a loss of service area. A (somewhat debated) plus point of price cap regulation is that such regulation induces firms to seek cost-reducing technologies because they offer a way to increase utility profits.

With technological changes over time, the nature of regulation changes in that some functions of the utility companies are "unbundled" and thrown open to free competition. New technologies might make it possible to break up the different stages of the electric generation process or natural gas transmission such that competition might be allowed to function in some stages. For example, in twenty-first-century United States and elsewhere the electricity generation market is relatively competitive and consumers are able to purchase electricity from competing vendors (generators). However, the transportation of electricity still remains a natural monopoly and continues to be regulated. Further, oftentimes the deregulation of some or all functions of public utilities might occur over time due to political-economic compulsions.

In practice, however, both deregulation and increased regulation are plagued by uncertainties, both for regulators and the firms they oversee. For instance, the firms do not know when and whether they will face additional regulation (or deregulation). The regulators, on the other hand, are unaware whether new technologies would mandate additional regulation. Another related issue facing nations involves how to make the regulations somewhat consistent across international borders so that utilities from one nation do not have undue advantages over utilities from other nations (U.S. and Canadian utilities have faced such issues following the North American Free Trade Agreement [NAFTA]).

There is some criticism of public utility regulation in that over time the regulated utilities tend to take over the regulatory agencies that oversee them (called the capture theory of regulation). Thus the societal interests that the regulatory agencies are supposed to further are somewhat compromised. The evidence regarding the capture of regulatory agencies is mixed, however. Further, some researchers, including John Galbraith in his 1973 work, have questioned the supposed underproduction by monopolies.

To summarize, whereas over time changes in environment and technology warrant changes in regulation of public utilities, the nature of markets that utilities serve generally warrants they be overseen in some form or another by government bodies.

SEE ALSO *Energy; Energy Industry; Public Sector*

BIBLIOGRAPHY

Berg, Sanford V., and John Tschirhart. 1998. *Natural Monopoly Regulation.* Cambridge, U.K.: Cambridge University Press.

Galbraith, John K. 1973. Power and the Useful Economist. *American Economic Review* 63: 1–11.

Kahn, Alfred E. 1971. *The Economics of Regulation: Principles and Institutions.* 2 vols. New York: Wiley.

Rajeev K. Goel

PUBLIC WELFARE

Welfare programs represent an effort on behalf of nation-states and international organizations to provide assistance to people who are otherwise unable to take advantage of market (primarily capitalist) relations. Welfare programs emerged as a public (meaning government-funded) phenomenon following historical periods of industrialization in Western nation-states during the eighteenth and nineteenth centuries and in Asian, Latin American, and African states in the twentieth century, following the decline of colonialism.

Prior to industrialization, explanations for poverty and other forms of political marginalization abounded, most of which emphasized the failings of poor individuals themselves rather than market-based, state-centered, or international explanations. Preindustrial explanations for the existence of the poor fall into two categories. The first category follows the logic of retribution. Poor individuals have committed sins or other values-based transgressions for which the penalty was poverty. In response to such explanations, programs developed first by private individuals and religious organizations were geared toward treating the poor as criminals in fact if not by law.

The second set, paternalistic explanations, evolved from two primary origins: (1) a response to the recognition of the harsh conditions industrialization brought to urban centers, which were increasingly teeming with rural poor who had migrated in search of work; and (2) a justification for the economic exploitation of indigenous populations in colonial contexts around the world. In response to the first origin, labor laws emerged in Great Britain, France, and later the United States first to protect children, who were the first to be seen as "innocent" victims of market fluctuations. Later, through the social movements of labor unions and the rise of Marxist ideology as a challenge to capitalism, women and, last, adult males found increased economic protection through widows' pensions, unemployment insurance, and better protected labor negotiations.

In response to the second origin, the logic of paternalism dictated an attention to the supposed "natural and primitive" state of the indigenous poor, who then must be "developed" or otherwise socialized into market-based civilization. A different set of programs arose that focused on the mollification of indigenous resistance to the economic exploitation of colonialism and, later in the postcolonial context, the enforced economic independence of new states with limited reparations from colonial conquerors who had benefited economically from previous arrangements. In response to the needs of newly independent states, an international development movement emerged to plug some of the holes required for economic integration into world markets and increased political stability. Many international development programs were premised on this prior paternalistic logic.

Both explanations of poverty remained salient during the rise of progressive movements in industrialized liberal democracies such as Great Britain and the United States. However, a third explanation emerged following the Industrial Revolution as part of reformist, progressive activism that emphasized the role of economic institutions that were either dependent upon or responsible for the creation of vast swaths of poverty. In Western nations, the emergence of socialism as an alternative to liberalism produced hybrid political-economic models such as social democracy, which emphasizes a balance between free markets and economic equality. Northern nations such as Sweden have emerged as the archetypical models of social democracy, where public welfare includes guarantees of financial assistance, generous child care and family leave policies, housing assistance, employment protections, and disability and old age insurance. More recent scholarship has emphasized four ideal types for public-welfare provision comparisons: social democratic, liberal democratic, conservative, and post-Communist regimes.

While social democracies are attractive in terms of the safety net for the economically disadvantaged, individual citizens carry a much heavier tax burden to cover such programs than they do in liberal democracies such as the United States, where programs are not nearly as comprehensive—financially or programmatically. This fact may help to explain why there is not a direct linear relationship between the level of public-welfare provision and general citizen support for such provision. The relationship is instead curvilinear, suggesting that citizens in high-spending, social democratic Scandinavian countries level off in support, while citizens in lower-spending liberal southern European nations continue to support such public-welfare expenditures. This trade-off is one that continues to be contested within each country, with welfare program popularity also based significantly on perceptions of program recipients.

Both liberal democracies and social democracies among Western nations, however, share a comparative advantage in terms of long-term political stability, gross domestic product, and other economic resources that enable nation-states to remain relatively independent of international organizations in terms of social safety-net provision. Newer democracies—many of which emerged in a postcolonial context of limited political stability, low gross domestic product, and low availability of cash-producing resources—face ongoing struggles to provide a social safety net of cash assistance, agricultural subsidies, child care and family leave policies, housing assistance, employment protection, or disability and old age insurance. In these contexts, international organizations, such as the World Health Organization, UNICEF, the International Monetary Fund, and the World Bank, have significant influence upon nation-states' ability to provide public welfare for their citizens.

For example, structural adjustment programs prescribed for what are called "developing" nations often require fiscal policies that substantially limit domestic public-welfare capabilities. For example, liberalizing a national economy often includes allowing significant amounts of foreign investment to enhance the economy. However, with such investments comes the provision of corporate incentives that can limit labor protections for workers—including less onerous minimum wage laws, worker safety regulations, and labor union protections. The trade-offs between public-welfare programs and economic stability for new nation-states is an ongoing challenge. However, a new framework promises to question some of these trade-offs and the paternalistic premises that undergird international development programs. The "empowerment" literature changes the social construction of public-welfare recipients—from either domestic or international programs—into one that focuses on the existing capabilities of the poor and more democratically includes them in program design and funding decisions. Still new, empowerment logic is widespread in the area of microlending, which encourages market integration one small business owner at a time.

In "developed" nations public-welfare programs are more commonly defined as protections against the vagaries of the market—cash assistance for those who do not work, whether because of unemployment, disability, or old age. The security of these programs is based on more domestic considerations than those of developing nations. In countries such as the United States, Great Britain, and France, public policy debates surrounding the shrinking of public-welfare programs boils down to debates that focus again on the people who might benefit—whether they are deserving of assistance or not. As one might expect, those who are deemed deserving of assistance—those, for example, who have "paid into a system" through decades of taxes on their wages—are less likely to have benefits cut than those who are presumed to receive "something for nothing." To the degree recipients are perceived as deserving, programs are more popular. When recipients are perceived as undeserving, programs are less popular. Such explanations continue to shed light upon the size and limits of welfare state disbursements to the poor and to debates surrounding the boundary lines between the "deserving poor" and the "undeserving poor."

SEE ALSO *Developing Countries; International Monetary Fund; Poverty; Public Health; Public Interest; Social Welfare System; Stability, Political; Structural Adjustment; United Nations; Welfare; Welfare State; World Bank, The; World Health Organization; World War II*

BIBLIOGRAPHY

Feldman, Stanley, and John Zaller. 1992. The Political Culture of Ambivalence: Ideological Responses to the Welfare State. *American Journal of Political Science* 36 (1): 268–307.

Friedmann, John. 1992. *Empowerment: The Politics of Alternative Development.* Cambridge, MA: Blackwell.

Girvetz, Harry K. 1968. Welfare State. In *International Encyclopedia of Social Sciences*, ed. David Sills, vol. 16, 512–520. New York: Macmillan/Free Press.

Hacker, Jacob. 2006. Inequality, American Democracy, and American Political Science: The Need for Cumulative Research. *PS: Political Science and Politics* 39: 47–49.

Hancock, Ange-Marie. 2004. *The Politics of Disgust: The Public Identity of the "Welfare Queen".* New York: New York University Press.

Jaeger, Mads Meier. 2006. Welfare Regimes and Attitudes towards Redistribution: The Regime Hypothesis Revisited. *European Sociological Review* 22 (2): 157–170.

Katznelson, Ira. 2005. *When Affirmative Action Was White: An Untold History of Racial Inequality in Twentieth Century America.* New York: Norton.

Lieberman, Robert. 2005. *Shaping Race Policy: The United States in Comparative Perspective.* Princeton, NJ: Princeton University Press.

Quadagno, Jill. 1994. *The Color of Welfare: How Racism Undermined the War on Poverty.* New York: Oxford University Press.

Skocpol, Theda. 1995. *Social Policy in the United States: Future Possibilities in Historical Perspective.* Princeton, NJ: Princeton University Press.

Vreeland, James Raymond. 2003. *The IMF and Economic Development.* New York: Cambridge University Press.

Ange-Marie Hancock

PULLMAN PORTERS

Ironically, the position of Pullman porter, which was designed to capitalize on the legacy of slavery, instead became the catalyst for both the formation of an African American middle class and the first major African American labor union (the Brotherhood of Sleeping Car Porters). In addition it was linked to the emergence of the U.S. civil rights movement in the twentieth century.

At the end of the Civil War, the Pullman Sleeping Car transformed travel in the United States. Though sleeping cars on trains had been used before, the Pullman was the first comfortable, indeed luxurious, sleeping car, and it ushered in a new era of comfortable cross-country train travel. The job of the Pullman porter included loading and unloading passengers and their luggage, keeping toilet and general-use areas and cabins clean, and turning down and putting up the folding upper and lower beds. The porter also took care of patrons' personal needs, such as boxing ladies' hats, sending letters and telegrams, setting up card tables, stocking coolers with ice, serving food and drinks in the dining car, and selling cigarettes, candy, and playing cards. When necessary he also took on the chores of the conductor, though he was never paid a conductor's wages. For many years porters were on call twenty-four hours. As envisioned by founder George Pullman (1831–1897), the porter's role was to supply the average traveler with the luxury of a servant for the duration of the trip. Pullman specifically modeled the Pullman porter after the plantation house servant, and he intended the jobs to be filled by the recently freed slaves.

The Pullman Company, headquartered just outside Chicago, quickly became the largest single employer of African Americans, and Pullman porter positions were among the most prestigious jobs available to them. However, the wages and working conditions were poor compared to those of white Americans. Porters represented the first foray for African Americans into the middle class, but this was due more to the perceived prestige of the position and the experience of being well traveled than to the economic gains. That said, many of the Pullman porters were highly educated. Nonetheless, this was the best employment they could obtain in Jim Crow–era America, and the company kept porter hours long and wages low, forcing them to rely upon tips as a significant part of their income. Until the formation of the Brotherhood of Sleeping Car Porters (BSCP) in 1925, porters were never paid more than office boys, the lowest ranking white employees.

In a degrading act of racism, whites routinely called all porters "George" after George Pullman, following an older racist custom of naming slaves after their masters. The Society for the Prevention of Calling Sleeping Car Porters "George" (SPCSCPG) was formed in 1916 to promote the elimination of the practice. The SPCSCPG lasted until 1941 and at its peak counted more than 31,000 members, including George Herman "Babe" Ruth and King George V. Although the SPCSCPG ostensibly was formed to eliminate a racist practice stemming from the slavery era, some scholars speculate that the society was formed as a way for white railway workers and frequent Pullman passengers to distance themselves from the African American Pullman porters.

In 1925 the Pullman porters formed the BSCP and chose A. Philip Randolph (1889–1979), the well-educated editor of Harlem's *Messenger Magazine*, as president. Randolph had never been employed as a porter and therefore could not be disciplined by the Pullman Company. Hence Randolph maintained complete control of the direction of BSCP throughout his long tenure as the organization's president and relied on his regional delegates, most notably Milton P. Webster of the Chicago chapter, to maintain the day-to-day activities of the union.

The most important issues for Randolph and the BSCP in the early years were to win recognition of the BSCP as the sole authorized representatives of the Pullman porters and then to deal with the industry's split labor market that placed African Americans in lower-paying positions or paid them less even when they were doing the same work as whites, such as conductor duties. After a long and contentious fight, the first goal was accomplished, and progress was made toward achieving the second goal.

The Pullman Company and other employers of the period were not alone in their determination to protect the split labor market. Labor unions were unwilling to embrace African Americans, typically seeing them as competitors rather than allies. However, by 1929 the BSCP was admitted into the American Federation of Labor (AFL). Randolph used his position in the AFL to push for greater acceptance of minority workers by stressing the common economic goals of workers rather than racial differences, and he was instrumental in gaining wider acceptance of African Americans in many industries.

In 1941 Randolph and other BSCP organizers called for African Americans to march on Washington, D.C., to protest racial discrimination in the defense industries. Randolph decided that the march had to be an African Americans–only protest, not to distance African Americans from supportive whites but to establish African American control over their own destinies. Once it became obvious to President Franklin D. Roosevelt that Randolph had succeeded in effectively organizing a massive protest, he signed Executive Order 8802, the Fair Employment Act (1941), which prohibited defense and other government-related industries from discriminating against African Americans. Although this order carried no punitive meas-

ures for those who did not comply, it officially acknowledged the need for the government to address racial issues. Randolph called off the march on Washington, but the group continued to work on civil rights issues.

In 1982 Jack Santino produced and directed *Miles of Smiles, Years of Struggle: The Untold Story of the Black Pullman Porter*, a documentary chronicling the organization of the BSCP and the impact this group had on the U.S. civil rights movement. In 1983 Santino followed up with a striking article in the *Journal of American Folklore* that documented through oral history the racial stereotypes, racial violence, and other forms of racial discrimination faced by African American porters, who were by then in their eighties and nineties. Interestingly many of the instances of racism and abuse discussed by the former porters occurred long after the formation of the BSCP.

SEE ALSO *Civil Rights Movement, U.S.; Discrimination, Racial; Labor; Racism; Roosevelt, Franklin D.; Social Movements; Unions*

BIBLIOGRAPHY

Bates, Beth Thompkins. 2001. *Pullman Porters and the Rise of Protest Politics in Black America, 1925–1945*. Chapel Hill: University of North Carolina Press.

Calliste, Agnes. 1995. The Struggles for Employment Equity by Blacks on American and Canadian Railroads. *Journal of Black Studies* 25: 297–317.

Harris, William H. 1979. A. Philip Randolph as a Charismatic Leader, 1925–1941. *Journal of Negro History* 64: 301–315.

Santino, Jack. 1982. *Miles of Smiles, Years of Struggle: The Untold Story of the Black Pullman Porter*. San Francisco: California Newsreel.

Santino, Jack. 1983. Miles of Smiles, Years of Struggle: The Negotiation of Black Occupational Identity through Personal Experience Narrative. *Journal of American Folklore* 96 (382): 393–412.

Valien, Preston. 1940. The Brotherhood of Sleeping Car Porters. *Phylon* 1: 224–238.

Paul Ketchum
David G. Embrick

PUNCTUATED EQUILIBRIUM

Punctuated equilibrium is a descriptive hypothesis in evolutionary biology concerned with macroevolutionary dynamics specifically at the level of speciation. Punctuated equilibrium holds that most species originate by the splitting of a population during brief geological periods (punctuations), and that subsequently species persist with only relatively moderate morphological change (stasis) for the remainder of their existences. "Evolution by jerks," as punctuated equilibrium has been lucidly labeled, is usually contrasted with *phyletic gradualism* ("evolution by creeps"), which states that species evolve uniformly and slowly by the gradual transformation of large populations. Proposed jointly by paleontologists Niles Eldredge and Stephen Jay Gould (1941–2002) in 1972, punctuated equilibrium immediately lit a scientific controversy that has smoldered ever since.

Punctuated equilibrium was, however, hardly controversial at its inception. As a general characterization of macroevolutionary processes, it was largely presaged by Hugh Falconer (1808–1865) and Charles Darwin (1809–1882) in the mid-nineteenth century and later echoed by Hermann J. Muller (1890–1967) and George Gaylord Simpson (1902–1984) in the early twentieth century. Eldredge and Gould postulated their version of the hypothesis as a logical extension (into paleontology) of Ernst Mayr's (1904–2005) ecological theory of *allopatric speciation* (1963), which was widely considered the dominant theory of speciation. Allopatric theory proposes that speciation occurs when a smaller subpopulation becomes geographically isolated from its parent population. Over time, this peripheral daughter population diverges in isolation until it can no longer interbreed with the parent. Speciation as such happens relatively quickly in a small population and in a limited geographic range. Due to the relative brevity of this localized speciation event, intermediate morphologies will be unlikely to fossilize and will be rare even if they do, producing an apparent paleontological pattern of stasis punctuated by discontinuous speciation events.

While born of an orthodox evolutionary theory, punctuated equilibrium has been associated throughout its existence with more radical evolutionary concepts. The scientific controversy over punctuated equilibrium is multifaceted, but it has largely coalesced around three related issues: (1) whether punctuated equilibrium is "Darwinian"; (2) whether stasis truly is the predominant mode of evolution in the fossil record; and (3) whether the proposed mechanisms for both stasis and punctuations are valid.

One of the easiest means to draw attention to an evolutionary concept is to pronounce it "anti-Darwinian," and punctuated equilibrium has been no exception. Both proponents and detractors of punctuated equilibrium often claim that Darwin explained the incompleteness of the paleontological record as solely the result of the imperfect geological preservation of fossils. However, as pointed out by Frank H. T. Rhodes (1983, 1987), Darwin in fact devoted the larger part of chapter 10 of *On the Origin of Species* (titled "On the Imperfection of the Geological Record") to explaining how "gaps" in the fossil record are a direct consequence of speciation processes and the nature of natural selection. Like Eldredge and Gould, Darwin thought it likely that most species exist in a state of morphological stasis, only intermittently broken by bursts of localized change and speciation. Darwin found this point so important for understanding the paleontological record that he reiterated the argument in three separate chapters (Darwin [1872] 1993, chap. 4, "Natural Selection," p. 152; chap. 10, p. 428; and chap. 15, "Recapitulation and Conclusion," p. 619).

Furthermore, in debates over punctuated equilibrium, the term *gradualism* has been used in at least two different senses. Eldredge and Gould's phyletic gradualism concerns the tempo of evolution, entailing evolutionary trajectories that are geologically slow, constant, and unidirectional—a concept pointedly contrasted with the rapid speciation described by punctuated equilibrium. For Darwin, however, *gradual* has little to do with rate ([1872] 1993, pp. 312–317). Rather, it means that evolution by natural selection advances in small "grades" that are dependent on a population's normal genetic variation. Morphological change therefore can be genetically gradual and geologically rapid. While phyletic gradualism may have been a widespread evolutionary assumption in the twentieth century, it cannot be pinned on Darwin himself. Thus, given the significant overlap between the tenets of punctuationism and Darwin's views, punctuated equilibrium is resolutely "Darwinian."

Whether the fossil record truly displays a predominant pattern of stasis continues to be an active area of paleontological research. Punctuated equilibrium is most readily tested when geological strata are well resolved temporally with abundant fossil preservation. Empirical studies have resulted in mixed appraisals, with a roughly equal spread among those supporting phyletic gradualism, punctuated equilibrium, or a third "hybrid" process that may be described as *punctuated gradualism* (Erwin and Anstey 1995). Probably the most tangible contribution of the punctuated equilibrium controversy has been the widespread acceptance of Gould and Eldredge's claim that "stasis is data." Lack of morphological change is an evolutionary pattern that warrants an explanation.

The assortment of mechanisms that Gould and Eldredge have proposed to explain stasis and rapid speciation is the most contentious aspect of the punctuated equilibrium debate (Coyne and Charlesworth 1997). Eldredge and Gould initially implied that punctuated equilibrium is explained adequately by Mayr's mainstream theory of allopatric speciation. However, they successively suggested numerous additional "non-Darwinian" mechanisms, including saltational mutations and species selection (Gould 1980, 2002), none of which have been broadly accepted. Emphasizing an antireductionist pluralism, Eldredge and Gould further claimed that each of these speculative mechanisms was significant for its potential to decouple lower-level genetic processes from upper-level macroevolutionary trends. Perhaps ironically, the punctuationist paradigm has been adopted more recently by molecular biologists, who have found within in vitro evolution experiments analogous patterns of stasis interleaved with rapid genetic change (Elena et al. 1996). Thus, punctuated equilibrium may ultimately find its *raison d'être* in the very reductionist realm so vigorously opposed by Gould: molecular evolution via the "selfish gene."

SEE ALSO *Anthropology, Biological; Archaeology; Darwin, Charles; Gould, Stephen Jay*

BIBLIOGRAPHY

Coyne, Jerry A., and Brian Charlesworth. 1997. On Punctuated Equilibria. *Science* 276 (5311): 338–341.

Darwin, Charles. [1872] 1993. *The Origin of Species by Means of Natural Selection.* 6th ed. New York: Modern Library.

Eldredge, Niles, and Stephen Jay Gould. 1972. Punctuated Equilibria: An Alternative to Phyletic Gradualism. In *Models in Paleobiology*, ed. Thomas J. M. Schopf, 82–115. San Francisco: Freeman, Cooper.

Elena, Santiago F., Vaughn S. Cooper, and Richard E. Lenski. 1996. Punctuated Evolution Caused by Selection of Rare Beneficial Mutations. *Science* 272 (5269): 1802–1804.

Erwin, Douglas H., and Robert L. Anstey. 1995. Introduction. In *New Approaches to Speciation in the Fossil Record*, 11–38. New York: Columbia University Press.

Gould, Stephen Jay. 1980. Is a New and General Theory of Evolution Emerging? *Paleobiology* 6 (1): 119–130.

Gould, Stephen Jay. 2002. *The Structure of Evolutionary Theory.* Cambridge, MA: Belknap.

Gould, Stephen Jay, and Niles Eldredge. 1977. Punctuated Equilibria: The Tempo and Mode of Evolution Reconsidered. *Paleobiology* 3: 115–151.

Mayr, Ernst. 1963. *Animal Species and Evolution.* Cambridge, MA: Harvard University Press.

Rhodes, Frank H. T. 1983. Gradualism, Punctuated Equilibria, and the Origin of Species. *Nature* 305 (5932): 269–272.

Rhodes, Frank H. T. 1987. Darwinian Gradualism and Its Limits: The Development of Darwin's Views on the Rate and Pattern of Evolutionary Change. *Journal of the History of Biology* 20 (2): 139–157.

Douglas L. Theobald

PUNISHMENT

The concept of punishment originates at least as far back in philosophy as Socrates (Cooper and Hutchinson 1997), and the practice of punishment as a social institu-

tion seems to go as far back as there have been human societies. While the histories of the institutions of punishment vary from society to society, country to country, and nation to nation, some questions about punishment seem to be nearly universal. Because of the importance of the institution of punishment, it is crucial that its conceptual underpinning be explored with precision and care. What is punishment? Is it ever morally justified? Can it play a role in maintaining and strengthening just political institutions?

There are at least three important philosophical and ethical questions concerning punishment. The first concerns its nature. Much confusion can result if the nature of punishment is not understood to amount to some kind of harsh treatment of the offender or the harmful wrongdoer. Although punishment is legitimate, institutionally implemented harsh treatment for the commission of a legal offense (Hart 1968; Feinberg 1970; Rawls 2000; Corlett 2006), it might well have side effects—even positive ones—such as moral education or rehabilitation. By "harsh treatment" is meant some form of corporal punishment, incarceration, fines, or the like. But it is important not to confuse punishment with deterrence, moral education, or rehabilitation. These are not forms of punishment, because punishment is not properly defined necessarily in terms of deterring, morally educating, or rehabilitating offenders. To think otherwise is to beg the question in favor of one of the theories of punishment considered below. This is not to say, however, that genuine punishment cannot deter future harmful wrongdoings, morally educate, or rehabilitate in some ways on some occasions.

A second question concerning punishment amounts to a set of questions raised by Anthony Quinton (1954), John Rawls (1955), and Stanley Benn (1958). The first pertains to the moral justification of the institution of punishment itself, while the second regards the moral justification of particular forms of punishment. Clearly, the belief that punishment is morally justified does not mean that all forms of punishment are justified, though it would seem that for any particular form of punishment to be justified, the institution of punishment itself must be justified. Attempts have been made to reconcile major theories of punishment by suggesting that one theory is best fit to answer the question of the morality of the institution of punishment, while another theory is best able to answer questions of how particular punishments ought to be meted out to offenders (Rawls 1955; Corlett 2006).

A third question regarding punishment is the extent to which it might serve to the betterment of just political institutions. The role that punishment might play in maintaining and strengthening just political institutions has been addressed in a myriad of ways in recent years, especially in the debate about the morality of the very institution of punishment. It has been argued by punishment abolitionists that punishment is morally wrong because of social and political inequalities of opportunity that make the imposition of the punishment unfair and hence unjust. Indeed, they argue, there exist significant degrees of unfairness in terms of racism and classism in the system of punishment that make punishment unjustified. Proponents of punishment argue that the system is often fair enough to justify the punishment of those who truly commit their crimes and are sufficiently responsible for them, assuming that adequate due process of law obtains.

Considering the nature of punishment as hard treatment, there are two main theories of punishment—that is, of the moral justification of the institution, particular forms, and the role of punishment. Although there are various hybrid forms of these theories, the two are called "utilitarianism" and "retributivism." The former was defended by Jeremy Bentham ([1789] 1948), among others, while the latter was formulated by Socrates (Cooper and Hutchinson 1997) and later made famous by Immanuel Kant ([1780] 1996). Each theory defends some form(s) of the principle of proportional punishment. While Bentham provides no fewer than thirteen principles of proportional punishment based in utilitarian reasoning, Kant and other retributivists subscribe to some notion that punishments ought to fit the crimes and that the choice of punishment does not depend solely on considerations of social utility.

More recently, retributivists such as Joel Feinberg have argued for a number of expressive functions of punishment: authoritative disavowal, symbolic nonacquiescence, vindication of the law, and absolution of others (Feinberg 1970). It would seem that these expressive functions are consistent with either a utilitarian or retributivist outlook.

Perhaps the most oft discussed issue of punishment is that of capital punishment. Some capital punishment abolitionists argue that the criminal justice system is so corrupted because of racism and classism that the administration of capital punishment is unfair and hence unethical. Others point to the prohibitive cost of imposing the penalty as well as the mitigating factors that seem to accrue with every capital case. Still others point to the intrinsic value of human life and argue that this prohibits the taking of life in any circumstances. Utilitarians who oppose capital punishment argue that it fails to deter violent crime and robs society of the opportunity to rehabilitate capital offenders (Corlett 2006).

However, proponents of capital punishment argue that while these considerations are important and ought to be taken seriously by anyone thinking about punish-

ment, it is unclear that the racism, classism, and other factors that make capital punishment unfair in one society make it necessarily unfair when imposed in another that lacks such factors. Also the administration of capital punishment can be made more economically efficient without threatening due process considerations of appeals and related factors necessary for a reasonably just legal system. Moreover considerations of alleged intrinsically valuable human life (in some absolute sense), deterrence, and rehabilitation each admit of dubious foundations apart from particular ethical standpoints, which themselves need independent argumentative support. In particular, it is argued, they do not seem to be able to account well for considerations of deservedness and proportional punishment, without which no theory of punishment can be properly construed as plausible.

For some, capital punishment is morally justified to the extent that it is administered without prejudice as to ethnicity, sexuality, and socioeconomic class and to the extent that the alleged offender is guilty of the capital offense; performed it with sufficient intent, voluntariness, and knowledge; and was at fault in what he or she did, failed to do, or attempted to do. That some are wrongfully charged and even convicted and sentenced to death in no way logically discounts the rightness of capital punishment for those who are guilty. However, no theory of punishment ought to take lightly the unforgivable evils of wrongful convictions—especially in capital cases. Thus these theorists desire to put in place legal rules punishing those responsible for wrongful convictions, where fault accrues.

But retributivism and utilitarianism differ from one another in other ways. According to utilitarianism, punishment is an evil and can only be justified insofar as it increases the overall happiness of society—either by deterrence of future harmful wrongdoings or by rehabilitation. Classic criticisms of this position on punishment's justification include that it fails to take into consideration what offenders deserve and thus minimizes if not nullifies personal and social responsibility for harmful wrongdoing. It is future oriented.

Retributivism, on the other hand, holds that harmful wrongdoers ought to get what they deserve in approximate proportion to their harmful wrongdoings caused to others. Classic concerns with this theory include that it does not clarify the allegedly primitive notion of desert and that it cannot provide an adequate account of proportional punishment. Those who defend retributivism have replied with robust conceptual analyses of the concepts of desert and proportionality, adding that any plausible theory of punishment must take seriously deservedness, proportionality, and responsibility (Corlett 2006). And insofar as utilitarian theories flounder along these lines, only retributivism serves as a plausible foundation of punishment's justification. For any plausible theory of punishment's justification must make adequate sense of deservedness, responsibility, and proportional punishment because denying the importance of these notions spells disaster for systems of punishment seeking to be just and fair. Retributivism has often been confused with vengeance theories of punishment. But as Feinberg (1965) and Robert Nozick (1981) have argued at some length and with precision, retributivism does not entail vengeance of any kind. There are also moral education theories of punishment (Hampton 1984), but they seem not to entail punishment (hard treatment) at all or unwarrantedly assume a version of utilitarianism to justify punishment. Hence they either are not theories of punishment at all or they beg important questions about punishment's justification.

Of course there are hybrid theories of punishment, especially between retributive and utilitarian theories. Indeed it might well be the case that most theories of punishment amount to some form of hybrid theory, as not even Kant (who many allege founded retributivism) held to a pure form of retributivism, as many believe he did (Corlett 2006).

Punishment theorists have written much on the matter of forgiveness, mercy, and punishment. Ought the state to forgive or show mercy to harmful wrongdoers by mitigating or even excusing punishments? Many utilitarian theorists have argued affirmatively to this complex question in that the future results of how society responds to harmful wrongdoers is more important than past harmful wrongdoings themselves. Some retributivists, however, have argued that taking responsibility seriously requires that a criminal justice system not permit the language and emotions of forgiveness to interfere with holding harmful wrongdoers responsible for their actions, failures to act, or attempted actions. The reason for this is that they must get what they deserve—nothing more and nothing less—for harmful wrongdoings they have wrought on others. The value of deservedness, responsibility, and proportionality are so strong for some retributivists that not to take them into account in punishment is to commit a most serious injustice. This implies that forgiveness and mercy have no legitimate place in a reasonably just criminal justice system. And this is true even if the wrongdoer offers a genuine apology. Apology, forgiveness, and mercy are irrelevant to a system of genuine criminal justice, though mitigation and excuse play pivotal roles in such a system where responsibility is, all relevant things considered, not full.

While collective forms of punishment do not take on forms of corporal punishment as in individual human cases, certain collectives can be legitimately held responsible for harmful wrongdoings as a kind of vicarious liability (Feinberg 1970; Corlett 2006). But unlike individual harmful wrongdoers, collective harmful wrongdoers are typically fined because they have "no soul to be damned, no body to be kicked" (Coffee 1981). Other forms of collective punishment might include adverse publicity (French 1984).

Among the many contemporary areas of investigation in punishment theory is the question of whether there ought to be similar punishments for both successful and failed crimes. Some have argued that certain theories of punishment demand by implication that they ought not to be punished differently simply because of differences in the consequences of the intended crimes. For insofar as the intentions of the harmful wrongdoers are the same, they ought to be punished similarly. Yet this places such theories of punishment in an embarrassing situation, as the result appears counterintuitive (Feinberg 2003). Others deny this point, arguing that no plausible theory of punishment would ever concede that punishment can rightly accrue to a harmful wrongdoer simply because of considerations of intent; that is, there are no purely anticonsequentialist theories of punishment that are even initially plausible. Thus any plausible theory of punishment must hold that a combination of criminal intent and the consequences of the harmful wrongdoing play roles in determining the just punishment of the criminal.

What is clear is that punishment entails hard treatment, and what justifies it on moral grounds must involve at least notions of deservedness, responsibility, and proportionality. To deny this much is implicitly to embrace claims that result in injustice and unfairness.

SEE ALSO *Ethics; Foucault, Michel; Imprisonment; Justice; Kant, Immanuel; Philosophy; Prisons; Rawls, John; Utilitarianism*

BIBLIOGRAPHY

Benn, Stanley I. 1958. An Approach to the Problems of Punishment. *Philosophy* 33: 325–341.

Bentham, Jeremy. [1789] 1948. *Introduction to the Principles of Morals and Legislation.* New York: Hafner.

Coffee, John. 1981. No Soul to Blame, No Body to Kick: An Unscandalized Inquiry into the Problem of Corporate Punishment. *Michigan Law Review* 79: 386–460.

Cooper, John M., and D. S. Hutchinson, eds. 1997. *Plato: Complete Works.* Indianapolis, IN: Hackett Publishing.

Corlett, J. Angelo. 2006. The Philosophy of Joel Feinberg. *Journal of Ethics* 10: 131–191.

Corlett, J. Angelo. 2006. *Responsibility and Punishment.* 3rd ed. Dordrecht, Netherlands: Springer.

Feinberg, Joel, ed. 1965. *Reason and Responsibility.* Belmont, CA: Dickenson Publishing.

Feinberg, Joel. 1970. *Doing and Deserving: Essays in the Theory of Responsibility.* Princeton, NJ: Princeton University Press.

Feinberg, Joel. 2003. *Problems at the Roots of Law*. Oxford: Oxford University Press.

French, Peter A. 1984. *Collective and Corporate Responsibility*. New York: Columbia University Press.

Hampton, Jean. 1984. The Moral Education Theory of Punishment. *Philosophy and Public Affairs* 13: 208–238.

Hart, H. L. A. 1968. *Punishment and Responsibility*. Oxford: Oxford University Press.

Kant, Immanuel. [1780] 1996. *The Metaphysical Elements of Justice*. Trans. and ed. Mary Gregor. Cambridge, U.K., and New York: Cambridge University Press.

Nozick, Robert. 1981. *Philosophical Explanations*. Cambridge, MA: Harvard University Press.

Quinton, Anthony. 1954. On Punishment. *Analysis* 14: 133–142.

Rawls, John. 1955. Two Concepts of Rules. *Philosophical Review* 64: 3–32.

Rawls, John. 1999. *Collected Papers*, ed. Samuel Freeman. Cambridge, MA: Harvard University Press.

J. Angelo Corlett

PURCHASING POWER PARITY

Purchasing power parity (PPP) is the theoretical proposition that national currencies have the same real purchasing power at home and abroad. This notion is best understood starting from the point at which two currencies trade at par. Suppose that the exchange rate of the U.S. dollar for the Canadian dollar is unity (as was approximately true for a good portion of the early 1970s). If PPP holds, goods and services sold within Canada (quoted in Canadian dollars) will have the same prices as goods and services sold within the United States (quoted in U.S. dollars). Assuming Canadian and U.S. dollars were both accepted as media of exchange, there would be no need to post prices in anything other than "dollars." And it would not matter which dollars were chosen.

Consider the following thought experiment. Suppose one or a combination of the three variables in the PPP equation—the prices charged by Canadian retailers, those charged by U.S. retailers, or the nominal exchange rate—changes such that Canadian goods become 10 percent more expensive than the same U.S. goods when all prices are expressed in the same units (i.e., a common currency). If so, consumer demand for the now more expensive Canadian goods would rapidly decline to zero.

Purchasing power parity may be thought of as ruling out this possibility. The literature has contrasted two ways in which this happens. First, arbitrageurs would take advantage of the fact that the market has two prices for

goods and services of the same quality. Specifically, arbitrageurs would buy the lower priced goods in America and resell them at the 10 percent higher price in Canada. However, the increased demand for goods and services sold in America will pull American prices up while the increased supply of goods and services sold in Canada will push Canadian prices down. Arbitrageurs will continue buying in America and selling in Canada until the prices in the two countries are equal. Some economists argue that instantaneous arbitrage prevents the departure from parity—departures from PPP would never be observed in the real world. The more likely case, however, is that the force of arbitrage would be quick enough that the temporary nature of the deviation would be a fleeting economic event, of minor consequence from a macroeconomic perspective.

The second scenario is that restoration of purchasing power parity takes a long time. During this time, consumers and firms are altering their demand and supply decisions. In the literature that uses the consumer price index to compute deviations from PPP, the amount of time is takes for a deviation of 10 percent to work its way down to only 5 percent—the so-called half-life of the deviation—is somewhere between three and five years. In contrast to the near instantaneous adjustment case, this is glacial and should be expected to put into motion seismic shifts in demand and supply across locations. Yet, we do not see this type of quantity reaction in the data. Large variations in real exchange rates (deviations from PPP) are not associated with large variations in trade balances or the overall business cycle.

Thus, purchasing power parity, one of the most intuitive of economic concepts, fails to hold in practice. Moreover, its failure to hold does not appear to lead to the type of quantity reactions we would anticipate from basic economic principles. These observations raise two key issues. The first issue is the conceptual validity of PPP. The second is the empirical validity of PPP measures relative to the theoretical concept.

The consumer basket of a modern industrialized country contains literally thousands of individual goods and services, and the cost of arbitrage varies significantly across them. When costs of arbitrage such as transportation costs arise, price differences across locations are expected to arise as well. These deviations are referred to as deviations from the law of one price (LOP). For items in the consumption basket that are not traded across countries, deviations from the LOP are expected to be large and may persist indefinitely. The classic example of a nontraded item is a haircut, which requires the purchaser and the seller to be at the same place at the same time. While the haircut is exchanged in this bilateral meeting, the market for haircuts is localized. Contrast this with heart surgery. Here again, the buyer and seller must be at the same place at the same time. While most major cities have impressive medical centers to meet local demand for high-quality care such as this, people do travel to the markets with the best heart surgeons, sometimes across a vast ocean. The combination of scarcity and high consumer benefit overcomes a large trade cost. Commodities, in contrast, often involve small trade costs and their physical depreciation is slow. This means that buyers and sellers do not have to be in the same place at the same time and inventories provide stocks of supply at or near consumption locations. The general message here is that services tend to be localized in trade while goods are globally mobile. We see these distinctions between goods and services in trade flow data, although the Internet is changing the manner in which some goods and a few services are produced and exchanged. While the PPP exchange rate may be thought of as a weighted average of LOP deviations of the individual items that underlie its construction, there is so much variation across those items that any broad-brushed economic interpretation of the PPP exchange rate are highly debatable.

Currently there are perhaps three or four competing theories that attempt to explain deviations from PPP. The simplest and most enduring explanation for the time series variation in relative prices is sticky prices. We know that the nominal exchange rate varies often by a percent or more over the course of a single day, while many retail prices remain fixed for months on end. This begs the question of why prices are so costly to adjust or why it is not in the firm's interest to adjust.

If two sellers are physically across the street from one another, we expect the prices of identical goods or services to hold up to a deviation associated with the cost of crossing the street. Otherwise, consumers would never visit the high-price location. Given that we do observe a price differential, we are led to associate the deviation with an impediment to spatial arbitrage. The impediments could take various forms: physical distance, branding, patents, or copyrights.

For example, restaurant menu prices need not adjust continuously in light of what competitors are doing because the menus contain differentiated products. Models of monopolistic competition have been developed to account for price differences across varieties of goods. Here the producer has the ability to charge different prices in the same market even when the cost of providing the different goods is the same.

Price differences could also arise under perfect competition and arbitrage because the cost of providing goods to final consumers involves both shipping costs and the costs of providing goods in the retail outlets. The price of bread in a grocery store must partly defray the cost of

labor, capital, and rent borne by the grocer. These costs often differ enormously across locations, particularly when the locations are in different countries. This contrasts starkly with the emergence of manufacturers who sell products online. In this case, everyone pays the same price up to a shipping cost, exactly as the trade cost model would predict.

As models develop in sophistication and the empirical data becomes available to make extensive cross-location comparisons of prices of individual goods and services, we will gain an increasingly clear picture of the reasons for the failure of purchasing power parity to hold at a point in time and over the long run. Inevitably this will involve models that incorporate a variety of goods, services, and market structures. Moreover, the empirical target of the theoretical literature is moving as locations of production and consumption change and as the technology for achieving the exchange of goods and services continues to evolve. Highly accessible introductions to the academic literature on purchasing power parity, the law of one price, international trade costs, and price dispersion in the European Union are, respectively, Rogoff (1996), Goldberg and Knetter (1997), Anderson and van Wincoop (2004), and Crucini, Telmer, and Zachariadis (2005).

SEE ALSO *Arbitrage and Arbitrageurs; Balance of Trade; European Union; Exchange Rates; Inflation; Interest Rates; International Monetary Fund; Trade; Trade Deficit; Trade Surplus*

BIBLIOGRAPHY

Anderson, James A., and Eric van Wincoop. 2004. Trade Costs. *Journal of Economic Literature* 43 (3): 691–751.

Crucini, Mario J., Chris I. Telmer, and Marios Zachariadis. 2005. Understanding European Real Exchange Rates. *American Economic Review* 95 (3): 724–738.

Goldberg, Pinelopi K., and Michael M. Knetter. 1997. Goods Prices and Exchange Rates: What Have We Learned? *Journal of Economic Literature* 35: 1243–1272.

Rogoff, Kenneth. 1996. The Purchasing Power Parity Puzzle. *Journal of Economic Literature* 34 (2): 647–668.

Mario J. Crucini

PURGATORY

Purgatory comes from the Latin word, *purgatio*, which means purification, cleansing or expiation. Many religions affirm the need for moral and spiritual purification. Purgatory, though, is chiefly identified with the Catholic doctrine that maintains, first, that some souls after death require purification (*purgatio*) before reaching heaven, and second, that the prayers and intercessions of the living can assist souls in purgatory.

The word *purgatory* as such, is not found in the Bible, though variations of *katharsis*, the Greek equivalent of *purgatio*, can be found (e.g., *katharoi*, Matt 5:8, and *katharismou*, 2 Pet. 1:9). Church fathers such as Augustine (354–430) found support for purgatory in 2 Maccabees 12:43–46, a passage (not considered canonical by Protestants) that mentions an expiatory sacrifice offered in the temple to atone for the sins of Jewish soldiers who died wearing pagan amulets. The inference is that there is expiation for some sins after death.

Various Church fathers, such as Gregory of Nyssa (c. 330–395), affirmed a postmortem purgation by "purifying fire" (*tou katharsiou purós*) based on 1 Corinthians 3:11–15 (some will be saved "only as through fire"). Patristic writers such as Augustine and Pope Gregory I (c. 540–604) also believed that Matthew 12:32 implies that certain sins will only be forgiven in the age to come (i.e., after death).

Under the influence of neo-Platonism, some early Christian writers, such as Origen (c. 185–254), suggested an ongoing purification after death leading to a universal restoration (*apokatastasis*) of all humans (and possibly demons) with God. The local Council of Constantinople condemned *apokatastasis* in 543.

The doctrine of purgatory underwent more systematic development in the West than in the East. As its penitential system developed, Latin theology saw purgatory as the postmortem expiation of the temporal punishment due to sins. According to this theology, temporal effects or "punishments" of sin (e.g., wounds to oneself and others) remain even after the guilt (*culpa*) of sin is taken away by confession. Such temporal "punishments" require penances for adequate purification, satisfaction, or expiation. When the temporal effects of sin have not been purified prior to death, the person must undergo purgatory.

Because penances during the Middle Ages were often severe, the Church offered various indulgences, that is, extrasacramental ways (e.g., prayers, pilgrimages, and almsgiving) for gaining remission of the temporal punishments due to sin. These indulgences were granted by the Church via her access to the "treasury" of the merits of Christ and the saints. The faithful could apply these indulgences to themselves for their own purification or to souls in purgatory by means of suffrage or intercession (*per modum suffragii*).

Although purgatory was often seen as a temporary hell, the Italian poet Dante Alighieri (1265–1321) offered a more positive understanding of the doctrine. In the *Purgatorio*, the second part of his *Divine Comedy*, Dante describes the purifying rather than penal aspects of pun-

ishment. The souls ascend "Mount Purgatory" while receiving penances, practicing virtues, and reciting prayers designed to purge the root causes of the seven capital sins. Those in "lower purgatory" are purified of sins or vices related to "love perverted," namely pride, envy, and wrath. Those in "mid-purgatory" overcome sloth, which is associated with "love defective." Finally, those in "upper purgatory" are purged of "love excessive," linked to the sins of avarice, gluttony, and lust. For Dante, the purpose of purgatory is the interior purification of one's love for God and neighbor before entering heaven.

Only the Roman Catholic Church teaches purgatory as dogma. The Profession of Faith, read before the Second Council of Lyons (1274), distinguished between the souls who go immediately to hell after death, those who go immediately to heaven, and those who die in charity but are cleansed after death by "purgatorial and cleansing penalties" (*poenis purgatoriis seu catharteriis*). The Council of Florence repeated this doctrine in 1439 and reaffirmed that sacrifices of the mass, as well as prayers and offerings of the faithful, can alleviate the penalties of those in purgatory. In the wake of the Protestant denial of the doctrine, the Council of Trent, in 1563, upheld the reality of purgatory but warned bishops to exclude from popular sermons "the more difficult and subtle questions" not useful for edification and to prohibit all that belongs to curiosity, superstition, or unseemly gain.

The Catholic Church has never defined purgatory as a specific place. The exact nature and duration of the purgatorial punishments is open to speculation, and some, such as Catherine of Genoa (1447–1510), describe the fire of purgatory as the fire of God's love. Traditional Catholic theology specifies two forms of suffering in purgatory: the pain of loss (*poena damni*), because of the temporary deprivation of heaven; and the pain of sense (*poena sensus*), experienced by souls in a manner analogous to sensible pain. Whatever suffering the souls in purgatory experience is mitigated by their assurance of heaven once their purification is complete. The common Catholic teaching is that, after the general judgment, there will be only heaven and hell, and purgatory will cease.

The Protestant Reformers of the sixteenth century rejected purgatory as an unscriptural doctrine that obscures the atonement of Christ as the only satisfaction for sin. Moreover, they linked purgatory to "false practices" such as indulgences, private masses, and prayers for the dead.

The Eastern Orthodox churches have prayers for the departed in their liturgies, but they have never defined purgatory as a doctrine. Several Orthodox confessions of faith, such as the original ones of Peter Moghila (1596–1647), the metropolitan of Kiev, and Dositheus (1641–1707), the patriarch of Jerusalem, affirmed the reality of postmortem purification. Some Orthodox theologians have also posited the existence of two hells, one for the damned and another for those needing further purification. Still others have mentioned a middle state of souls after death (*mesi katastasis*), where they receive comfort from the prayers of the living. In general, though, Eastern Orthodox churches regard the whole matter as too mysterious for dogmatic formulations.

The Catholic Church continues to teach the reality of purgatory. Vatican II (1962–1965) and the *Catechism of the Catholic Church* (1992/1997), however, limit themselves to general affirmations of postmortem purification through the grace of God (cf. Vatican II's *Lumen Gentium*, 49 and the *Catechism*, 1030 and 1472).

SEE ALSO *Christianity; Church, The; Greek Orthodox Church; Heaven; Hell; Protestantism; Punishment; Purification; Religion; Roman Catholic Church; Sin*

BIBLIOGRAPHY

Daley, Brian E. 2003. *The Hope of the Early Church: A Handbook of Patristic Eschatology.* Peabody, MA: Hendrickson Publishing.

Dante Alighieri. 1955. *The Divine Comedy.* Canto 2: *Purgatory.* Trans. Dorothy L. Sayers. London: Penguin Books.

Jugie, M. 1936. *Purgatoire dans l'Église Greco-Russe après le Concile de Florence.* In Vol. 13, Part 1 of *Dictionnaire de Théologie Catholique*, 1326–1352. Paris: Librairie Letouzey et Ané.

Michel, A. 1936. Purgatoire. In Vol. 13, Part 1 of *Dictionnaire de Théologie Catholique*, 1163–1326. Paris: Librairie Letouzey et Ané.

Ombres, Robert. 1978. *Theology of Purgatory.* Butler, WI: Clergy Book Service.

Tsirpanlis, Constantine N. 1991. *Introduction to Eastern Patristic Thought and Orthodox Theology.* Collegeville, MN: Liturgical Press.

Ware, Timothy. 1993. *The Orthodox Church*, 2nd ed. New York: Penguin Books.

Robert Fastiggi

PURIFICATION

The concept of purification, or the ritual cleansing of persons and objects, is found across cultures and religions. It is present in urban and rural settings, in sectarian and secularized societies, and in tribal and multiethnic communities. It has been a sociological feature of human existence from antiquity to modernity, one with an array of behavioral guidelines and consequences.

Purification is associated with two other socioreligious notions: purity and pollution. Purity is linked to sanctity, devotion, and safety; pollution is associated with impurity, irreligion, and danger. Purification is regarded as a means of transitioning from a polluted to a pure state. Personal and group activities are carefully regulated by rules and rites designed to protect and purify individuals, communities, the deity or deities venerated by those groups, and even the world itself from the impurity supposedly caused by pollution. These notions arise from within the context of religious worldviews, and they often have transgressions and demonology as causative factors and penitence and exorcism as resolutionary mechanisms. Modern notions of hygiene, disease, waste products, and environmental contaminants that appear to be reflected in the codes and practices of purity, pollution, and purification bear only an inadvertent correspondence to purification. Purity and pollution are usually not based on physical cleanness and uncleanness, but on holiness and the loss of that state through inadvertent and deliberate violations of socioreligious tenets that renders a believer devotionally impure or polluted, thereby excluding him or her from partaking in the activities of a confessional community.

IMPLICATIONS

The ideal of purity, the fear of pollution, and the quest for purification arose from the systemic ordering of the religious world. The problem of pollution became a subcategory of evil because ritual impurity was equated with moral disorder caused by the forces of evil. Thus, the holy had to be protected from defilement. As a result, purity and impurity came to be regarded as opposites within religious settings. There was a rejection of spiritual and physiological conditions regarded as inappropriate. These conditions came to be prohibited completely, and they were to be resolved via purification whenever present. In some religions, such as Zoroastrianism, Judaism, and Islam, prohibitions became codes whose breach, whether intentional or unintentional, causes pollution, which is to be corrected by purification and atonement. In other devotional systems, such as in Polynesian societies, items and actions that were holy became taboo, and any violation of the connection between what is *tabu* and the deities with which these items and actions are associated is believed to bring divine wrath upon the violator, and possibly upon his or her community. In each case, however, the shared notion is that of separation of the pure from the impure, based on a religious dichotomy between the holy and the profane (representing good and evil, respectively).

Also central to understanding purification is a widespread belief that pollution can cross physical and spiritual boundaries through transfer between individuals and objects, all of which would in turn become impure and capable of spreading the pollutant. The human body is one such domain where transition across a physical boundary creates pollution and requires acts of purification. Hair and nails, while attached to the body, are considered to be pure, as are blood, saliva, semen, and vaginal fluid when inside the body. But all these items are viewed as open to pollution by evil spiritual forces once separated from the body's protection, and they are all capable of causing impurity in any persons and objects with which contact occurs. Ultimately, therefore, it is not just a single person or item that is involved in the system of purity, pollution, and purification, but rather the entire society and environment in which the believers live.

ANALYSIS

Methodological dilemmas exist in the interpretation of purification rituals. Among the issues involved are cultural relativity, the notion that beliefs and rituals are personal and social phenomena having values and meanings assigned by practitioners, the necessity for interpretations to be based on particular contexts, and attention to the historical contexts in which beliefs and practices developed. For instance, the Hebrew Bible, or Old Testament, preserves an apparent distinction in belief, terminology, and praxes between ritual purity and moral purity. Israelites who were not *tahor* (pure) because of a deliberate or accidental transgression that had rendered them *tameh* (impure) could not enter the temple nor have contact with believers, activities, and items relating to the community's religious life. Purification with water, followed by isolation or at least refraining from contact with other persons and items was one prescribed means by which purity could be reestablished. In other situations, such as the purification of men after skin diseases and women after childbirth, sacrifices of burnt offerings (*'olah*) and sin offerings (*hatta'*) necessary for the atonement of sins were associated with the process of regaining purity. So a nexus took place between ritual and moral purity in Judaism. Another historically-based intertwining of concepts is seen in Roman praxis, where *lustrare* (lustration), which may have originated around the second century BCE as a propitiatory rite, came to involve sprinkling with pure water, and so was categorized by Greeks and then Romans as a purification ritual, or *katharmon*.

Perhaps most important to the study of purification is the variety of functions served. For example, purification and penance are viewed by Zoroastrians as necessary to counter evil, which is believed to function as a pollutant external to the holy. In Jewish, Christian, Muslim, Hindu, and Buddhist belief as well, purification can be used to negate impurity and defilement. But Hindu, Buddhist, and Jain penances, or *tapas*, do not negate impurity caused by contact with an external pollutant. Instead, they are undergone as a form of repentance. Self-

flagellation, a practice among European Christians during the Middle Ages and still performed by Shia during the Muslim month of Muharram, involve acts of suffering intended to provide an expiation of sin and spiritual pollution. Despite the differences, however, all such acts of purification are connected by the intent of ensuring physical and, even more importantly, spiritual purity. Therefore, rites of passage or important transitory stages in the life cycle—such as birth, puberty, marriage, initiation into confessional communities and clerical organizations, and death—came to be associated with purificatory rites, as did individual physiological acts, whether voluntary or involuntary, such as urination, defection, sexual intercourse, childbirth, menstruation, and sickness.

In certain communities, such as among the ancient Israelites, medieval Jews, and ancient and medieval Zoroastrians, participation in purification was obligatory. Among other groups, such as the ancient and classical Greeks, participation in the system of purity and purification, or *miasma*, appears to have been at least technically a voluntary one. Yet whether obligatory or voluntary, such systems operated on consensus and coercion, and being regarded as impure often resulted in exclusion from communal life.

SELECT INSTANCES

Often, but not always, purification involves an external cleansing of the person or object, an internal expiation of the person, a period of isolation, and atonement for having become impure. The sequence of events varies, as do the items utilized during the process. The Zoroastrian ritual of *barashnum i no shab*, or purification of the nine (days and) nights, which is now used only before induction as a magus, or priest, is emblematic of such cleansing. A variety of items have been utilized by different cultures as purificatory agents. Earth (dust), urine, and blood are some purificatory agents utilized by specific communities. Dust has often been employed among Zoroastrians and Muslims as a substitute for water. The blood of a sacrificial bull served to purify Roman men undergoing initiation into the mysteries of Mithras during late antiquity. Smoke via fumigation would be used to purify household items among Jews and Zoroastrians.

Water is the most widely used substance for purification. The Christian practice of dipping fingers into a water basin upon entering a church (now quite infrequent) is a remnant of the custom of purification before prayer. All Muslims, irrespective of gender and age, perform *wudu'* (or *vuzu'*), a washing of the face, hands, and feet prior to entering a mosque. Zoroastrians perform a *padyab*, or rite of protection by water, by washing all uncovered parts of the body and face before praying at a fire temple. Water, because it symbolizes life and fertility, is also the purificatory agent used prior to initiation in many religious communities—the Christian baptism is the most widely known example, continuing a Jewish and Gnostic tradition that was followed later by Mandeans and Manicheans. The Zoroastrian *sade nahn* (simple bath) and the Hindu *upanayana* (washing) serve similar purposes.

Purification rites using water are performed by orthodox male and female Jews, Muslims, Zoroastrians, Hindus, and Buddhists after sexual intercourse to purify themselves from contact with semen and vaginal fluid. Because water is associated with fertility, such purification may also occur prior to marriage to ensure that the new couple begins life together in ritual and moral purity. A Roman counterpart, the *lustration*, can also be mentioned in the context of purification before marriage. In Africa, washing a Yoruba bride's feet before entering the bridegroom's home is another such purification.

Menstruation and childbirth are two situations in which purification is widespread across cultures. The seclusion of menstruating women and the prohibition of sexual intercourse during menses and for a certain period of time thereafter (the time of menses plus one day for Zoroastrians, menses plus four days among Hindus, between three and ten days for Muslims, and seven days for Jews) has been practiced in order to ensure that the husband or male partner does not become polluted by the woman's ritual impurity. After childbirth, a period of separation or isolation of the mother is prescribed by many confessional groups—it would last for forty days among Jews, Zoroastrians, Hindus, and Buddhists. After menses and childbirth, Jewish women are required to undergo a ritual immersion, or *mikvah*, to regain purity, Zoroastrian women have to perform a *sade nahn*, and a ritual bath, or *ghusl*, is undergone by Muslim women. Only orthodox or orthopractic women follow the stipulations completely now. Most other Jewish, Muslim, and Zoroastrian women now regard menses, childbirth, and the blood associated with these conditions as merely physiological processes that have no moral connection, and so they simply bathe or shower in water as they would to routinely clean themselves. The Christian practice of churching—or reintroducing a new mother to the community after childbirth, isolation, and purification—has fallen into disuse.

Fears that sex, procreation, and menstruation were linked to evil and sin reinforced the concepts of impurity associated with them, generated gender-specific misogyny in beliefs and practices directed at women, and contributed to patriarchy in many ancient and medieval societies. Traditionalist communities in both Western and Eastern countries continue some of those dichotomies. One result, among orthodox Jews, Christians, and Zoroastrians, is the exclusion of women from the priesthoods.

Class and caste hierarchies were shaped in part by issues of purity, pollution, and purification as well. One example among Hindus, Buddhists, and Zoroastrians pertains to families that wash and transport corpses, and thus are often shunned as ritually impure due to their occupation. For Hindus, in particular, the *varnashrama dharma*, or system of endogamous classes, excludes persons who deal with corpses, bodily fluids, and bodily excrements in their work. Those individuals—called *dalit* (downtrodden), and more paternalistically *harijans* (children of the god Hari Vishnu)—have traditionally been social outcastes living apart from the other classes and unable to worship at temples. Any member of the three upper socioreligious classes—the Brahmins (priests and scholars), the Kshatriyas (warriors and politicians), and the Vaishyas (merchants, artisans, and landowners), all of whom are regarded as "twice born" and therefore permitted to study scripture—who has direct or indirect contact with an untouchable person, through touch, food, water, objects, or even the outcaste's shadow, becomes polluted. He or she is technically required to undergo a ritual bath for religious purity to be regained. Only in modern India (after 1949–1950) and Pakistan (after 1953) have secular national constitutions deemed the still fairly widespread practice of untouchability illegal.

CONCLUDING OBSERVATIONS

Vitiation of the efficacy of purification is thought to occur if the prescribed rites are not performed exactingly or if contact occurs again with impure persons and objects. Consequently, during antiquity and medieval times, the proper performance of purification rituals, specialization of individuals as purifiers, and an extensive literature on purification developed, as evidenced by the biblical *Leviticus* and the Iranian *Videvdad*. The violation of divine commandments and contact with evil spirits were said to be the ultimate sources of pollution. As a part of religion, purification was an important, widespread, socioreligious factor linked to good, evil, demonology, and even differential gender and class relations. Its sway began to attenuate slowly in Europe with the Enlightenment and the Industrial Age. From the eighteenth century onward, colonialism spread Western science, especially in connection with medicine, to other societies via secular education. As result, practices of purification have attenuated in the daily lives of many secularized women and men.

SEE ALSO *Buddhism; Caste; Christianity; Cultural Relativism; Hinduism; Humiliation; Islam, Shia and Sunni; Judaism; Magic; Purgatory; Religion; Rites of Passage; Rituals; Sanitation; Shame; Sin; Stigma; Vodou*

BIBLIOGRAPHY

Choksy, Jamsheed K. 1989. *Purity and Pollution in Zoroastrianism: Triumph over Evil.* Austin: University of Texas Press.

De Silva, David A. 2000. *Honor, Patronage, Kinship, and Purity: Unlocking New Testament Culture.* Downers Grove, IL: InterVarsity Press.

Douglas, Mary. 1969. *Purity and Danger: An Analysis of Concepts of Pollution and Taboo.* 2nd ed. London: Routledge and Kegan Paul.

Dumont, Louis. 1980. *Homo Hierarchicus: The Caste System and Its Implications.* Rev. English ed. Chicago: University of Chicago Press.

Eliade, Mircea. 1959. *The Sacred and the Profane: The Nature of Religion.* Trans. Willard R. Trask. New York: Harcourt Brace Jovanovich.

Gennep, Arnold van. 1960. *The Rites of Passage.* Trans. Monika B. Vizedom and Gabrielle L. Caffee. Chicago: University of Chicago Press.

Katz, Marion Holmes. 2002. *Body of Text: The Emergence of the Sunni Law of Ritual Purity.* Albany: State University of New York Press.

Maccoby, Hyam. 1999. *Ritual and Morality: The Ritual Purity System and Its Place in Judaism.* Cambridge, U.K.: University of Cambridge Press.

Parker, Robert. 1983. *Miasma: Pollution and Purification in Early Greek Religion.* Oxford: Clarendon Press.

Jamsheed K. Choksy

PUSH-PULL EFFECTS

SEE *Immigrants to North America; Migration.*

PUTIN, VLADIMIR
1952–

Vladimir Vladimirovich Putin succeeded Boris Yeltsin as president of the Russian Federation on December 31, 1999. A former KGB agent, Putin was appointed prime minister by Yeltsin in August 1999. When Yeltsin abruptly resigned at the end of 1999, he named Putin his successor. Putin subsequently won the presidency in elections in March 2000, and a second term in March 2004.

With the end of the Cold War and the collapse of the Soviet Union in 1991, Russia's international relevance ebbed. Consequently, Putin's presidency has been dominated by domestic concerns, such as the concentration of wealth and power in the hands of the new Russian entrepreneurial oligarchs and separatist violence in the province of Chechnya. The former problem arose when young Russian businessmen, taking advantage of a weak legal system that lacked adequate property rights and could not protect contracts, amassed huge amounts of money and influence in the 1990s when the Russian government began auctioning state-owned assets. Putin, in a crackdown on corruption and illegal business practices, embarked on a crusade against the "robber barons," resulting in the high-profile and controversial arrest of Mikhail Khordovsky, the head of the oil company Yukos, as well as the indictments of many others. While these attacks on Russia's megarich may have broken the power of the oligarchs, they have drawn criticism for leading to the consolidation of power in Putin's hands and the suppression of media outlets critical of Putin's administration.

The problem of Chechnya has plagued Russia since the first Chechen war began in December 1994. The first war ended in 1997 with a peace treaty that was violated when Chechen separatists invaded the neighboring Russian republic of Dagestan to consolidate power and establish Islamic rule. But the invasion and the subsequent bombing of buildings in Russian cities, allegedly by Chechen rebels, had a galvanizing effect on Russian public opinion, which simultaneously discredited Yeltsin's administration and strengthened Putin's image as a strong nationalistic leader, contributing to Putin's victory in the presidential elections in March 2000. By the end of 2006, the Russian military occupied much of Chechnya, but Chechen rebels had carried out several brutal attacks against civilian targets, including the seizure of a Moscow theater on October 23, 2002, which resulted in the deaths of 130 civilians, and the siege of a school in Beslan on September 1, 2004, in which 344 people, including 186 children, were killed.

While Putin's legacy in Russian politics remains unclear, he is trying to reestablish Russia's place on the world stage and to shepherd Russia through difficult political and economic transformations. Putin enjoys personal relationships with many Western leaders, including U.S. president George W. Bush, French president Jacques Chirac, and British prime minister Tony Blair. While Russia has been accommodating toward the West on issues such as counter-terrorism, other concerns such as domestic civil liberties have strained those connections. Putin has come under fire from Western observers for stepping back from Yeltsin's democratic reforms and moving Russia toward a semi-authoritarian regime. This domestic retrenchment has been accompanied by a halting rapprochement with the West, including acceptance of NATO's expansion into central Europe and the Baltic states, and gradual economic improvement. However, having failed to diversify Russia's domestic economy, the country's economic success rests mainly on the export of oil, casting doubts on the long-term viability of Putin's reform plan. Critics fear that ultimately Putin's failure to enact meaningful political reform will undermine Russia's economic future as well.

SEE ALSO *Russian Federation; Yeltsin, Boris*

BIBLIOGRAPHY

Jack, Andrew. 2004. *Inside Putin's Russia: Can There Be Reform Without Democracy?* New York: Oxford University Press.

Shevtsova, Lilia. 2005. *Putin's Russia.* Rev. ed. Trans. Antonina W. Bouis. Washington, DC: Carnegie Endowment for International Peace.

Seth Weinberger

PUTNAM, ROBERT
1941–

It has been a fundamental concern of the social sciences to understand the individual, societal, and governmental traits that enable a human community to thrive. The research of Robert D. Putnam is driven by a desire to understand the conditions for effective governance. Putnam has examined the question of how national traditions of ideological style affect political decision-making in books such as *The Beliefs of Politicians* (1973) and *Bureaucrats and Politicians in Western Democracies* (1981). In *Hanging Together* (1987) and *Double-Edged Diplomacy* (1995) he also looked at how political leaders negotiate within the constraints of domestic political opinion and national interest to develop international agreements that are beneficial to all signatories.

Putnam is best known, however, for his work on the ways in which an active community—one characterized by a high level of social capital—contributes to the welfare of society and the effectiveness of government. Following Putnam's lead, the Organisation for Economic Co-operation and Development (OECD) and the World Bank have each issued reports on how social capital can assist economic development in sub-Saharan Africa, East Asia, and eastern Europe. As Putnam noted wryly in the epilogue to his book *Bowling Alone* (2000), he went overnight from being an "obscure academic" to being a guest of presidents and prime ministers and appearing on talk shows and in the pages of *People* magazine.

In *Bowling Alone* Putnam defines social capital as "social networks and the norms of reciprocity and trustworthiness that arise from them" (p. 19). Like financial, physical, and human capital, stocks of social capital can be built up or drawn down. Putnam finds that the accumu-lation of social capital in America is rapidly dwindling. His metaphor for the reduction of organized social networks, that Americans are now "bowling alone," is emblematic of their reduced willingness to engage with others for purposes ranging from community improvement to pursuing a hobby.

Putnam's first sustained treatment of the effects of social capital centered on Italy. Despite the equalization of financial resources available to Italian regional governments, some are far better than others in developing effective policies. Putnam discovered that those regions with a high level of social capital—including active participation in politics, widespread feelings of solidarity, trust and tolerance, and a social structure rich in associational life—enjoy more effective governance because they create an active partnership between government and society. Where social networks are widespread, Putnam notes in *Making Democracy Work* (1993, p. 113), "light-touch government is effortlessly stronger because it can count on more willing cooperation and self-enforcement among the citizenry."

Putnam's work in Italy led him to consider declining social capital in the United States. Over the last generation, America has experienced sharp declines in citizen participation in politics, in active membership in all manner of clubs and associations, in church membership and attendance, in involvement in unions and professional associations, and even in social gatherings and family dinners. We have become a spectator society, more likely to support community purposes through our checkbooks than through direct involvement. In *Democracies in Flux* (2002), Putnam and his colleagues found that other countries have also experienced declines in social capital. The United States is distinctive because the loss of connectivity and participation began earlier and has been steeper than elsewhere.

The immediate impact of a growing disconnection among family, friends, and neighbors is to reduce the quality of social and political life. Growing levels of political distrust and alienation, declining satisfaction with one's life, the physical decay of cities, and increases in crime, teen pregnancy, and mortality rates are all associated with diminishing social capital. As Putnam notes in *Bowling Alone*, "Weak social capital fosters the symptoms of social disintegration, such as crime and poverty, and those symptoms in turn further undermine social connections" (p. 287).

Critics have pointed out that the concept of social capital levies a special responsibility to understand social networks in poor communities, and for that matter in any community not organized in ways characteristic of predominantly white, middle-class neighborhoods. The constraints of income, leisure, and social amenities make it likely that poor communities will lag in social capital formation compared to wealthier areas. There are alternative forms of social organization in poorer communities, though, and understanding social capital formation in such areas requires an appreciation of forms of association and collaboration that may be quite different from those characteristic of middle-class communities. Cultivating a broad understanding of social capital formation has always been an objective of Putnam's, implied in his juxtaposition of reading clubs with bowling leagues as two effective forms of association.

Some observers have pointed to a "dark side" of social capital. A tightly knit community is a community of control. When you know the religion, ethnic background, and political beliefs of everyone in your neighborhood, and when your neighbors know yours, there is pervasive pressure for homogeneity. One who does not (or cannot) conform remains an outsider. The same social networks identified by Putnam as creative of social capital—churches, clubs, social and civic organizations—are identified by Antonio Gramsci as structures that maintain the hegemony of the dominant group (Gramsci 1971).

Although communities with tightly knit social networks may be less tolerant, it is possible to combine highly developed social networks with collaborative attitudes toward people outside those networks. This is a phenomenon Putnam calls the "bridging" form of social capital. In *Better Together* (2003) Putnam recounts a number of strategies community leaders use to develop community networks that form bridges over existing social divides.

Given the significance of social capital for human welfare, it is important to know how stocks of social capital can be increased. Putnam's work on Italy demonstrated that regional variations in social capital remained strikingly similar for over 800 years, despite massive changes in government, society, and economy. His more recent work on the United States, however, emphasizes the positive effects of people's efforts to organize on behalf of some cause that will improve their lives. People do not set out to build social capital, but trust and social networks are nonetheless created as a by-product of person-to-person contacts that occur in the process of working for a common goal. Trends in social capital, like trends in financial or human capital, feature growth sectors even in a general context of stagnation or decline. Robert Putnam's work aids in the identification of what concerned citizens can do to increase the extent of interpersonal connectivity and trust in their societies.

SEE ALSO *Associations, Voluntary; Class; Communalism; Communitarianism; Democracy; Gramsci, Antonio; Hegemony; Networks; Networks, Communication; Social Capital; Social Movements; Trust*

BIBLIOGRAPHY

PRIMARY WORKS

Putnam, Robert D. 1973. *The Beliefs of Politicians: Ideology, Conflict, and Democracy in Britain and Italy.* New Haven, CT: Yale University Press.

Putnam, Robert D. 1993. *Making Democracy Work: Civic Traditions in Modern Italy.* With Robert Leonardi and Raffaella Nanetti. Princeton, NJ: Princeton University Press.

Putnam, Robert D. 1995. *Double-Edged Diplomacy: International Bargaining and Domestic Politics.* Edited with Peter Evans and Harold Jacobson. Berkeley: University of California Press.

Putnam, Robert D. 2000. *Bowling Alone: The Collapse and Revival of American Community.* New York: Simon and Schuster.

Putnam, Robert D., ed. 2002. *Democracies in Flux: The Evolution of Social Capital in Contemporary Society.* New York: Oxford University Press.

Putnam, Robert D. 2003. *Better Together: Restoring the American Community.* With Lewis Feldstein. New York: Simon and Schuster.

Putnam, Robert D., and Nicholas Bayne. 1987. *Hanging Together: Conflict and Cooperation in the Seven-Power Summits.* Rev. ed. Cambridge, MA: Harvard University Press.

SECONDARY WORKS

Aberbach, Joel, Robert D. Putnam, and Bert Rockman. 1981. *Bureaucrats and Politicians in Western Democracies.* Cambridge, MA: Harvard University Press.

Hoare, Quintin, and Geoffrey Nowell Smith, eds. and trans. 1971. *Selections from the Prison Notebooks of Antonio Gramsci.* New York: International Publishers.

Pharr, Susan, and Robert D. Putnam, eds. 2000. *Disaffected Democracies: What's Troubling the Trilateral Countries?* Princeton, NJ: Princeton University Press.

Thomas R. Rochon

PUTTING-OUT SYSTEM

The putting-out system was a system of domestic manufacturing that was prevalent in rural areas of western Europe during the seventeenth and eighteenth centuries. It evolved out of an early form of independent commodity production, constituting a *transitional phase* to what German social theorist Karl Marx (1818–1883) called the "formal" subordination of labor to capital.

The subordination of labor to capital refers to a situation in which the direct producers are *separated* from the means of production, depending on capitalists to provide them with the necessary tools, machinery, and raw materials to produce commodities. Such producers also receive a wage from the capitalists and have no control over the disposition of the products of their labor. Wage-earners who still retain considerable control over their own labor process, however, are subject merely to "formal subordination" rather than to the "real subordination" to capital that characterizes the fully developed factory system of industrial capitalism.

Domestic workers involved in the putting-out system typically owned their own tools (such as looms and spinning wheels) but depended upon merchant capitalists to provide them with the raw materials to fashion products that were deemed the property of the merchants. Semifinished products would be passed on by the merchant to another workplace for further processing, while finished products would be taken directly to market. The typical commodity product of the putting-out system was cloth (more specifically, wool textiles), although other commodities (notably ironware) were also produced under this system.

A salient feature of the putting-out system was the high degree of control that the direct producers retained over their own labor processes. Working at home (or near home) and at their own pace, domestic producers were well positioned to balance work-time and leisure-time in accordance with the pre-capitalist preference for leisure. The system also allowed adult family members to develop a domestic division of labor in which their children could contribute productive labor under direct parental supervision. These circumstances were conducive to the rise and consolidation of the nuclear family as a dominant family form—a form that was also encouraged by the earlier (and still-extant) system of independent commodity production.

With time, it became clear to the merchant "putter-outs" that their domestic employees required a greater degree of supervision to maximize their productivity and discourage "embezzlement" of raw materials or even finished products. Stephen Marglin argued in his 1974 article "What Do the Bosses Do? The Origins and Functions of Hierarchy in Capitalist Production," that it was these *social* considerations rather than any technological imperative that accounted for the rise of the factory system. By removing wage-earners from their own domestic environments and assembling them in a common workplace, merchant capitalists were in a better position to control the hours and pace of work and, through vigilant surveillance, to prevent embezzlement. By doing this, of course, many merchant capitalists transformed themselves into industrial capitalists, inaugurating the long transition to a "specifically capitalist" as opposed to an artisanal mode of commodity production.

Dan Clawson argued in his 1980 publication *Bureaucracy and the Labor Process* that Marglin's "social control argument" for the disappearance of the early putting-out system and the rise of the factory has many strengths but is one-sided in its dismissal of the important role played by new technologies (especially power-driven machinery) in facilitating the subordination of labor to capital. According to Clawson "It is much more fruitful, and obviously the only Marxist approach, to understand the process as one of class struggle: Capitalists tried to impose social control in the form of factories, while workers struggled to resist. In this struggle, technological innovations were crucial capitalist weapons to help change the balance of power" (p. 51). Furthermore, noted Clawson, by assembling workers in large factories and workshops, capital could significantly improve their productivity by imposing ever-more detailed divisions of labor and taking advantage of machinery requiring a central power source.

The putting-out system all but disappeared in western Europe by the nineteenth century. However, by the late twentieth century it experienced a revival, stimulated by the advent of new computer and information technologies. Thanks to computer technology, the Internet, and new systems of inventory control, it has become increasingly possible for capital to employ stay-at-home workers without sacrificing productivity, control over hours, or effective cost accounting. The products of this new putting-out system are varied, but its most typical product is information.

SEE ALSO *Autonomy; Capital; Computers: Science and Society; Conjunctures, Transitional; Division of Labor; Factory System; Internet; Labor; Machinery; Marx, Karl; Microelectronics Industry; Mode of Production; Productivity; Technological Progress, Economic Growth; Technological Progress, Skill Bias; Wages*

BIBLIOGRAPHY

Clawson, Dan. 1980. *Bureaucracy and the Labor Process.* New York: Monthly Review Press.

Marglin, Stephen A. 1974. What Do the Bosses Do? The Origins and Functions of Hierarchy in Capitalist Production. *Review of Radical Political Economics* 6: 60–92.

Marx, Karl. [1867] 1977. *Capital.* Vol. 1. New York: Vintage.

Murray Smith

PUTTY-CLAY MODELS
SEE *Vintage Models.*

PUTTY-PUTTY MODELS
SEE *Vintage Models.*

PUTTY-SEMI-PUTTY MODELS

SEE *Vintage Models.*

PYGMALION EFFECTS

The Pygmalion effect, which is an interpersonal form of a self-fulfilling prophecy, borrows its name from the myth by the Roman poet Ovid and the subsequent play by George Bernard Shaw. Pygmalion was a sculptor who carved a sculpture of a beautiful woman from a piece of flawless ivory. He fell in love with his creation and begged the goddess Aphrodite to intervene on his behalf. She was so moved by his devotion that she brought the statue to life, and they lived happily ever after. In social psychology, Pygmalion effects occur when one person's beliefs or expectations about another creates or elicits the expected behavior, much as Pygmalion created his perfect woman, or Professor Higgins transformed Eliza Doolittle into a lady in Shaw's play.

Psychological research on Pygmalion effects began with Robert Rosenthal's studies that showed that experimenters' expectations for their participants' behavior could operate as self-fulfilling prophecies. Self-fulfilling prophecies were first defined by Robert K. Merton (1948) as originally false definitions of the situation that evoke new behaviors that make the false definition come true. In a research context, this means that experimenters may obtain significant results not because their theories are correct, but because they unintentionally bias participants to respond in the hypothesized manner. For example, Rosenthal and Kermit Fode (1963) showed that rats whose experimenters believed them to be specially bred to be "maze bright" actually completed a test maze more quickly than rats believed to be "maze dull," although in reality the "maze bright" and "maze dull" labels had been randomly assigned.

These studies initially generated tremendous controversy because they raised the inevitable question of the extent to which research findings are merely an artifact of experimenter bias. Sufficient studies were conducted to confirm that experimenter expectancy effects can and do occur and that, consequently, steps should be taken in the design of experimental studies to prevent them. The simplest way to do so is to conduct a study in a *double-blind* manner, such that neither the participant nor the experimenter is aware of the participant's experimental condition. Today, the double-blind randomized experiment is considered the gold standard of experimental design.

Rosenthal and his colleagues then turned their attention to other domains where Pygmalion effects could be operating. In 1968 Rosenthal and Lenore Jacobson published *Pygmalion in the Classroom,* describing the results of an experiment in which teachers at an elementary school were informed that certain of their students had performed well on a test of "academic blooming" and could be expected to demonstrate dramatic spurts in academic performance in the upcoming school year. In reality, the students identified as "academic bloomers" had been randomly chosen. Results of IQ tests administered at the end of the school year showed, however, that students labeled "academic bloomers" did in fact demonstrate significantly greater gains in IQ across the school year compared to control students. This finding similarly generated tremendous controversy, owing to the inescapable implication that some children who do not thrive in school may underperform not because of limitations in natural ability but because their teachers do not expect them to do well. This implication is particularly socially problematic when one considers that teachers' expectations are not random, but are systematically related to the socioeconomic status and race of the students.

The controversy was laid to rest in 1978 when Rosenthal and Donald Rubin published a meta-analytic review of the 345 studies of Pygmalion effects conducted to date. This review showed, first, that the combined significance level for Pygmalion effects was highly statistically significant across all studies and, second, that the average effect size was a Pearson correlation coefficient of $r = .33$, an effect considered to be moderate in magnitude. The Rosenthal and Rubin review thus provided definitive evidence that Pygmalion effects occur across a wide range of domains and are of practical importance.

Subsequent research on Pygmalion effects has been concerned primarily with documenting their existence in other interpersonal contexts, including everyday interactions and the workplace, and with understanding their underlying mediating processes—in other words, identifying the specific verbal and nonverbal behaviors given off by expecters that elicit the expected behavior from the targets. For example, Mark Snyder, Elizabeth Tanke, and Ellen Berscheid (1977) showed that men spoke in a warmer and friendlier fashion during telephone conversations with women whom they had been led to believe were very attractive, which in turn elicited warmer, friendlier, and more appealing behavior from the women.

Efforts to eliminate Pygmalion effects have been largely ineffective, owing to the fact that the behaviors that cause these effects are often subtle and not under the conscious control of the expecters. Future research needs to focus more on ways in which we can harness the power of positive expectancies and minimize the destructive effects of negative expectancies.

SEE ALSO *Self-Fulfilling Prophecies*

BIBLIOGRAPHY

Merton, Robert K. 1948. The Self-Fulfilling Prophecy. *Antioch Review* 8: 193–210.

Rosenthal, Robert, and Kermit Fode. 1963. The Effect of Experimenter Bias on the Performance of the Albino Rat. *Behavioral Science* 8: 183–189.

Rosenthal, Robert, and Lenore Jacobson. 1968. *Pygmalion in the Classroom: Teachers' Expectations and Pupils' Intellectual Development.* New York: Holt, Rinehart, and Winston.

Rosenthal, Robert, and Donald Rubin. 1978. Interpersonal Expectancy Effects: The First 345 Studies. *Behavioral and Brain Sciences* 1 (3): 377–386.

Snyder, Mark, Elizabeth Tanke, and Ellen Berscheid. 1977. Social Perception and Interpersonal Behavior: On the Self-Fulfilling Nature of Social Stereotypes. *Journal of Personality and Social Psychology* 35 (9): 656–666.

Monica J. Harris

Q

QADHAFI, MUAMMAR AL
1942–

Muammar al Qadhafi was born in 1942 to a nomadic Bedouin family, which was part of the Qadhafa tribe. After completing his primary education, Qadhafi attended the Sebha secondary school in Fezzan, Libya, between 1956 and 1961, where he received a traditional Islamic religious education. The political events that took place during his school years—including the establishment of Israel and the defeat of the Arab armies and Gamal Abdel Nasser's (1918-1970) rise to power in Egypt—defined the fundamentals of his political philosophy and worldview. Likewise, his tribal background and Islamic education contributed to his piety and the high value he attached to family ties, egalitarianism, and personal honor.

Between 1961 and 1963 Qadhafi attended the University of Libya after which he joined the Military Academy in Benghazi, which was opened to members of low income classes and offered them an opportunity for upward economic and social mobility. During his stay at the military academy, together with a few of his fellow cadets Qadhafi formed a free officer movement, which four years later would depose the pro-western Libyan monarchy. After his graduation from the academy in 1965, he was sent to Britain for one year of military training at the Royal Military Academy at Sandhurst.

On September 1, 1969, in a bloodless coup, Qadhafi and a group of seventy young army officers seized control of the government and overthrew the Libyan monarchy.

The coup received enthusiastic backing from the Libyan people and the army. The Revolutionary Command Council abolished the monarchy and proclaimed Libya as the Libyan Arab Peoples Republic.

QADHAFI'S POLITICAL IDEOLOGY AND FOREIGN POLICY

While Qadhafi occupied the position of head of state and the commander-in-chief of the armed forces, he left the day-to-day administration of governmental tasks to his subordinates and devoted his time to his revolutionary views concerning pan-Arabism, Islam, and the struggle against pro-western Arab reactionary forces, imperialism, and Zionism (including support of the state of Israel). Official government statements and the Libyan press referred to Qadhafi as the "Brother Leader," "Guide of the Revolution," and "Philosopher of the Revolution."

Instead of using socialism or western liberalism, Qadhafi gave primacy to his own vision of Islamic socialism and pan-Arab Nationalism. He called his form of government a "direct, popular democracy" and "Islamic socialism." He formed public committees to increase the opportunities for the Libyan people to exercise direct political participation and supervision of the government.

In 1973 Qadhafi proclaimed his Third Universal Theory, which consisted of socialism, popular democracy, Arab unity, and progressive Islam. His political philosophy appeared in his 1976 *Green Book*. Qadhafi called for the nationalization and redistribution of domestic industries and large private landholding, including religious properties. He also imposed a system of Islamic morals and outlawed alcohol and gambling. He directed the public committees to supervise the mosques in order to undermine the influence of the clerics who were critical of the *Green Book* and his nationalization of private property.

Qadhafi advocated Arab and pan-Islamic unity and tried unsuccessfully to form unions with other Arab states including Egypt, Syria, and Tunisia. He has also been active in African politics and various pan-African organizations, and he has given extensive humanitarian aid to African states.

QADHAFI'S SUPPORT OF REVOLUTIONARY MOVEMENTS AND TERRORISM

Qadhafi also extended financial and military support to several liberation and opposition movements such as the Palestine Liberation Organization, Black September (another pro-Palestinian organization), and the Irish Republican Army (IRA) among others. His revolutionary committees were engaged in the assassination of some Libyan dissidents living abroad. By the mid-1980s he was widely regarded in the West as the key supporter of international terrorism.

In an attempt to force Qadhafi to abandon his support of terrorist groups, in March 1982 the United States declared a ban on the import of Libyan oil and the export to Libya of American oil technology. During January and March 1986, President Ronald Reagan (1911–2004) ordered the American navy to attack Libyan patrol boats, and on April 15, 1986, he directed the American air force to attack Qadhafi's headquarters in Tripoli and Benghazi. The United Nations also imposed upon Libya economic sanctions for Qadhafi's refusal to allow the extradition to the United States or Britain of two Libyans accused of planting a bomb on Pan Am Flight 103 over Lockerbie, Scotland, in December 1988.

QADHAFI'S ECONOMIC EXPERIMENT FALTERS

The 1990s witnessed increasing disapproval of Qadhafi's revolutionary experiment by Islamic clerics, the middle class, professionals, and students. Moreover, the Libyan economy experienced serious problems resulting from the international sanctions, the decline in the price of oil in the second half of the 1980s and the 1990s, and poor governmental economic planning. This economic downturn limited the capacity of the government to provide employment and social welfare benefits to the politicized youth and the urban poor. The economic crisis was made worse by the fact that half of the Libyan population at the time was below the age of 15.

Following years of international isolation and growing socioeconomic challenges, and despite the anti-impe-

rialist rhetoric against the West, Qadhafi's revolutionary ideals did not come to fruition. Not only did his Arab unity schemes fail, but also the various armed revolutionary movements he backed did not achieve their goals, and the demise of the Soviet Union left Qadhafi more vulnerable to his main archenemy, the United States.

In the wake of these developments, Qadhafi began to redirect Libya's domestic and foreign policy starting the second half of the 1990s. He initiated economic liberalization measures to revitalize the economy and to attract foreign capital and investments. In his effort to lift the United Nations sanctions, in 1999 Qadhafi pledged to fight Al-Qaeda and offered to open up Libya's weapons program to international inspection. Through the mediation of South African president Nelson Mandela, Qadhafi gave up the two accused Libyans for the bombing of Pan Am Flight 103 in order to be tried in the Netherlands. In August 2003 Libya formally accepted responsibility for the Lockerbie bombing and Qadhafi agreed to pay compensation of $2.7 billion to the families of the 270 victims.

The terrorist attacks of September 11, 2001, availed Qadhafi the opportunity to further normalize Libya's relations with the West. Qadhafi condemned the attacks and extended his condolences to the American people, and he supported the United States' right to retaliate. As a sign of his abandonment of supporting international terrorism, Qadhafi started sharing information about Al-Qaeda and other terrorist groups with British and American intelligence services. In 2003 he allowed international inspectors to dismantle Libya's weapons of mass destruction. Because of Qadhafi's moves, the UN sanctions were lifted, and in March 2004 British prime minister Tony Blair became the first western leader in decades to visit Libya to meet with Qadhafi.

SEE ALSO *Al-Qaeda; Arabs; Blair, Tony; Coup d'Etat; Green Book, The (Libya); Islam, Shia and Sunni; Nationalization; Organization of Petroleum Exporting Countries (OPEC); Pan-Africanism; Pan-Arabism; Petroleum Industry; Reagan, Ronald; Revolution; Socialism, Islamic; United Nations; Weapons of Mass Destruction*

BIBLIOGRAPHY

Bearman, Jonathan. 1986. *Qadhafi's Libya*. London: Zed Books.

Bleuchot, Herve. 1982. The Green Book: Its Context and Meaning. In *Libya Since Independence: Economic and Political Development*, ed. J. A. Allan. New York: St. Martin's Press.

Burgat, Francois. 1995. Qadhafi's Ideological Framework. In *Qadafi's Libya, 1969–1994*, ed. Dirk Vandewalle. New York: St. Martin's Press.

Deeb, Marius, and Mary Jane Deeb. 1982. *Libya Since the Revolution: Aspects of Social and Political Development.* New York: Praeger.

Middle East Reporter Weekly. 1998. Libya's Qadhafi Turns Attention to Black Africa. (September 19).

Middle East Reporter Weekly. 2002. Reforms: Libya Opening up at Long Last. (January 19).

Pargeter, Alison. 2002. Pariah No More. *The World Today* (London), June.

Takeyh, Ray. 1998. Qadhafi and the Challenge of Militant Islam. *Washington Quarterly* 21(3): 159–172.

Vandewalle, Dirk. Qadhafi's 'Perestroika': Economic and Political Liberalization in Libya. *Middle East Journal* 45 (2).

Emile Sahliyeh

QUALIA

SEE *Functionalism.*

QUALIFICATIONS

In any society where good (desirable) jobs and high social status positions are relatively scarce, elites put mechanisms into place to limit access. Whereas in traditional societies "proof of ancestry" served that gatekeeper function, in modern societies the gatekeeper mechanism is expected to be the system of *qualifications.* The German social theorist Max Weber famously noted the rise of education, and specifically certificates (diplomas), as the preeminent form of qualification in modern society. In delineating the distinction of a society/system dominated by bureaucratic form (as opposed to traditional or charismatic forms), Weber wrote that office holding in bureaucracy was a vocation that required at least a prescribed course of training and working experience and oftentimes specialized examinations. The system of examinations was, then, a way to ensure the qualifications of any applicant (of any social strata), and it took the place of the traditional selection by noble birth.

EDUCATIONAL CREDENTIALING

The sociologist Randall Collins, studying U.S. society closer to the turn of the millennium, noted that education and parent occupational level were indeed the most important predictors of occupational success. Yet Collins, in the influential book *The Credential Society: An Historical Sociology of Education and Stratification* (1979), challenged the notions that (1) education led to skills acquisition and that (2) skills were the main determinant of occupational success. Instead Collins posited that while

educational credentials were still the key to occupational achievement, this correlational path need not, and often did not, run through the intervening variable of skills acquisition. Collins noted that most skills could be learned on the job, but the best jobs were saved for the applicants with the best educational credentials. This line of thinking was presaged by the work of postwar French sociologists such as Georges Friedmann (1946) and Alain Touraine (1955) who claimed distinctions between the concepts of qualification (a social construction with historical specificity) and skill (job-specific mastery). Touraine was particularly concerned with how the Industrial Revolution increasingly caused "social" qualifications to replace technical competence as measures of worker value.

Support for the value of education as one of these new qualifications was also proffered in economics by the Nobel laureate A. Michael Spence. Spence argued in 1973 that in a (labor) market characterized by imperfect information, individuals possessing qualifications would need to signal such qualifications to potential employers. Spence noted that education worked as a signal of qualification in the labor market. Taken together, the arguments of Collins and Spence suggest that whether or not education actually bestows qualifications, it bestows the presumption of qualifications in a competitive labor marketplace. As such, it is often not the actual possession of qualifications that leads to a job but rather a credential or signal of employability that leads to a job. That such credentials or signals are not equitably accessible by all members of a given society has been a continuing source of social science inquiry and popular consternation.

Historically, in societies stratified by race, gender, and class, educational credentialing has stratified correspondingly. Human Rights Watch concludes that children across the globe face discrimination in access to education, and thus the educational imparting of qualifications, based on race, ethnicity, religion, and other status. A 2003–2004 UNESCO report confirms that gender disparity in education remains a deep concern for much of the developing world. This concern is exacerbated in societies that are increasingly characterized by the need for knowledge and technological expertise acquired through education.

Yet in many Western postindustrial societies, gender parity in access to education (and even higher education) has been largely achieved. While women in these societies have made great strides in educational credentialing, racial minorities have fared slightly less well, and lower social classes still less well, even though progress has been made. For example, racial discrimination embedded both inherently in a qualification vehicle and in that qualification's use as an exclusionary moving target was addressed directly by the Supreme Court of the United States in 1992. The U.S. Supreme Court, in *United States v. Fordice*, 505 U.S. 717 (1992), noted that the State of Mississippi had used minimum ACT test scores first as a way to racially segregate institutions of higher education and then, as black student scores on these exams rose, as a way to maintain segregation by setting minimums out of reach of even the highest performing students of color. In striking down Mississippi's sole dependence on a discriminatory qualifier, the court further noted that most other states used a variety of qualifications in order to compensate for discrimination embedded in any one indicator and thereby improve racial balance on higher education campuses. The case demonstrates both the progress made and the barriers still to overcome in the United States' use of qualification for selection purposes.

OPPORTUNITY AND OCCUPATIONAL OUTCOMES

But even if women and racial minorities (though not necessarily lower and working classes) increasingly have access to qualifications (taught skills or merely credentials) afforded by attendance at both non-elite and elite colleges and universities, there is still evidence that coveted jobs are not meted out by qualifications alone. Indeed, social capital theorists are quick to point out that many individuals may share the same qualifications (or human capital) when seeking jobs yet may not achieve the same occupational outcomes due to the scarcity of opportunities. Groundbreaking research by Mark Granovetter in 1974 empirically confirmed the common wisdom that in job placement, it is often not "what you know" (formal qualifications) but rather "who you know." Even in postindustrial, bureaucratized societies, then, traditional modes of meting out jobs based on social capital and networks oftentimes negate the value of educational qualifications.

Further, some occupational qualifications depend less on education and training and more on physical or biological traits. In the United States, for example, societal controversies have arisen over the stated qualifications for jobs such as firefighters and police officers: Admittance to these occupations typically entails passing physical ability and strength tests that have often discriminated on the basis of sex. U.S. statutes, such as Title VII of the 1964 Civil Rights Act, that prohibit discrimination in employment based on race, color, religion, sex, and national origin still allow exceptions in cases where an employer can demonstrate that sex, religion, or national origin is a bona fide occupational qualification (BFOQ). British law, under the sex Discrimination Act of 1975, also allows for limited discrimination in recruitment, training, promotion, and transfer in a job for which the sex of the work is a "genuine occupational qualification" (GOQ). As in the

U.S. law, the occupational qualification mandating preference for a particular social category exists when the essence of the job makes it unsuitable for persons in other social categories. In these cases, then, sex, religion, and national origin may denote actual job qualifications and not just mark inequitable access to job qualifications.

Due to the richness of the concept, social scientists have been interested in qualifications as both an independent and dependent variable. As noted above, there is a long social science tradition of trying to understand precursors and access to qualifications in the job market (often focusing on racial and gender disparity in possession of job qualifications). As well, newer literature is beginning to center questions of qualifications as independent variables in models of income and occupational prestige, for example. The French sociology of work tradition is a reminder that qualifications are often social constructions, manipulated in the interests of elites. And finally, a continuing challenge is the interchangeability of the constructs of job qualifications and KSAs (knowledge, skills, and abilities) in the management and sociological literature coming out of the United States.

SEE ALSO *Labor Market; Skill; Stratification*

BIBLIOGRAPHY

Collins, Randall. 1979. *The Credential Society: An Historical Sociology of Education and Stratification.* New York: Academic Press.

Friedmann, Georges. 1946. *Problèmes humains du machinisme industriel.* Paris: Gallimard.

Granovetter, Mark S. 1974. *Getting a Job: A Study of Contacts and Careers.* Cambridge, MA: Harvard University Press.

Spence, A. Michael. 1973. Job Market Signaling. *Quarterly Journal of Economics* 87(3): 355–374.

Touraine, Alain. 1955. La qualification du travail: Histoire d'une notion. *Journal de psychologie normale et pathologique* 13: 27–76.

Weber, Max. 1968. Bureaucracy. In *Economy and Society: An Outline of Interpretive Sociology,* eds. Guenther Roth and Claus Wittich; trans. Ephraim Fischoff et al. Berkeley: University of California Press: 956–1006.

Rikki Abzug

QUALITY CONTROLS

Quality control is a management process that provides information about the conformity of either products or services to prespecified standards of utility. This function first became professionalized during the nineteenth century as a means for addressing the growing problem of the asymmetric distribution of product information that attended the rise of giant business enterprise and the emergence of mass markets. On the firm level, the growing scale and scope of manufacturing created pressure for the development of new metrics for informing management decision processes. While cost accounting was effective in ascertaining profitability, it provided little insight into the factors that affected output quality. This represented a potentially serious informational shortcoming as the largest manufacturing entities sought the realization of economies of scale through long production runs of standardized products.

On the consumer level, industrialization changed the nature of the relationship between consumers and producers. Unlike the shop economy of the preindustrial era, the line of communication connecting these groups for resolving quality issues became attenuated by the intermediation of longer supply chains and more impersonalized distributional arrangements. Industrialization also displaced indirect modes for assuring quality through guild or craft union validation of artisan skills through apprentice, journeyman, or master status. Many firms following scientific management principles enhanced the efficiency of their production lines by systematizing work effort through worker time-and-motion studies. These initiatives de-emphasized the role of the skilled craft practitioner and encouraged the placement of greater reliance in mass production on cheaper un- or semiskilled labor.

Quality assessment had within its compass the ability to surmount the problems of informational asymmetries about product quality in two ways. First, firms could apply quality standards to define what constituted a steady-state condition in their manufacturing. This new firm-specific knowledge, used in conjunction with accounting and financial data, could enhance efficiency by extending organizational capacities for planning, coordinating, controlling, monitoring, and evaluating production activities. Such study was also important to corporations in determining the economic limits of product inspection. Second, the dissemination of reliable information about product standards helped to eliminate asymmetries in external markets, thus contributing to a reduction in consumer risk perceptions. Such knowledge also helped consumers weigh more objectively the trade-off between performance benefits and costs in project analysis. Moreover, quality standards affected producer reputations by providing consumers with a basis for making grading comparisons between the output of rival suppliers.

Initially the focus of quality assessment centered on products rather than processes. The measurement of key design attributes and their alignment with engineering design standards became paramount. This involved the use of such measurement devices as gauges, calipers, jigs, and meters to determine if products met physical and performance requirements detailed in specification documents and blueprints. Such evaluation also involved destructive testing to measure the physical limits of materials. These early approaches, however, proved insufficient because they lacked an effective means for assessing the significance of test data. The statistical summarizations of this period were mere enumerations, devoid of a scientific basis for defining the nature of quality or for determining whether it had been effectively controlled in production.

The Bell System in the United States achieved a major breakthrough in surmounting problems of quality definition and analysis in the 1920s by developing new approaches that emphasized process and probability theory. The initial focus of innovation centered on the captive manufacturing subsidiary Western Electric, which supplied most of the material requirements of the Regional Bell Operating Companies. Such methodological innovation responded to regulatory pressures to provide more economical and efficient communication services through the deployment of more reliable equipment. In 1925, quality-control research centered on the inspection engineering department of the Bell Laboratories. Prime movers in establishing what became known as "statistical quality control" included Walter A. Shewhart of the theory and special studies unit and Harold F. Dodge of the inspection methods and results unit. Working in close coordination with the firm's manufacturing departments, they defined a unifying theory and set of applied methodologies that revolutionized quality engineering by 1928.

The assessment of quality at Bell benefited from several new analytical constructs based in probability theory. The control chart, for example, exploited the properties of the normal curve to clarify the economic limits of control. It distinguished between "common causes of errors" that were random and uncontrollable and "assignable causes of error" that could be rectified through management action. The trade-offs inherent in sample selection and evaluation became better illuminated from the specification of consumer's risk (Type I) involving the incorrect acceptance of an unreliable sample and producer's risk (Type II) involving the incorrect rejection of a valid sample. Customer planning was facilitated by the determination of the "average outgoing quality limit," a steady-state metric indicating the maximum number of defects in product shipments. In these and other ways probability theory increased the analytical power, flexibility, and range of quality engineering.

The new knowledge subsequently gained higher professional status in the United States and abroad. Shewhart taught the first collegiate course in quality engineering at Stevens Institute of Technology during the late 1930s, and soon thereafter Armand V. Feigenbaum of General Electric wrote the first doctoral dissertation on the subject at the Massachusetts Institute of Technology. During World War II, the new techniques were applied extensively in the U.S. Army Ordnance Corps with the assistance of Bell System advisers. W. Edwards Deming was also instrumental in organizing training programs for national defense industries through the War Production Board. In the postwar era, engineers with the Civil Communication Service of Supreme Command Allied Powers helped to revive interest in the topic in Japan. The Japanese Union of Scientists and Engineers began sponsoring courses presented by Deming, Joseph Juran, and others. In 1947 a new professional association, the American Society for Quality Control (now the American Quality Society), was founded. In 1956 the European Organization for Quality Control was formed.

While manufacturing quality control has continued to evolve, the new frontier involves the use of its concepts to address problems of informational asymmetry for services. The U.S. General Accounting Office, for example, reflected a concern about quality in audits of federally financed projects by requiring the evaluation of program effectiveness and results. Studies of environmental pollution, for example, often employ the probabilistic tools initially developed for industry. The notion of quality has also affected professional governance, albeit in a less quantitative way. The American Institute of Certified Public Accountants since the 1980s has required accounting firms to evince compliance with practice-quality standards as a condition of membership.

BIBLIOGRAPHY

Bayart, Denis. 2000. How to Make Chance Manageable: Statistical Thinking and Cognitive Devices in Manufacturing Control. In *Cultures of Control*, ed. Miriam R. Levin, 153–176. Amsterdam, Harwood Academic Publishers.

Deming, W. Edwards. 1986. *Out of the Crisis*. Cambridge, MA: MIT Press.

Feigenbaum, Armand V. 1983. *Total Quality Control*, 3rd ed. New York: McGraw-Hill.

Juran, Joseph M. 2004. *Architect of Quality: The Autobiography of Dr. Joseph M. Juran*. New York: McGraw-Hill.

Miranti, Paul J., Jr. 2005. Corporate Learning and Quality Control at the Bell System, 1877–1929. *Business History Review* 79 (spring): 39–72.

Shewhart, Walter A. 1931, *Economic Control of Quality of Manufactured Product*. New York: Van Nostrand.

Paul J. Miranti

QUALITY OF SERVICE
SEE *Quality, Product.*

QUALITY, PRODUCT

The product quality concept is often surrounded by some vagueness. Sometimes it is associated with such imprecise notions as "goodness," "expensiveness," "having class," and "satisfying" (Robson 1986, p. 69), albeit all these notions of quality point to the broad idea of customer satisfaction.

Quality is also sometimes defined as freedom from deficiencies or conforming to specifications, or predetermined standards that remain largely assumptive and imprecise. Because quality is perceived as "freedom from deficiencies," the concept is often interpreted to mean quality control and thus the exclusive concern of a special unit of the organization that may be called the Quality Control Department.

In recent years, however, a new quality concept has emerged that appears to focus more on product aspects such as utility, functionality, brand, packaging, and after-sales service that meet the needs of customers in a wider way. Quality is perceived as "meeting the requirements of the customer, now and in the future" (Cole 1996, pp. 232, 237–238). The quality concept is therefore often related to the customer, and so in this sense we talk about not only quality of goods but also quality of services such as accounting, invoicing, and communication.

Customers also include internal customers, people in the production line who are supplied with or receive the product of another's work. The inclusion of internal customers has meant that theoretically as well as practically the quality concept covers those things that affect not only end users, who may not even be seen or known, but everyone involved. Consequently, it becomes incumbent on every worker to meet the requirements of his or her own customer(s).

This new dimension to the quality concept underscores a shift in emphasis from quality control to quality of service, from the culture of "appraise and react" to the prevention of defects. Quality improvement and emphasis on quality concern everyone in the organization, and so reflect a realization of the real importance of quality.

The quality policy of a company that aims at defect-free performance would probably rest on deficiency-prevention programs. Investment in preventing errors involving costs in getting things done right the first time or preventing things going wrong in the first place through proper training of workers, planning ahead, and investing in appropriate tools, techniques, and technologies can significantly reduce total costs of failure and quality. Theoretically, the economics of quality would probably state that reduction in the number of errors through prevention would tend to lead to reduction in total costs. Consequently, quality as a policy option may be warranted by solid commercial and financial considerations.

Technological changes and innovations have the potential to improve techniques of work, and by preventing mistakes and increasing productivity, a better way of doing work assures product quality. Other prevention activities capable of changing quality include monitoring worker efforts and efforts aimed at improving managerial quality or skills. Because the organization depends on the skills, knowledge, innovativeness, and motivation of workers, improved managerial skills and quality can integrate and align employee contributions with organization strategy for achieving results, increase problem-solving capacity, provide understanding and use for information systems to support decision-making and evaluation processes, and develop paradigms to understand and direct all parts of the organizational system in the same direction to achieve quality objectives.

Another factor capable of affecting changes in product quality is market conditions, particularly market pricing. Generally, organizations sell and people want to acquire the benefits of products. Much as other aspects of the product, quality has benefits that potential buyers want, such as long product life, absence of faults and subsequent breakdown, reliability, and increase in value. However, for some types of products such as disposable goods (syringes or plastic cutlery) whose one-time benefits may be immediate, quality may take a backseat to such characteristics as hygiene, functionality, durability, or aesthetics. Quality may be emphasized because of the need to sell benefits. Prices can be raised if the product can offer added benefits, and generally, depending on what is important to buyers, price changes arising from improved product quality affect customer buying behavior. For instance, if price is not a major factor in the buyer's analysis, a marginal increase in quality may prove more attractive.

Productivity studies tend to suggest that productivity increases improve quality, lower prices, and generally can affect society in significant ways. However, similar studies of the public sector show that there has been a lack of growth in the productivity in public services such as hospitals and public schools while, over time, the cost of providing public goods increases as a result of new technologies and better trained public service providers. Baumol's cost disease is often used to describe this lack of growth in productivity and inflation in the cost of bureaucracy. Baumol (2003) argues that because many public administration activities are heavily labor-intensive and take

place under relatively monopolistic market conditions, and because the demand for public goods is generally inelastic, there is little growth in productivity over time.

There is a widely held view that a high relative quality position (often incompatible with a low relative cost position) can be achieved through product differentiation. Product differentiation involves marketing or designing product that customers perceive as unique. Products may be differentiated along key features of the product or minor details, and at the market level, differentiation becomes the means by which the quality of goods is improved over time, mainly as a result of innovations such as introduction of new improved or better products. However, where goods presented in the market are ordered according to their objective quality so that one may be considered better than another, vertical differentiation occurs. This differentiation can be made along one definitive or decisive feature, along a few features each of which has a range of values, or across a large number of features each of which has only a presence or absence "lag." It is possible with the last two to have a product that is better than another using one set of criteria but worse than the other using a different set of criteria. Common with supplied goods, vertical differentiation, which produces perceived differences in quality by different customers, may play a key role in customer buying behavior. Though advertising can influence or bias customer perceptions of these differentiating features, what makes the big difference in comparing widely different goods fulfilling the same needs is the nature of the need fulfilled, as often is the case with necessities or luxury goods.

This model of vertical product differentiation regards buyers in competitive market situations basically as price insensitive, for customers without their own opinion or means of judging quality will often rely on price to make their calculations of quality, so the quality-price relationship is often upwardly sloped. This model has been used to study the market structures that emerge from differentiation and to demonstrate that better production has a higher price and more expected benefits for consumers. However, a neoclassical model of product differentiation has been developed to explain the probable exploitation of market situations where customers exhibit bounded rationality because they lack knowledge and information-processing capability for market choices they make so that not all highly priced goods are of high quality (Piana 2003). This neoclassical model shows that the customer, a hyper-rational agent, maximizes utility by choosing an optimal collection of things and thus exhausts his or her budget.

In contrast, when products are differentiated by minor details or features that cannot be ordered, horizontal differentiation occurs. A model of horizontal product differentiation captures consumer behavior for various versions of the market. For instance, ice cream flavors or a product with different colors or styles presents different versions of the same product. While consumers may have consistent preferences for one version or the other, it is common for a supplier of many versions of the same product to determine a unique price for all of them. Nevertheless, the rating of a product according to different measures of quality or taste depends on its physical and immaterial features. Manez and Waterson (2001) reviewed the implication of horizontal and vertical product differentiation on market structure under the assumption of single-product firms and also examined the major results of multiproduct firm models.

On the effects on product market and consumer behavior, Christou and Vettas (2003), in their study of advertising within a random-utility, nonlocalized competitive model of product differentiation, maintain that in a symmetric equilibrium, advertising is suboptional when product differentiation is small and excessive otherwise. They believe that increasing the number of firms may increase or decrease the market price. They believe that in a quasi-concavity, profits may fall because firms may prefer price deviation as they target only those customers who are informed about their product.

Differentiation by quality protects a business from competitive rivalry, for it creates customer loyalty, lowers sensitivity to price, and protects the business from other competitive forces that reduce price-cost margins (Phillips, Chang, and Buzzell 1983). Competition may exist in the context of product rivalry where differentiation is achieved by both quality and brand or from some specific product characteristics or brand. Ford and General Motors both sell lines of automobiles having specific product features such as economy compacts, luxury cars, and so forth, and within these limits both companies provide similar offers, but then customers typically remain aligned to each depending on their valuation of quality or other perceived product benefits.

In a relatively free competitive market, vertical differentiation may permit businesses to increase profits by offering products that appeal to different types of customers, though cutthroat or head-on rivalry may result if customers perceive these products as good substitutes. Where, however, the market is open but monopolistic—what is often described as a "contestable market"—transient or opportunistic firms may not worry about quality as they may move in, exploit the gains, and leave before market conditions turn sour. Quality of goods and services enables an organization to achieve excellence and engage in profitable activities. Harold Greneer of ITT once remarked that quality was their most profitable product line, whereas IBM's policy on quality has been one that seeks complete defect-free performance. In fact, IBM and ITT have in recent years invested millions of dollars on quality to reap immense benefits, which include cost reduction, increased profitability, and a reputation for excellence.

In spite of these apparent gains of quality, however, there appears to be inherent difficulties in measuring product/service quality. Quality is often perceived in relative terms and so presents the problem of determining how much good is "good," what level of satisfying is "satisfactory," or how high enough in the hierarchy of classes a product has to be before it is considered "classy." These difficulties of assessment have given rise to many companies establishing acceptable quality levels (AQLs) for their products and services, a level determined by what each company considers appropriate.

SEE ALSO *Competition, Monopolistic*

BIBLIOGRAPHY

Baumol, William J. 1986. *On Contestable Market Analysis.* The Conference Board Research Bulletin No. 195, Antitrust and New View of Microeconomics.

Baumol, William. J. 2003. Baumol's Disease: No Cure As Yet, But It Isn't Fatal. *Harvard Business Review* (July): 112–113.

Baumol, William J., and Hilda Baumol. 1985. *On the Cost Disease and Its True Policy Implications for the Arts.* In *Public Choice, Public Finance, and Public Policy,* ed. David Greenaway and G. K. Shaw, 67–77. London: Basil Blackwell.

Baumol, William J., and Alan S. Blinder. 1999. *Economics: Principles and Policy.* 8th ed. Fort Worth, TX: Dryden Press.

Cole, G. A. 1996. *Management Theory and Practice,* 5th ed. London: Continuum.

Christuo, Charalambos, and Nikolaos Vettas. 2003. Informative Advertising and Product Differentiation. Working Paper No. 3953, CEPR.

Manez, J. A., and M. Waterson. 2001. Multiproduct Firms and Product Differentiation: A Survey. The Warwick Economics Research Paper Series (TWERPS), 594, University of Warwick, Dept. of Economics.

Phillips, Lynn W., Dae R. Chang, and Robert D. Buzzell. 1983. Product Quality, Cost Position and Business Performance: A Test of Some Key Hypotheses. *Journal of Marketing* 47 (2): 26–43.

Piana, Valentino. 2003. Consumer Microdata: Incomes, Preferences, Purchase Timing. http://www.economicsewbinstitute.org/.

Robson, M. 1984. *Quality Circles in Action.* Aldershot, U.K.: Gower.

Robson, M. 1986. *Journey to Excellence.* Chichester, U.K.: John Wiley.

Triplett, Jack E., and Barry P. Bosworth. 2003. Productivity Management Issues in Services Industries: Baumol's Disease Has Been Cured. *Federal Reserve Bank of New York Economic Policy Review* (September): 23–33.

Fred Ozor

QUANTIFICATION

Quantification is the act of giving a numerical value to a measurement of something, that is, to count the quanta of whatever one is measuring. Quantification produces a standardized form of measurement that allows statistical procedures and mathematical calculations. Quantitative research methods are based on a natural science, positivist model of hypothesis testing. In the social sciences these methods attempt to collect and analyze numerical data on social phenomena, seeking to understand the links between a relatively small number of attributes across a wide variety of cases. Thus, quantification is especially useful in describing and analyzing social phenomena on a larger scale.

THE RISE OF QUANTIFICATION

During the last centuries quantification has become immensely prevalent in the social sciences. Practices of quantification have been widely used in the West since the thirteenth century, and even before that. But only in the first part of the seventeenth century did the idea that social topics may be subjected to systematic quantitative analysis begin to acquire real dominance in Europe. These tendencies grew stronger during the nineteenth century, and by the first half of the twentieth century the "quantitative paradigm" had become extremely dominant in most of the social sciences, including economics, psychology, sociology, and political sciences.

There are a few prominent explanations for this growing use of quantitative measures in western society and in the social sciences in particular. First, the growing prominence and success of the natural sciences, especially physics, drove social scientists to imitate their use of quantitative measures in the hope of acquiring similar success and precision (see for example the 2002 book *How Economics Became a Mathematical Science*, by Roy Weintraub).

A second explanation emphasizes the rise of capitalism and the rational spirit in western societies, described by sociologist Max Weber in his 1905 book *The Protestant Ethic and the Spirit of Capitalism*. Weber describes a move toward a more rational, bureaucratic, and calculative life, and the increased tendency to quantify social entities and behaviors is well explained in light of these changes. Some scholars ascribe the proliferation of quantification mainly to the rise of the modern centralized state, in which public officials face the need to efficiently manage increasing populations and large-scale social institutions. Finally, in his 1995 book *Trust in Numbers: The Pursuit of Objectivity in Science and Public Life*, Theodore Porter suggests another interesting explanation. Porter argues that the tendency toward quantification in modern society is not so much a response to the success of the natural sciences,

as it is an attempt of weak professional groups to pacify social and political pressures for greater accountability. In other words, according to Porter, the surge of quantification in the social sciences was driven mainly by the desire to create an appearance of professionalism and gain legitimacy for social research and public policies.

THE MERITS OF QUANTIFICATION

Quantification holds prominent advantages to scholars and policy makers. Its advocates believe that it increases precision and generalizability, while minimizing prejudice, favoritism, and nepotism in decision-making. According to this view, the decontextualized and value-free mathematical symbols used in statistical analyses assist in achieving objectivity, stability, and fair judgment as decisions become more businesslike. In this sense the quantification and standardization of the social life have liberating and emancipatory effects.

Quantification is also economical. Many feel that in today's world, with the inevitable avalanche of numbers that arises from the growing state apparatuses and with the fast advancing information revolution, there is simply too much information to be efficiently handled with detailed qualitative descriptions. Trying to make complicated decisions without finding a way to reduce the amount of information to be considered may be overwhelming. Quantification, therefore, serves as a necessary tool for organizing and discarding information, making the flux of data more manageable. It recognizes that people have bounded cognitive skills and can only process limited amounts of information. Quantification saves time, helps in making sense and analyzing large datasets, and facilitates large-scale research, planning, managing, and decision-making. In light of these advantages, some scholars believe that every aspect of the social world can, and in fact should be quantified. Psychologist Edward Thorndike, for example, claimed at the beginning of the twentieth century that "Anything that exists exists in a certain quantity and can be measured" (Custer 1996).

THE SHORTCOMINGS OF QUANTIFICATION

But many disagree with this approach. First, critics of quantification claim that it sacrifices the substance and authenticity of the information. Transforming social experiences into standardized numbers leads to alienation and distances many groups from these experiences. It also allows decision makers to escape accountability, as numbers and statistics become refuge from personal responsibility. In that sense, quantification is actually a way of making decisions without seeming to decide, as decisions are left to the numbers. Quantification, according to its opponents, symbolizes the takeover of the market economy over social life, eliminating values of recreation and spontaneity. Another problem is that quantification facilitates the emergence of new categories such as "the nation" or "public opinion." These terms are actually materializations of complex social actions and institutions, but in the process of quantification they turn into "things." In the process of quantification, important information is lost for the sake of simplicity and calculability. But in areas such as environmental preservation, intimate relationships, identities, rights, and religion, these attempts often distort the nature of the category and fundamental qualities disappear. At the same time, the dominance of quantification also erases existing objects and relations, making some social phenomena, which cannot be quantified, practically invisible.

Finally, critics of quantification claim that it is often extended into areas in which it does not make statistical sense. This is especially true when measuring social entities, which are often flexible and subject to revision and change. For example social scientists often criticize the quantification of categories such as race and ethnicity, claiming that these are not real and stable entities, but rather fluctuating social definitions and classifications. This problem is exemplified in population censuses, in which some categories are invented and imposed on people by state officials, even when they do not coincide with personal identities and perceptions of self. In addition the interpretation of quantitative representations of social realities, such as race, fails to place these realities in the social context of the real world. This failure, in turn, may lead to misconceptions and erroneous judgments.

Despite these problems, quantification is clearly a process that cannot be avoided. It is an important and viable component of today's social world, and there are few who would argue for returning to a prequantification world. Still, much more thought must be given to the problems of quantification and to its pitfalls. Researchers and policy makers must identify the places where it distorts the reality of social life and be much more cautious when applying it to social categories.

SEE ALSO *Alienation; Bureaucracy; Capitalism; Data; Demography; Ethnicity; Information, Asymmetric; Mathematics in the Social Sciences; Professionalization; Protestant Ethic; Race; Rationality; Science; Social Science; Social Science, Value Free; Weber, Max*

BIBLIOGRAPHY

Crosby, Alfred W. 1997. *The Measure of Reality: Quantification and Western Society 1250-1600*. Cambridge, U.K.: Cambridge University Press.

Custer, R. L. 1996. Qualitative Research Methodologies. *Journal of Industrial Teacher Education* 34(2): 3–6.

Espeland, Wendy N. 2002. Commensuration and Cognition. In *Culture in Mind: Toward a Sociology of Culture and Cognition*, ed. Karen A. Cerulo, 63–88. New York: Routledge.

Porter, Theodore M. 1995. *Trust in Numbers: The Pursuit of Objectivity in Science and Public Life*. Princeton, NJ: Princeton University Press.

Weber, Max. [1905] 2001. *The Protestant Ethic and the Spirit of Capitalism*. 3rd edition, intro. and trans. Stephen Kalberg. Los Angeles: Roxbury.

Weintraub, E. Roy. 2002. *How Economics Became a Mathematical Science*. Durham, NC: Duke University Press.

Woolf, Harry, ed. 1961. *Quantification: A History of the Meaning of Measurement in the Natural and Social Sciences*. Indianapolis, IN: Bobbs-Merrill.

Zuberi, Tukufu. 2000. Deracializing Social Statistics: Problems in the Quantification of Race. *The Annals of the American Academy* 568 (March): 172–185.

Eran Shor

QUANTITY INDEX

We begin our discussion of quantity indexes by setting up some basic notation: Let $p^0 = (p_1^0, \ldots, p_n^0)$ be a vector of prices for n goods in period 0. Let $p^1 = (p_1^1, \ldots, p_n^1)$ be a vector of prices for the same n goods in period 1. Similarly, let $q^0 = (q_1^0, \ldots, q_n^0)$ and $q^1 = (q_1^1, \ldots, q_n^1)$ represent quantity vectors for the n goods in periods 0 and 1, respectively.

Total expenditure in the two periods is the sum (across all n goods) of the prices multiplied by the corresponding quantities: $Y^0 = \sum_{i=1}^{n} p_i^0 q_i^0$ and $Y^1 = \sum_{i=1}^{n} p_i^1 q_i^1$. Thus, the ratio of total expenditures in the two periods equals Y^1/Y^0. If total expenditure is increasing from period 0 to period 1, then Y^1/Y^0 exceeds 1. If total expenditure is decreasing, then Y^1/Y^0 is less than 1. Total expenditure can increase from one period to another simply because prices are increasing. For example, suppose that the quantity vectors are identical in the two periods but the prices of all n goods increase from period 0 to period 1; then total expenditure will also increase.

Quantity indexes can be used to remove the effects of price changes in order to facilitate comparison of expenditures in different time periods. We will use the notation Q_{01} to denote a *quantity index* between periods 0 and 1. If the quantity index exceeds 1, then it means that expenditure is increasing from period 0 to period 1 after the effects of price changes have been removed. Similarly, if it is less than 1, then it means that expenditure is decreasing after the effects of price changes have been removed. In the context of national income accounting, quantity indexes can best be thought of as measuring changes in *real* or *inflation-adjusted* expenditure; see "How Do I Use Chain-Type Indexes (or Chained Dollar) Measures of Economic Activity, Such as Real GDP?" under FAQs at http://www.bea.gov/index.htm.

A simple and easy-to-interpret way to remove the effects of price changes and, therefore, to calculate a quantity index would be to compare the cost of the quantity vectors in the two periods using a common set of prices. The *Laspeyres quantity index*, for example, uses the prices from period 0 and is defined as follows: $Q_{01}^L = \dfrac{\sum_i p_i^0 q_i^1}{\sum_i p_i^0 q_i^0}$.

If Q_{01}^L exceeds 1, then it means that the period 1 quantity vector costs more than the period 0 quantity vector in period 0 prices. Similarly, if Q_{01}^L is less than 1, then it means that the period 1 quantity vector costs less than the period 0 quantity vector in period 0 prices.

The *Paasche quantity index* is analogous to the Laspeyres quantity index, but with the period 1 prices replacing the period 0 prices. The resulting index is defined as follows: $Q_{01}^P = \dfrac{\sum_i p_i^1 q_i^1}{\sum_i p_i^1 q_i^0}$. If the quantity vectors are identical in the two periods, then both Q_{01}^L and Q_{01}^P will equal 1 even though Y^1/Y^0 may well differ from 1.

Later, we will develop the concept of superlative quantity indexes, which are preferable to these simple quantity indexes.

PRICE INDEXES, QUANTITY INDEXES, AND THE WEAK FACTOR REVERSAL TEST

Price and quantity indexes are closely related concepts. A *price index*, P_{01}, is a function of the price and quantity vectors in periods 0 and 1, which measures the change in the prices of the *n* goods between the two periods. If it is greater than 1, it means that prices increased from period 0 to 1. If it is less than 1, it means that prices decreased.

A price index and a quantity index satisfy the *weak factor reversal test* if the following equation holds: $P_{01} Q_{01} = Y^1/Y^0$. Weak factor reversal can be used to formalize our interpretation of quantity indexes as removing the effects of price changes in order to facilitate comparison of total expenditure in two different time periods.

Assume, just for simplicity, that both total expenditure and prices are increasing between the two periods, so that $Y^1/Y^0 > 1$ and $P_{01} > 1$. If the percentage increase in prices, implied by the price index, is exactly the same as the percentage increase in total expenditure, then $P_{01} = Y^1/Y^0$ and, consequently, the quantity index will equal 1. If the percentage increase in prices exceeds the percen-

tage increase in total expenditure, then $P_{01} > Y^1/Y^0$, implying that the quantity index will be less than 1. Conversely, if the percentage increase in total expenditure exceeds the percentage increase in prices, then $Y^1/Y^0 > P_{01}$, implying that the quantity index will exceed 1.

COST OF LIVING, STANDARD OF LIVING, AND SUPERLATIVE INDEXES

Triplett discusses the connection between price and quantity indexes for a set of consumer goods and services and the concept of a cost-of-living index:

> A consumption price index should measure the change in the cost of maintaining a fixed, or constant, standard of living. If the price index holds the standard of living constant, then any increase in per capita consumption expenditures that exceeds the increase in the price index can be interpreted as an increase in the standard of living…. Thus, from the standard-of-living orientation, the price index measures the changing cost of a constant standard of living, and the quantity index measures increases or decreases in the standard of living. (1992, p. 49)

Diewert (1976) provided a strong rationale for preferring certain price and quantity indexes, which he termed *superlative*. Without focusing on technicalities, a price index is superlative essentially if it provides a good approximation to the changing cost of a constant standard of living using only the observed price and quantity data. A more extensive discussion of the concept of a cost-of-living index and its connection to superlative price indexes can be found in the entry Price Indices.

A pair of price and quantity indexes is said to be a *superlative pair* if one of them is a superlative index and the other is defined implicitly by the weak factor reversal test. Thus, for our purposes, it will suffice to interpret a superlative quantity index as one that satisfies the weak factor reversal test in conjunction with a superlative price index (we note, however, that superlative quantity indexes can be defined independently of superlative price indexes without reference to weak factor reversal; see Diewert 1976). In practical terms, following Triplett, this means that superlative quantity indexes can be interpreted as measuring increases or decreases in the standard of living. For an authoritative survey of index number theory, including superlative indexes, see Diewert (1981).

The Laspeyres and Paasche quantity indexes, discussed previously, are not superlative. There are, however, many price and quantity indexes that are known to be superlative. Among these, indexes based on Fisher's ideal formula have been widely used. *Fisher's ideal price index* is defined as $P_{01}^{FI} = \sqrt{\dfrac{\sum_i p_i^1 q_i^0}{\sum_i p_i^0 q_i^0} \dfrac{\sum_i p_i^1 q_i^1}{\sum_i p_i^0 q_i^1}}$.

The corresponding quantity index is defined as $Q_{01}^{FI} = \sqrt{\dfrac{\sum_i p_i^1 q_i^1}{\sum_i p_i^1 q_i^0} \dfrac{\sum_i p_i^0 q_i^1}{\sum_i p_i^0 q_i^0}}$, which is the geometric mean of the Laspeyres and Paasche quantity indexes. Together, these two indexes satisfy the weak factor reversal test, since

$$P_{01}^{FI} Q_{01}^{FI} = \frac{\sum_i p_i^1 q_i^1}{\sum_i p_i^0 q_i^0} = \frac{Y^1}{Y^0}.$$ Diewert (1976) proved that Fisher's ideal quantity and price indexes are both superlative and, in view of the weak factor reversal test, together they constitute a superlative pair.

In the same paper, Diewert also proves that the Tornqvist-Theil quantity index is superlative. The *Tornqvist-Theil quantity index*, Q_{01}^{TT}, is defined as

$$Q_{01}^{TT} = \prod_{i=1}^{n} \left(q_i^1 / q_i^0 \right)^{\frac{1}{2}(w_i^0 + w_i^1)},$$ where $w_i^0 = p_i^0 q_i^0 / Y^0$ and $w_i^1 = p_i^1 q_i^1 / Y^1$ are the expenditure shares for good i for periods 0 and 1 respectively. A corresponding implicit price index can be obtained for this index using the weak factor reversal test.

CHAIN-WEIGHTING

Suppose that we have price and quantity data for many periods denoted by p_t and q_t, where $t = 0, 1, \dots, T$ (for example, suppose we have annual data for twenty years). This allows us to compute quantity indexes from each period to the successive one, $Q_{t-1, t}$, for all t. We can produce a time series covering more than two periods using the concept of *chain-weighting*. A chain-weighted time series can be constructed as follows: The value of the series, I_t, for any period t is the previous value of the series, I_{t-1}, multiplied by the corresponding quantity index for the two periods, so that $I_t = I_{t-1} Q_{t-1, t}$ for all t (see Bureau of Economic Analysis 2006, Appendix 1). Thus, the growth rate of a chain-weighted index between adjacent periods is $(I_t - I_{t-1})/I_{t-1} = Q_{t-1, t} - 1$.

FROM THEORY TO PRACTICE

National statistical agencies, such as the Bureau of Economic Analysis (BEA), use chain-type quantity indexes to estimate changes in real or inflation-adjusted gross domestic product (GDP) and its components, which can be used when making comparisons over time. BEA (2006) discusses the background and history of the national income and product accounts (NIPAs) for the United States.

As noted by BEA (2006, p. 2), "in 1996, BEA introduced several major improvements to the NIPAs. BEA began estimating the changes in real GDP and its components by chaining together year-by-year quantity changes that were calculated using the Fisher index formula, rather than estimating real GDP on the basis of prices of a single, arbitrary base year." The previous method tended to cause an understatement of real GDP growth for periods prior to the reference year and an overstatement of real GDP growth for periods after the reference year, which is called *substitution bias* in real GDP growth. These and other problems are eliminated by the use of Fisher's ideal formula (see BEA 2006, p. 15).

Quantity indexes are useful in other contexts as well. For example, the Federal Reserve Bank of Saint Louis and the Bank of England both produce chain-weighted monetary aggregates based on the Tornqvist-Theil quantity index formula; see Anderson, Jones, and Nesmith (1997) and Hancock (2005), respectively. The Federal Reserve Bank of Saint Louis refers to its superlative monetary aggregates as *monetary services indexes*, while the Bank of England refers to its as *Divisia money*. Monetary aggregates include many different types of components—for example, currency, checking accounts, savings deposits, money market mutual funds, time deposits, and the like—which vary in terms of their usefulness for making transactions. As argued by Hancock (2005), Divisia money is a gauge of the money supply that gives the greatest weight to the components of the aggregate that are most used in transactions.

EMPIRICAL ILLUSTRATION

As noted above, the BEA estimates changes in real GDP and its components for the United States by employing chain-type quantity indexes based on Fisher's ideal formula. In this section, we show how real GDP growth is related to the U.S. business cycle to illustrate the use of quantity indexes.

We obtained the chain-type quantity index for real GDP from BEA and calculated its annualized quarterly growth rate from 1947 to 2006. As identified by the National Bureau of Economic Research (NBER) (see http://www.nber.org/cyclcs.html) there were ten recessions over the period from 1947 to 2006. These recessions are strongly associated with negative real GDP growth, whereas real GDP growth is usually, although not always, positive when the United States is not in a recession. Annualized quarterly real GDP growth averaged 3.4 percent over the entire period from 1947 to 2006. By comparison, averaging over just the recessionary quarters (peak to trough inclusive) yields average annualized quarterly real GDP growth of −1.2 percent.

As noted by the Business Cycle Dating Committee of the NBER (2001), the financial press often defines a recession as two consecutive quarters of decline in real GDP. While this is true of most of the recessions identified by NBER, it is not true of all of them.

SEE ALSO *Business Cycles, Real; Divisia Monetary Index; Economic Growth; Fisher, Irving; Price Indices; Recession*

BIBLIOGRAPHY

Anderson, R. G., B. E. Jones, and T. D. Nesmith. 1997. Building New Monetary Services Indexes: Concepts, Data, and Methods. Federal Reserve Bank of Saint Louis *Review* 79 (1): 53–82.

Bureau of Economic Analysis. 2006. *A Guide to the National Income and Product Accounts of the United States.* Available from http://bea.gov/bea/mp.htm.

Bureau of Economic Analysis. How Do I Use Chain-Type Indexes (or Chained Dollar) Measures of Economic Activity, Such as Real GDP? Frequently Asked Questions (FAQs). http://www.bea.gov/index.htm.

Business Cycle Dating Committee, National Bureau of Economic Research. 2001. The Business-Cycle Peak of March 2001. November 26. http://www.nber.org/cycles/november2001/.

Diewert, W. E. 1976. Exact and Superlative Index Numbers. *Journal of Econometrics* 4 (2): 115–145.

Diewert, W. E. 1981. The Economic Theory of Index Numbers: A Survey. In *Essays in the Theory and Measurement of Consumer Behaviour in Honour of Sir Richard Stone*, ed. A. Deaton, 163–208. London: Cambridge University Press.

Hancock, M. 2005. Divisia Money. Bank of England *Quarterly Bulletin* (spring): 39–46.

National Bureau of Economic Research. Business Cycle Expansions and Contractions. http://www.nber.org/cycles.html/.

Triplett, J. E. 1992. Economic Theory and the BEA's Alternative Quantity and Price Indexes. *Survey of Current Business* 72: 49–52.

Barry Jones

QUANTITY THEORY OF MONEY

The quantity theory of money (QTM) refers to the proposition that changes in the quantity of money lead to, other factors remaining constant, approximately equal changes in the price level. Usually, the QTM is written as $MV = PY$, where M is the supply of money; V is the velocity of the circulation of money, that is, the average number of transactions that a unit of money performs within a specified interval of time; P is the price level; and Y is the final output. The quantity theory is derived from an accounting identity according to which the total expenditures in the economy (MV) are identical to total receipts from the sale of final goods and services (PY). This identity is transformed into a behavioral relation once V and Y are assumed as given or known variables.

The QTM dates back to sixteenth-century Europe where it was developed as a response to the influx of precious metals from the New World, and in this sense it is one of the oldest theories in economics. Nevertheless, only in the writings of the late mercantilists does one start to find theoretical statements that justify the connection between M and P. David Hume (1711–1776) argued that assuming a case of equilibrium, an expansion in M (for example, through the discovery of new gold mines) would make a group of entrepreneurs richer, and their rising demand would increase the prices of products, thereby increasing the income of another group of entrepreneurs whose demand would increase the price level even further, and so forth. These chain effects at some point die out, and their end result would be the restoration of equilibrium, albeit at a higher price level. Hume and the mercantilists did not back up their claims by developing a theory of value and distribution; for them, the QTM was explained either mechanically or through the operation of competition.

In contrast to Hume, for classical economists the QTM became a constituent component of their theory of value and distribution. Invoking Say's Law of markets, according to which output can be taken as given, and assuming that V is also given for it is determined by the customs of payments and the institutional arrangements of society, it then follows that proportional changes in M will be reflected in P and vice versa. David Ricardo (1772–1823) in particular reversed the usual causal relationship of the QTM arguing that changes in P lead to changes in M and not the other way around. The idea is that the value of gold (money) is a kind of a *numéraire* for all other prices, which means that if the quantity of money becomes more abundant because of the rise in productivity of gold mines (because of the discovery of new gold mines or technological change), it follows that the price of gold falls and, therefore, the prices of all other commodities rise. Alternatively, if total output increases, the subsequent scarcity of money raises its price above the normal level, and the excess profits in gold production lead to the expansion of supply, thereby reducing the price of gold, which returns to its normal level, and equilibrium is restored at a higher price level. Thus, the normal price of gold is what actually determines the quantity of money in circulation. Consequently, the difference between Ricardo and the mercantilists is that the arrow of causality runs from P to M and, therefore, the quantity of money is endogenously determined—that is, it is determined within the economic system.

The quantity theory continued in the writings of the neoclassical economists, with the issue of exogeneity predominant in the work of Irving Fisher (1867–1947). The so-called Fisher's equation of exchange (1911) can be stated as follows: $MV + M'V' = PT$, where M is currency and M' is demand deposits; V and V' are the respective velocities; and T stands for total volume of transactions and not only of final goods. Another interesting development is that associated with Knut Wicksell (1851–1926), who stressed the endogenous character of the money supply, which is responsible for the variations in the price level. The advent of Keynesian economics in the 1930s rendered the QTM of minor importance, and it was used only for the determination of nominal magnitudes of real variables.

According to Keynesian analysis the quantity of money could not affect the real economy in any direct way but only indirectly through variations in the interest rate. In contrast, a characteristically different view has been expressed by economists at the University of Chicago. More specifically, Milton Friedman (1912–2006) claimed that money matters and is responsible for almost every economic phenomenon. In fact, Friedman argued that the major economic episodes in U.S. economic history—from the Great Depression of the 1930s to the inflation of 1970s—could be explained through variations in money supply. During the mid- to late 1960s the appearance of stagflation and the rejection of the usual Phillips curve were registered as a blow against Keynesian economics and facilitated the acceptance of monetarism and its establishment as a school of economic thought with significant appeal. Friedman not only showed the inadequacy of Keynesian economics to deal with stagflation but he also proposed an explanation based on the concept of the natural rate of unemployment—that an expansionary economic policy affects the economy only in the short run, while in the long run the economy returns to the natural rate of unemployment but this time with higher inflation.

Friedman and the monetarists express the QTM in terms of growth rates, which means that they consider as a given, in the beginning at least, the velocity of money circulation, and thus that the growth rate of money supply influences the growth rate of nominal output identified with the nominal gross domestic product (GDP), that is, the product of the real GDP times the general price level. Later, when Friedman introduced the notion of natural unemployment, it could be argued that in the long run, at least, the real GDP is equal to full employment GDP, which corresponds to the level of natural unemployment, and thus the growth rate of GDP is known in the long run. Consequently, in the long run the growth rate of the money supply—to the extent that it exceeds the growth rate of the real GDP—increases the growth rate of the price level, that is, the rate of inflation.

According to Keynesians the velocity of money is characterized by high volatility; consequently, changes in the supply of money can be absorbed by changes in the velocity of money with negligible effects either on output or on the price level. These arguments emphasize that the velocity of money depends on consumer and business spending impulses, which cannot be constant. A similar view is shared by economists of the neoclassical synthesis, especially in the case in which the economy is in the liquidity trap, whereby, regardless of the changes in the supply of money, the real economy is not affected at all. Changes in the supply of money are absorbed by corresponding changes in the velocity of money. Furthermore, the effect of money supply on prices may work indirectly through variations in interest rates, which in turn induce effects on aggregate demand.

The empirical evidence with respect to the effects of the money supply on the price level so far has been mixed and depends on the definitions of the money supply (narrow or broad) and the time period. As a consequence, the velocity of the narrow money supply, $V1 = GDP/M1$, for the U.S. economy has displayed a rising trend during the period 1920–1929, a falling trend during the period 1929–1946, an upward trend in the period 1947–1981, erratic behavior along a falling trend during the period 1981–1991, and an upward trend since then. The erratic behavior of the 1980s has been attributed to the deregulation of the banking industry and the appearance of new checkable accounts. Clearly, the overall movement of $V1$ is associated with the long-run upward or downward stage of the economy. The results with respect to the U.S. data prove somewhat better for the monetarist argument with regard to the velocity $V2 = GDP/M2$. A closer look at $V1$ or $V2$ in monthly or quarterly data reveals substantial fluctuations in the short run. The variability of the velocity of circulation has been attributed, among other things, to the frequency of payments, the efficiency of the banking system, the interest rate, and the expected inflation rate. From the above it follows that the causal relationship between money supply and price level—that is, the issue of exogeneity versus endogeneity—is not settled yet and, therefore, continues to attract the attention of economists. There is no doubt that the discussion will continue in the future as economists try to understand better the interrelations of monetary and real economic variables.

SEE ALSO *Economics, Keynesian; Fisher, Irving;*
  Friedman, Milton; Hume, David; Interest Rates;
  Keynes, John Maynard; Mercantilism; Monetarism;
  Monetary Theory; Money; Money, Demand for;

Neutrality of Money; Phillips Curve; Ricardo, David; Say's Law

BIBLIOGRAPHY

Fisher, Irving. 1911. *The Purchasing Power of Money: Its Determination and Relation to Credit, Interest, and Crises.* New York: Macmillan.

Friedman, Milton, and Anna Jacobson Schwartz. 1963. *A Monetary History of the United States, 1867–1960.* Princeton, NJ: Princeton University Press.

Green, Roy. 1982. *Classical Theories of Money, Output, and Inflation.* New York: St. Martin's.

Lefteris Tsoulfidis

QUASI-EXPERIMENTATION

SEE *Campbell, Donald.*

QUEBECOIS MOVEMENT

The Quebecois movement of the late twentieth century was the product of long-standing strained relations between the francophone (or French Canadian) and anglophone (or English Canadian) populations of Canada. From these deep historical roots, the Quebecois movement grew into an important force shaping Canada's current social, political, and economic conditions. Although the movement has at times sought sovereignty for Quebec, recent developments suggest that such an outcome is highly unlikely.

Tensions between anglo- and francophone settlers in colonial North America mirrored those among the imperial powers of the period but took on their own character. For example, French settlers interacted more easily with Native Americans than did the British, and this relationship both affected and reflected the balance of power each European group perceived in eighteenth-century North America. In fact, the war known variously as the French and Indian War (in the United States), the Seven Years War (in Europe and English Canada), or the War of Conquest (in French Canada) had been raging in North America for two years before European powers actually declared war on one another in 1756. One decisive element of that war was the rapid and thorough defeat of French forces by the English at the Plains of Abraham, upstream from Quebec City, on September 13, 1759. That defeat led to the withdrawal of French imperial gov-

ernance from Canada and set the stage for British domination. While the British did make some conciliatory gestures toward French Canadians, notably in the 1774 Quebec Act, cultural and economic competition and hostility between English and French Canadians continued unabated. In a report to the British government, Lord Durham, the governor general of British North America from 1837 to 1838, famously described the two groups as "two nations warring in the bosom of a single state." As a remedy, he suggested aggressive assimilation of French Canadians into the British system.

French Canadians balked at being anglicized and resisted repressive moves by English Canadians, such as abolition of bilingual and Catholic schools in New Brunswick and Manitoba, respectively, in the 1870s. By this time, Canada was independent from Britain, and French Canadians soon found themselves united in opposition to Ottawa's alignment with British military policy. The 1899 Boer War was particularly odious to French Canadians, who regarded it as simple British imperialism, a phenomenon they themselves had experienced as oppressive. In this political climate, French Canadians continued to experience everyday humiliations and bigotry at the hands of English Canadians, who generally regarded them as inferiors.

TWENTIETH-CENTURY DEVELOPMENTS

At the turn of the twentieth century, Prime Minister Wilfred Laurier emphasized that the Canadian confederation had been founded on the concept of "two nations." The obvious domination of one nation by the other was antithetical to the logic of confederation. When the Great Depression struck, French Canadians were much harder hit than their English counterparts, giving painful evidence of the terrible economic disadvantage under which the Quebecois labored. Crises over conscription in both world wars showed the depth of French Canadian distrust of Canadian military policy. For example, a 1942 plebiscite showed that nearly 80 percent of English Canadians supported entering World War II, while the same margin of French Canadians opposed doing so.

Arguably, the contemporary Quebecois movement began in the 1960s with the Quiet Revolution. This was a trend in French Canadian politics toward more aggressive political demands for special status within Canada and a new emphasis on the Quebec provincial government as the instrument of change. The Liberal provincial government of Jean Lesage began the process in 1960 under the slogan "*Maîtres chez nous*" ("Masters of our own house"), demanding that Ottawa recognize Quebec as having a "special status" that afforded the province economic and social powers unique in Canada. At the national level, the

Liberal Party under Prime Minister Lester Pearson responded to these developments in part by recruiting more French Canadians, including Pierre Elliott Trudeau, who would later serve as prime minister and be an important figure in Anglo–French relations. Trudeau entered federal politics in 1965, believing that neither Quebec separatism nor a special status for the Quebecois was in the best interest of Canada. He swiftly rose through the ranks of power, succeeded Pearson as leader of the Liberal Party, and in 1968 became prime minister. In the same year, several provincial parties advocating varying degrees of Quebecois separation from the rest of Canada joined forces to create the Parti Québécois (PQ, or *Péquistes*), under the forceful and charismatic leadership of René Lévesque. The *Péquistes* advocated a plan of sovereignty-association, in which Quebec would be politically independent from, but economically linked to, the rest of Canada.

Quebec's 1970 provincial elections were a watershed, passionately debated and anxiously watched throughout Canada. If Lévesque and the *Péquistes* gained control of the provincial legislature, separation seemed sure to follow. In fact, the provincial Liberals, led by Robert Bourassa, won handily, and the *Péquistes* took only 7 of 108 seats. Sparked by this loss, the terrorist Front de Libération du Québec (FLQ) kidnapped James Cross, Britain's trade commissioner in Montreal, and Pierre Laporte, a cabinet minister of the Quebec government. In exchange for the hostages, the FLQ demanded funds, the release of FLQ-sympathizing prisoners (whom Trudeau referred to publicly as "bandits"), and promulgation of their manifesto. This became known as the October Crisis. Trudeau's government responded by passing the War Measures Act, which gave police and government extra leeway to use force domestically and led to the unusual circumstance of tanks and armed soldiers in Canadian streets. When asked by a reporter how far he would go to defend his position, Trudeau famously responded, "Just watch me." While the majority of Canadians did not sympathize with the FLQ, the War Measures Act was highly controversial. The crisis ended when Cross was freed, Laporte was killed, some kidnappers were given safe passage to Cuba, and others were captured. Nonetheless, a significant minority of French Canadians sympathized with at least some of the FLQ's position, and the federal government still had to address Quebec's concerns.

In 1974 and 1976, Quebec's provincial legislature passed two laws—Bill 22 and Bill 101 (the latter also known as the Charter of the French Language)—declaring French the province's official language, mandating French-language schools for immigrants, and requiring the use of French in the workplace. These laws were generally well received by francophone residents of Quebec but were highly controversial among English-speaking and other Quebeckers and in Canada as a whole.

Trudeau's Liberal government was reelected in 1980, and the prime minister set a high priority on patriating the Canadian Constitution. Canada had been created in 1867 by the British North America Act, an act of the British Parliament. Arguably, then, Canada existed only with another state's permission. A true sovereign declares its own sovereignty, and Trudeau believed Canadians' own sense of nationality hinged on this distinction. For these and other reasons, Trudeau's government wished to change Canada's founding document from an act of the British Parliament to an act of the Canadian Parliament. The process of shifting from the British North America Act to a truly Canadian document was known as patriation of the Constitution.

Trudeau's government had reason to hope Quebec would not be a stumbling block in this process. Also in 1980, the Parti Québécois introduced a provincial referendum asking for a mandate to negotiate a new relationship between Quebec and the rest of Canada; the referendum failed. The Liberals' optimism must have vanished quickly, however, since the following year the Parti Québécois was reelected with substantially increased support. The referendum was not a clear indicator of the complex situation in Quebec. Ultimately, the federal government formulated a new Constitution (in the Constitution Act of 1982), with a Charter of Rights and Freedoms to address some of the human-rights concerns of, among others, French Canadians. The Constitution Act, which represented compromise by the national government as well as the provinces, was accepted by Ottawa and every provincial government except Quebec's.

In 1984, the Liberals lost control of Parliament to the Conservatives. Brian Mulroney, the new prime minister, made a priority of resolving constitutional tensions with Quebec and met with Robert Bourassa at Meech Lake, Ontario, in 1987. As a result of the Meech Lake conference, the national government agreed to propose constitutional changes recognizing Quebec as a "distinct society" within Canada; stating that the coexistence of French and English speakers is fundamental to Canadian society; and affording Quebec a role in choosing supreme court justices, making immigration policy, and vetoing constitutional amendments. Bourassa was satisfied with the Meech Lake Accord, but the agreement rankled some nonfrancophone Canadians by seemingly giving the Quebecois a privileged position ahead of other groups, such as aboriginals and women. Although Ottawa and eight provincial governments approved of the accord, holdouts in Manitoba and Newfoundland succeeded in killing the agreement in 1990.

The Quebec government announced another referendum on sovereignty for 1992. In hope of preempting separation, the national government proposed a new conference, this time at Charlottetown, Prince Edward Island, to work on constitutional issues. Ottawa hoped to reconcile Quebec's demands with those of aboriginal groups, social groups protected under the charter, and various economic demands of the provinces. This proved a monumental task, and the result pleased few parties. Ultimately, only four provinces approved the Charlottetown Accord, while six (including Quebec) rejected it.

In 1995, the Quebec government held its second referendum (the first being in 1980) on separation. The margin of victory was almost the smallest imaginable: 49.4 percent favoring sovereignty for Quebec, 50.6 percent opposing. The run-up to this vote spurred passionate discussion across Canada about what it means to be Canadian, and the reporting of election returns was both politically and emotionally fraught. In 1998, charismatic politician Lucien Bouchard of the Bloc Québécois (a political party with candidates at the national level, whereas the Parti Québécois stands candidates only at the provincial level) began calling for the people of Quebec to consider asking Ottawa for a new deal. The national government responded by requesting an opinion from the Supreme Court of Canada on the domestic and international legality of Quebec's secession. In 2000, the Court ruled that Quebec could not unilaterally secede from Canada and that the conditions facing Quebec did not constitute persecution under international law. However, a "clear expression of a clear majority of Quebeckers" for sovereignty would require a serious response from the national government or else would call into question the democratic legitimacy of the Canadian government. Since the Court's ruling, separation seems unlikely, although the Bloc and Parti Québécois remain important voices in Canadian politics.

SEE ALSO *Assimilation; Ethnocentrism; Identity; Minorities; Nationalism and Nationality; Parliaments and Parliamentary Systems; Partition; Secession; Separatism; Sovereignty; Terrorism*

BIBLIOGRAPHY

Bothwell, Robert. 1998. *Canada and Québec: One Country, Two Histories*, rev. ed. Vancouver, Canada: UBC Press.

Gougeon, Gilles. 1994. *A History of Québec Nationalism*. Trans. Louisa Blair, Robert Chodos, and Jane Ubertino. Toronto: James Lorimer.

Saywell, John. 1999. *Canada: Pathways to the Present*. Rev. ed. Toronto: Stoddart.

Thorburn, Hugh G., and Alan Whitehorn, eds. 2001. *Party Politics in Canada*. 8th ed. Toronto: Pearson/Prentice Hall.

Lisa L. Ferrari

QUEER STUDIES

Formed out of scholarly conferences in the 1980s, queer studies started as an elite academic movement of primarily humanities scholars who had taken a lead in developing lesbian and gay social constructionist studies in the 1980s (Fuss 1991). Social science scholars were largely absent from its beginning intellectual formations (see, for example, Fuss 1991; Abelove et al. 1993; Warner 1993).

Correcting for this absence, two important edited readers stand out in foregrounding a queer perspective for the social sciences and, conversely, a more social standpoint for queer studies. The first is *Queer Theory/Sociology* (1996). In his introduction to the volume, Seidman argues that queer theory wants to shift the study of sexuality "from explaining the modern homosexual to questions of the operation of the hetero/homosexual binary, from an exclusive preoccupation with homosexuality to a focus on heterosexuality as a social and political organizing principle, and from a politics of minority interest to a politics of knowledge and difference" (1996, p. 9). While this volume importantly situates the development of sexuality studies within earlier British sociological work on homosexuality (e.g., McIntosh 1996; Plummer 1996; Weeks 1996), its intersectional queer/sociology focus provides empirical studies that illustrate the postmodern critique of identity as multiple, exclusionary, and performative.

As Steven Epstein (1996) and Arlene Stein and Ken Plummer (1996) noted, earlier sociological work on sexuality as socially constructed was problematically absent from the new onslaught of queer studies scholarship. Instead, queer studies theoretically centered Michel Foucault's work (1978) and those of his followers, particularly Judith Butler (1990, 1993) and Eve Sedgwick (1990, 1993), making them the triumvirate benchmarks in the field. Setting the bar for analytical virtuosity, Sedgwick's statement in *Epistemology of the Closet* (1990) triumphs the need to make sexuality and the hetero/homo binary part of every analytical study of modern Western culture. Later historical studies, such as George Chauncey's (1994), date the rise of the closet to the 1930s and its intensification during the cold war, when state-sanctioned homosexual discrimination became patterned and systematic. Similarly, Seidman's (2002) sociological genealogy of the closet's rise and fall over the last half century empirically concretizes the closet's social shifts and changes. Interestingly, the theoretical acumen of Butler's work, and its ironically enabling programmatic framework, on identities as performative, specifically in their striving to perform idealized versions of heteronormative and gender-normative forms, serves as a theoretical cradle for empirical studies on intersectional identities of sexuality, gender, race, and class (e.g., Stein 1997; Esterberg 1997; Bettie 2002; Salzinger 2003).

Social Perspectives in Lesbian and Gay Studies (1998), edited by Peter Nardi and Beth Schneider, is the other key reader in sociology that highlights a queer perspective as the latest word in conceptualizing sexualities. However, in his afterword to the volume, Plummer (1998) notes the limitations of what he calls the "Foucauldian deluge" on sociology and is critical of its overemphasis on discourses and texts to the detriment of empirical social research more broadly (see Green [2002] for a similar critique of queer theory).

Contradictorily, since the mid-1990s, queer studies and the sociology of sexualities have converged in their analytical focuses while continuing to remain apart in their conversations and debates (see, for example, David Eng et al. [2005] on queer studies in a double issue of the journal *Social Text* and Joshua Gamson and Dawne Moon [2004] in their review of queer studies and its status in the sociology of sexualities). The fields converge, however, in their Foucauldian conceptualization of power as disciplinary, exclusionary, and normalizing, as well as in their studying of identities, institutions, and relations of state, nation, and globe. Still, queer studies' latest voices remain scholars from primarily the humanities (see Eng et al. 2005). And the sociology of sexualities, although drawing strongly on queer studies, remains distant from its emphasis on discourse/text, its poststructural antinormative theoretical presuppositions that typically eschew identity altogether, and its use of antihumanist language to problematize identity categories and the written text itself (see Butler's [1995] and Fraser's [1995] exchange as exemplars of these issues).

These contradictions notwithstanding, queer studies and the sociology of sexualities come together in their analysis of identities, from their gender and sexual interaction to the problematizing of heterosexual identities to the analyzing of the multiple ways race, class, and gender, in addition to sexuality, interact, and finally to the very limit of identity itself. Additionally, the two fields have made the relationships between processes of sexualities and nationalism, colonialism, and globalization key trends as well. This entry will briefly review some of these convergences in detail.

In rethinking sexual and gender-identity formations, Judith Halberstam's (1998) and R. W. Connell's (1987, 1995) works on female masculinity and hegemonic masculinity, respectively, help queer studies scholars to rethink conceptions of dominance and resistance. Female masculinity, for Halberstam, extends the concept of masculinity beyond men to include women, and views masculinity as a general form of gender expression and practice that lesbians, butch lesbians, butch women, as well as nonlesbian females, draw on to project authority, strength, and aggression in social life. Conceptualizing the intersection of compulsory heterosexuality and male dominance, Connell's concept of hegemonic masculinity links heterosexual male practices of homophobia and sexism to the subordination of femininities and dominated masculinities.

Building on the work of Monique Wittig (1992), Adrienne Rich (1980), and Connell, queer studies continues to make compulsory heterosexuality and heterosexual identities problematic and in need of social explanation. From Jonathan Katz's (1996) historical overview of the development of heterosexuality as an ideology and an identity over the nineteenth and twentieth centuries to Chyrs Ingraham's (1996, 1999) concept of the heterosexual imaginary and its ideological role in white weddings or Elizabeth Freeman's (2002) work on marriage, weddings, and heterosexualities, queer studies continues to attempt to undo compulsory heterosexuality's hegemony.

As Gamson and Moon note, "Long before queer theory began speaking of 'multiple identities,' black feminists had articulated an intersectional analysis of oppression that recognized race, gender, class, and sexual oppression as interlocking systems" (2004, p. 52). Since the early 1980s, scholarship on intersectionality has proliferated in the field. Stein's (1997) study of generational differences between two cohorts of lesbians makes age, history, and social conditions central aspects in explaining differences among lesbians who came out in the 1970s in comparison to the 1990s. Analyzing the racial, gender, class, and sexual intersections of mostly queer people of color on talk shows, Gamson's (1998) study demonstrates struggles over queer visibility and media representation. Furthermore, from humanities scholars like Tavia Nyong'o (2005), whose work illustrates the exclusions but also social necessities of intersectional identities like the pejorative *punk*, and intersectional sociologists like Roderick Ferguson (2004), who approaches the social through combining social theory, sociology, and literature, to Chet Meeks (2001), who theorizes the limits of sexual identity and liberation and develops a politics of antinormalization to underscore sexual differences beyond identity, scholarship on intersectionality demonstrates the hybrid importance of this research in queer studies.

The last key trend in queer studies is scholarship on nationalism, colonialism, and globalization and its relation to sexual practices. Important work by Joyti Puri

(1999) shows the continuities and discontinuities in transnational discourses of menstruation, marriage, pornography, and homosexuality for Indian women today. Focusing on the relationship between sexual and colonial practices, Ann Laura Stoler's (2002) study of Dutch colonial rule in nineteenth- and twentieth-century Indonesia demonstrates the way colonial practices organized sexuality, intimacy, and family in shaping the relationships between Dutch men and the native Indonesian women they had sex with and made "concubines." Finally, Chandan Reddy (2005) details the uses and abuses of gay Pakistani asylum seekers in the U.S. policy of "family reunification," which simultaneously makes asylees part of a class of low-wage workers in the United States.

In short, queer studies' focus on identity and its multifarious constructions, as well as its engagement with scholarship on nationalism, colonialism, and globalization, illustrates the field's intellectual efflorescence, contemporary relevance, and vanguardism.

SEE ALSO *Foucault, Michel; Gender; Gender, Alternatives to Binary; Gender Studies; Heteronormativity; Identity; Other, The; Said, Edward; Sexual Orientation, Determinants of; Sexual Orientation, Social and Economic Consequences; Sexuality*

BIBLIOGRAPHY

Abelove, Henry, Michèle Barale, and David Halperin. 1993. *The Lesbian and Gay Studies Reader*. New York: Routledge.

Bettie, Julie. 2003. *Women without Class: Girls, Race, and Identity*. Berkeley: University of California Press.

Butler, Judith. 1990. *Gender Trouble: Feminism and the Subversion of Identity*. New York: Routledge.

Butler, Judith. 1993. *Bodies that Matter: On the Discursive Limits of "Sex."* New York: Routledge.

Butler, Judith. 1995. Contingent Foundations. In *Feminist Contentions: A Philosophical Exchange*, 35–58. New York: Routledge.

Chauncey, George. 1994. *Gay New York: Gender, Urban Culture, and the Making of the Gay Male World, 1890–1940*. New York: Basic Books.

Chodorow, Nancy. 1976. Oedipal Asymmetries and Heterosexual Knots. *Social Problems* 23 (4): 454–468.

Chodorow, Nancy. 1978. *The Reproduction of Mothering: Psychoanalysis and the Sociology of Gender*. Berkeley: University of California Press.

Chodorow, Nancy. 1994. *Femininities, Masculinities, Sexualities: Freud and Beyond*. Lexington: University of Kentucky Press.

Connell, R. W. 1987. *Gender and Power: Society, the Person, and Sexual Politics*. Stanford, CA: Stanford University Press.

Connell, R. W. 1995. *Masculinities*. New York: Routledge. 2nd ed., 2005.

Eng, David, with Judith Halberstam and Jose Munoz. 2005. Introduction: What's Queer About Queer Studies Now? *Social Text* 23 (3–4): 1–15.

Epstein, Steven. 1996. A Queer Encounter: Sociology and the Study of Sexuality. In *Queer Theory/Sociology*, ed. Steven Seidman, 145–167. Cambridge, MA: Blackwell.

Esterberg, Kristin. 1997. *Lesbian and Bisexual Identities: Constructing Communities, Constructing Selves*. Philadelphia: Temple University Press.

Ferguson, Roderick. 2004. *Aberrations in Black: Toward a Queer of Color Critique*. Minneapolis: University of Minnesota Press.

Fraser, Nancy. 1995. False Antitheses. In *Feminist Contentions: A Philosophical Exchange*, 59–74. New York: Routledge.

Freeman, Elizabeth. 2002. *The Wedding Complex: Forms of Belonging in Modern America Culture*. Durham, NC: Duke University Press.

Foucault, Michel. 1978. *The History of Sexuality*, Vol. 1: *An Introduction*. New York: Vintage.

Fuss, Diana, ed. 1991. *Inside/Out: Lesbian Theories, Gay Theories*. New York: Routledge.

Gamson, Joshua. 1998. *Freaks Talk Back: Tabloid Talk Shows and Sexual Nonconformity*. Chicago: University of Chicago Press.

Gamson, Joshua, and Dawne Moon. 2004. The Sociology of Sexualities: Queer and Beyond. *Annual Review of Sociology* 30: 47–64.

Green, Adam. 2002. Gay but Not Queer: Toward a Post-queer Study of Sexuality. *Theory and Society* 31: 521–545.

Halberstam, Judith. 1998. *Female Masculinity*. Durham, NC: Duke University Press.

Ingraham, Chrys. 1996. The Heterosexual Imaginary: Feminist Sociology and Theories of Gender. In *Queer Theory/Sociology*, ed. Steven Seidman, 168–193. Cambridge, MA: Blackwell.

Ingraham, Chrys. 1999. *White Weddings: Romancing Heterosexuality in Popular Culture*. New York: Routledge.

Katz, Jonathan Ned. 1996. *The Invention of Heterosexuality*. New York: Plume.

McIntosh, Mary. 1996. The Homosexual Role. In *Queer Theory/Sociology*, ed. Steven Seidman, 33–40. Cambridge, MA: Blackwell.

Meeks, Chet. 2001. Civil Society and the Sexual Politics of Difference. *Sociological Theory* 19 (3): 325–343.

Nardi, Peter, and Beth Schneider, eds. 1998. *Social Perspectives in Lesbian and Gay Studies: A Reader*. New York: Routledge.

Nyong'o, Tavia. 2005. Punk'd Theory. *Social Text* 23 (3–4): 19–34.

Plummer, Ken. 1996. Symbolic Interactionism and the Forms of Homosexuality. In *Queer Theory/Sociology*, ed. Steven Seidman, 64–82. Cambridge, MA: Blackwell.

Plummer, Ken. 1998. Afterword: The Past, Present, and Futures of the Sociology of Same-sex Relations. In *Social Perspectives in Lesbian and Gay Studies: A Reader*, ed. Peter Nardi and Beth Schneider, 605–614. New York: Routledge.

Puri, Joyti. 1999. *Woman, Body, Desire in Post-colonial India: Narratives of Gender and Sexuality*. New York: Routledge.

Reddy, Chandan. 2005. Asian Diasporas, Neoliberalism, and Family: Reviewing the Case for Homosexual Asylum in the Context of Family Rights. *Social Text* 23 (3–4): 101–119.

Rich, Adrienne. 1980. Compulsory Heterosexuality and Lesbian Existence. *Signs* 5 (4): 631–660.

Salzinger, Leslie. 2003. *Genders in Production: Making Workers in Mexico's Global Factories.* Berkeley: University of California Press.

Sedgwick, Eve. 1990. *Epistemology of the Closet.* Berkeley: University of California Press.

Sedgwick, Eve. 1993. *Tendencies.* Durham, NC: Duke University Press.

Seidman, Steven. 1994. Symposium: Queer Theory/Sociology: A Dialogue. *Sexualities* 12 (2): 166–177.

Seidman, Steven, ed. 1996. *Queer Theory/Sociology.* Cambridge, MA: Blackwell.

Seidman, Steven. 2002. *Beyond the Closet: The Transformation of Gay and Lesbian Life.* New York: Routledge.

Stein, Arlene. 1997. *Sex and Sensibility: Stories of a Lesbian Generation.* Berkeley: University of California Press.

Stein, Arlene, and Ken Plummer. 1996. "I Can't Even Think Straight": "Queer" Theory and the Missing Sexual Revolution in Sociology. In *Queer Theory/Sociology*, ed. Steven Seidman, 129–144. Cambridge, MA: Blackwell.

Stoler, Ann Laura. 2002. *Carnal Knowledge and Imperial Power: Race and the Intimate in Colonial Rule.* Berkeley: University of California Press.

Warner, Michael. 1993. Introduction. In *Fear of a Queer Planet: Queer Politics and Social Theory*, ed. Michael Warner, vii–xxxi. Minneapolis: University of Minnesota Press.

Weeks, Jeffrey. 1996. The Construction of Homosexuality. In *Queer Theory/Sociology*, ed. Steven Seidman, 41–63. Cambridge, MA: Blackwell.

White, Kevin. 1993. *The First Sexual Revolution: The Emergence of Male Heterosexuality in Modern America.* New York: New York University Press.

Wittig, Monique. [1980] 1992. *The Straight Mind and Other Essays.* Boston: Beacon.

James J. Dean

QUEER THEORY

SEE *Politics: Gay, Lesbian, Transgender, and Bisexual; Queer Studies.*

QUESNAY, FRANÇOIS
1694–1774

François Quesnay was born in the village of Méré, Île de France, into a family of merchants and small landowners. As a child he received no formal training, but he learned to read and write from a gardener. Largely self-taught, in 1711 he began to study medicine and surgery in Paris. In 1717 he married; he had three children. He first earned a

living as a surgeon and contributed several essays to the controversy between surgeons and physicians in France in the 1740s. In 1734 he assumed the position of physician of the Duke of Villeroy and in 1749 of Madame the Pompadour, Louis XV's favorite, in Versailles. In 1752 he saved the dauphin from smallpox, which won him the king's favor, a noble title, and a significant amount of money. At the beginning of the 1750s he was elected a member of the Académie des Sciences, Paris, and the Royal Society, London. During this period Quesnay stopped publishing medical works and turned to economics. The years 1756 and 1757 saw the publication of his entries in the *Encyclopédie* on *Fermiers* (farmers) and *Grains* (corn). Three further entries devoted to *Hommes* (people), *Impôts* (taxes), and *Interét de l'argent* (money rate of interest) could not be published in the *Encyclopédie* after an attempt to assassinate the king, which was grist for the mill of the enemies of the *encyclopédistes* (d'Alembert, Diderot, and others) and brought the project to a standstill. The first two articles were published only at the beginning of the twentieth century, the third in 1766.

Of particular importance to Quesnay's works in economics and their impact on the contemporary political debates first in France and then beyond was his encounter with the Marquis de Mirabeau in 1757. Mirabeau became a close follower of Quesnay and untiringly spread the gospel of the new physiocratic school. In 1758 Quesnay composed the first edition of the *Tableau économique*, which contained the first schematic account of the intertwined processes of production, distribution, and disposition of the riches of an entire nation. Mirabeau compared the importance of the *Tableau* to that of the discovery of fire and the wheel; Marx called it the "most brilliant idea" of political economy up until then and the physiocrats "the true fathers of modern political economy" (Marx 1963, p. 44). Two further editions of the *Tableau* followed in 1759. In 1763 Mirabeau published the *Philosophie rurale* in three volumes, a work that was heavily influenced (and partly even written) by Quesnay. In the same year the physiocrats began to engage in economic policy debates. Their articles appeared first in the *Journal de l'agriculture* and then in *Éphémerides du citoyen*, the "sect's" main outlet. Quesnay contributed several essays on themes such as the natural law doctrine, the so-called sterility of industry, and, in 1766, a simplified version of the *Tableau* in an article titled "Analyse de la formule arithmétique du Tableau économique." The school's influence in France peaked in the late 1760s and then steadily declined. Quesnay died in December 1774 near Versailles.

Quesnay conceived the process of production as a circular flow, with the rent of land being traced back to the existence of surplus product (*produit net*) left over after all means of production have been used up and all means of subsistence in support of the laboring population have been deducted from annual gross outputs. With a social division of labor, the products have to be exchanged for one another in interdependent markets. In order for the process to be able to continue unhampered, prices must cover physical real costs of production, consisting of means of production and subsistence, plus, in agriculture, the rent of land. A major concern of Quesnay was with the system's potential for growth. This depended on whether the surplus was consumed productively or unproductively and whether new methods of production could be developed and introduced, which by increasing productivity increased the social surplus.

Quesnay's works had a major influence on the development of central concepts and analytical tools in economics. After him the idea of ubiquitous economic interdependence never left the realm of economics again. Marx's analysis of simple and extended reproduction in volume 2 of *Capital* drew on the *Tableau* (see Marx 1974, and Gehrke and Kurz 1995), as did Wassily Leontief's (1941) input-output analysis. Piero Sraffa's (1960) reformulation of the classical approach to the theory of value and distribution was inspired by the physiocrats' multisector analysis. Also inspiring Sraffa was the physiocrats' concern with the implications for the theory of value and distribution of the specific conditions of the transformation of matter and energy into new forms of matter and energy in given sociotechnical conditions. Quesnay's concept of production as a circular flow is in marked contrast with the view entertained by some marginalist economists such as Eugen von Böhm-Bawerk of production as a one-way avenue of finite duration leading from the services of original factors of production to final output. The concept of a closed system, as we encounter it in Quesnay, is employed in fields of economics that take into account the laws of thermodynamics, such as environmental economics.

SEE ALSO *Economics; Marx, Karl; Physiocracy; Surplus; Sraffa, Piero*

BIBLIOGRAPHY

Gehrke, Christian, and Heinz D. Kurz. 1995. Karl Marx on Physiocracy. *European Journal of the History of Economic Thought* 2 (1): 53–90.

Hecht, Jacqueline. 2005. La vie de François Quesnay. In *François Quesnay. Oeuvres économiques complètes et autres textes*. 2 vols. Ed. Christine Théré, Loic Charles and Jean-Claude Perrot. Paris: Institut National d'Études Démographiques. Vol. 2, pp. 1331-1420.

Institut National d'Études Démographiques. 2005. *François Quesnay. Oeuvres économiques complètes et autres textes*. 2 vols. Ed. Christine Théré, Loic Charles and Jean-Claude Perrot. Paris: Author.

Leontief, Wassily. 1941. *The Structure of American Economy, 1919–1929: An Empirical Application of Equilibrium Analysis.* Cambridge, MA: Harvard University Press.

Marx, Karl. 1963. *Theories of Surplus Value.* Part 1. Trans. Emile Burns. Moscow: Progress Publishers.

Marx, Karl. 1974. *Capital.* Vol. 2. London: Lawrence and Wishart.

Quesnay, François. 1972. *Tableau économique.* 3rd ed. Ed. and trans. Marguerite Kuczynski and Ronald Meek. London: Macmillan.

Sraffa, Piero. 1960. *Production of Commodities by Means of Commodities: Prelude to a Critique of Economic Theory.* Cambridge, U.K.: Cambridge University Press.

Vaggi, Gianni. 1987. *The Economics of François Quesnay.* London: Macmillan.

Heinz D. Kurz

QUESTIONNAIRES

SEE *Surveys, Sample.*

QUOTA SYSTEM, FARM

Farm commodity quotas are defined as government-administered area or quantity allotments restricting what a farmer can produce or market. Such supply controls in the United States initially rested on several presumptions, some or all of which are no longer valid. One was that farmers reacting to market forces were incapable of adjusting their resources and output in a timely manner to maintain their income at a socially acceptable level in response to shocks from weather, foreign markets, and rapid productivity advance. That presumption in turn implied that, in the absence of supply control, farmers were predestined to chronically produce too much and hence to experience perennially low farm prices, incomes, and rates of return on resources.

Another presumption was that the demand for farm commodities was inelastic. That is, a reduction in market quantity would reduce quantity proportionately less than it would raise commodity price, thereby raising commodity receipts and farm income.

Supply controls in the form of quotas or allotments can be voluntary or mandatory, on resources or commodities, whole farm or part farm, on crop area or output, and short term or long term. Under the Agricultural Adjustment Act of 1933, the grandfather of farm commodity programs, government rewarded farmers who voluntarily controlled how much of major crops they planted with commodity price supports or direct payments.

The Agricultural Adjustment Act of 1938 introduced mandatory supply control. The term mandatory, though widely used, was nonetheless misleading because area quotas became binding on all producers of the commodity only if a two-thirds majority supported quotas in a national referendum. Due to generous price supports attending these quotas, farmers widely accepted mandatory controls. However, controls were largely ineffective in boosting total farm income because the area reduced for basic farm program crops was offset by area and production expansion for other crops. Slippage also was large because crop price supports encouraged additional application of fertilizers, irrigation water, and other inputs so that higher yields offset area cuts. Despite ineffective supply control, production was not excessive because of droughts in 1934 and 1936, and demand expansion during World War II.

Generous commodity support prices introduced in the 1940s were continued after the war, generating surpluses in the absence of supply control. Consequently, the government in 1954 introduced a conservation reserve program (CRP) to convert cropland, even whole farms, to long-term soil conserving uses. By 1960, 29 million acres were under 10-year contracts.

Farmers idled inferior cropland under CRP. Surpluses continued to mount due to the slippage factors noted and to statutory limits on the minimum size of specific crop quotas. The U.S. Congress rejected industry-wide mandatory controls in 1962. The next year the government offered wheat farmers the opportunity to accept tight mandatory allotments coupled with high support prices versus free markets. Wheat farmers rejected controls in a hard fought national referendum in 1963.

The government deemed that farmers should not have free markets, however, and enacted voluntary short-term diversion programs whereby each farmer annually could choose to divert part of his land to soil conserving uses in return for price support and payments from the government. Such newly dominant short-term area diversion, of minimal size in previous decades, grew large and averaged 52 million acres in the 1960s, then reached the high-water mark of 78 million acres in 1983. Problems engendered by that 1983 diversion coupled with drought in the same year prompted a reexamination of commodity programs. Critics observed that voluntary area diversion programs were expensive for taxpayers. Furthermore, such programs, by raising commodity prices, lost markets to cheaper substitutes (for example, cotton to synthetics) and to foreign competition. Agribusiness firms that supply farm inputs and process and market farm products thrive on farms' raw material volume—and they were not getting volume. Livestock producers as well as food consumers were hurt by feed costs inflated by supply controls.

These and other factors led Congress to end most supply controls in the Freedom to Farm bill of 1996. By 2007, supply control remained only under the Conservation Reserve Program (for environmental purposes) and on a minor crop, sugar. The demand for farm output had become elastic due to a large biofuels market. Because quotas reduce farm income when demand is elastic, they are an anachronism of an earlier era.

Termination of controls pleased consumers, agribusiness firms, and livestock producers, but reliance on payments without supply controls introduced new problems. Payments without controls induce farm output to exceed levels in an unregulated market. Whereas programs prior to 1996 cut production by approximately 5 percent from unregulated competitive market levels in the 1960s and 1980s and lesser amounts in other years, the 1996 and 2002 farm bills without supply management raised farm output an estimated 3 percent over competitive market levels. Part of that excess production is being dumped on international markets. Thus, the United States has shifted from World Trade Organization (WTO) acceptable blue box policies (that support farm income but control production) to less acceptable amber box policies (that expand output and exports above competitive market levels). Supply control programs are fatally flawed and are dead, but other, current government programs to support farm income in the United States remain problematic.

SEE ALSO *Agribusiness; Agricultural Economics; Agricultural Industry; Great Depression; New Deal, The; Protectionism; Subsidies; Subsidies, Farm*

BIBLIOGRAPHY

Rasmussen, Wayne, Gladys Baker, and James Ward. 1976. *A Short History of Agricultural Adjustment.* Agricultural Information Bulletin No. 391. Washington, DC: Economic Research Service, U.S. Department of Agriculture.

Tweeten, Luther. 1989. *Farm Policy Analysis.* Boulder, CO: Westview Press.

Tweeten, Luther. 2002. Farm Commodity Programs: Essential Safety Net or Corporate Welfare? In *Agricultural Policy for the 21st Century,* eds. Luther Tweeten and Stanley Thompson, 2-34. Ames: Iowa State Press.

Luther Tweeten

QUOTA SYSTEMS

A quota system is one of two different ways in which a policy of affirmative action may be implemented; it is the alternative to a system of *preferential boosts.* Under an affirmative action policy, membership in an identity group recognized as marginalized and underrepresented increases one's chances of being selected to a desirable position—for example, admission into a prestigious educational institution, or employment in a respected organization. The increased access is accomplished under a quota system by reserving a certain share of the available positions for members of the relevant group, thus dividing the overall selection process into two separate competitions. Under a system of preferential boosts, by contrast, there is a single competition for access to the available positions, but some additional favorable consideration is given to group members in evaluating individual qualifications and thereby determining applicant rankings.

During the early period in which affirmative action policies were implemented in the United States—from the mid-1960s through the 1970s—quota systems were not uncommon, though affirmative action policies more often took the form of preferential boosts. In India, however, affirmative action has mainly taken the form of quota systems. In other countries where affirmative action is practiced, one can find varying combinations of the two systems.

Under a quota system, the number of available positions reserved for members of a marginalized identity group in a separate competition is most often set equal to the proportion of that group in the overall population of the country (or the relevant region or locality). Such proportionality need not necessarily, however, characterize a quota system of affirmative action; the number of reserved positions may be set at any level. Separate quotas and competitions may of course be established for members of more than one identity group. Whatever the criteria for ranking applicants, these criteria are applied separately to each group of applicants, and the highest-ranking applicants in each group are selected until the available positions are filled.

Under a quota system, the number of selected members of any group targeted by affirmative action will equal the size of the quota for that group—unless fewer group applicants actually apply. A variant of this kind of selection process is one that excludes from the reserved quota those applicants whose qualifications irrespective of group membership enable them to be selected in competition with all other applicants. In this case, all the group applicants who are selected to reserved seats rank lower, by the relevant ranking criteria, than those selected in the general competition, and the overall number of group applicants selected may well exceed the quota reserved for them.

A preferential boost system is applied somewhat differently to quantitative and to qualitative selection procedures. In a quantitative selection procedure, an applicant's qualifications are summarized in an overall point score in order to determine his or her position in the rank order,

and the preferential boost takes the form of a certain number of additional points credited to applicants from the targeted group. In the case of a qualitative selection procedure, a variety of applicant qualifications are taken into account but not formally aggregated into a single overall point score. In this case, the preferential boost takes a less precise form; for example, applicants from the targeted group could be viewed in a rosier light or given extra credit for signs of unrealized potential. Different degrees of preferential boost may of course be given to applicants from different groups. In any kind of preferential-boost system, one cannot be certain in advance how many applicants from each group will be selected.

The difference between a quota system and a preferential-boost system is not as great as it may first appear. Corresponding to a quota system that selects any given number of targeted group applicants for a particular position, there is bound to be some amount of preferential boost that leads to the same outcome. In the case of a selection process in which applicants' qualifications are summarized in a single point score, the amount of preferential boost that would do so is the number of points needed to bring the marginal group applicant's score up to the level that would make him or her the last applicant admitted in the general competition. (There is one minor exception to this rule: if the last applicant selected to fill a quota has qualifications equal to those of one or more of the top applicants who failed to be selected, then a preferential-boost system would have to either accept or reject all of the marginal applicants with equal qualifications.)

Notwithstanding the formal correspondence between quota and preferential-boost systems, there remains a substantive difference between the two systems insofar as the parameters of each kind of system—the size of the quota or the amount of the preferential boost—are held constant for a period of time. A preferential-boost system assures that the gap in conventional qualifications between targeted group applicants selected and other applicants selected does not vary much over time, while the number of the targeted group applicants selected will in all likelihood vary from one competition to the next. A quota system assures that the number (or the proportion) of targeted group applicants selected will remain constant, unless the quota is not filled, while the gap in conventional qualifications will likely vary considerably over time.

In practice, quota systems are often constrained by specification of minimum conventional qualifications (e.g., a minimum qualifying score) below which targeted group applicants will be rejected, even if their quota is not filled. Whenever such a minimum conventional qualifications requirement serves to keep the number of accepted applicants below or equal to the quota, this kind of constrained quota system has the same effect as a preferential-boost system in which the size of the preferential boost is equal to the gap between the minimum conventional qualifications required of a successful targeted applicant and the conventional qualifications of the last applicant admitted in the general competition. (If and when the preferential boost implied by a minimum qualifications requirement in a constrained quota system is not binding—that is, if it alone would allow more applicants to be selected than the size of the quota—then there is, of course, a difference in outcome as between the constrained quota system and the corresponding preferential-boost system.)

A pure quota system is considerably more arbitrary than either a constrained quota system or a preferential-boost system of affirmative action. By focusing on a target number (or proportion) of group applicants to be selected, a pure quota system ignores problems likely to arise if the conventional qualifications gap between targeted group and other applicants selected becomes substantial. At the same time, however, it should be clear that the choice among a pure quota system, a constrained quota system, and a preferential-boost system is not the most critical choice for an affirmative action policy. Arguably the most important factor is the size of the explicit or implicit preferential boost involved in the policy, for this will affect the likelihood that affirmative action beneficiaries can succeed in performing well in the positions to which they have gained access.

SEE ALSO *Affirmative Action*

BIBLIOGRAPHY

Fryer, Roland G., Jr., and Glenn C. Loury. 2005. Affirmative Action and Its Mythology. *Journal of Economics Perspectives* 19 (3): 147–162.

Weisskopf, Thomas. 2004. *Affirmative Action in the United States and India: A Comparative Perspective.* London: Routledge.

Thomas E. Weisskopf

QUOTAS

Quotas represent one method available to policymakers as a structural remedy for political or economic inequality. Put most succinctly, quotas have traditionally emerged from pragmatic discussions regarding the implementation of legislation or constitutional mandates to pursue equality among citizens. While citizens across nations have traditionally endorsed the political value of equality, there have been long-standing debates at the local, national, and international levels about the role of government in establishing or protecting citizens' equality.

Contemporary debates about quotas emerge most frequently in the context of affirmative action policies. Affirmative action policies are premised on the belief that government must not simply protect citizens from invidious discrimination but must also take "affirmative steps," as U.S. president Lyndon B. Johnson stated in his 1965 Executive Order 11246, to ensure that citizens have equal opportunity to obtain jobs in a labor market with a history of pervasive discrimination. Quotas have emerged around the world as one method to pursue and achieve equality in two ways: equality of opportunity to compete for jobs, education, or political power; and equality of outcome—the successful acquisition of such jobs, education, or political power.

One common use of quotas has enhanced the political power of women in legislatures around the world. Many parliamentary democracies have implemented quotas of women to stand for election, including Germany, France, Belgium, Bolivia, Rwanda, and Palestine. Such quotas have produced greater female representation in parliaments and changes in public policy and legislation that have an impact upon women's well-being. These quotas, while controversial at the time of implementation, seem relatively stable and unlikely to change in the foreseeable future.

The use of quotas in other sectors of government policy continues to be much more controversial as they attempt to enhance equality among various lines of difference in political society. Nigeria, at the time of its independence in 1979, attempted to counteract the ethnic inequality that was a legacy of colonialism by instituting policies of "ethnic balancing," many including hard numerical quotas for admissions into higher education and civil-service hiring. Yet ethnic tensions over access to wealth and ethnoreligious differences continue regularly to erupt into violence. Similarly, India included some forms of affirmative action at the time of its independence from Britain in 1947, yet political and economic inequality remains widespread in the world's largest democracy. The "reservation system," as India's quota system is known, sets numerical percentages as targets for the inclusion of lower-caste minorities. Despite its constitutional legitimacy, implementation remains uneven. For this and other reasons, some target quotas go unfulfilled each year. When framed as a policy of racial or ethnic incorporation, quotas remain subject to legal challenge and outright invalidation, as occurred in the United States.

The U.S. policy of affirmative action emerged out of the modern civil rights movement of the mid-twentieth century and has moved away from "hiring goals" as quotas into a still-controversial system of preferential boosts to women and minority candidates for federal contracts, jobs, and college admission. Presidents John F. Kennedy,

Lyndon B. Johnson, and Richard Nixon together were responsible for affirmative action's evolution into a system of quotas. Kennedy first established a Presidential Committee on Equal Employment Opportunity, chaired by then–vice president Johnson, which focused on a comprehensive remedy to racial inequality by focusing on both protecting black and other minority citizens from discrimination and taking positive steps to encourage greater access to fair employment and education. These two policy arenas—education and employment—became primary battlegrounds for the implementation of affirmative action in the United States.

Initially the executive orders of Johnson (1965, 1968) and Nixon (1970, 1971) focused on two aspects of affirmative action implementation: time and scope. As well, both presidents' administrations started with oversight of corporations that were federal contractors, and then sought further expansion of the policy in the private sector. Goals and timetables emerged as methods of enforcing compliance with both the letter and spirit of antidiscrimination laws. "Hiring goals" were set in cases where there was significant underutilization of certain racial groups in an industrial sector such as construction, and "admissions goals" were set in the domain of higher education. In the implementation of programs to achieve such goals, quotas were set as targets so that employers and educational institutions could demonstrate that they were taking the aforementioned affirmative steps.

These quotas were almost immediately challenged in court by white majority individuals who considered such programs a direct threat to their access to employment and higher education opportunities. The Supreme Court has spent a significant amount of time over the past forty years attempting to regulate the constitutionality of programs designed to implement the protection and promotion of equality. The court first contended with the Civil Rights Act of 1964, which created the Equal Employment Opportunity Commission as a federal agency charged with the oversight of public and private employers' policies to prevent discrimination. In *Griggs v. Duke Power* (1971), the Court developed the theory of disparate impact, allowing the definition of discrimination to expand to situations where malicious intent was not necessarily a factor. Enforced corrective action such as hiring goals were permissible in situations where a definitive mismatch existed between the availability of minority workers and their presence in a particular occupation. Later, in *United Steelworkers of America v. Weber* (1979), the Supreme Court allowed voluntary agreements, including quotas reserving half of all craft training positions for African Americans until the percentage of African American workers in the sector matched the percentage in the local labor force. This decision is consistent with the underlying assumption that affirmative action in general

is a time-bound policy; such policies will be obsolete once equality is achieved.

The Court also had a major impact on the scope of affirmative action programs. In 1978 the Court strictly limited the use of quotas as a tool of affirmative action programs in *Regents of the University of California v. Bakke*. Allan Bakke, a white applicant to the University of California at Davis medical school, successfully sued to remove the "hard" quota of reserving sixteen seats in each incoming first-year class for racial minorities. While the Court refused to allow this kind of quota, it continued to allow the use of race in a more vague way, "as a plus," in admissions decisions. Quotas were also restricted in terms of the types of actions employers could take to pursue them. In two cases—*Firefighters v. Stotts* (1984) and *Wygant v. Jackson Board of Education* (1986)—the Court refused to allow employers to take jobs away from whites via layoffs in order to increase the number of minority hires.

During this same period scholars have hotly debated both whether quotas are a just form of implementing affirmative action and chronicled the trajectory of marginalized groups who have been targeted by such programs. In elite levels of higher education, African Americans have been determined to benefit greatly from admissions policies that include affirmative action—whether quotas or more loosely defined "goals." On the other hand, though such policies have vastly contributed to the expansion of the black middle class, the persistently poor who have been left out of such benefits have become more economically insecure and isolated from the economic and political benefits of stable communities. As well, although little evidence suggests that affirmative action has produced "reverse discrimination" in the employment sector, the lack of structural investment in higher education over the past forty years and the emerging baby boomlet population have produced greater competition for a relatively stable number of college admissions slots in the United States, increasing public anxiety about affirmative action in general and political resistance to quotas of any kind—Supreme Court sanctioned or not.

Most recently the Supreme Court has continued to uphold the idea that the time for race to be considered a factor in college admissions and employment continues, despite numerous restrictions on the scope. In *Grutter v. Bollinger* (2003), Justice Sandra Day O'Connor, author of the majority opinion, restated the idea of a time limit to policies such as the constitutionally permissible law school admissions process. It is clear from the docket of the Court, however, that the scope of such policies is ever changing, and given political resistance to quotas in college admissions, their eventual reinstatement is highly unlikely in the United States.

The experience of the United States with quotas varies from that of other countries in terms of scope, policy domain, and timetable. While other nations have successfully implemented quotas to ensure proportional representation of women in their lawmaking bodies, the winner-takes-all quality of the U.S. electoral context makes such quotas more difficult, though not impossible, to implement. On the other hand, compared to such countries as France and Great Britain, which have both struggled to address racial inequality through either color-blind means or race-conscious means such as quotas, the United States spent more time during the mid-twentieth century directly confronting the lack of minority incorporation through various pieces of state and federal legislation.

While it is clear that persistent inequality is a challenge for nearly every country in the world, the responses to such inequality through the policy remedy of quotas has had mixed results and varying levels of political will to enforce them. As well, the scholarly analysis of such policies has not settled on a conventional wisdom as to their efficacy in producing the goal to which almost all of the quota programs aspire: equality among all citizens.

SEE ALSO *Affirmative Action; Discrimination; Hierarchy; Inequality, Gender; Inequality, Racial; Quota Systems; Stratification*

BIBLIOGRAPHY

Bowen, William, and Derek Bok. 1998. *The Shape of the River: Long-Term Consequences of Considering Race in College and University Admissions.* Princeton, NJ: Princeton University Press.

Deshpande, Ashwini. 2006. Affirmative Action in India and the United States. *World Development Report on Equity and Development.* Background Papers. Washington, DC: World Bank.

Katznelson, Ira. 2004. *When Affirmative Action Was White: An Untold History of Racial Inequality in Twentieth Century America.* New York: Norton.

Lieberman, Robert. 2005. *Shaping Race Policy: The United States in Comparative Perspective.* Princeton, NJ: Princeton University Press.

Moses, Michele S. 2002. *Embracing Race: Why We Need Race Conscious Education Policy.* New York: Teachers College Press.

Sowell, Thomas. 2004. *Affirmative Action around the World: An Empirical Study.* New Haven, CT: Yale University Press.

Weisskopf, Thomas. 2004. *Affirmative Action in the United States and India: A Comparative Perspective.* London and New York: Routledge.

Ange-Marie Hancock

QUOTAS, TRADE

Trade quotas are upper limits on the quantity of goods shipped between two nations in a particular category, for example, men's shirts. An export quota is administered by customs officials in the export nation, while import quotas are administered by the import nation. Prospective exporters or importers must first obtain a license to ship an agreed quantity, such as one unit. In practice many export quotas are set up at the request of importing nations, in which case they are voluntary export quotas (VERs). The most prominent example of VERs is the Multifibre Arrangement (MFA) that lapsed in 2005 and that set bilateral export quotas for textile and apparel trade, affecting some 10 percent of the value of trade of rich countries.

Quotas act similarly to tariffs in that trade is reduced, domestic prices are driven up, and exporter prices are driven down. In one very special case, quotas are fully equivalent to tariffs. The equivalence case requires that the importing country set the quota and that it sell the licenses to import at a competitive auction, thereby obtaining the revenue as it would with a tariff. When other qualifications are met, the price paid for a one-unit license is equivalent to a tariff, volume of trade and domestic and export nation prices are the same, and equivalence prevails.

QUOTAS VERSUS TARIFFS

Quotas in practice are more inefficient than tariffs. First, quotas strengthen monopoly power. For example, a sole domestic firm becomes a monopoly in its home when foreign firms are limited to a fixed quantity of sales whereas with a tariff, that firm potentially competes with many firms. Monopoly power raises prices above cost and thus imposes a loss on the economy.

Quotas are also inherently highly discriminatory, which adds to their cost. Discrimination arises because quotas are set individually for trade partners and for product lines. Even if the quotas initially are associated with uniform tariff equivalents, changes in economic conditions introduce nonuniformity. This produces dramatic discrimination across countries. Moreover, across product lines within a country, regulations typically prevent resale of quota licenses from low-payoff to high-payoff lines of sale, similarly preventing market forces from achieving nondiscrimination. Nations also use quotas to discriminate in favor of allies or against enemies, as with the U.S. sugar quota, which allows imports from high-cost Philippines and excludes low-cost Cuba.

Quotas may increase fluctuations in prices compared with tariffs, and this is costly. A fixed specific tariff will permit fluctuating amounts of trade when there are shocks to foreign supply or domestic demand. The average volume of trade anticipated should be compared with a fixed quota of the average amount. The fixed quota will produce fluctuating tariff equivalents, which in effect discriminates across situations (states of nature) with different realized shocks. This discrimination is costly: It is more efficient to have more trade in high-tariff-equivalent states and less trade in low-tariff-equivalent states. The tariff accomplishes this perfectly compared with the quota.

The allocation of quota licenses is a potent cause of corruption, imposing further costs on the economy as resources are diverted from production to the pursuit of quota licenses: Before its reforms of the 1990s, India's government was often called "the license Raj."

POLITICAL ECONOMY OF QUOTAS

Why have quotas been used when tariffs can also provide benefits to import-competing interests, apparently at lower cost? There must be some political advantage of quotas over tariffs in cases where they are used. Quotas are less transparent than tariffs because calculation of tax equivalents requires data on comparable domestic and foreign prices. The lack of price data often means no one outside the most closely concerned parties knows how costly the quota is. This may permit import-competing interests to obtain tighter limits on imports than they could obtain from tariffs. Because beneficiaries provide political support to politicians who set quotas, both the government and interest groups may gain from choosing quotas over tariffs.

An apparent disadvantage of quotas relative to tariffs is that the government's potential tariff revenue is dissipated as quota rent earned by the license holders. The apparent disadvantage may, however, be a political advantage. First, with a VER, the quota rent typically gets awarded to foreign exporters who are initially being restricted in their access to the market. This compensates the foreigners for their loss and eases the problem of international trade relations with the foreign government. (This advantage is temporary. Later on, the VER will

exclude exporters from other foreign countries and complicate trade relations with their governments.) Second, license holders are a very easily identified group of beneficiaries—easier to squeeze for political support than import-competing producers who may be hard to identify.

The apparent political advantage of quotas seems to argue that they should be very widespread. Politicians can play mutually beneficial games with producer groups in setting up market-share arrangements all over the international trading economy. Thus, limits on their use to a few areas of the world economy poses an important puzzle. To illustrate the importance of the puzzle, consider the MFA set of VERs that, until recently, controlled some 10 per cent of world trade. The MFA began in the 1950s and was gradually extended to cover more products and countries, so it looked durable. Yet the Uruguay Round of multilateral trade negotiations set an end date in January 2005. Despite the reversion to a temporary extension of VERs on China in fall 2005, the end of the MFA seems to be accomplished. Political economy should be able to say why. Moreover, political economy should be able to explain the use of tariffs as opposed to quotas in many other product categories.

SEE ALSO *Barriers to Trade; Tariffs*

BIBLIOGRAPHY

Anderson, James E. 1988. *The Relative Inefficiency of Quotas.* Cambridge, MA: MIT Press.

Krugman, Paul R., and Maurice Obstfeld. 2006. *International Economics.* 7th ed. Boston: Addison-Wesley.

James E. Anderson

QUOTATIONS FROM CHAIRMAN MAO
SEE *Little Red Book.*